THE BLACKWELL HANDBOOK OF ORGANIZATIONAL LEARNING AND KNOWLEDGE MANAGEMENT

THE BLACKWELL HANDBOOK OF ORGANIZATIONAL LEARNING AND KNOWLEDGE MANAGEMENT

Edited by

MARK EASTERBY-SMITH AND MARJORIE A. LYLES

Blackwell
Publishing

BLACKWELL PUBLISHING
350 Main Street, Malden, MA 02148-5020, USA
9600 Garsington Road, Oxford OX4 2DQ, UK
550 Swanston Street, Carlton, Victoria 3053, Australia

First published 2003
First published in paperback 2005 by Blackwell Publishing Ltd

4   2007

Library of Congress Cataloging-in-Publication Data

The Blackwell handbook of organizational learning and knowledge management / edited by
Mark Easterby-Smith and Marjorie A. Lyles.
        p. cm.
Includes bibliographical references and index.
ISBN 978-0- 631-22672-7 (hardback) – ISBN: 978-1-4051-3304-3 (paperback)
1. Organizational learning – Handbooks, manuals, etc.   2. Knowledge management –
Handbooks, manuals, etc.   I. Easterby-Smith, Mark.   II. Lyles, Marjorie A.
HD58.82 .B56 2003
658.3′124 – dc21

                                                                    2002013799

ISBN: 978-0-631-22672-7 (hardback) – ISBN: 978-1-4051-3304-3 (paperback)

A catalogue record for this title is available from the British Library.

Set in 10 on 12 pt Baskerville
by SNP Best-set Typesetter Ltd, Hong Kong

For further information on
Blackwell Publishing, visit our website:
www.blackwellpublishing.com

Contents

List of Figures

List of Tables

List of Contributors

Maryam Alavi
Goizueta Business School, Emory University, Atlanta, Georgia, USA

Paul Almeida
McDonough School of Business, Georgetown University, Washington DC, USA

Caroline A. Bartel
Stern School of Business, New York University, New York, USA

Richard A. Bettis
Kenan Flagler Business School, University of North Carolina at Chapel Hill, USA

Mikelle A. Calhoun
Stern School of Business, New York University, New York, USA

Rossella Cappetta
Department of Organization, Bocconi University, Milan, Italy

John S. Carroll
MIT Sloan School of Management, Boston, USA

Bala Chakravarthy
IMD, Lausanne, Switzerland

John Child
Birmingham Business School, University of Birmingham, Birmingham, UK

Kevin G. Corley
Penn State University, Philadelphia, USA

Rob Cross
University of Virginia, McIntire School of Commerce and IBM Institute for Knowledge-Based Organizations

Mary Crossan
Richard Ivey School of Business, University of Western Ontario, London, Canada

Robert DeFillippi
Sawyer School of Management, Suffolk University, Boston, USA

Anthony J. DiBella
Organization Transitions, Inc. East Greenwich, and Worcester Polytechnic Institute, Massachusetts, USA

Yves Doz
INSEAD, Fontainebleau, France

Mark Easterby-Smith
Lancaster University Management School, Lancaster, UK

Amy C. Edmondson
Harvard Business School, Boston, USA

Bente Elkjaer
Department of Educational Sociology, Danish University of Education, Copenhagen, Denmark

Stephen Fineman
School of Management, University of Bath, Bath, UK

Nicolai J. Foss
LINK, Department of Industrial Economics and Strategy, Copenhagen Business School, Frederiksberg, Denmark

Raghu Garud
Stern School of Business, New York University, New York, USA

Dennis A. Gioia
Penn State University, Philadelphia, USA

Rob Grant
McDonough School of Business, Georgetown University, Washington DC, USA

Sachi Hatakenaka
MIT Sloan School of Management, Boston, USA

Niall Hayes
Lancaster University Management School, Lancaster, UK

Andrew C. Inkpen
Thunderbird, American Graduate School of International Management, Glendale, Arizona, USA

Marjorie A. Lyles
Kelley School of Business, Indiana University, Indianapolis, USA

Volker Mahnke
LINK, Department of Industrial Economics and Strategy, Copenhagen Business School, Frederiksberg, Denmark

Shige Makino
Chinese University of Hong Kong, Hong Kong

Pablo Martin de Holan
School of Business and Faculté Saint-Jean, University of Alberta, Edmonton, Canada

Suc McEvily
Katz School, University of Pittsburgh, USA

Suzyn Ornstein
Sawyer School of Management, Suffolk University, Boston, USA

Joyce S. Osland
Dr. Robert B. Pamplin, Jr. School of Business Administration, University of Portland, Portland, Oregon, USA

Anupama Phene
David Eccles School of Business, University of Utah, Salt Lake City, USA

Nelson Phillips
Judge Institute of Management Studies, University of Cambridge, Cambridge, UK

Josh Plaskoff
Eli Lilly and Company, Indianapolis, USA

Laurence Prusak
IBM Institute for Knowledge-Based Organizations, Cambridge, Massachusetts, USA

Devaki Rau
Northern Illinois University, De Kalb, USA

Suzana Rodrigues
Birmingham Business School, University of Birmingham, Birmingham, UK

Jenny W. Rudolph
Carroll School of Management, Boston College, Boston, USA

Jane E. Salk
Graduate School of Industrial Administration, Carnegie Mellon University and School of Management, University of Texas at Dallas, USA

Harry Scarbrough
Warwick Business School, University of Warwick, Coventry, UK

Bernard L. Simonin
Fletcher School of Law and Diplomacy, Tufts University, Medford, Massachusetts, USA

Robin Snell
Lignan University, Hong Kong

William H. Starbuck
New York University, New York, USA

Jacky Swan
Warwick Business School, University of Warwick, Coventry, UK

Gabriel Szulanski
Department of Management, Wharton School, University of Pennsylvania, Philadelphia, USA

Sully Taylor
School of Business Administration, Portland State University, Portland, Oregon, USA

Amrit Tiwana
Goizueta Business School, Emory University, Atlanta, Georgia, USA

Haridimos Tsoukas
Athens Laboratory of Business Administration (ALBA), Greece and University of Strathclyde Graduate School of Business, Glasgow, UK

Frans A.J. Van Den Bosch
Department of Strategy and Business Environment, Rotterdam School of Management, Erasmus University Rotterdam, The Netherlands

Raymond Van Wijk
Department of Strategy and Business Environment, Rotterdam School of Management, Erasmus University Rotterdam, The Netherlands

Dusya Vera
Richard Ivey School of Business, University of Western Ontario, London, Ontario, Canada

Henk W. Volberda
Department of Strategy and Business Environment, Rotterdam School of Management, Erasmus University Rotterdam, The Netherlands

Georg von Krogh
University of St. Gallen, St. Gallen, Switzerland

Geoff Walsham
The Judge Institute of Management Studies, University of Cambridge, Cambridge, UK

Sidney G. Winter
Department of Management, The Wharton School, University of Pennsylvania, Philadelphia, USA

Sze-Sze Wong
Fuqua School of Business, Duke University, Chapel Hill, North Carolina, USA

Anita Williams Woolley
Harvard Business School, Boston, Massachusetts, USA

Maurizio Zollo
Department of Strategy and Management, INSEAD, France

Foreword

A handbook is a living embodiment of the well-known aphorism about scholars who stand on the "shoulders of giants." That imagery is even more apt for the present work because of its focus on discovering, enacting, cumulating, transmitting, and revising the knowledge that is associated with giants. Robert Merton has traced the origins of the "giants" aphorism back to the mid 12th century and to the French philosopher Bernard de Chartres. One of his students, writing in 1169, remembered de Chartres' original remark about giants this way:

> Bernard de Chartres used to compare us to [puny] dwarfs perched on the shoulders of giants. He pointed out that we see more and farther than our predecessors, not because we have keener vision or greater height, but because we are lifted up and borne aloft on their gigantic stature. (Sills and Merton, 1991: 19)

That image has changed slightly over the centuries, but perhaps nowhere has that change been as biting as in this comment by psychologist David Zeaman in 1959:

> One of the differences between the natural and the social sciences is that in the natural sciences, each succeeding generation stands on the shoulders of those that have gone before, while in the social sciences, each generation steps in the faces of its predecessors. (Sills and Merton, 1991: 259)

Contrary to what Zeaman suggests, the following discussions of social science are respectful and concerned as much with continuities as with breaks from the past.

In many ways this issue of continuities–discontinuities is at the core of learning and knowledge management. Put yourself in the place of the authors collected in this volume. Their task was to climb down from the shoulders of giants, go back to the choice points that the giants started with, rethink those choice points, and see if it might make sense to remake those early decisions differently on the basis of what we know about organizing and social life.

Sir Frederic Bartlett's serial reproduction exercise provides a suitable, if unexpected, vehicle to illustrate what it means to rework an earlier choice point. In Bartlett's exercise, which some of you know better as the parlor game "telephone," a person listens to a complex story such as the War of the Ghosts, tells it to a second person, who tells it to a third, and this continues until the final version is compared with the original version and is typically found to be a massive simplification of the original. Now, imagine that, after some lapse of time, the story is sent back through the same people who originally simplified it. Will the story regain its original complexity or will it be simplified even more? The answer, as Lance Kurke, Liz Ravlin, and I found is that nuance and complexity are restored.

The relevance of this demonstration for the future of our work on organizational learning and knowledge management is substantial. The concepts of learning that we now work with may seem more complex than their predecessors because we have made more refined differentiations of what we inherited. But it is also true that what we have inherited are simplified solutions to what originally were much more complex problems. The solutions have been simplified as they go from investigator to investigator and become farther removed from their origins. To go back to earlier work, to devolve from what we understand now, is not just an exercise in nostalgia that revisits earlier simplicities. Going back is also a chance to see in more detail a complex basic issue, a crucial turning point, a choice that turned out to result in the simplifications we now work with. The beauty of devolution is that we have a chance to remake the earlier choice. In the example of the Bartlett exercise, when the Ghosts story is restored back to something of its original form through reverse transmission, we then have the opportunity to transmit it a second time. But this time we do so in a different context, with a different awareness and aspiration, and with sensitivity to different features and different solutions. The editors of this handbook alert us to this potential for enrichment in their introductory chapter. The authors provide this enrichment in the remaining chapters.

Consider an example. If we devolve backward from our current concern with learning in the face of ambiguity, contradiction, and confusion and look for early efforts to frame these issues, one place we could stop is the very first statement of cognitive dissonance theory in class notes handed out at the University of Minnesota by Leon Festinger. If we look closely at these notes, we see two interesting things. First, we find that Festinger's notes were titled "Social communication and cognition: a very preliminary and highly tentative draft." The first three sentences of the notes are crucial. They read:

> In order to understand communication behavior in persons it is necessary to separate various kinds of communications. . . . We shall here concern ourselves with one conceptually defined subarea under the rubric of communication which seems to be important. Specifically, we shall present a theory together with some supporting data, to explain communication oriented toward acquiring or supporting one's cognition. (Festinger in Harman and Mills: 355)

Thus, somewhat to our surprise, we discover that dissonance theory is not really about cognition or discrepancy, but it is about communication and finding support. Originally, cognition was embedded in interaction and communication, not just in solitary information processing, although you'd never know that by reading current discussions of cognition in the context of learning and knowledge management.

Second, what's also interesting about Festinger's notes is that they are grounded in the real world, specifically in the empirical phenomenon of rumor. Festinger proposed that if a person's reactions with respect to some event are inconsistent with his cognition, that person will communicate with others in ways that are consonant with the reaction. Thus, he predicted that in an earthquake near Bihar India on January 15, 1934 (data were from Prasad), those who felt the shocks of the quake and were fearful but who saw no actual damage or destruction, would experience dissonance and would spread rumors that would make it appropriate for them to be afraid. Thus, those who were spared by the earthquake would communicate more fear-provoking rumors about the disasters that were or would be triggered by the earthquake than those who actually experienced the destruction. Consistent with the prediction there were widespread fear-provoking rumors among those who were spared. They were convinced that they would be overrun by floods, cyclones, and deluges within the next 3 to 5 days. The prediction that more disasters were imminent is consonant with the cognition of being afraid.

This finding clearly is subject to other interpretations than Festinger's. And that's my point. The outcomes of several data sets on rumor suggested to Festinger that a homeostatic communication process, shaped by pressures toward cognitive consonance, might be operating. Those same rumor data might suggest something quite different than dissonance to students of organizational learning whose informants live amidst a continuous stream of rumors concerning job loss, takeovers, divestments, firing, reorganization, or succession. Devolving toward the early stages of dissonance theory, and redoing what we find, might nudge us to give communication a more central place in our work on learning.

This volume suggests that part of our future as scholars interested in learning and knowledge management may lie in someone else's past, the recovery of that past, and remaking the choices they faced in ways that are more mindful of organizational phenomena. A clear strength of this volume is that its contributors explicitly stand on the shoulders of giants. And when they step down from those shoulders, they do not stamp on the faces of those giants. Instead, they try to stand in their shoes, reconstruct their choice points, and go backward in order to go forward differently.

These efforts enact a community of practice. And they do so in ways that are mindful of the ways in which learning and knowledge management unfold in universities. I am struck by the sense in which this handbook functions like a virtual university. That similarity is not trivial because, as John Gardner (1968) has said, what is crucial about a university is that it "stands for things that are forgotten in the heat of battle, for values that get pushed aside in the rough-and-tumble of everyday living, for the goals we ought to be thinking about and never do, for the facts we don't like to face, and the questions we lack the courage to ask" (1968: 90). To wade into these chapters is to confront things we forget, values we slight, goals we neglect, facts we avoid, and questions we fear. Those confrontations are jolts. But they are more than that. They are precisely the learning experiences that these authors are trying to explain. That's great because it provides repeated tests of the plausibility of the argument. But it's also not so great since these jolting moments of explicit learning are short-lived. Their transient quality is best captured by Cohen and Gooch who describe how quickly the lessons learned on a military battlefield vanish.

> In the chaos of the battlefield there is the tendency of all ranks to combine and recast the story of their achievements into a shape which shall satisfy the susceptibilities of national and

regimental vain-glory. . . . On the actual day of battle naked truths may be picked up for the asking; by the following morning they have already begun to get into their uniforms. (Cohen and Gooch, 1990: 44)

These chapters will trigger in readers the very phenomena of learning and knowledge acquisition that the chapters themselves seek to explain. When this happens, it means that temporarily new resources have been mobilized to understand the triggers and triggering. But, that potential for reflection and improvement may be short-lived. First impressions count. They count because it is not long before those first impressions are "tidied up" by tendencies to normalize the unexpected and by tendencies to confirm one's expectations of what is crucial. Both of these tendencies are akin to climbing back into the uniforms of prevailing paradigms. These authors have done what they can to point up "naked truths" close to scenes where people struggle for alertness and grasp. It is now up to the reader to linger over those truths, delay their flight back into accustomed uniforms, and clothe themselves differently. To do that is to enact the soul of this book.

Karl E. Weick
University of Michigan

REFERENCES

Cohen, E.A. and Gooch, J. (1990) *Military Misfortunes: The Anatomy of Failure in War*. New York: Vintage.

Gardner, J.W. (1968) *No Easy Victories*. New York: Harper.

Harmon-Jones, E. and Mills, J. (eds.) (1999) *Cognitive Dissonance: Progress on a Pivotal Theory in Social Psychology*. Washington, DC: American Psychological Assn.

Sills, D.L. and Merton, R.K. (eds.) (1991) *International Encyclopedia of the Social Sciences: Social Science Quotations*. New York: Macmillan.

1

Introduction: Watersheds of Organizational Learning and Knowledge Management

Mark Easterby-Smith and Marjorie A. Lyles

Introduction

The fields of organizational learning and knowledge management have developed quickly over the last decade, and the academic literature has demonstrated increasing diversity and specialization. Some people might therefore claim that it is foolhardy to seek to cover the full range of the literature within one volume. Our response is to highlight four features of the current literature which provide a general rationale for compiling this handbook.

First is the novelty and speed of development of the field. Across the patch there was very little activity before 1990, and in some sub-areas almost everything dates after 1995. The speed of development, coupled with the lead times of publishing, means it is hard to develop a cumulative sense to the field where studies and publications are able to build systematically on previous work. We have therefore encouraged the authors who have contributed to the handbook to locate their sub-fields within a time line which shows how the present position has evolved from prior work, and then to speculate on potential future directions.

The second feature is the increasing diversity and specialization of the field. This has led to tighter definitions and the isolation of problems such as the political implications of organizational learning and knowledge management; but it has also led to developments taking place in parallel which result in limited awareness of what is happening elsewhere at the same time. There is therefore a need to locate different sub-areas in relation to each other, so that overlaps and potential areas of synergy can be identified. In preparing the chapters of the book we have ensured that authors in related areas received copies of each other's drafts so that they could also identify potential commonalities and differences, whether they be overlaps of subject material, similar theoretical roots, or shared problem areas. This also implies a need for some mapping exercises, and several chapters (in addition to this one) aim to do just that.

The third feature is that debates and arguments have started to flourish largely as a consequence of this diversity. Debates have focused around the definition of terms and the meaning of concepts, the appropriateness of methods of inquiry, ways of influencing learning processes within organizations, and the purposes to which we should put our knowledge of organizational learning and knowledge management. These are highly desirable because they lead to clarification of terms, sharpening of distinctions, and development of new ideas. Consequently, we have encouraged authors to identify ongoing debates in their areas; in a number of places we have juxtaposed chapters that represent different perspectives on particular contemporary debates.

Fourth, despite the growing diversity we have also been surprised at the number of citations that appear repeatedly across the chapters of the Handbook, which suggests that there still remains considerable commonality in the field. If we reach back to some of the earlier papers, there are several common points of departure, which may have become a form of "tacit knowledge" that underlies the work of most scholars. Accordingly, we devote much of this chapter to looking at the sources of key concepts, and to the works that have had a disproportionate influence on the evolution of the field. We see these as being similar to the watersheds of rivers which provide essential starting points for distinct streams, but which may subsequently become forgotten as the downstream rivers gather both strength and importance.

This opening chapter has three main sections. In the first section we offer a preliminary mapping of the field that is covered by the Handbook, which is elaborated in the chapters that follow. In the second section we present an analysis of the citations given by the chapters, and since we are interested in the origins of the field we have concentrated publications primarily dating from before 1996. One reflection of the newness of the field is that there are less than 800 citations to publications predating 1996, out of a total of over 2,200 citations across the 30 invited chapters of the book. In the third section we develop the theme of watersheds by focusing on the older publications, some of which score well in our analysis of citations, and all of which appear to have had a significant impact on the evolution of the fields of organizational learning and knowledge management.

THE FIELD AND THE SCOPE OF THE HANDBOOK

For reasons of space, the title of the Handbook refers to organizational learning and knowledge management; but two other important topics, "the learning organization" and "organizational knowledge," are also covered here. At first glance they may all seem very similar, but there are a number of important distinctions which we will explain below (also see Vera and Crossan, in chapter 7). The distinction between the first two terms was clearly articulated by Tsang (1997) to the extent that *organizational learning* refers to the study of the learning processes of and within organizations, largely from an academic point of view. The aims of such studies are therefore primarily to understand and critique what is taking place. On the other hand, the *learning organization* is seen as an entity, an ideal type of organization, which has the capacity to learn effectively and hence to prosper. Those who write about learning organizations generally aim to understand how to create and improve this learning capacity, and therefore they have a more practical and performative agenda. We have gathered together papers in part II of this volume that reflect different aspects of the domain covered by these two terms.

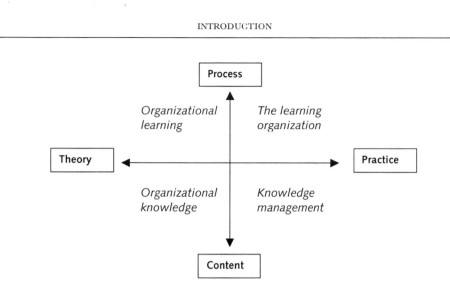

FIGURE 1.1   Mapping of key topics in the Handbook

A similar distinction can be made between the terms *organizational knowledge* and *knowledge management*. Those who write about the former often adopt a philosophical slant in trying to understand and conceptualize the nature of knowledge that is contained within organizations. Hence many of the discussions relate around distinctions between individual and organizational knowledge, or whether the distinction between tacit and explicit knowledge is useful. Those who write about the latter generally adopt a technical approach aimed at creating ways of disseminating and leveraging knowledge in order to enhance organizational performance. The role and design of information technology is often central to such discussions. Part III of the Handbook considers issues in the domain of organizational knowledge and knowledge management.

In figure 1.1 we offer an initial mapping of these four terms. We have used the dichotomies of theory–practice and content–process to organize the mapping. The first of these dichotomies follows the concerns of academics against those of practitioners, as described above. Even this is not necessarily straightforward. For example, a critical study of a learning organization would fit into the organizational learning box, and a study of the way knowledge is constructed within corporate knowledge management systems would belong to the organizational knowledge box.

The second dichotomy, the distinction between learning and knowledge, also seems fairly obvious: knowledge being the stuff (or content) that the organization possesses, and learning being the process whereby it acquires this stuff. Again, things are not quite so simple, as several of the chapters will demonstrate. For example, some chapters build on the paper by Cook and Brown (1999) which distinguishes between the epistemologies of possession and practice. In this case "possession" fits well with the view of knowledge as content, but the epistemology of practice (or knowing) fits more closely with the process of learning from experience. We mention these potential limitations in passing because we still believe that it is valuable to start with some clear organizing principles, as an initial map for the reader. But we would hope that those who get to the end of the book will become very clear about the inadequacies of such dichotomies!

There are also a number of themes and issues which cut across the whole field and therefore touch on all four quadrants of figure 1.1. Some of these are fundamental issues about the nature of knowledge (Tsoukas, chapter 21) and the processes of learning (Carroll et al., chapter 29); others relate to the role played by politics (Cross and Prusak, chapter 23), culture (Taylor and Osland, chapter 11), emotion (Fineman, chapter 28), forgetting (Martin de Holan and Phillips, chapter 20), social identity (Child and Rodrigues, chapter 27) and organizational identity (Corley and Gioia, chapter 31).

Many of the chapters review and update key concepts such as organizational capabilities (Zollo and Winter, chapter 30), knowledge creation (von Krogh, chapter 19; Bettis and Wong, chapter 17), communities of practice (Plaskoff, chapter 9), stickiness (Szulanski and Capetta, chapter 26) and absorptive capacity (Van Den Bosch et al., chapter 14). Not only is it possible to locate these concepts on the general map of figure 1.1, but it is also worth noting that they are often informed by different disciplinary and ontological assumptions (Easterby-Smith, 1997). That is why we have grouped a number of chapters into part I, which considers the disciplinary perspectives underlying current developments in the field. We therefore hope that these chapters will enable readers to locate more clearly the different chapters in subsequent parts of the book.

This brings us to the next section of our initial chapter. On the grounds that a knowledge of the past is useful in making sense of the present, our aim here is to consider some of the formative influences in the field from a historical perspective. Thereby we hope to explain both similarities and differences between distinct parts of the field.

MAJOR SOURCES

If we start with the four terms in figure 1.1, although all of them are relatively new, some are newer than others. Thus the idea of knowledge management only emerged in the mid 1990s, whereas the first references to organizational learning appeared as far back as the early 1960s (Cyert and March, 1963; Cangelosi and Dill, 1965). But all four areas draw on literature and ideas that are older than their immediate concerns, and in a number of places there are overlaps between these initial sources.

Moreover, the field as a whole has been characterized by sudden surges of interest in particular topics, often followed soon after by rapid decline. (See Scarbrough and Swan, chapter 25, for further discussion of fads and fashions). These surges can often be explained by the changes in the business or technological environment. But literature also plays a significant part, and a number of books or papers have managed to capitalize on latent interest which then creates a major sub-industry in its own right. One obvious example is the book by Senge (1990) which is one of the most cited texts in this volume, and amongst sources in this general field, within the Social Science Citation Index (SSCI), it is second only to Cyert and March. Although Senge was not the first person to coin the term "learning organization," it was the publication of his book which led to international awareness of the learning organization across both academic and practitioner communities. Thereafter, many large companies started claiming that they were learning organizations, or that they were aspiring to this status, and academics rushed to identify the characteristics of learning organizations, or to critique and deconstruct the very concept. As such, the publication of Peter Senge's book represents a watershed, in the same way that Peters and Waterman (1982) represented a watershed for academics, consultants and practitioners in the previous decade.

Our aim now is to examine systematically the chapters in this book to see if there are patterns that can be discerned. We do this by looking at all the citations for publications that predate 1996, where the content of the item has some relevance to the fields of organizational learning and management. In a few cases we have included references that are more recent because, as with knowledge management, the topic is so new that hardly any references exist before 1996.

In table 1.1 we list the authors of books or papers according to how many of the chapters in this handbook have cited them. For each cited work we give the author names and date, but we do not provide full bibliographical details at the end of this chapter because all are cited in subsequent chapters. The full citations for many of these papers can be found in chapter 2, and if not there, we indicate the next chapter in which details can be found.

There are a few points to note about this table. First, the list provides most of the names one would expect to see. If we take the total number of citations for authors then the leading figures in the field are James March, Ikujiro Nonaka, Chris Argyris, Peter Senge, and George Huber, along with the pairs of Brown and Duguid, Nelson and Winter, Cohen and Levinthal, and Kogut and Zander – no surprises here. Indeed the impact of these authors is also reflected in the SSCI which gives counts for each of these publications in excess of 250. The highest scores in the SSCI, each around 2,000, are achieved by Cyert and March (1963), Senge (1990) and Nelson and Winter (1982), as of July 2002.

Second, the dominance of the top publications is balanced by considerable diversity once one gets down to the level of detail. Thus, although the top 13 were cited by at least one-third of the authors contributing to this handbook, nearly half of the papers were only cited once or twice. This is because many of the authors are working in specialist areas which have limited overlap with others. And finally, the newness of the field is indicated by the fact that there are very few publications (only 12) which are cited more than twice and which appeared before 1980 (these have been highlighted in bold type in table 1.1). These older publications seem particularly interesting since they have stood the test of time and are continuing to influence leading contemporary scholars, and we will look further at some of them in the next section of the chapter.

WATERSHEDS

As mentioned above, we are using the term "watershed" to indicate a significant turning-point in the development of the subject area. In making sense of key watersheds we need to take account of (1) the absolute frequency of citation; (2) the timing of each publication; (3) the topic of the paper that does the citing; and (4) the text in which the citation is embedded. Given the natural tendency of academics to cite more recent work, there is

TABLE 1.1   Frequency of citations in this Handbook

16 hits	*15 hits*
Nonaka and Takeuchi (1995)	None
14 hits	*13 hits*
Brown and Duguid (1991)	Cohen and Levinthal (1990)
Nelson and Winter (1982)	Huber (1991)
	Kogut and Zander (1992) (ch. 5)
12 hits	*11 hits*
Levitt and March (1988) (ch. 3)	Senge (1990)
March (1991)	
10 hits	*9 hits*
Argyris and Schön (1978)	Grant (1996) (ch. 5)
8 hits	*7 hits*
Cyert and March (1963)	Leonard-Barton (1995) (ch. 11)
Daft and Weick (1984)	
Davenport and Prusak (1998) (ch. 4)	
Fiol and Lyles (1985)	
Hedberg (1981) (ch. 8)	
Nonaka (1994)	
Szulanski (1996) (ch. 12)	
6 hits	*5 hits*
Barney (1991) (ch. 5)	Cook and Yanow (1993) (ch. 3)
Lave and Wenger (1991)	**Dewey (1916, 1933, 1938)**
Miner and Mezias (1995)	**Duncan and Weiss (1979)** (ch. 8)
Nahapiet and Ghoshal (1998) (ch. 12)	Lyles (1988) (ch. 13)
Walsh and Ungson (1991)	Orr (1990)
	Penrose (1959) (ch. 15)
	Polanyi (1958/1962) (ch. 12)
	Simon (1991) (ch. 5)
	Weick (1995)
	Weick and Roberts (1993)
	Winter (1987) (ch. 5)
4 hits	*3 hits*
Argote, Beckman and Epple (1990) (ch. 20)	**Allen (1977)**
Boland and Tenkasi (1995) (ch. 4)	**Argyris (1977)**
Hamel (1991) (ch. 12)	Bohn (1994) (ch. 4)
Henderson and Clark (1990) (ch. 15)	**Candelosi and Dill (1965)** (ch. 7)
Inkpen and Crossan (1995) (ch. 12)	Cohen and Levinthal (1989) (ch. 13)
Kim (1993)	Darr, Argote and Epple (1994) (ch. 13)
Kogut (1988) (ch. 7)	de Geus (1988) (ch. 7)
Lave (1991)	Dougherty (1992) (ch. 10)
Leonard-Barton (1992) (ch. 7)	Dougherty (1996) (ch. 18)
March, Sproull and Tamuz (1995) (ch. 17)	Garvin (1993) (ch. 8)
Nicolini and Meznar (1995)	Hamel and Prahalad (1989) (ch. 15)
Spender (1996) (ch. 15)	**Hayek (1945/1949)** (ch. 5)

TABLE 1.1   *Continued*

Tsoukas (1996) (ch. 4)	Lave (1988)
Zander and Kogut (1995) (ch. 15)	Lipman and Rumelt (1982) (ch. 15)
	Lyles and Schwenk (1992) (ch. 5)
	March and Simon (1958) (ch. 18)
	Nevis, diBella and Gould (1995) (ch. 3)
	Pisano (1994) (ch. 7)
	Prahalad and Bettis (1986) (ch. 12)
	Prahalad and Hapsleigh (1990) (ch. 15)
	Ring and Van de Ven (1992) (ch. 21)
	Saxenian (1990) (ch. 12)
	Stehr (1994) (ch. 19)
	Williamson (1975) (ch. 21)
2 hits	*1 hit*
71 further papers	241 further papers
Total number of hits included in analysis: 797	Total number of citations in the Handbook: 2218

Note: Bold type indicates publications appearing before 1980.

a good case for giving extra weight to some of the older works which have been cited, especially where they are identified by authors working in different fields.

On this basis we may identify three main groups of literature as the timeline moves forward: (1) *classic* works, which pre-date the identification of the ideas of organizational learning and knowledge management per se; (2) *foundational* works, which represent some of the first writings that set the agenda for subsequent work; and (3) *popularizing* works, which have acted as the most visible watersheds in the development of the field. It is important to note in passing that we do not regard the third term as being in any way pejorative; indeed, some of the "popularizing" works were highly scholarly and all of them managed to generate streams of extremely valuable work. It is not possible to give a single time-band within which the three groups of literature appeared because different sub-areas have emerged at different times and at different rates; hence, the relevant watersheds come at slightly different times. We start with classic works, which are presented for the whole field; we then consider separately the time lines within each of the four sub-areas defined at the outset of this chapter.

Classic works

Here we identify four main authors who have had a significant influence and who were active before the earliest mentions of terms such as organizational learning appeared: John Dewey, Michel Polanyi, Edith Penrose, and Frederick Hayek. They are not the most frequently cited in the present volume, partly because they have been overlaid by more recent authors (and, as academics, we are encouraged to focus more on recent publications than on classic works). Nevertheless, each of them has a substantial rating in the SSCI (running to several thousand citations for Dewey, Polanyi, and Hayek). We comment briefly here on their contributions primarily in the light of chapters within this Handbook, and in a few cases we will also refer to other key works in the field, including those listed in table 1.1.

Dewey is the only one of these authors who explicitly focused his attention on learning. His ideas of learning from experience fit most easily into models of individuals learning within organizations (DeFillippi and Ornstein, chapter 2), and the notion of iterations between experience and reflection is frequently seen to underlie action learning, which is one of the key tools of the learning organization (Pedler et al., 1989). Dewey's view that learning takes place through social interaction and yet cannot be passed from person to person as if it were a physical object is also seen to underlie the social learning perspective (Elkjaer, chapter 3). Other authors who take a social constructionist approach to organizational knowledge (Cook and Brown, 1999; Nicolini and Meznar, 1995) rely on Dewey's heritage, and Nonaka and Takeuchi (1995) acknowledge the contribution of Dewey's philosophical contribution to "pragmatism" in asserting that there cannot be a clear distinction between the observer and the observed.

Polanyi is best known for his distinction between tacit and explicit knowledge. The key idea of "tacitness" has parallels to Dewey's experiential learning, because it is something that is held within the individual. Naturally, there are many different interpretations of what this all means. One version of tacit knowledge is that it is conscious, but not articulated; another version is that it is unconscious and hence unarticulable, as Tsoukas discusses (chapter 21). Polanyi's ideas are based on philosophical analysis and argument, rather than on any empirical investigation, and of course, some would argue that the notion of tacit knowledge cannot be examined empirically because it is unconscious.

The influence of Polanyi is most evident in contemporary discussions about the nature of organizational knowledge. The idea of tacit knowledge is important for those trying to understand the roots of competitive advantage because it is the unexpressed knowledge and experiences of organizations which provide the unique competencies that cannot easily be replicated by competitors (Barney, 1991). While tacit knowledge may give unique advantages to a company, it also poses problems because it cannot easily be moved across cultural boundaries (Makino and Inkpen, chapter 12), nor is it easy to move between different parts of the same organization (Szulanski and Capetta, chapter 26).

Penrose is cited less frequently, but her ideas on the significance of the internal (human) resources of the firm are fundamental and, as she puts it, "the dominant role that increasing knowledge plays in economic processes" (1959: 77). Chakravarthy, Doz, McEvily, and Rau (chapter 15) note the importance of "excess resources" within an organization which can lead to innovation, which parallels the need for slack to allow experimentation. There are many other points made by Penrose which mirror those made both by her contemporaries and by recent authors. Thus, in discussing the role of top teams, she comments that "the administrative group is more than a collection of individuals; it is a collection of individuals who have had experience in working together, for only in this way can teamwork be developed" (1959: 46). And "success depends upon a gradual building up of a group of officials experienced in working together" (1959: 52). These views anticipate the ideas of social constructionists who emphasize that organizations know more than the sum of the knowledge of individuals within them; it also emphasizes the role of experience and the fact that "Knowledge comes from formal teaching and from personal experience" (1959: 53), which is very close to the distinction that Polanyi was developing at the same time between explicit and personal (tacit) knowledge.

It is not surprising that the work of Hayek is seen to underlie the thinking of those who adopt an economics perspective on organizational learning and knowledge. In particular, his view that one of the fundamental problems of economics is to use the knowledge there is initially dispersed around different individuals in a way that contributes to producing good decisions for the organization or society as a whole (see Foss and Mahnke, chapter 5). But he has also had a wider influence, possibly because his 1945 paper was extensively quoted by March and Simon (1958). Here, the emphasis that he places on the knowledge held by individuals naturally focuses attention on "the knowledge of the particular circumstances of time and place" (Hayek, 1949: 80), which may be seen to anticipate the current attention given to "situated" knowledge. Moreover, it starts to provide a methodological justification for the use of qualitative methods that are sensitive to contextual factors, such as narrative method, in trying to understand processes of organizational learning (Bartel and Garud, chapter 16).

Not only are the contributions of these four authors still recognized by contemporary scholars, but we can also see that their ideas overlapped with each other in several respects. But all of this predates the invention of the idea of organizational learning, which we will discuss in the following section.

Organizational learning

The idea that an organization could *learn* in ways that were independent of the individuals within it was the key breakthrough, which was first articulated in Cyert and March (1963). Evidently the book was the product of much discussion and debate which had been going on among the team at Carnegie Tech during the 1950s (Augier, 2001) and it was foreshadowed, but not explicitly, by March and Simon (1958). Cyert and March propose a general theory of organizational learning as part of a model of decision making within the firm, and emphasize the role of rules, procedures, and routines in response to external shocks and which are more or less likely to be adopted according to whether or not they lead to positive consequences for the organization. A number of specific ideas were outlined in their book, which were subsequently developed further by other scholars. Noteworthy points in the book are: the idea that it is through "organizational learning processes [that] . . . the firm adapts to its environment" (1963: 84); the view that "the firm learns from its experience" (1963: 100); and an early version of the distinction between single and double-loop learning: "An organization . . . changes its behavior in response to short-run feedback from the environment according to some fairly well-defined rules. It changes rules in response to longer-run feedback according to some more general rules, and so on" (1963: 101/2).

The book by Cyert and March could perhaps be described as *the* foundational work of organizational learning. But others made fundamental contributions in the early days. Cangelosi and Dill (1965) produced the first publication in which the words "organizational learning" appeared in the title, and although the paper is based on tendentious data, it already makes a distinct contribution to debates in the field because it starts to argue against the neo rationality underlying the Cyert and March model. It is suggested that the model may be appropriate for established organizations in stable circumstances, but that it has limited relevance to organizations developing within dynamic circumstances.

Thus, Cangelosi and Dill propose a model based on tensions between individual and organizational levels of learning, which is similar to the notion of organizational learning being a discontinuous process (Argyris and Schön, 1978), and is reflected in the contemporary work of Crossan et al. (1999).

The book by Argyris and Schön (1978) was very important since it laid out the field as a whole very clearly, and the distinction between organizations with and without the capacity to engage in significant learning (Models II and I) received a great deal of attention. In it, the authors take a different critique of the rationalist assumptions of Cyert and March by pointing out that human behavior within organizations frequently does not follow the lines of economic rationality. Both individuals and organizations seek to protect themselves from the unpleasant experience of learning by establishing defensive routines. During the 1970s and 1980s there were a number of other *foundational* works, such as Hedberg (1981), Shrivastra (1983), Daft and Weick (1984) and Fiol and Lyles (1985), which made important contributions to the definitions of terminology, and to deeper perspectives on organizational learning, such as the distinction between learning and unlearning.

Perhaps the most significant *popularizing* force in the study of organizational learning was the publication of the Special Edition of *Organization Science* in 1991. This contains a number of highly cited articles including March (1991), Huber (1991), Epple et al. (1991), and Simon (1991) which have been very influential, and have essentially set the academic research agenda for much of the 1990s. These papers follow, in the main, the neo-rationalist tradition which suggests that it is desirable to maximize the efficient use of knowledge in organizations, while recognizing that there are substantial, largely human, obstacles in its way. Many of the chapters in the current volume build explicitly upon their foundations (for example, Salk and Simonin, chapter 13; Van Den Bosch et al., chapter 15; and Szulanski and Cappetta, chapter 26).

However, it is also interesting that the same issue of *Organization Science* included a paper by Brown and Duguid (1991) which has come to represent an alternative tradition that regards the social processes of organizational learning as pre-eminent. This tradition has been fuelled by the work of Lave (1988), Orr (1990), Lave and Wenger (1991), Cook and Yanow (1993) and Nicolini and Meznar (1995). In the current volume it is evident that it underpins the work of authors such as Hayes and Walsham (chapter 4), Taylor and Osland (chapter 11), von Krogh (chapter 19), Cross and Prusak (chapter 23), and Bartel and Garud (chapter 16). From the early 1990s these two traditions have developed largely independently and have had increasing difficulty in communicating with each other. We hope, therefore, that in this Handbook there is sufficient coverage of both traditions to encourage better mutual understanding and a new dialogue between the two communities.

The learning organization

The idea of the learning organization is of more recent provenance. It emerged towards the end of the 1980s largely on the basis of European work, with UK authors such as Garratt (1988) and Pedler et al. (1989) making early contributions, although the paper by de Geus (1988), which was published in the *Harvard Business Review*, brought the concept to wider attention. Nevertheless, the major watershed was the book by Senge (1990) which attracted enormous interest particularly because companies and consultants were search-ing for new ideas to replace the largely discredited concepts of corporate excellence (Peters and Waterman, 1982). Senge's book was both a *foundational* work and a *popularizer* because it rapidly became a key source for academics as well as an inspiration for practitioners. His ideas were highly attractive because they provided the potential for renewal and growth, with an underpinning of both technical and social ideas drawn from the systems dynam-ics developed by Jay Forrester at MIT, the psychodynamic organizational theory developed by Chris Argyris, and the process consultation of Ed Schein.

Despite the huge success of Senge's initial book, the idea has not been widely adopted by the North American academic community,[1] and it has continued to be primarily a Euro-pean affair (for example, Swieringa and Wierdsma, 1992; Burgoyne et al., 1994; Pearn et al., 1995; and Probst and Büchel, 1997). The few academics who write in the USA on this issue, for example, Dixon (1994) and Torbert (1994) are often influenced by European ideas, such as the work of Revans (1980) on action learning. In the present volume, DiBella (chapter 8) provides a valuable updating and development of the concepts related to the learning organization by proposing a more flexible method than that originally laid down by Senge. Plaskoff (chapter 9) describes strategies for implementing learning in organiza-tions using ideas drawn from the communities of practice literature, and Edmondson and Woolley (chapter 10) stress the importance of evaluating interventions because the success of learning innovations may vary considerably in different parts of the same organization.

Given the lack of a strong North American academic tradition, looking at the "learn-ing organization," it is not surprising that some of the best critical literature on the subject has come from European authors (Coopey, 1995; Coopey and Burgoyne, 2000; Snell and Chak, 1998). The chapters in this volume by Scarbrough and Swan (chapter 25) and by Fineman (chapter 28) also follow this tradition.

Organizational knowledge

Organizational knowledge as a subject of study has been around for a long time, but primarily within the economics community. Thus, as we have noted above, the "classical" influence of economists such as Hayek and Penrose, and the philosopher Polanyi, has been significant. One of the major *foundational* works, also from an economics perspective, is Nelson and Winter (1982), which is particularly strong on the importance of "tacit knowing" as a basis for individual and organizational competence. Other foundational works emerged in the early 1990s, especially from two special issues of the *Journal of Man-agement Studies* on knowledge work (Alvesson, 1993; Starbuck, 1992, 1993); the elaboration of six different forms of organizational knowing by Blackler (1995) was an important foun-dational work.

But the key *popularizing* influence was Ikujiro Nonaka, who produced a series of papers and a highly respected book (Nonaka and Takeuchi, 1995), that set the standard for the emergent field with a rich mixture of concepts and field data. Key ideas expounded in the book include: the notion of knowledge creation through transformations of tacit and explicit knowledge; the importance of national culture and philosophy to understanding the construction and communication of knowledge; the interrelationship between the policy domain and the operational levels in the creation of knowledge; and the general principle that most dichotomies, such as tacit/explicit and mind/body, are false.

The influence of Polanyi is therefore strongly evident in the works of dominant figures like Nelson and Winter, and Nonaka; his ideas are also central to recent debates about the nature of organizational knowledge (Spender, 1996) as well as the contributions in this Handbook by von Krogh (chapter 19), Szulanski and Capetta (chapter 26), Makino and Inkpen (chapter 12), Tsoukas (chapter 21), Calhoun and Starbuck (chapter 24), and indirectly in the work of Van Wijk et al. on knowledge networks (chapter 22). But it is also possible to see the influence of Hayek and other neoclassical economists in Nonaka's discussion about the problem of resolving the perspectives of the policy and operational domains – which, Nonaka argues, can be solved through the process of knowledge conversion.

Knowledge management

The idea of knowledge management has arrived very recently; indeed, as Davenport and Prusak (2000) comment, it was still in its infancy only in 1998. Thus, we are not able to see a linear development over time in this area; development has been rapid and chaotic, even though it is still possible to discern some decisive factors. To some extent, knowledge management has gained academic legitimacy on the back of Nonaka's work, but the driving force in the corporate world has come from major consultancy companies seeking to capitalize on the enormous potential of information technology in a period following disenchantment with the methods and prescriptions of re-engineering (Hammer and Champy, 1993; Grint and Case, 1998). The idea is pretty simple, since it starts with the neo-economic view of the strategic value of organizational knowledge and then uses familiar IT software such as databases and electronic conferencing to facilitate the acquisition, sharing, storage, retrieval, and utilization of knowledge. As such, the conceptual logic follows the technical view of organizational learning as expounded by Huber (1991) and colleagues.

However, there are now critiques being mounted of knowledge management initiatives precisely on the grounds that they ignore the social architecture of knowledge exchange within organizations (Hansen et al., 1999), and it is not surprising that some of these are coming from the "social" school of organizational learning theorists (for example, Brown and Duguid, 2000). Given the novelty of the area, it is hard to offer definitive influences other than Nonaka and the twin traditions within the literature on organizational learning. Perhaps the key formative work will come to be recognized as the book by Davenport and Prusak (1998) which has received eight citations among the 30 invited chapters in this Handbook, and at the time of writing had already clocked 150 hits in the SSCI. Naturally, both of these authors influence the contributions by Hayes and Walsham (chapter 4) and Alavi and Tiwana (chapter 6).

CONCLUSIONS

In this opening chapter we have offered a general mapping of the field covered by this Handbook and have also tried to demonstrate some of the inter-linkages both over time and between parallel, but apparently independent, areas of development. It has also been possible to identify some significant influences, which predate the invention of the concepts of organizational learning and knowledge management, and which might be seen as providing a common heritage, or similar watersheds.

It should be clear by now that the different sub-areas of the field are at different stages of maturity. Some of them are major rivers, which have flown gently for a long time; some are shorter streams, which flow very quickly; and others are sudden torrents, which emerge almost overnight – and which could disappear again equally quickly. The chapters which follow in this book attempt to locate current research perspectives and issues in their areas within a general time-line, which includes reviewing past trends and speculating briefly on future directions. All of the chapters are original, and most have been commissioned and written specifically for this Handbook. Those that are located within more established areas naturally have more material to draw on which is directly relevant to their current interests; those in the newer areas are often engaged in delineating their fields for the first time and trying to locate them in relation to older traditions.

It is our hope that many of the chapters will eventually become seen as "foundational works" because, in the former case, they manage to provide clear maps and overviews of their areas, and, in the latter case, they are able to establish the agendas for future research. As for the Handbook as a whole, we hope that it will be seen as a major statement of the state of the field at the start of the 21st century, and in the final chapter we speculate, based on some further research, about where it might be heading next.

NOTE

1. Even though James March uses the term "learning organization" in March (1988), it is without the normative implications that the term subsequently adopted following the work of Senge (1990).

REFERENCES

Alvesson, M. (1993) Organization as Rhetoric: Knowledge-intensive Firms and the Struggle with Ambiguity. *Journal of Management Studies*, 30: 997–1016.

Argyris, C. and Schön, D.A. (1978) *Organizational Learning: A Theory of Action Perspective*. Reading, MA: Addison-Wesley.

Augier, M. (2001) Simon Says: Bounded Rationality Matters. Introduction and Interview. *Journal of Management Inquiry*, 10 (3): 268–75.

Barney, J. (1991) Firm Resources and Sustained Competitive Advantage. *Journal of Management*, 17 (1): 99–120.

Blackler, F. (1995) Knowledge, Work and Organizations. *Organization Studies*, 16 (6): 1021–45.

Brown, J.S. and Duguid, P. (1991) Organizational Learning and Communities-of-practice: Toward a Unified View of Working, Learning and Innovation. *Organization Science*, 2 (1): 40–57.

Brown, J.S. and Duguid, P. (2000) *The Social Life of Information*. Boston, MA: Harvard Business School Press.

Burgoyne, J., Pedler, M., and Boydell, T. (1994) *Towards the Learning Company: Concepts and Practices*. London: McGraw-Hill.

Cangelosi, V.E. and Dill, W.R. (1965) Organizational Learning: Observations Toward a Theory. *Administrative Science Quarterly*, 10 (2): 175–203.

Cook, S.D.N. and Brown, J.S. (1999) Bridging Epistemologies: The Generative Dance between Organizational Knowledge and Organizational Knowing. *Organization Science*, 10 (4): 381–400.

Cook, S.D.N. and Yanow, D. (1993) Culture and Organizational Learning. *Journal of Management Inquiry*, 2 (4): 373–90.

Coopey, J. (1995) The Learning Organization: Power, Politics and Ideology. *Management Learning*, 26 (2): 193–213.

Coopey, J. and Burgoyne, J. (2000) Politics and Organizational Learning. *Journal of Management Studies*, 37 (6): 869–85.

Crossan, M., Lane, H.W., and White, R.E. (1999) An Organizational Learning Framework: From Intuition to Institution. *Academy of Management Review*, 24 (3): 522–37.

Cyert, R.M. and March, J.G. (1963) *A Behavioural Theory of the Firm*. Englewood Cliffs, NJ: Prentice-Hall.

Daft, R.L. and Wieck, K.L. (1984) Toward a Model of Organizations as Interpretation Systems. *Academy of Management Review*, 9 (2): 284–95.

Davenport, T.H. and Prusak, L. (1998/2000) *Working Knowledge: How Organizations Manage What They Know*. Boston, MA: Harvard Business School Press.

De Geus, A.P. (1988) Planning as Learning. *Harvard Business Review*, Vol 66 (2): 70–4.

Dewey, J. (1916) *Democracy and Education: An Introduction to the Philosophy of Education*. London: Collier-Macmillan.

Dixon, N. (1994) *The Organizational Learning Cycle: How We Can Learn Collectively*. London: McGraw-Hill.

Easterby-Smith, M. (1997) Disciplines of Organizational Learning. *Human Relations*, 50 (9): 1085–116.

Epple, D., Argote, L., and Devadas, R. (1991) Organizational Learning Curves: A Method for Investigating Inter-plant Transfer of Knowledge Acquired through Learning by Doing. *Organization Science*, 2 (1): 58–70.

Fiol, C.M. and Lyles, M.A. (1985) Organizational Learning. *Academy of Management Review*. 10 (4): 803–13.

Garratt, B. (1987) *The Learning Organization*. London: Fontana.

Grint, K. and Case, P. (1998) The Violent Rhetoric of Re-engineering: Management Consultancy on the Offensive. *Journal of Management Studies*, 35 (5): 557–77.

Hammer, M. and Champy, J. (1993) *Reengineering the Corporation*. London: Nicholas Brealey.

Hansen, M.T., Nohria, N., and Tierney, T. (1999) What's Your Strategy for Managing Knowledge? *Harvard Business Review*, March-April: 106–16.

Hayek, F.A. (1949) The Use of Knowledge in Society. In F.A. Hayek (ed.), *Individualism and Economic Order*. London: Routledge and Kegan Paul. Originally published in *American Economic Review* (1945), XXXV (4): 519–30.

Hedberg, B. (1981) How Organizations Learn and Unlearn. In P.C. Nystrom and W.H. Starbuck (eds.), *Handbook of Organizational Design*. London: Cambridge University Press.

Huber, G.P. (1991) Organizational Learning: The Contributing Processes and the Literature. *Organization Science*, 2 (1): 88–115.

Lave, J. (1988) *Cognition in Practice: Mind, Mathematics and Culture in Everyday Life*. Cambridge: Cambridge University Press.

Lave, J. and Wenger, E. (1991) *Situated Learning: Legitimate Peripheral Participation*. Cambridge: Cambridge University Press.

March, J.G. (1988) *Decisions and Organizations*. Oxford: Blackwell.

March, J.G. (1991) Exploration and Exploitation in Organizational Learning. *Organization Science*, 2 (1): 71–87.

March, J.G. and Simon, H.A. (1958) *Organizations*. New York: Wiley.

Nelson, R.R. and Winter, S.G. (1982) *An Evolutionary Theory of Economic Change*. Cambridge, Mass: Harvard University Press.

Nicolini, D. and Meznar, M.B. (1995) The Social Construction of Organizational Learning: Concepts and Practical Issues in the Field. *Human Relations*, 48 (7): 727–46.

Nonaka, I. and Takeuchi, H. (1995) *The Knowledge-Creating Company: How Japanese Companies Create the Dynamics of Innovation*. Oxford: Oxford University Press.

Orr, J. (1990) Sharing Knowledge, Celebrating Identity: War Stories and Community Memory in a Service Culture. In D.S. Middleton and D. Edwards (eds.), *Collective Remembering: Memory in Society*. Beverly Hills, CA: Sage.

Pearn, M., Roderick, C., and Mulrooney, C. (1995) *Learning Organizations in Practice*. London: McGraw-Hill.

Pedler, M., Boydell, T., and Burgoyne, J.G. (1989) Towards the Learning Company. *Management Education and Development*, 20 (1): 1–8.

Penrose, E.T. (1959) *The Theory of the Growth of the Firm*. Oxford: Blackwell.

Peters, T.J. and Waterman, R.H. (1982) *In Search of Excellence: Lessons from America's Best Run Companies*. New York: Harper and Row.

Polanyi, M. (1959) *The Study of Man*. London: Routledge and Kegan Paul.

Polanyi, M. (1966) *The Tacit Dimension*. London: Routledge and Kegan Paul.

Probst, G. and Büchel, B. (1997) *Organizational Learning: The Competitive Advantage of the Future*. London: Prentice-Hall.

Revans, R.W. (1980) *Action Learning: New Techniques for Management*. London: Blond and Briggs.

Senge, P.M. (1990) *The Fifth Discipline: The Art and Practice of the Learning Organization*. London: Century Business.

Shrivastava, P. (1983) A Typology of Organizational Learning Systems. *Journal of Management Studies*, 20 (1): 7–28.

Simon, H. (1991) Bounded Rationality and Organizational Learning. *Organization Science*, 2 (1): 125–34.

Snell, R. and Chak, A.M-K. (1998) The Learning Organization: Learning and Empowerment for Whom? *Management Learning*, 29 (3): 337–64.

Spender, J-C. (1996) Making Knowledge the Basis of a Dynamic Theory of the Firm. *Strategic Management Journal*, 19 (special issue): 45–62.

Starbuck, W.H. (1992) Learning by Knowledge-intensive Firms. *Journal of Management Studies*, 29: 713–40.

Starbuck, W.H. (1993) Keeping a Butterfly and an Elephant in a House of Cards: The Elements of Exceptional Success. *Journal of Management Studies*, 30: 885–922.

Swieringa, J. and Wierdsma, A. (1992) *Becoming a Learning Organization: Beyond the Learning Curve*. Wokingham, UK: Addison-Wesley.

Torbert, W.R. (1994) Managerial Learning, Organizational Learning: A Potentially Powerful Redundancy. *Management Learning*, 25 (1): 57–70.

Tsang, E.W.K. (1997) Organizational Learning and the Learning Organization: A Dichotomy between Descriptive and Prescriptive Research. *Human Relations*, 50 (1): 73–89.

Part I

DISCIPLINARY PERSPECTIVES

2

Psychological Perspectives Underlying Theories of Organizational Learning

ROBERT DEFILLIPPI AND SUZYN ORNSTEIN

CHAPTER OUTLINE

Five theoretical perspectives in psychology (biological, behavioral, cognitive, socio-cultural, and psychodynamic) are examined in terms of their usage in theories of organization learning. Analysis suggests the dominant role played by cognitive psychological perspectives. Also, psychological theory is most often employed meta-phorically within organization learning theories. Applied organization learning theories are most likely to incorporate multiple psychological perspectives. Future roles for psychology include neuro-psychological perspectives related to distributed learning and behavioral perspectives related to rewards, punishments, and learning from failure.

INTRODUCTION

The purpose of this chapter is to explore the ways in which psychological perspectives are used by scholars in the development and explanation of theories of organizational learning. This goal will be accomplished first by reviewing five dominant psychological perspectives that can be used to categorize psychological theories of learning. Next, four theoretical approaches to understanding organizational learning will be identified and then considered in terms of their reliance on underlying psychological perspectives. Finally, observations and future directions will be offered regarding the ways in which the concept of organizational learning can benefit from the discipline of psychology.

In examining the uses of psychological perspectives in theories of organizational learning, we are mindful that concepts and assumptions derived from one social science discipline may be used variously when applied within a second social science discipline. Thus, we will identify whether the theoretical concepts and assumptions dominant in the field of psychology are used in one or more of the following three ways in the field of organizational learning. First, theoretical assumptions regarding individual learning may be used reductionistically for building organization learning theories. Such reductionistic use of psychological theory largely assumes that organizational learning can be explained in terms of psychological learning principles. A second use of psychological theory is as a source of metaphors for identifying organizational learning processes that may or may not be similar to the same processes assumed for individual learning. Finally, some psychological assumptions may be embedded in organizational learning theories that presume organizational learning is an emergent process not reducible to individual learning processes, although individual learning may be a component of organizational learning.

DOMINANT THEORETICAL PERSPECTIVES IN PSYCHOLOGY

The field of psychology is devoted to understanding human behavior, mental processes, and the ways in which the interaction of these is impacted by an individual's physiology, mental state, and external environment. Not surprisingly, because humans are quite complex, many different types of explanations of behavior have been offered. These explanations come in the form of theories, models, and frameworks that can be categorized according to their underlying assumptions and explanations.

The primary assumptions and explanations that differentiate psychological models are ones that posit human behaviors ranging from (1) conscious to unconscious in origin; (2) impacted primarily by environment or heredity; (3) fixed to malleable in the future; (4) observable to inferable in interpretation; and (5) absolutist to relativist *vis-à-vis* the role of individual and society. Models and theories that share similar assumptions are classified as "perspectives." The five most distinctive perspectives are commonly referred to as "biological," "learning," "cognitive," "sociocultural," and "psychodynamic" (Tavris and Wade, 1995). Each of these five approaches will be described in turn and examples of representative theories of learning will be discussed. This information will serve as the basis for analyzing ways in which organizational learning is or is not predicated on the various theoretical perspectives in psychology.

The biological perspective

Theories and models that fit this perspective seek to explain human behavior as the result of physiology and anatomy. The underlying assumption is that "all actions, feelings, and thoughts are associated with bodily events" (Tavris and Wade, 1995: 20). New technologies that allow for the exploration of the brain (e.g., magnetic resonance imaging (MRI) and positron emission tomography scan (PET scan)) and advances in neurophysiology have contributed significantly to popularizing this perspective. This view of psychology holds that much of our appreciation of human behavior must rest on our understanding of "nature" rather than nurture (that is, heredity rather than environment).

The theories and models that exemplify this approach to understanding human behavior can most simply be classified as genetic or neurophysiological in scope. The genetic approach seeks to find universal explanations of human activities such as language, perception, emotion, and temperament. These explanations are predicated on studies of heredity (Kagan and Snidman, 1991), adaptation (Ekman and Heider, 1988), and human biology (Collins, 1991) as well as widespread observation of both human (e.g., Chomsky, 1957; Pinker, 1994) and animal behavior (cf. Harlow, 1958; Harlow and Harlow, 1966). The prime assumption underlying the learning models that fit this framework is that a complete understanding of human learning must rely on a comprehensive knowledge of the biochemistry and genetic make-up of the human brain.

The neurophysiological approach focuses explicitly on the brain and nervous system as providing the most valuable clues to understanding people's behaviors. This perspective posits that the "hardware" of the nervous system establishes boundaries and limits on behavior. A relevant area of focus within this perspective is the biology of memory. The dominant view within this area of study is that different types of information are stored in various parts of the brain (this is known as localization of function, Caramazza and Hillis, 1991). The minority view within the biology of memory is that information is distributed across wide areas of the brain (Lashley, 1950; John et al., 1986). Accordingly, brain damage or compromised neurotransmitters can severely limit an individual's memory – thereby impacting learning.

The learning perspective

This approach posits that all (or at least most) human behavior happens as the result of learning and therefore the best way in which to understand people is to examine how they learn. Behaviorism and social learning theory are the most prominent examples of this approach. Both share assumptions that learning is observable and conscious, while behaviorism takes an absolutist approach and social learning theory is more relativistic.

Behaviorism has a long and distinguished history in the field of psychology (Watson, 1925; Skinner, 1938). This approach to understanding behavior rests on the assumption that observable behaviors result from their consequences. In classical conditioning this happens as the result of pairing an unconditioned stimulus and its correspondent response (behavior) with a conditioned stimulus that comes to elicit a substantially similar response. In operant conditioning, behaviors increase or decrease in relation to their reinforcement schedule. Specifically, when a behavior is followed by a positive consequence, it increases (positive reinforcement). Behaviors followed by aversive consequences are reduced (punishment); while behaviors that are ignored tend to diminish over time (extinction) and those that help to avoid a negative consequence, increase (negative reinforcement).

Whereas the behaviorist view implies that an individual must personally experience the consequences of his/her behavior in order to "learn," the social learning model more broadly defines the process of learning. This model suggests that people can learn by watching others' behavior followed by observing and evaluating the consequences experienced by these others (Bandura, 1977). This approach differs from traditional behaviorism by suggesting that (1) people can learn by observation, (2) perception and interpretation play a role in learning, and (3) motivating beliefs can impact individual learning. Another distinction between behaviorism and social learning theory is that traditional behaviorism does not acknowledge cognitive processes, let alone try to explain them. Social learning theory on the other hand, does recognize that there is a cognitive mediation between observation and future behavior. Finally, behaviorism suggests that individual learning is solely a function of the individual whereas social learning theory posits reciprocal determinism (Bandura, 1979; also see Elkjaer's chapter 3 in this volume for a much more extensive review of social learning theory).

The cognitive perspective

Whereas the biological perspective is primarily concerned with explanations rooted in brain science, and the learning perspective focuses on observable behavior, the cognitive approach seeks to explain people by understanding their thinking, reasoning, and memory – in short, their cognitions. This approach rests on an appreciation for the mental processes from which are derived thought, belief, perception, and interpretation. The underlying assumption of this perspective is that an understanding of human behavior cannot be effective without a complete awareness of the "origins and consequences of people's cognitions" (Tavris and Wade, 1995: 22).

The most significant expressions of the cognitive perspective are multi-stage models of human development of thought and reasoning (which leads to learning). The more traditional of these models is represented by the work of Piaget (1929/1960). He proposed that all children develop their cognitive capacities across four developmental stages. During these stages learning is accomplished by developments in representational thinking, increased use of symbols and language, concrete understandings of the physical world, and abstract understandings of ideas and reasoning. A more recent theory of development is provided by the work of Kitchener and King (1990). These scholars have posited that the logical endpoint of cognitive development is the ability to use reflective or critical thinking. They have determined that there are seven stages to the development of this type of thought. Both of these models, as well as other cognitive theories not reviewed, rest on the assumption that people can best be understood by inferring their mode of thinking from observing their behaviors.

The sociocultural perspective

This perspective focuses on how the context in which people live can be examined to better understand them. The assumption underlying theories representative of this perspective is that we cannot fully understand human behavior until we appreciate everything about their social, cultural, and sociocultural environment. Whereas the three perspectives already discussed view the individual as separate from his/her environment, this approach takes full account of the relationship between an individual and his/her environment.

Three critical areas of study that share the assumptions on which this perspective is predicted are role theory, group dynamics, and cultural context. The impact of roles on human behavior has been classically demonstrated by Milgram (1974) and Zimbardo (Haney et al., 1973). In both of these studies, subjects were assigned a role (experimenter and prison guard, respectively) and given a task. In both cases, subjects behaved in ways that were at great odds with their normal behavior leading to the conclusion that their interpretation of the role they adopted had caused them to behave in these different ways.

Similarly, the study of group dynamics is replete with instances in which individuals behave differently in a group than they would on their own (Aronson, 1992). Finally, there is ample evidence that culture is a powerful influence on human behavior and learning (e.g., Hofstede, 1980; Toda et al., 1978).

The psychodynamic perspective

The psychodynamic perspective is predicated on assumptions that emphasize unconscious intrapsychic dynamics, fixed developmental stages of mental growth, a symbolic reality, subjective observations, and the belief that much present behavior is rooted in past unresolved experience. This perspective rests heavily on the groundbreaking work of Sigmund Freud (1935).

Although Freudian psychoanalysis provides the most (in)famous theory for describing human behavior, numerous other psychodynamic perspectives have been developed (Horney, 1950; Adler, 1964; Jung, 1967; Erikson, 1963). While these theories do not explicitly focus on individual learning, they all clearly imply that learning is predicated on previous experience (conscious and unconscious), based on developmental stage, and impacted by unresolved conflicts. Beyond their shared assumptions about the role of unconscious life and subjective interpretations, these models all look to integrate the whole of human experience. That is, they try to incorporate the biological, learning, cognitive, and sociocultural nature of human life into developing an understanding of human behavior (Tavris and Wade, 1995). Moreover, the psychodynamic perspective approaches understanding of human behavior from an interventionist, or clinical approach. As such, the psychodynamic perspective is the most integrative of the various approaches to understanding and as a result, the most complex and least understood.

DOMINANT THEORETICAL PERSPECTIVES IN ORGANIZATIONAL LEARNING AND THEIR USE OF PSYCHOLOGICAL EXPLANATIONS

Just as there are numerous perspectives from which to examine individual learning, multiple ways of thinking about organizational learning have been postulated. In order to evaluate the broadest spectrum of organizational learning views, we first undertook a review of the last 15 years of such theory. Rather than adopt an existing classification scheme, after reading over 70 articles, we inductively categorized the theoretical views into four broad theoretical approaches to organizational learning. Various conceptualizations were identified as sharing a common approach based on (1) the extent to which their authors cross-referenced one another, (2) shared assumptions about organizational learning, and (3) suggestions of other scholars. For example, Easterby-Smith et al. (1998) identify constructionist methods of inquiry which, along with suggestions of Nicolini and Meznar (1995), resulted in our identification of the "social construction" perspective of organizational learning. Our "information processing" perspective owes an intellectual debt to Huber (1991). Similarly, the "behavioral/evolutionary" perspective was greatly influenced by the work of Nelson and Winter (1982). The "applied learning" perspective is the category under which we subsume both action and experiential learning more generally associated with organizational learning consultation and organizational development interventions. (See table 2.1.)

Information processing

Information processing perspectives view organizations as systems of information. Their primary task is to reduce ignorance by improved organizational processes that mimic the processes of computation recognized in both humans and in computer systems. Hayes and Walsham explicitly review the role of information and information communication technologies in chapter 4 of this volume.

This view relies on two psychological learning assumptions. First, this approach assumes that information/knowledge/learning is stored in collective memory based on the cumulative experiences of individuals comprising the organization. Second, this approach is predicated on shared mental models of interpretation to give meaning to information. For example, Huber's (1991: 89) information processing perspective claims that "an organization learns if any of its units acquires knowledge that it recognizes as potentially useful to the organization." This perspective on information processing is also evident in writings by Daft and Weick (1984), whose model of organizations as interpretation systems assumes that organizations have both cognitive systems and memories. Moreover, they assert that, although individuals send and receive information, both individuals and organizations develop mental models. March (1991) similarly agues that organizations store knowledge accumulated over time from the learning of its members in the form of an organizational code that constitutes the organization's shared mental model.

Almeida et al. examine methods of information processing (scanning, scouring, and integration) in chapter 18 of this volume.

Cohen and Levinthal's (1990) writings on absorptive capacity also reflect an information processing perspective by asserting that an organization's ability to absorb new knowledge depends upon the absorptive capacities of its individual members. In both the case of individual and organization absorptive capacity, the assimilation and use of new knowledge depends upon the pre-existence of related knowledge. Van Den Bosch and associates update the absorptive capacity concept in chapter 15 of this volume.

In examining the psychological underpinnings of information processing, three approaches can be identified. First, the issue of whether memory is stored individually or collectively seems, metaphorically at least, to mirror the discussion in biological psychology about the location of memory. The neuropsychological perspective clearly argues two different views (localized and distributed) whereas the information processing approach to organizational learning clearly suggests that memory is distributed across the organization. Martin De Holan and Phillips discuss knowing and forgetting in service organizations in chapter 20 of this volume. Second, the information processing approach to organizational learning seems to rely on assumptions within the psychological cognitive perspective which suggest that sense making is a critical component of learning (for individuals and organizations). Third, the information processing perspective also evidences a strong behavioral

TABLE 2.1 Psychological perspectives in theories of organization

Psychological perspectives	Information processing	Behavioral/evolutionary	Social construction	Applied learning
Biological	Storage and memory are distributed across organization (March, 1991)			
Learning	Stimulus-response is lower level learning (Fiol and Lyles, 1985) Learning as computation (Huber, 1991)	Consequences shape learning (Lant and Mezias, 1990)	Social learning is embedded in relationships (Orr, 1990; Wenger, 1998)	Single-loop learning is driven by consequences (Argyris and Schön, 1974)
Cognitive	Sensemaking is higher level learning (Fiol and Lyles, 1985)	Trajectory results from cumulative prior learning (Nelson and Winter, 1982)	Cognition is socially mediated sensemaking (Weick, 1991)	Learning derives from experience processing (Kolb, 1984) and from action and reflection (Lewin, 1946) Cognition derives from shared mental models (Kim, 1993)
Sociocultural			Communities socially construct meaning (Brown and Duguid, 1991)	
Psychodynamic		Path dependence as initial state shaping future behavior. History matters (Nelson and Winter, 1982) Organizational learning perspectives		Individual and group defensiveness undermines organization learning (Argyris, and Schön, 1974)

orientation toward stimulus–response patterns of behavior. This is illustrated in Fiol and Lyles (1985), who distinguish between lower level learning, which consists of stimulus induced repetitions of past behavior, and higher level learning, which presumes the development of more cognitively complex patterns of association.

Behavioral

In general, behavioral theories focus on the antecedents to and changes in organizations' routines and systems as the organization responds to its own experience and that of other organizations. Nelson and Winter (1982) have the most well-developed theory of behavioral learning, which they describe as an "evolutionary model of the firm." Their theory presumes that organizations learn by encoding inferences from history into routines that guide behavior. These routines are independent of the individual actors who execute the routines and such routines are sustained even in the presence of considerable turnover of individual actors within the organization. Zollo and Winter further discuss organization routines in chapter 30 of this volume.

Two important constructs in the Nelson and Winter model are path dependence and trajectory. Path dependence is the principle that history matters and that initial conditions for the creation of an organization predetermine the repertoire of individual skills and organizational capabilities that constrain the organization's ability to adapt to environmental circumstances. Trajectory is the notion that a company's future learning of new capabilities will follow a path that builds on cumulative learning and capabilities of its past. Thus the two constructs are highly interdependent and suggest that organizational learning is constrained and not highly malleable.

Other research representing the behavioral school of organizational learning consists of computer simulations of complex patterns of evolving chains of behavior and their performance consequences (Herriott et al., 1985; Lant and Mezias, 1990). This type of research demonstrates how relatively simple assumptions about organizational goals and behavioral search and selection routines can produce over time entirely counterintuitive performance results. This research implies that organization learning and performance is not reducible to individual or group learning and behavior and thus it also views organizational learning as an emergent phenomenon.

A more extreme form of organization evolutionary learning emphasizes environmental selection and retention of organizations (Baum and Singh, 1994). In this way, population level learning occurs over time as adaptive routines are retained in surviving organizations (Miner and Haunschild, 1995). Such learning does not require any complex cognitive processing within the organizations, nor does it require that organizations themselves demonstrate adaptive behavior.

Although we have elected to call this family of organizational learning perspectives "behavioral," it has only a passing reliance on psychological principles of behaviorism – or other learning approaches. Specifically, these models of organizational learning do focus on consequences as the factor that most impacts learning. However, the organizational learning behavioral approach also relies on psychological models of cognition (e.g., the trajectory notion in Nelson and Winter's model) and on a psychodynamic notion that all current learning is influenced by the past (e.g., the path-dependence notion in the Nelson and Winter model).

Social construction

Social construction perspectives on organizational learning emphasize the social context. Such perspectives assume that learning is embedded in the relationships and interactions between people (Orr, 1990; Wenger, 1998). Learning is thus social and is grounded in the concrete situations in which people participate with others. Social construction perspectives complement information processing and behavioral perspectives by focusing on organization learning as involving socially mediated cognitive processes of interpretation and sense making. Weick (1991) conceives of the organization as a sense making system that engages in recurring cycles of enactment, selection and retention. These processes are the means by which the organization evolves as it makes sense of itself and its environment. Sense making involves reducing the equivocality (multiple meanings) of an ambiguous world to a more manageable set of meanings (Daft and Weick, 1984).

Two organizational learning theories rely on the enactment of sense making to build their models, namely the community of practice perspective and the SECI knowledge creation perspective. The community of practice perspective asserts that learning arises from within communities of practitioners sharing a common language, values and practices, and newcomers to such communities learn through legitimate peripheral participation in such communities (Lave and Wenger, 1993). Moreover, people within such communities socially construct meaning and learning during the course of their trajectory of participation as they become more deeply embedded within the community of practice (Brown and Duguid, 1991). Shared practice leads to "collective knowledge, shared sense making and distributed understanding that doesn't reduce to the content of individual heads" (Brown and Duguid, 1998: 96).

Plaskoff offers an innovative conceptual framework for communities of practice in chapter 9 of this volume.

The community of practice perspective is predicated on the "situated cognition" psychological view that learning arises by a process of enculturation in which neophyte members to a community acquire that particular community's subjective world view or collective memory (Brown et al., 1989). Enculturation thus includes learning the "stories" that constitute the collective memory of the community and learning to recognize those occasions where a specific story represents community knowledge applicable to the situation. The practice of storytelling in turn contributes to the construction and development of one's identity as a community member and a practitioner within that community (Brown and Duguid, 1991). These communities are not organizationally bounded or preordained groups such as task forces or project teams. Indeed, communities of practice are often not recognized by formal employing organizations and their boundaries are more fluid and may embrace people in geographically dispersed organizational and physical settings. Finally, the community of practice perspective emphasizes informal, improvisational practices that arise out of "making do" with what is available within the situation at hand (Orr, 1990). Such situation-specific improvisational practices enable their community members to socially construct their knowledge of effective practices out of the social and material circumstances of their specific practice situation (Lave, 1988). Situated learning through improvisational practices contrasts with the canonical practices by which formal organizations (i.e., schools and employers) seek to impart knowledge and generate learning through abstract knowledge and generic skill acquisition.

Nicolini and Meznar (1995) suggest that organizational members situated at the periphery may learn faster than members at the core of an organization. This is presumably because peripheral members are less completely socialized and embedded into the collective knowledge and sense making of a single community but instead are more likely to appreciate the sense making of other communities with divergent interests, knowledge and perspectives. By contrast, Weick and Roberts (1993) suggest that work settings such as the flight decks of aircraft carriers, induce its members to engage in shared sense making in which no individual understands fully the totality of the situation. However, their "heedful interrelating" in relation to specific cues of the situation allows them to act in concert. Similarly, each actor in a theater company or player on a sports team knows their part but it is the totality of the interactions among the players that collectively give meaning to the situation.

Nonaka and Takeuchi (1995) have also emphasized the social nature of organization learning in their writings on the knowledge creating company and organizational knowledge creation, which they explain in terms of four processes – socialization, externalization, combination and internalization (the SECI model) – by which explicit and tacit knowledge are transformed into each other. Socialization captures knowledge through physical proximity and direct interaction, thus facilitating the sharing of tacit knowledge between individuals, as when experts mentor apprentices in learning a craft. Externalization converts tacit knowledge into explicit knowledge by articulating ideas in symbolic form (e.g., metaphors, analogies or narratives). Combination occurs when explicit knowledge is collected, compiled, edited and disseminated. Finally, internalization occurs when explicit knowledge is embodied in actions and practices that facilitate experimentation and learning-by-doing. Tsoukas examines concepts of knowledge beyond the tacit-explicit dichotomy in chapter 21 of this volume.

Nonaka and Takeuchi (1995) view learning as largely occurring in teams, which provide the shared context where individuals can interact with each other, create new points of view through dialogue and discussion, pool their information and integrate diverse individual perspectives. These authors contrast the Western view of a company as a machine, with the Japanese view of the company as a living organism that enjoys a collective sense of identity and purpose. They insist that all new knowledge begins with the individual and suggest that organizational learning consists in making personal knowledge available to others.

In summary, social construction perspectives on organizational learning draw most explicitly upon sociocultural psychological perspectives for their core concepts and root metaphors. Situational determinants of learning play a major role in social construction perspectives. Secondarily, the social construction perspective embodies social cognition and individual cognition psychological principles to account for learning processes Again, these ideas are further developed in Elkjaer's chapter 3 of this volume. Writings on community of practice (e.g., Brown and Duguid, 1991) reveal the strongest grounding in sociocultural psychology and in social cognition theories of learning and therefore seem to embody a reductionistic relation between psychological theories of learning and organization learning. By contrast, writings on SECI knowledge creation (e.g., Nonaka, 1994) embody the spirit of social construction theories but seem not to have direct psychological ancestries. Rather, their Japanese philosophical roots suggest a more metaphoric relationship to Western theories of sociocultural psychology and social cognition views of learning.

Applied learning

Applied perspectives on organizational learning suggest that learning is grounded in direct experience and also requires active intervention by trained facilitators or consultants to improve organizational and individual learning practices. One variant of this perspective is project-based learning (PBL), which refers to the theory and practice of utilizing real-world work assignments on time-limited projects to achieve mandated performance objectives and to facilitate individual and collective learning (DeFillippi, 2001; Smith and Dodds, 1997). Project-based learning is partly related to the action learning writings of Reg Revans (1982) who theorized that learning resulted from the interaction between programmed instruction and the spontaneous questioning that arises from the interpretation of experience. Additionally, the project-based learning perspective draws upon notions of pragmatic learning associated with Dewey (1933) who argued for experimenting in the real world. Raelin (2000) examines the roots of his own variant of work-based learning in experiential learning (e.g., Kolb, 1984) and in the processes of reflection employed in adult learning (Mezirow, 1991). Another important foundational perspective for project learning is Lewin's (1946) action research perspective and its subsequent application to learning projects (e.g., Coghlan, 2001). The enormous intellectual contributions of action science theorists (Argyris and Schön, 1978) are addressed separately in this section.

Project-based learning in all its forms emphasizes the importance of reflective practices, which refer to the means by which project participants make sense of their project experience and ponder the meaning of the experience for themselves and others (Raelin, 2001). However, project-based learning traditions differ in the focal audience they target for reflection. Action learning interventions often emphasize problem-based reflections on behavior and taken-for-granted assumptions that interfere with individual learning and effective work performance (Smith, 2001). Action research projects, by contrast, are more oriented toward reflecting on how the organizational and social-cultural context impacts project performance and by implication, organization learning (Coghlan, 2001). Project-organized companies (e.g. construction, high technology) often employ project-learning interventions to capture "lessons learned" from completed projects into company knowledge management databases for re-use by team members on subsequent projects (Keegan and Turner, 2001). Finally, community-of-practice and network organization projects employ reflective practices oriented toward understanding how learning generated during projects is disseminated to external project sponsors and their relevant occupational and industry networks (Ayas and Zeniuk, 2001).

Psychologically, project-based learning theory and practice tends to draw upon cognitive learning perspectives. Smith (2001) identifies the following relevant schools of cognitive theory for action learning interventions: distributed cognition theory (Dede, 1996), cognitive flexibility theory (Spiro et al., 1988), situated cognition theory (Perret-Clermont,

1993), and metacognition theory (Flavell, 1976). Most action learning theorists cite the experiential learning models of Kolb (1984), who in turn draws upon the developmental psychology of Piaget (1981) for inspiration. Similarly, many action learning theorist-practitioners (e.g., Raelin, 2001; Smith, 2001) cite Mezirow (1991) and his writings on reflection, which draw explicitly upon cognitive developmental psychology (e.g., Kegan, 1982).

"Action science" is another action technology developed from the work of Kurt Lewin (1946). Implied in its moniker is the assumption that knowledge will be used in the service of action. As popularized by Argyris (Argyris and Schön, 1974, 1978, 1996; Argyris, 1977, 1992), action science is predicated on "the notion that people can improve their interpersonal and organizational effectiveness by examining the latent beliefs that spur their actions" (Raelin, 1997: 21). As such, action science involves clinical intervention whereby a skilled facilitator helps individual members of a group/organization surface their assumptions-in-use and espoused-assumptions, helps them to learn about and from their defenses, and thereby helps them to learn more effective means to interact with others.

Modern organizational learning models that are based on action science principles generally forego the clinical nature of the initial approach. Rather, these perspectives share the action science assumptions that people need to carefully reflect on their assumptions (mental models) in order to learn how and why they interpret the world as they do. Similarly, the constant testing of these assumptions against reality provides an opportunity for updating mental models – thereby learning. Additionally, contemporary organizational learning models are built on action science ideas of single- and double-loop learning. Single-loop learning refers to learning that occurs as a direct result of consequences. Double-loop learning adds the step of interpreting the consequences and deriving learning from this interpretation.

These ideas of action science have been applied to organizational learning by means of generalization. That is, as individuals learn more effective actions, this learning will aggregate/spillover to their employing organizations. The action science approaches to organizational learning all assume that organizations learn as a result of individual learning (Argyris and Schön, 1996).

For example, Kim's (1993) integrated model of organizational learning is premised on the assumption that "the mental models in individuals' heads are where a vast majority of an organization's knowledge (both know-how and know-why) lies" (p. 44). His conceptual model links individuals' mental models (frameworks and routines) to individual single- and double-loop learning and suggests that single loop learning has more the character of conditioned behavioral response whereas double-loop learning builds on the development of a higher level cognitive processing. At the organization level, it appears that the organizational *Weltanschauung* and organizational routines constitute the shared mental models that determine organizational action. However these shared mental models slowly evolve in response to the mental models of the individuals comprising the organization. Hence, organizational learning is an additive function of the legacy of those individuals who collectively have contributed to the creation and maintenance of a shared mental model. This may suggest that the organization's culture is an additive, accumulative function of the legacy of individuals' shared cognitive perspectives.

Other writings whose theorizing builds directly from Argyris and Schön's single- and double-loop learning perspective include Swieringa and Wierdsma (1992) and Torbert (1994). Stata (1989) provides a similar cognitive process perspective by defining organizational learning as occurring through shared insights, knowledge, and mental models, and building on past knowledge and experience.

Senge (1990) is also closely identified with the importance of clarifying and understanding mental models for effective organizational learning. However, his perspective is also more subtle and complex in its recognition of the impact of systemic feedback loops that lead to unanticipated consequences of self-defeating behavior. Hence, the Senge perspective also subsumes a behavioral psychological perspective (cf. Elkjaer, chapter 3).

Perhaps the popularity of the action science approach to understanding organizational learning can be attributed to the fact that this view is rooted in four different psychological perspectives. Single-loop learning is directly predicated on the behavioral models of learning whereas double-loop learning relies on a social learning approach to learning. The notion of shared mental models relies on the cognitive perspective. The notion of unearthed assumptions, that is unconscious or unstated assumptions and of defensiveness of these notions, relies on a psychodynamic perspective of understanding human behavior.

Another liberating aspect of applied learning perspectives is their willingness to embrace multiple levels of learning. Coghlan (1997) has offered a recent view of organizational learning as a dynamic inter-level process that inter-relates learning by individuals, teams, interdepartmental groups and organizations. He suggests that his approach is akin to Agryris and Schön's (1996) ladders of aggregation. Coghlan (1997) thus defines organizational learning as integrating learning at the individual, team and interdepartmental group levels with learning about the organization's relationship to its external environment and its strategic position vis-à-vis its stakeholders. Such a multi-level perspective on learning is also evident in other applied perspectives, such as Senge (1990) and Arthur et al. (2001).

Several examples of applied learning perspectives are found in chapters of this volume. DiBella discusses organizations as learning portfolios in chapter 8. Similarly, Edmondson and Woolley discuss a group level intervention in chapter 10. However, applied learning perspectives are also subject to criticism by Scarbrough and Swan's assessment (chapter 25) of the learning organization as a potential managerial fad.

OBSERVATIONS ON THE USE OF PSYCHOLOGICAL THEORY IN ORGANIZATIONAL LEARNING

Having identified and reviewed four major approaches and multiple theories of organizational learning, what can we say about the role played by psychological perspectives underlying these views? Clearly, cognitive learning perspectives dominate most organizational learning theories, including information processing, social construction, and applied learning. Whether grounded in individual or social cognitive learning theory, many organizational learning perspectives view sensemaking and understanding as well as computation and information processing as essential psychological processes that individuals must accomplish in order for organizational learning to occur. However, there also exists a strong behavioral learning psychological tradition reflected in the evolutionary view of organizational learning. The use of psychodynamic perspectives on individual learning is most evident in the applied organizational learning theories and practices that inform action science and related project-based learning perspectives.

The information processing approach to organizational learning seems most closely aligned with the biological psychology perspective due to its concerns with the storage of memory/information. Of course, the difference is that the psychological perspective assumes a single brain for storage purposes while the organizational learning perspective assumes information is stored in the minds of many individuals. It seems plausible that future refinements to cognitive information processing approaches will incorporate additional biological assumptions in much the same way that the fields of psychobiology and social psychology are finding areas of rapprochement (Berntson and Cacioppo, 2000).

Many organizational learning theorists have background/training in the fields of sociology and economics. As such, many of the underlying assumptions more closely match those associated with these disciplines. For example, the evolutionary learning perspective of Nelson and Winter (1982) explicitly reflects the influence of the economics backgrounds of its authors in its cognitive and information processing orientation, which also characterizes behavioral economics thinking applied to the behavioral theory of the firm (Cyert and March, 1963). Similarly, the sociological tradition is strongly reflected in the evolutionary learning perspective of Miner and Haunschild (1995) whose writings on population learning is largely grounded in population ecology and organization ecology sociological theories (Baum and Singh, 1994).

Overall, we observe that most organizational learning perspectives incorporate psychological theory perspectives more as background assumptions rather than as systematic underpinnings for their theory. As such, the use of psychological theory in organizational learning is often more a semantic, metaphoric device for talking about learning, rather than a systematic, reductionistic derivation of organization learning principles and processes from foundational psychological constructs and processes. Two schools of organizational learning appear to use psychological theory most explicitly. One surprising candidate is evolutionary theory, which derives hypotheses primarily grounded in non-cognitive behavioral learning theory. Perhaps because evolutionary organization theories make the most elementary of psychological learning assumptions, they are able to employ these assumptions most rigorously and systematically in their theorizing. The other organizational learning perspective with strong psychological roots in human cognition are the single- and double-loop organizational learning perspectives of Argyris and Schön (1978, 1996) and their followers.

Interestingly, the paradigmatic shift in psychology these days is toward integration of perspectives. For example, as suggested by Berntson and Cacioppo (2000), the areas of psychobiology and social psychology have great potential to positively impact one another with the adoption of various multi-level analytical tools. It appears that a similar shift is underway in the world of organizational learning. Applied learning approaches such as project-based learning cut across many areas of study and look to explain learning at multiple levels of analysis and from multiple perspectives (DeFillippi, 2001). Similarly, one of the most popularly acclaimed organizational learning models of the 1990s cuts across psychological perspectives and levels of analysis (Senge, 1990). Senge's "disciplines" of mental models and personal mastery are based on individual learning models whereas his discipline of shared vision is a group level phenomena that is based on cognitive assumptions. The discipline of team learning is clearly group focused and based on sociocultural assumptions while systems thinking can be applied at all levels of analysis as it shares assumptions across the psychological spectrum.

FUTURE DIRECTIONS

As organizations increasingly rely on information technology systems to generate and store information, we'd expect that organizational learning scholars would increasingly turn to the neurological aspects of psychology to find metaphors and possible explanations. Certainly, the metaphor of brain and central nervous system as a large computer network has already made its way into the popular culture. The ways in which this system duplicates information, shares information and develops transmission problems seem ripe for organizational extrapolation. Hayes and Walsham's chapter in this volume on the role of information communication technologies addresses some of these themes.

In terms of suggestions, we recommend two areas for future studies of organizational learning. First, there is a void in the organizational learning literature that appropriately and systematically looks at rewards and punishments (i.e., a behavioral approach to learning). Much in organizational life is predicated on rewards and punishments. For example, evaluation systems, merit compensation plans, bonus pay plans, promotions based on accomplishment, mentoring provided to the most capable are all means that organizations formally employ in order to "teach" or at least reinforce desired behaviors to individuals (in other words, these formalized mechanisms are devised so that people will learn and perform desired behaviors). However, as Kerr (1975) so aptly pointed out a quarter century ago, people learn to perform the behaviors that are rewarded rather than those that are espoused as desired. It seems to us that much of today's literature on organizational learning espouses learning (at individual, group, and organizational level) without accounting for the fact that much organizational practice may not be consistent with these suggestions.

Second, the role that both individual and organizational failure plays in subsequent organizational learning has received scant attention in the theoretical realm although it has been a topic of much popularity in publications oriented toward practitioners (e.g., Hamm, 2001; Kessler et al., 2001). Implied in the cognitive and behavioral approaches are the mechanisms through which learning as a result of the failure experience may occur. Integrating these approaches with the practical facts of failure may lead to an enhanced theoretical understanding of organizational learning.

REFERENCES

Adler, A. (1938/1964) *Social Interest: A Challenge to Mankind*. New York: Capricorn.
Anand, V., Manz, C., and Glick, W. (1998) An Organization Memory Approach to Information Management. *Academy of Management Review*, 231: 796–809.

Argyris, C. (1977) Double-loop Learning in Organizations. *Harvard Business Review*, 55 (5): 115–25.

Argyris, C. (1992) *On Organizational Learning*. Oxford: Blackwell.

Argyris, C. and Schön, D.A. (1974) *Theory in Practice: Increasing Professional Effectiveness*. San Francisco, CA: Jossey-Bass.

Argyris, C. and Schön, D.A. (1978) *Organizational Learning: A Theory of Action Perspective*. Reading, MA: Addison-Wesley.

Argyris, C. and Schön, D. (1996) *Organizational Learning II*. Reading, MA: Addison-Wesley.

Aronson, E. (1992). *The Social Animal*, 6th edn. New York: W.H. Freeman.

Arthur, M.B., DeFillippi, R.J., and Jones, C. (2001) Project-based Learning as the Interplay of Career and Company Non-financial Capital. *Management Learning*, 32 (1): 99–117.

Ayas, K. and Zeniuk, N. (2001) Project-based Learning: Building Communities of Reflective Practitioners. *Management Learning*, 32 (1): 61–76.

Bandura, A. (1977) *Social Learning Theory*. Englewood Cliffs, NJ: Prentice-Hall.

Bandura, A. (1979) The self-system in reciprocal determinism. *American Psychologist*, 34: 344–58.

Baum, J.A.C. and Singh, J.V. (1994) *Evolutionary Dynamics of Organizations*. New York: Oxford University Press.

Berntson, G.G. and Cacioppo, J.T. (2000) Psychobiology and social psychology: Past, present, and future. *Personality and Social Psychology Review*, 4: 3–15.

Brown, J.S., Collins, A., and Duguid, P. (1989) Situated Cognition and the Culture of Learning. *Education Researcher*, 18 (1): 32–42.

Brown, J.S. and Duguid, P. (1991) Organization Learning and Communities of Practice: Towards a Unified View of Working, Learning, and Innovation. *Organization Science*, 2: 40–57.

Brown, J.S. and Duguid, P. (1998) Organizing Knowledge. *California Management Review*, 40 (3): 90–111.

Caramazza, A and Hillis, A. (1991) Lexical Organization of Nouns and Verbs in the Brain. *Nature*, 349: 788–90.

Chomsky, N. (1957) *Syntactic Structures*. The Hague, Netherlands: Mouton.

Coghlan, D. (1997) Organizational Learning as a Dynamic Interlevel Process. *Current Topics in Management*, 2: 27–44.

Coghlan, D. (2001) Insider Action Research Projects: Implications for Practising Managers. *Management Learning*, 32 (1): 49–60.

Cohen W.M. and Levinthal, D.A. (1990) Absorptive Capacity: A New Perspective on Learning and Innovation. *Administrative Science Quarterly*, 35: 128–52.

Collins, R.L. (1991) Reimpressed Selective Breeding for Lateralization of Handedness in Mice. *Brain Research*, 564: 194–202.

Cyert, R.M. and March, J.G. (1963) *A Behavioral Theory of the Firm*. Englewood Cliffs, NJ: Prentice-Hall.

Daft, R.L. and Weick, K.E. (1984) Toward a Model of Organizations as Interpretation Systems. *Academy of Management Review*, 9 (2): 284–95.

Dede, C. (1996) Emerging Technologies and Distributed Learning. *American Journal of Distance Education*, 10 (2): 4–36.

DeFillippi, R.J. (2001) Project-based Learning, Reflective Practices and Learning Outcomes. *Management Learning*, 32 (1): 5–10.

Dewey, J. (1933) *How We Think*. Chicago: Henry Regnery.

Easterby-Smith, M., Gherardi, S., and Snell, R. (1998). Organizational Learning: Diverging Communities of Practice? *Management Learning*, 29 (3): 259–72.

Ekman, P. and Heider, K.G. (1988) The Universality of a Contempt Expression: A Replication. *Motivation and Emotion*, 12: 303–08.

Erikson, E.E. (1950/1963) *Childhood and Society*. New York: W.W. Norton.

Fiol, C.M. and Lyles, M.A. (1985) Organizational Learning. *Academy of Management Review*, 10 (4): 803–13.

Flavell, J.H. (1976) Metacognitive Aspects of Problem Solving. In L.B. Resnick (ed.) *The Nature of Intelligence*. Hillsdale, NJ: Erlbaum.

Freud, S. (1935) *A General Introduction to Psychoanalysis* (trans. Joan Riviere). New York: Washington Square Press.

Goldstein, J. (1999) Emergence as a Construct: History and Issues. *Emergence: A Journal of Complexity Issues in Organizations and Management*, 1 (1): 49–72.

Hamm, S. (2001). Less ego, more success. *Business Week*, July 23: 56–9.

Haney, C., Banks, C., and Zimbardo, P. (1973) Interpersonal Dynamics in a Simulated Prison. *International Journal of Criminology and Penology*, 1: 69–97.

Harlow, H. (1958) The Nature of Love. *American Psychologist*, 13: 673–85.

Harlow, H. and Harlow, M.K. (1966) Learning to Love. *American Scientist*, 54: 244–72.

Herriott, S.C., Levinthal, D.A., and March, J.G. (1985) Learning from Experience in Organizations. *American Economic Review*, 75: 298–302.

Hofstede, G. (1980) *Culture's Consequences: International Differences in Work-Related Values*. Beverly Hills, CA: Sage.

Horney, K. (1950) *Neurosis and Human Growth*. New York: W.W. Norton.

Huber, G.P. (1991) Organizational Learning: The Contributing Processes and the Literatures. *Organization Sciences*, 2(1): 88–115.

John, E.R., Tang, Y., Brill, A.B., Young, R., and Ono, E. (1986). Double-labeled Metabolic Maps of Memory. *Science*, 233: 1167–75.

Jung, C. (1967) *Collected Works*. Princeton, NJ: Princeton University Press.

Kagan, J. and Snidman, N. (1991) Infant Predictors of Inhibited and Uninhibited Profiles. *Psychological Science*, 2: 40–4.

Keegan, A. and Turner, J.R. (2001) Quantity versus Quality in Project-based Learning Practices. *Management Learning*, 32 (1): 77–98.

Kegan, R. (1982) *The Evolving Self*. Cambridge, MA: Harvard University Press.

Kerr, S. (1975). On the Folly of Rewarding A While Hoping for B. *Academy of Management Journal*, 18: 769–83.

Kessler, E.H., Bierly, P.E., and Gopalarkrishman, S. (2001) Vasa Syndrome: Insight from a 17th-century New Product Disaster. *Academy of Management Executive*, 15 (3): 80–91.

Kim, D.H. (1993). The Link between Individual and Organizational Learning. *Sloan Management Review*, 35 (1): 37–50.

Kitchener, K.S. and King, P.M. (1990) The Reflective Judgment Model: Ten Years of Research. In M.L. Commons (ed.) *Adult development*. Vol. 2 of *Models and Methods in the Study of Adolescent and Adult Thought*. Westport, CT: Greenwood.

Kolb, D.A. (1984) *Experiential Learning as the Source of Learning and Development*. Englewood Cliffs, NJ: Prentice-Hall.

Lant, T.K. and Mezias, S.J. (1990) An Organization Learning Model of Convergence and Reorientation. *Strategic Management Journal*, 11: 147–9.

Lashley, K.S. (1950) In Search of the Enegram. In *Symposium for the Society of Experimental Biology*, Vol. 4, New York: Cambridge University Press.

Lave, J. (1988) *Cognition in Practice: Mind, Mathematics, and Culture in Everyday Life*. New York: Cambridge University Press.

Lave, J. and Wenger, E. (1993) *Situated Learning: Legitimate Peripheral Participation*, New York: Cambridge University Press.

Lewin, K. (1946) Action Research and Minority Problems. *Journal of Social Issues*, 2 (4): 34–46.

March, J.G. (1991) Exploration and Exploitation in Organizational Learning. *Organization Science*, 2 (1): 71–87.

Mezirow, J. (1991) *Transformative Dimensions of Adult Learning*. San Francisco: Jossey-Bass.

Milgram, S. (1974) *Obedience to Authority: An Experimental View*. New York: Harper & Row.

Miner, A.S. and Haunschild, P. (1995) Population Level Learning. In B.M. Staw and L.L. Cummings (eds.), *Research in Organizational Behavior*. Greenwich, CN: JAI Press.

Miner, A.S. and Mezias, S.J. (1996) Ugly Duckling No More: Pasts and Futures of Organizational Learning Research. *Organizational Science*, 7 (1): 88–99.

Mischel, W. (1979) On the Interface of Cognition and Personality: Beyond the Person-Situation Debate. *American Psychologist*, 34: 740–54.

Nelson, R.R. and Winter, S.G. (1982) *An Evolutionary Theory of Economic Change*. Cambridge, MA: Harvard University Press.

Nicolini, D. and Meznar, M.B. (1995) The Social Construction of Organizational Learning: Conceptual and Practical Issues in the Field. *Human Relations*, 48 (7): 727–46.

Nonaka, I. (1994) A Dynamic Theory of Organizational Knowledge Creation. *Organization Science*, 5 (1): 14–37.

Nonaka, I. and Konno, N. (1998) The Concept of "Ba": Building a Foundation for Knowledge Creation. *California Management Review*, 40 (3): 40–54.

Nonaka, I. and Takeuchi, H. (1995) *The Knowledge Creating Company*. New York: Oxford University Press.

Orr, J. (1990) Sharing Knowledge, Celebrating Identity: War Stories and Community Memory in a Service Culture. In D.S. Middleton and D. Edwards (eds.), *Collective Remembering: Memory in Society*. Beverly Hills, CA: Sage Publications.

Perret-Clermont, A.N. (1993) What Is it that Develops? *Cognition and Instruction*, 11: 197–205.

Piaget, J. (1929/1960) *The Child's Conception of the World*. Paterson, NJ: Littlefield, Adams.

Piaget, J. (1981) *Intelligence and Affectivity*. California: Annual Reviews.

Pinker, S. (1994) *The Language Instinct: How the Mind Creates Language*. New York: Morrow.

Raelin, J.A. (1997) A Model of Work-Based Learning. *Organization Science*, 8 (6): 563–78.

Raelin, J.A. (2000) *Work-Based Learning: The New Frontier of Management Development*. Englewood Cliffs, NJ: Prentice Hall.

Raelin, J.A. (2001) Public Reflection as the Basis of Learning. *Management Learning*, 32 (1): 11–30.

Revans, R.W. (1982) *The Origin and Growth of Action Learning*. Brickley, UK: Chartwell-Bratt.

Senge, P.M. (1990) *The Fifth Discipline: The Art and Practice of the Learning Organization*. New York: Doubleday Currency.

Skinner, B.F. (1938) *The Behavior of Organisms: An Experimental Analysis*. New York: Appleton-Century-Crofts.

Skinner, B.F. (1969) *Contingencies of Reinforcement: A Theoretical Analysis*. New York: Alfred Knopf.

Skinner, B.F. (1971) *Beyond Freedom and Dignity*. New York: Alfred Knopf.

Smith, B. and Dodds, R. (1997) *Developing Managers through Project-Based Learning*. Aldershot, VT: Gower.

Smith, P.A.C. (2001) Action Learning and Reflective Practice in Project Environments that are Related to Leadership Development. *Management Learning*, 32 (1): 31–48.

Spiro, R.J., Coulson, R.L., Feltovich, P.J., and Anderson, D.K. (1988) Cognitive Flexibility: Advanced Knowledge Acquisition in Ill-Structured Domains. *Proceedings of the Tenth Annual Conference of the Cognitive Science Society*, Hillsdale, NJ: Erlbaum.

Stata, R. (1989) Organizational Learning: The Key to Management Innovation. *Sloan Management Review*, Spring, 12 (1): 63–74.

Swieringa, J. and Wierdsma, A. (1992) *Becoming a Learning Organization*. Wokingham, UK: Addison-Wesley.

Tavris, C. and Wade, C. (1995) *Psychology in Perspective*. New York: HarperCollins.

Toda, M., Shinotsuka, H., McClintock, C.G., and Stech, F.J. (1978) Development of Competitive Behavior as a Function of Culture, Age, and Social Comparison. *Journal of Personality and Social Psychology*, 38, 825–39.

Torbert, W.R. (1994) Managerial Learning, Organizational Learning: A Potentially Powerful Redundancy. *Management Learning*, 25 (1): 57–70.

Walsh, J. and Ungson, G. (1991) Organization Memory. *Academy of Management Review*, 16: 57–91.

Watson, J. B. (1925) *Behaviorism*. New York: W.W. Norton.

Weick, K.E. (1991) The Nontraditional Quality of Organizational Learning. *Organization Science*, 2 (1): 116–24.

Weick, K.E. (1995) *Sensemaking in Organizations*. Thousand Oaks, CA: Sage Publications.

Weick, K.E. and Roberts, K.H. (1993) Collective Mind in Organizations: Heedful Interrelating on Flight Decks. *Administrative Science Quarterly*, 38 (3): 357–81.

Wenger, E. (1998) *Communities of Practice: Learning, Meaning and Identity*. New York: Oxford University Press.

3

Social Learning Theory: Learning as Participation in Social Processes

CHAPTER OUTLINE

This chapter is a review of social learning theory in organizational learning literature. The review is made by way of comparing individual learning theory in organizational learning literature with that of social learning theory on three issues. These are: (1) the content of organizational learning; (2) the method of organizational learning; and (3) the relation between the individual and the organization. An important difference is that social learning theory encompasses both the epistemology and ontology of learning, and individual learning theory delimits itself to the epistemological part of learning. This has consequences for how organizational learning may be understood and facilitated. In the chapter, however, it is shown that in order to conceptually bind the epistemology and the ontology of learning together, a theory of pragmatism is needed. Thus, John Dewey's concepts of inquiry, reflection and experience are included to do just that.

INTRODUCTION

Many reviews have over the years been made to create an overview of literature on organizational learning (Dodgson, 1993; Easterby-Smith, 1997; Fiol and Lyles, 1985; Henriksson, 1999; Huber, 1991; Levitt and March, 1988; Miner and Mezias, 1996; Shrivastava, 1983). The amount of reviews has led to the following remark: ". . . there appear to be more reviews of organizational learning than there is substance to review" (Weick and Westley, 1996: 440). This chapter is, nevertheless, yet another review of literature on organizational learning. This literature review is, however, a review that is primarily focused on literature on organizational learning in which the understanding of learning is based on social learning theory. Social learning theory in organizational learning literature has been coined under several names such as "situated learning" (Brown and Duguid, 1991; Richter, 1998), as "practice-based learning" (Gherardi, 2000), and "learning as cultural processes" (Cook and Yanow, 1993; Henriksson, 2000; Yanow, 2000).

I prefer the term *social learning theory* to indicate that we are in the field of social theory, and that the point of departure for learning is the living experience of everyday life. All social learning theory, however, view learning as participation in social processes emphasizing both issues of knowing, and issues of being and becoming. This means that social learning theory encompasses both the epistemology and the ontology of learning. Thus, social learning theory considers both the issue of human existence and development (ontology), and the issue of people coming to know about themselves and what it means to be part of world and history (epistemology). In social learning theory, development and learning are, in other words, inseparable processes; and they constitute each other in an understanding of learning as participation in social processes.

The overall governing question for this review is: How does social learning theory contribute to an understanding of organizational learning, which differs from a point of departure in individual learning theory? Most of the literature on organizational learning and its counterpart, the Learning Organization, departs from individual learning theory; and social learning theory in organizational learning literature has grown out of a criticism of just that departure (see, for example, Elkjaer, 1999, and the references mentioned in note 1). The criticism is elaborated later, but, in short, it is that individual learning theory focuses on learning as inner mental processes related to the acquisition and processing of information and knowledge. It leads to mind being the locus of learning, and as a consequence, a separation of the individual learner and the context, in this case, the organization, for learning. This, in turn, means that the learning focus is on how people get to know – in a very narrow sense – and not on how the organizational context is a key element in the learning, socialization and development of organizational members. In other words, individual learning theory is criticized for neglecting the ontological dimension of learning and only focusing on the epistemological dimension.

Having said that, it may be argued that social learning theory in organizational learning literature is not fully explicit about how to bind conceptually the two dimensions of learning together, those for human development and human knowing. This is the background for introducing *John Dewey*'s concepts of inquiry, reflection and experience in this review (Dewey, 1933/1986, 1938/1986). Dewey's concepts of inquiry and reflection are not to be confused with plain communication skills (Senge et al., 1999), but to be related with the overall creation of individual and collective, cultural and historical knowledge. Likewise, Dewey's concept of experience is not to be confused with the concept of experience found in humanistic and individual-oriented psychology in which experiencing is viewed as intrinsically psychical, mental and private processes. Dewey's notion of experience is a non-dualist concept covering the individual and the world, and experience is always culturally mediated (see also Miettinen, 2000). I return to Dewey's concepts of inquiry, reflection, and experience as notions that hold potentials for bridging conceptual gaps in developing a social learning theory for organizational learning.

A word about method for making this review is needed. The review is made by reading a selected number of texts that all claim to rest upon social learning theory, and to be critical of individual learning theory.[1] The way of reading the texts was inspired by a phenomenological approach (Giorgi, 1975). This means bracketing any theoretical knowledge the reader/interpreter may have in order to read the text as a text, that is, as a phenomenon of words put together in order to give meaning. After this the interpreters apply their own theoretical framework or structure in order to give the texts new meaning according to the purpose of the phenomenological reading. In this case, the purpose is to explore the contribution of social learning theory to the field of organizational learning. Because social learning theory builds upon individual learning theory, I find it helpful to introduce the two learning theories along the same structure.

Jean Lave's pioneering work on coining the essence of learning has served as an important source of inspiration (Lave, 1997). These are the telos or direction of learning, the learning mechanism, and the subject–world relation. In my adoption of these issues, they have become the purpose and content of organizational learning, the methods for organizational learning, and the relation between the individual and the organization. In other words, what do individual learning theory and social learning theory regard as the purpose and content of organizational learning; how is organizational learning to come about; and how is the individual and the organization understood and conceptualized?

The chapter starts with an introduction to organizational learning based upon individual learning theory, which is followed by an introduction of social learning theory in organizational learning literature. Then follows a section called "inspiration from pragmatism" in which John Dewey's concepts of inquiry, reflection and experience are introduced as a way to bridge the conceptual gap between the ontological and the epistemological dimension of learning. Finally, in the conclusion, implications for organizational learning of a social learning theory are suggested.

ORGANIZATIONAL LEARNING BASED UPON INDIVIDUAL LEARNING THEORY

The literature on organizational learning was based initially on theories of organizational behaviour within the field of management science (Cyert and March, 1963; Easterby-Smith, 1997; Gherardi, 1999; March and Simon, 1958). These early contributions to the emerging field of organizational learning dealt with information processing and decision-making in organizations. The purpose was to help organizations learn to adapt to changes in the environment and to provide prescriptive managerial techniques. About 30 years later, with the publication of Senge's book, the counterpart of organizational learning, the learning organization, appeared as yet another way to create organizational learning (Senge, 1990). Judging from the many books and guidelines that have been published on how to develop a learning organization and pave the way for organizational learning, the learning organization and organizational learning have proved to be powerful models for organizational development (Argyris and Schön, 1978/1996; Nevis et al., 1995; Pedler and Aspinwall, 1998; Senge et al., 1999).

The learning theory in much of the literature on organizational learning and the learning organization is inspired by the field of individual-oriented psychology. Enhancing information processing and decision-making in organizations is seen as something that is done by individuals' learning, and processes that can be enhanced by individuals' learning. Individuals' learning outcomes can then, by way of individuals acting on behalf of an organization, be crystallized in organizational routines and values and become organizational learning. The idea is that individuals hold a mental model in their mind, which is an abstract representation of their actions. It is the mental model, which can be enhanced in order for individuals, and subsequently for organizations, to enhance information processing and lead to better decision-making in organizations.

Thus, learning is, according to individual learning theory, identical to the enhancement of individuals' mental models, and happens when individuals acquire information and knowledge, which subsequently can guide their – and, thus, the organization's – behaviour. The focus on mental modeling as the essence of learning in individual learning theory is the reason for naming individual learning theory as that of "cognitive" learning theory. Similarly, mental models may also be termed "cognitive structures." It is a focus on learning, which is directed towards what goes on in the minds of people.

A cognitive learning theory privileges abstract and general verbal and conceptualized knowledge over and above the thinking that derives from practice (Lave, 1988; Nicolini and Meznar, 1995). An example is when Senge talks about the importance of learning to think of organizations as systems, that is to learn "systems thinking" in order to develop learning organizations (Senge, 1990). It is a way for organizations to learn, which first coins the organization as an abstract entity, a "system," which then the organizational member must learn to relate to understand in order to behave in adequate ways. Another way to conceptualize learning is to begin with the concrete and work-related organizational actions and practice. This would demand a development of organizational members' awareness to sense and act upon the uncertain situations that they encounter in their lived everyday organizational life and work. Uncertain situations are those that arouse doubts and disturb habitual actions. Developing an awareness of situations of uncertainty among organizational members would include a view of the organization as a context affording specific actions and inhibiting other.

However, the process of abstraction is viewed as a necessary condition for learning in cognitive learning theory. To the learner, learning is the acquisition of a body of data, facts and practical wisdom accumulated by former generations. Learning is for the learner to come to know the world and to learn about practice. Learning is a process of knowledge delivery from a knowledgeable source to a target lacking that knowledge. Knowledge is out there somewhere, stored in places (books, databases, minds) waiting to be transferred to and acquired by another mind for future use (Gherardi et al., 1998).

In the organizational learning literature that rests upon individual learning theory, learning is regarded as a specific activity, something to be initiated, motivated, and stimulated. Learning happens when a discontinuity is introduced, when there is a problem to be solved. It is assessed on the basis of change in the organizational routines and values, which are to be secured in the organizational memory (for example, an information system, work descriptions, and the like). Organizational learning based upon individual learning theory is actually individual learning in organizations, which creates the problem of transferring individual learning outcomes to that of the organization.

The individual–organization split has been one of the major problems in the organizational learning literature that rests upon individual learning theory (Argyris and Schön, 1978/1996; Mumford, 1991) and also the target of much criticism (Cook and Yanow,

TABLE 3.1   Individual learning theory

	Individual learning theory
Content	Cognitive structures
	Know about practice
Method	Discontinuity
	Knowledge acquisition
	In the mind
Relation between individual–organization	Separated ("soup and bowl")

1993; Gherardi et al., 1998). The answer given in the organizational learning literature itself has been, as earlier mentioned, to view individuals as acting on behalf of the organization (Argyris and Schön, 1978/1996; Senge, 1990). This view of the relation between individual and organization creates a separation between individuals and organization. To use a metaphor, it is a relation as that between soup and bowl, the soup does not shape the bowl, and the bowl does not alter the substance of the soup. Thus, individual and organization, soup and bowl, "can be analytically separated and studied on their own without doing violence to the complexity of the situation" (McDermott, 1993: 282).

In sum, in organizational learning literature based upon individual learning theory, learning is about changing cognitive structures. Learning is a specific activity, which happens by acquisition of abstract and general knowledge acquisition initiated by a discontinuity. The acknowledged problem in organizational learning based upon individual learning theory is the individual–organization dissociation, that is, how to make individual learning become organizational. See table 3.1 for a summary.

Organizational learning that rests upon individual learning theory separates epistemology, to come to know about the world, from ontology, to be and become part of the world. It is a split between learning and human development – and growth – and it is a separation between thinking and acting. In the next section, social learning theory in organizational learning is explored. This, too, is not without problems, maybe because social learning theory has been formulated as a negation of individual learning theory in organizational learning literature.

SOCIAL LEARNING THEORY IN ORGANIZATIONAL LEARNING LITERATURE

The emergence of organizational learning literature based upon social learning theory grows, as mentioned, out of a critique of the organizational learning (and the learning organization) literature based upon individual learning theory. But the appearance of social learning theory in organizational learning literature coincides with a social constructivist turn in social science and in educational studies (Berger and Luckmann, 1991/1966; Bredo, 1997; Larochelle et al., 1998). The individual mind as the locus of learning is, in other words, questioned from many fields of research. The main criticisms are that if learning is indicated by change in cognitive structures, how is it possible to learn on the basis of actions that may or may not be verbally representative as specific mental models but may instead be emerging through taking action? Further, if learning is a specific activity delimited to certain initiated events like problem-solving, how does one account for what is not learning? Finally, if it is possible to separate the individual from the organization, how does one account for the fact that people can be knowledgeable in one situation, and not in another comparable situation (Lave, 1988)?

Instead, the argument from the view of social learning theory is that a situation posits certain possibilities for some actions and not for others depending on individuals' former experiences and power in a specific context. Individuals are at one and the same time to be regarded as "products" of their social and cultural history and "producing" situations mirroring that. The individuals interact with selves, others, artifacts and contexts as just that, "products" and "producers" of situations. This – situated – view of learning moves learning away from the individual mind to the social sphere of interaction, activity, and practice, and this has paved the road for another view on learning and on knowledge (Cook and Brown, 1999). It is, however, a view that has earlier roots in American pragmatism, and in the work of the early 20th century Russian psychologist Vygotsky and the tradition of the cultural-historical activity theory (Bredo, 1997; Elkjaer, 2000; Popkewitz, 1998). I will return to that, but first social learning theory in organizational learning literature is introduced with regard to the what and how of learning as well as the relation between the individual and the organization.

Content and method in social learning theory

In organizational learning literature based upon social learning theory, learning is not regarded as a specific, delimited and intentional activity. Rather, learning is regarded as ubiquitous and part of human activity as such. In other words, learning cannot be avoided; it is not a choice for or against learning. Learning is an integral part of the practice in everyday organizational life and work (Nicolini and Meznar, 1995).

Learning is not restricted to taking place inside individuals' minds but as processes of participation and interaction. In other words, learning takes place among and through other people (Gherardi et al., 1998). Learning is a relational activity, not an individual process of thought. This view changes the locus of the learning process from that of the mind of the individual to the participation patterns of individual members of organizations in which learning takes place.

In individual learning theory, the learning content is to come to know about practices; in social learning theory, the learning content is to become a practitioner. In social learning theory, learning is a way of being and becoming part of the social worlds that comprise an organization, and in which the central issue of learning is to become a practitioner (Brown and Duguid, 1991; Richter, 1998). Learning is a practical rather than an epistemic accomplishment, and it is a matter of identity development. Changing the content of learning from knowledge acquisition to identity formation expands the concept of learning to include an ontological dimension. It also involves a change of the term "knowledge" as knowledge becomes the embedded or situated knowledge of the organization, and not something stored in books, brains and information systems (Cook and Brown, 1999; Gherardi et al., 1998).\Knowledge becomes the active process of knowing – or getting to know – the way to participate and interact in organizations.|Learners are to construct their own knowledge and to make sense of their participation in the social processes of the organization. It is not just the individuals who solely retain knowledge, rather knowledge is distributed within and among colleagues (Cook and Brown, 1999; Richter, 1998).

The learning content is context specific, and it implies discovery of what is to be done, when and how according to the specific organizational routines, as well as knowing which specific artifacts to use where and how. Learning also involves being able to give a reasonable account of why things are done and of what sort of person one must become in order to be a competent member of a specific organization. In social learning theory, to know is to be capable of participating with the requisite competence in the complex web of relationships among people and activities. Learning implies acquisition of a "situated curriculum," which denotes the pattern of learning opportunities available to newcomers in their encounter with a specific community inside a specific organization. Learning is that which enables actors to modify their relations to others while contributing to the shared activity. When the locus of learning moves away from inside the mind to social relations it also moves into the areas of conflict and power. This makes the issue of empowerment essential, as learning requires access and opportunity to take part in the ongoing practice. The social structure of this practice, its power relations and its conditions for legitimacy, define the possibilities for learning (Gherardi et al., 1998).

Language is, according to social learning theory, a central element of any process of learning since language is conceived as the main way of acting in contemporary organizations. Language is, however, not merely a medium of knowledge transmission. Language is the medium of culture and as such it constitutes a crucial element in the process of learning, when the latter is conceived as the result of interaction among individuals in a specific occupational and organizational culture. The study of organizational learning is to explore the specific contexts of activities and social practices in which learning may occur. Only by understanding the circumstances and how the participants construct the situation can a valid interpretation of a learning activity be made (Gherardi et al., 1998).

In sum, with regard to the what and how of social learning theory in organizational learning, a social learning theory emphasizes informality, improvisation, collective action, conversation and sense making, and learning is of a distributed and provisional nature. According to this view the aim of learning is not to acquire already known knowledge and to solve externally defined problems. It should be about moving into unknown territory, to "face mystery" (Gherardi, 1999), and to make a journey into the land of discovery rather than following an already paved road. In the next part, the issue of the relation between the individual and the organization is taken up.

Relation between individual and organization

According to social learning theory, learners are social beings that construct their understanding and learn from social interaction within the specific socio-cultural settings of an organization. The role of individual learners is to be engaged in sense making, and to create knowledge within and among their trajectory of participation. The individual in social learning theory is to be understood as a participant in the social processes of everyday life of an organization. The organization provides occasion for interpretations of what goes on in an organization (Richter, 1998).

Continuing the metaphorical image from individual learning theory, the separation of soup and bowl may be replaced by the melting together of individuals and organizations as that of a rope. "The fibers that make up the rope are discontinuous; when you twist them together, you don't make *them* continuous, you make the *thread* continuous . . . The thread has no fibers in it, but, if you break up the thread, you can find the fibers again" (McDermott, 1993: 274). Thus, one cannot talk of the relation between individuals and organizations, or individual and context, as individuals in an organization, but individuals as part of a specific organizational practice as well as of patterns of participation and interaction.

There are, however, two views of context represented in social learning theory in organizational learning literature. The two understandings of context are whether context is a historical product of which persons are a part, or whether context is constructed as persons interact. To quote:

> One argues that the central theoretical relation is historically constituted between persons engaged in socioculturally constructed activity and the world with which they are engaged . . . The other focuses on the construction of the world in social interaction; this leads to the view that activity is its own context. Here the central theoretical relation is the intersubjective relation among coparticipants in social interaction. (Lave, 1993: 17)

The first view is represented in activity theory (Blackler, 1993; Engeström, 2001) and American pragmatism. The second is inspired by social constructionism and phenomenological social theory. The latter is represented in the following much cited definition of learning in organizational learning literature based upon social learning theory, namely that learning is "the acquiring, sustaining, or changing of intersubjective meanings through the artifactual vehicles of their expression and transmission and the collective actions of the group" (Cook and Yanow, 1993: 384; see also Corley and Gioia, chapter 31 of this volume; Weick and Westley, 1996). The group – or the collective actions of the group, and not the individual, is suggested here as the primary level of analysis. This is a social constructionist view on the relation between the individual and the organization. In the organizational learning literature, this view is also called a cultural approach to organizational learning (Cook and Yanow, 1993; Henriksson, 2000; Yanow, 2000). The focus is on "situated meaning (in this case, what is meaningful to those actors engaged in organizational learning activities)" (Yanow, 2000: 248). Context as a historical product in organizational learning literature can be expressed like this:

> The context must . . . be conceived as a historical and social product which is co-produced together with the activity it supports: agents, objects, activities, and material and symbolic artefacts all constitute a heterogeneous system that evolves over time. (Gherardi et al., 1998: 275)

Whether one views context as either socially constructed *in situ* or as a historical and social product, is, I believe, a complicated matter consisting of many circumstances like political attitudes, academic traditions, "taste," etc. For my part, I have a hard time not to view situations as consisting of people and contexts with a history mirroring social and cultural backgrounds. My major problem is that a view of context as nothing other than a process of construction in social interaction and by the use of artifacts restrict the interventionist activities to ways of interacting with artifacts (in the broadest meaning of this term, which means that language is also an artifact that is a tool for action and interaction). With activity as its own context, it is difficult to see how change can be directed at changing contexts themselves that is of changing the conditions for learning and development. But, naturally, I also subscribe to a view of context as that of historically and culturally produced because I have my theoretical roots in American pragmatism. This connection is elaborated on shortly.

To sum up, in social learning theory individuals' mind and actions are regarded as related to their participation in social processes formed by culture and history. This means that knowing, according to social learning theory, is always an integral part of broader changes of being, which can be traced to learners' participation in social worlds (Star, 1992; Strauss, 1993), communities of practice (Lave and Wenger, 1991) or activity systems (Blackler, 1993; Engeström, 2001). A social world

> posits circumscribed practices for its members, possible ways of being human, possible ways to grasp the world – apprehended first with the body, then with tools and symbols – through participation in social practices and in relationship with other people. Knowing is this grasping that is at the same time a way of participating and of relating. (Packer and Goicoechea, 2000: 234)

Thus, in social learning theory it is not possible to separate knowing from being and becoming. To be and become – or emerge as – a knowledgeable person demands participation in social processes, which also involves relating to other beings and to (and with) the cultural and historically produced artifacts of the social worlds. In table 3.2, individual and social learning theory in organizational learning is summarized.

In the following section, I introduce the work of John Dewey (1916/1966, 1933, 1938) because his concepts of inquiry, reflection and experience help bind the processes of epistemology and ontology in learning together. These are, as I have argued, at the heart of social learning theory in organizational learning literature but lack the conceptual elaboration here. Dewey's notions of inquiry, reflection and experience help to see that the ontological dimension of learning – how humans become humans – and the epistemological dimension – how humans become knowledgeable – cannot be separated. Human development and human learning are inseparable processes that can be better understood by way of these Deweyan concepts.

INSPIRATION FROM PRAGMATISM

In the Deweyan universe, there are no universal cognitive structures that shape human experience of reality. Dewey argued against Cartesian dualism and Kant's *a priori* and

TABLE 3.2   Individual and social learning theory

	Individual learning theory	*Social learning theory*
Content	Cognitive structures Know about practice	Identity formation Become a practitioner
Method	Discontinuity Knowledge acquisition In the mind	Ubiquitous Participation and interaction Part of everyday practice

Relation between
individual and organization
	Separated ("soup and bowl")	Weaved together ("a rope")
		Two understandings of context:
		— individual and context as
		    historically produced
		— organizational activity as
		    its own context

innate categories (space, time, causality, and object) as structuring human thinking. For Dewey, knowledge always refers directly to human experience and the origin of knowledge is living experience and not the other way around, as if logical theorems might govern thinking (McDermott, 1973/1981; Sleeper, 1986). This does not, however, mean that pragmatism rejects cognition as "thinking is a process of inquiry, of looking into things, of investigating. *Ac*quiring is always secondary, and instrumental to the act of *in*quiry. It is seeking, a quest, for something that is not at hand" (Dewey, 1916/1966: 148).

In pragmatism, ideas, theories, and concepts – that is, different forms of thinking and abstraction – function as instruments for actions. The nature of actions is always delimited or selective, because humans cannot act in general, nor in a vacuum. The essence of action is irremediably contextual. It follows that thinking and ideas or meanings developed through thinking are contextual as well. Thus, a reflected action is created in relation to a specific situation or problem.

The concept of *inquiry* in pragmatism developed out of the criticism leveled at the concept of knowledge in formal logic with its references to a priori knowledge above and beyond the human world of experience. Dewey's development of logic as a theory of inquiry is based on everyday life experiences. Inquiry cannot be reduced to a response to purely abstract thoughts as it is anchored in situations as part of our everyday life. It is part of life to inquire, turn things around intellectually, come to conclusions and make evaluations. People do that all the time whether conscious of it or not. This is how people learn and become cognizant human beings.

Inquiry is a process that starts with a sense that something is wrong. Intuitively, the inquirer suspects there is a problem. The suspicion does not necessarily arise from an intellectual wit. It is not until the inquirer(s) begin to define and formulate the problem that inquiry moves into an intellectual field by using the human ability to reason and think verbally. In other words, the inquirer(s) use their previous experiences from similar situations. According to Dewey, the inquirer(s) try to solve the problem by applying different working hypotheses and conclude by testing a model of solution. The initial feeling of uncertainty, the uncertainty that started the inquiry process must disappear before a problem has been solved. If the inquiry is to lead to new experiences, to learning, it requires thoughts or reflection over the relation between the problem's definition and formulation and the solution. It is not until reflection has established a relation between the action and the consequence(s) of the action that learning takes place.

The provocative element in the development of *experience* is when habitual actions are upset, that is when people face uncertainties. This feeling cannot be forced upon anybody from the outside, and must be within the individual's capacity of solving problems. As a result of inquiries into problematic situations, people gain new experiences and construct new knowledge. However, some experiences may not be apprehended as such; that is, they do not enter the conscious and verbal sphere. Dewey talks a great deal about the aesthetics of experiences and the sensation that they perfect or complete – at least for a time. Any delight and comfort in a situation is also an experience, and knowing is just one way of experiencing (McDermott, 1973/1981). There is little distinction between an intellect that knows and a body that acts. Along the continuum of experience, there is a vague transfer between non-cognitive and cognitive experiences that is crucial to learning. If people want to learn from their experiences, however, they must get them out of the physical and non-discursive field and turn them into acknowledged and conscious experiences.

> To "learn from experience" is to make a backward and forward connection between what we do to things and what we enjoy or suffer from things in consequence. Under such conditions, doing becomes a trying; an experiment with the world to find out what it is like; the undergoing becomes instruction – discovery of the connection of things. Two conclusions important for education follow. (1) Experience is primarily an active–passive affair; it is not primarily cognitive. But (2) the *measure of the value* of an experience lies in the perception of relationships or continuities to which it leads up. It includes cognition in the degree in which it is cumulative or amounts to something, or has meaning. (Dewey 1916/1966: 140)

People gain experiences as a result of how they live their lives and how they associate with other people. This, in turn, depends on who they are as persons and how they enter into these relations, but it is difficult to avoid gaining any experiences. But if people are going to learn from their experiences, they have to use their ability not only to contemplate the relation between their actions and their consequences, but also to relate them to their present experiences. Only at this point do people's experiences turn into reflective experiences – learning experiences.

In sum, pragmatism is a reminder of humans' agency but this agency is grounded in and part of context as well as individual capacities. Thinking is useful as it can act as a guideline for actions by way of working hypotheses, and reflection is necessary in order to produce learning. The organizational member and the organization are weaved together in a social world in which acting and thinking goes on as a continuous process. In table 3.3, I have summarized what the inspiration from pragmatism contributes to an understanding of organizational learning in the light of social learning theory.

In pragmatism, the learning content may be coined as the development of human experience, which at the same time is to come to know about the world and become part of it.

TABLE 3.3 Individual, social, and pragmatic learning theory

	Individual learning theory	*Social learning theory*	*Pragmatic learning theory*
Content	Cognitive structures Know about practice	Identity formation Become a practitioner	Development of human experience Know about world and become part of world
Method	Discontinuity Knowledge acquisition In the mind	Ubiquitous Participation and interaction Part of everyday practice	Inquire to acquire Thinking as instrumental for action Reflection as necessary for learning
Relation between individual–organization	Separated ("soup and bowl")	Weaved together ("a rope") Two understandings of context: — individual and context as historically produced — organizational activity as its own context	Impossible to separate Human knowing is part of human being Individual and context "products" of human being and knowing

In this way, social learning theory for organizational learning inspired by pragmatism does not make a separation between coming to know about practice and coming to be a practitioner. It is not possible to develop experience as either processes of knowledge or processes of becoming. Experience encompasses both processes.

The learning method is inquiry, which includes thinking as a way to define problems, and reflection as a way to move learning outcome into the verbal and conscious area, which make it possible to share it with others. Thus, inquiry is a way to acquire knowledge but it is a way that does not begin with language and conscious reflection. Rather, inquiry starts in the senses, the bodily feelings and emotions, which may be turned into words in order to provide a way to learn from inquiry. These processes cannot be restricted to mind or bodies, thinking or actions, but encompass both. And their consequences are not to be restricted to knowledge acquisition but to include development of experience, that is growth.

It is not possible to separate the individual and the social, the context and/or the organization in pragmatism. The two are mutually constituted as human beings and human knowing, and as such they are products of history and culture.

CONCLUSION

Applying a social learning theory in organizational learning takes the focus of learning away from the individual mind and "places" it in the organizational context as a setting for organizational learning. This means that the organizational actions directed to develop

organizational learning cannot be solely focused on changing individuals' ways of thinking but should be focused on the organizational context, its patterns of participation
and interaction. Social learning theory also takes the focus away from knowledge as the
learning input to that of developing organizational members so that they become capable
practitioners.

A point of departure in social learning theory for organizational learning means
that learning is viewed as an ongoing activity, which cannot be controlled; only the environments, the organization, can be made to facilitate organizational learning to a larger
or lesser degree. One critique of social learning theory is that it focuses too much on the
organizational context, and thus cannot, for example, encompass the mobile, knowledgeable and potentially influential individual. This may be the transformational leader
or the ordinary professional who imports new ideas to the work and who perhaps gets
changed by outside encounters. The answer to this criticism is that the focus on context
does not omit the individual as the two are viewed as mutually constituted and continuously changing with the participants "moving" in and out of the specific context at
hand. Thus, one cannot just change the organizational context without including the
concrete and present participants in this context. The essence of applying a social learning theory is that it is not possible to work with ideal-typical individuals who learn by way
of changing their ways of thinking. Organizations consist of real people, each with their
own experiences, history and hopes for the future. This embodies the organizational
context together with the specific work practice, the artifacts or organizational rules and
regulations. And it is from this starting-point that learning and organizational learning
begins to occur.

The contribution to social learning theory from pragmatism is to stress the coexistence
between epistemology and ontology in learning. This is done by focusing on the development of human experience as both encompassing processes of knowledge acquisition and
of being and becoming part of world. And it also stresses the interconnectedness of the
development of individuals and organizations. The most beneficial contribution from pragmatism for organizational learning is, however, the notion of inquiry, which provides a
method in which thinking is regarded as a tool, a way to define problems, and reflection
is included as a way of sharing learning outcomes.

Given the widespread contemporary interest in viewing learning as participation in
social processes, I think that future research on organizational learning will bring more
emphasis on the importance of "organizing" the organizational context for organizational
learning. This will, I think, bring forward issues of a return to the studies of work processes
and to how learning and organizational learning may be furthered by making a stronger
connection between the development of work and work learning. Issues of power, division
of labor and the organization of work will follow from this and enter the organizational
learning literature of the future (see also Easterby-Smith et al., 2000).

I also think that the literature on organizational learning will become more informed
by the learning literature in general – especially the literature on adult and vocational education. There are some signs of "mergers" but they are few and far between (Boud and
Garrick, 1999; Tight, 2000). It is my hope that this interest will contribute to see learning
not as a debate between thinking or action/practice, but will be inspired by American
pragmatism to see these processes as a mutually co-existing.

Acknowledgments

I would like to thank two younger colleagues of mine, Jens Broendsted and Jonna Kangasoja, for having made good comments on an earlier version of this chapter. Also thanks to the book reviewers, Mark Easterby-Smith and – in my case – Robin Snell. The latter for having challenged (in a kind and supportive way) the very idea of the validity of a social learning theory.

Note

1. The main texts are, in alphabetical order: Brown and Duguid, 1991; Cook and Brown, 1999; Cook and Yanow, 1993; Easterby-Smith et al., 1998; Gherardi, 1999; Gherardi, 2000; Gherardi et al., 1998; Nicolini and Meznar, 1995; Richter, 1998; Yanow, 2000. Other texts have been included and are mentioned in the text.

References

Argyris, C. and Schön, D.A. (1978/1996) *Organizational Learning II: Theory, Method, and Practice.* Reading: Addison-Wesley.

Berger, P.L. and Luckmann, T. (1991/1966) *The Social Construction of Reality: A Treatise in the Sociology of Knowledge.* Harmondsworth: Penguin.

Bernstein, R.J. (ed.) (1960) *John Dewey: On Experience, Nature and Freedom: Representative Selections.* New York: The Liberal Arts Press.

Blackler, F. (1993) Knowledge and the Theory of Organizations: Organizations as Activity Systems and the Reframing of Management. *Journal of Management Studies,* 30 (6): 863–84.

Boud, D. and Garrick, J. (eds.) (1999) *Understanding Learning at Work.* London: Routledge.

Bredo, E. (1997) The Social Construction of Learning. In G. Phye (ed.), *Handbook of Academic Learning: Construction of Knowledge.* San Diego: Academic Press, 3–43.

Brown, J.S. and Duguid, P. (1991) Organizational Learning and Communities-of-Practice: Toward a Unified View of Working, Learning, and Innovation. *Organization Science,* 2 (1): 40–57.

Cook, S.D.N. and Brown, J.S. (1999) Bridging Epistemologies: The Generative Dance between Organizational Knowledge and Organizational Knowing. *Organization Science,* 10 (4): 381–400.

Cook, S.D.N. and Yanow, D. (1993) Culture and Organizational Learning. *Journal of Management Inquiry,* 2 (4): 373–90.

Cyert, R. and March, J. (1963) *A Behavioral Theory of the Firm.* Englewood Cliffs, NJ: Prentice Hall.

Dewey, J. (1916/1966) *Democracy and Education: An Introduction to the Philosophy of Education.* New York: The Free Press.

Dewey, J. (1933/1986) *How We Think: A Restatement of the Relation of Reflective Thinking to the Educative Process.* Boston: D.C. Heath and Company.

Dewey, J. (1938/1949) *Logic: The Theory of Inquiry.* New York: Henry Holt and Company.

Dodgson, M. (1993) Organizational Learning: A Review of Some Literatures. *Organization Studies,* 14 (3): 375–94.

Easterby-Smith, M. (1997) Disciplines of Organizational Learning: Contributions and Critiques. *Human Relations,* 50 (9): 1085–1113.

Easterby-Smith, M., Crossan, M., and Nicolini, D. (2000) Organizational Learning: Debates Past, Present and Future. *Journal of Management Studies,* 37 (6): 783–96.

Easterby-Smith, M., Snell, R., and Gherardi, S. (1998) Organizational Learning: Diverging Communities of Practice? *Management Learning*, 29 (3): 259–72.

Elkjaer, B. (1999) In Search of a Social Learning Theory. In M. Easterby-Smith, L. Araujo and J. Burgoyne (eds.), *Organizational Learning and the Learning Organization: Developments in Theory and Practice*. London: Sage, 75–91.

Elkjaer, B. (2000) The Continuity of Action and Thinking in Learning: Revisiting John Dewey. *Outlines: Critical Social Studies*, 2: 85–101.

Engeström, Y. (2001) Expansive Learning at Work: Toward an Activity Theoretical Reconceptualization. *Journal of Education and Work*, 14 (1): 133–56.

Fiol, M.C. and Lyles, M.A. (1985) Organizational Learning. *Academy of Management Review*, 10 (4): 803–13.

Gherardi, S. (1999) Learning as Problem-driven or Learning in the Face of Mystery. *Organization Studies*, 20 (1): 101–24.

Gherardi, S. (2000) Practice-based Theorizing on Learning and Knowing in Organizations. *Organization*, 7 (2): 211–23.

Gherardi, S., Nicolini, D., and Odella, F. (1998) Toward a Social Understanding of How People Learn in Organizations: The Notion of Situated Curriculum. *Management Learning*, 29 (3): 273–97.

Giorgi, A. (1975) An Application of Phenomenological Method in Psychology. In A. Giorgi, C.T. Fischer, and E.L. Murray (eds.), *Duquesne Studies in Phenomenological Psychology II*, Pittsburgh: Duquesne University, 82–103.

Henriksson, K. (1999) *The Collective Dynamics of Organizational Learning: On Plurality and Multi-Social Structuring*. Lund Studies in Economics and Management 49: The Institute of Economic Research. Lund: Lund University Press.

Henriksson, K. (2000) *When Communities of Practice Came to Town: On Culture and Contradiction in Emerging Theories of Organizational Learning*. Working Paper Series. Institute of Economic Research: Lund University.

Huber, G.P. (1991) Organizational Learning: The Contributing Processes and the Literatures. *Organization Science*, 2 (1): 88–115.

Larochelle, M., Bednarz, N., and Garrison, J. (eds.) (1998) *Constructivism and Education*. Cambridge: Cambridge University Press.

Lave, J. (1988) *Cognition in Practice: Mind, Mathematics and Culture in Everyday Life*. Cambridge: Cambridge University Press.

Lave, J. (1993) The Practice of Learning. In S. Chaiklin and J. Lave (eds.), *Understanding Practice: Perspectives on Activity and Context*. Cambridge: Cambridge University Press, 3–32.

Lave, J. (1997) Learning, Apprenticeship, Social Practice. *Nordisk Pedagogik*, 17 (3): 140–51.

Lave, J. and Wenger, E. (1991) *Situated Learning: Legitimate Peripheral Participation*. Cambridge: Cambridge University Press.

Levitt, B. and March, J.G. (1988) Organizational Learning. *Annual Review of Sociology*, 14: 319–40.

March, J. and Simon, H.A. (1958) *Organizations*. New York: Wiley.

McDermott, J.J. (1973/1981) *The Philosophy of John Dewey*. Chicago: University of Chicago Press.

McDermott, R.P. (1993) The Acquisition of a Child by a Learning Disability. In S. Chaiklin and J. Lave (eds.), *Understanding Practice: Perspectives on Activity and Context*. Cambridge: Cambridge University Press, 269–305.

Miettinen, R. (2000) The Concept of Experiential Learning and John Dewey's Theory of Reflective Thought and Action. *International Journal of Lifelong Education*, 19 (1): 54–72.

Miner, A.S. and Mezias, S.J. (1996) Ugly Duckling No More: Pasts and Futures of Organizational Learning Research. *Organization Science*, 7 (1): 88–99.

Mumford, A. (1991) Individual and Organizational Learning: The Pursuit of Change. *Industrial and Commercial Training*, 23 (6): 24–31.

Nevis, E.C., DiBella, A.J., and Gould, J.M. (1995) Understanding Organizations as Learning Systems. *Sloan Management Review*, 36 (2): 73–85.

Nicolini, D. and Meznar, M.B. (1995) The Social Construction of Organizational Learning: Conceptual and Practical Issues in the Field. *Human Relations*, 48 (7): 727–46.

Packer, M.J. and Goicoechea, J. (2000) Sociocultural and Constructivist Theories of Learning: Ontology, not just Epistemology. *Educational Psychologist*, 35 (4): 227–41.

Pedler, M. and Aspinwall, K. (1998) *A Concise Guide to the Learning Organization*. London: Lemos and Crane.

Popkewitz, T.S. (1998) Dewey, Vygotsky, and the Social Administration of the Individual: Constructivist Pegagogy as Systems of Ideas in Historical Spaces. *American Educational Research Journal*, 35 (4): 535–70.

Richter, I. (1998) Individual and Organizational Learning at the Executive Level: Towards a Research Agenda. *Management Learning*, 29 (3): 299–316.

Senge, P.M. (1990) *The Fifth Discipline: The Art and Practice of the Learning Organization*. New York: Doubleday Currency.

Senge, P., Kleiner, A., Roberts, C., Ross, R., Roth, G., and Smith, B. (1999) *The Dance of Change: The Challenges of Sustaining Momentum in Learning Organizations: A Fifth Discipline Resource*. London: Nicholas Breadley Publishing.

Shrivastava, P. (1983) A Typology of Organizational Learning Systems. *Journal of Management Studies*, 20 (1): 7–28.

Sleeper, R.W. (1986) *The Necessity of Pragmatism: John Dewey's Conception of Philosophy*. New Haven and London: Yale University Press.

Star, S.L. (1992) The Trojan Door: Organizations, Work, and the "Open Black Box". *Systems Practice*, 5 (4): 395–410.

Strauss, A.L. (1993) *Continual Permutations of Action*. New York: Aldine de Gruyter.

Tight, M. (2000) Critical Perspectives on Management Learning: A View from Adult/Continuing/Lifelong Education. *Management Learning*, 31 (1): 103–19.

Weick, K.E. and Westley, F. (1996) Organizational Learning: Affirming an Oxymoron. In S.R. Clegg, C. Hardy, and W.R. Nord (eds.), *Handbook of Organization Studies*. London: Sage, 440–58.

Yanow, D. (2000) Seeing Organizational Learning: A Cultural View. *Organization*, 7 (2): 247–68.

4

Knowledge Sharing and ICTs: A Relational Perspective

Niall Hayes and Geoff Walsham

Chapter Outline

Information communication technologies (ICTs) have been closely associated with the development of the great majority of knowledge management initiatives. However, most accounts have focused on technical aspects, while few have considered the use of information technology in relation to its social context. This chapter examines some of the challenges and opportunities that surround the use of ICTs in knowledge management initiatives from a relational perspective, which views knowledge as being processual, provisional and highly context dependent. Specifically we review the lessons arising within the relational literature that has considered this theme, and compare and contrast these insights with the issues that arose in a UK pharmaceuticals company which introduced a groupware application to support its knowledge management initiative. The chapter concludes by eliciting some lessons for both theory and practice, and prioritizing future research themes that consider ICTs and knowledge management.

Introduction

Knowledge work is a relatively new and dynamic area of research that has emerged as a direct response to the changing organizing processes that pervade many contemporary organizations. Hayman and Elliman (2000) define knowledge workers as people who enrich given information and who learn from the information that is communicated. They also view knowledge workers as being educated to a high level, having career loyalty to an area of expertise and being "given" significant autonomy in how they perform their tasks. Due to the emphasis on communication and information in knowledge work, information and communication technologies (ICTs) have been closely associated with the development of knowledge management initiatives (Zuboff, 1996; Hayes, 2001). Indeed, Easterby-Smith et al. (2000) estimate that 70 percent of publications on knowledge management have focused on the design of information technologies. In the commercial arena, most knowledge management initiatives have a strong IT focus, where knowledge is seen as capable of being leveraged through the development of shared databases and "knowledge warehouses." Zack (1999) distinguishes between two types of ICTs that assist in knowledge management projects: integrative and interactive applications. Integrative applications take the form of structured databases that allow employees to store and retrieve information on past projects, through best practice, contact records and working papers for example. Interactive applications take the form of discussion forums or desk-top conferencing, allowing for lessons, views and experiences to be shared regardless of physical location (Leidner, 2000; Whitley, 2000).

Within the academic literature, two contrasting epistemological approaches have underpinned knowledge management: the content and relational perspective (Scarbrough and Burrell, 1997; Tsoukas, 1996). This chapter adopts the latter perspective. From the content perspective, knowledge is defined as being a predicative truth as it prescribes what to do (Nonaka and Takeuchi, 1994; Galliers and Newell, 2000). Knowledge is viewed as being able to be codified and stored in knowledge repositories, which allows for knowledge to be shared, built upon and retained regardless of employee turnover (Wasko and Faraj, 2000). Much of this literature has a practitioner orientation and has focused on collecting, distributing, reusing and measuring existing codified knowledge (Cohen, 1998; Knock and McQueen, 1998). Many writers within this tradition have argued that there are knowledge markets, with knowledge buyers, sellers and brokers in organizations, who seek a personal gain in knowledge transactions (Prusak, 1997; Davenport and Prusak, 1998; Holsapple et al., 1996). Thus to summarize, from the content perspective, knowledge can be viewed as an economic asset that allows for predictive truth to be codified, stored, and exchanged between individuals within a firm (Bohm, 1994; Pan and Scarbrough, 1999; Shin et al., 2001).

Relational writers are critical of this dominant view of knowledge (Lave, 1988; Blackler et al., 1997), and suggest that instead of treating knowledge as being a largely cerebral and tradable entity, knowledge should be viewed as being relative, provisional, and primarily context-bound (Orr, 1990; Blackler et al., 1993; Barley, 1996). Rather than knowledge, relational writers argue that the focus of enquiry should be on the process of knowing and the capability to act (Blackler, 1995; Brown and Duguid, 1998; Schultze, 2000). Furthermore, many are critical of the content approach for its weak empirical base and prescriptive standpoint (Pan and Scarbrough, 1999). They suggest that exchanging knowledge as if it were an economic asset via ICTs does not relate to the actual experience of the use of knowledge management applications within specific contexts (Schultze, 2000). Relational writers also argue that it is important to view knowledge as reflecting one group or individual's viewpoint of the truth, which may be misunderstood, unjustified or contentious outside its own specific locality (Galliers and Newell, 2000).

The objective of this chapter is to examine some of the challenges and opportunities that surround the use of ICTs in intra-organizational knowledge management initiatives. To examine this theme, we will compare and contrast the issues that have been reported in the relational literature, with the issues that arose in a knowledge management initiative undertaken by a UK pharmaceuticals company, in order to garner some lessons primarily for theory, but also for practice (chapter 9 in this volume adopts a more

practitioner-oriented focus). The chapter is structured as follows. Following this introduction, we will review some of the key issues that have been reported in the relational
literature. The third section outlines the challenges that a pharmaceuticals company
encountered when introducing a leading groupware technology to support a knowledge
management initiative. The following sections then draw on the review of the literature
and the case study to consider implications for theory development and implications
for practitioners respectively. The final section presents some conclusions.

LITERATURE REVIEW

This section reviews some key themes in the relational literature concerned with the role
of ICTs in knowledge management initiatives. Table 4.1 highlights these themes, specific
issues pertinent to each theme, and some relevant references from the literature. Table 4.1
also outlines the structure of this section.

Knowledge and practice

One theoretical position that has had considerable influence in conceptualizing the relationship between ICTs and knowledge management has been the communities of practice approach. Indeed, Easterby-Smith et al. (2000) view the emergence of practice as a
unit of analysis as one of the most promising developments within organizational learning in recent times. Brown and Duguid (1998) argue that knowledge is socially embedded
within communities, and as such is inseparable from practice. They term this "knowledge
stickiness." Brown and Duguid (1998) suggest that through practice, a community develops a shared sense of what it does, its language, its prejudices and how it relates to other
·communities and their practices (Lave and Wenger, 1991; Boland and Tenkasi, 1995).
A community of practice consists of specialized knowledge workers, and includes divisions,
functional areas, product lines, professional specialities, project teams, and issue-based
committees (Boland and Tenkasi, 1995). Boland and Tenkasi (1995) explain that these
communities interweave with each other across various levels of the organization as, "individuals will find themselves as members of several communities of knowing operating
within a firm and its environment." Plaskoff, in chapter 9, provides a more detailed discussion of the composition of groups that justify the term "community." Furthermore,
though most writers see ICTs as being a useful aid in collaboration, due to the socially
embedded nature of knowledge, and its inseparability from practice, a reliance on the use
of ICTs to transfer knowledge is problematic (Brown, 1998; McDermott, 1999). The following subsections will review the extent and nature of the problems reported to occur
when sharing knowledge within communities, while the subsequent subsection will review
the problematic issues between communities.

Knowledge sharing within communities   Within communities, knowledge is viewed as circulat-
ing easily due to the shared sense of what practice is and what the standards for judgement are (King and Star, 1990; Brown and Duguid, 1998). Zack (1999) argues that due to
the shared understanding of practice, integrative applications that allow access to data

TABLE 4.1 Themes and issues in the relational literature on ICTs and knowledge work

Key theme	Issues arising within this theme	Indicative references
Knowledge/practice	Knowledge is socially embedded within practice	Easterby-Smith et al. (2000); Brown and Duguid (1998); Lave and Wenger (1991); Brown (1998); McDermott (1999)
	A reliance on ICTs to transfer knowledge is problematic	
Knowledge sharing within communities	Knowledge circulates relatively easily due to shared professional backgrounds	Brown and Duguid (1998); King and Star (1990)
	One view is that integrative applications are sufficient to support knowledge sharing	Zack (1999); Boland and Tenkasi (1995); McDermott (1999)
	IT may disrupt the ability of newcomers to learn from those with more expertise	Ruhleder (1994); Orlikowski (1996)
Knowledge sharing between communities	The emergence of new work arrangements	Schultze and Boland (2000a)
	IT may hinder understandings being shared across professional domains	Brown (1998); McDermott (1999); Schultze (2000); Hislop et al. (2000)
	Interactive applications are more suitable than integrative ones	Zack (1999); Olivera (2000); Ruhleder (1994)
	New facilitating roles are required	Zack (1999); Storck and Hill (2000)
Norms and culture	A strong IT focus is often at the expense of engendering an appropriate organizational climate	Liebowitz (2001)
	Culture should encourage co-operation, trust, innovation and enterprise	Zack (1999); Pan and Scarbrough (1999)
	Financial and career incentives may assist or hinder culture	Quinn et al. (1996); Orlikowski (1993)
Power and politics	Expertise is used to support the interests of specific groups	Hislop et al. (2000); Newell et al. (2000)
	Individualistic motivations for participation	Wasko and Faraj (2000)
	Visibility can lead to positive, negative or unexpected implications for participation	Wasko and Faraj (2000); Schultze and Boland (2000b)
	Knowledge management as a normative slogan	McDermott (1999); McKinley (2002); Knights et al. (1993)

stored centrally are sufficient to support work between employees from the same community, though others still advocate more interactive applications (Boland and Tenkasi, 1995; McDermott, 1999).

However, though ICT support within communities is generally viewed as being less problematic than working across community groups, Ruhleder (1994) warns that the introduction of an ICT may disrupt the ability of newcomers to learn from those with more expertise. She warns that when older members of the community do not understand how to use new systems, or do not use them effectively, then this may disrupt the transmission of domain expertise that had traditionally occurred through problem solving within the context of actual practice. This fear was borne out in Orlikowski's (1996) study of customer service analysts in a software company. She found that, after the introduction of shared databases that were used to assist analysts to respond to calls, work practices became increasingly dependent on the database. When the records on the database did not match the specific problem they were engaged in solving, or when the technology was not available, less experienced employees were incapable of responding to customer problems.

Knowledge sharing between communities As was noted in the previous subsection, sharing knowledge between employees with different professional backgrounds is viewed as more complex than within well-established communities (Ruhleder, 1995; Brown and Duguid, 1998; Newell et al., 2000). Schultze and Boland's (2000a) study of US Company, a manufacturer of building materials, found that the introduction of KnowMor, a knowledge management application that bridged the different functions and locations, led to changing temporal and spatial work arrangements. They provide an example of the Notes administrators being required to perform not only technical activities, as previously, but also to write accounts of their actions into shared databases. Work practice changed in that they would now point users to these entries rather than deal with requests themselves. Schultze and Boland (2000a) explain that the new work practices required them to perform a dual role of an acting (in terms of the technical change) and accounting self (in terms of making explicit their technical work).

A further challenge relates to the limited understandings that can be developed when reliance is placed on ICTs to share knowledge between communities. Brown's (1998) insightful study of the use of the Internet to support knowledge working found that a reliance on technology as a means of transferring knowledge is insufficient. Instead he contended that abstractions recorded and shared on the Internet need to be considered as being inseparable from their own historical and social locations of practice. McDermott (1999) provided a detailed analysis of why reliance on abstractions is problematic. He cited the case of a diverse group of systems designers to illustrate what he termed the difficulties of thinking "outside an expert's own territory." He ascertained that, rather than needing each other's documentation stored on a common database, the system designers needed to understand the logic that other designers used in practice, such as the rationale behind the combination of specific software, hardware, and service plans. Similarly, Schultze's (2000) case study of experts across US Company discovered that each group had their own conventions. She explained that the information technology professionals emphasized the importance of documentation, while the competitive intelligence analysts emphasized secrecy and selective dissemination. Hislop et al.'s (2000) study of Cent Co., an international manufacturing company, found that domain expertise could not be encoded in documents and policies or ICT infrastructures. Instead, they discovered that social networks were developed to transfer the domain specific information. The above studies have all indicated that, as knowledge is tied to disciplinary practice, crossing professional boundaries is highly problematic when an emphasis is placed on ICTs.

Thus, due to the difficulties of working between communities, many suggest that attention needs to be given to the nature of ICT support. When there is no shared history of working together, Zack (1999) argues that integrative applications are unsuitable. Instead he recommends the use of interactive applications that support *ad hoc* collaboration (such as discussion databases and video conferencing) as being more appropriate. Olivera's (2000) study of a consulting company found that users preferred interacting with people rather than computer-based systems such as the intranet. Though he notes this preference is not atypical, in this case he viewed it as surprising due to the consultants being highly sophisticated technology users. Further to this, writers in this tradition have suggested that the formality demanded by technologies can leave little room for the more productive informal and unexpected relations to occur (Ruhleder, 1994; Brown and Duguid, 1998; Hayes, 2000). Brown and Duguid (1998) suggest that, when technology constrains work practices, this often results in users subverting formal designs so that they may allow for more expansive interaction (Hayes, 2000).

In addition to emphasizing the importance of developing social networks between communities and the careful design of electronic support, several authors have suggested that working between communities requires the creation of new facilitating roles. Zack (1999) emphasizes the importance of the appointment of facilitators who are charged with encouraging, interpreting and evaluating participation in cross-community electronic forums. Storck and Hill (2000) found that Xerox unit managers undertook facilitating roles so as to encourage knowledge sharing. They would present talks on their initiatives and question participants about what they had learned. They would then record and circulate the key messages electronically to the broader community. Storck and Hill (2000) also discovered that facilitators in Xerox looked for mutual interests that masked differences in hierarchical status among members, so as to encourage commitment and reduce uncertainty. Schultze and Boland's (2000a) case also indicated that facilitators could assist in alleviating the difficulties arising from "information overload." They found that a particular knowledge management system, KnowMor, circulated information widely in US Company, which resulted in staff feeling they could not respond to or keep up-to-date with the amount of information they received. Schultze and Boland suggested that, prior to the introduction of KnowMor, analysts had performed a key-facilitating role, by disseminating information continuously, and on a "who needs to know basis."

Norms and culture

One pervasive theme in the information systems literature is that many knowledge management initiatives have focused exclusively on technology at the expense of creating an appropriate organizational culture (Liebowitz, 2001). Based on his case studies of Technology Research Inc. and Buckman Laboratories, Zack (1999) argued that the technology focus was a major obstacle to engendering an organizational climate that valued and encouraged cooperation, trust, and innovation. Pan and Scarbrough's (1999) study of

Buckman laboratories similarly argued that in addition to the K'netix knowledge network (which comprised customer and manufacturing databases as well as email, discussion forums and virtual conference rooms) an enterprising culture needed establishing whereby associates felt motivated and rewarded. Storck and Hill's (2000) study of Xerox found that in addition to technology, the climate also contributed to the success of the knowledge management initiative. They described how Xerox had relaxed the centralized control structure, so as to allow participants to identify with, and be committed to, their community rather than to Xerox as a whole. They concluded that within communities, this engendered a climate that allowed for openness, trust and commitment.

In addition, several writers have suggested that reward structures require change to provide an incentive for employees to work collaboratively. Quinn et al.'s (1996) study of Merrill Lynch and NovaCare discovered that groupware, in tandem with new incentive systems and the inversion of the traditional hierarchical structure, allowed both organizations to tailor themselves to the particular way in which their professional intellectual capital creates value. Orlikowski's (1993) study of a US consulting company argued that both the competitive promotion and financial reward structure led to Lotus Notes, the leading groupware technology, remaining largely unused by consultants. However, she found that between the technologists and senior consultants who were not subject to the competitive culture, Notes was used to share their knowledge and experience in order to aid them in conducting their work. The view emerging from these studies is that rewards based on individual effort should be replaced by those that reward reciprocity and entrepreneurship to encourage extensive use of ICTs (Pan and Scarbrough, 1999; Zack, 1999).

Political issues and knowledge sharing

A final important theme to emerge in the literature relates to the inseparability of knowledge management initiatives from issues of power and politics. Surprisingly, within the organizational learning literature, issues of power and politics were noted by Easterby-Smith et al. (2000) to have been somewhat neglected in the past. In relation to ICTs, however, some studies have considered this theme. Hislop et al. (2000) identified that in Pharma Co., a UK company concerned with the development and production of nuclear medicine, external expertise and information were utilized by groups as a political resource to reinforce and support their particular visions for change. They also described how groups supporting the interests of senior managers received the authoritative support and financial resources to bring about changes. Newell et al.'s (2000) study found that the introduction of communication forums reinforced the 'powerful centrifugal forces' in their firm. Wasko and Faraj's (2000) study of discussion groups on the Internet showed that many participated in the discussion databases as a means to further their own individualistic agendas. They discovered that discussion databases were viewed as an important resource to gain a name for themselves, to generate job opportunities or to try to gain customers for their consulting firm.

Several studies have also indicated that the visibility technology provides of the views and work practices of participants may result in negative, positive or unexpected implications. In Wasko and Faraj's (2000) study, the visibility had negative consequences. They describe how some people who did not feel confident with their level of ability would not contribute to the Usenet group as they feared being ridiculed about any inaccurate or unso-phisticated views they recorded. Wasko and Faraj described occasions when employees engaged in personal attacks as a means of trying to demonstrate their superior expertise. In contrast, Schultze and Boland's (2000b) study of US Company indicated how the infor-mation technology consultants would visibly record their work in the databases as a means to protect themselves from any blame that may subsequently be leveled by their clients or other consultants. Schultze and Boland's case further indicated how the visibility that KnowMor provided could unintentionally have a negative effect on relationships within US Company. For example, one analyst felt that his role had inadvertently been threat-ened due to the way another employee had harnessed the visibility KnowMor provided. KnowMor had allowed this latter employee to be aware of and widely circulate some details about a merger that the analyst should have been aware of. The analyst resented the implication that he was not doing his job well, and responded to the issue by revoking the employee's access to KnowMor.

McDermott (1999) argued that, due to the pervasiveness of politics in knowledge working, one key challenge is not to homogenize views, but to encourage diverse collabo-ration, and an appreciation of the context specific insights of members from other com-munities. McKinley (2000) supports this view and warns against ICTs being used in knowledge management projects for surveillance and control activities. Knights et al. (1993) are highly critical about ICT's role in knowledge management. They suggest that studies on technologically focused organizational developments such as knowledge man-agement are merely normative slogans which have, "tended to be heavy on notion of nego-tiation and trust between members of the network and exceptionally light on domination and power-relations-interdependent relationships based on reciprocity and mutual trust, where self interest is sacrificed for the communal good." They further argue that the dom-inant views of knowledge work are superficial as they neglect their embeddedness in institutional power relations that are hierarchical, competitive, coercive, and exploitative (Aldrich and Whetten, 1981; Walsham, 1993).

This brief review of the literature has highlighted some important areas of study that have arisen due to the use of ICTs in knowledge management initiatives. ICTs have been seen to have been used relatively unproblematically within communities, but have raised significant challenges between communities, in part due to the new work practices that they engender between members of different professional domains. This requires new roles and skills, as well as the interaction of different normative contexts, and different finan-cial and career structures. Finally, these new forms of working and the visibility that the technology provides engender new forms of political activity. These themes will be explored, in varying degrees, in the following section, through the detailed discussion of the use of a groupware technology in a UK pharmaceuticals company.

KNOWLEDGE SHARING IN COMPOUND UK

This section presents in detail some issues concerning knowledge working across bound-aries that arose in Compound UK, the UK selling division of a multinational pharma-ceuticals company (see also Hayes and Walsham, 2000a, 2000b; Hayes, 2001). The first subsection outlines the background to the company, and the main uses of Lotus Notes, which was introduced to support knowledge management. The second subsection discusses how the reliance on the use of Notes to work collaboratively between communities restricted the degree to which employees could ascertain the views and experiences of others, and utilize them in their day-to-day practices. The final subsection will consider how the visibility that resulted from the reliance on the use of Lotus Notes to work between functional boundaries led to some employees adopting different political strategies.

Compound UK

Compound UK is concerned primarily with selling pharmaceutical products to hospitals and general practices, while also undertaking clinical trials of new drugs with participating doctors in Great Britain and Northern Ireland. The UK pharmaceuticals sector saw major change over the late 1980s and 1990s as a result of reforms in the UK healthcare sector. These reforms sought to achieve cost savings by introducing an internal market place (Flynn and Williams, 1997). The introduction of these market reforms split the healthcare sector between primary care and specialist care. The primary care sector covers general practices, while the specialist care sector covers hospital markets. Since the reforms, many primary care doctors are fund-holders. They have budgetary responsibilities for drugs, hospital referrals and staff as well as for their fixed costs. Hospitals are also more autonomous from the Department of Health than they were prior to the reforms, and are responsible for their own budgets (Connah and Pearson, 1991). As a consequence, specialist care doctors are part of a large group of decision-makers, including managers and accountants. From the point of view of Compound UK, this meant not only that purchasers were looking for cost savings, but also that sales situations now included a wider range of stakeholders having an influence in purchasing decisions.

As figure 4.1 indicates, Compound UK consisted of five departments. Our research study focused on the commercial function. In 1996, the commercial function consisted of its director, 8 regional managers, 12 area managers, and around 150 sales representatives (reps). All members of the commercial function, apart from the director, worked from their own homes, while employees working in other departments were located at the head office, Compound Square. These functions included the medical function, which undertook clinical trials, and the marketing department, which performed market analysis, compiled the sales material and arranged conferences. As part of the response to the sectoral changes outlined above, Lotus Notes was introduced as a means to encourage employees to draw on all areas of the organization to work and share information and knowledge across functional and geographic boundaries.

In addition to an electronic mail (e-mail) facility, there were three main uses of Lotus Notes, as summarized in table 4.2. First, it was used to create a database to support the cooperative activities involved in strategic selling. Strategic selling was a sales approach that helped employees to identify those individuals within a hospital or general practice that had an influence on the purchasing decisions. The shared databases supported this process by allowing views and contributions to be structured and shared between those involved in securing a particular sales account. The second and most prevalent use of Notes

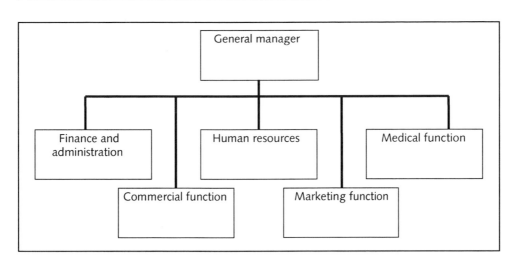

Figure 4.1   Organizational structure of Compound UK

TABLE 4.2   Key uses of Lotus Notes in Compound UK

Lotus Notes component	Intended opportunity for participation
E-mail	To enable one-to-one communication between individuals
Strategic selling	To enable employees in different functions to input their views and information in a structured way with the aim of bringing together the employees' shared knowledge so that they might contribute to a successful sale
Contact recording	To enable employees to record and review the views, interests and requirements of particular doctors
Discussion databases	To enable employees to review the thread of discussions that had emerged on a particular issue

was the contact recording database. In addition to recording the number of doctors that reps visited, as had been the case since the 1970s, the Lotus Notes databases also required employees to record specific details about doctors such as the outcome of the meeting, the doctor's personal and medical interests, and their involvement in clinical trials. Together, the strategic selling and contact recording databases soon built up a vast chronology of details that allowed employees in all functions an increased awareness of a particular customer and their interactions with Compound UK. This was viewed as being particularly beneficial for new reps or medics joining the company, or existing employees changing their job.

The final use of Notes was the provision of a wide variety of shared databases which allowed employees with the same and different professional backgrounds to discuss issues that were of interest or concern. They typically focused on issues, products or a particular role such as the ways that the products were marketed and sold. Finally, as reps were mostly unavailable during the day, when they were travelling to visit doctors and other stakeholders, Notes also bridged the different times of working between members of the sales force and employees located at Compound Square. Notes allowed reps to review and respond to their electronic mail and the shared databases before they left home in the morning or when they returned in the evening.

A qualitative research approach underpinned the longitudinal empirical work undertaken in Compound UK. The aim was to gain a detailed understanding of the activities employees undertook, and the meanings they attributed to them in the course of their everyday interactions (Van Maanan, 1979; Hammersley and Atkinson, 1983). The research was carried out in two phases over a two-and-a-half year period. Phase 1 lasted between October 1995 and February 1996. During this phase, 33 in-depth interviews were carried out. Phase 2 took place between February 1997 and May 1997. During this phase 21 follow-up interviews were conducted in order to try to understand the use of cooperative systems over time. In both phases, interviews would typically last between one and three hours each, and were supplemented by social interactions in the cafeteria and during drinks in the evening with employees. These extensive interactions were intended to further reveal a "rich under life" that is usually seen as being masked to quantitative researchers (Geertz, 1973), and to those qualitative researchers that place their emphasis solely on undertaking interviews.

Sharing knowledge explicitly across boundaries

Though recording views and details on the shared databases presented considerable opportunities for employees to work across boundaries, it was not without difficulties. One difficulty that pervaded crossing functional boundaries was the *limited awareness of what it was to occupy the role of another employee.* Historically, formal and informal meetings tended to be function specific, and this continued to be the case after the introduction of Lotus Notes. This left the organization-wide databases as the main way for employees located in the different functions to collaborate together. However, due to the lack of experience and understanding of the backgrounds and assumptions of employees in different disciplines, many employees felt considerable uncertainty about what they required from each other, and exactly how they could draw on each other's expertise. This led to animosity, particularly between staff based at Compound Square and the field force. Those located centrally were scathing of the sales force as they saw many problems which they encountered arising from the limited quantity and quality of details recorded by reps on the contact recording and strategic selling databases. As an information technology developer mentioned: "They [reps] do not see the wider picture, and as such do not see the benefits of their extra work [sic] to the rest of the company."

However, reps were furious that often they received e-mail requests from those working centrally for information that they had already recorded on the shared databases. This left them feeling ill disposed to recording detailed information in the future. These misunderstandings were compounded by the differing times of working between the field force and Compound Square. As reps were away from home all day, and sometimes at night, they were often unable to respond as promptly to messages or complete the shared databases as staff in Compound Square may require.

Working across functional boundaries was restricted further due to the *highly personal or profession specific information staff were required to codify on the various components of the cooperative technology*. Several employees portrayed the information recorded on Notes as being highly personal and meaningless unless it was read by people in the same locality and/or from the same background. As one medical expert mentioned: "I can put letters onto the database, but not my whole diary. You can not put this level of detail into a Notes database, and much of what I do input must be meaningless to others."

Many reps were adamant that no amount of information they recorded on Lotus Notes would provide either new reps or employees located in other functions with the extent of access to doctors that many of them enjoyed. They suggested that their extensive access to doctors arose from their long-established relationships rather than the details that they recorded on Notes. Other less confident employees feared that what they recorded may be misunderstood or might appear stupid or irrelevant to other employees. The preclusion of recording personal information about stakeholders due to the Data Protection Act (1989) compounded these limitations. For example, though many reps wanted to record a particular doctor's model of car and registration number, as it indicated which doctors were working that day, the legislation prohibited this. This limited participation resulted in many experts' views, experiences and activities being invisible to other employees. Thus, much of what employees were able to make discursive on the shared databases was only felt to be a simplistic representation of what they sought to convey.

Sharing views on the role or functional specific databases was generally less problematic. This was due to the *intimate understandings and experience of working with others in the same function*. This local mastery was sustained not only through the use of Notes, but also through the regular formal and informal face-to-face discussions and interactions. This meant that the challenges reported in this subsection were not as significant within communities, as compared to between communities.

Compounding the difficulties reported in this subsection were *the increased workloads* that many employees associated with using the different components of Notes. The collaborative activities that Notes was intended to support were in addition to their existing activities and responsibilities. In addition, many reps felt overwhelmed with the diversity and number of requests that they received, and the number of databases that they felt they should review. Consequently, reps in particular had little time to develop relationships with employees located within Compound Square.

Visibility and politicizing

In addition to the challenges arising from the reliance on the use of Notes to ascertain the views and experiences of others, the political and non-political motivations that different employees had for participation also presented significant challenges to working across professional boundaries. Our study highlighted how several *senior managers harnessed the surveillance capacity Lotus Notes provided* to try to ensure that reps worked in the ways that they promoted. Not long after Notes was introduced, the commercial director instructed the

Notes developer to devise a league facility which could indicate centrally how many contact records and strategic selling sheets had been completed by each sales representative. The strategic selling manager would then send out electronic messages to field force managers to inform them about their reps' position in the league tables. Area managers felt obliged to inform members of their sales team that their low contact recording rates had been noticed centrally.

In addition to using the contact records for league tables, some senior managers would regularly review the detailed comments and observations that reps had recorded, so that they could gain an insight into how Compound UK's products were faring. The strategic selling database also allowed monitoring by senior managers of how reps were planning their more complex sales. If this was not in the way advocated by senior management, the strategic selling manager would contact the reps' area manager to inform them. This confirmed many of the reps' suspicions about the intention behind the electronic contact recording and strategic selling databases, namely to increase central surveillance and control.

Some reps welcomed the extensive surveillance capacity and harnessed it as a means to *further their careers rather than to share knowledge*. With regards to contact recording, reps were advised by their senior managers to only input relevant calls (i.e. only those stakeholders that could make a purchasing decision or if something of significance had occurred prior to their previous visit) into the contact recording database. However, regardless of this, some ambitious reps continued to register a high position in the league table as they viewed this as a good opportunity to prove to senior managers that they were working hard. In addition, many career-orientated reps would seek to gain favor with the strategic selling manager, by working on a considerable number of strategic selling sheets at any moment in time.

Many *non-careerist reps were quite resentful of those reps that used Notes to try to further their careers* rather than to share knowledge. Non-careerist reps were generally those that had been doing the job for some time, and had mostly given up any hopes they had for further advancement, while careerist reps were ambitious, and tended to be younger. Non-careerist reps did not see the point of entering every visit they made unless there was something worthwhile that other members of the company could benefit from. Nor did they mind completing strategic selling sheets when sales situations were truly complex, but felt that careerist reps merely completed them to gain favor with the strategic selling manager. As one rep mentioned: "There are not that many complex sales situations in my area, and I only need to keep active a few strategic selling accounts at a time, unlike some of the shining stars!"

Due to the extensive use careerist reps made of the contact recording and strategic selling databases, non-careerist reps felt normatively obliged to complete a "satisfactory" amount of contact records and strategic selling sheets so as not to be singled out by the strategic selling manager, regardless of their relevance. Though this was kept to as minimal a level as they thought was acceptable, they felt frustration with their peers for having to undertake what they saw as being a futile and time-consuming task.

Ambitious employees also viewed the *national discussion databases as providing a means to further their careers*. They would respond positively to any views and comments that senior managers recorded on the discussion databases. As a result of this politicizing, many non-careerist employees did not see any benefit from participating in discussions that were dominated by what one rep described as: "ambitious people competing with each other about who could shout the loudest."

Though all the company-wide databases that were deemed highly political, *some discussion databases were considered to be safe from heavy politicizing*. Some non-careerist employees did include themselves in the functional or regional specific shared databases. On these databases, many non-ambitious reps would discuss the ways that they had approached sales situations and other areas of interest that they shared. In addition, those employees that had experience of working with members of other functions would discuss and provide advice to less experienced members of their own community on how they could best interact with members of other functions. However, ambitious reps did not make much use of these local forums, as they viewed their time being better spent on career-enhancing national discussion forums.

THEORIZING KNOWLEDGE SHARING

This section will compare and contrast the issues in the literature review with the case study in order to garner some lessons primarily for researchers to consider concerning the role of ICTs in knowledge sharing. We will first examine how existing theorizations may be extended in relation to the changing work practices that arise from a reliance on textual narratives to share knowledge within and between professional domains. Second, we will suggest that existing theoretical insights do not sufficiently recognize that sharing knowledge on electronic forums is a highly political process.

Narrative and working between and within communities

This subsection will examine why and how work practices change as a result of the use of ICTs in knowledge management initiatives. Though this theme was highlighted in the literature review, only Schultze and Boland's (2000b) study of US Company explicitly considered the detailed content of these new work arrangements. They found that new work arrangements arose due to the reliance on the use of ICTs to work across spatial, temporal and functional boundaries (Walsham, 1998). They described how these new work practices required employees to perform a dual role of both an "acting" and "accounting" self. This conceptual distinction was apparent in Compound UK. Employees "acted" in terms of selling products or undertaking clinical trials, and then "accounted" for their practice by making explicit their activities and views on the various databases that bridged the spatial, temporal and functional boundaries. However, in trying to make explicit their sales and medical work, employees needed to make sense of their own activities in a way that was comprehensible to others, and also make sense of and utilize the accounts of others. This involved them continually engaging themselves in a highly reflexive sensemaking process. Consequently, though we consider Schultze and Boland's (2000b) two constructs as being insightful, we suggest that they have not explicitly recognized the on going reflexive sensemaking processes that underpin the acting and accounting self. We suggest

TABLE 4.3   Acting, accounting and sensemaking processes when working between professional
groups

- ◆ Reflexively monitor and make sense of their own on-going activities so that they can account
  for them in linear prose
- ◆ Account for their activities on shared forums in a way that is comprehensible to members of
  their own or other professional domains
- ◆ Make sense of the accounts recorded by members of other professions on shared forums and
  then utilize them in their own activities
- ◆ Facilitators can assist in acting, accounting and sensemaking processes

that sensemaking processes comprise three interrelated work practices, which collectively
represent a significant challenge to the use of ICTs in knowledge management initiatives.
This is discussed more fully below and key points are summarized in table 4.3.

One central challenge for acting and accounting processes relates to how in accounting for the activities employees undertake, they are required to *reflexively monitor and make
sense of their own on-going activities* (what they have done, how they achieved this in specific
contexts, what their views are etc.), *so that they can account for them in linear prose*. Making their
activities explicit on an on-going basis is alien to most employees who are typically only
required to account for what they have done when problems have arisen (Giddens, 1984:
6). Furthermore, the work practices and views that employees are able to make discursive
in textual form are not fully representative of the histories, activities, and assumptions that
underpin their formulation, and as such, are only likely to be partial rationalizations of
the complexity that underpins their practice (Brown, 1998; Hayes, 2001). In addition to
these new sensemaking skills, staff may not have the writing skills required to clearly convey
in textual form the meaning that they intended. In Compound UK, many feared that what
they recorded may be misinterpreted, particularly by employees in other professional
domains. Thus we suggest that future studies need to be sensitive to the on-going reflexive
sensemaking processes that people engage in when rationalizing their activities, and the
extent to which they have the writing skills to account for their activities in textual form.
Neither of these points have been made explicit in Schultze and Boland's acting and
accounting concepts, or in the wider literature.

A further challenge for acting and accounting processes arising from the underlying
construct of sensemaking relates to how employees are required to *account for their activities
on shared forums in a way that is comprehensible to members of their own or other professional domains.*
In Compound UK, formulating accounts so that they were meaningful to others involved
staff monitoring the extent, tone and nature of the accounts that other staff had made
available on the shared forums, and to a much lesser extent, any in-depth interactions that
had taken place. Based on our case, and the findings of Brown (1998), we suggest that a
reliance on reflexively monitoring and making sense of the accounts others have recorded
on shared forums so as to account for their activities in a way that is accessible to members
of other professional domains will always be limited. This is due to the inseparability of
these abstractions from their own historical and social locations of practice. Understanding and providing theoretical insights into the reflexive sensemaking processes that people

engage in when endeavoring to account for their own activities' textual form so that they are accessible and meaningful to others, is perhaps one of the most significant challenges that arises in knowledge sharing.

A third and related challenge to acting and accounting processes concerns how knowledge management initiatives typically require people to *make sense of the accounts recorded by members of other professions on shared forums and then utilize them in their own activities*. Our case and several of the empirical studies reviewed above have indicated that a reliance on accounts recorded on discussion forums to collaborate across professional disciplines does not provide a sufficient insight into the "path of thinking" or different conventions that underpins the logic that other professions draw upon in their practice (Schultze, 2000; McDermott, 1999). Indeed, Hislop et al.'s (2000) study found that domain expertise could not be encoded on ICTs, and instead was transferred via social networks. Thus, we suggest that making sense of the conventions of others and taking this into account in their activities requires reflexive engagement in practice, in addition to the use of shared forums, with members of different professional domains. This ongoing sensemaking process provides the basis for people to develop a deeper understanding of the assumptions that underpin the work practices and formulation of accounts recorded by members of different professional groups (Brown, 1998). We suggest that further theoretical developments should examine how people make sense of the narratives recorded by members of other professions and utilize them in their ongoing practice.

Furthermore, though some of the literature has focused on the importance of facilitators, we suggest that these accounts can be developed further by considering *how facilitators assist in acting, accounting and sensemaking processes* that the use of ICTs require employees to undertake when engaging in knowledge sharing. Indeed, the facilitators in Storck and Hill's (2000) study of Xerox undertook activities that could assist with this. Examples included the presentations that were made by members of the different professional domains, and how they questioned staff about what they had learned.

The above issues arising from work between professional groups are likely to be less severe when working within professional domains. Our study and some of the literature has indicated that this is due to the well established shared assumptions, rationales, premises and work practices (King and Star, 1990; Hayes, 2001), within specific professional domains. However, considering the first point in table 4.3, the challenges surrounding rationalizing the complexity that underpins practice is as relevant within as it is between professional domains. Also, the issue reported in the literature review section above, concerning the disruption that a reliance on ICTs may present to newcomers to learn from those with more expertise, remains a challenge to acting, accounting and specifically sensemaking processes (Ruhleder, 1994; Orlikowski, 1996).

Political motivations for cross-community participation

This subsection focuses on how political and normative issues shape and are shaped by the use of shared electronic forums. An initial observation arising from the literature review is that theoretical and empirical insights in this area have not been as plentiful as the issues warrant. One theoretical approach, developed by Hayes and Walsham (2000b, 2001),

TABLE 4.4   Key themes arising in relation to political and normative issues

♦ The visibility of political enclaves may exacerbate careerist motivations arising from an individualistic reward structure

♦ Senior managers may harness the surveillance capacity that political enclaves provide to reinforce their dominant positions

♦ Acting, accounting and sensemaking processes are viewed as being inseparable from their political and normative context

♦ Views that are homogenized to reflect senior management perspectives limit knowledge management initiatives

♦ The maintenance of safe enclaves is a fragile process

involves the constructs of political and safe enclaves. Political enclaves describe contexts for participation that resembles a public façade, while safe enclaves describe contexts for participation that allow for more genuine views and assumptions to be exposed. We will draw on these two constructs below to discuss the challenges that knowledge management initiatives face in relation to political and normative issues. The discussion is summarized in table 4.4.

Reward structure   A first theme relates to how the reward structure, and the visibility which political enclaves provide, may influence the motivations that people have for participation. In Compound UK, careerist employees harnessed the visibility that the contact recording and strategic selling databases provided to indicate to senior managers that they were working hard and in the ways advocated. On the discussion databases, they could indicate to senior managers that they were contributing to the development of new insights, while also concurring with the views of senior managers. Though several studies have made a cursory reference to the importance of the reward structure in knowledge management initiatives, very few have explicitly considered how the career reward system can influence the nature of participation. Of those that have, Orlikowski's (1993) study found that consultants did not make any use of Lotus Notes as it was not associated with either the career or the financial reward structure, while Quinn et al. (1996) discovered that modifying the reward structure to emphasize reciprocity was vital to the success of Merrill Lynch's and NovaCare's knowledge management initiatives. However, neither study highlighted how the visibility that political enclaves provide may exacerbate careerist motivations that arise from an individualistic reward structure, and how this may assist or hinder knowledge management initiatives. We suggest this is an important issue for future studies to examine.

Domination and control   A second important theme concerns the way that senior managers may harness the surveillance capacity that political enclaves provide to reinforce their dominant positions (McKinley, 2000; Newell et al., 2000; Walsham, 2001). In Compound UK, senior managers used the information all employees recorded (especially careerist employees) to coordinate and control much more of their employees' day-to-day activities. This was evident in the way that the contact recording and strategic selling databases were used by some senior managers. This had the effect of simultaneously increasing the dominance of senior management, while reducing the autonomy of middle managers dealing directly with the sales force. This effect was in contrast to the espoused intention surrounding the introduction of Lotus Notes, and indeed the majority of knowledge management initiatives reported in the literature, which envisage a relaxing of hierarchical control so as to engender trust and cooperation (Pan and Scarbrough, 1999; Zack, 1999; Storck and Hill, 2000). We suggest that though several studies have considered how the surveillance capacity that political enclaves provide may limit the nature and extent of participation, few accounts to date have considered the implications for knowledge management initiatives arising from the reduced authority of middle managers.

Acting, accounting and sensemaking   The construct of political enclaves can further sensitize the ideas developed in the previous subsection concerning the acting, accounting and sensemaking self. In Compound UK, when staff made sense of their own activities and then decided how they would represent these to others, they did this by considering what would be politically and normatively acceptable to others. For example, careerist reps formulated their activities and accounted for them in ways that they thought would meet senior management approval, and with this enhance their career prospects. Furthermore, when non-careerist reps made sense of the representations others recorded on the cross-functional discussion databases, many were aware of the political undertones that lay behind them. This sensemaking process led to their non-participation. In relation to the contact recording and strategic selling databases, even though non-careerist reps saw much of the use they made of them as being futile, they were conscious to account for their activities in a way that would be normatively acceptable to senior managers. Thus we suggest it is vital that acting, accounting and sensemaking processes are viewed as being inseparable from their political and normative context.

Homogenization   A further theme in relation to political enclaves concerns how homogenizing views so that they reflect senior management perspectives limits knowledge management initiatives (McDermott, 1999). This was apparent in the Compound UK case study in the nature of interaction in all organization-wide shared forums. We suggest that examining the latitude which employees have to distance themselves from received wisdom is a fundamental challenge for future studies to investigate (Brown and Duguid, 1991). Furthermore, we suggest that this will require future work to move beyond utopian accounts that hypothesize what the appropriate culture for knowledge management initiatives may be, to being more sensitive to the hierarchical, coercive and competitive nature of knowledge work (Knights et al., 1993).

Safe enclaves   With respect to the construct of safe enclaves, the use made of role or function specific forums in the Compound UK case study lived up to many of the criteria for success that have been reported in the literature. These include trust, openness and reciprocity (Pan and Scarbrough, 1999; Zack, 1999; Storck and Hill, 2000). However, our case also indicated that their relative success in knowledge sharing rested precariously upon several important features. First they were all domain specific, which meant that employees felt confident that their representations would be understood by members of their own professional domain, and that they could easily be made sense of as being genuine. Second, they were all optional, which meant they were not associated with the normative control structure. Third, senior managers were not privy to the discussions that occurred on safe enclaves. Finally, and relatedly, many careerist reps optionally excluded themselves from using them, as they saw their time as being better spent using the community wide political enclaves to further their own career aspirations. We suggest that the maintenance of safe enclaves is a fragile process, as the removal or change of one or more of the elements listed above may result in a change in the extent and nature of their use.

NORMATIVE GUIDELINES FOR THE DEVELOPMENT OF ICT APPLICATIONS TO SUPPORT BOUNDARY CROSSING

What does this review of the literature, our case, and our conclusions imply for the design of ICT support for knowledge management? This penultimate section draws upon the analysis presented in the previous section to establish guidelines for developers to consider, first when ICTs are used to support work between communities, and second for work within communities. The term "developers" is a deliberately broad category to refer to all those involved in the creation, introduction and review of shared forums.

First and foremost, we suggest that developers need to establish education programs to assist in countering the difficulties that have been reported to arise in relation to acting, accounting and sensemaking processes. These programs should aim to provide staff an insight into the conventions and rationales of members of other professional domains, and furthermore a detailed understanding of their work practices. To achieve this, the program should first consist of experts from different professional backgrounds making presentations that outline the typical tasks they perform and the logic that they use to undertake their work. They should also present examples of the different types of information and expertise that they would like members of other functions to contribute. Second, to solidify their sensemaking processes, participants should undertake exercises on the knowledge management application with program participants from different professional domains, so as to provide them with feedback about how they could improve their accounting processes. Third, developers should rebuff access to organization-wide shared databases until they are satisfied that each employee's accounting and sensemaking processes have reached an adequate level of competence. We further suggest that developers need to develop one-off programs when there are any significant changes in the ways that specific professional domains undertake their work, and especially if any large-scale restructurings take place. Education programs of this sort will require levels of ongoing investment and senior management commitment that is typically not associated with groupware implementations (Grudin, 1990), which may be one of the most difficult issues to address.

A final guideline for developers to consider is the need for mentors to be assigned to less experienced staff. Mentors should be staff that are experienced in working with employees in the varying professional domains. First, mentors should review the contributions made by less experienced staff and advise them how they could better meet the needs of members of other professions. Second, mentors should assist their charges in making sense of the representations recorded by members of other professions. Finally, mentors should highlight circumstances where in-depth face-to-face interactions may be more beneficial than relying on representations recorded on the ICT.

In relation to countering the difficulties arising from political and normative issues, due to the complexity that surrounds how the political and normative context is continually produced and reproduced, generating guidelines in the relatively prescriptive form described so far in this subsection is more difficult (see chapter 9 for more detailed guidelines). However, there are several issues relating to the symbolism that senior managers exhibit in their on-going use of shared discussion forums that organizations should bear in mind. We suggest that senior managers need to recognize that when people account for their activities on shared forums, they endeavor to do so in a way that they deem to be politically and normatively acceptable to senior managers. They do this by continually monitoring the use that senior managers have made of the discussion forums. This will include the consistency of the tone and nature of views recorded, how the visibility that the technology provides has been harnessed to monitor and control their subordinates' practice, which discussion forums they have participated in or utilized, and their conduct and directives outside the discussion forums. It is important for senior managers to recognize that when the symbolism they exhibit leads to participation in discussion forums being of a highly political nature, then many staff will exclude themselves from participating in those forums that they consider to be normatively optional. Furthermore, it is also worth noting that sensemaking processes are highly dependent on the history of previous organizational restructurings in specific contexts, which are often associated with increased workloads and new forms of control, rather than valuing professional autonomy. Finally, the above political issues need to be considered carefully when modifying the career or financial reward structure to emphasize reciprocity, as has been suggested in several previous studies (Pan and Scarbrough, 1999; Zack, 1999), to analyze how this is likely to affect different forms of careerist and non-careerist activity.

CONCLUSION

ICTs are likely to continue to have an ever-increasing role to play in knowledge management initiatives due to the emphasis placed on information and communication. We have outlined two approaches to conceptualizing knowledge management in this chapter, the content and relational perspectives, and have argued that it is important for both academics and practitioners to recognize the underpinnings and assumptions that categorize the approach they adopt to the study or development of knowledge management technologies. This chapter has focused on the relational approach, and has highlighted some of the difficulties that arise from adopting a content view of knowledge management, and specifically, thinking of knowledge management initiatives as being technical projects. From a relational perspective, we argue that knowledge cannot be conceived of as being an entity that can be possessed, codified, organized and shared in the same way that data and information have been in the past. Instead, we have highlighted the importance for both academics and practitioners to view knowledge as being socially embedded and inseparable from practice.

We have indicated that what is represented on the screen is merely a snapshot, reflecting an author's accounting and sensemaking abilities, which are necessarily limited and inseparable from his or her own historical and social locations of practice (Brown, 1998; Walsham, 2001). Similarly, making sense of the representations that others record is also a provisional, highly reflexive and context bound process. Furthermore, we have illustrated how the nature and extent of knowledge sharing is influenced by and influences each professional domain's socio-political context. Without recognizing that knowledge is provisional and context bound, it is likely that all that will transpire in knowledge management initiatives is the circulation of more and more information that will merely magnify the problems that employees already encounter in their acting, accounting, and sensemaking processes. Thus, we suggest that there are two important priorities for future research on the role of ICTs in knowledge management initiatives to consider. First, to examine how people account for and make sense of their own and others' activities and experiences in textual form across diverse professional domains. Second, we suggest that future studies should also address how the use of ICTs maintain or change the political and normative context, and what implications for knowledge working arise. This chapter has aimed to provide a substantial review of the literature, and has used the Compound UK case to reinforce and extend existing conceptualizations of the role of ICTs in knowledge management. We suggest that this may provide a useful basis for future theoretical and practical developments to build upon.

REFERENCES

Aldrich, H. and Whetten, D. (1981) Organisation-sets, Action-sets, and Networks: Making the Most of Simplicity. In P.C. Nystrom and W.H. Starbuck (eds.), *Handbook of Organizational Design*, Oxford: Oxford University Press, 385–408.

Barley, S. (1996) Technicians in the Workplace: Ethnographic Evidence for Bringing Work into Organization Studies. *Administrative Science Quarterly*, 41 (1): 146–62.

Blackler, F. (1995) Knowledge, Knowledge Work and Organisations: An Overview and Interpretation. *Organisation Studies*, 16 (6): 1021–46.

Blackler, F., Crump, N. and McDonald, S. (1997) Knowledge, Organisations and Competition. In G. Kroght, J. Roos and D. Kleine (eds.), *Knowing in Firms: Understanding, Managing and Measuring Organisational Knowledge*. London: Sage.

Blackler, F., Reed, M. and Whitaker, A. (1993) Editorial: Knowledge and the Theory of Organisations. *Journal of Management Studies*, 30 (6): 851–61.

Bohm, R.E. (1994) Measuring and Managing Technological Knowledge. *Sloan Management Review*, 26 (1): 61–73.

Boland, R.J. and Tenkasi, R. V. (1995) Perspective Making and Perspective Taking in Communities of Knowing. *Organization Science*, 6 (4): 350–72.

Brown, J.S. (1998) Internet Technology in Support of the Concept of "Communities-of-practice": The Case of Xerox. *Accounting, Management and Information Technologies*, 8 (4): 227–36.

Brown, J.S. and Duguid P. (1991) Organisational Learning and Communities of Practice: Towards a Unified View of Working, Learning and Innovation. *Organization Science*, 2 (1): 40–57.

Brown, J.S. and Duguid, P. (1998) Organizing Knowledge, *California Management Review*, 40 (3): 90–111.

Cohen, D. (1998) Toward a Knowledge Context: Report on the First Annual UC Berkeley Forum on Knowledge and the Firm. *California Management Review*, 40 (3): 22–39.

Connah, B. and Pearson, R. (1991) *NHS Handbook*. London: Macmillan Press Ltd.

Davenport, T.H. and Prusak, L. (1998) *Working Knowledge: How Organizations Manage What They Know*. Boston: Harvard Business School Press.

Easterby-Smith, M., Crossan, M., and Nicolini, D. (2000) Organizational Learning: Debates Past, Present and Future. *Journal of Management Studies*, 37 (6): 783–96.

Flynn, R. and Williams, G. (1997) *Contracting for Health: Quasi-Markets and the National Health Services*. Oxford: Oxford University Press.

Galliers, R.D. and Newell, S. (2000) Back to the Future: From Knowledge Management to Data Management. London School of Economics, Information Systems Department, Working Paper No. 92.

Geertz, C. (1973) *The Interpretation of Cultures*. New York: Basic Books.

Giddens, A. (1984) *The Constitution of Society*. Cambridge: Polity Press.

Grudin, J. (1990) Groupware and Co-operative Work: Problems and Prospects. In B. Laurel (ed.), *The Art of Human Computer Interface Design*. Cambridge: Addison Wesley.

Hammersley, M. and Atkinson, P. (1983) *Ethnography: Principles in Practice*. London: Tavistock Publications.

Hayes, N. (2000) Work-arounds and Boundary Crossing in a High Tech Optronics Company: The Role of Co-operative Work-flow Technologies. *Computer Supported Co-operative Work: An International Journal*, 9 (3/4): 435–55.

Hayes, N. (2001) Boundless and Bounded Interactions in the Knowledge Work Process: The Role of Groupware Technologies. *Information and Organization*, 11 (2): 79–101.

Hayes, N. and Walsham, G. (2000a) Competing Interpretations of Computer Supported Co-operative Work. *Organization*, 7 (1): 49–67.

Hayes, N. and Walsham, G. (2000b) Safe Enclaves, Political Enclaves and Knowledge Working. In C. Prichard, R. Hull, M. Chumer, and H. Willmott (eds.), *Managing Knowledge: Critical Investigations of Work and Learning*. London: Macmillan.

Hayes, N. and Walsham, G. (2001) Participation in Groupware–mediated Communities of Practice: A Socio-political Analysis of Knowledge Working. *Information and Organization*, 11 (4): 263–88.

Hayman, A. and Elliman, T. (2000) Human Elements in Information Systems Design for Knowledge Workers. *International Journal of Information Management*, 20 (4): 297–309.

Hislop, D., Newell, S., Scarbrough, H., and Swan, J. (2000) Networks, Knowledge and Power: Decision Making, Politics and the Process of Innovation. *Technology Analysis and Strategic Management*, 12 (2): 399–411.

Holsapple, C., Johnson, L., and Waldron, V. (1996) A Formal Model for the Study of Communication Support Systems. *Human Communication Research (International Communication Research)*, 22 (3): 422–47.

King, J.L. and Star, S.L. (1990) Conceptual Foundations for the Development of Organisational Decision Support Systems. In *Proceedings of the Twenty-third Annual Hawaiian International Conference on Systems Science*. III, IEEE Computer Society Press, 143–51.

Knights, D., Murray, F., and Willmott, H. (1993) Networking as Knowledge Work: A Study of Strategic Inter-organisational Development in the Financial Services Industry. *Journal of Management Studies*, 30 (6): 975–95.

Knock, N. and McQueen, R. (1998) Knowledge and Information Communication within Organizations: An Analysis of Core, Support and Improvement Process. *Knowledge and Process Management*, 5 (1): 29–40.

Lave, J. (1988) *Cognition in Practice: Mind, Mathematics and Culture in Everyday Life*. Cambridge: Cambridge University Press.

Lave, J. and Wenger, E. (1991) *Situated Learning: Legitimate Peripheral Participation*. Cambridge: Cambridge University Press.

Leidner, D. (2000) Editorial. *Journal of Strategic Information Systems*, 9 (2-3): 101–105.

Liebowitz, J. (2001) Knowledge Management and its Link to Artificial Intelligence. *Expert Systems With Applications*, 20 (1): 1-6.

McDermott, R. (1999) Why Information Technology Inspired but Cannot Deliver Knowledge Management. *California Management Review*, 41 (4): 103–17.

McKinley, A. (2000) The Bearable Lightness of Control: Organisational Reflexivity and the Politics of Knowledge Management. In C. Prichard, R. Hull, M. Chumer, and H. Willmott (eds.), *Managing Knowledge: Critical Investigations of Work and Learning*. London: Macmillan.

Newell, S., Scarbrough, H., Swan, J., and Hislop, D. (2000) Intranets and Knowledge Management: De-centred Technologies and the Limits of Technological Discourse. In C. Prichard, R. Hull, M. Chumer and H. Willmott (eds), *Managing Knowledge: Critical Investigations of Work and Learning*. London: Macmillan.

Nonaka, I. and Takeuchi, H. (1994) *The Knowledge Creating Company: How Japanese Companies Create the Dynamics of Innovation*. Oxford: Oxford University Press.

Olivera, F. (2000) Memory Systems in Organizations: An Empirical Investigation of Mechanisms for Knowledge Collection, Storage and Access, *Journal of Management Studies*, 37 (6): 811–32.

Orlikowski, W.J. (1993) Learning from Notes: Organisational Issues in Groupware Implementation. *The Information Society*, 9 (3): 237–50.

Orlikowski, W.J. (1996) Evolving with Notes: Organisational Change around Groupware Technology. In C.U. Ciborra (ed.), *Groupware and Teamwork: Invisible Aid or Technical Hindrance?* Chichester: Wiley Series in Information Systems.

Orr, J.E. (1990) Sharing Knowledge, Celebrating identity: Community Memory in a Service Culture. In D. Middleton and D. Edwards (eds), *Collective Remembering*. Newbury Park, CA: Sage, 169–89.

Pan, S.L. and Scarborough, H. (1999) Knowledge Management in Practice: An Exploratory Case study. *Technology Analysis and Strategic Management*, 11 (3): 359–74.

Prusak, L. (1997) *Knowledge in Organizations: Resources for the Knowledge-Based Economy*. London: Butterworth-Heinemann.

Quinn, J.B., Anderson, P., and Finkelstein, S. (1996) Managing Professional Intellect: Making the Most of the Best. *Harvard Business Review*, 74 (2): 71–82.

Ruhleder, K. (1994) Rich and Lean Representations of Information for Knowledge Work: The Role of Computing Packages in the World of Classical Scholars. *ACM Transactions on Information Systems*, 12 (2): 208–30.

Ruhleder, K. (1995) Computerisation and Changes to Infrastructures for Knowledge Work. *The Information Society*. 11 (2): 131–44.

Scarbrough, H. and Burrell, G. (1997) The Axeman Commeth. In S. Clegg and G. Palmer (eds), *The Politics of Management Knowledge*. London: Sage.

Schultze, U. (2000) A Confessional Account of an Ethnography about Knowledge Work. *MIS Quarterly*, 24 (1): 3–41.

Schultze, U. and Boland, R.J. (2000a) Place, Space and Knowledge Work: A Study of Outsourced Computer Systems Administrators. *Accounting, Management and Information Technologies*, 10 (3): 187–219.

Schultze, U. and Boland, R.J. (2000b) Knowledge Management Technology and the Reproduction of Knowledge Work Practices. *Journal of Strategic Information Systems*, 9 (2-3): 193–212.

Shin, M., Holden, T., and Schmidt, R. (2001) From Knowledge Theory to Management Practice: Towards an Integrated Approach. *Information Processing and Management*, 37 (2): 335–55.

Storck, J. and Hill, P.A. (2000) Knowledge Diffusions through Strategic Communities, *Sloan Management Review*, 41 (2): 63–74.

Tsoukas, H. (1996) The Firm as a Distributed Knowledge System: A Constructionist Approach. *Strategic Management Journal*, 17 (Winter Special Issue): 11–25.

Van Maanen, J. (1979) The Fact of Fiction in Organisational Ethnography. *Administrative Science Quarterly*, 24 (4): 539–49.

Walsham, G. (1993) *Interpreting Information Systems in Organizations*. Chichester: John Wiley and Sons.

Walsham, G. (1998) IT and Changing Professional Identity: Micro-studies and Macro-theory. *Journal of the American Society for Information Science*, 49 (12): 1081–89.

Walsham, G. (2001) *Making a World of Difference: IT in a Global Context*. Chichester: John Wiley and Sons.

Wasko, M. and Faraj, S. (2000) "It's What One Does": Why People Participate and Help Others in Electronic Communities of Practice. *Journal of Strategic Information Systems*, 9 (2-3): 155–73.

Whitley, E.A. (2000) Tacit and Explicit Knowledge: Conceptual Confusion around the Commodification of Knowledge. London School of Economics, Information Systems Department, Working Paper Number 90.

Zack, M.H. (1999) Managing Codified Knowledge. *Sloan Management Review*, 40 (4): 45–58.

Zuboff, S. (1996) Foreword. In C.U. Ciborra (ed.), *Groupware and Teamwork: Invisible Aid or Technical Hindrance?* Chichester: Wiley.

5

Knowledge Management: What Can Organizational Economics Contribute?

Nicolai J. Foss and Volker Mahnke

Chapter Outline

Knowledge management has emerged as a very successful organization practice and has been extensively treated in a large body of academic work. Surprisingly, however, organizational economics (i.e., transaction cost economics, agency theory, team theory and property rights theory) has played no role in the development of knowledge management. We argue that organizational economics insights can further the theory and practice of knowledge management in several ways. Specifically, we apply notions of contracting, team production, complementarities, hold-up, etc. to knowledge management issues (i.e., creating and integrating knowledge, rewarding knowledge workers, etc.), and derive refutable implications that are novel to the knowledge management field from our discussion.

KNOWLEDGE MANAGEMENT: PERILS AND PROMISES

During the last decade or so, knowledge management (KM) – a set of management activities aimed at designing and influencing processes of knowledge creation and integration including processes of sharing knowledge – has emerged as one of the most influential new organizational practices. Numerous companies have experimented with KM initiatives in order to improve their performance. At the same time, the literature on KM has virtually exploded (e.g., Nonaka and Takeuchi, 1995; Boisot, 1998; Choo, 1998; Easterby-Smith et al., 2000; von Krogh et al., 2000).

KM would thus seem to be one of those areas where managerial practice and the academic literature develop simultaneously and perhaps even co-evolve. Here KM is not much different from many other management fads of the recent decades, such as business process reengineering or total quality management that also promise to contribute to competitive advantage – although this is asserted rather than carefully demonstrated. The analogy goes further, for KM is also akin to these fads in that there is no clear disciplinary foundation of KM. Indeed, the underpinnings of KM are a mixed bag, ranging from Eastern philosophical traditions over ideas from organizational behavior to notions from information science. Strikingly (to us, at least), organizational economics plays no role in the disciplinary base of KM. However, the KM literature neglects organizational economics at its peril.

Organizational economics looks inside the firm by examining the tasks of motivating and coordinating human activity. It is taken up with explaining the nature of efficient organizational arrangements, and the determinants of such arrangements. Efficiency is understood in the sense of maximizing the joint surplus from productive activities, including processes of creating, sharing and exploiting knowledge. A basic proposition is that the costs and the benefits of productive activities – and therefore joint surplus – is influenced by the incentives, property rights and ways of disseminating and processing information that structure productive activities. Perhaps as a result of organizational economics playing at best a small role in the evolution of KM, there is seldom any sustained attention to the *cost* of KM activities. For example, when von Krogh et al. (2000) in a major survey of the KM literature mention cost, they devote four pages (out of more than 250) to it, and then only treat costs of searching for knowledge, a category of cost that is only one among a multitude of relevant costs of KM.[1] This neglect of organizational costs is quite representative of the whole KM literature. Moreover, we would argue that even the potential *benefits* of alternative ways of organizing KM are ill-understood in the literature. On the managerial level, something similar may be observed. This is, perhaps, best expressed in the words of a knowledge manager, who recently stated to us that the

> concept of KM for mutual benefit seems self-evident for the enthusiasts, which only increases their puzzlement when others in their organization show apathy of even negative interest in the concept. If there is no offsetting benefit for sharing knowledge in terms of money and recognition, or the process by which one does so is arcane or bureaucratic, or it is difficult to find the right fora, then organizational costs rise and participation drops proportionally.

Because neither the relevant costs of alternative ways of organizing knowledge in organizations, nor their benefits are addressed in any systematic manner in the KM literature, the attendant trade-offs, and how these may be influenced by managerial action also remain ill-understood. The result is that the literature does not allow propositions about *optimal* KM strategies, and how these vary with changes in the relevant parameters, to be made. In other words, in its present manifestation, the KM literature does not constitute a managerially relevant contingency framework; it may supply inspiration (and entertainment) for managers, but not much in the nature of firm guidance.

Lest this be taken as a wholesale condemnation of KM, let us state immediately that the KM literature contains numerous salient observations on knowledge processes, that is, processes of creating, sharing and exploiting knowledge (e.g. Lyles and Schwenk, 1992; Nonaka and Takeuchi, 1995; von Krogh et al., 2000). In addition, the literature does much to identify key characteristics of knowledge structures that surround knowledge processes in terms of knowledge type, knowledge distribution, complexity and relatedness (e.g. Lyles and Schwenk, 1992; Weick and Roberts, 1993; Galunic and Rodan, 1998). In this chapter, we take some of these ideas as grist for a theoretical mill consisting of organizational economics. In particular, we focus on the *coordination* and *incentive* problems that processes of creating, sharing and exploiting knowledge inside firms may give rise to, and how various aspects of governance may be understood as a response to such problems. We thus take steps towards meeting the challenge contained in the recent observation that "the time is ripe to start addressing learning and knowing in the light of inherent conflicts between shareholders' goals, economic pressure, institutionalized professional interest and political agendas" (Easterby-Smith et al., 2000: 793).

The remainder of this chapter is structured as follows. First, we highlight key insights from organizational economics, and briefly sketch general implications for the understanding of KM practices. Second, we show that novel propositions about KM may be derived from organizational economics. We also address from an organizational economics perspective a number of central phenomena (e.g. firm specific learning, teamwork, communities of practice, knowledge integration) that have been discussed in the KM literature and conclusions follow in the final section. A final reservation. Our chosen subject in this chapter is a vast one. Considerable narrowing of the issues is necessary for space reasons. Thus, in the following we disregard KM issues that relate to the issue of the boundaries of the firm (e.g., make-or-buy decisions, joint ventures, networks, etc.), and focus solely on KM as it pertains to internal organization.[2]

ORGANIZATIONAL ECONOMICS: A NOVEL PERSPECTIVE IN KNOWLEDGE MANAGEMENT

Overall

Although organizational economics began as a theory of the existence and optimal scope of the firm (Coase, 1937; Williamson, 1975), during the last twenty years or so it has increasingly been applied to internal organization issues. In particular, organizational economics has directed attention to the coordination and incentive problems that are caused by the pathologies that unavoidably accompany an internal division of labor, such as asymmetric information, diluted performance incentives, measurement difficulties, bargaining problems, moral hazard, duplicative (redundant) efforts, etc. In turn, organizational economists have explained how a host of organizational arrangements, such as various kinds of authority, payment schemes, delegation of decision rights, etc., serve to alleviate the severity of such problems.

Beginning our brief sampling of organizational economics perspectives, *agency theory perspectives* have predominantly addressed issues related to payment schemes (Holmström, 1979, 1982) delegation of decision rights (Fama and Jensen, 1983; Jensen and Meckling, 1992; Aghion and Tirole, 1997), multi-tasking (Holmström and Milgrom, 1991), and managerial commitment (Baker et al., 1999) under assumptions of moral hazard and asymmetric information. *Transaction cost economics* (Williamson, 1985, 1996), and *property rights insights* (Hart, 1995) have been brought to bear on issues related to allocation of rights and design of contracts when investments in human capital are firm-specific, agents may behave in an opportunistic manner, and contracts are incomplete. *Team theory* (Marschak and Radner, 1972; Casson, 1994) has addressed the optimal design of organizational structures, given the bounded rationality of individuals (but absent conflicts of interest). Finally, work on *complementarities* between organizational elements (e.g., payment schemes, delegation of rights, supervision methods, etc.) (Milgrom and Roberts, 1990, 1995) has lent strong formal support to the traditional notion that there are stable, discrete governance structures that combine organizational elements in predictable ways (Thompson, 1967; Williamson, 1996). It is fair to say that the empirical base of organizational economics, in terms of the number of corroborations of predictions of these theories, is fairly strong (Shelanski and Klein, 1995; Prendergast, 1999).

Although organizational economics is constituted by a number of different theories, nevertheless there are a number of common threads in the literature (cf. Foss, 2000). On the method level, all of organizational economics is unabashedly *individualistic* in the sense that all organizational phenomena should be explained as the outcome of the choice behavior of individual agents. At the theoretical base, the whole literature is concerned with *efficiency*, that is to say, how resources are allocated so that they yield the maximum possible value. Two closely related implications follow immediately. First, the organizational economics perspective is intimately taken up with value-creation; as noted, maximizing the value that can be created is the meaning of economic efficiency. Second, since the allocation of resources is (also) a matter of how the relevant resources are governed and organized and since value-creation is dependent upon governance and organization, it follows that an efficiency perspective allows one to discriminate between alternative forms of economic organization in terms of efficiency. Rational actors will choose those organizational forms, contracts and governance structures that maximize their joint surplus and will find ways to split this surplus among them.

In turn, the influence of alternative organizational arrangements on value-creation may be analyzed in terms of motivation, knowledge, information, and complementarity – and how alternative arrangements embody different ways of influencing these variables (cf. also Buckley and Carter, 1996). Motivation, etc. are all in different ways related to those *transaction costs* that (in various guises) are central in all organizational economics theories, and whose size influences the value that may be created from organizing and governing scarce resources in particular ways. The value that can be created, in the presence of transaction costs, fall short of what may be created in a world with no problems of motivation, etc. (a "first-best" situation), and, hence, no transaction costs. While such a world may be imagined, it is not the world of managers and other inhabitants of organizations. However, motivation, etc. may be manipulated so that the organization approaches it. We discuss motivation, knowledge and information, and the coordination of complementary actions *seriatim* in the following.

Motivation

The motivational assumptions of organizational economics have been subject to a good deal of scrutiny and critical discussion. Many scholars in, for example, organizational behavior, have been critical of the seemingly cynical assumptions with respect to human nature that drive much of organizational economics analysis. To these critics, opportunism ("self-interest seeking with guile," Williamson, 1996) and moral hazard (i.e., using asym-

metric information to one's advantage and the other party's disadvantage after a contract
has been concluded) are not descriptively accurate. They may furthermore be "bad for
practice" to the extent that managerial action based on prescriptions from these theories
may, by treating people as would-be opportunists, lead to self-fulfilling prophecies (Ghoshal
and Moran, 1996). However, such motivational assumptions fundamentally serve to highlight the – presumably undisputed – fact that actors often have very different interests;
opportunism and similar assumptions are stark ways of highlighting this. Moreover, the
motivational assumptions serve to emphasize that economic organization needs to be
designed with an eye to the possibility that some (by no means all) actors may act in a
morally hazardous or opportunistic manner.

In the context of internal organization, the largest effort so far may well have been
devoted to exploring how various aspects of internal organization – from accounting
principles over payment methods to the nature and function of hierarchy itself – may be
explained as efficient responses to various principal–agent problems. Thus, particular
attention has been paid to differences between input and output-based payment, and how
the choice between these is determined by the observability of effort and states of nature;
the role of monitoring and of subjective and objective performance measurement
(Prendergast, 1999); and of how a hierarchical structure may constrain "rent-seeking," that
is, attempts to influence superiors to one's own advantage (Milgrom, 1988).

One perspective on all this is that various aspects of internal organization arise to curb
the resource costs of agents pursuing their own interests in a way that is harmful to the
organization. Under an organizational division of labor, management (and the owners of
the firm) delegate some rights to employees, ranging from the trivial (the right to work with
the company's vacuum cleaner) to the all-important (the right to make decisions on major
investment projects). Management wishes these delegated rights to be exercised in an
optimal manner. However, since the right holders cannot be constantly monitored, and
since performance pay schemes trade-off incentives and risk, some losses (compared to
a full-information situation) are usually unavoidable. Internal organization arises as a
trade-off between these losses and the costs of designing monitoring schemes, incentive
contracts, etc.

A particular set of incentive problems is caused by problems of managerial commitment. For example, often employees wish to specialize their human capital to the firm,
thus becoming more productive and hoping to capture some of the marginal productivity created. In other words, they expect to be compensated for their investment. However,
by specializing in this way, employees become subject to a potential hold-up problem
(Williamson, 1985, 1996; Hart, 1995). To be sure, the possession of specialized knowledge
may be a strong bargaining lever. However, there is another strong party to the bargain
situation, namely the firm to which the employee specializes. The implication is that
employees cannot expect to capture all or even most of the quasi-rent from their specialized human capital investments, which harms incentives to undertake the investments
(Hart, 1995). Strong and credible managerial commitment to not using the hold-up option
may solve the problem (Kreps, 1990). Another way of solving the problem is to allocate
(more) decision rights to employees who undertake human capital investments (Rajan and
Zingales, 1998). Thus, in professional service firms, often employees with a long tenure
and good demonstrated performance become partners. A final managerial problem has to

do with managerial interference in the business of agents to whom the same management have delegated rights (e.g., to run their own projects). This "problem of selective intervention" (Williamson, 1985) arises because it is often hard for management to commit to not interfere. For example, it is not possible to make a court-enforceable contract to prevent managerial interference once decision rights have been delegated. However, arbitrary intervention, the breaking of promises to not intervene, etc., all of which will often be very tempting for management, are very destructive for motivation (Baker et al., 1999; Foss, 2002).

These incentive problems are clearly relevant to the understanding of the costs of KM practices. To the extent that agents' human capital investments consist in the gathering and building up of specialized knowledge and skills, they are not likely to be willing to share the relevant knowledge and skills with other agents, unless they are properly compensated. They are not going to give up a strong bargaining lever without compensation. However, it is often difficult to contract over knowledge and skills. Moreover, there is a fundamental problem of managerial commitment: since it is difficult to write and enforce contracts between those employees who possess important specialized knowledge and the firm on the sharing of the knowledge and the compensation to the employees, it is tempting for management to renege on the promise after the sharing of knowledge has actually taken place. Two implications of direct relevance for KM follow. First, forced KM initiatives may well be experienced as hold-ups by those agents inside the firm who control specialized knowledge and skills. Their future investment incentives are harmed accordingly. Second, unless these agents can expect to be compensated they are unlikely to share their knowledge at all. It is likely that the best way to handle this (i.e., to invest in human capital *and* to share knowledge embodied in this capital) is by giving the relevant employees appropriate incentives, perhaps even making them partners through providing ownership rights.

Asymmetric knowledge and information

Even if agents can be motivated to take actions (i.e., exploit their decision rights) that are "incentive-compatible" with those of other agents or principals, there is still no guarantee that they also make optimal (i.e., value maximizing) choices. Willingness is not the same as ability. To some extent this is a problem of information transmission: Under an organizational division of labor, no agent inside the firm is likely to have all the information needed for making an optimal choice, and transmitting all of this information to him is prohibitively costly. Delegation may arise as a cost economizing response to this. However, it is also a matter of the often fleeting, subjective and tacit character of knowledge – a favorite theme of the KM literature. As Hayek (1945: 77–78) famously argued:

> The peculiar character of the problem of a rational economic order is determined precisely by the fact that the knowledge of the circumstances of which we must make use never exists in concentrated or integrated form but solely as the dispersed bits of incomplete and frequently contradictory knowledge which all the separate individuals possess. The economic problem of society is thus not merely a problem of how to allocate "given" resources – if "given" is taken to mean given to a single mind which deliberately solves the problem set by these "data". It is rather a problem of how to secure the best use of resources known to any

of the members of society, for ends whose relative importance only these individuals know. Or, to put it briefly, it is a problem of the utilization of knowledge which is not given to anyone in its totality.

Arguably, firms face this problem of dispersed knowledge to a smaller extent than societies do; however, it is still relevant to them. Firms may cope with the problem in different ways. Again, they may delegate decision rights so that these rights are co-aligned with those who possess the relevant knowledge, balancing the attendant benefits with the agency costs that are caused by delegation (Jensen and Meckling, 1992). However, knowledge sharing is an alternative to this. Thus, rather than delegating decisions rights in order to better utilize local knowledge, the existing rights structure (i.e., existing authority relations, payment schemes, organizational structures, etc.) remains unchanged and the relevant knowledge is gathered and shared among those who can make profitable use of this knowledge. Such knowledge sharing is, of course, a key focus of KM.

However, in the KM literature, knowledge sharing is often discussed and endorsed without any examination of the *alternative* of delegating rights so that knowledge is better utilized in this way. An organizational economics perspective not only identifies the relevant (organizational) alternatives, but also allows us to say something about the costs and benefits of these alternatives. Thus, one obvious advantage of the knowledge-sharing alternative is that it does not necessarily involve any delegation of decision rights. Knowledge sharing, as portrayed in the KM literature, may therefore impose smaller agency costs on an organization than the alternative of delegating decision rights. However, there are *other* costs to consider when the choice has to be made between the two alternatives of knowledge sharing and delegating decision rights. For whereas knowledge sharing that takes place within an existing organizational structure may not impose the same agency costs as delegating decision rights does, knowledge sharing is likely to impose higher costs of communicating, storing, and retrieving knowledge than the delegation alternative. The point is not here that specialized IT systems have to be set up in order to reach the goal of knowledge sharing. Rather, the point is that knowledge sharing may introduce costs that are caused by the bounded rationality of individuals, that is, their limited ability to identify, absorb, process, and remember knowledge. And, of course, there are costs associated with trying to transform knowledge that only exists in tacit form into an articulate form. As Hayek (1945) argued, decentralization economizes on these costs. In firms, delegation may be an attractive means of economizing on the costs associated with bounded rationality and tacit knowledge (Jensen and Meckling, 1992). The bottom line is that a full assessment of what alternative is superior in a specific situation – the improved utilization of knowledge by means of knowledge sharing or by means of delegation of decision rights – turns on a number of costs that have to be balanced against the relevant benefits. In its present manifestation, the KM literature does identify neither the relevant alternatives, nor the relevant net benefits.

The coordination of complementary actions

Even if agents can be motivated to take incentive-compatible actions and even if they possess the right information or knowledge (because they are specialists or because this information or knowledge is somehow transmitted to them), there is still a problem of coordinating actions inside the firm. In particular, the more complementary actions are, the more closely they need to be coordinated. Through the use of the price mechanism, markets cope well with the coordination problem (Hayek, 1945). However, the more complementary actions are, the more necessary it is to supplement the use of the price mechanism with other mechanisms, such as communication (Richardson, 1972). Firms have only limited access to the price mechanism, but they may have privileged access to the mechanism of communication (relative to markets). In this perspective, one advantage of KM may actually be that it assists the coordination of complementary actions by spreading knowledge, effectively bringing about common knowledge conditions. KM thus reduces what Koopmans (1957: 162–3), referred to as "secondary uncertainty":

> In a rough and intuitive judgment the secondary uncertainty arising from a lack of communication, that is, from one decision maker having no way of finding out the concurrent decisions and plans made by others . . . is quantitatively at least as important as the primary uncertainty arising from random acts of nature and unpredictable changes in consumers' preferences.

When the acquisition (creation, sourcing) of knowledge in a firm is delegated to specialist knowledge workers, the firm is facing this kind of secondary uncertainty (cf. Buckley and Carter, 1996: 82). One possible function of KM is thus to reduce secondary uncertainty, although this is not one that is identified in the KM literature.

Summing up: organizational economics aspects of knowledge management

In the frictionless world that dominated microeconomics before the revolution in information, property rights and transaction costs economics about three decades ago, there are no problems of motivation, knowledge, information, and coordination. In this Nirvana, resources, including knowledge resources, are allocated in the best possible way ("first-best"). Contracts can be written and enforced costlessly and information is free. Therefore, there are no losses from lacking motivation, defective or missing knowledge, or coordination that goes wrong. There are no problems of exchanging knowledge either, so that markets are as efficient for this purpose as firms are. However, in a more realistic world, contracts are imperfect, for example, so that it is hard and perhaps impossible to write contracts that compensate those who "give up" (i.e., share) valuable knowledge; commitment (including managerial commitment) may be broken; employees may be held up by management so that their incentives to invest in and share knowledge are harmed, etc. Lest managers live in a Paradise or Nirvana, KM practices are subject to these incentive costs.

The argument so far is therefore that organizational economics is able to illuminate the practice of KM in important ways. In particular, by focusing on incentive compatibility problems, particularly as these relate to issues of investing in the production and sharing of knowledge, organizational economics identifies important, but hitherto neglected incentive costs and benefits of KM practices. This is the reason why organizational economics should be seen as an indispensable part of the disciplinary foundation of KM. In the following section we deal further with processes of knowledge creation and integration in an organizational economics perspective.

KNOWLEDGE MANAGEMENT: ORGANIZATIONAL ECONOMIC INSIGHTS

In this section, we shall more concretely apply specific organizational economics insights to two clearly central aspects of KM: knowledge creation and knowledge integration. The former category encompasses learning (by doing, using, being instructed, etc.) and innovation processes, while the latter refers to how to make best use of existing knowledge in the firm. We develop propositions based on organizational economics regarding how firms may stimulate investments by employees in firm specific knowledge, resolve incentive problems in knowledge creating teams, and make choices between alternative means in the integration of knowledge, including knowledge sharing.

Knowledge creation

It is now almost an axiom that knowledge creation in firms lies at the heart of competitive advantage (Nonaka and Takeuchi, 1995; von Krogh et al., 2000). That "firms learn," "firms know," etc. have become commonplace expressions in much of the strategy and KM literature.[3] However, it is not firms as such that learn, and firms themselves do not possess knowledge. So-called "firm knowledge" is composed of knowledge sets controlled by individual agents. We stress this admittedly basic methodological individualist point in order to emphasize the point that by focusing on the level of the individual agent, rather than the firm, organizational economics highlights questions that are neglected in the KM literature *because* much of this literature operates on the firm level and does not have an explicitly individualistic starting point.

   In particular, an organizational economics perspective directs attention to the possible incentive conflicts that may arise in connection with issues such as: How can employees be induced to making their human capital firm specific when this puts them at a risk? What are the complications of knowledge creation in teams? Do individual incentives enable or impede knowledge creation in teams? And so on. Perhaps somewhat contrary to intuition, such questions are central to successful KM in practice and they are particularly prone to an organizational economics treatment. This is because processes of creating knowledge – for example, in the form of innovation projects – are typically risky, unpredictable (the knowledge-to-be-created can only be partly foreseen), often long term, labor intensive, idiosyncratic (that is, hard to compare to other processes), and often require substantial human capital investments (Holmström, 1989: 309). A number of these characteristics are the basic stuff that contracting problems are made of.[4] In the following we discuss a number of ways in which firms may motivate employees to expend effort in the production of new knowledge. In this connection, we discuss how the return stream from such new knowledge is shared between the firm and the employee. Thus, the problems of motivating employees and capturing rents from new knowledge are two sides of the same coin.

We assume throughout that an asymmetric information setting obtains, and that incentive conflicts are present. To see why these assumptions are appropriate ones, consider a world where asymmetric information and incentive conflicts (agency problems, hold-up problems) are absent. Here, the interests of the various agents involved in the creation of new knowledge can be easily aligned. First, employees and employers would assess the value of new knowledge in the same way (because information about this is symmetric). Second, bargaining will be efficient immediately, because the symmetry of information means that there will be no strategic behavior. Third, the employee's reward for any learning investments will be guaranteed, since the employer will not attempt to hold-up the employee. In such a Nirvana world, where both employee and employer access the same information on the value of ideas and each other's outside options, inducing optimal human capital investment can be achieved by writing complete contracts. If more realistic assumptions are introduced, an incentive perspective on knowledge creation is particularly appropriate, because it stresses not only that agents making learning investments must somehow share in the extra surplus from those investments to be properly motivated, but also that providing such motivation is no easy matter under asymmetric information, incomplete contracts, and self-interested behavior.

Earning rents from knowledge creation   The KM literature seldom makes clear exactly how the mechanism from knowledge creation to new rents works. However, the resource-based view in strategic management has gone some way towards clarifying this by identifying a set of criteria that resources must meet to be sources of (sustained) competitive advantages, such as being valuable, rare and costly to imitate (Barney, 1991). Moreover, the relevant resources should not be fully mobile (Peteraf, 1993). Knowledge assets, particularly newly created ones, are particularly likely to meet these criteria (Winter, 1987). Given this, managers may wish to induce knowledge creation by means of providing incentives to employees to upgrade their own knowledge capital and by spending corporate resources on having employees do this (e.g., training, setting up incentives, etc.). From the perspective of the firm, earning rents from employee upgrading of knowledge is far from trivial. In particular, whether of not firms are likely to earn rents from employees' knowledge, depends on (1) the type of learning investment (e.g., firm specific or general knowledge); (2) the resolution of agency conflicts in firms (e.g., remuneration schemes, and promotion rules); and (3) transaction costs in labor markets (e.g., signaling and screening). We consider these *seriatim*.

Types of learning investments   Firms' investments in augmenting the knowledge of their employees may be of two kinds, namely general and firm-specific ones. Both may increase an employee's productivity, but they have different implications with respect to who is likely to appropriate the returns and who will carry the costs of the investment. General learning investments may increase an employee's productivity in a range of employment opportunities. Such general investments include the learning of languages and generic skills, such as learning word processing programs, that are equally useful for current and potential employers. Becker (1962) suggests that employees will pay for their general training, because in competitive markets they are the sole beneficiaries of the improvements of their productivity. A firm will not pay for an employee's learning of general knowledge, because of the weakness of its bargaining position after having made the investment. In contrast, the learning of firm-specific knowledge restricts an employee's possibility to capture returns on this knowledge outside of the firm that undertakes the investment. Becker (1962) argues that to the extent that an employee's productivity increase exceeds his wage increase after learning, the firm can earn rents even if it alone incurs the costs of firm-specific learning investments. As far as such investments are concerned, the relative bargaining position of firms is strong because employees cannot credibly threaten to leave the firm to bargain for higher wages that reflect their productivity increase after specific learning investments. Thus, it is very likely that firms will appropriate a substantial part of the relevant rents. Of course, firms that undertake more specific learning investments will also create more rents, because the benefits (e.g., in terms of productivity or increased innovativeness) are larger to the firm in the case of specific than in general learning investments. Thus, the following refutable proposition may be put forward:

PROPOSITION 1:   *Firms with a high ratio of specific to general learning investments will earn and appropriate relatively more rents than firms with a low ratio.*

Inducing firm specific learning: incentive conflicts and their resolution   Consider next the situation from the perspective of employees. From their point of view, learning is an investment of effort for which they wish to be compensated. Firms will have to provide inducements for such investments. However, as we have seen, making firm-specific learning investments restricts an employee's outside employment options (and therefore his bargaining power), which will tend to reduce firm-specific learning investments below the optimal level. This is because of the incentive problem that undertaking these investments means becoming more vulnerable to managerial hold-ups. Resolving this problem turns on management's ability to credibly signal that it will not take advantage of employees who by making firm-specific learning investments have put themselves at risk. An organizational economics interpretation of (beneficial) corporate culture is that it is essentially an embodiment of such signals (Kreps, 1990). Thus, firms with corporate cultures that credibly signal that management is committed to a non-opportunistic approach in dealing with subordinates will induce higher learning investments on the part of employees. Such a corporate culture makes the provision of incentives credible, so that employees correctly believe that management will not renege on promises with respect to compensation.

With respect to the issue of providing incentives for employees' investment in firm specific knowledge, organizational economics suggests at least three possibilities: high-powered incentives (i.e., making employees residual claimants to a higher degree), promotion rules, and conferring access to critical resources. Consider these in turn.

1   *High-powered incentives* – often represented as the contingent portion of pay – may be used to induce contributions through providing larger shares of quasi-rents to employees (Williamson, 1996). Firm-specific learning investments may be induced by providing equity to employees (e.g. in the firm of stock options or equity) or other high-powered incentives, such as performance pay (Demsetz and Lehn, 1989; Williamson, 1985).

However, offering such high-powered incentives may also lead to a number of distortions. This is the case, for example, when the corresponding costs (e.g., of using the firms' assets) are not borne by those to whom high-powered incentives are offered (Holmström, 1989). Thus, as Williamson (1985) argues, this is exactly why incentives in firms are often comparatively low powered. Another problem with high-powered incentives is that they expose employees to considerable risks. For example, performance (e.g., the value of stock options) may fluctuate for reasons beyond an employee's control. In addition, employees may be highly dependent on the fixed, risk-free part of their income if they lack alternative sources of income. Risk-averse employees may therefore shy away from high-powered incentives. On the other hand, risk estimates may be in the eye of the beholder, and more highly skilled employees may judge risk differently from other employees. Moreover, for incentive pay to be effective, either observability of output or behavior must obtain. If behaviors or output for tasks cannot be specified because cause–effect relationships are not well understood, high performance ambiguity poses a problem because neither behaviors nor outputs can be related to specific skill acquisition with any precision. Thus, the less output and behavior can be pre-specified so as to reflect employees specific skill development, the less effective high-powered incentives become (Ouchi, 1980). Thus, the following refutable proposition may be put forward:

PROPOSITION 2: *The use of high-powered incentives to induce firm-specific learning will be more common in firms with higher skilled, wealthier employees, and pre-specified output.*

2   The design of *promotion rules* is an alternative way of inducing firm-specific learning investments. Consider inducing investments in firm-specific knowledge by means of "up-or-stay" rules (e.g., the worker is either promoted or stays in the original job) relative to "up-or-out" rules (e.g., the worker is promoted or fired) (Prendergast, 1993; Gibbons, 1998; Huberman and Kahn, 1988). Generally, when workers bear the costs of acquiring specific skills they will do so only if the wage (W^s) obtainable after skill acquisition minus their opportunity costs (C^s) exceeds current payment (W^{ns}). The principal will pay the wage (W^s) only if the productivity difference ($P^s - P^{ns}$) exceeds the wage difference ($W^s - W^{ns}$). With "up-or-stay" rules principals distinguish jobs and attach different wages to it. This promotion rule creates a tension between needing a large enough wage gap to induce the worker to invest and keeping the gap small enough so that the principal is willing to promote the worker after the worker has invested (Prendergast, 1993). Gibbons (1998: 126) illustrates this point.

For example, suppose that an untrained worker produces 10 in the easy job, that a trained worker produces 20 in the easy job and 30 in the difficult job, and that the opportunity cost of training is 15. Then training is efficient (30 − 10 > 15) but we cannot find wages that simultaneously induce the worker to invest (wage difference greater than opportunity cost, 15) and induce the firm to promote a trained worker (wage difference smaller than productivity difference, 30 − 20). As a consequence, employees' investment in firm-specific skills may be low, *although* such investments would be efficient. Huberman and Kahn (1988) suggest that "up-or-out rules" can solve this incentive problem. For example, with this rule the principal makes a commitment to promote the worker after a pre-specified time span or otherwise fire him (e.g. tenure in academic jobs, moving up career ladders in consultancies). Because of the resulting rat-race, this creates incentives for investments in firm-specific knowledge. To illustrate, consider the example above. As before, specific learning investments lead to firm rents only when they are efficient ($P^s - P^{us} > 15$). If a worker expects promotion, he will invest at any wage (W^*) which exceeds his opportunity costs plus best alternative (e.g. $W^* > W^{ALT} = 15$). The principal promotes the worker if his productivity (P^s) exceeds his high wage ($P^s > W^*$). Although with up-or-out rules there is always a wage (W^*) that is low enough to induce the principal to promote the worker who has made sufficient investments in firm-specific capital, up-or-out rules come at a cost. Because it is not possible to keep the worker in the firm when the productivity after investment does not exceed his high salary, this up-or-out rule may waste investments in firm-specific skills. This is especially obvious when there are different layers where such up-or out rules apply and workers survive the first rounds but drop out at a higher level (cf. Gibbons, 1998).[5] Thus, the following refutable proposition may be put forward:

PROPOSITION 3:   *Firms utilizing up-or-out rules will induce higher investments in firm-specific human capital than firms using up-or-stay rules.*

Additionally, once employees have invested in firm-specific capital, a firm also needs to tie employees long enough to the firm, so that firm-specific human capital investments can be recouped. Turnover of key knowledge carriers is a major problem in this respect. Typically, to prevent turnover from happening firms use deferred rewards and pensions, which benefit employees only in the distant future (Milgrom and Roberts, 1990).

3   *Providing access to assets.* Firms may positively influence learning investments by conferring access to critical resources (Rajan and Zingales, 1998), such as critical knowledge resources. Access may be defined as the ability to use or work with a critical resource including other human resources. It provides an opportunity for employees to specialize relative to these assets. We earlier analyzed this as giving rise to a potential hold-up problem, since the firm may hold up the specialized employee. However, the other side of the coin is that specialization to a critical asset in combination with an employee's right to withdraw her, also critical, human capital gives her considerable bargaining power with respect to the sharing of the surplus from productive activities, that is, bargain for a higher salary. It can be shown that when investments are additive (i.e., the total surplus is dependent on the sum of the investments), granting access and, as it were, giving away bargaining power, may be a superior incentive mechanism to induce firm-specific learning. In contrast, when investments are complementary (i.e., the marginal return of one investment rises in the level of the other investment), which is likely to take place in team-based firms, we are back to the familiar hold-up problem (Williamson, 1985; Hart, 1995). Not only will the employee directly influence the size of the surplus if she withdraws her human capital; she will also influence it indirectly, because her human capital investments are complementary to the human capital investments of other employees. In this situation, it will not be advantageous to grant the employee (too much) access (see Rajan and Zingales, 1998 for details).

The three mechanisms above may be substitutes or complements, depending on the circumstances. Thus, tournaments in the form of up-or-out rules may substitute for performance pay when employees are sufficiently risk-averse. Access may substitute for incentives in the same situation. Promotion rules and incentives may substitute for access, when giving an employee access would be giving her too much bargaining power. On the other hand, all three mechanisms are often seen together; for example, in consultancies, partners have obtained their position through a tournament that works according to certain promotion rules, they granted access to assets contingent on learning investments, and they are usually residual claimants. We may now put forward the following proposition:

PROPOSITION 4: *Firms that resolve incentive conflicts in knowledge production by means of incentives, and/or promotion rules and/or deferred payment and/or access will gain competitive advantage relative to firms that do not use these means.*

Transaction costs in labor markets In the above, analysis of firm-specific human capital has made the simplifying assumption that costs of concluding labor market transactions can be neglected. This is, of course, not the case, as such costs aggravate complications of inducing firm-specific investments. Asymmetric information between current and potential employers is one source of switching costs in labor markets (Akerlof, 1970). Employees must search for new job opportunities and firms must search for fitting employees. In this search process, there may be several complications. For example, a current employer usually knows more about employees' human capital and learning ability than potential employers do (Spence, 1973, 1974). In wage negotiations employees will have to credibly signal to new employers their ability to perform. However, because some employees will overstate their ability in order to drive up wages, employers will not only incur costs of screening employees, but may also reduce wages offered to account for the risk of picking a wrong employee (i.e., a lemon). If this is the case, employees willing to switch from their current employer would find the wage offered by new employers unattractive. The higher transaction costs in labor markets are, the more difficult it is for employees to switch between employers. By implication, high transaction costs in labor markets lower incentives for employees to invest in firm-specific knowledge without appropriate safeguarding and compensation. Thus, firms operating in labor markets with high transaction costs incur greater costs to induce employee's firm-specific learning compared to firms that do not.

One particular interesting way to induce firm-specific learning in such situations is to offer employees the possibility to engage in the acquisition of certified general knowledge such as management training, language and computer skills (Laing, 1994). Employees might face lower lock-in as a result, because the acquisition of certified general skills reduces labor market transaction costs such as screening and matching (Spence, 1974; Barzel, 1982). None the less, a firm offering such general training possibilities to its employees can benefit in several ways. First, investments in general skills can increase the productivity effects of firm-specific skill investments because common knowledge between employees facilitates the combination and blending of specific skills (Kogut and Zander, 1992; Foss, 2001b). Second, sponsoring general training as a form of pay also signals the commitment of employers to their employees (Kreps, 1990) that their investments in firm-specific knowledge will not be opportunistically exploited. Thus, the following refutable proposition may be put forward:

PROPOSITION 5: *Firms sponsoring certified acquisition of general skills as a form of merit pay will induce higher employee investments in firm-specific human capital.*

Complications of providing incentives for knowledge creation in teams Many contributions to the KM literature recommend the use of teams in the form of work groups, inter-disciplinary and cross-functional teams to foster knowledge creation (e.g. Brown and Eisenhardt, 1995; Meyer and Tore, 1999; von Krogh et al., 2000). Teamwork may bring knowledge together that hitherto existed separately, resulting in "new combinations" (Schumpeter, 1950), it may facilitate cross-functional communication, cross-fertilization of ideas and enhance worker involvement. Through the integration of knowledge of individual members, teams may not only blend knowledge and insights beyond what individual members may achieve; the development of new knowledge may also be stimulated by conversations and language-based learning in teams (Brown and Duguid, 1991; Nonaka and Takeuchi, 1995). However, while knowledge creation in teams has its virtues, there are special difficulties associated with aligning interests of team members (Scott and Einstein, 2001). Not only will teams be particularly prone to moral hazard, notably in the form of shirking, but the right form of incentives may also be contingent on the type of team at hand. Questions arise that remain neglected in the KM-literature such as: Who should be rewarded – teams or individuals? Who should evaluate contributions of team members – other team members, a specialized monitor, or an external manager? What measures of performance should be used and when? An organizational economics perspective suggests that the success of teams' knowledge creating efforts depend, *inter alia*, on (1) the size of the team, (2) trade-offs between individual and team incentives, (3) exclusion rules, and (4) the matching varying degrees of uncertainty to incentive design.[6]

1 *Free-rider problems and team size.* Alchian and Demsetz provide a classic treatment of incentive problems in team-production – a process "wherein individual cooperating inputs do not yield identifiable, separate outputs" (1972: 779). Where measuring individual input productivity and rewarding accordingly becomes difficult, team members may free-ride on other team members' contributions to knowledge creation. This is so because the benefits of withholding marginal effort accrues to each shirking member while the resulting losses accrue to the team as a whole. In principle, knowledge production in teams could be organized through a set of bilateral agreements between team members who promise best effort and ensure mutual control. However, such agreements are difficult to manage and will most likely incur large resource costs; for example, time spent on negotiation and haggling means that less time is available for knowledge creation. As teams grow in size, the larger these costs become, in fact, they increase exponentially with the number of team members (Rosen, 1991). In addition, free-rider problems become more prevalent, the larger the knowledge-creating team becomes. Thus, one can derive the following refutable proposition:

PROPOSITION 6:   *Knowledge creation in teams will be less effective the larger the team size because shirking and free-riding will increase.*

2 *Individual and/or team incentives.* Team size problems are aggravated if incentives are exclusively allocated to a team as a whole rather than also considering incentives for individuals (Laursen and Mahnke, 2001). When capable and willing team members are forced to support free-riders, they often withdraw effort or else leave the team. On the other hand, relying exclusively on individual incentives can inhibit cooperation in teams – especially

when task performance crucially depends on the exchange of information and mutual adaptation (Thompson, 1967; Balkin and Gomez-Mejia, 1992). None the less, many recommendations in the KM literature are mistaken when they note that individual rewards may be the antithesis to teamwork. An organizational economics perspective urges managers not to neglect possibilities to induce individual contributions on which team performance ultimately rests.

One possibility to resolve incentive conflicts in the knowledge creating team is that a team member specializes in monitoring other members' contributions to generate reliable information based on which rewards may be distributed (Alchian and Demsetz, 1972). A positive effect of monitoring is that knowledge about talents is discovered that can be used to reduce shirking but also a better recombination or new uses of skills and talent. However, as specialized monitors become increasingly removed from actual teamwork, possible knowledge gaps between those creating new knowledge and those specializing in monitoring may increase over time to eventually compromise effective monitoring. As an alternative management may provide incentives for achievements of the group as a whole and let the group members distribute team rewards among themselves based on subjective performance evaluation (e.g., 360-degree reviews).[7] This utilizes the fact that team members will often have information about each other's contributions, behavior, and ability that is superior to that of external management (Gibbons, 1998). Thus, specialized incentive procedures may cope with some of the incentive problems by combining incentives to teams with incentives to individual team members. This leads us to the following refutable proposition:

PROPOSITION 7: *Knowledge creation in teams will be more effective in firms that use combinations of team-based and individual incentives.*

3 *Exclusion rules.* We mentioned earlier that firms often use promotion rules in order to solve incentive conflicts through setting up competition between employees. Similar mechanisms may reduce incentive problems in teams. Lazear (1989) suggests that tournaments may involve self-selection and exclusion mechanisms. These drive up effort levels, because only those are attracted who believe in their survival and exercise effort and skills in a team's knowledge creation effort (Dillard and Fisher, 1990). In particular, giving teams the right to exclude team members (Lazear, 1989; Malcomson, 1998) on the basis of subjective performance measures (e.g., peer evaluation, group leader assessment, or a combination), is clearly relevant in this context.

Setting up tournaments inside firms may be a viable control mechanism in team-based knowledge creation. But they also have their dangers. If tournament rules cannot exclude sabotage among team members they may lead to outright breakdown of knowledge creation in teams (Lazear, 1989). An exaggerated emphasis on competition may also drive out exploration by team members who prefer to make quick wins through exploiting ideas of others rather than to explore new ideas on their own. This has two harmful effects on the knowledge creating team (March, 1994). First, explorers benefit from developing absorptive capacity based on which they can pick up good ideas that others engaged in the same team process cannot exploit on their own. The less others involved in the knowledge creating team are able to develop and exploit ideas themselves, the more important it becomes that others can relate to their ideas. Second, as team members increasingly engage in exploitation to the neglect of exploration, the fewer ideas are available for exploitation. When competition provides disincentives for exploration and revealing ideas openly, the loss of relative absorptive capacity (Lane and Lubatkin, 1998) among team members diminishes the capacity for knowledge creation in the team as a whole.[8] Thus we suggest the following refutable proposition:

PROPOSITION 8:   *Knowledge creation in teams will be more effective the more team members are entitled to exclude non-exploring team-members by self-selection.*

4   *Uncertainty and team types.* Knowledge creating teams may operate under varying degrees of means and end uncertainty. To illustrate, the KM literature distinguishes two types of knowledge creating teams: "communities of practice" and learning in "epistemic groups." The former denotes a team of peers who learn during and about the execution of pre-specified tasks with defined outcomes (Lave and Wenger, 1990; Brown and Duguid, 1991; Brown, 1998).[9] They key problem is to create knowledge about means whose ends are well known. Examples include how to fix a working process that has broken down, how to deal with customer demands more quickly etc. By contrast, "epistemic communities" deal with knowledge creation for non-routine problems whose ends and means cannot be specified ex ante (Cohen, 1998). Here the key problem is to discover means for ends that are unknown at the time the team starts developing knowledge. An example comes from a KM team at a software security firm that described their situation as follows: "In 2–3 years' time, our company will be designing security products we don't know, incorporating technologies which haven't been invented, made in processes yet to be defined, by people we have not yet recruited."

One complication of means and ends uncertainty is that both complicate the provision of incentives in team. This is because measurement bases for the provision of incentives become increasingly noisy the less means and ends can be pre-specified ex ante. In other words: uncertainty leads to performance ambiguity, which complicates the provision of incentives (Ouchi, 1980). Only if performance ambiguity is low does performance pay seem effective in aligning conflicting interest. If this is not the case, variable rewards might be appropriate if pay and control can relate to specified behavior or to other forms of standardization (e.g. processes), which can serve as a basis for measuring performance. Unfortunately, to the extent that standardization of behavior or processes is prevented, such as in the case of many epistemic communities, neither behaviors nor outputs can be determined with precision. In this case, Ouchi (1980) suggests, clan control might be the solution to promote cooperation and mitigate conflict of interest: the basis of control becomes a set of internalized values and norms. In should be noted, however, that clan control can lead to normative fixation and group think that are both detrimental rather than conducive to knowledge creation in teams (e.g., Grandori, 2001). Comprehensive empirical research regarding managerial control dilemmas in knowledge-creating teams remains sparse and inconclusive. However, contrary to popular recommendations in the literature to abandon incentives in favor of normative control altogether,[10] recent evidence shows that incentives for knowledge creating teams seem to prevail in practice across a number of industries (Laursen and Mahnke, 2001; Laursen and Foss, 2002). An organizational economics perspective on knowledge creation would not expect otherwise. Thus we suggest the following refutable proposition:

PROPOSITION 9: *Teams employing combinations of individual incentives, team incentives, and exclusion rules will be more effective at knowledge creation than teams relying on clan control.*

None the less, as we move from inducing individual learning to knowledge creation in teams complications of providing incentives vastly increase. Given these complications of knowledge creation in teams, an organizational economics perspective suggests that team-based learning is a particularly expensive knowledge creation mechanism that is riddled with many problems that include, but are not limited to, providing incentives. Seen this way, organizational economic insights might serve as a reminder that knowledge creation in teams yields benefits at substantial costs. These may be compared to the benefits and costs of individual learning in firms as well as hiring of external expertise in the form of employment or contingent work – two alternative mechanisms of organizational learning (Simon, 1991).

Integrating knowledge: insights from organizational economics

Organizational economic insights (Coase, 1937; Demsetz, 1988; Jensen and Meckling, 1992; Williamson, 1985) have already substantially fertilized the literature on knowledge in organization that characterizes the firm as a knowledge-integrating institution (Conner and Prahalad, 1996; Grant, 1996; Kogut and Zander, 1992, 1993).[11] Therefore, this section is restricted to briefly reviewing the key insights on knowledge integration needs and mechanisms.[12]

Specialization of tasks leads to focused learning in narrowly defined domains. However, because the division of tasks also leads to the division of knowledge, knowledge-integration may be required when several activities are interdependent and individuals need to adapt their action to each other (Thompson, 1967). If individuals are specialized in different knowledge domains this will limit the rate at which knowledge that lies outside a narrow specialization can be assimilated, accumulated, and applied (Simon, 1957; Lane and Lubatkin, 1998). Three coordination mechanisms may be conducive to address such knowledge-integration problems – direction, common knowledge, and autonomous adaptation – but their efficacy may vary with varying task-dependencies at hand.

Autonomous adaptation is the marvel of market. As Hayek (1945: 527) argues, markets (be they between or in companies) make individuals do desirable things without anyone having to tell them to do them. While the price mechanisms economizes on investments in shared knowledge, it only facilitates thin communication among individuals that coordinate their tasks and action. Its applicability may also be limited to situations where task coordination is signified by low uncertainty and low interdependence between tasks that makes autonomous adaptation possible (Grandori, 2001). Moreover, pricing knowledge in exchange faces a fundamental paradox: the value of knowledge to a purchaser is not known until after the knowledge is revealed; however, once revealed, the purchaser has no need to pay for it (Arrow, 1984). Second, Arrow also argues that "authority, the centralization of decision-making, serves to economize on the transmission and handling of knowledge" (1974: 69). Demsetz (1988) agrees when he suggests that "[d]irection substitutes for education (that is, for the transfer of the knowledge itself)." For example, employees transfer reports and memos rather than the knowledge on which they are crafted; superiors give advice on what to do and intervene at times rather than to transfer knowledge on which their judgement is based. Building on this argument, Conner and Prahalad (1996) stress that authority not only provides a low cost method of communicating, but also allows the flexible blending of expertise when contingencies emerge that were not foreseeable when, for example, an employment contract was concluded. This nicely corresponds to Coase (1937) who makes coordination by entrepreneurial direction based on employment contracts the distinguishing mark of the firm as an institution. Like price coordination, direction economizes on investments in common knowledge. In addition direction saves communication cost not because communication is restricted to thin communications as was the case with price coordination, but because communication (be it thin or thick) is restricted to top–down interaction on particular occasions. However, the application of top–down direction to coordinate knowledge, finds its limits when superiors do not understand what and how results are achieved at a lower level – as is often the case with knowledge work (Foss, 1999, 2001a). Finally, common knowledge (Grant, 1996) in the form of combinative capabilities, routines, shared context or codes or social capital (Kogut and Zander, 1992; Nelson and Winter, 1982; Nahapiet and Ghoshal, 1998) may ease coordination, particularly when tasks are highly interdependent. However, as a discussion of knowledge-codification tools illustrates, investments in common knowledge and knowledge-sharing – both in terms of managerial effort (see Zollo and Winter, 2002) and in terms of aligning diverging interest (Mahnke, 1998) – is particularly expensive. Thus, an organizational economics perspective suggests:

PROPOSITION 10:   *Firms investing in shared knowledge and engaging in substantial knowledge-sharing only in the presence of high task interdependence will outperform firms that do so even under conditions of low task uncertainty.*

CONCLUSIONS

Since its take-off in the beginning of the 1970s (e.g., Alchian and Demsetz, 1972), organizational economics has been centrally concerned with what is a very recent recognition in the KM literature, namely "that social relations and learning processes do not happen in a political vacuum and, on the contrary, take place in a landscape of interests and differential power positions and relations" (Easterby-Smith et al., 2000: 793). Fundamentally, organizational economics represents a body of theory that allows the theorist to understand the nature of the obstacles to coordination within and between firms, as well as such issues as how the allocation of incentives and property rights influence the actions and investment decisions of individual agents (i.e., their human capital investments). It does so on the basis of precise assumptions about technologies (e.g., team production, complementarities), the distribution of information, the allocation of incentives and property rights, the degree of rationality and foresight possessed by agents, etc. In other words, organizational economics is taken up with the benefits as well as the costs of alternative contractual, organizational, and institutional structures. It puts forward comparative propositions on this basis.

Organizational economics advances research on KM by allowing the derivation of novel refutable propositions of direct relevance for the practice of KM. We have provided a number of examples. More fundamentally, it provides a micro-foundation (much needed, in our view) that allows focused research regarding the relation between KM, value creation, and value appropriation by the involved stakeholders. We are confident that further research along these lines will continue to be fruitful.

Notes

1. Von Krogh et al. (2000: 122) further observe that "search costs are the total costs incurred by an organization's efforts to get individual members or a group to act effectively." It is not so: search cost is a category that is entirely different from the incentive and coordination costs of getting "members or a group to act effectively." More on this later.

2. We have dealt with the issue of the boundaries of the firm in the context of knowledge management in Foss (2002, 2003) and Mahnke (2001).

3. Part of the motivation for the interest in, and growth of, various knowledge-oriented approaches to organizations appears to be the widespread belief that organizational economics approaches to organizations have very little to offer with respect to an understanding of learning processes in firms (Kogut and Zander 1992; Madhok, 1996). This is, in our view, something of a misunderstanding. It is true that organizational economics approaches do not conceptualize firms as knowledge-based entities *per se*. However, that does not mean that it has little to offer of the processes whereby knowledge is created in firms.

4. For example, incentives need to be provided so that agents are motivated to supply an efficient (i.e., second-best) level of effort, and undertake the required human capital investments; care must be exercised in connection with multi-stage projects where the firm may wish to stop projects at a certain stage and the project leader (who may be better informed) may not; risk-allocation is particularly pertinent here; etc. This is not to say that understanding knowledge creation is trivial in the context of organizational economics – far from it. In fact, because processes of knowledge creation are more uncertain in terms of the variance of the benefit distribution, and because the distribution of those benefits over time is harder to anticipate, than in the case of more routine investment projects, analysis is comparatively more complicated.

5. This argument holds important lessons for remuneration practices and career paths in consultancies, which employ up-or-out rules. When senior consultants do not make enough investments to be qualified as a partner, they are fired, but their value to the firm may exceed their value in the best alternative due to previously acquired firm-specific skills. Firing thus means that firms waste firm-specific investments in human capital. Thus, although up-or-out rules may be better than up-or-stay rules, they are still inefficient compared to the first-best.

6. A further complication obtains when intrinsic motivation is an important consideration. In that case, high-powered (extrinsic) incentives may be counter-productive (Kreps, 1997). Moreover, social comparison processes may complicate the situation further. When such processes are strong, team members may be rewarded as a unit, rather than individually because differential individual rewards impede cooperation (Ouchi, 1980, Jones, 1987; Balkin and Gomez-Mejia, 1992). However, sometimes differentiated incentives may be used, particularly when it

is up to the team itself to reward performance. Pfeffer and Langton (1993) add that distributive justice relates to individuals' perception of whether they are receiving a fair share of the available rewards proportionately to their contribution to the group, personal risk and responsibility assumed.

7. Such exercises can be associated with 360-degree feedback mechanisms.

8. In the words of March (1994: 248): "Since returns from exploration are preliminary returns from absorbing ideas [generated by others], those returns are insignificant if no one else is engaging in exploration. As long as nobody else is engaging in exploration, there is inadequate incentive for any individual participant – or potential new entrant to do so."

9. For example, Brown and Duguid (1991) in a study of informal networks among Xerox repair representatives illustrate how informal "war stories" about painstaking customers and unusual repairs helped its members to deal with situations in their daily practices that were nowhere in the official manuals of the company. Learning in communities of practice is task-oriented, in the sense that there is less uncertainty about what should be achieved than about how to achieve it.

10. Recent contributions to the knowledge management literature have suggested creating a knowledge-creating atmosphere (Prusak and Davenport, this volume), to generate corporate spirit, or to enhance a climate of mutual care based on reciprocity (von Krogh, 1998). Additionally, appeals are made to intrinsic motivation (McGregor, 1960; Deci, 1975), peer recognition, or symbolic rewards such as Texas Instrument's annual "best practice celebration and sharing day" (O'Dell and Grayson, 1998). We agree. However, while these possibilities play their part in stimulating knowledge creation, explicit forms of incentives may also supplement them.

11. There are also several studies on product development that have argued that varying degrees of knowledge integration is conducive to explain firm performance (e.g., Clark and Fujimoto, 1991, Iansiti, 1997). Others suggest that patterns of common knowledge in the guise of combinative capabilities, routines, or core competencies are conducive in explaining differences in which firms can do well and how they perform (Hoopes and Postrel, 1999; Grant, 1991).

12. For a more detailed review on the relation between organizational economic insights and claims associated with the "new" knowledge-based theory of the firm see Foss (1996a, b) and Foss and Foss (2000).

References

Aghion, P. and Tirole, J. (1997) Formal and Real Authority in Organization. *Journal of Political Economy*, 105: 1–29.

Akerlof, G.A. (1970) The Market for Lemons: Quality and the Market Mechanism. *Quarterly Journal of Economics*, 84: 488–500.

Alchian, A.A. and Demsetz, H. (1972) Production, Information Costs, and Economic Organization. In A.A. Alchian, *Economic Forces at Work*. Indianapolis: Liberty Press.

Arrow, K.J. (1974) *The Limits of Organization*. New York: W.W. Norton and Co.

Arrow, K.J. (1984) Information and Economic Behaviour. In *Collected Papers of Kenneth Arrow*, Vol. 4. Cambridge, MA: Belkamp Press.

Baker, G., Gibbons, R., and Murphy, K.J. (1999) Informal Authority in Organizations. *Journal of Law, Economics and Organization*, 15: 56–73.

Balkin, D. and Gomez-Mejia, L. (1992) Matching Compensation and Organizational Strategies. *Strategic Management Journal*, 11: 153–69.

Barney, J. (1991) Firm Resources and Sustained Competitive Advantage. *Journal of Management*, 17: 99–120.

Baron, J.N. (1988) The Employment Relation as a Social Relation. *Journal of the Japanese and International Economies*, 2: 492–525.

Barzel, Y. (1982) Measurement Cost and the Organization of Markets. *Journal of Law and Economics*, 25 (April): 27–48.

Becker, G.S. (1962) Investment in Human Capital: A Theoretical Analysis. *Journal of Political Economy*, 70: 7–44.

Boisot, M. (1998) *Knowledge Assets: Securing Competitive Advantage in the Information Economy*. Oxford: Oxford University Press.

Bolton, P. and Farrell, J. (1990) Decentralization, Duplication, and Delay. *Journal of Political Economy*, 98: 803–26.

Brown, J.S. (1998) Organizing Knowledge. *California Management Review*, 40 (3): 90–112.

Brown, J.S. and Duguid, P. (1991) Organizational Learning and Communities-of-practice: Towards a Unified View of Working, Learning, and Innovation. *Organization Science*, 2 (1): 40–57.

Brown, S.L. and Eisenhardt, K.M. (1995) Product Development: Past Research, Recent Findings, and Future Directions. *Academy of Management Review*, 20 (3): 342–83.

Brynjolfsson, E. (1994) Information Assets, Technology, and Organization. *Management Science*, 40: 1645–62.

Buckley, P.J. and Carter, M.J. (1996) The Economics of Business Process Design: Motivation, Information and Coordination within the Firm. *International Journal of the Economics of Business*, 3: 5–24.

Burns, T. and Stalker, G.M. (1961) *The Management of Innovation*. London: Tavistock.

Casson, M. (1994) Why are Firms Hierarchical? *International Journal of the Economics of Business*, 1: 47–76.

Cheung, S.N.S. (1983) The Contractual Nature of the Firm. *Journal of Law and Economics*, 26: 1–22.

Choo, C.W. (1998) *The Knowing Organization*. Oxford: Oxford University Press.

Chow, C. (1983) The Effects of Job Standard Tightness and Compensation Scheme on Performance: An Exploration of Linkages. *Accounting Review*, 58: 667–85.

Clark, K. and Fujimoto, T. (1991) *Product Development Performance*. Boston: Harvard University Press.

Coase, R.H. (1937) The Nature of the Firm. In N.J. Foss (ed.) (2000) *The Theory of the Firm: Critical Perspectives in Business and Management*, Vol. 2. London: Routledge.

Coff, R.W. (1999) When Competitive Advantage Doesn't Lead to Performance: The Resource-based View and Shareholder Bargaining Power. *Organization Science*, 10: 119–34.

Cohen, D. (1998) Towards a Knowledge Context. *California Management Review*, 40 (3): 22–30.

Conner, K.R. and Prahalad, C.K. (1996) A Resource Based Theory of the Firm: Knowledge Versus Opportunism. *Organization Science*, 7 (5): 477–501.

Deci, E. (1975) *Intrinsic Motivation*. New York: Plenum Press.

Demsetz, H. (1988) The Theory of the Firm Revisited. *Journal of Law, Economics, and Organization* 4: 141–61.

Demsetz, H. and Lehn, K. (1989) The Structure of Corporate Ownership: Causes and Consequences. *Journal of Political Economy*, 93 (6): 1155–77.

Dillard, J. and Fisher, J. (1990) Compensation Schemes, Skill Level and Task Performance: An Experimental Examination. *Decision Sciences*, 21: 121–37.

Easterby-Smith, M., Crossan, M., and Nicolini, D. (2000) Organizational Learning: Debates Past, Present and Future. *Journal of Management Studies*, 38 (6): 783–96.

Fama, E. and Jensen, M.C. (1983) Separation of Ownership and Control. *Journal of Law and Economics* 26: 301–25.

Foss, N.J. (1996a) Knowledge-based Approaches to the Theory of the Firm: Some Critical Comments. *Organization Science*, 7: 470–76.

Foss, N.J. (1996b) More Critical Comments on Knowledge-Based Theories of the Firm. *Organization Science* 7: 519–23.

Foss, N.J. (1999) The Use of Knowledge in Firms. *Journal of Institutional and Theoretical Economics*, 155: 458–86.

Foss, N.J. (2000) The Theory of the Firm. In idem. (ed.), *The Theory of the Firm: Critical Perspectives in Economic Organization* (4 vols.), London: Routledge.

Foss, N.J. (2002) "Hayek vs Coase": Economic Organization and the Knowledge Economy," *International Journal of the Economics of Business*, 9: 9–36.

Foss, N.J. (2003) Selective Intervention and Internal Hybrids, forthcoming in *Organization Science*.

Foss, N.J. and Foss, K. (2000) Competence and Governance Perspectives: How Much Do They Differ? And How Does It Matter?" In N.J. Foss and V. Mahnke (eds.), *Competence, Governance, and Entrepreneurship*. Oxford: Oxford University Press.

Galunic, D.C. and Rodan, S. (1998) Resource Re-combinations in the Firm: Knowledge Structures and the Potential for Schumpeterian Innovation. *Strategic Management Journal*, 19: 1193–201.

Ghoshal, S. and Moran, P. (1996) Bad for Practice: A Critique of the Transaction Cost Theory, *Academy of Management Review*, 21: 13–47.

Gibbons, R. (1998) Incentives in Organizations. *Journal of Economic Perspective*, 12: 115–32.

Grandori, A. (1997) Governance Structures, Coordination Mechanisms and Cognitive Models. *Journal of Management and Governance*, 1: 29–42.

Grandori, A. (2001) *Organizations and Economic Behavior*. London: Routledge.

Grant, R. (1991) Resource-based Theory of Competitive Advantage: Implication for Strategy Formulation. *California Management Review*, 33 (3): 114–35.

Grant, R. (1996) Toward a Knowledge-based Theory of the Firm. *Strategic Management Journal*, 17: 109–22.

Harryson, S.J. (2000) *Managing Know-who Based Companies*. Cheltenham: Edward Elgar.

Hart, O. (1995) *Firms, Contracts, and Financial Structure*. Oxford: Oxford University Press.

Hayek, F.A. (1945) The Use of Knowledge in Society. In idem (1948) *Individualism and Economic Order*. Chicago: University of Chicago Press.

Helper, S., MacDuffie, J.P., and Sabel, C. (2000) Pragmatic Collaborations: Advancing Knowledge While Controlling Opportunism. *Industrial and Corporate Change*, 9: 443–87.

Henderson, R.I. (2000) *Compensation Management in a Knowledge-Based World*. London: Prentice-Hall.

Holmström, B. (1979) Moral Hazard and Observability. *Bell Journal of Economics*, 10: 74–91.

Holmström, B. (1982) Moral Hazard in Teams. *Bell Journal of Economics*, 13: 324–41.

Holmström, B. (1989) Agency Costs and Innovation. *Journal of Economic Behavior and Organization*, 12: 305–27.

Holmström, B. (1999) The Firm as a Subeconomy. *Journal of Law, Economics, and Organization*, 15: 74–102.

Holmström, B. and Milgrom, P. (1991) The Firm as an Incentive System. *American Economic Review*, 84: 972–91.

Holmström, B. and Roberts, J. (1998) The Boundaries of the Firm Revisited. *Journal of Economic Perspectives*, 12: 73–94.

Hoopes, D. and Postrel, S. (1999) Shared Knowledge, Glitches, and Product Development Performance. *Strategic Management Journal*, 9: 837–65.

Huberman, G. and Kahn, C. (1988) Limited Contract Enforcement and Strategic Renegotiation. *American Economic Review*, 78 (3): 471–84.

Iansiti, M. (1997) *Technology Integration: Making Critical Choices in a Dynamic World*. Boston: Harvard Business School Press.

Jensen, M.C. and Meckling, W.H. (1992) Specific and General Knowledge and Organizational Structure. In L. Werin and H. Wijkander (eds.), *Contract Economics*. Oxford: Blackwell.

Jones, G.R. (1987) Organization-client Transactions and Organizational Governance Structures. *Academy of Management Journal*, 30: 197–218.

Kogut, B. and Zander, U. (1992) Knowledge of the Firm, Combinative Capabilities, and the Replication of Technology. *Organization Science*, 3: 383–97.

Kogut, B. and Zander, U. (1993) Knowledge of the Firm and the Evolutionary Theory of the Multinational Corporation. *Journal of International Business Studies*, 24: 625–45.

Koopmans, T. (1957) *Three Essays on the State of Economic Science*. New York: McGraw-Hill.

Kreps, D. (1990) Corporate Culture and Economic Theory. In J. Alt and K. Shepsle (eds.), *Perspectives on Positive Political Economy*. New York: Cambridge University Press.

Kreps, D. (1997) Intrinsic Motivation and Extrinsic Incentives. *American Economic Review*, 87 (2): 359–64.

Laing, E. (1994) Accounting Tools Really Can Help: Product Profitability Analysis. *Management Accounting*, 72 (9): 50–1.

Lane, P.J. and Lubatkin, M. (1998) Relative Absorptive Capacity and Inter-organizational Learning. *Strategic Management Journal*, 19 (8): 461–77.

Laursen, K. and Foss, N.J. (2002) New HRM Practices, Complementarities, and the Impact on Innovation Performance. *Cambridge Journal of Economics* (forthcoming).

Laursen, K. and Mahnke, V. (2001) Knowledge Strategies, Firm Types, and Complementarity in Human-Resource Practices. *Journal of Management and Governance*, 5 (1): 1–27.

Lave, J. and Wenger, E. (1990) *Situated Learning: Legitimate Peripheral Participation*. Cambridge: Cambridge University Press.

Lazear, E. (1989) Pay, Equality and Industrial Politics. *Journal of Political Economy*, 97: 561–80.

Lyles, M.A. and Schwenk, C.R. (1992) Top Management, Strategy and Organizational Knowledge Structures. *Journal of Management Studies*, 29: 155–74.

Madhok, A. (1996) The Organization of Economic Activity: Transaction Costs, Firm Capabilities, and the Nature of Governance. *Organization Science*, 7 (5): 577–90.

Mahnke, V. (1998) The Economies of Knowledge Sharing. IVS/CBS working paper.

Mahnke, V. (2001) The Process of Vertical Dis-integration: An Evolutionary Perspective on Outsourcing. *Journal of Management and Governance*, 5: 353–79.

Malcomson, J. (1998) Incentive Contracts in Labor Markets. In O. Ashenfelter and D. Card (eds.), *Handbook of Labor Economics*, Vols. III and IV. New York. North Holland.

March, J.G. (1991) Exploration and Exploitation in Organizational Learning. *Organization Science*, 2: 71–87.

March, J.G. (1994) *A Primer on Decision Making*. New York: Free Press.

Marschak, J. and Radner, R. (1972) *The Theory of Teams*. New Haven: Yale University Press.

Matusik, S.F. and Hill, C.W.L. (1998) The Utilization of Contingent Work, Knowledge Creation, and Competitive Advantage. *Academy of Management Review*, 23: 680–97.

McGregor, D. (1960) *The Human Side of the Enterprise*. New York: McGraw-Hill.

Mendelson, H. and Pillai, R.R. (1999) Information Age Organizations, Dynamics, and Performance, *Journal of Economic Behavior and Organization*, 38: 253–81.

Meyer, C. (1994) How the Right Measures Help Teams Excel. *Harvard Business Review* (May–June): 95–103.

Meyer, M. and Tore, D. (1999) A Product Development for Services. *The Academy of Management Executive*, 13: 64–76.

Milgrom, P. (1988) Employment Contracts, Influence Activities and Efficient Organization Design. *Journal of Political Economy*, 96. 42–60.

Milgrom, P. and Roberts, J. (1990) The Economics of Modern Manufacturing: Technology, Strategy and Organization. *American Economic Review*, 80: 511–28.

Milgrom, P. and Roberts, J. (1995) Complementarities and Fit Strategy, Structure, and Organizational Change in Manufacturing. *Journal of Accounting and Economics*, 19: 179–208.

Miller, G. (1992) *Managerial Dilemmas*. Cambridge: Cambridge University Press.

Myers, P.S. (ed.) (1996) *Knowledge Management and Organizational Design*. Boston: Butterworth-Heinemann.

Nahapiet, J. and Ghoshal, S. (1998) Social Capital, Intellectual Capital and the Organizational Advantage. *Academy of Management Review*, 382: 242–66.

Neef, D. (ed.) (1998) *The Knowledge Economy*. Boston: Butterworth-Heinemann.

Nelson, R. and Winter, S. (1982) *An Evolutionary Theory of Economic Change*. Cambridge, MA: The Belknap Press.

Nonaka, I. and Takeuchi, H. (1995) *The Knowledge-Creating Company*. Oxford: Oxford University Press.

O'Dell, C. and Grayson, J.C. (1998) If Only We Knew what We Know: Identification and Transfer of Internal Best Practices. *California Management Review*, 40 (3): 183–97.

Osterloh, M. and Frey, B. (2000) Motivation, Knowledge Transfer and Organizational Form. *Organization Science*, 11: 538–50.

Ouchi, W. (1980) Markets, Bureaucracies and Clans. *Administrative Science Quarterly* 25: 129–41.

Peteraf, M.A. (1993) The Cornerstones of Competitive Advantage: A Resource-based View. *Strategic Management Journal*, 14: 179–91.

Pfeffer, J. and Langton, N. (1993) The Effect of Wage Dispersion on Satisfaction, Productivity, and Working Collaboratively: Evidence from College and University Faculty. *Administrative Science Quarterly*, 38: 382–408.

Prendergast, C. (1993) The Role of Promotion in Inducing Specific Human Capital Acquisition. *Quarterly Journal of Economics*, 108 (2): 523–34.

Prendergast, C. (1999) The Tenuous Tradeoff of Risk and Incentives. Working paper.

Prusac, L. (1998) Introduction to Series – Why Knowledge, Why Now? In D. Neef (ed.), *The Knowledge Economy*. Boston: Butterworth-Heinemann.

Putterman, L. (1995) Markets, Hierarchies and Information: On a Paradox in the Economics of Organization. *Journal of Economic Behavior and Organization*, 26: 373–90.

Rabin, M. (1993) Information and the Control of Productive Assets. *Journal of Law, Economics and Organization*, 9: 51–76.

Radner, R. (1993) The Organization of Decentralized Information Processing. *Econometrica*, 61: 1109–46.

Rajan, R.G. and Zingales, L. (1998) Power in a Theory of the Firm. *Quarterly Journal of Economics*, 113: 387–432.

Richardson, J.B. (1972) The Organization of Industry. *Economic Journal*, 82: 883–96.

Rosen, S. (1991) Transaction Costs and Internal Labor Markets. In O.E. Williamson and S.G. Winter (eds.), *The Nature of the Firm*. Oxford: Basil Blackwell.

Schumpeter, J.A. (1950) *Essays on Entrepreneurs, Innovations, Business Cycles, and the Evolution of Capitalism*. New Brunswick: Transaction Publishers.

Scott, S. and Einstein, W. (2001) Strategic Performance Appraisal in Team Based Organization: One Size Does Not Fit All. *Academy of Management Executive*, 15 (2): 107–16.

Shelanski, H. and Klein, P.G. (1995) Empirical Research in Transaction Cost Economics: A Review and Assessment. *Journal of Law, Economics, and Organization*, 11: 335–61.

Simon, H.A. (1957) *Models of Man*. New York: John Wiley & Sons.

Simon, H. (1991) Bounded Rationality and Organizational Learning. *Organization Science*, 2: 125–34.

Spence, A.M. (1973) Job Market Signalling. *Quarterly Journal of Economics*, 87: 355–77.

Spence, A.M. (1974) Market Signaling Informational Transfer in Hiring and Related Screening Processes. *Harvard Economic Studies*, 143.

Thompson, J.D. (1967) *Organizations in Action*. New York: Wiley.

Von Krogh, G. (1998) Care in Knowledge Creation. *California Management Review*, 40 (3): 133–53.

Von Krogh, G., Ochijo, K., and Nonaka, I. (2000) *Enabling Knowledge Creation*. Oxford: Oxford University Press.

Weick, K.E. and Roberts, K.H. (1993) Collective Mind in Organizations: Heedful Interrelating on Flight Decks. *Administrative Science Quarterly*, 38: 357–81.

Williamson, O.E. (1975) *Markets and Hierarchies: Analysis and Antitrust Implications*. New York: Free Press.

Williamson, O.E. (1985) *The Economic Institutions of Capitalism*. New York: Free Press.

Williamson, O.E. (1996) *The Mechanisms of Governance*. Oxford: Oxford University Press.

Winter, S. (1987) Knowledge and Competence as Strategic Assets. In D. Teece (ed.), *The Competitive Challenge*. Cambridge, MA: Ballinger, 159–84.

Zollo, M. and Winter, S. (2002) Deliberate Learning and the Evolution of Dynamic Capabilities. *Organization Science*, 13: 339–44.

6

Knowledge Management: The Information Technology Dimension

Maryam Alavi and Amrit Tiwana

Chapter Outline

In this chapter, we discuss the role of information technology (IT) in enabling key organizational knowledge management processes. We review the potential role of IT in supporting knowledge creation, codification and retrieval, transfer, and integration and application. While highlighting the divides in the literature, we use existing organization theory as a lens for examining what we believe to be promising applications of distributed learning systems, communication support systems, and expert systems for enabling these knowledge management processes. The choice of enabling IT, considered as a portfolio of tools, will be different depending on whether an organization's context is suited for the knowledge stock or network model. We illustrate each facet with cases and identify the aspects of the IT dimension of knowledge management that remain theoretically understudied.

Introduction

Organizational knowledge management is a broad and multi-faceted topic involving socio-cultural, organizational, behavioral, and technical dimensions. Subsumed under the knowledge management rubric is a large set of behavioral strategies (e.g., learning organization and communities of practice), information-based approaches (e.g., best practices and competitive intelligence), and technologies (e.g., data mining and expert systems). Knowledge and knowledge management are not new phenomena and organizations are continuously engaged in the creation/acquisition, accumulation and application of knowledge. According to Penrose (1959) the accumulation of knowledge is built into the very nature of firms. Recently, however, interest in and emphasis on organizational knowledge and knowledge management has increased among developed economies. This interest has been attributed to several factors including globalization of the economy and markets, volatility of business and competitive environments, and a trend toward knowledge intensive products and services as well as rapid progress in information technologies (Alavi, 2000). Effective knowledge management in organizations involves a combination of technological and behavioral elements. Considering the complexity and variety of knowledge management technologies, this chapter focuses on the technological components of knowledge management and the potential relationships between technical and behavioral dimensions. This focus is based on the premise that large-scale and complex knowledge management initiatives in organizational settings can be greatly enhanced and facilitated through the application of advanced information technologies. In fact, it has been argued that the availability of certain new technologies such as the World Wide Web and communication support systems "has been instrumental in catalyzing knowledge management" (Davenport and Prusak, 1998:123).

In this chapter, we first provide an overview of categories of knowledge management technologies, which correspond to four knowledge management processes: knowledge creation, knowledge storage and retrieval, knowledge transfer, and knowledge application. For each category, we present a case example of organizational application of information technology (IT). We focus our discussion on the organizational knowledge management implications of these technologies and highlight the dimensions of organizational characteristics, knowledge task domains, and the IT component itself. We also discuss the complementary choices that are available to managers when they select specific technologies in building a larger and comprehensive knowledge management system. The extant literature has treated information technologies for knowledge management and strategic/behavioral approaches for managing organizational knowledge separately. We believe that exploring the linkages between these two parallel streams of work offers promising avenues for research and practice and extends the insights gleaned from the IT implementation and design literatures. Finally, we discuss various research issues and research questions pertaining to design and implementation of knowledge management technologies in organizational settings.

The Role of Information Technology in Organizational Knowledge Management

Organizations routinely engage in the generation, capture, and use of knowledge in order to develop and deliver their products and/or services, and to compete effectively in the marketplace. Recently, however, there has been a trend toward the application of advanced information technologies (e.g., the Internet, intranets, web browsers, data warehouses, data mining and software agents) to systematize, facilitate, and expedite firm-wide knowledge management. Consider the following examples at Hewlett-Packard (HP), provided by Davenport and Prusak (1998). HP uses a variety of computerized systems to support its knowledge management activities. One such system is the company's Electronic Sales Partners (ESP). ESP is a web-based system that contains white papers, sales presentations, technical manuals, and product information. ESP also provides links to other relevant knowledge resources on HP's worldwide intranet. The system is used extensively by the sales force in support of various sales activities and is perceived to be highly successful. In addition to ESP, HP also uses a software system called Notes to support large-scale internal and external knowledge sharing. For example, an internal Notes-based application called "Trainers' Trading Post" enables trainers throughout the company to share their experiences with various educational programs and offers by participating in discussion data bases. Externally, HP uses Notes to share product and service information with the resellers of its computer systems.

Considering the plethora of information technology tools that may be applied to the management of organizational knowledge, it is useful to adopt a framework to categorize these tools and to relate them to the primary organizational KM processes. By drawing on knowledge management and information technology research literatures, this section identifies such a framework and describes the key IT tools which support various organizational knowledge management processes.

We adopt the knowledge management framework developed by Alavi and Leidner (2001a), which is based on the view of organizations as "knowledge systems." According to this view, organizations consist of four "knowledge processes": creation, storage/retrieval, transfer, and application (Alavi and Leidner, 2001a; Holzner and Marx, 1979). These knowledge processes are described in the next section.

Knowledge creation process

Knowledge creation refers to the development of "new" organizational know-how and capability (Nonaka, 1994; Nonaka and Nishiguchi, 2001). Knowledge originates within individuals or social systems (groups of individuals) (Alavi, 2000). Some organizations allocate dedicated resources to the knowledge creation process. A useful example is employee training and development programs that aim to generate knowledge at the individual levels. Another example is the establishment of units or groups (e.g., R&D departments) for the purpose of creating new knowledge. At the individual level, knowledge is created through cognitive processes such as reflection and learning. Social systems (i.e., groups) generate knowledge through collaborative interactions and joint problem solving. Information technology can thus play a role in the knowledge creation process through its support of the individuals' learning processes as well as support of collaborative interactions among individuals. The next section discusses this category of knowledge management technologies consisting of e-learning and collaboration support systems as well as examples of their organizational applications.

Information technology support of knowledge creation.   *E-learning systems* are computerized systems in which the learner's interactions with learning materials (e.g., assignments and exercises), instructors, and/or peers are mediated through technology. Due to the promise of flexibility and reduced downtime and travel expenses, there has been a recent flux of e-learning activities (in the form of distributed learning) in corporations as well as educational institutions. In distributed learning environments, learning interactions are dispersed over time and/or distance. Two models of distributed e-learning have been identified: (1) synchronous and (2) asynchronous (Alavi and Leidner, 2001c).

The synchronous model resembles a classroom in which the instructor and the students are located in two or more remote locations. In the asynchronous (or online) model, students are provided with remote access to course material through information and communication technologies. In the second model, the student is largely in charge of his/her learning, thus experiencing great flexibility in choosing the time, pace, frequency and form of learning activities (Alavi and Leidner, 2001c).

A variety of studies have illustrated the use and outcome of different forms of e-learning systems. These studies have collectively illustrated the effectiveness of e-learning and its impact on learning dynamics and outcomes (see Alavi and Leidner, 2001c for the review of research in this area). Web-based integrated software packages for e-learning have recently been developed that provide two sets of capabilities: (1) assembling multimedia content created by a variety of authoring/publishing software programs into a course; and (2) managing course registration, administering and recording tests online, and tracking course and program completion. Companies are making asynchronous Web-based e-learning increasingly available to their employees in order to save the travel expenses and loss of work hours associated with traditional classroom training and development. For example, Ernst and Young, LLP has developed a web-based learning system called Learning Environment to Accelerate Performance (LEAP). The LEAP system provides internal as well as client training and development programs through web-based interactive distance learning approaches. About 85 percent of Ernst and Young's professional employees work outside of their offices on any given day. Using their laptops to access the LEAP system, this mobile work force benefits greatly from timely and efficient delivery of training programs. IDC estimates that the US corporate market for e-learning will grow from an estimated $1.1 billion in 2000 to $11.4 billion in 2003.

Another category of IT for support of knowledge creation consists of *collaboration support systems*. These systems refer to integrated information and communication technologies designed to facilitate interactions among individuals in support of organizational collaboration during task performance. New knowledge is created through collaboration – by combining and amplifying the individual group members' knowledge. This joint creation of knowledge is usually accomplished through the group members' exposure to each other's thoughts, opinions, and beliefs, while also obtaining and providing feedback from others for clarification and comprehension. Collaboration support systems aim at improving group collaborative interactions by providing techniques for structuring task interactions and systematically directing the pattern, timing, content, and recall of group discussions. Consider the following example, adapted from Malhotra et al. (2001), of a collaboration support system used in the design of a new product. Boeing-Rocketdyne, a US manufacturer of liquid fueled rocket engines, initiated an inter-organizational team to design a new and highly efficient rocket engine. A computerized system specially designed for the team provided the forum and the supportive environment for collaboration necessary for the development of the new product. The system consisted of communication and messaging capabilities and an electronic whiteboard, as well as an easy-to-search information repository. All team members were easily and securely able to access the system capabilities remotely. The content of the information repository could consist of various forms of entries including sketches, snapshots, hotlinks to desktop applications, and documents or templates. Each team member was able to create, comment on, modify, search, and reference-link the entries in the data repository. The team decided that when extensive changes to the existing information repository entries are needed, a new entry should be created and linked to the existing one in order to preserve and observe the evolution of the team's thoughts and ideas. The electronic whiteboard allowed real-time access to and manipulation of the same entry. Furthermore, modeling tools enabled real-time illustration and analysis of ideas. Malhotra et al. (2001) provide an interesting example of the use of the system: during a teleconference, while all the team members were logged into the system, one of the engineers sketched an idea on the whiteboard. The idea involved drilling a certain number of holes into a metal plate. As the debate about the number and location of the holes continued, another engineer at a remote location used his desktop CAD (computer assisted design) tool to develop a more accurate and detailed drawing of the sketch. The analysis of the CAD drawing revealed that the metal plate was not large enough for all the required holes. The team then proceeded to modify the design in real-time and to develop a new feasible solution.

Knowledge storage and retrieval process

Knowledge storage and retrieval refers to development of organizational memory (i.e., stocks of organizational knowledge) and the means for accessing its content. We can identify two types of organizational memory: internal and external. Internal memory refers to the stocks of knowledge that reside within the individuals or groups of individuals in an organization. Internal organizational memory as defined here consist of individuals' skills as well as the organizational culture (Walsh and Ungson, 1991). External memories contain codified and explicit organizational knowledge and include formal policies and procedure, and manual and computer files. The development of external memory in organizations involves three key activities: (1) determining the knowledge content of the memory; (2) determining the sources of the content and specifying the means of collecting the targeted knowledge; and (3) developing the content of the external memory and specifying the means of accessing its content. Most IT initiatives for the creation of organizational memory have focused on the third activity – the development of the explicit knowledge stocks and mechanisms for retrieval of the contents. In the next section we discuss the key technologies for the storage and retrieval of codified organizational knowledge: data warehousing/data mining and repositories.

Information technology for support of knowledge storage and retrieval.   Many organizations collect large volumes of transactional data even though raw data is rarely of direct benefit (Fayyad and Uthurusamy, 1996). Grocery stores, for example, capture data on customer purchases, dates, times, and quantities at cash registers. Automotive manufacturers collect data on retail sales, and customers, on potential leads at the front-end, and on suppliers, logistics, and engineering designs at the back-end. Much of this data tends to be locked in functional silos and functionally separated databases. A data warehouse is a centralized repository that integrates, summarizes, and creates a historical profile of such data, which would otherwise remain fragmented (Inmon, 1996). Data warehouses therefore help convert large volumes of raw data into smaller chunks of interlinked information. The assumption underlying data warehousing is that valuable information is embedded in large volumes of objective data (Fayyad and Uthurusamy, 1996). Data mining is a useful technique for uncovering such information. Data mining is defined as the process of automatically searching for unknown correlations in the data by looking for interesting patterns, anomalies, and clusters (Loeb et al., 1998). Although such integrative repositories can be mined to discern information and patterns in the data, they also afford the opportunity to delve into the granular detail underlying that pattern (Loeb et al., 1998). A data warehouse provides a central access point for real-time transactional data across the entire enterprise. Summaries and aggregations of transactional data available in a data warehouse provide inputs for the various other knowledge management tools which support other knowledge management processes.

Sears, Roebuck and Company, a large US conglomerate of loosely coupled businesses, provides an illustrative example of the application of data warehousing for knowledge storage and retrieval. Although its many businesses such as automotive services, retail operations, termite extermination, and consumer credit target overlapping pools of customers, the customers' records were maintained and managed independently in business-specific databases. Such fragmentation of customer records prevented Sears from creating a unified profile of individual customers. Complex and idiosyncratic data structures, multiple lines of business, and multiple indexing mechanisms made coordination of such data challenging (Johnson, 1999). In some lines of business Sears used customers' home telephone numbers, in others their last names, and in others their social security numbers. In 1999, Sears implemented a data warehouse to connect its many fragmented databases to create a unified view of the customer across all product lines and business categories. Such an integrated store of knowledge about each customer's history of purchases, interactions, and transactions now allows the company to build a comprehensive picture of each customer to target new offerings to its existing clientele more effectively.

Another technical approach to organizational knowledge storage and retrieval is *information repository*. In most organizations, codified knowledge is often fragmented in many databases (Zack, 1999). Repositories bring together content from various data sources, providing a unified access point and reducing knowledge search costs (Hansen, 1999). Repositories can store highly structured content such as transactional data, customer records, and financial information, or relatively unstructured content such as multimedia content and conversational discussion threads. Web-based data warehouses, which integrate content from several distributed databases, are perhaps the most common form of repositories among contemporary organizations. Repositories for unstructured content complement those built primarily for highly structured content. Such repositories allow for the storage and retrieval of unstructured content that fosters knowledge sharing both internally and with customers. For example, Dell, the computer hardware manufacturer located in Austin, Texas, uses a repository to facilitate knowledge storage for customers and its technical support staff. When a customer is faced with a specific problem – say a problem with a device driver software application on a recently purchased system – he or she can search a repository of the "frequently asked questions" for a solution. If a similar problem was previously addressed, the repository can immediately provide a possible solution. If no solution can be retrieved from the repository, posting the query can elicit troubleshooting suggestions from Dell's support staff who continually monitor this repository. By storing and reusing knowledge in the form of the solutions to frequently encountered problems, Dell is able to reduce the overhead of providing technical support to customers.

Knowledge transfer process

The knowledge transfer process involves the transmission of knowledge from the initial location to where it is needed and is applied. Although the concept of knowledge transfer is simple, its execution in organizational settings is not. This is because organizations often do not know what they know and often possess weak systems for locating and transmitting different forms of knowledge within their various locations (Huber, 1991). The ability to transfer existing knowledge to the point of application is a key detriment to organizations' realization of the full value of their knowledge assets (Argote and Ingram, 2000).

We can identify three modes of knowledge transfer in organizations: (1) transfer of knowledge between individuals; (2) transfer between individuals and knowledge repositories (e.g., downloading a report from a document repository, or developing a report and storing it in a document repository); and (3) transfer among existing knowledge repositories (e.g., using information filtering software to locate and transfer pre-specified knowledge items among existing knowledge repositories). Considering the various modes of knowledge transfer, we can identify two models of IT applications in this area: (1) the network model; and (2) the knowledge stock model. The network model focuses on facilitating person-to-person transfer of knowledge via electronic communication channels. The stock model, on the other hand, focuses on the electronic transfer of codified knowledge to and from computerized knowledge repositories. Next we discuss communication support systems and information portals representing the network and the stock models of knowledge transfer respectively.

Information technology support of knowledge transfer process.   The network model of knowledge transfer draws heavily on *communication support systems* to establish electronic channels for the efficient transfer of knowledge among individuals. Some communication support systems enable synchronous (i.e., near real-time) exchange of messages among the communicating parties, while others enable only asynchronous (time-delayed) message exchange. The synchronous communication support systems include online chat, audio- and videoconferencing; and the asynchronous communication support systems for knowledge transfer consist of email, voice mail, and computer conferencing. Consider the use of communication support systems, video and audio conferencing, to enhance the efficiency of knowledge transfer at British Petroleum (Davenport and Prusak, 1998). In one instance, the operations on a North Sea mobile drilling ship came to a halt as a result of equipment failure. Through the use of a satellite link, an ad hoc video and audio conferencing network was established between the engineers on the ship and drilling equipment engineers in Aberdeen in eastern Scotland. The engineers in Aberdeen, visually examining the broken equipment through the video link and synchronous interactions and discussions with the remotely located ship engineers, were able to diagnose the problem and lead ship engineers through the necessary repairs in a few short hours. Diagnosing the problem and fixing the broken part without the video and audio links that enabled transfer of know-how between the expert engineers in Aberdeen and the engineers on the ship would have required dispatching the experts to the ship and would have caused considerable delay and cost.

The stock model of knowledge transfer draws on information and communication technology to transmit codified information between knowledge repositories and individuals. The dominant technical tool employed to implement the stock model of knowledge transfer is the enterprise information portal. An *enterprise information portal* (also referred to as a corporate portal) enables the transfer of knowledge from knowledge repositories to and from individuals through a central access point and a web browser interface. A key advantage of portals lies in their ability to transfer knowledge to and from a diverse array of knowledge resources and backbone information systems from any place and at any time. Consider the application of information portals at Frito-Lay, a $8.5 billion division of PepsiCo that manufactures and sells snacks throughout North America and through its subsidiaries on five other continents. Frito-Lay relies on information about private-label competitors and market trends in order to manage marketing and advertising strategies. Information about sales in different regions and product categories was readily available locally in scattered systems and databases but was difficult to share widely across the entire company's distributed operations. The company felt the need for a technical solution that would allow a salesperson to share interesting insights and information instantaneously with his/her peers in other locations. A portal was implemented on an existing corporate intranet with two overarching goals: (1) streamline knowledge transfer among the sales force across Frito-Lay, and (2) to exploit customer- and market-specific knowledge. The portal system included access to sales information, analysis, market-specific news, and a directory of area experts in the company. A natural language search facility was also implemented as part of the portal. The system was pilot tested across 10 geographic locations and delivered promising results. Within a few months, Frito-Lay doubled its growth rate in the test markets as internal marketing specialists started to share sales tips, best practices, and market insights.

Knowledge application process

Knowledge application refers to the use of knowledge for decision-making and problem-solving by individuals and groups in organizations. Knowledge in and of itself does not produce organizational value. Its application for taking effective action does. On the other hand, absorption and application of "new" knowledge by individuals is complex. For example, work in the area of individual cognition and knowledge structures has demonstrated that, in most cases individuals in organizational settings enact cognitive processes (problem-solving and decision-making) with little attention and by invoking only pre-existing knowledge and cognitive "routines" (Gioia and Pool, 1984). While this tendency leads to a reduction in cognitive load and is therefore an effective strategy for dealing with individual cognitive limitations, it creates a barrier to the search for and application of new knowledge in organizations. Thus, information technology tools that facilitate knowledge application can potentially lead to significant organizational value. We next discuss information technology tools, consisting of expert systems and decision support systems designed for the purpose of applying pertinent knowledge to the execution of organizational tasks.

Information technology support of knowledge application. Managers often use rules of thumb, tricks of the trade, heuristics, and tacitly developed criteria to make decisions. *Rule-based expert systems* facilitate routine application of such knowledge through codification of the decision rules. Existing expertise is embedded in the software and use of the embedded knowledge is automated (George and Tyran, 1993; Lado and Zhang, 1998). The embedded knowledge frees knowledge workers from the monotonous reapplication of knowledge when such knowledge is relatively stable. Five conditions must be simultaneously satisfied in order to achieve the development of a rule-based expert system for the purpose of knowledge application (Tiwana, 1999: 222). First, the variables relevant to a problem should be known. Second, these variables should be expressed in quantitative terms. Third, the rules covering most if not all of these variables should exist. Fourth, rules that are applied simultaneously to solve a decision problem should not overlap. Fifth, the rules must have been validated in practice. Expert knowledge is extracted and applied in solving a problem although universal criteria for judging good solutions are unavailable. A rule-based expert system is a valuable tool for knowledge application when an expert's tacit knowledge can be converted into codified rules. Under this condition, application of the codified knowledge becomes programmatic and frees the human expert to focus on other organizational activities that are more resistant to automata.

Dhar and Stein (1997) describe the use of a rule-based expert system at NYNEX Inc., a leading provider of telephone services in New York and New England. Approximately 50 percent of NYNEX's 60,000 employees are devoted to maintenance and repair of its extensive network of telephone lines. When a customer reports a problem with a telephone line, a service representative collects information and remotely initiates a set of electrical tests known as the *mechanized loop test* (MLT). Based on this diagnosis, a decision is made whether to send a service technician to the customer site. It is important to reduce the erroneous dispatching of service personnel because a one percent error rate adds approximately $3 million to NYNEX's annual maintenance costs. The company developed an expert system to handle over 30 percent of all support calls across NYNEX's 55 call centers. Every reported problem is matched against the rule-based expert system to find a solution. Use of the system by field technicians helps to validate and refine these rules constantly and adapts them to new types of equipment and technologies (e.g., telephones, modems, and other networking) that customers adopt.

Another form of expert systems, a *case-based reasoning system*, facilitates the application of semi-structured knowledge through the intelligent reuse of previous problem-solving experiences. A case-based reasoning system documents each problem-solving initiative as a separate case. Over time, a collection of problem cases and solutions to the problems emerges. Each case is classified using pre-specified attributes. The user specifies a new problem and assigns weights to several attributes to indicate their relative importance in problem-solving. A case-based reasoning system then uses past cases to aid in solving new problems through an intricate process of pattern matching. Cases that are the closest matches are retrieved from the case base and this subset can be further refined to find the closest match. A distinguishing characteristic of this approach is that the contextual details of each case are retained and retrieved with it. A case-based reasoning system is designed with the expectations that the domain will change, that new cases will be added over time, and that the initial set of attributes will be less than precise (Dhar and Stein, 1997). A downside of this approach is that it requires advance planning and pre-specification of the attributes that will be used in the system. Further, as the number of cases in the system increase, its performance degrades.

Compaq Computer Corporation, a leading manufacturer of computer systems, provides an illustrative example of a case-based reasoning system (Dhar and Stein, 1997: 236). In the face of intense price-based competition and commoditization of computer hardware, Compaq decided to use customer support as a differentiating component of its product offering. Although this approach seemed simplistic on the surface, Compaq realized that logging a customer problem, analyzing it, and providing a solution to it were less than straightforward for three reasons. First, the range of Compaq's products required that technical support staff possess a wide breadth of expertise. Second, frequently changing models and technologies led to rapid obsolescence of that expertise. Third, Compaq's systems built on a wide range of other hardware and software developed by its partners such as Microsoft. This widened the scope of knowledge needed by Compaq's technical staff. Moreover, the frequency of customer support calls was typically very high during the early phases of a new product's introduction. Since many customers were unable to articulate the problem precisely, the technical support staff would require the ability to cope with imprecise information from the customers. It was crucial but challenging for Compaq to maintain high levels of service quality with limited resources. Compaq implemented a case-based reasoning system, SMART, to address these challenges. The system was initially populated with a prototypical set of problems from past customer support incidences. When a new problem was reported, the system matched its attributes with the attributes of the cases contained in the system; and the closest case was retrieved. The search-and-retrieval process was based largely on natural language descriptions of the problem. If no match was found for a given problem, the problem was immediately flagged as being unresolved. Domain experts then produced a solution to the problem, which was then entered into the system as a new case. Compaq realized the payoffs from automating the application of technical support knowledge within the first year of implementation. The success rate of problem resolution encounters was 50 percent higher when Compaq's staff used SMART to respond to the customer query. The savings in customer support costs within the first year were estimated at about $20 million (Dhar and Stein, 1997).

Another form of IT system that can support knowledge application in organizations is decision support systems. *Decision support systems* are defined as computer-based systems that support unstructured decision-making in organizations through direct interactions with data and analytical models (McNurlin and Sprague, 2001: 368). The primary strength of decision support systems is their ability to combine highly structured information with unstructured information in a problem-specific context. Decision support systems filter aggregate information (such as total sales per week by region) from the data captured through pervasive transaction processing systems (such as cash registers, bar-code scanners, and ATMs). Three components define a decision support system: dialogue, data, and models. The dialogue represents the interactions between the user and the system. The data represents aggregated data such as that obtained from a data warehouse. Models represent the analytical conceptualizations by which data are manipulated to address tasks.

Decision support systems are increasingly being integrated with web-based interfaces to capture data about specific customers. For example, a decision support system can capture click-stream data from a customer's navigation patterns on a website and then aggregate that data to draw inferences about the products that a customer might be interested in. This provides the opportunity of presenting the customer with customized offers that is likely to be relevant to his/her interests. Sara Lee uses a decision support system for knowledge application in the domain of sales forecasting. The company repeatedly faced excessive inventories because of the quality of sales forecasts that were derived from its sales force's hunches. Moreover, with over 200 versions of its key products in grocery stores, it was increasingly difficult for Sara Lee to keep its forecasting model up to date. A decision support system was introduced along with a policy decision to reduce the total number of versions of its products from 200 to 36. The decision support system used time-series data from the preceding time periods and extrapolated the patterns into the future to predict sales of specific products over the next several periods. The forecasts are then distributed every two weeks to Sara Lee's sales force to create shared understanding among the larger group. As a result, the company has reduced its forecast errors from about 10–20 percent to about 1–2 percent. It has also helped reduce inventories and increase service levels to greater than the industry average of about 97 percent (McNurlin and Sprague, 2001: 372–3).

Summary: role of information technology in support of knowledge management processes

Consistent with some other authors (e.g., Alavi and Leidner, 2001a; Davenport and Prusak, 1998; Zack, 1999) we contend in this section that organizational knowledge management can be enhanced and supported through applications of advance IT tools to create an infrastructure and a "field" for support of the timing, scope, dynamics, and efficiency of the underlying knowledge management processes. IT tools for support of various KM processes of creation, storage and retrieval, transfer, and application described in this section are summarized and displayed in table 6.1. Organizational knowledge management is not a discrete and monolithic phenomenon or at any point in time individuals and groups may be involved in several different phases and processes of knowledge management (Alavi and Leidner, 2001a).

Knowledge management technology is a broad concept and technical tools are not limited to those described in this chapter. Furthermore, knowledge management technologies displayed in each of the columns of table 6.1 are not mutually exclusive. In some large-scale organizational knowledge management initiatives, a combination of various technologies are used synergistically.

INFORMATION TECHNOLOGIES AND KNOWLEDGE MANAGEMENT: DIRECTIONS FOR RESEARCH

Implementation research in the IT literature has traditionally focused on the issues and processes that facilitate applications of IT in various organizational settings. This

TABLE 6.1 Information technology tools for support of KM processes

	Knowledge management processes			
	Creation	Storage and retrieval	Transfer	Application
Information technology tools	E-learning Collaboration support systems	Data warehousing and data mining Repositories	Communication support systems Enterprise information portals	Expert systems Decision support systems

literature, however, has not explicitly studied IT implementation in the context of organizational knowledge processes of knowledge creation, storage and retrieval, transfer, and application as conceptualized in this chapter. In this section we discuss some of the research issues in relation to the role of some of the specific IT tools for support of the knowledge management processes described in this chapter.

The knowledge management and IT research literatures have identified a number of cultural, organizational, strategic, and technical factors that can influence the design and implementation of IT systems for support of organizational knowledge management. A useful area of future research would be to focus on the factors that may create specific opportunities and/or challenges in the deployment of various categories of IT tools to support the corresponding knowledge management processes. Once these factors are identified, further research can identify specific organizational and technical initiatives that may address these challenges/opportunities and thus enhance the effectiveness of knowledge management tools.

Next, for illustrative purposes, we will briefly discuss some of the organizational issues faced in the design and implementation of the technology tools corresponding to the four knowledge management processes displayed in table 6.1.

E-learning systems

E-learning was identified as a tool for the support of the knowledge creation process. Despite the growing interest and enthusiasm for development and application of e-learning systems, little theoretically grounded and rigorous research guides the development and implementation of these systems in organizational settings. Previous research in the IS area over the last decade has investigated the learning effectiveness of various forms of synchronous and online e-learning systems. The investigations of e-learning systems collectively indicate that (1) no "best" e-learning system configuration exists (i.e., a variety of forms and approaches to design effective e-learning systems can be used); and (2) e-learning systems positively impact individual learning and knowledge acquisition (Alavi et al., 1995; Butler, 1990, Leidner and Jarvenpaa, 1993). Recently, researchers (e.g., Alavi and Leidner, 2001b, 2001c; Kozma, 1994) have called for an investigation of the ways by which technology features can engage psychological processes of learning that in turn result in highly effective knowledge acquisition.

One of the challenges in the deployment of e-learning systems as knowledge creation tools in organizational settings is requirements determination. E-learning requirement determination consists of three complex steps: (1) developing a knowledge model that specifies the structure, types, and levels of skills and competencies required for particular jobs; (2) rating the performance of individual employees by job competencies; and (3) linking the competency model to specific e-learning courses. These steps are highly complex and their execution in organizational settings is by no means trivial, calling for an extensive and sustained research effort.

Knowledge repositories

Knowledge repositories constitute a prominent technical approach to the storage and retrieval of codified organizational knowledge. However, it is not clear what specific knowledge (i.e., content, domain, type and scope of knowledge) should be stored in repositories. Thus, a useful line of inquiry would be to identify factors that influence the knowledge storage and retrieval requirements of the firm to develop effective and efficient methodologies for determining these requirements in a given firm.

Further research is also needed to determine whether and how pointers to tacit knowledge can be incorporated into the content brought together in repositories. As new patterns and correlations are inferred from mining a data warehouse, how can organizations assess whether those patterns hold over time? In other words, how can the perishability of that knowledge be determined? Short of mechanisms to facilitate such referential checks, organizations are not immune to inappropriate applications of pre-existing solutions to entirely new problems (Robey and Boudreau, 1999). In repositories, especially those that span multiple partner organizations, the issues of knowledge ownership and appropriability are open research issues. Indeed, technology research offers worthy avenues for further exploration of the issues in inter-organizational contexts where the contribution of specific information cannot be quantifiably traced to a given firm in a network.

Communication support systems

Communication support systems in the form of e-mail, discussion databases, and audio/video conferencing systems can greatly enhance knowledge transfer in firms. However, research needs to investigate the relative effectiveness of various communication support systems for the transfer of different types of knowledge. For example, we might assert that "rich" communication media (e.g., videoconferencing) may be more appropriate for transfer of complex or ambiguous knowledge (for example, beliefs, impressions, and hunches) between individuals. On the other hand "lean" communication media (e.g., e-mail) may be more effective for transfer of explicit and factual knowledge. Yet one might hypothesize that the application of communication support systems can expand the reach and scope of knowledge transfer in organizational settings by augmenting the face-to-face communication channels among individuals. Research needs to investigate these hypotheses and test the validity of these assertions. Furthermore, a number of organizational factors are believed to impact the level, speed, and intensity of organizational knowledge transfer. The interplay between the organizational factors and communication support systems and their impact on the rate and scope of knowledge transfer needs to be investigated. For example, the strength of relationships between the source of knowledge and the intended recipient of knowledge may impact the frequency, ease of use, and effectiveness of communication systems in the knowledge transfer process. Furthermore, communication support systems cannot overcome cultural factors that may inhibit knowledge transfer in organizations. Examples of these inhibitors include a lack of trust, intolerance for mistakes, the not-invented-here syndrome, and a highly individualistic versus collaborative organizational culture. Research investigating the role of these and other contextual variables can ultimately facilitate organizational implementation of communication support systems for knowledge transfer.

Expert systems

Expert systems facilitate the routine application of codifiable knowledge by embedding it in software-based systems. Although valuable knowledge emerges through the interaction among disparate knowledge bases (for a review, see Kogut and Zander, 1992), as previously discussed, expert systems are not robust in using interacting rules. Once specialized knowledge is embedded in an expert system, its ongoing validity and applicability is difficult to assess. Future research should explore how to maintain the knowledge embedded in expert systems and how to identify inconsistencies with its context. Future empirical work should also explore how a turbulent context (and knowledge perishability) influences users' perceptions and trust in the recommendations provided by an expert system.

Most expert systems are designed to assist with individual decision-making. However, knowledge work is now increasingly collaborative, involving group rather than individual decision-making. We believe that future research can provide valuable insights into the confluence of expert systems and decision support systems. One fruitful area of research may explore how the insights gleaned from the cumulative tradition in group decision support can help design expert systems that facilitate knowledge integration and decision-making in groups. Furthermore, as Yoo and Alavi (2001) have shown, differences among the effectiveness of different types of collaborative systems might be contingent on whether a group has history. Future work should therefore explicitly model group history (or lack thereof) into empirical research.

An important line of research in the implementation of various types of IT systems for knowledge management would be the development of approaches to quantification of the benefits of these systems. Benefits of knowledge management result from the use of knowledge and not from the IT system directly. Thus, this line of work should focus on the organizational outcomes and consequences of the systems rather than system performance metrics such as the size of knowledge repositories or the number of user queries processed by a given system. According to some authors (Alavi, 2000; Davenport and Prusak, 1998) the benefits of IT systems for the support of knowledge management tend to be subjective, context-dependent, and imprecise. This in turn implies that multiple metrics and

approaches to the measurement of IT system benefits may be needed. These assertions
need to be validated through research.

We believe that real options theory might provide one way to evaluate investments
in knowledge management technology (for a review and application see Benaroch and
Kauffman, 1999; McGrath, 1999). The balanced scorecard approach provides an alternative mechanism for measuring both the financial and non-financial impacts of such
investments (Kaplan and Norton, 1996). For a recent application of this approach to IT
evaluation, see Martinsons et al. (1999).

SUMMARY AND CONCLUSIONS

In this chapter we have explored the information technology dimension of knowledge
management. Our discussion complements other work that has explored the strategic and
organizational facets of knowledge management and enabling technologies in largely parallel streams of research. We adopted Alavi and Leidner's (2001c) framework that views
knowledge management processes through a systemic lens. Using various lenses, we highlighted how information technology can create value when the specific knowledge management processes that they support are explicitly considered.

Organization theorists have described knowledge creation as the cornerstone of knowledge management. In our discussion of knowledge management technologies for knowledge creation, we presented two perspectives on knowledge creation. First, technologies
such as e-learning systems and collaboration support systems bring together diverse but
specialized expertise and facilitate novel recombinations of that knowledge. Such lateral
combinations of previously unconnected knowledge can provide new insights and can
create new knowledge. Without such enabling technologies, the contributing knowledge
components are less likely to interact and combine to create new knowledge. Second,
information technology can facilitate knowledge creation by converting large volumes
of objective, transactional data into more discernible insights that can be acted on by
organizations.

Although organizations might own or have access to knowledge, its use is often hindered by the inability of individuals to find it. Information technologies that facilitate
knowledge storage and retrieval provide mechanisms to search and retrieve knowledge efficiently both within organizations and across the larger business networks in which they
participate. Such IT tools facilitate the storage and retrieval of knowledge that cannot be
stored in individuals' internal memories. We illustrated information technologies that
facilitate this process by drawing on data warehousing and knowledge repositories as exemplars. The former brings together highly structured data that is otherwise fragmented
across organizational, functional, and geographic boundaries. When such fragmented data
is brought together, it can be mined for actionable nuggets of knowledge. Knowledge
repositories complement such highly structured content by providing mechanisms for
storing and retrieving less structured content such as conversational threads and multimedia content. We also noted that the widespread adoption of the Internet holds promise
for knowledge storage and retrieval technologies because it overcomes the financial risk
and compatibility constraints that have plagued large-scale distributed information systems.

Scholars have described knowledge transfer as an important facet of knowledge management and have argued that it provides a firm grounding for developing a sustainable competitive edge in business environments characterized by high levels of turbulence and innovation (see Argote and Ingram, 2000 for a review). We described two models for knowledge transfer: the network model and the knowledge stock model. The network model implicitly assumes that the most valuable knowledge cannot be codified and embedded in systems. Instead of attempting to store specialized knowledge in a software system, IT tools then facilitate spontaneous connections between the individuals who possess the necessary knowledge. The knowledge stock model is better suited to contexts in which valuable knowledge can be made explicit and codified in repositories. Consequently, the focus of this model is to facilitate the electronic transfer of knowledge to and from repositories. The two models are not mutually exclusive, and a KM strategy may draw on both models. We suggest that future research focuses on bringing together the two in contextually ideal combinations.

The value of knowledge assets is determined primarily by their use. The fourth process that we discussed was knowledge application. We described two approaches for enabling knowledge application through IT. First, existing and relatively stable knowledge can be codified and embedded in software. We described rule-based expert systems as an exemplar. Embedded rules derived from the process of codifying expert knowledge allow application of domain-specific knowledge by others who lack expertise in that domain. It also reduces the overhead of routine reapplication of that knowledge. Such information technologies in turn free up individuals to perform other knowledge tasks that are more difficult to automate. When rules cannot be explicated but patterns are discernible in problem-solving tasks, case-based reasoning systems facilitate the application of knowledge that is created through a process of learning-by-doing. A second approach for IT-enabled knowledge application is exemplified by decision support systems. Such systems bring together structured and unstructured content and analytical models in formats that are conducive to their use by decision-makers.

Overlaps clearly exist across the four knowledge management processes we discuss. Any given technology might support more than one knowledge management process. Based on this recognition, we described several avenues for future research on the information technology dimension of knowledge management. We also identified opportunities for bringing together the insights gleaned from the strategy and technology literatures. We described several empirical research questions that might contribute to our understanding of both facets of knowledge management by drawing on these largely independent streams.

The information technology dimension of knowledge management remains understudied. Further empirical research on this facet of knowledge management offers unprecedented opportunities for connecting and unleashing the potential of the most original source of new knowledge: the human mind.

REFERENCES

Alavi, M. (1994) Computer-Mediated Collaborative Learning: An Empirical Evaluation. *MIS Quarterly*, 18 (3): 159–74.

Alavi, M. (2000) Managing Organizational Knowledge. In R.W. Zmud (ed.), *Framing the Domains of IT Management*. Cincinnati, OH: Pinnaflex Educational Resources.

Alavi, M. and Leidner, D. (2001a) Knowledge Management and Knowledge Management Systems: Conceptual Foundations and Research Issues. *MIS Quarterly*, 25 (1): 107–36.

Alavi, M. and Leidner, D. (2001b) Research Commentary: Computer-Mediated Learning: A Call for Greater Depth and Breadth for Research. *Information System Research*, 12: 1–10.

Alavi, M. and Leidner, D. (2001c) Virtual Learning Systems. Working paper, Goizueta Business School, Emory University, Atlanta, GA.

Alavi, M., Wheeler, B.C., and Valacich, J.S. (1995) Using IT to Reengineer Business Education: An Exploratory Investigation of Collaborative Telelearning. *MIS Quarterly*, 19 (2): 293–311.

Argote, L. and Ingram, P. (2000) Knowledge Transfer: A Basis for Competitive Advantage in Firms. *Organizational Behavior and Human Decision Processes*, 82 (1): 150–69.

Benaroch, M. and Kauffman, R.J. (1999) A Case for Using Real Options Pricing Analysis to Evaluate Information Technology Project Investments. *Information Systems Research*, 10 (1): 70–86.

Butler, W. (1990) The Construction of Knowledge in an Electric Discourse Community. Working Paper, University of Texas at Austin, Austin, TX.

Davenport, T.H. and Prusak, L. (1998) *Working Knowledge*. Cambridge, MA: Harvard Business School Press.

Dhar, V. and Stein, R. (1997) *Intelligent Decision Support Methods: The Science of Knowledge Work*. Upper Saddle River, NJ: Prentice-Hall.

Fayyad, U. and Uthurusamy, R. (1996) Data Mining and Knowledge Discovery in Databases, *Communications of the ACM*. 39 (11): 24–6.

George, J.F. and Tyran, C.K. (1993) Expert Systems and Organizations: Predictions and Evidence. *Accounting, Management and Information Technologies*, 3 (3): 173–89.

Gioia, D.A. and Pool, P.P. (1984) Scripts in Organizational Behavior. *Academy of Management Review*, 9 (3): 449–59.

Hansen, M. (1999) The Search-Transfer Problem: The Role of Weak Ties in Sharing Knowledge across Organizational Subunits. *Administrative Science Quarterly*, 44: 83–111.

Hansen, M.T., Nohira, N. and Tierney, T. (1999) What's Your Strategy for Managing Knowledge? *Harvard Business Review*, March–April: 106–16.

Holzner, B. and Marx, J. (1979) *The Knowledge Application: The Knowledge System in Society*. Boston: Allyn-Bacon.

Huber, G. (1991) Organizational Learning: The Contributing Processes and the Literatures. *Organizational Science*, 2 (1): 88–115.

Inmon, W. (1996) The Data Warehouse and Data Mining. *Communications of the ACM*, 39 (11): 49–50.

Johnson, A. (1999) Viewing Data in Real Time. *CIO Magazine*, December, http://www.cio.com/archive/120199/et.html (accessed September 26, 2002).

Kaplan, R. and Norton, D. (1996) Using the Balanced Scorecard as a Strategic Management System. *Harvard Business Review*, January–February: 75–85.

Kogut, B. and Zander, U. (1992) Knowledge of the Firm, Combinative Capabilities, and the Replication of Technology. *Organization Science*, 3: 383–97.

Kozma, R.B. (1994) Will Media Influence Learning? Reframing the Debate. *Educational Technology Research and Development*, 37 (1): 67–80.

Lado, A. and Zhang, M. (1998) Expert Systems, Knowledge Development and Utilization, and Sustained Competitive Advantage: A Resource-Based Model. *Journal of Management*, 24 (4): 489–509.

Leidner, D. and Jarvenpaa, S. (1993) The Information Age Confronts Education: Case Studies on the Electronic Classroom. *Information Systems Research*, 4 (1): 24–54.

Leidner, D. and Jarvenpaa, S. (1995) The Use of Information Technology to Enhance Management School Education: A Theoretical View. *MIS Quarterly*, 19 (3): 265–91.

Loeb, K.A., Rai, A., Ramaprasad, A. and Sharma, S. (1998) Design, Development and Implementation of a Global Information Warehouse: A Case Study at IBM. *Information Systems Journal*, 8 (4): 291–311.

Malhotra, A. Majchrzak, A. Carmen, R. and Lott, V. (2001) Radical Innovation without Collocation: A Case Study at Boeing-Rocketdyne. *MIS Quarterly*, 25 (2): 229–49.

Martinsons, M., Davison, R. and Tse, D. (1999) The Balanced Scorecard: A Foundation for the Strategic Management of Information Systems. *Decision Support Systems*, 25 (1): 71–88.

McGrath, R. (1999) Failing Forward: Real Options Reasoning and Entrepreneurial Failure. *Academy of Management Review*, 24 (1): 13–30.

McNurlin, B. and Sprague, R. (2001) *Information Systems Management in Practice 5/E*. Upper Saddle River, NJ: Prentice Hall.

Nonaka, I. (1994) A Dynamic Theory of Organizational Knowledge Creation. *Organization Science*, 5: 14–37.

Nonaka, I. and Nishiguchi, T. (2001) Social, Technical, and Evolutionary Dimensions of Knowledge Creation. In I. Nonaka and T. Nishiguchi (ed.), *Knowledge Emergence: Social, Technical, and Evolutionary Dimensions of Knowledge Creation*. New York: Oxford University Press: 286–9.

Penrose, E.T. (1959) *The Theory of the Growth of the Firm*. New York: Wiley.

Robey, D., and Boudreau, M. (1999) Accounting for Contradictory Organizational Consequences of Information Technology: Theoretical Directions and Methodological Implications. *Information Systems Research*, 10: 167–85.

Tiwana, A. (1999) *The Knowledge Management Toolkit: Practical Techniques for Building a Knowledge Management System*. Upper Saddle River, NJ: Prentice-Hall.

Walsh, J.P. and Ungson, G.R. (1991) Organizational Memory. *Academy of Management Review*, 16 (1): 57–91.

Webster, J. and Hackley, P. (1997) Teaching Effectiveness in Technology-Mediated Distance Learning. *Academy of Management Journal*, 40 (6): 1282–13.

Yoo, Y. and Alavi, M. (2001) Media and Group Cohesion: Relative Influences on Social Presence, Task Participation, and Group Consensus. *MIS Quarterly*, 25 (3): 371–90.

Zack, M. (1999) Managing Codified Knowledge. *Sloan Management Review*, Summer: 45–58.

7

Organizational Learning and Knowledge Management: Toward an Integrative Framework

Dusya Vera and Mary Crossan

Chapter Outline

The literature on organizational learning (OL) and knowledge management (KM) is characterized by the use of very diverse terminology, where concepts are often employed but rarely discussed together. Recognizing that no single overarching framework has been proposed to clear up this conceptual confusion, this chapter proposes a framework that integrates OL and KM and establishes a theoretical link between these constructs and performance. Our integrative model acknowledges the distinct roots of each field, identifies conceptual boundaries, and establishes relationships between the constructs and firm performance. We propose this framework as an instrument to facilitate communication between researchers working on various facets of the phenomenon.

"Organizational learning" and "knowledge management" are terms commonly used in today's business environment and usually associated with large-budget projects pursued by firms convinced that the only competitive advantage the company of the future will have is its ability to learn faster than its competitors (DeGeus, 1988). Although early academic discussions about these concepts date to the 1960s (Cangelosi and Dill, 1965; Polanyi, 1967), it was not until the 1990s that these topics dramatically captured the attention of managers, when Senge (1990) popularized the concept of the "learning organization" and Nonaka and Takeuchi (1995) described how to become a "knowledge-creating company." It was also in the 1990s when the rapid evolution of information technology and the Internet allowed the development of sophisticated knowledge management tools.

But, while consultants provide learning and knowledge management solutions to managers, academics (e.g., Huber, 1991; Simon, 1991; Weick, 1991) have expressed their concern about the lack of consistent terminology, cumulative work, and a widely accepted framework that connects the learning and knowledge fields. Miner and Mezias (1996: 88) even called the organizational learning theory "an ugly duckling in the pond of organizational theory: interesting, but living on the fringes." Furthermore, although organizational learning (OL) and knowledge management (KM) are closely interrelated, they are rarely discussed together. The motivation for this chapter comes from the recognition that too many terms have been created to describe and prescribe learning and knowledge in firms and that no framework has been presented to clear up this conceptual confusion. We see great potential for the cross-fertilization of ideas between these two fields and believe that there are important opportunities for dialogue between researchers interested in understanding the role and the impact of learning and knowledge in firms.

Efforts to distinguish the fields of organizational learning and knowledge management are rare. The language becomes confusing when authors such as Nonaka and Takeuchi (1995) insist that organizational learning and the knowledge creation process are different concepts. Also, while researchers in each field often fail to acknowledge the other – as when researchers in organizational learning exclude the term "knowledge" from their studies and researchers in knowledge management do the same with the term "learning" – other researchers use the terms learning, knowledge, and knowledge management interchangeably. The apparent distinction between OL and KM has led to the creation of different leadership roles in firms, where chief learning officers have an HR focus and build on training, education, leadership development, and change management, while chief knowledge officers have an IT focus and build on knowledge worker productivity, knowledge repositories, and networks (Stuller, 1998).

The purpose of this chapter is to provide a conceptual framework that defines and integrates OL and KM and establishes a theoretical link between these constructs and performance. Our research questions are: (1) *How do OL and KM fit together?* and (2) *How do they impact performance?* To answer these questions, we begin by defining the two constructs and acknowledging their distinct roots. Then, we establish the fields' domains and their boundaries. It is important to note that since these fields are in flux, the term "boundary" should be interpreted as the salient differences that distinguish the fields given the current dialogue. Third, propositions that integrate OL and KM and link them to performance are offered. Finally, we present conclusions and directions for future research.

DEFINITION OF CONSTRUCTS

In defining *organizational learning*, we agree with the growing group of theorists (e.g., Argyris and Schön, 1978; Duncan and Weiss, 1979; Miller, 1996), who emphasize the interrelationship between cognition and behavior and conclude that the learning process encompasses both cognitive and behavioral change. Individuals and groups learn by understanding and then acting or by acting and then interpreting (Crossan et al., 1995). The definition of OL adopted for this chapter incorporates this thinking: organizational learning is the process of change in individual and shared thought and action, which is affected by and embedded in the institutions of the organization. When individual and group learning becomes institutionalized, organizational learning occurs and knowledge is embedded in non-human repositories such as routines, systems, structures, culture, and strategy (Crossan et al., 1999; Nelson and Winter, 1982; Walsh and Rivera, 1991). The organizational learning system is comprised of the continually evolving knowledge stored in individuals, groups, and the organization and constitutes the fundamental infrastructure that supports a firm's strategy formulation and implementation processes.

Early work in organizational learning, spearheaded by James March (Cohen and Sproull, 1996) made use of learning concepts that were translated from the psychology literature on individual learning (e.g. choice, decision making, information processing). For example, Argyris and Schön (1978) proposed that organizations learn through individuals acting as agents for firms. When defining single-loop and double-loop learning, they explained learning in terms of individual level error detection and error correction. Today, authors offer more comprehensive frameworks of OL that link the different levels of learning and that study learning from a systemic view. Furthermore, the study of the OL phenomenon has been enriched by the contributions from diverse disciplines (Easterby-Smith, 1997) and new perspectives such as interpretive systems (Daft and Weick, 1984), communities of practice (Brown and Duguid, 1991), dialogue (Isaacs, 1993), and memory (Casey, 1997; Walsh and Rivera, 1991). Finally, because of its intrinsic notion of change, organizational learning research has been associated with questions of how organizations evolve, transform (e.g., Barnett et al., 1994; MacIntosh, 1999), and renew themselves (e.g., Crossan et al., 1999; Lant and Mezias, 1992; Mezias and Glynn, 1993) in order to face the challenges of a continuously changing environment.

When defining organizational learning, it is important to note its relationship to *the learning organization* (LO). Senge (1990: 1) defines a learning organization as "a place where people continually expand their capacity of creating results they really want, where patterns of thinking are broadened and nurtured, where collective aspiration is free and where people are continually learning to learn." Organizational learning and the learning organization belong to different streams of theorizing in the field (Easterby-Smith et al., 1998). OL is a descriptive stream, with academics who pursue the question "how does an organization learn?" In contrast, LO is a prescriptive stream, targeted at practitioners who are interested in the question "how should an organization learn?"

In defining knowledge management, a major source of confusion arises from the failure to differentiate *knowledge management* and *organizational knowledge* (OK). Although the term knowledge management is often used in conference calls and book titles, it is seldom defined and incorporated in academic papers, where the concept of organizational knowledge is the one frequently used. We argue that in an effort to clear up this confusion, it is not only important to distinguish knowledge from the process of trying to manage it, but as in the case of OL and LO, it is necessary to distinguish between descriptive and prescriptive streams of research.

Knowledge management has been defined as "the explicit control and management of knowledge within an organization aimed at achieving the company's objectives" (Van der Spek and Spijkervet, 1997: 43), "the formal management of knowledge for facilitating creation, access, and reuse of knowledge, typically using advanced technology" (O'Leary, 1998: 34), "the process of creating, capturing, and using knowledge to enhance organizational performance" (Bassi, 1999: 424), and "the ability of organizations to manage, store, value, and distribute knowledge" (Liebowitz and Wilcox, 1997: i). We recognize in these definitions a strong prescriptive element, where KM is understood as "managed learning" and is assumed to have a positive impact on performance. In addition, consultants suggest KM is closely linked to the management of information technology. Common examples of KM tools and solutions are intranets, datawarehousing/knowledge repositories, electronic document systems, yellow pages catalogs, best practices/lessons databases, groupware, and decision support systems (Hansen et al., 1999; Ruggles, 1998).

In contrast to the knowledge management concept, which is seldom discussed in management academic journals (see Hedlund, 1994 and Sanchez, 1996 for exceptions), organizational knowledge is an established theoretical construct. Knowledge has been proposed as a key firm resource and a source of competitive advantage. This research is rooted in the resource-based view of the firm (Barney, 1991; Penrose, 1959). Several authors argue for a *"knowledge-based theory of the firm"* as a theory that explains the organizational advantage of firms over markets (Ghoshal and Moran, 1996; Grant, 1996; Kogut and Zander, 1992).

To develop a theory where the creation, transfer, and application of knowledge is the reason why firms exist, researchers have engaged in a passionate debate about what knowledge is and what forms or types of it are available (Collins, 1993). Whereas the term learning has not been bound up in questions of veridicality and accuracy, the term knowledge has witnessed many debates. Different philosophical views and conceptual paradigms offer different perspectives about what knowledge is and how it can be studied. For example, based on their distinct epistemological and ontological assumptions, positivists argue that reality is objective and can be comprehended accurately, while for post-modernists all meanings are context specific. While it is impossible to integrate these theories or resolve their disagreements, Gioia and Pitre (1990) propose that there is "similarity despite disparity" across paradigms, and that a multiparadigm approach to theory building would help researchers to achieve a more comprehensive understanding of organizational phenomena. In the study of knowledge, although the positivist view ("knowledge as justified true belief") is the predominant one in Western culture and a generally accepted assumption in organizational theory (Nonaka and Takeuchi, 1995), it has been increasingly challenged and complemented by more constructivist perspectives that argue that knowledge cannot be conceived independently from action, shifting the notion of *knowledge* as a commodity that individuals or organizations may acquire, to the study of *knowing* as something that they do (Blackler, 1995; Cook and Brown, 1999; Nicolini and Meznar, 1995; Polanyi, 1967). Polanyi's (1967) work, in particular, has been highly influential in defining knowledge as dynamic, when he argues that knowledge is an activity, which could be better described as a process of knowing.

Although the knowledge (explicit and tacit) and knowing constructs come from different paradigms, we believe that efforts towards integrating them are consistent with Gioia and Pitres' (1990) call for more multiparadigm research. According to Polanyi (1967), explicit knowledge is articulated and specified either verbally or in writing, while tacit knowledge is unarticulated, intuitive, and non-verbalizable. "Perception" – the process of getting to know an external object by the impression made by it on our senses – underlies the paradigm of tacit knowledge (Polanyi, 1967). In perceiving a simple object, there are clues that are unspecifiable, thus, all empirical knowledge has an indeterminate content. Building on this work, Cook and Brown (1999) propose that explicit and tacit knowledge are not enough to understand the nature of knowledge and that to account for all somebody knows, it is necessary to add the notion of knowing. For them, while explicit and tacit knowledge are "possessed" by people, knowing is not about possession, but about

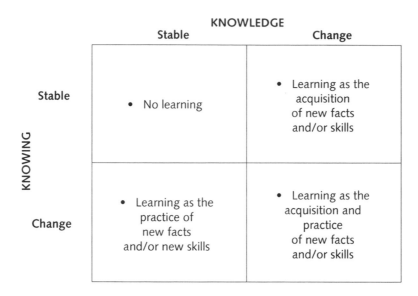

FIGURE 7.1   Knowledge–knowing–learning matrix

"practice" and about interacting with the things of the social and physical world. For example, when riding a bike, people use their explicit knowledge about the parts of a bike and the tacit knowledge about how to keep balance on a bike. People possess this knowledge even when they are not riding a bike. The difference is that while biking, people practice their knowing, that is, they put knowledge into action.

In figure 7.1 we summarize the relationships we observe between knowledge, knowing, and learning. First, knowledge can be obtained through the mind (learning by reflection, anticipatory learning) and through the body (learning by doing, experimental learning). Second, knowledge is accumulated in our minds (know what, declarative knowledge) and also in our bodies (know how, procedural knowledge). Third, knowing is practice, it is something we do. Knowing is not knowledge *used in* action, but knowledge that is *part of* action (Cook and Brown, 1999). Last, learning is the change in knowledge and the change in knowing, which involves, as mentioned before, changes in cognition and changes in behavior. Knowledge and knowing are the content of the learning process, in other words, what we learn or get to know. The main distinction between knowledge and knowing is that knowledge is mainly cognitive, including the facts and the skills we possess, while knowing is mainly behavioral, it is knowledge as action.

In addition to understanding what knowledge is and how it can become a source of sustainable competitive advantage, the organizational knowledge literature also studies the processes through which knowledge is created, developed, retained, and transferred (e.g., Argote and Ingram, 2000; Nonaka and Takeuchi, 1995; Pisano, 1994; Szulanski, 1996). Thus, this second branch of research steps back from the questions about knowledge types and forms and emphasizes the need to understand the micro-processes by which knowledge is created or acquired, communicated, applied, and utilized in organizations. Similarly,

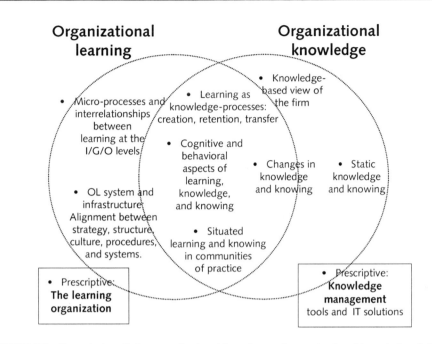

FIGURE 7.2   Boundaries of the organizational learning and organizational knowledge fields

there is a growing interest in studying the alignment between the firm's knowledge and its strategy, structure, environment, and leadership (e.g., Bierly and Chakrabarti, 1996; Hedlund, 1994; Sanchez, 1996; Zack, 1999). In a later section of this chapter, we will discuss how this process view of knowledge relates to the organizational learning process.

In summary, OL focuses on learning as a process of change, while OK stresses knowledge as a resource that provides competitive advantage and studies the processes associated with its management. LO and KM share prescriptive views of how firms should effectively learn and manage knowledge. The remainder of the chapter focuses on integrating the descriptive streams of research (OL and OK), briefly referencing the insights coming from prescriptive work (LO and KM).

Definition of Boundaries

Figure 7.2 summarizes our conclusions about the domains and boundaries of the OL and OK fields. We see these boundaries as fluid. They will evolve as the dialogue between members of these fields continues.

In figure 7.2 we show OL and OK as overlapping fields of research, but we recognize that there are topics that are dealt with primarily in one of the two fields, and topics in which one field is more advanced in its thinking than the other. For example, we see OL as the most advanced in terms of providing a multilevel theory of learning in organizations. We also note that OL advances the view of an OL system or infrastructure where organizational-level storehouses of knowledge – strategy, structure, systems, culture, and procedures – are aligned. In contrast, we see the OK field focused on creating a knowledge-based view of the firm, where the creation and integration of knowledge is the reason why firms exist. The following ten points summarize our observations from figure 7.2:

1   Each of the fields has a component of prescriptive literature. One aspect in which the OK literature can learn from the evolution of the OL field is in terms of differentiating descriptive and prescriptive work. While the OL literature has cleared up the confusion between the concepts of "organizational learning" and "learning organization," the terms "organizational knowledge" and "knowledge management" still mean different things to different communities. We observe in OK strong academic roots. In contrast, we conclude that KM is mainly concerned with providing managers with information technology solutions and prescriptions about how to proactively manage knowledge in organizations.

2   From a positivist perspective, one basic difference between OL and OK is that where OK is mainly centered on understanding the nature of knowledge as an asset or a stock, OL primarily emphasizes the processes through which knowledge changes or flows. That is, there is a distinction between studying *what* is learned and studying the *process* of learning, or between studying *content* and *process*. Schendel (1996: 6), for example, emphasizes the need to understand learning as a process, when he states that "the capacity to develop organizational capability may be more important in creating competitive advantage than the specific knowledge gained." OK views knowledge as a firm resource that can lead to sustainable competitive advantage. Thus, we position the knowledge-base view of the firm in figure 7.2 within the boundaries of the OK domain. The discussion is focused on trying to understand what knowledge is, on defining knowledge typologies, and contrasting knowledge to concepts such as data and information. We conclude that OK has a more static (content) view of knowledge, while OL is primarily interested in the changes (processes) in knowledge.

3   Although we have made a distinction between the study of static knowledge (OK) and the study of how knowledge changes (OL), we show in figure 7.2 that the two fields have some overlap, since there is research in OK (e.g., knowledge conversion and knowledge development processes) that examine the evolution of knowledge over time (e.g., Argote and Ingram, 2000; Nonaka and Takeuchi, 1995).

4   There is a growing agreement in the OL literature that for learning to occur changes in cognition and in behavior must happen. In the case of the OK literature, although it has a strong cognitive side, it also discusses knowledge and knowing as grounded in action and as processes that require both cognitive and physical activity. Furthermore, constructivist approaches to knowledge emphasize that knowledge is constructed in interaction with the world, that knowledge is situated in practice, and that knowledge is relational, mediated by artifacts, contextualized, and dynamic (Blackler, 1995). We conclude that, although the OL field has been the most explicit in explaining the cognitive and behavioral aspects of the learning phenomenon, OK has extended its focus on cognition, to incorporate the action-orientation and utilization of the knowledge acquired.

5   As suggested earlier in this paper, OL and OK also overlap, because learning has been increasingly defined in terms of knowledge processes. For example, Argote (1999) defines learning as "knowledge acquisition" and states that learning involves the processes through

which members share, generate, evaluate, and combine knowledge. In addition, as mentioned in the previous point, knowledge is not viewed as purely cognitive anymore. Thus, when the notion of static knowledge is replaced by dynamic knowing and the agenda switches from managing knowledge assets to studying the knowledge-associated processes, such as creation, retention, and transfer, there is a powerful opportunity to unify the insights from both the organizational learning and organizational knowledge communities.

6   When studied from a social constructivist perspective, OL and OK share the recognition that learning and knowing are situated in practice. This research includes the study of community of practices (Brown and Duguid, 1991) and activity systems (Blackler, 1995; Spender, 1996). The fundamental idea is that it is impossible to separate learning from working (Brown and Duguid, 1991) and that knowledge exists in socially distributed activity systems, where participants employ their situated knowledge in a context which is itself constantly developing (Gherardi et al., 1998). In response to this changing situation, participants learn, that is, their knowledge and behavior will also inevitably develop (Blackler, 1995).

7   In terms of the levels of analysis, several authors in the OL and OK fields (e.g., Crossan et al., 1999; Kogut and Zander, 1992; Nonaka and Takeuchi, 1995) have proposed that learning occurs and that knowledge exists at the individual, group, organizational, and inter-organizational or network levels. This fourth level of analysis has attracted a great deal of attention from researchers interested in the role of learning in alliances, joint ventures, strategic groups, and inter-firm relationships in general (e.g., Doz, 1996; Inkpen and Crossan, 1995; Lyles and Salk, 1996). However, other scholars associate learning and knowledge with only the individual level or with a specific subset of these four levels. The debate in the literature mostly focuses on the organizational level, because of concerns about anthropomorphism. On one side, Simon (1991: 176) states that "all learning takes place inside individual human heads; an organization learns in only two ways: (a) by the learning of its members; or (b) by ingesting new members who have knowledge the organization didn't previously have." On the other side, Hedberg (1981: 6) argues that "although organizational learning occurs through individuals, it would be a mistake to conclude that organizational learning is nothing but the cumulative result of their members' learning . . . Members come and go, and leadership changes, but organizations' memories preserve certain behaviors, mental maps, norms and values over time." Furthermore, work by Nelson and Winter (1982) describes knowledge at the organizational level and refers to organizational routines as the organization's genetic material, some explicit in bureaucratic rules, some implicit in the organization's culture. In our analysis, we observe the two fields moving in this second direction and authors agreeing that organizations are more than the sum of individuals and that by acknowledging the existence of non-human repositories of knowledge and organizational learning systems (Shrivastava and Grant, 1985), the capacity to learn, to know, and to have a memory (Walsh and Rivera, 1991) can be attributed to firms.

8   Once the different levels of analysis are recognized, the next step is to provide a theory that links the levels, explaining the microprocesses by which learning and knowledge at one level become learning and knowledge at another level. Schwandt's (1995) Dynamic Organizational Learning Model, for example, moves in this direction. In this model, organizational learning is a dynamic social system defined as "a system of actions, actors,

symbols, and processes that enables an organization to transform information into valued knowledge, which, in turn, increases its long-run adaptive capacity" (Schwandt, 1995: 370). Four learning subsystems (environmental interface, action-reflection, dissemination and diffusion, and meaning and memory) and its associated processes explain how individuals and groups in organizations collectively engage in social actions of learning. Crossan et al.'s (1999), Nonaka and Takeuchi's (1995), and Spender's (1994, 1996) work are other examples of ambitious efforts towards multilevel research. From our analysis of this work, we argue that OL is more advanced than OK in terms of providing this multilevel theory of how learning occurs at the individual, group, and organizational levels, how learning at one level impacts learning at other levels, and how knowledge flows from one level to the others. When discussing multiple levels of knowledge, the OK agenda has centered around tacit versus explicit knowledge and person to person transfer. For example, Spender (1994, 1996) has integrated the tacit and explicit taxonomy with the individual and social levels of analysis to present a matrix of four types of organizational knowledge: conscious, automatic or non-conscious, objectified or scientific, and collective. He discusses the "action-domains" of each of the four types of knowledge and describes learning as the conversion from one type of knowledge to another. Still, the cognitive and behavioral processes involved in these learning flows need to be identified in order to provide useful prescriptions to firms.

9   To develop a multilevel theory of knowledge in organizations, OK also needs to establish relationships between the different knowledge-associated processes at different levels. For example, what for one individual is knowledge sharing may be knowledge acquisition (learning) for a group, or what for one individual is knowledge creation (learning) may be knowledge access for a group. In addition, when, for example, knowledge transfer process is discussed at the group level, what is viewed as a transfer of current knowledge in the eyes of the sender may be seen as the acquisition of new knowledge in the eyes of the receiver. These examples show that OL and OK involve many knowledge processes and that there are significant opportunities for the two fields to work together to build a theory that relates the processes at different levels of analysis.

10   Finally, we propose in figure 7.2 that the OL literature has most explicitly discussed the development of a learning system or infrastructure, which consists of embedded learning in the strategy, structure, culture, systems, and procedures of the firm. This learning infrastructure affects and is affected by learning processes and the different elements of the systems need to be aligned with each other for the firm to be successful.

Building on the conclusions from this initial review, the following section presents propositions that relate the learning and knowledge constructs to firm performance.

INTEGRATIVE FRAMEWORK

In this section, we integrate existing work on organizational learning and organizational knowledge and propose relationships between these constructs and firm performance. We define performance as the organization's success or failure in achieving its financial and non-financial (e.g., quality, reputation, growth) goals. The goal of our two propositions is to create a bridge between the OL and OK areas and to suggest a way in which authors in each field can build on the work of the other.

The feedback relationship between learning and knowledge

Learning and knowledge are intertwined in an iterative, mutually reinforcing process: While learning (the process) produces new knowledge (the content), knowledge impacts future learning. Two theories, in particular, clearly differentiate between learning processes and learning content or objects: Nonaka and Takeuchi's (1995) knowledge spiral and Crossan et al.'s (1999) 4I framework of organizational learning. These two theories will be discussed in the following paragraphs.

Using the distinction between tacit and explicit knowledge, Nonaka and Takeuchi (1995) suggest four basic modes of knowledge creation – socialization, externalization, internalization, and combination – and four types of content: sympathized knowledge, conceptual knowledge, operational knowledge, and systemic knowledge. Mintzberg et al. (1998: 211) summarize these "four modes of knowledge conversion":

> *Socialization* describes the implicit sharing of tacit knowledge, often even without the use of language – for example, through experience . . . *Externalization* converts tacit to explicit knowledge, often through the use of metaphors and analysis – special uses of language. *Combination* combines and passes formally codified knowledge from one person to another . . . *Internalization* takes explicit knowledge back to the tacit form, as people internalize it, as in "learning by doing". Learning must therefore take place with the body as in the mind.

In their 4I framework of organizational learning, Crossan et al. (1999) argue that learning takes place on the individual, group, and organizational levels, and that four sub-processes link the three levels, involving both behavioral and cognitive changes. According to this model, the process of OL can be conceived as a dynamic interplay among the organization belief system, the behaviors of its members, and stimuli from the environment, where beliefs and behaviors are both an input and a product of the process as they undergo change. Mintzberg et al. (1998: 212) summarize the four sub-processes embedded in the 4I framework:

> *Intuiting* is a subconscious process that occurs at the level of the individual. It is the start of learning and must happen in a single mind. *Interpreting* then picks up on the conscious elements of this individual learning and shares it at the group level. *Integrating* follows to change collective understanding at the group level and bridges to the level of the whole organization. Finally, *institutionalizing* incorporates that learning across the organization by imbedding it in its systems, structures, routines, and practices.

To describe the relationship between learning and knowledge, the concepts of flows and stocks have been frequently used (Appleyard, 1996; Bontis et al., 2002; Decarolis and Deeds, 1999). These metaphors were introduced by researchers of the resource-based view of the firm (Itami, 1987). In the OK literature, Spender (1994) talks about the "flow of learning" to describe the conversion of automatic knowledge to collective knowledge and of collective knowledge to objectified knowledge. Furthermore, Bontis et al. (2002) operationalize the 4I framework of OL in the form of the Strategic Learning Assessment Map (SLAM) and introduce the terms "stocks of knowledge" and "flows of knowledge". They differentiate between knowledge that is static and resides at the individual, group, and organizational levels, and knowledge that is dynamic and moves across levels. There are two flows of knowledge, the feed-forward from the individual and group to the organization – representing the four sub-processes of learning: intuiting, interpreting, integrating, and institutionalizing – and the feedback from the organization to the individual and group. Knowledge stocks and flows interact with one another in a comprehensive organizational learning system and need to be aligned with each other.

In our integrative framework, we use the stock metaphor to identify our knowledge construct, which includes all the human and non-human repositories of knowledge in the organization. Then, we apply the flow metaphor to our learning construct, where the flow of learning represents the different processes that take place at different levels so that new knowledge is created and institutionalized. We also assert in our model that both the knowledge stocks and the learning flows have cognitive and behavioral dimensions. Miller (1996: 486) summarizes the link between learning, knowledge, and action when he states that "organizational learning is the acquisition of new knowledge by actors who are able and willing to apply that knowledge in making decisions or influencing others in organizations." For Miller, if knowledge were unrelated to organizational action or decision-making, it would be relevant only to individual learning, and not to organizational learning. However, it is important to recognize that there can be a time gap between the points in time when knowledge is created and used (Sitkin et al., 1998).

In our first proposition, we also argue that while learning creates new knowledge, knowledge affects future learning. Learning processes are ongoing and iterative and existing knowledge impacts learning, because it governs what gets noticed and flagged as a problem (Tiemessen, 1997). This tension between learning and knowledge is represented in Crossan et al.'s (1999) feed-forward and feedback flows of learning. The firm innovates and renews itself through the feed-forward process and new knowledge is created and institutionalized. At the same time, organizational level systems, structures, strategies, and routines guide the future learning of individuals and groups through the feedback process, exploiting what the firm has already learned. Kogut and Zander (1992), in their model of how knowledge grows, also argue that firms learn in areas closely related to their existing practice. Using a path dependency argument, they state that new learning does not occur in abstraction from current abilities and that it depends on the firm's combinative capabilities to generate new applications from existing knowledge. Finally, Nelson and Winter (1982) explain how previous choices made by individuals, which are embedded in organizational routines – organizational knowledge – shape and constrain further individual choices.

The previous discussion leads to the following proposition about the relationship between learning and knowledge:

PROPOSITION 1:   *Learning is the process through which knowledge is created and developed. Current knowledge impacts future learning.*

The moderating role of a learning/knowledge strategy

Researchers have opposite views about the impact of learning and knowledge on firm performance. On one side of this discussion are those scholars who establish a positive link between these constructs. In their pioneer work, Cangelosi and Dill (1965) mention that improved performance is learning. Later, Fiol and Lyles (1985: 803) propose that, irrespective of the underlying interpretations of organizational learning, "in all instances the assumption that learning will improve future performance exists." The perspective of the knowledge-based view further stresses a positive link between knowledge and performance. It is expected that a particular sub-category of knowledge, which is valuable, rare, inimitable and non-substitutable (Barney, 1991), would lead to competitive advantage.

On the other side of the discussion are authors (Argyris and Schön, 1978; March and Olsen, 1975), who do not see a direct relationship between learning, knowledge, and performance. For example, Levitt and March (1988: 335) state that "learning does not always lead to intelligent behavior" and Huber (1991: 89) adds that "learning does not always increase the learner's effectiveness, or even potential effectiveness... Entities can incorrectly learn, and they can correctly learn that which is incorrect." Complementary to this view is Leonard's (1992) description of how core rigidities are deeply embedded knowledge sets that hinder innovation. Arthur's (1989) law of increasing returns also supports the equivocal link between knowledge and performance. While having a good base of knowledge means that a company can leverage it and increase its advantage over competitors, having a poor base of knowledge means that the company that is losing advantage can only lose further advantage. Finally, from their review of the OL literature, Crossan et al. (1995) conclude that good performance is not a sign of learning and that learning may negatively impact performance in the short term.

In conclusion, OL, and OK views of the impact of learning and knowledge on performance are diverse. While the OL literature presents an equivocal link between the learning process and performance, the knowledge literature suggests that knowledge – if recognized as a source of competitive advantage – explains differences in performance.

Recent empirical efforts have found support for the direct impact of learning, knowledge, and human and social capital on performance (e.g., Appleyard, 1996; Bontis et al., 2002; Decarolis and Deeds, 1999; Hitt et al., 2001; Yeoh and Roth, 1999). It is important to note that the conclusion of these studies is not that "the more learning the better" or "the more knowledge the better," but that learning that is effective, and that knowledge that is relevant may have positive effects on performance. In our model, we emphasize that when studying learning and knowledge as antecedents of firm outcomes, it is critical that contextual variables, and in particular strategic variables, be included. The effectiveness of learning can only be assessed on the basis of its utility in guiding behavior relative to the organization's relevant domain (Crossan, 1991).

Capturing this thinking, we include in our integrative framework a construct called "co-alignment," which represents the "mutual alignment" between a firm's business strategy and a firm's learning/knowledge strategy. The notion of co-alignment has been useful to study fit among organizational factors such as the environment, the structure, the culture, the leadership, and the strategy of firms (e.g., Thomas et al., 1991; Venkatraman and

Prescott, 1990). In our second proposition, co-alignment is a moderator of the impact of learning and knowledge on performance. We propose that if learning and knowledge are not relevant to, and consistent with the firm's purpose, they do not guarantee positive results. For knowledge to become a source of competitive advantage, firms need to match their learning/knowledge strategy with their business strategy. When a firm's learning/knowledge strategy matches its business strategy, the impact of knowledge and learning is positive. If this match is not achieved, knowledge and learning may have no impact or even have a negative impact on performance.

In recent years, authors in the OL and OK field have started to develop the "learning strategy" and "knowledge strategy" constructs. These learning/knowledge strategies can be explicit or implicit. Bierly and Chakrabarti (1996) define a knowledge strategy as the set of strategic choices that shape and direct the organization's learning process and determine the firm's knowledge base. In contrast to Bierly and Chakrabarti's definition, Zack's (1999) definition of knowledge strategy explicitly includes the notion of fit to the firm's business strategy. He suggests that a knowledge strategy describes the overall approach an organization intends to take to align its knowledge resources and capabilities to the intellectual requirements of its business strategy. Through a knowledge strategy, organizations identify the knowledge required to execute the firm's strategic intent, compare that to its actual knowledge, and recognize its strategic knowledge gaps (Zack, 1999).

There are also initial efforts in the OL and OK fields towards understanding the dimensions of a learning/knowledge strategy. As part of their knowledge strategy taxonomy, Bierly and Chakrabarti (1996) describe four tensions in the learning process: the tension between external and internal learning, radical and incremental learning, fast and slow learning, and a narrow and wide knowledge base. Building on this work, Zack (1999) adds that a knowledge strategy includes decisions regarding the creation, development, and maintenance of a firm's knowledge resources and capabilities. These decisions are the choices between internal and external knowledge, and between exploration and exploitation. These two pieces of research cut across the OK and the strategy fields. In addition, Argote (1999) lists several tensions or tradeoffs in the learning process, which define a learning strategy. These are the tensions between group and organizational learning, heterogeneity and standardization, learning by planning and learning by doing, and the tension between fast and slow learning. Argote's (1999) work cuts across the OL and OK fields.

Given that these three lists of learning/knowledge choices barely overlap each other, it appears that neither list is comprehensive. However, for the purposes of this paper, we are not interested in providing a comprehensive list of the dimensions of a learning/knowledge strategy, but in emphasizing the importance of studying the impact of learning and knowledge on performance within the strategic context of the firm. In addition to Bierly and Chakrabarti's (1996), Argote's (1999), and Zack's (1999) work, other authors have introduced similar concepts such as "learning styles" (Ribbens, 1997), "learning modes" (Miller, 1996), "learning orientations" (Nevis et al., 1995), and "knowledge management styles" (Jordan and Jones, 1997). Table 7.1 summarizes the dimensions discussed in these conceptualizations. There is ample room for future research in the integration of these concepts.

The previous discussion leads to our second proposition:

TABLE 7.1   Examples of dimensions incorporated into learning/knowledge strategies

Author	Typology/Taxonomy	Dimensions
Bierly and Chakrabarti (1996)	Four knowledge strategies	♦ External–Internal learning ♦ Incremental–Radical learning ♦ Fast–Slow learning ♦ Breadth of knowledge base
Argote (1999)	Four tensions in the learning process	♦ Group–Organizational learning ♦ Heterogeneity–Standardization ♦ Learning by planning–Learning by doing ♦ Fast–Slow learning
Zack (1999)	Six knowledge strategies	♦ External–Internal knowledge ♦ Exploration–Exploitation
Miller (1996)	Six modes of learning	♦ Degree of strategic choice (voluntarism-determinism) ♦ Mode of thought and action (methodological-emergent)
Nevis et al. (1995)	Seven learning orientations	♦ Knowledge source (internal–external) ♦ Product-process focus ♦ Documentation mode (personal–public) ♦ Dissemination mode (formal–informal) ♦ Incremental-radical learning ♦ Value-chain focus (design-deliver) ♦ Skill development focus (individual-group)
Ribbens (1997)	Four organizational learning styles	♦ Random–Sequential knowledge ♦ Abstract–Concrete knowledge
Jordan and Jones (1997)	Knowledge management styles	♦ Knowledge acquisition ♦ Focus: internal–external ♦ Scarch: opportunistic-focused ♦ Problem-solving ♦ Location: individual–team ♦ Procedures: trial and error–heuristics ♦ Activity: experimental–abstract ♦ Scope: incremental–radical ♦ Dissemination ♦ Processes: informal–formal ♦ Breath: narrow–wide ♦ Ownership ♦ Identity: personal–collective ♦ Resource: specialist–generalist ♦ Storage/memory ♦ Representation: tacit–explicit

PROPOSITION 2:   *The co-alignment between a firm's learning/knowledge strategy and its business strategy positively moderates the relationship between learning/knowledge and performance.*

In the next section, we provide conclusions and directions for future research based on this study.

CONCLUSIONS AND DIRECTIONS FOR FUTURE RESEARCH

The objective of this chapter has been to reduce the conceptual confusion in the organizational learning and knowledge management fields by providing synthesis and integration of these closely related concepts. To achieve this purpose, we have critically reviewed previous research in an effort to understand how these literatures fit together and how they can be integrated into a more meaningful conceptual model for both academics and practitioners. We propose the present framework as an instrument to facilitate communication between researchers. It is not our intent to force fit the model, but to build on previous research to open up the possibility for provocative and creative dialogue that will further develop this integrative model.

One contribution of this chapter is to make a distinction between the "organizational knowledge" and the "knowledge management" literatures and to propose that studies in the first stream of research are descriptive and targeted to academic audiences, while studies in the second stream are mainly prescriptive and targeted to managers. Although academic forums have started to incorporate knowledge management in their discussions (e.g., conferences and books), this topic has a strong practitioner orientation and is heavily associated with the use of technology solutions and information systems that capture and distribute knowledge in firms.

A second contribution of this chapter has been to sketch the boundaries of each of the field's domains. The conclusion from figure 7.2 was that the fields greatly overlap. Although there are topics that are mainly being studied by one field (e.g., the knowledge-based view of the firm in OK) and topics, in which one community is more advanced in its theoretical development (e.g., a multilevel theory of learning in OL), there are also multiple topics that are being studied by OL and OK researchers at the same time. We believe there are significant opportunities for each of the communities to learn from the experience and developments of the other.

One step towards more common work is for authors to acknowledge multiple literature bases. Currently, researchers tend to draw on literature from only one area. This is clearly recognized when researchers in organizational learning exclude the term "knowledge" from their studies and researchers in organizational knowledge do the same with the term "learning." The current body of research on learning and knowledge includes theories focused on understanding types of knowledge and knowledge conversion processes (e.g., Nonaka and Takeuchi, 1995; Spender, 1994, 1996) and theories focused on understanding learning processes (e.g., Argyris and Schön, 1978; Crossan et al., 1999). The next step is to integrate the vocabulary and the findings to provide more comprehensive descriptions of the phenomenon. Efforts in this direction are the studies by Miller (1996), Argote (1999), and Bontis et al. (2002).

We also emphasized in our discussion the strong link between learning processes and knowledge-associated processes. In our model we recognize that learning can be defined in terms of the processes of knowledge creation, retention, transfer, etc. That is, authors studying organizational learning and researchers studying knowledge acquisition, knowledge creation, and knowledge development are likely to be studying the same phenomenon from different perspectives and with the use of different terminology. In addition, as mentioned earlier, when knowledge-associated processes are studied at different levels of analysis, learning is linked to processes such as knowledge sharing, transfer, access, and storage.

A final conclusion from our model is that learning and the accumulation of knowledge only lead to better performance, when they support and are aligned with the firm's strategy. We argue in this paper that researchers interested in studying the impact of OL and OK on performance need to be more specific about the characteristics of the knowledge that enhances performance and the conditions under which learning leads to competitive advantage. We have proposed the co-alignment between a firm's learning/knowledge strategy as a moderator of the impact of learning and knowledge on performance. We see potential in the further theoretical development of the "learning/knowledge strategy" construct and invite researchers in the two fields to work together to define the critical decisions or tradeoffs that managers need to address regarding learning and knowledge resources in their firms.

One important direction of future theoretical work is to build on Gioia and Pitre's (1990) call for a multiparadigm approach to theory building and to link, or at least juxtapose, the multiple views about knowledge and learning that have been created by different paradigms. Although researchers are likely to root their work in the assumptions of one paradigm, it is important to acknowledge and incorporate some of the insights coming from multiple perspectives. In our case, we come from a positivist perspective, but have tried to emphasize in our analysis the value of incorporating insights from social constructivist and interpretivist paradigms.

A final direction for future empirical work is to test the two propositions. In testing them, future research needs to address the choice of appropriate measures and methodology. Several instruments are available in the academic and managerial OL and OK literatures. In particular, it will be important to find or to develop measures that capture the nature of learning as a process and knowledge as the content of learning. Furthermore, future research can build on Bierly and Chakrabarti's (1996) operationalization of a knowledge strategy in the pharmaceutical industry. To operationalize the co-alignment between a firm's business strategy and a firm's learning/knowledge strategy, researchers can build on empirical work in contingency and configurational theories (e.g., Thomas et al., 1991; Venkatraman and Prescott, 1990) that study fit among constructs and how this fit impacts performance outcomes.

To conclude, we hope this study provides researchers in organizational learning and knowledge management with a preliminary map of how these fields relate to one another. There is much to be learned from each domain and we are hopeful that researchers will seek to expand the literature bases from which they draw to advance the field as a whole.

References

Appleyard, M. (1996) How Does Knowledge Flow? Interfirm Patterns in the Semiconductor Industry, *Strategic Management Journal*, 17: 137–54.

Argote, L. (1999) *Organizational Learning: Creating, Retaining, and Transferring Knowledge*, Norwell, MA: Kluwer.

Argote, L. and Ingram, P. (2000) Knowledge Transfer: A Basis for Competitive Advantage in Firms, *Organizational Behavior and Human Decision Processes*, 82: 150–69.

Argyris, C. and Schön, D. (1978) *Organizational Learning: A Theory of Action Perspective*, Reading, MA: Addison-Wesley.

Arthur, W. (1989) Competing Technologies, Increasing Returns, and Lock-in by Historical Events, *Economic Journal*, 99: 116–31.

Barnett, W., Greve, H., and Park, D. (1994) An Evolutionary Model of Organizational Performance, *Strategic Management Journal*, 15: 11–28.

Barney, J. (1991) Firm Resources and Sustained Competitive Advantage, *Journal of Management*, 17: 99–120.

Bassi, L. (1999) Harnessing the Power of Intellectual Capital. In J. Cortada and J. Woods (eds.), *The Knowledge Management Yearbook 1999–2000*, Boston: Butterworth Heinemann: 422–31.

Bierly, P. and Chakrabarti, A. (1996) Generic Knowledge Strategies in the US Pharmaceutical Industry, *Strategic Management Journal*, 17: 123–35.

Blackler, F. (1995) Knowledge, Knowledge Work, and Organizations: An Overview and Interpretation, *Organization Studies*, 16: 1021–46.

Bontis, N., Crossan, M., and Hulland, J. (2002) Managing an Organizational Learning System by Aligning Stocks and Flows, *Journal of Management Studies*, 39: 437–69.

Brown, J.S. and Duguid, P. (1991) Organizational Learning and Communities of Practice: Toward a Unified View of Working, Learning, and Innovation, *Organizational Science*, 2: 40–57.

Cangelosi, V. and Dill, W. (1965) Organizational Learning Observations: Toward a Theory, *Administrative Sciences Quarterly*, 10: 175–203.

Casey, A. (1997) Collective Memory in Organizations. In J.P. Walsh and A.S. Huff (eds.), *Advances in Strategic Management*. Vol. 14, *Organizational Learning and Strategic Management*. Greenwich, CT: JAI Press, 111–51.

Cohen, D. and Sproull, D. (1996) *Organizational Learning*. Thousand Oaks, CA: Sage Publications.

Collins, H. (1993) The Structure of Knowledge. *Social Research*, 60: 95–116.

Cook, S. and Brown, J.S. (1999) Bridging Epistemologies: The Generative Dance between Organizational Knowledge and Organizational Knowing. *Organization Science*, 10: 381–400.

Crossan, M. (1991) Organization Learning: A Sociocognitive Moel of Strategic Management. Unpublished doctoral dissertation, University of Western Ontario.

Crossan, M., Lane, H., and White, R. (1999) An Organizational Learning Framework: From Intuition to Institution. *Academy of Management Review*, 24: 522–38.

Crossan, M., Lane, H., White, R., and Djurfeldt, L. (1995) Organizational Learning: Dimensions for a Theory, *The International Journal of Organizational Analysis*, 3: 337–60.

Daft, R. and Weick, K. (1984) Towards a Model of Organizations as Interpretation Systems. *Academy of Management Review*, 9: 284–95.

Decarolis, D.M. and Deeds, D. (1999) The Impact of Stocks and Flows of Organizational Knowledge on Firm Performance: An Empirical Investigation of the Biotechnology Industry. *Strategic Management Journal*, 20: 953–68.

DeGeus, A. (1988) Planning as Learning. *Harvard Business Review*, March–April: 70–4.

Doz, Y. (1996). The Evolution of Cooperation in Strategic Alliances: Initial Conditions or Learning Processes? *Strategic Management Journal*, 17: 55–79.

Duncan, R. and Weiss, A. (1979) Organizational Learning: Implications for Organizational Design. In B. Staw (ed.), *Research in Organizational Behavior*, Greenwich, CT: JAI Press: 75–124.

Easterby-Smith, M. (1997) Disciplines of Organizational Learning: Contributions and Critiques, *Human Relations*, 50: 1058–113.

Easterby-Smith, M., Snell, R., and Gherardi, S. (1998) Organizational Learning: Diverging Communities of Practices?, *Management Learning*, 29: 259–72.

Fiol, C. and Lyles, M. (1985) Organizational Learning. *Academy of Management Review*, 10: 803–13.

Gherardi, S., Nicolini, D., and Odella, F. (1998) Toward a Social Understanding of How People Learn in Organizations, *Management Learning*, 29: 273–97.

Ghoshal, S. and Moran, P. (1996) Bad for Practice: A Critique of the Transaction Cost Theory, *Academy of Management Review*, 21: 13–47.

Gioia, D. and Pitre, E. (1990) Multiparadigm Perspectives on Theory Building. *Academy of Management Review*, 15: 584–603.

Grant, R. (1996) Toward a Knowledge-based Theory of the Firm, *Strategic Management Journal*, 17: 109–22.

Hansen, M., Nohria, N., and Tierney, T. (1999) What Is your Strategy for Managing Knowledge?, *Harvard Business Review*, March–April: 106–16.

Hedberg, B. (1981) How Organizations Learn and Unlearn. In P.C. Nystrom and W.H. Starbuck (eds.), *Handbook of Organizational Design*, Oxford: Oxford University Press: 3–27.

Hedlund, G. (1994) A Model of Knowledge Management and the N-form Corporation, *Strategic Management Journal*, 15: 73–90.

Hitt, M., Bierman, L., Shimizu, K., and Kochhar, R. (2001) Direct and Moderating Effects of Human Capital on Strategy and Performance in Professional Service Firms: A Resource-based Perspective, *Academy of Management Journal*, 44: 13–28.

Huber, G. (1991) Organizational Learning: The Contributing Processes and the Literatures, *Organization Science*, 2: 88–115.

Inkpen, A. and Crossan, M. (1995) Believing is Seeing: Joint Ventures and Organizational Learning. *Journal of Management Studies*, 32: 595–619.

Isaacs, W. (1993) Taking Flight: Dialogue, Collective Thinking, and Organizational Learning, *Organizational Dynamics*, 22: 24–39.

Itami, H. (1987) *Mobilizing Invisible Assets*, Cambridge, MA: Harvard Business Press.

Jordan, J. and Jones, P. (1997) Assessing your Company's Knowledge Management Style, *Long Range Planning*, 30: 392–8.

Kogut, B. and Zander, U. (1992) Knowledge of the Firm, Combinative Capabilities, and the Replication of Technology, *Organization Science*, 3: 383–97.

Lant, T. and Mezias, S. (1992) An Organizational Learning Model of Convergence and Reorientation, *Organization Science*, 3: 47–71.

Leonard, D. (1992) Core Capabilities and Core Rigidities: A Paradox in Managing New Product Development. *Strategic Management Journal*, 13: 111–25.

Levitt, B. and March, J. (1988) Organizational Learning, *Annual Review of Sociology*, 14: 319–40.

Liebowitz, J. and Wilcox, L. (1997) *Knowledge Management and its Integrative Elements*, Boca Raton: CRC Press.

Lyles, M. and Salk, J. (1996) Knowledge Acquisition from Foreign Parents in International Joint Ventures: An Empirical Examination in the Hungarian Context, *Journal of International Business Studies*, 27: 877 903.

MacIntosh, R. (1999) Conditioned Emergence: A Dissipative Structures Approach to Transformation, *Strategic Management Journal*, 20: 297–316.

March, J. and Olsen, J. (1975) Organizational Learning under Ambiguity, *European Journal of Policy Review*, 3: 147–71.

Mezias, S. and Glynn, M.A. (1993) The Three Faces of Corporate Renewal: Institution, Revolution, and Evolution. *Strategic Management Journal*, 14: 77–101.

Miller, D. (1996) A Preliminary Typology of Organizational Learning: Synthesizing the Literature. *Journal of Management*, 22: 485–505.

Miner, A. and Mezias, S. (1996) Ugly Duckling no More: Pasts and Futures of Organizational Learning Research. *Organization Science*, 7: 88–99.

Mintzberg, H., Ahlstrand, B., and Lampel, J. (1998) *Strategy Safari: A Guided Tour through the Wilds of Strategic Management*. New York: The Free Press.

Nahapiet, J. and Ghoshal, S. (1998). Social Capital, Intellectual Capital, and the Organizational Advantage. *Academy of Management Review*, 23: 242–66.

Nelson, R. and Winter, S. (1982) *An Evolutionary Theory of Economic Change*. Cambridge, MA: Harvard University Press.

Nevis, E., DiBella, A., and Gould, J. (1995) Understanding Organizations as Learning Systems, *Sloan Management Review*, Winter: 73–85.

Nicolini, D. and Meznar, M. (1995) The Social Construction of Organizational Learning: Conceptual and Practical Issues in the Field, *Human Relations*, 48: 727–40.

Nonaka, I. and Takeuchi, H. (1995) *The Knowledge-creating Company: How Japanese Companies Create the Dynamics of Innovation*, New York: Oxford University Press.

O'Leary, D. (1998) Using AI in Knowledge Management: Knowledge Bases and Ontologies, *IEEE Intelligent Systems*, 13: 34–9.

Penrose, E. (1959) *The Theory of the Growth of the Firm*, Oxford: Blackwell.

Pisano, G. (1994) Knowledge, Integration, and the Locus of Learning: An Empirical Analysis of Process Development, *Strategic Management Journal*, 15: 85–100.

Polanyi, M. (1967) *The Tacit Dimension*, London: Routledge.

Ribbens, B. (1997) Organizational Learning Styles: Categorizing Strategic Predispositions from Learning, *The International Journal of Organizational Analysis*, 5: 59–73.

Ruggles, R. (1998) The State of the Notion: Knowledge Management in Practice, *California Management Review*, 40: 80–9.

Sanchez, R. (1996) Modularity, Flexibility, and Knowledge Management in Product and Organizational Design. *Strategic Management Journal*, 17: 63.

Schendel, D. (1996) Knowledge and the Firm, *Strategic Management Journal*, 17: 1–4.

Schwandt, D.R. (1995) Learning as an Organization: A Journey into Chaos. In S. Chawla and J. Renesch (eds.), *Learning Organizations: Developing Cultures for Tomorrow's Workplace*, Portland, OR: Productivity Press: 365–79.

Senge, P. (1990) *The Fifth Discipline: The Art and Practice of the Learning Organization*, New York: Doubleday/Currency.

Shrivastava, P. and Grant, J. (1985) Empirically Derived Models of Strategic Decision making Processes, *Strategic Management Journal*, 6: 97–114.

Simon, H. (1991) Bounded Rationality and Organizational Learning, *Organization Science*, 2: 125–34.

Sitkin, S.B., Sutcliffe, K.M., and Weick, K.W. (1998) Organizational Learning. In R. Dorf (ed.), *The Technology Manager Handbook*. Boca Raton, FL: CRC Press, chapter 7, 70–6.

Spender, J. (1994) Knowing, Managing, and Learning, *Management Learning*, 25: 387–412.

Spender, J.C. (1996) Making Knowledge the Basis of a Dynamic Theory of the Firm, *Strategic Management Journal*, 17: 45–62.

Stuller, J. (1998) Chief of Corporate Smarts, *Training*, 35: 28–34.

Szulanski, G. (1996) Exploring Internal Stickiness: Impediments to the Transfer of Best Practice within the Firm. *Strategic Management Journal*, 17: 27–43.

Thomas, A., Litschert, R., and Ramaswami, K. (1991) The Performance Impact of Strategy-manager Coalignment: An Empirical Examination, *Strategic Management Journal*, 12: 509–22.

Tiemessen, I. (1997) *The Knowledge Management Process in International Collaborations*, Thesis, Richard Ivey School of Business, University of Western Ontario, London, ON.

Van der Spek, R. and Spijkervet, A. (1997) Knowledge Management: Dealing Intelligently with Knowledge. In J. Liebowitz and L. Wilcox (eds.), *Knowledge Management and its Integrative Elements*. Boca Raton: CRC Press: 31–59.

Venkatraman, N. and Prescott, J. (1990) Environment-strategy Coalignment: An Empirical Test of its Performance Implications, *Strategic Management Journal*, 11: 1–23.

Walsh, J.P. and Rivera, G. (1991) Organizational Memory, *Academy of Management Review*, 16: 57–91.

Weick, K.E. (1991) The Nontraditional Quality of Organizational Learning, *Organization Science*, 2: 116–24.

Yeoh, P. and Roth, K. (1999) An Empirical Analysis of Sustained Advantage in the US Pharmaceutical Industry: Impact of Firm Resources and Capabilities, *Strategic Management Journal*, 20: 637–53.

Zack, M. (1999) Developing a Knowledge Strategy, *California Management Review*, 41: 125–45.

Part II

ORGANIZATIONAL LEARNING AND LEARNING ORGANIZATIONS

8

Organizations as Learning Portfolios

ANTHONY J. DIBELLA

CHAPTER OUTLINE

The labels and names we give to constructs reflect our underlying assumptions and theories yet shape their practical implications and our research agendas. This chapter advocates a view of "organizations as learning portfolios" and contrasts its characteristics with the image of "the learning organization." In the former, learning is considered an innate aspect of all organizations whose learning styles represent an acquired capability. A firm's investments in learning can be allocated and managed within the context of its portfolio. Learning portfolios can be managed to maximum effect when the impact and time value of learning are considered. The role of chief learning officers is to oversee a firm's learning portfolio or architecture. A set of research implications is presented.

INTRODUCTION

Metaphors and images are powerful tools that shape how we perceive and interact with the world (Morgan, 1986, 1993). The presumptions we carry about people, places, and things guide our expectations and actions; and the words we use to label, characterize, or describe our world embed or reflect what those presumptions are. It is no different in the domain of organization studies. The labels we give to our constructs carry with them meanings and assumptions that, although usually unstated, guide our hypothesis-making and testing, and the actions of those who apply our theories.

In this chapter I examine images and characterizations that pertain to the nature of learning in and of organizations. In particular I offer and advocate a view of "organizations as learning portfolios" by specifying presumptions necessary to substantiate this image and identifying critical dimensions and their implications, both theoretical and practical. Part of this elaboration is to differentiate the image from that of "the learning organization" which has become a customary way to juxtapose the words "learning" and "organization." To exemplify an organization as a learning portfolio, I include and draw from a case study of Fiat-Auto.

An image of "organizations as learning portfolios" affirms the multi-dimensionality of learning in and of organizations. This perspective has significant implications for the design of interventions to promote learning and change. Instead of viewing organizations as monoliths and prescribing singular learning practices that are universally viewed as optimal (i.e. "best practices"), advocates for organizational effectiveness respond to the particularities that exist within complex organizations by choosing to manage multiple learning activities. Specific activities are valued for their unique contributions and for the synergistic possibilities created through their complementarity with other supported activities. What is valued is not a search for the best form or type of learning but a breadth of learning activities, their complementarity and relative effectiveness.

IMAGES OF ORGANIZATIONS AND LEARNING

Organizations as learning portfolios

In recent years, the work of Howard Gardner (1993) and Daniel Goleman (1995) has shown that an understanding of the learning capability of individuals requires more than just testing for IQ. Learning and intelligence are multi-dimensional concepts that cannot be determined with a single measure. Reliance on single measures simplifies reality but, more critically, devalues ways of learning and forms of intelligence that deviate from social norms.

Much as individuals learn in different ways (Kolb, 1974), so too with organizations. To some extent these differences are a function of the diverse environments in which organizations must operate. For example, in stable environments with established products like ketchup or cement, what and how organizations learn will be very different from what occurs in industries that are volatile and involve new products or evolving technologies, such as computer hardware and software. Learning differences between organizations also occur as a result of differences in history, culture, size, and age. New, entrepreneurial firms are apt to learn differently from larger, established firms. This creates opportunities for firms, like Apple in the 1970s and 1980s, to take market share away from IBM. However, more critically the social complexity of organizations supports multiple cultural realities or segments (Van Maanen and Barley, 1985), and how learning occurs in one segment will differ from how it occurs in another segment (DiBella, 2001).

Organizational learning style is a function of how organizations learn as represented by the different learning activities that they undertake (DiBella and Nevis, 1998). An organization's pattern of learning activities reflects its learning style (Shrivastava, 1983). Such styles do not indicate how well an organization is learning nor judge the value of what is learned, but they do indicate a great deal about what is learned and how learning takes place. In aggregate, a complex organization is bound to support numerous learning practices that represent different learning styles. These practices and styles constitute the raw elements of an organization's learning portfolio. By recognizing a range of learning styles within an organization, we can focus on how certain styles are matched to work demands and provide complementary or strategic advantages.

Learning styles represent an organization's acquired capability. To use that capability for competitive advantage, organizational members must first recognize what that capability consists of. Identifying current capabilities provides a starting point for strategic action to change, augment, or enhance one's style or portfolio of styles. Rather than presume no existing competence and the need to build it from the bottom up, managers work with, and from what already exists.

Research has revealed that some organizations have a dominant learning style, while many more use a variety of styles, each of which provide some learning capability (DiBella et al., 1996). Companies with a large portfolio of styles are apt to have multiple competencies and a greater capacity to adapt to change than companies that rely on a single learning style. By focusing on a company's learning portfolio in its entirety, learning advocates re-orient themselves from wondering whether the company has the right learning style (or is, or is not, a learning organization) to considering the complementarity of its styles. Instead of evaluating the style of a particular part of a company, the learning advocate takes a systems view to consider the synergistic possibilities. Recognizing the presence of multiple styles within a company can also explain inter-group conflicts and barriers to learning. If different parts of a company learn in different ways, then it is highly unlikely that knowledge will be transferred across functional or project boundaries. Once we recognize such differences, they can be managed as a potential source of competitive advantage.

One possible reason why managers often ignore existing capabilities is their attention to the plea that organizations must first unlearn before they can learn (Hedberg, 1981; McGill and Slocum, 1993). However, to develop learning capability organizations must distinguish between unlearning *what* they know and do, from *how* they learn as represented by their learning portfolio. Managers can then make more informed assessments about how present capabilities realize or inhibit learning and whether barriers to improved performance exist because of what is being learned versus how learning takes place.

Table 8.1 contains a set of characteristics about learning and organizations. I start with the major presumption that learning is an essential process of all organizations. From this core, a set of related characteristics can be derived.

- *All organizations learn.* Rather than face a bi-modal world consisting of organizations that learn and those that do not, I make the presumption that all organizations learn. Hence the notion of the learning organization is as redundant as the notion of hot steam or a breathing mammal. Organizations don't have to be developed so they can learn, they already do.
- *Source of learning.* Learning occurs through the natural social interaction of people being and working together (Brown and Duguid, 2000). Organizations as contexts for social interaction naturally induce learning. Learning occurs through the very nature of organizational life.
- *Learning is rooted in culture.* As cultures, all organizations have embedded learning processes. For example, acculturation, which every organization must have to integrate

TABLE 8.1   Organizations as learning portfolios

Uni-modal world	All organizations have learning capability
Source of learning	Organizational existence
Culture	Culture is created and survives through embedded learning processes
Organizations are heterogeneous	Complex organizations house different structural units and sub-cultures
Learning style	Multiple and complementary, or in conflict
Managerial focal point	Understanding and appreciating current capability

new employees (Van Maanen and Schein, 1979), is an embedded learning process. As organizational culture evolves, so too does the nature and process of learning.

♦ *Organizations are differentiated structures.* Different organizational units promote different behaviors and forms of interaction. There is differentiation in behaviors and social interaction both vertically and horizontally in organizations (Trice and Beyer, 1993). Types and forms of learning vary between these different units. The cacophony of differences is consistent with a view of complex system as organized anarchies (Cohen et al., 1972).

♦ *Learning styles.* Organizations learn in divergent ways. There is no one way to learn or better ways for organizations to learn. Learning styles will vary across an organization that may house multiple styles in different organizational units.

♦ *Managerial focal point.* Managers need to understand the nature of social interaction in their organizations and how existing behavior and routines engender learning. Once management understands how their organizations learn, they can direct those learning processes towards what is strategically desirable.

To understand the distinctiveness of the "organization as learning portfolio" metaphor or framework, I now review the quite popular view of the learning organization. Those who advocate for the learning organization carry, like the rest of us, a set of presumptions about learning and organizations (Edmondson, 1996). These are infrequently stated and may be subconscious but can be deduced from the nature of their writing and its implications.

The "learning organization"

During the past ten years the learning organization has become synonymous with long-term success and ability. As elaborated by Arie deGeus (1988) and Peter Senge (1990), the learning organization is a template for an organization that continually creates its future by adapting to environmental change and proactively shaping its environment. The learning organization has become a very powerful vision and metaphor for change, but what does this juxtaposition of the words "learning" and "organization" represent?

Table 8.2 contains a set of characteristics derived from some of the writing on learning organizations. Whether those who have conceptualized or written about the learning

TABLE 8.2 The learning organization

Bi-modal world	There are organizations that learn and those that do not
Source of learning	Strategic action promotes the prerequisite conditions
The role of culture	Organizations must have the right culture for learning to occur
Organizations are homogeneous	Organizations learn systemically or they do not
Learning style	Learning processes are singular and specific
Managerial focal point	Innate organizational disabilities which prevent learning

organization would agree with this list is difficult to say. The key is that presumptions may be derived from the connotations of the term itself.

Bi-modal world   By conceiving of "learning organizations" and advocating for their creation or development, theorists effectively bifurcate the world of organizations. When learning is used as an adjective to describe a particular type of organization, one underlying assumption is that some organizations learn, others do not. Such a division suggests that learning is optional and not indigenous to the life of organizations.

Source of learning   Why do some organizations learn and others do not? Learning, as a mechanism to foster organizational improvement, does not occur through chance or random action but through the development and use of specific skills. Without disciplined action or intervention from their leaders, organizations fail to learn due to the impact of the many forces that constrain learning. For example, Senge (1990) states that it takes five component technologies or disciplines to establish a learning organization – personal mastery, mental models, shared vision, team learning, and systems thinking. What distinguishes learning organizations (from non-learning organizations) is their mastery or focus on these five disciplines. Another normative modeler (Garvin, 1993) claims that learning organizations are skilled at systematic problem-solving, experimentation, learning from their own experiences and from others, and transferring knowledge.

Culture and learning   For organizations to learn, they must have the right culture, a learning culture. Mayo and Rick (1993) claim that a learning organization can be recognized by the interdependence of language and culture. In a similar manner, Beckhard and Pritchard (1992) discuss building a learning organization by creating a culture that values learning and rewards progress, not just results.

Organizations as homogeneous, structured systems   Duncan and Weiss (1979) explain that learning occurs when organizations match their structures to their environments in order to maximize the understanding of members of action-outcome relationships. Purser and Pasmore (1992) claim that learning is dependent on the design of knowledge work. To maximize learning, the design of knowledge work must be formalized and aligned with the influence of decision-makers. These theoreticians base their argument on the presumption that becoming a learning organization is predicated on having the right organization structure or design. Adler and Cole (1993), argue that this is so empirically as well.

They claim that the work design at NUMMI Motors, the Toyota–GM joint car manufac-turing venture, provided greater learning opportunities than did the design of Volvo's Uddevalla plant. Through standardization of work methods, NUMMI was able to identify problems and areas for improvement that led to learning.

Learning style   An oft-cited theoretical distinction in learning styles is Argyris and Schön's familiar contrast (1978) between single- and double-loop learning. More recently, "triple-loop learning," learning about learning, has been identified as yet another learning style (Bartunek and Moch, 1987; Torbert, 1994). Learning organizations promote double- and triple-loop learning since those styles are considered more advanced.

Managerial focal point   Learning disabilities occur due to the fundamental ways in which individuals have been trained to think and act (Argyris and Schön, 1974, 1978; Senge, 1990) and from organizational barriers to discover and utilize solutions to organizational problems (Tucker et al., 2002). Snyder and Cummings (1992) identify the problems of amnesia (lack of organizational memory), superstition (biased interpretation of experi-ence), paralysis (inability to act), and schizophrenia (lack of coordination among organi-zational constituencies). Watkins and Marsick (1993) address three barriers to learning – learned helplessness, truncated learning, and tunnel vision – with the latter paralleling Senge's call for a systems perspective. To avoid or solve learning disabilities, organizational leadership must establish the normative conditions essential for learning to take place. The focus may be on enhancing competencies of individual members or teams, changing the organizational culture, or redesigning structure or systems (Edmondson, 1996).

CONTRASTING IMAGES: IMPLICATIONS

To talk about developing "learning organizations" means focusing on certain prescribed organizational and managerial characteristics. With its emphasis on managerial initiatives to establish the preconditions or skills for learning, a research agenda based on the need for "learning organizations" would be oriented towards micro or individual-based factors. Another key issue pertains to establishing a vision and moving the firm towards that vision. In invoking the need for "learning organizations," theorists lay out a prescription for organizational improvement. While visions are powerful tools that motivate, one effect is to denigrate rather than appreciate the strengths of the organization as it now exists. To regard learning as somehow antithetical to organizations is contrary to appreciative inquiry (Srivastva et al., 1999).

To consider "organizations as learning portfolios" produces a view of learning and organizations that is fundamentally different from the prescriptive vision of the "learning organization." Instead of focusing on some future state to be attained through manage-rial action and executive leadership, any desire to enhance an organization's learning must focus on understanding the organization as it now exists through its culture and differen-tiated structures. Organizations house diverse learning activities and styles that ideally are complementary but may, in fact, be in conflict.

Instead of perceiving organizations as some unified, homogeneous, or monolithic entity that does or does not learn, one can view learning as innate to all organizations but allow for its different manifestation in different parts of the organization. Instead of focusing on the dilemmas – why don't organizations learn, or how do we build learning organizations? – the focusing questions become: what do organizations learn and in how many different ways? More specific research questions can then be derived, such as: what's in the portfolio?; how are the contents of the portfolio aligned with the mission/vision of the organization?; what are the complementarities of learning styles across the organization?; how are learning processes aligned across the organizations?; what are the ROIs (returns on investment) of the different learning styles?

The notion of an "organization as a learning portfolio" helps us recognize that firms may simultaneously support multiple and diverse learning activities (DiBella and Nevis, 1998, 2001). Rather than view the organization as a monolith that progresses in sync through a series of learning stages, different components of a firm can function in different stages. Instead of learning stages being regarded or treated as sequential stages (Carroll, this volume), they are seen as concurrent ones; and learners themselves function simultaneously in multiple learning environments (Plaskoff, this volume).

FIAT: CASE EXAMPLE OF A COMPANY'S LEARNING PORTFOLIO

The following case was produced from field research I conducted over the course of two trips to Italy to understand the nature of learning. Data were collected through structured and unstructured interviews, participant observation and content analysis of internal documents. Additional background on this case was previously reported elsewhere (Nevis, 1995; DiBella et al., 1996; DiBella and Nevis, 1998). The case shows how learning takes place through multiple activities supported at FIAT Auto.

FIAT AUTO'S LEARNING PORTFOLIO

FIAT Auto designs, manufactures, and markets automobiles worldwide under a variety of trademarks including Fiat, Lancia, and Alfa Romeo. Staffed by approximately 3,000 managers and professionals, Direzione Technica (DT) is FIAT's engineering division responsible for the design of new automobiles. DT is organized into functional departments which each specialize in a particular aspect of car design, such as body style or engines.

FIAT once produced vehicles under the Fiat trademark only. Subsequently, it acquired Lancia and then Alfa Romeo. Each trademark was produced in separate companies, which gave FIAT Auto a product-focused organization structure. In 1991, the three car companies were reorganized as FIAT Auto into a functionally based structure with a heavy emphasis on project management. Trademark models are designed by new product development teams that reside in staff groups (*piattaforma*) responsible for the new models of a certain size or cost, e.g. subcompact, luxury. Staff from functional units are assigned to the *piattaformas* on a full-time basis to develop new models.

In 1989, FIAT Auto had one of its most successful years ever. In the same year its CEO authorized benchmarking studies to compare FIAT's performance to that of other world automobile manufacturers and a few consumer, durable goods companies. Approximately 50 of FIAT's top managers participated in this study by visiting other firms and their plants worldwide. The study group discovered that not only was the marketplace changing due to different consumer tastes and expectations, but the processes whereby firms designed and manufactured products were also rapidly changing. The group became convinced that, although FIAT was having a successful year, unless it changed how it worked and how it learned, it would lose its ability to compete with global companies.

One of the process changes DT made was to simultaneous engineering. New product development teams now work together in "*co-location*" in common, open work areas to facilitate communication and coordination. Staff from the Direzione Technica and other FIAT Auto divisions, such as manufacturing and marketing, who are also assigned to the *piattaformas*, work in "*co-location*." Where engineers and other functional staff once worked sequentially on related tasks, now they work concurrently in parallel rather than in series. In this form of "*simultaneous engineering*," new models are completed without the time delays that occurred when components were designed sequentially or when newly designed components had to pass from function to function.

In describing the roots of FIAT's organizational culture, staff often refer to Italy's tradition of paternalistic, religious, and militaristic organization forms. Particular reference is made to the heavy reliance on authority that stems from rigid, hierarchical structures and the acceptance of formal authority. There is significant concern at DT that FIAT's traditional culture generated too much of a Taylorian division between those staff who did the thinking and those who acted. During the last two years, DT has learned about making the transition to a more open and flexible organization. This transition is reflected in the desire to shift the style of management from "*capo*" (head, commander) to "*leader.*" In the former, the framework is to command and obey; in the new framework of management the focus is cooperation and integration.

While discrete projects aimed at improvement and learning have been completed or are still underway, management's aim is to spawn institutionalized processes that facilitate continuous improvement. It is expected that changing the culture, structure, and management style at DT will accomplish this. Among the formal mechanisms to spawn learning is the use of Total Quality Planning (PQT) to identify areas needing improvement. PQT is required of all organizational units to identify both product and process issues that can be improved upon.

Staff also expect learning to occur through the very mechanisms whereby work is accomplished. DT's functional departments learn through the acquisition of "*Know-How Engineering*" and the establishment and improvement of "*Shelf Engineering.*" Each functional unit is also expected to build a *Memoria Technica*, a database containing knowledge about components and processes. Learning also occurs in the *piattaformas* through the application and utilization of *"know-how engineering"* in car design. In solving design problems for specific models, functional staff may generate solutions that, once communicated back to the function, may subsequently be applied in the design of other models.

Learning at Fiat-Auto

The experiences at FIAT indicate a concerted effort to build learning capability by enhancing and extending the firm's learning portfolio. FIAT has learned through acquisition (of Lancia and Alfa Romeo), through adaptation (of best practices obtained through its benchmarking studies), and through correction via its PQT process. Now shifts in work process will create new learning capabilities. For example, the *Memoria Technica* represents a bureaucratic learning style; the shift to concurrent engineering will create communities of practice; and the change in leadership style represents a shift from a learning style of authorized expert to role modeling.

ANALYZING LEARNING PORTFOLIOS

When an organization's learning portfolio is examined in its entirety, several questions and concerns come to mind. First, what's in the portfolio now? Answering this question requires having an inventory of the learning practices and profiles that exist throughout the organization or firm. This inventory of data about learning provides the basic building block for analysis. At FIAT Auto, knowledge acquisition, adaptation, correction, and communities-of-practice are all supported and used.

A second concern pertains to the relatedness of the items in the inventory. To what extent are the learning practices and styles complementary, in conflict, or redundant? We should expect, for example, that what gets learned at FIAT Auto through its internal methods of self-correction and communities-of-practice would complement the more externally focused activities of acquisition and adaptation. In another work context, nuclear power plants, we would expect to see incremental learning taking place among operations staff which would complement the learning of a research and development unit engaged in transformative learning. (A transformative or double-loop style, which may lead to unanticipated consequences, would be inappropriate in an environment like nuclear power operations where controls are needed to avoid disastrous outcomes.)

A third concern about learning portfolios is the extent to which current practices or styles align with or match learning needs and work demands. Consider a team or organization that is in a new industry where innovation is critical to success. If it has an overemphasis on learning practices that support formal dissemination or incremental learning, then what's getting learned (and the speed whereby that learning is disseminated) is apt to not be as helpful to the firm's competitiveness as practices that support transformative learning. In another scenario, if a firm wants to emphasize teamwork, then it should give more support to learning practices that promote group rather than individual learning. In the auto industry where product innovation is becoming increasingly more critical to success, FIAT Auto's relative emphasis on learning through communities-of-practice should outweigh its investments in learning through correction.

The idea that a firm's learning portfolio might be misaligned with its learning needs or competitive demands raises the possibility of portfolio management. How can a firm manage its portfolio for maximum advantage? What criteria should be followed in making portfolio management decisions? How would a managed learning portfolio differ from an unmanaged one? These questions suggest that instead of blindly supporting learning practices or not supporting them at all, companies allocate their learning resources within their portfolio in such a way so as to maximize their effectiveness. Learning capability and learning effectiveness must go hand in hand.

LEARNING PORTFOLIO MANAGEMENT

Managing a learning portfolio requires a sensitivity and appreciation for outcomes; and traditionally in most business environments, outcomes or outputs are examined in the light of inputs. Return on investment, or ROI, has been a key measure or statistic that reflects the ratio of outputs to inputs. Since business people aim to maximize the returns on their investments, they make management decisions about their investments using ROI as a guiding indicator.

Using ROI as a singular criterion for making management or investment decisions is a limiting approach. To determine the value of outputs and expected returns requires that assumptions be made about the future; and these assumptions can turn out to be invalid. Assumptions are also made about linear associations, that an investment (usually financial resources) will be converted to some measurable amount of inputs (material, labor, process technology) that will be converted to an expected set of outputs (products, services, benefits). Over time unanticipated events or circumstances occur which thwart the realization of the presumed causal linkage, as when the cost of material or labor increases. Consequently, many management decisions end up being based on projections that turn out to be inaccurate.

This problem is especially prevalent with learning investments since the period during which the returns from learning are realized can be quite lengthy; and the lengthier the period of returns to be gained from an investment, the more tenuous our assumptions. Also the usefulness of learning pertains to its timeliness. When employees learn something in a formal training program, such as how to use new software for group collaboration, it is often because they expect to use those new skills right away. In that scenario, the benefits and outcomes from the learning have immediate value. On the other hand, employees sometimes learn behaviors (such as how to deal with angry customers or aggressive competitors) that they hope they never have to use. If we never use such behaviors, does that mean they have no value and were not worth the initial learning investment? Of course not, but what criteria should be used to make decisions among learning investments that lead to uncertain outcomes?

Another difficulty in using ROI as a criterion to manage learning investments is that it only takes into account tangible assets or returns. When an employee learns a new skill, a work team learns how to work better together, or a firm develops a new process technology, nothing tangible is created, but obviously the learning has produced something of value. When managers take the customary route of basing investment decisions and allocating learning resources among practices that generate tangible benefits and hence promise a higher ROI, they neglect to account for several characteristics of learning.

INVESTMENT DIMENSIONS TO LEARNING

There are two critical aspects or dimensions to learning that have direct bearing on learning portfolio management. The first of these, which I have come to name "Learning Use," came to my direct attention while researching and working with clients in the healthcare field. The second, "Learning Impact," came from my consulting work in the education industry.

Learning Use

Some of the learning that takes place in healthcare involves practices or techniques that are used immediately to care for sick patients. Healthcare is a unique context in which the effect of not learning (possible death) is so devastating, that medical practitioners and caregivers continually explore new procedures and protocols to help their patients. Consequently, they learn new techniques because they are needed immediately to address a patient's condition and thereby improve their well-being, if not their very survival. Yet as part of their formal training, medical practitioners also learn about illnesses and diseases they may encounter at some future date.

One can think of this comparison as reflecting a time dimension to the value of learning. For some practices the usefulness of what's been learned is realized immediately in the short term, while for other uses the benefit comes later on. In industry this contrast is reflected in a manager's choice between focusing on production activities that create valued outcomes and benefits in the short term and investment activities that lead to benefits in the long term. This contrast may be depicted in the following continuum:

LEARNING USE: *immediate* ↔ *future*

The relative timeliness of when we use or apply what we have learned is an important criterion to weigh in choosing between alternative learning investments. Considering a practice in light of its learning use (immediate versus future) is a helpful marker.

Learning Impact

It is one thing to use or apply what we have learned, it is another to realize the benefits from that use. For example, while a healthcare practitioner may learn and then use a new protocol to assist someone with poor health, whether the use of that protocol actually adds value or creates benefit to the patient may not be known for some time. In effect, there are time lags between the use of learning and its resultant benefits. Consequently, we can't be certain, at the outset, of the value of what we're learning.

For some uses of learning, the benefits are unambiguous, as when emergency room staff use new protocols to save a patient. In other cases, whether a new form of surgery or a new protocol of radiation therapy will extend the life of a cancer patient may not be known until some time has passed. Whenever learned attitudes or behaviors are used without controls or comparisons, there should always be uncertainty over their impacts. Without controls, we cannot be sure whether the outcomes should be attributed to what had been learned or some other factor, such as chance or merely the passage of time. For example, if a sick patient is treated in some new way recently learned by medical staff and then feels better, medical staff cannot be sure that the patient would not have felt better without the new treatment.

Thus while learning may be used immediately, the payoff from that use may be uncertain or lag behind in time. Often we learn and use new behaviors because the impact is empirically known. At other times the impact is unknown, but we invest in learning just the same because we believe that the payoff or benefit will ultimately be positive. This contrast may be depicted in the following continuum:

LEARNING IMPACT: *certain* ↔ *uncertain*

The field of education is forever having to cope with the challenges of this dichotomy. In our large research universities, scholars who teach focus on developing theory whose impact is uncertain, while many of their students prefer learning which they perceive to have a certain impact. In primary and secondary education we invest in the schooling of our children with the hope and expectation that they will learn how to lead meaningful and productive lives as adults. Of course, support for education also comes from competitive pressures that our children be as successful as possible (even as other competitive pressures lead investors to expect that our corporations be as profitable as possible). The uncertain but expected payoffs from elementary and secondary education help fuel the coffers of many local school committees.

Yet when it comes to supporting education or learning in corporate environments, decision-makers aren't quite so generous as they rely on ROI and other business measures to assess the returns and value of investments in learning. Learning portfolio management aims to maximize that value. Considering the Learning Use and Learning Impact of a given practice can guide that management process and ensure the effectiveness of learning efforts.

Assessing learning effectiveness

To be learning effectively means investing and allocating resources with an organization's learning portfolio to maximize value. Assessing learning effectiveness involves identifying the relative value of practices in one's learning portfolio. Learning Use and Learning Impact can be used as indicators for such an assessment. Any learning practice can be scored on the basis of these two dimensions to determine *relative* value. (Relative is highlighted for emphasis since absolute value cannot be determined; and the focus should be on weighing the value of learning investments compared to one another.) Once practices are scored, learning resources can be allocated on the basis of those scores.

GUIDING LEARNING PORTFOLIOS: THE ROLE OF CHIEF LEARNING OFFICER

After a company allocates its learning investments, patterns of learning activity are created which culminate in the establishment of the company's learning portfolio. As an organization's learning portfolio takes shape, a learning architecture is created with the hope that what gets learned adds value. Many firms have come to recognize the need to take a systems view of learning and to proactively shape their learning architecture. Many firms have created corporate universities to oversee all learning activities, while others have developed roles for learning strategists and chief learning officers (CLO).

Companies that are oriented towards the use of computers or information technology to promote learning have created the role of the chief knowledge officer. In some cases the transition to this role merely involved relabeling previous job titles such as chief information officer or director of management information systems. In general, their focus is on managing and utilizing existing, computerized databases through data mining rather than learning portfolio management.

The role of the CLO is, in effect, to oversee a company's learning architecture and ensure that what's in the portfolio actually matches the architecture. To do so involves several activities to design, develop, and maintain learning. First is the task of designing the learning architecture in the light of the organization's culture and learning demands. A CLO should take a comprehensive view of the entire organization or firm to understand learning requirements and to profile current and desired learning. The second task is supporting those learning practices required to meet the firm's strategic needs; and the third task is to evaluate practices for their quality and impact and redesign the learning architecture as necessary.

Many firms have given their CLOs the role of running their corporate universities. Unfortunately, the activities of corporate universities emphasize practices that engender formal learning such as training and classroom teaching. The domain of a strategically focused CLO should be on all learning practices that exist within the firm's learning portfolio and on how best to allocate resources among them.

With a systems view, a CLO looks comprehensively at an organization's learning portfolio, sees how it aligns with the strategic demands on the firm, and allocates resources accordingly. Yet perhaps, more importantly the role of the CLO is to be an organization's or firm's learning advocate. As economies transition more and more into the post-industrial age with an emphasis on services, companies are placing greater emphasis on knowledge management. When firms learn by creating or acquiring knowledge, they develop a growing capacity for effective action. It is difficult to place a value on that capacity since it is an intangible asset; a CLO must champion the allocation and use of resources that produce such intangible assets.

Learning Use and Learning Impact are important markers to look at in allocating resources among alternative learning practices. Yet it is the value created from learning practices that many managers view as the ultimate criterion. A challenge of many CLOs is to promote learning, which in many cases creates intangible assets, in contexts that may only value what is tangible.

In Conclusion

The image of a firm, company, or organization as a learning portfolio is an alternative paradigm to the more popular notion of the learning organization. Its characteristics lead us to frame the issue and challenge of learning in and of organizations in different ways. It also provides a bridge from the processes of learning to the content of the knowledge that is generated and used in our organizations. For if knowledge is in the notes, learning makes the music.

The result is different research questions and different avenues and approaches for interventions. For example, what types of knowledge are valued across an organization's portfolio and how is that knowledge aligned with its strategic direction? What are the diverse ways in which knowledge is acquired, disseminated, and used? How do various forms or styles of learning across an organization conflict or complement one another? Finally, how are resources allocated within the portfolio and how might they be reallocated to increase a firm's return on its learning investments?

As theorists and practitioners struggle to make their organizations more adaptable and more resilient (Deevy, 1995), the call to learning will endure. Until a proven formula for learning is found or generated, alternative paradigms will be needed to explore what does or does not help executives make their organizations learn. The "organization as learning portfolio" broadens the view about how learning and organizations can best fit together.

References

Adler, P.S. and Cole, R.E. (1993) Designed for Learning: A Tale of Two Auto Plants. *Sloan Management Review*, 34: 85–94.

Argyris, C. (1985) *Strategy, Choice, and Defensive Routines*. Boston: Putnam.

Argyris, C. and Schön, D.A. (1974) *Theory in Practice: Increasing Professional Effectiveness*. San Francisco: Jossey-Bass.

Argyris, C. and Schön, D.A. (1978) *Organizational Learning*. Reading, MA: Addison-Wesley.

Bartunek, J.M. and Moch, M.K. (1987) First-order, Second-order, and Third-order Change and Organization Development Interventions: A Cognitive Approach. *Journal of Applied Behavioral Science*, 23: 483–500.

Beckhard, R. and Pritchard, W. (1992) *Changing the Essence: The Art of Creating and Leading Fundamental Change in Organizations*. San Francisco: Jossey-Bass.

Brown, J.S. and Duguid, P. (2000) *The Social Life of Information*. Boston: Harvard Business School Press.

Cohen, M.D., March, J.D., and Olsen, J.P. (1972) A Garbage Can Model of Organizational Choice. *Administrative Science Quarterly* 17: 1–25.

Deevy, E. (1995) *Creating the Resilient Organization: A Rapid Response Management Program.* Englewood Cliffs, NJ: Prentice-Hall.

deGeus, A.P. (1988) Planning as Learning. *Harvard Business Review*, March–April: 70–4.

DiBella, A.J. (2001) *Learning Practices: Assessment and Action for Organizational Improvement.* Upper Saddle River, NJ: Prentice-Hall.

DiBella, A.J. and Nevis, E.C. (1998) *How Organizations Learn: An Integrated Strategy for Building Learning Capability.* San Francisco: Jossey-Bass.

DiBella, A.J., Nevis, E.C., and Gould, J.M. (1996) Understanding Organizational Learning Capability. *Journal of Management Studies* 33: 361–79.

Duncan, R. and Weiss, A. (1979) Organizational Learning: Implications for Organizational Design. *Research in Organizational Change and Development*, 1: 75–123.

Edmondson, A.C. (1996) Three Faces of Eden: The Persistence of Competing Theories and Multiple Diagnoses in Organizational Intervention Research. *Human Relations*, 49: 571–5.

Gardner, H. (1993) *Multiple Intelligences: Theory in Practice.* New York: Basic Books.

Garvin, D.A. (1993) Building a Learning Organization. *Harvard Business Review*, July–August: 78–91.

Goleman, D. (1995) *Emotional Intelligence.* New York: Bantam Books.

Hedberg, R. (1981) How Organizations Learn and Unlearn. In P. Nystrom and W. Starbuck (eds.), *Handbook of Organizational Design.* Oxford: Oxford University Press: 3–27.

Kolb, D.A. (1974) On Management and the Learning Process. In D. Kolb, I. Rubin, and J. McIntyre (eds.), *Organizational Psychology: A Book of Readings* (2nd edn.). Englewood Cliffs, NJ: Prentice-Hall, 27–42.

Mayo, A. and Rick, S. (1993) Recognising a Learning Organization. *European Forum for Management Development*, 93 (1): 14–17.

McGill, M.E. and Slocum, J.W. (1993) Unlearning the Organization. *Organizational Dynamics*, 22: 67–78.

Morgan, G. (1986) *Images of Organization.* Newbury Park, CA: Sage.

Morgan, G. (1993) *Imaginization.* Beverly Hills, CA: Sage.

Nevis, E.C., DiBella, A.J., and Gould, J.M. (1995) Understanding Organizations as Learning Systems. *Sloan Management Review*, 36 (Winter): 73–85.

Purser, R.E. and Pasmore, W.A. (1992) Organizing for Learning. *Research in Organizational Change and Development*, 6: 37–114.

Senge, P.M. (1990) *The Fifth Discipline.* New York: Doubleday.

Shrivastava, P. (1983) A Typology of Organizational Learning Systems. *Journal of Management*, 20: 7–28.

Srivastva, S., Cooperrider, D.L., and Associates (1990) *Appreciative Management and Leadership: The Power of Positive Thought and Action in Organizations.* San Francisco: Jossey-Bass Publishers.

Srivastva, S., Cooperrider, D.L., and Associates (1999) *Appreciative Management and Leadership: The Power of Positive Thought and Action in Organizations* (revised edn.). Euclid, OH: Williams Custom Publishing.

Snyder, W.M. and Cummings, T.G. (1992) Organizational Learning Disabilities. Paper presented at the annual meeting of the Academy of Management, Las Vegas.

Torbert, W.R. (1994) Managerial Learning, Organizational Learning: A Potentially Powerful Redundancy. *Journal of Management Learning* 1: 57–70.

Trice, M. and Beyer, J. (1993) *The Cultures of Work Organizations.* Englewood Cliffs, NJ: Prentice-Hall.

Tucker, A.L., Edmondson, A.C., and Spear, S. (2002) When Problem Solving Prevents Organizational Learning. *Journal of Organizational Change Management*, 15 (2): 122–37.

Van Maanen, J. and Barley, S. (1985) Cultural Organization: Fragments of a Theory. In P.J. Frost, L.F. Moore, M.R. Louis, C.C. Lundberg, and J. Martin (eds.) *Organization Culture.* Beverly Hills: Sage, 31–53.

Van Maanen, J. and Schein, E.H. (1979) Toward a Theory of Organizational Socialization. In B.M. Staw and L.L. Cummings (eds.) *Research in Organizational Behavior*, Vol. 1. Greenwich, CT: JAI Press.

Watkins, K.E. and Marsick, V.J. (1993) *Sculpting the Learning Organization*. San Francisco: Jossey-Bass.

9

Intersubjectivity and Community Building: Learning to Learn Organizationally

Josh Plaskoff

CHAPTER OUTLINE

Communities of practice have recently become key components in an organizational learning toolkit. Building communities requires that individuals learn how to learn organizationally. A key to developing powerful communities is developing expanding circles of intersubjectivity, or common understanding, about how to be a community. Community work at Eli Lilly and Company, a multinational pharmaceutical company, has produced both a philosophy and a methodology for developing communities of practice called the APPLE process (Assess, Plan, Prepare, Launch, and Establish). The purpose of this process is to develop three attributes of community: common beliefs, common behaviors, and a sense of belonging. This work derives from the socio-cultural work of Vygotsky and Leontiev, and develops a way to bridge the theoretical with the practical.

INTRODUCTION

Communities of practice (CoPs) have recently become key components in an organizational learning toolkit. Rumizen (2001) dubbed them, not portals or best practice databases, the knowledge management "Killer App." Communities, the core of the human social system, have been studied for decades in anthropology, sociology, and psychology. Tönnies (2001), the 19th-century sociologist, distinguishes between *Gemeinschaft* (the personal community as a living organism) and *Gesellschaft* (society as a mechanical aggregate). Dewey (1916) treats the community's relationship to a public education system. Marx, Weber, and Durkheim embrace the collective as the foundation for their philosophical systems.

Communities as business constructs are new, however, and a new set of constraints and opportunities arise in this setting. Most published research on CoPs is theoretical and descriptive. Lave and Wenger (1991), for example, provide a good descriptive account of communities, while Wenger (1998a) is the most comprehensive theoretical foundation on the subject. This chapter takes a different perspective. It derives from my work as chief architect for a community infrastructure between 1999 and 2001 at Eli Lilly and Company, a major pharmaceutical company. The purpose of this project was to seek ways to expedite the building of a shared history in communities through stable membership. What proved critical was building intersubjectivity, or a shared understanding, both concerning the practice and communities in general. This chapter will examine this work and its outcomes. The presentation will be integrative and multi-faceted, both practical and theoretical in focus, sourcing a multitude of fields including organizational learning, sociology, religion, psychology, philosophy, and education. The plan for this chapter is to show the linkages between theory and practice. First, key foundational elements about knowledge, learning, and CoPs will be summarized. The community-building frameworks based on these principles will then be presented.

KNOWLEDGE, COGNITION, AND ORGANIZATIONAL LEARNING

To understand why CoPs have attained such visibility in organizational learning, we must start with the core epistemological questions of what constitutes knowledge and how (and perhaps whether) it is transferred.

The individualist view

Until recently, behaviorist and cognitive models have been the primary underlying forces influencing learning and organizational epistemologies (von Krogh and Roos, 1995). According to these theories, knowledge is an object that can reside outside individuals and can be delivered to a learner as one would deliver food as nourishment (Gherardi et al., 1998). The primary emphasis has been on individual minds and explicit knowledge (Baumard, 1999; Cook and Brown, 1999), knowledge that is easily represented through a formal symbol system (Nonaka and Takeuchi, 1995; Polanyi, 1966).

Employee development, which has embodied this epistemology, has taken the form of event-driven training mechanisms for the individual (corporate universities, training, seminars, computer-based self-studies, etc.). In addition, knowledge management and organizational learning champions have emphasized best practice capture, codification, and distribution (Fahey and Prusak, 1998; Hansen et al., 1999; O'Dell and Grayson, 1998), even when the results are questionable, such as best practice databases that are merely "information junkyards" (McDermott, 1998). Though these tools are worthwhile, they represent only a small fraction of the knowledge that exists and learning that can and does take place in an organization. To see this potential requires a paradigmatic shift in thinking.

A social view of knowledge and cognition

Recent epistemological and psychological theories have moved focus away from the individual. Building on Marx's and Hegel's historical materialism, the Russian psychologists

Vygotsky and Leontiev formulated a socio-historical theory of activity and higher mental functions (see Leontiev, 1978; Vygotsky, 1978). This revolutionary approach to knowledge and cognition spawned current constructivist thinking, which posits the social and constructive nature of knowledge.

Knowledge, from this perspective, is not an object that is "passed physically from one to another, like bricks; [it] cannot be shared as persons would share a pie by dividing it into physical pieces" (Dewey, 1916: 4). Rather, it is socially constructed through collaborative efforts with common objectives or by dialectically opposing different perspectives in dialogic interaction (Bakhtin, 1981; Pea, 1993). Knowledge is built into – or perhaps better stated, is equivalent to – the patterns inherent in culture: in the reifications of artifacts, the behavioral patterns, and actions set in history. Thus, explicit knowledge only represents the "tip of the iceberg" (Nonaka and Takeuchi, 1995), since most knowledge is tacit. Cook and Brown (1999) have even postulated that beyond tacit knowledge there is a knowledge inherent in practice itself which they call "knowing." In this sense, knowledge is a diffused and emergent property rather than a discrete entity unto itself.

If knowledge is distributed, then cognition and intelligence are distributed as well. Studies of airline pilots and ship navigation have shown that completion of actions and problem-solving (or cognition) is based on distributed access to information and knowledge and a coordinated shared understanding amongst participants (Hutchins, 1995, 1996; Hutchins and Klausen, 1998). No person alone can complete an action – it must always be the "person plus" (Perkins, 1993), a collective phenomenon. Cognitive resources are by no means restricted to people; they can also be embedded in tools, as a calculator has the ability to compute a square root. The resources to complete any action is distributed amongst people, environments, and situations (Pea, 1993), in fact all cultural resources, and the coordination and configuration of those resources is the collective task of those completing the action.

Implications for organizational learning

The organizational learning implications of this alternative epistemology are profound. First, learning is situated (Brown et al., 1989; Gherardi et al., 1998; Lave and Wenger, 1991) and contextual, closely tied to the situation in which knowledge is being created and used. It is situated in context of the activity or practice, part and parcel of the work itself. Learning does not only happen in the classroom; in fact, most learning results from interaction with co-workers during shared collaborative tasks. Learning and meaning are constructed from participation in social practice (Star, 1998). Lave and Wenger (1991) describe this learning phenomenon as legitimate peripheral participation (LPP). According to this model, learning is not a matter of obtaining individual, objective knowledge or formal expertise. Rather, it is the attainment of the subjective perspective of a group of individuals engaged in a shared enterprise (a CoP) that is contained within artifacts, behaviors, and language. Individuals become encultured (Brown et al., 1989) to the group, acting like physicians, cabinetmakers, or insurance claims adjusters in the eyes of the other practitioners in the community. Thus, learning is more about developing an identity and becoming a practitioner through social interaction with others than about learning objectively about the practice (Brown and Duguid, 1991).

If learning is situated in practice, then practice precedes knowledge (Hedegaard, 1995). Higher mental functions as social processes within the practice manifest themselves externally first and then are internalized through a transformational process. As Vygotsky (1981: 162) states:

> It is necessary that everything internal in higher forms was external, that is, for others it was what it now is for oneself. Any higher mental function necessarily goes through an external stage in its development because it is initially a social function.

For Vygotsky, learning appears in two planes, the social plane and the psychological plane, first interpsychological then intrapsychological. Internalization occurs as a result of a genetic relationship in which those possessing less mature cultural forms of behavior interrelate with those more culturally mature (Wertsch, 1985). Vygotsky calls the distance between the actual development level of individuals using their own means and the potential development level of individuals under the guidance of those more capable, *the zone of proximal development*. The apprenticeship model from which Lave and Wenger derive the concept of CoPs demonstrates these Vygotskian principles in action. The longevity and evolution of the community is dependent on the perpetuation of the practice (see von Krogh in this volume). This requires moving novices to the status of full practitioners through a social process of scaffolding by experienced practitioners, shrinking the zone of proximal development to enable the novice to become a contributing member of the community. As we will see later, the zone of proximal development will also come into play in building communities.

Since knowledge is socially constructed, focus on knowledge creation, rather than knowledge transfer, becomes paramount for organizational learning. Knowledge creation has been described as a cyclical conversion process between tacit and explicit knowledge comprised of four conversion steps: socialization, externalization, combination, and internalization (Nonaka, 1994; Nonaka and Takeuchi, 1995). Socialization is key to knowledge creation. During socialization, individuals share experiences and develop common mental models. Often this happens through dialogue and observation. The concepts generated during this socialization process are then externalized through the use of metaphor and analogy, which helps to "understand the unknown through the known and bridges the gap between the image and a logical model" (Nonaka and Takeuchi, 1995: 67). The model derived from externalization is then systematized through combination. Finally, the concept is re-embodied into tacit knowledge through "learning-by-doing." By segmenting these processes, Nonaka seems to differ from Vygotsky in specifying a gap (combination) between internalization and externalization. He points out, however, that knowledge creation is a continuous and dynamic interaction between tacit and explicit knowledge, and that conversion modes shift depending on the triggers. Taking this into account, Nonaka and Vygotsky, who both give primacy to socialization and the dialectic of internalization and externalization, are complementary in the understanding of learning and knowledge creation.

Intersubjectivity: The Key to Communities and Community-Building

From the discussion above, it should be clear that Nonaka's model of knowledge creation, the constructivist view of knowledge, and Vygotsky's internalization–externalization model and zone of proximal development are dependent on a shared situational understanding. This shared understanding is known as intersubjectivity (Crossley, 1996; Rogoff, 1990; Rommetveit, 1974; Wertsch, 1985).[1] Intersubjectivity is the act of transcending the private and becoming one with the other. As Rommetveit (cited in Wertsch, 1985: 160) states:

> The basic problem of human intersubjectivity becomes ... a question concerning in what sense and under what conditions two persons who engage in a dialogue can transcend their different private worlds. And the linguistic basis for this enterprise, I shall argue, is not a fixed repertory of shared "literal" meanings, but very general and partially negotiated drafts of contracts concerning categorization and attribution inherent in ordinary language.

Individuals bring different perspectives and preliminary interpretations to a situation and, through semiotically mediated negotiation, attain a state of intersubjectivity (Wertsch, 1985). Language and other cultural tools that mediate shared activity serve as a means of creating this temporary shared social reality. Thus, one way to view intersubjectivity is the result of an alignment of cultural elements.

Identifying common reference points for an activity (experiences and frameworks) helps develop intersubjectivity (Rogoff, 1990). Metaphors and analogies, for example, serve as good intersubjectivity-building tools. They develop understanding of a new concept through comparison with one that is already well understood. The depth of intersubjectivity reached, however, can vary. According to Crossley (1996), intersubjectivity can take two forms: radical and egological. In the radical form, relationships involve an unconditional communicative openness between parties and a lack of self-awareness of each individual. The self and other become one. In the egological form, the individual empathizes with the other by transposing him/herself into the other's position. Both forms emerge in communities.

If intersubjectivity is responsible for the efficiency and effectiveness by which learning and activity are carried out, then the converse would also be true; breakdowns in intersubjectivity lead to inefficiencies in activity. This is only partially true. Activity theory argues that contradictions occur among various elements of an activity (or cultural) system. Rules, division of labor, and tools may be at odds with the overarching objectives or with each other. Though contradictions lead to breakdowns in intersubjectivity, they are also catalysts for change. If "holes" in intersubjectivity are explored and new views of reality are constructed as a result, the system progresses. If they remain obstacles to activity, then they negatively impact the system.

The impact on practice participation is obvious, but how does this impact building of communities? First, community building involves developing a stronger sense of intersubjectivity around practice. This may consist of merely surfacing what is latent, or it may require developing a completely new understanding of the practice itself. Addressing the intersubjectivity of the practice leads to the identity of the community.

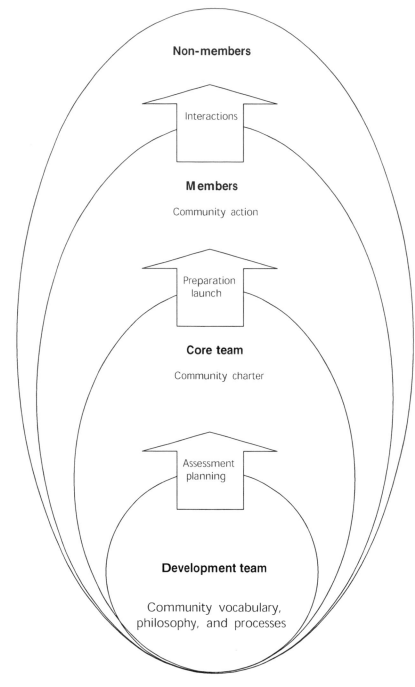

FIGURE 9.1   Expansive intersubjectivity in community development

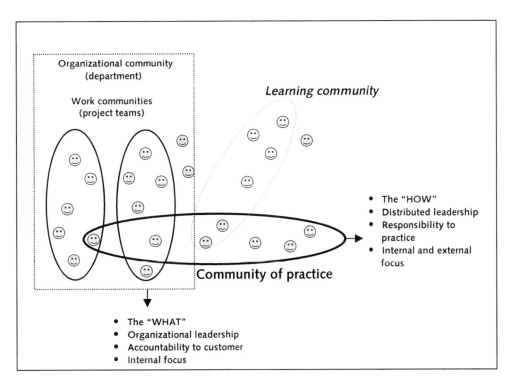

FIGURE 9.2   Types of social structures

community activities and growth. This is not the case with the photography club. The scientists' community offers a much more complex development challenge than does the photography club.

Consistency in terminology can also become a problem. As CoPs proliferate around a company, multiple memberships become commonplace. If the concept of community differs radically from group to group, intersubjectivity about community life and expectations of participation within the corporation will break down. This disconnect can lead to a disintegration of the community infrastructure and an inability of communities to connect with each other.

Arguing semantics in a company is difficult: people will continue to use the term *community* for any social group in the corporation. To address this issue, two approaches can be taken to labeling communities: (1) distinguish among departments, teams, learning communities, and CoPs with those willing to carefully consider terminology; or (2) define community types for each social structure in the company for those who indiscriminately use terminology. No matter which method is chosen, distinguishing structure types is critical. Figure 9.2 depicts the four organizational structures in this framework. Descriptions of these categories expand on work by Wenger and Snyder (2000).

Most departments (organizational communities) are hierarchical in nature, driven by a reporting structure from employee to management to executive leadership. In general, they provide employee accountability structures and focus for the project work that creates company profits. Employees identify with departments through their reporting structure and are driven by compliance systems, such as performance management, succession planning, and reviews. The primary departmental knowledge activities are communication and coordination concerning events, projects, promotions, strategy, and vision.

The project team is unified by a very specific goal – the creation of deliverables. Members are associated with the team through their accountability for a portion of the project. Management systems for teams are similar to departments – performance directly affects succession, reviews, and salary increases; management is often hierarchical, with the project manager the ultimate decision-maker. Though some teams have elements of community (common beliefs, for example), many, influenced by systems of individual accountability rather than team responsibility, still have departmental trappings. The primary team knowledge activities are coordination of tasks, timelines, and resources and communication about constraints, changes, and barriers.

A learning community in this framework is an informal group that shares knowledge about a topic. The topic can be a computer program, a hobby, or a job task. The topic, however, is not the members' dominant work activity, but rather a peripheral, supplemental, or even unrelated domain. This community is not an organizational structure and is generally free from ties to management structures (performance management, salary increases, etc.), and leadership is distributed among the members. The primary learning community knowledge activities are learning and connection: sharing techniques or ideas, and networking expertise. The photography club treated earlier would be an example of a learning community.

The community of practice addresses critical work processes. Though some theorists see the fundamental purpose of a community of practice as learning (Wenger, 1998a, for example), they should also be considered engines for practice innovation and diffusion, since knowledge creation and learning are inseparable (Brown and Duguid, 1991; Nonaka and Takeuchi, 1995; von Krogh et al., 2000). Project teams within departments produce the "what," the deliverable that ultimately provides profit, either directly or indirectly, for the company. The community of practice is orthogonal to the project team (see figure 9.2), providing a venue in which practitioners from a variety of company settings commit to defining and refining their practice, or addressing the "how." This relationship forges a double-knit organizational structure (McDermott, 1999).

CoPs are the identity containers for members of the corporation. While a learning community focuses on a supplementary skill, task, or interest, the community of practice focuses on the dominant work done by its members. Members identify themselves both inside and outside the corporation through their practice ("I am a cardiologist," "I am an engineer," "I am a chemist"), and take ownership for their practice, driven by feelings of responsibility and passion for its quality and integrity. Table 9.1 summarizes the attributes of departments, teams, learning communities, and CoPs.

DEVELOPING THE COMMUNITY BUILDING PROCESS

Once these discriminations have been made, the development team can then set its sights on developing a community-building process designed to foster intersubjectivity. The

TABLE 9.1 Attributes of organizational structure

Attribute	Department (organizational community)	Project team (work community)	Interest group (learning community)	Community of practice
Primary activities	Communication, coordination	Coordination, communication	Learning, connection	Innovation, learning
Member association	"I report into X"	"I am accountable for part of X"	"I am interested in X"	"I am an X"
Leadership	Organizational	Organizational	Distributed	Distributed
Purpose	Accountability to customer	Accountability to customer	Responsibility to self and community	Responsibility to practice and community
Motivation	Charge for career	Drive for deliverables	Interest in ideas	Passion for practice

process presented here has three components: a stage model for community development, the three dimensions of intersubjectivity, and the APPLE development process. The stage model identifies how a community evolves over time. The three intersubjectivity dimensions describe relationships within communities and serve as the guideposts for all the activities in both developing and maintaining a community. The APPLE development process provides a step-by-step framework for moving a community along the development stages, building the three dimensions. Each of the development components will be treated below.

Stages of community development

Wenger (1998b) defines five stages of development for a community: potential, coalescing, active, dispersed, and memorable. During the potential stage, individuals begin to find others with common interests but have no structure in which to share their experience. During the coalescing stage, the members begin to come together to define their practice, to define the function of their community, and to recognize the potential of their interconnections. During the active stage, the members develop the practice by defining artifacts, tools, creating relationships, and enhancing the practice. When members no longer engage in the practice, the community enters the dispersed stage. The members stay in contact and call each other for advice, but the community relationships dissipate. When the community is no longer viable, it enters the memorable stage, in which it completely dissipates, but the knowledge and experience still resides in its members who tell stories about the experience in the community and collect "memorabilia" from it.

Wenger's stage model provides a useful tool for educating potential community members and leaders, creating in them a sense of common goals and a common understanding of the development direction. An expansion to Wenger's work is that the active stage can be divided into two parallel streams. Some communities are solely internally focused (Active I). The members create commitment and connection to each other and

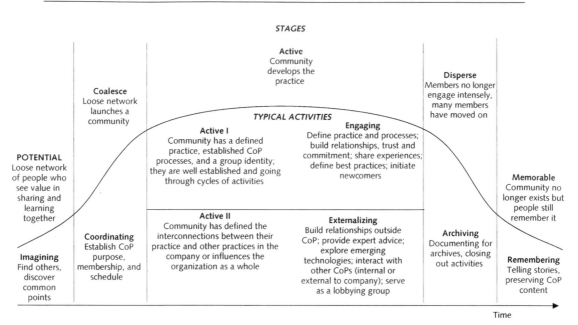

FIGURE 9.3   Stages of community development (adapted from Wenger, 1998a)

develop the practice, but the community scope is limited to its boundaries. They often remain anonymous or understated in the company. Some communities, on the other hand, see their role not only as innovating on their practice, connecting with others, and building competency, but also as influencing the company by publicly defining the role of their practice in the greater activities and business goals of the corporation (Active II). Their influencing may include changing work processes to better enable their effectiveness, lobbying for retaining or attracting staff, or even altering high-level decision-making. They may also actively seek to partner with other communities to enhance their collaboration and the potential for radically changing their practice. Active II is not more evolved or advanced than Active I. These descriptors are merely used to help communities define their goals and needs. Figure 9.3 summarizes these stages of development.

Dimensions of intersubjectivity: the three Bs

Communities are founded upon relationships built on common understandings, vision, values, and beliefs, or intersubjectivity. The three pathways to intersubjectivity are intellectual, social, and emotional (Rogoff, 1990). Based on these three dimensions, this model puts forward the three Bs of community: believing, behaving and belonging.[2] Each of these three dimensions informs activities from community start up to its continuing growth and evolution. These three components form a system; none can truly exist alone. The dimensions, however, can exist in varying degrees. The key is proper balance for the needs of the group. Segmenting community cohesion and intersubjectivity in this way enables members to identify existing imbalances and needed changes in community dynamics.

TABLE 9.2 Believing questions

♦ What are the boundaries of the practice? What is "in" and what is "out"?
♦ How is this practice relevant to the success of the enterprise as a whole?
♦ What are our values?
♦ What is our practice responsible for?
♦ What types of problems do the community wish to address?

Believing Believing encompasses the cognitive, thinking components of intersubjectivity. Key to believing is the establishment of the community identity and an understanding of the practice. The belief structure creates a common value system for the members, defines the community boundaries, and specifies how the practice holds strategic relevance for the enterprise in which it resides. Believing generally surfaces the specific problems that the community wishes to address and the mental models and body of knowledge needed to solve them. The focus areas should be both long-term and short-term, providing both a framework to strive for in the future and a specific set of problems to address in the present.

Behaving As the community develops, members establish ways of working with each other, tools in the domain, and processes and procedures in their practice. These behaviors become accepted by the community and guide communication, actions, and problem-formulation for members. Behaving focuses on two components: behavioral norms and artifacts. First, there is a socially accepted way of performing tasks that, though they can be challenged by innovation, are solidly entrenched in the community members. Second, in performing these behaviors, members generate and use artifacts – tools, documentation, knowledge bases, websites, and applications – that can facilitate or expedite processes. The knowledge of the community is passed on to existing and future members by becoming embedded in these artifacts.

Belonging What people believe and how they behave creates a sense of belonging – an emotional feeling that they are part of a joint enterprise with others of the same mind. Belonging is nurtured through personal relationship that must be developed and supported. Relationships, in this model, thrive on three elements: trust, equal representation, and understanding.

At the heart of productive work relationships and extensive knowledge sharing stands trust (Bukowitz and Williams, 1999; Handy, 1995; Lesser and Prusak, 2000). Accountability models drive most organizations. This type of model is built on an individualistic reward and punishment system, which, by creating an environment of judgment, often stifles risk-taking and discourages sharing behaviors. Communities need to foster a sense of trust to counter these external forces, providing a safe environment for innovation, testing ideas, and knowledge sharing. Trust is fostered through deep relationships and through personal interaction and a personal "testing" and understanding process.

Most organizations are hierarchically structured, with certain positions imbued with a level of power to direct, evaluate, decide, hire, and fire. With this stratification of power comes the potential for dissolution of trust at multiple levels and barriers to creating

TABLE 9.3 Behaving questions

- What knowledge should be shared, created, and documented?
- How should members share their insights with each other and collaborate on community work?
- What tools do members of the community currently use in participating in the practice and what tools need to be created to enable it further?
- How does the community determine what practices should be standardized?
- How does the community operate outside the boundaries of the company and the community?

TABLE 9.4 Belonging questions

- What kinds of activities generate a sense of unity and trust?
- How can members help each other?
- How can the community become a safe place for members to try out ideas?
- What conflicts exist and how can they seed conversations?
- Do all members have an equal say? Are some members excluded?
- How are new members brought into the community?
- How does the community operate outside the boundaries of the company and the community?

personal relationships required to develop a sense of belonging. Communities, by adopting a distributed leadership model, eliminating corporate "castes" within their walls, and allowing all members of the practice to participate equally, develop thriving relationships.

Because multiple voices characterize the community structure, conflict and disagreement is a norm rather than an exception. Good communities turn disagreements into learning experiences and chances to foster understanding. Through managed conversations (von Krogh et al., 2000), members express different opinions, approaches, and philosophies and find ways to reconcile differences, combine approaches, and create new knowledge.

APPLE process

Communities form naturally and will do so at the stage at which they are most comfortable (Wenger, 1999). A community-building process, however, can help catalyze the evolutionary process and provide guidance for more quickly reaching levels of interaction and involvement (Active I or II). Loosely based on traditional system design models, the development model presented here leads the developer and the community from identification of the situation through establishment of the community. The process bears the acronym APPLE to represent the five steps of the process: Assessment, Planning, Preparation, Launch, and Establishment and evolution.

Assessment The purpose of the assessment phase is to gather information about the current state of the existing or potential community to determine whether community building is necessary, and if so, what direction to take. Generally, communities develop initiators – practitioners who have been exposed to the community concept and have taken it upon themselves to either spark conversations among practitioners or to seek out help in developing a community. These initiators serve as good information sources about the potential members and the practice. Education is also a significant activity during this step in the process. Dialogue between the development team and the initiators serves as the first opportunity to develop intersubjectivity about communities with potential members, positioning them to do the same later with new members.

Several criteria determine community readiness: the maturity level (according to the stages presented earlier), geographic dispersion, technological comfort (if technology is to be used), and value to the business (if sponsorship needs to be gained). In addition to these criteria, the assessment should focus on the current levels of the three Bs. The perceived identity should be examined. Excitement and passion for the practice and certain domain topics can serve as entry points for community conversations. Questions about behaving can reveal the current tools and ways that potential members interact, share knowledge, collaborate, and learn. Belonging questions can uncover current levels of trust and relationship among practitioners and how the various members or sites view each other. In some cases this data is difficult to gather directly from practitioners, especially if the relationships are negative. In these cases, observation of work processes is helpful as well as interviews with individuals who interact with the practitioners that are more objective and able to help describe the relationships they have observed. From the collected data, a determination must then be made as to whether a community of practice is the right solution, if there is enough desire for community and passion for practice to sustain a community effort, and whether the current situation can be changed enough to allow the community to be successful.

Planning and preparation   Once the initiators have determined that building a community would benefit the practice, they enter the most important and most intensive community-building activity – planning. During this phase the foundations for the community are laid. When this strategic phase is completed, the community prepares for launch, specifying the tactical steps necessary for this event. Because the preparation phase is comprised of relatively mundane tasks, it will not be covered in depth here.

The planning phase is critical to community success. Because this work lays the foundation for the future of the community, commitment and attention to this phase cannot be overemphasized. It involves three major tasks: building the core of the community, developing the community charter, and developing strong community relationships.

The first task during this phase is to build a core group. The core group serves as the generators of the community charter and as the engine for the community. The core group can be analogized to the founders of a company. As the founding leadership of a company determines its culture (Schein, 1992), so does the core group of the community determine the culture of the community. Therefore, extreme care must be taken in bringing members into the core.

Core group members should have a number of characteristics. The core group should represent a mix of experienced (five years' tenure) and inexperienced members of the practice. Also, if the community spans multiple organizations, and most do, the core group should represent a mix of these organizations. This composition provides an innovative spirit that is informed and balanced by experience. Second, core group members should have a passion for the community enterprise, be personally willing to participate actively, share willingly, and influence and network with others. Finally, some core group members should be well-respected members of the practice to give legitimacy to the enterprise.

As with any organization, involving too many members too fast prevents efficient development of intersubjectivity and relationship. Between five and ten core group members is optimal. During their recruitment, they should be educated about the development process, what their role will be, and how they can help contribute to community success.

To both build relationship and to develop the common understanding about community work, the community development staff conducts an all-day session, the result of which is the community charter. During this all-day session, the key points and benefits of CoPs are reviewed. Learning about communities and surfacing community values is aided by analogies. Communities in the workplace have much in common with communities outside of it. Business people participate in communities on a regular basis outside of work. Yet, they often do not make the connection between these communities and communities in the workplace. Analogies help to make this connection.

One analogy compares building a community to creating a city. Most large cities were formed near rivers that provide a lifeline of trade and a source of water and food. In the same way, communities in corporations congregate around a "river" – a passion or need, either that enhances the social environment or ensures the "survival" of workers by enabling them to do their jobs better. For community developers, the surveyors of the land, the task is to discover the "rivers" where people congregate. Once discovered, the task is to survey the land, discovering the enabling peaks and distracting valleys, the dangerous mysteries of difficult relationships and the hidden treasures of passionate advocates and storehouses of knowledge. Once the terrain is determined, the boundaries are laid – the purpose and domain of the community. Finally, the social norms of the city are established – the behaviors and ground rules of the community. In the same way that a city's life evolves and is socio-historical in nature, so is the development of a community. The city continues to grow and change, and so does the community. This analogy helps the core group clearly understand the process of community development.

The second analogy provides a discussion activity during the all-day session. Core group members mentally leave the workplace and examine communities outside of work. First, they think of a community to which they currently belong. They then list what keeps them engaged in that community. Then, they think of a community that they consciously left, and they list why they left. In debriefing these attributes of community, the core group becomes aware of some of the key enablers and barriers that create or prevent communal relationships. Not only does this align core group members about the definition of community, but it also begins creating belief in a set of core values for their own community.

Once the core group is established, the charter is developed in an all-day session. This charter serves as the community's externalization of its three Bs. Active brainstorming activities and negotiation by the entire core group generates the charter, which helps it possess the fingerprints of all members. It is comprised of six components. The *Description of the Practice* provides a concise description of the practice on which the community is based. *Boundaries* contain a brief listing of who (or what) is part of the community (within its boundaries) and who or what is not (outside its boundaries). *Reason for Existence* describes

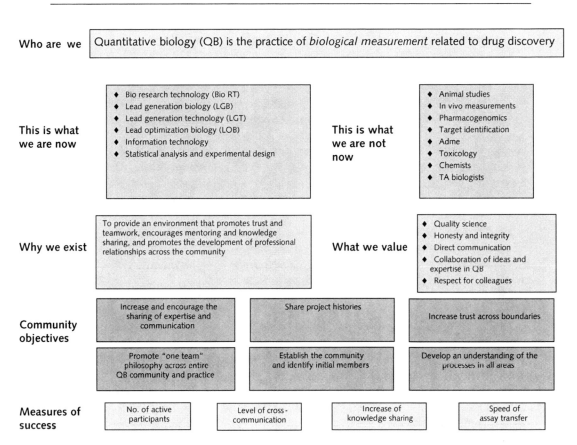

FIGURE 9.4   Quantitative biology community charter

an overarching statement about the purpose of the community. *Values* holds a concise statement or list of what the community believes is important and what value it brings to the company. *Objectives* enumerate a list of specific, measurable objectives that the community wishes to achieve. Generally these address specific issues in the practice. *Measures of Success* list indicators that the community is achieving its objectives. Figure 9.4 is a sample charter from one community.

The activities that generate the charter naturally develop relationships among members. Following the creation of the charter, a number of activities can continue this process. Beginning to work on specific projects to benefit the practice, conducting sharing meetings, continuing to strategize how to build the community, and working collaboratively on work projects can not only help to build the relationship, but can begin to demonstrate and embody the principles and desired behaviors of the community prior to launch. Launch should not occur until the core group members have established strong relationships and had time to behave as community members, since at this point, responsibility for developing intersubjectivity is being transitioned from the development team to the core group. A strong and cohesive understanding and relationship is critical to maintain the foundations of the culture as new members begin to participate.

Once the blueprint and the core group relationships have been established, the group prepares to share its work with the rest of the community and to involve other members. The preparation phase educates the extended world of practitioners with the value of community. If the group decides to launch the community with a meeting, the meeting agenda is prepared, the activities are identified, and the logistics are addressed.

Launch The launch of the community has four major purposes. First, it serves as a way of recruiting new members into the community – of bringing those from the periphery toward the core. Second, it tests whether the charter is compelling. If feedback from potential members shows confusion or resistance, the core group may need to revisit the community charter. Third, it educates the organization about communities and how they can benefit the organization. Finally, it represents an intersubjectivity transition point. The core group members take over responsibility for community education and developing intersubjectivity about communities and their specific community with potential members. The community developer transitions into a consultant and coach.

The launch can take a variety of forms. A "metaphoric event" is very effective, more effective than a standard business meeting. Instead of formally presenting the charter, the core group communicates the charter in the context of a particular metaphor. One of our communities, for example, created a small neighborhood. Participants followed a "bus pass" that directed them to different venues (decorated tables), at which core group members explained a portion of the charter. The optometrist's office housed the vision. At the bank, participants learned about values. By the time participants completed the trip, they were well acquainted with the purpose, activities, vision, and members of the community. Another group used the Olympics as its context, with each game serving as a discussion point. Others have used a presentation format. The preparation phase mentioned earlier is used to delegate tasks and design this event.

Certain messages should be delivered at launch. First and foremost, the community values and member commitment must be clearly communicated. Potential members need to understand that community is commitment to a set of values, a vision, and relationships. Second, management's expression of support can give the community legitimacy. Because communities are a different way of working, some individuals need to know that it is acceptable for them to participate. A message from a member of management (however, not an insistence on participation) is helpful in sending this message. Third, core group members should make clear that active participation in the community is optional, yet desired. Finally, the core members should ensure that potential members of the community know that the charter and the community can and must evolve and change. The work done by the core group only serves as a base from which to grow. All members have a say in that evolution.

The launch meeting often results in attracting a few to the community concept. Immediate involvement of these individuals is critical. Growth, however, needs to be monitored carefully. Some may still not be attracted to the concept. This resistance naturally helps to control growth. Community growth and evolution is a complex topic worthy of its own treatment.

DISCUSSION: SOME KEY LEARNINGS FROM APPLYING THE MODEL

Communities provide an enabling context for knowledge creation. The organic and informal nature of the environment needed is often different from that which exists in American corporations today (Wenger and Snyder, 2000). The clashing of the new model with old and entrenched ways of working result in three major issues that should be specifically highlighted in the development and nurturing of CoPs:

♦ Creating communities is an emotional endeavor driven by passion in an environment that generally suppresses emotions.
♦ Communities thrive on responsibility; organizations drive through accountability.
♦ Communities hand control to the practitioners; management is often expected and seeks to control.

These are not independent issues, and to overcome them requires significant adjustment in the organization and in management's attitudes toward the structures within those organizations.

Communities and commitment

According to von Krogh et al. (2000: 12), the "key quality of knowledge workers is their humanness"; the goal of organizational learning, therefore, is to bring out this humanness by creating the proper *ba* (see Nonaka, 1998, for a treatment of this concept). Humanness arises in our relationships with others through communities. Dewey (1916: 4) defines this relationship in this way:

> [People] live in a community in virtue of the things which they have in common ... What they must have in common in order to form a community or society are aims, beliefs, aspirations, knowledge – a common understanding ... The communication which insures participation in a common understanding is one which secures similar emotional and intellectual dispositions – like ways of responding to expectations and requirements.

As mentioned earlier, the pathway to this sense of intersubjectivity is an emotional, social, and intellectual endeavor. Common understanding of aims and beliefs is achieved through emotional commitment, active empathy, personal responsibility for the self and others, honesty, and trust.

Unfortunately, though corporations are often good at reaching *cognitive* consensus, their recognition of the primacy of relationships and the importance of *emotional* connection is lacking. Humphrey and Ashford (1994) have shown that many organizations possess a set of "feeling rules" – procedures for addressing emotional issues within company guidelines that suppress the individual's expression of personal emotions. Thus, public expression of frustration and enthusiastic celebrations are taboo and are often taken as signs of weakness or lack of control. At the same time, corporations invest significant funds in digital infrastructures assuming that relationships can be built and enhanced through computer networking. Yet, "information systems are of limited usefulness in facilitating a group's commitment to a concept, sharing emotions tied to tacit experience, or embodying the knowledge related to a certain task" (von Krogh et al., 2000: 27). So, to create this environment, a corporation must change some of its fundamental beliefs about the relationships between workers and what is acceptable and not acceptable in the workplace.

Responsibility versus accountability

What drives the current environment differs significantly from what drives communities. Companies operate under an individual accountability model. For the pay that each individual receives, he or she is expected to deliver a certain amount of production for the corporation. To foster this accountability, corporations have developed and implemented a system of rewards and punishments, of monitoring and feedback. This carries forward the same accountability model inherent in the school system in which children are educated as well as the Judeo-Christian religious frameworks that are infused in many cultures. Management's role is to monitor and enforce this accountability and to ensure delivery of the desired product (thus meeting their accountabilities) for the management above them.

Accountability is a control system that enforces with fear from without. Responsibility, on the other hand, is commitment established through caring and passion from within (for a description of the difference between accountability and responsibility, see Dunne and Legge, 2001). Unlike the accountability model, individuals driven by responsibility feel an emotional tie and commitment to other individuals or entities in their joint enterprise, who, in turn, have the same emotional tie. They are driven by a common objective and inter-subjectivity, which determines their coordinated actions.

What many companies do in their implementation of CoPs is turn to what they know best, and overlay an accountability model on the community, tying participation and performance in the community to organizational performance metrics, to end-of-year evaluations, and to salary increases. While this may build accountability to the organization, it creates a conflict for the community members and an inability to fully develop a sense of commitment and responsibility within the community. In imposing these systems, management often tries to make explicit the commitments and relationships with the hopes of measuring their contribution to the company and use the results to evaluate the individual. As Baumard (1999: 204) points out, however, "commitment cannot be reduced to its explicitation." In support of this thesis, he describes two examples of companies that created commitment of groups of employees from another corporate culture not by lecturing them about compliance, making their agreements explicit, or insisting on changing their behaviors, but by allowing them to work through their own choices through discussion. While this approach is critical for the development and nurturing of communities, it often creates discomfort for corporate management.

Leadership and management

The implications for management of the two issues previously covered are profound. In this new community model, management must remove the control hat and put on a hat of facilitator and environment creator. The accountability for the deliverables associated with the department lies in the hands of the management, but the responsibility for the practice that determines how those projects are achieved lies in the hands of the practitioners. Management must trust the wisdom of practitioners and "work for those practitioners" in creating a knowledge-enabling environment that nurtures communities, encourages and legitimizes, but does not require, participation and values direction-setting at all levels.

Some companies have tried establishing a new position called global practice leader – an individual, generally an executive, who is accountable for the performance of the practice at the company. This role can prove problematic for two reasons. First, a title attached to a role in the corporation immediately creates a different relationship between practitioners at the individual contributor level and the holder of the title. It creates an accountability relationship that has all the trappings of a reporting relationship. This relationship often stifles risk-taking, challenges to the establishment, and creative thought, since there is fear of being perceived as confrontational, incompetent, or emotional (see above). Second, it prevents commitment and responsibility from being established at the level of the practitioner, which would more likely produce effective results. What this position does is confuse organizational leadership (the vertical plane in figure 9.2) with community leadership (the horizontal plane).

Leadership in a community of practice is distributed and takes two forms. The first form is administrative leadership. The tasks undertaken in this type of leadership ensure the continuity of the community from a tactical point of view – setting up meetings, distributing information, setting agendas, and facilitating gatherings. It does not carry with it the ability to reward or punish, and feedback is provided solely to enhance and enable community function. The second form is leadership by mentoring. In this role, those who step up to leadership in the community lead by encouraging participation in the community, connecting individuals who need knowledge from each other, transitioning new members and members on the periphery into the core of the community, and being a spokesperson or advocate of the community outside its boundaries. Leadership must be examined carefully in an organization seeking to develop a community culture.

CONCLUSION

As organizational learning takes hold in individualistic companies, employees must learn not only the content and techniques of their domain, but also new ways of interacting in the company – new cultural forms. CoPs are one such structure that promotes learning and at the same time requires its members to learn a new way of behaving.

Communities are houses of intersubjectivity. They are infused with common understanding of both the practice and communal activity. Though community creation, which seeks to create something from nothing, is unproductive, community building, which catalyzes intersubjectivity, the development of social norms, and the determination of the identity of a practitioner group, is crucial to achieving a strong organizational learning strategy.

Building communities and organizational learning for that matter is more about removing barriers instituted by the organization that prohibit employees' natural tendencies to socially construct knowledge, negotiate meaning, and internalize cultural enablers than creating specialized learning programs or processes to codify and distribute all organizational knowledge. Communities are one step toward allowing people to interact naturally.

The work presented here introduces a number of topics for future work. First, as mentioned earlier, these frameworks only treat community startup. How communities evolve and change over a period of time, adopt new members, and adapt to outside organizational changes are rich areas for investigation. Intersubjectivity can provide a key to these activities as well, but research on this phenomenon is also sorely needed. Intersubjectivity literature is primarily philosophical, though many related ideas appear in the psychological and sociological literature. Synthesis of these concepts into a unified genetic conceptual framework and its application to community evolution could be very fruitful.

The continued work on this framework will focus on answering three questions. First, what type of leadership in the organization enables communities to thrive? Second, how can we further design technological solutions to enable intersubjective relationships in communities? Finally, how do the human systems (succession, promotions, and performance management systems) need to change in an organization with highly intersubjective communities? The foundation already created, however, can allow communities to continue to slowly reintroduce missing elements of humanness and belonging to meaning-seeking companies.

Acknowledgments

Many thanks to my community team and my management at Lilly, Tom Schwen, the CPSquare Consortium (especially Etienne Wenger, Richard McDermott, and Bill Snyder), Marjorie Lyles, Mark Easterby-Smith and especially my wife Robyn.

Notes

1. Intersubjectivity derives from the phenomenology of Husserl (1965) and later appears in the writing of Buber (1974) and the existential system of Sartre (1966).
2. My study of Reconstructionist Judaism uncovered the three Bs, but I have been unsuccessful identifying the specific source. They may be the work of Mordecai Kaplan, the philosopher behind Reconstructionism.

References

Bakhtin, M. (1981) *The Dialogic Imagination*. Austin: University of Texas Press.

Baumard, P. (1999) *Tacit Knowledge in Organizations*. London: Sage Publications.

Brown, A., Ash, D., Rutherford, M., Nakagawa, K., Gordon, A., and Campione, J. (1993) Distributed Expertise in the Classroom. In G. Salomon (ed.), *Distributed Cognitions: Psychological and Educational Considerations*, Cambridge: Cambridge University Press, 188–228.

Brown, J.S., Collins, A., and Duguid, P. (1989) Situated Cognition and the Culture of Learning. *Educational Researcher*, 18 (1): 32–42.

Brown, J.S. and Duguid, P. (1991) Organizational Learning and Communities of Practice: Toward a Unified View of Working, Learning, and Innovating. *Organization Science*, 2 (1): 40–56.

Buber, M. (1974) *I and Thou*. New York: MacMillan Publishing.

Bukowitz, W. and Williams, R. (1999) *The Knowledge Management Fieldbook*. New York: Prentice-Hall.

Cook, S. and Brown, J.S. (1999) Bridging Epistemologies: The Generative Dance between Organizational Knowledge and Organizational Knowing. *Organization Science*, 10 (4): 381–400.

Crossley, N. (1996) *Intersubjectivity: The Fabric of Social Becoming*. London: Sage Publications.

Dewey, J. (1916) *Democracy and Education*. New York: The Free Press.

Dunne, D. and Legge, J. (2001) US Local Government Managers and the Complexity of Responsibility and Accountability in Democratic Governance. *Journal of Public Administration Research and Theory*, 11 (1): 73–88.

Fahey, L. and Prusak, L. (1998) The Eleven Deadliest Sins of Knowledge Management. *California Management Review*, 40 (3): 265–76.

Gherardi, S., Nicolini, D., and Odella, F. (1998) Toward a Social Understanding of How People Learn in Organizations. *Management Learning*, 29 (3): 273–97.

Handy, C. (1995) Managing the Dream. In S. Chawla and J. Renesch (eds.), *Learning Organizations: Developing Cultures for Tomorrow's Workplace*, Portland, OR: Productivity Press, 45–56.

Hansen, M., Nohria, N., and Tierney, T. (1999) What's Your Strategy for Managing Knowledge? *Harvard Business Review*, 77 (2): 106–16.

Hedegaard, M. (1995) The Qualitative Analysis of the Development of a Child's Theoretical Knowledge and Thinking. In L. Martin, K. Nelson, and E. Tobach (eds.), *Sociocultural Psychology: Theory and Practice of Doing and Knowing*, Cambridge: Cambridge University Press, 293–325.

Humphrey, R. and Ashford, B. (1994) Cognitive Scripts and Prototypes in Service Encounters. In T. Swartz, D. Bowen, and S. Brown (eds.), *Advances in Service Marketing and Management: Research and Practice*. Greenwich, CT: JAI Press.

Husserl, E. (1965) *Philosophy as Rigorous Science*. New York: Harper Torchbook.

Hutchins, E. (1996) Learning to Navigate. In S. Chaiklin and J. Lave (eds.), *Understanding Practice: Perspectives on Activity and Context*, Cambridge: Cambridge University Press, 35–63.

Hutchins, E. (1995) *Cognition in the Wild*. Cambridge, MA: The MIT Press.

Hutchins, E. and Klausen, T. (1998) Distributed Cognition in an Airline Cockpit. In Y. Engeström and D. Middleton (eds.), *Cognition and Communication at Work*, Cambridge: Cambridge University Press, 15–34.

Lave, J. and Wenger, E. (1991) *Situation Learning: Legitimate Peripheral Participation*. Cambridge: Cambridge University Press.

Leontiev, A. (1978) *Activity, Consciousness, and Personality*. Englewood Cliffs, NJ: Prentice-Hall.

Lesser, E. and Prusak, L. (2000) Communities of Practice, Social Capital and Organizational Knowledge. In E. Lesser, M. Fontaine, and J. Slusher (eds.), *Knowledge and Communities*, Boston: Butterworth Heinemann, 123–32.

McDermott, R. (1998) Why Information Technology Inspired but Cannot Deliver Knowledge Management. *California Management Review*, 41 (4): 103–17.

McDermott, R. (1999) How to Build Communities of Practice in Team Organizations: Learning across Teams. *Knowledge Management Review*, 2 (2): 32–6.

Nonaka, I. (1994) A Dynamic Theory of Organizational Knowledge Creation. *Organization Science*, 5 (1): 14–37.

Nonaka, I. (1998) The Concept of "ba": Building a Foundation for Knowledge Creation. *California Management Review*, 40 (3): 40–54.

Nonaka, I. and Takeuchi, H. (1995) *The Knowledge-Creating Company: How Japanese Companies Create the Dynamics of Innovation*. Oxford: Oxford University Press.

O'Dell, C. and Grayson, C.J. (1998) If Only We Knew What We Know: Identification and Transfer of Internal Best Practices. *California Management Review*, 40 (3): 154–74.

Pea, R. (1993) Practices of Distributed Intelligence and Designs of Education. In G. Salomon (ed.), *Distributed Cognitions: Psychological and Educational Considerations*, Cambridge: Cambridge University Press, 47–82.

Perkins, D. (1993) Person-plus: A Distributed View of Thinking and Learning. In G. Salomon (ed.), *Distributed Cognitions: Psychological and Educational Considerations* Cambridge: Cambridge University Press, 88–110.

Polanyi, M. (1966) *The Tacit Dimension*. Garden City, NY: Doubleday.

Rogoff, B. (1990) *Apprenticeship in Thinking: Cognitive Development in Social Contexts*. Oxford: Oxford University Press.

Rommetveit, R. (1974) *On Message Structure: A Framework for the Study of Language and Communication*. London: John Wiley and Sons.

Rumizen, M. (2001) *The Complete Idiot's Guide to Knowledge Management*. New York: Macmillan Publishing.

Ryan, S. (1995) Learning Communities: An Alternative to the "Expert Model." In S. Chawla and J. Renesch (eds.), *Learning Organizations: Developing Cultures of Tomorrow's Workplace*, Portland, OR: Productivity Press, 279–91.

Sartre, J. (1966) *Being and Nothingness*. New York: Washington Square Press.

Schein, E. (1992) *Organizational Culture and Leadership* (2nd edn). San Francisco: Jossey-Bass.

Smith, M. and Kollock, P. (1998) *Communities in Cyberspace*. London: Routledge.

Star, S. (1998) Working Together: Symbolic Interactionism, Activity Theory, and Information Systems. In Y. Engeström and D. Middleton (eds.), *Cognition and Communication at Work*, Cambridge: Cambridge University Press, 296–318.

Tönnies, F. (2001) *Community and Civil Society*. Cambridge: Cambridge University Press.

Von Krogh, G. and Roos, J. (1995) *Organizational Epistemology*. New York: St. Martin's Press.

Von Krogh, G., Ichijo, K., and Nonaka, I. (2000) *Enabling Knowledge Creation: How to Unlock the Mystery of Tacit Knowledge and Release the Power of Innovation*. Oxford: Oxford University Press.

Vygotsky, L. (1978) *Mind in Society: The Psychology of Higher Mental Functions*. Cambridge, MA: Harvard University Press.

Vygotsky, L. (1981) The Genesis of Higher Mental Functions. In J. Wertsch (ed.). *The Concept of Activity in Soviet Psychology*. Armonk, NY: M.E. Sharpe.

Wenger, E. (1998a) *Communities of Practice: Learning, Meaning, and Identity*. Cambridge: Cambridge University Press.

Wenger, E. (1998b) Communities of Practice: Learning as a Social System. *Systems Thinker*, 9 (5): 1–5.

Wenger, E. (1999) Communities of Practice: The Key to Knowledge Strategy. *Knowledge Directions: The Journal of the Institute for Knowledge Management*, 1: 48–63.

Wenger, E. and Snyder, W. (2000) Communities of Practice: The Organizational Frontier. *Harvard Business Review*, 78 (1): 139–45.

Wertsch, J. (1985) *Vygotsky and the Social Formation of Mind*. Cambridge, MA: Harvard University Press.

10

Understanding Outcomes of Organizational Learning Interventions

Amy C. Edmondson and Anita Williams Woolley

Chapter Outline

Organizational learning interventions, like other planned change efforts, often fail to meet their stated goals. This chapter suggests that part of this failure is due to a tendency to evaluate success or failure as a dichotomous, organization-level outcome. We argue instead that change initiatives can reach different degrees of success in different parts of an organization, depending on interpersonal context. Early work on organizational change suggested that psychological safety is a critical factor in reducing resistance and enabling people to cope with change. Recent research has shown that psychological safety varies significantly across work groups in the same organization. Building on these observations, we theorize that the same organizational learning intervention can achieve different results across organizational groups due to variance in psychological safety. To further explore this proposition, we investigated outcomes of a change program designed to promote organizational learning in a large manufacturing company. The study sheds light on why different parts of an organization might have different responses to the same program. We discuss implications for research and practice related to organizational learning interventions.

Introduction

Efforts by managers and consultants to produce organizational learning and change face persistent hurdles. A range of psychological, interpersonal, and structural factors make organizations resistant to change (e.g., Walton, 1975; Goodman et al., 1980; Argyris, 1993; Garvin, 2000). Skepticism about planned organizational interventions is both widespread and understandable, following numerous documented failures in implementing such desired changes as self-managed teams, high commitment work systems, total quality management, or organizational learning (e.g., Roth and Kleiner, 2000; Hackman, 1998; Beer

and Spector, 1992; Turner and Crawford, 1998; Walton, 1975). Other researchers have
argued forcefully that change programs fail due to inadequate attention to what is needed
to produce change in human behavior in organizational settings (Beer and Eisenstat, 1996).
In this chapter, we build on this observation to suggest that resistance to change is unlikely
to be uniform, even within a single organization. We argue instead that the presence and
extent of resistance to organizational interventions is likely to vary within an organization.
More specifically, variance in interpersonal climate and behavioral norms across different
work groups is likely to affect responses to a change program or other intervention, even
when consistent training and implementation methods are developed and delivered. Previous research has found that interpersonal climate and behavior both vary across groups
within the same organization (Edmondson, 1999); however, the implications of this for
efforts to implement an organizational learning intervention have not been explored.

We propose that results of an organizational learning intervention cannot be assessed
adequately at the organizational level of analysis, where important within-organization
variance cannot be detected. Moreover, we suggest that understanding how different parts
of an organization respond differently to the same intervention may shed light on sources
of resistance to organizational change that would otherwise be missed. To elaborate this
proposition further, in this chapter we describe a case study in which we explored responses
to an organizational learning intervention and tested specific hypotheses related to within-
organization variance in these responses. We conclude by outlining the implications that
our findings have for managers who wish to implement and evaluate the effectiveness of
interventions.

Resistance to organizational learning interventions

Many recent change efforts are focused on creating learning organizations (Senge, 1990;
Watkins and Marsick, 1993; Senge et al., 1994; DiBella and Nevis, 1998; Roth and Kleiner,
2000). We define an organizational learning intervention (OLI) as a deliberate effort on
the part of managers or consultants to implement organizational learning mechanisms,
which are institutionalized structures and procedures that support the collection, analysis,
use, or dissemination of information relevant to the organization's performance (Popper
and Lipshitz, 1998). A central feature of an OLI is the goal of increasing an organization's ability to foster productive, learning-oriented conversations that allow the effective
transfer of accurate and relevant information between individuals and groups (Argyris,
1993; Schein, 1993). The underlying premise of such efforts is that by increasing the quality
of conversations among members about important issues, organizations are more likely to
accomplish challenging goals and accomplish them efficiently. For example, the skillful
exchange of ideas in a product development project, in which people from different functions must work together to design, manufacture and market a new product, is critical to
the success of the project and of the organization, as organizational performance depends
on successful new products for future revenues (Schoonhoven et al., 1990; Roth and
Kleiner, 2000).

To describe an OLI in more specific terms, we focus our discussion on interventions
that focus on enhancing dialogue (Isaacs, 1993; Ford and Ford, 1995). This approach

explicitly uses dialogue as an organizational learning mechanism (Popper and Lipshitz, 1998), such as by implementing a series of dialogue sessions to engage organization members in a learning process that focuses on the organization's goals (Isaacs, 1993). Dialogue has long been recognized as important to organizational learning. For example, Daft and Huber (1987) emphasize the importance of dialogue among managers to enable learning in organizations, without explicitly considering the role of intervention to facilitate this. The purpose of interventions that use dialogue, as described thoughtfully by Schein (1993) and by Senge and his colleagues (1994), is to foster productive conversation in which organization members learn from each other and thereby create positive outcomes for the organization.

Clearly, this is easier said than done. Productive conversation is open, honest, and thorough, which introduces an element of risk because it requires people to discuss potentially threatening issues. People often believe that they have much to lose in being open in organizations (Cannon and Edmondson, 2001). Moreover, asking people to examine and change the ways they interact with others requires fighting against well-worn defenses, including tacit theories of how to behave (Argyris, 1993). Consultants or internal training programs often attempt to teach interpersonal skills or conversational abilities to overcome these barriers. None the less – despite compelling theory and considerable consulting effort and skill – it is likely that the quality and sincerity of conversation will vary within an organization using such a program, based on a variety of factors including personal motivation, interpersonal skill, and structural factors such as reward systems.

An organizational intervention designed to alter how people talk to each other may be particularly vulnerable to resistance. Such programs can put people in a bind (Isaacs, 1992). For example, employees may think that if they openly commit to the program, they risk appearing too eager to those who may be skeptical, and they also risk wasting valuable work time. Yet, if they do not commit, they may be seen as resisting change and they risk not benefiting from what the program has to offer. A way to cope with such dilemmas is to speak up about their concerns and ask for others' thoughts and suggestions (e.g., Argyris and Schön, 1978). This is unlikely to happen if people believe their peers or supervisors are not supportive or do not have their best interests in mind. The default response in this situation is to fail to commit, thereby avoiding risk – a safe path that may constitute one source of resistance to change. However, those who are able to openly discuss their concerns may find a way to get involved in the change process in enthusiastic and productive ways. What factors within the interpersonal context separate those who commit to a change initiative and experiment with new behaviors from those who remain cynical or resistant? This chapter suggests a starting point in answering this question.

Variegated versus coordinated responses to an OLI

An implicit assumption in the literature on planned organizational change is that change efforts succeed or fail uniformly throughout an organization. The organization is thus treated as the appropriate unit of analysis for assessing the results of an intervention such as a change program (e.g., Turner and Crawford, 1998). Resistance to change also has been characterized as an organizational-level phenomenon (e.g., Hannan and Freeman,

1984; Levitt and March, 1988). Even Kurt Lewin's frequently referenced model of producing change through unfreezing, changing and refreezing, originally proposed as applicable to individuals and groups, is often used to describe an organization-level response (Dawson, 1999). Given this organization-level perspective, top management – which oversees the entire organization – is often seen as responsible for a program's failure, and lack of top management commitment – or top management's failure to "walk the talk" – are typical culprits identified by consultants and internal change agents attempting to lead a change effort. Similarly, top management commitment is often cited as the reason change efforts succeed (e.g., Kilmann et al., 1988; Kotter, 1996).

An alternative view is that while the goal of a change program such as an OLI may be to enhance the performance of the organization as a whole, organizational-level outcomes are achieved through numerous local changes throughout an organization. Organization change starts with new behaviors and decisions on the part of individuals, who are influenced by proximal interpersonal factors as well as by organization-level factors (Salancik and Pfeffer, 1978; Edmondson, 1996b). If a preconceived notion of organization-wide success is emphasized, local, interim changes may take place in parts of an organization and be missed by those evaluating the effects of an intervention. To understand more about the effects of interventions designed to enhance organizational learning, it is important to investigate whether different parts of an organization respond and change differently in response to such interventions and, if so, under what conditions desired change outcomes are more likely to occur.

Past research and theory and new empirical data both support the idea that OLIs are likely to be resisted or embraced by groups within an organization rather than by the organization as a whole. First, people who work closely together develop shared perceptions of the organization and shared norms for behavior that influence their discussions of salient issues such as new policies in the workplace (Pfeffer and Salancik, 1978). Co-located peers, such as members of the same team or small department, are thus likely to develop similar responses to an organizational learning initiative. Second, the views of managers or supervisors are likely to influence subordinates, such that people who report to the same manager may view an intervention similarly. At the same time, people who neither interact nor report to the same person often have widely discrepant views of the way things are in an organization; for example, different functions, such as engineering and marketing, have been said to live in different "thought worlds" (Dougherty, 1992). Third, the tendency for different work groups in the same organization to vary in attitudes, behavior and performance is well established in the research literature (e.g., Edmondson, 1999; Batt, 1999; Cohen and Ledford, 1996), making organizations unlikely to have a single coordinated response to a change initiative. In other words, the quality of the "soil" is likely to vary from one location to another in an organization. Given these local variations, the same "seed" may differ in its ability to take root and grow.

The influence of psychological safety on implementation of an OLI

Members of organizations are subject to a variety of influences – intrapersonal, interpersonal, and organizational. The kinds of behavioral changes most organizational learning programs promote are particularly affected by interpersonal factors, such as power dynamics (Lee, 1997) and group norms (Hackman and Morris, 1975), because the desired changes must take place in face-to-face interaction. As people consider experimenting with new behaviors, their beliefs about how proximal others will respond are likely to affect their willingness to take the risk of this experimentation. Moreover, the fear of looking foolish can lead people to choose the easier paths of avoidance or cynicism. In short, when experimenting with new behaviors and skills, what others (peers and managers) think is particularly salient. Therefore, we propose that such change efforts are resisted or accepted differently by different groups in an organization, who are likely to have varying norms and expectations about interpersonal behavior. This is because people who interact face to face often share common assumptions and beliefs, which are likely to affect willingness to embrace a proposed change (Edmondson, 1999). Of particular relevance is the degree of psychological safety.

Psychological safety is the perception that one's work environment is safe for interpersonal risk-taking, such that proximal others will not reject or embarrass those who make mistakes or speak up about difficult issues (Edmondson, 1999). Psychological safety stems from mutual respect and trust among co-workers (Kahn, 1990). The construct has roots in early research on organizational change in the 1960s, in which Schein and Bennis (1965) discussed the need to create psychological safety if organization members are to feel secure and capable of changing. More recently, Schein (1993) argued that psychological safety helps people overcome the defensiveness, or "learning anxiety," that occurs when people are presented with data that disconfirm their expectations or hopes, which can thwart productive learning behavior. Psychological safety does not mean positive affect or mutual liking but, rather, describes a sense of confidence that the interpersonal consequences of well-intentioned risk will not be negative. Finally, recent empirical research has shown that perceptions of psychological safety in the workplace are similar among people who work closely together in a group and vary greatly across groups (Edmondson, 1999).

Although expectations about peers' attitudes and behaviors affect psychological safety, dyadic relationships between subordinates and supervisors/managers are centrally important in this construct. Managers have more power – defined as relative dependencies between people for valued resources (Emerson, 1962) – than subordinates, often leading to subordinates' concerns about appearing competent if they are to gain access to resources and career rewards (Lee, 1997; Winter 1973, 1993). Risking failure or appearing incompetent can be particularly costly for individuals who believe their managers will evaluate them negatively. Thus, employees' perceptions of their managers' intentions and attitudes play a central role in shaping the degree of psychological safety that employees experience at work (Edmondson, 1996b). If subordinates believe that managers are unwilling to act as advocates, or cannot be counted upon to provide help, then the dilemmas faced by individual employees, such as those introduced by OLIs as describe above, are extremely difficult to cope with productively. This is equally true if the interpersonal climate in a work unit is characterized by fear of being rejected for making a mistake – making experimentation with new behaviors especially risky. In contrast, if the interpersonal climate is characterized by psychological safety, individuals are more likely to experiment with new behaviors, ideas, or tools. Thus, an interpersonal climate in which it is safe to take the risks involved for learning is critical to encouraging new behaviors. We propose that where there is psychological safety, the open, learning-oriented conversation advocated by a dialogue intervention is likely to occur, increasing the chances of desired outcomes, and where psychological safety is lacking this is unlikely to occur. Thus, the psychological safety experienced by individuals in a given part of an organization may be a critical influence on how such an intervention is received. These general propositions, derived from the literature, are explored in a case study described below.

Psychological safety and learning-oriented dialogue   First, we anticipate that employees will be more likely to embrace an organizational learning intervention if they view the interpersonal climate at work as safe. In contrast, feeling unsafe, they would be likely to carry on an inauthentic conversation, such as by saying what they think managers want to hear, or by holding back and failing to reveal their true thoughts. Thus, implementation success, defined as the acceptance and routine use of a novel tool or program (Yin, 1977), is likely to be predicted by psychological safety.

> HYPOTHESIS 1:   *Psychological safety is positively associated with successful implementation of an OLI.*

Furthermore, we expect that the degree of learning-oriented conversations taking place as a result of an OLI – one measure of implementation success – will be positively associated with outcomes attributable to the OLI. For example, individuals might be able to make more informed decisions, or improve their job performance. Thus, we anticipated the following.

> HYPOTHESIS 2:   *The degree of learning-oriented conversation occurring as part of an OLI is positively associated with achieving positive outcomes.*

Hypotheses 1 and 2 can be combined to suggest a model in which psychological safety increases the chance of organizational members successfully using an OLI to engage in learning-oriented conversations, which in turn increases the chances of achieving business results or outcomes. These hypotheses do not pertain to events that take place before and after the overall intervention; instead, they focus on social factors affecting the actual use of the tools and processes an OLI might introduce into the workplace. Our argument is simply that psychological safety conditions affect an organization's ability to produce tangible outcomes by affecting how well the OLI tools and processes are used.

Alignment of perceptions of OLI implementation   The implementation of an OLI is typically a multi-party phenomenon. Often, two or more participants in a conversation view what is said or done differently. Such discrepancies are an indication of the quality of the conversation, particularly in terms of the degree of shared learning. Discrepancies that are associated with power differences also provide an indication of the quality of learning. For example, if a manager believes that a conversation is effective in dealing with the concerns of subordinates, while subordinates believe the same conversation was ineffective or problematic, the conversation was clearly not of optimal quality. The direction of the discrepancy is important due to the nature of power relationships, as described above. Previous research has shown that those who are in the lower power position in a relationship attend more to and are more accurate in decoding the non-verbal behavior of their higher-powered partner (Elfenbein et al., 2002; Henley, 1973) than vice versa. Thus, managers are likely to miss cues indicating dissatisfaction and discomfort on the part of the subordinate if they are subtle, and the extent to which a manager had a more positive assessment of a given conversation than her subordinate had is one indication of how comfortable the subordinate was in revealing concerns to the manager. The degree to which a subordinate's view is less positive than the manager's, which we refer to as a power-related *perceived discrepancy*, can be used as an index of the quality of dialogue implemented as part of an OLI. We then predict that psychological safety on the part of subordinates facilitates their speaking openly, which will reduce the likelihood of a power-related perceived discrepancy.

HYPOTHESIS 3:   *Subordinate psychological safety is negatively associated with the power-related perceived discrepancy in perceptions of dialogue quality.*

Similarly, this perceived discrepancy is likely to have a negative effect on outcomes of the OLI.

HYPOTHESIS 4:   *The power-related perceived discrepancy is negatively associated with positive outcomes of the OLI.*

Summary

This chapter argues that the efficacy of an intervention can vary within a single organization as a function of psychological safety. Our core argument is that an OLI can lead to different outcomes in different groups, even with consistent training and implementation methods. Our thinking draws from pioneering work on organizational change published decades ago suggesting that psychological safety reduces defensiveness and enables change, as well as from very recent research showing that psychological safety varies in striking ways across groups within the same organization. Finally, we note that this discussion applies particularly to efforts to produce change in interpersonal behavior, which is typically the focus of an OLI (e.g., Argyris, 1993; Isaacs, 1993; Schein 1993).

A CASE STUDY: THE CHANGE PROGRAM AT ELECTRONICO

Research site and project history

To explore these ideas, we studied an OLI in a multinational manufacturing company in the consumer electronics industry, which we call Electronico. In this section we describe the program and illustrate the range of responses we discovered by interviewing managers and their subordinates. Consistent with the perspective that achieving programmed organizational change is difficult (Beer et al., 1990), we found substantial evidence of cynicism among employees about management's motives in implementing the program, along with pessimism about the company's ability to change. However, we also found pockets of enthusiasm, and we wanted to understand the conditions under which OLIs might be embraced by managers and employees.

The purpose of the program at Electronico was to enhance organizational learning and employee empowerment through "dialogue." To do this, consultants designed a process that required managers and their subordinates to meet quarterly to discuss current work, as well as mutual hopes and expectations for the future. The goal of the intervention was to foster productive, open conversations about issues relevant to both task accomplishment and to individuals' career and personal aspirations, by mandating these quarterly dialogue sessions. The Electronico Dialogue Program (EDP) was thus designed to foster learning between managers and subordinates and to promote employee empowerment and better performance outcomes. As explained in a recent annual report, Electronico holds as one of its cornerstones "the dignity and respect of each individual." EDP was conceptualized and put in place by the company's CEO in an effort to realize this value for each employee in the workplace.

Once implemented, EDP consisted of two steps to be carried out quarterly by every employee in the organization. First, all employees would respond to a survey asking formal questions related to the meaningfulness of their job, the degree to which the workplace was meeting their needs, the sensitivity of the organization to their personal circumstances, and their career path in the organization. The directionality of their answers (positive versus negative) was entered into a computer system, and subordinates' responses to each question were documented and distributed to their managers. This was called "the metric." Second, after filling out the metric, each employee met with his or her manager to have a "dialogue," which could be structured according to the formal questions or unstructured and focused on topics of the employee's choice. EDP included a process for managers to "escalate" issues that arose in the course of the dialogues that could not be handled locally; this meant bringing an issue to the attention of more senior managers. In this way, the program was designed to serve a dual purpose: first, to improve the relationships between managers and subordinates at the local level through dialogues and, second, to provide a mechanism for the organization to learn about any systemic issues that needed to be addressed at the organizational level. As part of the implementation process, a core team made up of managers from all business units was created to review and address issues that emerged from the metric or were escalated from dialogues, with the intention that solutions would be developed to address common concerns. We refer to this group as the EDP team.

In spite of high-level management support for EDP, one year after its launch many experienced considerable frustration with how it was going. As summarized by an EDP team member we interviewed, some people saw the dialogues as an unnecessary requirement – something that "good managers should be doing anyway." Many managers claimed that their employees were not committed to, or were even resistant to, the idea of engaging in a dialogue each quarter, while many subordinates made the same claim about their managers. Many employees believed that it was another management fad lacking real commitment from the organization. In addition, some subordinates expected that all issues formally "escalated" after a dialogue would receive a formal response, and when this did not occur they often became cynical and dissatisfied.

We were invited to study EDP 18 months after its implementation to see if we could learn more about how people viewed the program. Our primary contact at Electronico was a senior manager who had been charged by the CEO to continue to expand and improve EDP throughout the company. Each step of this study was designed to understand what factors affected the program's success, so as to identify actions that could be taken to improve this or other OLIs. In the course of our research, various EDP team members served as our contacts for generating employee samples and collecting data.

Field research activities

This study had two phases. The first phase involved exploratory interviews with managers and subordinates in a variety of business units to learn more about how EDP was being used. We used these data to design a survey instrument with which we could collect quantitative data from a larger sample of Electronico employees to explore potential influences on differences identified in the interviews. At the end of the first phase, we ran a pilot test of the new survey and analyzed the data to revise the instrument before wider distribution. The second phase of the study involved preliminary tests of the guiding hypotheses, using data obtained from distribution of the revised survey to a larger sample of employees.

Interviews and dialogue sessions   Over the course of two months, we conducted 35 interviews with 17 managers and 18 subordinates, each lasting 30 minutes to an hour. The interviews encompassed 17 manager-subordinate dyads; two different subordinates of one manager were involved and two other managers were included without their subordinates. Participants represented all major business units of the company and ranged in position from factory production-line worker to vice president. Volunteers were solicited by the EDP team, and we followed up to conduct interviews and distribute the pilot survey. The manager–subordinate dyads were also asked to supply a tape recording of an upcoming dialogue.

The objectives of this phase of the study were to understand participants' views about what constitutes a productive dialogue with their manager or subordinate, as well as to explore factors that might affect the chances of having a good dialogue. Additionally, the interviews allowed us to observe the extent to which dyads in different parts of the organization were receptive to EDP and were achieving its stated goals. We used what we learned to develop meaningful survey items for this context, as well as to explore the central questions of our study: Did the success of this intervention vary across the company? Was there a relationship between psychological safety and the degree to which the dialogues were perceived as valuable? And finally, was there a relationship between the perception of dialogue quality and the degree to which action was taken – thereby helping to achieve the intervention's organizational goals? All interviews were taped. We also requested that each dyad supply a tape of their dialogue for that quarter, and we received six tapes. Initial qualitative analyses were conducted by the interviewer through the analysis of field notes and memo writing (Glaser and Strauss, 1967), and later verified through the reading of a random selection of interview transcripts by an independent analyst.

Survey measures   Survey measures included *psychological safety*, *dialogue quality*, and *outcomes* (the degree to which dialogues led to actions or results). The survey measured psychological safety using Likert scales for items such as "If I make a mistake in this job, it is often held against me" (reverse scored) and "If I had a problem in this company, I could depend on my manager to be my advocate." Dialogue quality was measured in the survey by asking respondents to reflect specifically upon their most recent dialogue with their manager; a typical item was "I felt free to say that I did not understand something my manager said and ask him/her to explain further." The degree to which dialogues led to effective action was assessed by a third survey measure, outcomes, which included items such as "Between dialogues, there is progress made on issues that we discuss." This scale measured outcomes from the subordinate's perspective in each dyad, consistent with the focus of EDP of providing a supportive context for subordinate development. A complete list of survey items is in the appendix.

To pilot the instrument, we mailed it to the 35 participants interviewed. Nineteen surveys (54 percent) were returned. Although this was a low response rate and a small N, the variance on all key variables was sufficiently large to allow us to assess intercorrelations among survey items and conduct preliminary psychometric analyses of the measures. These data also allowed us to compare interview and survey data for the same respondents, as a rough index of external validity. The interviewer – blind to the survey scores – rated the tapes of interviews from 1 to 5 on *psychological safety*[1] and assessed *outcomes* from 1 to 5 based on the existence of follow-up action or insight[2] resulting from the dialogue. Lastly, she rated the tapes of the dialogues themselves to assess dialogue quality; here, we used a scale from 1 to 5 based on the balance and quality of advocacy and inquiry (see Argyris and Schön, 1978), and the extent of involvement of both participants. These ratings were compared with survey scales to provide a rough index of the survey's external validity, as described below.

We then distributed the survey to 166 Electronico employees. Members of the EDP team helped to compile lists of participants, based on our request for a sample that was representative of the different job levels and divisions across the worldwide organization. Eighty-four surveys (51 percent) were returned. The appendix summarizes survey psychometric analysis, demonstrating the adequacy of the survey measures. Because EDP was implemented at all levels of the organization, all respondents were asked to answer questions from their perspective as a subordinate, such that they rated their relationship with their own manager. Additionally, those managers surveyed whose subordinates were also included in the sample were asked to fill out a separate short instrument, asking them to rate their most recent dialogue with that subordinate. Overall, therefore, the survey data provided perceptions of individuals and dyads scattered throughout the company; these respondents served as representatives of over 80 work groups at Electronico. The resulting data allow us to check for variance in key measures, such as psychological safety and dialogue quality, but not to draw conclusions about the level of analysis that best characterizes these variables.

FINDINGS AND IMPLICATIONS

Variance in intervention effectiveness

Interview data and transcripts of actual dialogue sessions at all levels of the organization revealed substantial variance in perceptions of and behaviors related to EDP – despite using identical materials and training sessions throughout Electronico as part of the intervention. The data suggested that manager–subordinate dyads tended to follow one of two distinct paths. In some dyads, participants appeared to view the program as a "complaint channel," rather than seeing it as an opportunity to take responsibility for problems and enlist managers' help in thinking through or solving them. Not surprisingly, for these dyads EDP was not seen as an effective tool. The inclusion of a formal process through which managers could "escalate" issues raised by subordinates to human resources or upper management was intended to be a minor or rarely used feature. In practice, however, many dyads habitually relied on the escalation process, thus shifting responsibility for action elsewhere, counter to the intention of EDP. In dyads in which the dialogues were viewed as ineffective, this escalation process – and its failure – often became the focus of the dialogue session's conversation, instead of a thoughtful and open exchange about problems, opportunities and potential actions.

In contrast, we found that other dyads interviewed saw the program as useful and effective. These informants viewed the dialogues as a valuable opportunity to get to know their manager or subordinate better, to remove intangible barriers to work productivity, and to develop a better shared understanding of their work and their environment. We also found that in all of the positive cases, both members of the dyad viewed the dialogue program similarly. In sum, dyads adopted strikingly different stances toward the program – with some reporting tangible benefits and viewing the program as helpful to them in doing their jobs and others, in contrast, reporting cynicism and frustration about the failure of the company to address escalated issues. For example, when asked about the dialogues, one manager focused her comments on the failures of the escalation process; she explained that dialogues do not go well because subordinates "feel like they didn't get an answer before, [and] they will show that they are dissatisfied and that they don't feel like they are going to get a straight answer to the question . . . they'll be more cynical." This focus, in turn, was shared by her subordinate, who commented, "I don't mind dialoguing with my manager at all. [She and] I kind of share the same skepticism, which is [about] what is going to become of the issues that I bring up." Because both believed that nothing would get done about "escalated" issues, they reinforced each other's belief that the program was ineffective.

A pattern emerged in these interviews in which participants tended to view the program negatively when they focused on the "escalation" process. As another manager explained, after a token statement of the program's value, "The process in the dialogues itself has been pretty good . . . There are a lot of concerns, though, about the issues that are brought up being escalated . . . they don't get answers back. So there's a real negative connotation because of that." These statements reveal a tacit assumption that the purpose of EDP is to report problems elsewhere so that they can be fixed by others, which itself may be a powerful barrier to learning – and to a dialogue's ability to have a positive impact on work outcomes.

In contrast, other managers and subordinates viewed the intervention as useful, in particular by benefiting their working relationships. For example, one manager explained:

> There was always plenty of face time [before EDP] but it was . . . always focused on the task at hand. I never had time for the other further discussions that went outside of the range of [immediate] projects. So what we are able to do now is to actually differentiate, and employees can come in and say "Listen, I want to have a conversation with you specifically about [this issue] . . .". It used to take them weeks to say, "Look the real issue here is XYZ."

Those who viewed the program as effective rarely or never escalated issues, tending instead to view themselves as responsible for addressing them. To illustrate, later in the interview, this manager went on to say, "The moment of truth for me is when employees realize that, at the heart of most of the [issues] is some initiative that the employee has to take. The manager then becomes the coach, the supporter, the sponsor."

A subordinate in another dyad gave a concrete example of how the program helped him to learn more about his boss's non-verbal behavior and improve their relationship:

> With [my boss], I paid a lot of attention to her facial expressions – sometimes to her lack of expression . . . lack of giving feedback, or lack of responsiveness . . . [then with EDP] I said "you know I need to give you some feedback about [how] I'm interpreting you" and I gave her some examples, and it wasn't just stuff that came up in dialogue, it was other situations too . . . She was quite surprised when I gave her that feedback and then she explained to me what she was probably thinking at that time, which had nothing to do with displeasure, she was focusing very intently on my thought and [didn't intend to communicate] displeasure.

Finally, another subordinate expressed his appreciation of the honesty he believed his manager demonstrated during their dialogues: "I don't think [my boss] says something just to make you happy, either. If the answer would be no, then that answer would be no. And you have to respect that . . . I like that, too."

In summary, striking differences in perceptions about the effectiveness of EDP provided general support for our proposition that responses to a change program can vary greatly across parts of an organization. Next, we wanted to examine the relationship between psychological safety and the quality of dialogues taking place, as well as how dialogue quality, in turn, was related to outcomes.

The relationship between psychological safety and dialogue quality

In analyzing the interview data, we sought to understand what factors differentiated those who had successful experiences as a result of the intervention from those who did not. Comments from the former group suggested that things went well from the start. Subordinates in these dyads reported feeling immediately comfortable using the dialogues as an opportunity to talk about issues of importance to them. For instance, one subordinate told us:

The dialogues have gone very well; it's just so comfortable. I mean I'm not nervous when I go in . . . I could be myself, I don't have to put on an act or anything, [I don't] worry about saying the wrong thing because something [bad] may happen if I do . . . I feel like I could just talk more about it and raise issues or concerns and not feel like I'm rushed to get out of the room because I knew he had to be somewhere else in a certain time frame.

Another subordinate expressed a similar level of comfort being open:

[The program is helpful] because I have been able to tell [my manager] exactly what I wanted to do, what my interests were, where I wanted to go . . . [I've been] able to have candid conversations with him . . . I was able to tell him [what I was thinking] and be open and honest with him and not feel threatened and not feel like they're going to say "well this guy is leaving, so let's not pay attention to him."

Interestingly, these subordinates imply that the program is itself a useful tool, in contrast to those quoted above, who saw the tool as difficult or impossible to use. At the same time, both comments suggest that a certain level of psychological safety was present in the manager–subordinate relationship – providing fertile soil for new growth of the same seed. Consistent with this observation, no one reported that their relationship with their manager or subordinate was altered by the intervention; psychological safety was in place, or not in place, prior to its introduction. Thus, being able to speak openly without fear of sanction appeared to make it possible for people to utilize the dialogue sessions in the spirit in which the CEO and the EDP team intended. Moreover, being able to engage in conversation in this way early in the process established a foundation from which a dyad could continue to build positive attitudes and behaviors going forward.

In contrast to these satisfied employees, a subordinate experiencing frustration with EDP explained that he felt that "personal issues" have no place in his dialogues with his manager:

I'd say I could pretty much discuss anything (with my manager), other than something on a personal level. I think if I had a personal problem with another person in there, I would not discuss it, because I think it would be something that I should handle on my own.

His manager appears to agree:

I've had people tell me that they're mentally ill. Just everything from soup to nuts, problems at home . . . [and] I try and avoid the personal problems because I really don't own those . . . I don't encourage someone to open up about personal issues. If they do want to discuss them, that's fine. I'll certainly listen, but I think as managers we've got to realize that we're not in the business of psychology. What we're here to do is improve the employee's ability to perform on the job, remove barriers and so forth and build a good workplace with a team environment.

Given how explicitly addressing personal issues and employee development was part of the stated intent of EDP (indeed, "sensitivity to personal circumstances" is an item in their dialogue guide), it was perplexing to us why this manager and subordinate came to a joint conclusion that these were things that should not be discussed. We were left to conclude that they probably did not feel comfortable raising such issues, which (along with other corroborating evidence) suggested a lack of psychological safety. Evidence of a lack of psychological safety is present in additional comments made by this manager in the same interview: "I have not had a lot of luck in escalating issues that emerge from the dialogues . . . I've been stepped on a few times for being too straightforward . . . I'm not real comfortable that there wouldn't be repercussions [for escalating issues]."

Another manager's comment further supports our hypothesis that a lack of psychological safety may hamper the success of this kind of OLI:

> I think people are still a little hesitant to think that there's a real honest discussion process that could go on and I wonder about that sometimes myself . . . and you know, I just run out of stuff to talk about . . . and, of course they [the subordinates] are not going to argue with you.

This manager's view that the dialogues are unlikely to be worthwhile because subordinates "are not going to argue with you" when you are a manager reveals something of his own tacit theory of power relationships, and may unwittingly foster a kind of self-fulfilling prophecy among his subordinates.

The variance in the experiences of the dyads is quite striking, particularly given the identical training and support for the program supplied to all employees at its introduction. Such data illustrate how Hypothesis 1 might play out, such that psychological safety could foster taking the interpersonal risks that allow the conversation in a dialogue to be candid and genuine – itself fostering subsequent successful dialogues. Survey data provide further insight and speculative support for this hypothesis. Psychological safety is correlated with both self-reported and observer-rated dialogue quality ($r = 0.58$ ($p < 0.01$, $n = 83$) and $r = 0.58$ (not significant, $n = 8$), respectively). Table 10.1 presents illustrative quotes for the small sample of eight dyads for whom we have both interview and dialogue transcript data. In summary, both qualitative and quantitative data suggest that subordinates with high levels of psychological safety are also more likely to have productive, learning-oriented dialogues, following an OLI.

The relationship between dialogue quality and outcomes

To explore Hypothesis 2, that the quality of conversation is positively associated with achieving results from the dialogues, we examined the association between survey measures of dialogue quality and work outcomes ($r = 0.70$, $p < 0.01$, $n = 83$). As both variables come from the same survey, this correlation is likely to be inflated by common method bias, and further research is needed to establish a conclusive relationship. We thus draw upon qualitative data to further explore this relationship between dialogue quality and work outcomes.

One manager's description showed how psychological safety and dialogue quality might work together to enable positive results:

> The fact is, we have never had to escalate [an issue] . . . there hasn't been an issue raised that we didn't have the resources right on the team to deal with. Even pretty significant changes

in people's jobs. If you listen to the conversation between [my subordinate] and I, [you will see that] she has dramatically changed her job responsibilities. And before, under the manager that she had a year ago, she really believed that she was going to have to leave the team to do what she wanted to do. During the dialogue process, not this one but the previous one, I was able to discover what her skills were and we started finding projects that were more challenging given her skills. It is very hard to come to your boss, especially when you are a fairly recent employee, and say "I am lot more talented than this and you guys are wasting a lot of – you are not really using a tenth of what you can get out of me."

The subordinate's willingness to openly talk to her new manager allowed them to have a productive dialogue in which they jointly discovered skills and opportunities and thereby made changes. Similarly, in another dyad, a subordinate who had previously assumed that he would have to leave Electronico to find a more interesting job, also reported the dialogues producing benefits:

[My boss] is trying to open doors for me . . . he's allowing me to go and meet with some of our senior executives in different parts of the company and have a conversation with them to allow me to share my interests with them . . . [the dialogues] helped us to, I think, build a relationship.

Another manager commented that the intervention had helped her create new opportunities for her subordinates:

I think [EDP] has opened up a lot of subjects that typically would not have been as much a part of the [conversations] and I think that there have been a lot of positives in respect to, for instance, talking about career planning. People started opening up, and there's been a good discussion about meaningful jobs and helping people move on in their careers, too. So in two of my subordinates' dialogues, we covered that situation . . . one has already moved on to another position, and the other one is moving to another position [in a few months].

In contrast to these positive comments, subordinates in dyads reporting lower quality dialogues said little about outcomes. Although some noted the possibility of identifying training opportunities, no comments were volunteered about improvement in work relationships or other career outcomes. Complaints focused on the failure of others in the organization – those to whom issues were escalated – to do anything to fix situations.

The relationship between psychological safety and power-related discrepant views

Our data allow us to examine certain relationships unencumbered by common method bias. Specifically, to explore Hypothesis 3, that psychological safety is negatively correlated with a power-related discrepancy in ratings of the quality of the dialogues, we analyzed a subset of the phase two survey data at the dyadic-level. Specifically, the sample ($n = 83$) included 27 manager–subordinate dyads who conduct quarterly dialogues with one another. While previous analyses utilized all respondents' views of their relationship with their own manager (who may or may not have also been involved in the study), in this section we look only at the data for complete dyads that participated ($n = 27$ dyads,

TABLE 10.1 Psychological safety, dialogue quality, and quality of outcomes in six dyads

Dyad	Psychological safety[a] (with illustrative data)	Dialogue quality[b] (with illustrative data)	Quality of outcomes[a] (with illustrative data)
1	Low The subordinate recently had an incident that resulted in disciplinary action and seemed reluctant to speak negatively in the interview about his manager. He also reported frustration about changes in policies that were not discussed in advance (e.g., removal of telephones from factory floor) The manager failed to show up three times for mutually scheduled appointments for interviews with one of the researchers. The interview finally took place but was very short, consisting of brief "yes/no" answers	Low Manager tends to discount/shut down concerns raised by subordinate: Manager: OK, hmmm, question five. Do you receive candid feedback at least every 30 days? Subordinate: Not really. Manager: OK. It could be because we had documented . . . [goes on to provide an elaborate reason. No concrete action is agreed upon to address the issue]	Low Only actions discussed were related to getting information about training courses; no follow-up on other issues raised by subordinate "[My manager is] great for scheduling training classes . . . [and] writing down action items [during the dialogues]"
2	High* The subordinate reported that EDP dialogues were very comfortable right from the beginning: "I could be myself, I don't have to put on an act or anything, worry about saying the wrong thing because something [bad] may happen if I do"	High* The manager asked a lot of questions about subordinate's perspective: e.g., "How did you feel about these goals when we set them? Did they give you energy?" And, "So you're moving yourself from a very administrative role 12 months ago . . . How does it feel?" Later: "What do we need to do about that?	High* The subordinate reported that she was more satisfied in her job because of the ability to raise concerns with her boss, and that "Everything I brought up has been acted upon" The manager explained that the program really raises productivity: "The barriers to more productivity are very

#						
	The manager commented that EDP is a success because "[personal] stuff comes up, because they honestly believe (a), that they can trust me, but also (b) that there is a process for dealing with these kinds of issues"		". . . is there anything we need to do about it?" And finally: "Did we hit everything you wanted to hit during this particular dialogue?"		small issues that we could deal with very quickly [when they are talked about] . . ."	
3	The subordinate described his relationship with a previous manager as "excellent" and very open, and said that EDP was facilitating a similarly strong relationship with his new boss The manager explained that positive dialogues happen because of "trust on both sides. And being able to communicate honestly with each other, and not being afraid to tell the good *and* not so good news. A willingness to share fears, obviously, and concerns"	High	The manager encourages sharing of feelings and problems during the dialogue. Subordinate: I am aware of the competitiveness between [colleague] and I, I feel like I want to win at [his] expense, or that [he] wins at my expense . . . Manager: I understand where you are coming from with your comment about . . . being in [colleague's] shadow . . . And I'm glad that you talked to me about it	High	The subordinate reported learning to understand the manager's non-verbal communication better, and said he had paid attention to her "lack of facial expression," thinking she intended to communicate displeasure, but learned instead that she "was focusing very intently on my thought . . ." The manager said that a lot of issues were raised in the dialogue that "typically would not have been as much a part of the conversations [without EDP]"	High
4	The subordinate reported that there was a high level of trust before EDP started and that his manager is "very open, very	High*	[tape of dialogue was inaudible] The subordinate reported that he can share positive or negative views	—	The subordinate reported that, as a result of EDP, more issues are brought out and discussed.	High*

Continues

TABLE 10.1 *Continued*

Dyad	Psychological safety[a] (with illustrative data)	Dialogue quality[b] (with illustrative data)	Quality of outcomes[a] (with illustrative data)
	approachable, and solicits feedback of any kind" Manager: I think we tend to be pretty open around here, but I appreciate the chance to sit down and do a checkpoint every quarter	with his boss and "know she will keep it issue-specific and not take it personally. She doesn't internalize what I tell her"	Subordinate: I think [EDP] is a good process. I think it's, you know, absolutely necessary to . . . discuss the undiscussable Manager: It's a good way to get to know (some associates) . . . before, you might get a [quick aside] here or there. This gives you a chance to sit down and really focus on it
5	Low Subordinate: . . . the recent down-sizing made it difficult to talk about whether I have a meaningful job . . . there's one [manager] that I don't want to talk to about anything I am supposed to talk to him about, let alone all of these other things. I don't have that trust . . .	Low Subordinate reported asking about someone five levels above her getting a promotion which changed the way she thought about her own career plan. The manager's response was, "That's a pretty high level position; I don't know that you should be concerned about that yet." "So, that led me to believe that we are not ready to have a conversation about [my career plan] yet"	Low Subordinate asks manager to track down information about something she had "escalated" on her last EDP activity report, related to domestic partner benefits. She says she doesn't know if that "ever did or didn't happen . . . I know the answer from corporate benefits, I just wonder if they discussed it at all"

| 6 | High* | Subordinate: . . . I'd say I could pretty much discuss anything . . .

Manager: I guess the key issues are, one, the employee trusts the manager and, two, timing, such that you schedule the dialogue at a time that you're not going to be rushing to get it done, and that you sit down with this employee to . . . let them determine . . . what time they need for their inputs | High* | Manager: Did you have any formal training on the dialogue process?

Subordinate: No, well we had a book. . . . [but] I don't think we had any kind of class. That's why, when we first did it, I used to answer all yes, because everything was always mostly or partly yes, then you said, well, no, if it's any bit no, then the answer is no. That's when this became more useful, when I began to understand how it works

Manager: How do you feel about the [EDP] process?

Subordinate: I'm liking it more every time, now . . . I can see it doing something. I think of lot of it has to do with the fact that you are on board with it . . . | High* | Subordinate: [With] the previous supervisor, it was just something we had to do, and I was not getting anything out of it. Now I'm really getting something out of it . . . .

Manager: [when I raise an issue with him], he'll make an action plan and he'll act upon it |

---

[a] Overall rating derived from researchers' assessment of qualitative data from *individual interviews*.

[b] Overall rating derived from researchers' assessment through coding of the manager–subordinate dyad's audio-taped dialogue.

* Coding of these qualitative data is corroborated by survey measures (above or below sample median of 3.8 on a five-point Likert scale).

TABLE 10.2   Descriptive statistics and Pearson correlations for manager/subordinate dyad survey scores ($n = 27$)

	1	2	3	4
1. Psychological safety	1.00	0.59**	−0.02	0.52**
2. Subordinate rating of dialogue quality		1.00	0.35*	0.61**
3. Manager rating of dialogue quality			1.00	0.36*
4. Outcome				1.00
Mean	3.73	3.74	3.85	3.60
Standard deviation	2.33	2.38	2.4	2.00
Range	0.63	0.54	0.57	0.55

* Correlation is significant at the 0.05 level (1-tailed).
** Correlation is significant at the 0.01 level (1-tailed).

52 individuals). In this sample, managers in each dyad were asked to reflect on specific dialogues that took place with the particular subordinate who was also in the study sample.[3] Table 10.2 displays descriptive statistics and correlations for the survey scales specific to these 27 dyads. Note, first, that the correlation between manager and subordinate ratings of the same dialogue session is significant at the $p < 0.05$ level, as is the correlation between manager ratings of dialogue quality and outcome.

Curiously, however, the correlation between manager ratings of dialogue quality and subordinate psychological safety is close to zero. Insight about this is provided by examining the *difference* in dialogue quality ratings between the manager and subordinate within each dyad. The degree to which managers and subordinates differ in their perceptions of dialogue quality is significantly associated with psychological safety as rated by the subordinate; thus, regressing this difference score (manager rating minus subordinate rating of dialogue quality) on subordinate psychological safety reveals a significant relationship, accounting for substantial variance in the dependent variable ($\beta = -0.52$, $p = 0.005$; $R^2 = 0.27$). This finding is particularly compelling, because as noted above the relationship is not subject to the common method variance that otherwise affects the correlation among survey variables. Finally, in addition to managers' and subordinates' direct ratings of their own dialogues, this difference score provides an implicit measure of dialogue quality. Further, the extent to which the manager, the more powerful member of the dyad, rates the dialogue more positively than the subordinate is associated with low subordinate ratings of psychological safety in their relationship. Both low psychological safety and low dialogue quality ratings from a subordinate signal that he or she does not feel able to speak openly to the manager, which may be why the manager is unaware that the dialogue is not going well, as indicated by his or her higher dialogue quality rating.

Negative relationship between power-related discrepancy and outcome

Consistent with Hypothesis 4, we also found that the difference in dialogue quality scores between the manager and subordinate in each dyad was negatively correlated, although not significantly, with outcomes achieved by the intervention ($r = -0.21$, $p = 0.15$). This is another example of an implicit measure, in a finding that is consistent with the previous results; when the dialogues are not going well – or when managers think they are going better than subordinates think they are going – the quality of the outcomes associated with the program may suffer. This also helps us understand a little more about the difficulty managers face in discovering why such change programs are not going well and how to improve them; it is possible for managers to believe that they are engaging in perfectly good dialogues that fail to yield tangible results. We might expect a manager in such a situation to infer that the problem lies in a lack of commitment on the part of his or her subordinates, which is precisely the type of explanations we were given by managers.

The Electronico data are consistent with our proposition that OLIs are influenced by interpersonal perceptions among people who work closely together, particularly in a manager–subordinate relationship. In these data, it is possible to understand how the proposition that psychological safety would affect local responses to an organizational intervention might play out. Attitudes and actions of proximal others – especially managers – affect how people view specific materials, events or tools, such that the same intervention can be seen and used in fundamentally different ways and lead to different and varied outcomes. This particular field study provides highly suggestive data for the notion that the psychological safety characterizing manager – subordinate relationships is associated with both the quality of the dialogues implemented as part of the intervention and reports of positive outcomes.

These data also suggest that in situations in which supportive conditions are not in place managers may mistakenly believe that things are going well when they are not. When subordinates did not feel psychologically safe, their managers were more likely to report that things were going well in dialogues than were subordinates. Although these correlational data do not allow causal inferences, we can speculate that, in conditions of low psychological safety, subordinates would not feel able or willing to give their managers the feedback needed for the intervention to work. Understandably, managers in such situations may interpret the absence of feedback from the subordinate as a sign that all is going smoothly, and thus make no effort to improve or change their own behavior. Further, when good outcomes are not achieved, these managers may attribute this to the readily accessible explanation of a lack of commitment on the part of subordinates. This interpretation of the data is one of many possible explanations for the variance in EDP effectiveness, however, and additional research is needed to better understand potential mechanisms at work that lead to the kinds of within-organization variance we found at this company.

Finally, there are several limitations of this study in addition to the use of cross-sectional data. The sample was small and not scientific and the survey response rate was low, limiting the confidence we can have in the quantitative data. Fortunately, however, respondents were not a self-selected sample of enthusiasts; in contrast, there was substantial variance on the key measures of interest, such that we were able to conduct preliminary tests of association for variables that help illustrate our broader theoretical propositions. The use of qualitative and quantitative data to investigate this program provides a strength of the study, allowing us to achieve a fuller understanding of how a process implemented as part of an OLI was received and used. In sum, these data are presented to conduct preliminary tests of plausibility and to illustrate how our theory might play out in an organizational intervention process, rather than to test formal hypotheses. Future research will have to be done to extend these ideas and develop more precise measures and comprehensive samples.

CONCLUSION

This chapter argues that the efficacy of an intervention can vary within a single organization as a function of psychological safety. Our core argument is that an OLI can lead to different outcomes in different groups, even with consistent training and implementation methods. Past theory, together with a case study of an OLI in a single, large company, contributes to a perspective that contrasts with the notion of organization-wide program success or failure. In this field site, we found substantial variance in the use and outcomes of the program. As expected, many participants reported a lack of behavioral or organizational change coupled with pronounced cynicism about the intervention; however, we also found individuals and dyads reporting meaningful success attributable to it. This leads us to speculate that interventions are more likely to produce real learning if work groups and manager–subordinate relationships are characterized by psychological safety – providing a fertile soil in which the seeds of an intervention can bear fruit.

We offer three concluding ideas for researchers and practitioners to keep in mind when designing and evaluating OLIs within companies. First, as observed in this case, substantial local variation can exist in the extent to which individuals resist or embrace an intervention. Tools and ideas can be embraced in some parts of the organization while simultaneously rejected elsewhere. Thus, it is important to evaluate the efficacy of an intervention at the appropriate level of analysis, which we argue is the level of the work group for behavioral change related to organizational learning. Although an intervention may appear at one level to be a failure, pockets of success may be present, and we suggest these successes may be attributable to fertile soil rather than to better seeds (or interventions). Second, certain antecedent factors such as psychological safety influence the quality of the soil, which can vary across parts of an organization and consequently so can the quality of implementation of a change effort and nature of the outcomes. We argue that this is important for both researchers and practitioners to keep in mind when assessing results of an intervention, or looking for the "cause" of a seemingly failed one. Although putting more money and time into training might seem like the answer, such efforts can be wasted when carried out in an environment that is not conducive to change, suggesting that initial work might have to be done to prepare the soil.

Third, the nature of the interrelationships of these factors can easily lead to faulty causal inferences regarding why a change program does not appear to be working. What looks like failure at the organizational level might actually be a complex pattern of local successes and failures; what looks like a successful dialogue to a manager might be a useless and uncomfortable exchange to a subordinate, and finally what looks like a poorly designed intervention might actually be a perfectly good one in an unreceptive environment. Therefore, we suggest that both practitioners and researchers investigate outcomes and processes of OLIs at the work unit level of analysis, in addition to the organization level, incorporating combined perspectives of all participants, investigating antecedent conditions as well as program implementation and outcomes. This more detailed implementation planning and analysis ultimately may help cultivate the soil throughout the organization so that the seeds of change, once planted, can take root and grow.

NOTES

1. These ratings were based on respondents' reports of how easy it was to discuss difficult issues with the manager, on their willingness to give and receive feedback with their manager, and on the environment surrounding the dialogue (e.g., privacy and a perceived lack of being rushed or hurried in the session).
2. For example, achieving some tangible outcome was illustrated by such statements as "The issue that was bothering me got resolved" and achieving insight by "I understood more how my body language was misleading."
3. Although these managers also answered questions about dialogues with their own managers, these data are not relevant for the dyadic analyses.

APPENDIX: SURVEY ITEMS AND PSYCHOMETRIC ANALYSIS

Preliminary analyses

We assessed psychometric properties of the survey variables in two ways. Cronbach's alpha provides a measure of internal consistency reliability of the measures to be used in testing hypotheses, and comparisons of pilot survey data with coded qualitative data from the interviews and dialogues were used to assess external validity. Table 10.A2 displays correlations and descriptive statistics for the survey scales from phase two data ($n = 83$) and shows that Cronbach's alpha was at or above 0.75 for all three variables.

As shown in table 10.A3, ratings of individual interviews and tapes of manager–subordinate dialogues were significantly correlated with scores obtained from the same individuals on the survey instrument.

TABLE 10.A1   Survey items

Scale	Item
Psychological safety (Subordinate)	If I make a mistake in this job, it is often held against me (R)
	It is difficult to ask others in this department for help (R)
	My manager often encourages me to take on new tasks or to learn how to do things I have never done before
	If I was thinking about leaving this company to pursue a better job elsewhere, I would talk to my manager about it
	If I had a problem in this company, I could depend on my manager to be my advocate
	Often when I raise a problem with my manager, s/he does not seem very interested in helping me find a solution (R)

Continues

TABLE 10.A1   *Continued*

Scale	Item
Dialogue (Subordinate)	I would like to have another conversation like this one I felt free to say that I did not understand something my manager said and ask him/her to explain further I thought my manager was genuinely curious about my ideas and what I had to say My manager did not provide support for what s/he was saying (R) My manager stated what s/he thought about something and what s/he hoped to see done The conversation dealt mostly with broad or abstract issues (R) My manager asked a lot of questions s/he seemed to already know the answers to (R) It was not clear what I should do next based on what was said (R)
Dialogue (Manager)	I would like to have another conversation like this one We talked about very specific issues During the dialogue, the subordinate stated what s/he thought and why s/he thought it We thoroughly discussed the thinking behind any action items we decided to initiate The conversation dealt mostly with broad or abstract issues (R)
Outcomes	In between dialogues, there is progress made on issues that we discuss The opportunity to discuss my career path and my training opportunities has had a positive impact on my job performance It is not worth raising any issues during the dialogues; not much happens as a result of raising them anyway (R) My manager follows up on the action items s/he takes on during dialogues

TABLE 10.A2   Descriptive statistics and Pearson correlations for survey scales ($n = 83$)

	1	2	3
1. Psychological safety	1.00	0.58**	0.63**
2. Dialogue quality		1.00	0.70**
3. Outcome			1.00
Mean	3.67	3.62	3.39
Standard deviation	0.62	0.51	0.69
Range	2.83	2.38	2.75
Cronbach's alpha	0.75	0.77	0.79

** Correlation is significant at the 0.01 level (1-tailed).

TABLE 10.A3   Descriptive statistics and correlations of survey scores with ratings of psychological safety and outcome based on interviews ($n = 19$) and dialogue scores based on ratings of taped dialogues ($n = 8$)

	1	2	3	4	5	6
1. Psychological safety (survey)	1.00	0.21	0.57*	0.45*	0.58	0.01
2. Dialogue quality (survey)		1.00	0.32	0.64*	0.64*	0.28
3. Outcome (survey)			1.00	0.15	0.62*	0.47*
4. Psychological safety (interview)				1.00	0.54	0.59*
5. Dialogue quality (tape)					1.00	0.60*
6. Outcome (interview)						1.00
Mean	3.74	4.13	3.82	3.71	3.50	3.58
Standard deviation	0.46	0.36	0.70	1.10	0.71	0.73
Range	1.80	1.25	2.67	3.00	3.00	3.00
Cronbach's alpha	0.53	0.56	0.71	—	—	—

* Correlation is significant at the 0.05 level (1-tailed).

REFERENCES

Argyris, C. (1993) *Knowledge for Action: Changing the Status Quo.* San Francisco: Jossey-Bass

Argyris, C. and Schön, D. (1978) *Organizational Learning: A Theory of Action Perspective.* Reading, MA: Addison-Wesley.

Batt, R. (1999) Work Organization, Technology, and Performance in Customer Service and Sales. *Industrial and Labor Relations Review*, 52 (4): 539–64.

Beer, M., and Eisenstat, R. (1996) Developing an Organization Capable of Implementing Strategy and Learning. *Human Relations*, 49 (5): 597–620.

Beer, M., Eisenstat, R.A., and Spector, B. (1990) *The Critical Path to Corporate Renewal.* Boston, MA: Harvard Business School Press.

Beer, M., and Spector, B. (1993) Organizational Diagnosis: Its Role in Organizational Learning. *Journal of Counseling and Development*, 71 (6): 642–50.

Cannon, M.D. and Edmondson, A.C. (2001) Confronting Failure: Antecedents and Consequences of Shared Beliefs about Failure in Organizational Work Groups. *Journal of Organizational Behavior*, 22: 161–77.

Cohen, S.G. and Ledford, G.E. (1994) The Effectiveness of Self-managing Teams: A Quasi-experiment. *Human Relations*, 47 (1): 13–43.

Daft, R.L. and Huber, G.P. (1987) How Organizations Learn: A Communications Framework. *Research in the Sociology of Organizations*, 5: 1–36.

Dawson, P. (1999) Towards a Processual Framework for Understanding Change. Paper presented at the Academy of Management annual meetings in Chicago, August.

DiBella, A.J. and Nevis, E.C. (1998) *How Organizations Learn: An Integrated Strategy for Building Learning Capability.* San Francisco: Jossey-Bass.

Dougherty, D. (1992) A Practice-Centered Model of Organizational Renewal through Product Innovation. *Strategic Management Journal*, 13: 77–93.

Edmondson, A. (1996a) Three Faces of Eden: The Persistence of Competing Theories and Multiple Diagnoses in Organizational Intervention Research. *Human Relations*, 49 (5): 597–620.

Edmondson, A. (1996b) Learning from Mmistakes is Easier Said than Done: Group and Organizational Influences on the Detection and Correction of Human Error. *Journal of Applied Behavioral
Science*, 32 (1): 5–32.

Edmondson, A. (1999) Psychological Safety and Learning Behavior in Work Teams. *Administrative
Science Quarterly*, 44 (2): 350–83.

Elfenbein, H.A., Marsh, A., and Ambady, N. (2002) Emotional Intelligence and the Recognition of
Emotion from the Face. In L.F. Barrett and P. Salovey (eds.), *The Wisdom of Feelings: Processes Underlying Emotional Intelligence*. New York: Guilford Press.

Emerson, R.M. (1962) Power-dependence Relations. *American Sociological Review*, 27: 31–40.

Ford, J.D. and Ford, L.W. (1995) The Role of Conversations in Producing Intentional Change in
Organizations. *The Academy of Management Review*, 20: 541–70.

Garvin, D.A. (2000) *Learning in Action*. Boston: Harvard Business School Press.

Glaser, B.G. and Strauss, A.L. (1967) *The Discovery of Grounded Theory: Strategies for Qualitative Research*.
New York: Aldine de Gruyter.

Goodman, P.S., Bazerman, M. and Conlon, E. (1980) Institutionalization of Planned Organizational
Change. *Research in Organizational Behavior*, 2: 215–46.

Hackman, J.R. (1998) Why Groups Don't Work. In R.S. Tindale and L. Heath (eds.), *Theory and
Research on Small Grops: Social Psychological Applications to Social Issues*. New York: Plenum Press:
245–67.

Hackman, J.R. and Morris, C.G. (1975) Group Tasks, Group Interaction Process, and Group
Performance Effectiveness. In H.H. Blumberg, A.P. Hard, V. Kent, and M. Davies (eds.), *Small
Groups and Social Interaction*, Vol. 1. Chichester, UK: John Wiley & Sons.

Hannan, M. and Freeman, J. (1984) Structural Inertia and Organizational Change. *American Sociological Review*, 49: 149–64.

Henley, N.M. (1973) Power, Sex and Nonverbal Communication. *Berkeley Journal of Sociology*, 18: 1–26.

Isaacs, W.N. (1992) The Perils of Shared Ideals, Unpublished DPhil dissertation, Oxford University.

Isaacs, W.N. (1993) Taking Flight: Dialogue, Collective Thinking and Organizational Learning. *Organizational Dynamics*, 22: 24–40.

Kahn, W.A. (1990) Psychological Conditions of Personal Engagement and Disengagement at Work.
Academy of Management Journal, 33 (4): 692–724.

Kilmann, R.H., Covin, T.J., and Associates (1988) *Corporate Transformation*. San Francisco: Jossey-Bass,
435–50.

Kotter, John P. (1996) *Leading Change*. Boston: Harvard Business School Press.

Lee, F. (1997) When the Going Gets Tough, Do the Tough Ask for Help? Help Seeking and Power
Motivation in Organizations. *Organizational Behavior and Human Decision Processes*, 72 (3): 336–63.

Levitt, B. and March, J. (1988) Organizational Learning. *Annual Review of Sociology*, 14: 319–40.

Lewin, K. (1951) *Field Theory in Social Science*. New York: Harper & Row.

Pfeffer, J. and Salancik, G.R. (1978) *The External Control of Organizations*. New York: Harper & Row.

Popper, M. and Lipshitz, R. (1998) Organizational Learning Mechanisms: A Structural and Cultural Approach to Organizational Learning. *Journal of Applied Behavioral Science*, 34 (2): 161–79.

Roth, G. and Kleiner, A. (2000) *Car Launch: The Human Side of Managing Change*. New York: Oxford
University Press.

Salancik, G. and Pfeffer, J. (1978) A Social Information Processing Approach to Job Attitudes and
Task Design. *Administrative Science Quarterly*, 23: 224–53.

Schein, E.H. (1993) On Dialogue, Culture, and Organizational Learning. *Organizational Dynamics*, 22
(2): 40–51.

Schein, E.H. and Bennis, W. (1965) *Personal and Organizational Change through Group Methods*. New York:
Wiley.

Schoonhoven, C.B., Eisenhardt, K.M., and Lyman, K. (1990) Speeding Product to Market: Waiting Time to First Product 1. *Administrative Science Quarterly*, 35 (1): 177–207.

Senge, P. (1990) *The Fifth Discipline: The Art and Practice of the Learning Organization.* New York: Doubleday.

Senge, P., Kleiner, A., Roberts, C., Ross, R., and Smith, B. (1994) *The Fifth Discipline Field Book: Strategies and Tools for Building a Learning Organization.* New York: Doubleday.

Turner, D. and Crawford, M. (1998) *Change Power: Capabilities that Drive Corporate Renewal.* Mona Vale, NSW: Woodslande Pty Ltd.

Walton, R.E. (1975) The Diffusion of New Work Structures: Explaining Why Success Didn't Take. *Organizational Dynamics*, Winter: 3–21.

Watkins, K.E. and Marsick, V.J. (1993) *Sculpting the Learning Organization: Lessons in the Art and Science of Systemic Change.* San Francisco: Jossey-Bass.

Winter, D.G. (1973) *The Power Motive.* New York: Free Press.

Winter, D.G. (1993) Power, Affiliation, and War: Three Tests of a Motivational Model. *Journal of Personality and Social Psychology*, 65 (3): 532–45.

Yin, R.K. (1977) "Production Efficiency versus Bureaucratic Self-interest: Two Innovative Processes?" *Policy Sciences*, 8: 381–99.

11

The Impact of Intercultural Communication on Global Organizational Learning

SULLY TAYLOR AND JOYCE S. OSLAND

CHAPTER OUTLINE

This chapter provides a look at organizational learning through the lens of intercultural communication. Since the organizational learning research seldom considers the impact of intercultural communication, we have written a conceptual piece based on reviews of both literatures and our own experience with global organizations. The chapter begins by first examining the role of communication in organizational learning. Next, we introduce the basic concepts of intercultural communication. We identify those aspects of intercultural communication that most directly affect knowledge transfer: marginality, stereotypes, style differences, linguistic ability, cosmopolitanism, satisficing, and intercultural sensitivity. We explore the relationship between stages of intercultural sensitivity and the readiness to learn, focusing on the trigger events that can move people and organizations to higher levels of sensitivity. Finally, we describe and discuss the practical implications an understanding of intercultural communication has for organizational learning and questions that need to be addressed by future research.

INTRODUCTION

In a global economy, success depends on accurately reading and responding to environmental complexity and competition (Bartlett and Ghoshal, 1989; 2000). Organizational learning would appear to be a prerequisite for surviving in the global context (de Geus, 1988; Hamel and Prahalad, 1994). Moreover, the diversity of peoples and environments in which multinational firms (MNCs) operate should increase the potential number and sources of innovations and learning. As Cohen and Levinthal (1990: 133) note, "interactions across individuals who each possess diverse and different knowledge structures will augment the organization's capacity for making novel linkages and associations – innovating – beyond what any one individual can achieve." The MNC can thus be seen as a set of networked repositories of knowledge and capabilities (Leonard-Barton, 1995; Kogut and Zander, 1992; Gupta and Govindarajan, 1991). Makino and Inkpen's chapter in this book focus attention on the fact that potential for learning – what they term "exploration" – can in fact lead MNCs to invest in other countries. While there has been recent research into how MNCs can tap the knowledge potential of their global networks of people and units (e.g., Nohria and Ghoshal, 1997), the examination of the processes that enhance global knowledge transfer is at a relatively early stage.

The need to understand the processes of global knowledge transfer is especially important because there is some evidence to suggest that many MNCs fail to tap the knowledge or leverage the learning that occurs within them (Nohria and Ghoshal, 1997; Bartlett and Ghoshal, 1989). Many expatriates, for example, find that the knowledge they have gained during their sojourns abroad concerning the foreign environment is ignored once they return to HQ, with little or no attempt to archive and distribute the learning that has occurred (Osland, 1995; Kamoche, 1996). One of the major challenges facing global firms is to develop processes and policies that will more effectively integrate the knowledge and experience of repatriates (Bernhut, 2001; Birkinshaw, 2001).

Given the limited success of MNCS in transferring knowledge and the paucity of research on global organizational learning, this chapter will introduce one of the key barriers to global organizational learning: intercultural communication. Intercultural communication is defined as a "symbolic process in which people from different cultures create shared meanings" (Lustig and Koester, 1999: 52). The basic research question posed in this chapter is: What factors in the intercultural communication process affect organizational learning and prevent global organizations from sharing and transferring the information and knowledge at both the individual and group level?

There are very few studies that deal with the link between intercultural communication and organizational learning (e.g. Heavens and Child, 1999). Therefore, this chapter is a conceptual piece based on a review of both literatures and our own experience with global organizations. The chapter begins by first examining the role of communication in global organizational learning. Next, we introduce the basic concepts of intercultural communication and identify those aspects of intercultural communication that most directly affect knowledge transfer. We explore the relationship between stages of intercultural sensitivity and the readiness to learn, and we focus on the trigger events that can move people and organizations to higher levels of sensitivity. Finally, we discuss the practical implications an understanding of intercultural communication has for organizational learning, and offer directions future research can follow in addressing this aspect of global organizational learning.

COMMUNICATION IN GLOBAL ORGANIZATIONAL LEARNING

At the base of all theories concerning organizational learning, albeit from the information processing perspective (e.g., Huber, 1991) or the social construction perspective (Brown and Duguid, 1991; Cook and Yanow, 1993), lies the assumption that communication must occur in order for knowledge to be created or disseminated. When examining organizational learning in MNCs, it is particularly important to examine the impact of culture on communication because of the need to share knowledge across individuals and groups located in highly divergent cultural environments. Regardless of the type of knowledge to be transferred (tacit versus explicit; operational versus strategic) or the manner of transfer (archival versus verbal; experiential versus cognitive), the communication process will be affected by culture. While both knowledge creation and knowledge transfer are important, in MNCs it can be argued that transfer is particularly important because if MNCs can simply leverage all the knowledge that they have within the global networks, they will greatly enhance their ability to respond to environmental changes and increase performance (Bartlett and Ghoshal, 1989).

Organizational learning theorists usually include within their definitions of the phenomenon the capability of organizations to not only create new knowledge, but to transfer it (Senge, 1990; Garvin, 1993; Huber, 1991). Huber calls this "information distribution," and observes that it is "a determinant of both the occurrence and breadth of organizational learning" (1991: 100). In other words, in order for organizations to learn, they must first have access to the knowledge that is available within the company. He goes on to observe the potential impediments to the effective distribution of knowledge in organizations, which includes such factors as the perception of personal characteristics of the receiver (e.g., power and status), the workload of the sender, and the number of sequential links in the communication chain linking the sender and the receiver (Huber, 1991: 101). Thus, Huber (1991) makes salient the role of communication in information and knowledge transfer, but he does not address the potential barriers represented by differences in ethnic or national cultural patterns of communication.

National or ethnic cultural background of individuals has long been recognized as a major influence on communication, and hence it is reasonable to expect that knowledge transfer within MNCS will be affected by national culture. There are many definitions of national culture – around 200 of them (Adler, 2002). We have chosen to use a representative definition: "the shared beliefs, values, and practices of a group of people. A group's culture includes the language or languages used by group members as well as the norms and rules about how behavior can appropriately be displayed and how it should be understood" (O'Hair et al., 1997: 9).

Communication of knowledge in MNCs can occur between different types of actors – between individuals, between individuals and groups, and among groups, internally or externally, nationally or internationally. In this chapter we will focus on the internal transfer of knowledge among these various actors. While the sharing of knowledge with the external environment may be of some importance to business success, the major learning that the MNC can capture and turn into a distinctive competence (Barney, 1991) is most likely to be internal. Illustrations of such internal learning are knowledge about new markets, improvements in business processes, recent competitor behavior and relevant technological innovations.

Individuals are usually seen as the basis of learning within organizations (Inkpen and Dinur, 1998; Kim, 1993; Nonaka and Takeuchi, 1995). "The prime movers in the process of organizational knowledge creation are the individual members of an organization" (Nonaka, 1994: 17). Individuals hold internal images of how the world works. These are called "mental models." The mental models arbitrate what new information we acquire, retain, use and delete, but most important, "they not only help us make sense of the world we see, they can also restrict our understanding to that which makes sense within the mental model" (Kim, 1993: 39). Through learning gathered by interaction with the environment, an individual's mental model changes, and these changes become embedded in the organization's mental model. "The cycles of individual learning affect learning at the organizational level through their influence on the organization's shared mental models" (Kim, 1993: 43). Individual learning is combined, amplified and changed into group mental models in the intermediate step of group learning, as emphasized by Nonaka (1994) and Inkpen and Crossan (1995). The process of embedding the individual's new mental model into the organization is never simple. Much knowledge, particularly tacit knowledge, can be lost in the process due to lack of connections between people or parts of the organizational structure.

Organizations as a whole, as well as their sub-units, are thus also important learners and communicators (Inkpen and Crossan, 1995; Kim, 1993). Organizations can be seen as interpretation systems (Daft and Weick, 1984; Inkpen and Crossan, 1995) that scan the environment, interpret events, and develop concepts to guide future action. The mental models that the organization collectively holds help it in decision-making through the schemas, scripts, and causal maps that result from the mental models. Very often this learning is embedded in the knowledge structure of the top management team and in the organizational structures and processes they create based on their shared mental models (Kim, 1993). The organization communicates its mental models internally through established standard operating procedures, organizational culture, assumptions, artifacts and overt behavior rules that characterize the organization (Kim, 1993). Thus, communication becomes a key factor both in how the organization learns from the individuals within it and how it communicates its mental models to these same individuals.

Based on this framework of the interdependent and interactive nature of individual and organizational learning, we will examine the impact of intercultural communication on knowledge transfer. Before proceeding, however, the distinction between the mental models of individuals and organizations on the one hand, and national culture on the other, warrants clarification. While national culture can be seen as a type of mental model, it is a much broader and more deeply rooted "way of seeing the world." In this chapter, we will make the distinction that the term "mental model" refers to a more narrow, organizationally relevant perspective that focuses on an image or perception of what makes the organization successful. National culture refers to the broader, life-encompassing group-influenced mental picture that people acquire early in life from membership in a particular ethnic group or culture.

INTERCULTURAL COMMUNICATION

When examining organizational learning in MNCs, it is clear that a strong intercultural component must be included in order to study and understand how organizations can be successful. MNCs by their very nature are engaged in business in a number of countries with often widely divergent cultures. This leads to increased ambiguity concerning meaning "It is the ambiguity of meaning that marks the boundaries of culture" (Cohen, 1985: 55) – "the boundary is where the ambiguity begins, where managers can no longer be sure of the correctness of their interpretation of what is going on" (Apfelthaler and Karmasin, 1998: 8). Ambiguity can lead to anxiety. Communicating with strangers (people from other cultures) is both a source of anxiety and a means for diminishing it. "Reducing anxiety is one of the major functions of communication when we interact with strangers" (Gudykunst and Kim, 1997: 27) because it can lead to more accurate predictions and expectations about a stranger's meaning and behavior.

Ting-Toomey emphasizes the interactive nature of intercultural communication in this definition, "the symbolic exchange process whereby individuals from two (or more) different cultural communities negotiate shared meanings in an interactive situation"(1999: 16–17). *Cultural communities* are "groups of interacting individuals within a bounded unit who uphold a set of shared traditions and way of life" (Ting-Toomey, 1999: 18). The *symbols* they use are verbal and non-verbal. The *exchange process* is an interdependent one – two cultural strangers find themselves in a mutually interdependent, transactional relationship in which they are simultaneously encoding and decoding messages that influence the other person's communication. Furthermore, the intercultural process is irreversible (Barnlund, 1962) because receivers may not form the same impression to repeated messages, and they may not change their reaction to a communication the sender wants to "take back" and edit. Shared meanings are *negotiated* in a creative, give-and-take process that involves adaptation and multiple levels of meaning (Ting-Toomey, 1999). The *interactive situation* refers to both concrete (physical setting, equipment, seating arrangements) and intangible or psychological features (such as behavioral scripts, goals, motivations, norms, roles, social skills, etc.) (Burgoon et al., 1996).

The interaction of cross-cultural communication often faces barriers to success. "Unfortunately, more often than not, intercultural encounters are filled with misunderstandings and second guesses because of language problems, communication style differences, and value orientation differences" (Ting-Toomey, 1999: 18). Accordingly, Gudykunst and Kim's (1997) well-accepted intercultural communication model highlights the filters present in intercultural communication. Their model depicts messages and feedback flowing between Person A and Person B that are transmitted and interpreted through the filters of cultural, sociocultural (e.g., social identity) and psychocultural (e.g., attitudes) influences. These filters are mechanisms that delimit the number of alternatives used to transmit and interpret messages, thereby limiting the predictions made about how people from another culture might respond to communication behavior. The filters also delimit what stimuli are attended to and how incoming messages are interpreted. In the next section of the chapter we turn to how these filters affect the communication process in global organizational learning.

INTERCULTURAL COMMUNICATION BARRIERS TO ORGANIZATIONAL LEARNING

Based on our experiences with MNCs and an examination of the intercultural literature, we will address those factors or barriers in cross-cultural communication in the following sections that most directly influence organizational learning, generally by delimiting how messages are perceived and interpreted. The transactional nature of intercultural

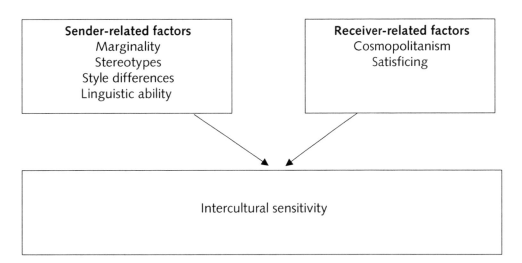

Figure 11.1   Intercultural communication factors that affect organizational learning

communication indicates that the parties involved are simultaneously senders and receivers, but for ease of categorization, we have divided the factors into sender- and receiver-related categories as shown in figure 11.1. The sender-related factors consist of marginality, stereotypes, style differences that distinguish senders and receivers, and the linguistic ability of the sender. The receiver-related category includes the receivers' cosmopolitanism and their tendencies toward satisficing and plateauing of cultural knowledge. The aggregate of the factors that affect senders and receivers can be seen as their degree of intercultural sensitivity (M. Bennett, 1993), which in turn relates to an MNC's "level of readiness" and potential for organizational learning. While we have chosen these factors carefully based on the cross-cultural communication literature, because this is a pioneering conceptual work, there is no way to gauge the relative weight and validity of these factors in global organizational learning without future empirical research.

Sender-related intercultural communication barriers to organizational learning

Marginality of the sender   Marginality plays an important role in intercultural interactions. Cultural marginality refers to people who have internalized two or more cultural frames of reference (Stonequist, 1932). This can lead to internal culture shock as two cultural voices vie for attention (J. Bennett, 1993). Marginal people are often ideally suited to boundary spanning or mediating roles between cultures (Bochner, 1982), since they understand both cultures objectively and subjectively. For example, some expatriates interpret the actions of the foreign subsidiaries to headquarters and vice versa, thereby contributing to organizational learning. There is, however, a less positive aspect to marginality. "Marginal people [such as expatriates] feel that they live on the periphery rather than at the center of a group or community" (Osland, 1995: 113). This can translate into less opportunity to speak or be heard because they are not members of the dominant coalition. They may also consciously or unconsciously monitor their communication to reflect their marginal role.

With regard to organizational learning in MNCs, perceived marginality affects perception and, thus, the influence of the sender. This is reminiscent of Huber's (1991) reference to the status and power of the receiver as a potential barrier to information transfer. In many MNCs, employees who are not in the home country of the firm are seen as "marginal." Even well-respected expatriates who have been sent from the home country can become marginalized by their physical absence from the corporate office. Ironically, people on the margins of organizations sometimes have a more accurate view of events and circumstances than central decision-makers. Their position on the margin may bring them access to broader sources of information, and in high power distance cultures (Hofstede, 1980), information is sometimes less censored in their presence. Yet, because the MNC views senders as marginal, the information or knowledge they transmit is considered of less value or relevance than similar information from a member within the home country. An organizational norm becomes established that discourages either seeking information from the marginal members, or from granting much attention when such people volunteer information. A classic example is the well-known 19th-century incident of a low-level US Navy lieutenant on a posting in the China Seas who proposed a radical and extremely beneficial modification of sea fighting that was assiduously ignored by the War Department in Washington until Abraham Lincoln personally intervened to champion the innovation (Tushman and O'Reilly, 1997).

Perceived marginality can hamper both individuals and organizational units. The organization as a whole can marginalize all managers operating in foreign affiliates, including host-country, third-country, and expatriate managers, as well as certain affiliates (Inkpen and Dinur, 1998). In particular, affiliates in smaller foreign countries that neither command nor produce significant resources (Gupta and Govindajaran, 1991) are likely to be marginalized. Information and knowledge flowing from them is likely to have little influence on the knowledge base or decision-making of either the home office or other units.

Generally speaking, marginality has to do with lack of membership in the dominant coalition of the organization, but it can also pertain to horizontal relations and individual communications. For example, a Japanese manager employed by an American MNC in Tokyo may be very receptive to information provided by the home office. He may, however, discount the same kind of information if it is received from a Korean manager in the company's affiliate in Seoul. This perceived marginality of the Korean is due to the historical animosity between Korea and Japan and the cultural superiority that many Japanese feel they have over Koreans. This example points to the relationship between marginality and stereotypes.

Stereotypes concerning the stranger   Stereotyping is "an exaggerated set of expectations and beliefs about the attributes of a group membership category . . . an overgeneralization without any attempt to perceive individual variations" (Ting-Toomey, 1999: 161). According to research, stereotypes are based on relatively little information, are resistant to change even in light of new information, and are rarely accurately applied to specific individuals (Christensen and Rosenthal, 1982; McCauley et al., 1980). Stereotypes affect the senders' ability to communicate their messages because they interfere with their ability to be "heard" and accurately judged. In a similar fashion, the senders' marginality interferes with their ability to be seen and heard. The senders' stereotype about receivers determines how much and what type of information they will share with them.

Stereotypes combine with attitudes (such as prejudice) to create expectations of how strangers will behave. These expectations, in turn, influence the way in which people interpret incoming stimuli and the predictions they make about strangers' behavior. "Using our frame of reference invariably leads to misinterpretations of the strangers' messages, as well as inaccurate predictions about their future behavior" (Gudykunst and Kim, 1997: 48). While stereotyping is very normal behavior, it can inhibit organizational learning, particularly across organizational boundaries. If HQ staff does not expect to hear solid, innovative ideas from certain nationalities, they may not pay careful attention to all the information coming from the field. Subsidiaries can also discount input coming from headquarters if they do not perceive corporate staff as competent.

It should be noted that stereotyping is not always viewed as negative behavior in intercultural communication. Adler (2002) writes that stereotypes can be helpful if they are consciously held, descriptive rather than evaluative, accurate, and viewed as a "first best guess" about a group or person, which means they are subject to modification once first-hand experience is obtained. When people are willing to continue learning about strangers, stereotypes are not necessarily harmful. In the absence of learning, however, stereotyping leads to a reduction in intercultural communication effectiveness.

Like individuals, organizations may hold stereotypes in the form of mental maps and shared assumptions. An organizational norm may exist, for example, in a Japanese MNC that Americans are so individualistic that no knowledge concerning effective team functioning could possible exist in the company's US subsidiary. Even if the US subsidiary were to share codified or tacit knowledge about techniques for creating effective team functioning, the HQ in Japan is likely to ignore this knowledge because of stereotypes about Americans that are reflected in organizational values and norms.

Individual behavior can be affected by stereotypes as well, with negative consequences for organizational learning. A US HQ staff person may receive a report from a French manager concerning dangerous moves by competitors in Europe and dismiss the news as an overreaction by "those emotional French." Thus, the stereotypes that individuals hold within the MNC can seriously, and negatively, affect the ability of senders to have their messages heard by key processors of information and knowledge.

Communication style differences Another factor that has an effect on communication in global organizational learning is the area of communication style differences. The potential effect of communication style on organizational learning has received only passing attention in research on global organizational learning. Yet there is no doubt that it exists. In their study of organizational learning in a new intercultural team, Heavens and Child (1999) found that the Japanese members failed to communicate important information to British members. In this case, the Japanese communication reticence and formality with strangers led to a slowdown in reaching the team's goal.

Cultural and ethnic identities influence verbal and non-verbal communication styles (Ting-Toomey, 1999: 100). Mutual clarity is extremely hard to achieve without an

TABLE 11.1   Cultural communication styles

Verbal style	Major characteristic
High- versus low-context	Meaning conveyed in context versus explicit verbal message
Direct versus indirect	Explicit versus implicit, camouflaged message
Person-oriented versus status-oriented	Emphasis on unique, personal identities versus honoring prescribed power-based membership identities
Self-enhancement versus self-effacement	Emphasis on boasting about accomplishments and abilities versus humility and self-deprecation
Succinct – exacting – elaborate	Low to moderate to high quantities of talk

understanding of these style differences, but a limited number of MNCs make the effort to educate their employees in intercultural communication. Table 11.1 presents the most common style differences that affect organizational learning: high versus low context, direct versus indirect, person-oriented versus status-oriented, self-enhancing versus self-effacing, and elaborate versus succinct styles.[1]

1   *High- versus low-context communication.* According to Hall (1976), low-context communication relies on explicit verbal messages to convey intention or meaning. In contrast, high-context communication tends to transmit intention or meaning via the context (such as social roles or positions) and the non-verbal channels (such as pauses, silence, tone of voice). High-context communication involves multi-layered contexts (e.g. historical context, social norms, roles, situational and relational contexts), and the listener is expected to "read between the lines" of indirect messages. In contrast, the onus lies on the sender in low-context communication to transmit a clear, direct message that listeners can easily decode (Ting-Toomey, 1999: 101). Knowledge transfer occurs differently and may be misinterpreted between high- and low-context communicators.

2   *Direct versus indirect verbal styles.* These styles are differentiated by "the extent to which intentions are revealed by tone of voice and the straightforwardness of the content message"(Ting-Toomey, 1999: 103). In the direct style, the speaker's intentions are specified in a forthright tone of voice; in the indirect style, in contrast, verbal statements hide the speaker's meaning, which is conveyed in nuances. Failure to understand these style differences allows for misinterpretation. Westerners, who prefer a direct style, often perceive the indirect style of the Chinese as "insincere and untrustworthy" (Graf, 1994). The indirect style, characterized by an unwillingness to say "no" directly or to force others into that position, allows for greater face-saving. People from cultures using indirect styles may perceive those with a direct style as both blunt and obtuse (Ting-Toomey, 1999). People and organizations with a direct style may be unaware that an indirect communicator is even trying to transfer knowledge to them.

3   *Person-oriented versus status-oriented verbal styles.* The person-oriented verbal style is individual centered and emphasizes the importance of informality and role suspension. The status-oriented verbal style is role centered and emphasizes formality and large power

distance (Ting-Toomey, 1999: 106). Power distance is the extent to which a society accepts the fact that power in institutions and organizations is distributed unequally (Hofstede, 1980). Koreans and Japanese are status-oriented whereas US Americans are person-oriented. This style difference sometimes makes for uncomfortable interactions and misinterpretations; it may also determine who talks with whom in the hierarchy, who is allowed to come up with new knowledge and pass it along, and how much information and knowledge is shared.

4   *Self-enhancement versus self-effacement verbal styles.* "The self-enhancement verbal style emphasizes the importance of boasting about one's accomplishments and abilities. The self-effacement verbal style, on the other hand, emphasizes the importance of humbling oneself via verbal restraints, hesitations, modest talk, and the use of self-deprecation concerning one's effort or performance" (Ting-Toomey, 1999: 107). Collectivist Asian cultures are generally self-effacing while Arab and African-American cultures are self-enhancing (Ting-Toomey, 1999). A person from a self-effacing culture may be so modest about knowledge they have acquired that people from self-enhancing cultures pay no attention. In contrast, the self-enhancers' boastful mode of transferring knowledge may be so distasteful to people from self-effacing cultures that they ignore or sabotage an effort at organizational learning.

5   *Succinct versus elaborate verbal styles.* This style refers to the amount of talk with which people feel comfortable. The continuum of speech quantity ranges from *succinct* (low quantity) to *exacting* (precision and "just the right" amount of words) to *elaborate* (high quantity) (Gudykunst and Ting-Toomey, 1988). The elaborate style, found in Arab cultures, also includes detailed descriptions, repetition, verbal elaboration and exaggeration, and the use of metaphor, similes, and proverbs. The exacting style, typical of England, Germany, and Sweden, emphasizes clarity and precise meanings. These cultures perceive the use of too many words as exaggeration while the use of too few words is viewed as ambiguous. The succinct style, manifested in China, Japan, Korea, and Thailand, is characterized by understatements, and meaningful pauses and silences (Gudykunst and Ting-Toomey, 1988). Rather than simply noting that another culture uses more or fewer words to communicate, these style differences are often the cause of cultural misattributions. People with a succinct style may discount elaborate speakers as illogical or inefficient and even stop listening to them. Elaborate speakers may assume succinct communicators have very little to say or contribute. Both these scenarios impact the effective transfer of knowledge. In multicultural meetings and teams, highly verbal US Americans sometimes fill in the silences and do not allow enough room for people with a more succinct style (or for non-native speakers) to talk.

Ting-Toomey concludes, "In individualistic cultures, people find themselves in numerous contexts that call for direct talk, person-oriented verbal interaction, verbal self-enhancement, and talkativeness. In contrast, in collectivistic cultures, people tend to encounter more situations that emphasize the preferential use of indirect talk, status-oriented verbal interaction, verbal self-effacement, and silence" (1999: 103).

Linguistic ability   The lack of language comprehension and fluency constitute other barriers to organizational learning. In addition to the obvious obstacles of mutual understanding and ease of transaction, people tend to restrict their communication to those who speak their own language. When large MNCs buy local companies in another country, they sometimes appoint as their liaison or local manager the host-country national who is most fluent in the language of the home country of the MNC. This person is not necessarily the most competent or best able to teach them about the local subsidiary and context; however, the transaction costs of communicating with them are the lowest.

Receiver-related intercultural communication barriers to organizational learning

While the sender may encounter barriers to communicating information and knowledge to others for the reasons outlined above, the other part of the communication dyad is the receiver. Both the organization and individuals within the organization are potential receivers of information and knowledge critical to organizational learning.

There are two major factors that can affect the receptivity of both organizations and individuals: cosmopolitanism and satisficing behaviors.

Cosmopolitanism   Cosmopolitanism is an attitudinal stance or mindset that indicates an orientation toward the outside world (Merton, 1957). As originally conceived, it emphasized people who are oriented towards the outside world, and contrasted them with "locals" who are more focused on local affairs (Merton, 1957). While later this was expanded to include a distinction between those in organizations who are oriented to a reference group outside the firm (Gouldner, 1957, 1958), it is this original external orientation to the world upon which we will draw. With increasing globalization, the concept of cosmopolitanism has received renewed attention, with an added emphasis on a willingness to engage with the external world. Hannerz (1996: 103) describes it in this fashion.

> A more genuine cosmopolitanism is first of all an orientation, a willingness to engage with the Other. It entails an intellectual and esthetic openness toward divergent cultural experiences, a search for contrasts rather than uniformity. To become acquainted with more cultures is to turn into an *aficionado*, to view them as artworks. At the same time, however, cosmopolitanism can be a matter of competence, and competence of both a generalized and more specialized kind. There is the aspect of a state of readiness, a personal ability to make one's way into other cultures, through listening, looking, intuiting, and reflecting. And there is cultural competence in the stricter sense of the term, a built-up skill in maneuvering more or less expertly with a particular system of meanings.

Cosmopolitanism can thus be seen as related to a key concept in intercultural communication called mindfulness. According to Thich (1991), this term means attending to one's internal assumptions, cognitions, and emotions, and simultaneously being attuned to the other's assumptions, cognitions, and emotions. It also involves being open to novelty and unfamiliar behavior (Ting-Toomey, 1999: 267–8). Langer wrote that mindfulness involves learning to (1) see behavior or information presented in the situation as novel or fresh; (2) view a situation from several vantage points or perspectives; (3) attend to the context and the person in which we are perceiving the behavior; and (4) create new categories through which this new behavior may be understood (1997: 111). In addition, cosmopolitanism at the organizational level can be seen as related to Kim's (1993) concept of organizational intrusiveness, or the willingness of the organization to look outside itself, as well as to Cohen and Levinthal's (1990) concept of absorptive capacity, which is the ability of an organization to recognize the value of new, external information and integrate it into existing knowledge.

In sum, the cosmopolitanism of the receiver is an important attitude that can influence the effectiveness of communication in global organizational learning. If a receiver at headquarters (or headquarters as a whole) is not interested in the external environment and not willing to engage with it, it is likely that she will ignore incoming communication as irrelevant to her local concerns, whether those are headquarters politics or knowledge produced at headquarters. It is not that she has a prejudice per se against externally generated knowledge, but simply a lack of interest in it. Equally, those in local operations may be so locally oriented that they are uninterested in external operations and even if exposed to potentially useful information or knowledge generated elsewhere in the firm, ignore it. In either case, the receiver is certainly not seeking information relevant to organizational learning from external (i.e. external to their own site) sources due to a lack of interest and curiosity, and thus miss potentially valuable input.

Satisficing Satisficing is the second factor that influences receivers. In decision-making this term refers to accepting a decision that is "good enough" because the costs of maximizing are too great (Simon, 1976). In an intercultural context, we find satisficing in two areas – the plateauing that occurs in both language acquisition and cultural understanding (Osland, 1995: Osland and Bird, 2000). When these skills are good enough to get by, some people stop learning. There is no motivation to reach a higher level of fluency or understanding until a trigger event occurs, which initiates another round of cultural sensemaking (Osland and Bird, 2001) or a return to the dictionary or language teacher.

In terms of organizational learning, satisficing occurs when firms or individuals assume they understand enough to get by and be effective in a global context. MNCs that are not experiencing negative business results in foreign markets, or who are protected from the consequences of negative business results by subsidies at home, may feel satisfied with the level of cultural knowledge they have. It can be argued that until the late 1980s many Japanese MNCs had high levels of satisficing behavior with regard to intercultural communication. The economic recession of the 1990s and the problems many Japanese MNCs have faced with overseas operations, such as Matsushita's troubles in Hollywood, have caused a re-examination of their level of intercultural understanding.

Individuals can also exhibit satisficing behaviors, particularly when their focus is restricted to short-term business goals. A US technical manager in a US MNC's subsidiary in China may have learned enough language and cultural knowledge to get by on a day-to-day basis when that country was still at an early stage of market opening, with few highly qualified engineers available. He may not realize 15 years later that the skills and knowledge of the young Chinese engineers he is working with are considerably more sophisticated. Because the US technical manager is still using a set of behaviors that was good enough to get by in the short term, he is unlikely to recognize that the information environment around him has changed unless a trigger event, such as widespread resignations, occurs to jolt him out of his complacency. Whether the manager responds to the trigger event depends in part on his level of readiness to continue learning about his work setting and the other culture.

Intercultural sensitivity and levels of readiness

The third box in figure 11.1 represents an overall level of readiness to communicate in ways that are beneficial to global organizational learning. We have labeled this "intercultural sensitivity," and it can be seen in this instance as a composite of the individual receiver and sender factors described above. We posit that both MNCs as a whole as well as the individuals within them have differing levels of "readiness to transfer" information and knowledge across borders The readiness to learn and transfer knowledge in a global organization rests on a threshold level of intercultural sensitivity. The highest level of cross-cultural adaptation involves conscious efforts to learn from the stranger. Cross-cultural adaptation and organizational learning are discrete, but linked, forms of learning (Levinson and Asahi, 1995).

> Apparently, a party's ability to take advantage of the learning opportunities in an IJV [international joint venture] may depend partially on its propensity to engage with an alien culture, an area of responsibility often left to the host country. For example, joint learning is rare in US–Chinese IJVs because US partners tend to force unilateral learning on their Chinese counterparts (Child and Markoczy, 1993). This is unfortunate; if US IJV managers only play the role of teacher, they can hardly acquire cultural knowledge such as organizational networking and supplier/customer relations . . . Presumably, the greater the cultural learning, the greater is the skill transfer and the better is the IJV performance (Lin and Germain, 1999: 17).

The overall willingness to engage the other culture is best described in Milton Bennett's (1993) developmental model of intercultural sensitivity (DMIS). This taxonomy describes the stages that people move through in their acquisition of intercultural competence. The model assumes that as one's experience of cultural difference becomes more sophisticated, one's competence in intercultural relations increases (Bennett and Bennett, 2002: 13). Among other uses, it assesses the "developmental readiness" of students to pursue certain kinds of intercultural learning by placing them in one of the six categories shown in figure 11.2 (Bennett and Bennett, 2002). These six stages can be usefully applied to understand how a composite of the various factors discussed above can describe the level of readiness of either an individual or an organization to effectively engage in global organizational learning.

The DMIS model is used to describe both individuals and organizations. "When a significant number of people in an organization have worldviews at one of the DMIS stages, the organization can be said to be characterized by that stage. What constitutes a "significant number" may depend on a number of factors, such as the formal and informal power of those particular people and the extent to which they constitute a critical mass in the organization (Bennett and Bennett, 2002: 16).

The model has six stages that are grouped into two major categories: ethnocentric and ethnorelative. Both individuals and companies falling within the ethnocentric level "can

Figure 11.2   Bennett's developmental model of intercultural sensitivity

be seen as . . . avoiding cultural difference, either by denying its existence, by raising defenses against it, or by minimizing its importance" (Bennett and Bennett, 2002: 14). In all three stages, one's own culture is experienced as central to reality – hence the term "ethnocentric." In contrast, people experience their own culture in the context of other cultures in the ethnorelative stages (Bennett and Bennett, 2002: 14). Companies and individuals seek cultural difference, "either by accepting its importance, by adapting a perspective to take it into account, or by integrating the whole concept into a definition of identity" (ibid.).

We hypothesize that there is a correlation between intercultural sensitivity and the readiness to transfer knowledge in global organizational learning. The willingness to question assumptions, the openness to knowledge regardless of its origin, and the high level of multidirectional communication necessary for organizational learning is more likely to be found in organizations that have reached the ethnorelative stages. Based on our examination of the factors listed above, we would expect ethnocentric organizations and individuals to show a greater tendency to marginalize other organizational members and units, to be more prone to stereotyping, and to be less conscious and tolerant of communication style differences and less flexible in adapting to other styles. We would also expect them to be less cosmopolitan and show a greater tendency toward satisficing.

In order to increase organizational learning in MNCs, it is necessary to move both organizations and individuals toward the ethnorelative level of readiness. Attempting to change only one of these will result in either the organization instituting organizational policies and espousing a set of values it cannot implement, or creating a large set of employees whose higher level of ethnorelativism is not matched by organizational structures, policies and norms.

Trigger events and increased readiness to learn   We argue that both organizations and individuals are unlikely to move from the ethnocentric to the ethnorelative level of readiness without a disruption of some sort. These disruptions can be viewed as trigger events (Griffith, 1999) that cause the actors to become consciously engaged and question previous schemas of interpretation. Louis and Sutton (1991) identified three types of triggers. First, switching to a conscious mode is provoked when one experiences a situation as *unusual or novel* – when something "stands out of the ordinary," "is unique," or when the "unfamiliar" or "previously unknown" is experienced. Second, switching is also provoked by *discrepancy* – when "acts are in some way frustrated," when there is "an unexpected failure," a "disruption," "a troublesome . . . situation," when there is a significant difference between expectations and reality. The third trigger event refers to *deliberate initiatives*, usually in response to an internal or external request for an increased level of conscious attention – as when people are "asked to think" or "explicitly questioned" (Louis and Sutton, 1991: 60).

For an organization, the first kind of situation – an unusual or novel experience – can occur when a group or unit within the global network makes a positive and unexpected contribution of information or knowledge that has an impact on organizational performance. Hewlett-Packard, for example, had to re-examine its organizational view of the capabilities of its Singaporean affiliate when presented with a clear example of the ability of the Singaporean design team to move beyond adaptation to innovation. When such questioning leads to changes in attitude about the marginality of a particular unit, as well as a re-examination of the organization's view of its foreign operations, the trigger event moves the firm toward a more ethnorelative level of readiness.

For individuals, a similar trigger can occur when they are presented with valuable information or knowledge from an organizational member previously stereotyped as incapable of providing valuable input. A manager in the HQ of a Spanish telecommunications MNC might receive a report from its Chilean subsidiary on an innovative approach to billing customers for mobile services. Realizing that the innovation greatly enhanced return on investment and is applicable world-wide could force the Spanish manager to re-examine her stereotypes about Chileans and other Latin American nationals, thus moving her toward greater ethnorelativism and openness to learning from international colleagues.

A trigger event can also be negative, a discrepancy between what is desired and what is obtained. For an organization, this could be the success of competitors' moves in its overseas markets and a consequent fall in its own performance. The experience of Procter & Gamble in Japan in the 1970s illustrates this kind of trigger. When P&G first acquired a medium-sized Japanese firm to manufacture its disposable diapers, it held 100 percent of the Japanese market due to its first mover status. However, it ignored the input from the managers in its Japanese subsidiary and failed to adjust the product to fit the smaller size of Japanese babies and other considerations of Japanese mothers. It soon found that Japanese competitors flooded the market with their own disposable diapers, which led to a drop of more than 70 percent in P&G's market share in Japan. The company had been satisficing, basing its behavior on a superficial understanding of Japanese employees and the local context and failing to re-examine its assumptions. The reduced market share was a trigger event that led to a change in the way the company interacted with its Japanese subsidiary.

For individuals, such as the HQ-based leader of a global team, a discrepancy could include the inability to reach the goals set for the team. The leader could be facing possible negative impacts on his compensation or promotion. Examination of the hindrances to effective team performance could make the leader more aware of his tendency to discount important information or ideas because they were couched in elaborate descriptions rather than the succinct style he preferred. As a result, he might be motivated to learn more about communication style differences and attempt to reconcile his own language style with that of other team members.

Finally, an outside event such as a corporate initiative or training program can lead people to re-examine aspects of their intercultural communication. For organizations, this could include a change in corporate leadership, with a subsequent change in vision and norms. The CEO of a chemical company with a global strategy decided that international experience should be a prerequisite for promotion to senior management. The corporation's heroes became those people who worked abroad. Repatriates were promoted and given strategic responsibilities, which made it easier to transfer their knowledge back to headquarters. The firm acquired global expertise and transformed a formerly parochial mindset to a global mindset in a relatively short time frame.

For individuals, a deliberate initiative and important disruption often involves training. Hult et al. (2000), for example, found in their international study of organizational learning among supply chain managers that those who had received training in understanding and using organizational learning concepts had better supply chain relationships. One could argue that the training enhanced the cosmopolitanism of these individuals, leading to greater effectiveness in intercultural communication and learning with others in the supply chain.

DISCUSSION

To summarize, the process of intercultural communication affects organizational learning at both the individual and the organizational level. Sender- and receiver-related factors influence how messages are perceived and interpreted, and they filter the exchange of ideas in a global organization. This results in both individuals and organizations having varying levels of intercultural sensitivity that can be characterized as either ethnocentric or ethnorelative (M. Bennett, 1993). Trigger events – novelty, discrepancy, and deliberate initiatives (Louis and Sutton, 1991) – can help move people and firms to higher stages of ethnorelativism and global organizational learning.

On the surface, there appear to be linkages between intercultural sensitivity and the capacity for organizational learning. Further research is needed to test whether ethnorelative organizations are more successful at organizational learning and whether people with high levels of intercultural communication competence are more skilled at organizational learning.

To move individuals to higher levels of intercultural sensitivity, Bennett and Bennett (2002) recommend different types of training and experience for each stage. Their work provokes several questions for organizational learning scholars. Is it possible to identify discrete stages of organizational readiness to learn globally and, if so, do we have the knowledge to move organizations up these stages? We can readily borrow the ethnocentric and ethnorelative terms and apply them to an organization's openness to knowledge that is created with and outside corporate headquarters, similar to Perlmutter's (1969) taxonomy. Would the identification of more narrow and discrete stages lead us to more systematic ideas for increasing organizational readiness to learn?

When we turn our attention to practical implications, the most obvious way to diminish the effects of intercultural communication filters is more training and emphasis on intercultural communication for members of global organizations. Research could determine whether more intercultural training and intercultural sensitivity correlates with a higher level of both global organizational learning and firm performance, a relationship suggested by prior research. For example, individual communication-related factors discussed in this chapter, such as stereotyping and prejudice have been found to decline as a result of contact with other racial and ethnic groups (Williams, 1947; Allport, 1954). Contact is needed not only between national groups, but also between different organizational cultures and different professions. In addition, more managerial attention could focus on the effects of marginality versus inclusion, and on policies and practices that unwittingly reinforce unequal status. Managers must also recognize that while the diversity inherent in an MNC can be a positive factor in organizational learning, as mentioned previously, stress is inherent in intercultural encounters, as evidenced in the literature on culture shock (Furnham and Bochner, 1986; Kim, 1988, 1989a) and intergroup anxiety (Barna, 1983; Gudykunst and Ting-Toomey, 1988; Stephan and Stephan, 1985). Learning to anticipate and deliberately manage this stress and anxiety could facilitate the transfer of knowledge.

Future research must also answer some important questions raised by this chapter. First and foremost is to determine whether the set of intercultural communication factors chosen for discussion here are indeed the complete set of those most relevant to global organizational learning. While drawn from prior research into intercultural communication in general, in the absence of prior research the authors have chosen this set as because that most likely to affect organizational learning based their own knowledge of and experience with MNCs. Along with this must come a determination of the relative weights each of these factors has in affecting successful transfer of knowledge in global firms. Again, without empirical research specific to this research question, it is difficult to even predict which factors might be most important in explaining successful intercultural communication in global organizational learning.

A further question pertains to the relative importance of individual versus organizational actors in the intercultural communication process. Are highly ethnorelative firms in which most individual employees lag behind more or less successful than firms in which the opposite is true? The challenge of finding firms with these various configurations will make research into this area difficult and requiring of creative research methodologies. Yet answering the question could be an important task as the answer is likely to influence how scarce managerial resources are allocated in global firms wishing to increase their global organizational learning.

Finally it is important to note that this chapter does not argue that effective intercultural communication is the most important determinant of global organizational learning. While we have argued that communication is extremely important, particularly for transfer of tacit knowledge between individuals and groups, in MNCs, it may be that other mechanisms are just as important to global organizational learning, such as information systems. Given the nature of global competition today we believe that it is unlikely that a mechanistic system that rests on the transfer of largely archival or explicit knowledge can be a substitute for individual and organizational communication as described in this chapter. However, we recognize that establishing the veracity of this belief is an empirical question requiring future research.

A second suggestion for decreasing stereotyping and prejudice in MNCs comes from research on intergroup contact theory, which maintains that prejudice declines as a result of contact with other racial and ethnic groups (Williams, 1947; Allport, 1954). A recent meta-analysis of hundreds of studies concluded that contact does reduce prejudice when it is facilitated by (1) equal status; (2) group interdependent efforts toward common goals; (3) high potential for cross-group friendship; (4) positive experiences that counter negative stereotypes; and (5) authority sanction (Pettigrew and Tropp, 2000). MNCs could devote more attention and energy to these facilitating factors. Contact is needed not only between national groups, but also between different organizational cultures and different professions. More managerial attention, as well as research, could focus on the effects of marginality versus inclusion and on policies and practices that unwittingly reinforce unequal status.

The greater heterogeneity and diversity of viewpoints and experiences found in MNCs can be a positive factor in organizational learning. There are, however, transaction costs to multicultural work that affect global learning. First, relationships among different national or professional groups involve "intergroup postures" that often cause "in-group loyalties" and "out-group discrimination" (Brewer and Miller, 1984; Brown and Turner, 1981). "We-they" groups accentuate the perceived differences that divide them and are subject to attribution errors – inaccurate assumptions about the behavior of strangers, which are closely related to ethnocentrism and prejudice (Brewer and Miller, 1984). These tendencies are more pronounced when the groups involved have a history of dominance/subjugation or wide discrepancies in power and prestige (Kim, 1989b). In MNCs, employees' expectations and interpretations of the behavior of people and groups from other cultures are frequently inaccurate, which can affect work performance as well as organizational learning.

An awareness of these transaction costs and a deliberate effort to manage them could facilitate the transfer of knowledge. This leads us back to the theme of mindfulness. If the intercultural communication process is both transactional and irreversible, that argues for paying more attention to the way employees of global firms, as well as the firms themselves, communicate and working to ensure that communications elicit more rather than less organizational learning. Mindfulness also involves increased awareness of the ethnocentric tendencies manifested in attitudes, policies, and procedures. Finally, mindfulness means identifying intercultural competence knowledge in the firm and transferring and institutionalizing that knowledge throughout the organization. By doing so, MNCs can eliminate some of the filters that impede organizational learning.

NOTE

1. There are other communication differences related to culture, such as monochronic versus polychronic time schedules and instrumental versus affective styles, but they appear to have less potential direct impact on organizational learning.

REFERENCES

Adler, N. (2002) *International Dimensions of Organizational Behavior*, 4th edn. Cincinnati, OH: South-Western.

Allport, G.W. (1954) *The Nature of Prejudice*. Reading, MA: Addison-Wesley.

Apfelthaler, G. and Karmasin, M. (1998) Do You Manage Globally or Does Culture Matter All? Paper presented at the *Academy of Management Conference*, San Diego, CA.

Barna, L. (1983) The Stress Factor in Intercultural Relations. In D. Landis and R. Brislin (eds.), *Handbook of Intercultural Training*. Vol. 2: *Issues in Training Methodology*. New York: Pergamon, 19–49.

Barney, J. (1991) Firm Resources and Sustained Competitive Advantage. *Journal of Management*, 17: 99–120.

Barnlund, D. (1962) Toward a Meaning-centered Philosophy of Communication. *Journal of Communication*, 2: 197–211.

Bartlett, C. and Ghoshal, S. (1989) *Managing Across Borders*. Boston: Harvard Business School Press.

Bartlett, C. and Ghoshal, S. (2000) *Transnational Management*. Boston: Irwin McGraw-Hill.

Bennett, J. (1993) Cultural Marginality: Identity Issues in Intercultural Training. In R.M. Paige (ed.), *Education for the Intercultural Experience*. Yarmouth, ME: Intercultural Press, 109–35.

Bennett, J.M. and Bennett, M.J. (2002) Developing Intercultural Sensitivity: An Integrative Approach to Global and Domestic Diversity. In D. Landis, J.M. Bennett, and M.J. Bennett (eds.), *The Handbook of Intercultural Training*. Thousand Oaks, CA: Sage (in press).

Bennett, M. (1993) Towards Ethnorelativism: A Developmental Model of Intercultural Sensitivity. In R.M. Paige (ed.), *Education for the Intercultural Experience*. Yarmouth, ME: Intercultural Press, 21–71.

Bernhut, S. (2001) Measuring the Value of Intellectual Capital. *Ivey Business Journal*, 65 (4): 16–20.

Birkinshaw, J. (2001) Making Sense of Knowledge Management. *Ivey Business Journal*, 65 (4): 32–6.

Bochner, S. (ed.) (1982) *The Mediating Person: Bridges between Cultures*. Boston: Hall.

Brewer, M.B. and Miller, N. (1984) Beyond the Contact Hypothesis: Theoretical Perspectives on Desegregation. In N. Miller and M. Brewer (eds.), *Groups in Contact: The Psychology of Desegregation*. New York: Academic Press, 281–302.

Brown, J.S. and Duguid, P. (1991) Organizational Learning and Communities-of-practice: Toward a Unified View of Working, Learning, and Innovation. *Organization Science*, 2 (1): 40–57.

Brown, R. and Turner, J. (1981) Interpersonal and Intergroup Behavior. In J. Turner and H. Giles (eds.), *Intergroup Behavior*. Chicago: University of Chicago Press, 33–65.

Burgoon, J., Buller, D., and Woodall, W.G. (1996) *Nonverbal Communication: The Unspoken Dialogue*, 2nd edn). New York: McGraw-Hill.

Child, J. and Markoczy, L. (1993) Host-country Managerial Behavior and Learning in Chinese and Hungarian Joint Ventures. *Journal of Management Studies*, 30 (4): 611–31.

Christensen, D. and Rosenthal, R. (1982) Gender and Nonverbal Decoding Skill as Determinants of Interpersonal Expectancy Effects. *Journal of Personality and Social Psychology* 42: 75–87.

Cohen, A.P. (1985) *The Symbolic Construction of Community*. London/New York: Routledge.

Cohen, W. and Levinthal, D. (1990) Absorptive Capacity: A New Perspective on Learning and Innovation. *Administrative Science Quarterly*, 35 (1): 128–52.

Cook, S. and Yanow, D. (1993) Culture and Organizational Learning. *Journal of Management Inquiry*, 2: 373–90.

Daft, R. and Weick, K. (1984) Toward a Model of Organizations as Interpretation Systems. *Academy of Management Review*, 3: 546–63.

De Geus, A. (1988) Planning as Learning. *Harvard Business Review*, 66 (2): 70–4.

Furnham, A. and Bochner, S. (1986) *Culture Shock: Psychological Reactions to Unfamiliar Environments*. London: Methuen.

Garvin, D. (1993) Building a Learning Organization. *Harvard Business Review*, 71 (4): 78–92.

Gouldner, A.W. (1957) Cosmopolitans and Locals: Toward an Analysis of Latent Social Roles – I. *Administrative Science Quarterly*, 2: 281–306.

Gouldner, A.W. (1958) Cosmopolitans and Locals: Toward an Analysis of Latent Social Roles – II. *Administrative Science Quarterly*, 2: 444–80.

Graf, J. (1994) Views on Chinese. In Y. Bao (ed.), *Zhong guo ren, ni shou le shen me zhu zhou? [Chinese People, What Have You Been Cursed With?]* Taipai, Taiwan: Xing Guang Ban She.

Griffith, T.L. (1999) Technology Features as Triggers for Sensemaking. *Academy of Management Review*, 24 (3): 472–88.

Gudykunst, W. and Kim, Y.Y. (1997) *Communicating with Strangers: An Approach to Intercultural Communication.* Boston: McGraw-Hill.

Gudykunst, W. and Ting-Toomey, S. with Chua, E. (1988) *Culture and Interpersonal Communication.* Newbury Park, CA: Sage.

Gupta, A. and Govindarajan, V. (1991) Knowledge Flows and the Structure of Control within Multinational Corporations. *Academy of Management Review*, 16 (4): 768–92.

Hall, E.T. (1976) *Beyond Culture.* Garden City, NY: Anchor Press/Doubleday.

Hannerz, U. (1996) Cosmopolitans and Locals in World Culture. In U. Hannerz, *Transnational Connections: Culture, People, Places.* London: Routledge, 102–11.

Hamel, G. and Prahalad, C.K. (1994) *Competing for the Future.* Boston, MA: Harvard Business School Press.

Heavens, S. and Child, J. (1999) Mediating Individual and Organizational Learning: The Role of Teams and Trust. Paper presented at the 1999 Organization Learning Conference, Lancaster University, Lancaster, UK, June.

Hofstede, G. (1980) *Culture's Consequences.* Beverly Hills, CA: Sage.

Huber, G. (1991) Organizational Learning: The Contributing Processes and the Literatures. *Organization Science*, 2 (1): 88–115.

Hult, T., Nichols, E., Giunipero, L., and Hurley, R. (2000) Global Organizational Learning in the Supply Chain: A Low versus High Learning Study. *Journal of International Marketing*, 8 (3): 61–83.

Inkpen, A.C. and Crossan, M. (1995) Believing is Seeing: Joint Ventures and Organizational Learning. *Journal of Management Studies*, 32 (5): 595–618.

Inkpen, A.C. and Dinur, A. (1998) Knowledge Management Processes and International Joint Ventures. *Organization Science*, 9 (4): 454–68.

Kamoche, K. (1996) Strategic Human Resource Management within a Resource-Capability View of the Firm. *Journal of Management Studies*, 33 (2): 213–34.

Kim, D. (1993) The Link between Individual and Organizational Learning. *Sloan Management Review*, 35 (1): 37–50.

Kim, Y. (1988) *Communication and Cross-cultural Adaptation: An Integrative Theory.* Clevedon, England: Multilingual Matters.

Kim, Y. (1989a) Intercultural Adaptation. In M. Asante and W. Gudykunst (eds.), *Handbook of International and Intercultural Communication.* Newbury Park, CA: Sage, 275–99.

Kim, Y. (1989b) Explaining Interethnic Conflict. In J. Gittler (ed.), *The Annual Review of Conflict Knowledge and Conflict Resolution*, Vol. 1. New York: Garland, 101–25.

Kogut, B. and Zander, U. (1992) Knowledge of the Firm, Combinative Capabilities, and the Replication of Technology. *Organization Science*, 3: 383–97.

Langer, E. (1997) *Mindfulness.* Reading, MA: Addison-Wesley.

Leonard-Barton, D. (1995) *Wellsprings of Knowledge.* Boston: Harvard Business School Press.

Levinson, N. and Asahi, M. (1995) Cross-national Alliances and Interorganizational Learning. *Organizational Dynamics* 24 (2): 50–63.

Lin, X. and Germain, R. (1999) Predicting International Joint Venture Interaction Frequency in US–Chinese Ventures. *Journal of International Marketing* 7 (2): 5–23.

Louis, M.R. and Sutton, R. (1991) Switching Cognitive Gears: From Habits of Mind to Active Thinking. *Human Relations*, 44: 55–76.

Lustig, M. and Koester, J. (1999) *Intercultural Competence. Interpersonal Communication across Cultures.* New York: Longman Addison-Wesley.

McCauley, C., Stitt, C.L., and Segal, M. (1980) Stereotyping: From Prejudice to Prediction. *Psychological Bulletin*, 29: 195–208.

Merton, R.K. (1957) Patterns of Influence: Local and Cosmopolitan Influentials. In R.K. Merton, *Social Theory and Social Structure*. Glencoe, IL: Free Press, 368–80.

Nohria, N. and Ghoshal, S. (1997) The Differentiated Network. San Francisco: Jossey-Bass.

Nonaka, I. (1994) A Dynamic Theory of Organizational Knowledge Creation. *Organization Science*, 5 (1): 14–37.

Nonaka, I. and Takeuchi, H. (1995) *The Knowledge-Creating Company*. New York: Oxford University Press.

O'Hair, D., Friedrich, G., Wiemann, J., and Wiemann, M. (1997) *Competent Communication*. New York: St. Martin's Press.

Osland, J. (1995) *The Adventure of Working Abroad: Hero Tales from the Global Frontier*. San Francisco, CA: Jossey-Bass.

Osland, J. and Bird, A. (2000) Beyond Sophisticated Stereotyping: Cultural Sensemaking. *Academy of Management Executive*, 14 (1): 65–77.

Osland, J. and Bird, A. (2001) Trigger Events in Cultural Sensemaking. Paper presented at the Institute for Research on Intercultural Cooperation Conference, The Netherlands.

Perlmutter, H. (1969) The Tortuous Evolution of the Multinational Corporation. *Columbia Journal of World Business*, January–February: 9–18.

Pettigrew, T.F. and Tropp, L.R. (2000) Does Intergroup Contact Reduce Prejudice? Recent Meta-analytic Findings. In S. Oskamp (ed.), *Reducing Prejudice and Discrimination*. Mahwah, NJ: Erlbaum, 93–113.

Senge, P. (1990) *The Fifth Discipline*. London: Century.

Simon, H.A. (1976) *Administrative Behavior*. New York: Free Press.

Stephan, W. and Stephan, C. (1985) Intergroup Anxiety. *Journal of Social Issues*, 41 (3): 157–75.

Stonequist, E. (1932) *The Marginal Man: A Study in the Subjective Aspect of Cultural Conflict*. Chicago (n.p.).

Thich, N.H. (1991) *Peace Is Every Step: The Path of Mindfulness in Everyday Life*. New York: Bantam Books.

Ting-Toomey, S. (1999) *Communicating across Cultures*. New York: Guilford.

Tushman, M. and O'Reilly III, C. (1997) *Winning through Innovation*. Boston, MA: Harvard Business School Press.

Williams, R.M. Jr. (1947) *The Reduction of Intergroup Tensions*. New York, NY: Social Science Research Council.

12

Knowledge Seeking FDI and Learning across Borders

Shige Makino and Andrew C. Inkpen

Chapter Outline

Competing across borders provides firms with a variety of learning opportunities. This chapter discusses knowledge seeking foreign direct investment (FDI) and learning across borders. FDI is viewed as a dynamic process of exploitation and exploration of capabilities. Using organizational learning theory, we examine how firms use FDI to facilitate cross-border learning and improve innovative outcomes. We discuss the conditions under which knowledge seeking FDI is likely to occur. In considering how learning occurs, we examine knowledge acquisition through individual channels (employment and personal ties) and through organization channels (alliances and acquisitions). In developing the chapter, we show that processes of exploitation and exploration are dynamically linked by multiple loops between a parent and a subsidiary, between a subsidiary and local firms, and between subsidiaries.

Introduction

Competing across borders provides multinational corporations (MNCs) with a variety of learning opportunities. Geographic diversity exposes a firm to a diverse set of environments, which have the potential to lead to innovation and enhanced organizational capabilities (Ghoshal, 1987). In this chapter we focus on MNC learning opportunities created by foreign direct investments (FDIs). FDIs have increased dramatically over the past few decades. We examine FDI that is intended to source strategic assets such as technological, marketing, management expertise, or other intangible assets owned by other firms in locations abroad. We refer to this type of activity as knowledge seeking FDI. Our view of knowledge seeking FDI is based on organizational learning theory and suggests that firms use FDI to facilitate cross-border learning and improve innovative outcomes. Building on March's (1991) concept of exploitation and exploration in learning, we examine how

MNCs use FDI not only as a means to exploit existing capabilities but also as a means to explore new ones. In developing the chapter, we show that processes of exploitation and exploration are dynamically linked by multiple loops between a parent and a subsidiary, between a subsidiary and local firm(s), and between subsidiaries.

EXPLOITATION AND EXPLORATION

Organizations both exploit existing capabilities and explore for new ones. Maintaining a balance between exploitation and exploration has important implications for resource allocation and hence, long-term performance and survival. March (1991) noted that exploitation of known alternatives has more certain outcomes, short time horizons, and more precise effects than exploration. Exploration of new alternatives has less certain outcomes, longer time horizons, and more diffused effects. Although organizations must allocate resources between exploitation and exploration, the allocation and tradeoffs are difficult. Reliance on exploiting known alternatives may result in missing opportunities to explore new advantages, whereas reliance on exploring new alternatives may result in short-term loss of efficiency (March, 1991). The key consideration for sustainable success of the firm is a balance between exploitation and exploration in organizational development process. All too often, however, firms tend to substitute exploitation of known alternatives for the exploration of unknown ones. As March stated:

> The essence of exploitation is the refinement and extension of existing competencies, technologies, and paradigms. Its returns are positive, proximate, and predictable. The essence of exploration is experimentation with new alternatives. Its returns are uncertain, distant, and often negative. Thus, the distance in time and space between the locus of learning and the locus for the realization of returns is generally greater in the case of exploration than in the case of exploitation, as is the uncertainty. Such features of the context of adaptation lead to a tendency to substitute exploitation of known alternatives for the exploration of unknown ones, to increase the reliability of performance rather more than its mean (1991: 85).

The view that firms tend to substitute exploitation of existing capabilities for exploration of new ones has also been addressed in different academic disciplines. In economics, Arrow (1974) argued that organizational behavior and decisions are history dependent and the very pursuit of efficiency may lead to rigidity and unresponsiveness to changes. Arrow argued that the essence of organizational decisions involves two types: terminal acts (decisions to act using existing information) and experiments (decisions to collect information for action). As a corollary to March's concepts of exploitation and exploration, Arrow argued that both types of decisions, terminal acts and experiments, have implications for resource utilization. Terminal acts are based on sets of information that are already possessed and, thus, are less costly. Experiments are costly and yield no benefits directly, but have the instrumental value of improving the terminal act by supplying more information. Thus, in situations where the degree of external environmental uncertainty is high, organizations tend to focus on more certain activities than exploration of new information (experiments). Consequently, organizations become more rigid, rather than responsive, when faced with external changes.

In strategic management, researchers have suggested that firms can build competitive advantages through exploitation of existing firm-specific capabilities and skills (Wernerfelt, 1984; Barney, 1991). Recent studies, however, have argued that as, or even more, important than exploiting existing capabilities, organizations must understand how to develop and renew competencies to respond to changes in external environments (Kogut and Zander, 1992; Henderson and Cockburn, 1994; Teece et al., 1997). These studies emphasized the importance of a firm's ability to configure dynamic processes of capability exploitation and building. Such ability is referred to as dynamic capability (Teece et al., 1997), combinative capability (Kogut and Zander, 1992), and architectural competence (Henderson and Cockburn, 1994). Although the importance of capability building in the face of environmental change has been frequently cited in the literature (for example, Ghemawat, 1993), research suggests that responses to external changes are difficult because firms are often bound by existing routines and sunk costs, and remain committed to existing, or sometimes outmoded, know-how and capabilities (Nelson and Winter, 1982; Tushman and Anderson, 1986; Levitt and March, 1988). Leonard-Barton (1992) studied new product and process development projects and found that primary sources of core rigidities or routines lie in the difficult-to-change nature of the value systems embodied in a firm's existing core capabilities, suggesting that obstacles to innovation are not only technical but also organizationally embedded barriers to changes. In the international arena, which is the focus of this chapter, the process of internationalization has been described as a search for new knowledge as the basis for developing new capabilities (for example, Barkema et al., 1996; Chang, 1995; Inkpen and Beamish, 1987).

In short, the above literature suggests that both exploitation and exploration are essential for firms' survival and development of competitive advantages. However, since firms can perform a limited number of actions due to limited available resources, uncertainty, or bounded rationality, they tend to focus more on exploitation of existing capabilities than exploration of new ones. How to create the mechanism that facilitates exploration of new capabilities is therefore a critical issue to any contemporary enterprise. In this chapter, we examine the idea of exploitation and exploration in the MNC context and propose that learning in MNCs has both exploitation and exploration aspects. Below, we discuss theoretical foundations of both exploitation and exploration aspects of a firm's international expansion strategy. We first briefly review two traditional theories of MNCs, which focus on exploitation aspects of international expansion strategy. Then, we move to detailed discussions of conceptual issues pertaining to exploration aspects of international expansion strategy, which we call "knowledge seeking FDI."

FDI AS EXPLOITATION

Two major perspectives in the international business literature attempt to explain why firms engage in international activities through FDI. The first perspective suggests that foreign firms invest in foreign countries to gain greater market power in a host country (Hymer, 1976). Hymer proposed that firms engage in international operations when they possess certain forms of advantages over local competitors that outweigh their disadvantages of being foreign. The second perspective suggests that foreign firms invest in foreign countries as a means to minimize market transaction costs. This perspective is referred to as internalization theory (Buckley and Casson, 1976; Rugman, 1981; Hennart, 1982). The basic principle of internalization is that imperfections (or market failures) in intermediate product markets and the need for foreign firms to exploit the economies of interdependent activities lead to the replacement of the market mechanism of cross-border transactions by internal hierarchy (Dunning, 1988: 18). Teece (1981) identified three categories of international markets that foreign firms internalize through FDI: intermediate product markets; markets for know-how; and international capital markets.

The two conventional theories of FDI focus mainly on the questions of why MNCs exist. They share four common underpinnings. First, the theories assume that firms can transfer between sub-units intangible assets such as know-how, or advantages that are embodied in these assets, across borders without incurring costs and without losing their value. However, this assumption hardly holds for real situations in transactions within an MNC. Indeed, the internal transfer of intangible assets such as know-how is much more costly than is often assumed due to the tacit nature of the assets and organizationally embedded barriers to this transfer (Teece, 1977; Kogut and Zander, 1992; Kostova, 1999; Kostova and Zaheer, 1999). Studies that have examined international knowledge transfers (for example, Inkpen and Dinur, 1998) have found that the type and complexity of knowledge impact the ease of transfer. In a study of learning about new host countries, Lord and Ranft concluded that "learning . . . appears to be a complex process that varies significantly between firms due to variations in internal flows of local market knowledge" (2000: 584).

Second, the theories tend to focus on one-way flow of intangible assets that typically move from a home country of the parent to a host country in which its subsidiary operates. The underlying assumption is that FDI is used to exploit the capabilities or other assets developed by the parent in its home country. The theories cannot clearly explain, however, the case in which intangible assets move from a subsidiary to its parent, or to other subsidiaries, as the result of capability building initiated by that subsidiary. The traditional theories provide little insight regarding how patterns in two-way interactions among the parent and other subsidiaries develop or change over time and thus fail to develop a dynamic process of the MNC growth. In reality, MNCs involve a network of knowledge flows to, from, and between subsidiaries. The ability to manage these knowledge flows is fundamental for MNC advantage, as Bartlett and Ghoshal (1989) made clear.

Third, the theories view locations as exogenous entities, and, typically, as sources of undefined uncertainties. The conventional MNC theories focus on two types of uncertainties: contextual and behavioral. The contextual uncertainty comes from the MNC's lack of knowledge about local market conditions, changes in customer demand, volatility in exchange rates, and interventions by local governments. The behavioral uncertainty comes from potential opportunistic behaviors of prospective transacting parties. The main idea underlying this view is that uncertainties are threats to the MNC, rather than opportunities, although uncertainties themselves simply imply that future events are not predictable. The conventional theories of FDI tend to neglect the learning opportunities created by diverse locational conditions.

Finally, the conventional theories are somewhat restrictive because they neglect more behavioral issues and imply too strongly a tractable economic analysis in understanding

FDI and, especially, cooperative relationships. As Robins (1987: 83) argued, the effort to explain structural change solely on the basis of microeconomic processes obscures the role of historical and social forces that influence the competitive environment. In addition, the emphasis on structural arrangements and tangible assets (Lorenzoni and Lipparini, 1999) makes some implicit assumptions that organization design can be equated with structure when in fact, organization design includes variables besides the physical structure. These include the people, task, reward systems, and decision and information processes and in particular, the intangible assets associated with learning and knowledge. For an MNC to capitalize on a sub-unit's knowledge, that knowledge will have to be amplified and internalized as part of an organization's knowledge base. This process has similarities with the knowledge creation process, which Nonaka (1994) described as one that involves various organizational levels, carriers of knowledge, and specific learning processes at work at each level.

FDI as Exploration: Knowledge Seeking FDI

Various studies have discussed FDI as a means of capability building (Hedlund, 1986; Bartlett and Ghoshal, 1989; Cantwell, 1989; Dunning, 1993, 1998; Birkinshaw, 1997; Birkinshaw and Hood, 1998; Kuemmerle, 1999; Frost, 2001). Although there is some overlap in ideas discussed, the studies tend to focus on specific phenomena of knowledge seeking FDI and have not been organized under a broader conceptual framework. The following discussion links MNC behaviors with organizational learning perspectives in three key areas: (1) conditions under which firms engage in cross-border learning activities through FDI; (2) locations of cross-border learning; and (3) the rationale for MNC learning.

Learning conditions: absorptive capacity

In the MNC literature, there is a consensus that for FDI to occur, firms should possess firm-specific advantages that can be exploited in the host country. Furthermore, this literature posits that a variation in foreign activities among firms can be explained partly because firms possess different levels of firm-specific advantages. However, since foreign expansion is motivated not only by exploitation of existing advantage but also for exploration of new advantage in the host country, the observed variation in the extent of foreign activities among firms can also be explained by the fact that firms possess different levels of capabilities to search, acquire, and integrate new advantages from external sources. Such capability is often referred to as absorptive capacity and is closely related to the concept of learning effectiveness (Inkpen, 2000). Cohen and Levinthal (1990) suggested that absorptive capacity is a function of prior related knowledge, including knowledge of the most recent scientific or technological developments, which confers an ability to recognize the value of new information, assimilate it, and apply it to commercial ends.

Two ideas are implicit in the notion that absorptive capacity is a function of prior related knowledge: learning is cumulative and learning performance is greatest when the object of learning is related to what is already known (Cohen and Levinthal, 1990: 131). The notion that learning is cumulative suggests that the development of absorptive capacity requires a path-dependent process of knowledge accumulation. Firms may differ in how they accumulate knowledge and, hence, possess unique absorptive capacity, which leads to a variation among firms in their motivations and capabilities to engage in knowledge seeking FDI and, more generally, learning within the MNC. The notion that learning performance is greatest when learning extends existing knowledge suggests that learning will be most difficult in novel domains, as is often the case in foreign market expansion. In extending Cohen and Levinthal's (1990) ideas, firm should be more likely to engage in knowledge seeking FDI when they possess a strong competence base related to the new market. However, it can also be argued that firms engage in knowledge seeking FDI to explore a new competence base and, therefore, engage in knowledge seeking FDI to go beyond local search, or incremental extension of their existing capability base, to acquire new technological capabilities that they lack (Rosenkopf and Nerkar, 2001).

The likelihood that firms would engage in knowledge seeking FDI also depends on the presence of neighboring business operations, or co-specialized assets (Teece, 1986). Such neighboring business operations are typically embodied in the network of related functional activities such as manufacturing and distribution. The availability of a local manufacturing and distribution network is the key for successful knowledge seeking FDI. Not only is such a network a source of new ideas for innovation (von Hippel, 1988), it also enables the firms to capitalize on acquired strategic assets such as technological capabilities for both production and commercial application in the local market (Teece, 1986; Nobel and Birkinshaw, 1998). The presence of neighboring business operations facilitates firms' capability building in two ways. First, firms can gain access to both public and private sources of new strategic assets through their network of local affiliates. Second, firms can overcome the liability of foreignness and gain legitimacy among key local industrial players and political agents, which makes access to external sources less difficult and costly. If we can assume that the primary goal of foreign R&D subsidiaries is to source new technological capabilities in a host country, and manufacturing subsidiaries to exploit the existing technological capabilities in local production, the process of exploitation and exploration of technology should co-evolve in feedback effects among affiliates in neighboring functional activities in the host country (Levinthal and Myatt, 1994).

Learning locations: external sources

The economic geography literature suggests that FDI is concentrated in particular locations due to positive externalities such as technological spillover, pooled skilled labour, and other industry specific inputs (Smith and Florida, 1994; Head, Ries, and Swenson, 1995). In the international business literature, Dunning (1981) provided an exhaustive list of location specific factors that influence the location of FDI. Both literatures define location- (or country-) specific conditions as *exogenous* factors that constrain or encourage inward FDI. In the logic of knowledge seeking FDI, some forms of location factors should be considered *endogenous* factors that directly constitute a firm's capabilities. The basic idea underlying knowledge seeking FDI is that critical resources and capabilities sought by firms are more often spatially determined than simply existing within any single firm (Enright, 1998). Such resources and capabilities are often located in inter-firm networks in particular geographical locations, which are referred to as network resources (Gulati, 1999). A firm's network resources results from "the informational advantages they obtain from their participation in inter-firm networks that channel valuable information" (Gulati, 1999: 399). Unlike natural resources or other country-specific tangible resources, these resources are often tacit, owned by a group or network of firms in particular locations of the host country. Unlike the public good nature of firm-specific assets, they are immobile across borders because they are embedded in social relations among network members that operate in nearby locations. In fact, they are both firm-specific *and* location-specific in nature (Cantwell, 1989).

The strategic assets available in a particular location are often embedded in a *social network* of local firms or other organizations such as universities that share common cultures, values, and norms. Teece (1992) and Saxenian (1990), for example, observed that the new entrants in Silicon Valley have built not only on Silicon Valley's technical infrastructure but also on its institutional infrastructure and its dense social and professional networks. In this social network, proximity creates a unique collaborative culture which facilitates collective learning and flexible adjustment among specialist producers of complex or related technologies (Saxenian, 1990). A social network in a particular location is further embedded in a broader system of industry structure and social relations in a national environment (Porter, 1990; Kogut, 1990), resulting in heterogeneous distribution of innovative activities across nations (Cantwell, 1989), and hence, increased concentration of knowledge seeking FDI in particular host countries.

The perspective that views locations as sources of strategic knowledge assets has been empirically supported. Researchers reported that the proportion of cross-border acquisition of US technology assets has been growing significantly (Teece, 1992; Inkpen et al., 2000). Research has found that foreign firms were often motivated to invest in the United States to gain access to US-based technology (Almeida, 1996; Chang, 1995; Shan and Song, 1997; Frost, 2001). While most research on knowledge seeking FDI is limited to the case of firms from developing countries (DCs), a growing number of studies have reported that firms from less developed countries and newly industrializing economies invest in DCs to source new technologies (Kumar, 1998; van Hoesel, 1999; Makino, Lau and Yeh, 2002).

Learning rationale: dominant logic and internationalization

The above arguments suggest that absorptive capacity and external sources for strategic assets are the driving forces leading to knowledge seeking FDI. However, these two forces alone cannot explain why firms *decide* to engage in knowledge seeking FDI. Why, in circumstances in which firms could learn through FDI, do some firms engage in FDI and others do not? A firm's decision to engage in knowledge seeking FDI may depend on the MNC manager's mindset about the business and its basis for advantage. This mindset has been referred to as dominant logic (Prahalad and Bettis, 1986). Dominant logic is the shared cognitive map of the top managers and is expressed as learned, problem-solving behavior that guides firm actions. Dominant logic often inhibits the firm's learning process.

Because dominant logic builds on top managers' knowledge of the core business and the businesses they are familiar with, managers may avoid making decisions outside the boundaries of their knowledge. Consequently, preference in learning tends to be given to exploitation of existing, familiar capabilities, rather than to exploration of new, novel ones, even when firms notice the opportunities to do so (Levitt and March, 1988).

Dominant logic is also embedded in a particular country context. First, most firms tend to hire more domestic managers than foreign managers, at least in the initial stage of internationalization of the firm, and these domestic managers tend to have a common (home country) national identity and share similar cultural background and, perhaps, similar ethnocentric orientations (Perlmutter, 1969). Second, firms normally start business operations in their home country and then expand into foreign countries, which means managers tend to be familiar more with domestic than international business practices. Third, most firms do business primarily with other domestic suppliers and customers and deal with governments, labor unions, trade associations, and other interest groups that also base their key activities in the same home country.

Because the dominant logic of many MNCs is embedded in a home country context, three important observations can be made: (1) Many firms find it difficult to search learning opportunities outside the boundaries of their home country; (2) Firms may actually see learning opportunities in foreign countries but are unable to explore them (Inkpen and Crossan, 1995, discussed the difficulty firms often have in exploiting learning opportunities); (3) Some firms do explore learning opportunities in foreign countries, but their prior domestic experience may significantly influence what to search for, what to experience, and how to interpret what is learned in the host countries. For the first two observations, dominant logic inhibits firms from exploring cross-border learning opportunities. The third observation involves the case in which a firm's prior domestic business experience, or "congenital knowledge" (Huber, 1991), limits its subsequent learning in foreign countries.

In order for knowledge seeking FDI to be considered a legitimate strategy for capability building, firms need to change, or unlearn (Hedberg, 1981), the dominant logic created by domestic operational experience. As Prahalad and Oosterveld (1999) maintained, MNC managers need to shift from a zone of comfort to a zone of opportunity in how they view international markets. One major factor that makes unlearning of dominant logic difficult is uncertainty stemming from the firm's lack of operational experience in and knowledge about local market conditions in a foreign country. Several researchers have developed the model of international expansion under uncertainty. Johanson and Vahlne (1977, 1990) proposed that as firms accumulate local experience and overcome psychic distance, they will choose a mode of investment with successively greater resource commitment, which typically starts with non-regular export, exports via agents, establishment of a sales subsidiary, and finally establishment of a manufacturing subsidiary. They also proposed that as firms accumulate local experience, they enter host country markets with successively greater psychic distance. Chang (1995) studied Japanese electronics firms' sequential investment in the United States and found that when Japanese firms entered a new business, they typically started with a small investment into an area related to their core business. They then moved into other, less related areas and the scale of investment grew over time. Other research (Erramilli, 1991) found that foreign direct investment tended to occur from nearby and familiar foreign markets to more distant and unfamiliar ones. These studies generally suggest that a firm's international expansion might be best characterized as an incremental expansion process of dominant logic of MNC managers rather than as mere physical transfer of domestic operations in foreign countries.

LEARNING CHANNELS

This section discusses MNC acquisition of knowledge through individual and organization channels.

Acquisition through individual channels

Subsidiary learning is conducted by individuals who are either locally hired managers or expatriates sent from the parent (Almeida and Kogut, 1999). Subsidiary managers use their own personal network and socialized methods to acquire knowledge from external sources and then may transfer the acquired knowledge to the parent firm or other affiliates within an MNC. Ideally, subsidiary managers play a dual role in cross-border learning by: (1) searching and acquiring knowledge from external sources in a host country; and (2) transferring the acquired knowledge to parent or other affiliated subsidiaries within the MNC. In reality, intrafirm knowledge transfers are as problematic, expensive, and difficult as they are critical to organizational survival. Many large MNCs encounter difficulties in transferring practices across organizational units (Cerny, 1996).

The recognition of subsidiary managers' dual learning roles leads to the issue of whether MNCs should use local managers or expatriates. Local managers will be socially better connected to the business community but expatriates will share similar social relations with other MNC units. One view suggests that cross-border learning requires subsidiary managers to share common communication codes with external sources and gain legitimacy from them (Westney, 1994). The other view suggests that cross-border learning requires subsidiary managers to share common communication codes with their parent firm (and other affiliates) and achieve efficiency in internal-transfer of knowledge within the MNC (for example, Boyacigiller, 1990). The problem is that both external and internal communication codes may be incompatible and difficult to integrate under common organizing principles and identity (Tushman, 1977). Consequently, subsidiary managers face a dilemma: if they accept more expatriates (locals), internal communication will become more (less) efficient, yet external communication with local business communities may become less (more) efficient. Research has examined whether and when foreign affiliates adopt parent-firm HRM practices and local HRM practices in different national contexts (Rosenzweig and Nohria, 1994, reviewed this research stream). This research generally suggests that subsidiary HRM practices tend to conform more closely to those of local organizations than to those of the parent in its home country, although this tendency varies across types of HRM practices.

This evidence suggests that MNCs may initially focus on the internal efficiency of knowledge transfer by using more expatriates than locals. However, in subsequent subsidiaries, MNCs should use more locals than expatriates. One possible explanation is that

MNCs develop internal and external communication codes in a sequential manner. They first develop internal communication codes by extending the existing code to the subsidiary through the use of expatriates. Once internal systems of communication are established, MNCs successively use more local managers who are well connected to the external sources and start exploring personal ties and networks in a host country.

Acquisition through organizational channels

This section considers how MNCs can acquire new knowledge by grafting, which means learning through acquisition of knowledge associated with others' experience (Huber, 1991). At the organizational level, MNC grafting can occur through strategic alliances and acquisitions.

Strategic alliances   There is an extensive literature examining strategic alliances and learning (see Inkpen, 2002 for a summary). Both equity and non-equity strategic alliances provide a platform for organizational learning. Through the shared execution of the alliance task, mutual interdependence and problem solving, and observation of alliance activities and outcomes, firms can learn with and from their partners. This learning can encompass both competitive and cooperative behaviors of alliance partners (Khanna et al., 1998). The competitive aspect of interpartner learning arises from a firm's incentive to acquire the partner's skills faster than the partner (Hamel, 1991). The unintended loss of knowledge by Western firms in technology sharing alliances with Japanese firms has been considered by various studies (for example, Reich and Mankin, 1986; Pucik, 1988). The cooperative aspect of interpartner learning arises from a firm's incentive to combine its competence base with the partner's and to produce something new that is beneficial to all members (Kogut 1988).

In the international context, a key issue associated with alliance learning is the bargaining power between the MNC partner and the local partner. Inkpen and Beamish (1997) examined the root causes of instability in international joint ventures and argued that once the alliance is formed, if the foreign partner attaches a high value to the acquisition of local knowledge and has the ability to acquire the knowledge, the probability of alliance instability increases. Once a foreign partner has acquired local knowledge, unless the local partner is contributing other valuable and non-imitable skills to the alliance, the rationale for cooperation will be eliminated. Instability may be the result, although relationship attributes between the partners may moderate the shifts in bargaining power. Thus, the acquisition of local knowledge is an enabling device for the foreign partner to operate autonomously. Yan and Gray's (1994) case study of bargaining power and control identified both resource-based and context-based components of bargaining power and found that local knowledge in areas such as local sourcing, domestic distribution, and personnel management was the main resource contributed by the local partners.

Another international issue, and one that is unresolved, involves partner diversity and its impact on learning. Parkhe (1991) proposed that diversity between the partners in international strategic alliances could lead to learning. In contrast, Pitts and Lei (1997) argued that alliances designed to learn and absorb tacit knowledge are harder to manage among partners that come from different cultural contexts than from partners from a similar cultural context. Phan and Peridis (2000) took the notion of diversity one step further and proposed that conflict between the partners supports the learning process. The authors' rationale was that attempts to reduce partner conflict can block the second order learning process triggered by such conflict.

Acquisitions The acquisition of a local organization is another way to acquire organizationally embedded knowledge (Vermeulen and Barkema, 2001). There are several potential advantages of acquisitions over alliances. First, the firm can obtain new knowledge relatively quickly and generally faster than via internal development. Second, the firm can safeguard unwanted spillover of its proprietary knowledge since there is no partnership. However, acquisitions also have potential disadvantages. First, an acquisition may result in the ownership of unnecessary assets. Second, integration between acquiring and acquired units' may result in a time consuming process of adjustment and may lead to cultural clash between the units. Third, the evaluation of the value of target firms is difficult due to information asymmetry between the acquiring and acquired firms.

There is a limited amount of research on international acquisitions as the basis for learning. Hennart and Park (1993) argued that firms with strong technological abilities have less need to buy existing firms and are more likely to enter foreign markets through start-ups. Barkema and Vermeulen (1998) found that a firm's strategic posture at the time of an international expansion, in terms of multinational and multiproduct diversity, influenced strategic choice. This diversity offered opportunities for learning but also created a possible constraint. Barkema and Vermeulen found a curvilinear relationship between product diversity and the propensity to expand through start-ups versus acquisitions, which led to the conclusion that learning continues until organizational limits on learning are reached.

MNC LEARNING AS A DYNAMIC PROCESS

This section discusses a dynamic process of learning activity within an MNC (figure 12.1). Each arrow in the figure indicates the direction in knowledge flow. An MNC's capability building first occurs in its home country. The MNC then establishes its subsidiary in a host country and exploits its capabilities in the local market (①). On a parallel path, the subsidiary starts exploring new capabilities in the host country and then shares the explored capabilities with its parent MNC (②). The process of exploitation and exploration subsequently occurs between the parent firm and a subsidiary in a different host country (③) and then between subsidiaries in different host countries within the MNC (④). In this chapter, the type of learning that takes place at subsidiary levels (②, ③, ④) is called subsidiary learning. Subsidiary learning involves both acquisition and transfer of the acquired knowledge to the parent firm and other affiliates within an MNC. Geographical diffusion of affiliate learning is encompassed in a higher order learning process, which we call MNC learning (⑤). MNC learning involves configurations of separate sets of subsidiary learning within an MNC, which guide subsequent subsidiary learning.

Subsidiary learning is analogous to single-loop learning and MNC learning to double-loop learning (Argyris, 1976). At the subsidiary level, learning occurs in multiple dyadic relationships in internal and external network of the MNC (Ghoshal and Bartlett, 1990).

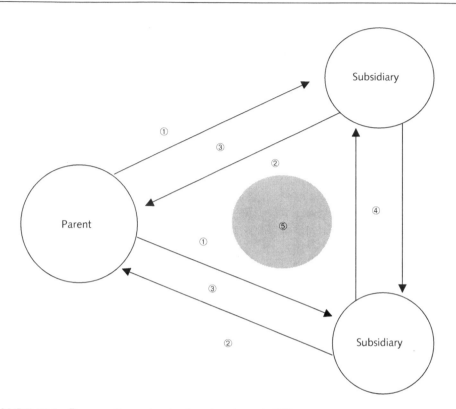

FIGURE 12.1   Process of cross-border learning through FDI

The relationships are linked in a loop of exploitation and exploration of knowledge, which eventually becomes routinized and stable, resulting in increased specialization and localization. At an MNC level, learning involves configuration of dispersed, localized learning activities across nations, which requires considerable institutionalizing efforts for the MNC to manage the dispersed learning processes under a coherent social context (Inkpen and Crossan, 1995). A tension between subsidiary learning and MNC learning lies in the fact that, as local search goes on, learning at subsidiary levels becomes more localized and the localized learning process makes MNC learning more difficult. The more localized the local knowledge, the more sticky it becomes and the more likely the recipient is to reject the knowledge (Szulanski, 1996).

A key task of MNC managers is balancing subsidiary and MNC learning. On the one hand, MNCs need to promote search for new capabilities from a broad array of subsidiary learning. On the other hand, they need to maintain coherent organizational contexts in order to achieve a certain degree of efficiency in coordinating dispersed cross-border learning activities. The literature suggests that MNCs can manage this tension in three ways: (1) through organizational structural approaches; (2) through social capital approaches; and (3) through "ba" approaches.

Organizational approaches

Barkema and Vermeulen (1998) concluded that learning from multinational diversity was subject to organizational constraints on information sharing. Possible organizational solutions can be viewed as either hierarchical or network in nature. The main idea underlying the hierarchical solution is that MNC learning outcomes can be enhanced by enforcing hierarchical control over geographically dispersed subsidiary learning. An MNC typically adopts a middle-layer structure such as a regional headquarters structure (Ohmae, 1999) or a matrix structure (Galbraith and Nathanson, 1978) in which subsidiary learning is grouped into separate units of activities according to geographical regions or product category. The head office of each unit is responsible for establishing what subsidiaries should learn, allocating scarce resources among subsidiaries, and minimizing redundancies in subsidiary learning within the unit.

The second organizational option is a network solution in which MNCs enhance learning outcomes by enforcing lateral relationships among subsidiaries. In this solution, MNCs are viewed as an integrated interorganizational network, in which a subsidiary has a relatively high degree of freedom in subsidiary initiative and one subsidiary's learning activities are embedded in others' activities in the network (Ghoshal and Bartlett, 1990). As interactions and exchanges between subsidiaries become intense, subsidiary learning initiated by separate subsidiaries becomes more interdependent and subsidiary managers start sharing common understandings about what they are expected to learn for the MNC as a whole. Consequently, convergent patterns in subsidiary learning emerge.

The role of social capital

The development of social capital among sub-units within an MNC can be the basis for balancing subsidiary and MNC learning. Social capital is defined as "the sum of the actual and potential resources embedded within, available through, and derived from the network of relationships possessed by an individual or social unit" (Nahapiet and Ghoshal, 1998: 243). Nahapiet and Ghoshal (1998) suggested that knowledge can be transferred and disseminated more efficiently between sub-units when managers of the sub-units possess strong social interaction ties, develop trusting relationship, and share common values and norms. Social capital facilitates knowledge transfer and dissemination in two ways. First, social capital creates a set of higher-order organizing principles that act as mechanisms by which to codify knowledge into a common language accessible to a wider group of individuals (Kogut and Zander, 1992) and enforces organizational identity (Kogut and Zander, 1996; Child and Rodrigues, 1996). Second, social capital increases the efficiency of actions of both sources and recipients of knowledge and reduces the probability of opportunism as well as the need for costly monitoring processes and, hence, the costs of transactions (Nahapiet and Ghoshal, 1998). Researchers have suggested that successful development of social capital would facilitate creation and transfer of knowledge within an MNC (Bartlett and Ghoshal, 1989; Nonaka and Takeuchi, 1995; Kostova, 1999) and facilitate combination and exchange of resources and thus, value creating activities of the MNC (Nahapiet and Ghoshal, 1998; Tsai and Ghoshal, 1998). In a study of learning and international alliances, Inkpen and Dinur (1998) identified critical knowledge management processes that acted as knowledge connections. The knowledge connections created the potential for individuals to share their observations and experiences. Inkpen and Dinur concluded that knowledge creation is a dynamic process involving interactions at various organizational levels and an expanding community of individuals that enlarge, amplify, and internalize the alliance knowledge.

An issue associated with the development of social capital is that it requires extensive and systematic socializing processes (Edström and Galbraith, 1977; De Meyer, 1991), which involve time consuming and costly interactions and communications among individuals. Another critical issue is that while development of strong social capital creates a high degree of internal consistency within an MNC, it may preclude a subsidiary's access to external sources of knowledge and thus increase the MNC's dependence on the subsidiary's boundary spanning roles. Where to position the center of gravity in the continuum between the quest for internal consistency within an MNC and the quest for effective boundary spanning roles by subsidiaries is the key issue in the social capital solution for managing the subsidiary-MNC learning tension.

MNC as a ba or knowledge creation

Nonaka and Konno (1998) introduced the concept of ba to describe the organizational context in which knowledge creation emerges. The concept of ba is defined as a shared space for emerging relationships, which provides a platform for advancing individual and/or collective knowledge. The ba exists in interactions between individuals at any level of intra- or inter-organization relations and can be physical, virtual, mental, or any combination of them. Nonaka and Konno identified four types of ba, which correspond to each stage of knowledge creation within an organization. Originating ba, the space where individuals share feelings, emotions, experiences, and mental models, facilitates the sharing of tacit knowledge between individuals. Interacting ba, the space where individuals interact through dialog and integrate their mental models and skills into common terms and concepts, facilitates the translation of tacit knowledge into explicit knowledge. Cyber ba is the space where individuals exchange and disseminate the common terms and concepts with other individuals in different organizational units and, hence, facilitates synthesis of explicit knowledge within an organization. Exercising ba, the space where individuals learn by continuous self-refinement through exercise of the shared terms and concepts, facilitates the conversion of explicit knowledge into the organization's tacit knowledge.

The concept of ba provides a framework for understanding the interactions between subsidiary learning and MNC learning. For successful subsidiary learning, a subsidiary needs to develop an originating ba to acquire tacit knowledge from external sources, which will be primarily through individual channels. The subsidiary then needs to develop an interacting ba where subsidiary managers translate tacit knowledge into explicit knowledge through personal interactions. The network of affiliates within an MNC works as a cyber ba in which explicit knowledge is transferred from the source subsidiary to other affiliates within the MNC (the parent firm and other subsidiaries), thus facilitating MNC learning. The shared explicit knowledge is then accumulated and internalized as tacit knowledge in an exercising ba both at a subsidiary and at a parent firm through the process of applying the knowledge into practice, which in turn becomes the basis for further subsidiary learning.

Viewing an MNC as a ba, or a platform for knowledge creation, emphasizes the importance of the subsidiary's ability to both encode and decode tacit knowledge acquired through subsidiary learning. Since tacit knowledge is of no value if it is not used at a specific time in a specific place, the use of knowledge requires the configuration, or "organic concentration," of the knowledge resources at a certain time space and time (Nonaka and Konno, 1998: 41). The role of top managers in creating the right ba at the right time and place within an MNC is therefore critical for successful MNC learning. Although the concept of ba in an MNC context is underdeveloped, the idea that views an MNC as a space for knowledge creation through learning warrants further development.

CONCLUSION

This chapter discussed key conceptual issues that pertain to knowledge seeking FDI and learning across borders. We first discussed some of the conditions in which knowledge seeking FDI is likely to occur. We suggested that firms engage in knowledge seeking FDI when they possess absorptive capacity that involves related technological knowledge and business activities. However, the MNC's actual engagement in knowledge seeking FDI is dependent upon, and often inhibited by, the dominant logic shared among MNC managers. Managers' ethnocentric attitudes and the prior international experience of the MNC may also inhibit knowledge seeking. With regard to the where question, we suggested that MNCs tend to conduct learning activities in locations where knowledge spillover exists or where there is a potential for spillover. Since target knowledge is often location specific and firm specific in nature, MNCs need to locate their learning activities in locations close to the firms (or the network of the firms) that possess that knowledge. With regard to the how question, we suggested that MNCs acquire target knowledge either through individual channels (employment and personal ties) or through organization channels (alliances and acquisitions). As target knowledge becomes more tacit, MNCs are more likely to use an FDI, rather than licensing, as a means of knowledge acquisition. As target knowledge becomes more organizationally embedded, organization channels will assume a greater role. Finally, we discussed the tension between the MNC's search for new capabilities and the need to maintain coherent organizational contexts.

Although increasing numbers of studies have focused on explaining questions pertaining to MNCs and learning, we believe there are many interesting opportunities to study FDI from an organizational learning perspective. As we discussed throughout the chapter, organization learning theory provides a useful framework for development of a comprehensive model of FDI. Not only does learning theory explain exploration aspects of FDI more effectively than traditional economics based theories, it also views FDI as a dynamic process of exploitation and exploration of capabilities across borders.

ACKNOWLEDGMENT

The work described in this chapter was partially supported by a grant from the Research Grants Council of the Hong Kong Special Administration (Project No. CUHK4052/99H).

REFERENCES

Almeida, P. (1996) Knowledge Sourcing by Foreign Multinationals: Patent Citation Analysis in the US Semiconductor Industry. *Strategic Management Journal*, 17 (Winter special issue): 155–65.

Almeida, P. and Kogut B. (1999) Localization of Knowledge and the Mobility of Engineers in Regional Networks. *Management Science*, 45 (7): 905–17.

Argyris, C. (1976) Single-loop and Double-loop Models in Research on Decision Making. *Administrative Science Quarterly*, 21: 363–77.

Arrow, K.J. (1974) *The Limits of Organization*. New York: W.W. Norton & Company.

Barkema, H.G. and Vermeulen, F. (1998) International Expansion through Start-up or Acquisition: A Learning Perspective. *Academy of Management Journal*, 41: 7–26.

Barkema, H.G., Bell, J.H.J., and Pennings, J.M. (1996) Foreign Entry, Cultural Barriers, and Learning. *Strategic Management Journal*, 17: 151–66.

Barney, J. (1991) Firm Resources and Sustained Competitive Advantage. *Journal of Management*, 17 (1): 99–120.

Bartlett, C.A., and Ghoshal, S. (1989) *The Transnational Solution: Managing Across Borders*. New York: Free Press.

Birkinshaw, J.M. (1997) Entrepreneurship in Multinational Corporations: The Characteristics of Subsidiary Initiatives. *Strategic Management Journal*, 18 (3): 207–29.

Birkinshaw, J.M. and Hood, N. (1998) Building Firm-specific Advantages in Multinational Corporations: The Role of Subsidiary Initiative. *Strategic Management Journal*, 19: 221–41.

Boyacigiller, N. (1990) The Role of Expatriates in the Management of Interdependence, Complexity and Risk in Multinational Corporations. *Journal of International Business Studies*, 21(2): 357–81.

Buckley, P.J. and Casson, M. (1976) *The Future of the Multinational Enterprises*. London: Macmillan.

Cantwell, J.A. (1989) *Technological Innovation and Multinational Corporations*. Oxford: Basil Blackwell.

Cerny, K. (1996) Making Local Knowledge Global. *Harvard Business Review*, 74, May/June: 22–38.

Chang, S.J. (1995) International Expansion Strategy of Japanese Firms: Capability Building through Sequential Entry. *Academy of Management Journal*, 38 (2): 383–407.

Child, J. and Rodrigues, S. (1996) The Role of Social Identity in the International Transfer of Knowledge. In S.R. Clegg and G. Palmer (eds.), *The Politics of Management Knowledge*. London: Sage Publications, 46–68.

Cohen, M.W. and Levinthal, D.A. (1990) Absorptive Capacity: A New Perspective on Learning and Innovation. *Administrative Science Quarterly*, 35: 128–52.

De Meyer, A. (1991) Tech Talk: How Managers are Stimulating Global R&D Communication. *Sloan Management Review*, 33 (Spring): 49–58.

Dunning, J.H. (1981) *International Production and the Multinational Enterprise*. London: Allen & Unwin.

Dunning, J.H. (1988) The Eclectic Paradigm of International Production: A Restatement and Some Possible Extensions. *Journal of International Business Studies*, 19 (1): 1–32.

Dunning, J.H. (1993) *Multinational Enterprises and the Global Economy*. New York: Addison-Wesley.

Dunning, J.H. (1998) Location and the Multinational Enterprise: A Neglected Factor? *Journal of International Business Studies*, 29 (1): 45–66.

Edström, A. and Galbraith, J.R. (1977) Transfer of Managers as a Coordination and Control Strategy in Multinational Organizations. *Administrative Science Quarterly*, 22 (2): 248–63.

Enright, M.J. (1998) Regional Clusters and Firm Strategy. In A.D. Chandler, P. Hagström and Ö. Sölvell (eds.), *The Dynamic Firm: The Role of Technology, Strategy, Organization, and Regions*. New York: Oxford University Press, 315–42.

Erramilli, M.K. (1991) The Experience Factor in Foreign Market Entry Behavior of Service Firms. *Journal of International Business Studies*, 22 (3): 479–502.

Frost, T.S. (2001) The Geographic Sources of Foreign Subsidiaries' Innovation. *Strategic Management Journal*, 22: 101–23.

Galbraith, J.R. and Nathanson, D.A. (1978) *Strategy Implementation: The Role of Structure and Process*. St. Paul: West Publisher.

Ghemawat, P. (1993) The Risk of Not Investing in a Recession. *Sloan Management Review*, 34 (2): 51–8.

Ghoshal, S. (1987) Global Strategy: An Organizing Framework. *Strategic Management Journal*, 8: 425–40.

Ghoshal, S. and Bartlett, C.A. (1990) The Multinational Corporation as an Interorganizational Network. *Academy of Management Review*, 15 (4): 603–25.

Gulati, R. (1999) Network Location and Learning: The Influence of Network Resources and Firm Capabilities on Alliance Formation. *Strategic Management Journal*, 20 (5): 397–420.

Hamel, G. (1991) Competition for Competence and Inter-partner Learning within International Strategic Alliances. *Strategic Management Journal*, 12 (Summer special issue): 83–103.

Head, K., Ries, J. and Swenson, D. (1995) Agglomeration Benefits and Location Choice: Evidence from Japanese Manufacturing Investments in the United States. *Journal of International Economics*, 38 (3–4): 223–47.

Hedberg, B. (1981) How Organizations Learn and Unlearn. In P.C. Nystrom and W.H. Starbuck, (eds.), *Handbook of Organizational Design*, New York: Oxford University Press, 3–27.

Hedlund, G. (1986) The Hypermodern MNC – A Heterarchy? *Human Resource Management*, 25 (1): 9–25.

Henderson, R. and Cockburn, I. (1994) Measuring Competence? Exploring Firm Effects in Pharmaceutical Research. *Strategic Management Journal*, 15 (Winter Special Issue): 63–84.

Hennart, J.F. (1982) *A Theory of Multinational Enterprise*. Ann Arbor: University of Michigan Press.

Hennart, J.F. and Park, Y.R. (1993) Greenfield versus Acquisitions: The Strategy of Japanese Investors in the United States. *Management Science*, 39: 1054–70.

Huber, G.P. (1991) Organizational Learning: The Contributing Processes and the Literatures. *Organization Science*, 2: 88–115.

Hymer, S.H. (1976) *The International Operations of National Firms: A Study of Direct Foreign Investment*. Cambridge, MA: The MIT Press.

Inkpen, A.C. (2000) Learning through Joint Ventures: A Framework of Knowledge Acquisition. *Journal of Management Studies*, 37: 1019–43.

Inkpen, A.C. (2002) Learning, Knowledge Management and Strategic Alliances: So Many Studies, so Many Unanswered Questions. In P. Lorange and F. Contractor (eds.), *Cooperative Strategies and Alliances: What We Know 15 Years Later*, forthcoming.

Inkpen, A.C. and Beamish P.W. (1997) Knowledge, Bargaining Power and International Joint Venture Stability. *Academy of Management Review*, 22: 177–202.

Inkpen, A.C. and Crossan, M.M. (1995) Believing Is Seeing: Joint Ventures and Organization Learning. *Journal of Management Studies*, 32 (5): 595–618.

Inkpen, A.C. and Dinur, A. (1998) Knowledge Management Processes and International Joint Ventures. *Organization Science*, 9: 454–68.

Inkpen, A.C. Sundaram, A.K. and Rockwood, K. (2000) Cross-border Acquisitions of US Technology Assets. *California Management Review*, 42 (3): 50–71.

Johanson, J. and Vahlne, J.E. (1977) The Internalization Process of the Firm: A Model of Know-ledge Development and Increasing Foreign Market Commitment. *Journal of International Business Studies*, Spring/Summer: 22–32.

Johanson, J. and Vahlne, J.E. (1990) The Mechanism of Internationalisation. *International Marketing Review*, 7 (4): 11–24.

Khanna, T., Gulati, R. and Nohria, N. (1998) The Dynamics of Learning Alliances: Competition, Cooperation, and Relative Scope. *Strategic Management Journal*, 19 (3): 193–210.

Kogut, B. (1988) Joint Ventures: Theoretical and Empirical Perspectives. *Strategic Management Journal*, 9 (4): 319–32.

Kogut, B. (1990) Country Capabilities and the Permeability of Borders. *Strategic Management Journal*, 12: 33–47.

Kogut, B. and Zander, U. (1992) Knowledge of the Firm, Combinative Capabilities, and the Repli-cation of Technology. *Organization Science*, 3 (3): 383–97.

Kogut, B. and Zander, U. (1996) What Firms Do? Coordination, Identity, and Learning. *Organization Science*, 7: 502–18.

Kostova, T. (1999) Transnational Transfer of Strategic Organizational Practices: A Contextual Perspective. *Academy of Management Review*, 24 (2): 308–24.

Kostova, T. and Zaheer, S. (1999) Organizational Legitimacy under Conditions of Complexity: The Case of the Multinational Enterprise. *Academy of Management Review*, 24 (1): 64–81.

Kuemmerle, W. (1999) The Drivers of Foreign Direct Investment into Research and Development: An Empirical Investigation. *Journal of International Business Studies*, 30 (1): 1–24.

Kumar, N. (1998) Emerging Outward Foreign Direct Investments from Asian Developing Countries: Prospects and Implications. In N. Kumar (ed.), *Globalization, Foreign Direct Investment and Technology Transfers: Impacts on and Prospects for Developing Countries*. New York: Routledge, 177–94.

Leonard-Barton, D. (1992) Core Capabilities and Core Rigidities: A Paradox in Managing New Product Development. *Strategic Management Journal*, 13: 111–25.

Levinthal, D.A. and Myatt, J. (1994) Co-evolution of Capabilities and Industry: The Evolution of Mutual Fund Processing. *Strategic Management Journal*, 13: 363–80.

Levitt B. and March, J.G. (1988) Organizational Learning. *Annual Review of Sociology*, 14: 319–40.

Lord, M.D. and Ranft, A.I. (2000) Organizational Learning about New International Markets: Exploring the Internal Transfer of Local Market Knowledge. *Journal of International Business Studies*, 31: 573–90.

Lorenzoni, G. and Lipparini, A. (1999) The Leveraging of Interfirm Relationships as a Distinctive Organizational Capability: A Longitudinal Study. *Strategic Management Journal*, 20 (4): 317–38.

Makino, S., Lau, C.M. and Yeh, R.S. (2002) Asset Exploitation versus asset seeking: Implications for location choice of foreign direct investment. *Journal of International Business Studies*, 33, 3, 403–21.

March, J.G. (1991) Exploration and Exploitation in Organizational Learning. *Organization Science*, 2 (1): 71–87.

Nahapiet, J. and Ghoshal, S. (1998) Social Capital, Intellectual Capital, and the Organizational Advantage. *Academy of Management Review*, 23 (2): 242–66.

Nelson, R.R. and Winter, S.G. (1982) *An Evolutionary Theory of Economic Change*. Cambridge: Harvard University Press.

Nobel, R. and Birkinshaw, J. (1998) Innovation in Multinational Corporations: Control and Communication Patterns in International R&D Operations. *Strategic Management Journal*, 19: 479–96.

Nonaka, I. (1994) A Dynamic Theory of Organizational Knowledge. *Organization Science*, 5: 14–37.

Nonaka, I. and Konno, N. (1998) The Concept of "*Ba*": Building a Foundation for Knowledge Creation. *California Management Review*, 40(3): 40–54.

Nonaka, I. and Takeuchi, H. (1995) *The Knowledge-Creating Company: How Japanese Companies Create the Dynamics of Innovation.* New York: Oxford University Press.

Ohmae, K. (1999) *The Borderless World: Power and Strategy in the Interlinked Economy.* New York: Harper-Business.

Parkhe A. (1991) Interfirm Diversity, Organizational Learning and Longevity in Global Strategic Alliances. *Journal of International Business Studies,* 22: 579–602.

Perlmutter, H.V. (1969) The Tortuous Evolution of the Multinational Corporation. *Columbia Journal of World Business,* 4 (January–February): 9–18.

Phan, P.H. and Peridis, T. (2000) Knowledge Creation in Strategic Alliances: Another Look at Organizational Learning. *Asia Pacific Journal of Management,* 17: 201–22.

Pitts, R.A. and Lei, D. (1997) Building Cooperative Advantage: Managing Strategic Alliances to Promote Organizational Learning. *Journal of World Business,* 32: 203–23.

Porter, M. (1990) The Competitive Advantage of Nations. *Harvard Business Review,* March/April: 73–93.

Prahalad, C.K. and Bettis, R.A. (1986) The Dominant Logic: A New Linkage between Diversity and Performance. *Strategic Management Journal,* 7: 485–501.

Prahalad, C.K. and Oosterveld, J.P. (1999) Transforming Internal Governance: The Challenge for Multinationals. *Sloan Management Review,* Spring: 31–9.

Pucik, V. (1988) Strategic Alliances, Organizational Learning, and Competitive Advantage: The HRM Agenda, *Human Resource Management,* 27: 77–93.

Reich, R.B. and Mankin, E.D. (1986) Joint Ventures with Japan Give Away our Future. *Harvard Business Review,* 64 (March/April): 78–86.

Robins, J.A. (1987) Organizational Economics: Notes on the Use of Transaction-cost Theory in the Study of Organizations, *Administrative Science Quarterly,* 32: 68–86.

Rosenkopf, L. and Nerkar, A. (2001) Beyond Local Search: Boundary-spanning, Exploration, and Impact in the Optical Disk Industry. *Strategic Management Journal,* 22: 287–306.

Rosenzweig, P.M. and Nohria, N. (1994) Influences on Human Resource Management Practices in Multinational Corporations. *Journal of International Business Studies,* 25 (2): 229–51.

Rugman, A.M. (1981) *Inside the Multinationals: The Economics of Internal Markets.* New York: Columbia University Press.

Saxenian, A. (1990) Regional Networks and the Resource of Silicon Valley. *California Management Review,* 33 (1): 89–112.

Shan, W. and Song, J. (1997) Foreign Direct Investment and the Sourcing of Technological Advantage: Evidence from the Biotechnology Industry. *Journal of International Business Studies,* 28 (2): 267–84.

Smith, D.F. Jr., and Florida, R. (1994) Agglomeration and Industrial Location: An Econometric Analysis of Japanese-affiliated Manufacturing Establishments in Automotive-related Industries. *Journal of Urban Economics,* 36 (1): 23–41.

Szulanski, G. (1996) Exploring Internal Stickiness: Impediments to the Transfer of Best Practice within the Firm. *Strategic Management Journal,* 17 (Special Issue): 27–43.

Teece, D.J. (1977) Technology Transfer by Multinational Firms: The Resource Cost of Transferring Technological Know-how. *Economic Journal,* 87 (346): 242–61.

Teece, D.J. (1981) The Multinational Enterprise: Market Failure and Market Power Considerations. *Sloan Management Review,* 22 (3): 3–17.

Teece, D.J. (1986) Profiting from Technological Innovation: Implications for Integration, Collaboration, Licensing and Public Policy. *Research Policy,* 15 (6): 285–305.

Teece, D.J. (1992) Foreign Investment and the Technological Development in Silicon Valley. *California Management Review,* 34 (2): 88–106.

Teece, D.J., Pisano, G., and Shuen, A. (1997) Dynamic Capabilities and Strategic Management. *Strategic Management Journal*, 18 (7): 509–33.

Tsai, W. and Ghoshal, S. (1998) Social Capital and Value Creation: The Role of Intrafirm Networks. *Academy of Management Journal*, 41 (4): 464–76.

Tushman, M.L. (1977) Special Boundary Roles in the Innovation Process. *Administrative Science Quarterly*, 22: 587–605.

Tushman, M.L. and Anderson, P. (1986) Technological Discontinuities and Organizational Environments. *Administrative Science Quarterly*, 31 (3): 439–65.

Vermeulen, F. and Barkema, H. (2001) Learning through Acquisitions. *Academy of Management Journal*, 44: 457–76.

von Hippel, E. (1988) *The Sources of Innovation*. New York: Oxford University Press.

van Hoesel, R. (1999) *New Multinational Enterprises from Korea and Taiwan: Beyond Export-Led Growth*. New York: Routledge.

Wernerfelt, B. (1984) A Resource Based View of the Firm. *Strategic Management Journal*, 5 (2): 171–80.

Westney, D.E. (1994) Institutionalization Theory and the Multinational Corporation. In S. Ghoshal and D.E. Westney (eds.), *Organization Theory and the Multinational Corporation*. New York: St. Martin's Press, 53–76.

Yan, A. and Gray, B. (1994) Bargaining Power, Management Control, and Performance in United States–China Joint Ventures: A Comparative Case Study. *Academy of Management Journal*, 37: 1478–1517.

13

Beyond Alliances: Towards a Meta-Theory of Collaborative Learning

Jane E. Salk and Bernard L. Simonin

Chapter Outline

Much recent research and theorizing identifies learning in and from inter-organizational alliances as their *raison d'etre* and as a critical factor contributing to their performance. Joint ventures (JVs) and strategic alliances among firms garner much of the attention in the literature, although many other types of inter-organizational collaboration occur where learning potential and needs also are strong. Similarly, many influential studies focus almost exclusively on organizational or inter-organizational level data and phenomena, additionally with a structural orientation, despite the implicit or explicit importance accorded to group and individual level social processes and mechanisms in the learning theories drawn upon. The time has come for a broader conceptualization and more elaborated map of the domain. To that end, we offer a meta-framework to systematize and encapsulate learning and knowledge-driven issues rooted in diverse organizational settings.

INTRODUCTION

While organizational learning and strategic alliances constitute two separate and equally rich domains of research, there is a growing interest in how organizations learn from their network of alliances and partners, in how knowledge gained from collaborative endeavors can become a source of competitive advantage, and in how one can develop superior collaborative know-how. This chapter builds upon, while pushing beyond, prior attempts to identify and organize the contributions to date (e.g., Tiemessen et al., 1997; Inkpen, 2001; Lyles and Dhanaraj, 2003). Our view and proposed model of alliances constitute an attempt to develop a meta-theory of collaborative learning, one that accounts for, and is meaningful to, all types of organization (from non-profit to for-profit), all levels of learning and knowledge management (at the level of individuals, teams, organizations, and networks), and for different collaborative foci (from intra-organizational to inter-organizational).

Mapping the Collaborative Learning Field

Upon hearing about the recent remarriage of a friend, Samuel Johnson declared: "This is the triumph of hope over reason." Like Johnson's hopeful friend, more and more firms engage in repeated alliances with, at best, mixed success. In the corporate world, the number of alliances has increased greatly over the latter half of the 1980s and 1990s (Bleeke and Ernst, 1991; Hennart, 1991; Lorange and Roos, 1993; Mjoen and Tallman, 1997). Although firms form alliances for a variety of reasons, inter-organizational learning has been deemed an important rationale for their creation (Hamel, 1991; Kogut, 1988; Lyles, 1988; Pucik, 1991). Though public information and experience in the practice and research domains, and in individual firms, accumulates, the press continues to be full of stories of under-performing inter-firm collaborations or discontinued ones, where it is doubtful that learning opportunities were exploited.

A general problem with the organizational learning literature, and the literature on learning and knowledge management in alliances more specifically, is a bewildering proliferation of definitions and approaches. Inter-firm alliances have been defined as purposive linkages between independent organizations (Kale et al., 2000), or as independently initiated inter-firm linkages that cover any intentional informal or formal inter-firm collaborations involving exchange, sharing or co-development (Gulati, 1995). What all definitions have in common is that collaborative alliances entail investment of time and resources by all partners, interactivity across the partners and some defined or envisioned product or output. Thus, inter-firm collaborations include franchises, licensing agreements, loose alliances for R&D, marketing, but also arrangements where a new joint entity or interface is created, including consortia, equity JVs, and, ultimately, mergers and acquisitions (M&A). Research mostly focuses upon the business world, ignoring nonprofit and for profit–nonprofit collaborations, public sector alliances, and intra-organizational, not just inter-firm, collaborations. Though some scholars treat alliances as if they constitute particular organizational forms (Khanna et al., 1998), in practice the organizational and human resource arrangements are highly variable, and variable in ways that are likely to be related to learning intents, capabilities and outcomes (Inkpen, 1995b).

Our objective is to provide a new, more encompassing meta-framework that will help map the inter-organizational collaborative learning and knowledge management field more rationally and systematically. Our contention is that learning and knowledge-driven issues rooted in diverse organizational settings can be encapsulated under this single, unifying paradigm. Now that our intentions are clear, from now on, when referring to alliances, we mean organizational collaborations of all types.

In the following sections we map the field, outlining where research and theory has been focused, identifying lacunae and highlighting where more attention is needed. We organize our inquiry via the following questions that arose from our readings and discussions. Why should inter-organizational collaborations be viewed as platforms for learning? What is inter-organizational learning; who learns (the levels of analysis engaged)? Where does knowledge in inter-organizational collaborations accumulate, get transferred and stored? What is the role of time (when)? How does learning occur? And how much learning does or should occur to reap benefits? We then synthesize from this exploration a framework of collaborative learning.

Why is learning important for collaborative alliances?

Many scholars, including Grant and Baden-Fuller (2001), Khanna et al. (1998), Mitchell and Singh (1996) Kogut (1988), and Kogut and Zander (1992) view knowledge acquisition and learning as primary reasons for the formation of collaborative alliances. The "learning race" perspective (Hamel et al., 1989; Khanna et al., 1998) assumes a strategic intent to learn from the partner, and advances the idea that competitive advantage accrues to the entity that learns faster and more effectively than the other. However, Zeng and Hennart (2001), Hagedoorn and Sadowski (1999) and Inkpen (2000) all suggest that few partners have "racing" intents and call into question the assumption that many or most alliances have clear learning objectives. Zeng and Hennart (2001: 1) go a step further to suggest that "many learning races are alliances 'gone bad' rather than the normal and desirable way alliances should evolve." In fact, Grant and Baden-Fuller (2001) argue that the main advantage of alliances over firms and markets is in *accessing* knowledge (rather than *acquiring* knowledge). They propose that the distinction between the acquisition and accessing of knowledge is similar to the difference between knowledge exploration and exploitation – thus the main issue with alliances is the efficiency and effectiveness of knowledge utilization and the learning race, in itself, is immaterial.

If there can be learning races, there can also be *"teaching races."* In particular situations, the knowledge holder (rather than the knowledge seeker) is the one motivated to accelerate the diffusion of knowledge to partners. Franchising (see Darr et al., 1995), internal corporate JVs (Shortell and Zajac, 1988), multinationals rolling out best practices across foreign subsidiaries, and consortia members eager to establish a dominant technology or product standard in the market, are settings where teaching races might occur. In the public sector, the numerous partnerships engaged by the World Bank are examples of teaching races. For instance, on projects of National Health Accounts (NHA) systems, the World Bank collaborates with the Inter-American Development Bank, the Pan-American Health Organization, the United States Agency for International Development, and the Latin-American and Caribbean NHA consortium of representative countries, not only to pool and maximize technical and financial resources, but also to effectively disseminate existing knowledge and standard practices. The teaching race perspective, as another arm of sustainable competitive advantage, deserves our attention.

Assuming learning intents or motives seems more clear for cases of R&D collaborations (Decarolis and Deeds, 1999; Lane and Lubatkin, 1998) and in the transitional economy context of the early to mid 1990s (Lyles and Salk, 1996), though in neither instance should these contexts be seen as naturally setting up learning races. Whichever view one sympathizes with, however, the issue of strategic intent to acquire knowledge and learn in alliances remains under-specified and under-studied in the literatures reviewed in this article.

Attention to whether a strategic intent to learn exists, whether it simultaneously entails concerns about protecting one's own know-how, and what specific types of skills or knowledge are sought should be a vital concern in studies of collaborative alliances for several reasons. First, there is the question of whether the focal entity can and does a priori define a set or domain of knowledge to expropriate and incorporate. The nature of those learning targets matters greatly for how the process plays itself out and the sorts of structures and capabilities necessary to facilitate a positive outcome. For example, the knowledge targeted might relate to minimizing or sharing risks and exploitation of skills and knowledge already possessed by the focal organization; in other cases, exploration for innovation and recombination of knowledge might be sought. March (1991) notes that the nature of these two types of knowledge acquisition intents differs: for exploitation the processes and outcomes are more certain and the time horizon shorter, while unpredictability of outcomes and longer time horizons characterize exploration (also see Makino and Inkpen, chapter 12).

Second, top management and members of a negotiating team often frame strategic intents, while groups and individuals actually responsible for the implementation and management of the collaboration are often different and might or might not fully understand and share these intents (Harrigan, 1986). Hence, understanding how and whether actors understand and communicate strategic intents involving knowledge and learning across different levels of analysis is important.

Third, knowledge acquisition and use occurs even when not specifically targeted by a priori strategic intents. This can occur due to changing contexts and circumstances, leakage of employees or know-how from partners that was not anticipated, serendipity, entrepreneurial orientations of those involved in, or exposed to, the collaboration or from carry-overs of knowledge and skills acquired from one collaborative context into another.

Learning, at any level, requires some level of stress and motivation (Schein, 1998). Moreover, the nature and substance of such motivations are variable, across cases of collaboration and often across levels and stakeholders within focal organizations in a collaboration. Much in the alliance literatures *assumes* that learning intents are present and primary (not superimposed by the researcher), that an intent signaled by one level of the organization holds for other levels of the organization and that learning intents that might be very different in substance and nature can be lumped together for analysis. This might largely be appropriate for some research questions. However, understanding in the field broadly defined entails paying more attention to actors' intents and their relationship to incentive systems, organizational structures, and other context factors.

What is learning and what is learned?

Turning to the "What?" question, four areas of interest have attracted attention: knowledge types; knowledge characteristics; cognitive versus behavioral manifestations of learning; and collaborative know-how as both a type of knowledge in itself and a possible moderator of the learning process in alliances.

Knowledge types   In alliances, whether or not organizations have a well-defined learning agenda and a clear strategic intent for seeking knowledge transfer, types of knowledge that may ultimately be developed or transferred in the context of an alliance remain constant. In the business world, knowledge related to markets, internationalization, marketing activities, R&D, design, procurement and logistics, production and manufacturing processes, human resource management practices, finance and accounting, and strategy have the potential to become sources of competitive advantage. As such, they may be both coveted and protected. In nonprofit organizations, fundraising and grant proposal development skills represent valuable knowledge-based counterparts. In the public sector, knowledge ranging from diplomatic *savoir-faire* to institutional and administrative expertise also represents critical assets. Alliances can be the stage for the deployment of, or exposure to, any of these knowledge types, some of which are more or less vital to a given organization. The same holds in intra-firm alliances. For instance, foreign subsidiaries of a multinational organization operating in various countries can benefit from the sharing of best practices, technologies, manufacturing processes, and new product development initiatives through collaborative programs.

Attempts not only to recognize, but also to isolate and measure different types of knowledge are rare. In their study of learning by international joint ventures (IJVs), Lane et al. (2001) look at the knowledge acquired from foreign parents, explicitly identifying the types of knowledge under consideration: managerial techniques, technological expertise, marketing expertise, manufacturing and production processes, and product development expertise. To date, a strong focus on technology dominates research related to organizational learning and alliances, be it a target for learning or a context for studying knowledge transfer. Among the numerous studies of technology-based alliances (e.g. Dodgson, 1996; Eisenhardt and Schoonoven, 1996; Hagedoorn and Schakenraad, 1994; Khanna et al., 1998) some have focused on R&D issues (e.g. Olk, 1997; Sampson, 2001) while others have looked at specific industries ranging from biotechnology (e.g. Pisano, 1988; Powell et al., 1996) to semiconductors (e.g. Appleyard 1996, 2001). The less plentiful studies focusing on non-technology related knowledge include the study of marketing know-how (Simonin, 1999b; Aulakh et al., 1996), franchising skills (Darr et al., 1995), and collaborative know-how (Simonin, 2000). Much remains unexplored in light of this imbalance between research focus and the diversity of knowledge types.

Knowledge characteristics Understanding knowledge characteristics (and the organizational structures that support them) is key to understanding knowledge flows, transfers, storage, and lack thereof. In alliances, beyond the characteristics of knowledge seekers and knowledge providers, and the nature of their interrelationship, knowledge-specific variables shape the transferability of any given form of know-how (Simonin, 1999b). Alliance researchers overwhelmingly point to knowledge characteristics of tacitness and the work of Polanyi (1967), often ignoring all other facets or, at best, collapsing them into a single, uni-dimensional variable. Tacitness has been the proxy of choice for assessing the difficulty (or ease) of accumulating and transferring knowledge. However, since there are many types of knowledge, there are also many other distinct characteristics of knowledge to account for. Some characteristics are completely knowledge-intrinsic whereas others are also linked to the situation of both the knowledge seeker and provider.

Besides tacitness, complexity and specificity have been considered antecedents of causal and knowledge ambiguity (Reed and DeFillippi, 1990; Simonin, 1999a, 1999b). Complexity captures the number of interdependent routines, technologies, resources, and individuals linked to a specific asset or knowledge. More complex human or technological systems generate higher levels of ambiguity and, therefore, restrain imitation (Reed and DeFillippi, 1990). Research on these aspects yields mixed results. Zander and Kogut (1995) find no significant direct relationship between complexity and the speed of transfer of manufacturing related knowledge. Likewise, Simonin (1999b) observed no effect of complexity on the transferability of marketing know-how between alliance partners. On the other hand, he found significant effects in the case of the transfer of technology and manufacturing process know-how between partners (Simonin, 1999a). Moreover, specificity was significant in the transfer of marketing know-how, particularly when collaborative experience of the knowledge seeker is limited and the alliance is not yet mature, but not in the case of the transfer of technology and process knowledge. Here, specificity captures notions of durable investments and specialized knowledge undertaken or developed in the context of particular collaborative relationship.

Other knowledge characteristics likely to impact the pace, depth, and meaningfulness of learning in alliances include validity, novelty, relatedness, uniqueness, value, and actionability. Validity means that the knowledge is given accurately and reliably. Novelty captures the time dimension of knowledge; is it new, timely, or obsolete? Relatedness refers to the degree to which a knowledge seeker is familiar or has prior experience with a given knowledge platform, principles, or context – does it fit the existing knowledge base and portfolio? Uniqueness refers to the presence or absence of alternate, substitutable bodies of knowledge. Uniqueness differs from specificity in that the focus is not on the co-specialization of knowledge with the alliance, but rather on the presence of competing knowledge bases. Value can be construed as market value (absolute value) or as the value of knowledge to a partner given its specific capabilities, history, context, and ambitions (relative value). Finally, actionability relates to the readiness, receptivity (Hamel, 1991), and ability of the organization to utilize and leverage particular knowledge. Obviously, we would expect new, valid, unique, related, and actionable knowledge to be more valuable.

Cognitive versus behavioral   The proper operationalization and measurement of learning and learning outcomes remains a challenge (Inkpen, 2001). At the heart of this challenge lies the dual manifestation of learning: both behavioral and cognitive (Fiol and Lyles, 1985). For instance, learning might be inferred from witnessing the adoption of a new product testing procedure inspired by an alliance partner (behavioral), or from observing the rise of a common and consistent conceptual understanding by JV managers about how to lobby in foreign markets (cognitive). Both manifestations of learning deserve research attention. Changes in routines, procedures, processes, actions, physical output, and structures (behavioral side) must be reconciled with changes in cognitive maps, conceptual representations, mental associations, shared beliefs, and understanding (cognitive side).

Collaborative know-how   In the context of alliances and organizational learning research, collaborative know-how plays an important role. By focusing on alliances and collaborative know-how, one draws and controls specific research boundaries under which to study organizational learning. Simonin (2002) argues that collaborative know-how can be considered a unique type of competence, one that may help explain why some alliances succeed brilliantly while others fail dramatically, and why some organizations are able to leverage their network of collaborative arrangements more effectively than others. Likewise, Kanter (1994), considering intercompany relationships as key business assets, maintains that the know-how to create and sustain fruitful collaboration, or collaborative advantage, "gives companies a significant leg up." In short, collaborative know-how is to collaborative advantage what a firm's core competency is to competitive advantage (Simonin, 2001). This alliance capability has increasingly captured the attention of researchers (e.g. Lyles, 1988; Simonin, 1997; Dyer and Singh, 1998; Gulati, 1999; Lorenzoni and Lipparini, 1999; Anand and Khanna, 2000; Appleyard, 2001; Kale et al., 2001).

Thus, identifying, mapping, and measuring a firm's level of collaborative know-how constitutes a critical first step in understanding organizational learning processes and performance in alliances. Most research to date has focused on prior experience as a proxy to actual knowledge and evidence of learning. Research results pertaining to the effects of experience remain mixed. Lei and Slocum (1992) trace the root-causes of failures and alliance problems to ignorance and lack of experience. On the other hand, Barkema et al. (1997) conclude that past JV experience does not favor alliance survival. Powell et al. (1996) argue that collaborative experience is necessary not only to manage a diverse portfolio of alliances, but also to develop the capability to extract value from these alliances. Anand and Khanna (2000) report mixed results with a significant effect of experience in the case of JVs but not in the case of licensing agreements. More recently, using an event study methodology on US companies, Reuer et al. (2001) found that prior experience with international IJVs has no apparent effect on the performance of new IJVs (measured by the firm's valuation effects of the venture's announcement). Likewise, in her study of R&D alliances in the telecom equipment industry, Sampson (2001) found that prior experience increases collaborative benefits up to a point; whereas some degree of experience helps performance, extensive experience does not.

While collaborative experience is a construct of great theoretical importance in its own right, it nevertheless represents a concept distinct from collaborative know-how. In general, experience is considered a key antecedent of know-how. Studying US multinationals, Simonin (1997) showed that collaborative know-how fully mediates the effect of collaborative experience on performance. At the same time, many organizations multiply alliance endeavors without extracting proper lessons and without fully developing distinct collaborative competences. Future research should account for both collaborative experience and know-how concepts, isolate their respective effects, and clearly specify their interrelationship. Potentially, this can shed some additional light on the role of experiential versus non-experiential learning.

Research initiatives that have attempted to isolate the higher-order construct of collaborative know-how and its development include Appleyard (2001) and Simonin (2000). Simonin (2000) delineates empirically a multidimensional construct of collaborative know-how that singles out five distinct factors: partner search and selection; negotiating; managing and monitoring; knowledge and skill transfers; and exiting. Each one of these factors encompasses various specialized activities and types of skills. It is still unclear how collaborative know-how accumulates and decays, how it impacts performance, and why it varies across organizations. Of further interest, the comparison between inter-organizational and intra-organizational collaborative know-how represents a promising research area.

Who knows and who learns? Units of analysis, governance and organization forms

Learning and knowledge acquisition occur at individual, group, organizational and inter-organizational levels of analysis (Nonaka and Takeuchi, 1995; Kogut and Zander, 1992).

Learning also can occur via and in networks at any of these levels. Extended discussion of debates surrounding levels of analysis and their incorporation into models of learning can be found in Vera and Crossan (chapter 7). Alliance research has emphasized the inter-organizational level of analysis (cf. Inkpen and Crossan, 1995; Lyles and Salk, 1996; Lane et al., 2001). That said, the mechanisms through which learning is realized and potentially converted into performance, often indirectly inferred rather than directly observed, imply structures and processes at the organizational and sub-organizational levels. These include social network interactions and proximity of groups and individuals and will be enumerated and described in the section below on how learning occurs.

It is important for researchers and research streams focusing narrowly on JVs, alliances, M&A, franchising, licensing, etc. to track approaches and developments in research looking at other specialties. One reason is that a licensing arrangement might lead to a JV or acquisition, a JV might end with one partner buying out the other as the end game – hence over time these forms can be interrelated in a developmental sense. Second, though human resources are critical factors in many types of learning, it is outside the "mainstream" of managerial alliance research that one finds exemplars focusing on the role of individuals (cf. Darr et al., 1995; Metiu, 2002; Kane et al., 2002). Clearly, individuals are conduits of, or sensors for, learning and knowledge in a collaborative setting (cf. Nonaka and Takeuchi, 1995) and the effect of context can interact with individual characteristics to affect learning (Dickson and Weaver, 1997). The practice of sending expatriates and secondees to alliances reflects the recognition by managers that individuals play a vital role in scanning, sensemaking and learning in alliances (Kogut et al., 1995; Almeida and Kogut, 1999; Salk and Shenkar, 2001). Almeida and Kogut traced movements of individuals across firms and within and across geographic areas, linking movements of personnel to knowledge acquisition. The classic literature on boundary-spanners further underscores the vital role individuals and groups play in channeling flows of knowledge and as learners themselves (cf. Allen, 1977; Tushman, 1977).

Groups can be particularly important influences in socialization of members (Van Maanen and Schein 1979), and in providing social support and norms to push knowledge residing in individuals or subgroups toward institutionalization. If we want to understand the role of individuals and social groups in bearing, transferring and transforming knowledge that ultimately becomes organizational, it is critical to examine the role of extrinsic and intrinsic motivation (Osterloh and Frey, 2000) and factors affecting psychological contracts (Rousseau, 1995). Salk and Shenkar (2001) and Salk (1996) describe highly affect-charged environments found in at least some multinational alliance teams, with rampant stereotyping and in-group out-group dynamics. A network perspective would suggest that these dynamics should affect communication and motivation and, hence, knowledge and learning transfer processes. Social identity theory predicts that perceptual group boundaries should affect which groups and individuals are chosen as referents for knowledge and as sources of learning. Kane et al. (2002) assigned groups to superordinate and sub-group identity conditions and found that when members were rotated between groups, learning of superior production techniques was significantly higher when the member rotated into the group shared a common superordinate identity. Hence, research on the role of social identity processes and emotional climate in organizational learning in alliances would contribute greatly to illuminating this heretofore dark corner. As developed in the next section, it is logical that the key to understanding alliances is not choosing one level of analysis, but seeking to develop and test cross-level models and constructs of learning and learning processes.

Governance forms likely hold a key to understanding how levels of analysis relate to one another, and the capacity and motivation of various participants to learn. Governance form as a mechanism shaping structures and flows of knowledge will be discussed in the section on "How learning occurs" below. Centralized organizations might not learn effectively in alliances in the same way that an N-form or simply more decentralized organization might. Centralized organizations might also tend to choose modally different forms of collaboration with other firms. While the dominant conduits and repositories of knowledge might tend to pull toward the center in hierarchies, hence suggesting the importance of thoroughly accounting for learning occurring at the organizational level, in network organizations, inter-individual and inter-group networks might be the dominant loci of learning and knowledge repositories. Beyond simple structural typologies, the degree to which bureaucratic structures and rules or strong, shared cultures dominate as governance mechanisms matter. The roles of individuals, groups and the organization might well differ in their roles vis-à-vis knowledge recognition, acquisition, driving change based on learning and acting as repositories in bureaucratically versus culturally driven organizations (Schein, 1998).

Learning in M&As, alliances among governmental entities or non-governmental organizations (NGOs), and forms such as franchising, only marginally considered in the literatures devoted to for-profit business alliances, might greatly enrich understanding of how governance affects learning and knowledge transfer. For example, Haspeslaugh and Jemison (1991: 145) in their work on M&A, develop a framework for mapping strategic intents onto the mode of implementation. They distinguish between intents that have high needs for interdependence (high to low) and needs for organizational autonomy (high to low). High autonomy/low interdependence strategic rationales occur when what is being acquired are skills and knowledge embedded in a particular organizational context; in such a scenario, a governance approach that buffers the acquired organization to preserve its special capabilities is required. By contrast, a strategic intent to rationalize capacity would fall into a high integration, low autonomy needs category. Unlike the previous example, hierarchies and systems need to be either subsumed or merged. Harrigan (1986) made a similar qualitative observation that, depending on the goals, a JV culture and way of operating sometimes needs to diverge greatly from those of the parents. Such distinctions might help push discussions of sticky-bleeding, tacit-explicit toward a more nuanced way of viewing the role between governance structures and learning, though it has yet to be picked up and further developed.

Where does learning occur and where is it stored in collaborative alliances?

Learning can occur and knowledge can be stored at multiple levels or analysis. The concept of organizational memory (Walsh and Ungeson, 1991) focuses attention upon non-human repositories, such as systems, structures, rules, routines. Other theorists focus upon individuals as bearers of, and repositories for, knowledge and organizational change more

generally (Schein, 1998; Simon, 1991). Individuals play a vital role in creating tacit organizational knowledge by converting tacit into explicit knowledge (Nonaka and Takeuchi,
1995: 64–73). Especially in new alliances, where norms, rules and routines are to be established and tested, what will one day indeed be institutionalized and persist independently
of certain constellations of members may reside for some period of time primarily in individuals and groups (see discussion of life cycles below).

Learning occurs by entities throughout cooperative systems. Zeng and Hennart (2001:
7) correctly point out that much research focuses on one participant's learning rather than
the behavior of partners simultaneously or a network as a whole. The majority of studies
reviewed focused on learning by partners; learning by the joint organization formed by
the collaboration (Inkpen, 1995a; Lyles and Salk, 1996; Lane et al., 2001) has received
more limited attention. The following comments from Osborn and Hagedoorn (1997)
remain true today:

> The potentially important role of individuals in operating alliances remains virtually unex-
> plored . . . Emergent patterns of relationships appear more salient in alliances and networks
> than the more traditional vertical and lateral placement within a hierarchy. A simple transfer
> of accumulated knowledge gained in studying individuals and groups in organizational set-
> tings may be highly questionable if one presumes that both setting and individual character-
> istics interact (Dickson and Weaver, 1997). It may be necessary to revisit an older tradition in
> organizational behavior that stresses developing and managing nonhierarchical relationships.
> (Sayles, 1964)

Variables such as power and influence, motivation and individual skills of those involved
in collaborations would likely moderate the relationship between alliance structure and
learning. Szulanski (1996), studying intra-firm transfers of best practice, found that in addition to the nature of the knowledge to be transferred (especially causal ambiguity), the
characteristics of the knowledge recipient and the nature of the relational context (arduous
relationships; laborious and distant relationships) were major impediments to transferring
knowledge.

Focusing upon a particular cooperation or focal organization also leads to potentially
missing secondary effects entailing changes located in institutional fields. Collaborative
know-how entails accruals of knowledge about how to manage relations across time and
different specific partnerships. Lawrence et al. (forthcoming) found that NGO collaborations in Palestine varied in their degree of involvement and embeddedness. This accounted
for differences in the degree to which a collaboration resulted in proto-institutions: "new
practices, rules and technologies that transcend the particular collaborative relationship
and may become new institutions if they diffuse sufficiently." Thus, there might be
dynamics of innovation and change missed by researchers that might have very important
ramifications for future behavior and other outcomes associated with performance over
time. This applies to research and business alliances as well. For example, in a highly
embedded field of firms, it is possible that collaborative practices not only evolve from the
direct partnering experiences of firms, but also via diffusion and mimesis across the field
that might ultimately transform practices and create innovations.

When does learning occur and when can we observe its effects?

Though a majority of studies looking at learning in cooperative alliances tends to be cross-sectional, time is most certainly a critical dimension to understand any change or learning process (Ancona et al., 2001a). Alliances evolve and change over time (Salk, 1996; Inkpen and Beamish, 1997). Moreover, the degree to which such changes are anticipated in practice or predictable is highly variable. Looking at the same IJVs in 1993 and 1996, Lane et al. (2001) found that the modal types of learning and variables most strongly associated with learning from the foreign parent changed over that period. The learning races and bargaining power perspectives (Yan and Gray, 1994; Inkpen and Beamish, 1997) suggest that alliances can be unstable over time and, when they do not end, the nature and content of the relationships can be expected to change. The nature of the relationship and the context (environments faced by the partners) likely co-evolve (Koza and Lewin, 1998). However, process remains a sorely understudied aspect of alliances (Doz, 1996).

Though emphasis on time and timing in the organization studies and strategy literatures has been increasing, there is a lack of definitional and methodological coherence (Ancona et al., 2001b). In terms of organizational learning, the question of time raises fundamental questions. One approach to studying organizational learning over time has entailed tracing learning curves (Argote, 1999). While learning curves suit settings and questions, and potentially could be incorporated and applied in more studies of alliances, it so far leaves a number of other time-related issues unexplored. Among these issues are timing and sequences of interdependence and dependence of factors underpinning learning and the acquisition and transformation of that learning. Does one map learning and knowledge processes in alliances in terms of critical incidents and events, in terms of transitions in networks, group dynamics, in terms of looking at feedback loops into the system or systems, or measurable changes in routines, behaviors, and outputs? Do firm, functional and culture-specific differences in approaches to time (Hall, 1983; Ancona et al., 2001) entail different approaches to learning, embedding, using, and storing knowledge? To what extent, and on which dimensions and levels, might a lifecycle model of organizational learning be plausible and researchable and how might co-evolution of contexts and alliances relate to this? Salk (1996) found that developmental patterns of multicultural IJV top teams follow a sort of punctuated equilibrium (see Gersick, 1989); issues of social identity and role investment often impede coordination and communication flows until a critical incident creates shared performance pressures, giving team members an incentive for role investment and motivation to adapt.

In short, while the dimension of time and timing is implicit in most theories and frameworks of organizational learning in alliances, this aspect has so far received inadequate attention in empirical research. The degree to which this is possibly the most fundamental gap in studies of alliances and organizational learning (and perhaps much of the organizational learning literature more generally) is further highlighted by looking in the next section at approaches to the question of how organizational learning is thought to occur in alliances.

How can and does learning occur in alliances?

Research focused upon understanding the processes of learning and knowledge transfer in alliances include Hamel (1991), Inkpen and Dinur (1998), Lane et al. (2001) and Simonin (1999a, 1999b). Most empirical studies in this area focus on a few specific explanatory variables, sometimes on an *ad hoc* basis, providing only a partial explanation to the overall phenomenon. While each study has the potential to add to our comprehension of a given facet of alliance learning, it also contributes to the fragmentation of our understanding. The big picture is lost.

To address this problem, we propose a generic taxonomy of variables related to the "how?" question in figure 13.1. Four distinct blocks of explanatory variables compose this conceptual framework and help organize logically variables of interest: (1) alliance-specific variables; (2) partner-specific variables; (3) knowledge-specific variables; and (4) context-specific variables.

For each block, we provide a list of pertinent variables. Lists are illustrative rather than exhaustive. The first block, alliance-specific variables, refers to many of the variables we already introduced and discussed that may facilitate or impede the learning process. For instance, the importance of the form of the alliance (e.g. equity versus non-equity based) on learning constitutes a significant research question to many researchers.

Partner-specific variables, the model's second block, subsume many critical research variables such as absorptive capacity, prior experience, strategic intent, trust, protectiveness, and collaborative know-how. Much attention has been paid to issues surrounding trust and protectiveness, a major concern being proprietary know-how bleeding to partners (Hamel et al., 1989; Hamel, 1991; Khanna et al., 1998; Kale et al., 2000).

Effective management of networks at the inter-organizational level also serves as a vital mechanism for knowledge acquisition. There are different kinds of networks and different schools of thought about the types of networks most conducive to learning. Some theorists emphasize exploiting structural holes in inter-firm networks to limit redundancy and to have a unique combination of access to information and knowledge by virtue of a distinctive position. Social network theory stressing cohesion and strength of ties suggests that the trust and social capital built up through dense repeated relations increases knowledge flows within these networks. These approaches have divergent views concerning the mechanisms and operationalizations of their transmission. Both are promising avenues, though we believe they probably will prove to explain effectiveness of different types of learning and knowledge exploration.

A key concept underpinning both approaches so far and the concept underlying the "how" in organizational learning more generally is that of absorptive capacity: the ability to identify, assimilate and exploit knowledge (Cohen and Levinthal, 1989). To study knowledge transfers, it is helpful to distinguish between knowledge-seekers and knowledge-providers (Simonin, 1999a) or learning versus teaching partners (Inkpen, 2001). In the IJV literature, Lyles and Salk (1996) identified structures and processes contributing to an IJV's capacity to absorb knowledge from the foreign parent. These included a flexible organization, written business plans and goals, a clear division of labor and training by the foreign parent. These variables suggest (albeit indirectly) a mode of human resource management and organizing that shapes cognitive orientations and informational networks

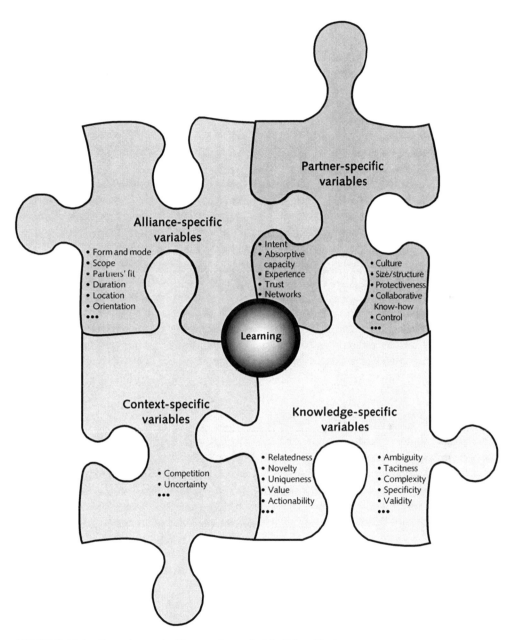

FIGURE 13.1   Learning and alliances: theoretical building blocks

within the alliance organization itself. Since then, Lane and Lubatkin (1998) introduced the notion of relative absorptive capacity: the relatedness of the partnering firms' knowledge bases, organizational structure and compensation as proxies for similarity in the norms and learning processes in the organizations, and dominant logics as a proxy for the motivation and ability to use the knowledge acquired. Lane et al. (2001) found support for the relative absorptive capacity construct in their study of IJVs. In their study, the relatedness of knowledge and organizational characteristics of flexibility and training by the foreign parent predicted knowledge acquisition by the foreign parent, while the dominant logic (differentiation) and training in the IJV (a diffusion mechanism) predicted performance.

Experiential (through training, learning-by-doing) as well as non-experiential learning (via proximity, observation) are implied by these studies. In other research that looks at learning by firms in geographic clusters, flows of personnel are viewed as mechanisms for the grafting of new knowledge and skills from one firm to another (Almeida and Kogut, 1999). Moreover, proximity provides opportunities for mimetic learning.

The third block, knowledge-specific variables, was discussed earlier under the "What?" section. The central point here is the determination of knowledge characteristics that create ambiguity and value. Ambiguity affects comprehension and transferability. Value stimulates learning intent for the knowledge seeker and encourages protective behaviors by the knowledge holder. Finally, context-specific variables, the fourth building block of our model, subsume non-controllable variables that may be sources of noise, but also motivation enactment of strategic intent to become an active, focused, or better learner or teacher.

How much learning? How much performance?

The performance outcomes imputed to learning (whether or not that learning has been directly measured or traced) vary greatly in the literature. Decarolis and Deeds (1999), for example, look at co-citation as a measure of knowledge acquisition. Lane and Lubatkin (1998) have used patents as a way of assessing how much is learned. Others, such as Anand and Khanna (2000) and Chan et al. (1997) use stock market performance (abnormal stock returns as a possible proxy for investors' assessment of learning) to measure performance. Argote (1999) discusses the use of learning curves as a measure of performance. Finally, Lyles and Salk (1996) and Lane et al. (2001) use perceptual responses of IJV general managers, along a variety of dimensions, to measure both the amount learned and performance of the IJV.

When modeling performance, there is a research tradition distinguishing between learning-driven and financially driven objectives in strategic alliances (e.g. Crossan and Inkpen, 1994; Dodgson, 1996; Hamel, 1991; Pucik, 1988). Ohmae (1989: 153) argues "most of the time, the financials don't capture the real benefits of alliances." In an attempt to account for both types of benefits, Simonin (1997) showed empirically that collaborative know-how affects both tangible collaborative benefits (financial and market outcomes; measured by both perceptual scales and objective financial indicators: ROA and ROI) and intangible collaborative benefits (learning outcomes, based on perceptual measures).

This may explain why some studies fail to identify a significant relationship between experience and performance when it may seem counterintuitive. For instance, Shortell and

Zajac (1988) found no significant effect of past experience on the profitability of new internal corporate JVs. Likewise, Inkpen (1995a) found that neither the experience of having previously managed a JV nor the experience of having worked before with a particular partner affects learning efforts. Meanwhile, Reuer et al. (2001) found that prior IJV experience and also the heterogeneity of that experience impact performance (measured with abnormal returns). The bottom line is that past experience may not be a reliable proxy for learning; whenever possible, researchers should try to assess levels of know-how as well. Depending on context and competencies, some organizations may learn well from experience, others may not.

Beyond learning and performance by partners, learning's relationship to performance of alliances constitutes a promising research avenue, particularly given the interest in alliance stability and longevity. Inkpen (2001) notes that the direct link between learning and alliance performance has received limited attention and further warns that too much research has focused on alliance learning as an end itself, rather than as a means to organizational performance. We believe that it is necessary to recognize different types of learning and their respective impact on performance. In light of Reuer et al.'s (2001) findings regarding the importance of experience heterogeneity and of the continuing fascination with the notion of single-loop versus double-loop learning (Argyris and Schon, 1978), more precision is needed in calibrating collaborative learning so that the link to performance is more meaningful.

Whatever approach taken, the general view has been that the more an organization learns the better its performance. While there has been some empirical support for this hypothesized relationship, learning also has personal and organizational costs. The benefits of alliance learning is emphasized, though very little is understood of the drawbacks of learning. Here we distinguish the possible drawbacks associated with alliances (e.g. Trojan horse effects, nurturing a competitor) from those associated specifically with learning. More attention should be given to categorizing and evaluating the actual cost of learning (investment cost, operating costs, opportunity cost, human cost, knowledge dissipation cost). Learning for the sake of learning may lead to "*learning paralysis*." We were reminded of this learning paralysis by the acute case of an IJV in Hungary between a local company and a Western partner. The IJV's top priority was for the local partner to learn and raise the technology and manufacturing to acceptable levels and production standards. A year later, learning was still the main activity with no sign of production on the horizon. Ultimately, the IJV dissolved without having ever manufactured a thing.

TOWARD A META-FRAMEWORK OF COLLABORATIVE LEARNING

Figure 13.2 presents our mapping of the field. We discuss its dimensions below.

Alliances: specifying the boundaries

We have contended that definitional ambiguities render assessing cooperation, particularly inter-firm cooperation, difficult. Early on, O'Brien and Tullies (1989), Root (1988) and

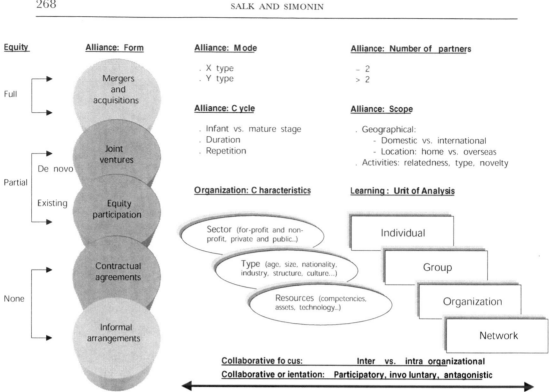

FIGURE 13.2   Mapping the collaborative field

Shenkar and Zeira (1987) recognized that the term "strategic alliances" already was becoming little more than a buzzword. These definitional ambiguities are a major source of difficulty when comparing the results of different studies (Terpstra and Simonin, 1993). Although many definitional propositions exist, their practical value may be quite limited. Rather, researchers should focus on the key variables that help frame the boundaries of collaboration. In figure 13.2, these key variables are: alliance form, mode, scope, number of partners, and cycle. Alliance *form* (Terpstra and Simonin, 1993) refers to the structural organization of the alliance along an equity continuum from no equity involved to full equity participation in the case of an acquisition or a merger. Past research has focused essentially on three forms: contractual agreements (e.g. licensing, franchising; no equity is involved), equity participation (e.g. equity swaps and partial acquisition; here, no new legal entity is created), and JVs (formation of a new and separate legal entity).

At the extremes of the equity continuum, two other forms of collaboration deserve attention. First, informal arrangements correspond to the case when no equity, but also no contract, is involved (e.g. exchange of personnel, benchmarking). Often unnoticed in the literature, this form of cooperation appears to be widely used. Hakansson and Johanson (1988), report in a study of cooperation between firms involved in technical development that more than two-thirds of the arrangements were informal. Second, the case of full equity (as opposed to no and partial equity) represents another, often ignored, case of cooperation. M&A, thus, is an ultimate form of collaboration where partners fully fuse their structures, legal existence, processes, cultures, and knowledge platforms. Likewise, the multinational organization's network of subsidiaries and affiliates fits our expanded definition. Over a decade ago, Hamel et al. (1989) warned that ownership structure seems to capture managers' attention when, in fact, the learning between partners is more important. Today, due to the growing interest in the learning organization and knowledge management, this impetus may have shifted. When looking at the alliance form, more is in play beyond the desire for control. The different structural forms of cooperation just identified may vary in their conduciveness to learning and types of prominent learning issues.

As *form* refers to the structural component of an alliance, *mode* focuses on the function of the collaboration (Terpstra and Simonin, 1993). These modes fall into two general categories: Type X and Type Y (Porter and Fuller, 1986). Type X corresponds to joint activities (partners perform activities at the same level of the value chain (e.g., joint R&D) while Type Y relates to complementary activities (partners perform activities at different levels of the value chain; e.g., one partner provides the manufacturing capability whereas the other provides marketing). From a learning point of view, Type X is more propitious to maintenance and single-loop learning due to the likely presence of a common knowledge base. Type Y alliances may be a source of greater knowledge gaps between partners resulting in possible shifts of expertise (accumulation of radically different knowledge, double-loop learning), but, conversely, it is less likely that learning occurs due to the specialization and partitioning of knowledge across partners.

Next, geography and activities define the *scope* of an alliance. In terms of geographical scope, one should differentiate domestic from international alliances on the basis of the national and linguistic origin of the partners (Meschi, 1997) and the location of the alliance itself or its interface (home or overseas) particularly when the focus is on knowledge transfer. Turning to the scope of alliance activities, one can distinguish the type of activities contributed (e.g., marketing, product development), their relatedness to the partners' expertise and core competencies (central or peripheral), and the valence of their overall novelty (e.g., breakthrough or routine). The *number of partners* can influence learning processes and utilization. The case of two partners differs from cases with three or more partners as the degree of complexity in interactions grows in a non-linear way. While most alliance research deals with dyadic relationships, studying consortia-like arrangements, particularly when assessing learning outcomes, processes, and performance levels, would contribute to the field.

Finally, when specifying alliance boundaries, one must isolate the components of an *alliance cycle*. Different challenges and problems exist at different stages of an alliance life (e.g., infant vs. mature stage). Cooperation evolves and co-evolves over time and requires re-examination at various stages. More generally, an alliance should be understood in light of its duration. Over the years, cultural (national) distances might decrease (Meschi, 1997), trust might intensify (Gulati, 1995), attachment between partners develops (Inkpen and Beamish, 1997), partners become more familiar with each other's expertise and unique practices, and different intervening variables can affect the transferability of knowledge (Simonin, 1999a, 1999b). Lastly, repetition provides another facet of a collaborative cycle. It encapsulates the degree and frequency at which partners collaborated in the past: is the alliance a first encounter between specific partners or, rather, another episode of a long collaborative history between them?

Learning: specifying the unit of analysis

Our model of collaborative learning identifies four distinct units of analysis: individuals, teams, organizations, and networks. These different levels of analysis also correspond to different learning foci and outcomes that are interrelated. This approach is consistent with Tiemessen et al.'s (1997) organizational learning framework that recognizes three levels of learning (individual, group, organization). The alliance literature needs investigations into how to reconcile individual and organizational learning. Likewise, more research pertaining to knowledge structures and processes, with networks taken as a unit analysis, is needed. Overall, paying attention to units of analysis equates to more precision in the coverage and understanding of collaborative learning.

Organization: specifying the key characteristics

Beyond drawing alliance boundaries and the units of analysis, specifying key organizational characteristics that help to further classify alliances and identify boundary conditions for learning outcomes and processes is necessary. Our model focuses on three categories: sector, type, and resources. *Sector* is a reminder that alliances go beyond business-to-business collaborations. Future research needs to address the full collaborative spectrum and, as such, what we coin "non-traditional alliances." Of particular interest, alliances between non-profit organizations, public agencies, and hybrids with business organizations deserve greater attention. Under *type*, we regroup variables that characterize an organization and are likely to impact learning (e.g., age, size, nationality, industry, structure, culture, etc.). Finally, *resources* captures aspects of an organization pertaining to knowledge (competencies, technology, intangible assets).

Collaboration: specifying the focus and orientation

Finally, we turn to two other key collaborative dimensions: collaborative focus and collaborative orientation. *Collaborative focus* draws a distinction between inter and intra-organizational collaborations. The bulk of alliance research deals with inter-firm collaborations. Our contention is that they are only a subset of the overall collaborative phenomenon. In a multinational enterprise, for instance, foreign subsidiaries or research teams from different strategic business units (SBUs) collaborate with one another on specific projects. Best practices and global campaigns need to be shared within a network of affiliates. In a sense, we argue that the study of organizational learning and knowledge transfer in the context of multinationals and FDI (see chapter 12 by Makino and Inkpen) is not so different from that in the context of traditional alliances: both fit under our model of collaborative learning. In one case the knowledge seeker may be a subsidiary in Spain and the knowledge holder/provider another subsidiary in Germany or headquarters; in the other case (traditional alliance) two unrelated companies play these roles.

Collaborative orientation depicts the nature and climate of a given collaboration: participatory, involuntary, and antagonistic. This is particularly important when looking at knowledge flows across partners. Under a *participatory* setting, one would expect the most favorable conditions for learning. The roles of the teaching partner and learning partner (Inkpen, 2001) are well specified, harmonized, and accepted. At the opposite, under an *antagonistic* setting, partners fight or co-habit at best. Learning is difficult. Partners adopt explicit protective measures, deploy shielding mechanisms, and engage in defensive actions to protect the transparency of their competencies, particularly when the embodied knowledge is explicit and held by only a few experts (Hamel, 1991; Inkpen and Beamish, 1997, Simonin, 1999a, 1999b). The last category, *involuntary collaboration*, depicts a situation where one organization may not even be aware of its role as a contributing partner. Then, learning is likely to be moderate and truncated through partial access only. As an extreme form of involuntary collaboration, reverse engineering and hiring of competitors' talents open a window on learning. Assessing collaborative orientation will provide a reliable gauge on the boundaries of learning opportunities and challenges ahead.

WHERE NEXT TO BETTER UNDERSTAND COLLABORATIVE ALLIANCES? – CONCLUDING REMARKS

Throughout we repeatedly have highlighted a number of aspects and avenues of inquiry that to our mind remain obscure and ripe for inquiry. To begin with, we repeat that there is much to be gained by viewing a far broader range of collaborative settings, including franchises, NGOs, MNCs, M&A and hybrid arrangements as learning contexts that should be studied, compared and contrasted to create common theory and knowledge about learning in collaborative alliances. Our analysis confirms once again the reflection that the alliance literature in general pays insufficient attention to social processes (Doz, 1996). Research on learning in inter-organizational alliances remains overwhelmingly structural and macro in focus. One of the biggest gaps revealed time and again above is a relative lack of studies that look at inter-organizational collaborative learning at the intra-organizational, group and individual levels of analysis. The work by Lyles and Salk (1996) and Lane et al. (2001) attempts to find rough and ready proxies for inter-group and inter-personal contact and things that might affect it. For example, their findings highlight the importance of training in inter-organizational collaborative learning, a finding congruent with those of Inkpen (1998). Their perceptual measures, however, while suggestive, need to be followed up by studies that dig deeper into the role of human resource management and organizational governance.

Though treated in detail in chapter 22 of this volume, we want to lend our support to the contention that using network approaches and theory to study processes of knowledge transfer and learning in such settings, especially across levels of analysis should reap rich dividends for the field. Collecting network and other original multi-level survey data admittedly is time consuming since it cannot be generated from secondary sources. However, Darr et al. (1995) reveal the (intentional) advantages from creatively selecting a bounded group of organizations (pizza restaurants) for which reasonable metrics for learning curves can be established. Their sort of study would be difficult to do for "messier" though

important outcomes such as developing collaborative capabilities or other access or appro-
priations of knowledge. There are many exogenous and contextual factors that could
impinge upon changes in such things as speed to market, quality, production efficiency,
market share – all things that firms might be learning through their alliance activities.
However, one could study and possibly identify internal morphologies or network configurations of groups and individuals and particular ways of organizing personnel in alliance
activities that could contribute both to learning within and from a collaborative alliance
as well as to performance within and across alliances. This, in turn, could help address
issues important to managers. Among these are: how to structure units managing alliance
activity; how to reward individuals to provide incentives for importing knowledge from
alliances; and how to manage assignments of managers involved in alliances so that managers involved do not leave. Anecdotal evidence suggests that managers returning from
alliance assignments in some firms feel their experiences are underutilized and that they
often leave. This observation also underscores the importance of the time or lifecycle
dimensions of the collaborative learning phenomenon, at the same time highlighting that
not enough is known about it.

Another ongoing gap is the lack of rigorously conducted case studies and comparative
case studies. It would be highly informative for theory building to seek out and conduct
studies of "best practice" and "worst practice" in developing collaborative know-how.
Comparing outliers offers different benefits for expanding our knowledge of collaborative
learning than focusing, as does virtually all of the current research, on averages.

In conclusion, while learning in alliances has deservedly captured the attention of management scholars, the boundaries of the phenomenon and the variables that need to be
assessed to understand it holistically have not been encapsulated in one place. This is where
we hope our inquiry will be of use. We have laid a foundation for new avenues of research
and for more cross-fertilization and dialogue across research paradigms and communities
who, without explicitly acknowledging it, want to understand the same things.

References

Allen, T.A. (1977) *Managing the Flow of Technology: Technology Transfer and The Dissemination of Techno-logical Information Within the R&D Organization*. Cambridge, MA: MIT Press.
Almeida, P. and Kogut, B. (1999) Localization of Knowledge and the Mobility of Engineers in Regional Networks. *Management Science*, 45 (7): 905–17.
Anand, B.N. and Khanna, T. (2000) Do Firms Learn to Create Value? The Case of Alliances. *Strategic Management Journal*, 21 (Special Issue): 295–315.
Ancona, D., Goodman, P., Lawrence, B., and Tushman, M. (2001a) Time: A New Research Lens. *Academy of Management Review*, 26 (4): 645–63.
Ancona, D., Okhysen, G., and Perlow, L. (2001b) Taking Time to Integrate Temporal Research. *Academy of Management Review*, 26 (4): 512–29.
Appleyard, M. (1996) How Does Knowledge Flow? Interfirm Patterns in the Semiconductor Indus-try. *Strategic Management Journal*, 17: 137–54.
Appleyard, M. (2001) Cooperative Knowledge Creation: The Case of Buyer-supplier Co-development in the Semiconductor Industry. Paper presented at IMD's conference on *Cooperative Strategies and Alliances: What We Know 15 Years Later*.

Argote, L. (1999) *Organizational Learning: Creating, Retaining and Transferring Knowledge*. Norwell, MA: Kluwer.

Argyris, C. and Schön, D. (1978) *Organizational Learning: A Theory of Action Perspective*. Reading, MA: Addison-Wesley.

Aulakh, P.S., Kotabe, M., and Sahay, A. (1996) Trust and Performance in Cross-border Marketing Partnerships. *Journal of International Business Studies*, 27 (5): 1005–32.

Barkema, H., Vermeulin, F., Shenkar, O., and Bell, H. (1997) Working Abroad, Working with Others: How Firms Learn to Operate International Joint Ventures. *Academy of Management Journal*, 40 (2): 426–42.

Bleeke, J. and Ernst, D. (1991) The Way to Win in Cross Border Alliances. *Harvard Business Review*, 69 (6): 127–35.

Chan, S., Kensinger, J., Keown, A., and Martin, J. (1997) Do Strategic Alliances Create Value? *Journal of Financial Economics*, 46: 199–221.

Cohen, W.M. and Levinthal, D.A. (1989) Innovation and Learning: The Two Faces of R&D. *The Economic Journal*, 99: 569–96.

Cohen, W.M. and Levinthal, D.A. (1990) Absorptive Capacity: A New Perspective on Learning and Innovation. *Administrative Science Quarterly*, 35 (1): 128–52.

Crossan, M. and Inkpen, A.C. (1994) Promise and Reality of Learning through Alliances. *International Executive*, 36: 263–73.

Darr, E., Argote, L., and Epple, D. (1995) The Acquisition, Transfer and Depreciation of Knowledge in Service Organizations: Productivity in Franchises. *Management Science*, 41: 1750–62.

Decarolis, D.M. and Deeds, D. (1999) The Impact of Stocks and Flows of Organizational Knowledge on Firm Performance: An Empirical Investigation. *Strategic Management Journal*, 20 (10): 953–68.

Dickson, P.H. and Weaver, K.M. (1997) Environmental Determinants and Individual-level Moderators of Alliance Use. *Academy of Management Journal*, 40 (2): 404–25.

Dodgson, M. (1996) Learning, Trust and Inter-firm Technological Linkages: Some Theoretical Associations. In R. Coombs, A. Richards, P. Saviotti, and V. Walsh (eds.), *Technological Collaboration*. Cheltenham, UK: Edward Elgar.

Doz, Y. (1996) The Evolution of Cooperation in Strategic Alliances: Initial Conditions or Learning Processes? *Strategic Management Journal*, 17: 55–83.

Doz, Y. and Prahalad, C.K. (1987) *The Multinational Mission*. New York: The Free Press.

Dyer, J.H. and Singh, H. (1998) The Relational View: Cooperative Strategy and Sources of Interorganizational Competitive Advantage. *Academy of Management Review*, 23 (4): 660–79.

Eisenhardt, K.M. and Schoonhoven, C.B. (1996) Resource-based View of Strategic Alliance Formation: Strategic and Social Effects in Entrepreneurial Firms. *Organization Science*, 7 (2): 136–50.

Fiol, M. and Lyles, M.A. (1985) Organizational Learning. *Academy of Management Review*, 10 (4): 803–13.

Gersick, C. (1989) Marking Time: Predictable Transitions in Task Groups. *Academy of Management Journal*, 32 (2): 274–309.

Grant, R. and Baden-Fuller, C. (2001) A Knowledge Accessing Theory of Interfirm Alliances. Paper presented at IMD's conference on *Cooperative Strategies and Alliances: What We Know 15 Years Later*.

Gulati, R. (1995) Structure and Alliance Formation Patterns: A Longitudinal Analysis. *Administrative Science Quarterly*, 40 (4): 619–52.

Gulati, R. and Gargiulo, M. (1999) Where Do Interorganizational Networks Come From? *American Journal of Sociology*, March: 177–231.

Hagedoorn, J. and Sadowski, B. (1999) The Transition from Strategic Technology Alliance to Mergers and Acquisitions: An Exploratory Study. *Journal of Management Studies*, 36 (1): 87–107.

Hagedoorn, J. and Schakenraad, J. (1994) The Effect of Strategic Technology Alliances on Company Performance. *Strategic Management Journal*, 15: 291–309.

Hakansson, H. and Johanson, J. (1988) Formal and Informal Cooperation Strategies in International Industrial Networks. In F. Contractor and P. Lorange (eds.), *Cooperative Strategies in International Business*. Lexington, MA: Lexington Books.

Hall, E. (1983) *The Dance of Life*. New York: Anchor Books/Doubleday.

Hamel, G. (1991) Competition for Competence and Inter-partner Learning within International Strategic Alliances. *Strategic Management Journal*, 12 (special issue): 83–103.

Hamel, G., Doz, Y. and Prahalad, C.K. (1989) Collaborate with Your Competitors and Win. *Harvard Business Review*, 67 (1): 133–39.

Harrigan, K.R. (1986) *Managing for Joint Venture Success*. Lexington, MA: Lexington Books.

Haspeslaugh, P.C. and Jemison, D.B. (1991) *Managing Acquisitions: Creating Value Through Corporate Renewal*. New York: Free Press.

Hennart, J.F. (1991) A Transaction Costs Theory of Equity Joint Ventures: An Empirical Study of Japanese Subsidiaries in the United States. *Management Science*, 37 (4): 483–97.

Inkpen, A. (1995a) Organizational Learning and International Joint Ventures. *Journal of International Management*, 1: 165–98.

Inkpen, A. (1995b) *The Management of Joint Ventures: An Organization Learning Perspective*. New York: Routledge Press.

Inkpen, A. and Dinur, A. (1998) Knowledge Management Processes and International Joint Ventures. *Organization Science*, 9: 454–68.

Inkpen, A. (2000) A Note on the Dynamics of Learning Alliances: Competition, Cooperation, and Relative Scope. *Strategic Management Journal*, 21: 775–9.

Inkpen, A. (2001) Learning, Knowledge Management and Strategic Alliances: So Many Studies, so Many Unanswered Questions. Paper presented at IMD's conference on 'Cooperative Strategies and Alliances: What We Know 15 Years Later'.

Inkpen, A. and Beamish, P. (1997) Knowledge, Bargaining Power and International Joint Venture Stability. *Academy of Management Review*, 22: 177–202.

Kale, P., Dyer, J., and Singh, H. (2001) Alliance Capability, Stock Market Response, and Long Term Alliance Success. Paper presented at IMD's conference on 'Cooperative Strategies and Alliances: What We Know 15 Years Later'.

Kale, P., Singh, H., and Perlmutter, H. (2000) Learning and the Protection of Proprietary Assets in Strategic Alliances: Building Relational Capital. *Strategic Management Journal*, 21: 217–37.

Kane, A., Argote, L., and Levine, J. (2002) Knowledge Transfer between Groups via Personnel Rotation: Effects of Social Identity and Knowledge Quality. GSIA Working Paper, 2002–01, Carnegie Mellon University.

Kanter, R.M. (1994) Collaborative Advantage. *Harvard Business Review*, July–August: 96–108.

Khanna, T., Gulati, R., and Nohria, N. (1998) The Dynamics of Learning Alliances: Competition, Cooperation and Relative Scope. *Strategic Management Journal*, 19(3): 193–210.

Kogut, B. (1988) Joint Ventures: Theoretical and Empirical Perspectives. *Strategic Management Journal*, 9: 319–32.

Kogut, B., Walker, G., Shan, W., and Kim, D.J. (1995) Platform Technologies and National Industrial Networks. In J. Hagedoorn (ed.), *Technical Change and the World Economy*. Brookfield, VT: E. Elgar, 58–82.

Kogut, B. and Zander, U. (1992) Knowledge of the Firm, Combinative Capabilities, and the Replication of Technology. *Organization Science*, 3: 383–97.

Koza, M.P., and Lewin, A.Y. (1998) The Co-evolution of Strategic Alliances. *Organization Science*, 9 (3): 255–64.

Lane, P. and Lubatkin, M. (1998) Relative Absorptive Capacity and Interorganizational Learning. *Strategic Management Journal*, 19: 461–77.

Lane, P., Salk, J.E., and Lyles, M. (2001) Absorptive Capacity, Learning and Performance in International Joint Ventures. *Strategic Management Journal*, 22 (12): 1139–62.

Lawrence, B., Hardy, C., and Phillips, N. (forthcoming) Institutional Effects of Interorganizational Collaboration: The Emergence of Proto-institutions. *Academy of Management Journal*.

Lei, D. and Slocum, J. (1992) Global Strategy, Competence-building and Strategic Alliances. *California Management Review*, 35 (1): 81–7.

Lorange, P. and Roos, J. (1993) *Strategic Alliances: Formation, Implementation, and Evolution*. Cambridge, MA: Blackwell.

Lorenzoni, G. and Lipparini, A. (1999) The Leveraging of Interfirm Relationships as a Distinctive Organizational Capability: A Longitudinal Study. *Strategic Management Journal*, 20 (4): 317–38.

Lyles, M. (1988) Learning among Joint Venture Sophisticated Firms. *Management International Review*, 28 (Special Issue): 85–98.

Lyles, M. and Dhanaraj, C. (2003) Learning across Borders: Organizational Learning and International Alliances. In V. Mahnke and T. Pedersen (eds.), *Governing Knowledge in MNCs*. New York: Oxford University Press, forthcoming.

Lyles, M. and Salk, J.E. (1996) Knowledge Acquisition from Foreign Parents in International Joint Ventures: An Empirical Examination in the Hungarian Context. *Journal of International Business Studies*, 29 (2): 154–74.

March, J.G. (1991) Exploration and Exploitation in Organizational Learning. *Organization Science*, 2 (1) Special Issue: 71–87.

Meschi, P.X. (1997) Longevity and Cultural Differences of International Joint ventures: Toward Time-based Cultural Management. *Human Relations*, 50 (2): 211–27.

Metiu, A. (2002) Group Engagement across Status Differences and Physical Distance. Paper presented at the 2002 Academy of Management Meetings, Denver, CO, August 12.

Mitchell, W. and Singh, K. (1996) Survival of Businesses Using Collaborative Relationships to Commercialize Complex Goods. *Strategic Management Journal*, 17 (3): 169–95.

Mjoen, H. and Tallman, S. (1997) Control and Performance in International Joint Ventures. *Organization Science*, 8 (3): 257–74.

Nonaka, I. and Takeuchi, H. (1995) *The Knowledge-creating Company*. New York: Oxford University Press.

O'Brien, P. and Tullis, M. (1989) Strategic Alliances: The Shifting Boundaries between Collaboration and Competition. *Multinational Business*, Winter, 4: 10–17.

Ohmae, K. (1989) The Global Logic of Strategic Alliances. *Harvard Business Review*, 67 (2): 143–54.

Olk, P. (1997) The Effect of Partner Differences on the Performance of R&D Consortia. In P. Beamish and J. Killing (eds.), *Cooperative Strategies, American Perspectives*. San Francisco: The New Lexington Press.

Osborn, R.N. and Hagedoorn, J. (1997) The Institutionalization and Evolutionary Dynamics of Interorganizational Alliances and Networks. *Academy of Management Journal*, 40 (2): 261–78.

Osterloh, M. and Frey, B. (2000) Motivation, Knowledge Transfer and Organizational Forms. *Organization Science*, 11 (5): 538–50.

Pisano, G. (1988) Innovation through Markets, Hierarchies, and Joint Ventures: Technology Strategy and Collaborative Arrangements in the Biotechnology Industry. Dissertation, University of California, Berkeley.

Polanyi, M. (1967) *The Tacit Dimension*. Garden City, NY: Anchor.

Porter, M. and Fuller, M. (1986) Coalitions and Global Strategy. In M. Porter (ed.), *Competition in Global Industries*. Boston, MA: Harvard Business School Press.

Powell, W., Koput, K., and Smith-Doerr, L. (1996) Interorganizational Collaboration and the Locus of Innovation: Networks of Learning in Biotechnology. *Administrative Science Quarterly*, 41: 116–45.

Pucik, V. (1988) Strategic Alliances, Organizational Learning, and Competitive Advantage. *Human Resource Management*, 27: 77–93.

Pucik, V. (1991) Technology Transfer in Strategic Alliances: Competitive Collaboration and Organizational Learning. In T. Agmon and M. von Glinow (eds.), *Technology Transfer in International Business*. Oxford University Press: New York, 121–42.

Reed, R. and DeFillippi, R. (1990) Causal Ambiguity, Barriers to Imitation, and Sustainable Competitive Advantage. *Academy of Management Review*, 15: 88–102.

Reuer, J., Park, K.M., and Zollo, M. (2001) Experiential Learning in International Joint Ventures: Obstacles and Opportunities. Paper presented at IMD's conference on 'Cooperative Strategies and Alliances: What We Know 15 Years Later'.

Root, F. (1988) Some Taxonomies of International Cooperative Arrangements. In F. Contractor and P. Lorange (eds.), *Cooperative Strategies in International Business*. Lexington, MA: Lexington Books.

Rousseau, D.M. (1995) *Psychological Contracts in Organizations: Written and Unwritten Agreements*. Thousand Oaks, CA: Sage.

Salk, J.E. (1996) Partners and other Strangers: Cultural Boundaries and Cross-cultural Encounters in International Joint Venture Teams. *International Studies of Management and Organization*, 26 (4): 48–72.

Salk, J.E. and Brannen, M.Y. (2000) National Culture, Networks and Individual Influence in a Multinational Management Team. *Academy of Management Journal*, 43 (12): 191–202.

Salk, J.E. and Shenkar, O. (2001) Social Identities and Cooperation in an International Joint Venture: An Exploratory Case Study. *Organization Science*, 12 (2): 161–78.

Sampson, R. (2001) Experience, Learning, and Collaborative Returns in R&D Alliances. Paper presented at IMD's conference on 'Cooperative Strategies and Alliances: What We Know 15 Years Later'.

Sayles, L.R. (1964) *Managerial Behavior: Administration in Complex Organizations*. New York: McGraw-Hill.

Schein, E.H. (1998) *Process Consultation*. Reading, MA: Addison-Wesley.

Shenkar, O. and Zeira, Y. (1987) Human Resources Management in International Joint Ventures: Direction for Research. *Academy of Management Review*, 12 (3): 546–57.

Shortell, S. and Zajac, E. (1988) Internal Corporate JVs: Development Processes and Performance Outcomes. *Strategic Management Journal*, 9: 527–42.

Simon, H. (1991) Bounded Rationality and Organizational Learning. *Organization Science*, 2: 125–34.

Simonin, B. (1997) The Importance of Developing Collaborative Know-how: An Empirical Test of the Learning Organization. *Academy of Management Journal*, 40 (5): 1150–74.

Simonin, B. (1999a) Ambiguity and the Process of Knowledge Transfer in Strategic Alliances. *Strategic Management Journal*, 20: 595–623.

Simonin, B. (1999b) Transfer of Marketing Know-how in International Strategic Alliances: An Empirical Investigation of the Role and Antecedents of Knowledge Ambiguity, *Journal of International Business Studies*, 30 (3): 463–90.

Simonin, B. (2000) Collaborative Know-how and Collaborative Advantage, *Global Focus*, 12 (4): 19–34.

Simonin, B. (2002) The Nature of Collaborative Know-how. In P. Lorange and F. Contractor (eds.), *Cooperative Strategies and Alliances: What We Know 15 Years Later*, forthcoming.

Szulanski, G. (1996) Exploring Internal Stickiness: Impediments to the Transfer of Best Practice within the Firm. *Strategic Management Journal*, 17 (Winter Special Issue): 27–43.

Terpstra, V. and Simonin, B. (1993) Strategic Alliances in the Triad: An Exploratory Study. *Journal of International Marketing*, 1 (1): 4–25.

Thorelli, H. (1986) Networks: Between Markets and Hierarchies. *Strategic Management Journal*, 7: 37–51.

Tiemessen, I., Lane, H., Crossan, M., and Inkpen, A. (1997) Knowledge Management in International Joint Ventures. In P. Beamish and J. Killing (eds.), *Cooperative Strategies, North American Perspectives*. San Francisco: New Lexington Press, 370–99.

Tushman, M.L. (1977) Special Boundary Roles in the Innovation Process. *Administrative Science Quarterly*, 22 (4): 587–605.

Van Maanen, J. and Schein, E.H. (1979) Toward a Theory of Organizational Socialization. In B.M. Staw and L.L. Cummings (eds.), *Research in Organizational Behavior*, Vol. 1. Greenwich, CT: JAI Press.

Walsh, J.P. and Ungeson, G.R. (1991) Organizational Memory. *Academy of Management Review*, 16 (1): 57–92.

Yan, A. and Gray, B. (1994) Bargaining Power, Management Control, and Performance in United States–China Joint Ventures: A Comparative Case Study. *Academy of Management Journal*, 37 (6): 1478–517.

Zander, U. and Kogut, B. (1995) Knowledge and the Speed of the Transfer and Imitation of Organizational Capabilities: An Empirical Test. *Organization Science*, 6 (1): 76–92.

Zeng, M. and Hennart, J.F. (2001) Learning Races and Cooperative Specialization: Reconciling Two Views of Alliances. Paper presented at IMD's conference on 'Cooperative Strategies and Alliances: What We Know 15 Years Later'.

14

Absorptive Capacity: Antecedents, Models, and Outcomes

FRANS A.J. VAN DEN BOSCH, RAYMOND VAN WIJK AND
HENK W. VOLBERDA

CHAPTER OUTLINE

This chapter focuses on the gap between the speed of proliferation of theoretical and empirical contributions and the speed of accumulation of the acquired scientific knowledge regarding absorptive capacity. To contribute to narrowing this gap, we will in particular review the *conceptual* developments of the absorptive capacity construct. Based on the seminal contributions of Cohen and Levinthal (1989, 1990) we will provide a brief overview of the various conceptual attributes of this construct, like the definition, antecedents and consequences, and levels of analysis involved. Next, we will assess the refinements, extensions and reconceptualizations of this construct in the literature. Furthermore, from the perspective of viewing models as mediating instruments between theory and empirical phenomena (Morgan and Morrison, 1999), we will analyze efforts to build conceptual models. Finally, we will address the progress made, select key problems and we will formulate future research directions to improve the *multilevel* and *transdisciplinary* characteristics of absorptive capacity.

INTRODUCTION

Absorptive capacity is defined as the ability to recognize the value of new external knowledge, assimilate it, and apply it to commercial ends (Cohen and Levinthal, 1990). Key antecedents discerned that influence absorptive capacity are both prior related knowledge (including basic skills and learning experience) and organizational factors, such as the structure of communication and distribution of knowledge. Several social science disciplines like psychology, sociology, economics and political science may contribute to the understanding of how these key antecedents influence absorptive capacity. Absorptive capacity is, therefore, potentially a powerful *multilevel* and *transdisciplinary construct*. In both theory building and empirical research, therefore, this construct is in principle able to bridge and

TABLE 14.1   Issues addressed in this chapter

Absorptive capacity construct: definition, antecedents, and organizational outcomes
- ♦ Definitions and levels of analysis
- ♦ Key antecedents and organizational outcomes
- ♦ The absorptive capacity construct as mediator between related literatures

Absorptive capacity: refinements, extensions, and reconceptualizations
- ♦ Definitions and levels of analysis
- ♦ Dimensions of absorptive capacity
- ♦ Antecedents and outcomes

Models of absorptive capacity: extensions
- ♦ Models as mediators
- ♦ Illustrative examples of absorptive capacity models
- ♦ Learning from modeling absorptive capacity

Progress, problems, and future research directions
- ♦ Progress and problems
- ♦ Future research directions

to enrich various related literatures, such as organizational learning and the knowledge-based view of the firm.

We will point out, however, that there is a *gap* between the speed of proliferation of theoretical and empirical contributions and the speed of accumulation of the acquired scientific knowledge regarding absorptive capacity. Efforts aimed at recognizing and narrowing this gap deserve more attention. To contribute to narrowing this gap, we will in particular focus on *an overview of the conceptual developments*. This chapter is, therefore, structured as follows (see table 14.1). First, based on the seminal contributions of Cohen and Levinthal (1989, 1990) the following section provides a brief overview of the various conceptual attributes of this construct, like the definition, antecedents and consequences, and levels of analysis involved. Second, we assess the refinements, extensions and reconceptualizations of this construct in the literature. Third, from the perspective of viewing models as mediating instruments between theory and empirical phenomena, we will analyze efforts to build conceptual models. In the final section we address the progress made and select key problems. We will formulate future research directions to improve the multilevel and transdisciplinary characteristics of absorptive capacity.

ABSORPTIVE CAPACITY CONSTRUCT: DEFINITIONS, ANTECEDENTS, AND ORGANIZATIONAL OUTCOMES

The absorptive capacity construct evolved from prior research in the 1980s, for example regarding the role of R&D in firm performance and organizational learning (Fiol and Lyles, 1985; Hedberg, 1981; Levitt and March, 1988). Another example is Kedia and Bhagat (1988) who already used the term "absorptive capacity" in the context of technology transfers across nations. We will limit ourselves here, however, to the contributions of Cohen and Levinthal (1989, 1990). They introduced the term of a firm's "learning" or "absorptive capacity" (Cohen and Levinthal, 1989: 569) and proposed to consider prior related knowledge as a key antecedent. By doing so, this section provides a kind of template that will be used to assess the contributions of subsequent research on absorptive capacity in the next sections.

Definitions and levels of analysis

As Cohen and Levinthal (1989, 1990) coined the term "absorptive capacity" (Lane and Lubatkin, 1998: 463) it makes sense to start with their definition and to focus in the next section on extensions or reconceptualizations of their definition. Cohen and Levinthal (1989: 569–70) introduced the absorptive capacity construct as follows: "the firm's ability to identify, assimilate and exploit knowledge from the environment." In their widely cited paper in *Administrative Science Quarterly*, Cohen and Levinthal (1990: 128) defined a firm's absorptive capacity as "an ability to recognize the value of new information, assimilate it, and apply it to commercial ends." Although in this definition the emphasis is on new information, and information is not the same as knowledge (Boisot, 1998), on the same page Cohen and Levinthal (1990: 128) refer to absorptive capacity as "the ability to evaluate and utilize outside knowledge." We therefore suggest using the following definition of absorptive capacity as a firm level construct: *the ability to recognize the value of new external knowledge, assimilate it, and apply it to commercial ends.*

This definition introduces *three capabilities*: (1) recognizing the value; (2) assimilating; and (3) applying new external knowledge to commercial ends. These three capabilities have been labeled as components or dimensions of absorptive capacity. For example Lane et al. (2001) distinguish three components of absorptive capacity and each of these components refers to one of the three capabilities mentioned above. Zahra and George (2002) use the term "dimensions of absorptive capacity," like Lane and Lubatkin (1998), to distinguish the three capabilities involved in absorbing new external knowledge.

In discussing their definition of absorptive capacity, Cohen and Levinthal (1990: 131) pointed out two important issues: (1) the level of analysis, and (2) the impact of the organizational context on absorptive capacity by emphasizing that "an organization's absorptive capacity will depend on the absorptive capacity of its individual members," however a firm's absorptive capacity is not "simply the sum of the absorptive capacity of its employees, and it is therefore useful to consider what aspects of absorptive capacity are distinctly organizational." Both issues gave rise to extensions and reconceptualizations regarding the definition, the antecedents, dimensions, and outcomes of absorptive capacity.

As the definition of absorptive capacity makes clear, absorptive capacity is a multilevel construct. The lowest level to apply absorptive capacity is *the individual level*. It is at this level that the link between absorptive capacity and learning is most evident. In this connection, Cohen and Levinthal (1990) refer to memory development, in which accumulated prior knowledge enables the ability to store new knowledge into one's memory and to recall and use it. This dynamic process gives rise to a key notion of absorptive capacity that prior related knowledge facilitates the learning or absorption of new related knowledge. Based on a review of the literature on learning and problem-solving processes at the individual level, Cohen and Levinthal (1990: 130) suggest that both these processes develop similarly: "the prior possession of relevant knowledge and skill is what gives rise to creativity . . ." and that these processes require time and an intensity of effort. A final observation at the individual level about learning or the absorption of new related knowledge is that the diversity or breadth of knowledge domains is important. In this connection Cohen and Levinthal (1990: 131) point out: "knowledge diversity also facilitates the innovative process by enabling the individual to make novel associations and linkages."

Having founded the absorptive capacity construct at the individual level, the next level of analysis discussed by Cohen and Levinthal (1990) is *the organizational level*. Simply adding the absorptive capacity of the organizational members, however, will not give rise to the absorptive capacity at organizational level. What is missing in such a naive approach is to pay attention to the (organizational) context, or as Cohen and Levinthal (1990: 131) point out (italics added): "it is therefore useful to consider *what aspects of absorptive capacity are distinctly organizational.*"

Although Cohen and Levinthal (1990) primarily focus on absorptive capacity at the firm level, several observations are made regarding *the inter-firm level*. For example, critical remarks are made regarding a firm "buying" absorptive capacity through hiring new personnel or corporate acquisitions. The path dependent and often tacit nature of a firm's idiosyncratic prior related knowledge and organizational context limits the quick integration of outside acquired absorptive capacity. Referring to the definition of absorptive capacity, considerable efforts and time are involved to assimilate and apply to commercial ends these types of external knowledge. Another observation deals with cooperative research ventures or strategic alliances emphasizing: "the simple notion that it is important to consider the costs of assimilating and exploiting knowledge from such ventures . . ." (Cohen and Levinthal, 1990: 149). This notion stresses the importance of absorptive capacity of the partners involved in interorganizational relations. This has been elaborated in subsequent research in, for example, the relative absorptive capacity construct (Lane and Lubatkin, 1998).

Having touched upon the individual, firm and interorganizational levels of analysis it is important to point out the multilevelness characteristic of absorptive capacity, like Cohen and Levinthal (1990: 128, italics added) do: "Outside sources of knowledge are often critical to the innovation process, *whatever the organizational level at which the innovating unit is defined.*" Therefore, other relevant levels of analysis are a particular industry, cluster of related industries, such as an emerging industrial complex – e.g. multimedia (De Boer et al., 1999) and financial services (Volberda et al., 2001) – region or nation (Wegloop, 1995) or even clusters of institutionally linked countries, like the European Union (Meyer-Krahmer and Reger, 1999).

Key antecedents and organizational outcomes

Cohen and Levinthal (1990) describe prior related knowledge as various related knowledge domains, basic skills and problem-solving methods, prior learning experience and learning skills, and a shared language. This encompassing view on prior related knowledge

TABLE 14.2   Two key clusters of antecedents of a firm's absorptive capacity

Prior related knowledge as the first cluster of antecedents	Internal mechanisms influencing a firm's absorptive capacity as the second cluster of antecedents
Examples: ♦ General knowledge of related domains ♦ Basic skills and problem-solving methods ♦ Prior learning experience ♦ Shared language	♦ *Structure of communication* (both intra- and inter-organizational) Examples: centralized versus decentralized interface functions, shared internal language etc. ♦ *Character and distribution of expertise and knowledge* within organization Examples: cross-function interfaces, internal and external networks etc.

Source: Based on Cohen and Levinthal (1990), see also Van Den Bosch et al. (1999: 553).

means that this construct relates to a cluster of antecedents of absorptive capacity. Several of these examples, like learning experience, problem-solving methods and in particular a shared language, however, refer directly to the "distinctive organizational aspects" of absorptive capacity. We will label these aspects as "*internal mechanisms* that influence the organization's absorptive capacity" (Cohen and Levinthal, 1990: 135, italics added) giving rise to a second cluster of antecedents. We suggest, therefore, considering *two clusters of antecedents*: (1) prior related knowledge and (2) internal mechanisms, namely distinctly organizational aspects of absorptive capacity. Table 14.2 shows both clusters of antecedents and the partial overlap of these clusters. For instance, in each cluster the importance of shared language is mentioned. Furthermore, as Cohen and Levinthal (1990: 132) have also emphasized, the internal mechanisms discerned in table 14.2 are mutually related: "designing communication structures cannot be disentangled from the distribution of expertise in the organization."

The distinction of two key clusters of antecedents of absorptive capacity makes several developments in the literature clear. First, as these two clusters of antecedents of absorptive capacity address rather encompassing phenomena, scholars working with the absorptive capacity construct will tend to select a subset of the antecedents from one or from both clusters as shown in table 14.2. In empirical research, this selection of a subset of antecedents will be influenced in particular by the availability of data. In a more general sense, theoretical and/or empirically driven selection processes regarding antecedents and outcomes to be addressed in research gave rise to several absorptive capacity models. Second, considering the broad and important organizational phenomena covered by the two clusters of antecedents, the absorptive capacity construct could in principle be used to integrate research regarding these phenomena. We will come back to this issue in the final section.

To understand the importance and usefulness of the absorptive capacity construct, besides the definition and antecedents, paying attention to the consequences of organizational outcomes is helpful as well. Cohen and Levinthal (1990) related absorptive

TABLE 14.3   Examples of literatures the absorptive capacity construct might bridge and enrich

- ◆ Organizational learning literature
- ◆ Managerial cognition literature
- ◆ Innovation and national systems of innovation literature
- ◆ Organizational change, strategic renewal and entrepreneurship literature
- ◆ Knowledge-based view of the firm literature
- ◆ Dynamic capability literature
- ◆ Co-evolutionary literature
- ◆ Inter-organizational relations and network literature

capacity to organizational outcomes such as innovative capabilities and innovative performance. Furthermore, they pointed out that absorptive capacity affects expectation formation ". . . permitting the firm to predict more accurately the nature and commercial potential of technological advances" (Cohen and Levinthal, 1990: 136). Related to expectation formation is the impact that the level of absorptive capacity may have on a firm's aspiration level as organizational outcome. In this connection Cohen and Levinthal (1990: 137) suggest that the higher the level of absorptive capacity, the more likely a firm will be proactive in "exploiting opportunities present in the environment, independent of current performance." Obviously, this type of organizational outcome is of great importance in, among others, strategy research, co-evolutionary research and entrepreneurship research. We expect, therefore, that in these fields of inquiry the absorptive capacity construct will be used.

The absorptive capacity construct as mediator between related literatures

Table 14.3 provides a brief overview of the various related literatures that could be bridged and enriched by using the absorptive capacity construct. The selection of these literatures is based on assessing to what extent these literatures are directly related to either the key antecedents of absorptive capacity and/or to the organizational outcomes associated with this construct. For several of the literatures mentioned in table 14.3 we will briefly illustrate these links. The link between absorptive capacity and the organizational learning and innovation literatures can be illustrated by referring, for example, to the dual role of R&D. R&D generates not only innovations and new knowledge, but also enhances learning. This phenomenon is illustrated by the title of Cohen and Levinthal (1989) paper: "Innovation and learning: the two faces of R&D." Another example is provided by Cockburn and Henderson (1998) who pointed out that firms have to invest in absorptive capacity in the form of in-house basic research, to be able to access and learn from upstream basic research.

An example of a link between the organizational learning and managerial cognition literatures is among others provided by Dijksterhuis et al. (1999) who emphasize that a change in shared managerial schemas – that is a firm's idiosyncratic application of a single or multiple management logic(s) being shared among a firm's key decision makers influence a firm's absorptive capacity. Examples of management logics are a classical and a modern management logic (Volberda, 1998). In a classical management logic, the environment is considered as a closed system while in a modern management logic, an open systems approach is used. Obviously, firms associated with a classical management logic do not consider the environment as a source of valuable knowledge to be absorbed and, therefore, lack absorptive capacity.

Another example of how absorptive capacity might link several of the literatures mentioned in table 14.3, is provided by research on strategic renewal. Strategic renewal can take place by external actions like strategic alliances aimed at creating an organizational competitive advantage in which the absorptive capacities of the firm involved are important (Dyer and Singh, 1998). Internal actions, like starting up new businesses and launching new products and services, require substantial exploration activities and an absorptive capacity to facilitate these activities (Volberda et al., 2001). In co-evolutionary research, absorptive capacity is considered as one of the main mediating factors between micro- and macro-evolution (Lewin et al., 1999). For an overview of knowledge and internal, external and social networks including the relationship with absorptive capacity see Van Wijk et al. (2002).

ABSORPTIVE CAPACITY: REFINEMENTS, EXTENSIONS, AND RECONCEPTUALIZATIONS

We will discuss briefly here illustrative research that extends the definition and levels of analysis of absorptive capacity. Next, we elaborate the dimensions of absorptive capacity discerned in subsequent research and we will illustrate how the required dimensions at firm level depend on the external context.

Definitions and levels of analysis: extensions

The lowest level of analysis of absorptive capacity within a *focal firm* is the individual level. Examples of intermediate levels are the team, organizational unit, business unit, division and subsidiaries within multidivisional enterprises. Finally, at the corporate level the focal firm's absorptive capacity may be assessed. Of these levels of analysis, the majority of the publications on absorptive capacity address either the business unit level (for example Tsai, 2001) or the subsidiary level (for instance Gupta and Govindarajan, 2000), but in particular the firm level (for instance Pennings and Harianto, 1992). Several scholars analyzing the absorptive capacity of a focal firm, however, emphasize different aspects of Cohen and Levinthal's (1990) definition and adapt these aspects to the appropriate level of analysis or add new aspects as well. For example, Kim (1998) focused on learning capability and problem-solving skills, being part of prior related knowledge as the first cluster of antecedents (see table 14.2), and analyzes absorptive capacity at the firm level by investigating prior knowledge bases and the intensity of effort. Gupta and Govindarajan (2000) analyzed the absorptive capacity of subsidiaries in multinational enterprises by focusing on the prior related knowledge of these organizational units.

Research on absorptive capacity in an *interorganizational context* such as strategic alliances and joint ventures have been performed by, for example, Inkpen and Dinur (1998), Lyles and Salk (1996), and Kamien and Zang (2000); see Van Wijk et al. (2002) for an overview. Lane and Lubatkin (1998) reconceptualized the firm level definition of Cohen and Levinthal (1990) and suggested the construct of *relative absorptive capacity*. Relative absorptive capacity is defined as "the ability of a firm to learn from another firm" in a student–teacher pairing, namely a learning dyad (Lane and Lubatkin, 1998: 462). Relative absorptive capacity is, like in Cohen and Levinthal's definition of absorptive capacity, dependent on "the ability of the student firm to recognize and value new external knowledge, to assimilate that knowledge, and to commercially utilize it" (Lane and Lubatkin, 1998: 464). The importance of considering the absorptive capacity of the partner in interorganizational relations has been pointed out earlier by, for instance, Veugelers and Kesteloot (1996). They investigated, among others, asymmetries in absorptive capacity between partners and the likelihood of establishing successful R&D joint ventures.

In the context of national systems of innovations (NSI), research on the level of analysis of the absorptive capacity of *nations* has also been conducted. For example, Carlsson and Jacobsson (1994) investigated technological systems in Sweden. They pointed out that increasing the absorptive capacity of the economy becomes an important aspect of public policy. Another interesting example is provided by Wegloop (1995: 419) who suggested distinguishing National Absorptive Capacity defined as "those institutions and actions that allow firms within the NSI to recognize the value of new external information, assimilate it, and apply it to commercial ends." Keller (1996) investigated a country's implementation of technologies invented abroad and mentions the importance of raising the absorptive capacity of the economy. See also Mowery and Oxley (1995) and Montresor (2001) on related topics and Meyer-Krahmer and Reger (1999), who discussed the importance of raising the absorptive capacity of national systems of innovations in a European context.

Dimensions of absorptive capacity: extensions

Several authors have pointed out that absorptive capacity is a multidimensional construct. Based on Cohen and Levinthal's (1990) definition of absorptive capacity and the distinction of three types of abilities, we will provide some examples below. Lane and Lubatkin (1998) suggested distinguishing three dimensions: (1) the ability to recognize and value new external knowledge; (2) the ability to assimilate new external knowledge; and (3) the ability to commercialize new external knowledge. Based on Grant (1996), who discussed three dimensions of knowledge integration, Van Den Bosch et al. (1999) suggested distinguishing similar dimensions of knowledge absorption: respectively the *efficiency*, *scope*, and *flexibility dimension*. Van Wijk et al. (2001) highlighted the depth and breadth dimension of absorptive capacity. The *depth dimension* of absorptive capacity facilitates the absorption of new, additional knowledge in a domain in which knowledge is already present. Deep knowledge gains from specialization. Specialization enhances rationalization and routinization. The depth of absorptive capacity is, therefore, associated with the efficiency dimension of knowledge absorption. The *breadth dimension* of absorptive capacity enables the absorption of new knowledge in domains other than but related to what is currently known. This dimension is associated with the scope dimension of knowledge absorption and with exploration. Zahra and George (2002) suggested distinguishing four dimensions of absorptive capacity, each playing different but complementary roles in explaining how absorptive capacity can influence organizational outcomes. These *four dimensions* are respectively: the acquisition, assimilation, transformation and exploitation dimension. Zahra and George (2002) relate these dimensions to corresponding capabilities. To emphasize the contingent character of the relevance of the dimensions of absorptive capacity, below we will illustrate how a particular type of external knowledge environment may influence the required dimensions of absorptive capacity.

Dimensions of absorptive capacity and changing external contexts

As indicated above, building on Grant's (1996) three characteristics of knowledge integration, Van Den Bosch et al. (1999) distinguished three dimensions of knowledge absorption: efficiency, scope, and flexibility. Efficiency of knowledge absorption refers to the activities, procedures, and routines that firms use to identify, assimilate, and exploit new knowledge. The efficiency dimension focuses on the cost and economies of scale perspective on knowledge absorption. The scope dimension of knowledge absorption is associated with the breadth of knowledge a firm draws upon. Flexibility of knowledge absorption refers to the extent to which a firm can access additional, and reconfigure existing knowledge. March's (1991) distinction between exploration and exploitation in the development of organization knowledge can be related to these three dimensions of knowledge absorption. The efficiency dimension of knowledge absorption is associated with the exploitation of a firm's knowledge configuration, as "the essence of exploitation is the refinement and extension of existing competencies, technologies, and paradigms" (March, 1991: 85). Furthermore, the scope and flexibility dimension of knowledge absorption can be associated with the exploration of a firm's knowledge configuration.

How do firms cope with the peculiarities of their (knowledge) environment? This question has been raised earlier by Starbuck (1992). In the following application based on Van Den Bosch et al. (1999), we elaborate on this question by investigating how *key contingencies in the external knowledge environment* do influence the required presence or absence of the dimensions of knowledge absorption. We will distinguish two contingencies: a stable and a turbulent knowledge environment, see table 14.4. In a stable knowledge environment, like a mature single industry, existing firms have a strong focus on the exploitation of knowledge. The knowledge domain the incumbent firm wishes to exploit is closely related to its current knowledge base (Cohen and Levinthal, 1990). This phenomenon is associated with "local search," for instance when a firm's R&D activity is closely related to its previous R&D activity (Huygens at al., 2001).

Within the context of exploitation of knowledge, a firm's interface function – capturing the structure of communication between the external environment and the firm and between sub-units within the firm and being one of the antecedents of absorptive capacity – will have a tendency to become more centralized, increasing the efficiency of internal communication. Following Cohen and Levinthal (1990), we point out that this centralization tendency is supported by a well-developed shared knowledge and an internal language, creating a more inward-looking absorptive capacity. Cohen and Levinthal

TABLE 14.4   Types of knowledge environments, focus of knowledge absorption, and requirements regarding three dimensions of knowledge absorption

Types of knowledge environment	Focus of knowledge absorption on	Requirements regarding three dimensions of knowledge absorption		
		Efficiency	Scope	Flexibility
(1) Stable knowledge environment Example: Mature single industry	Exploitation	High	Low	Low
(2) Turbulent knowledge environment Example: Emerging industrial complex	Exploration	Low	High	High

Source: Van Den Bosch et al. (1999).

(1990:133) pointed out that both inward-looking and outward-looking absorptive capacities are necessary for effective organization, but that "excessive dominance by one or the other will be dysfunctional." Over time, an efficiency focus on knowledge absorption is likely to result in a low diversity of knowledge structures, few cross-functional relationships and a low absorptive capacity. Firms operating in stable knowledge environments, therefore, are likely to become more reactive. This reactive firm behavior can be considered as an example of an organizational outcome moderated by absorptive capacity.

Contrary to firms in stable knowledge environments, firms in turbulent knowledge environments, however, are likely to dedicate efforts exclusively to increasing their absorptive capacity. In such environments, a firm's knowledge absorption is likely to be more focused on exploration. The scope and flexibility dimension of knowledge absorption are important in such a context. Contrary to the situation in a stable knowledge environment, the interface function is likely to be more decentralized in a turbulent knowledge environment. This decentralization of the interface function is reflected in an increasing diversity or breadth of knowledge structures and a growing importance of cross-functional relations (Jones and Craven, 2001). Table 14.4 summarizes the impact these different knowledge environments are likely to have on the requirements regarding the three dimensions of knowledge absorption. Another example of how the required dimensions of absorptive capacity are influenced by the external environment is provided by Zahra and George (2002), who discuss the impact of various appropriability regimes on their acquisition dimension of absorptive capacity. They suggest that when a firm is confronted with a weak regime of appropriability, the acquisition of new external knowledge will be low because imitation of innovative products or services by rivals might be the case.

Antecedents and organizational outcomes: extensions

In the previous section we suggested that scholars are likely to focus on a particular subset of antecedents selected from the two clusters of antecedents discerned in table 14.2. Furthermore, depending on the level of analysis, particular variables within these two clusters are likely to be selected or refined. Table 14.5 illustrates this selection process by

TABLE 14.5   Antecedents of absorptive capacity

Level of analysis	Examples of antecedents	Illustrative references
Intra-firm level	◆ A unit's R&D intensity	Tsai (2001)
	◆ Knowledge flow configuration (horizontal versus vertical)	Van Wijk et al. (2001)
	◆ Prior related knowledge and similarity of certain attributes (for example sharing similar common meanings, a mutual subcultural language)	Gupta and Govindarajan (2000)
Firm level	◆ Prior related knowledge, and internal mechanisms (see table 15.2)	Cohen and Levinthal (1990)
	◆ Prior related knowledge, organizational form, combinative capabilities	Van den Bosch et al. (1999)
	◆ External sources, knowledge complementarity, and experience	Zahra and George (2002)
Inter-firm level	◆ Specific type of new knowledge; similarity of compensation practices and organizational structures; familiarity with organizational problems	Lane and Lubatkin (1998)

providing a brief overview of the types of antecedents used at various levels of analysis. At the intra-firm level the antecedents used in the three examples provided in table 14.5 address different selections from the two clusters of antecedents. For example, Tsai (2001) selected a content dimension of prior related knowledge by using R&D expenditure (divided by sales). For a more encompassing approach of prior related knowledge see, for example, Shane (2000). In the other two examples an operationalization is used of both prior related knowledge and a subset of internal mechanisms influencing the unit's absorptive capacity. Van Wijk et al. (2001) used the knowledge flow configuration as antecedent addressing general knowledge and prior learning experience. The knowledge flow configuration also reflects the character and distribution of expertise and knowledge (Van Wijk and Van Den Bosch, 1998, 2000). The knowledge flow configuration therefore addresses parts of the two clusters of antecedents of absorptive capacity as shown in table 14.2. Furthermore, in the survey used, the structure of the communication – another internal mechanism influencing absorptive capacity mentioned in table 14.2 – is addressed as well.

Gupta and Govindarajan (2000) used Cohen and Levinthal's (1990) definition to operationalize the antecedents of absorptive capacity of subsidiaries of multinational enterprises, see table 14.5. The antecedents used at firm level in Van Den Bosch et al. (1999) and Zahra and George (2002) will be discussed in the section on absorptive capacity models below. At inter-firm level Lane and Lubatkin (1998) used three antecedents for explaining the relative absorptive capacity construct. These *interorganizational antecedents* are the similarity of both firms' knowledge bases (but different specialized knowledge), organizational

TABLE 14.6 Absorptive capacity as moderator of various organizational outcomes

Examples of organizational outcomes	Illustrative references
◆ Innovative performance; exploration/ exploitation; new product development	Cohen and Levinthal (1990); Tsai (2001); Van Wijk et al. (2001); Stock et al. (2001)
◆ Expectation formation; reactive/proactive strategy formation	Cohen and Levinthal (1990); Volberda (1998); Van den Bosch et al. (1999)
◆ Organizational adaptation; co-evolution; strategic renewal	Lewin and Volberda (1999); Lewin et al. (1999); Volberda et al. (2001)
◆ Transfer of best practice and knowledge flows within the firm	Szulanski (1996); Gupta and Govindarajan (2000)
◆ New wealth creation; entrepreneurial wealth; competitive advantage; financial performance	Lewin et al. (1999); Deeds (2001); Zahra and George (2002); Tsai (2001)
◆ Knowledge transfers; organizational learning in alliances and IJV performance	Ahuja (2000); Kim (1998); Koza and Lewin (1998); Lane and Lubatkin (1998); Lyles and Salk (1996); Mowery et al. (1996)
◆ Diversification	Kumar and Seth (2001)

structures and compensation policies, and dominant logics. The first antecedent refers to the relative relationship between the student firm's knowledge and that of its teacher. Regarding the second antecedent, both organizational structures and compensation policies serve as proxies for the similarity of the knowledge-processing systems and norms of the firms involved. The third antecedent is based on the assumption that a firm's dominant logic determines why it applies the acquired knowledge to which commercial objectives. These three antecedents refer to, respectively, the know-what, know-how and know-why portion of the knowledge bases involved. Their dependent variable is a firm's success regarding inter-organizational learning.

Organizational outcomes

Many scholars recognize that a firm's absorptive capacity is not a goal in itself, but that it moderates important organizational outcomes. For example, Cohen and Levinthal (1990) relate absorptive capacity to, among others, innovative capabilities, innovative performance and expectation formation. In subsequent research efforts several related organizational outcomes have been addressed. In table 14.6 we give some examples of organizational outcomes and illustrative references.

For three examples in table 14.6 we will briefly discuss how absorptive capacity influences the organizational outcome. Van Wijk et al. (2001) found that vertical knowledge transfers appeared to relate to increases in the depth dimension of absorptive capacity but have no significant relation with the degree of exploration over exploitation. Horizontal knowledge transfers were found to have a positive relationship with the breadth dimension of absorptive capacity. The breadth of absorptive capacity appeared to be positively related to the level of exploration over exploitation. Stock et al. (2001) investigated the influence of absorptive capacity (operationalized by R&D intensity) and new product development performance in the computer modem industry. Their results indicated an "inverted-U" shape, suggesting that increasing absorptive capacity results in increasing performance but only up to a certain level. Deeds (2001) studied the relationship between absorptive capacity and the amount of entrepreneurial wealth creation using as a proxy for absorptive capacity, the aggregate number of research communities in which a firm participates measured by co-citation analysis. The results indicated a positive relationship between absorptive capacity and entrepreneurial wealth creation in pharmaceutical biotechnology firms in the USA.

ABSORPTIVE CAPACITY MODELS

To enhance the development of absorptive capacity models, we will emphasize the importance of considering models both as mediators between theories and the real world and as learning mechanisms. To this end, we will discuss examples of absorptive capacity models each addressing different antecedents, outcomes and levels of analysis.

Models as mediators

Morgan and Morrison (1999) introduce the perspective of viewing models as mediators or mediating instruments between theory and empirical phenomena. In this perspective, models are considered as "autonomous agents" that can function as an instrument of investigation. In this connection, Morgan and Morrison (1999: 10) point out: "It is precisely because models are partially independent of both theories and the world that they have this autonomous component and so can be used as instruments of exploration in both domains." In elaborating this perspective they address *four questions*. These questions deal with respectively: how models are constructed, how models function, what models represent and finally how we can learn from models. Morgan and Morrison (1999: 11–12) emphasize that: "We do not learn much from looking at a model – we learn more from building the model and from manipulating it." Learning from building models stimulates finding out what "will work to represent certain aspects of the theory or the world or both" (Morgan and Morrison, 1999: 386). Below, three recent efforts in model building will be discussed as illustrative examples. These three models all address antecedents and organizational outcomes of absorptive capacity, albeit by focusing on different subsets of antecedents (in terms of table 14.2) and dimensions and on particular outcomes (in terms of table 14.6). The models also differ regarding empirical research methodology. The first model is illustrated in longitudinal case research; the second model is advanced as a conceptual model, while the third model is tested in quantitative research.

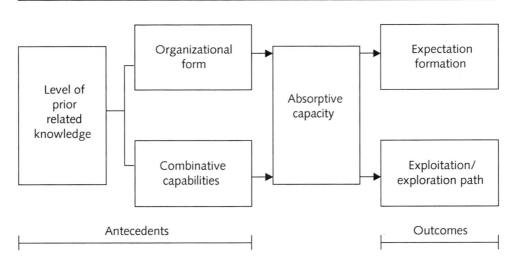

FIGURE 14.1   A model of a firm's absorptive capacity: antecedents and outcomes (adapted from Figure 1 in Van Den Bosch et al., 1999)

Illustrative examples of absorptive capacity models

Figure 14.1 portrays a model of absorptive capacity distinguishing major antecedents and outcomes that are closely related to the ones discerned by Cohen and Levinthal (1990). The model depicts how absorptive capacity is largely a function of prior related knowledge and how two complementary antecedents reflect key examples of "internal mechanisms influencing a firm's absorptive capacity" as described in table 14.2. The model portrays how these two internal mechanisms moderate prior related knowledge and absorptive capacity. In the context of this model, prior related knowledge can be considered as a kind of distributed organizational knowledge system (Tsoukas, 1996), while the two internal mechanisms enable the connection and integration of the various parts, domains and skills of prior related knowledge. These two internal mechanisms emphasize the fundamentally organizational character of a firm's knowledge (Zollo and Winter, 2002).

This way of modeling suggests that, for example, *ceteris paribus*, prior related knowledge, a change in organizational form for example from a functional to a matrix form (Volberda, 1998), or from a functional form to internal network forms of organizing (Van Wijk et al., 2002), has an influence on the level of absorptive capacity. The third antecedent refers to combinative capabilities. This construct is used in the model to investigate the capabilities associated with the internal mechanisms influencing a firm's absorptive capacity. A firm's combinative capabilities synthesize and apply current and acquired knowledge (Kogut and Zander, 1992). The use of the term "combination" by Kogut and Zander is associated with "integration," as used by Grant (1996). Van Den Bosch et al. (1999) build on these contributions by distinguishing between three types of combinative capabilities a firm has at its disposal: systems capabilities, coordination capabilities, and socialization capabilities. Systems capabilities refer to procedures and manuals often used to integrate explicit knowledge. Coordination capabilities enhance knowledge absorption through relations between members of a team, an organization unit or organization units; for an interesting account of team learning and the role of team leader coaching see Edmondson (2001). Socialization capabilities refer to a shared ideology as well as collective interpretation of the reality and enable absorptive capacity by specifying broad, tacitly understood rules for appropriate action under unspecific contingencies (Camerer and Vepsalainen, 1988).

In using the combinative capability construct, both the structure of communication and the distribution of expertise and knowledge – representing the second cluster of antecedents – are introduced in the model. Systems, coordination, and socialization capabilities address several aspects of the structure of communication and the ways in which the distribution of expertise and knowledge are involved in knowledge absorption. For example, systems capabilities enable the combination of explicit knowledge available within the distribution of knowledge across the organizational units, while coordination and socialization capabilities enable the externalization of tacit knowledge. In this regard, Jones and Craven (2001) provide empirical evidence on how, in particular, coordination capabilities can positively influence a firm's absorptive capacity. The model depicts two related types of organizational outcomes: expectation formulation and the exploitation/exploration path. Both outcomes contribute to the path dependent character of absorptive capacity, giving rise to dynamic effects such as a feedback loop from the level of expectation formation to a change in organizational form, enhancing the absorptive capacity.

The model sketched above has been illustrated by two longitudinal case studies (Van Den Bosch et al., 1999). The primary purpose of these case studies is obtaining insights into how the firms' absorptive capacity, at the time of transformation of the industry from traditional publishing firms moving into the emerging multimedia industrial complex, moderated and co-evolved with the firms' adaptations in organizational form and combinative capabilities. The case studies illustrated how the organizational form and combinative capabilities interact over time and what their combined effect was on the level of absorptive capacity. The case studies also highlighted the stickiness of socialization capabilities and the struggle with changing organizational forms, aimed at forms that facilitate the scope and flexibility dimension of knowledge absorption.

A second example of the absorptive capacity model

Figure 14.2 portrays another example of a model of absorptive capacity at firm level, in which the distinction between a firm's *potential* and *realized capacity* to absorb knowledge is introduced. Potential capacity comprises knowledge acquisition and assimilation, while realized capacity is determined by transformation and exploitation. In this connection Zahra and George (2002: 3) point out that outcomes reflect a firm's realized capacity and that the potential capacity component "has received disproportionally less empirical scrutiny when compared to realized capacity." They suggest both types of capabilities have separate, but complementary roles and propose to take into account *the efficiency factor*: the ratio of realized to potential absorptive capacity. Firms with a high efficiency factor are likely to increase their performance.

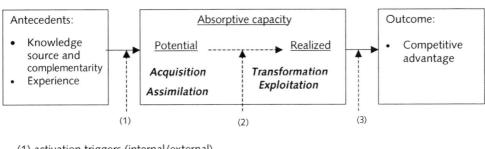

(1) activation triggers (internal/external)
(2) social integration mechanisms
(3) regimes of appropriability

FIGURE 14.2   A model of a firm's absorptive capacity: antecedents and outcomes (adapted from Figure 1 in Zahra and George, 2002)

Zahra and George (2002) distinguish as key antecedents external sources of knowledge, such as inter-organizational relationships like alliances, knowledge complementarity and experience. External sources of knowledge must be complementary to the knowledge a firm already possesses. In comparison to the two clusters of antecedents depicted in table 14.2, in this model the antecedents do not address the second cluster of antecedents being the internal mechanisms influencing a firm's absorptive capacity. Instead, internal (for example, an organizational crisis) and external (for example, regulatory change) triggers are introduced, moderating the antecedents, potential and realized absorptive capacity and outcomes. In the model, so-called social integration mechanisms are supposed to reduce the gap between potential and realized absorptive capacity and thereby increase the efficiency factor. Both informal and formal social integration are discerned. These mechanisms are expected to lower the barriers to information sharing and are, therefore, related to one of the key antecedents, being structure of communication, discerned in table 14.2. The model explicitly takes into account the external context to explain the relationship between absorptive capacity and outcomes by introducing the regimes of appropriability as a moderating factor. Under a strong regime of appropriability it is expected that there will be a significant and positive relationship between realized absorptive capacity and sustainable competitive advantage as outcome, because of higher costs of imitation by rivals. Zahra and George (2002) advanced the above sketched conceptual model but did not test the model.

A third example of the absorptive capacity model

Figure 14.3 portrays an absorptive capacity model (Lane et al., 2001) of learning in international joint ventures (IJV) from knowledge held by foreign parents. The model segments absorptive capacity into the three types of capabilities proposed by Cohen and Levinthal (1990). The first two capabilities enable knowledge learned from foreign partners, while the third is directly associated with the realization of organizational outcome and is,

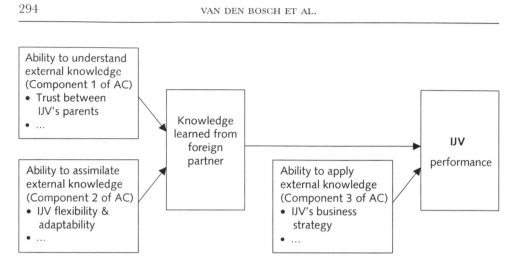

FIGURE 14.3   An absorptive capacity model of learning in international joint ventures (IJV): components, antecedents and outcome (adapted from Figure 1 in Lane et al., 2001)

therefore, in a sense related to realized absorptive capacity discussed in the previous model. In this model, the antecedents are distributed along each of the three components of absorptive capacity. The antecedents of the first component are trust between an IJV's parents and the IJV's relative absorptive capacity *vis-à-vis* its foreign parent. The second component, the ability to assimilate new knowledge from the parents, is determined by an IJV's flexibility and in particular its learning structure and processes (Lyles and Salk, 1996). The IJV's strategy and training competences (in particular relevant for tacit knowledge) are the antecedents of the third component. By segmenting the model in this way, the relationship between the first two components and IJV performance is moderated by the amount of knowledge learned from the foreign parents. The model was tested in a sample of established Hungarian IJVs surveyed in 1993 and again in 1996. The results provide support for the above indicated antecedents of each of the three components. The results, however, suggest that of the three components of absorptive capacity, the antecedents of the first two, do affect learning but not performance. The antecedents of the third component, the ability to apply external knowledge, however, do influence performance.

Learning from modeling absorptive capacity

In reflecting on the three examples of models of absorptive capacity, we briefly address the questions raised by Morgan and Morrison (1999). Regarding the first question of how the models are constructed, the three examples above show that the construction process can be triggered by the absorptive capacity theory or associated theories and/or by the empirical problems addressed by the model. All these examples, however, incorporated a subset of antecedents and dimensions or components of absorptive capacity in the model, and a particular organizational outcome as well. The selection of the subset of antecedents of absorptive capacity chosen, or of its components, is, however, not extensively discussed or justified in these three examples. In addressing the second question, this suggests that the three models function partly to illustrate absorptive capacity theories, partly to address the selected organization outcomes and partly to integrate and reconceptualize previous modeling efforts and empirical findings. Reflecting on the third question about what the models represent, this variety in functions of the models discussed emphasizes that these models represent neither absorptive capacity theories nor empirical realities. Indeed, these models try to mediate both.

How can we learn from these modeling efforts? First, it seems important in ongoing research efforts to recognize the mediating role of absorptive capacity models. Second, to learn from the various ways in which this role can be performed, it is important to justify more clearly what theoretical and empirical aspects are selected and how they are addressed in the proposed model. Third, as absorptive capacity, due to its cumulative and path dependent character, by definition requires a dynamic model, in further model building efforts this issue deserves serious attention. Although progress has been made in conceptual absorptive capacity models, in most empirical research there is less or no room for assessing, for example, how changes in antecedents influence absorptive capacity over time, including feedback loops such as how an increase of absorptive capacity may influence internal organizational factors (Van Den Bosch et al., 1999). Fourth, considering the multi-level and transdisciplinary character of the absorptive capacity construct, in papers using absorptive capacity models it is important to discuss the contribution of the proposed model to (1) addressing the multilevel characteristic; and (2) to what extent the model might help bridging and enriching which literatures.

PROGRESS, PROBLEMS AND FUTURE RESEARCH DIRECTIONS

To benefit from the templates used in the preceding sections, in the first column of table 14.7 we discern important conceptual attributes and characteristics of absorptive capacity.

Table 14.7 contains three columns in which we *tentatively indicate the progress*, and select some problems and topics for future research. In doing so, we hope to contribute to the purpose of this chapter as indicated in the introduction.

Progress and problems

In our assessment of the progress of the development of the absorptive capacity construct, models, and applications, *two observations* are evident. First, considering the relatively large number of publications on absorptive capacity dealing with a variety of levels of analysis, the multilevelness characteristic of absorptive capacity has clearly been recognized by researchers in various related fields of inquiry. Second, in literature search using different search programs, it is amazing to observe the variety of journals associated with different literatures (see, for example, the references section below), publishing papers on absorptive capacity using this construct as either the independent variable or dependent variable. In the context of the analysis in the preceding sections, these two observations give rise to our *third observation*. The proliferation of models and applications of the absorptive capacity construct to various levels of analysis and in various related literatures did not

TABLE 14.7   Absorptive capacity: progress, problems, and future research

Absorptive capacity	Progress	Problems: a selection	Future research directions
◆ Definition and measurement	Low	✓ ⎫	Construct development
◆ Dimensions	Medium	⎬	and measurement
◆ Levels of analysis/multilevel construct	High	⎭	Emphasis on multilevel theory
◆ Intra-organizational antecedents		✓ ⎫	
– prior related knowledge	Low		
– internal mechanisms	Low	⎬	Emphasis on model
◆ Inter-organizational antecedents	Medium	✓	building
◆ Outcomes	Medium	✓	
◆ Models	Low	✓ ⎭	
◆ Transdisciplinary construct	High	✓	Bridging and enriching literatures

substantially contribute yet to cumulative learning and scientific knowledge accumulation about the theoretical and empirical underpinnings of the absorptive capacity construct. To the extent this third observation is correct, this *gap* between the speed of proliferation of theoretical and empirical *applications* and the speed of *accumulation of the acquired scientific knowledge* might weaken over time the multilevel and transdisciplinary characteristics of absorptive capacity. In an effort to narrow this gap we will first discuss the progress made and select problems regarding the conceptual attributes.

Although the definition of absorptive capacity is, generally speaking, not disputed in the literature, its contribution to the measurement of absorptive capacity appears to be more problematic in the sense that for the measurement of the absorptive capacity construct its antecedents are often used. For example, in empirical research R&D spending as a percentage of sales is often used as a proxy for a firm's absorptive capacity. But R&D is also a part of the antecedent prior related knowledge (see table 14.2). As Mowery et al. (1996: 82) pointed out: "R&D intensity measures inputs to the creation of capabilities and indicates little if anything about resultant changes in capabilities." Lane and Lubatkin (1998) provided empirical evidence about the relatively low explanatory power of R&D spending in comparison to the explanatory power of their three dimensions of absorptive capacity. We believe these problems gave rise to efforts aimed at operationalizing the dimensions or components of absorptive capacity (see the section on "Absorptive Capacity: Refinements, Extensions, and Reconceptualizations"). These efforts resulted in, for example, distinguishing complementary dimensions like potential and realized capacity (Zahra and George, 2002) and in empirically assessing separate dimensions or abilities to absorb external knowledge in empirical research. For example, the findings of Lane et al. (2001) suggest that the first two components of absorptive capacity, being the ability to recognize and the ability to assimilate new external knowledge, affect learning while the third component, the ability to apply new external knowledge, did not influence learning but affected performance.

The progress made regarding operationalizing the antecedents and determining their impact on absorptive capacity is in our view not substantial. At intraorganizational and firm level, the internal mechanisms influencing absorptive capacity still deserve attention in terms of assessing their impact on absorptive capacity. At interorganizational level, however, substantial progress has been made by the introduction of the relative absorptive capacity construct (Lane and Lubatkin, 1998), the measurement of this construct by expert evaluations and the empirical assessment of the influence of the antecedents. The relationships between the antecedents at firm level and at dyad or interorganizational levels still deserve attention. A systematic account of antecedents of absorptive capacity beyond the dyad, for example at national level, is up till now missing. The progress made pertaining to the organizational outcomes of absorptive capacity can be discussed along two lines: (1) the number of various types of outcomes discerned; and (2) the empirical evidence found to the extent that absorptive capacity indeed contributes to these outcomes. The empirical assessment has made some progress.

In discussing the progress, we pointed out our third observation: the gap between the speed of proliferation of theoretical and empirical applications and the speed of accumulation of the acquired scientific knowledge about absorptive capacity. The problems we have selected in the third column of table 14.7 have in common that we perceive them as important *barriers* to the accumulation of scientific knowledge. The first issue mentioned in table 14.7 deals with the definition and measurement of the construct. The definition provided by Cohen and Levinthal (1990) discerns three types of abilities constituting the absorptive capacity construct. In empirical research some researchers focus on trying to measure the construct on the basis of company data or by evaluations by outsiders, or instead of the construct measuring the associated outcome, while other researchers focus on the three abilities. There is no general agreement, therefore, on how to measure absorptive capacity. The antecedents of absorptive capacity at the various levels of analysis and in particular how they are related to each other is still another serious problem. For example, how are the absorptive capacities of employees related to a firm's absorptive capacity? As discussed above, internal organizational mechanisms operationalized by, for example, the type of organizational form and combinative capabilities in use (Van Den Bosch et al., 1999) do play a role, but to what extent is this the case for other levels of analysis as well? And how are organizational antecedents related to interorganizational antecedents? Is the relationship between independent and dependent variables similar at different levels of analysis (Rousseau, 1985)? These questions address the issue of multilevel research (Klein et al., 1994, 1999; Morgeson and Hofman, 1999). Another barrier is the lack of attention regarding the question of what we can learn from absorptive capacity model building efforts. Investigating these problems is in particular important for the underpinning of absorptive capacity as a multilevel and transdisciplinary construct.

Future research directions

Building on the discussions of the progress and problems, we selected four promising future research directions, see the fourth column of table 14.7. In terms of research priorities, more emphasis on construct development and measurement and on model building is mostly needed. Hopefully, these efforts will enable the third future research direction, the emergence of multilevel theory building regarding absorptive capacity. These research directions will give rise to an even more fruitful bridging and enriching of related literatures. We will briefly elaborate each of these future research directions below.

In further developing the absorptive capacity construct, it seems useful to focus on how the various capabilities, dimensions or components discerned from absorptive capacity can be helpful for the operationalization and measurement of the construct. Regarding *measurement*, utilizing and comparing complementary methods are clearly needed. For example, by using a survey filled out by employees of the firm involved, but also by using a survey aimed at industry experts assessing the firm involved and/or by using quantitative proxies and case study research. Reflecting on different measurement methods of absorptive capacity and by clearly distinguishing the measurement of the construct and the measurement of its antecedents and consequences will create further progress. The construct development will also be triggered by a strong emphasis on model building efforts as well. From the perspective of models as mediators between theories and empirical phenomena, complementary absorptive capacity models may highlight different aspects of the absorptive capacity construct and stimulate the search for corresponding aspects of the empirical phenomena investigated.

The development of dynamic models is also needed. In particular the development of a co-evolutionary research approach to explain the change in a firm's absorptive capacity (Lewin and Volberda, 1999). The incorporation of variables addressing *managerial intentionality* to influence the level of absorptive capacity is also needed. Therefore, paying attention to managerial cognition (Calori et al., 1994), managerial knowledge integration (Van Den Bosch and Van Wijk, 2001) and managerial competences (Sanchez, 2001) will be important in future model building efforts. By juxtaposing both complementary models and their findings at various levels of analysis we can learn more about the absorptive capacity construct and its dimensions, the antecedents, outcomes and measurement methods as well. On the basis of these research efforts, it may become clear to what extent absorptive capacity models have the characteristics of multilevel models. In multilevel models "the relationship between the independent and dependent variables is generalizable across organizational entities" (Klein et al., 1994: 223). In doing so, the multilevel and transdisciplinary characteristics of absorptive capacity might be further explored and developed.

Acknowledgments

This research was funded by a "Payment to a Centre of Excellence" awarded by the Royal Dutch/Shell Group and is a part of the research program of the Erasmus Strategic Renewal Centre (ESRC) and of the Erasmus Research Institute of Management (ERIM). We would like to thank Erik J. de Boer and Ancella de Boer for their able research assistance.

References

Ahuja, G. (2000) The Duality of Collaboration: Inducements and Opportunities in the Formation of Interfirm Linkages. *Strategic Management Journal*, 21 (3): 317–43.

Boer, M. de, Van Den Bosch, F.A.J., and Volberda, H.W. (1999) Managing Organizational Knowledge Integration in the Emerging Multimedia Complex. *Journal of Management Studies*, 36 (3): 379–98.

Boisot, M.H. (1998) *Knowledge Assets*. Oxford: Oxford University Press.

Calori, R., Johnson, G., and Sarnin, Ph. (1994) CEOs' Cognitive Maps and the Scope of the Organization. *Strategic Management Journal*, 15: 437–57.

Camerer, C. and Vepsalainen, A. (1988) The Economic Efficiency of Corporate Culture. *Strategic Management Journal*, 9: 115–26.

Carlsson, B. and Jacobsson, S. (1994) Technological Systems and Economic Policy: The Diffusion of Factory Automation in Sweden. *Research Policy*, 23 (3): 235–49.

Cockburn, I.M. and Henderson, R.M. (1998) Absorptive Capacity, Coauthoring Behavior, and the Organization of Research in Drug Discovery. *The Journal of Industrial Economics*, 46 (2): 157–83.

Cohen, W.M. and Levinthal, D.A. (1989) Innovation and Learning: The Two Faces of R&D. *The Economic Journal*, 99: 569–96.

Cohen, W.M. and Levinthal, D.A. (1990) Absorptive Capacity: A New Perspective on Learning and Innovation. *Administrative Science Quarterly*, 35 (1): 128–52.

Cohen, W.M. and Levinthal, D.A. (1994) Fortune Favors the Prepared Firm. *Management Science*, 40: 227–51.

Cohen, W.M. and Levinthal, D.A. (1997) Reply to Comments on Fortune Favors the Prepared Firm. *Management Science*, 43: 1463–8.

Deeds, D.L. (2001) The Role of R&D Intensity, Technical Development and Absorptive Capacity in Creating Entrepreneurial Wealth in High Technology Start-ups. *Journal of Engineering and Technology Management*, 18: 29–47.

Dijksterhuis, M.S., Van Den Bosch, F.A.J., and Volberda, H.W. (1999) Where Do New Organizational Forms Come From? Management Logics as a Source of Coevolution. *Organizational Science*, 10 (5): 569–82.

Dyer, J.H. and Singh, H. (1998) The Relational View: Cooperative Strategy and Resources of Interorganizational Competitive Advantage. *Academy of Management Review*, 23: 660–79.

Edmondson, A. (2001) Psychological Safety and Learning Behavior in Work Teams. *Administrative Science Quarterly*, 44 (2): 350–84.

Fiol, M. and Lyles, M. (1985) Organizational Learning. *Academy of Management Review*, 10 (4): 803–13.

Grant, R.M. (1996) Prospering in Dynamically Competitive Environments: Organizational Capability as Knowledge Integration. *Organization Science*, 7 (4): 375–87.

Gupta, A.K. and Govindarajan, V. (2000) Knowledge Flows within Multinational Corporations. *Strategic Management Journal*, 21 (4): 473–96.

Hedberg, B.L.T. (1981) How Organizations Learn and Unlearn. In P.C. Nystrom and W.H. Starbuck (eds.), *Handbook of Organizational Design*, Vol. 1. New York: Oxford University Press, 3–27.

Huygens, M., Baden-Fuller, Ch., Van Den Bosch, F.A.J., and Volberda, H.W. (2001) Coevolution of Firm Capabilities and Industry Competition: Investigating the Music Industry 1877–1997. *Organization Studies*, 22 (6): 971–1011.

Inkpen, A.C. and Dinur, A. (1998) Knowledge Management Processes and International Joint Ventures. *Organization Science*, 9: 454–68.

Jones, O. and Craven, M. (2001) Expanding Capabilities in a Mature Manufacturing Firm: Absorptive Capacity and the TCS. *International Small Business Journal*, 19: 39–55.

Kamien, M.I. and Zang, I. (2000) Meet Me Halfway: Research Joint Ventures and Absorptive Capacity. *International Journal of Industrial Organization*, 18: 995–1012.

Kedia, B.L. and Bhagat, R.S. (1988) Cultural Constraints in Transfer of Technology across Nations: Implications for Research in International and Comparative Management. *Academy of Management Review*, 13 (4): 559–71.

Keller, W. (1996) Absorptive Capacity: On the Creation and Acquisition of Technology in Development. *Journal of Development Economics*, 49: 199–227.

Kim, L. (1998) Crisis Construction and Organizational Learning: Capability Building in Catching-up at Hyundai Motor. *Organization Science*, 9: 506–21.

Klein, K.J., Damereau, F., and Hall, R.J. (1994) Levels Issues in Theory Development: Data Collection and Analysis. *Academy of Management Review*, 19 (2): 195–229.

Klein, K.J., Tosi, H., and Cannella, A.A. (1999) Multilevel Theory Building: Benefits, Barriers, and New Developments. *Academy of Management Review*, 24 (2): 243–8.

Kogut, B. and Zander, U. (1992) Knowledge of the Firm, Integration Capabilities, and the Replication of Technology. *Organization Science*, 3: 383–97.

Koza, M.P. and Lewin, A.Y. (1998) The Coevolution of Strategic Alliances. *Organization Science*, 9 (3): 255–64.

Kumar, S. and Seth, A. (2001) Knowledge, Absorptive Capacity, and the Theory of the Diversified Firm. *Academy of Management Proceedings*, 2001, Best Papers BPS, BPS:E1–E6.

Lane, P.J. and Lubatkin, M. (1998) Relative Absorptive Capacity and Inter-organizational Learning. *Strategic Management Journal*, 19: 461–77.

Lane, P.J., Salk, J.E., and Lyles, M.A. (2001) Absorptive Capacity, Learning and Performance in International Joint Ventures. *Strategic Management Journal*, 22: 1139–61.

Levitt, B. and March, J.G. (1988) Organizational Learning. *Annual Review of Sociology*, 14: 319–40.

Lewin, A.Y. and Volberda, H.W. (1999) Prolegomena on Coevolution: A Framework for Research on Strategy and New Organizational Forms. *Organization Science*, 10 (5): 519–34.

Lewin, A.Y., Long, Ch.P., and Carroll, T.N. (1999) The Coevolution of New Organizational Forms. *Organization Science*, 10 (5): 535–50.

Lyles, M.A. and Salk, J.E. (1996) Knowledge Acquisition from Foreign Parents in International Joint Ventures: An Empirical Examination in the Hungarian Context. *Journal of International Business Studies*, 27 (5): 877–904.

March, J.G. (1991) Exploration and Exploitation in Organizational Learning. *Organization Science*, 2 (1): 71–8.

Meyer-Krahmer, F. and Reger, G. (1999) New Perspectives on the Innovation Strategies of Multinational Enterprises: Lessons for Technology Policy in Europe. *Research Policy*, 28: 751–76.

Montresor, S. (2001) Technological-globalism, Technological-nationalism and Technological systems: Organizing the Evidence. *Technovation*, 21: 399–412.

Morgan, M.S. and Morrison, M. (eds.) (1999) *Models as Mediators, Perspectives on Natural and Social Sciences*. Cambridge: Cambridge University Press.

Morgeson, F.P. and Hofmann, D.A. (1999) The Structure and Function of Collective Constructs: Implications for Multilevel Research and Theory Development. *Academy of Management Review*, 24 (2): 249–65.

Mowery, D.C. and Oxley, J.E. (1995) Inward Technology Transfer and Competitiveness: The Role of National Innovation Systems. *Cambridge Journal of Economics*, 19: 67–93.

Mowery, D.C., Oxley, J.E., and Silverman, B.S. (1996) Strategic Alliances and Interfirm Knowledge Transfer. *Strategic Management Journal*, 17: 77–91.

Pennings, J.M. and Harianto, F. (1992) Technological Networking and Innovation Implementation. *Organization Science*, 3: 356–82.

Rousseau, D.M. (1985) Issues of Level in Organizational Research: Multi-level and Cross-level Perspectives. In L.L. Cummings and B.M. Staw (eds.), *Research in Organizational Behavior*, vol. 7, Greenwich, CT: JAI Press, 1–37.

Sanchez, R. (ed.) (2001) *Knowledge Management and Organizational Competence*. Oxford: Oxford University Press.

Shane, S. (2000) Prior Knowledge and the Discovery of Entrepreneurial Opportunities. *Organization Science*, 11 (4): 448–69.

Starbuck, W.H. (1992) Learning by Knowledge-intensive Firms. *The Journal of Management Studies*, 29 (6): 713–41.

Stock, G.N., Greis, N.P., and Fischer, W.A. (2001) Absorptive Capacity and New Product Development. *The Journal of High Technology Management Research*, 12 (1): 77–91.

Szulanski, G. (1996) Exploring Internal Stickiness: Impediments to the Transfer of Best Practice within the Firm. *Strategic Management Journal*, 17: 27–43.

Tsai, W. (2001) Knowledge Transfers in Intra-Organizational Networks. *Academy of Management Journal*, 44 (5): 996–1004.

Tsoukas, H. (1996) The Firm as a Distributed Knowledge System: A Constructionist Approach. *Strategic Management Journal*, 17 (Winter Special Issue): 11–25.

Van Den Bosch, F.A.J., Volberda, H.W., and Boer, M. de (1999) Coevolution of Firm Absorptive Capacity and Knowledge Environment: Organizational Forms and Combinative Capabilities. *Organization Science*, 10 (5): 551–68.

Van Den Bosch, F.A.J. and Van Wijk, R. (2001) Creation of Managerial Capabilities through Managerial Knowledge Integration: A Competence-Based Perspective. In R. Sanchez (ed.), *Knowledge Management and Organizational Competence*, Oxford: Oxford University Press, 159–76.

Van Wijk, R.A. and Van Den Bosch, F.A.J. (1998) Knowledge Characteristics of Internal Network-based Forms of Organizing. In S. Havlovic (ed.), *Academy of Management Best Paper Proceedings*, B1–7.

Van Wijk, R.A. and Van Den Bosch, F.A.J. (2000) The Emergence and Development of Internal Networks and their Impact on Knowledge Flows: The Case of Rabobank Group. In A.M. Pettigrew and E.M. Fenton (eds.), *The Innovating Organization*, London: Sage, 144–77.

Van Wijk, R., Van Den Bosch, F.A.J., and Volberda, H.W. (2001) The Impact of the Depth and Breadth of Knowledge Absorbed on Levels of Exploration and Exploitation. *Academy of Management Meeting*, BPS Division, Insights into Knowledge Transfer, Washington DC, USA, August 3–8.

Van Wijk, R., Van Den Bosch, F.A.J., and Volberda, H.W. (2003) Knowledge and Networks. In M. Easterby-Smith and M.A. Lyles (eds.), *Companion to Organizational Learning and Knowledge*, Oxford: Blackwell Publishers.

Veugelers, R. and Kesteloot, K. (1996) Bargained Shares in Joint Ventures among Asymmetric Partners: Is the Matthew Effect Catalyzing? *Journal of Economics*, 64 (1): 23–51.

Volberda, H.W. (1998) *Building the Flexible Firm: How to Remain Competitive*. Oxford: Oxford University Press.

Volberda, H.W., Baden-Fuller, C., and Van Den Bosch, F.A.J. (2001) Mastering Strategic Renewal: Mobilizing Renewal Journeys in Multi-unit Firms. *Long Range Planning*, 34 (2): 159–78.

Volberda, H.W., Van Den Bosch, F.A.J., Flier, B., and Gedajlovic, E. (2001) Following the Herd or Not? Patterns of Renewal in The Netherlands and the UK. *Long Range Planning*, 34 (2): 209–29.

Wegloop, P. (1995) Linking Firm Strategy and Government Action: Towards a Resource-based Perspective on Innovation and Technology Policy. *Technology in Society*, 17 (4): 413–28.

Zahra, S.A. and George, G. (2002) Absorptive Capacity: A Review, Reconceptualization, and Extension. *Academy of Management Review*, 27 (2): 185–203.

Zollo, M. and Winter, S.G. (2002) From Organizational Routines to Dynamic Capabilities. *Organization Science*, 13 (3): 339–51.

Part III

ORGANIZATIONAL KNOWLEDGE AND KNOWLEDGE MANAGEMENT

15

Knowledge Management and Competitive Advantage

Bala Chakravarthy, Sue McEvily, Yves Doz, and Devaki Rau

CHAPTER OUTLINE

Knowledge-based competition is an area of intense interest to both strategic management scholars and practitioners alike. Researchers investigating this topic often anchor their work in the resource-based theory of the firm, which argues that distinct knowledge should give the firm a competitive advantage. The theory emphasizes barriers to imitation, such as the tacitness or complexity of knowledge, as the basis for sustained competitive advantage. Another stream of research maintains that the way in which firms manage their knowledge resources is crucial to persistent advantages. We suggest that characteristics of knowledge are primarily valuable for defending existing advantages, while the processes it uses to accumulate and leverage knowledge have greater implications for creating new sources of advantage. This chapter develops propositions to highlight central relationships between knowledge characteristics, knowledge management processes, and competitive advantage. We also explore tensions between distinct processes for acquiring, protecting, and leveraging knowledge.

INTRODUCTION

In a recent special issue on knowledge, Spender (1996) lamented that despite the popular preoccupation with knowledge and associated ideas, it is too problematic a concept to make the task of building a dynamic knowledge-based theory of the firm easy. Knowledge is most commonly treated as a stock – the content and volume of understanding that exists at any given point in time. However, there is debate in the literature on whether it is knowledge *per se* or rather knowledge management, which is at the source of a firm's competitive advantage. We argue, in this chapter, that it is the latter. By knowledge management, we mean the accumulation, protection and leverage of knowledge. The value of the three knowledge management processes to a firm's strategic advantage is not well understood.

Even the research on learning, which we view as just one of the three knowledge management processes – knowledge accumulation – has been hampered by fragmented efforts without an overall framework to pull all the findings together (Huber, 1991).

To clarify relationships between knowledge and competitive advantage, we first distinguish knowledge from learning, and then discuss how knowledge accumulation, protection, and knowledge leverage influence a firm's competitive advantage. We offer propositions highlighting how these activities may influence a firm's current competitive advantage, and its ability to create new sources of advantage. To conclude, we discuss tensions between the three knowledge management processes.

Knowledge versus learning

The distinction between knowledge and learning is at times fuzzy in the literature. This confusion appears to stem, in part, from the fact that evidence of knowledge and learning can each be found in better performance, and both learning and knowledge have been defined in terms of new or greater understanding. Further, both have been measured as stocks – e.g. cumulative experience or investment, but conceptualized as processes (Spender, 1996; Argote, 1999; Eisenhardt and Santos, 2001). It is most common, however, for authors to define knowledge as a type or degree of understanding that exists at a point in time, and learning as the process of acquiring this comprehension.

A variety of learning processes have been described, and the processes associated with accumulating new knowledge tend to differ according to how distant new understanding is from an organization's current knowledge base. Levitt and March (1988) note that "Organizations learn by encoding inferences from history into routines that guide behavior." This may call for systematically repeating an action and studying its consequences (Argote and Epple, 1990). But knowledge accumulation need not be restricted to the experiences of the firm. Organizations can also learn vicariously by carefully studying the consequences of others' behaviors and by experimenting with novel technologies, markets, and processes. They can acquire the knowledge of others by merging with or acquiring another firm or access the knowledge of others through strategic alliances. We view all forms of knowledge accumulation as learning.

While we acknowledge that the genesis of all knowledge may be in the minds of individuals, our focus here is not on the intrapersonal processes of knowledge accumulation. Fiol and Lyles (1985) show that organizational learning is multi-level, occurring at the individual, group and organizational levels. We are interested in knowledge accumulation at the organizational level of analysis. So, what exactly is being accumulated when an organization learns?

Nonaka (1994) defines knowledge as *justified true belief.* He argues that knowledge cannot be equated with truth, even though the purpose of learning may in fact be to seek the truth. Knowledge can be superficial or deep. Thus knowledge may be mere insights and heuristics that provide an understanding of the effectiveness of past actions (Fiol and Lyles, 1985), or be more tangible routines to guide organizational actions (Levitt and March, 1988; Nelson and Winter, 1982). Given the complex and dynamic environments confronting many businesses today, the "truth" about how to compete successfully may be hard to discern. When the intentions and capabilities of the organizations that populate a firm's industry shift rapidly, it may rely on the hunches and intuitive understanding of its members (Quinn, 1992). We define knowledge as beliefs that guide organizational action; it is causal understanding that may or may not fully reflect the realities of the environments a firm faces.

KNOWLEDGE MANAGEMENT AND COMPETITIVE ADVANTAGE

The distinctive role that each of the three knowledge management activities play in providing a firm its competitive advantage can be seen in figure 15.1 (Chakravarthy et al., 2002). Assuming that a firm has already accumulated distinctive knowledge, protecting and extending that knowledge is the first step in its fight to sustain competitive advantage. We describe characteristics of a firm's knowledge that protect it and allow it to remain distinctive later in this chapter. If the firm can then leverage its distinctive knowledge base and apply it to new market opportunities, it ensures its growth. But no knowledge base can be distinctive forever, and a firm's forays into new markets will eventually call for new knowledge as well. The cycle repeats again when the firm seeks to accumulate new knowledge. Sustaining profitable growth calls for continuous iterations between these three knowledge management activities of protect, leverage, and accumulate (Chakravarthy, 1996, 1997).

Knowledge accumulation

The resource-based view of the firm attributes the competitive advantage of a firm to the unique knowledge that it has over its competitors (Lippman and Rumelt, 1982). Based on the definition of knowledge we have adopted, *knowledge is accumulated when units within the firm or the organization as a whole gains new understanding.* Comprehension may develop through deliberate efforts to learn something, such as through experimentation, or as a byproduct of activities that have other outcomes. In either case, learning requires some type of feedback, or the ability to observe the effect or outcome of one's efforts. While experience and choice create opportunities for learning, knowledge is only generated when this is accompanied by reflection and abstraction.

We agree with Nonaka (1994: 15) when he notes, "although the terms 'information' and 'knowledge' are used interchangeably, there is a clear distinction between information and knowledge . . . information is a flow of messages, while knowledge is created and organized by the very flow of information, anchored on the commitment and beliefs of its holder." In other words, while information may be more ubiquitous, the conversion of this information into knowledge is special. Of course, some of the generally available information may in fact have been established through test of proof, for example, scientific theories, market surveys and so on. The test of proof does not make external information, knowledge to a firm. Only knowledge that is proprietary to a firm is of competitive advantage to it. For example, the discovery that silicon has a particular molecular structure (a fact) does not provide any direct competitive advantage to a firm. However, an

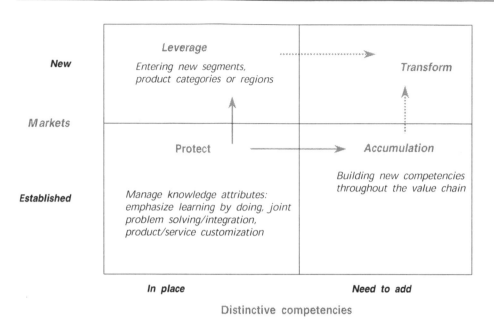

FIGURE 15.1   A typology of knowledge management activities

understanding of how certain molecular structures conduct energy is competitively useful knowledge. Knowledge accumulation activities encompass the acquisition of novel facts. The acquisition of new information often serves to qualify (refine) extant understanding, such as the precise conditions under which conductivity breaks down. Data are critical to the ability to use and develop new action/attribute–outcome associations that expand the firms' range of potential behaviors and choices.

Depth of knowledge   New knowledge is developed when there is a cognitive association (Hedberg, 1981) that is drawn between actions and their consequences. When this individual knowledge is communicated to others it becomes a loose cause map for guiding that sub-group's actions (McCaskey, 1982). The application of this loose cause map to a class of problems is not defined explicitly and the cause map may not solve all of the organization's problems successfully (Reitman, 1964). When the causal structure of a heuristic is better understood, it can be abstracted into a script. A script retains knowledge of expected sequences of behaviors, actions, and events (Gioia and Poole, 1984). It provides cues to organizational members on how to act in a given context. When a script can unambiguously specify what action should be taken under a prescribed condition it is called a tight script. Rules and standard operating procedures (Cyert and March, 1963; Levitt and March, 1988; Nelson and Winter, 1982) are examples of tight scripts. A tight script improves the efficiency with which the organization responds to a problem. Based on this, we expect:

PROPOSITION 1:   *The deeper the knowledge base that a firm enjoys, the stronger is its competitive advantage.*

The learning processes of building new heuristics and scripts encompass variation, selection, and retention mechanisms (Weick, 1979). Retained knowledge is validated over time through planned actions, and eventually stored in routines where it takes on a habitual character. Organizational members take action based on this knowledge without thinking, which is efficient as long as conditions do not change. A failed plan, on the other hand, should engender questions about the future value of the underlying knowledge base (Lyles, 1988). Existing knowledge may no longer be useful for achieving certain objectives or a firm's objectives may change. Each may require the firm to understand new phenomena. In either case, divesting existing knowledge is often a precursor to effective learning (Huber, 1991). For example, Intel's metamorphosis from memories to processors, unlearning was required. Hence:

PROPOSITION 2:   *But unless the usefulness of this deep knowledge is periodically questioned, a core competence can become core rigidity.*

Types of knowledge   Two broad types of knowledge often underlie a firm's competitive advantage: *resource conversion and market positioning. Resource conversion knowledge* refers to the ability of a firm to use generic resources, which are also available to its competitors, and yet create distinctive products and services from these, through product and/or process innovation. The patents, copyrights and trade secrets that a firm owns are the most articulated aspects of its resource conversion knowledge (Friedman et al., 1991). The hunches, speculations and beliefs that are the forerunners to a successful patent or copyright application or a well-established trade secret, are also part of this knowledge base, albeit more tacit and less justified aspects of it.

Resource conversion knowledge is used to create value by transforming the characteristics of the inputs a firm uses, or bringing them together in unique ways. This knowledge is a likely source of superior performance when the attributes of the system – those elements of a firm's products or processes that underlie its cost or differentiation advantage, cannot be discerned by merely investigating the inputs to it. If resource conversion knowledge is firm specific, a system's meaning may not be discernable without access to the organization's "deep collective knowledge," which places its components and their relationships to one another in an idiosyncratic social and technological context (Spender, 1996). However, resource conversion knowledge alone is not enough for competitive success. Xerox is a firm that had resource conversion knowledge, albeit without always having the ability to turn its innovation into working products at an efficient cost, but its poor ability to position this knowledge in appropriate markets meant it gained very little competitive advantage from its many inventions.

The ability of a firm to see opportunities in its environment and avoid threats is also a form of knowledge. We call this its *market positioning knowledge.* The firm may not have access to any special information over its competitors, and yet may be able to see patterns in this information that others are unable to. Canon, in its early years, is a good example of this. It focused initially on its ability to exploit the unmet market needs for a low price copier, albeit with a product that was simple and unsophisticated. Spender (1996) offers three heuristics that can be useful in this regard: interpretive flexibility, boundary management, and identification of institutional influences. Interpretive flexibility refers to the richness of the interpretations that the firm's actors are able to make of its environment. Boundary management refers to the firm's ability to define its boundaries and interactions with others and help attenuate consideration of its endless externalities. Finally, recognizing the power and influence of a firm's stakeholders in forging its own strategy is another important knowledge heuristic. Superior *market positioning knowledge* is thus a composite of rich sensing, sensible boundary management and effective stakeholder management. The above discussion suggests:

PROPOSITION 3:   *Resource conversion knowledge must be complemented by market positioning knowledge in order for a firm to achieve competitive success.*

Knowledge protection

Protection encompasses activities that seek to maintain the proprietary nature of a firm's knowledge stocks. This includes seeking legal protection, such as patents and non-compete agreements, designing policies to limit turnover, and educating employees about the types of knowledge they should not share with their peers in other organizations (Appleyard, 1996). In addition, firms can also take a variety of actions to shape characteristics of their knowledge base in an effort to slow imitation. Three characteristics of knowledge have been repeatedly linked to the height of imitation barriers: tacitness, complexity, and specificity (Dierickx and Cool, 1989; Reed and DeFillippi, 1990; Doz, Santos and Williamson, 2001; McEvily and Chakravarthy, 2002). These attributes increase "stickiness" – the costs to transfer knowledge across organizational boundaries and the degree to which it resists identification (Zander and Kogut, 1995; Szulanski, 1996; von Hippel, 1998).

There are a variety of ways that firms can manage these knowledge attributes. Firms might maintain the tacitness of their knowledge, for example, by emphasizing learning by doing, overlapping problem solving, and job rotation to transfer lessons gleaned through experience (Nonaka, 1991). On the other hand, Nonaka and Takeuchi (1995) suggest that one way of protecting tacit knowledge is to actively foster its articulation and to encourage individuals to recombine it in novel ways. This shared knowledge then becomes the basis for future learning and the accumulation of new tacit knowledge. Alternatively, a firm may wish to codify employee knowledge to prevent its loss through turnover and to disseminate it such that no individual has a complete understanding. When knowledge is embedded in the complex interaction of many people it is firm specific and thus difficult to copy. Similarly, a firm may tailor its products to suit the needs of certain customers, such that the "meaning" of their design requires access to the firm's particular experience with the application context, making it tougher to imitate.

Tacitness, complexity, and specificity have received more attention in the literature than knowledge management activities as potential barriers to imitation, and policies such as patents appear only to be effective in a few industries (Mansfield et al., 1981). Unfortunately, little is known about the relative efficacy of these knowledge management practices. Moreover, since knowledge resides in many forms, including databases, individuals, management practices, and artifacts, the processes a firm uses to protect it will be equally diverse. Therefore, we focus on the degree to which a firm's knowledge has these characteristics, rather than specific activities for manipulating tacitness, complexity, and specificity.

Tacitness   Two dimensions of tacitness are discussed in the literature. The first is the *inability to articulate* what one knows about how to achieve an observed performance outcome (Polanyi, 1962; Nelson and Winter, 1982; Winter, 1987). The *procedures* one relies on may be inaccessible either because they have been learned implicitly or because they have become second nature, taken for granted and or forgotten (Reber, 1993). Moreover, even if the steps a firm follows can eventually be articulated, this may be insufficient for another firm to achieve the same level of performance. For example, competitors may follow the same basic procedures to make pianos or violins, but be unable to achieve quality or product performance that is comparable to that embodied in a Steinway or Stradivarius (Garud, 1997). Experts might subconsciously attend to cues and make judgments that are not communicated or observable.

On the other hand, if the causal mechanisms that influence performance are known, these may be acted on in a variety of ways, so even if a competitor cannot imitate the same procedures, it may be able to replicate the firm's performance. Thus the second dimension of tacitness is the *personal nature* of knowledge (Polanyi, 1962; Nonaka and Takeuchi, 1995; Teece et al., 1997), which derives from an inability to articulate the *principles* that affect the level of performance one achieves. Both dimensions help to describe knowledge that cannot be communicated sufficiently to enable others to achieve the same level of performance.

The more tacit a firm's knowledge, the less employees can communicate to suppliers, customers, or their peers, who might deliberately or inadvertently share information with the firm's competitors. If few of the reasons for a product's superior performance can be articulated, competitors only acquire partial knowledge through their intelligence gathering activities. Also, it is hard for a competitor to assess the true value of an individual's tacit knowledge. Often such knowledge is valuable only in the specific context of a firm. Employees that are hired away might be less productive in another firm (Barney, 1992; Arora and Gambardella, 1994). Thus:

PROPOSITION 4:   *The more tacit the knowledge base of a firm, the easier it is for a firm to defend a competitive position based on that knowledge.*

Complexity   This is usually defined according to dimensions that increase the difficulty of comprehending how a system (i.e. an organization, organism, device) functions or produces some outcome. Simon (1962) defines a complex system as one that consists of *many unique* and *interacting* elements, which have *equally important* effects on the outcomes produced by the system. Elements are distinct when an individual cannot use the same knowledge to understand them; so increasing the number of unique elements raises the amount of information that must be processed to understand the system's behavior. If each element is equally important to the achievement of a performance outcome, knowing how one element functions reveals very little about how the system as a whole works. In addition, if individual elements are interdependent, then one must understand their joint effects on the performance outcome, and the number of interactions increases geometrically with the number of elements. In other words the embeddedness of specific knowledge elements in a systemic context renders the value and transferability of specific knowledge components difficult to assess.

Complexity may slow performance replication by obscuring the sources of superior performance. The costs of transfer may increase with complexity, to the extent that competitors must design all product components identically to copy an individual design change (Dierickx and Cool, 1989), or copy every element of a firm's marketing strategy. Accordingly, MacMillan et al. (1985) argue that competitors find it harder to compete with products and services when their development and marketing relies on a complex knowledge set. Therefore:

PROPOSITION 5: *The more complex the knowledge base of a firm, the easier it is for a firm to defend a competitive advantage based on that knowledge.*

Specificity This is the loss in value that occurs when a resource or information is applied in a new context. Yet, there may be more than one context across which a firm could transfer or simultaneously apply its knowledge, and the degree to which knowledge loses value may depend upon the destination one considers. For instance, a firm might use its knowledge to serve many customers within an application, and to serve multiple applications. To the extent its knowledge loses value from one customer to the next, or across applications, it is more specific to a product's end use. Knowledge may also be specific to the inputs a firm uses to develop a product, and this does not have to co-vary with end use. What a firm knows about how to exploit the core component of a product may be more or less specific to the peripheral components it is used with, for example. These distinct loci of transfer or application could be considered different facets of specificity. Most discussions linking specificity to the persistence of a performance advantage have focused on firm-specificity. However, to the extent that a firm's design choices require knowledge of the application context, specificity may also hinder their identification and transfer.

Products supported by highly specific knowledge are challenging to reverse engineer because idiosyncratic features of the application context moderate the relationships between design parameters and product performance. Thus, competitors that lack contextual knowledge will find it difficult to discern the reasons for a product's superior performance. Intelligence gathering is also difficult for competitors unfamiliar with the application. Suppliers are unlikely to possess the detailed knowledge of the application that a firm has, and customers might take the idiosyncrasies of their own needs for granted and fail to communicate them to competitors. Further, there are fewer sources of potential knowledge leak, since each product is designed for a narrow set of customers. While it is possible to hire away key employees, these experts may not apply their specialized knowledge to a competitor's product components and architecture with the same proficiency. Hence the proposition:

PROPOSITION 6:   *The more specific the knowledge base of a firm, the easier it is for a firm to defend a competitive position based on that knowledge.*

Limits to imitation barriers   Performance advantages based on knowledge that is tacit, complex and specific might be harder to replicate because the causes of superior performance are more ambiguous to outside observers than to members of the focal firm (Reed and DeFillippi, 1990; Barney, 1991). However, barriers to imitation will only explain persistence when imitation is the best way for rivals to close a performance gap. Tacitness, complexity and specificity will be stronger predictors of persistence to the extent knowledge flowing through the aforementioned channels are valuable inputs to competitors' development activities. We expect a firm's knowledge to be more useful for closing major performance gaps than it is for matching minor improvements.

Since major improvements are unlikely to be matched by simple changes to extant designs, the alternative to imitation is for competitors to initiate their own search for new technologies. Competitors face substantial uncertainty about the prospects for this to yield a substitute technology with sufficient potential to close the performance gap. Not only is their prior technological experience likely to be less useful in this process, any time lost responding to the innovator may put competitors further behind, as the innovator moves down the learning curve with the new technology. Thus, imitation is likely to be a more expeditious and reliable way to close major performance gaps. It is important to note that this does not mean an imitator incurs less time than the innovator did to introduce a major improvement. It does mean we expect imitation to reduce the time competitors incur to close a major performance gap, compared to the time it would take them if they started from scratch. Along similar lines, Wilson (1977) argues that radical innovations are more likely to be licensed than are relatively minor product changes because licensing minor innovations saves the licensee fewer of the costs associated with product development.

Since many incremental changes are difficult to transfer across firms, and competitors frequently have alternative means of achieving the same level of improvement, companies are less likely to devote resources to gathering detailed information about the sources of minor improvements. The effort required to gather the intelligence about minor improvements may actually be greater than that required to identify the sources of major improvements. The design changes responsible for minor improvements will be less obvious, so reverse engineering may not be as efficient. Information gathering may also be harder, as the source of improvement could reside at more places thoughout the development organization. Further, since small changes require less effort, they are more likely to be forgotten and the contextual factors that made them feasible may be taken for granted and not communicated to others. Consequently, a better use of a firm's resources may be to accelerate its own efforts to extract the most out of its individual design and marketing approaches. We therefore propose:

PROPOSITION 7:   *The tacitness, complexity and specificity of a firm's knowledge base are of greater relevance to a firm in defending a competitive advantage that is based on a major technological (or other design) change.*

Knowledge leveraging

Leveraging is the use of existing knowledge for commercial ends. When knowledge is applied to existing ends, the size and durability of a firm's competitive advantage will be defined by how well protected its knowledge is, as suggested in the previous section. New challenges must be addressed in order to apply existing knowledge to new ends, and that is our focus in this section.

More specifically, we focus on leverage as the application of knowledge to new tasks (e.g., reusing proven practices in a new organizational unit) or objectives (e.g., improving existing products or developing new ones). Leveraging a firm's knowledge across a wide range of its businesses has two advantages. First, it maximizes the return on that knowledge. Second, it can also accelerate the knowledge articulation process, by providing more application opportunities. By providing different but related application opportunities, leveraging allows not just the repetitive honing of that knowledge, but its enrichment and synthesis with other knowledge resources in response to new needs or problems. In other words, leveraging can help both knowledge protection and accumulation.

Despite its obvious advantages, leveraging faces two difficulties: (1) the discovery of new opportunities and the mobilization of resources towards them; and (2) the validation of the opportunity/resource match.

Discovery of new opportunities Most companies are prisoners of existing definitions of customers and markets (Hamel and Prahalad, 1991). While the elements and sources of corporate creativity are known, their application to the discovery of new applications remains difficult. First, the diffusion and sharing of knowledge between businesses, in itself, seems to improve the likelihood of discovering new opportunities by exposing organizational members to one another's resources, and allowing these to be matched with possible opportunities. Second, applying the business logic of one product, or one industry to another may also help. Some observers would argue, for example, that Canon did not transform the photocopier industry through strategic brilliance but more through a routine application of the business logic of its camera business. Third, moving from the fixation on product-markets, to grasping underlying needs and functionalities may also facilitate the discovery of unmet or poorly served needs. New opportunities are likely to draw on a mix of knowledge resources, which have been cultivated in various parts of the organizations; and need to be combined in new ways. Accessing these resources and getting the various sub-units to contribute to the new opportunity may not be easy. Issues of sub-unit politics and failure to identify the proper sub-units that can provide the necessary support can stifle the exploitation of new opportunities.

In the earlier subsection we described how complex, specific and tacit knowledge offers the best protection to a firm from imitation by its competitors. Ironically, the very same characteristics that prevent external imitation also inhibit internal sharing (Chakravarthy et al., 2001; Galunic and Rodan, 1998; Szulanski, 1996). When the knowledge held by an organizational unit is tacit, it is hard for other units within the firm to even know of its existence. When this knowledge is specific or complex, it adds to the cost of its transfer and thus deters sharing.

If the sharing involves product technology, the use of core platforms and modular designs can help minimize this problem. If the changes in the materials and fundamental principles used to design components can be embedded in modules, the user needs to know only the functionality of the module and not how this functionality is achieved (Henderson and Clark, 1990). In other words, tacitness, complexity and specificity can be contained within the module. Leveraging a knowledge module for a new application may not require a full understanding of the underlying knowledge, only the performance that it enables. However, if the knowledge that needs to be shared is process know-how or an administrative heuristic, sharing is facilitated only if the organization facilitates frequent exchange of people. Even if the knowledge held by an expert is tacit, his/her rotation between organizational units increases the probability of this expertise being noticed. In addition, if there is an open exchange of information between organizational units, through apprenticeships, even specific and complex knowledge can be transferred and adapted to suit the new opportunity.

The experiences of Sharp are informative in this regard. The company used three approaches for resource mobilization. First, a monthly meeting of the corporate director of technology with marketing and technology executives from the various divisions combines the newly identified needs of the marketplace with the technologies of the various divisions, in a process of matching opportunities with technologies and knowledge. Second, the "urgent project process" allowed key technical personnel from the various divisions to work together under a carefully selected project leader on projects enjoying corporate-wide priority (set by the CEO, suggested by the divisions, and screened in the monthly meeting). Participants in these "urgent" project teams had complete freedom of action, but were also submitted to extreme pressures for results. Third, the top 3 percent of engineers (in a professional achievement rating system) were rotated between labs every third year, to promote cross-fertilization of skills across the company's labs.

Unfortunately, the cost of establishing such a social network is often seen as prohibitive. Based on these observations, we suggest:

PROPOSITION 8: *The tacitness, complexity and specificity of a firm's knowledge base can make its leveraging towards new market opportunities difficult, unless the social network of the firm encourages frequent exchange of experts and dissemination of their expertise.*

Matching knowledge with opportunity Previous studies suggest that two forces within organizations can hinder firms' abilities to recognize valuable opportunities to apply existing knowledge in new ways. First, firms often define their served markets too narrowly, thus ruling out a number of potential uses for their knowledge. For example, it has been argued that IBM's focus on mainframes and its concept of being a proprietary hardware company may have made the firm oblivious to emerging opportunities in networked microcomputers. Similarly, Apple's narrow concept of its businesses did not allow the company to leverage its operating system knowledge, thus leaving the door open for Microsoft (Rappaport and Halevi, 1991). Second, a company may push its reliance on core knowledge too far (Levitt and March, 1988).

But the good news in any organization is that there are different thought worlds (Dougherty, 1992) within it. Despite the efforts to homogenize the thinking around its opportunities and competencies, there is diversity. In better-managed organizations this diversity is even encouraged and nurtured. However, challenge to the mainstream thinking will only come under two conditions: performance failure or stretch ambition. Failure prompts a rethink within the organization of its opportunity space and/or a critical re-examination of the value of its core knowledge. Unfortunately, failure also brings with it time pressure, preventing those within the organization with different knowledge or alternate thought from participating effectively. On the other hand, if the organization has a purpose that is stretching, it provides a more conducive context for the continuous and more leisurely questioning of its market position and core knowledge. In addition to a stretch ambition, this evolutionary process requires a diversity of mindsets and knowledge bases. Top management ensures the organization's self-renewal by encouraging a healthy competition between rival ideas and knowledge, but always through experimentation close to the firm's current market position and core knowledge.

Matching opportunities and knowledge requires a delicate balance between stretch and proximate search. Canon, for instance, had a tremendous ambition ("to be as big as IBM and Matsushita combined") but also a very disciplined process of proximate search, whereby the company ventured only in areas where most of its existing knowledge applied – and reduced entry risks, and where only a few (most often one) new knowledge was required. Within that broad policy, growth is a mushrooming process, in which the overall trajectory of the company is not predetermined. While industry discontinuities – e.g., recent "digitalization" – are spotted as early as possible, and massive resources committed to turn them into opportunities rather than threats, the exact composition of the core knowledge bundle and the product market portfolio are largely emergent from a series of "autonomous" initiatives, some emphasizing reach, some capitalizing on mobilizing related knowledge (Burgelman and Doz, 2001). Hence:

PROPOSITION 9:   *Successful leveraging requires a careful blend of a stretching ambition and proximate search.*

TRADEOFFS BETWEEN THE KNOWLEDGE MANAGEMENT ACTIVITIES

We distinguished three distinct types of knowledge management activities (see figure 15.1), protecting, leveraging, and accumulating new knowledge. As distinctive knowledge is an important source of competitive advantage, knowledge accumulation is central to a firm's long-term performance. If valuable knowledge is hard to procure, imitate or substitute, the advantage is sustained over a longer period. When a firm's distinctive resources are shared and leveraged across its multiple businesses, it is able to economize on the assets and skills that it uses to defend existing advantages and may enjoy greater opportunities to create new sources of advantage (Prahalad and Hamel, 1990). Thus, we expect knowledge accumulation, protection, and leverage to all have a positive impact on a firm's sustained superior performance. While each is important, there may be tensions among these three knowledge management activities (figure 15.2).

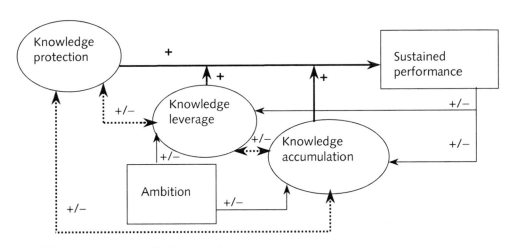

FIGURE 15.2   An integrative framework

Knowledge accumulation versus leverage

Accumulating knowledge is a key to competitive advantage, and yet business logics are often so intensely inertial as to make the leveraging of knowledge in new ways unlikely. The company may develop excess resources (Penrose, 1959), yet remain dependent on old management logics to exploit them. Conversely, aggressive attempts at leveraging knowledge can inhibit knowledge accumulation because the latter may typically not offer financial returns in the short run whereas the former often does.

A firm's own performance can drive the need for knowledge accumulation and create opportunities for leverage, but may act on these processes in opposing ways. Superior performance provides the slack resources that are needed to invest in knowledge accumulation (Chakravarthy, 1986); however, this can also breed a sense of complacence, lowering incentives to overcome the organizational and political barriers that obstruct leverage. On the other hand, continued poor performance can increase motivation within the firm to exploit knowledge in new ways, but limited resources and a loss of focus due to too much urgency can hinder efforts to accumulate knowledge.

In multi-site operations where knowledge development may occur in parallel, relatively tight frameworks are used to diffuse existing knowledge and to further their strengthening locally. For example, local managers of McDonald's in the restaurant business or Banc One in the banking business are not allowed to deviate much from standard practice. However, exhaustive specification of procedures, and strict adherence to them stifles learning. Either procedures are blindly adhered to and learning stops, or procedures are increasingly ignored and informal "communities of practice" develop, often fostering significant collective "learning by doing" within the local "community" but making results from that learning increasingly difficult to share with other sub-units which have developed other practices. Therefore, a key issue for management of this tension is to create a "tight–loose" process for knowledge leveraging, leaving enough freedom for learning to take place but imposing sufficient communality for comparing performance and sharing results to facilitate later diffusion.

Ambition (Hamel and Prahalad, 1989) may also help to achieve the right balance between knowledge accumulation and leverage. Stretch goals motivate a stronger emphasis on leveraging knowledge in new ways. On the other hand, a very strong ambition may also lead the firm to move away from its existing knowledge and accumulate new knowledge. As noted earlier, when a firm's performance is very good, its managers have little incentive to use knowledge in new ways or to accumulate new knowledge. Ambition can be used to recalibrate the value of performance by continuously moving the hurdle upwards. As Kaku in Canon would note: "Today Mount Fuji, tomorrow Mount Everest." What was adequate for the former would be inadequate knowledge when scaling the latter. A stretching ambition may help improve knowledge accumulation and leverage, compensating for the effects on them of a firm's performance. Ambition is thus an important moderating variable in establishing the right tradeoffs between knowledge accumulation and leverage.

Knowledge protection versus accumulation

Experience is intrinsically conservative, and leads to strong emotional and organizational commitment. This may assist in protecting existing knowledge, by embedding it deeper into complex social relationships and tacit mindsets. First, successful "learning by doing" requires time slack – continuity of task and constancy of performance criteria. But as cumulative learning is achieved, and cumulative excellence develops, commitment to this skill set grows and vested interests build. Second, knowledge results from, and reinforces, specific mindsets. Successful procedures and what they deliver are sources of satisfaction. These cannot be questioned without questioning the worth of the individuals and communities that bred them. The skills and tools that individuals possess shape how they think and perceive their environment. This reliance leads to strong value judgments and orthodoxies. Third, organizational routines are the result of a satisfactory compromise between stakeholders in an organization and they implicitly reflect the relative credibility and relative power of various categories of stakeholders (Leonard-Barton, 1992). A shift in the relative criticality of knowledge may threaten the balance of power in the organization, and question the continued validity of existing knowledge. Dominant groups and coalitions commit to tangible and intangible assets, and the product markets that have shaped existing knowledge, in order to perpetuate their greater influence within the organization. These commitments may extend to powerful outsiders, such as important current customers who have vested interests in the continuation of the firm's current business portfolio and technological trajectory.

These forces lead firms to favor protection of existing knowledge rather than the accumulation of new knowledge. It is striking, for example, to see how IBM masterfully achieved "architectural" control over mainframes in the 1960s and 1970s and let Microsoft and Intel take such control away from IBM in personal computers in the 1980s. To encourage effective knowledge accumulation, management needs to shake up existing patterns of behavior, values, and tacit mindsets. Since this typically requires articulation of tacit knowledge, it sacrifices some protection of that knowledge. To maintain an appropriate balance between knowledge protection and leverage, managers must encourage employees to cycle between working within existing knowledge and ambitions, and articulating and challenging them. This may be accomplished through periodic formalized processes to initiate major changes, or by building subtle mechanisms for generating continuous variation within organizational routines.

Knowledge leverage versus protection

Knowledge leverage and protection can also be in conflict. Effective protection of knowledge often requires segregating or embedding knowledge within the organization, while leverage demands integration and articulation. The dynamics among different parts of an organization can hinder leverage. Groups and individuals may prefer to hone their skills on local problems and small groups will try to deepen their local knowledge rather than transfer it to other parts of the organization. Moving skills and knowledge from the individual to the collective level requires several activities, the articulation of the knowledge (or a collective apprenticeship) and its diffusion to other units (Hedlund and Nonaka, 1993). However, articulation of knowledge is unlikely to be ever fully feasible, because knowledge cannot be entirely captured in explicit procedural knowledge. Direct diffusion of tacit knowledge and skills is also possible, but their transfer is likely to place a greater burden on the transferor (Szulanski, 1996). Articulation of knowledge makes it easy to transfer it internally, but also makes it vulnerable to external pilferage. Additionally, characteristics of knowledge that protect it from imitation can hinder its transformation and recombination, making leverage difficult (Galunic and Rodan, 1998; McEvily and Chakravarthy, 2002).

Sustaining superior performance

The above discussion suggests why it is difficult for a firm to sustain superior performance over time. Knowledge leverage is necessary for growth; knowledge accumulation to ensure that this growth is profitable; and knowledge protection to sustain this profitable growth. The three knowledge management activities have to be kept in a delicate balance, which is not always easy. Discovering how to attain this balance is a potentially fruitful issue for future research.

CONCLUSION

In this chapter we have offered several testable propositions about the links between knowledge management and competitive advantage. We have also highlighted key tradeoffs deserving of further research. We address one final issue in closing.

A question that we believe warrants attention is whether firms should seek a balance between the three knowledge management activities or whether they stand a better chance of gaining and sustaining advantage by maximizing their attention to just one of them, perhaps sequentially.

March (1991) has argued that to survive, firms need to engage in both exploitation and exploration. Exploration has to do with the degree to which an organization *accumulates* new knowledge, while exploitation is the *leverage* of old knowledge. Others have suggested a more contingent approach. For instance, researchers have suggested that in environments with greater volatility (e.g., heterogeneous or fickle customer preferences and expanding technological opportunities) knowledge accumulation should be emphasized over knowledge protection. Although this clearly makes intuitive sense, little empirical evidence has been gathered to relate turbulence, knowledge management and competitive advantage. In fact Sorenson (2001) found the exact opposite relationship, where superior knowledge accumulators performed better when their environment was more stable but did not have a survival advantage over their competitors when environmental volatility increased. So is knowledge accumulation helpful in volatile or stable environments? Does this depend on how volatility is measured? Do other characteristics of the environment have a say?

Knowledge protection was shown to help in environments dominated by incremental technological change (McEvily and Chakravarthy, 2002). How about other environments? Is knowledge leverage more important in these? Or does the environment dictate which type of knowledge, resource conversion or market positioning, is more important to a company's competitive success?

In order to make progress in this area, we need to identify how to characterize environmental change, how to assess a firm's knowledge management activities; and to make comparisons across industries and markets. A challenge here is the difficulty of relating environmental change to knowledge management. For example, one measure of environmental turbulence is the frequency of new product introductions; however, new products may embody very incremental changes in the underlying knowledge. A case in point is Bayus's (1998) study of personal computers. The study showed that new products embodied very incremental technological change; suggesting that refinement may be most valuable here. Yet, this is an industry we typically consider to be volatile.

Finally, we need to address the "value of knowledge" question that the resource-based view takes as given. It starts with the assumption that knowledge is valuable for a firm but perhaps misses the point that it is not knowledge *per se*, rather knowledge management activities that provide the firm with its competitive advantage. Compared to knowledge, which can be held intra personally, in groups, as well as organizationally; knowledge management activities are all organizationally embedded. Consequently, it is easier to measure them. This chapter thus offers renewed hope for empirically testing the links between knowledge management, learning and competitive advantage.

References

Appleyard, M. (1996) How Does Knowledge Flow? Interfirm Patterns in the Semiconductor Industry. *Strategic Management Journal*, 17(Winter Special Issue): 137–54.

Argote, L. (1999) *Organizational Learning: Creating, Retaining, and Transferring Knowledge*, Norwell, MA: Kluwer.

Argote, L. and Epple, D. (1990) Learning Curves in Manufacturing. *Science*, 247: 920–4.

Arora, A. and Gambardella, A. (1994) The Changing Technology of Technological Change: General and Abstract Knowledge and the Division of Labor. *Research Policy*, 23: 523–32.

Barney, J. (1991) Firm Resources and Ssustained Competitive Advantage. *Journal of Management*, 17: 99–120.

Bayus, B.L. (1998) An Analysis of Product Lifetimes in a Technologically Dynamic Industry. *Management Science*, 44 (6): 763–75.

Burgelman, R. and Doz, Y. (2001) The Power of Strategic Integration. *Sloan Management Review*, Spring, 42 (3): 28.

Chakravarthy, B.S. (1986) Measuring Strategic Performance. *Strategic Management Journal*, 7: 437–58.

Chakravarthy, B.S. (1996) Flexible Commitments. *Strategy and Leadership*, 24: 14–20.

Chakravarthy, B.S. (1997) A New Strategy Framework for Coping with Turbulence. *Sloan Management Review*, Winter, 38 (2): 69–82.

Chakravarthy, B.S., Lorange, P., and Cho, H. (2002) The Growth Imperative for Asian Firms. *Nanyang Business Review*, 1 (1): 69–76.

Chakravarthy, B.S., Zaheer, A., and Zaheer, S. (2001) Knowledge Sharing in Organizations: A Field Study. Paper presented at the Strategic management Society Conference, San Francisco.

Cyert, R.M. and March J. (1963) *A Behavioral Theory of the Firm*. Englewood Cliffs, NJ: Prentice-Hall.

Daft, R.L. and Weick, K.E. (1984) Toward a Model of Organizations as Interpretation Systems. *Academy of Management Review*, 9: 284–96.

Dierickx, I. and Cool, K. (1989) Asset Stock Accumulation and Sustainability of Competitive Advantage. *Management Science*, 35(12): 1504–11.

Dougherty, D. (1992) Interpretive Barriers to Successful Product Innovation in Large Firms. *Organization Science*, 3 (2): 179–202.

Doz, Y., Santos, J., and Williamson, P. (2001) *From Global to Metanational: How Companies Win in the Knowledge Economy*. Boston, MA: Harvard Business School Press.

Eisenhardt, K.M. and Santos, F. (2001) Knowledge-based View: A New Theory of Strategy. In A. Pettigrew, H. Thomas, and R. Whitington (eds.), *Handbook of Strategy and Management*. London: Sage Publications.

Fiol, C.M. and Lyles, M.A. (1985) Organizational Learning. *Academy of Management Review*, 10 (4): 803–13.

Friedman, D.D., Landes, W.M., and Posner, R.A. (1991) Some Economics of Trade Secret Law. *Journal of Economic Perspectives*, 5: 61–72.

Galunic, D.C. and Rodan, S. (1998) Resource Recombination in the Firm: Knowledge Structures and the Potential for Schumpeterian Innovation. *Strategic Management Journal*, 19 (12): 1193–201.

Garud, R. (1997) On the Distinction Between Know-how, Know-why, and Know-what. In J.P. Walsh and A.S. Huff (eds.), *Advances in Strategic Management*, Vol. 14. Greenwich, CT: JAI Press, 81–101.

Gioia, D.A. and Poole, P.P. (1984) Scripts in Organizational Behavior. *Academy of Management Review*, 9: 449–59.

Hamel, G. and Prahalad, C.K. (1989) Strategic Intent. *Harvard Business Review*, 67: 63–76.

Hamel, G. and Prahalad, C.K. (1991) Corporate Imagination and Expeditionary Marketin., *Harvard Business Review*, 69 (4): 81–92.

Hedberg, B.L.T. (1981) How Organizations Learn and Unlearn. In Nystrom and Starbuck, *Handbook of Organizational Design*, Oxford.

Hedberg, B. (1981) How Organizations Learn and Unlearn. In P.C. Nystrom and W.H. Starbuck (eds.), *Handbook of Organizational Design*, Vol. 1. New York: Oxford University Press, 3–27.

Henderson, R. and Clark, K.B. (1990) Architectural Innovation: The Reconfiguration of Existing Product Technologies and the Failure of Established Firms. *Administrative Science Quarterly*, 35: 9–30.

Huber, G.P. (1991) Organizational Learning: The Contributing Processes and the Literatures. *Organization Science*, 2: 88–115.

Leonard-Barton, D. (1992) Core Capabilities and Core Rigidities: A Paradox in Managing New Product Development. *Strategic Management Journal – Special Issue: Strategy Process: Managing Corporate Self Renewal*, 13: 111–27.

Levitt, B. and March, J. (1988) Organizational Learning. *Annual Review of Sociology*, 14: 319–40.

Liebeskind, J.P. (1996) Knowledge, Strategy, and the Theory of the Firm. *Strategic Management Journal*, 17 (Winter Special Issue): 93–108.

Lippman, S.A. and Rumelt, R. (1982) Uncertain Imitability: An Analysis of Interfirm Differences in Efficiency under Competition. *Bell Journal of Economics*, 13: 418–38.

Lyles, M.A. (1988) Learning among Joint Venture Sophisticated Firms. *Management International Review*, 28: 85–98.

MacMillan, I., McCaffery, M., and Van Wijk, G. (1985) Competitors' Responses to Easily Imitated New Products – Exploring Commercial Banking Product Introductions. *Strategic Management Journal*, 6: 75–86.

Mansfield, E., Schwartz, M., and Wagner, S. (1981) Imitation Costs and Patents: An Empirical Study. *Economic Journal*, 91: 907–18.

March, J.G. (1991) Exploration and Exploitation in Organizational Learning. *Organization Science*, 2: 71–87.

McCaskey, M.B. (1982) *The Executive Challenge: Managing Change and Ambiguity*. Marshfield, MA: Pittman.

McEvily, S. and Chakravarthy, B.S. (2002) The Persistence of Knowledge-Based Advantage: An Empirical Test for Product Performance and Technological Knowledge. *Strategic Management Journal*, 23 (4): 285–305.

Nelson, R. and Winter, S. (1982) *An Evolutionary Theory of Economic Change*. Cambridge, MA: The Belknap Press of Harvard University.

Nonaka, I. (1991) Toward Middle-up Down Management: Accelerating Information Creation. *Sloan Management Review*, 29 (3): 9–18.

Nonaka, I. (1994) A Dynamic Theory of Organizational Knowledge Creation. *Organization Science*, 5: 14–37.

Nonaka, I. and Takeuchi, H. (1995) *The Knowledge-Creating Company: How Japanese Companies Create the Dynamics of Innovation*. New York: Oxford University Press.

Penrose, E.T. (1959) *The Theory of the Growth of the Firm*. Oxford: Basil Blackwell.

Polanyi, M. (1962) *Personal Knowledge: Towards a Post-Critical Philosophy* (corrected edn). Chicago, IL: University of Chicago Press.

Prahalad, C.K. and Hamel, G. (1990) The Core Competence of the Corporation. *Harvard Business Review*, May–June: 79–91.

Quinn, J.B. (1992) *Intelligent Enterprise*. New York: The Free Press.

Rappaport, A.S. and Halevi, S. (1991) The Computerless Computer Company. *Harvard Business Review*, July–August: 69–80.

Reed, R. and DeFillippi, R.J. (1990) Causal Ambiguity, Barriers to Imitation, and Sustainable Competitive Advantage. *Academy of Management Review*, 15 (1): 88–102.

Reber, A.S. (1993) *Implicit Learning and Tacit Knowledge: An Essay on the Cognitive Unconscious*. New York: Oxford University Press.

Reitman, W.R. (1964) Heuristic Decision Procedures, Open Constraints, and the Structure of Ill-Defined Problems. In N.W. Shelley and G. Bryan (eds.), *Human Judgments and Optimality*. New York: John Wiley & Sons, 282–315.

Simon, H. (1962) The Architecture of Complexity. *Proceedings of the American Philosophical Society*, 106 (December): 467–82.

Sorenson, O. (2001) Interdependence and Adaptability: Organizational Learning and the Long-term Effect of Integration. Working paper, Los Angeles, CA.: University of California at Los Angeles.

Spender, J.C. (1996) Making Knowledge the Basis of a Dynamic Theory of the Firm, *Strategic Management Journal*, 17 (Special Issue): 45–62.

Szulanski, G. (1996) Exploring Internal Stickiness: Impediments to the Transfer of Best Practice Within the Firm. *Strategic Management Journal*, 17(Winter Special Issue): 27–43.

Teece, D.J., Pisano, G., and Shuen, A. (1997) Dynamic Capabilities and Strategic Management. *Strategic Management Journal*, 18 (7): 509–33.

Von Hippel, E. (1998) *Sources of Innovation*. New York: Oxford University Press.

Weick, K.E. (1979) *The Social Psychology of Organizing*. Reading, MA: Addison-Wesley.

Wilson, R.W. (1977) The Effect of Technological Environment and Product Rivalry on R&D Effort and Licensing of Inventions. *Review of Economics and Statistics*, 59 (2): 171–8.

Winter, S.G. (1987) Knowledge and Competence as Strategic Assets. In D. Teece (ed.), *The Competitive Challenge: Strategies for Industrial Innovation and Renewal*. New York: Harper and Row.

Zander, U. and Kogut, B. (1995) Knowledge and the Speed of Transfer and Imitation of Organizational Capabilities: An Empirical Test. *Organization Science*, 6 (1): 76–92.

16

Narrative Knowledge in Action: Adaptive Abduction as a Mechanism for Knowledge Creation and Exchange in Organizations

Caroline A. Bartel and Raghu Garud

Chapter Outline

Narratives are important vehicles for creating and disseminating knowledge in organizations. In this chapter, we propose a process through which actors generate knowledge from narratives, which we label "adaptive abduction." Adaptive abduction leverages the temporal and contextual structure that orders the persons, objects, and events in a narrative, allowing a person to confirm, amend, or construct some set of inferences about past events and their own current situations. It is this process that affords narratives interpretive flexibility across time and space, enabling different people in different situations to use the same narrative for their own purposes. In this way, narratives bring together people that operate in different organizational realities, enabling them to interpret each other's experiences and formulate possible applications to their own work contexts. Moreover, the narrative itself is transformed in the process of adaptive abduction as people recount the narrative and incorporate their interpretations and implications. Thus, narratives are dynamic entities that take on new forms as they are translated and retold in organizational settings, thereby allowing knowledge for creation and transformation.

Introduction

With the advent of new intellectual tools (e.g., Internet and intranets) and organizational practices aimed at knowledge management, there is renewed interest in the organizational literature as to how knowledge is represented and applied. Two contrasting perspectives on these issues are representative of the variety of positions held by organizational scholars. One perspective suggests that valid knowledge takes the form of abstract principles or rules (often involving causal relationships), whereas a second perspective contends that knowledge is context dependent and best captured in rich descriptions or narratives. In this chapter, we refer to these forms of knowledge as "propositional knowledge" and "narrative knowledge," respectively.

We consider both perspectives on knowledge to be valid, each representing and probing the world in different ways for different purposes. Abstract principles are typically derived from formal and empirical evidence to provide individuals with a set of *if–then* rules that inform particular interpretations of events or courses of action under certain circumstances. Such generalizations enable swift information processing and action in organizations as individuals can utilize them without reassessing a decision situation in detail each time it arises.

However, even if people can and do think about their experiences and knowledge in terms of these context-free abstractions, more often than not, specific incidents told in narrative form are triggered when people think about themselves and others (Baumesiter and Newman, 1994). Prior research has suggested that individuals have an inherent ability and predisposition to use narratives (Fisher, 1987; Lounsbury and Glynn, 2001; Polkinghore, 1987) and that information in memory tends to be stored and recalled in narrative form more often than in propositional form (see Fiske and Taylor, 1991). These ideas are consistent with Weick's (1995: 127) assertion that "most organizational realities are based on narrative" (see also Tsoukas and Hatch, 2001) and Lounsbury and Glynn's (2001) position that entrepreneurs rely on narratives in interactions with potential investors to mobilize resources for ventures. Moreover, narrative knowledge includes tacit understandings that are sometimes obscured in generalizations, which can affect a person's understanding of past, present, and anticipated future events substantially. Examples include contextual and historical knowledge, such as an organization's culture and its deeply held assumptions about organizational life, including those pertaining to employees, competitors, customers, and relationships among individuals or organizational sub-groups (i.e., departments, work groups).

Hayek (1945) pointed out that circumstances of time and place may be highly significant for a given situation and that generalizations, by their nature, cannot take direct account of such details. As a result, Hayek argued that the "man on the spot" must find some other way in which to generate the decisions left to him. That is, generalizations need to be augmented with alternative forms of knowledge to fully inform a person's thoughts and actions in organizational settings. In this regard, an important question is: *How can actors create and apply knowledge in the course of their daily work lives?* Thick descriptions in the form of narratives, we suggest, are an important means. However, if narratives themselves have to gain legitimacy as vehicles for knowledge, it is important to explicate their epistemological and ontological status and specify the mechanisms that enable people to create and apply knowledge to their current or future situations. It is to this task that we dedicate ourselves in this chapter.

The remainder of this chapter is organized as follows. We first provide a brief summary of the nature of narrative knowledge, emphasizing how a narrative's capacity to preserve the complexity, ambiguity and dynamism of a particular set of events enables knowledge exchange and generation. This is not intended as a review chapter, but, rather, we aim to extend contemporary theorizing about narratives to better understand how knowledge is created and exchanged in organizations. Our position is that individuals constitute much of the knowledge creation that takes place in organizations. We therefore propose a process through which individuals generate knowledge from narratives, which we label "adaptive abduction." This process celebrates the interpretative flexibility (Pinch and Bijker, 1987) of narratives as different people use the same narrative to generate different implications for navigating the flow of current and anticipated events. Such adaptive abduction is important, because if there is no interpretive flexibility, the knowledge system is "inactive, asocial and purely machine-like" (Spender, 1996: 59). Although our discussion is focused primarily on individual actors, we recognize that knowledge creation occurs through other means that transcend individuals (Garud and Nayyar, 1994; Grant, 1996; Kogut and Zander, 1996). We therefore describe how narrative knowledge and adaptive abduction affect knowledge creation in the broader organizational context. We conclude this chapter by raising possible research questions for organizational scholars interested in how individuals use narratives to generate and act on knowledge within their organizations.

Nature of Narrative Knowledge

We suggest that knowledge creation and transformation in organizations results from individuals' active participation and interactions with tasks, technologies, resources, and people within a particular organizational context (Bourdieu, 1990; Brown and Duguid, 1991; Garud and Rappa, 1994; Hutchins, 1991; Tsoukas, 1996). This perspective has several noteworthy concepts. First, knowledge is situated in a particular context and consists of understandings that are created or transformed with ongoing experience in a given work context (Lant, 1999). Orr (1990) and Lave and Wenger (1994), for example, describe how exposure to and immersion in the activities of a work community (e.g., work group, department, occupation, organization) produce an inseparable mixture of both abstract, technical understandings and tacit, informal practices that shape how people take action within a work community on an everyday basis.

Another key concept is that knowledge results from both individual and collective processes. To this point, Tsoukas (1996: 14) noted, "individual knowledge is possible precisely because of the social practices within which individuals engage – the two are mutually defined." Hence, social interactions and the sharing of information contribute not only to individual knowledge but also to shared knowledge (see also von Krogh in this volume). Shared knowledge helps form the "unarticulated background" (Tsoukas, 1996) that underlies individual thought and behavior and enables coordinated action among people in a given work context. Accordingly, narratives are often vehicles for communicating aspects of an organization's culture and turning points in its history (Boje, 1995; Czarniawska, 1997; Trice and Beyer, 1993) during the socialization of newcomers. For instance, Van Maanen (1975, 1998) documented changes in attitudes and knowledge held by police recruits as a function of early career experiences and powerful socialization process where they learn proper approaches to urban policing through stories told by seasoned officers.

The foregoing ideas that knowledge is inextricably tied to contexts and practices and is shared through social interactions point to the potential importance of narratives in organizational settings. Organizational scholars have argued that knowledge is embedded in conversations and, particularly, the narratives or stories that individuals exchange with one another (Boje, 1991; Brown and Duguid, 1991; Orr, 1990; Weick and Roberts, 1993; Zuboff, 1988). As Searle (1995: 60) noted, "language (and in this case narrative) is partly constitutive of institutional facts."

In this chapter we use the terms "narratives" and "stories" interchangeably. Narratives are "thick descriptions" that provide a holistic account of a set of events and contain a mixture of beliefs, intentions, actions, and contextual details that are temporally ordered and have an implied "plot" that connects them in terms of causality. The plot suggests a meaningful synthesis of interrelated activities by situating them in a historical and social context and by highlighting the contribution of individual events (Bal, 1985; Czarniawska, 1998). In this way, narratives impart meaning to the people, events, and actions that individuals encounter in their organizational lives (Weick, 1995). Narratives therefore are not to be reduced into a series of propositional statements that specify necessary and sufficient conditions (Mohr, 1982; Van de Ven, 1992). As Boje (1995: 1008) suggested, narratives or stories should be treated as "one totalizing account, one set of universals, one set of essentials, and one construction."

Brown and Duguid (1991: 45) argue that narratives complement other forms of knowledge, such as propositional knowledge, and enable people to develop understandings from their experiences to enhance "the impoverished directive route that they have been furnished by the corporation." That is, the if-then mechanisms (e.g., rules and procedures, routines, and directives) indicative of propositional knowledge are often limited in use and narratives may serve to overcome those limitations. Consider the widely shared narrative of the invention of the Post-It® Note at 3M. The narrative describes a chain of events detailing Spence Silver's development of the technology in 1968 and Art Fry's application of the adhesive to a bookmark, which ultimately led to the creation and release of the Post-It® Note in 1980. 3M has a written account of these events, which appears in its *Innovation Chronicles* – an internal publication containing 20 narratives capturing critical lessons for innovation at 3M.

The Post-It® Note narrative outlines a sequence of events involving key organizational actors and a plot that emphasizes how innovation requires a blend of curiosity, practicality and persistence, and a collective effort among people from various organizational domains (e.g., research and development, marketing). For instance, the Post-It® Note narrative starts off with a caption "The 3M dedication to innovation is always a team effort. Innovators learn that *it's better to ask for forgiveness than for permission.*" In some other context, the message contained here would be considered to be an act of insubordination. However, a reason for this aphorism becomes clear as an understanding of 3M's context emerges from a read of the rest of the narrative and other narratives contained in the *Innovation Chronicles*. 3M encourages employees to "bootleg" and promotes an understanding that "technology belongs to the corporation." Given such a "collateral context" (March et al., 1991) the message *"it's better to ask for forgiveness than for permission"* is interpreted as a signal to be entrepreneurial and creative. To reinforce this message, the Post-It® Note narrative highlights how "a team of tenacious innovators at 3M created the product that permanently changed the way we communicate."

The underlying plot that is woven into the Post-It® Note narrative essentially provides a process theory that helps the recipient of the narrative to navigate the unfolding flow of events. That is, it allows employees to garner practical insight into the creative process within a given organizational context. The plot suggests how the actions of actors and how specific events should be interpreted, given what has transpired previously. In this way, events are appreciated in terms of their embedding context, which is conveyed through details pertaining to time, place, attributes of actors, and attributes of the context.

For instance, the Post-It® Note narrative points out "Despite the initial 'kill the program' efforts, Nicholson convinced Joe Ramey, the Division Vice President, to come with him to Richmond, VA and walk up and down the streets on 'cold' calls to see if they could sell the product – they did, and this almost-killed program was resurrected." As Pentland (1999: 713) offered, such details provide information that is essential to the interpretation of the unfolding narrative. For 3M employees, this detail reinforces the importance of tenacity and persistence, a theme that runs through all the narratives of discovery in the *Innovation Chronicles*. Indeed, through such accounts, 3M hopes to preserve memories of past accomplishments and the conditions surrounding their development. The expectation is that a holistic recounting of the Post-It® Note encapsulates processes that fuel innovation within the organization. Such processes would be difficult, if not impossible, to communicate through context-free generalizations.

The holistic accounts that narratives provide are thus an important means for capturing path dependencies associated with human choice (Arthur, 1988; David, 1985). Path dependence suggests that it would be futile to interpret events in isolation of their historical moorings. This point is consistent with Cohen and Levinthal's (1990: 128) notion of "absorptive capacity": the use of prior related knowledge to recognize the value of new knowledge, assimilate it, and apply it toward some end. Consider a narrative that has generated considerable controversy – the origins of the letters of the typewriter keyboard. According to the narrative by David (1985), the specific arrangements of the keyboard, as manifest in QWERTY, emerged to prevent typebars from clashing and jamming if struck in rapid succession as well as to create a promotional gimmick which involved placing "R" in the first row so that the a salesman could impress customers by rapidly pecking out the brand name: TYPE WRITER. At that time, according to David, other layouts existed that did not imply the jamming of keys. But happenstance, in combination with human habituation, resulted in the perpetuation of an inferior alternative (QWERTY). That is, technological change and human agency are path dependent (David, 1985).

The implications that David derives from the QWERTY narrative are so important that the narrative itself and its implications have not gone unchallenged. Liebowitz and Margolis (1990), for instance, have dismissed David's narrative as being a "fable," challenging both its completeness as well as its implications.[1] As we will discuss later, the controversy and debate that narratives such as the QWERTY story can generate are important mechanisms for knowledge creation. For the moment, however, we want to point to a major implication of the QWERTY narrative that even Liebowitz and Margolis accept – choices and investments can be durable, and path dependencies arise from such durability. Durability and the wider notion of path dependence suggest that events have to be seen within their historical contexts. It would be committing a fallacy of generalization to ignore the complex and holistic processes within which activities are situated. And it is here that we can see the benefits of narratives over propositional forms of knowledge in their ability to capture the path dependent nature of events.

How Do Individuals Generate and Apply Narrative Knowledge?

To argue that narratives capture path dependencies associated with human choice, we encounter the issue of generalization. That is, if each narrative is an idiosyncratic account of a particular set of processes, how can we learn from them? Do the details of the narrative itself obscure and destroy the knowledge generalization process?

These questions, though important, are relevant from an epistemological and ontological position that attempts to generalize and validate knowledge using inductive and deductive logic. By inductive logic we mean the generation of abstract principles or causal rules through a process of grounded theorizing that connect two or more constructs through a process of constant comparison (Dyer and Wilkins, 1991; Eisenhardt, 1989; Glaser and Strauss, 1967). By deductive logic we mean the application of these rules to arrive at "testable" propositions about social phenomena. At the heart of both approaches is the notion of covariation, whereby individuals infer necessary and sufficient causation between independent and dependent variables (Mohr, 1982; Van de Ven, 1992). Both approaches are attempts at creating linkages between samples and populations. Individuals who hold either perspective are therefore likely to develop variance theories explicating efficient causation between two or more constructs (Mohr, 1982; Van de Ven, 1992).

For those who subscribe to a different ontology and epistemology, questions about how individuals might arrive at generic conclusions from particularized accounts miss the point about how narratives enable individuals to create and apply knowledge. Although a narrative may have a particular plot that connects a series of actors and events, an ability to abstract and apply embedded knowledge is ultimately left to the recipient's interpretation. Such a process of interpreting narratives and generating knowledge *in situ* is neither inductive nor deductive, but rather, is abductive (Eco, 1979; Dunbar et al., 1996; Peirce, 1931; Truzzi, 1976).

Abductive processes

Peirce (1931) originally described abduction as a process that is different from deduction and induction. Deduction involves arriving at a "result" based on applying a "rule" to a "case." For instance, the rule might state "all athletes are strong" and when applied to a case "Mary is an athlete" produces a result "Mary is strong." Induction, on the other hand, is to infer a rule given a case and a result. Abduction, in contrast to deduction and induction, involves inferring a case based on a result to which a rule is applied. For instance, the result may be "Mary is strong" to which we apply a rule such as "all athletes are strong" and from this we infer that "Mary is an athlete."

We suggest that abductions lie at the heart of the inferences that individuals draw from everyday work phenomena. In an organizational setting, abductions involve using existing frameworks to draw inferences from narratives. Allison (1971) illustrates such a process in his use of three "lenses" to explain the Cuban missile crisis. As Allison showed, each lens highlighted certain facets of the phenomenon while obscuring others. In a similar way, individuals bring multiple perspectives and experiences to bear on a narrative to generate inferences that then informs their actions (Dunbar et al., 1996). These perspectives can include schemas, mental models, belief systems, or values and norms, which help organize generic knowledge about a particular stimulus and include a blend of abstract principles and specific incidents. These shape attention (what information is noticed), encoding of information (the structure, evaluation, interpretation, and transformation of information into a representation), memory for old information, and information integration (generating inferences) (Massaro and Cowan, 1993; Neisser, 1976; Weick, 1979). Individuals observe certain events in a narrative and use their perspectives to make sense of the events and derive conclusions about how to behave in their current or anticipated future situations.

Thus, whereas induction and deduction entail establishing links between samples and populations, or between particulars and general rules, abduction is a process whereby actors infer and apply implications from a narrative to their particular context. It is a process of articulating and consolidating a listing of events, information about the historical and social context, and the thoughts and feelings of actors into a schematic whole that attributes significance to individual elements according to their effect on the whole (Polkinghore, 1987). Simply put, abduction is the process of reconstructing the implied plot of a story as conveyed by the narrator. Often, abduction can yield multiple interpretations that provide a meaningful synthesis for a single set of events and actions. These can be reconciled according to the principle of best fit where an individual compares proposed plot structures with the narrative, eliminates or revises different plots accordingly, and ultimately selects an interpretation that can be applied to his/her particular context. The onus of generalization therefore lies not only with the narrator, but also with the recipient who has the responsibility to abstract the essence of a narrative and recontextualize it to generate valid implications. In this way, abduction involves a process of mindful replication (Garud, 1999).

This view stands in contrast to traditional perspectives that view knowledge as being devoid of ambiguity and subjectivity (Schwab, 1980). With traditional perspectives, individuals may reduce complex realities with ever-narrower classifications and framing to remove ambiguity and subjectivity. Classification and framing are "powerful technologies" (Bowker and Star, 2000: 319) and are key mechanisms for the constitution of "social facts" within an epistemic community (Searle, 1995). In this way, the constructs that we create to probe reality often become the basis for reality (Latour and Woolgar, 1979: 240). For instance, IQ tests have become so institutionalized that we now consider a person to be intelligent or not based on his or her score on the IQ test. As Bowker and Star (2000) pointed out, these classifications become embedded in working infrastructures and become relatively invisible without losing any of their power. Eventually, if we are not careful, rather than mindful replication, we begin pursuing a process of mindless replication as we become prisoners of the very constructs and language that we have created (von Krogh and Roos, 1995; Wittgenstein, 1958).

It is here that we can see the benefits that narratives have to offer in their capacity to spawn multiple interpretations. Abduction as a mechanism for generalizing from narratives suggests that interpretative flexibility (Pinch and Bijker, 1987) rather than rigidity has value. By interpretative flexibility we mean that narratives have the power to evoke different meanings for the participants involved (Thachankary, 1992). The meaning given to actors and events in a narrative can differ between individuals and can change over time for a specific individual as he/she reinterprets their roles and attaches different significance. Thus, on different occasions, a person may derive different implications from the same narrative. And, in fostering interpretative flexibility, it allows individuals to escape the forces of history even while benefiting from them, thereby generating a dynamic rather than a static world.

Adaptive abduction

So far, we have suggested that narratives offer a contextualized holistic account of events and that the onus for generalization from such narratives lies with the person who wants to learn from the narrative. The process of abduction that we have offered as a mechanism implies that different participants may derive different meanings from the same story. As Lave and Wenger (1994: 34) pointed out:

> In this sense, any "power of abstraction" is thoroughly situated, in the lives of person and in the culture that makes it possible . . . That is why stories can be so powerful in conveying ideas, often more so than any articulation of the idea itself. What is called general knowledge is not privileged with respect to other "kinds" of knowledge. It too can be gained only in specific circumstances. And it too must be brought into play in specific circumstances. The generality of any form of knowledge always lies in the power to renegotiate the meaning of the past and future in constructing the meaning of present circumstances.

For instance, General Electric's (GE's) Jack Welch's narrative on "boundary-less behavior" may have different implications for those who work in different parts of the world and thus operate with different perspectives on organizational life. This transformative property of narratives suggests that there is a duality (Giddens, 1979) rather than a dichotomy between objects and subjects. Appreciative of this duality abduction, Eco (1979: 132) quotes Peirce: "the various sounds made by the instruments of an orchestra strike upon the ear, and the result is a peculiar musical emotion, quite distinct from the sounds themselves." Eco (1979: 132) goes on to add:

> What has to be retained from this quotation is not the picture of a particular emotional state, but, rather, the idea that the hearer, hearing music, grasps more than the single "meaning" of each sound. If this interpretive movement stopped at the enjoyment of such an imprecise emotion, there would be neither abduction nor anything else relevant to our present purposes. But, the hypothetical movement is fulfilled when a new sense (a new combinational quality) is assigned to every sound, inasmuch as they compose the new contextual meaning of the musical piece. This example is a very complex instance of aesthetic interpretation.

As this quote suggests, there is an active process of inferencing and, similarly, narrative knowledge requires active participation (Boland et al., 2001). Individuals infer implications from a narrative and then develop their own recounting of it to guide their actions. Through recounting, a narrative becomes a part of an individual's experience – it no longer exists as a separate entity apart from the individual. As Boje (1991) stated, listeners are co-producers with the narrator of a story, using their own perspectives and experiences to fill in gaps and develop their own interpretation. Individuals are therefore engaged in a dynamic process of refinement to the plot and resulting implications of narratives, even for those narratives that are widely shared and accepted. Consequently, "learning neither resides in the minds of individuals, nor is entirely socially constructed" (Lant, 1999: 177). It is resident in interactions (Garud, 1997; Lant, 1999).

Given the transformative nature of this process, we use the term "adaptive abduction" to describe how individuals generate and apply knowledge and action from narratives. As individuals extract implications and develop their own recounting of a narrative, they adapt not only themselves but the narrative itself. In this sense, narratives not only capture path dependencies but are path creative as well (Garud and Karne, 2001). For instance, narratives can transform knowledge by generating impulses that unfold in self-fulfilling ways. Shaw et al. (1998) recently described how organizations craft "strategic stories" as part of the planning process to mobilize people to move the organization in a desired direction. These researchers note "when people can locate themselves in the story, their sense of commitment and involvement is enhanced" (1998: 50). While adaptive abduction can yield future actions that refine, elaborate or somehow build on prior organizational actions, it can also generate dynamics that undo or somehow prevent a set of actions from occurring. If nothing is more practical than a good theory (Lewin, 1945; Van de Ven, 1989), then, certainly Orwell's *1984* and Huxley's *Brave New World* are powerful narratives precisely because they have the power to generate impulses that preclude certain outcomes from coming to fruition.

March (1998) stated that people who respect the future of the organization have to respect the past, and we claim that adaptive abduction associated with the interpretation of narratives is a fundamental mechanism bridging the two. Understanding this dual role of narratives, one of capturing the role of history in shaping human choice, and the other, the role of human choice in shaping history, is a key part of the transformative power of narratives. In this way, the process of adaptive abduction helps to further expose the link between storytelling and organizing suggested by organizational scholars (Boje, 1991; Browning, 1991; Czarniawska, 1997; Martin et al., 1983). We revisit the Post-It® Note narrative to illustrate this point.

The account of an innovation that occurred nearly thirty years ago continues to galvanize action within 3M. In a study of 3M's micro-replication technology platform in 1998 (Garud, 1999), practitioners at 3M freely drew upon examples from Post-It® Note to support institutionalized ways of operation at 3M. These included the "15% bootlegging" rule, "going to the smoke-stacks" (a metaphor for connecting with the customer) and an ability to "build upon 3M's technology platforms" that belong to the company and not to any specific division. It was interesting to see practitioners apply principles contained in the original Post-It® Note narrative in mindful ways to the micro-replication technology, a fast-growing business at 3M. For instance, a practitioner suggested, "going to the smoke stacks" in today's electronic age meant connecting with the customer using the World Wide Web. Indeed, others at 3M offered their own contextualized application of the principles embodied in the Post-It® Note narrative and, in the process, their own narratives. In the process, they were preserving and modifying 3M's unique culture. In this way, narratives are not only accounts *of* past events but also serve as catalysts *for* future outcomes (Geertz, 1973).

Adaptive abduction and boundary objects

The degree to which an organization is able to generate and apply knowledge will depend on the degree to which individual members generate knowledge in the course of their daily work. However, organizational knowledge is not simply the sum of individual members' insights garnered through adaptive abduction, it depends on the transfer of such knowledge within and across organizational subgroups. We see narratives as instrumental in promoting such exchanges and thus view them as "boundary objects."

The notion of "boundary objects" was developed by Star (1989) to describe mechanisms that coordinate distributed work among heterogeneous actors who hold different goals, values, and languages. Boundary objects can take explicit forms (e.g., contracts, standard operating procedures, and newsletters) as well as more abstract and social forms (e.g., conferences, workshops, cross-functional teams) that bring people from diverse worlds together. The critical feature is that they act as common information spaces that enable interaction and coordination without consensus or shared goals. That is, boundary objects provide a common reference point that enables interaction between disparate subgroups. Boundary objects provide a bridge between different work communities in that they are pliable enough to accommodate and retain heterogeneous goals and points of view, yet robust enough to provide a common basis for interaction across groups. For example, Star gives the example of maps of geographical areas as boundary objects due to their capacity to cover identical physical territories but also focus on different knowledge interests (e.g., life zones of interest to biologists versus trails identified by museum conservationists).

We suggest that narratives also function as boundary objects. The act of exchanging narratives within a specific work community can foster shared perspectives (frames of reference) among its members. However, the fact that narratives represent those perspectives suggests that when a narrative is shared with a different work community, it can encourage perspective taking by its members (Boland and Tenkasi, 1995). This is the essential function of a boundary object: to enable different work communities to come together to share information, ideas, or coordinate actions. To act as boundary objects, useful narratives have to be at an appropriate degree of abstraction such that they possess degrees of freedom to allow different work communities to become engaged while, at the same time, offering a given work community enough of a common core to abstract from. Particularly powerful narratives are those that can be retold, reinterpreted, and applied to a broad range of situations and work communities. Conceiving narratives as boundary objects allows us to understand how narratives and the process of adaptive abduction affect knowledge creation in the broader organizational context.

Let us return to the narrative about QWERTY to explicate this point. The fact that there is a controversy around this narrative makes this an appealing boundary object that has brought together historians, economists, and organization theorists. The QWERTY narrative and the controversies it has ignited can simultaneously galvanize future action as they evoke introspection about past choices. The power of the QWERTY narrative does not lie in suggesting that humans are perpetually stuck in the choices that we have made in the past, but, rather, lies in provoking us to think of ways by which we might escape such path dependence once we become aware of the stickiness of historical choices. Humans have the power to set in motion a sequence of events that result in the creation of new paths. After all, the human condition is Lamarckian rather than Darwinian (Gould, 1980; March, 1997). As March (1997: xi) pointed out, a Lamarckian perspective embraces the possibility that "innovations and history (are) attributable to willful human action and possibly susceptible to some degree of intentional management . . . and the possibilities for shaping and predicting historical change."

RESEARCH IMPLICATIONS FOR NARRATIVES AND ADAPTIVE ABDUCTION

We have offered a perspective on narratives emphasizing their richly textured and dynamic qualities. Narratives provide a holistic account of events that have a temporal ordering and an embedding context, and, thus, the potential to capture information about how and why certain outcomes were obtained. In capturing history, narratives also possess the power to unleash human agency to create new realities. This power comes from an interpretive process that we label as adaptive abduction. Through adaptive abduction, actors generate inferences from narratives and apply the knowledge to their own unique settings. Because people examine narratives through their own frames, different people derive different implications for action. To the degree that people then act upon these implications, the narrative itself is transformed as actors recount the narrative and incorporate their interpretations and implications. Thus, narratives are dynamic entities that take on new forms as they are translated and retold in an organizational setting. This perspective holds several implications for research that we explore.

Composition issues related to path dependence and path creation

We recommend that research further explicate the attributes that constitute a powerful knowledge-generating narrative. From narratives, individuals develop knowledge of past events and also develop implications for their future actions. It is therefore possible that distinct compositional properties are associated with different outcomes.

For instance, it would be useful to identify elements that allow a narrative to richly capture the path dependencies of actors and actions (David, 1985). By this we mean an identification of the elements that enable individuals and groups to comprehend, and thus generate knowledge related to, historical events. Pentland (1999) recently outlined several important properties of narratives for generating meaning. These include a sequential structure that orders events, identities and relationships of focal actors that reveal role structures and social networks in which events are embedded, an evaluative context that gives indications of the values and culture that define the situation, and other contextual indicators that provide a further backdrop for events. Research could explore more or less effective ways to structure these properties when communicating a narrative to others or when developing a personal recounting of it for oneself.

In addition to elements conveying path dependencies, a second objective for future research is to identify those elements of narratives that fuel path creation (Garud and Karne, 2001). It is possible that some narratives operate to trap people in the past where certain perspectives on situations and preferred modes of action are mindlessly replicated rather than transformed. In March's (1991) terms, such narratives promote "exploitation" whereby individuals maximize their use of pre-existing knowledge. We would expect that such narratives are highly prevalent when new organization members are socialized, for example. In these situations the objectives of the narrative are to convey an image of what the organization represents or stands for (i.e., its identity) as well as normative guidelines about appropriate modes of action for organization members. In contrast, other narratives provide an impetus for pursuing new knowledge, insights and actions, which is more indicative of "exploration" (March, 1991). For instance, Lampel (2001) pointed out how dramaturgical narratives can generate adaptive expectations that are able to overcome the shadow of the past. Such narratives are often told during organizational change efforts to promote awareness of the organization's past but also encourage others to question it and develop a new vision of what the future could hold (Conger, 1991; Corley and Gioia, in this volume; Lounsbury and Glynn, 2001; Reger et al., 1994).

At present, we know little about the properties of narratives that promote path creation. By this we mean the ways in which a narrative achieves interpretative flexibility and stimulates people to apply their own inferences to their particular settings. Potentially powerful narratives are those that allow people to question the meanings and implications of past events. Questioning is central to adaptive abduction as knowledge creation requires individuals to reflect on their understandings of events contained in a narrative and then extend it to develop solutions, decisions, or plans that are original, cogent and effective for their situation. The questioning process includes probing a narrative's assumptions (why would an actor do or say that?), consequences (why did that happen in that way?), contextual contingencies (what was it about the context that can explain the event?), and viewpoints (why did other actors view the decision as being effective?). Path creation hinges on such analyses because the development of new possibilities often requires "unlearning" (Hedberg, 1981; Lyles, 1998) and "discrediting" prior ways of thinking and acting (Weick, 1979), with the goal of letting go of the past in order to create a new future. Toward this end, questioning clarifies understandings, suggests alternative explanations and implications, creates links between information and ideas, and defines new situations to apply these learnings.

Although a person may be personally motivated to engage in questioning or be encouraged to do so by others, the narrative is the raw material that he or she will work with. Thus, an important issue concerns the properties of narratives that prompt a person to engage in questioning. For example, we suspect that active engagement in a narrative and in the knowledge creation process occurs when narratives contain paradoxes or controversies inherent in organizational life, or when narratives focus on extreme cases as a way to capture individuals' attention. For example, Martin and colleagues (1983) claimed that widely circulated stories in organizations often express tensions, such as between organizational values and individual values, inequality and equality, security and insecurity, and control and lack of control. We recommend additional work to explore the ways in which properties of narratives provoke questioning and active engagement.

Composition issues related to boundary objects

Another research issue that we highlight is the need to understand the properties of narratives that allow them to be effective boundary objects between work communities. For instance, a narrative containing properties that give rise to substantial interpretative flexibility could potentially produce multiple, contradictory accounts in a work community. Interpretive flexibility enables individuals to hold multiple interpretations for a set of events and thus develop different inferences for future action. This could have potential beneficial and harmful consequences when individuals must coordinate closely to accomplish a shared task. Coordination takes multiple forms, including coordination of action to achieve temporal and spatial synchronization of individuals' behaviors, coordination of understanding to attain agreement regarding meanings for information and events, and coordination of goals to achieve mutual adjustment of individuals' purposes, interests and intentions (Arrow et al., 2000). We see narratives as an important vehicle for achieving such coordination.

To the extent that individuals draw different inferences and implications for action from a narrative that is shared within their work community, then interpretative flexibility could serve to build and sustain a community of inquiry. Multiple plans or decisions would be available for a given task or problem, which could ultimately bolster a group's performance. However, this is contingent on a group's ability to assess alternatives and collectively agree on an appropriate course of action so that individual efforts can be coordinated. Thus, an important question becomes, *how do work communities manage multiple, conflicting accounts arising from narratives?* Following Garud and Rappa (1994), the research question is to identify the conditions under which such discrepancies exist and the dynamics involved when individuals vie for interpretive dominance. Explicating the social and psychological processes through which a narrative's capacity for interpretive flexibility affects coordinated action within or across work communities would further enrich our understanding of how narratives shape behavior within an organization.

In this regard, it would be useful to identify structural properties of narratives that allow actors sufficient interpretive flexibility even while providing them with a common core to abstract from. A property identified by Pentland (1999) seems especially relevant: an evaluative frame of reference. We suspect that particularly effective narratives contain an evaluative frame of references that explicitly, rather than implicitly, articulates cultural values and assumptions of the context in which the events occurred. Such information provides a common core for individuals working within that context, but also supplies individuals working in different contexts from the narrative (e.g., a marketing person interpreting a narrative of events that transpired in the finance group) with some standards against which to evaluate actions and actors.

When such information is not made explicit, it is unlikely that individuals in other work communities will be able to glean an understanding of these past events. Moreover, individuals are lacking critical data needed to engage in questioning, which is essential for generating new insights and courses of action for their own situations. For example, lack of awareness of the outcomes that are valued (and why) in a given work community makes it difficult for a person outside that community to generate inferences from the narrative and apply them to his or her work context where valued outcomes may differ substantially.

We suggest that researchers track the transmission of narratives that remain localized (within its originating work community) and those that cross community lines and then interview individuals to determine the ways in which they found certain narratives more or less useful for their own work situations.

Methodologies for narratives

What are some of the appropriate strategies for investigating narratives in organizational settings? Our perspective suggests that the process of adaptive abduction can uncover how and why past events transpired and also provide new inferences and implications for a given situation. Thus, knowledge generated through narratives occurs through a process of translation rather than diffusion. Knowledge is not imposed on or distributed to people in narrative form, but, rather, we see individuals as active participants in creating the knowledge that they hold. We therefore suggest that researchers approach the study of narratives from a process perspective, examining how individuals translate narratives and apply inferences garnered from them to their own situations.

Taking a process approach to the study of narratives requires a longitudinal approach, such that a researcher can capture both the dynamics of how knowledge is generated through adaptive abduction and how such knowledge then affects subsequent actions undertaken by an individual or work community. This implies that a central goal should include mapping the trajectory of a narrative over time. We construe the trajectories of narratives as an outcome of the interactions among individuals within specific work communities, which are shaped and constrained by their own contextual and historical forces as well as those of the organization as a whole. Research could identify how narratives are shared within or between work communities, how they are reinterpreted and retold, and how these processes impact organizational action.

Such efforts could employ field methods that examine pre-existing narratives in an organization or specific work community or field methods that use an experimental design. For example, researchers could work with an organization to identify some knowledge or learning point that it expects individuals across work communities to know and use. This knowledge could then be represented in abstract form (rule-like statements) with various caveats (qualifications) and in narrative form, which are then shared within different work communities. Researchers could execute a three-way comparison (proposition only, narrative only, both proposition and narrative) to assess the impact of different forms of knowledge on different groups of people in the organization. Important outcomes include retention of the information or learning points, application to other work situations, and the effectiveness of such applications. A tentative hypothesis is that, especially in dynamic environments, narrative knowledge will generate action that is more appropriate for the context in which a person is operating and, thus, more effective than knowledge communicated in propositional form.

For any study where narratives are a focal unit of analysis, we suggest that the researcher's charge is similar to the work of a journalist (Dunbar et al., 1996). We adopt the perspective of other ethnographers (Barley, 1986; Kunda, 1992; Van Maanen, 1975) who argue that a researcher must become a "semi-native" to achieve tacit understanding

of a particular work community or organization. Our discussion has placed special importance on the embedding context in which narratives are created and shared. Therefore, a
researcher needs intimate knowledge of the actors and context to interpret how actors use
narratives *in situ* and to articulate an account of observed events that uses their language.

For example, an area where research can add to the development of our perspective is
to explore how people apply their multiple perspectives to interpret narratives. For
researchers to have informed understandings of the inferences that individuals create and
then apply to organizational tasks or problems, they must be able to recognize the multi-
faceted lenses that these individuals use to interpret narratives. This requires a research
approach that adopts contextual realism as a primary objective. However, we stress that
researchers must not lose their own academic lens in the process. This is a danger if
researcher becomes "fully native."

CONCLUSION

Today's rapidly changing environment requires that individuals in organizations create and
apply knowledge at a faster rate than they did in the past. More than ever, organizations
are poised for constant change and learning and we argue that narratives enable individuals to develop deeper insights about past, present, and anticipated future events that
promote effective action. Researchers have long argued that narratives are valuable repositories for knowledge in organizations. We aimed to advance this line of argument by
describing a mechanism by which individuals generalize from narratives and apply what
they learn in the course of their daily work lives. Thus, we offer a perspective for *how* the
"actor on the spot" uses narratives as part of the knowledge creation process.

We made a case for adaptive abduction as a critical process that enables individuals to
create, transform, and mobilize knowledge. Adaptive abduction leverages the temporal and
contextual structure that orders the persons, objects, and events in a narrative, allowing a
person to confirm, amend, or construct some set of inferences about past events and their
own current situations. It is this process that affords narratives interpretative flexibility
across time and space, enabling individuals in different parts of the organization, facing
different situations, and at different points in time to use the same narrative for their own
purposes. In this way, narratives bring together multiple communities of actors that operate
in different organizational realities, enabling them to interpret each other's experiences
and formulate possible applications to their work contexts. As organizations continue to
become flatter (less hierarchical) and less dependent on formal rules, policies, and managerial intervention to guide individuals' actions, then informal means of sharing and
creating knowledge are likely to become increasingly important. This implies that the ways
in which narratives contribute to the knowledge creation process will become especially
relevant for future research.

NOTE

1.   These researchers argue that there is only suspect data regarding the superiority of an alterna-
     tive keyboard arrangement, Dvorak Simplified Keyboard (DSK), over the QWERTY layout.

Liebowitz and Margolis also point out that it is philosophically impossible for people to choose an inferior alternative ex-ante. With this argument, Liebowitz and Margolis attack the major implication of the QWERTY narrative offered by David regarding the perpetuation of market inefficiency.

REFERENCES

Allison, G.T. (1971) *Essence of Decision: Explaining the Cuban Missile Crisis.* Boston: Little Brown and Co.

Arrow, H., McGrath, J.E., and Berdahl, J.L. (2000) *Small Groups as Complex Systems: Formation, Coordination, Development, and Adaptation.* Thousand Oakes, CA: Sage.

Arthur, B. (1988) Self-reinforcing Mechanisms in Economics. In P.W. Anderson, K.J. Arrow and D. Pines (eds.), *The Economy as an Evolving Complex System.* Reading, MA: Addison-Wesley.

Bal, M. (1985) *Narratology: Introduction to the Theory of Narrative.* Toronto: University of Toronto Press.

Barley, S. (1986) Technology as an Occasion for Restructuring: Evidence from the Observations of CT Scanners and the Social Order of Radiology Departments. *Administrative Science Quarterly*, 31: 78–108.

Baumeister, R.F. and Newman, L.S. (1994) How Stories Make Sense of Personal Experiences. *Personality and Social Psychology Bulletin*, 20: 676–90.

Boje, D.M. (1991) The Storytelling Organization: A Study of Storytelling Performance in an Office Supply Firm. *Administrative Science Quarterly*, 36: 106–26.

Boje, D.M. (1995) Stories of the Storytelling Organization: A Postmodern Analysis of Disney as "Tamara-Land." *Academy of Management Journal*, 38: 997–1035.

Boland, R.J. and Tenkasi, R.V. (1995) Perspective Making and Perspective Taking in Communities of Knowing. *Organization Science*, 6: 350–72.

Boland, R.J., Singh, J., Salipante, P., Aram, J., Fay, S.Y., and Kanawattanachai, P. (2001) Knowledge Representation and Knowledge Transfer. *Academy of Management Journal*, 44: 393–417.

Bourdieu, P. (1990) *The Logic of Practice.* Cambridge, England: Polity Press.

Bowker, G.C. and Star, S.L. (2000) *Sorting Things Out: Classification and its Consequences.* Cambridge, MA: The MIT Press.

Brown, J.S. and Duguid, P. (1991) Organizational Learning and Communities of Practice: Toward a Unified View of Working, Learning, and Innovation. *Organization Science*, 2: 40–57.

Browning, L.D. (1991) Organizational Narratives and Organizational Structure. *Journal of Organizational Change Management*, 4: 59–67.

Cohen, W.M., and Levinthal, D.A. (1990) Absorptive Capacity: A New Perspective on Learning and Innovation. *Administrative Science Quarterly*, 35: 128–52.

Conger, J.A. (1991) Inspiring Others: The Language of Leadership. *Academy of Management Executive*, 5: 31–45.

Czarniawska, B. (1997) *Narrating the Organization: Dramas of Institutional Identity.* Chicago, IL: The University of Chicago Press.

Czarniawska, B. (1998) *A Narrative Approach in Organization Studies.* Thousand Oaks, CA: Sage.

David, P. (1985) Clio and the Economics of QWERTY. *Economic History*, 75: 227–332.

Dunbar, R., Garud, R., and Raghuram, S. (1996) Deframing in Strategic Analyses. *Journal of Management Inquiry*, 5: 23–34.

Dyer, W.G., and Wilkins, A.L. (1991) Better Stories, not Better Constructs, to Generate Better Theory: A Rejoinder to Eisenhardt. *Academy of Management Review*, 16: 613–19.

Eco, U. (1979) *A Theory of Semiotics.* Bloomington: Indiana University Press.

Eisenhardt, K.M. (1989) Building Theories from Case Study Research. *Academy of Management Review*, 14: 532–50.

Fisher, W.R. (1987) *Human Communication as Narration: Toward a Philosophy of Reason, Value, and Action.* Columbia, SC: University of South Carolina Press.

Fiske, S.T. and Taylor, S.E. (1991) *Social Cognition* (2nd edn). New York: McGraw-Hill.

Garud, R. (1997) On the Distinction between Know-how, Know-why and Know-what in Technological Systems. In J. Walsh and A. Huff (eds.), *Advances in Strategic Management*, Vol. 14, Greenwich, CT: JAI Press, 81–101.

Garud, R. (1999) 3M Innovation as a Process of Mindful Replication. Case presented at the Annual Meeting of the Academy of Management, Chicago, IL.

Garud, R. and Karne, P. (2001) Path Creation as a Process of Mindful Deviation. In R. Garud and P. Karne (eds.), *Path Dependence and Creation*, Mahwah, NJ: Lawrence Erlbaum Associates, 1–40.

Garud, R. and Nayyar, P. (1994) Transformative Capacity: Continual Structuring by Intertemporal Technology Transfer. *Strategic Management Journal*, 15: 365–85.

Garud, R. and Rappa, M.A. (1994) A Socio-cognitive Mode of Technology Innovation: The Case of Cochlear Implants. *Organization Science*, 5: 344–62.

Geertz, C. (1973) *The Interpretation of Cultures.* New York: Basic Books.

Glaser, B. and Strauss, A. (1967) *The Discovery of Grounded Theory: Strategies for Qualitative Research.* Chicago: Aldine.

Giddens, A. (1979) *Central Problems in Social Theory.* Los Angeles: University of California Press.

Gould, S. (1980) *The Panda's Thumb.* New York: W.W. Norton and Co.

Grant, R.M. (1996) Towards a Knowledge-based Theory of the Firm. *Strategic Management Journal*, 17: 109–22.

Hayek, F.A. (1945) The Use of Knowledge in Society. *American Economic Review*, 35: 519–30.

Hedberg, B. (1981) How Organizations Learn and Unlearn. In P.C. Nystrome and W.H. Starbuck (eds.), *Handbook of Organizational Design*, Vol. 1. New York: Oxford University Press, 3–27.

Hutchins, E. (1991) Organizing Work by Adaptation. *Organization Science*, 2: 14–29.

Kogut, B. and Zander, U. (1996) What Firm's Do? Coordination, Identity, and Learning. *Organization Science*, 5: 502–18.

Kunda, G. (1992) *Engineering Culture: Control and Commitment in a High-Tech Corporation.* Philadelphia: Temple University Press.

Lampel J. (2001) Show and Tell: Product Demonstrations and Path Creation of Technological Change. In R. Garud and P. Karnoe (eds.), *Path Dependence and Creation*, Mahwah, NJ: Lawrence Erlbaum Associates, 303–28.

Lant, T. (1999) A Situated Learning Perspective on the Emergence of Knowledge and Identity in Cognitive Communities. In J. Porac and R. Garud (eds.), *Cognition, Knowledge and Organizations*, Stamford, CT: JAI Press, 195–214.

Latour, B. and Woolgar, S. (1979) *Laboratory Life: The Social Construction of Scientific Facts.* Beverley Hills: Sage.

Lave, J. and Wenger, E. (1994) *Situated Learning: Legitimate Peripheral Participation.* Cambridge, England: Cambridge University Press.

Lewin, K. (1945) The Research Center for Group Dynamics at Massachusetts Institute of Technology. *Sociometry*, 8: 126–35.

Liebowitz, S.J. and Margolis, S.E. (1990) The Fable of the Keys. *Journal of Law and Economics*, 22: 1–26.

Lounsbury, M. and Glynn, M.A. (2001) Cultural Entrepreneurship: Stories, Legitimacy and the Acquisition of Resources. *Strategic Management Journal*, 22: 545–64.

Lyles, M.A. (1988) Learning among Joint Venture Sophisticated Firms. *Management International Review*, 28: 85–98.

March, J.G. (1991) Exploration and Exploitation in Organizational Learning. *Organization Science*, 2: 71–87.

March, J.G. (1997) Forward. In R. Garud, P. Nayyar, Z. Shapira (eds.), *Technological Innovation: Oversights and Foresights* Cambridge, UK: Cambridge University Press, ix–xii.

March, J.G. (1998) Research on Organizations: Hopes for the Past and Lessons from the Future. Lecture delivered at the SCANCOR Conference, *Samples for the Future*, September 20–22.

March, J.G., Sproull, L.S., and Tamuz, M. (1991) Learning from Samples of One or Fewer. *Organization Science*, 2: 1–13.

Martin, J., Feldman, M.S., Hatch, M.J., and Sitkin, S.B. (1983) The Uniqueness Paradox in Organizational Stories. *Administrative Science Quarterly*, 28: 438–53.

Massaro, D.W. and Cowan, N. (1993) Information Processing Models: Microscopes of the Mind. *Annual Review of Psychology*, 44: 383–425.

Mohr, L.B. (1982) *Explaining Organizational Behavior: The Limits and Possibilities of Theory and Research.* San Francisco, CA: Jossey-Bass.

Neisser, U. (1976) *Cognition and Reality.* San Francisco: W.H. Freeman.

Orr, J.E. (1990) Sharing Knowledge, Celebrating Identity: Community Memory in a Service Culture. In D. Middleton and D. Edwards (eds.), *Collective Remembering*, London: Sage, 168–89.

Peirce, C.S. (1931–58) *Collected Papers.* Cambridge: Harvard University Press.

Pentland, B.T. (1999) Building Process Theory with Narrative: From Description to Explanation. *Academy of Management Review*, 24: 711–24.

Pinch, T.J. and Bijker, W.E. (1987) The Social Construction of Facts and Artifacts: Or How the Sociology of Science and the Sociology of Technology Might Benefit Each Other. In W.E. Bijker, T.P. Hughes, and T.J. Pinch (eds.), *The Social Construction of Technological Systems: New Directions in the Sociology and History of Technology*, Cambridge: MIT Press.

Polkinghore, D.E. (1987) *Narrative Knowing and the Human Sciences.* Albany, NY: State University of New York Press.

Reger, R.K., Gustafson, L.T., DeMarie, S.M., and Mullane, J.V. (1994) Reframing the Organization: Why Implementing Total Quality Is Easier Said than Done. *Academy of Management Review*, 19: 565–84.

Schwab, D.P. (1980) Construct Validity in Organizational Behavior. In B.M. Staw and L.L. Cummings (eds.), *Research in Organizational Behavior*, Vol. 2. Greenwich, CT: JAI Press Inc, 3–43.

Searle, J. (1995) *The Construction of Social Reality.* New York: The Free Press.

Shaw, G., Brown, R., and Bromiley, P. (1998) Strategic Stories: How 3M Is Rewriting Business Planning. *Harvard Business Review*, May-June: 41–50.

Spender, J.C. (1996) Making Knowledge the Basis of a Dynamic Theory of the Firm. *Strategic Management Journal*, 17: 45–62.

Star, S.L. (1989) The Structure of Ill-structured Solutions: Heterogeneous Problem-solving, Boundary Objects and Distributed Artificial Intelligence. In M. Hans and L. Gasser (eds.), *Distributed Artificial Intelligence*, Vol. 2. Menlo Park, CA: Morgan Kauffman, 37–54.

Thachankary, T. (1992) Organizations as "texts": Hermeneutics as a Model for Understanding Organizational Change. *Research in Organizational Change and Development*, 6: 197–233.

3M Innovation Chronicles (1998) St. Paul, MN: 3M General Offices.

Trice, H., and Beyer, J.M. (1993) *The Cultures of Work Organizations.* Englewood Cliffs, NJ: Prentice-Hall.

Truzzi, M. (1976) Selective Attention: Sherlock Holmes: Applied Social Psychologist. In W. Sanders (ed.), *The Sociologist as Detective: An Introduction to Research Methods*, New York: Praeger Press, 67.

Tsoukas, H. (1996) The Form as a Distributed Knowledge System: A Constructionist Approach. *Strategic Management Journal*, 17: 11–25.

Tsoukas, H. and Hatch, M.J. (2001) Complex Thinking, Complex Practice: The Case for a Narrative Approach to Organizational Complexity. *Human Relations*, 54: 979–1014.

Van de Ven, A.H. (1989) Nothing Is Quite so Practical as a Good Theory. *Academy of Management Review*, 14: 486–9.

Van de Ven, A.H. (1992) Suggestions for Studying Strategy Process: A Research Note. *Strategic Management Journal*, 13: 169–88.

Van Maanen, J. (1975) Police Organization: A Longitudinal Examination of Job Attitudes in an Urban Police Department. *Administrative Science Quarterly*, 20: 207–28.

Van Maanen, J. (1998) Identity Work: Notes on the Personal Identity of Police Officers. Paper presented at the annual meeting of the Academy of Management, San Diego, CA.

von Krogh, G. and Roos, J. (1995) *Organizational Epistemology*. New York, St. Martin's Press.

Weick, K. (1979) *The Social Psychology of Organizing*. New York: Random House.

Weick, K.E. (1995) *Sensemaking in Organizations*. Thousand Oaks, CA: Sage.

Weick, K.E. and Roberts, K. (1993) Collective Mind in Organizations: Heedful Interrelating on Flight Decks. *Administrative Science Quarterly*, 38: 357–81.

Wittgenstein, L. (1958) *Philosophical Investigations*. Oxford, UK: Blackwell.

Zuboff, S. (1988) *In the Age of the Smart Machine: The Future of Work and Power*. New York: Basic Books.

17

Dominant Logic, Knowledge Creation, and Managerial Choice

RICHARD A. BETTIS AND SZE-SZE WONG

CHAPTER OUTLINE

Dominant logic is a conceptual framework for thinking about the process and results of cognitive simplification in top management teams. It develops and evolves due to the characteristics of the firm's industry and strategy. With experience and successes, the dominant logic condenses into a variety of familiar organizational features where it takes on a highly durable and self-reinforcing nature. This mutually reinforcing web of "visible" organizational features and a largely "invisible" value system suppresses variance in the firm because the emphasis on current goals, strategic activities, and structures precludes the consideration of alternatives. Organizational learning also becomes focused on current competencies because the dominant logic biases knowledge, know-how and skill accumulation into path dependent knowledge pathways "preferred" by the dominant logic. In light of the tendency of dominant logic toward condensation, we suggest two ways that may counter its simplification. One way is to develop multiple dominant logics so that different interpretations can co-exist and grow. Another way is to focus on process logics so as to understand and improve how managers make decisions. By managing the decision-making process more effectively, managers may be able to guard against the development of rigid ways of thinking.

INTRODUCTION

The purpose of this chapter is to discuss the nature of the general management dominant logic concept (generally referred to below as simply "dominant logic") and to connect it with key issues in learning, knowledge creation, and managerial choice. We also speculate on some potentially fruitful avenues for applying and extending the theory of dominant logic. This is not intended primarily as a review article although many important aspects of a review are necessary to the fundamental purpose of the chapter. What is intended is to extend the usefulness of the dominant logic concept in understanding/exploring various organizational phenomena and to connect it more firmly to various other concepts and literatures. Those interested in a thorough review are referred to the original source (Prahalad and Bettis, 1986) and to a variety of other sources (e.g., Bettis 2000; Bettis and Prahalad, 1995; Ginsberg 1990; Grant, 1988; Powell, 2000; Ramanujan and Varadarajan, 1989; Scott, 2000; von Krogh and Grand, 2000; von Krogh and Roos, 1996).

The concept of a general management dominant logic arose in response to the need to examine why firms find it so hard to manage: (1) diversification (even "related" diversification) and/or (2) rapid or discontinuous change in a core or base business (Prahalad and Bettis, 1986). Although superficially different, the issues of diversification and change in the core business both involve the necessity to change the mental models of managers. Such changes go far beyond the intellectual recognition of the need to change and have proven very difficult to accomplish in practice. Recent practitioner-oriented work by Sull (1999) and by Foster and Kaplan (2001) testify to the difficulties involved.

Dominant logic provides a simple and potentially powerful way of thinking about various strategic issues. There are certainly other frameworks for thinking about these issues, and we claim no particular advantage for dominant logic. We do believe that it is one useful way for organizing reflection about and thoughtful inquiry into issues related to strategic change.

In what follows we first discuss the fundamental nature of the dominant logic concept. We then discuss the "condensation" of dominant logic into visible and invisible organizational features. Next we discuss the variance suppression that occurs at the dominant logic level, and how it is affected by variance suppression effects at other levels of analysis. Then, we briefly discuss the implications of dominant logic on core competence and organizational learning. We end with a couple of speculative sections on: (1) the possibility of having multiple dominant logics in an organization and (2) the nature of "process" logics.

The Nature of Dominant Logic

The theory of a general management dominant logic is one conceptual framework for thinking about the process and results of cognitive simplification in top management teams. As Schwenk (1984) suggests, strategic decision-making in top management teams is subject to cognitive simplification. Top management, as with all humans, employ simplifying decision-making heuristics, such as prior hypothesis bias, adjustment and anchoring, illusion of control and representativeness, that decrease their ability to appreciate the true complexity of problems and select the best solution.

The dominant logic represents the shared cognitive map (Prahalad and Bettis, 1986) and strategic mindset of the top management team or the dominant coalition, and is closely associated with the processes and tools used by top management. There may be minor variations in the details of the individual cognitive maps among top management team members, but the major features conform. From a managerial viewpoint, the congruence in cognition among top management team members offers advantages of efficiencies, but inevitably, it also introduces the disadvantages of rigidity. For example, the dominant logic may be inappropriately applied in diversification moves or when there are

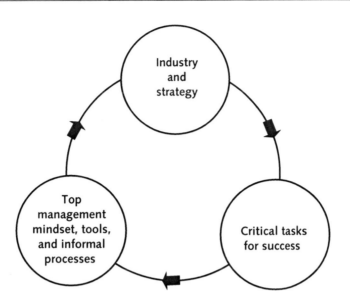

FIGURE 17.1   Evolution of general management dominant logic

changes in the core industry. As Sull (1999) has observed, good companies go bad because they insist only on doing what worked in the past.

As shown in figure 17.1, the dominant logic develops and evolves due to the characteristics of the industry and the strategy (or business model) the firm uses to compete in this industry. Essentially, experience and success in the presence of reasonable environmental stability breed shared patterns of thinking about key strategic and managerial issues. These shared cognitive patterns typically involve beliefs about issues such as causality in the industry, appropriate product cost structures, and desirable customer characteristics. As discussed below, this cognitive representation of the dominant logic eventually condenses or even ossifies into a variety of familiar organizational features where it takes on a highly durable and self-reinforcing nature. After condensation the dominant logic defines as much what the organization cannot do as it defines what the organization can do (discussed below). The theoretical foundations of the shared mental encoding process lie in a variety of literatures including operant conditioning, decision heuristics, pattern recognition, cognitive simplification and paradigms. The reader is referred to Prahalad and Bettis (1986) for an introductory discussion of some major foundation literatures.

The dominant logic concept also connects closely to the literature on complex adaptive systems (e.g., Axelrod and Cohen, 1999; Holland, 1995; Waldrop, 1992). Bettis and Prahalad (1995) point out that the dominant logic can be viewed as an emergent property of organizations. Such a view is entirely consistent with the cognitive mechanisms of individuals mentioned above. These cognitive mechanisms can be viewed as driving the microdynamics of agents in an organization. The outcome of these agents interacting with each other and with the common environment and common business model (or strategy) is seen at the aggregate level in the emergence of a dominant logic (and many other organizational properties). This emergence process is analogous to the way in which the particle mechanics of a large number of individual atoms within a gas interact with each other and the environment to produce emergent properties such as pressure and various thermodynamic relationships.

As an emergent property, it should be noted that the dominant logic is inherently an adaptive property as long as neither the domain of application nor the environment changes significantly. It allows the organization to "anticipate" the environment by specifying the nature of cause and effect relationships. It economizes on managerial resources by simplifying and speeding decision making. However, this adaptive ability has obvious limitations and carries with it toxic side effects discussed below and in various references.

CONDENSATION OF DOMINANT LOGIC

This section examines how the dominant logic becomes embedded in the major features of organization over time. As with all theoretical discussion there is considerable simplification. The objective is to characterize the essential features of what we call the "condensation process." The objective is not to capture the complete complexity of this process and its relationship to a myriad of other issues.

The dominant logic develops over time. As mentioned above and illustrated in figure 17.1, there is an initial period during which the characteristics of the environment and firm strategy drive the formation of a shared mindset among the top management team. Obviously, in the presence of success (stability) this mindset becomes more uniform across managers and stronger over time. Up to this point the issue of significant change of the dominant logic is largely a matter of individual cognitive change across the top management team. This does not mean that change will be easy. However, it is likely to be much easier than when the dominant logic has condensed into a matrix of mutually reinforcing features within the organization.

As this mindset continues to develop, certain concepts and informal processes become associated with it within the top management team. For example, the authors have seen a firm in which "cost plus" pricing became the only accepted way of thinking about pricing within the top management team. Also, the authors have observed firms in which the informal capital budgeting decision process among the top management team centered on rationing a percentage of sales proportionally across functions (e.g., manufacturing and sales). Increasingly the dominant logic places constraints on: (1) the search spaces associated with problems; (2) the conceptual frameworks used to help make decisions; and (3) the key features of acceptable solutions. The dominant logic at this point still remains largely invisible. It is cognitive with few or no obvious physical manifestations in the organization. It can only be examined through discussion with top managers and their direct reports.

As organizations grow and become more complex it becomes necessary and important to establish formal structure, procedures, systems, and processes. These are usually designed in at least rough congruence with the dominant logic. In this sense the dominant logic begins to condense into "visible" organization features. It also becomes "invisibly" embodied as a significant part of the organization value system or culture. Formal structure, procedures, systems, processes and controls are the hallmark of competent professional management. They standardize, simplify, and expedite decision making in line with the needs of the business. They focus attention on what are to be considered key issues. They establish priorities that conform to the strategic imperatives of the firm. In sum, they embody the dominant logic in the organizational features that direct attention and shape decisions for managers and employees throughout the organization.

By their very nature systems, procedures, controls and processes are designed to be inflexible and difficult to change. Significant change in these features is undertaken only rarely, after considerable analysis, and at significant cost. Furthermore, they form a reinforcing web of relationships. For example, the job recruitment and selection, and organizational socialization processes often result in the employment of individuals who share the organization's beliefs and values. Like a form of social control (O'Reilly and Chatman, 1996), employees' beliefs and interpretations of events, attitudes and behaviors become increasingly aligned with the dominant logic. This reinforces the existing systems, procedures, controls and processes, which in turn, fortifies the dominant logic.

Significant change in any one system, procedure, control or process is likely to require significant change in all or others to maintain alignment. The recent popularity of certain techniques of change management, especially process re-engineering has led many managers to conclude that changes are not only possible, but not all that difficult. However, as Christensen and Overdorf (2000) have observed, processes and systems are not nearly as flexible and adaptable as the proponents of these techniques suggest.

This process of condensation may take place over a considerable period of time with the dominant logic becoming more and more condensed. Once it has proceeded very far the problem of changing dominant logics becomes substantially more complex. As with physical solids, the process of moving back to a fluid state can require enormous amounts of energy if it can be accomplished at all. The condensation of a dominant logic is an irreversible process. One obviously cannot step backwards along the same path to the organization as it existed before condensation of the dominant logic. Change must involve creating a new path in the presence of a cognitive dominant logic and a mutually reinforcing web of "visible" organizational features and a largely "invisible" value system. Ultimately, this must involve unlearning of the inappropriate dominant logic. Success here is usually much more the exception than the rule. Dominant logics are extraordinarily resistant to unlearning.

As illustrated in figure 17.2, as the process of condensation moves forward, a reinforcing feedback loop is established. The structure, systems, and processes designed largely to conform to the dominant logic now provide information, controls, incentives, values and decision rules that mirror the dominant logic to a substantial degree. Top management receives information and decision agendas congruent with the dominant logic. Information systems insure that attention is allocated to issues deemed important by the dominant logic. Decision rules are established to conform to the dominant logic. Metrics are those deemed important by the dominant logic. Controls assure compliance with the dominant logic. Hence the entire organization becomes a reinforcing system built largely around the dominant logic.

The focus narrows throughout the organization. Thoughtful action and creative analysis are increasingly displaced by "unconscious" rules, processes, values, and systems

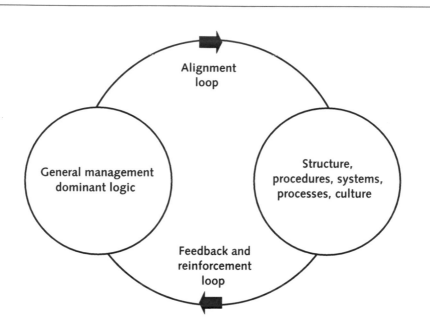

FIGURE 17.2   Condensation of general management dominant logic

(Ashforth and Fried, 1988). The capability for thoughtful independent action atrophies and decisions increasingly become automatic and habitual. Doing different things or even doing things differently becomes more and more difficult for the organization. This is suggestive of the common observation that the more successful organizations become the more difficult they find it to change. Of course as long as there is no necessity to make significant change, the condensed dominant logic can provide a highly effective and efficient means of managing the organization. The organization tends toward simplification, where it gradually weeds out "unsuccessful" practices and builds "architectures of simplicity" (Miller, 1993). In an earlier era, aligning organizational characteristics with strategy was considered the major mechanism of strategy implementation. In fact this paradigm of tight and long-term alignment of organizational characteristics with a "semi-permanent" strategy is still followed pedagogically in many MBA programs.

With continuous reinforcement in place, condensation may move to a stage best described as "fossilization." The organization becomes merely a rigid physical imprint of something that was once alive and able to move and to respond to the environment. In this state performance must decline catastrophically before an attempt is made to respond. The usual result is the dissolution or acquisition of the organization.

VARIANCE SUPPRESSION

The condensation process essentially suppresses variance within the organization. As discussed above, organizations increasingly emphasize *a* goal, strategic activity, structure and/or set of procedures and processes, and preclude the consideration of others. This downward spiral toward simplification is likely to be the result of an interaction among several variance suppression processes existing at different levels of analysis, ranging from the cognitive top management level to the organizational field level.

Variance suppression occurs at several levels of analysis (Bettis, 2000). At the industrial and organizational field level, forces of competition and selection (Hannan and Freeman, 1977) and isomorphism (DiMaggio and Powell, 1983) result in increasingly homogenization among firms. At the strategic group level (Reger and Huff, 1993), homogenization also occurs as firms in the same industry increasingly share similar beliefs and behaviors (Porac et al., 1989). At the top management team level, the dominant logic also suppresses variance by directing top management decision making, among many things, into certain heuristics, models, concepts, beliefs, and types of analysis. Therefore, variance suppression is a general phenomenon that is prevalent in many different levels of analysis.

Variance suppression at each of these levels is unlikely to be independent, but is likely to impact one another. As discussed in the earlier section, dominant logic tends toward variance suppression as top management increasingly adopts a certain worldview (e.g., heuristic, beliefs, paradigm). How much variance it suppresses is likely a function of the variance the organization faced in the organizational field when the dominant logic was developing among the top management team. To the extent that more variance was faced during this period, the dominant logic is likely to be more robust, but even this has obvious limits. Furthermore, variance is not uniform and generic. It has a qualitative component. Different variables can be involved, such as technology, customer needs, or social values. Hence the dominant logic may be more robust to some variables than others. However, early in their lives, firms themselves may also be the source of environmental variance for others in an established industry. This is not the same as having to respond to variance caused by other factors. For instance Digital Equipment, as a new entrant, increased the variance in the computer environment by introducing the minicomputer. Incumbents (e.g., IBM, Burroughs, and NCR) found it hard to respond since their logics (and core competencies) were organized around mainframe computing. However, Digital Equipment subsequently developed a strong dominant logic based on the minicomputer. This logic prevented them from responding adequately when variance again was increased by the PC.

At the same time that environmental variance affects variance in the dominant logic, it also affects the adaptability of the dominant logic. One way to think about this is the requisite variety principle from cybernetics, which suggests that the variety within a system (or the variety the system is capable of exhibiting or producing) must be matched to the environmental variety that the system faces (Ashby, 1956). The principle of requisite variety plainly suggests that organizations today must be capable of a greater variety of actions or variance, including learning, during a period of increased environmental variance. To illustrate this metaphorically, consider the design of airplanes. Fighter planes must be designed for more rapid, frequent, severe, and unscripted maneuvers than passenger planes because they operate in a rapidly changing, unpredictable, and hostile environment. The tradeoff is that they are much less stable than passenger planes and, hence, rather unsafe, even in peacetime.

A second way to think about the implications of variance suppression for organizational change is in terms of ecological models of random variation and selective retention. In recent years these models, originating in biology, have shown considerable explanatory power in many fields. The models have been applied to a variety of organizational issues. For our purposes we will only mention two specific areas where they have been applied: learning (e.g., Campbell, 1960) and research and development (R&D) (e.g., Nelson and Winter, 1982). (It should be noted that R&D is obviously a very specific kind of organizational learning.) In the former of these two cases suppression of variance reduces the rate of learning. In the latter it reduces the likelihood of a significant innovation. Obviously, if variation is suppressed there are profound implications for the random variation/selective retention model as it has been applied to various phenomena. Again, the implications for dominant logic should be obvious.

What this all suggests is that we need to give more attention to the non-recursive relationships between variance generation and variance suppression at different levels of analysis, and the issues of "fit" between variance generation and suppression at these different levels. It is not a simple issue of more variance increases adaptive capability. Too little variance limits adaptation, but too much variance will simply swamp any organization. As such, we have to be cognizant of the tradeoffs, and explore ways in which they play out in different situations.

Relevance of Dominant Logic to Core Competence and Learning

Recently discussions about strategy in both academia and practice have often centered on learning, know-how, experience, skill and wisdom (e.g., Kogut and Zander, 1992; Pisano, 1994; Szulanski, 1996). It is in this context that the concept of core competence has become popular and influential. Core competence was originally defined by Prahalad and Hamel (1990: 82) as "the collective learning in the organization, especially how to coordinate diverse production skills and integrate multiple streams of technologies." In popular managerial usage it has increasingly become associated with those key organizational skills and supporting resources and capabilities that form the basis for competitive advantage of complex firms. It should be noted that this popular usage is not necessarily in line with the way in which it was originally defined.

One important impact of a dominant logic in an organization is in terms of how it structures and directs what the organization learns. For example, Daft and Weick (1984) argue that when organizations view their environment as not analyzable, they would scan their environments more actively, and pursue prospector strategies. In contrast, when they view their environment as analyzable and benevolent, they engage in less scanning and pursue defender strategies. Therefore, by shaping management's perception of reality, the dominant logic influences their interpretations of events, and the actions they take. Cognitively, it directs top management attention, and hence learning to those issues, that are deemed important. In addition, once in condensed form, it can at least partially focus organizational learning throughout the organization. Condensed into a subset of organizational values it defines at least partially the essence of what is important and valuable to the organization. Learning is most likely to be directed to those things that the value set deems important. Condensed into systems, processes, procedures and structures it can severely restrict the focus of attention and hence the focus of learning.

The overall impact is that learning priorities are likely to be substantially influenced by the dominant logic. Ultimately this means that the "collective learning" of the organization that Prahalad and Hamel (1990) discuss is at least partially, if not largely, determined by the dominant logic. In this sense the dominant logic is a precursor that helps drive development of a core competence, or, alternatively impede development of other core competencies. More broadly, it biases knowledge, know-how and skill accumulation into path dependent knowledge pathways "preferred" by the dominant logic. Path dependence of knowledge accumulation then reinforces the efficiency of these pathways to the organization. It should be noted that under conditions of relative stability this is a desirable feature. It focuses learning on those areas of importance to the strategy. It is only when other knowledge pathways (e.g., disruptive technologies) become important that new knowledge pathways are needed.

The relationship between dominant logic and learning, however, is unlikely to be unidirectional. Research on organizational learning posits that the development of knowledge about action–outcome relationships is a learned process (Daft and Weick, 1984; Fiol and Lyles, 1985) through mechanisms of experience (Levitt and March, 1988), feedback (Daft and Weick, 1984), information processing (Huber, 1991), and negotiation of meaning (Brown and Duguid, 1991). This suggests that a learning process mediates the development of dominant logic (e.g., beliefs about action–outcome relationships) in the top management team. For example, how the top management team members jointly make sense of the environment is likely to affect the content of the dominant logic that emerges. Collaborative inquiry among members could adaptively change "theories-in-use" (Argyris and Schön, 1978), and therefore, adjust the dominant logic. Similarly, how the top management team processes information (e.g., scan and acquire information) could also impact their interpretation of the environment (Daft and Weick, 1984), and therefore, the dominant logic. Hence, the way that the top management team learns could affect the type of dominant logic that emerges.

We believe that the relationships between dominant logic, and learning and core competence (or learning more generally) is a highly potential avenue for further research. Furthermore, we suggest that the issue of how firms develop new competencies can only be effectively addressed academically and practically by considering the constraints imposed by the dominant logic and how it can be changed.

FUTURE DIRECTIONS FOR THE STUDY OF DOMINANT LOGIC

Multiple dominant logics?

By its very nature, dominant logic represents the *dominant* way in which managers think and act. It economizes on cognitive processing by offering a schema to classify environmental cues, and interpret their meanings. However when the meaning of environmental cues change or the cues themselves change, it is inappropriate. Classification and interpretation of cues become inappropriate either because new cues are not recognized or categorized in inappropriate categories, or strategies to deal with these new cues are incompatible. A dominant logic that was once well adapted becomes non-adaptable.

Ashby (1956) argued that requisite variety in the internal environment is required to match variety in the external environment. Applied in the context of logics, this suggests that organizations in rapidly changing environments have to move beyond a dominant logic, and toward what is best characterized as multiple logics. As population ecologists have advocated (Hannan and Freeman, 1977), generalization is preferred over specialization in changing environments. Having a range of logics would not only allow organizations to scan and recognize a broader spectrum of environmental cues, but also select responses from a repertoire of logics. It is both easier and speedier to switch among multiple logics than to "unfreeze" a deeply ingrained dominant logic and develop a new dominant logic. In the ideal (and perhaps unrealistic case), the organization can flexibly change to another logic that is more appropriate as conditions change. Maintaining and executing a variety or continuum of logics might also mitigate against the condensation process that deeply and firmly embeds a dominant logic. By cultivating several logics and a meta-logic for choosing among them, organizations ostensibly could develop multiple ways of perceiving the environment.

Can organizations develop multiple logics? If organizations can develop multiple logics, then how do they do it? As discussed earlier in the previous section, organizations tend toward simplification. Success focuses top management attention on fewer issues and well-worn paths to solutions. In other words, a dominant logic emerges. This process suggests the inevitable development of a single dominant logic, and highlights the difficulties of managing the development of multiple logics and a meta-logic for facilitating them.

Our thinking about the development of multiple logics is motivated by recent advances in complexity theory (Holland, 1995; Waldrop, 1992). One of the main principles of complexity theory is that there is a phase lying between chaos and order where complex, adaptive behavior persists. Unlike the chaotic phase where interactions are random, or the order phase where interactions are stable, the complex phase generates interactions that are adaptive to different conditions. This strongly suggests that organizations must generally decrease their inherent level of stability and move closer to a disequilibrium state. Furthermore, Holland's research suggested that simple rules are capable of producing complex behavior. Although the application of complexity theory to organizational research is fairly recent, the use of simple rules to produce complex behavior dates back to Herbert Simon's (1996) architecture of complexity. He explained how simple rules of assembly are capable of producing the required complex behaviors that match complex environments. The origins of complex adaptive behavior can, therefore, be surprisingly simple.

Drawing from this line of argument, we offer a way to think about the implications of this theory on the cultivation and maintenance of multiple logics. Like the production of complex behavior, we argue that *multiple logics can evolve from simple rules that are robust*. We can think of organizations as having a meta-level dominant logic that is characterized by very simple but robust rules. Being simple, the meta-dominant logic offers organizational members wide room for discretion and imagination. In contrast to dense and complicated dominant logics, that try to consider all contingencies, simple meta dominant logics allow different interpretations to grow, and even allow conflicting interpretations to co-exist. Furthermore, these simple logics must be robust to both the environment and organizational responses to it. The ambiguity associated with simple rules permits multiple logics to flourish because the rules are flexible enough to accommodate the different meanings. An example would be General Electric's Jack Welch's famous dictum of "be number 1 or number 2 in your market". Under this simple rule, different strategic logics are acceptable, as long as they propel GE's businesses to the top of their respective industry field. This rule can be thought of as GE's meta dominant logic. Because of its simplicity, it can be translated into different strategic logics. The simplicity and robustness of the rule allows organizational sub-units to develop their own logic or change logic without unnecessary constraint from above. However the condensation of this logic at sub-unit level remains a problem when environmental conditions change significantly.

How a management team can move to such a simple meta-logic is unclear and represents a potentially interesting research avenue. One thing is clear. The process of condensation of a dominant logic specific to one set of environmental conditions, as discussed earlier, must be strongly resisted. This suggests, at a minimum, the frequent deconstruction and reconstruction of various formal structures, procedures, systems, processes and controls. In other words the organization must take positive steps to ensure some level of instability. Given the natural tendency of managers (and all human beings) to seek stasis, enormous leadership efforts would have to be exerted to accomplish such a task on a periodic basis. We cannot be overly optimistic about the prospects.

Process dominant logics

Discussions of dominant logic thus far have focused at a general level. We use the term to refer to the mindset, casual map, or mental model of the top management team. However, the exact contents in the dominant logic are usually left unspecified. Most of the time, we assume dominant logic represents the strategic concepts and causal relations among these concepts because it is mostly applied to illustrate the strategies used by management teams. Of course, given strategic success, this logic condenses into many other visible and invisible features of the organization.

We want to focus briefly on the processes that top management teams develop to make decisions. Top management teams often develop stable ways of making strategic decisions. Like most other teams, top management team members over time develop a process logic that guides how they voice opinions, seek information, resolve differences, and make the final decision. Previous experiences, political dynamics, preference of the CEO, and interactions among members influence the process logic that emerges. Once created, the process logic as a component of the dominant logic endures and guides how strategic decisions are made. Unlike the issue-oriented aspects of a dominant logic that focuses on strategic concepts and their causal relationships, a process dominant logic focuses on the team processes involved in the top management team.

Considering the process aspects of dominant logic suggests a richer construct than is often envisioned. In addition to strategic issues logic, it also relates to the management team's model of how decision-making should take place, and/or how information should be processed within the team. For instance, in Eisenhardt's (1989) study of decision-making in high velocity environments, she found that top management teams in successful firms use more information, develop more alternatives, engage in a two tiered advice process, and employ quick conflict resolution methods.

We believe that the study of the process aspects of dominant logic in top management teams represent a productive ground for future research. As shown in Eisenhardt's study, the decision-making process in top management teams is a key differentiator of successful and unsuccessful firms. So far, most of the discussion of dominant logic has mostly been focused on how heuristics that capture rules of dealing with strategy develop and persist. We believe that it would be equally rewarding to turn research attention to the process aspects of logics that prevail in top management teams. By determining how information is sought and processed, process logics influence how information, knowledge, and opinions are combined to form the final strategic decision. Hence, the process logic of a top management team could help to explain why a particular decision is reached. More importantly, as we move toward more turbulent environments, it would be interesting to explore the types of process dominant logics that would allow members to more accurately sense new changes in the environment, and effectively integrate members' expertise to invent new responses.

References

Argyris, C. and Schön, D. (1978) *Organizational Learning*. Reading, MA: Addison-Wesley.

Ashby, W.R. (1956) *An Introduction to Cybernetics*. New York: John Wiley & Sons.

Ashforth, B.E. and Fried, Y. (1988) The Mindlessness of Organizational Behaviors. *Human Relations*, 41 (4): 305–29.

Axelrod, R.M. and Cohen, M.D. (1999) *Harnessing Complexity: Organizational Implications of a Scientific Frontier*. New York: Free Press.

Bettis, R.A. (2000) The Iron Cage Is Emptying, the Dominant Logic No Longer Dominates. In J. Baum and R. Dobbins (eds.), *Economics Meets Sociology in Strategic Management*. Stamford: JAI Press.

Bettis, R.A. and Prahalad, C.K. (1995) The Dominant Logic: Retrospective and Extension. *Strategic Management Journal*, 16 (1): 5–14.

Brown, J.S. and Duguid, P. (1991) Organizational Learning and Communities-of-practice: Toward a Unified View of Working, Learning, and Innovation. *Organization Science*, 2: 40–57.

Campbell, D.T. (1960) Blind Variation and Selective Retention in Creative Thought as in Other Knowledge Processes. *The Psychological Review*, 67: 380–400.

Christensen, C.M. and Overdorf, M. (2000) Meeting the Challenge of Disruptive Change. *Harvard Business Review*, 78 (2): 67–76.

Cyert, R.M. and March, J.G. (1963) *A Behavioral Theory of the Firm*. Englewood Cliffs, NJ: Prentice-Hall.

Daft, R.L. and Weick, K.E. (1984) Toward a Model of Organizations as Interpretation Systems. *Academy of Management Review*, 9: 284–95.

DiMaggio, P. and Powell, W. (1983) The Iron Cage Revisited: Institutional Isomorphism and Collective Rationality in Organizational Fields. *American Sociological Review*, 48: 147–60.

Eisenhardt, K.M. (1989) Making Fast, Strategic Decisions in High-velocity Environments. *Academy of Management Journal*, 32: 543–76.

Fiol, C.M. and Lyles, M.A. (1985) Organizational Learning. *Academy of Management Review*. 10 (4): 803–13.

Foster, R. and Kaplan, S. (2001) *Creative Destruction*. New York: Currency.

Ginsberg, A. (1990) Connecting Diversification to Performance: A Sociocognitive Approach. *Strategic Management Journal*, 15 (5): 514–35.

Grant, R.M. (1988) On Dominant Logic, Relatedness and the Link between Diversity and Performance. *Strategic Management Journal*, 9 (6): 639–42.

Hannan, M.T. and Freeman, J. (1977) The Population Ecology of Organizations. *American Journal of Sociology*, 82 (5): 929–64.

Holland, J.H. (1995) *Hidden Order: How Adaptation Builds Complexity*. Reading, MA: Addison-Wesley.

Huber, G.P. (1991) Organizational Learning: The Contributing Processes and Literatures. *Organization Science*, 2: 88–115.

Kogut, B. and Zander, U. (1992) Knowledge of the Firm, Combinative Capabilities, and the Replication of Technology. *Organization Science*, 3 (3): 383–97.

Levitt, B. and March, J.G. (1988) Organizational Learning. *Annual Review of Sociology*, 14: 319–40.

March, J.G. (1991) Exploration and Exploitation in Organizational Learning. *Organization Science*, 2 (1): 71–87.

Miller, D. (1993) The Architecture of Simplicity. *Academy of Management Review*, 18 (1): 116–38.

Nelson, S.G. and Winter, R.R. (1982) *An Evolutionary Theory of Economic Change*. Cambridge, MA: Harvard University Press.

O'Reilly, C.A. III and Chatman, J.A. (1996) Culture as Social Control: Corporations, Cults, and Commitment. *Research in Organizational Behavior*, 18: 157–200.

Pisano, G.P. (1994) Knowledge, Integration, and the Locus of Learning: An Empirical Analysis of Process Development. *Strategic Management Journal*, 15: 85–100.

Porac, J.F., Thomas, H., and Baden-Fuller, C. (1989) Competitive Groups as Cognitive Communities: The Case of Scottish Knitwear Manufacturers. *Journal of Management Studies*, 26: 397–416.

Powell, W.W. (2000) The Sources of Managerial Logics. In J. Baum and R. Dobbins (eds.), *Economics Meets Sociology in Strategic Management*, Stamford: JAI Press.

Prahalad, C.K. and Bettis, R.A. (1986) The Dominant Logic: A New Linkage between Diversification and Performance. *Strategic Management Journal*, 7: 485–501.

Prahalad, C.K. and Hamel, G. (1990) The Core Competence of the Corporation. *Harvard Business Review*, 68 (3): 79–91.

Ramanujam, V. and Varadarajan, P. (1989) Research on Corporate Diversification: A Synthesis. *Strategic Management Journal*, 10: 523–51.

Reger, R.K. and Huff, A.S. (1993) Strategic Groups: A Cognitive Perspective. *Strategic Management Journal*, 1: 103–24.

Schwenk, C.R. (1984) Cognitive Simplification Processes in Strategic Decision-making. *Strategic Management Journal*, 5: 111–28.

Scott, R.W. (2000) The Structuration and Destructuration of Organizations and Organization Fields. In J. Baum and R. Dobbins (eds.), *Economics Meets Sociology in Strategic Management*. Stamford: JAI Press.

Simon, H.A. (1996) *The Sciences of the Artificial*. Cambridge, MA: The MIT Press.

Sull, D.N. (1999) Why Good Companies Go Bad. *Harvard Business Review*, 77 (4): 42–56.

Szulanski, G. (1996) Exploring Internal Stickiness: Impediments to the Transfer of Best Practice within the Firm. *Strategic Management Journal*, 17 (Winter Special Issue): 27–43.

Von Krogh, G. and Grand, S. (2000) Justification in Knowledge creation: Dominant Logic in Management Discourses. In G. Von Krogh, I. Nonaka, and T. Toshihiro (eds.), *Knowledge Creation: A Source of Value*, New York: St. Martin's Press, 13–35.

Von Krogh, G. and Roos, J. (1995) *Organizational Epistemology*. New York: St. Martin's Press.

Von Krogh, G. and Roos, J. (1996) A Tale of Unfinished Research. *Strategic Management Journal*, 17: 729–37.

Waldrop, M.M. (1992) *Complexity: The Emerging Science at the Edge of Order and Chaos*. New York: Simon and Schuster.

18

Innovation and Knowledge Management: Scanning, Sourcing, and Integration

PAUL ALMEIDA, ANUPAMA PHENE, AND ROB GRANT

CHAPTER OUTLINE

This chapter seeks to examine firm capabilities in knowledge management that are conducive to innovation. We attempt to unbundle the process of knowledge management by identifying its components – *search*, *transfer*, and *integration*. We further examine firm capabilities associated with each stage of the knowledge management process. We suggest that the *search* for knowledge is influenced by firm scanning capabilities that assist the firm in identifying useful knowledge in proximate and distant contexts. Once the firm has identified useful external knowledge, we determine how it can *transfer* the knowledge, delineating the role of firm sourcing capability and identifying the mechanisms that are used to facilitate transfer. Finally, we examine how firms *integrate* external knowledge with internal knowledge, by examining firm combinative capability, through field interviews of personnel engaged in R&D in semiconductor companies.

KNOWLEDGE AND INNOVATION

The quest for identifying and assimilating knowledge critical to innovation poses a very real challenge for today's firms. Knowledge is now recognized as a key competitive asset, that forms the basis of firm growth (Grant and Baden Fuller, 1995) and sustainable competitive advantage (Kogut, 1993). Since organizational innovation can be viewed as a result of the combination of existing and new knowledge (Kogut and Zander, 1992), firms that are adept at both sourcing and integrating new and existing knowledge are likely to be successful innovators.

Firms themselves are crucibles of knowledge – managerial, operational, and technical. However, they must exploit this internal knowledge in conjunction with external knowledge to compete successfully, gain profitability, and grow. Yet, which firm can claim to harness the potential of its knowledge fully and effectively? Which organization does not re-invent the wheel almost on a daily basis? Which organization thoroughly exploits its "best practices" or rejects its "worst practices"? Which firm can always find (within the organization or outside it) all the knowledge needed for innovation? Few, if any. Until the answers to all these questions are in the affirmative, there will always be opportunities for firms to increase their operational efficiency, manage risk and learn, by further developing the capabilities to manage knowledge available within the organization or within their competitive environment.

This chapter seeks to examine firm capabilities in knowledge management that are conducive to innovation. We analyze the process of knowledge management by identifying its components – *search*, *transfer*, and *integration* and the associated firm capabilities – *scanning*, *sourcing*, and *combinative*. Thus we address both the external sourcing of knowledge and the internal management. First, we review the existing literature that documents the role of external knowledge in innovation. Then we examine how firms *search* for knowledge in the environment by identifying the path dependent patterns of knowledge search which lead to technologically and geographically proximate search. We examine how firm scanning capabilities can assist the firm in searching for knowledge in proximate and distant contexts. Once the firm has identified useful external knowledge, we determine how it can *transfer* the knowledge, delineating the role of firm sourcing capability and identifying the mechanisms that are used to facilitate transfer. Finally we examine how firms *integrate* external knowledge with internal knowledge, by examining firm combinative capability, through field interviews of personnel engaged in R&D in semiconductor companies. Thus this chapter attempts to unbundle the process of knowledge management and analyze its components to determine how firms can develop capabilities in search, transfer and integration that enhance innovation and thus create competitive advantage.

EXTERNAL KNOWLEDGE AND INNOVATION: WHY EXTERNAL KNOWLEDGE?

The resource-based view of the firm suggests that internal knowledge, embodied within a firm's resources is an important source of competitive advantage (Barney, 1991; Wernerfelt, 1984). The firm is often the source of much of the knowledge used in innovation. However, few firms possess all the inputs required for successful and continuous innovation. This is partly due to technological dynamism, reflected in an environment punctuated by competence destroying or altering technologies, that has forced firms to maintain a wide range of technological knowledge and skills (Tushman and Anderson, 1986). Very few firms can independently develop and master the wide range of knowledge and skills needed to compete in ever-changing innovative environments (D'Aveni, 1994; Lane et al., 1998). Consequently, most organizations will develop a deficit within their boundaries as regards the critical knowledge needed to prosper and grow (Coase, 1937; Dussauge et al., 1998). Thus although a firm's own research efforts play an important role in innovation, firms must turn to external sources of knowledge to maintain their innovative processes.

The notion that firms must often turn to external sources to fulfill their knowledge requirements is hardly new (Jewkes et al., 1958) and has been extensively examined. Early research identifies that major contributions to a firm's knowledge base, often come from outside sources. In a classic study of 17 R&D laboratories, Allen and Cohen (1969) found that vendors, "unpaid outside consultants" and informal contacts with government bodies and universities are important sources of R&D knowledge. Research of major product and process innovations at Du Pont between 1920 and 1950 by Mueller (1966) showed that the original knowledge sources of the most critical inventions were outside the firm.

Current research in strategy supports these arguments, suggesting that knowledge existing outside a firm's boundaries may be critical to firm success (Dyer and Singh, 1998; Gulati, 1999). Access to a broader knowledge base through external learning increases the flexibility of the firm, critical in a dynamic environment (Grant, 1996). The "Yale" survey on appropriability, the results of which have been discussed in a series of papers by Klevorick et al. (1995), addresses the issue of external learning by examining inter-firm knowledge spillovers. In their survey of 650 R&D executives, the authors found that though own R&D was rated the most important channel of learning, external knowledge was also extremely important in most industries. Theoretical approaches are also being extended to incorporate the importance of external knowledge, the resource-based view of the firm, which originally focused on the role of internal capabilities, now encompasses resources that span firm boundaries – often embedded in inter-firm relationships (Dyer and Singh, 1998). Given the significant importance of external knowledge, established by our discussion, an important question remains on the table: how can firms direct the knowledge management process to effectively and efficiently search for, transfer, and integrate this knowledge?

THE STAGES (AND CAPABILITIES) OF KNOWLEDGE MANAGEMENT

We suggest here that the knowledge management process can be unbundled into three distinct stages. The first stage involves the firm scanning the environment as it searches for external knowledge useful to innovation. Thus the first stage is concerned solely with identifying useful knowledge. Once useful knowledge has been identified, the next challenge is to access and transfer the knowledge from the external constituent to the firm. It is in the second stage of transfer that knowledge actually crosses firm boundaries, and becomes a part of the firm's internal knowledge stock. Finally, the firm must integrate the transferred knowledge with its existing stock of internal knowledge to create value. In this last stage of the knowledge management process, we are concerned with the recombination of knowledge within firm boundaries that results in innovation. We proceed to examine each of these steps and the capabilities that the firm requires at each stage to shape the knowledge management process so that it culminates in innovation.

The search for external knowledge

How do firms search for external knowledge? An important idea emerging from the evolutionary perspective is that learning and search for external knowledge is "path dependent" (Nelson and Winter, 1982). This idea implies that a firm's past experience and expertise shapes its future decisions and hence the patterns of its knowledge search. The notion of path dependence is intertwined with that of local search. The concept of local search, embedded in evolutionary theory (Dosi, 1988; Winter, 1987) suggests that a firm, when seeking to innovate, will consider options in the neighborhood of its current activities, thus making radical change less likely. Research in organizational learning (March and Simon, 1958; Cyert and March, 1963) also makes a similar point regarding the search for new knowledge. This literature suggests that boundedly rational decision-makers rely on established organizational practices to drive the search for knowledge. Organizational theorists see learning as a process that involves trial, feedback, and evaluation. If too many parameters in the learning process are changed simultaneously the ability of the firm to engage in meaningful learning is attenuated (Teece et al., 1997).

Further the evolutionary perspective suggests that routines, or "socially constructed programs of action" drive organizational behavior. These routines are relatively stable and greatly influenced by the experience and history of the firm and the individuals therein (Nelson and Winter, 1982; Baum et al., 2000). Firms thus recognize and absorb external knowledge close to their existing knowledge base (Cohen and Levinthal, 1990). Hence even as firms seek to expand their knowledge stocks by looking externally, the resultant search processes are restricted to familiar and proximate areas. Thus the search for new knowledge is often restricted to a firm's current area of expertise and experience.

The local search argument assumes significant importance in the innovatory activities of the firm. Given the great size and uneven topography of all research projects that the firm is faced with, it turns to the "neighborhood concept" to create an optimal strategy to allocate innovative effort across different technologies (Nelson and Winter, 1982). Technological learning tends to be local and opportunities for learning will be "close in" to previous activities (Teece, 1988). Industry case studies support this notion as demonstrated in aviation (Miller and Sawers, 1968) and petroleum refining (Enos, 1962). The technological opportunity of a particular field of investigation will determine the strength of local search. Cantwell (1992) demonstrates that technological diversification has been greater for chemicals and pharmaceuticals than for electrical and electronic-related fields. He attributes this to the greater opportunities for innovation within the electrical and electronic fields than in chemicals and pharmaceuticals. For industries like semiconductors that are characterized by tremendous technological opportunities, technological search can be expected to remain fairly local.

It is not just technological search that is local but also geographic search. Studies of innovation and technology diffusion point to the geographic localization of knowledge. Jaffe et al. (1993) analyzed patent citation data to demonstrate that firms and universities acquire knowledge from others in geographically proximate locations. A key reason for geographically localized knowledge flows, research suggests, is the establishment of interfirm linkages between firms in the region (Saxenian, 1990). These relational linkages may be formalized, such as alliances and supply relationships (von Hippel, 1988) or informal, such as regional social networks (Rogers and Larsen, 1984) and mobility of engineers (Almeida and Kogut, 1999). Firms exploit these regional relationships to access knowledge from other local firms. Thus, the underlying reason for geographically local search is both organizational and relational in nature.

There are some advantages to local, contextually bounded search – it restricts the breadth and therefore the cost of the search process. Geographically and technologically proximate search also results in the acquisition of knowledge that can be more easily recognized and managed by the organization's existing routines and members. However, local search restricts the possibilities for innovation through recombinations, since it blocks out the acquisition of novel and more distant knowledge. Indeed, Levitt and March (1988) warn of competence traps and Leonard-Barton (1995) suggests that core capabilities associated with existing routines can become core rigidities as circumstances change. Recent studies in the area of strategic management share the view that, given technological change and the dynamic nature of competition, firms must move beyond local search to compete successfully over time. Porter (1990) points to the emergence of geographically dispersed but specialized regions, in various technologies and industries, emphasizing the need for geographically distant search. Kim and Kogut (1996) show that the dynamic of competition has encouraged semiconductor firms to diversify across technological sub-fields to maintain their competitive edge. Rosenkopf and Nerkar (2001) demonstrate that external exploration in distant technological domains yields innovations with more impact on a broader set of technological areas. No wonder March (1991) suggests that firms balance local search (exploitation) with more distant search (exploration).

Scanning capability   One of the ways to achieve such a balance is by extending the firms' scanning capabilities. A firm's scanning capability enables it to scan the environment and to recognize potentially useful knowledge in both local and distant contexts. This capability primarily stems from the firm's existing knowledge stock, arising from cumulative investments in R&D (Cohen and Levinthal, 1989). We posit that scanning capability is the outcome of the interaction of two dimensions of knowledge stock – its scale and scope. Firms typically focus on the scale of their knowledge stock that often results in the possession of a large volume of knowledge, that is technologically or geographically limited. This in turn limits the firm's scanning capability to proximate contexts. When breadth or scope of knowledge stock is increased, a firm will be more cognizant of knowledge from distant contexts. Consequently, to enhance scanning capabilities of the firm, particularly in the light of the path dependent processes that may limit external learning, it is important that firms make deliberate investments to enhance the breadth of their innovative activity. An emphasis on the development of the breadth of scanning capabilities permits firms to better recognize external knowledge from a variety of technological and geographic contexts. Combinations of existing and "new" or novel knowledge may subsequently enhance the value of the firm's innovation.

The sourcing and transfer of external knowledge

Recognizing the importance of outside knowledge does not necessarily permit a firm to access and transfer it. Nor does it explain which firms are best able to access knowledge or why firms are attentive to knowledge from certain sources and less attentive to others. To facilitate knowledge transfer firms must develop linkages to outside sources of knowledge that act as conduits for knowledge transfer (Almeida, 1996; Dyer and Nobeoka, 2000;

Gulati et al., 2000). It is these conduits that channel the externally available knowledge, and determine which knowledge the firm actually uses in the innovative process.

Prior research suggests that firms use a number of mechanisms that enable them to create conduits to external sources of useful knowledge. Besides traditional supply arrangements, these mechanisms include the hiring of scientists and engineers (Almeida and Kogut 1999; Zucker, 1998), the forming of strategic alliances (Mowery et al., 1996; Rosenkopf and Almeida, 2001) and the appropriation of informal networks in geographically proximate locations (Almeida and Kogut 1997; Liebeskind et al., 1996; Rosenkopf and Tushman 1998). Indeed, Rosenkopf and Almeida (2001) use patent citation data to evaluate the three mechanisms of learning, and find that all three mechanisms play a role in facilitating external learning by semiconductor startups.

Alliances   A central idea in the literature on alliances is that they are useful mechanisms for knowledge acquisition and learning (Hamel et al., 1989). The explosive growth of strategic alliances over the years, especially in high technology industries such as semiconductors and commercial aircraft, supports the view of the increasing importance of collaborative agreements in accessing and transferring external knowledge (Contractor and Lorange, 1988; Dyer and Singh, 1998; Mowery et al., 1998). Recent empirical research provides some support for the notion that the repeated use of alliances may result in increasing firm capabilities for learning from these mechanisms (Anand and Khanna, 2000). Powell et al. (1996) postulate the existence of "networks of learning," and suggest that participation in networks of R&D alliances facilitates the growth of new biotechnology firms because these networks create access to knowledge.

In-depth case studies provide us with a rich illustration of learning between alliance or network partners demonstrating overall knowledge flows across networks. Doz (1996) explores how alliances may be construed as learning processes, where learning occurs in multiple dimensions – environment, task, process, skill, and partner goals – and the amount of learning is facilitated or constrained by initial conditions. Dyer (1997) suggests that the breadth and intensity of the relationship between alliance partners will grow over time. Though there is considerable literature relating learning and alliances, few studies explicitly measure inter-firm knowledge transfers associated with alliances.

However, studies rooted in patent data have begun to explore this issue. In Stuart and Podolny's (1996) study of the major Japanese semiconductor firms, the authors suggest that Matsushita accomplished a technological transition through the strategic use of alliances. In two studies of alliances between multinational firms in 1985–86, spanning a variety of industries, Mowery et al. (1996, 1998) demonstrate that certain alliances are followed by rises in the cross-citation and common-citation patterns between the firms, suggesting some transfer of knowledge.

Mobility   Another mechanism for the transfer of knowledge across firm boundaries is through the mobility of people. Several primarily descriptive studies suggest that people are an important conduit of inter-firm knowledge transfer (Malecki, 1991). However, most research suggests only a connection between mobility and knowledge flows, offering at best indirect evidence. For instance, Markusen et al. (1986) find that regions with high concentrations of technical workers attract new high technology investment. In technology intensive industries as well, there are numerous descriptive studies of people carrying knowledge across firms (Hanson, 1982). In the semiconductor industry, interviews with engineers reveal many anecdotes of inter-firm knowledge flows associated with the mobility of engineers (Rogers and Larsen, 1984; Saxenian, 1990).

As was the case for alliance research, the most direct evidence linking mobility of engineers to inter-firm knowledge transfers may be accomplished through patent records. Almeida and Kogut (1999) show that after a semiconductor firm hired a new engineer, there was a significantly greater tendency for the hiring firm to cite the prior patents of the newly employed engineer than would be expected given its technology profile. In addition, Song, Almeida, and Wu (2001) demonstrate that during the early stage of development of Korean semiconductor firms, the practice of bringing US-educated and US-employed nationals back home leads to similar patenting practices.

Informal mechanisms associated with geographic regions   Research points to the importance of geographically clustered social networks in facilitating the informal diffusion of knowledge across firms (Rogers and Larson, 1984). Localized knowledge sharing was common between firms in the steel industry in nineteenth-century England (Allen, 1983). Case studies of regional clusters in Italy (Piore and Sabel, 1984) and Baden-Wuerttemberg in Germany (Herrigel, 1993) indicate extensive knowledge flows through networks in these regions. Why does co-location matter to the transfer of knowledge? Common to Alfred Marshall's (1920) "industrial districts" and Porter's (1998) localized, industry "clusters" is the idea that industry-specific knowledge develops in geographically concentrated locations. This phenomenon is true not only of traditional, craft-based industries, but also high-technology industries. This in turn leads to greater knowledge transfers between firms, due to the similarity in their knowledge bases and due to the extensive linkages that develop within a region.

Though linkages between firms could develop across geographic distances, proximity enhances the development of complex networks (Graham, 1985; Almeida and Kogut, 1999). Locational proximity reduces the cost and increases the frequency of personal contacts which serve to build social relations between players in a network (Almeida and Kogut, 1997; Dorfman, 1987; Saxenian, 1990; Zucker, 1998) that can be appropriated for learning purposes. Further proximity builds common institutional and professional ties that help build a context for knowledge transfers (Saxenian, 1990). There is a significant amount of research that offers evidence to support this. Saxenian (1990) relates the dynamism and the vitality of Silicon Valley to the extensive networking both at the firm level (between firms and universities, buyers and suppliers, venture capitalists etc.) and also between individuals within the region. Porter's (1990) description of the localized Italian ceramic tile industry points to close and repeated interactions between the various small businesses in the region. Almeida and Kogut (1999) show that the flow of knowledge within many of the semiconductor regions within the United States is facilitated by the mobility of engineers across firms within the region.

Thus, recent empirical research suggests that the mechanisms of alliances, mobility and geography offer firms the opportunity to access knowledge. Perhaps the most interesting opportunities for further investigation lie in evaluating the conditions under which this knowledge sourcing is most successful, and the relative merits and uses of the different conduits of knowledge acquisition. For instance, current research suggests that the usefulness of these conduits may vary depending on firm characteristics – Almeida et al. (2001) show that firms of various sizes indeed access knowledge through various mechanisms. However, as firms grow larger, they increasingly lose the ability to learn from informal channels such as the hiring of engineers and the informal channels associated with geographic proximity. Another interesting question relates to the relative roles played by these conduits in the knowledge sourcing process. Song et al. (2001) show that Korean and Taiwanese firms rely on different channels of knowledge sourcing through their technological development cycles. Similarly, Rosenkopf and Almeida (2001) show that firms can use the mechanisms of knowledge sourcing specifically to plug gaps in their technological knowledge base. The authors show that the mechanisms of alliances and mobility are most useful when used to source knowledge from distant technological settings. Thus though recent research has increased our insights into how firms use mechanisms of knowledge sourcing, there are still opportunities to further investigate the conditions and the manner in which these mechanisms are used.

Sourcing capability   The utilization of mechanisms to access knowledge from external organizations (formal and informal) is facilitated by the possession of valuable internal knowledge, since a firm's knowledge base makes it more attractive to other organizations for the sharing of knowledge. For instance, von Hippel (1988) describes how possession of knowledge serves as a prerequisite to arriving at inter-firm technology agreements that permit knowledge sharing and transfer. Thus the ability of the firm to build and actively utilize mechanisms for external knowledge transfer is termed sourcing capability. Similar, to scanning capability, it stems from the firm's internal knowledge base. However, unlike in the case of scanning capability, both the scale and scope of the firm's knowledge base contribute to enhancing its sourcing capability.

Sourcing capability reflects the firm's ability to internalize knowledge existing in the environment, and bring it within the scope of its own boundaries. For a firm to be successful at sourcing knowledge, it must understand the knowledge to be transferred, articulate it by coding it to facilitate transfer and transfer it by using well-established reliable routines and then decode it, once it has been transferred. A large scale and scope of knowledge ensures greater likelihood of the firm's ability to understand the knowledge. However, in addition to an existing knowledge stock, the firm needs routines that have been established to code and decode knowledge. A large scale of internal knowledge implies the existence of reliable and durable intra-firm knowledge transfer routines. Thus, while scale implies the reliability and durability of knowledge transfer routine, extensive scope indicates that versatility of these routines suggesting that the underlying ability to articulate, code, and decode can be extended or applied to many types of knowledge. Firms with significant sourcing capabilities can transfer external knowledge from the environmental context to the firm. This leads to the last stage in the knowledge management process, integration.

Integrating knowledge

The final stage in gainfully using the knowledge that has been determined to be useful and transferred within firm boundaries is its integration with knowledge existing in other parts of the firm, which results in innovation. It was Schumpeter (1934: 65) who first pointed out that innovation takes place by "carrying out new combinations." Henderson and Clark's (1992) concept of architectural knowledge reinforces this idea, suggesting that a critical feature of a firm's innovative ability may be the broader managerial capability to combine or link together knowledge within the firm. Thus integration appears to be an important stage in the knowledge management process since it results in value creation.

To shed some light on the knowledge integration process, we discuss our insights from field interviews carried out by the authors with research personnel in semiconductor firms to obtain their views on the process of integration of knowledge within the firm. These interviews involved two sets of research personnel involved in innovation. First, the inventors or architects of the innovation and secondly, design managers and directors of technology development – people that managed the innovation process – at seven semiconductor companies: Philips, Siemens, National Semiconductors, Fujitsu, Texas Instruments, IBM, and Samsung.

The interviews with managers suggested that managers emphasized the integration stage of the knowledge management process as opposed to the stages of knowledge search and transfer. The critical issue for each of our semiconductor firms was the integration of specialized knowledge from different parts of the company. This emphasis seems logical considering that the value creation aspect comes into play only at this stage in the knowledge management process. Thus, the former director of Texas Instruments' (TI) Tokyo R&D lab outlined the lab's role in accessing the knowledge bases of TI's Japanese customers, developing technologies where Japan was particularly strong (notably algorithms for image compression), and linking these technologies with ongoing research in Austin, Texas. Similarly, Fujitsu's 3D geometry processor was the result of closely integrated development involving both Fujitsu Laboratories in Japan and Fujitsu Microelectronics Inc. in San José, California. The need for integration of knowledge within the firm is a direct outcome of the increasing globalization of firm activity resulting in a dispersed knowledge base. This is evident in the case of National Semiconductor, that explained how closeness to customers necessitated dispersion of semiconductor activity, with semiconductors for games machines being developed in Japan, computer processors in the US, and digital wireless chips in Europe. Compounded with the dispersion of knowledge bases, there is increasing specialization of these bases. Siemens, Philips, Fujitsu, and National Semiconductor all noted that the increased specialization of knowledge in different parts of the firm has greatly increased the need to bring together specialist chip design knowledge from multiple locations.

How do firms engage in integration? The processes by which this geographically distributed knowledge was brought together by the companies was very different from the continual, intense knowledge sharing that been advocated by some exponents of "the learning company." In relation to semiconductor design, our interviewees identified the key process as *integrating* specialized knowledge drawn from different locations – what Nonaka and Takeuchi (1995: 67–69) refer to as "knowledge combination" to create "systemic knowledge." The key to efficient integration was the use of loosely coupled modular designs that permitted different individuals and groups to input their knowledge into the chip design without overloading channels of communication and learning capacity of every other design unit. Fujitsu told us that its VLIW (very long instruction word) processor chip (used primarily for mobile phones, video compression, and other media-rich processing) was developed jointly by design teams in Tokyo, San José and Frankfurt, but with each team working on specific modules and subsystems (these included a 16-bit instruction set, a 32-bit instruction set, a media instruction set, digital signal instruction set, and floating point instruction set). Hitachi reported that a similar modular architecture facilitated knowledge combination between its designers in Japan and California in its range of combined microcontroller and DSP (digital signal processing) chips.

Segmented modular designs did not mean, however, that cross-border knowledge flows could be reduced to codified knowledge capable of electronic transmission. Engineers and managers whom we interviewed confirmed the importance of different types of knowledge in determining the pattern and effectiveness of cross-border knowledge integration. The critical characteristic was the codifiability of knowledge: technical information tends to be highly codifiable and its transmission can be reduced to mere data transfer. Certainly, computer-based information systems for transferring electronic data formed the backbone of the knowledge management systems for all seven of the companies we spoke to.

However, our interviews with engineers emphasized that increasing chip densities (up to over a million transistors being packed into a single chip) and increasingly fine circuitry (approaching 0.1 microns), indicated that semiconductor design was pushing at the limits of physics. The result was that experience, intuition, creativity, and problem solving became increasingly important. The design engineers spoke of chip design as a continual battle against the limits imposed by the materials used and the fabrication processes that required a constant quest for experience and scientific knowledge with the addition of intuition and creativity. Successful problem solving required linking with multiple knowledge bases: with university researchers on fundamental science, with customers on the functional and technical requirements of new products, with manufacturing engineers over fabrication issues, with different design teams in order to access parallel experience and stimulate creative thinking. Most of these knowledge bases required accessing experience-based, intuitive knowledge of the tacit kind. The head of technology development at National Semiconductor pointed to the importance of integrating both explicit and tacit knowledge. A key characteristic of successful design teams was the ability to make full use of the form of computerized design tools and the company's library of designs, while exploring new opportunities through drawing upon the deeply ingrained know-how of seasoned engineers and the creativity and persistence of younger team members. Tacit knowledge is accumulated through experience and is inherently uncodifiable. Our interviews confirmed that the transfer of tacit knowledge depends not only upon trial-and-error imitation but also cultural and social context. This cultural and contextual knowledge is a function of socialization, often over a substantial period of time.

Our research revealed a wide range of media through which knowledge moves between the national units of the firm. All our interviewees put heavy emphasis on the importance of communicating internationally through electronic media. All the companies had invested considerably in information technology for the purposes of increasing the extent and efficiency of global knowledge management. In relation to semiconductor design, initiatives included standardized design tools and file formats, shared databases, common communications software, and design libraries, with users linked by company intranets.

National Semiconductor's head of technology development explained how its integrated design system with common naming conventions, UNIX file structures, and design tools had been driven by the vision of concurrent chip design where design teams were capable of working closely together regardless of geographical separation. Similarly, Fujitsu's "IP Highway" launched in 1998 was an internet-based infrastructure allowing the transfer of intellectual property and design data across all Fujitsu's subsidiaries.

However, the very nature of the knowledge integration – whereby individual country units were engaged in simultaneously receiving, creating, transmitting and integrating knowledge – revealed the limitations of electronic communication systems, especially in communicating experiential and intuitive know-how. At Siemens, engineers working on optoelectronic components explained that e-mails and file transfers only worked when supplemented by frequent telephone conversations, videoconferences and personal visits to other labs. National Semiconductor pointed to the importance of company-wide desktop videoconferencing facilities and the authority given to individual engineers to make overseas visits to meet with colleagues without the need for supervisory or budgetary approvals. Our interviewees confirmed prior research concerning the need for "rich" communication media to overcome the limits of electronic media with regard to complexity of language, flexibility of format, degree of personalization, and the extent of interactivity (Daft and Lengl, 1986). So what capabilities should the firm emphasize to enable knowledge integration within its boundaries? Just as scanning capability and sourcing capability enhance search and transfer stages of the knowledge management process, we posit combinative capability improves the stage of integration.

Combinative capability   The firm's combinative capability is its ability to combine existing knowledge for innovation. This managerial ability, of course, requires the transfer of knowledge from the points of access, with the boundary spanners and gatekeepers (Allen, 1977) to other locations within the firm where this knowledge can be usefully exploited. How do organizations develop this combinative capability?

The scale and scope of the firm's knowledge stock increase the potential for recombinations within the firm. However, to capitalize on this potential, firms need to develop internal mechanisms that enable recombinations. The role of internal communication systems (Cohen and Levinthal, 1989) is crucial in this regard. Zenger and Lawrence (1989) point out that the ability to communicate knowledge across organizational sub-units depends in part on the prevalence of a shared language and culture. But mere communication of knowledge may not be sufficient to ensure its exploitation. The nature of innovation, and the tacit and complex nature of knowledge may require that several sub-units interact actively across extended periods of time to build new products or processes (Westney and Sakakibara, 1986). To facilitate this knowledge integration process, firms must establish intra-organizational mechanisms, processes and systems to link various sub-units across time (Almeida et al., 1998). Our field interviews suggested the firm's ability to ensure internal compatibility of information systems; sharing of intellectual property; and common software, protocols, and methodologies were viewed as significant in enabling knowledge integration within the firm.

Another mechanism to enhance integration was mobility within the organization. Field interviews indicated the extensive use by the companies of transfer of personnel, either for short visits or for longer-term assignments (several years in some cases) means by which deeply embedded tacit knowledge could be transferred and integrated within the firm. However, international personnel transfers also served to improve integration through two other methods. First, they contributed to internationalizing the company's culture thereby overcoming some of the language and cultural barriers that might inhibit cross-border knowledge integration. The semiconductor divisions of Hitachi, Fujitsu, and IBM put considerable emphasis on building collaborative company cultures and behavioral norms that transcended national differences. Second, international transfers helped to build informal cross-national mechanisms for knowledge integration. The engineers at Philips and Siemens and R&D managers at IBM gave considerable weight to the role of the interpersonal networks that employees established during their careers in a company.

KNOWLEDGE AND INNOVATION: NEXT STEPS

We have identified the knowledge management process as the central process through which firms create innovation. Our inquiry into this process offers further insights into the literature on knowledge and innovation. We believe our study sheds new light on this process by unbundling it into its components. The knowledge management process consists of three related yet distinct sub-processes – the search for external knowledge, its subsequent sourcing and transfer, and finally its integration. We suggest that it may be worthwhile for researchers in the area of innovation to study not just the processes but the firm-specific capabilities associated with each stage. The capabilities associated with each stage of knowledge management become more complex as the process gets closer to culminating in value creation to innovation. While scanning capabilities are a result of the firm's knowledge stock, sourcing and combinative capabilities arise from a combination of the firm's knowledge stock and its routines, processes, and structure.

The identification of each stage and the associated capabilities enables us to offer prescriptions to managers in developing specific capabilities that improve the overall knowledge management capabilities of the firm. Better management of the knowledge management process is a chief concern of most firms. All the companies we spoke to recognized the need to improve their handling of this process. Identifying the capabilities necessary to search for, transfer, and integrate knowledge is only a starting point. The critical issues for management practice relate to the design and use of these knowledge management systems. Based on field research findings, we have argued that the knowledge managing advantages of the firm lie in its ability to use rules to standardize procedures and formats, directives to administer coordination between units, inter-personal relationships between employees, and a common culture to facilitate communication and cooperation. The design and choice of different mechanisms of knowledge transfer must take careful account of the nature of the knowledge management process (e.g. the extent to which it seeks to replicate knowledge, to combine knowledge, or to create new knowledge through problem solving), and the types of knowledge being transferred (in particular, the less codifiable the knowledge, the richer the communication medium needs to be). While firms have made huge strides in the use of IT to transfer information and support communication worldwide, the next level of knowledge management lies in the design and operation of organizational structures, management systems, and shared values and behavioral norms that can facilitate the movement of complementary knowledge types and link together the different modes of communication and knowledge transfer. Subsequent research needs to investigate in greater detail the design and performance of specific knowledge management practices, particularly those that use multiple communication modes.

References

Allen, R.C. (1983) Collective Invention. *Journal of Economic Behavior and Organization*, 4 (1): 1–24.

Allen, T. (1977) *Managing the Flow of Technology*. Cambridge, MA: MIT Press.

Allen, T. and Cohen, S. (1969) Knowledge Flow in Research and Development Laboratories. *Administrative Science Quarterly*, 14: 12–19.

Almeida, P. (1996) Knowledge Sourcing by Foreign Multinationals: Patent Citation Analysis in the US Semiconductor Industry. *Strategic Management Journal*, 7 (special issue): 155–65.

Almeida, P., Grant, R., and Song, J. (1998) The Role of International Corporations in Cross Border Knowledge Transfer in the Semiconductor Industry. In M. Hitt, E. Ricart, and D. Nixon (eds.), *Managing Strategically in an Interconnected World*. Chichester, UK: John Wiley & Sons.

Almeida, P., Grant, R., and Song, J. (2002) Are Firms Superior to Alliances and Markets? An Empirical Test of Cross Border Knowledge Building. *Organization Science*, 13: 147–61.

Almeida, P. and Kogut, B. (1997) The Exploration of Technological Diversity and the Geographic Localization of Innovation. *Small Business Economics*, 9 (1): 21–31.

Almeida, P. and Kogut, B. (1999) The Localization of Knowledge and the Mobility of Engineers in Regional Networks. *Management Science*, 45: 905–17.

Anand, B.N. and Khanna, T. (2000) Do Firms Learn to Create Value? The Case of Alliances. *Strategic Management Journal*, 21 (3) (Special Issue: Strategic Networks): 295–315.

Barney, J. (1991) Firm Resources and Sustained Competitive Advantage. *Journal of Management*, 17 (1): 99–120.

Baum, J., Calabrese, T., and Silverman, B. (2000) Don't Go It Alone: Alliance Network Composition and Startups' Performance in the Canadian Biotechnology Industry. *Strategic Management Journal*, 21 (3): 267–94.

Cantwell, J. (1992) The Internationalisation of Technological Activity and its Implications for Competitiveness. In O. Granstrand, L. Hakanson, and S. Sjolander (eds.), *Technology Management and International Business: Internationalization of R&D and Technology*. Chichester: Wiley.

Coase, R.H. (1937) The Nature of the Firm. *Economica*, 4: 386–405.

Cohen, W. and Levinthal, D. (1989) Innovation and Learning: The Two Faces of R&D. *The Economic Journal*, 99: 569–96.

Cohen, W. and Levinthal, D. (1990) Absorptive Capacity: A New Perspective on Learning and Innovation. *Administrative Science Quarterly*, 35: 128–52.

Contractor, F. and Lorange, P. (1988) Why Should Firms Cooperate? The Strategy and Economic Basis for Cooperative Ventures. In F. Contractor and P. Lorange (eds.), *Cooperative Strategies in International Business*. New York: Lexington.

Cyert, R. and March, J.G. (1963) *A Behavioral Theory of the Firm*. Englewood Cliffs, NJ: Prentice Hall.

Daft, R.L. and Lengl, R. (1986) Organizational Information Requirements, Media Richness and Structural Design. *Management Science*, 32: 554–71.

D'Aveni, R. (1994) *Hypercompetition: Managing the Dynamics of Strategic Maneuvering*. New York: Free Press.

Dorfman, N.S. (1987) *Innovation and Market Structure: Lessons from the Computer and Semiconductor Industries*. Cambridge, MA: Ballinger.

Dosi, G. (1988) Sources, Procedures and Microeconomic Effects of Innovation. *Journal of Economic Literature*, 26 (3): 1120–72.

Doz, Y. (1996) The Evolution of Cooperation in Strategic Alliances: Initial Conditions or Learning Processes? *Strategic Management Journal* (special issue), 17: 55–83.

Dussauge, P., Garrette, B., and Mitchell, W. (1998) Acquiring Partners' Capabilities: Outcomes of Scale and Link Alliances between Competitors. In M. Hitt, E. Ricart, and D. Nixon (eds.), *Managing Strategically in an Interconnected World*. Chichester, UK: John Wiley & Sons.

Dyer, J. (1997) Effective Interfirm Collaboration: How Transactors Minimize Transaction Costs and Maximize Transaction Value. *Strategic Management Journal*, 18: 535–56.

Dyer, J. and Nobeoka, K. (2000) Creating and Managing a High Performance Knowledge Sharing Network: The Toyota Case, *Strategic Management Journal*, 21: 345–67.

Dyer, J. and Singh, S. (1998) The Relational View: Cooperative Strategy and Sources of Interorganizational Competitive Advantage. *Academy of Management Review*, 23: 660–79.

Enos, J. (1962) *Petroleum Progress and Profits*. Cambridge, MA: MIT Press.

Graham, M. (1985) Industrial Research in the Age of Big Science. In R. Rosenbloom (ed.), *Research on Technological Innovation, Management and Policy*, Vol. 2. Greenwich, CT: JAI Press.

Grant, R.M. (1996) Prospering in Dynamically Competitive Environments: Organizational Capability as Knowledge Integration. *Organization Science*, 7: 375–87.

Grant, R.M. and Baden-Fuller, C. (1995) A Knowledge-based Theory of Inter-firm Collaboration. *Academy of Management Best Papers Proceedings*.

Gulati, R. (1999) Network Location and Learning: The Influence of Network Resources and Firm Capabilities on Alliance Formation. *Strategic Management Journal*, 20 (5): 397–420.

Gulati, R., Nohria, N., and Zaheer, A. (2000) Strategic Networks. *Strategic Management Journal*, 21: 203–15.

Hamel, G., Doz, Y., and Prahalad, C.K. (1989) Collaborate with your Competitors and Win. *Harvard Business Review*, 67 (1): 133–40.

Hanson, D. (1982) *The New Alchemists: Silicon Valley and the Microelectronics Revolution*. Boston, MA: Little, Brown.

Henderson, R. and Clark, K. (1992) Architectural Innovation: The Reconfiguration of Existing Competencies. *Administrative Science Quarterly*, 35: 9–31.

Herrigel, G. (1993) Large Firms, Small Firms, and the Governance of Flexible Specialization: The Case of Baden Wuttemberg and Socialized Risk. In B. Kogut (ed.), *Country Competitiveness: Technology and the Organizing of Work*. New York: Oxford University Press.

Jaffe, A., Trajtenberg, M., and Henderson, R. (1993) Geographic Localization of Knowledge Spillovers as Evidenced by Patent Citations. *Quarterly Journal of Economics*, 108: 577–98.

Jewkes, J., Sawers, D., and Stillerman, R. (1958) *The Sources of Invention*. London: Macmillan.

Kim, D.-J. and Kogut, B. (1996) Technological Platforms and Diversification. *Organization Science*. 7: 283–301.

Klevorick, A., Levin, A., Nelson, R., and Winter, S. (1995) On the Sources and Significance of Interindustry Differences in Technological Opportunities. *Research Policy*, 24 (2): 185–206.

Kogut, B. (1993) Introduction. In B. Kogut (ed.), *Country Competitiveness: Technology and the Organizing of Work*. New York: Oxford University Press.

Kogut, B. and Zander, U. (1992) Knowledge of the Firm, Combinative Capabilities and the Replication of Technology. *Organization Science*, 3 (3): 383–96.

Lane, P., Lyles, M., and Salk, J. (1998) Relative Absorptive Capacity, Trust and Interorganizational Learning in International Joint Ventures. In M. Hitt, E. Ricart, and D. Nixon (eds.), *Managing Strategically in an Interconnected World*. Chichester, UK: John Wiley & Sons.

Leonard-Barton, D. (1995) *Wellsprings of Knowledge. Building and Sustaining the Sources of Innovation*. Boston, MA: Harvard Business School Press.

Levitt B. and March, J. (1988) Organizational Learning. *Annual Review of Sociology*, 14: 319–40.

Liebeskind, J.P., Oliver, A.L., Zucker, L., and Brewer, M. (1996) Social Networks, Learning, and Flexibility: Sourcing Scientific Knowledge in New Biotechnology Firms. *Organization Science* 7 (4): 428–43.

Malecki, E.J. (1991) *Technology and Economic Development*. New York: John Wiley.

March, J.G. (1991) Exploration and Exploitation in Organizational Learning. *Organization Science*, 2 (1): 71–87.

March, J. and Simon, H. (1958) *Organizations*. New York: John Wiley.

Markusen, A., Hall, P., and Glasmeier, A. (1986) *High Tech America*. Boston, MA: Allen and Unwin.

Marshall, A. (1920) *Principles of Economics*. London: Macmillan.

Miller, R. and Sawers, D. (1968) *The Technical Development of Modern Aviation*. London: Routledge and Kegan Paul.

Mowery, D., Oxley, J., and Silverman, B. (1998) Technological Overlap and Interfirm Cooperation: Implications for the Resource-based View of the Firm. *Research Policy*, 27 (5): 507–23.

Mowery, D.C., Oxley, J.E., and Silverman, B.S. (1996) Strategic Alliances and Interfirm Knowledge Transfer. *Strategic Management Journal*, 17 (Winter Special Issue): 77–91.

Mueller, W.F. (1966) The Origins of the Basic Inventions Underlying DuPont's Major Process and Product Innovations, 1920–50. In R. Nelson (ed.), *The Rate and Direction of Inventive Activity*. Princeton: National Bureau of Economic Research.

Nelson, R. and Winter, S. (1982) *The Evolutionary Theory of the Firm*. Cambridge, MA: Harvard University Press.

Nonaka, I. and Takeuchi, H. (1995) *The Knowledge Creating Company: How Japanese Companies Create the Dynamics of Innovation*. New York: Oxford University Press.

Piore, M. and Sabel, C. (1984) *The Second Industrial Divide: Possibilities for Prosperity*. New York: Basic Books.

Porter, M. (1998) Clusters and the New Economics of Competition. *Harvard Business Review*, 76 (6): 77–90.

Porter, M.E. (1990) *The Competitive Advantage of Nations*. New York: Free Press.

Powell, W., Koput, K., and Smith-Doerr, L. (1996) Interorganizational Collaboration and the Locus of Innovation: Networks of Learning in Biotechnology. *Administrative Science Quarterly*, 41: 116–45.

Rogers, E. and Larsen, J. (1984) *Silicon Valley Fever*. New York: Basic Books.

Rosenkopf, L. and Almeida, P. (2001) Overcoming Local Search through Alliances and Mobility. Working Paper, University of Pennsylvania.

Rosenkopf, L. and Nerkar, A. (2001) Beyond Local Search: Boundary-spanning, Exploration and Impact in the Optical Disc Industry. *Strategic Management Journal*, 22: 287–306.

Rosenkopf, L. and Tushman, M.L. (1998) The Coevolution of Community Networks and Technology: Lessons from the Flight Simulation Industry. *Industrial and Corporate Change* 7 (2): 311–46.

Saxenian, A. (1990) Regional Networks and the Resurgence of Silicon Valley. *California Management Review*, Fall: 39–112.

Schumpeter, J.A. (1934) *The Theory of Economic Development*. Cambridge, MA: Harvard University Press.

Song, J., Almeida, P., and Wu, G. (2001) Mobility of Engineers and Cross-border Knowledge Building: The Technological Catching-up Case of Korean and Taiwanese Semiconductor Firms. In H. Chesbrough and R. Burgelman (eds.), *Research in Technology and Innovation Management*. New York: Elsevier, 59–84.

Stuart, T. and Podolny, J. (1996) Local Search and the Evolution of Technological Capabilities. *Strategic Management Journal* (summer special issue), 17: 21–38.

Teece, D. (1988) Capturing Value from Technological Innovation: Integration, Strategic Partnering and Licensing Decisions. *Interfaces*, 18 (3): 46–62.

Teece, D., Pisano, G., and Shuen, A. (1997) Dynamic Capabilities and Strategic Management. *Strategic Management Journal*, 18 (7): 509–33.

Tushman, M. and Anderson, P. (1986) Technological Discontinuities and Organizational Environments. *Administrative Science Quarterly*, 31: 439–65.

Von Hippel, E. (1988) *Sources of Innovation*. New York: Oxford University Press.

Wernerfelt, B. (1984) A Resource-based View of the Firm. *Strategic Management Journal*, 5 (2): 171–81.

Westney, E. and Sakakibara, K. (1986) The Role of Japan Based R&D in Global Technological Strategy. In M. Hurowitch (ed.), *Technology in the Modern Corporation*. London: Pergamon, 217–32.

Winter, S. (1987) Knowledge and Competence of Strategic Assets. In D. Teece (ed.), *The Competitive Challenge: Strategies for Industrial Innovation and Renewal*. Cambridge, MA: Ballinger, 159–84.

Zenger, T. and Lawrence, B. (1989) Organizational Demography: The Differential Effects of Age and Tenure. *Academy of Management Journal*, 32 (2): 353–77.

Zucker, L.G. (1998) Geographically Localized Knowledge: Spillovers or Markets? *Economic Inquiry* 36 (1): 65–86.

19

Knowledge Sharing and the Communal Resource

Georg von Krogh

Chapter Outline

This chapter construes knowledge sharing as "sequential collective action," discusses the problem of knowledge sharing in organizations and outlines various solutions offered in the literature to overcome this problem. In particular, the concept of "communal resource" for knowledge sharing is developed. Communal resources rely on opportunities for knowledge sharing and social norms, such as care in relationships and the search for authenticity in knowledge. The chapter ends with a discussion of important research questions for studies in organizational learning and knowledge management.

Introduction

We have come far in the field of "knowledge management"[1] research. There is an increasing body of work in organization behavior, organization theory, strategic management, information systems, technology and innovation management, marketing, and in the fundamental disciplines of economics, psychology, and sociology, which all make knowledge a central construct in theory and research. Common to most of these contributions is their intent to demonstrate the power that knowledge has for explaining and predicting behavior, at the level of societies and economies (Stehr, 1994), industries (Arthur, 1997), firms and institutions (for example, Nelson and Winter, 1982; Cohen and Levinthal, 1990; Grant, 1996; Spender, 1996; Kogut and Zander, 1992), networks (Dyer and Nobeoka, 2000), groups (Osterloh and Frey, 2000), and individuals (for example Cziksezentmihalyi, 1988). For the purpose of this chapter, I describe knowledge as having three important features, of which the first is justified true beliefs. An individual justifies the truthfulness of his or her observations based on observations of the world, which, in turn, depend on a unique viewpoint, personal sensibility, and individual experience (Nonaka and Takeuchi, 1995). Second, knowledge enables action. Third, knowledge is both explicit and tacit (Nonaka,

1994). Some knowledge can be put on paper, formulated in sentences, or captured in drawings. Other kinds of knowledge are tied to the senses, movement skills, physical experiences, rules of thumb, and intuition (Merleau-Ponty, 1995). Such tacit knowledge can be costly to describe to others. While the idea of tacit knowledge makes sense intuitively for most people, managers in particular often have a hard time coming to grips with it on a practical level. Recognizing the value of tacit knowledge, that is, figuring out how to use it to enhance task performance, has become the key challenge for knowledge management practice in many organizations (Choo, 1998).

The central quest for knowledge management research became performance enhancement through various dimensions of activities, enabling conditions, and information and communication technology tools that took into account the serendipitous and ambiguous nature of knowledge (Kluege et al., 2001). The research opportunities along these dimensions are still vast, but in order to progress fruitfully, we need to pay more attention to one of the core problems that bridge the chasm between the individual and collective levels: why, and under what circumstances do people share knowledge in organizations? The ability to carve out a research niche with a prosperous future depends on the ability to define the sharing problem and to deliver parsimonious theories and rich research based on a multiplicity of methods. In this short essay, I will elucidate the issue of knowledge sharing through a collective action framework, and identify two possible solutions to the sharing problem: the use of exogenous agency and the nurturing of a communal resource.[2] If there is some evolutionary stability of contributing to and benefiting from the community, over time, people may explore opportunities for joint learning in accordance with their interests. In this chapter I will discuss some conditions enabling this stability.

THE PROBLEM OF KNOWLEDGE SHARING

In capturing and localizing knowledge in the firm, the intent is to enhance the potential for and the efficiency of linking and integrating knowledge dispersed throughout the organization (Davenport and Prusak, 1996; Choo, 1998). Knowledge and best-practice transfer within and between organizations is not a one-way activity, but a process of sharing involving trial and error, feedback, and the mutual adjustment of both the sender and receiver of knowledge (Szulanski, 1996; Powell, 1998; Kaeser, 2001). Whereas the early literature on knowledge and technology transfer between and within organizations hinged on a simple model of the communication of information, new contributions in this area understand knowledge and technology transfer as a model of knowledge sharing and local knowledge (re)-creation (for a review, see von Krogh and Koehne, 1998). In theories of knowledge creation and innovation, the sharing of tacit knowledge among participants in an innovation process precedes the articulation of new concepts, the appraisal and justification of these concepts, and product prototyping (Leonard and Sensiper, 1998; von Krogh et al., 2000; Kaeser, 2001).

The sharing of tacit knowledge entails as much self-observation, reflection, and indwelling in the routines of the master, as it does observation and imitative learning by the apprentice of the master (Polanyi and Prosch, 1975). The sharing of tacit knowledge involves a transformation in the cognition of the master as well, as the training of the apprentice confronts the master with new experiences that are tightly connected to, if not caused by, the performance of the master's own routines. In this system of master and apprentice, the master's routines will change as a result of the master's reflection on his or her own routines as well as observation and reflection, but to what extent and in which direction, is dependent on the individual master's interest and willingness to adopt a shared identity with the apprentice (see A.P. Cohen, 1985). In effect, some authors claim that good apprenticeship training can only be achieved when the routines of the master include the observation and reflection that comes with training (Dreyfus and Dreyfus, 1986).

This example of tacit knowledge sharing brings forth an important insight. If knowledge sharing is knowledge re-creation in the manner outlined, rather than a simple communication of information and representation of tasks and procedural knowledge, knowledge sharing could be construed as a sequenced collective action problem. Knowledge sharing in this sense involves alteration in cognition and action both of the master and of the apprentice. In a master–apprentice relationship, the presence of another during task performance becomes an integral part of the task performance, cognition and action, by knowing that there is a master or apprentice observing, commenting, helping, or maybe even ignoring the other who performs tasks.[3] Knowledge sharing in this sense involves a collective change in cognition and action both of the master and of the apprentice.

Had it not been for the variation in individual interest throughout an organization, knowledge sharing would have been a straightforward activity without much shirking, guile or resistance. In an organization populated only by altruists, who are interested beyond all else in helping others to learn, knowledge sharing would not represent a major concern to researchers concerned with organizational efficiency and innovation (Collard, 1978). However, empirical studies show that there are diverse and distributed interests behind knowledge production, barriers to knowledge sharing and people who find ways to teach less than they learn from others (e.g., Latour, 1993; 1987). Paul Carlile (2002) has shown that people's long-term investments in areas of expertise make them reluctant to share knowledge with representatives from other areas, and they tend to be very conscious of "boundaries" and diverse interests, which separate their work practices from those of other disciplines. Darrah's (1995) ethnography of a high-tech manufacturing firm is also interesting in this respect. Fearing the loss of authority, manufacturing engineers who possessed full information about the product design and manufacturing specifications, were reluctant to share this with front-line workers. As a negative result, the firm's attempt at lowering quality costs in manufacturing by training led to more frustration than skill enhancement among the workers. These studies, that pay explicit attention to diverse and distributed interests in organizations, conclude that knowledge sharing is a fragile and uncertain activity.[4]

A theory that explains why and under what conditions the collective act of knowledge sharing occurs, must therefore take into account a variety of interest and personality traits including self-interest and individuals who seek to maximize their own utility (see Ostrom, 2000).[5] Given the sequencing of activities and self-interest, free-riding on other's knowledge is also of some concern. In the context of this chapter, free-riding on knowledge means that one individual learns while hiding the learning process from the one who bestows the knowledge. Under certain circumstances, the free-rider will be able to obtain benefits from the knowledge that are equal to those a contributor can obtain (see von

Hippel and von Krogh, 2001). Hence, if someone gives knowledge, why should someone else be interested in reciprocating?

It should be observed that diverse interests in the organization are not necessarily negative. Since knowledge and interest are connected, also in the sense that individual interest influences an individual's learning, it stands to reason that the distribution of diverse interests gives rise to the miscellany and creativity organizations need in order to extract value from sharing knowledge. Moreover, when the mean level of knowledge is not sufficient in a group for solving a particular problem, diverse interests can facilitate knowledge sharing (e.g., Oliver, 1993). At times, the only way to realize individual interests is to jointly learn, especially under time pressure.

Given distributed and diverse interests, there are several ways to theorize why, and under what circumstances people share knowledge in organizations. Two fruitful areas are concerned with agency and the communal resource.

AGENCY IN KNOWLEDGE SHARING

Collective action problems in general could be resolved by an agency,[6] such as management, enforcing a regime of cooperation while being exogenous to the process. Whereas the agency might enforce a regime of knowledge sharing in the organization, it might have limited concern for the details of the knowledge shared, and hence its control might focus more on the structure for sharing, effectiveness of sharing, fairness and distributive justice, punishing of free-riders and so on.

The agency can make structural choices where changes are intended to increase the points of contacts or networks of organization members (Kransdorf, 1998). On the modest end of the scale, as Grant (1996) suggested, knowledge can be shared by forming a group that engages in problem solving and decision-making. This alternative is particularly relevant if the task's complexity is very high, and the face-to-face interaction of people is needed for performing it. Moreover, management might create a unit that directs and oversees knowledge sharing. A comparison of manufacturing costs among a firm's activities in various countries might reveal strong differences. Case studies have shown that in order to exploit these differences, management typically creates a new knowledge management unit, or a knowledge and technology transfer unit whose task is to identify the "best practices" among selected plants, and then foster the transfer and leverage of these practices throughout the firm on a worldwide basis (Dixon, 2000; von Krogh et al., 2000).

On the back of large-scale organization changes, Nonaka and Takeuchi's (Nonaka and Takeuchi, 1995) case studies showed that the management can choose a multi-layered organization structure, which they call the "hypertext organization"; a business system layer that covers the main tasks and business processes of the firm; a project layer where people collaborate to create new knowledge and innovate; and a knowledge-base layer which comprises the memory of the organization (e.g., positions, databases, organization culture, etc.).

Between these two extreme structural solutions to the sharing problem, we typically find the agency choosing matrix organization structures that combine business activities with a regional focus, or a functional focus with an industry or customer focus. The matrix structure is intended to increase the interconnectedness of functions, departments, groups, and regional centers. However, as Bartlett and Ghoshal (1987) point out, the "matrix" is more than a structure, it is a "frame of mind." By this, they imply that performance expectations for both vertical and horizontal activities require extensive sharing of knowledge, but that in order for such structures to work, local individual interests must be reflected in the overall corporate agenda, and an effective human resource management must be put in place. The knowledge management literature comes to similar conclusions. Because human interest and tacit knowledge are often involved, there are strong limitations in the structural solutions to the knowledge-sharing problem (see also Boisot, 1998; Grant, 1996). Simply increasing people's exposure to functions, projects, and knowledge, and even to other people, does not safeguard the collective learning in the firm. Hence, within the agency solution, the knowledge management literature suggested that well-functioning human resource management systems are imperative. Case studies have shown, in modern organizations, although information and communication technologies enable people to connect more effectively, the performance of teams and their knowledge sharing are linked with individual and team-based incentives (Govindarajan and Gupta, 2001).

In those instances where tacit knowledge cannot be codified, sharing it between people is slow, costly, and uncertain (Kogut and Zander, 1992). In an important paper, Osterloh and Frey (2000) discussed the question whether self-interested individuals are motivated to share knowledge extrinsically, through material incentives such as money, or intrinsically, through the actual activity itself. Intrinsically motivated individuals act for their immediate need satisfaction. In particular, the authors argue that if knowledge to be shared is tacit, the role of intrinsic motivation outweighs the role of extrinsic motivation. No material incentive can make people change their interest to codify and share their tacit knowledge, and no contract can assure effective and efficient knowledge sharing. Intrinsic motivation, by which team members realize immediate need satisfaction by working together with others in order to solve complex tasks, is a prerequisite for (tacit) knowledge sharing.

THE COMMUNAL RESOURCE

The remainder of this chapter will be devoted to the role of a "community" in explaining why people share knowledge in organizations. First, I provide a brief review of some of the central literature on communities within and outside the organizational context. Then I will proceed to discuss how diverse and distributed interests influence knowledge sharing in communities. Assuming that organizations are populated with people whose interests are dynamic rather than static, I finally discuss how opportunity structures and the social norms of care and authenticity could positively impact knowledge sharing.

The term "community" can be derived from a classical sociological premise that people form social bonds through shared norms, traditions, identity, and solidarity. By intense and sustained communication, members develop a shared sense of identity. Interestingly, this deep sense of identity, tradition, solidarity, and long-standing norms can make a binding commitment among community members to mobilize large-scale societal changes. If people experience grievances or entrepreneurs see opportunities for action, feelings of solidarity can bind people together in collective action (Calhoun, 1994; 1986; J.L. Cohen, 1985; Fantasia, 1988).

Building on a long tradition in sociology, anthropology, and economics, a growing number of authors have focused on the role of communities in knowledge sharing. For an overview, see table 19.1.

A very important stream of work on occupational communities has shown how people who practice similar work develop a shared identity related to their occupations. Shared identity and work practice enables mutual learning, as well as solidarity (e.g., Van Maanen and Barley, 1984; Orr, 1990a).

With the increasing importance of the Internet for communication within and between organizations, another group of authors have studied the nature of virtual communities, where keeping the anonymity of individuals often takes precedence over membership selection based on social categories such as occupation. Anonymity should enable a free-flow of information between the members since individual sharing will not be inhibited by the fear of possible future retaliation due to the contents of their messages (Myers, 1994). Research on communities of interest has focused on groups with shared interest in topics as well as personal relationships. However, in these communities, anonymity might be less pronounced than for virtual communities. Learning and exchange of information are central activities in communities of interest, and interactions are mostly limited to the personal needs of members to obtain explicit knowledge and information at low cost and high speed. In contrast to the two community types that will be discussed next, virtual and interest communities do not bind people together by occupation or socialization into a village, rural district, or peasant group.

An interesting stream of work relates to "imagined communities." Here, people "imagine oneness" with others they have never met or seen. The foundation of this solidarity is a set of effective and simple socially transmitted constructs, such as an area of expertise or nationality. Imagined communities can be powerful in terms of large-scale social change (Anderson, 1983; Calhoun, 1991). In case studies of micro-communities for knowledge sharing, it was observed that people tend to identify with similar groups of experts throughout the organization, even though they have never met face-to-face. This identification, in turn, could positively impact on the helping behavior across organizational boundaries (von Krogh et al., 1997). Studies on communities of work practice provide insight into the social fabric of communities in organizations, how they work, and the conditions that enable or constrain them. A community of practice is characterized by having members who share work activities and engagement, and by working together over a certain period of time, develop a shared identity, language, artifacts, norms and values.

Returning to our initial problem, although communities are certainly interesting for the purpose of studying how individuals behave apolitically and altruistically (Wolin, 1961), systematic attention must also be paid to the collective action problem of knowledge sharing resulting from distributed and diverse interests. A community acts collectively without outside intervention from an agency. A community has a certain stability of affiliation over time,[7] it has multiplex and direct relations between the actors (Taylor and Singleton, 1993), and there is some level of common information (or cues) about the

TABLE 19.1 Different concepts of "community" (based on and adapted from von Krogh and Wicki, 2001)

Concept of community	Characteristics	Authors
Rural/peasant communities	◆ People live in a shared space and have shared tasks ◆ Romantic and idealistic view ◆ Opposing the trend toward anonymity in modern industrial societies	Foster (1965) Bell/Newby (1971) Cohen (1985) Frankenberg (1969)
Occupational communities	◆ People share occupation ◆ Individual identity is influenced by the occupation ◆ Creation and nurturing of autonomous work cultures	Van Maanen and Barley (1984) Orr (1990a, 1990b) Bechky (1999)
Virtual communities	◆ Based in the Internet ◆ Often formed around shared interests ◆ Limited face-to-face interaction and no shared physical workspace ◆ Attributes such as status, gender, or occupation are irrelevant for interaction ◆ Strong focus on technical performance among members	Rheingold (1993) Jones (1995) Komito (1998) Kozinets (1999) Hildreth and Kimble (2000) Castells (1996) Fernback (1997) Poltrock and Engelbeck (1997) Anderson (1983) Calhoun (1991)
Communities of interest	◆ Based on shared interests and relationships (e.g. inline-skating, cooking, investing) ◆ Focus on shared learning ◆ Sporadic social interaction ◆ No collective engagement	Amstrong and Hagel (1995) Hagel and Amstrong (1997)
Imagined communities	◆ Community as symbolically constructed set of ideas ◆ Political/religious activities ◆ Solidarity in the community is constructed and projected, not really lived	
Micro-communities of knowledge	◆ Ideal for sharing tacit knowledge ◆ A collective identity emerges through collective engagement in the process of knowledge creation	Von Krogh, Nonaka, and Ichijo (1997) Von Krogh, Ichijo, and Nonaka (2000)
Communities of practice	◆ Shared identity, language, artifacts, norms, and values ◆ Collective engagement and activities ◆ Shared knowledge ◆ Shared learning through narration and story-telling ◆ Members are "experts" in the area of practice	Lave and Wenger (1981) Brown and Duguid (1991) Weick and Roberts (1993) Boland and Tenkasi (1995) Wenger (1998) Snyder (1999) Glynn (1999) Hildreth and Kimble (2000)

knowledge of the other members. However, the negative returns to size apply. A community is different from the production team (Alchian and Demsetz, 1972). The community is established, developed and maintained by its affiliates in a manner of "self-production." The production team to some extent relies on the agency that allocates a complex production task and external inputs, performs outside monitoring of output of production, and sanctions the team. Communities and production teams face the same challenge of self-monitoring. Internal processes are at work in the production team where members, who can observe others, can sanction these processes as well.

Because communities can be conducive for sharing knowledge, the term "resource" can be appropriate to use for communities.[8] Taylor and Singleton (1993) suggest that in the case where the community displays a high degree of collective interests, the community can lower social (transaction) costs. First, affiliates of a community have access to information (cues) about others' knowledge. Hence, it is a resource. Second, bargaining costs are lower in a community because beliefs, preferences, and interests are shared. Third, the level of shared interests, the expectations of continued interaction, and the direct and manifold relations among individuals all reduce monitoring costs involved in enforcement of compliance in knowledge sharing. Here it is important to note the multiplex character of relationships. For the organization in question, the lack of need for an agency and reduced monitoring costs could potentially make the community a valuable resource. For example, for a well-functioning community, management does not have to design a formal system for knowledge sharing, monitoring behavior of organization members, and enforcing compliance with the procedures and rules of the system. The community is also a resource because it attracts individuals to identifiable social and virtual gatherings where people share interests, tasks and knowledge.

A common thread in the literature on communities in organizations seems to be that organizational members have a collective interest in sharing knowledge. In organizations that comprise communities, people are rewarded not only for sharing knowledge in communities, but also for being self-interested, rational, and free-riding, in order to advance their career and improve their monetary position. A community will be comprised of people who may have diverse and distributed interests, and individual interests will not be stable over time. Therefore, the "community" should not be defined by its level of shared interests, but rather by its evolutionary stability. That is, the community is not a communal resource per se. Depending on the context of community interactions, a person's interests, namely motivational focus, definition of a situation, personal objectives, and guidelines for conduct, evolve over time. As Massey (1994) points out in her criticism of Taylor and Singleton (1993), because of these possible changes in people's interests, some communities are more inauspicious towards collective action. The point of departure for defining a community should be to what extent it is able to maintain its community characteristics over time despite its diversity, and for defining a communal resource, whether this community shares knowledge without the prerequisite of an agency that monitors and enforces cooperation.

It follows that communities can be resources, perhaps even "liabilities," and there is a need to examine the conditions for the communal resource, where knowledge sharing can happen without the agency.[9] I would suggest there are at least three factors associated with knowledge sharing in the community: opportunity structures, care, and authenticity.

Opportunity structures

First, opportunity structure refers to the occasion and benefits of sharing knowledge in the community. Since interest and knowledge are intimately connected, and since it takes more effort to identify sharing possibilities if affiliates have diverse interests (irrespective of community size), the opportunity structure of a community is a particularly important factor for the problem of knowledge sharing. The community is an arena, or in Nonaka and Konno's (1998) understanding, multiple "places," where affiliates can realize diverse interests over time as they see fit. Narrow opportunity structures imply that knowledge sharing benefits can only be realized through a limited number of relationships with affiliates, and sharing very specific knowledge at both a very specific time and place. In contrast, broad opportunity structures involve more relationships in the community that share broader knowledge, in a continuous manner, and in several places that are both virtual and physical (see Diemers, 2001).

The concept of "opportunity structures" does not assume that affiliates have "full knowledge" of other's knowledge, which by our definition of knowledge would be impossible. As found by MacKenzie (1998) in his studies of the transfer of tacit knowledge involved in the design and manufacture of highly complex technologies, for the interests in sharing to be evoked at a particular time and place, all that is needed is a *cue* about what the other affiliates are capable of. This cue is both a stimulus to perception and a hint on how to behave in certain circumstances. Although cues about knowledge can elucidate opportunities for sharing, it is also likely that much sharing will be improvised in the community. A history of interaction among affiliates allows the community to deeply improvise knowledge sharing. People will send and interpret cues as to when, where, and how knowledge sharing is appropriate. A system of cues allows sharing in a community to proceed without unnecessary interruption. It allows individuals to coordinate the realizations of their interests at a particular time and place; for example, avoiding every affiliate intruding on each other's activities at all times. In this sense there is a relationship between the system of cues in a community and the social cost, both in terms of searching for knowledge and in terms of bargaining about when sharing it is suitable. In particular, the system of cues guides the sharing of tacit knowledge because it affects the level, time, and type of interaction needed for this sharing.

In order to sustain collective action of knowledge sharing under adverse conditions, the opportunity structures could rely less on a system of cues and deep improvisation, and more on behavioral rituals. In this case, the community will attempt to create a routine for its own knowledge sharing and expect everyone to engage in it. Opportunity structures may be costly to identify and realize as the community grows in size. A large community will have an abundance of cues, more attempts at spontaneous sharing, and many rituals that serve the interests of powerful individuals. The community's efforts to monitor free-riding can be important too, for its ability to sustain knowledge sharing. The context here is that free-riding on knowledge means that one individual learns while hiding the learning process from the one who bestows the knowledge. Several solutions to the free-rider problem have been suggested. However, it is generally noted in contributions to the concept of collective action, that the free-rider problem can be overcome in the creation and deployment of selective incentives (Friedman and McAdam, 1992; Oliver, 1980).

Selective incentives can be monetary like a fine paid for not participating, but they can also be non-monetary. As argued above, especially if the knowledge to be shared is tacit, self-interested individuals cannot be motivated to share knowledge through extrinsic means and no contract can assure effective and efficient sharing of tacit knowledge. Selective monitoring of individual efforts is easier in a sufficiently small group where people meet and communicate face to face (Ostrom, 1998). Selective incentives are positive (reinforcing behavior) or negative (changing behavior) and they are directed not at the group as a whole, but to each individual within it (Olson, 1967: 43–52; Fireman and Gamson, 1979; Taylor and Singleton, 1993).

In order to mobilize people for collective action, a typical immaterial selective incentive is membership in social categories (Friedman and McAdam, 1992; Tajfel, 1982). Empirical studies show that people tend to classify themselves and others in terms of cognitive categories (Tajfel and Turner, 1979). A collective identity can be defined as a "people's sense of who they are in terms of some meaningful social category (for example occupational, gender, status, age, [Community of Practice] member, presence on the intranet, tech-clubs, etc.) that distinguishes how they interact with those inside than from those outside the category" (Roy and Parker-Gwin, 1999: 206).[10] Individuals derive utility from credentials bestowed on them as affiliates if these give privileged access to resources, knowledge, social relations, status reputation, and so on. Hence, a value can be assigned to the social category that will be affected by past and current community affiliation. The higher the category's value, the more effective is the non-monetary selective incentive.

In the larger community, opportunity structures tend to be less robust. Therefore, the value of credentials might decrease with the increasing community size. Also, when the community increases in size, the impact of any individual's participation in knowledge sharing is negligible and a self-interested, rational individual will choose to free-ride under these conditions (Hardin, 1971). The cost of an individual's decision to free-ride is spread over a greater number of people, and the cost of organizing and using selective immaterial incentives to induce cooperation of individuals increases as well (Marwell and Oliver, 1993). Eventually, as the group grows, the monitoring costs outgrow the costs of sharing, and jointly they could outweigh the rewards from knowledge sharing itself. The expected outcome is that the opportunity structure will be underprovided and the value of the communal resource will decrease.

Affiliates' limited attention and cognition and the cost of realizing knowledge sharing, make opportunity structures a constraint on the communal resource. Regarding the practice of knowledge management, a popular way of facilitating knowledge sharing in many organizations is through so-called "technical share fairs" or "knowledge fairs" (e.g., Davenport and Prusak, 1998). These are large exhibitions over several days where research teams, engineering teams, technical groups, etc., can exhibit information about their projects, areas of expertise, and technical pursuits. Through these fairs, organizations enlarge the opportunity structure for knowledge sharing. The fair might also contribute to the evolutionary stability of the community, whereby social relations are reinforced and new ones are created. However, in spite of the abundant opportunities found in such fairs, it is not clear at all that individuals will coordinate the sharing of knowledge. For sharing to be enabled in an evolutionary stable manner, it might be that the right social norms have to be in place.

Care

A non-monetary selective incentive would result from members creating and enforcing social norms that compel affiliates to knowledge sharing in a customary fashion (e.g., Heckatorn, 1993). In effect, strong socialization and loyalty to the social norm could moderate free riding in the group (Ferre, 1992; Hirschamn, 1970; Ostrom, 1999).

Care is a social norm in human relationships, and involves the dimensions of trust, active empathy, access to help, lenience in judgment, and the extent to which the former four dimensions are shared in the community (von Krogh, 1998).[11] In caring for another, a care provider may provide information and support for valuable knowledge for task execution, may integrate a person socially, give guidance, enhance social bonds, as well as helping to choose what output of task performance is to be presented to a larger audience. The only requirement for care to be a social norm is that more than one individual, even those self-interested, derives utility from complying with it.

Let us look more carefully at the dimensions of care and how they relate to knowledge sharing. First, the more the affiliates trust each other to share knowledge, the lower the social costs as mentioned by Taylor and Singleton (1993).[12] Second, the more lenience in judgment of other's knowledge, experience, and behavior, the more likely that diverse and distributed interests can persist among affiliates in the community. Interaction can happen in spite of diverse interest, while realizing that some opportunities for sharing knowledge might emerge at some later point in time, and where affiliates suspend their immediate realization of their own interests for the benefit of the community. Active empathy, the third component of care, is the attempt to "put yourself in the shoes of the other," understanding his or her particular situation, interests, skills levels, successes, failures, opportunities, and problems (von Krogh et al., 2000). "Active empathy" is the proactive attempt among community affiliates to understand the interests of others. It allows many different interests to co-exist over time, and should positively impact the learning and the use of subtle cues needed for the sharing of tacit knowledge.

Fourth, care in the community also has to develop into "real and tangible help." In the relationship between a master and apprentice, for instance, the master will teach the design of a tool, how to use a tool, how to maintain the tool, where to acquire the tool, and so forth. Help among affiliates might be given based on an affiliate's own experience, by sharing that knowledge, or simply by sharing the burden of the task, and thereby learning together. As a social norm, care, through helping behavior, should moderate the free-rider problem in larger communities where knowledge sharing plays out as a deep improvisation rather than a ritual. Where opportunity structures are narrow due to an affiliate's lack of interest in helping, his or her future community status might be endangered, yet if it matters to him, he is likely to change his behavior.

As mentioned above, in the communal resource, the natural sequence of the collective activities of (tacit) knowledge sharing must be preserved. When affiliates exhibit strong trust, active empathy towards each other, a strong inclination to help, as well as lenience in judgment, all these should have a positive impact on the suspended satisfaction of individual needs and the realization of interests. It is care that allows for evolutionary stability, that is, for the community to persist as a resource for knowledge sharing.

Authenticity

When interests are collective in the community, one can assume that the "best knowledge" will be shared. In the absence of self-interested people or free riders, there is no reason why people should pass on false information, sub-optimal procedures, etc. However, where interests are diverse and distributed it is possible that the social norm "authenticity" could have an impact on the community as a resource for knowledge sharing. "Authenticity" means that legitimate knowledge in the community is shared directly from the source in a way that ensures its genuineness, accuracy, validity, and reliability. The master-apprentice is a good example to help illustrate what this means. An apprentice observes the genuine know-how of the master first-hand. Accuracy of the shared knowledge depends on the apprentice's ability to observe a certain level of detail in the work of the master. Validity, in turn, refers to the apprentice's ability to appraise observations, interpretations, and one's own understanding of task performance with the master. Validity also refers to the extent to which the knowledge shared with the apprentice can be extended to the same or different tasks of the apprentice as well. Reliable knowledge enables the apprentice to resolve repeated tasks. Reliability, in turn, depends on the interest of affiliates to apply the knowledge shared in the collective action process. Hence, we will have to revisit the system of social norms outlined thus far.

Care is a social norm from which people derive utility by giving. However, if care is the only norm in social relationships, the community might end up with more knowledge giving, with limited collective action of knowledge sharing, or in other words, little learning and using. In the case of authenticity, people derive utility from searching out valid and genuine knowledge, but since sharing is a matter of collective action, people also derive utility from making this knowledge reliable by using it.

At the extreme, communities, can be self-preserving, conforming, retaliating, and punishing people who try to branch out and be inventive. Massey (1994) found that in groups with strong social norms and diverse interests, collective action can be highly unlikely due to the social costs faced by individuals pursuing their own courses of action. Further, a community might have affiliates that detest any new, superior knowledge, even if the benefits are immediate and collective. Rejection could be warranted from the cost resulting from bargaining about what is "really superior knowledge," or the unlearning of previous lessons learned. Individual interests in rejecting superior knowledge could quickly transform into a collective protest against any new knowledge that someone tries to introduce into the community. For example, the newcomer to the engineering community might find that in some areas of practice, it is worthwhile learning the lessons from experienced engineers. However, there might be new methods that are more productive and will enhance the performance of the whole community, such as the use of a computer-aided design (CAD) system. The experienced engineer might take cues about the newcomer's extraordinary, repeated ability to finish technical designs in a fraction of the time that it used to take. The newcomer may provide documents and manuals on the use of these systems to the other engineers. If care is strong, he might even personally teach the use of these systems to other engineers. In turn, some may take great interest in learning and using the newly shared knowledge. This sharing requires cues about capable behavior, and assumes

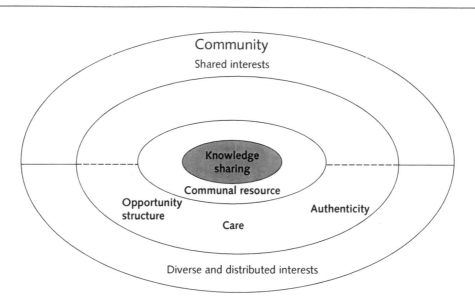

FIGURE 19.1   Factors influencing knowledge sharing in communities

that most community affiliates would be content to receive genuine, accurate, valid, and reliable solutions from those who have experience and insight. These experienced individuals in turn must be willing to share, as those who learn, must be willing to share what they experience with the new systems.

An overview of the argument is provided in figure 19.1. Communal resources are impacted by a community's characteristics, including the degree to which interests are diverse and distributed among affiliates. In particular, three factors taken together, opportunity structure, care, and authenticity, should impact knowledge sharing where interests are diverse and distributed. Opportunity structures here work as a constraint on knowledge sharing. As a social norm, care positively impacts an affiliate's ability to suspend the immediate satisfaction of needs and realization of opportunities for knowledge sharing, and to search for opportunities in spite of diverse interests. As a social norm, authenticity positively impacts the ability of affiliates to realize "better knowledge" within opportunity structures, to learn, and to improve. It is important to note that even if interests are shared, the community can be characterized by opportunity structures, care, and authenticity. However, I do not assume a priori collective interests in sharing knowledge among the affiliates, although the more collective the interests, the more powerful the communal resource for solving the social costs problem involved in the sequential collective action of knowledge sharing.

CONCLUSION AND RESEARCH IMPERATIVES

Knowledge sharing is a key process in many knowledge management activities, including the capture, transfer, and creation of knowledge. It might be more appropriate for future theory and research in knowledge management and organizational learning to consider knowledge sharing a problem of collective action among actors with diverse and distributed interests. The literature proposes two different solutions to this problem that are worthwhile examining. The first is to instate an agency, exogenous to the knowledge sharing, that structures, incentivizes, and monitors knowledge sharing, and punishes defiant behavior. Several problems are associated with this solution, such as choosing the right incentives for sharing and obtaining sufficient information for overseeing sharing activities with some degree of certainty.

Second, the communal resource reduces the social costs of sharing knowledge, thereby not needing to resort to an agency or to large numbers. However, where interests are diverse and distributed, the effectiveness of the community as a "communal resource" depends on its opportunity structures and social norms. Opportunity structures for knowledge sharing works on cues observed among people in the community. In terms of behavior, communities can "deeply improvise" or provide rituals. Care is a social norm that gives rise to trust, active empathy, helping behavior, and lenience in judgment. Authenticity is a social norm that gives credence to knowledge directly observed in action, as well as the willingness to be taught lessons of people with superior knowledge. If we assume people in an organization hold diverse and distributed interests that change over time, the evolutionary stability of the community matters for a theory of knowledge sharing in organizations. Several poorly understood factors gain significance for whether or not the community will reduce the social costs of knowledge sharing. Hence, the role of the community as a resource has still to be determined.

A number of research questions arise out of this discussion that should interest any knowledge management and/or organizational learning scholar, who cares about the communal resource. In the vein of the literature on communities within and outside organizations, we have assumed the existence of community a priori. However, as Wenger (1998) argues, there are distinct phases in the formation of a community that should be taken into account. Future research might investigate further what are the characteristics of the formation processes of communities, which support knowledge sharing? A related question concerns the composition of communities. Upon formation of communities, a central question to pursue would be if the new affiliate's background, diversity and distribution of interests influences the effectiveness of knowledge sharing, as well as the duration of the community.

A consequence of basing the definition of a community on concepts of collective action (e.g., Olson, 1967; Taylor and Singleton, 1993) is that researchers should consider the activities going on within the community as well as its evolutionary stability. Therefore, a community that ceases to operate is equally interesting as those that survive over long periods of time. Related to the evolutionary stability, a number of important questions emerge. How are opportunities for knowledge sharing found in the initial stage of community formation? What are the changes in opportunity structures as the community ages? One could argue that the inflow of newcomers refreshes viewpoints and regenerates the interest in and urge for new insights. How does the opportunity structure change with fluctuations in affiliation? Does a constant inflow of newcomers *actually* refresh viewpoints and regenerate the urge for new insights? What is the optimal turnover rate of affiliates, and how does this relate to the size of the community?

Furthermore, as Brown and Duguid (1991), and Wenger (1998) argue, communities of practice need available resources and time to develop. A similar argument is found in studies of collective action. Meeting in so-called free-spaces where resources and time are available, affiliates can act without being subject to agency monitoring, they can build social ties outside the existing social structures, and develop particular shared norms (Polletta, 1999). Some of these free-spaces might initially develop on the Inter- or Intranet (Townsend, 2000).

Care is a social norm in the community from which individuals derive utility. It would be interesting to investigate further the emergent rewards related to caring. What factors impact on the evolving care in community relationships? Do some caring people lead by example? What is the relationship between care and the integration of newcomers into the community? Previous work has identified costs to this social norm as well (von Krogh, 1998). Care can be misused as a strategy of over-helping by ignoring what people really need. Care can be used as a strategy of taking others to their own party. What is the relationship between care and over-helping behavior, and what is the consequence of over-helping for knowledge sharing in the community? Researchers working on issues in human resources management observe that studies of "caring occupations," such as nursing, have identified potential burnout of people who are expected to act both compassionately and effectively (Pines and Aronson, 1988; see also Sarason, 1985). Would a community among people who are expected to trade in emotions be related in any significant way to negative conditions, such as burnout or high personnel turnover? How does the pressure for externally oriented care relate to the emergence of social norms in such communities? Moreover, an issue that deserves attention in the research on learning in service organizations is the effect of externally and internally oriented care on the individual worker, in other words, how much care can people take? In my view, research on knowledge management and organizational learning in service organization, particularly those trading in sentiments, blind to the role of social norms and individual emotions, will be neither very insightful nor quite practical.[13]

Schwart and Tomz (1997) show formally that over time, agency can have great advantages over the community in terms of securing superior expertise and knowledge. The reason is that social norms maintained by the community but not questioned by the outside agency could have an adverse impact on accepting and integrating superior knowledge (see the argument above). This finding also raises questions regarding the potential negative impact of error-tolerance or lenience in judgment. What is the interplay between lenience in judgment and the cost of identifying "superior" knowledge? Also, there might be a difference between tacit and explicit knowledge worth noting. If authenticity is at work, how can affiliates deal with the difference in quality and robustness between ready-made explicit knowledge and tacit knowledge which evolves through learning?

And finally, as mentioned initially, most knowledge management researchers are interested in performance of both communities and firms. What are the best measures for community performance? How should we empirically study the performance of communities? Researchers, in particular those interested in strategic management, should investigate what characteristics of a community impact firm performance. Moreover, in some industries such as investment banking and management consulting, firms have hired whole teams rather than single individuals (human resources). If these teams display community characteristics outlined in this essay and in other works (see table 19.1), it would interesting to investigate and explain changes in the communal resource as it moves to a new organizational "home." Related to such investigations, what are the characteristics of capabilities that make firms outperform the industry average in terms of picking, developing and deploying communal resources (Makadok, 2001)? Do some firms actually learn to distinguish communal resources from communal liabilities, and do they have some particular capabilities of nurturing communities internally that make these more effective at reducing the social costs of knowledge sharing than in other firms?

A starting-point for answering these questions could be to investigate community performance and the interaction effects of human resource management systems. Communities and human resource management systems can pull employees in two directions: Individuals derive utility from both being self-interested, hoarding knowledge, and sharing knowledge in accordance with social norms emerging in community. Are there particular characteristics of human resource management systems, beyond incentives that are conducive to knowledge sharing in communities? In those instances when communities change their organizational home, and individuals change their exposure to human resource management systems, these interaction effects could be more pronounced.

Knowledge and organizational learning as a field of inquiry is here to stay. As a construct "knowledge" offers a powerful bridge between cognition and action, which improves the understanding of how organizations work, and how individuals operate within, with, and without organization. Hence, for those who take a serious interest in knowledge, learning, and organization, the future is filled with opportunities, challenges, and questions.

ACKNOWLEDGMENTS

I am grateful for comments from Marla Kameny, Marjorie Lyles, Margit Osterloh, Petra Kugler, Mattaeus Urwyler, Sebastian Spaeth, and one anonymous reviewer.

NOTES

1. Throughout the chapter I use the term "knowledge management" as a metaphor for activities aimed at reaching the organization's goal through the activities of capturing, sharing, and creating knowledge. It follows from the definition of knowledge that it cannot really be managed as such, but organizations can enable these activities in various forms.
2. When the master ignores the apprentice this could be a sign of disinterest, dissatisfaction, or doubt. In any event, the apprentice who wants to look good in the eyes of the master will most certainly be affected in his task performance and learning.
3. Similar conclusions have been reached in other studies of collective action in an organization setting, such as Monge et al. (1998), as well as McCaffrey et al. (1995).
4. A similar discussion is ongoing in economics where the topic is how psychological research modifies conceptions of an individual's utility function. An important insight is that people occasionally depart from pure self-interest to pursue "other-regarding" goals like altruism, fairness, and retaliation (Rabin, 1998).
5. An agent here means a person or group that exerts the power to produce an effect, and the agency refers to the activities of this person or group. The agency is exogenous to the

community. It is key to think of this solution as more encompassing than management in a company, since individuals in the organization may find various ways to actually enforce regimes of cooperation, like another colleague or a entity outside the organization.

6. I think the word "affiliation" is more appropriate than "membership" here in order to highlight the informal nature of the communal resource.

7. The word "communal resource" was first introduced by Taylor and Singleton (1993) although I use it differently here.

8. Interestingly, in their analysis of the community's ability to solve environmental problems, McCay and Jentoft (1998) come to very similar conclusions. Some environmental problems can be tracked back to community failure rather than a failure of the market or environmental agencies. Although their analysis tackles a different complex of problems, their study shows that researchers need to show care in identifying both positive and negative factors associated with collective action in communities.

10. I used "collective identity" here in a rather narrow sense. Some would include social norms, tradition, social relationships, and processes in identity (Stoecker, 1995).

11. An observer of the open source software development projects, such as operating system Linux, Himanen (2001) suggests that care is one of the most important social norms of communities of open source software developers. Care involves experienced programmers helping newcomers to learn, and improving the code others have made by debugging it. Although people normally are located at sites far apart, they work cooperatively over the Internet. Social norms make interactions easier and expectations to individual programmers easier to express and comply with.

12. Given the definition of interests in the paper, shared interests is not a prerequisite for trust.

13. The work of Sandelands (1988), Foner (1995), Fisher et al. (1983) provides a starting-point for further exploration of this issue.

REFERENCES

Alchian, A.A. and Demsetz, H. (1972) Production, Information Costs, and Economic Organization. *American Economic Review*, 62: 777–95.

Anderson, B.R. (1983) *Imagined Communities: Reflections on the Origin and Spread of Nationalism*. London: New Left Books.

Armstrong, A.G. and Hagel, J. (1995) Real Profits from Virtual Communities. *McKinsey Quarterly*, 5: 128–41.

Arthur, W.B. (1997) *Increasing Returns and Path Dependence in the Economy*. Ann Arbor, MI: The University of Michigan Press.

Bartlett, C.A. and Ghoshal, S. (1987) Tap Your Subsidiaries for Global Reach. *Harvard Business Review*, 64 (6): 87–94.

Bechky, B. (1999) Creating Shared Meaning across Occupational Communities: An Ethnographic Study of a Production Floor. Working paper, Philadelphia.

Bell, C. and Newby, H. (1971) *Community Studies*. London: Unwin Hyman.

Boisot, M. (1998) *Knowledge Assets: Securing Competitive Advantage in the Information Economy*. New York: Oxford University Press.

Boland, R.J. and Tenkasi, R.V. (1995) Perspective Making and Perspective Taking in Communities of Knowing. *Organization Science*, 4: 350–72.

Brown, J.S. and Duguid, P. (1991) Organizational Learning and Communities of Practice: Toward a Unified View of Working, Learning, and Innovation. *Organization Science*, 2: 40–57.

Calhoun, C. (1986) The Radicalism of Tradition: Community Strength or Venerable Disguise and Borrowed Language? *American Journal of Sociology*, 88 (5): 886–924.

Calhoun, C. (1991) Indirect Relationships and Imagined Communities: Large Scale Social Integration and the Transformation of Everyday Life. In P. Bordieu and J.S. Coleman (eds.), *Social Theory for a Changing Society*, Boulder, CO: Westview Press, 95–120.

Calhoun, C. (1994) Social Theory and the Politics of Identity. In C. Calhoun (ed.), *Social Theory and the Politics of Identity*. Oxford: Blackwell, 9–36.

Carlile, P. (2002) A Pragmatic View of Knowledge and Boundaries: Boundary Objects in New Product Development. *Organization Science*, 13 (4): 442–55.

Castells, M. (1996) *The Rise of the Network Society*. Malden: Blackwell.

Choo, C.W. (1998) *The Knowing Organization: How Organizations Use Information to Construct Meaning, Create Knowledge, and Make Decisions*. New York: Oxford University Press.

Cohen, A.P. (1985) The Symbolic Construction of Community. London: Tavistock.

Cohen, J.L. (1985) Strategy or Identity: New Theoretical Paradigms and Contemporary Social Movements. *Social Research*, 52 (4): 663–717.

Cohen, W. and Levinthal, D. (1990) Absorptive Capacity: A New Perspective on Learning and Innovation. *Administrative Science Quarterly*, 35: 128–52.

Collard, D. (1978) *Altruism and Economy: A Study in Non-selfish Economics*. New York: Oxford University Press.

Czikszentmihalyi, M. (1988) The Flow of Experience and its Significance for Human Psychology. In M. Czikszentmihalyi and I.S. Czikszentmihalyi (eds.), *Optimal Experience: Psychological Studies of Flow in Consciousness*. Cambridge: Cambridge University Press, 15–35.

Darrah, C.N. (1995) Workplace Training, Workplace Learning. *Human Organization*, 54: 31–41.

Davenport, T. and Prusak, L. (1998) *Working Knowledge*. Cambridge, MA: Harvard Business School Press.

Diemers, D. (2001) Virtual Knowledge Communities: Unpublished doctoral dissertation. Seminar for Sociology, St. Gallen: University of St. Gallen.

Dixon, N. (2000) *Common Knowledge*. Cambridge, MA: Harvard Business School Press.

Dreyfus, H.L. and Dreyfus, S.E. (1986) *Mind over Machine*. New York: MacMillan/Free Press.

Dyer, J. and Nobeoka, K. (2000) Creating and Managing a High-performance Knowledge-sharing Network: The Toyota Case. *Strategic Management Journal*, 21: 345–68.

Fantasia, R. (1988) *Cultures of Solidarity*. Berkeley: University of California Press.

Fernback, J. (1997) The Individual with the Collective: Virtual Ideology and the Realization of Collective Principles. In S.E. Jackson (ed.), *Creating Tomorrow's Organizations*. New York: John Wiley & Sons, 269–91.

Ferre, M.M. (1992) The Political Context of Rationality: Rational Choice Theory and Resource Mobilization. In A.D. Morris and C. McClurg (eds.), *Frontiers in Social Movement Theory*, New Haven: Yale University Press, 29–53.

Fireman, B. and Gamson, W.H. (1979) Utilitarian Logic in the Resource Mobilization Perspective. In M.N. Zald and J.D. McCarthy (eds.), *The Dynamics of Social Movements*. Cambridge, MA: Winthrop.

Fischer, J.D., Nadler, A., and De Paolo, B.M. (1983) *New Directions in Helping*. New York: Academic Press.

Foner, N. (1995) The Hidden Injuries of Bureaucracy. *Human Organization*, 54: 229–37.

Foster, G.M. (1965) Peasant Society and the Image of the Limited Good. *American Anthropologist*, 67: 289–315.

Frankenberg, R. (1969) *Communities in Britain: Social Life in Town and Country*. Harmondsworth: Ashgate Publishing Co.

Friedman, D. and McAdam, D. (1992) Collective Identity and Activism: Networks, Choices, and the

Life of a Social Movement. In A.D. Morris and C. McClurg (eds.), *Frontiers in Social Movement Theory*. New Haven: Yale University Press, 156–73.

Glynn, M.A. (1999) A Situated Learning Perspective on the Emergence of Knowledge and Identity in Cognitive Communities. *Advances in Management Cognition and Organizational Information Processing*, 6: 171–94.

Govindarajan, V. and Gupta, A. (2001) Building an Effective Global Business Team. *Sloan Management Review*, 42 (4): 63–71.

Grant, R.M. (1996) Towards a Knowledge-based Theory of the Firm. *Strategic Management Journal*, 17: 109–22.

Hagel, J. and Amstrong, A.G. (1997) Net Gain: Expanding Markets through Virtual Communities. Boston: Harvard Business School Press.

Hardin, R.R. (1971) Collective Action as an Aggregate N-prisoner's Dilemma. *Behavioral Science*, 16: 472–81.

Heckatorn, D. (1993) Collective Action and Group Heterogeneity: Voluntary Provision versus Selective Incentives. *American Sociological Review*, 58 (3): 329–50.

Hildreth, P. and Kimble, C. (2000) Communities of Practice in the Distributed International Environment. *Journal of Knowledge Management*, 4: 27–38.

Himanen, P. (2001) *The Hacker Ethic*. New York: Random House.

Hirschman, A.O. (1970) *Exit, Voice, and Loyalty*. Cambridge, MA: Harvard University Press.

Jones, S.G. (1995) Understanding Community in the Information Age. In S.G. Jones (ed.), *Computer Mediated Communication and Community*. London: Sage Publications, 10–35.

Kaeser, P. (2001) Knowledge Activists, Knowledge Transfer and Creation: Unpublished PhD dissertation. University of St. Gallen.

Kluege, J., Stein, W., and Licht, T. (2001) *Knowledge Unplugged*. Basingstoke: Palgrave.

Kogut, B. and Zander, U. (1992) Knowledge of the Firm, Combinative Capabilities, and the Replication of Technology. *Organization Science*, 3: 383–97.

Komito, L. (1998) The Net as a Foraging Society: Flexible Communities. *The Information Society*, 14: 97–106.

Kozinets, R.V. (1999) *E-tribalizing Marketing? The Strategic Implications of Virtual Communities*. Boston.

Kransdorf, A. (1998) *Corporate Amnesia: Keeping Know-how in the Company*. Oxford: Butterworth-Heinemann.

Latour, B. (1987) *Science in Action*. Cambridge: Harvard University Press.

Latour, B. (1993) *The Pasteurization of France*. Cambridge: Harvard University Press.

Lave, J. and Wenger, E. (1991) Situated Learning: Legitimate Peripheral Participation. Cambridge: Cambridge University Press.

Leonard, D. and Sensiper, S. (1998) The Role of Tacit Knowledge in Group Innovation. *California Management Review*, 40 (3): 112–32.

MacKenzie, D. (1998) *Knowing Machines: Essays on Technical Change*. Cambridge, MA: MIT Press.

Makadok, R. (2001) Towards a Synthesis of the Resource-based and Dynamic Capability View of Rent Creation. *Strategic Management Journal*, 22: 387–402.

Marwell, G. and Oliver, P. (1993) *The Critical Mass in Collective Action: A Micro-social Theory*. Cambridge: Cambridge University Press.

Massey, R.I. (1994) Impediments to Collective Action in a Small Community. *Politics and Society*, 22 (3): 421–35.

McCay, B.J. and Jentoft, S. (1998) Market or Community Failure? Critical Perspectives on Common Property Research. *Human Organization*, 57: 21–9.

McCaffrey, D.P., Faerman, S.R., and Hart, D.W. (1995) The Appeal and Difficulties of Participative Systems. *Organization Science*, 6 (6): 603–27.

Merleau-Ponty, M. (1995) *Phenomenology of Perception*. Trans. Colin Smith. London: Routledge.

Monge, P.R., Fulk, J., Kalman, M.E., Flanagin, A.J., Parnassa, C., and Rumsey, S. (1998) Production of Collective Action in Alliance-based Inter-organizational Communication and Information Systems. *Organization Science*, 9 (3): 411–33.

Myers, D.J. (1994) Communication Technology and Social Movements: Contributions.

Nelson, R. and Winter, S.G. (1982) *An Evolutionary Theory of Economic Change*. Cambridge, MA: Belknap.

Nonaka, I. (1994) A Dynamic Theory of Organizational Knowledge Creation. *Organization Science*, 5: 14–37.

Nonaka, I. and Konno, N. (1998) The Concept of "Ba": Building a Foundation for Knowledge Creation. *California Management Review*, 40: 40–54.

Nonaka, I. and Takeuchi, H. (1995) *The Knowledge Creating Company*. New York: Oxford University Press.

Oliver, P.E. (1980) Rewards and Punishment as Selective Incentives for Collective Action: Theoretical Investigations. *American Journal of Sociology*, 85: 1356–75.

Oliver, P. (1993) Formal Models of Collective Action. *Annual Review of Sociology*, 19: 271–300.

Oliver, P. and Marwell, G. (1988) The Paradox of Group Size in Collective Action: A Theory of Critical Mass II. *American Sociological Review*, 53: 1–8.

Oliver, P.E., Marwell, G., and Teixeira, R. (1985) Theory of the Critical Mass I: Interdependence, Group Heterogeneity, and the Production of Collective Goods. *American Journal of Sociology*, 91: 522–56.

Olson, M. (1967) *The Logic of Collective Action*. Cambridge, MA: Harvard University Press.

Orr, J. (1990a) *Talking about Machines: An Ethnography of a Modern Job*. Ithaca, NY: Cornell University Press.

Orr, J. (1990b) Sharing Knowledge, Celebrating Identity: War Stories and Community Memory in a Service Culture. In D. Middleton and D. Edwards (eds.), *Collective Remembering, Memory in Society*. Beverly Hills: Sage Publications, 169–89.

Osterley, M. and Frey, B.S. (2000) Motivation, Knowledge Transfer, and Organizational Forms. *Organization Science*, 11 (5): 538–50.

Ostrom, E. (1998) A Behavioral Approach to the Rational Choice Theory of Collective Action. *American Political Science Review*, 92 (1): 1–22.

Ostrom, E. (1999) Coping with the Tragedies of the Commons. *Annual Review of Political Science*, 2: 493–535.

Ostrom, E. (2000) Crowding Out Citizenship. *Scandinavian Political Studies*, 23 (11): 3–16.

Pines, A.M. and Aronson, E. (1988) *Career Burnout*. New York: Free Press.

Polanyi, M. and Prosch, H. (1975) *Meaning*. Chicago: University of Chicago Press.

Polletta, F. (1999) Free-spaces in Collective Action. *Theory and Society*, 28: 1–38.

Poltrock, S. and Engelbeck, G. (1997) Requirements for a Virtual Collocation Environment. In S.C. Hayne and W. Prinz (eds.), *Group '97 Proceedings of the International ACM SIG Group Conference on Supporting Group Work*. Phoenix: 61–70.

Powell, W. (1998) Learning from Collaboration: Knowledge and Networks in the Biotechnology and Pharmaceutical Industries. *California Management Review*, 40 (3): 228–40.

Rabin, M. (1998) Psychology and Economics. *Journal of Economic Literature*, XXXVI: 11–46.

Rheingold, H. (1993) A Slice of Life in my Virtual Community. In L.M. Harasim (ed.), *Global Networks, Computers and International Communication*. Cambridge, MA: MIT Press, 57–80.

Roy, W.G. and Parker-Gwin, R. (1999) How Many Logics of Collective Action? *Theory and Society*, 28: 203–37.

Sandelands, L.E. (1988) The Concept of Work Feeling. *Journal for the Theory of Social Behavior*, 18: 437–57.

Sarason, S. (1985) *Caring and Compassion in Clinical Practice*. San Francisco: Jossey-Bass.

Schwart, E.P. and Tomz, M.R. (1997) The Long-run Advantages of Centralization for Collective Action. *American Political Sciences Review*, 92 (3): 685–93.

Snyder, W.M. (1999) Organization and World Design. Working paper, Social Capital Group. Cambridge, MA.

Spender, J.-C. (1996) Making Knowledge the Basis for a Dynamic Theory of the Firm. *Strategic Management Journal*, 17: 45–62.

Stehr, N. (1994) *Knowledge Societies*. London: Sage.

Stoecker, R. (1995) Community, Movement, Organization: The Problem of Identity Convergence in Collective Action. *Sociological Quarterly*, 36: 111–21.

Szulanski, G. (1996) Exploring Internal Stickiness: Impediments to Transfer of Best Practice within the Firm. *Strategic Management Journal*, 17: 27–44.

Tajfel, H. (1982) *Social Identity and Integroup Relations*. Cambridge: Cambridge University Press.

Tajfel, H. and Turner, J.C. (1979) An Integrative Theory of Inter-group Conflict. In W.G. Austin and S. Worchel (eds.), *The Social Psychology of Inter-group Relations*. Monterey, CA: Brooks/Coole.

Taylor, M. and Singleton, S. (1993) The Communal Resource: Transaction Cost and the Solution to Collective Action Problems. *Politics and Society*, 21 (2): 195–214.

Townsend, A.M. (2000) Solidarity.com? Class and Collective Action in the Electronic Village. *Journal of Labor Research*, XXI (3): 393–405.

Van Maanen, J. (1991) The Smile-Factory: Work at Disneyland. In P. Frost, L.F. Moore, M.R. Louis, C.C. Lundberg, and J. Martin (eds.), *Rethinking Organizational Culture*. Newburry Park, CA: Sage, 58–76.

Van Maanen, J. and Barley, S.R. (1984) Occupational Communities: Culture and Control in Organizations. In L. Cummings and B. Staw (eds.), *Research in Organizational Behavior*. Greenwich, CT: JAI Press, 287–365.

Von Hippel, E. and von Krogh, G. (2001) Open Source Software Development: Issues for Organization Research. Working paper.

Von Krogh, G. (1998) Care in Knowledge Creation. *California Management Review*, 40: 133–54.

Von Krogh, G. and Koehne, M. (1998) Der Wissenstransfer in Unternehmen: Phasen des Wissenstransfer und Einflussfaktoren. *Die Unternehmung*, 52: 235–52.

Von Krogh, G. and Wicki, Y. (2001) Organisationales Wissen und Praktikergemeinschaften. In N. Thom and R.J. Zaugg (eds.), *Excellence durch Personal und Organisationskompetenz*. Berne: Paul Haupt, 269–90.

Von Krogh, G., Ichijo, K., and Nonaka, I. (2000) *Enabling Knowledge Creation*. New York: Oxford University Press.

Von Krogh, G., Nonaka, I., and Ichijo, K. (1997) Develop Knowledge Activists! *European Management Journal*, 15 (5): 133–54.

Weick, K.E. and Roberts, K.H. (1993) Collective Mind in Organizations: Heedful Interrelating on Flight Decks. *Administrative Science Quarterly*, 38: 357–81.

Wenger, E. (1998) *Communities of Practice: Learning, Meaning, and Identity*. Cambridge: Cambridge University Press.

Wolin, S. (1961) *Politics and Vision*. London: Allen and Unwin.

20

Organizational Forgetting

Pablo Martin de Holan and Nelson Phillips

Chapter Outline

Although the creation and transfer of organizational knowledge have been the focus of intensive investigation by management researchers, one aspect of the dynamics of knowledge – "organizational forgetting" – has received comparatively little attention. In this chapter, we explore the notion of organizational forgetting and relate it to the associated processes of knowledge transfer and creation. We go on to argue that forgetting is the necessary counterpart of learning and that attempts to manage knowledge must also include attempts to manage forgetting. We conclude with a discussion of an agenda for research on organizational forgetting.

Introduction

The imposing architecture of the Hotel Lutetia dominates the corner of Rue de Sevres and Rue de Babylone in Paris. The hotel has been renowned for over a century for its exquisitely decorated rooms, its impeccable service, and, as one would expect for a Parisian luxury hotel, for its gourmet restaurant. Yet this fine luxury hotel has not always been merely a hotel. When the German army entered Paris during World War II, its commanders requisitioned it to act as the Headquarters of the l'Abwehrleitstelle, the French branch of the German army's secret service (see Delarue, 1962), and to keep it operating at its usual standard of excellence, the German soldiers kept a significant part of the hotel staff on in their usual jobs.

This created a number of conflicts of interest. One of the most critical problems centered on the restaurant's impressive wine cellar that included some of the most prestigious and expensive French wines to be found in the city. The hotel staff took pride in the quality and variety of the cellar. So much pride, in fact, that when it became clear that the German army would requisition the Lutetia, they decided they had to do something to protect it. The decision was quickly made to eradicate all traces of the cellar, believing that if it were forgotten, it would survive the war. Accordingly, the staff proceeded to remove the door that led to the cellar, and to build and paint a wall to completely hide the entrance. From an organizational point of view, the cellar was "forgotten": while individuals remembered the cellar, from the Lutetia's perspective it was gone, and for the German soldiers it had never existed.

But it was not quite so simple. The new occupants of the building became suspicious when the staff claimed they did not have the wines selected by the German officers for their meals, and their suspicions grew stronger when menus and winelists dating from the pre-occupation days were found. Upset by this evidence, a German officer ordered a thorough search for the wine cellar and then demanded to see the building's blueprints. To his great frustration, he could find neither and, faced with more pressing problems than a missing wine cellar, soon dropped the matter.

After the war, and a brief stint as a sorting center for returning French prisoners of war, the Lutetia once again became a luxury hotel. As the staff had hoped, the cellar had survived the war unscathed, and once the door was restored, the restaurant once again had one of the finest wine cellars in Paris. However, by that time all copies of the old wine list had disappeared and the hotel had to embark on the time-consuming task of making a new inventory of the cellar.[1]

The story of the Hotel Lutetia raises a number of interesting questions for researchers interested in organizational knowledge. First, the decision to organizationally "forget" the wine cellar highlights the fact that although the focus in the literature has been on organizational *learning*, in some situations organizations may need to *eliminate* knowledge rather than develop new knowledge; in other words, to forget rather than to learn (e.g., Bettis and Prahalad, 1995; Lyles and Schwenk, 1992). Second, the difficulty the Lutetia experienced when it tried to eliminate all traces of its cellar points to the fact that forgetting may not be an easy task to manage. Forgetting may require significant management effort to succeed and how forgetting should be managed remains unclear. Third, the accidental loss of the wine list is a good example of the less positive kind of forgetting where an organization forgets something that it needs to remember. Research and experience show that organizational knowledge generally decays over time and that valuable knowledge can be lost, often involuntarily. How this process works, how this kind of forgetting can be minimized, and how to reduce the organizational impact of forgetting are not well understood yet.

In this chapter, we focus on the idea of organizational forgetting in all three of the above senses. We argue that the focus on "learning" has led to an under-emphasis on the equally important process of organizational forgetting and that the ongoing discussion of organizational learning needs to be complemented by a much clearer idea of how organizations "forget" or "unlearn." In focusing on organizational forgetting, we make three contributions to current thinking on knowledge management and organizational learning. First, we begin to answer the call from a number of academic (e.g. Bettis and Prahalad, 1995; Hedberg, 1981; Nystrom and Starbuck, 1984) and popular sources (e.g. Peters, 1992, 1994) to include a consideration of forgetting in discussions of organizational learning and knowledge management. Second, we provide a model linking organizational memory, learning, and forgetting. Finally, we begin a discussion of a future research agenda for the investigation of organizational forgetting. We believe that forgetting has the potential to add an important new dimension to our understanding of the dynamics of organizational knowledge, but this will require an extensive and dedicated program of research.

We present our argument in four steps. First, we review existing work on organizational knowledge, learning, and memory as a frame for discussing forgetting. Second, we introduce the idea of forgetting and present a model drawing on our research in the area. Third, we discuss the dynamics of organizational forgetting and its consequences for the organization. Finally, we conclude with some of the ramifications of a theory of forgetting for management research and practice and discuss directions for future research.

ORGANIZATIONAL LEARNING

The concept of organizational knowledge has proven to be a powerful tool in explaining the nature and behavior of firms (e.g., Kogut and Zander, 1996; Miles et al., 1998; Nahapiet and Ghoshal, 1998). Firms can be described as "repositories of knowledge" (Conner, 1991; Conner and Prahalad, 1996) that is embedded in assets, rules (Levitt and March, 1988), routines (Nelson and Winter, 1982), standard operating procedures (Cyert and March, 1963) and dominant logics (Bettis and Prahalad, 1995; Prahalad and Bettis, 1986).

Furthermore, researchers have gone on to argue that possessing organizational knowledge, and being able to produce new knowledge, are fundamental to sustained competitive advantage (Kogut and Zander, 1992; Prahalad and Hamel, 1990; Rumelt et al., 1994; Teece et al., 1997). As Grant argues, "the primary role of the firm, and the essence of organizational capability, is the integration of knowledge" (Grant, 1996; Spender and Grant, 1996). Firms exist because they can integrate and coordinate specialized knowledge held by individuals in a more efficient way than markets, and can transform that individual knowledge into collective, organizational knowledge (see also Barnard, 1938; Grant, 1996; Miles et al., 1998). In turn, that knowledge leads to advantage, because – all things being equal – knowledge is difficult to copy, is causally ambiguous, and typically beyond the grasp of rivals. When that knowledge is valuable and used appropriately, firms can enjoy sustained competitive advantage. Therefore, possessing knowledge and being capable of producing new knowledge are keys to organizational competitiveness.

It is not surprising, therefore, that the topic of organizational learning has received significant attention in the literature (e.g., Crossan et al., 1999; Daft and Huber, 1987; Dodgson, 1993; Duncan and Weiss, 1979; Easterby-Smith et al., 2000; Fiol and Lyles, 1985; Levitt and March, 1988; Miner and Mezias, 1996). While reviewing the entire literature on organizational learning is beyond the scope of this chapter, it is important to define the central concepts that appear in the literature – knowledge, learning, and momory – as a foundation for our discussion of forgetting. Learning theorists such as Huber (1991) and Levitt and March (1998) understand knowledge as a collective set of assumptions about organizational actions and their consequences (Schulz, 2001) and learning as the process that allows organizations to produce knowledge from their experiences (Huber, 1991). Accordingly, it can be claimed that at a broad organizational level, learning involves the development and testing of knowledge, insights, and associations regarding causal relations, and ultimately the selection of courses of action that satisfy organizational objectives. Learning, thus, can be thought of as the development of associations between actions and their consequences (Fiol and Lyles, 1985; Lyles, 1988).

Regardless of the method of production, it is generally accepted that organizational knowledge is embedded in some sort of organizational memory that does not disappear as individuals come and go. Rather than belonging to individual members, organizational knowledge is a distinct attribute of the organization as a social actor, distinguishable – and substantively different – from the knowledge of individuals (Ghoshal and Moran, 1996; Nahapiet and Ghoshal, 1998; Nelson and Winter, 1982; Selznick, 1957). Levitt and March (1988), for example, claim that organizational learning is codifying experiences into rules that guide behavior; these rules, and the routines that they create are the "crystallization of (organizational) knowledge" (Nelson and Winter, 1982). Although is it clear that not all new rules or routines emerge from learning processes, nor is all learning automatically translated into new rules (Schulz, 1998) and/or routines, it remains clear that learning and storing are intrinsically related, and that storing systems are essential for the successful completion of learning processes.

Thus, organizational memory acts as the central organizational system involved in the storage of the results of the knowledge produced by processes of organizational learning; learning can be seen as "organizational memory development" (Cross and Bayrd, 2000). Current conceptualizations of organizational memory (Moorman and Miner, 1998; Stein, 1995) are principally based on Walsh and Ungson's (1991) seminal work, which defined memory as stored information from an organization's history that can be brought to bear on present decisions. Memory is composed of a series of decisional stimuli kept in various "storage bins" which have behavioral consequences when retrieved (Walsh and Ungson, 1991). In this chapter, we will follow Olivera's conceptualization of memory as the "sets of knowledge retention devices . . . that collect, store and provide access to the organization's experience" (Olivera, 2000: 815), concluding that organizational learning produces organizational knowledge that is in turn stored in organizational memory. But how and under what circumstances do organizations lose things from their memory systems? Put another way, when and why do they "forget"?

FORGETTING: AN OVERVIEW

Contrasting definitions of learning aside, the focus of existing research on organizational knowledge tends to be on knowledge production and transfer (Schulz, 2001), rather than on how, and under what circumstances, knowledge is lost or purposefully removed from memory. Processes of forgetting or "unlearning" have been mentioned explicitly by a few researchers (e.g. Bettis and Prahalad, 1995; Day, 1994a, 1994b; Nystrom and Starbuck, 1984), but seldom as the main object of the research. Anand and associates, for example, present a clear example of forgetting, although the notion itself is not subsequently developed in their discussion (Anand et al., 1998: 798).

Similarly, Peters (1994: 128) is clear on the fact that forgetting (or "unlearning") is important, but doesn't take it much further than this vivid vignette:

The issue for Ford Motor Co., home of the original whiz kids, and others in the 1980s was forgetting – that is, unlearning the habits attached to a once-viable way of life . . . In 1938 the company tried to build a small car and failed miserably. "Small car" was translated by Ford's engineers into "shrunken big car". A stubby, expensive, over-engineered product emerged. Not only was Ford snared by yesterday's routines (big-car design was the only variety the firm's engineers knew), but it then overlearned from its 1938 error – that is, "We don't know how to build small cars."

Building on anecdotes, researchers have generally taken one of two approaches to forgetting. On the one hand, researchers have argued that organizations may forget accidentally, resulting in serious negative consequences for competitiveness. Some have gone on to document how an organization's pool of knowledge may dissipate rapidly (Argote et al., 1990; Darr et al., 1995; Epple et al., 1991) due to processes of knowledge loss caused by faulty or inadequate memory systems. This phenomenon can obviously have serious negative effects on productivity, profitability, and competitiveness (Argote, 1999).

The general perspective on this process in the literature is summarized by Day (1994a): "Organizations without practical mechanisms to remember what has worked and why will have to repeat their failures and rediscover their success formulas over and over again." Avoiding forgetting how to do valuable things is therefore as important as learning new things in retaining competitiveness. But, while the importance of not forgetting critical knowledge has been emphasized in the literature, the causes of forgetting have not been explored in any detail. The one exception is found in the work of Argote, who hypothesized that knowledge depreciation may happen because "products or processes change and render old knowledge obsolete . . . organizational records are lost or become difficult to access . . . [because of] member turnover" (Argote, 1999). However, while this work is a good starting-point, it does not get us very far in developing a theory of this sort of forgetting.

On the other hand, a number of writers adopt Peters' approach and point to the importance of "unlearning" to effective organizational learning and to the negative consequences of inertia (Miller, 1990, 1993). It is argued that organizations must forget old habits in order to learn new and more appropriate ways of doing things. Anand and colleagues (1998), for example, state that there are circumstances (such as environmental turbulence) when "the existing memory may be an obstruction rather than an aid to information management. Disruption and recreation of portions of the organization's memory may be required." Similarly, Crossan and her associates (1999) argue that "the tension between assimilating new learning (feed forward) and using what has already been learned (feedback) arises because the institutionalized learning (what has already been learned) impedes the assimilation of new learning." They are not alone. Many researchers (e.g., Bettis, 1991, Miller, 1990, 1994) have argued that the failure to discard or "unlearn" old dominant logics is one of the main reasons why organizations find it so difficult to change, even if they see clear evidence of changes in their environment. Unlearning, in this case the ability to discard an old logic in order to provide room for a new one, is seen as an essential part of learning: "strategic learning and unlearning of the kind involved in the dominant logic are inextricably intertwined" (Bettis, 1991). Others (Hedberg, 1981) have pointed out that an inability to unlearn can be a major organizational weakness, and some will go as far as

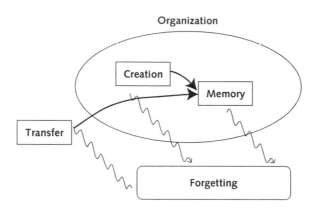

FIGURE 20.1   Modes of organizational forgetting

claiming that "firms that can unlearn and reframe their past success programs to fit with changing environmental and situational conditions will have a greater likelihood of survival and adaptation" (Lyles, 1988).

Combining these two streams of argument – that forgetting is both necessary and positive and unnecessary and negative – it is clear from the literature that forgetting is an important part of the dynamics of knowledge in organizations. In some contexts and at some times forgetting is a good thing for an organization; in other contexts and at other times the exact same loss of knowledge will be a very bad thing indeed. At the most fundamental level, we can assume that the relationship between organizational forgetting and other dynamics of knowledge are dependent on a variety of contingent factors. In the remainder of this chapter we will summarize what we know to date in order to answer an important questions: how do organizations forget?

MODES OF ORGANIZATIONAL FORGETTING

Our model of the relationship between knowledge creation, knowledge transfer, and forgetting is shown in figure 20.1.

The model in figure 20.1 summarizes our understanding of the varieties of organizational forgetting, which we divide in three modes. First, organizations can fail to successfully integrate knowledge transferred from another organization, or created internally, into its memory system. In figure 20.1, knowledge transfer processes are allowing some knowledge to make its way from an external organization to organizational memory, but some part (the wavy line) is being lost. Similarly, knowledge creation activities are producing knowledge on an ongoing basis, but some of that knowledge is dissipating before it is successfully integrated into memory. In both cases, knowledge enters the organization but then there is a failure to integrate it into the memory system and so it is lost. The second mode occurs when knowledge is successfully integrated into memory, but is lost due to a failure of the memory system. When this occurs, the organization loses some capability and some effort will be required to recreate the knowledge that was lost. The example of the lost wine list at the Lutetia Hotel is an excellent example of this kind of forgetting. The final mode involves knowledge that has made its way successfully into the memory system, but then is purposively forgotten. There are several possible reasons why an organization may want to forget. For example, organizations may need to forget some kinds of knowledge as part of an organizational change effort. Alternatively, it may be simply that the ongoing maintenance of the knowledge is consuming valuable organizational resources despite the fact that the organization no longer requires the knowledge.

In the remainder of the section we will explore each of the three modes of forgetting shown in the model in more detail. We will draw on existing literature and use a number of examples from a study of joint venture hotels that we conducted (Martin de Holan, 1998, 1999; Martin de Holan and Phillips, 1997). The research focused on six hotels operated by a major Cuban hotel chain and two of its international partners. The Cuban hotel chain is owned by a large, vertically integrated conglomerate, operating principally but not exclusively in the tourism industry; its two foreign partners are large Western companies, well known for their extensive experience in the hotel industry. All of the hotels we studied were either newly constructed at the time of the initiation of the strategic alliance, or had been reopened after several years of remodeling and revamping. This has the effect of creating a consistent low level of organizational memory and organizational performance in each hotel at the beginning of the study. It was therefore an ideal place to study the processes of knowledge mobilization, organizational learning and organizational forgetting.

The Importance of Organizational Forgetting

The need to mobilize (that is, to transfer and to create) knowledge was the primary rationale behind the strategic alliances we studied; these were learning alliances (Koza and Lewin, 2000; March, 1991) whose explicit objective was to help both partners learn to provide state-of-the-art tourism facilities in Cuba by creating new knowledge based on the existing knowledge base of each partner. As both partners firmly believed that only the combination of their expertise could provide the basis for rapid learning, the roles assigned to each were distinct and complementary: the international partner was in charge of providing the much-needed expertise and market knowledge necessary to run a world-class hotel; the role of the Cuban partner was to provide qualified labor, managerial systems and knowledge about the peculiarities of doing business in the Cuban context.

While learning was the primary motivation of the alliances, forgetting rapidly appeared as an important activity that needed to be addressed by managers. Two interrelated dimensions of learning emerged, complemented by equal but opposite dimensions of forgetting. The first dimension of learning and forgetting is linked to the pre-existing knowledge of individuals, who come to the organization with their own sets of skills, knowledge, and worldviews or "cosmogonies" (Weick, 1994). For example:

[The Cuban employees] are used to working in a certain way. Their attitude is . . . very difficult to change, they do it always the same way. So you show them something and you say:

do it this way because it is much better, and you show them. If you do not follow up every day to see what they do, in a week they are back to the system they are used to, a system where things are easy. So, you have to follow up on their work, . . .

Q – Do you have any examples of this?

They, they . . . it is small things, maybe the front desk, just taking messages, or answering the phone, making sure the guest receives the call. These are small things they do in a certain way, and sometimes they just forget, they go back to their system. (Housekeeping manager, Withwind Hotel,[2] French Canadian)

The second dimension of learning and forgetting is organizational, and involves the presence and renewal of dominant logics (Bettis and Prahalad, 1995; Lyles and Schwenk, 1992; Prahalad and Bettis, 1986). We consider these dominant logics as the organizational equivalent of the cosmogony, as they translate in systems of procedures that modify both behaviors and justifications for these behaviors. When these dominant logics are inadequate to the requirements of the context, they act as barriers to learning.

At the beginning my work was too schematic, managers said that everything had to be done according to the manual, and I had an idea to improve the way we did the bed, to give better service, we found a better way with one of the maids. Well, we couldn't implement it because everything was so schematic, everything was done by the book. (Housekeeping manager, Cuban, Montelimar)

In that sense, forgetting pre-existing organizational knowledge (that is, dropping some of the rules and procedures that were part of the partner's knowledge base) appeared as a necessary first step to *initiate* processes of knowledge creation. Whereas it was assumed that an organization initiating operations *tabula rasa* needed only to start accumulating knowledge, forgetting knowledge that pre-existed the organization became an important task. It appeared that although the business units did not have established procedures and routines, the individuals in charge had clear views about how it was to operate and what activities were needed, and the partners in the alliance had entrenched procedures and routines and ideas about how things ought to be done and why. For example,

[I came here] to train and to run the room side of the hotel as I would do it at home, as close as possible, to follow Alpha's policies and procedures, to implement Alpha's privileges here and finally, to implement Alpha's signature services on the third floor . . . I came to implement the basic programs that would be common at home, from a managerial perspective I came to implement things such as employee empowerment, which is a quite foreign concept here. (Special project manager, Canadian, Alpha Corporation)

and also,

[CorpCo's] manual says a four-star hotel must serve four juices in four different jars every morning. That may be OK in Canada, where the only thing you have to do is open the darn container and pour the liquid in the jar, but here we just don't have four kinds of juice, and if we do, it is too expensive. So we offer four juices, but one of them is orange, the other carrot, and the third orange-carrot, and the fourth, tropical punch, which is orange, carrot and I dunno, banana or whatever we have that day. But we make sure we have juices with and without sugar, so people who are watching their weight can drink the sugarless one. So what do you know? We have now six juices instead of four, but the basic flavors are the same. (Food and beverage manager, male, Cuban, Hotel Caribbean)

Forgetting at the individual and organizational level appeared as an important activity, even more so as the environment of the firm and the nature of the service provided was different from what the partners expected. Everything happened as if learning and forgetting could not be practically dissociated; forgetting, even when there seemed to be no pre-existing organizational knowledge in the business unit, appeared as a necessary first step to start learning processes in the organizations. We observed in our study both the omnipresence of forgetting, and the close relationship it maintains with processes of organizational learning and with the memory system of the organizations. In fact, these three building blocks – learning, forgetting, and storage of knowledge – are all equally important parts of the knowledge system in organizations.

With that initial insight, our goal then was to distinguish among different types of forgetting, and to identify the context in which they appeared. Three main dimensions emerged from the analysis of our case studies. The first dimension of forgetting involved the incapacity by the organization to retain a piece of knowledge that had been previously available to it. The second dimension deals with knowledge that has been stored in memory, but that degrades over time, causing the quality of the performance enabled by that knowledge to diminish. Our final dimension involves purging knowledge from memory. We discuss each of them in detail below.

Mode 1: the inability to integrate new knowledge

This dimension involves the inability to integrate new knowledge into the knowledge system. That is, knowledge that was either transferred to the organization from another organization or created by the organization itself but was not retained by it. In general, something is known or done for the first time, but becomes impossible in subsequent iterations. In this case, knowledge dissipates rapidly, disappearing from the organization almost immediately after the particular piece of knowledge has entered it. In our case, this situation appeared in several instances. For example, "if you do not follow-up, it is back to step 1," "you go on vacation, and when you are back, the standards are gone."

The flows of knowledge in the organizations studied had two loci. External knowledge was made available to the organizations through transfer; internal knowledge was produced by the organization. Successful instances of knowledge transfer and production were observed in the organizations; yet, we also observed that in several of these instances, knowledge would not remain available to the organization. Although initially we hypothesized that these were examples of failure to transfer or to create knowledge, we later realized that the organization had been able to use that knowledge, but only for short periods of time.

In Hotel Belltolls, a gala event for the elite of the country and the diplomatic corps was organized with great success: the general impression was that the quality of the premises,

the food and the service was impeccable. Yet, a few weeks later, a much more modest
gathering failed, as the quality of the food and service was mediocre. Subsequent failures
moved the organization to cancel its plans to introduce receptions to the product catalogue, depriving it of a profitable source of income. Says a manager,

> I think it's easy to get to a high standard; it's not difficult. I can go to another hotel and
> we can have the best meal tomorrow there, without a problem, the best service for one day.
> But to keep it, to keep the standard is very difficult. (Food and beverage manager, Dutch,
> Withwind Hotel)

And also,

> That is follow-up, and that can be annoying, it can give you a headache because the sauce
> that was supposed to be there since the beginning isn't there, and I know that it is supposed
> to be there and it was there since the beginning. It is the sauce, it is a saucer, and a little dish
> on top with a little spoon and a big spoon. Well, they are details, but that is the work we do
> . . . If not, they will change the pasta or they will put something that does not taste the same,
> and we need it to be always the same. (General manager, French, Withwind Hotel)

Together, these quotes suggest that the transfer of knowledge that has been created or
mobilized in the organization to the organization's memory system is a difficult task, with
often imperfect results. We can hypothesize that the rates of knowledge dissipation are
closely related to the quantity and quality of the efforts applied by the organization to store
that knowledge. More intense organizational effort and attention will lead to lower rates
of dissipation.

Our findings and the hypothesized relationships formalize Day's idea: "once knowledge
has been captured . . . it won't necessarily be retained or accessible. Retention requires that
the insights, policies, procedures and on-going routines that demonstrate the lessons are
regularly used and refreshed to keep up-to-date" (Day, 1994b). We explore this notion
further in the next section.

Mode 2: the deterioration of stored knowledge

We propose that moving knowledge to the organization's memory requires effort and attention, but also that it is critical to avoid rapid dissipation. Also we propose that failure to
store knowledge accelerates decay rates to the point where knowledge dissipates very
quickly after having been created. Complementing that first dimension, we focus here on
the degradation of knowledge after it has entered the organizational memory system.

We observed several instances of knowledge degradation. That is, where the quality of
the outputs diminished over time after having reached a level that was deemed satisfactory. In these situations, knowledge behaved quite differently from the predictions made
under learning curve assumptions, which state that the marginal cost of an additional unit
of output will diminish as the cumulative volume increases, up to the point where no more
learning occurs regardless of additional units produced. Here, instead, knowledge behaves
according to theory, but after having reached a plateau, quality of outputs decreases as the

organization forgets how to optimally perform the set of activities that led to the output in question. Says a manager,

> We calculate the daily cost of food and beverages. As soon as a new manager starts, he starts well, and then there is a phase where you have to watch that closely (or cost of food will increase again). In a kitchen the cost depends on how closely you watch everything, that is fundamental, you have to see what goes out, what comes in, and you have to monitor that very closely, as soon as [the chef] stops checking that, his performance (cost of food in relation to quality) goes down. We have seen that with our Cuban chefs, we hire one of them and in two weeks the cost of food is sky-high, and only then it stabilizes, we haven't been lucky with them. (Resident manager, Key Hotel, Cuban)

While some researchers have already presented findings about depreciation of organizational knowledge (Darr et al., 1995; Argote et al., 1990), it is still common to conceptualize learning as linear, cumulative processes that do not allow for deterioration. Yet, based on our evidence, we can suggest that for traditional learning effects to occur, organizations need to initiate activities that "maintain" the stock of knowledge of the organization. Again, we can hypothesize that, ceteris paribus, more and better maintenance activities will be correlated with lower rates of forgetting, and vice versa.

So far, we have presented instances where forgetting a piece of knowledge is undesirable, depriving the organization of a valuable resource. Nevertheless, there are situations where the issue faced by the organization is not simply retention of knowledge, but the ability to discard unwanted knowledge. We turn to that dimension next.

Mode 3: forgetting as knowledge management

The third dimension of forgetting identified in our cases involves voluntary forgetting, that is, forgetting that is actively desired by the organization, although not always achieved. For example:

> the Canadian (managers of the hotel) act as if this were some suburb of Montreal, they still have to understand that we are in Cuba and that certain things cannot be done their way. They want us to use their system, and that system does not work here, we need new ways of doing things that take into account the specificities of the country. (Resident manager, Montelimar Hotel, Cuban)

and

> [the Cuban employees' behavior] is normal, they treat customers just like they are treated when they are customers themselves, except that our customers are foreigners and have much higher expectations, here we have service à la Cuban, and that does not work. (Front desk manager, Canadian, Belltolls Hotel)

In these situations, forgetting was needed primarily as a way to make room for new knowledge, discarding knowledge that had once been functional for the organization but was now seen as a hindrance. Says a manager,

> [At first] we imported the structure [sets of rules and procedures and formal descriptions of jobs] of Superb Hotel, and very quickly we realized that it did not work well here, perhaps it was because there were no foreigners among us, or maybe because our managers were not prepared for it. And we saw contradictions appearing at all levels, and our operating procedures were not implemented, and the same hierarchical level that decided on their implementation had to check to make sure they were actually applied. Then we decided to change the structure, to work differently so we would not drown in meetings that did not get the problems solved. (General manager, Cuban, Caribbean hotel, non joint venture)

One insight of this statement is the presence of forgetting as a moderating factor in the process of learning. From our findings, we hypothesize that the rate of learning is influenced by the presence of forgetting, by helping the organization eliminate old knowledge that is no longer needed. The overall effectiveness of the processes of knowledge mobilization (including knowledge creation and knowledge transfer) is likely to be influenced by the presence or absence of forgetting, defined here as the capacity to discard old knowledge that is no longer needed. As organizational learning requires that new routines and new standard operating procedures replace old ones, processes of forgetting can influence the success of these learning processes.

Also, the need for organizational forgetting can be related to the strength and the quality of the memory systems of the organization. We hypothesize that a strong, well-developed memory system in the organization will require a higher degree of effort for forgetting to appear, whereas a weak memory system will require less effort. We hypothesize that holding effort constant, the quality of the organizational memory system will have a strong influence on the rates of learning and forgetting. In addition, the type of knowledge that is to be forgotten influences the amount of effort that will be needed to forget it. Says a manager,

> [she] came and gave us her advice, she has a lot of experience as housekeeping manager, and she gave us a procedure to make the rooms very different from the one that we had before, and the room ends up being just the same. Now we do the work much quicker and it has the same level of quality . . . [Alpha's standard operating procedures] make our work much quicker, and the customer is happier that way, when he goes to bed there is no inconvenience while undoing the bed, when he goes to bed the pillow stays put; with CorpCo it flies off. (Housekeeping manager, Cuban, Montelimar Hotel)

and also,

> I asked them (the employees) why on earth do you think that we are here? Why do you think the government has built this hotel? And for them, if this hotel is here is for customers and tourists to come, they didn't even mention that our objective was to be productive, to be profitable and to make money, that was a tough one. (Marketing manager, female, Nut Hotel)

Finally, it is common to distinguish between types of knowledge according to its degree of abstraction or concreteness, or, in Nonaka's conceptualization, between tacit and explicit knowledge (Nonaka, 1991, 1994). Under our hypothesis that the nature of the knowledge influences the rate of retention, we hypothesize that different kinds of knowledge require different levels of effort to be retained and to be forgotten.

Conclusions and New Avenues for Research

The idea of organizational knowledge has proven very fruitful in organization and management studies and has led researchers to understand different sources of organizational capabilities and competitiveness. While we are gaining a better understanding of how knowledge is created and transferred, there are still important dynamics of knowledge that remain unexplored. In this chapter, we have begun to discuss one of these dynamics, forgetting, and its role in knowledge processes in organizations.

Based on our research, and a number of examples and discussions drawn from the literature, it is clear that forgetting plays an important role in the dynamics of knowledge, a much more important role than its current status in the literature would indicate. The organizations we studied spent considerable time either trying to forget something that was no longer (or never had been) functional or trying not to forget things that were highly valued but in danger of being lost. In fact, they spent much more time on these activities than they devoted to knowledge creation or transfer. Managing forgetting was a major management concern and consumed a surprising amount of time and effort to forget things that needed to be forgotten, to avoid forgetting things that shouldn't be forgotten, and to recreate critical knowledge that was forgotten.

Our study also highlights the contextual nature of forgetting: while forgetting was a constant in these organizations, the effect of forgetting is context-dependent. If critical knowledge was forgotten, then competitiveness was lost and forgetting would have been better avoided. But, if the forgotten knowledge was extraneous or was actively interfering with the application of more appropriate knowledge, then forgetting was a positive occurrence. In some cases, managing to avoid organizational forgetting is critical; in others, managing to maximize the loss of organizational knowledge is equally adaptive. In other words, while learning is critical for organizational success, forgetting plays an equally important role. The ramifications of our study for research are clear. Management researchers must begin to pay more attention to forgetting if they wish to understand the dynamics of knowledge in organizations. In particular, we feel that there are three areas of particular importance for understanding organizational knowledge.

First, while we have discussed the fact that new knowledge may fail to be integrated into memory, we really have no idea why some new knowledge is successfully integrated when other new knowledge is not. While it is obviously useful to understand the different processes that affect learning outcomes, we should explore the different causes of forgetting, and in particular, the different organizational factors that prevent knowledge from being stored. A promising avenue for researchers would be to study where knowledge is embedded in the organization (i.e., routines, structures, understandings, assets), and to explore the factors that prevent knowledge from being embedded in each one of these dimensions. Knowledge may well crystallize in routines, but why and how remain to be explored.

A second promising area involves the study of errors in memory systems. More specifically, we need to explain why knowledge that is stored deteriorates with time, and what mechanisms prevent different parts of the organization from retrieving stored knowledge. Also, some researchers (see, for example, Argote, 1999) have shown that rates of knowledge depreciation vary across industries, hypothesizing that higher technological sophistication leads to lower depreciation rates. Nevertheless, it would be useful to know whether rates of knowledge dissipation differ between organizations in the same industry, or even within the same multi-unit organization, and why. In short, we need to pay more attention to the causes of memory errors, and try to understand under what circumstances they appear, increase or disappear.

The third area involves forgetting as knowledge management. It is clear from the literature that organizations often need to forget, and that managerial agency often involves forgetting. But, how does it work? Under what conditions should an organization forget? These are critical questions for researchers interested in the theory and practice of knowledge management.

In sum, how organizations can forget the things they want to forget, and avoid forgetting the things they do not want to forget, is an important question for management researchers. Furthermore, it is a question that has not been well studied to date, but that stands to make a significant contribution to our understanding of the dynamics of organizational knowledge. Our discussion in this chapter begins to draw together a number of threads from the literature but much further research and writing is required to come to a deeper understanding of organizational forgetting.

NOTES

1. We thank Mr. Eric Calcagno y Maillman for pointing out this story to the first author during a conversation in Paris, and Ms. Virginie de La Fresnaye, Chargée de la Communication of the Hotel Lutetia for corroborating significant parts of the vignette.
2. Names have been changed.

REFERENCES

Anand, V., Manz, C., and Glick, W. (1998) An Organizational Memory Approach to Information Management. *Academy of Management Review*, 23 (4): 796–809.
Argote, L. (1999) *Organizational Learning: Creating, Retaining, and Transferring Knowledge*. Boston: Kluwer Academic.
Argote, L., Beckman, S.L., and Epple, D. (1990) The Persistence and Transfer of Learning in Industrial Settings. *Management Science*, 36 (2): 140–55.
Barnard, C. (1938) *Functions of the Executive*. Boston, MA: Harvard University Press.
Bettis, R.A. (1991) Strategic Management and the Straightjacket: An Editorial Essay. *Organization Science*, 2 (3): 315–19.
Bettis, R. and Prahalad, C.K. (1995) The Dominant Logic: Retrospective and Extension. *Strategic Management Journal*, 16: 5–14.
Conner, K.R. (1991) A Historical Comparison of Resource-Based theory and Five Schools of Thought within Industrial Organization Economics: Do We Have a New Theory of the Firm? *Journal of Management*, 17: 121–54.
Conner, K.R. and Prahalad, C.K. (1996) A Resource-based Theory of the Firm: Knowledge versus Opportunism. *Organization Science*, 7 (5): 477–501.

Cross, R. and Bayrd, L. (2000) Technology Is Not Enough: Improving Performance by Building Organizational Memory. *Sloan Management Review*, Spring: 69–79.

Crossan, M., Lane, H., and White, R.E. (1999) An Organizational Learning Framework: From Intuition to Institution. *Academy of Management Review*, 24 (3): 522–37.

Cyert, R.M. and March, J.G. (1963) *A Behavioral Theory of the Firm.* Englewood Cliffs, NJ: Prentice-Hall.

Daft, R. and Huber, G. (1987) How Organizations Learn: A Communication Framework. In B. Staw and L. Cummings (eds.), *Research in the Sociology of Organizations*, Vol. 5. Greenwich, CT: JAI Press, 1–36.

Darr, E., Argote, L., and Epple, D. (1995) The Acquisition, Transfer and Depreciation of Knowledge in Service Organizations: Productivity in Franchises. *Management Science*, 41 (11): 1750–62.

Day, G.S. (1994a) The Capabilities of Market-driven Organizations. *Journal of Marketing*, 58 (October): 37–52.

Day, G.S. (1994b) Continuous Learning about Markets. *California Management Review*, 36 (Summer): 9–31.

Delarue, J. (1962) *Histoire de la Gestapo.* Paris: Arthème Fayard.

Dodgson, M. (1993) Organizational Learning: A Review of Some Literatures. *Organization Studies*, 14 (3): 375–94.

Duncan, R.B. and Weiss, A. (1979) Organizational Learning: Implications for Organizational Design. In B.M. Staw (ed.), *Research in Organizational Behavior*, Vol. 1. Greenwich, CT: JAI Press, 75–124.

Easterby-Smith, M., Crossan, M., and Nicolini, D. (2000) Organizational Learning: Debates Past, Present and Future. *Journal of Management Studies*, 37 (6): 783–96.

Epple, D., Argote, L., and Devadas, R. (1991) Organization Learning Curves: A Method for Investigating Intra-plant Transfer of Knowledge Acquired Trough Learning by Doing. *Organization Science*, 2: 58–70.

Fiol, C. and Lyles, M. (1985) Organizational Learning. *Academy of Management Review*, 10 (4): 803–13.

Ghoshal, S. and Moran, P. (1996) Bad for Practice: A Critique of the Transaction-cost Economics. *Academy of Management Review*, 21: 13–47.

Grant, R.M. (1996) Toward a Knowledge-based Theory of the Firm. *Strategic Management Journal* 17 (Winter): 109–22.

Hedberg, B. (1981) How Organizations Learn and Unlearn. In P. Nystrom and W. Starbuck (eds.), *Handbook of Organizational Design*, Vol. 1. Oxford: Oxford University Press, 3–27.

Huber, G.P. (1991) Organizational Learning, The Contributing Processes and the Literatures. *Organization Science*, 2: 88–115.

Kogut, B. and Zander, U. (1992) Knowledge of the Firm, Combinative Capabilities and the Replication of Technology. *Organization Science*, 3 (3): 383–97.

Kogut, B. and Zander, U. (1996) What Firms Do? Coordination, Identity, and Learning. *Organization Science*, 7 (5): 502–18.

Koza, M. and Lewin, A. (2000) Managing Partnerships and Strategic Alliances: Raising the Odds of Success. *European Management Journal*, 18 (2): 145–51.

Levitt, B. and March, J.G. (1988) Organizational Learning. *Annual Review of Sociology*, 14: 319–40.

Lyles, M. (1988) Learning among Joint Venture-Sophisticated Firms. In F. Contractor and P. Lorange (eds.), *Cooperative Strategies in International Business*. Lexington, MA: D.C. Heath.

Lyles, M.A. and Schwenk, C.R. (1992) Top Management, Strategy and Organizational Knowledge Structures. *Journal of Management Studies*, 29 (2): 155–74.

March, J.G. (1991) Exploration and Exploitation in Organizational Learning. *Organization Science*, 2 (1): 71–87.

Martin de Holan, P. (1998) The Dynamics of Knowledge in International Strategic Alliances: A Study of Foreign Run Hotels in Cuba. Paper presented at the Strategic Management Society Meetings, Orlando, FL.

Martin de Holan, P. (1999). Knowledge Creation, Mobilization and Maintenance in International Strategic Alliances. Paper presented at the Academy of Management, Chicago, IL.

Martin de Holan, P. and Phillips, N. (1997) Sun, Sand and Hard Currency: The Cuban Tourism Industry. *Annals of Tourism Research*, 24 (4): 1–33.

Miles, G., Miles, R.E., Perrone, V., and Edvinsson, L. (1998) Some Conceptual and Research Barriers to the Utilization of Knowledge. *California Management Review*, 40 (3): 281–8.

Miller, D. (1990) *The Icarus Paradox*. New York: Harper Business.

Miller, D. (1993) The Architecture of Simplicity. *Academy of Management Review*, 18 (1): 116–38.

Miller, D. (1994) What Happens after Success: The Perils of Excellence. *Journal of Management Studies*, 31 (3): 327–58.

Miner, A.S. and Mezias, S.J. (1996) Ugly Duckling No More: Pasts and Futures of Organizational Learning Research. *Organization Science*, 7 (1): 88–99.

Moorman, C. and Miner, A. (1998) Organizational Improvisation and Organizational Memory. *Academy of Management Review*, 23 (4): 698–724.

Nahapiet, J. and Ghoshal, S. (1998) Social Capital, Intellectual Capital, and the Organizational Advantage. *Academy of Management Review*, 23 (2): 242–66.

Nelson, R. and Winter, S. (1982) *An Evolutionary Theory of Economic Change*. Cambridge, MA: Harvard University Press.

Nonaka, I. (1991) The Knowledge Creating Company. *Harvard Business Review*, 69 (November–December): 96–105.

Nonaka, I. (1994) A Dynamic Theory of Organizational Knowledge Creation. *Organization Science*, 5 (1): 14–37.

Nystrom, P.C. and Starbuck, W. (1984) To Avoid Organizational Crises, Unlearn. *Organizational Dynamics*, 12 (4): 53–76.

Olivera, F. (2000) Memory Systems in Organizations: An Empirical Investigation of Mechanisms for Knowledge Collection, Storage and Access. *Journal of Management Studies*, 37 (6): 811–32.

Peters, T. (1992) *Liberation Management: Necessary Disorganisation for the Nanosecond Nineties*. New York: Alfred A. Knopf.

Peters, T. (1994) To Forget Is Sublime. *Forbes*, April 11, 128–30.

Prahalad, C.K. and Bettis, R.A. (1986) The Dominant Logic: A New Linkage between Diversity and Performance. *Strategic Management Journal*, 7: 485–502.

Prahalad, C.K. and Hamel, M. (1990) The Core Competence of the Corporation. *Harvard Business Review*, 68 (3): 79–92.

Rumelt, R., Schendel, D., and Teece, D. (eds.) (1994) *Fundamental Issues in Strategy*. Boston, MA: Harvard Business School Press.

Schulz, M. (1998) Limits to Bureaucratic Growth: The Density Dependence of Organizational Rules. *Administrative Science Quarterly*, 43 (December): 845–76.

Schulz, M. (2001) The Uncertain Relevance of Newness: Organizational Learning and Knowledge Flows. *Academy of Management Journal*, 44 (4): 661–81.

Selznick, P. (1957) *Leadership in Administration: A Sociological Interpretation*. Evanston, IL: Harper & Row.

Spender, J.-C. and Grant, R.M. (1996) Knowledge and the Firm: Overview. *Strategic Management Journal*, 17 (Winter): 5–9.

Stein, E.W. (1995) Organizational Memory: Review of Concepts and Recommendations for Management. *International Journal of Information Management*, 15 (1): 17–33.

Teece, D.J., Pisano, G., and Shuen, A. (1997) Dynamic Capabilities and Strategic Management. *Strategic Management Journal*, 18 (7): 509–33.

Walsh, J.P. and Ungson, G.R. (1991) Organizational Memory. *Academy of Management Review*, 16 (1): 239–70.
Weick, K. (1994) The Collapse of Sensemaking in Organizations: The Mann Gulch Disaster. *Administrative Science Quarterly*, 38 (4): 628–53.

21

Do We Really Understand Tacit Knowledge?

HARIDIMOS TSOUKAS

CHAPTER OUTLINE

This chapter advances the claim that tacit knowledge has been greatly misunderstood in management studies. Nonaka and Takeuchi's widely adopted interpretation of tacit knowledge as knowledge awaiting "translation" or "conversion" into explicit knowledge is erroneous: contrary to Polanyi's argument, it ignores the essential ineffability of tacit knowledge. In the chapter I show why the idea of focusing on a set of tacitly known particulars and "converting" them into explicit knowledge is unsustainable. However, the ineffability of tacit knowledge does not mean that we cannot discuss the skilled performances in which we are involved. We can discuss them provided we stop insisting on "converting" tacit knowledge and, instead, start recursively drawing our attention to how we draw each other's attention to things. Instructive forms of talk help us to re-orientate ourselves to how we relate to others and the world around us, thus enabling us to talk and act differently. Following Wittgenstein and Shotter, I argue that we can command a clearer view of our skilled performances if we "re-mind" ourselves of how we do things, so that distinctions, which we had previously not noticed, and features, which had previously escaped our attention, may be brought forward. We cannot operationalize tacit knowledge but we can find new ways of talking, fresh forms of interacting and novel ways of distinguishing and connecting. Tacit knowledge cannot be "captured," "translated," or "converted," but only displayed and manifested, in what we do. New knowledge comes about not when the tacit becomes explicit, but when our skilled performance is punctuated in new ways through social interaction.

INTRODUCTION

Nisi credideritis, non intelligitis ("Unless ye believe, ye shall not understand"). (St. Augustine, cited in Polanyi, 1962: 266)

Something that we know when no one asks us, but no longer know when we are supposed to give an account of it, is something that we need to *remind* ourselves of. (Wittgenstein 1958: No.89; italics in the original)

The act of knowing includes an appraisal; and this personal coefficient, which shapes all factual knowledge, bridges in doing so the disjunction between subjectivity and objectivity. (Polanyi, 1962: 17)

It is often argued that knowledge is fundamental to the functioning of late modern economies (Drucker, 1993; Stehr, 1994; Thurow, 2000). "What's new here?," a critique might ask. "Knowledge has always been implicated in the process of economic development, since anything we do, how we transform resources into products and services, crucially depends on the knowledge we have at our disposal for effecting such transformation. An ancient artisan, a medieval craftsman and his apprentices, and a modern manufacturing system all make use of knowledge: certain skills, techniques, and procedures are employed for getting things done."

What is distinctly new, then, in the contemporary so-called "knowledge economy"? Daniel Bell answered this question more than 30 years ago: theoretical (or codified) knowledge has acquired a central place in late modern societies in a way that was not the case before. Says Bell (1999: 20):

Knowledge has of course been necessary in the functioning of any society. What is distinctive about the post-industrial society is the change in the character of knowledge itself. What has become decisive for the organization of decisions and the direction of change is the centrality of *theoretical knowledge* – the primacy of theory over empiricism and the codification of knowledge into abstract systems of symbols that, as in any axiomatic system, can be used to illustrate many different and varied areas of experience. (italics in the original)

Indeed, it is hard today to think of an industry that does not make systematic use of "theoretical knowledge". Products increasingly incorporate more and more specialized knowledge, supplied by R&D departments, universities, and consulting firms; and production processes are also increasingly based on systematic research that aims to optimize their functioning (Drucker, 1993; Mansell and When, 1998; Stehr, 1994).

Taking a historical perspective of the development of modern market economies, as Bell does, one can clearly see the change in the character of knowledge over time. To simplify, modernity has come to mistrust intuition, preferring explicitly articulated assertions; it is uncomfortable with *ad hoc* practices, opting for systematic procedures; it substitutes detached objectivity for personal commitment (MacIntyre, 1985; Toulmin, 1990, 2001). Yet if one takes a closer look at how theoretical (or codified) knowledge is actually *used* in practice, one will see the extent to which theoretical knowledge itself, far from being as objective, self-sustaining, and explicit as it is often taken to be, it is actually grounded on personal judgements and tacit commitments. Even the most theoretical form of knowledge, such as pure mathematics, cannot be a completely formalised system, since it is based for its application and development on the *skills* of mathematicians and how such skills are used in practice. To put it differently, codified knowledge necessarily contains a "personal coefficient" (Polanyi, 1962: 17). Knowledge-based economies may indeed be making great use of codified forms of knowledge, but that kind of knowledge is inescapably used in a *non-codifiable* and *non-theoretical* manner.

The significance of "tacit knowledge" for the functioning of organizations has not escaped the attention of management theorists. Ever since Nonaka and Takeuchi (1995) have published their influential *The Knowledge-Creating Company*, it is nearly impossible to find a publication on organizational knowledge and knowledge management that does not make a reference to, or use the term "tacit knowledge." And quite rightly so: as common experience can verify, the knowledge people use in organizations is so practical and deeply familiar to them that when people are asked to describe how they do what they do, they often find it hard to express it in words (Ambrosini and Bowman, 2001; Cook and Yanow, 1996: 442; Eraut, 2000; Nonaka and Takeuchi, 1995; Harper, 1987; Tsoukas and Vladimirou, 2001: 987). Naturally, several questions arise: what is it about organizational knowledge that makes it so hard to describe? What is the significance of the tacit dimension of organizational knowledge? What are the implications of tacit knowledge for the learning and exercise of skills? If skilled knowing is tacit, how is it possible for new knowledge to emerge?

The purpose of this chapter is to explore the preceding questions. My argument will be that popular as the term "tacit knowledge" may have become in management studies, it has, on the whole, been misunderstood. By and large, tacit knowledge has been conceived in opposition to explicit knowledge, whereas it is simply its other side. As a result of such a misunderstanding, the nature of organizational knowledge and its relation to individual skills and social contexts has been inadequately understood. In this chapter I will first explore the nature of tacit knowledge by drawing primarily on Polanyi (the inventor of the term), an author who is frequently referred to but little understood. Then I will explore how Polanyi's understanding of tacit knowledge has been interpreted by Nonaka and Takeuchi, the two authors who, more than anyone else, have helped popularize the concept of "tacit knowledge" in management studies and whose interpretation has been adopted by most management authors (see for example, Ambrosini and Bowman, 2001; Baumard, 1999; Boisot, 1995; Davenport and Prusak, 1998; Devlin, 1999; Dixon, 2000; Leonard and Sensiper, 1998; Spender, 1996; von Krogh et al., 2000; for exceptions, see Brown and Duguid, 2000; Cook and Brown, 1999: 385 and 394–5; Kreiner, 1999; Tsoukas, 1996: 14; 1997: 830–1; Wenger, 1998: 67). Finally, I will end this chapter by fleshing out the implications of tacit knowledge, properly understood, for an epistemology of organizational practice.

POLANYI FOR BEGINNERS: A GUIDE

One of the most distinguishing features of Polanyi's work is his insistence on overcoming well-established dichotomies such as theoretical versus practical knowledge, sciences versus the humanities or, to put it differently, his determination to show the common structure underlying all kinds of knowledge. Polanyi, a chemist turned philosopher, was categorical that all knowing involves *skillful action* and that the knower necessarily participates in all acts of understanding. For him the idea that there is such a thing as "objective" knowledge, self-contained, detached, and independent of human action, was wrong and pernicious. "*All* knowing," he insists, "is personal knowing – participation through indwelling" (Polanyi and Prosch, 1975: 44; italics in the original).

Take for example, the use of geographical maps. A map is a representation of a particular territory. As an explicit representation of something else, a map is, in logical terms, not different from that of a theoretical system, or a system of rules: they all aim at enabling purposeful human action, that is, respectively, to get from A to B, to predict, and guide behavior. We may be very familiar with a map per se but to *use* it we need to be able to relate it to the world outside the map. More specifically, to use a map we need to be able to do three things. First, we must identify our current position in the map ("you are here"). Second, we must find our itinerary on the map ("we want to go to the National Museum, which is there"). And third, to actually go to our destination, we must identify the itinerary by various landmarks in the landscape around us ("you get past the train station and then turn left"). In other words, a map, no matter how elaborate it is, cannot read itself; it requires the judgment of a skilled reader who will relate the map to the world through both cognitive and sensual means (Polanyi and Prosch, 1975: 30; Polanyi, 1962: 18–20).

The same personal judgment is involved whenever abstract representations encounter the world of experience. We are inclined to think, for example, that Newton's laws can predict the position of a planet circling round the sun, at some future point in time, provided its current position is known. Yet this is not quite the case: Newton's laws can never do that, only *we* can. The difference is crucial. The numbers entering the relevant formulae, from which we compute the future position of a planet, are readings on our instruments – they are not given, but need to be worked out. Similarly, we check the veracity of our predictions by comparing the results of our computations with the readings of the instruments – the predicted computations will rarely coincide with the readings observed and the significance of such a discrepancy needs to be worked out, again, by us (Polanyi, 1962: 19; Polanyi and Prosch, 1975: 30). Notice that, like in the case of map reading, the formulae of celestial mechanics cannot apply themselves; the personal judgment of a human agent is necessarily involved in applying abstract representations to the world.

The general point to be derived from the above examples is this: insofar as a formal representation has a bearing on experience, that is the extent to which a representation encounters the world, personal judgment is called upon to make an assessment of the inescapable gap between the representation and the world encountered. Given that the map is a representation of the territory, I need to be able to match my location in the territory with its representation on the map, if I am to be successful in reaching my destination. Personal judgment cannot be prescribed by rules but relies essentially on the use of our senses (Polanyi, 1962: 19; 1966: 20; Polanyi and Prosch, 1975: 30). To the extent this happens, the exercise of personal judgment is a skilful performance, involving both the mind and the body.

The crucial role of the body in the act of knowing has been persistently underscored by Polanyi (cf. Gill, 2000: 44–50). As said earlier, the cognitive tools we use do not apply themselves; we apply them and, thus, we need to assess the extent to which our tools match aspects of the world. Insofar as our contact with the world necessarily involves our somatic equipment – "the trained delicacy of eye, ear, and touch" (Polanyi and Prosch, 1975: 31) – we are engaged in the art of establishing a correspondence between the explicit formulations of our formal representations (be they maps, scientific laws or organizational rules)

TSOUKAS

and the actual experience of our senses. As Polanyi (1969: 147) remarks, "the way the body participates in the act of perception can be generalized further to include the bodily roots of all knowledge and thought . . . Parts of our body serve as tools for observing objects outside and for manipulating them."

If we accept that there is indeed a "personal coefficient" (Polanyi, 1962: 17) in all acts of knowing, which is manifested in a skillful performance carried out by the knower, what is the structure of such a skill? What is it that enables a map-reader to make a competent use of the map to find his/her way around, a scientist to use the formulas of celestial mechanics to predict the next eclipse of the moon, and a physician to read an X-ray picture of a chest? For Polanyi, the starting point towards answering this question is to acknowledge that "the aim of a skilful performance is achieved by the observance of a set of rules which are not known as such to the person following them" (Polanyi, 1962: 49). A cyclist, for example, does not normally know the rule that keeps her balance, nor does a swimmer know what keeps him afloat. Interestingly, such ignorance is hardly detrimental to their effective carrying out of their respective tasks.

The cyclist keeps herself in balance by winding through a series of curvatures. One can formulate the rule explaining why she does not fall off the bicycle – "for a given angle of unbalance the curvature of each winding is inversely proportional to the square of the speed at which the cyclist is proceeding" (Polanyi, 1962: 50) – but such a rule would hardly be helpful to the cyclist. Why? Partly because, as we will see below, no rule is helpful in guiding action unless it is assimilated and lapses into unconsciousness. And partly because there is a host of other particular elements to be taken into account, which are not included in this rule and, crucially, are not known by the cyclist. Skills retain an element of opacity and unspecificity; they cannot be fully accounted for in terms of their particulars, since their practitioners do not ordinarily know what those particulars are; even when they do know them, as for example in the case of topographic anatomy, they do not know how to integrate them (Polanyi, 1962: 88–90). It is one thing to learn a list of bones, arteries, nerves and viscara and quite another to know how precisely they are intertwined inside the body (Polanyi, 1962: 89)

How then do individuals know how to exercise their skills? In a sense they don't. "A mental effort", says Polanyi (1962: 62), "has a heuristic effect: it tends to incorporate any available elements of the situation which are helpful for its purpose." Any particular elements of the situation which may help the purpose of a mental effort are selected insofar as they contribute to the performance at hand, without the performer knowing them as they would appear in themselves. The particulars are subsidiarily known insofar as they contribute to the action performed. As Polanyi (1962: 62) remarks,

> this is the usual process of unconscious trial and error by which *we feel our way* to success and may continue to improve on our success without specifiably knowing how we do it – for we never meet the causes of our success as identifiable things which can be described in terms of classes of which such things are members. This is how you invent a method of swimming without knowing that it consists in regulating your breath in a particular manner, or discover the principle of cycling without realizing that it consists in the adjustment of your momentary direction and velocity, so as to counteract continuously your momentary accidental unbalance. (italics in the original)

There are two different kinds of awareness in exercising a skill. When I use a hammer to drive a nail (one of Polanyi's favourite examples – see Polanyi, 1962: 55; Polanyi and Prosch, 1975: 33), I am aware of both the nail and the hammer but in a different way. I watch the effects of my strokes on the nail, and try to hit it as effectively as I can. Driving the nail down is the main object of my attention and I am focally aware of it. At the same time, I m also aware of the feelings in my palm of holding the hammer. But such awareness is subsidiary: the feelings of holding the hammer in my palm are not an object of my attention but an instrument of it. I watch hitting the nail by being aware of them. As Polanyi and Prosch (1975: 33) remark: "I know the feelings in the palm of my hand *by relying on them for attending to the hammer hitting the nail*. I may say that I have a *subsidiary* awareness of the feelings in my hand which is merged into my *focal awareness* of my driving the nail" (italics in the original).

If the above is accepted, it means that we can be aware of certain things in a way that is quite different from focusing our attention to them. I have a subsidiary awareness of my holding the hammer in the act of focusing on hitting the nail. In being subsidiarily aware of holding a hammer I see it as having a meaning that is wiped out if I focus my attention on how I hold the hammer. Subsidiary awareness and focal awareness are mutually exclusive (Polanyi, 1962: 56). If we switch our focal attention to particulars of which we had only subsidiary awareness before, their meaning is lost and the corresponding action becomes clumsy. If a pianist shifts her attention from the piece she is playing to how she moves her fingers; if a speaker focuses his attention to the grammar he is using instead of the act of speaking; or if a carpenter shifts his attention from hitting the nail to holding the hammer, they will all be confused. We must rely (to be precise, we must learn to rely) subsidiarily on particulars for attending to something else, hence our knowledge of them remains *tacit* (Polanyi, 1966: 10; Winograd and Flores, 1987: 32). In the context of carrying out a specific task, we come to know a set of particulars without being able to identify them. In Polanyi's (1966: 4) memorable phrase, "we can know more than we can tell."

From the above it follows that tacit knowledge forms a triangle, at the three corners of which are the *subsidiary particulars*, the *focal target*, and the *knower* who links the two. It should be clear from the above that the linking of the particulars to the focal target does not happen automatically but is a result of the *act* of the knower. It is in this sense that Polanyi talks about all knowledge being *personal* and all knowing being *action*. No knowledge is possible without the integration of the subsidiaries to the focal target by a person. However, unlike explicit inference, such integration is essentially tacit and irreversible. Its tacitness was earlier discussed; its irreversible character can be seen if juxtaposed to explicit (deductive) inference, whereby one can unproblematically traverse between the premises and the conclusions. Such traversing is not possible with tacit integration: once you have learned to play the piano you cannot go back to being ignorant of how to do it. While you can certainly focus your attention on how you move your fingers, thus making your performance clumsy to the point of paralyzing it, you can always recover your ability by casting your mind forward to the music itself. With explicit inference, no such break-up and recovery are possible (Polanyi and Prosch, 1975: 39–42). When, for example, you examine a legal syllogism or a mathematical proof you proceed orderly from the premises, or a sequence of logical steps, to the conclusions. You lose nothing and you recover nothing –

there is complete reversibility. You can go back to check the veracity of each constituent statement separately and how it logically links with its adjacent statements. Such reversibility is not, however, possible with tacit integration. Shifting attention to subsidiary particulars entails the loss of the skillful engagement with the activity at hand. By focusing on a subsidiary constituent of skillful action one changes the character of the activity with which one is involved. There is no reversibility in this instance.

The structure of tacit knowing has three aspects: the functional, the phenomenal and the semantic. The functional aspect consists in the *from–to* relation of particulars (or subsidiaries) to the focal target. Tacit knowing is a from – to knowing: we know the particulars by relying on our awareness of them for attending to something else. Human awareness has a "vectorial" character (Polanyi, 1969: 182): it moves from subsidiary particulars to the focal target (cf. Gill, 2000: 38–9). Or, in the words of Polanyi and Prosch (1975: 37–8), "subsidiaries exist as such by bearing on the focus *to* which we are attending *from* them" (italics in the original). The phenomenal aspect involves the transformation of subsidiary experience into a new sensory experience. The latter appears through – it is created out of – the tacit integration of subsidiary sense perceptions. Finally, the semantic aspect is the meaning of subsidiaries, which is the focal target on which they bear.

The above aspects of tacit knowing will become clearer with an example. Imagine a dentist exploring a tooth cavity with a probe. Her exploration is a from–to knowing (the functional aspect): she relies subsidiarily on her feeling of holding the probe in order to attend focally to the tip of the probe exploring the cavity. In doing so the sensation of the probe pressing on her fingers is lost and, instead, she feels the point of the probe as it touches the cavity. This is the phenomenal aspect whereby a new coherent sensory quality appears (i.e., her sense of the cavity) from the initial sense perceptions (i.e., the impact of the probe on the fingers). Finally, the probing has a semantic aspect: the dentist gets information by using the probe. That information is the meaning of her tactile experiences with the probe. As Polanyi (1966: 13) argues, the dentist becomes aware of the feelings in her hand in terms of their meaning located at the tip of the probe, to which she is attending.

We engage in tacit knowing through virtually anything we do: we are normally unaware of the movement of our eye muscles when we observe, of the rules of language when we speak, of our bodily functions as we move around. Indeed, to a large extent, our daily life consists of a huge number of small details of which we tend to be focally unaware. When, however, we engage in more complex tasks, requiring even a modicum of specialized knowledge, then we face the challenge of how to assimilate the new knowledge – to interiorize it, dwell in it – in order to get things done efficiently and effectively. Polanyi gives the example of a medical student attending a course in X-ray diagnosis of pulmonary diseases. The student is initially puzzled:

> he can see in the X-ray picture of a chest only the shadows of the heart and the ribs, with a few spidery blotches between them. The experts seem to be romancing about figments of their imagination; he can see nothing that they are talking about. (Polanyi, 1962: 101)

At the early stage of his training the student has not assimilated the relevant knowledge; unlike the dentist with the probe, he cannot yet use it as a tool to carry out a diagnosis. The student, at this stage, is a remove from the diagnostic task as such: he cannot think about it directly; he rather needs to think about the relevant radiological knowledge first. If he perseveres with his training, however,

> he will gradually forget about the ribs and begin to see the lungs. And eventually, if he perseveres intelligently, a rich panorama of significant details will be revealed to him: of physiological variations and pathological changes, of scars, of chronic infections and signs of acute disease. He has entered a new world. (Polanyi, 1962:101)

We see here an excellent illustration of the structure of tacit knowledge. The student has now interiorized the new radiological knowledge; the latter has become tacit knowledge, of which he is subsidiarily aware while attending to the X-ray itself. Radiological knowledge exists now not as something unfamiliar which needs to be learned and assimilated before a diagnosis can take place, but as a set of particulars – subsidiaries – which exist as such by bearing on the X-ray (the focus) *to* which the student is attending *from* them. Insofar as this happens, a phenomenal transformation has taken place: the heart, the ribs and the spidery blotches gradually disappear and, instead, a new sensory experience appears – the X-ray is no longer a collection of fragmented radiological images of bodily organs, but a representation of a chest full of meaningful connections. Thus, as well as having functional and phenomenal aspects, tacit knowledge has a semantic aspect: the X-ray conveys information to an appropriately skilled observer. The meaning of the radiological knowledge, subsidiarily known and drawn upon by the student, is the diagnostic information he receives from the X-ray: it tells him what it is that he is observing by using that knowledge.

It should be clear from the above that for Polanyi, from a gnosiological point of view, there is no difference whatsoever between tangible things like probes, sticks, or hammers on the one hand, and intangible constructions such as radiological, linguistic, or cultural knowledge on the other – they are all *tools* enabling a skilled user to get things done. To use a tool properly we need to assimilate it and dwell in it. In Polanyi's (1969: 148) words, "we may say that when we learn to use language, or a probe, or a tool, and thus make ourselves aware of these things as we are our body, we *interiorize* these things and *make ourselves dwell in them*" (italics in the original). The notion of *indwelling* is crucial for Polanyi and turns up several times in his writings. It is only when we dwell in the tools we use, make them extensions of our own body, that we amplify the powers of our body and shift outwards the points at which we make contact with the world outside (Polanyi, 1962: 59; 1969: 148; Polanyi and Prosch, 1975: 37). Otherwise our use of tools will be clumsy and will get in the way of getting things done.

For a tool to be unproblematically used it must not be the object of our focal awareness; it rather needs to become an instrument through which we act – of which we are subsidiarily aware – not an object of attention. To dwell in a tool implies that one *uncritically* accepts it, is unconsciously committed to it. Such uncritical commitment is a necessary presupposition for using the tool effectively and, as such, cannot be asserted. Presuppositions cannot be asserted, says Polanyi (1962: 60), "for assertion[s] can be made only *within* a framework with which we have identified ourselves for the time being; as they are themselves our ultimate framework, they are essentially inarticulable" (italics in the original).

The interiorization of a tool – its instrumentalization in the service of a purpose – is beneficial to its user for it enables him/her to acquire new experiences and carry out more competently the task at hand (Dreyfus and Dreyfus, 2000). Compare, for example, one who learns driving a car to one who is an accomplished driver. The former may have learned how to change gear and to use the brake and the accelerator but cannot, yet, integrate those individual skills – he has not constructed a coherent perception of driving, the phenomenal transformation has not taken place yet. At the early stage, the driver is conscious of what he needs to do and feels the impact of the pedals on his foot and the gear stick on his palm; he has not learned to unconsciously correlate the performance of the car with the specific bodily actions he undertakes as a driver. The experienced driver, by contrast, is unconscious of the actions by which she drives – car instruments are tools whose use she has mastered, that is interiorized, and is therefore able to use them for the purpose of driving. By becoming unconscious of certain actions, the experienced driver expands the domain of experiences she can concentrate on as a driver (i.e., principally road conditions and other drivers' behavior).

The more general point to be derived from the preceding examples is formulated by Polanyi (1962: 61) as follows:

> we may say . . . that by the effort by which I concentrate on my chosen plane of operation I succeed in absorbing all the elements of the situation of which I might otherwise be aware in themselves, so that I become aware of them now in terms of the operational results achieved through their use.

This is important because we get things done, we achieve competence, by becoming unaware of how we do so. Of course one can take an interest in, and learn a great deal about, the gearbox and the acceleration mechanism but, to be able to drive, such knowledge needs to lapse into unconsciousness. "This lapse into unconsciousness," remarks Polanyi (1962: 62),

> is accompanied by a newly acquired consciousness of the experiences in question, on the operational plane. It is misleading, therefore, to describe this as the mere result of repetition; it is a structural change achieved by a repeated mental effort aiming at the instrumentalization of certain things and actions in the service of some purpose.

Notice that, for Polanyi, the shrinking of consciousness of certain things is, in the context of action, necessarily connected with the expansion of consciousness of other things. Particulars such as "changing gear" and "pressing the accelerator" are subsidiarily known, as the driver concentrates on the act of driving. Knowing something, then, is always a contextual issue and fundamentally connected to action (the "operational plane"). My knowledge of gears is in the context of driving, and it is only in such a context that I am subsidiarily aware of that knowledge. If, however, I were a car mechanic, gears would constitute my focus of attention, rather than being an assimilated particular. Knowledge has, therefore, a *recursive* form: given a certain context, we blackbox – assimilate, interiorize, instrumentalize – certain things in order to concentrate – focus – on others. In another context, and at another level of analysis (cf. Bateson, 1979: 43), we can open up some of the previously blackboxed issues and focus our attention to them. In theory this is an endless process, although in practice there are institutional and practical limits to it. In this way we can, to some extent, "vertically integrate" our knowledge; although, as said earlier, what pieces of knowledge we *use* depends, at any point in time, on context. If the driver happens to be a car mechanic as well as an engineer he will have acquired three different bodies of knowledge, each having a different degree of abstraction, which, taken together, give his knowledge depth and make him a sophisticated driver (cf. Harper, 1987: 33). How he draws on each one of them, however – that is, what is focally and what is subsidiarily known – depends on the context-in-use. Moreover, each one of these bodies of knowledge stands on its own, and cannot be reduced to any of the others. The practical knowledge I have of my car cannot be replaced by the theoretical knowledge of an engineer; the practical knowledge I have of my own body cannot be replaced by the theoretical knowledge of a physician (cf. Polanyi, 1966: 20). In the social world, specialist, abstract, theoretical knowledge is necessarily refracted through the "lifeworld" – the taken-for-granted assumptions by means of which human beings organize their experience, knowledge, and transactions with the world (cf. Bruner, 1990: 35).

THE APPROPRIATION OF "TACIT KNOWLEDGE" IN MANAGEMENT STUDIES: THE GREAT MISUNDERSTANDING

As was mentioned in the introductory section of this chapter, "tacit knowledge" has become very popular in management studies since the mid 1990s, owing, to a large extent, to the publication of Nonaka and Takeuchi's (1995) *The Knowledge-Creating Company*. The cornerstone of Nonaka and Takeuchi's theory for organizational knowledge is the notion of "knowledge conversion" – how tacit knowledge is "converted" to explicit knowledge, and vice versa. As the authors argue,

> our dynamic model of knowledge creation is anchored to a critical assumption that human knowledge is created and expanded through social interaction between tacit knowledge and explicit knowledge. We shall call this interaction "knowledge conversion" (Nonaka and Takeuchi, 1995: 61).

Nonaka and Takeuchi distinguish four modes of knowledge conversion: from tacit knowledge to tacit knowledge (socialization); from tacit knowledge to explicit knowledge (externalization); from explicit knowledge to explicit knowledge (combination); and from explicit knowledge to tacit knowledge (internalization). Tacit knowledge is converted to tacit knowledge through observation, imitation and practice, in those cases where an apprentice learns from a master. Tacit knowledge is converted to explicit knowledge when it is articulated and it takes the form of concepts, models, hypotheses, metaphors, and analogies. Explicit knowledge is converted to explicit knowledge when different bodies of explicit knowledge are combined. And explicit knowledge is converted into tacit knowledge when it is first verbalized and then absorbed, internalized by the individuals involved.

The organizational knowledge-creation process proceeds in cycles (in a spiral-like fashion), with each cycle consisting of five phases: the sharing of tacit knowledge among the members of a team; the creation of concepts whereby a team articulates its commonly shared mental model; the justification of concepts in terms of the overall organizational purposes and objectives; the building of an archetype which is a tangible manifestation of the justified concept; and the cross-leveling of knowledge, whereby a new cycle of knowledge creation may be created elsewhere (or even outside of) the organization.

To illustrate their theory, Nonaka and Takeuchi describe the product development process of Matsushita's Home Bakery, the first fully automated bread-making machine for home use, which was introduced to the Japanese market in 1987. There were three cycles in the relevant knowledge-creation process, with each cycle starting in order to either remove the weaknesses of the previous one or improve upon its outcome. The first cycle ended with the assemblage of a prototype which, however, was not up to the design team's standards regarding the quality of bread it produced. This triggered the second cycle which started when Ikuko Tanaka, a software developer, took an apprenticeship with a master baker at the Osaka International Hotel. Her purpose was to learn how to knead bread dough properly in order to "convert" later this know-how into particular design features of the bread-making machine under development. Following this, the third cycle came into operation whereby the commercialization team, consisting of people drawn from the manufacturing and marketing sections, further improved the prototype that came out of the second cycle, and made it a commercially viable product.

To obtain a better insight into what Nonaka and Takeuchi mean by "tacit knowledge" and how it is related to "explicit knowledge," it is worth zooming into their description of the second cycle of the knowledge-creation process, since this is the cycle most relevant to the acquisition and "conversion" of tacit knowledge. In the section below I quote in full the authors' description of this cycle (references and figures have been omitted) (see Nonaka and Takeuchi: 1995: 103–6).

A Case Study: The Second Cycle of the Home Bakery Spiral

The second cycle began with a software developer, Ikuko Tanaka, sharing the tacit knowledge of a master baker in order to learn his kneading skill. A master baker learns the art of kneading, a critical step in bread making, following years of experience. However, such expertise is difficult to articulate in words. To capture this tacit knowledge, which usually takes a lot of imitation and practice to master, Tanaka proposed a creative solution. Why not train with the head baker at Osaka International Hotel, which had a reputation for making the best bread in Osaka, to study the kneading techniques? Tanaka learned her kneading skills through observation, imitation, and practice. She recalled:

> At first, everything was a surprise. After repeated failures, I began to ask where the master and I differed. I don't think one can understand or learn this skill without actually doing it. His bread and mine [came out] quite different even though we used the same materials. I asked why our products were so different and tried to reflect the difference in our skill of kneading.

Even at this stage, neither the head baker nor Tanaka was able to articulate know-ledge in any systematic fashion. Because their tacit knowledge never became explicit, others within Matsushita were left puzzled. Consequently, engineers were also brought to the hotel and allowed to knead and bake bread to improve their under-standing of the process. Sano, the division chief, noted, "If the craftsmen cannot explain their skills, then the engineers should become craftsmen."

Not being an engineer, Tanaka could not devise mechanical specifications. However, she was able to transfer her knowledge to the engineers by using the phrase "twisting stretch" to provide a rough image of kneading, and by suggesting the strength and speed of the propeller to be used in kneading. She would simply say, "Make the propeller move stronger", or "Move it faster." Then the engineers would adjust the machine specifications. Such a trial-and-error process continued for several months.

Her request for a "twisting stretch" movement was interpreted by the engineers and resulted in the addition inside the case of special ribs that held back the dough when the propeller turned so that the dough could be stretched. After a year of trial and error and working closely with other engineers, the team came up with product specifications that successfully reproduced the head baker's stretching technique and the quality of bread Tanaka had learned to make at the hotel. The team then materialized this concept, putting it together into a manual, and embodied it in the product. . . .

In the second cycle, the team had to resolve the problem of getting the machine to knead dough correctly. To solve the kneading problem, Ikuko Tanaka apprenticed herself with the head baker of the Osaka International Hotel. There she learned the skill through *socialization*, observing and imitating the head baker, rather than through reading memos or manuals. She then translated the kneading skill into explicit knowledge. The knowledge was *externalized* by *creating the concept of "twisting stretch."* In addition, she *externalized* this knowledge by expressing the movements required for the kneading propeller, using phrases like "more slowly" or "more strongly." For those who had never touched dough before, understanding the knead-ing skill was so difficult that engineers had to *share experiences* by spending hours at the baker to experience the touch of the dough. Tacit knowledge was *externalized* by lining special ribs inside the dough case. *Combination* took place when the "twisting stretch" concept and the technological knowledge of the engineers came together to produce a prototype of Home Bakery. Once the prototype was *justified* against the concept of "Rich," the development moved into the third cycle. (Nonaka and Takeuchi, 1995:103–6; italics in the original)

How Should We Understand Tacit Knowledge?

The preceding account of tacit knowledge has very little in common with that of Polanyi. Nonaka and Takeuchi assume that tacit knowledge is knowledge-not-yet-articulated: a set of rules incorporated in the activity an actor is involved, which is a matter of time for him/her to first learn and then formulate. The authors seem to think that what Tanaka learned through her apprenticeship with the master baker can be ultimately crystallized in a set of propositional "if–then" statements (Tsoukas, 1998: 44–8), or what Oakeshott (1991: 12–15) calls "technical knowledge" and Ryle (1963: 28–32) "knowing that." In that sense, the tacit knowledge involved in kneading that Tanaka picked up through her apprenticeship – in Oakeshott's (1991: 12–15) terms, the "practical knowledge" of kneading, and in Ryle's (1963: 28–32) terms, "knowing how" to knead – the sort of knowledge that exists only *in use* and cannot be formulated in rules, is equivalent to the set of statements that articulate it, namely it is equivalent to technical knowledge.

Tacit knowledge is thought to have the structure of a syllogism and as such can be reversed and, therefore, even mechanized (cf. Polanyi and Prosch, 1975: 40). What Tanaka was missing, the authors imply, were the premises of the syllogism, which she acquired through her sustained apprenticeship. Once they have been learned, it was a matter of time before she could put them together and arrive at the conclusion that "twisting stretch" and "the [right] movements required for the kneading propeller" (Nonaka and Takeuchi, 1995: 103–6) were what was required for designing the right bread-making machine.

However, although Nonaka and Takeuchi acknowledge that Tanaka's apprenticeship was necessary because "the art of kneading" (Nonaka and Takeuchi, 1995: 103) could not be imparted in any other way (e.g., "through reading memos and manuals", op. cit., p. 105), they view her apprenticeship as merely an alternative mechanism of transferring knowledge. In terms of content, knowledge acquired through apprenticeship is not thought to be qualitatively different from knowledge acquired through reading manuals, since in both cases the content of knowledge can be articulated and formulated in rules – only the manner of its appropriation differs. The mechanism of knowledge acquisition may be different, but the result is the same.

The "conduit metaphor of communication" (Lakoff, 1995: 116; Reddy, 1979; Tsoukas, 1997) that underlies Nonaka and Takeuchi's perspective – the view of ideas as objects which can be extracted from people and transmitted to others over a conduit – reduces practical knowledge to technical knowledge (cf. Costelloe, 1998: 325–26). However, while clearly Tanaka learned a technique during her apprenticeship, she acquired much more than technical knowledge, without even realizing it: she learned to make bread in a way which cannot be formulated in propositions but only manifested in her work. To treat practical (or tacit) knowledge as having a precisely definable content, which is initially located in the head of the practitioner and then "translated" (Nonaka and Takeuchi, 1995: 105) into explicit knowledge, is to reduce what is known to what is articulable, thus impoverishing the notion of practical knowledge. As Oakeshott (1991: 15) remarks,

> a pianist acquires artistry as well as technique, a chess-player style and insight into the game as well as a knowledge of the moves, and a scientist acquires (among other things) the sort of judgement which tells him when his technique is leading him astray and the connoisseurship which enables him to distinguish the profitable from the unprofitable directions to explore.

As should be clear from the preceding section, by viewing all knowing as essentially "personal knowing" (Polanyi, 1962: 49), Polanyi highlights the skilled performance that all acts of knowing require: the actor does not know all the rules he/she follows in the activity in which he/she is involved. Like Oakeshott (1991), Polanyi (1962: 50) notes that "rules of art can be useful, but they do not determine the practice of an art; they are maxims, which can serve as a guide to an art only if they can be integrated into the practical knowledge of the art. They cannot replace that knowledge." It is precisely because what needs to be known cannot be specified in detail that the relevant knowledge must be passed from master to apprentice.

> To learn by example is to submit to authority. You follow your master because you trust his manner of doing things even when you cannot analyse and account in detail for its effectiveness. By watching the master and emulating his efforts in the presence of his example, the apprentice unconsciously picks up the rules of the art, including those which are not explicitly known to the master himself. These hidden rules can be assimilated only by a person who surrenders himself to that extent uncritically to the imitation of another. (Polanyi, 1962: 53)

Like Polanyi's medical student discussed earlier, Tanaka was initially puzzled by what the master baker was doing – "at first, everything was a surprise" (Nonaka and Takeuchi, 1995: 104), as she put it. Her "repeated failures" were due not to lack of knowledge as such, but due to not having interiorized – dwelled in – the relevant knowledge yet. When, through practice, she begun to assimilate the knowledge involved in kneading bread – namely, when she became subsidiarily aware of how she was kneading – she could, subsequently, turn her focal awareness to the task at hand: *kneading* bread, as opposed to imitating the master. Knowledge now became a tool to be tacitly known and uncritically used in the service of an objective. "Kneading bread" ceased to be an object of focal awareness and became an instrument for actually kneading bread – a subsidiarily known tool for getting things done (Winograd and Flores, 1987: 27–37). For Tanaka to "convert" her kneading skill into explicit knowledge, she would need to focus her attention on her subsidiary knowledge, thereby becoming focally aware of it. In that event, however, she would no longer be engaged in the same activity, namely bread kneading, but in the activity of thinking about bread kneading, which is a different matter. The particulars of her skill are "logically unspecifiable" (Polanyi, 1962: 56), in the sense that their specification would logically contradict and practically paralyze what is implied in the carrying out of the performance at hand.

Of course, one might acknowledge this and still insist, along with Ambrosini and Bowman (2001) and Eraut (2000), that Tanaka could, *ex post facto*, reflect on her kneading skill, in the context of discussing bread-kneading with her colleagues – the engineers – and articulate it into explicit knowledge. But this would be an erroneous claim to make for, in such an event, she would no longer be describing her kneading skill *in toto* but only its technical part: that which is possible to articulate in rules, principles, maxims – in short, in propositions. What she has to say about the "ineffable" (Polanyi, 1962: 87–95) part of her skill, that which is tacitly known, she has said already in the bread she kneads and cannot put it in words (cf. Oakeshott, 1991: 14; Janik, 1992: 37). As Polanyi so perceptively argued, you cannot view subsidiary particulars as they allegedly are in themselves for they exist always in conjunction with the focus to which you attend from them, and that makes them unspecifiable. In his words:

> Subsidiary or instrumental knowledge, as I have defined it, is not known in itself but is known in terms of something focally known, to the quality of which it contributes; and to this extent it is unspecifiable. Analysis may bring subsidiary knowledge into focus and formulate it as a maxim or as a feature in a physiognomy, but such specification is in general not exhaustive. Although the expert diagnostician, taxonomist and cotton-classer can indicate their clues and formulate their maxims, they know many more things than they can tell, knowing them only in practice, as instrumental particulars, and not explicitly, as objects. The knowledge of such particulars is therefore ineffable, and the pondering of a judgement in terms of such particulars is an ineffable process of thought. (Polanyi, 1962: 88)

If the above is accepted, it follows that Tanaka neither "transferred" her tacit knowledge to the engineers, nor did she "convert" her kneading skill into explicit knowledge, as Nonaka and Takeuchi (1995: 104, 105) suggest. She could do neither of these things simply because, following Polanyi's and Oakeshott's definitions of tacit and practical knowledge respectively, skillful knowing contains an ineffable element; it is based on an act of personal insight that is essentially inarticulable.

Well, so far so good, but how are we to interpret Tanaka's concept of "twisting stretch," which turned out to be so useful for the making of Matsushita's bread-making machine? Or, to put it more generally, does the ineffability of skillful knowing imply that we can never talk about a practical activity at all? That the skills involved in, say, carpentry, teaching, ship navigation, or scientific activity will ultimately be mystical experiences outside the realm of reasoned discussion?

Not at all. What we do when we reflect on the practical activities we engage in, is to re-punctuate the distinctions underlying those activities, to draw the attention of those involved to certain hitherto unnoticed aspects of those activities – to see connections among items previously thought unconnected (cf. Weick, 1995: 87, 126). Through instructive forms of talk (e.g. "look at this," "have you thought about this in that way?," "try this," "imagine this," "compare this to that") practitioners are moved to *re*-view the situation they are in, to relate to their circumstances in a different way. From a Wittgensteinian perspective, Shotter and Katz (1996: 230) summarize succinctly this process as follows:

> to gain an explicit understanding of our everyday, practical activities, we can make use of the very same methods we used in gaining that practical kind of understanding in the first place – that is, we can use the self-same methods for drawing *our* attention to how people draw each other's attention to things, as they themselves (we all?) in fact use!

Notice what Shotter and Katz are saying: we learn to engage in practical activities through our participation in social practices, under the guidance of people who are more experienced than us (MacIntyre, 1985: 181–203; Taylor, 1993); people who, by drawing our attention to certain things, make us "see connections" (Wittgenstein, 1958: No. 122), pretty much like the master baker was drawing Tanaka's attention to certain aspects of bread-kneading. Through her subsequent conversations with the engineers, Tanaka was able to form an explicit understanding of the activity she was involved in, by having her attention drawn to how the master baker was drawing her attention to kneading – hence the concept of "twisting stretch." It is in this sense that Wittgenstein talks of language as issuing reminders of things we *already* know: "Something that we know when no one asks us, but no longer know when we are supposed to give an account of it, is something that we need to *remind* ourselves of" (Wittgenstein, 1958: No. 89; italics in the original).

In her apprenticeship, Tanaka came eventually to practice "twisting stretch" but she did not know it. She needed to be "reminded" of it. When we recursively punctuate our understanding, we see new connections and give "prominence to distinctions which our ordinary forms of language easily makes us overlook" (Wittgenstein, 1953: No. 132). Through the instructive (or directive) use of language we are led to notice certain aspects of our circumstances that, due to their simplicity and familiarity, they remain hidden ("one is unable to notice something – because it is always before one's eyes": Wittgenstein, 1953: No. 129). This is, then, the sense in which although skillful knowing is ultimately ineffable, it nonetheless can be talked about: through reminding ourselves of it, we notice certain important features which had hitherto escaped our attention and can now be seen in a new context. Consequently, we are led to relate to our circumstances in new ways and thus see new ways forward.

Conclusions

Tacit knowledge has been greatly misunderstood in management studies – or so I have argued in this chapter. Nonaka and Takeuchi's interpretation of tacit knowledge as knowledge-not-yet-articulated – knowledge awaiting for its "translation" or "conversion" into explicit knowledge – an interpretation that has been widely adopted in management studies, is erroneous: it ignores the essential ineffability of tacit knowledge, thus reducing it to what can be articulated. Tacit and explicit knowledge are not the two ends of a continuum but the two sides of the same coin: even the most explicit kind of knowledge is underlain by tacit knowledge. Tacit knowledge consists of a set of particulars of which we are subsidiarily aware as we focus on something else. Tacit knowing is vectorial: we know the particulars by relying on our awareness of them for attending to something else. Since subsidiaries exist as such by bearing on the focus *to* which we are attending *from* them, they cannot be separated from the focus and examined independently, for if this is done, their meaning will be lost. While we can certainly focus on particulars, we cannot do so in the context of action in which we are subsidiarily aware of them. Moreover, by focusing on particulars after a particular action has been performed, we are *not* focusing on them as they bear on the original focus of action, for their meaning is necessarily derived from their connection to that focus. When we focus on particulars we do so in a new context of action which itself is underlain by a new set of subsidiary particulars. Thus the idea that somehow one can focus on a set of particulars and convert them into explicit knowledge is unsustainable.

The ineffability of tacit knowledge does not mean that we cannot discuss the skilled performances in which we are involved. We can – indeed, should – discuss them provided we stop insisting on "converting" tacit knowledge and, instead, start recursively drawing our attention to how we draw each other's attention to things. Instructive forms of talk help us re-orientate ourselves to how we relate to others and the world around us, thus enabling us to talk and act differently. We can command a clearer view of our tasks at hand if we "re-mind" ourselves of how we do things so that distinctions that we had previously not noticed, and features that had previously escaped our attention, may be brought forward. Contrary to what Ambrosini and Bowman (2001) suggest, we do not so much need to operationalize tacit knowledge (as explained earlier, we could not do this, even if we wanted) as to find new ways of talking, fresh forms of interacting, and novel ways of distinguishing and connecting. Tacit knowledge cannot be "captured," "translated," or "converted," but only displayed, manifested, in what we do. New knowledge comes about not when the tacit becomes explicit, but when our skilled performance – our praxis – is punctuated in new ways through social interaction (Tsoukas, 2001).

REFERENCES

Ambrosini, V. and Bowman, C. (2001) Tacit Knowledge: Some Suggestions for Operationalization. *Journal of Management Studies*, 38: 811–29.

Bateson, G. (1979) Mind and Nature: A Necessary Unity. Toronto: Bantam Books.

Baumard, P. (1999) Tacit Knowledge in Organizations (trans. S. Wauchope). London: Sage.

Bell, D. (1999) The Axial Age of Technology Foreword: 1999. In D. Bell, *The Coming of the Post-Industrial Society*. New York: Basic Books, Special Anniversary Edition, ix–lxxxv.

Boisot, M.H. (1995) *Information Space: A Framework for Learning in Organizations, Institutions and Culture*. London, UK: Routledge.

Brown, J.S. and Duguid, P. (2000) *The Social Life of Information*, Boston: Harvard Business School Press.

Bruner, J. (1990) *Acts of Meaning*, Cambridge, MA: Harvard University Press.

Cook, S.D.N. and Brown, J.S. (1999) Bridging Epistemologies: The Generative Dance between Organizational Knowledge and Organizational Knowing, *Organization Science*, 10: 381–400.

Cook, S.D.N. and Yanow, D. (1996) Culture and Organizational Learning. In M.D. Cohen and L.S. Sproull (eds.), *Organizational Learning*, Thousand Oaks, CA: Sage, 430–59.

Costelloe, T. (1998) Oakeshott, Wittgenstein, and the Practice of Social Science. *Journal for the Theory of Social Behaviour*, 28: 323–47.

Davenport, T.H. and Prusak, L. (1998) *Working Knowledge*. Cambridge, MA: Harvard University Press.

Devlin, K. (1999) *Infosense*. New York: W.H. Freeman & Co.

Dixon, N.M. (2000) *Common Knowledge*. Boston: Harvard Business School Press.

Dreyfus, L.H. and Dreyfus, S.E. (2000) *Mind over Machine*. New York: Free Press.

Drucker, P. (1993) *Post-Capitalist Society*. Oxford: Butterworth/Heinemann.

Eraut, M. (2000) Non-formal Learning and Tacit Knowledge in Professional Work. *British Journal of Educational Psychology*, 70: 113–36.

Gill, J.H. (2000) *The Tacit Mode*. Albany: State University of New York Press.

Harper, D. (1987) *Working Knowledge*, Berkeley: University of California Press.

Janik, A. (1992) Why Is Wittgenstein Important? In B. Goranzon and M. Florin (eds.), *Skill and Education*. London: Springer-Verlag, 33–40.

Kreiner, K. (1999) Knowledge and Mind. *Advances in Management Cognition and Organizational Information Processing*, 6: 1–29.

Lakoff, G. (1995) Body, Brain, and Communication (interviewed by I.A. Boal). In J. Brook and I.A. Boal (eds.), *Resisting the Virtual Life*. San Francisco: City Lights, 115–29.

Leonard, D. and Sensiper, S. (1998) The Role of Tacit Knowledge in Group Innovation. *California Management Review*, 40 (3): 112–32.

MacIntyre, A. (1985) *After Virtue*, 2nd edn. London: Duckworth.

Mansell, R. and When, U. (1998) *Knowledge Societies*. New York: Oxford University Press.

Nonaka, I. and Takeuchi, H. (1995) *The Knowledge-Creating Company*. New York: Oxford University Press.

Oakeshott, M. (1991) *Rationalism in Politics and Other Essays*, new and expanded edn. Indianapolis: Liberty Press.

Polanyi, M. (1962) *Personal Knowledge*. Chicago: The University of Chicago Press.

Polanyi, M. (1966) *The Tacit Dimension*. London: Routledge & Kegan Paul.

Polanyi, M. (1969) *Knowing and Being*, M. Grene (ed.). Chicago: The University of Chicago Press.

Polanyi, M. and Prosch, H. (1975) *Meaning*. Chicago: The University of Chicago Press.

Reddy, M.J. (1979) The Conduit Metaphor: A Case of Frame Conflict in our Language about Language. In A. Ortony (ed.), *Metaphor and Thought*. Cambridge: Cambridge University Press, 284–324.

Ryle, G. (1963) *The Concept of Mind*. London: Penguin.

Shotter, J. and Katz, A.M. (1996) Articulating a Practice from within the Practice Itself: Establishing Formative Dialogues by the Use of a "Social Poetics". *Concepts and Transformation*, 1: 213–37.

Spender, J.-C. (1996) Making Knowledge the basis of a Dynamic Theory of the Firm. *Strategic Management Journal*, 17 (Special Winter Issue): 45–62.

Stehr, N. (1994) *Knowledge Societies*. London: Sage.

Taylor, C. (1993) To Follow a Rule . . . , In C. Calhoun, E. LiPuma, and M. Postone (eds.), *Bourdieu: Critical Perspectives*. Cambridge, UK: Policy Press, 45–59.

Thurow, L. (2000) *Creating Wealth*. London: Nicholas Brealey Publishing Ltd.

Toulmin, S. (1990) *Cosmopolis*. Chicago: University of Chicago Press.

Toulmin, S. (2001) *Return to Reason*. Cambridge, MA: Harvard University Press.

Tsoukas, H. (1996) The Firm as a Distributed Knowledge System: A Constructionist Approach. *Strategic Management Journal*, 17 (Winter Special Issue): 11–25.

Tsoukas, H. (1997) The Tyranny of Light: The Temptations and the Paradoxes of the Information Society. *Futures*, 29: 827–43.

Tsoukas, H. (1998) Forms of Knowledge and Forms of Life in Organized Contexts. In R.C.H. Chia (ed.), *In the Realm of Organization*. London: Routledge, 43–66.

Tsoukas, H. (2001) Where Does New Organizational Knowledge Come From? Keynote address at the International Conference *Managing Knowledge: Conversations and Critiques*, Leicester University, April 10–11, 2001.

Tsoukas, H. and Vladimirou, E. (2001) What Is Organizational Knowledge? *Journal of Management Studies*, 38 (7): 973–93.

Von Krogh, G., Ichijo, K. and Nonaka, I. (2000) *Enabling Knowledge Creation*. New York: Oxford University Press.

Weick, K. (1995) *Sensemaking in Organizations*. Thousand Oaks: CA: Sage.

Wenger, E. (1998) *Communities of Practice*. Cambridge: Cambridge University Press.

Winogrand, T. and Flores, F. (1987) *Understanding Computers and Cognition*. Reading, MA: Addison-Wesley.

Wittgenstein, L. (1958) *Philosophical Investigations*. Oxford: Blackwell.

22

Knowledge and Networks

RAYMOND VAN WIJK, FRANS A.J. VAN DEN BOSCH,
AND HENK W. VOLBERDA

CHAPTER OUTLINE

Reviewing the growing body of literature on how networks facilitate the management and organization of knowledge, this chapter discusses three types of networks: social, external, and internal networks. Studies of social networks have mainly focused on how knowledge transfers in networks facilitate network formation, and on how tie strength influences these knowledge transfers. Research on external networks has mainly concentrated on how complementary knowledge bases of firms are brought together, and on how learning processes between firms work out. Studies of internal networks have centered on how different structures and management processes facilitate knowledge creation and transfer. Since each of the three perspectives has contributed uniquely to the study of knowledge and networks, this chapter emphasizes the facets on which the perspectives complement each other. Finally, studies examining performance implications of knowledge and networks, as well as those considering networks as knowledge, are reviewed.

INTRODUCTION

Knowledge and networks are crucial to many organizations. Transformations in the competitive landscape propel firms to innovate and explore new opportunities, so as to outmaneuver competitors and achieve a competitive edge. Since knowledge is a bedrock ingredient of innovation, it has become significant to success (Grant, 1996). However, the knowledge required to innovate is not always readily available within a firm. To meet such deficiencies, firms can create knowledge internally (Nonaka, 1994), or they can acquire knowledge through external constituents (Cohen and Levinthal, 1990). Research has shown that network organization is rewarding for firms to gain access to knowledge, to facilitate learning processes, and to foster knowledge creation. In this chapter, state-of-the-art and received insights of how networks facilitate the management and organization of knowledge and learning are reviewed and consolidated, while prospective research avenues are discussed.

The study of organizational learning, knowledge, and networks in the management field traces its origins back to the 1950s and 1960s, with seminal sociological and economic contributions such as those of Cangelosi and Dill (1965) on organizational learning, of Penrose (1959) on the role of knowledge in the growth of the firm, and of Evan (1965) on organization sets. Strongly establishing themselves as individual streams of inquiry, over the years, these research streams have made major advancements. Research in which knowledge and networks are examined conjointly, on the other hand, has gained momentum predominantly during the past decade or so, since firms have been establishing the latter largely to gain access to and facilitate the organization and management of the former.

Networks are characterized by linkages between actors that are created in a temporal or semi-temporal fashion, commonly centering around a problem or issue (Baker, 1992). Actors in the network can learn from each other and integrate each other's knowledge until the problem is solved or the issue is past, and a new series of linkages can be formed with a different set of actors. The term "network" is fashionable, however. It suffers from semantic ambiguity, and has come to be an evocative metaphor ascribed to many collaborative ventures or relationships (Baker, 1992; Jarillo, 1988; Jones et al., 1997; Nohria, 1992; Parkhe, 1993; Quinn et al., 1996; Salancik, 1995).

The inconsistency surrounding the application of networks has two main antecedents.[1] First, multiple units and levels of analysis are involved in the study of networks. Second, by extension, networks have advanced both as an analytical tool employed by researchers and as a governance mode adopted by organizations (Nohria, 1992; Powell and Smith-Doerr, 1994). The disparity in units and levels of analysis at which networks have been studied, and the different applications of networks have brought about three distinct perspectives on networks: social networks, external networks, and internal networks. Mainly used as an analytical tool, a social network perspective considers every organization or set of organizations as a network regardless of governance mode. External and internal networks, on the other hand, have emerged as discrete modes of governance. Although the three perspectives are non-mistakenly concerned with network organization, each has contributed uniquely to the study of knowledge and networks. In this chapter, therefore, the facilitatory role of networks in creating and integrating knowledge will be reviewed by heeding these three perspectives on networks. Because some perspectives have recently appeared instrumental to others, additionally, facets are heeded on which these perspectives complement one another.

The chapter is organized as follows. In the next section, the main conclusions that can be drawn from research on the manifestation of knowledge in external, internal and social networks are presented. In the third section, the performance implications of networks and knowledge are heeded. Then, it is considered that networks by themselves may be a form of knowledge. In the final section, current understanding of knowledge and networks is discussed and future research directions are suggested.

Knowledge in Networks

The study of how networks foster the management and organization of knowledge centers around three perspectives: social networks, external networks, and internal networks. The origins of the three banners under which research into knowledge and networks has developed, as well as their applications, contributions to knowledge research, main parameters and performance implications are listed in table 22.1.

Knowledge in social networks

Having its origins in sociology and anthropology, the study of social networks goes by the notion that "the structure of any social organization can be thought of as a network" (Nohria and Eccles, 1992: 288), and that the actions of network actors are shaped and constrained because of their position and embeddedness in the network (Nohria, 1992). Or, as Lincoln (1982: 26) argues, "to assert that an organization is not a network is to strip of it that quality in terms of which it is best defined: the pattern of recurring linkages among its parts." A social network perspective entails not only that all organizations are social networks, but that the environment is a network of other organizations. With that, social network analysis provides management scholars a tool to be used to examine relations between actors, such as individuals, groups of individuals, and firms (Burt, 1982; Marsden, 1990; Tichy et al., 1979; Wasserman and Faust, 1994), in which "network" is essentially a construct created by the investigator. In that vein, social network analysis has been used to examine relations among individuals and units within and across organizations, as well as among organizations in organizational fields (e.g. Amburgey et al., 1996; Galaskiewicz and Wasserman, 1989), business groups (Gerlach and Lincoln, 1992; Granovetter, 1994), and regions (Grabher, 1993). Moreover, this view has led to the economics critique that, like any other actor, firms are far from atomistic agents, and embedded in networks that influence competitive actions (Granovetter, 1985, 1992; Burt, 1992).

Centering on the ties between actors, the contribution of social network research to the study of knowledge is twofold. First, tie content may be (1) assets, (2) information, and (3) status (Galaskiewicz, 1979). With the emergence of knowledge as a strategic asset (Grant, 1996; Winter, 1987), much research in social networks has come to center on knowledge transfer through ties. Second, ties have information benefits that occur in three forms: access, timing, and referrals (Burt, 1992). Access means that network ties influence access to parties. Timing allows actors to obtain information sooner than it becomes available to actors without such contacts. Referrals constitute processes which provide information to actors in the network on available opportunities. Hence, the information benefits of ties influence network formation, and consequently, opportunities to combine and exchange knowledge (see also, Dyer and Singh, 1998; Nahapiet and Ghoshal, 1998).

Main parameters Social network analysis describes the network of ties by considering actors' structural and relational embeddedness in the network (Granovetter, 1992). Relating to network density, network cohesion, and with that, the extent to which networks are open or closed, structural embeddedness refers to the structure of the network an actor

TABLE 22.1 Three network perspectives

	Social networks	External networks	Internal networks
Origin	Sociology and anthropology	Economics, mainly socio-economics and institutional economics	Management, mainly international business
Application	Network as an analytical tool to examine social relations and ties between individuals and organizations	Network as a governance mode intermediating markets and hierarchies	Network as a form of organizing alternative to multidivisional and functional organizations
Relation to study of knowledge	– Provide timely access to knowledge and information, either directly or indirectly through referrals, about potential partners – Vehicle to transfer knowledge directly	– Combination of complementary knowledge bases – Internalization of external knowledge	– Increase internal knowledge transfer so as to foster internal knowledge creation and integration processes
Main parameters	– Structural versus relational embeddedness – Positional embeddedness – Structural equivalence – Structural autonomy – Tie strength – Social capital versus structural holes	– Governance structure – Competition – Learning races	– Organization structure – Management – Knowledge flow configuration
Performance consequences	– Increased innovation – Increased value creation – Increased financial performance	– Increased innovation – Increased product development – Increased financial performance	– Increased innovation – Increased product development – Increased financial performance
Key studies	Ahuja (2000a; 2000b); Dyer and Singh (1998); Gulati (1995a; 1995b; 1998; 1999); Gulati and Gargiulo (1999); Hansen (1998); Powell et al. (1996); Tsai (2000; 2001); Tsai and Ghoshal (1998)	Badaracco (1991); Doz and Hamel (1998); Dyer (1996; 1997); Dyer and Nobeoka (2000); Hagedoorn (1993); Hagedoorn and Schakenraad (1994); Hamel (1991); Inkpen (1995); Inkpen and Crossan (1995); Inkpen and Dinur (1998); Lyles (1988); Parkhe (1991); Powell (1990); Pucik (1991)	Ghoshal and Bartlett (1997); Hedlund (1994; 1996); Miles and Snow (1994; 1996); Nohria and Ghoshal (1997); Pettigrew and Fenton (2000); Van Wijk and Van den Bosch (1998)

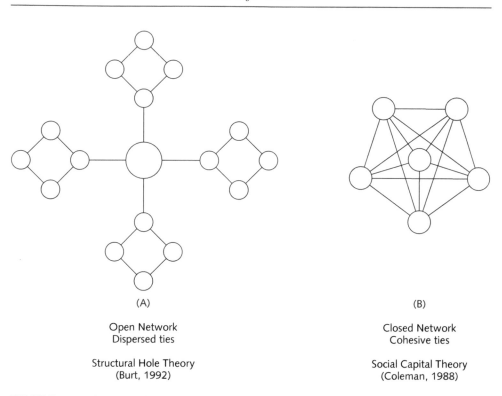

(A)   (B)

Open Network   Closed Network
Dispersed ties   Cohesive ties

Structural Hole Theory   Social Capital Theory
(Burt, 1992)   (Coleman, 1988)

FIGURE 22.1   Structural hole perspective versus social capital perspective on networks

finds itself in terms of mutual contacts to one another. Relational embeddedness indicates
the kind of relationships actors have developed, and is associated with tie strength or intensity (Gnyawali and Madhavan, 2001; Nahapiet and Ghoshal, 1998; Rowley et al., 2000).
In a study on the origins of inter-organizational networks, Gulati and Gargiulo (1999)
added to these two dimensions an actor's positional embeddedness, which provides information about the information benefits of the ties and network itself.

On the basis of these dimensions, two views have emerged on how knowledge and information flow through a network (Burt, 1997, 2000; Gargiulo and Benassi, 2000; Hite and
Hesterly, 2001; Uzzi, 1996, 1997; Walker et al., 1997). The first view, structural hole theory
(figure 22.1a), stresses that the information benefits accruing to an actor are highest when
that actor is central to the network and has a key role in linking multiple smaller actor networks between which no direct links exist. In other words, every piece of information and
knowledge must go through the central actor if it travels from one network to the other,
making the central actor structurally autonomous (Burt, 1992). Structural hole theory
views the network as an opportunity for entrepreneurs to exploit by seeking partners that
are unique or non-redundant and bring new information to be used in, for example, negotiating. Structural hole theory thus concerns the brokering of knowledge and information
flows.

The second view, social capital theory (figure 22.1b), maintains that actors should be linked as much as possible, so as to increase their social capital, which is defined as the set of social resources embedded in relationships. Actors in such a dense network enjoy information benefits since many actors in such a network share the same direct and indirect ties, and are therefore structurally equivalent. Thus, social capital theory stresses that the network is reproduced due to its value in preserving the social capital of an individual. Nahapiet and Ghoshal (1998: 250) argue that "social capital facilitates the development of intellectual capital by affecting the conditions necessary for exchange and combination [of knowledge] to occur." Social capital can therefore act as a resource, but also as a constraint in enforcing norms and values among network members (Burt, 2000; Coleman, 1988).

Corroborating Uzzi's (1997) "paradox of embeddedness," Gargiulo and Benassi (2000) found that actors positioned in structural holes were better able to adapt to environmental changes, and that the network closure produced by cohesive ties fostered stability. Walker et al. (1997) argue that structural hole theory best applies to networks of market transactions, while social capital theories best suit networks of cooperative relationships. This is echoed in Hite and Hesterly's (2001) study, who found that in the early growth stages of firms networks are likely to be dense, closed and socially embedded. In later growth stages, firms are likely to exploit structural holes in a balance of embedded, arm's-length relations.

Using Granovetter's (1973) distinction between weak ties, which are distant and infrequent, and strong ties, which are close and frequent, in a study of regional network development in the German Ruhr area, Grabher (1993) found that strong ties may lead to functional, cognitive and political lock-ins. A similar effect has been argued by Lyles and Schwenk (1992) who assert that a loosely coupled knowledge structure (cf. Orton and Weick, 1990) fosters adaptation. Conversely, the studies of Ahuja (2000a), Kraatz (1998), and Walker et al. (1997) found support that cohesive and strong ties, which are information-rich, fostered adaptiveness by increasing innovation. Hansen (1999) concluded that cohesive ties are less likely to allow firms to adapt to changes in coordination requirements. Strong ties require increased resources to maintain and are prone to network inertia, where nodes in the network stay within their network. In a study of interunit knowledge transfer, he found that a trade-off exists in the use of ties when searching for relevant knowledge and transferring knowledge. This search-transfer problem indicates that weak ties are most effective for searching knowledge and transferring non-complex, easy-to-codify knowledge, but that strong ties, characterized by close interaction and communication, are necessary for transferring complex, difficult-to-codify knowledge. Complexity of knowledge is thus an important moderator in the decision of optimal linkages (see also, Nonaka and Takeuchi, 1995; Winter, 1987; Zander and Kogut, 1995).

Complex knowledge, however, is a strong contributor to the novelty of innovation, and thus adaptation (cf. Galunic and Rodan, 1998). Using a social capital perspective, which emphasizes cohesion of ties, Tsai and Ghoshal (1998) also found that social capital contributes to value creation, as measured by product development performance. Following Nahapiet and Ghoshal (1998), they identified three dimensions of social capital: structural social capital, relational social capital and cognitive social capital. Structural social capital emerges from structural embeddedness, while relational social capital emerges from relational embeddedness. The cognitive dimension of social capital is embodied in shared codes and paradigms that facilitates common understanding of collective goals and proper conduct in the system of relations. Tsai and Ghoshal (1998) found that both structural and cognitive social capital contributed to relational social capital, which in turn increased knowledge and resource combinations, and value creation.

Similar to Stuart's (1998) finding that technological relatedness contributed to alliance formation, Tsai (2000) found that relatedness of resources and knowledge contributes to intraorganizational linkage formation. From an opposite viewpoint, technological distance between network partners has been found to relate negatively to innovation (Ahuja, 2000b). These findings suggest that absorptive capacity is important in network relations. Likewise, Szulanski (1996) found that lack of absorptive capacity with the recipient of knowledge was the most important barrier in intrafirm transfers of best practices. Absorptive capacity is built on prior knowledge endowments: the more knowledge a firm possesses in a certain knowledge domain, the easier it is to learn new things in that domain (Cohen and Levinthal, 1990). When the knowledge stocks of actors in a network overlap, learning and knowledge transfer are fostered. Van Wijk et al. (2001) found that broad knowledge, which facilitates the absorption of knowledge in a broad domain and thus increases the chance that the knowledge of network actors overlap, increased the ratio of exploration to exploitation. At the dyad level, the capacity to absorb knowledge from one partner is different from capacity to absorb knowledge from another partner, because the relevant knowledge bases of actors differ (Inkpen and Crossan, 1995; Dyer and Singh, 1998; Lane and Lubatkin, 1998). In that vein, Kumar and Nti (1998) suggested that firms leverage absorptive capacity so that knowledge absorbed from one partner may increase the ability to absorb knowledge from another partner.

Social network analysis has also been deployed to increase our understanding of how firms obtain information about the competencies, needs and reliabilities of potential partners in alliances (Gulati, 1995a, 1995b; Gulati and Gargiulo, 1999). Earlier studies found that personal ties between members of different organizations are important to the creation of new alliances (Ring and Van de Ven, 1992, 1994; Doz, 1996). Doz et al. (2000) studied two types of alliance formation processes: emergent and engineered processes. The existence of personal ties was found crucial in engineered processes, because in these alliance formation processes a triggering entity exists which actively recruits new partners. Emergent network formation processes develop when changes in the environment take place and trigger shared views and interest in an alliance among the partners involved.

In a longitudinal study of firms in the semiconductor industry, Stuart (1998) found that the alliance opportunity sets of prestigious organizations and organizations in crowded positions were highest. Organizations with crowded network positions are those that participate in networks in technological segments in which many firms actively innovate. Prestigious organizations are those organizations that have a track record of producing innovations that turn out to be dominant designs. A similar result was found by Ahuja (2000a), which indicates that linkage formation in networks is dependent on the technical, commercial and social capital of the actors in the network, and the occurrence of a major invention or breakthrough.

The possibility surfaces that information is imperfect, which raises search costs. Reliable information may be difficult to obtain before the alliance is initiated, and thus faces concerns of moral hazard and opportunistic behavior. One way firms can overcome the possibility of opportunism to occur and obtain reliable information is by considering the reputation of partners. As Granovetter (1985: 490) argues, individuals have "widespread preference for transacting with individuals of known reputation." As such, trust is found important to network formation and maintenance: trust enables network formation, it preserves the network through repeated ties, and repeated ties contribute to the development of trust (Bradach and Eccles, 1989; Gulati, 1995a).

Knowledge in external networks

Stemming from economics disciplines, mainly from socio-economics and institutional economics, external network research focuses on network organization as a governance mode interjacent to market organization and firm organization, extending the make-or-buy decision with the decision to cooperate (Powell, 1987, 1990; Williamson, 1975, 1985). In sociology, it was found already that repeated non-contractual ties could substitute for contractual ones (Macaulay, 1962). Research in this tradition focuses on the networks that firms maintain in the shape of joint ventures and strategic alliances that allow firms to reduce risk, to enjoy economies of scale, to block competitors, to obtain initial international presence and overcome trade barriers, and to have access to complementary resources and technologies (e.g., Contractor and Lorange, 1988; Doz and Hamel, 1998; Hagedoorn, 1993; Jarillo, 1988; Kogut, 1988; Pucik, 1991; Teece, 1986).[2]

From a knowledge perspective, external networks are initiated (1) to gain access to new knowledge and internalize that knowledge or (2) to pool knowledge together (Inkpen and Dinur, 1998; see table 22.1). Knowledge and product domains of a firm may not overlap, preventing firms from developing new products. Such inconsistencies trigger firms to look outside for knowledge and internalize it through alliances (Grant and Baden-Fuller, 1995). Firms may also have knowledge bases that are complementary or co-specialized, in such a way that innovation can only occur when those complementary knowledge bases are brought together in a separate entity, such as a joint venture (cf. Dyer, 1996a, 1996b; Larsson et al., 1998; Shenkar and Li, 1999; Teece, 1986). When built on relation-specific assets and knowledge sharing routines, idiosyncratic inter-firm linkages may emerge that allow firms to combine knowledge and other resources in unique ways, and lead to the generation of relational rents (Dyer and Singh, 1998). The ground for networks of alliances and joint ventures emerging is that a diverse set of cooperations provides a firm access to a broader knowledge base, which it potentially can tap into (Mitchell and Singh, 1996). For example, exemplar to Japanese "Alliance Capitalism" (Gerlach, 1992), Toyota and its suppliers cooperate in a diverse network to learn from each other and about new industry trends.

Main parameters Accounts have emerged that the Japanese are more successful in reaping the benefits from external networks than, for example, US firms, partly because of their history in external networks. Hamel (1991) portrayed the US–Japanese situation as US companies believing they are "masters" and Japanese companies behaving as "students," but by acting as "students" they proved to be the "masters" in reaping benefits from external networks. However, two studies have disconfirmed this. In their study covering the entire set of US–Japanese alliances in operation since 1980, Hennart et al. (1999) found no support for Hamel's (1991) thesis that Japanese firms are better learners than their US partners. They came to that finding by adopting the thesis that such learning race behavior would be reflected in changes in the equity stakes by the Japanese, which was not the case. Similarly, Mowery et al. (1996) found no support that Japanese firms were better learners in strategic alliances.

Alliance duration is one indicator of alliance success, but if the purpose of an alliance is internalizing the partners' knowledge, longevity may not be the right indicator (Hamel, 1991). Learning in external networks is fraught with competitive motivations (Gnyawali and Madhavan, 2001). Mowery et al. (1996) found that knowledge transfers between network partners would be higher when they share a common knowledge base, as this increased the capacity to absorb knowledge (see also Lane and Lubatkin, 1998). However, they also found that competition moderates this relationship, since firms operating in industries with the same primary Standard Industrial Classifications (SICs) tended to transfer less knowledge among each other.

Competition may also result in learning races. Learning races do contribute to the extent to which firms can reap private benefits from an alliance. Khanna et al. (1998) and Khanna (1998) have argued that learning races and the ability to internalize knowledge is dependent on the relative scope of the partnering firms and the alliance. The more the scope of the alliance overlaps with the scope of the firms involved, the more common benefits would accrue to both firms. Overlap in scope increases overlap in knowledge bases, and thus increases relative absorptive capacity (Lane and Lubatkin, 1998; Kumar and Nti, 1998), allowing both firms to internalize knowledge. When the scope does not overlap, private benefits would accrue to the partnering firm, since knowledge outside the scope of the alliance has only use to the focal firm.

On the basis of case studies at 11 firms, Hamel (1991) found that learning outcomes were dependent on the intent of a firm, the transparencies of the partners, and the receptivities of the partners. Intent refers to the initial propensity of firms to learn through their collaborations. Transparency refers to the openness of each partner. Receptivity denotes the capacity to learn, and closely relates to absorptive capacity (Cohen and Levinthal, 1990; Lane and Lubatkin, 1998). From this perspective, private benefits accruing to a firm would be high when that firm's intent is high, whereas the partners' is low; when the transparency of that firm is low, whereas the partners' is high; and when the focal firm's receptivity is high, and the partners' is low.

In a study covering the alliances of 147 multinational corporations (MNCs), Simonin (1999) found that ambiguity has a significant negative impact on knowledge transfer. He also found that the level of ambiguity is positively related to the tacitness of knowledge (see also Hansen, 1999), and complexity as to the interrelatedness of technologies, routines, individuals and resources. Cultural and organizational distance between partner firms was found to increase the ambiguity associated with interpartner learning (see also Szulanski, 1996). Simonin also found that higher levels of previous experience with the knowledge were negatively associated with ambiguity. As mentioned, higher levels of prior knowledge increases absorptive capacity.

Further, Simonin (1999) found that the effects of tacitness and ambiguity were independent of alliance duration, but that the effects of complexity and experience disappeared for older alliances and that the effect of cultural and organizational distance disappeared for younger alliances. Partners in older alliances may be more adapted to each other so that complexity and lack of previous experience are less problematic to knowledge transfer. Because of stronger ties, partners in older alliances may also have developed partner-specific collaborative knowledge (cf. Dyer and Singh, 1998; Kumar and Nti, 1998) that enables them to overcome issues of complexity and lack of previous experience. Simonin showed that collaborative knowledge contributed to knowledge transfer in alliances, but did not examine the independent effects of collaborative knowledge and alliance duration. Partners in younger alliances may be subject to a cultural adjustment curve that was seen by the partners as necessary to overcome before the alliance was initiated.

Distinct interdependencies and complexities inherent in tasks lead to coordination costs (Gulati and Singh, 1998). External networks are essentially incomplete contracts with the risks of opportunistic behavior and knowledge leakage emerging (Baum et al., 2000). Therefore, firms use different governance structures for their alliances (Grandori and Soda, 1995), which are differentiated by the amount of hierarchical controls (Dyer and Singh, 1998). When appropriation or opportunistic behavior is an issue, firms were found to use joint ventures and other equity-based arrangements as the inter-organizational governance mode (Baum et al., 2000). Dyer and Singh (1998) argue that effective governance can also occur through third-party enforcement or self-enforcement, either formally through hostages (Williamson, 1985) or informally through trust and reputation (Granovetter, 1985; Gulati, 1995b). For example, Kale et al. (2000) found that the development relational capital based on mutual trust creates a basis for knowledge transfer, and restricts opportunistic behavior. Thus, as in studies of social networks, as an alternative to the price mechanism of markets and the control mechanism of hierarchies, trust was found crucial in external networks (Bradach and Eccles, 1989).

Knowledge in internal networks

Being the first strain of research on networks that originated in the management field, internal network research centers on network organization as a form of organizing alternative to, for example, functional and multidivisional organization forms (Hedlund, 1994; Nohria and Ghoshal, 1997). When firms enter into external networks, little or no change takes place as to internal organization. Hierarchical logics and routines of organizing, such as those of the functional and multidivisional organization (Chandler, 1962; Williamson, 1975), remain unimpaired and prevent firms from deploying knowledge acquired externally as ambitiously internally (Ghoshal and Bartlett, 1997).

Since "knowledge is a resource that is difficult to accumulate at the corporate level . . . [and] those with the specialized knowledge and expertise most vital to the company's competitiveness are usually located far away from the corporate headquarters" (Bartlett and Ghoshal, 1993: 32), these developments have triggered the emergence of an alternate corporate model that marks "the selective infusion of market mechanisms into hierarchy and hierarchy into markets" (Zenger and Hesterly, 1997: 210). That is to say, alongside a large reliance on external networks, this corporate model relies on intra-organizational or internal networks to foster knowledge creation and integration inside a firm's boundaries. Research on this corporate model has developed most notably in the field of International Business to understand how MNCs can benefit from their distributed knowledge stocks, and has received a wide variety of labels, for example, differentiated network (Nohria and Ghoshal, 1997), integrated network (Ghoshal and Bartlett, 1997), cellular form (Miles et al., 1997), and simply internal network or network organization (Miles and Snow, 1995). For the mnemonics of "New" and "Novel" – as the successor to the multidivisional M-form – this corporate model has been more generally labeled the N-form corporation (Hedlund, 1994). However, owing to the N-form's network characteristics, "N" could also stand for "Network" (Ferlie and Pettigrew, 1996; Hedlund, 1996; Nohria, 1996; Perrone, 1997).

Most of the research on internal networks can be traced to the literature on new forms of organizing, since many new forms of organizing share common features that resemble network characteristics. This is not to say that internal networks are truly "new" forms of organizing. Burns and Stalker (1961) already compared the characteristics of organic systems of management, which illustrate close resemblance to internal networks. Likewise, Thompson (1965) was early to report that bureaucracies are moving in the direction of looser structures, decentralization, project organization, and freer communication to foster innovation. Also, Hedberg et al. (1976) laid down the foundations of self-designing organizations, showing close resemblance to internal networks. However, the proportion of firms with the characteristics indigenous to internal networks has been rising progressively during the 1990s (Pettigrew et al., 2000).

Pettigrew and Fenton (2000: 3) observe, however, that the "literature has yet to be united under an overarching theory or perspective and therefore may only be weakly classified as a research focus." Empirical studies of internal networks are largely limited to case studies of firms that seem to have been the first experimenting with internal network forms of organizing (Ghoshal and Bartlett, 1997; Pettigrew and Fenton, 2000). The insights gained on how internal networks facilitate internal knowledge transfer and creation has mostly emerged from studies explicitly examining knowledge creation and transfer (e.g., Grant, 1996; Kogut and Zander, 1992; Szulanski, 1996; Zander and Kogut, 1995).

Main parameters   Nohria and Ghoshal (1997: 208) argue that a differentiated network's advantage is its "ability to create new value through the accumulation, transfer, and integration of different kinds of knowledge, resources, and capabilities across its dispersed organizational units." To that end, the structure of internal networks embraces a dense network of dispersed, differentiated but interdependent organizational units with operational and strategic responsibility, in which knowledge is purposefully retained at lower levels.

Hedlund (1994) has labeled such a structure a "heterarchy," which is based on the principles of multiplication and combination rather than on the principle of division so characteristic of hierarchies. The presence of heterarchy is not to say, however, that hierarchical organization has disappeared in internal networks. Hierarchy remains indispensable to reach certain decisions quickly, resolve disputes, motivate allegiance to the internal network's mission and objectives, and to control activities of exploitation (Powell, 1990; Quinn et al., 1996). Furthermore, Gupta and Govindarajan (2000) found that the central organization of MNCs generally continue to play an important role in knowledge transfer in MNCs. In a study of a business transitioning into an internal network, Van Den Bosch and Van Wijk (2000) illustrated how a firm may move from a hierarchical form towards an internal network form, and that, although the number of organizational layers decreased, hierarchy remains existent and necessary. Nonaka and Takeuchi (1995) have captured this duality of structure in their "hypertext organization" model, which consists of a business-system layer that closely resembles a hierarchy, a project-system layer where people meet in teams and projects, and a knowledge base layer where the knowledge of the entire organization resides.

Changing the formal organization only will not give rise to heterarchy, but subtler changes in management are required as well to effectuate interdependencies among organizational units (Hedlund, 1994). In line with Burns and Stalker's (1961: 121) organic form in which "a network structure of control, authority, and communication" is present, several scholars have recently pointed out that internal networks require a different management philosophy compared to traditional forms (e.g., Ghoshal and Bartlett, 1997; Miles and Snow, 1994). Rather than a monitor or commander, the role of executive management in internal networks is that of an architect, catalyst, and facilitator of network processes (Hedlund, 1994). Instead of *allocating* resources based on formal control mechanisms, Ghoshal and Bartlett (1997) have pointed out that executives facilitate the *leveraging* of resources by institutionalizing common norms and values that breed a culture of trust, reciprocity and collaboration (see also Powell, 1990). Senior managers in internal networks are horizontal knowledge brokers "linking and leveraging the company's widely distributed resources and capabilities," rather than vertical information brokers (Bartlett and Ghoshal, 1993: 33).

In order to be of value to the firm in forming organizational capability knowledge needs to be integrated (Grant, 1996; Hedlund, 1994) and replicated (Kogut and Zander, 1992). The transfer and integration of knowledge across organizational units requires that knowledge flows connect stocks of knowledge of organizational units. Whereas in many other organization forms knowledge flows are primarily vertical from headquarters to units, in internal network forms horizontal knowledge flows between units supplant and supplement vertical ones (cf. Aoki, 1986). Although hierarchy remains existent in internal networks as an integration mechanism, and therefore vertical knowledge flows, the proportion of horizontal to vertical knowledge flows is likely to increase in internal networks (Van Wijk and Van Den Bosch, 1998).

NETWORK RESEARCH: INDIVIDUAL STREAMS OR COHERENT BODY?

Does the development of research on knowledge and networks under three banners mean that they are mutually exclusive? As can be observed in the previous discussion, streams of network research have already been used to develop others. This applies especially to those that are grounded in social network analysis, since the concepts used in social network analysis have general application to all kinds of organizations, including internal and external networks. Moving beyond the exogenous rationales for entering into external networks that characterize so many studies on external networks, most notably, social network analysis has been instrumental to explain endogenous aspects of network formation (Gulati and Gargiulo, 1999), as well as benefits of external networks (Dyer and Singh, 1998). Most recently, social network analysis has also been employed to understand intra-organizational linkage formation (Tsai, 2000) and benefits (Tsai and Ghoshal, 1998).

More generally, concepts used in one stream of inquiry can be used to develop another. For example, for many studies in inter-organizational networks, the level of analysis is adjustable to the intra-organizational level without any far-reaching consequences for the insights obtained from the study. For example, Lane and Lubatkin (1998) argue that relativity of absorptive capacity not only applies to inter-organizational networks, but could also explain intra-organizational learning processes between units. Indeed, absorptive capacity has been found important in social networks (Ahuja, 2000b; Tsai, 2001), external networks (Cohen and Levinthal, 1990; Dyer and Singh, 1998) and internal networks (Szulanski, 1996; Van Wijk et al., 2001), underscoring the power of the construct to transcend disciplines (Van Den Bosch et al., this volume). Others (e.g., Jones et al., 1997) have contributed to developing more general network theories. In certain cases, however, substitution of level of analysis entails implications. Part of this is the result of different contexts in which networks manifest themselves. For example, external networks are generally influenced by competitive forces between firms, which are less likely to play a crucial role or may even be absent in social and internal networks.

Given that every organization is essentially a social network (Lincoln, 1982), that firms listed on *Fortune*'s top 500 had on average 24 joint ventures in operation over the period 1978–92 (Nohria, 1996), and that the proportion of firms experimenting with internal networks seems to be rising (Pettigrew et al., 2000), firms, too, are likely to be involved in a variety of networks simultaneously. By way of illustration, in figure 22.2 it is portrayed that an organization can be involved in all three types of networks and that they operate in coexistence. In the center of the figure is the focal firm, firm A, which itself is an internal network. Firm A has an alliance set up with firm B, a hierarchical organization, which is illustrated as a formal network which is star-shaped with a couple of informal linkages. This alliance has come into existence because an employee working at unit A_1 of firm A was acquainted with a manager working for unit B_1 of firm B, and obtained knowledge of firm B's capabilities, which proved to be complementary to firm A's capabilities. The knowledge obtained from this social network was communicated to the headquarters of firm A, HQ_A, which initiated the alliance. A similar social relationship was present between unit A_2 of firm A and unit B_2 of firm B. In this case, it led to an alliance between unit A_2 of firm A with unit C_1 of firm C. The alliance was only established between the units of the respective firms, since the domain of the alliance was limited to the domains of the units and unit C_1 appeared to possess knowledge that was valuable to unit A_2, the information of which was obtained via the informal relationship between unit A_2 and unit B_2. Finally, the informal relationship between unit A_3 of firm A with unit D_1 of competing firm D resulted in the initiation of a joint venture between firm A and firm E. Unit D_1 had a close relationship with unit E_1, which in turn was on a friendly basis with a person

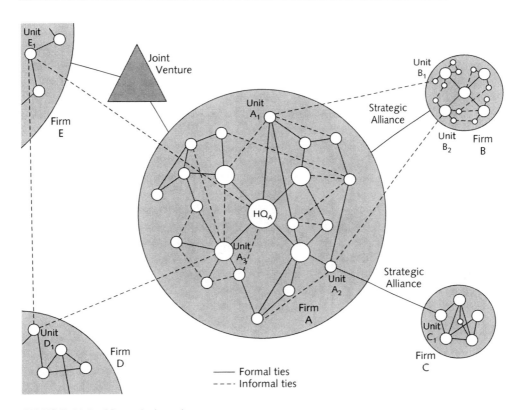

FIGURE 22.2   Networks in action

in the headquarters of firm A, HQ_A. This set of relationships allowed knowledge about the capabilities of firm A and firm E to flow through the social network, and resulted in a joint venture in which knowledge and resources were pooled to develop a new product. In that vein, firm A found itself in social networks, external networks, and internal networks, and the presence of one, at times, led to the creation of another.

NETWORKS, KNOWLEDGE, AND PERFORMANCE

Since networks and knowledge are employed in environments that put a premium on exploration rather than exploitation (March, 1991), studies examining the performance implications of knowledge and networks have mainly used innovation-based or product development performance measures. Others have used survival and growth rates as performance measures. Most of these studies have found positive performance implications.

Corroborating Powell et al.'s (1996) finding that the locus of innovation in high-technology industries lies often within the alliance, in a study of the hospital software systems industry, Mitchell and Singh (1996) found that, in general, collaborating firms were less likely to shut down than independent firms. However, they also found that, following a sudden environmental shock, firms with collaborative partnerships for activities central to the shock were more likely to shut down, while firms with collaborative partnerships for activities outside the shock were more likely to survive. In related studies Singh (1997) and Singh and Mitchell (1996) found that chances of firm survival were increased if a focal firm continued to build alliances with firms after existing partners shut down, or when new partnerships were formed by those partners. In that vein, inter-firm collaboration appeared to contribute to survival at one time, but inhibited the ability to adapt to environmental circumstances at another time. As they argue, "businesses that are able to work closely with current partners while at the same time identifying possible new partners are likely to succeed in an industry marked by ongoing technological change" (Singh and Mitchell, 1996: 112).

Likewise, in a study of the Canadian biotechnology industry, following the findings of Baum and Oliver (1992), Baum et al. (2000) found that startups can enhance performance by entering into alliances and by configuring them into a network through which access to diverse information and capabilities is provided. In this study, performance was measured by innovation-based measures which seemed crucial to increased survival rates in high-technology industries. Similar findings were found by Deeds and Hill (1996), Hagedoorn and Schakenraad (1994), and Stuart (2000).

A related finding was found in social network analysis, in reference to the "paradox of embeddedness," which denotes the trade-off of maintaining cohesive and diverse ties at the same time (Gargiulo and Benassi, 2000; Uzzi, 1997). Uzzi (1996) found that in stable environments increased embeddedness decreased failure rates, as it makes interaction more extensive and allows for transfer of fine-grained, complex knowledge (Hansen, 1999), which in turn fosters innovation and survival. In more turbulent environments, however, where selection processes operate with greater force, Uzzi (1996) found that a firm is more likely to survive if it has a diverse set of ties to a variety of partners. Similarly, Rowley et al. (2000) examined the combined role of structural and relational embeddedness – network density and tie strength – on performance in exploitation and exploration favoring environments. They found that network density was negatively related to firm performance in exploitation-favoring environments, but that strong ties have a positive influence on performance in such environments. They also found that the number of weak ties a firm has is positively related to performance in environments demanding exploration. No support was found, however, for their hypothesis that strong ties are negatively related to firm performance in an environmental context favoring exploration. Continuous formation of new relationships with diverse partners thus allows firms to maintain access to a broad knowledge base, which was found to contribute to innovation and exploration, but depth of knowledge, gained through strong ties, is crucial as well. Having both deep and broad knowledge facilitates knowledge absorption in a variety of domains, and allows for both exploration and exploitation (Van Wijk et al., 2001).

In a study of an internal network, Tsai (2001) found that a central network position providing access to a diverse set of knowledge and the presence of absorptive capacity increased not only innovative but financial performance. Likewise, Hoopes and Postrel (1999) found that shared knowledge brought about by cross-functional meetings, teams and participation by boundary-spanning individuals increased product development performance. In case a firm experienced "glitches," or absence of shared knowledge, it incurred excess costs. On the basis of that finding, Hoopes and Postrel (1999) submitted that the optimal amount of shared knowledge is determined by offsetting the cost of sharing knowledge against the cost of glitches.

KNOWLEDGE OF NETWORKS

The study of knowledge and networks is not limited to how knowledge manifests itself in networks. Networks themselves may be considered knowledge as well. In the context of external networks, following Lyles (1988), Kale and Singh (1999) advanced that firms can develop an "alliance capability" which facilitates the formation and use of alliances. Similarly, on the basis of a longitudinal case study, Lorenzoni and Lipparini (1999) proposed that the capability to interact with other firms improves learning as well as knowledge access and transfer. In a study of 147 MNCs, Simonin (1999) found that collaborative knowledge mitigated the negative effects of knowledge complexity, as well as cultural and organizational distance on learning. In other words, alliance capabilities may overcome barriers in inter-organizational knowledge transfer. In their study of alliances in the manufacturing sector, Anand and Khanna (2000) found support for the same hypotheses and found that firms learn to create more value as experience in joint venturing and alliances accumulated. From a similar learning perspective, Gulati (1999) also found that greater network alliance formation capabilities increase the chance that firms enter into alliance in the future (see also Amburgey et al., 1996; Dyer and Singh, 1998; Lyles, 1988). As such, the presence of alliance capabilities facilitates both the formation of new alliances and the transfer of knowledge via alliances.

Kale and Singh (1999) found that this "alliance capability" is determined, among other things, by a firm's internal knowledge sharing process, in which experiences of previous alliances can be shared. The sharing of knowledge that networks facilitate, at the same time facilitates the development of new networks. In that vein, besides the view that knowledge manifests itself *in* networks, the view has emerged recognizing that networks must be considered essentially *as* knowledge. As Kogut et al. (1993: 77) argue, "knowledge consists . . . also of the know-how regarding cooperation. Information of the network consists of identifying who will cooperate and who has what capabilities." Adopting that view, in a later paper, Kogut (2000: 423) argued that "because they are the outcome of generative rules of coordination, networks constitute capabilities that augment the value of firms" Therefore, grounded in the notion that capabilities are formed by knowledge (Grant, 1996), the social construction of a network is also an expression of knowledge.

PROGRESS AND PROSPECTS

Research into knowledge and networks has made substantial progress the past decade. As firms have progressively entered into networks, by now, networks are everywhere. Research into networks has developed under three banners. A social network can hardly be considered a governance mode or form of organizing, since the thrust of social network

analysis is that every organization is a social network, and that a social network can be
used to disseminate knowledge and information. External networks have been established
as a governance mode to gain access to knowledge unavailable within a firm's boundaries.
However, network governance modes are not limited to external networks. Internal networks have emerged to facilitate the management of that knowledge internally. Therefore,
the question addressed by Powell (1987), whether networks are a new form or a transitional mode of organizing, is not as straightforward and calls for further studies.

Despite the insights and understanding gained, still a substantial number of avenues for
future research remain. The essence of most of such research avenues is to provide further
cross-fertilization of the concepts employed by the three streams of research on knowledge
and networks. Social network analysis has addressed many issues of the networks of firms,
especially formation patterns and the effect of tie strength, however independent of governance mode. Many of the concepts deployed in social networks analysis may be determined by governance mode requiring cross-fertilization of research. For example, received
insights indicate that centrality in a social network provides benefits to information and
knowledge access (Burt, 2000; Tsai and Ghoshal, 1998). But actors may be central in a
hierarchy, as a CEO or headquarters is, or may be central in an internal network with only
one layer, where an individual other than the CEO or a unit other than headquarters may
be the most central actor. Insights into networks as a governance mode indicated that a
hierarchy is a less effective option to create, transfer and organize knowledge than a
network is, because of bounded rationality constraints (Ghoshal and Bartlett, 1997). In
that vein, the informational benefits a central actor has may be moderated by the degree
of hierarchy.

Other characteristics of organization form and governance mode may be incorporated
as well. As in social network analysis, the nodes comprising internal networks can be considered as organizational units, activities, and resources. Since each of the dispersed organizational units controls unique resources giving rise to differentiated activities and abilities,
these three classes of variables are related to each other in the overall structure of the
network. The question that arises here is how specialist units and generalist units can
absorb knowledge from each other. Absorptive capacity was found to be an important
determinant of knowledge transfer (Lane and Lubatkin, 1998; Tsai, 2001). However, since
absorptive capacity is a function of prior knowledge endowments, firms face a trade-off
in investing in deep specialist, and broad generalist knowledge (Cohen and Levinthal, 1990;
Van Wijk et al., 2001). Two specialists having non-overlapping knowledge bases may experience difficulty in transferring knowledge. Also, because the units are different, the activities of one unit may to some extent be dependent on activities of other units (Powell,
1990), as is the case when the resources held by units are complementary. This gives rise
to the question to what extent interdependence between units guides knowledge transfers.

A related prospect for future research is the examination of barriers to knowledge transfer and learning in networks. Szulanski (1996) found that a lack of absorptive capacity,
causal ambiguity, and arduous relationships between recipients and sources of knowledge
were the most important barriers to internal sharing of best practices. In a case study of
a financial services firm, Van Wijk and Van Den Bosch (2000) found that because of autonomy, organizational sub-units were involved in power issues and viewed each as competitors instead of cooperators. This was found to inhibit the transfer of knowledge, and led

to learning races of a similar kind as those portrayed in external networks. In a study of franchising, Darr et al. (1995) found that knowledge was shared between stores of the same franchisee, but not of different franchisees. One reason for this finding may be legal and power issues, another distance. In a related study, intra-plant transfers were found more common than interplant transfers, especially when the geographical dispersion of plants increased (Argote et al., 1990; see also, Schulz, 2001). Research in this area may be informed by studies on regional networks, in which firms have chosen to be co-located in order to allow knowledge to be transferred (Saxenian, 1994).

Another prospect for research is whether firms with an internal network form of organizing engage in external networks more than, for example, functional and multidivisional organization forms do, and whether they are more efficacious in so doing. It has been found that firms can develop an "alliance capability" that allows them to create more value as experience in networking and transferring knowledge increases (Anand and Khanna, 2000; Kale and Singh, 1999; Lyles, 1988). Similarly, it has been submitted that networks constitute knowledge (Kogut, 2000). From that viewpoint, knowing how to network internally may make firms more adept to network externally as well, because the processes involved are similar. Lane and Lubatkin (1998) found that similarity between organization structures and incentive systems fostered inter-organizational learning. A related question to investigate is whether firms that have both internal network structures are in a better position to learn from each other than when those firms have, for example, a multidivisional structure.

Given that networks also essentially are knowledge (Kogut, 2000; Kogut et al., 1993), a promising avenue for future research is the differentiation of knowledge into know-what, know-how, know-when, know-where, know-who, and know-why components (cf. Garud, 1997). This differentiation essentially relates to transactional knowledge content in social network analysis (cf. Tichy et al., 1979). For example, Tyler and Steensma (1998) found that executives with technical experience were more favorable to entering into a technology alliance than executives without that experience. Such issues may be investigated by considering the different components of knowledge. Van Den Bosch and Van Wijk (2001) argue that different kinds of knowledge components manifest themselves in distinct ways at different organizational levels. The knowledge-set of executive managers is different from that of functional managers. Future studies of knowledge and networks may differentiate between these knowledge components and examine how actors in a network transmit that knowledge, and how the integrated sets of knowledge operate in a firm.

Another question that is still open in the context of studies on networks as knowledge is how network capabilities contribute to performance. Simonin (1999) found that collaborative know-how mitigated the positive effects of complexity and cultural and organizational distance on ambiguity in alliance learning. As such, the presence of network capabilities may overcome the barriers of knowledge transfer in networks, and as such increase performance. However, further studies are necessary to become more conclusive. One way future research could obtain further insight into the performance implications of networks, as well as other network phenomena, is by studying dynamics and network transition processes, and viewing network capabilities as dynamic capabilities. At the same time, such longitudinal studies may also contribute to further understand the extent to which networks increase performance.

In sum, research into knowledge and networks has made substantial progress. The field of study is wide, however, and in its current state has left investigators with a variety of open terrains that deserve academic pursuit. Although first attempts to cross-fertilization have emerged in earlier research, the three perspectives on networks heeded in this chapter have been dealt with mostly separately. One of the main avenues to gain further understanding of how networks facilitate learning and knowledge creation and integration is by considering the three perspectives in a complementary way. By studying how networks as governance modes at the inter-organizational and intra-organizational level coexist and how social networks operate within those two governance modes, valuable further understanding could be obtained how knowledge and learning manifest themselves in networks.

NOTES

1. Two alternative uses of the term "network" exist that confound its meaning, but are beyond the scope of this chapter. First, by mentioning "networks" in economics, scholars are often referring to "network economies" or "network externalities," which are present when goods interface with other goods, entailing conversion, consumption and imitation effects. Of these, imitation effects especially impact on knowledge-related considerations, as they occur when mimetic behavior brought about by inter-firm information flows drives firms to imitation (Majumdar and Venkataraman, 1998). Second, when considering the implementation of networks, often reference is made to information technology networks that link computers throughout an organization. While these networks certainly contribute to the sharing of information and knowledge within and across firms, and even contribute to the development of a "network firm" (Antonelli, 1988), they go completely by on richer face-to-face communications, which are essential to network organization (Nohria and Eccles, 1992).
2. For a detailed review of learning and knowledge transfer in strategic alliances, see Lampel (this volume).

REFERENCES

Ahuja, G. (2000a) The Duality of Collaboration: Inducements and Opportunities in the Formation of Interfirm Linkages. *Strategic Management Journal*, 21 (Special Issue): 317–43.

Ahuja, G. (2000b) Collaboration Networks, Structural Holes, and Innovation: A Longitudinal Study. *Administrative Science Quarterly*, 45 (3): 425–55.

Amburgey, T.L., Dacin, T., and Singh, J.V. (1996) Learning Races, Patent Races, and Capital Races: Strategic Interaction and Embeddedness within Organizational Fields. In J.A.C. Baum and J. Dutton (eds.), *Advances in Strategic Management*, Greenwich, CT: JAI Press, 303–22.

Anand, B.N. and Khanna, T. (2000) Do Firms Learn to Create Value? The Case of Alliances. *Strategic Management Journal*, 21 (Special Issue): 295–315.

Antonelli, C. (1988) The Emergence of the Network Firm. In C. Antonelli (ed.), *New Information Technology and Industrial Change: The Italian Case*, Dordrecht: Kluwer Academic, 13–32.

Aoki, M. (1986) Horizontal vs. Vertical Information Structure of the Firm. *American Economic Review*, 76 (5): 971–83.

Argote, L., Beckman, S., and Epple, D. (1990) The Persistence and Transfer of Learning in industrial Settings. *Management Science*, 36 (2): 140–54.

Badaracco, J.L. (1991) *The Knowledge Link*. Boston, MA: Harvard Business School Press.

Baker, W.E. (1992) The Network Organization in Theory and Practice. In N. Nohria and R.G. Eccles (eds.), *Networks and Organizations: Structure, Form, and Action*, Boston, MA: Harvard Business School Press, 397–429.

Balakrishnan, S. and Koza, M.P. (1993) Information Asymmetry, Adverse Selection and Joint Ventures: Theory and Evidence. *Journal of Economic Behavior and Organization*, 20 (1): 99–117.

Bartlett, C.A. and Ghoshal, S. (1993) Beyond the M-form: Toward a Managerial Theory of the Firm. *Strategic Management Journal*, 14 (Summer Special Issue): 23–46.

Baum, J.A.C., Calabrese, T., and Silverman, B.S. (2000) Don't Go It Alone: Alliance Network Composition and Startups Performance in Canadian Biotechnology. *Strategic Management Journal*, 21 (Special Issue): 267–94.

Baum, J.A.C. and Oliver, C. (1992) Institutional Embeddedness and the Dynamics of Organizational Behavior. *American Sociological Review*, 57 (3): 540–59.

Bradach, J.L. and Eccles, R.G. (1989) Price, Authority, and Trust: From Ideal Types to Plural Forms. *Annual Review of Sociology*, 15: 97–118.

Burns, T. and Stalker, G. (1961) *The Management of Innovation*. London: Tavistock.

Burt, R.S. (1982) *Toward a Structural Theory of Action: Network Models of Social Structure, Perception, and Action*. New York: Academic Press.

Burt, R.S. (1987) Social Contagion and Innovation: Cohesion versus Structural Equivalence. *American Journal of Sociology*, 92 (6): 1287–335.

Burt, R.S. (1992) *Structural Holes: The Social Structure of Competition*. Cambridge, MA: Harvard University Press.

Burt, R.S. (1997) The Contingent Value of Social Capital. *Administrative Science Quarterly*, 42 (2): 339–65.

Burt, R.S. (2000) The Network Structure of Social Capital. In R.I. Sutton and B.M. Staw (eds.), *Research in Organizational Behavior*. Greenwich, CT: JAI Press.

Cangelosi, V.E. and Dill, W.R. (1965) Organizational Learning: Observations toward a Theory. *Administrative Science Quarterly*, 10 (2): 175–203.

Chandler, A.D. Jr. (1962) *Strategy and Structure*. Cambridge, MA: MIT Press.

Cohen, W.M. and Levinthal, D.A. (1990) Absorptive Capacity: A New Perspective on Learning and Innovation. *Administrative Science Quarterly*, 35 (1): 128–52.

Coleman, J.S. (1988) Social Capital in the Creation of Human Capital. *American Journal of Sociology*, 94 (Supplement): S95–S120.

Conner, K.R. and Prahalad, C.K. (1996) A Resource-based Theory of the Firm: Knowledge versus Opportunism. *Organization Science*, 7 (5): 477–501.

Contractor, F.J. and Lorange, P. (1988) Why Should Firms Cooperate? The Strategy and Economics Basis for Cooperative Ventures. In F.J. Contractor and P. Lorange (eds.), *Cooperative Strategies in International Business*, Lexington: Lexington Books, 3–30.

Darr, E.D., Argote, L., and Epple, D. (1995) The Acquisition, Transfer, and Depreciation of Knowledge in Service Organizations: Productivity in Franchises. *Management Science*, 41 (11): 1750–62.

DeCarolis, D.M. and Deeds, D.L. (1999) The Impact of Stocks and Flows of Organizational Knowledge on Firm Performance: An Empirical Investigation of the Biotechnology Industry. *Strategic Management Journal*, 20 (10): 953–68.

Deeds, D.L. and Hill, C.W.L. (1996) Strategic Alliances and the Rate of New Product Development: An Empirical Study of Entrepreneurial Biotechnology Firms. *Journal of Business Venturing*, 11 (1): 41–55.

Doz, Y.L. (1996) The Evolution of Cooperation in Strategic Alliances: Initial Conditions or Learning Processes? *Strategic Management Journal*, 17 (Summer Special Issue): 55–83.

Doz, Y.L. and Hamel, G. (1998) *Alliance Advantage*. Boston, MA: Harvard Business School Press.

Doz, Y.L., Olk, P.M., and Ring, P.S. (2000) Formation Processes of R&D Consortia: Which Path to Take? Where Does it Lead? *Strategic Management Journal*, 21 (Special Issue): 239–66.

Dyer, J.H. (1996a) Does Governance Matter? *Keiretsu* Alliances and Asset Specificity as Sources of Japanese Competitive Advantage. *Organization Science*, 7 (6): 649–66.

Dyer, J.H. (1996b) Specialized Supplier Networks as a Source of Competitive Advantage: Evidence from the Auto Industry. *Strategic Management Journal*, 17 (4): 271–92.

Dyer, J.H. and Nobeoka, K. (2000) Creating and Managing a High-Performance Knowledge-Sharing Network: The Toyota Case. *Strategic Management Journal*, 21 (3): 345–67.

Dyer, J.H. and Singh, H. (1998) The Relational View: Cooperative Strategy and Sources of Interorganizational Competitive Advantage. *Academy of Management Review*, 23 (4): 660–79.

Eisenhardt, K.M. and Schoonhoven, C.B. (1996) Resource-based View of Strategic Alliance Formation: Strategic and Social Effects in Entrepreneurial Firms. *Organization Science*, 7 (2): 136–50.

Evan, W.M. (1965) Toward a Theory of Inter-Organizational Relations. *Management Science*, 11 (10): B217–30.

Ferlie, E. and Pettigrew, A.M. (1996) Managing through Networks: Some Issues and Implications for the NHS. *British Journal of Management*, 7 (Special Issue): S81–99.

Galaskiewicz, J. (1979) *Exchange Networks and Community Politics*. Beverly Hills: Sage.

Galaskiewicz, J. and Wasserman, S. (1989) Mimetic Processes within an Interorganizational Field: An Empirical Test. *Administrative Science Quarterly*, 28 (1): 22–39.

Galunic, D.C. and Rodan, S. (1998) Resource Recombination in the Firm: Knowledge Structures and the Potential for Schumpeterian Innovation. *Strategic Management Journal*, 19 (12): 1193–1201.

Gargiulo, M. and Benassi, M. (2000) Trapped in your own Net? Network Cohesion, Structural Holes, and the Adaptation of Social Capital. *Organization Science*, 11 (2): 183–96.

Garud, R. (1997) On the Distinction between Know-how, Know-why and Know-what in Technological Systems. In J. Walsh and A. Huff (eds.), *Advances in Strategic Management*. Greenwich, CT: JAI Press, 81–101.

Gerlach, M.L. (1992) *Alliance Capitalism: The Social Organization of Japanese Business*. Berkeley, CA: University of Berkeley Press.

Gerlach, M.L. and Lincoln, J.R. (1992) The Organization of Business Networks in the United States and Japan. In N. Nohria and R.G. Eccles (eds.), *Networks and Organizations: Structure, Form, and Action*, Boston, MA: Harvard Business School Press, 491–520.

Ghoshal, S. and Bartlett, C.A. (1990) The Multinational Corporation as an Interorganizational Network. *Academy of Management Review*, 15 (4): 603–25.

Ghoshal, S. and Bartlett, C.A. (1997) *The Individualized Corporation*. San Francisco, CA: Harper Business.

Ghoshal, S., Korine, H., and Szulanski, G. (1994) Interunit Communication in Multinational Corporations. *Management Science*, 40 (1): 96–110.

Ghoshal, S. and Moran, P. (1996) Bad for Practice: A Critique of Transaction Cost Theory. *Academy of Management Review*, 21 (1): 13–47.

Gnyawali, D.R. and Madhavan R. (2001) Cooperative Networks and Competitive Dynamics: A Structural Embeddedness Perspective. *Academy of Management Review*, 26 (2): 431–45.

Gomes-Casseres, B. (1994) Group versus Group: How Alliance Networks Compete. *Harvard Business Review*, 72 (4): 62–74.

Grabher, G. (1993) The Weakness of Strong Ties: The Lock-in of Regional Development in the Ruhr Area. In G. Grabher (ed.), *The Embedded Firm: On the Socioeconomics of Industrial Networks*, London: Routledge, 255–77.

Grandori, A. and Soda, G. (1995) Inter-firm Networks: Antecedents, Mechanisms and Forms. *Organization Studies*, 16 (2): 183–214.

Granovetter, M.S. (1973) The Strength of Weak Ties. *American Journal of Sociology*, 78 (6): 1360–80.

Granovetter, M.S. (1985) Economic Action and Social Structure: The Problem of Embeddedness. *American Journal of Sociology*, 91 (3): 481–510.

Granovetter, M.S. (1992) Problems of Explanation in Economic Sociology. In N. Nohria and R.G. Eccles (eds.), *Networks and Organizations: Structure, Form, and Action*, Boston, MA: Harvard Business School Press, 25–56.

Granovetter, M.S. (1994) Business Groups. In N.J. Smelzer and R. Swedberg (eds.), *The Handbook of Economic Sociology*, Princeton, NJ: Princeton University Press, 453–75.

Grant, R.M. (1996) Prospering in Dynamically-competitive Environments: Organizational Capability as Knowledge Integration. *Organization Science*, 7 (4): 375–87.

Grant, R.M. and Baden-Fuller, C. (1995) A Knowledge-based Theory of Inter-firm Collaboration. *Academy of Management Best Paper Proceedings*, 17–21.

Gulati, R. (1995a) Does Familiarity Breed Trust? The Implications of Repeated Ties for Contractual Choice in Alliances. *Academy of Management Journal*, 38 (1): 85–112.

Gulati, R. (1995b) Social Structure and Alliance Formation Pattern: A Longitudinal Analysis. *Administrative Science Quarterly*, 40 (3): 610–52.

Gulati, R. (1998) Alliances and Networks. *Strategic Management Journal*, 19 (4): 293–318.

Gulati, R. (1999) Network Location and Learning: The Influence of Network Resources and Firm Capabilities on Alliance Formation. *Strategic Management Journal*, 20 (5): 397–420.

Gulati, R. and Gargiulo, M. (1999) Where do Interorganizational Networks come from? *American Journal of Sociology*, 104 (5): 1439–93.

Gulati, R. and Singh, H. (1998) The Architecture of Cooperation: Managing Coordination Costs and Appropriation Concerns in Strategic Alliances. *Administrative Science Quarterly*, 43 (4): 781–814.

Gupta, A.K. and Govindarajan, V. (2000) Knowledge Flows within Multinational Corporations. *Strategic Management Journal*, 21 (4): 473–96.

Hagedoorn. J. (1993) Understanding the Rationale of Strategic Technology Partnering: Interorganizational Modes of Cooperation and Sectoral Differences. *Strategic Management Journal*, 14 (5): 371–85.

Hagedoorn, J. and Schakenraad, J. (1994) The Effect of Strategic Technology Alliances on Company Performance. *Strategic Management Journal*, 15 (4): 291–309.

Hamel, G. (1991) Competition for Competence and Inter-partner Learning within International Strategic Alliances. *Strategic Management Journal*, 12 (Summer Special Issue): 83–103.

Hansen, M.T. (1999) The Search-Transfer Problem: The Role of Weak Ties in Sharing Knowledge across Organization Subunits. *Administrative Science Quarterly*, 44 (1): 82–111.

Hansen, M.T., Podolny, J.M., and Pfeffer, J. (2001) So Many Ties, So Little Time: A Task Contingency Perspective on the Value of Social Capital in Organizations. Working paper, Harvard Graduate School of Business, Boston, MA.

Hedberg, B.L.T., Nystrom, P.C., and Starbuck, W.H. (1976) Camping on Seesaws: Prescriptions for a Self-designing Organization. *Administrative Science Quarterly*, 21 (1): 41–65.

Hedlund, G. (1994) A Model of Knowledge Management and the N-form Corporation. *Strategic Management Journal*, 15 (Summer Special Issue): 73–90.

Hedlund, G. (1996) The Intensity and Extensity of Knowledge: Implications for Possible Futures of the Global Firm. *CEMS Business Review*, 1 (1): 111–26.

Hennart, J-F, Roehl, T., and Zietlow, D.S. (1999) "Trojan Horse" or "Workhorse"? The Evolution of US-Japanese Joint Ventures in the United States. *Strategic Management Journal*, 20 (1): 15–29.

Hite, J.M. and Hesterly, W.S. (2001) The Evolution of Firm Networks: From Emergence to Early Growth of the Firm. *Strategic Management Journal*, 22 (3): 275–86.

Hoopes, D.G. and Postrel, S. (1999) Shared Knowledge, "Glitches," and Product Development Performance. *Strategic Management Journal*, 20 (9): 837–65.

Inkpen, A.C. (1995) *The Management of International Joint Ventures: An Organizational Learning Perspective.* London: Routledge.

Inkpen, A.C. and Crossan, M.M. (1995) Believing is Seeing: Joint Ventures and Organizational Learning. *Journal of Management Studies*, 32 (4): 595–618.

Inkpen, A. and Dinur, A. (1998) Knowledge Management Processes and International Joint Ventures. *Organization Science*, 9 (4): 454–68.

Jarillo, J.C. (1988) On Strategic Networks. *Strategic Management Journal*, 9 (1): 31–41.

Jones, C., Hesterly, W.S. and Borgatti, S.P. (1997) A General Theory of Network Governance: Exchange Conditions and Social Mechanisms. *Academy of Management Review*, 22 (4): 911–45.

Kale, P. and Singh, H. (1999) Alliance Capability and Success: A Knowledge-based Approach. *Academy of Management Best Paper Proceedings*, BPS: O1–O6.

Kale, P., Singh, H., and Perlmutter, H. (2000) Learning and Protection of Proprietary Assets in Strategic Alliances: Building Relational Capital. *Strategic Management Journal*, 21 (3): 217–37.

Khanna, T. (1998) The Scope of Alliances. *Organization Science*, 9 (3): 340–55.

Khanna, T., Gulati, R., and Nohria, N. (1998) The Dynamics of Learning Alliances: Competition, Cooperation and Relative Scope. *Strategic Management Journal*, 19 (3): 193–210.

Kogut, B. (1988) Joint Ventures: Theoretical and Empirical Perspectives. *Strategic Management Journal*, 9 (4): 319–32.

Kogut, B. (2000) The Network as Knowledge: Generative Rules and the Emergence of Structure. *Strategic Management Journal*, 21 (Special Issue): 405–25.

Kogut, B., Shan, W., and Walker, G. (1993) Knowledge in the Network and the Network as Knowledge: The Structuring of New Industries. In G. Grabher (ed.), *The Embedded Firm: On the Socioeconomics of Industrial Networks*, London: Routledge, 67–94.

Kogut, B. and Zander, U. (1992) Knowledge of the Firm, Combinative Capabilities, and the Replication of Technology. *Organization Science*, 3 (3): 383–97.

Kraatz, M.S. (1998) Learning by Association? Interorganizational Networks and Adaptation to Environmental Change. *Academy of Management Journal*, 41 (6): 621–43.

Kumar, R. and Nti, K.O. (1998) Differential Learning and Interaction in Alliance Dynamics: A Process and Outcome Discrepancy Model. *Organization Science*, 9 (3): 356–67.

Lane P.J. and Lubatkin, M. (1998) Relative Absorptive Capacity and Interorganizational Learning. *Strategic Management Journal*, 19 (5): 461–77.

Larsson, R., Bengtsson, L., Henriksson, K., and Sparks, J. (1998) The Interorganizational Learning Dilemma: Collective Knowledge Development in Strategic Alliances. *Organization Science*, 9 (3): 285–305.

Liebeskind, J.P., Oliver, A.L., Zucker, L., and Brewer, M. (1996) Social Networks, Learning, and Flexibility: Sourcing Scientific Knowledge in New Biotechnology Firms. *Organization Science*, 7 (4): 428–43.

Lincoln, J.R. (1982) Intra- (and Inter-) Organizational Networks. In S.B. Bacharach (ed.), *Research in the Sociology of Organizations*, Vol. 1. Greenwich, CT: JAI Press, 1–38.

Lorenzoni, G. and Baden-Fuller, C. (1995) Creating a Strategic Center to Manage a Web of Partners. *California Management Review*, 37 (3): 146–63.

Lorenzoni, G. and Lipparini, A. (1999) The Leveraging of Interfirm Relationships as a Distinctive Organizational Capability: A Longitudinal Study. *Strategic Management Journal*, 20 (4): 317–38.

Lyles, M.A. (1988) Learning among Joint Venture Sophisticated Firms. In F.J. Contractor and P. Lorange (eds.), *Cooperative Strategies in International Business*. Lexington: Lexington Books, 301–16.

Lyles, M.A. and Schwenk, C.R. (1992) Top Management, Strategy and Organizational Knowledge Structures. *Journal of Management Studies*, 29 (2): 155–74.

Macaulay, S. (1962) Non-Contractual Relations in Business. *American Sociological Review*, 28 (1): 55–67.

Majumdar, S.K. and Venkataraman, S. (1998) Network Effects and the Adoption of New Technology: Evidence from the US Telecommunications Industry. *Strategic Management Journal*, 19 (11): 1045–62.

March, J.G. (1991) Exploration and Exploitation in Organizational Learning. *Organization Science*, 2 (1): 71–87.

Marsden, P.V. (1990) Network Data and Measurement. *Annual Review of Sociology*, 16: 435–63.

Miles, R.E. and Snow, C.C. (1994) *Fit, Failure and the Hall of Fame*. New York: Free Press.

Miles, R.E. and Snow, C.C. (1995) The New Network Firm: A Spherical Structure Built on a Human Investment Philosophy. *Organizational Dynamics*, 23 (4): 4–18.

Miles, R.E., Snow, C.C., Mathews, J.A., Miles, G., and Coleman, H.J. Jr. (1997) Organizing in the Knowledge Age: Anticipating the Cellular Form. *Academy of Management Executive*, 11 (4): 7–20.

Mitchell, W. and Singh, K. (1996) Survival of Businesses using Collaborative Relationships to Commercialize Complex Goods. *Strategic Management Journal*, 17 (3): 169–95.

Mowery, D.C., Oxley, J.E., and Silverman, B.S. (1996) Strategic Alliances and Interfirm Knowledge Transfer. *Strategic Management Journal*, 17 (Winter Special Issue): 77–91.

Nahapiet, J. and Ghoshal, S. (1998) Social Capital, Intellectual Capital, and the Organizational Advantage. *Academy of Management Review*, 23 (2): 242–66.

Nohria, N. (1992) Is a Network Perspective a Useful Way of Studying Organizations? In N. Nohria and R.G. Eccles (eds.), *Networks and Organizations: Structure, Form, and Action*, Boston, MA: Harvard Business School Press, 1–22.

Nohria, N. (1996) From the M-form to the N-form: Taking Stock of Changes in the Large Industrial Firm. Working Paper, Graduate School of Business, Harvard University, MA.

Nohria, N. and Eccles, R.G. (1992) Face-to-Face: Making Network Organizations Work. In N. Nohria and R.G. Eccles (eds.), *Networks and Organizations: Structure, Form, and Action*, Boston, MA: Harvard Business School Press, 288–308.

Nohria, N. and Ghoshal, S. (1997) *The Differentiated Network*. San Francisco, CA: Jossey-Bass.

Nonaka, I. (1994) A Dynamic Theory of Organizational Knowledge Creation. *Organization Science*, 5 (1): 14–37.

Nonaka, I. and Takeuchi, H. (1995) *The Knowledge-Creating Company*. New York: Oxford University Press.

Oliver, C. (1990) Determinants of Interorganizational Relationships: Integration and Future Directions. *Academy of Management Review*, 15 (2): 241–65.

Orton, D.J. and Weick, K.E. (1990) Loosely Coupled Systems: A Reconceptualization. *Academy of Management Review*, 15 (2): 203–23.

Parkhe, A. (1991) Interfirm Diversity, Organizational Learning, and Longevity in Global Strategic Alliances. *Journal of International Business Studies*, 22 (4): 579–601.

Parkhe, A. (1993) Messy Research, Methodological Predispositions and Theory Development in International Joint Ventures. *Academy of Management Review*, 18 (2): 227–68.

Penrose, E.T. (1959) *The Theory of the Growth of the Firm*. New York: Oxford University Press.

Perrone, V. (1997) The Coevolution of Contexts and Structures: The N-form. In T. Clark, *Advancement in Organizational Behavior: Essays in Honour of Derek S. Pugh*, Ashgate: Aldershot, 145–64.

Perrow, C. (1992) Small-Firm Networks. In N. Nohria and R.G. Eccles (eds.), *Networks and Organizations: Structure, Form, and Action*, Boston, MA: Harvard Business School Press, 445–70.

Pettigrew, A.M. and Fenton, E.M. (eds) (2000) *The Innovating Organization*. London: Sage.

Pettigrew, A.M., Massini, S., and Numagami, T. (2000) Innovative Forms of Organizing in Europe and Japan. *European Management Journal*, 18 (3): 259–73.

Pfeffer, J. and Nowak, P. (1976) Joint Ventures and Interorganizational Interdependence. *Administrative Science Quarterly*, 21 (3): 398–418.

Podolny, J.M., Stuart, T.E., and Hannan, M.T. (1996) Networks, Knowledge, and Niches: Competition in the Worldwide Semiconductor Industry, 1984–1991. *American Journal of Sociology*, 102 (3): 659–89.

Powell, W.W. (1987) Hybrid Organizational Arrangements: New Form or Transitional Arrangement? *California Management Review*, 30 (1): 67–87.

Powell, W.W. (1990) Neither Market nor Hierarchy: Network Forms of Organization. *Research in Organizational Behavior*, 12: 295–336.

Powell, W.W., Koput, K., and Smith-Doerr, L. (1996) Interorganizational Collaboration and the Locus of Innovation: Networks of Learning in Biotechnology. *Administrative Science Quarterly*, 41 (1): 116–45.

Powell, W.W. and Smith-Doerr, L. (1994) Networks and Economic Life. In N.J. Smelzer and R. Swedberg (eds.), *The Handbook of Economic Sociology*, Princeton, NJ: Princeton University Press, 368–402.

Pucik, V. (1991) Technology Transfer in Strategic Alliances: Competitive Collaboration and Organizational Learning. In T. Agmon and M.A. Von Glinow (eds.), *Technology Transfer in International Business*, New York: Oxford University Press, 121–42.

Quinn, J.B., Anderson, P., and Finkelstein, S. (1996) New Forms of Organizing. In H. Mintzberg and J.B. Quinn (eds.), *The Strategy Process*, New York: Prentice Hall, 350–62.

Ring, P.S. and Van de Ven, A.H. (1992) Structuring Cooperative Relationships between Organizations. *Strategic Management Journal*, 13 (8): 483–98.

Ring, P.S. and Van de Ven, A.H. (1994) Developmental Processes of Interorganizational Relationships. *Academy of Management Review*, 19 (1): 90–118.

Rowley, T., Behrens, D., and Krackhardt, D. (2000) Redundant Governance Structures: An Analysis of Structural and Relational Embeddedness in the Steel and Semiconductor Industries. *Strategic Management Journal*, 21 (Special Issue): 369–86.

Ruggles, R. (1998) The State of the Notion: Knowledge Management in Practice. *California Management Review*, 40 (3): 80–9.

Salancik, G.R. (1995) WANTED: A Good Network Theory of Organization. *Administrative Science Quarterly*, 40 (2): 345–49.

Saxenian, A. (1994) *Regional Advantage: Culture and Competition in Silicon Valley and Route 128*. Cambridge, MA: Harvard University Press.

Schulz, M. (2001) The Uncertain Relevance of Newness: Organizational Learning and Knowledge Flows. *Academy of Management Journal*, 44 (4): 661–81.

Shenkar, O. and Li, J.T. (1999) Knowledge Search in International Cooperative Ventures. *Organization Science*, 10 (2): 134–43.

Simonin, B.L. (1999) Ambiguity and the Process of Knowledge Transfer in Strategic Alliances. *Strategic Management Journal*, 20 (7): 595–623.

Singh, K. (1997) The Impact of Technological Complexity and Interfirm Cooperation on Business Survival. *Academy of Management Journal*, 40 (2): 339–67.

Singh, K. and Mitchell, W. (1996) Precarious Collaboration: Business Survival after Partners Shut Down or Form New Partnerships. *Strategic Management Journal*, 17 (Summer Special Issue): 99–115.

Smith, K.G., Carroll, S.J., and Ashford, S.J. (1995) Intra- and Interorganizational Cooperation: Toward a Research Agenda. *Academy of Management Journal*, 38 (1): 7–23.

Steensma, H.K. and Lyles, M.A. (2000) Explaining IJV Survival in a Transitional Economy through Social Exchange and Knowledge-based Perspectives. *Strategic Management Journal*, 21 (8): 831–51.

Stuart, T.E. (1998) Network Positions and Propensities to Collaborate: An Investigation of Strategic Alliance Formation in a High-technology Industry. *Administrative Science Quarterly*, 43 (3): 668–98.

Stuart, T.E. (2000) Interorganizational Alliances and the Performance of Firms: A Study of Growth and Innovation Rates in a High-Technology Industry. *Strategic Management Journal*, 21 (8): 791–811.

Szulanski, G. (1996) Exploring Internal Stickiness: Impediments to the Transfer of Best Practice within the Firm. *Strategic Management Journal*, 17 (Winter Special Issue): 27–43.

Teece, D.J. (1986) Profiting from Technological Collaboration: Implications for Integration, Collaboration, Licensing, and Public Policy. *Research Policy*, 15 (6): 285–305.

Thompson, V.A. (1965) Bureaucracy and Innovation. *Administrative Science Quarterly*, 10 (1): 1–20.

Tichy, N.M., Tushman, M.L., and Fombrun, C. (1979) Social Network Analysis for Organizations. *Academy of Management Review*, 4 (4): 507–19.

Tsai, W. (2000) Social Capital, Strategic Relatedness and the Formation of Intraorganizational Linkages. *Strategic Management Journal*, 21 (8): 925–39.

Tsai, W. (2001) Knowledge Transfer in Intra-organizational Networks. *Academy of Management Journal*, 44 (5): 996–1004.

Tsai, W. and Ghoshal, S. (1998) Social Capital and Value Creation: The Role of Intrafirm Networks. *Academy of Management Journal*, 41 (4): 464–76.

Tyler, B.B. and Steensma, H.K. (1998) The Effects of Executives' Experiences and Perceptions on their Assessment of Potential Technological Alliances. *Strategic Management Journal*, 19 (10): 939–65.

Uzzi, B. (1996) The Sources and Consequences of Embeddedness for the Economic Performance of Organizations: The Network Effect. *American Sociological Review*, 61 (4): 674–98.

Uzzi, B. (1997) Social Structure and Competition in Interfirm Networks: The Paradox of Embeddedness. *Administrative Science Quarterly*, 42 (1): 35–67.

Van Den Bosch, F.A.J. and Van Wijk, R. (2000) Transition Processes towards the N-form Corporation: Implications for Knowledge Flows. In M.A. Hitt, R.D. Nixon, K. Coyne, and P. Clifford (eds.), *Dynamic Resources*, New York: John Wiley.

Van Den Bosch, F.A.J. and Van Wijk, R. (2001) Creation of Managerial Capabilities through Managerial Knowledge Integration: A Competence-based Perspective. In R. Sanchez (ed.), *Organizational Competence and Knowledge*, New York: Oxford University Press, 159–76.

Van Wijk, R. and Van Den Bosch, F.A.J. (1998) Knowledge Characteristics of Internal Network-based Forms of Organizing. In S. Havlovic (ed.), *Academy of Management Best Paper Proceedings*. BPS: B1–B7.

Van Wijk, R. and Van Den Bosch, F.A.J. (2000) The Emergence and Development of Internal Networks and their Impact on Knowledge Flows: The Case of Rabobank Group. In A.M. Pettigrew and E.M. Fenton (eds.), *The Innovating Organization*. London: Sage, 144–77.

Van Wijk, R., Van Den Bosch, F.A.J. and Volberda, H.W. (2001) Absorptive Capacity, Knowledge Flows and Innovative Performance: A Study of their Relationships. Working Paper, Rotterdam School of Management, Erasmus University.

Walker, G., Kogut, B., and Shan, W. (1997) Social Capital, Structural Holes and the Formation of an Industry Network. *Organization Science*, 8 (1): 109–25.

Wasserman, S. and Faust, K. (1994) *Social Network Analysis: Methods and Applications*. Cambridge: Cambridge University Press.

Williamson, O.E. (1975) *Markets and Hierarchies*. New York: Free Press.

Williamson, O.E. (1985) *The Economic Institutions of Capitalism*. New York: Free Press.

Winter, S.G. (1987) Knowledge and Competence as Strategic Assets. In D. Teece (ed.), *The Competitive Challenge*. New York: HarperCollins, 159–84.

Zander, U. and Kogut, B. (1995) Knowledge and the Speed of the Transfer and Imitation of Organizational Capabilities: An Empirical Test. *Organization Science*, 5 (1): 76–92.

Zenger, T.R. and Hesterly, W.S. (1997) The Disaggregation of Corporations: Selective Intervention, High-powered Incentives, and Molecular Units. *Organization Science*, 8 (3): 209–22.

23

The Political Economy of Knowledge Markets in Organizations

Rob Cross and Laurence Prusak

CHAPTER OUTLINE

Over the past 30 or so years scholars have invested significant effort in understanding processes and performance implications of learning in organizations. Through this research we have developed a great deal of insight into the acquisition and use of declarative (know-what) and procedural (know-how) knowledge. In contrast, we have less understanding of learning as a function of interaction among organizational actors embedded within a political and social system. Following Miner and Mezias's (1996) call for new approaches to the study of organizational learning, we have written this chapter to suggest some parameters and important dimensions of internal markets for knowledge that impact both individual and collective learning. Specifically we propose a model of internal knowledge markets with three distinguishing features: (1) knowledge market actors; (2) a knowledge market price system; and (3) knowledge market signals. We conclude this chapter with a specific example of how social network analysis can be employed to model knowledge markets within organizations.

INTRODUCTION

A significant and growing body of literature addressing the topic of organizational learning has evolved over the past 30 years or so. Perhaps most basically, theory and research in this tradition diverge as to the importance of cognitive or behavioral forms of learning (Fiol and Lyles, 1985). Early work in the cognitive tradition helped us consider learning at an individual level as a process of revising assumptions in thought (e.g., Argyris and Schön, 1978; Argyris, 1982; Schön, 1990) or at an organizational level as environment interpretation (e.g., Daft and Weick, 1984; Cohen and Levinthal, 1990). Alternatively, many researchers in the behavioral tradition have considered learning to be a product of change in behavior resulting from modification to an organization's programs, goals, decision rules, or routines (e.g., Cyert and March, 1963; Nelson and Winter, 1982; Levitt and March, 1988). Such characteristics of organizations serve both as retention facilities and constraints on future learning as past precedents shape organizational attention.

While influential, a good deal of this early work was distant from the day-to-day operations of real organizations. More recently scholars have begun to consider where important learning might happen within organizations as well as processes by which this learning occurs and/or impacts organizational performance.[1] As a result, we have gained a great deal of insight into mid-range theories of organizational learning that focus heavily on processes and occasionally performance implications of the acquisition of declarative (know-what) or procedural (know-how) knowledge (e.g., Walsh, 1995; Cohen and Sproull, 1996; Moingeon and Edmondson, 1996; Sanchez and Heene, 1997; Walsh and Huff, 1997; Argote, 1999; Van Den Bosch and Van Wijk, 2001) and occasionally know-why (Walsh and Ungson, 1991; Garud, 1997).

In contrast, we have seen less focus on individual and organizational learning as a function of social interaction among organizational actors embedded within a specific political and social system (see Plaskoff, and Van Wijk, Van Den Bosch and Volberda in this volume for exceptions).[2] We find this an interesting point of inquiry given the extent to which people rely on relationships for informational and learning purposes (Granovetter, 1973; Allen, 1977; Rogers, 1995). To be sure, we have evidence of how cultural norms and patterns of interaction evolve as a form of social memory among a collective (e.g., Middleton and Edwards, 1990; Barley, 1986 and 1990; Pentland, 1992; Cook and Yanow, 1993; Casey, 1997). Similarly, ethnographic evidence has demonstrated the importance of social interaction in learning how to do one's work and be part of a group (Lave and Wenger, 1991; Brown and Duguid, 1991; Orr, 1996; Chaiklin and Lave, 1996; Wenger, 1998). However, though rich in description, these efforts provide little ability to model knowledge markets within organizations for either descriptive or prescriptive purposes.

Following Miner and Mezias's (1996) call for new approaches to the study of organizational learning, we have written this chapter to suggest some parameters and important dimensions of internal markets for knowledge that impact both individual and collective learning over time. Throughout, we prefer the old-and-new term, political economy, when talking about internal knowledge markets. This term, which is enjoying a new lease on life (Lindbloom, 2001), helps point out that economic and exchange activities are embedded in social relations and structures (Arrow, 1974; Granovetter, 1985; Uzzi, 1997). This is especially true for what we term knowledge markets. As we will show, the very substance of this exchange – knowledge – is such a scarce and valued resource that its value in any market will draw social dynamics into whatever "perfect" market arrangements might exist.

KNOWLEDGE MARKETS

We start from the perspective that there is a genuine market for knowledge in organizations. Like markets for goods and services, the knowledge market has buyers and sellers who negotiate to reach a mutually satisfactory price for the goods exchanged. It has brokers who bring buyers and sellers together and even entrepreneurs who use their market knowledge to create internal power bases. Knowledge market transactions occur because all of the participants in them believe that they will benefit in some particular way. In economists' jargon, they expect the transactions to provide "utility." However, there really are no such things as "pure" markets: markets that can be understood solely in economic terms. As analysts from John Stuart Mill to Karl Marx to Thorstein Veblen to James March have argued, every market system is embedded in and affected by social and political realities.

In highly efficient markets, buyers and sellers find each other and exchange their goods readily. A clear pricing system enables them to agree on the value of the goods being sold with the least possible friction. Markets for knowledge, however, are notably inefficient in most organizations. The right seller is often hard to locate, and can be hard to reach even if we know her location. For example, she might not want to sell at the price we offer. Also, it is difficult, if not impossible, to judge the quality of knowledge before we "purchase" it. Both the knowledge value and likelihood of eventual payment are uncertain.

To get a feel for the inefficiencies of the knowledge market, compare it to the market for new cars. In the car market, we can easily get information about the sellers and products. The *Yellow Pages* list all car dealers. Newspapers regularly print information about what cars are available, where to buy them, and what they cost. Consumer reports and a host of other publications provide detailed independent evaluations of cars and reveal dealer costs. In many cases, a buyer will have a choice of vendors for the same product. The shopper has opportunities to examine and test cars before buying one. A written contract defines what is being bought and how much we must pay for it. Warranties and laws protect the buyer if the product is defective. Sellers have legal recourse if the buyer fails to pay.

Knowledge markets are obviously much murkier. The value of knowledge is rarely as tangible or explicit as the value of a car. There are no consumer reports on knowledge sellers and brokers. As our discussion of the price system makes clear, payment is much less certain and less tangible than in the new car market. Information about where knowledge resides in the organization is highly imperfect. In fact, much of the current interest in knowledge management derives from the fact that organizations lack good information about where their knowledge is and, therefore, have difficulty getting it and making use of it. Our studies show that three factors in particular often cause knowledge markets to operate inefficiently in organizations: the incompleteness of information about the knowledge market; the asymmetry of knowledge; and the localness of knowledge. We touch on each of these briefly below.

♦ *Incompleteness of information.* Firms very often do not know where to find their own knowledge. The lack of maps to guide a knowledge buyer to a seller is a fundamental problem that even the most advanced skill profiling systems have not begun to address adequately. The absence of explicit information about the pricing structure is also a source of inefficiency, with knowledge transactions inhibited by uncertainty about what the likely return on shared knowledge will be.

♦ *Asymmetry of knowledge.* There often is abundant knowledge on a subject in one department of an organization and a shortage somewhere else. Marketing may have extensive knowledge about a particular set of customers that Sales needs but lacks. Strategic knowledge that resides at the top may not be available to middle managers. A certain amount of asymmetry must exist in any market as they cannot exist without scarcity.

But strong asymmetry prevents knowledge from getting where it is needed as buyers and sellers don't meet.

◆ *Localness of knowledge.* People usually get knowledge from their organizational neighbors. The knowledge market depends on trust, and individuals generally trust the people they know. Also, mechanisms for getting access to distant knowledge tend to be weak or non-existent. As a result, people will buy whatever knowledge the person in the next office may have rather than deal with the effort and uncertainty of trying to discover who in the company may know more. Simon and March (1958) use the term "satisficing" to describe the human tendency to settle for the knowledge or information that is good enough for their purposes. Localness adds to market inefficiency because it causes people to make do with less than optimal knowledge while a much better product goes unsold and unused.

Sociologist Harrison White (1981) said that sociology, economics and political science are the three lenses needed to see organizations fully. We continue to find that these three realities must be taken fully into account to understand markets for knowledge. If the political reality of an organization is such that calculating and secretive hoarders of knowledge thrive, then potential knowledge buyers will have no currency valuable enough to tempt them to share their expertise. If it is considered a sign of weakness or incompetence within the culture of an organization to admit to a problem you can't solve on your own, then the social cost of "buying" knowledge will be too high. Once again, the knowledge market won't operate well. We suggest that to truly understand an organization's knowledge market, attention must be paid to three distinguishing features: (1) knowledge market actors; (2) a knowledge market price system and (3) knowledge market signals.

KNOWLEDGE MARKET ACTORS

First let us review the players in the knowledge market: the buyers, sellers, and brokers who take part in knowledge transactions and drive knowledge markets. An individual can perform all three roles in a single day and sometimes can play more than one role simultaneously. It is quite common, for instance, to be a knowledge buyer, seller, and broker during the same conversation. However, for clarity in the following discussion, we will look at the roles separately.

Buyers

Knowledge buyers or seekers are usually people trying to resolve an issue whose complexity and uncertainty precludes an easy answer. They are people engaged in a semi-bounded search. Clearly, asking for the GNP of France or a list of the 20 largest US banks is not a knowledge search; it is a request for data. Knowledge seekers are looking for insights, judgments, and understanding. They want answers to questions such as "What is this particular client like?," or "How did we manage to win that sale?" Such questions require complex answers that are often imbued with emotional subtexts so important to our sensemaking. Thus, buyers seek knowledge because it has distinct value to them. It will help them make a sale or accomplish a task more efficiently; it will improve their judgments and skills and help them make better decisions. In short, it will make them more successful at their work as this task of searching for knowledge accounts for a fairly substantial part of most managers' and executives' jobs (Mintzberg, 1973).

Sellers

Knowledge sellers are people in an organization with an internal market reputation for having substantial knowledge about a process or subject. They may sell their knowledge by the piece or, more likely, in a "bundle," in exchange for a salary. Although virtually everyone is a knowledge buyer at one time or another, not everyone is necessarily a seller. Some people are skilled but unable to articulate their tacit knowledge. Others have knowledge that is too specialized, personal, or limited to be of much value on the knowledge market.

Some potential knowledge sellers keep themselves out of the market because they believe they benefit more from hoarding their knowledge than they would from sharing it. In many organizations, of course, this is a rational belief. If knowledge is power, then the owners of knowledge have power that may dissipate if other people come to know what they know. This is a reality of knowledge politics that managers need to deal with in designing knowledge initiatives. For a knowledge market to work at all, knowledge sharing must be rewarded more than knowledge hoarding.

Brokers

Knowledge brokers (also sometimes known as "gatekeepers" or "boundary spanners") make connections between buyers and sellers: those who need knowledge and those who have it. Such people often serve a key dissemination and bridging function but can play their role in the organization in two markedly different ways: (1) from a self-interested perspective as delineated in the work of Ron Burt (2000) or (2) from the perspective of an "honest broker" as portrayed in the work of James Coleman (1988) or Nan Lin (2001). According to a study we developed for a client, about 10 percent of managers across industries are boundary spanners and therefore potential knowledge brokers. They enjoy exploring their organizations, finding out what people do and who knows what. They like to understand the big picture, which puts them in a position to know where to go for knowledge, especially if it falls outside their official area of responsibility.

Librarians frequently act as covert knowledge brokers, suited by temperament and their role as information guides to the task of making people-to-people as well as people-to-text connections. For instance, when someone in a high-tech firm asks the corporate librarian to do research on the next generation of reduced instruction set chips, the librarian is likely to say "Did you know that John Smith has been asking about the same subject? You might want to talk to him." Because corporate libraries often serve the whole organization, librarians are among the few employees who have contact with people from many departments. In the course of their work, they come to understand a great deal about the various knowledge needs and resources of the company. Traditionally librarians value customer service and have highly developed techniques for finding out what they don't already know. All of these factors make them natural knowledge brokers.

A KNOWLEDGE MARKET PRICE SYSTEM

All markets have a price system so that value exchanges can be efficiently rendered and recorded. What is the price system of the knowledge market? What sort of currency do participants exchange? When firms buy knowledge from outside of their organizations, they frequently (though not invariably) pay with cash. A lawyer, an investment banker, or a consultant can make several thousand dollars per day because the client perceives that his or her special knowledge is worth that much. Within organizations, the medium of exchange is seldom money but there are agreed-upon currencies that drive the knowledge market. We have come to the conclusion that there are at least three factors at work. In order of significance from greatest to least, they are reciprocity, repute, and altruism.

Reciprocity

A knowledge seller will spend the time and effort needed to share knowledge effectively if he expects the buyers to be willing sellers when he is in the market for their knowledge. Due to norms of reciprocity, asking contacts for significant amounts of help may place a person in their debt (Blau, 1986; Coleman, 1990). How much debt will vary from contact to contact and from person to person depending on such factors as relative status and attitude. Time, energy, and knowledge are finite. They are very scarce resources in most people's workdays. The choices people make, particularly before a relationship has developed sufficient history to make it expressive and valued in its own right, will usually depend on some calculation and perceived self-interest embedded within a given incentive system.

Reciprocity may be achieved less directly than by getting knowledge back from others as payment for providing it to them. In firms structured as partnerships, knowledge sharing that improves profitability will return a benefit to the sharer, now and in the future. Individuals who have significant stock options in a firm are in a similar position. Whether or not a knowledge seller expects to be paid with equally valuable knowledge from the buyer, he may believe that his being known for sharing knowledge readily will make others in the company more willing to share with him. That is a rational assumption, since his reputation as a seller of valuable knowledge will make others confident of his willingness to reciprocate when he is the buyer and they have knowledge to sell. Often this willingness makes it more likely that people throughout the company will respond in kind at a later date. So reciprocity and repute are related.

Repute

A knowledge seller usually wants her colleagues to know her as a knowledgeable person with valuable expertise that she is willing to share with others in the company. Whether developed via joint effort on a task, reputation alone or as a product of perception established in direct contact and then reinforced through third party interaction, people develop understandings of other's skills and knowledge. Repute may seem intangible, but it often produces tangible results. For example, people develop a reputation for being good in a specific field, and this becomes valuable in its own right as it defines how they come to be involved in important projects during their careers. Further, having a reputation for knowledge sharing makes achieving reciprocity more likely; being known as a knowledge seller makes one a more effective knowledge buyer.

Having a reputation as a valuable knowledge source can also lead to the tangible benefits of job security, promotion, and other corporate rewards. In service businesses such as consulting, investment banking, and entertainment, success often hinges on repute. In fact, in many businesses today, the importance of repute is increasing as the old social contract between firm and worker based on length of service and loyalty erodes. As the promise of continued employment in exchange for long, loyal service fades, workers at all levels feel considerable pressure to heighten individual repute for their demonstrated knowledge, skills, and competencies.

Altruism

It is possible, of course, that a knowledge sharer may be a nice person who wants to help whether or not he gets anything beyond a "thank you" in return. Or he may be so passionate about his knowledge that he is happy to share it whenever he gets a chance. Such people do exist. Many knowledge sharers are motivated in part by a love of their subject and to some degree by altruism, whether "for the good of the firm" or based on a natural impulse to help others. We all know individuals who simply like helping.

Mentoring is a form of knowledge transfer based in part on altruism. Erik Erikson, among others, has pointed out that people go through a "generative stage" (usually in later middle age) when it becomes important to them to pass on what they have learned to others. Firms cannot create this impulse, but they can surely encourage or discourage it.

Formally recognizing mentoring relationships, giving managers time to pass on their knowledge, and understanding that experienced employees have valuable and often tacit knowledge are ways to foster mentoring. Many firms ignore the contribution that older workers can make to their younger colleagues because they have no way of evaluating or efficiently capturing exactly what it is that the older worker knows. Knowledge altruism is real and can be encouraged. It tends to flourish in organizations that hire "nice" people and treat them nicely. We constrain it, though, by increasing demands on the time and energy of employees. Political theorist C.B. MacPherson argues that our national culture is one of "possessive individualism" and this is also just as true within organizations. It clearly doesn't make sense to depend entirely on goodwill to cultivate something as important as knowledge sharing.

Social context of price system

As outlined earlier, it is well known that most economic and exchange activities are embedded in a social context (Granovetter, 1985; Uzzi, 1997). Our price system mechanisms are no exception – they both derive from, and are heavily conditioned by, various structural, relational, and political dynamics within an organizational setting. Myriad features of an organization's context can enable or constrain the knowledge market price system in various ways. Quite frequently, unique circumstances such as institutional forces, culture and history of a given organization result in context that conditions the price system in various ways. However, at least two contextual dimensions are consistently at play: power and trust.

Power

We now know that knowledge does not flow freely or uniformly in organizations. Sociologists have poignantly demonstrated how correct information can have little or no impact on critical decision processes. Organizational theorists have shown that a person's knowledge can be constrained by role or not acted upon due to motivational or cognitive impediments when introducing knowledge into diverse social contexts. A key social mechanism that can impede, distort, highlight or call attention to certain information or knowledge is power. Powerful members in a given social context have significant ability to denote what new knowledge or information is worth attending to and so constrain the direction of learning in a given setting.

Such power can accrue both formally and informally. From a formal perspective, we know that a defining characteristic of almost any organization is a hierarchy or formal chain of command. As a product of hierarchy, power inheres in official positions (Astley and Sachdeva, 1984). These authority relations are often characterized by unilateral exchange, with people in "authority ranking" relationships tending to perceive each other as differing in social importance and status. From this perspective, access to powerful others is limited and often reliant on the generosity or self-interest of the superior. Alternatively, more powerful recipients likely enjoy greater access to an organization's distributed expertise (e.g., witness the extent to which a subordinate will go to provide a superior with information).

Of course, power also derives from position in informal structure. To the extent that an actor is located at tightly coupled interconnected nodes in the network, they gain power as their immersion in multiple interdependencies makes them indispensable. Alternatively, it can also accrue by virtue of certain forms of centrality within informal networks (Freeman, 1979; Burt, 1992). Having access to information itself is a privilege that can connote power (Pettigrew, 1972; Pfeffer, 1994) as we have evidence that centrality in advice networks has been related to an individual actor's influence (Burkhardt and Brass, 1990; Ibarra and Andrews, 1993). Again, such people play influential, though often covert, roles in knowledge sharing and exchange. Powerful people tend to stay in power due to increasing returns to power.

Trust

We also suggest that trust – at both a dyadic and cultural level – is a second important element of social context. One's trust in another is likely to shape the extent to which people will be forthcoming about their lack of knowledge.[3] Without trust, knowledge initiatives will fail, regardless of how thoroughly they are supported by technology and rhetoric and even if the survival of the organization depends on effective knowledge transfer. The members of the organization must see people get credit for knowledge sharing. There must be direct evidence of trust; a declaration of the importance of trust in the corporate mission statement is not sufficient. If part of the internal knowledge market is untrustworthy, the market becomes asymmetric and less efficient. Our experience is that in large part, trustworthiness must start at the top. Trust tends to flow downward through organizations. Upper management's activities and examples often define norms and values. If top managers are trust-worthy, trust will tend to seep through and come to characterize the whole firm. If they cynically exploit others' knowledge for personal gain, distrust will propagate throughout the company.

Personal contact and trust are intimately related. The US army recognizes what it calls "face time" (the amount of time members in a unit spend together) as an essential element in building trust within groups and measures it as one of the determinants of success. In addition to being a necessary condition for knowledge exchange, trust can be a product of it as well. British Petroleum's Virtual Teamworking project succeeded because of the atmosphere of mutual trust established by management, the VT project team, and the participants. Face-to-face meetings among participants established rapport, understanding and an intuitive basis for evaluating a person's trustworthiness. The frequent videoconferences during which participants exchanged knowledge raised the level of trust and led to measurable improvements in honoring commitments to meet the delivery dates of promised work.

Trust is an essential condition of a functioning knowledge market, as it is of any market that does not depend on binding and enforceable contracts. Of course, even transactions bound by written contracts entail some degree of trust. But the knowledge market – with no chance of appeals – is very much based on credit, not cash. The word "credit" means "to believe" or "to trust," and mutual trust is at the heart of knowledge exchange. When we sell knowledge within an organization, our receiving adequate payment now, or in the future, depends on the trustworthiness of the buyer and of management. In most cases, we will gain repute for a knowledge transaction only if the buyer gives us credit for it. If he pretends the knowledge was his all along, we gain nothing. If someone claims our research results as his own, we are no more likely to make further knowledge available to him than we are to offer our house to someone who stole our car. A buyer who fails to give credit and recognize his debt to us is also unlikely to reciprocate when we need knowledge. Similarly, management that pays lip service to the value it attaches to knowledge sharing but rewards employees who hoard knowledge will not create the level of trust needed to make the knowledge market effective.

The role of trust in knowledge transactions helps explain why knowledge initiatives based solely on the belief that infrastructure creates communication seldom deliver the expected benefits. The impersonality of groupware allows anyone to post information and invites anonymous access to that information. However, it does not create the same confidence in the quality of knowledge that personal acquaintance and reputation can inspire. The promise of reciprocity in such a system is also weak. The buyer who downloads an item from a server does not feel the same obligation to the provider that he would if he got the same material through a phone call or meeting. This is why the most successful groupware systems are moderated to assure that posted material is accurate and timely. Some even have mechanisms for metering the use of posted items and crediting the suppliers.

KNOWLEDGE MARKET SIGNALS

By "market signals," we mean information that indicates both where knowledge actually resides in the organization and how to gain access to it. There are formal and informal signals in knowledge markets. Title or position is the most common formal signal, indicating who has or should have valuable knowledge. If we need to learn about a particular research project, it makes sense to go to the project manager; if we need to know what is happening in marketing, why not ask the director of the marketing department? This commonsense approach can work, but in fact, the organizational chart is generally not that effective as a guide to company knowledge. The project director may be unwilling to share his knowledge or have had no direct involvement with the aspects of the project we need to understand. It may be that the marketing director once knew a lot about marketing but now knows mainly about the politics of running a marketing department. Clearly, advancement within a firm is not based solely on knowledge – even tacit or social knowledge – but influenced by other key variables such as drive, ambition, energy, intuition, judgment, ego (or lack thereof), and luck. The expert who knows exactly what we need to learn and would be willing to tell us may be sitting in one of the cubicles we pass on the way to the director's office.

Probably the best knowledge market signals occur within the informal networks of practice that always develop in organizations. Within these webs, people ask each other who knows what or who is a useful resource. If the person you ask where to go for specific knowledge doesn't know an appropriate seller, she probably knows someone else who does know. Much of the work that goes on in firms gets done because people continually ask one another, through informal networks who knows how to do things. The informal networks of buyers, brokers, and sellers move knowledge through the organization. Knowledge markets cluster around formal and informal networks, so providing information about these networks is a good way to make knowledge visible.

Informal networks have the benefits and drawbacks of their informality. Because they function through personal contact and word of mouth, they engender the trust that is an essential engine of successful knowledge exchange. A recommendation that comes from someone we know and respect within the firm is more likely to lead us to a trustworthy seller with appropriate knowledge than would a cold call based on the organizational chart or corporate phone directory. Such informal networks are also dynamic. Because they consist of people more or less continually in communication with one another, they tend to update themselves. People share information about who has left the company or moved to new projects, who has recently become surprisingly useful sources of knowledge, and who has become unexpectedly reticent.

More and more, our own research and the research of others leads us to believe that the most salient unit of analysis when working with knowledge markets is these informal networks or communities. Given their importance, we have conducted a research program over the past two years trying to better understand how to facilitate knowledge creation and sharing in informal networks. Our belief is that social network analysis (SNA) provides a unique set of methods that can further empirical inquiry into knowledge markets. As a set of methods, SNA provides an ability to model content moving in networks, roles in these networks and characteristics of relationships (or signals) that define who is sought out for what.

For example, one avenue of inquiry we have been focused on over the past two years is determining predictors of who is sought out for what kinds of knowledge. The first step in our research was to understand the characteristics of individual relationships that yield effective knowledge creation and sharing (Cross and Borgatti, 2000; Cross et al., 2001). We interviewed 40 managers and asked them to reflect on a project completed within the past six months and identify the three relationships they relied on most during that project for knowledge creation and sharing. We then had them carefully delineate why each of these people was sought out and uniquely beneficial on that project in helping to solve problems.[4] Four features emerged that seemed to determine who was sought out for informational purposes (and thus reflect market signals of a sort). These included: (1) knowing what another person knows and, thus, when to turn to them;[5] (2) being able to gain timely access to that person; (3) willingness of the person sought out to engage in problem solving rather than dump information; and (4) a degree of safety in the relationship that promotes learning and creativity.

The managers we interviewed indicated that these four dimensions were key characteristics of relationships that were effective for learning and knowledge sharing. In contrast, they also recounted numerous times when learning or knowledge sharing did not happen due to one of the above dimensions not existing in the relationship (e.g., someone knew what they needed to know but did not make themselves accessible). Quantitatively, these relational dimensions have consistently predicted who people seek out for informational purposes across a wide variety of networks we have assessed via social network analysis (even after controlling for typical variables of gender, physical proximity, time in organization and formal hierarchical position).

Thus, using social network analysis to map these dimensions of relationships that in many ways are market signals and lead to information seeking provides a unique ability to model and understand one aspect of knowledge markets and organizational learning more generally. First, one can analyze the knowledge, access, engagement, and safety networks separately to determine where a given group might be experiencing problems. For example, if it is discovered that a specific *knowledge* network is sparse, it might make sense to consider a skill profiling system or action learning sets – technical and social interventions designed to help a network know what it knows. In contrast, if the *access* network is sparse, then it might make sense to consider peer feedback, emphasizing collective rather than individual incentives or technical means of connecting distributed workers (e.g., video conferencing). In general, we have found that analyzing the networks individually provides more precise means of improving a group's ability to share and create knowledge than implementing a broad cultural intervention or distributed technology.

In addition, we have also found it helpful to assess relationships cumulatively to get a better understanding of a network's knowledge creation and sharing potential. In doing this, we can analyze networks where pairs of relationships exist (e.g., both know and access) or networks where all of the relationships exist (e.g., know, access, engagement and safety). For example, we conducted a social network analysis of 38 members within a practice of a consulting organization. The first network question asked each person to indicate the extent to which they understood and valued the knowledge and skills of their colleagues. A network diagram of this question can be found in figure 23.1a.

The *know* picture demonstrates who in this practice indicated that they knew and valued other people's knowledge and skills. Though relatively sparse compared to similar networks we have assessed, this network does show a healthy core/periphery pattern without distinct subgroups (which might represent a variety of information flow problems). An interesting point to note in this diagram is the central people – B, C, D, M and T – as these are the individuals most likely to be tapped for informational purposes by the group.[6] Just as importantly, it is interesting to note the people around the edges of the network who are less connected. Ultimately, these people are relatively less utilized by the group and raise important questions for managers to consider regarding why this might be.

The network diagram takes on added life when we consider the remaining dimensions of importance (access, engagement, and safety). By combining the networks, we get a view of relationships that contain all dimensions – ones where people value what someone else knows, are able to gain access to each other, are willing to engage in problem solving and feel a degree of safety. This network diagram can be found in figure 23.1b. Several things are interesting in this network. First, we notice a fairly marked decline in the number of connections among the group in comparison to the *knowledge* network (which suggests an important extension to the study of transactive memory in less constrained field settings). While many central people remained central, it is important to note that several people higher in the hierarchy shifted out to the periphery of the network. For example, we now see that D, J, and G (the three partners in this group) are all out on the periphery of the network. Intuitively this makes sense, though it is often a surprise to those people in higher hierarchical positions. As people move higher within an organization, their work begins to entail more administrative tasks which makes them both less accessible and less knowledgeable about the day-to-day more operational work of their subordinates.

Just as importantly, we now see a marked increase in the number of people on the periphery of the network as well as five people who have become completely disconnected. It might be that people in these positions do not know what people in the organization thought they knew when they were hired. Alternatively, it might be that these people are peripheral because they are relatively new and the organization's hiring and orientation practices do little to help them integrate into a network of colleagues. Regardless, using social network analysis to map these market signals allows us to understand why a given party might be heavily sought out or not on a systematic basis.

Also of interest in the combined network, is the sub-group that has formed at the bottom right-hand corner of the network. The mere existence of a sub-group is not necessarily a bad thing. On the one hand, a group that has splintered off from the main network can represent untapped knowledge and occasionally political problems that must be addressed. However, it might also be the case that to develop new products or services, management will make room and time for people to innovate, as General Motors did with their Saturn division or IBM with development of the PC at Boca Raton. A common practice among

(a)

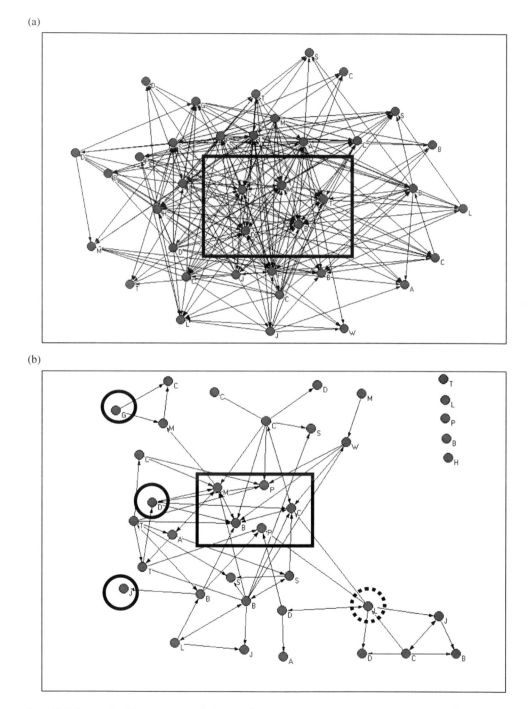

(b)

FIGURE 23.1   (top) Know network; (bottom) Know × access × engage × safety network

many organizations seeking creativity is to allow such a group to form and be creative outside of the requirements of day-to-day work and the pressure that often exists to conform to current ways of doing things.

This was the case in this scenario. Roughly one year prior to this analysis, L had been asked to develop a new service line in a technical network application. To do so, he hired several uniquely skilled people and spent a good bit of time pursuing development of the service offering and sales opportunities, activities that had little to do with the work of this group of consultants. As a result, the smaller group became isolated from the main group over time. In and of itself, this was not bad given the group's unique charter. What was a problem was that this group became linked back to the main network entirely through L. This put L in a particularly influential position and also made the group susceptible to his leaving, which in fact did happen when he was lured away by a high tech startup. Of course the consulting practice was able to integrate these people over time, but interviews indicated that this was a costly process in terms of lost billable hours (and could have been avoided).

A quick review of the example above provides the reader with a rudimentary appreciation of the application of social network analysis to developing and testing knowledge market models within organizations. In this example, we simply demonstrated through visual means how one might think of modeling knowledge marker signals. In a similar fashion, it is feasible to better understand payment mechanisms from a network perspective within organizations. And of course, the more advanced analytics that can be brought to bear via social network analysis can be quite useful in understanding roles or clustering within informal networks (e.g., Wasserman and Faust, 1994; Scott, 1990). For example, it is possible to employ brokerage roles, centrality measures (Freeman, 1979) or even notions of structural equivalence (Burt, 1987) to assess roles in knowledge markets.

In addition to modeling knowledge markets, we think the application of social network analysis to the study of organizational learning can be significant. For example, the combined network view outlined above should begin to provide insight into organizational learning as reflected in social network patterns. Huber (1991: 89) claimed that an organization has learned when "through its processing of information its range of potential behaviors has changed." Thus if we are interested in promoting an organization's ability to react to new opportunities, we need to account for the ways in which people in networks become able to leverage each others' knowledge. Changes in the knowledge, access, engagement, and safety relations underlying a network's future information processing behavior provides the means of both descriptive and prescriptive purchase on this phenomena.

Given the extent to which people rely on their contacts for information (e.g., Granovetter, 1973; Allen, 1977; Burt, 1992), this is not trivial and raises ways of thinking about the impact that highly central people have on the trajectory of a group over time. It has been claimed that organizations are path dependent or constrained by what they know. Such notions as absorptive capacity, core rigidities or architectural knowledge have been described as leading to this path dependence over time (Cohen and Levinthal, 1990; Henderson, 1992; Leonard-Barton, 1995). While important, this work has often been done at a level of abstraction that makes interventions questionable. In contrast, various uses of social network analysis might help us to better understand precisely whose knowledge is primarily responsible for what a group is likely to learn over time.

CONCLUSION

Where is the critical knowledge in the firm? Nelson and Winter (1982) proposed that it lay primarily in organizational routines. We propose that it also lies in the dynamic web of relationships existent in all organizations and which in many ways can be understood as a market. Appreciating that knowledge does not simply flow through an organization but is bartered, blocked, exchanged, and modified alters our thinking about knowledge. We suggest that one productive view is an internal market for knowledge that begins to account for critical actors, pricing mechanisms, and signals.

Understanding characteristics of this market can inform our awareness of social models of organizational learning whereby we are concerned not just with acquisition of declarative and procedural knowledge but processes by which people learn from others and how to tap into them in an effective fashion. Perhaps the strongest lesson we have learned from twentieth-century history is that command and control, centralized, political economies dramatically underperform, in many ways, more market-oriented approaches. While acknowledging the need for some central coordination within a firm, we would still advocate "letting a thousand flowers bloom" in knowledge markets as well.

NOTES

1. For example, we have seen evidence of organizational learning from operating experience (e.g., Argote et al., 1990; Epple et al., 1996; Argote, 1999), innovation efforts (e.g., Van de Ven and Polley, 1990; Pisano, 1994); unique events (March et al., 1991; Cross and Baird, 2000), strategic alliances (e.g., Barley et al., 1992; Inkpen, 1995); teams (Edmondson, 1996, 1999); improvement initiatives (e.g., Leonard-Barton, 1985; Winter, 1996), and individuals (Cohen, 1991; Kim, 1993).
2. Although more recent work in transactive memory and distributed cognition is providing insight into this form of learning.
3. While trust can refer to the ability to accurately predict another's behavior, we use trust to mean the belief that one will not be taken advantage of (Porter et al., 1975).
4. Interviews generally lasted between two and three hours and followed a two-step process common in ego network studies (Scott, 1990; Wasserman and Faust, 1994). First, the composition of each respondent's advice network was determined using a name generator technique (Burt, 1984; Marsden, 1990). Then the characteristics of each relationship were further explored using name interpreter questions. In terms of theory development, we employed a case-based logic in data collection by doing semi-structured interviews guided by a pre-existing theoretical model (Yin, 1994) that we held "loosely" to allow for inductive theory development (Glaser and Strauss, 1967; Lincoln and Gubba, 1985). Our initial framework was informed by streams of research in social exchange theory and social capital, social network analysis, transactive memory and distributed cognition, cognitive and social theories of learning and communication studies. Interviews were transcribed, coded and assessed for inter-rater reliability using typical content

analysis procedures (Diesing, 1971; Lincoln and Gubba, 1985; Strauss, 1987; Miles and Huberman, 1994). A third party independently coded interview transcripts with 93 percent agreement.

5. This of course is subject to bias (Fiske and Taylor, 1984). However, one's perception of another's knowledge and skills, even if inaccurate, informs who is turned to for what.

6. This assertion was validated by interviews in this setting and quantitative models of knowledge seeking in several organizations.

REFERENCES

Allen, T. (1977) *Managing the Flow of Technology*. Cambridge, MA: MIT Press.

Argote, L. (1999) *Organizational Learning: Creating, Retaining and Transferring Knowledge*. Norwell, MA: Kluwer Academic Publishers.

Argote, L., Beckman, S.L., and Epple, D. (1990) The Persistence and Transfer of Learning in Industrial Settings. *Management Science*, 36 (2): 140–54.

Argyris, C. (1982) *Reasoning, Learning and Action*. San Francisco, CA: Jossey-Bass.

Argyris, C. and Schön, D. (1978) *Organizational Learning: Theory, Method and Practice*. Reading, MA: Addison-Wesley.

Arrow, K.J. (1974) *The Limits of Organization*. New York: Norton.

Astley, G. and Sachdeva, P. (1984) Structural Source of Intraorganizational Power: A Theoretical Synthesis. *Academy of Management Review*, 9: 104–13.

Barley, S.R. (1986) Technology as an Occasion for Structuring: Evidence from Observations of CT Scanners and the Social Order of Radiology Departments. *Administrative Science Quarterly*, 31: 78–108.

Barley, S. (1990). The Alignment of Technology and Structure through Roles and Networks. *Administrative Science Quarterly*, 35: 61–103.

Barley, S.R., Freeman, J., and Hybels, R.C. (1992) Strategic Alliances in Commercial Biotechnology. In N. Nohria, *Networks and Organizations*, Boston, MA: Harvard Business School Press, 311–45.

Blau, P. (1986) *Exchange and Power in Social Life*. New Brunswick, NJ: Transaction Publishers.

Brown, J.S. and Duguid, P. (1991) Organizational Learning and Communities-of-practice: Toward a Unified View of Working, Learning and Innovation. *Organization Science*, 2 (1): 40–57.

Burkhardt, M. and Brass, D. (1990) Changing Patterns or Patterns of Change: The Effects of a Change in Technology on Social Network Structure and Power. *Administrative Science Quarterly*, 35: 104–27.

Burt, R. (1984) Network Items and the General Social Survey. *Social Networks*, 6: 293–339.

Burt, R. (1987) Social Contagion and Innovation: Cohesion versus Structural Equivalence. *American Journal of Sociology*, 92: 1287–335.

Burt, R. (1992) *Structural Holes*. Cambridge, MA: Harvard University Press.

Burt, R.S. (2000) The Network Structure of Social Capital. In R.I. Sutton and B.M. Shaw (eds.), *Research in Organization Behavior*. Greenwich, CT: JAI Press, 345–423.

Casey, A. (1997) Collective Memory in Organizations. In J. Walsh and A. Huff (eds.), *Advances in Strategic Management*, vol. 14. Greenwich, CT: JAI Press, 111–46.

Chaiklin, S. and Lave, J. (eds.) (1996) *Understanding Practice: Perspectives on Activity and Context*. Cambridge: Cambridge University Press.

Cohen, M.D. (1991) Individual Learning and Organizational Routines: Emerging Connections. *Organization Science*, 2 (1): 135–9.

Cohen, W. and Levinthal, D. (1990) Absorptive Capacity: A New Perspective on Learning and Innovation. *Administrative Science Quarterly*, 35: 128–52.

Cohen, M.D. and Sproull, L.S. (eds.) (1996) *Organizational Learning*. Thousand Oaks, CA: Sage Publications.

Coleman, J. (1990) *Foundations of Social Theory*. Cambridge, MA: Harvard University Press.

Coleman, J.S. (1988) Social Capital in the Creation of Human Capital. *American Journal of Sociology*, 94, Supplement, 95–120.

Constant, D., Sproull, L., and Kiesler, S. (1996) The Kindness of Strangers. The NSNA Social Networks Conference, Vancouver.

Cook, S.D. and Yanow, D. (1993) Culture and Organizational Learning. *Journal of Management Inquiry*, 2 (4): 112–34.

Cross, R. and Baird, L. (2000) Technology Is Not Enough: Improving Performance by Building Organizational Memory. *Sloan Management Review*, 41 (3): 41–54.

Cross, R. and Borgatti, S. (2000) The Ties that Share: Relational Characteristics that Facilitate Knowledge Transfer and Organizational Learning. Paper presented at the 2000 INSNA Social Networks Conference, Vancouver.

Cross, R., Parker, A., Prusak, L., and Borgatti, S. (2001) Knowing What We Know: Supporting Knowledge Creation and Sharing in Social Networks. *Organizational Dynamics*, 30 (2): 100–20.

Cyert, R.M. and March, J.G. (1963) *A Behavioral Theory of the Firm*. Englewood Cliffs, NJ: Prentice-Hall.

Daft, R. and Weick, K. (1984) Toward a Model of Organizations as Interpretive Systems. *Academy of Management Review*, 9 (2): 284–95.

Diesing, P. (1971) *Patterns of Discovery in the Social Sciences*. Chicago, IL: Aldine-Atherton.

Edmondson, A. (1996) Learning from Mistakes Is Easier Said than Done: Group and Organizational Influences on the Detection and Correction of Human Error. *Journal of Applied Behavioral Science*, 32 (1): 5–28.

Edmondson, A. (1999) Psychological Safety and Learning Behavior in Work Teams. *Administrative Science Quarterly*, 44 (2): 350–83.

Epple, D., Argote, L., and Murphy, K. (1996) An Empirical Investigation of the Microstructure of Knowledge Acquisition and Transfer through Learning by Doing. *Operations Research*, 44 (1): 77–86.

Fiol, C.M. and Lyles, M.A. (1985) Organizational Learning. *Academy of Management Review*, 10 (4): 803–13.

Fiske, S. and Taylor, S. (1984) *Social Cognition*. New York: McGraw-Hill.

Freeman, L.C. (1979) Centrality in Social Networks: I. Conceptual Clarification. *Social Networks*, 1: 215–39.

Garud, R. (1997) On the Distinction between Know-how, Know-why and Know-what in Technological Systems. In J. Walsh and A. Huff (eds.), *Advances in Strategic Management*. Greenwich, CT: JAI Press, 81–101.

Glaser, B. and Strauss, A. (1967) *The Discovery of Grounded Theory: Strategies for Qualitative Research*. Hawthorne, NY: Aldine de Gruyter.

Granovetter, M. (1973) The Strength of Weak Ties. *American Journal of Sociology*, 78: 1360–80.

Granovetter, M. (1985) Economic Action and Social Structure: The Problem of Embeddedness. *American Journal of Sociology*, 91 (3): 481–510.

Henderson, R.M. (1992) Technological Change and the Management of Architectural Knowledge. In T.A. Kochan and M. Useem (eds.), *Transforming Education*. Boston, MA: Sloan School of Management.

Huber, G. (1991) Organizational Learning: The Contributing Processes and Literatures. *Organization Science*, 2 (1): 88–115.

Ibarra, H. and Andrews, S. (1993) Power, Social Influence and Sensemaking: Effects of Network Centrality and Proximity on Employee Perceptions. *Administrative Science Quarterly*, 38: 277–303.

Inkpen, A.C. (1995) Believing Is Seeing: Joint Ventures and Organizational Learning. *Journal of Management Studies*, 32 (5): 595–618.

Kim, D. (1993) The Link between Individual and Organizational Learning. *Sloan Management Review*, 35: 37–50.

Lave, J. and Wenger, E. (1991) *Situated Learning: Legitimate Peripheral Participation*. Cambridge, UK: Cambridge University Press.

Leonard-Barton, D. (1995) *Wellsprings of Knowledge: Building and Sustaining the Sources of Innovation*. Boston, MA: Harvard Business School Press.

Levitt, B. and March, J.G. (1988) Organizational Learning. *Annual Review of Sociology*, 14: 319–40.

Lin, N. (2001) *Social Capital: A Theory of Social Structure and Action*. Cambridge: Cambridge University Press.

Lincoln, Y. and Guba, E. (1985) *Naturalistic Inquiry*. Beverly Hills, CA: Sage.

Lindbloom, C. (2001) *The Market System*. New York: Yale University Press.

March, J.G. and Simon, H.A. (1958) *Organizations*. New York: Wiley.

March, J., Sproull, L., and Tamuz, M. (1991) Learning from Samples of One or Fewer. *Organization Science*, 2 (1): 1–13.

Marsden, P. (1990) Network Data and Measurement. *Annual Review of Sociology*, 16: 435–63.

Middleton, D. and Edwards, D. (eds.) (1990) *Collective Remembering*. Thousand Oaks, CA: Sage Publications.

Miles, M. and Huberman, A. (1994) *Qualitative Data Analysis*, 2nd edn. Thousand Oaks, CA: Sage.

Miner, A. and Mezias, S. (1996) Ugly Duckling No More: Pasts and Futures of Organizational Learning Research. *Organization Science*, 7 (1): 88–99.

Mintzberg, H. (1973) *The Nature of Managerial Work*. New York: Harper Row.

Moingeon, B. and Edmondson, A. (eds.) (1996) *Organizational Learning a Competitive Advantage*. Thousand Oaks, CA: Sage Publications.

Nelson, R. and Winter, S. (1982) *An Evolutionary Theory of Economic Change*. Cambridge, MA: Belknap Press.

Orr, J.E. (1996) *Talking about Machines: An Ethnography of a Modern Job*. Ithaca, NY: Cornell University Press.

Pentland, B.T. (1992) Organizing Moves in Software Support Hot Lines. *Administrative Science Quarterly*, 37 (4): 527–48.

Pettigrew, A.M. (1972) Information Control as a Power Resource. *Sociology*, 6 (2): 187–204.

Pfeffer, J. (1994) *Power in Organizations*. Boston, MA: Harvard Business School Press.

Pisano, G. (1994) Knowledge Integration and the Locus of Learning: An Empirical Analysis. *Strategic Management Journal*, 15: 85–100.

Porter, L., Lawler, E., and Hackman, J. (1975) *Behavior in Organizations*. New York: McGraw Hill.

Rogers, E. (1995) *Diffusion of Innovations*, 4th edn. New York: Free Press.

Sanchez, R. and Heene, A. (eds.) (1997) *Strategic Learning and Knowledge Management*. New York: John Wiley.

Schön, D. (1990) *Educating the Reflective Practitioner*. San Francisco: Jossey Bass.

Scott, J. (1990) *Social Network Analysis*. Thousand Oaks, CA: Sage Publications.

Strauss, A. (1987) *Qualitative Analysis for Social Scientists*. New York: Cambridge University Press.

Uzzi, B. (1997) Social Structure and Competition in Interfirm Networks: The Paradox of Embeddedness. *Administrative Science Quarterly*, 42: 35–67.

Van de Ven, A. and Polley, D. (1990) Learning while Innovating. *Organization Science*, 3 (1): 92–116.

Van Den Bosch, F.A.J. and Van Wijk, R. (2001) Creation of Managerial Capabilities through Managerial Knowledge Integration. In R. Sanchez (ed.), *Knowledge Management and Organizational Competence*. New York: Oxford University Press, 159–76.

Walsh, J.P. (1995) Managerial and Organizational Cognition: Notes from a Trip Down Memory Lane. *Organization Science*, 6 (3): 280–321.

Walsh, J. and Huff, A. (eds.) (1997) *Organizational Learning and Strategic Management*. Greenwich, CT: JAI Press.

Walsh, J.P. and Ungson, G.R. (1991) Organizational Memory. *Academy of Management Review*, 16 (1): 57–91.

Wasserman, S. and Faust, K. (1994) *Social Network Analysis: Methods and Applications*. Cambridge: Cambridge University Press.

Wenger, E. (1998) *Communities of Practice*. Oxford, UK: Oxford University Press.

White, H.C. (1981) Where Do Markets Come From? *American Journal of Sociology*, 87, 517–47.

Winter, S. (1996) Organizing for Continuous Improvement: Evolutionary Theory Meets the Quality Revolution. In M.D. Cohen and L.S. Sproull (eds.), *Organizational Learning*. Thousand Oaks, CA: Sage Publications.

Yin, R.K. (1994) *Case Study Research: Design and Methods*, rev. edn. Newbury Park, CA: Sage.

24

Barriers to Creating Knowledge

MIKELLE A. CALHOUN AND WILLIAM H. STARBUCK

CHAPTER OUTLINE

This chapter focuses on institutionalized processes for creating knowledge, especially methods that academics and professionals espouse publicly when they create objective knowledge. Knowledge creation also blocks discovery, because when people decide that an explanation or observation is true, they create barriers to the acceptance of alternative truths. Whether people see knowledge as being objective depends upon consensus, so the chapter next considers the development of consensus. What kinds of knowledge elicit general agreement? Because knowledge creation suffers from many human dysfunctions, the chapter's final section considers the usefulness of knowledge creation. How essential is it to create knowledge? Are barriers to knowledge creation actually harmful or might they be beneficial?

INTRODUCTION

> We have met the enemy and he is us. (Walt Kelly, Earth Day poster, 1970)

The US Food and Drug Administration (FDA) approves drugs for sale, then doctors prescribe those drugs and people take them, believing them to be safe and effective. However, such beliefs may result from persuasion by critical proponents more than from conclusive research, and they may turn out to be inaccurate, as adverse reactions occur.

After being introduced in 1985, Seldane became a marketing success as the most popular non-sedating antihistamine (Hall, 2001). Then, in 1989, a woman experienced serious heartbeat irregularities, and her doctor conjectured that her heartbeat irregularities had been caused by interaction between Seldane and another drug. Subsequent investigation disclosed previous reports of dangerous heartbeat irregularities related to Seldane. Nine months later, the FDA ordered Seldane's maker to notify doctors of Seldane's potentially fatal interactions with at least two widely used drugs. In 1992, the FDA ordered

Seldane's maker to print a prominent warning at the top of Seldane's label. Early in 1997, the FDA threatened to withdraw its approval of Seldane because it had recently approved the sale of a safer drug, Allegra, which was produced by the same company. In 1998, Seldane's maker voluntarily withdrew it from the market, and the FDA banned the sale of all products containing Seldane's active ingredient. At that time, the FDA announced that there had been 396 deaths among users of Seldane. Thus, the interaction phenomena that led to Seldane's removal had been identified by 1990, but it took eight years to develop consensus that the drug should not be sold. Agreement about Seldane's properties developed gradually through a process that seems to have favored the economic interests of the drug's maker.

As concerns were escalating about Seldane, Schering-Plough was seeking approval of an alternative antihistamine, Claritin. To obtain approval to sell a new drug, its manufacturer must convince the FDA that the drug is both safe and effective. Schering-Plough supported its application to the FDA with statistics from double-blind field trials indicating that Claritin has weak effects. In one study, 46 percent of those taking Claritin experienced improvement but 35 percent of those taking a placebo also experienced improvement. In another study, 43 percent of those taking Claritin experienced improvement but 32 percent of those taking a placebo also experienced improvement. Physicians concluded that 37–47 percent of people who took placebos had shown "good to excellent response to treatment."

The FDA medical examiner who had been assigned to review Claritin became a skeptic about its effectiveness. He opined the proposed 10-milligram dose "is not very different than placebo clinically." The "minimum effective dose," he said, ought to be 40 milligrams, but Claritin would act as a sedative at such dosage levels. Schering-Plough's 1981 patent application had stated that Claritin had "little or no sedative effects." This FDA examiner's skepticism disappeared from the evaluation process when he became very seriously ill.

In May 1988, the FDA stated that a 10-milligram dose of Claritin is not sedating, and the General Accounting Office reported that "a consensus had developed at FDA that 10 milligrams was effective" by July 1989. Later that year, the FDA reorganized and transferred the evaluation of Claritin to another division. A reviewer in the new division raised the possibility that Claritin might be carcinogenic at high dosages. This issue mired Claritin in further debate until 1993, when, after 77 months of evaluation, the FDA finally approved it for sale. A major reason for this approval was concern about the safety of Seldane. According to the General Accounting Office, the FDA had "started to believe that it would be beneficial to have Claritin for sale."

Hall (2001) remarked that "Claritin had gone from being a me-too drug, to one that looked possibly unapprovable, to the only game in town." During 1998 and 1999, Schering-Plough spent a remarkable $322 million to advertise Claritin to consumers. The drug now brings its maker $2 billion annually.

Again, pharmaceutical knowledge developed gradually over many years, during which the issues shifted somewhat erratically. Most of what people thought they knew about Claritin came from research that had been conducted or financed by Schering-Plough. The research had produced ambiguous findings, some of which were made less ambiguous by Schering-Plough's aggressive advertising. The FDA's evaluation process reflected the personal characteristics of the evaluators as well as the organization of the

FDA. Had Seldane not appeared dangerous, the FDA might never have judged Claritin acceptable. Yet, Claritin's market success indicates that it is now widely seen as a safe and very effective drug.

What did the FDA or Schering-Plough learn from this series of experiences? Since the recommended dosage that FDA finally approved was the one requested in the initial licensing application, the FDA's questions had not been reinforced by consequences. One of the key FDA evaluators left the agency, taking his idiosyncratic knowledge with him. Partly because of the agency's reorganization, many FDA personnel moved to jobs where their experience with Claritin was irrelevant. Schering-Plough had persisted in the face of discouraging prospects for six-and-a-half years, and the FDA's eventual approval likely reinforced such perseverance. Never before had a pharmaceutical company spent so much money to advertise a product, and Claritin's subsequent success likely reinforced the future use of heavy advertising. Claritin's long-term success also likely reinforced the idea of selling marginally effective medications for prevalent ailments.

What Is Creation of Knowledge?

> History warns us, however, that it is the customary fate of new truths to begin as heresies and to end as superstitions. (Thomas Henry Huxley, 1880: 1)

Anyone with the temerity to write about knowledge has to confront pervasive disagreement about the meaning of knowledge. In the early 1990s, New York University faculty participated in a knowledge management seminar. Successive speakers adopted diverse viewpoints, discussed diverse issues, and proposed diverse applications. So varied were the contributions that one could say the speakers agreed on only one point: None of them agreed with the others about the proper definition of knowledge. Indeed, every single speaker began by explaining his or her distinctive definition of knowledge.

Thus, our first reaction was to seek cover in legitimate authority. We found that *Webster's Third International Dictionary* offers eight definitions, but these are variations on two basic themes: (1) thorough familiarity and (2) perception of facts or truth. The second of these themes strikes us as being especially interesting because it poses the questions: What is fact? What is truth?

The dictionary offers little help on the questions of what is fact or truth: It defines fact as knowledge of truth, and truth as fact. The dictionary's reticence is understandable, for philosophers have been debating these questions for ages. The proper definitions of knowledge, fact, and truth have also been the foci of many legal battles (Black, 1990). We have no intention of entering such discussions. But we are intrigued by another version of these questions: Under what circumstances do people decide that some perception or belief constitutes knowledge? In deciding that something is true, people create barriers to the acceptance of other potential truths.

Knowledge is what people say it is. It is people, individually and collectively, that determine what is or is not classified as knowledge. Although people disagree about the existence of absolute truths, if such truths exist, people have to observe them through human perceptual systems, so human understanding of facts or truths is molded by human bodies and human social systems. Polanyi (1962) argued that because observations always depend on the humans who make them, notions about complete scientific objectivity are delusive.

Social systems are central because social processes elevate perceptions into facts, beliefs into truths. What one person regards as fact another may classify as superstition or myth. This implies that processes of communication, social influence, and consensus building play central roles in knowledge creation. Brunsson (1982) pointed out that a perception or belief held by only one person has the status of being subjective, and its effects are limited to that person's actions. On the other hand, a widely shared perception or belief acquires the status of being objective; not only can it affect the actions of many but these many act with the support of objective fact. Indeed, to motivate collective action, a perception or belief must be widely shared. When a perception or belief is supported by consensus, it gains the status of truth.

Thus, knowledge always reflects social construction, even the knowledge that is supposed to be highly dependable. Legal juries afford an example of this molding of truth, and several researchers have observed processes of social construction during scientific research. Mitroff (1974) studied scientists participating in the Apollo moon-landing project, Latour and Woolgar (1979) observed scientists at the Salk Institute, Zukav (1979) studied research on quantum mechanics, and Knorr-Cetina (1981) observed laboratory physicists. Their analyses portray scientists as social beings who develop their observations interactively. Other investigations have looked at competition among researchers, secrecy, and misrepresented results (Gaston, 1971; Gilbert, 1977; Over, 1982; Samuelson 1980).

People and organizations acquire information through social networks, and a portion of this information becomes knowledge. However, the gathering of information is not equivalent to the creation of knowledge, and indeed, people may gather information without the intention of creating knowledge. For example, evidence suggests that business firms use alliances mainly to gather information that never rises to the level of knowledge (Porrini, 2001). Eisenhardt and Schoonhoven (1996) observed that firms are more likely to form alliances if they are in highly competitive industries or they are attempting to lead technologically, and Stuart (1998) inferred that alliances occur at the highest rates in industries where many firms innovate and invent. In such situations, ambiguity prevails, very few beliefs have wide consensus, and beliefs grow obsolete too rapidly to become truths.

In a social world, nearly all facts are descriptions of social behavior. The "laws" of economics, the "facts" of history, the "norms" of society, and religious principles are all descriptions of human actions, habits, or beliefs. As behavior changes, knowledge of this behavior also changes, and it is possible that phenomena change faster than researchers can understand them. Consider, for example, the challenges of creating knowledge about the effectiveness of leadership. Managers with more education use different leadership styles, and subordinates with more education react differently to leadership styles (Dreeben, 1968; Haire et al., 1966; Kunda, 1992). In the US, median educational level of workers over 25 has risen from 8.6 years in 1940 to 12.7 years in 1991. In 1940, less than 5 percent of the workforce had completed four years of college or more, but this percentage rose to 17 by 1980 and to 26 by 2000. These changes have concentrated in and paralleled changes in employment (Cummings and Schmidt, 1972). Employment in government, finance, and professional services rose from 17 percent in 1950 to 46 percent in 2001. The fastest-growing occupations have been professional and technical workers and managers and administrators. Thus, the practices that constitute effective leadership have been evolving even as researchers have been attempting to develop understanding of what constitutes effective leadership.

Even when principles remain stable, they have to be restated in today's language. For example, an ancient Chinese document states a contingency theory of leadership that was probably transcribed before 2200 BCE (Rindova and Starbuck, 1997). Not only are the principles in this ancient theory still valid today, but they may offer more insight than today's theories. However, the ancient document lacks the symbols that make today's contingency theories appear credible to contemporary managers and academics: The document is terse, it reports no statistical analyses, and it does not explain how the principles might apply to today's situations.

People not only define "knowledge" but what it means to "create" knowledge. Some experts say they create knowledge. Starbuck (1992) found the distinctions experts make between creating knowledge, applying knowledge, and preserving knowledge to be very difficult to draw or to defend. Although experts characterize their activities differently, the experts' actual behaviors are very similar. Experts who say they are creating new knowledge highlight the newness of their data and the differences between their findings and those of earlier investigators. However, such innovations are almost always marginal, and experts imbed their creations in the context of related investigations and familiar knowledge. The distinction between creation and application seems to be especially obscure in the context of complex systems because people may only be able to create valid knowledge about complex systems by testing their beliefs through application (Starbuck, 1976: 1100–3). Ambiguity about the meaning of "creation" nurtures theories about knowledge creation that seek to encompass everything and that seem absurd when taken to the extremes.

Creation is nearly always a social process, even when the participants perceive themselves as acting independently, and one result may be controversy over who created what. Consider the debate over who "invented" the concept of packet switching, the operating scheme for the Internet (Circuits, 2001; Hafner, 2001). In 1963, J.C.R. Licklider wrote a memo that proposed the creation of a large network for the US Defense Department's Advanced Research Projects Agency. At Licklider's suggestion, the Agency asked Larry Roberts to develop a design for this network. Roberts' design incorporated ideas from several people, including Leonard Kleinrock who had analyzed traffic flows in "message-switched" networks, Thomas Marill who had built a two-node network, and Wes Clark who had proposed that minicomputers could serve as routing devices. In October 1967, a committee reviewed a draft design for the network, which described the proposed system as "store and forward," not as "packet switching." But shortly after, Larry Roberts attended a technical conference where he learned that both Paul Baran and Donald Davies had been developing ideas similar to his own. During 1968–69, a group of people at an engineering firm built the proposed network; the system designer for this project was Robert E. Kahn. However, not until 1971 did documentation for the network incorporate the term "packet switching," drawn from Davies's 1967 presentation. Thirty years later, a small storm of controversy arose over who had created the most essential knowledge. Some books and articles had credited Baran and Davies alone with having created packet switching. In 2000, the Institute of Electrical and Electronics Engineers recognized Baran, Davies, Kleinrock, and Roberts "For their early, preeminent contributions in conceiving, analyz ing and demonstrating packet-switching networks, the foundation technology of the Internet." Davies then published an article in which he said "I can find no evidence that [Kleinrock] understood the principles of packet switching." In 2001, the US National Academy of Engineering honored four people for having created the Internet – Roberts, Kleinrock, Kahn, and a man who had made later contributions, Vinton G. Cerf.

Certainly, someone who seeks to create knowledge has to attempt to influence processes of social construction. Davis (1971) analyzed the properties that make contributions to sociology "interesting," hence attracting attention and exerting influence. He inferred that interesting contributions exhibit similar presentational characteristics that create tension. However, to create knowledge, one must do more than merely attract attention and elicit discussion; one must build widespread consensus. Thus, Peter and Olson (1983) argued that science is a sub-field of marketing – "the marketing of ideas in the form of substantive and methodological theories."

Since the topic of barriers to the creation of knowledge could have immense scope, we have had to make some rather arbitrary choices about what to discuss. One of these choices is to focus on systematic, institutionalized processes of knowledge creation. This chapter considers only intentional processes used by academics and professionals. The next part of the chapter focuses on research methods that recognized experts espouse publicly when they say they are creating objective knowledge. What kinds of methods receive wide use? The ensuing part of the chapter examines the development of consensus about propositions. On what propositions do people agree? Because the foregoing sections suggest that knowledge creation suffers from many human dysfunctions, the final section considers the usefulness of knowledge creation. How essential is it to create knowledge? Are barriers to knowledge creation actually harmful or might they be beneficial?

Barriers in the Methods that Experts Use to Create Knowledge

> Science is simply setting out on a fishing expedition to see whether it cannot find some procedure which it can call the measurement of space and some procedure which it can call the measurement of time, and something which it can call a system of forces, and something which it can call masses, so that these formulae may be satisfied . . . The theory, so far from founding science on a sound observational basis, forces everything to conform to a mere mathematical preference for certain simple formulae. (Whitehead, 1926: 139–40)

There is considerable evidence that research does not actually occur in the fashion that scientists allege, and there is some evidence that much research about human behavior fails to produce any knowledge whatever. Of course, research methods vary considerably among fields, but all scientific fields endorse a few principles: (1) Researchers are supposed to make the creation of knowledge an overriding goal that supercedes all others. (2) Researchers are supposed not only to be honest and truthful but to tell the whole truth.

(3) Researchers are supposed to build on the work of their predecessors, so that knowledge accumulates over time. (4) Results are supposed to speak for themselves.

Some research methods have been making considerably more progress than others. In a classic article, Platt (1964) pointed out that some natural sciences had made substantial progress whereas others had bogged down. Platt argued that more progress has occurred in fields that formulated critical tests that excluded potential hypotheses. That is, science has made progress mainly by showing that some hypotheses are incorrect, not by showing "new" hypotheses might be correct (Popper, 1959). The problem with showing a hypothesis is consistent with observations is that this only indicates the hypothesis might be correct. Since many hypotheses might possibly be correct, not merely the hypothesis tested, negligible progress occurs. Indeed, research that supports hypotheses decreases knowledge by increasing ambiguity.

However, many research fields focus their efforts on methods that attempt to generate many new hypotheses without excluding any potential hypotheses. An obvious instance is the social and economic sciences, where journals regularly refuse to print studies that fail to reject null hypotheses, and where many published articles reject null hypotheses that are probably true (Blaug, 1980; Greenwald, 1975). In such a research context, the only effective way to expose inferential errors is through studies that fail to replicate prior findings and publishing the contradictory results. Yet, journals in these fields also decline to publish replications. Thus, there is reason to wonder about the amount of knowledge creation occurring in the social and economic sciences.

One clue to the true value of research results lies in the rarity with which empirical research produces clear answers. All data describe specific instances, which are always somewhat unique, often context driven, and potentially deceptive. Social science researchers periodically raise questions about disconnects between research questions and real-world contexts in which the phenomena actually occur. For instance, Cappelli and Sherer (1991: 97) detailed examples in support of their complaint that "research in OB has systematically abandoned contextual arguments in order to remain consistent with theoretical developments in the field of psychology." Records and surveys always contain biases and errors, so data drawn from such sources inherit their defects. Self-reporting problems and the use of certain "facts" as proxies for other "facts" render most data inaccurate and the links between data and theories tenuous at best. Samples often violate the assumptions made in analyses, rendering the analyses speculative and often very misleading. Researchers are frequently aware that several hypotheses are consistent with their data or that missing data could alter their inferences. Thus, almost all empirical studies call, implicitly or explicitly, for better studies. Someone who has observed such behavior for a time should think it unlikely that empirical research can create knowledge.

As well, empirical research often produces misleading answers. Hayek (1975) criticized social scientists for focusing on phenomena that can be measured quantitatively and for using causal models where they lack adequate understanding of causation. Quantitative measures describe rather limited aspects of phenomena and may not include the central aspects of phenomena. In the study of complex phenomena, determinants of outcomes can rarely be known or measured and the partial derivative thinking that pervades most empirical studies substitutes fewer, larger effects for complete understanding. One result, Hayek (1975) alleged, is that economic policy-makers, focusing on what they could measure and ignoring what they could not, inadvertently modified national economies in ways that gave economies undesirable new properties.

Research about social systems has very restricted opportunities to experiment usefully. To run controlled experiments, researchers generally have to study very artificial situations, with the result that experimental findings probably do not extrapolate to realistic situations. Experiments with real social systems lack controls and occur mutatis mutandis, so findings are very difficult to interpret. As a result, researchers must draw conclusions about general principles from observations of specific instances. For example, who is a successful manager? What is a best practice? Such inferences can be not merely wrong, but harmful, as Hayek observed.

At the same time, research about social systems very much needs experiments that perturb normal behaviors and question their ordinary assumptions (Starbuck, 1976). Existing social systems operating as they naturally do are very capable of creating misleading impressions. Existing social systems rarely violate critical constraints, and indeed, they are unlikely to come close to violating them. Existing social systems are nearly always close to equilibrium in almost all dimensions, so they do not exhibit the full range of behaviors of which they are capable. Thus, studies of the existing social systems misrepresent dynamics and conceal many causal factors. Only by intervening and attempting to produce unnatural changes can researchers discover latent potentialities. Consider the revolutionary idea of Joseph Lister that post-surgery infections might be caused by living organisms in the air, and hence that it might be necessary to kill these organisms. To test this idea, Lister tried to persuade doctors and nurses to behave differently, but he met indifference and hostility. Then, German doctors experimented with antiseptic methods during the Franco–Prussian War, and found good results.

Webster and Starbuck (1988) examined the progress made by researchers toward understanding nine focal relations in organizational behavior. These relations have been the targets of as many as 4,000 studies, and one series of studies extended for 55 years, others for 11 to 40 years. Webster and Starbuck found that researchers appeared to have made no progress toward accurately describing four of the relations and that they had made negative progress toward describing the other five relations. That is, in five instances, studies had been producing effect sizes that had trended gradually toward zero. Furthermore, in four instances, researchers had been making comparisons that probably overstated the strengths of effect sizes.

Webster and Starbuck proposed five reasons for their depressing discoveries. (1) Researchers may be adhering to incorrect hypotheses despite disconfirming evidence. (2) Researchers may be continuing to use older research methods after these cease to produce added knowledge. (3) Most studies may be building on misinterpretations of poorly conducted studies. As researchers make better measurements and obtain better data over time, they discover that studied relations do not exist or are very weak. (4) Studies that produced large effect sizes and became the objects of imitation may have had unreported idiosyncracies. In particular, researchers tend to use confirmatory data-gathering strategies and to attribute effects to the relations they expected to see. (5) People's characteristics may be changing faster than psychologists' theories or measures improve.

Knowledge is difficult to improve and extend partly because the espoused goals of research are self-defeating. Researchers set self-defeating goals in at least four ways.

First, most researchers want to understand the present and future, but all researchers study the past, and all data come from the past, sometimes the distant past. Even studies that gather current information produce data about what happened at the time of data gathering, which may no longer be current information by the time the data have been analyzed. People and social systems change constantly, and from time to time, they change dramatically. Dramatic examples of this phenomenon occurred with the design of highway systems for major metropolitan areas. The designers started with surveys of drivers' sources and destinations and analyzed these to develop idea routes that would benefit the most drivers. But it took from 5 to 20 years to build the actual highways, by which time the original data were very obsolete.

In general, people have developed almost no ability to forecast social phenomena long into the future. Although almost everyone can make accurate forecasts about the short-run future by extrapolating recent trends, no one has shown that they can predict accurately beyond a few periods ahead. In his classic book on forecasting, Armstrong (1985: 9) advised: "Do not hire the best expert you can – or even close to the best. Hire the cheapest expert." Elliott (1973) compared the four complex economic forecasting models with two naive forecasts. One naive forecast says that GNP in three months will be the same as GNP today. This no-change forecast was as accurate as three of the four computer models. The more accurate naive forecast says that the GNP trend over the last three months will continue for the next three months. This linear-trend forecast was as accurate as the best computer model, which was the simplest one. Makridakis and various colleagues (1982) compared 24 statistical forecasting methods by forecasting 1,001 series of observations. They found that no-change forecasts beat all others 38–64 percent of the time, and that a variant of straight-line extrapolation made the most accurate forecasts at least 50 percent of the time.

Second, researchers strive to create generally valid theories, but a theory that is true everywhere has to be tautological. One example is microeconomic theory, which its users regard as axiomatic. Because users insist that this theory cannot be incorrect, they use it to reinterpret observations retrospectively. But such reinterpretations mean that microeconomic theory can neither be disproved nor confirmed. Another example is afforded by the macroeconomic analysis that brought Solow the Nobel Prize. Seeking to describe the relation between labor, capital, and output, Solow (1957) introduced technology as the missing ingredient. He then estimated the effects of technology by calculating the amounts that would be necessary for there to exist an almost perfect relationship between labor, capital, and output. He assumed that this relationship might take one of five algebraic forms, and table 24.1 shows the multiple correlations he obtained with each of these forms. Obviously, the fits were very close with every algebraic form. Indeed, the only reason the multiple correlations were not all 1.00 is that Solow used an approximation when calculating the effects of technology. As a result, the high correlations give no information about the correspondence between Solow's theory and his data.

Third, researchers strive to create theories that describe their observations very accurately, but a theory that represents observations with extreme accuracy is just as incomprehensible as the situation observed. Dutton and Starbuck (1971: 4) called this effect "Bonini's paradox" because it appeared in Bonini's (1963) computer simulation of a hypothetical business firm. Bonini used computer simulation so that his theory could

TABLE 24.1   Correlations in Solow's analysis of the aggregate production function

Model (assumed algebraic function)	Multiple correlation
$\Delta q = \alpha + \beta k$	0.9982
$q = \alpha + \beta \log k$	0.9996
$q = \alpha - \beta / k$	0.9964
$\log q = \alpha + \beta \log k$	0.9996
$\log q = \alpha - \beta / k$	0.9980

incorporate complex, realistic assumptions. The resulting simulation model exhibited behavior that Bonini (1963) judged to be realistic, but he found his model very difficult to understand. He said:

> We cannot explain completely the reasons why the [simulated] firm behaves in a specific fashion. Our model of the firm is highly complex, and it is not possible to trace out the behavior pattern throughout the firm . . . Therefore, we cannot pinpoint the explicit causal mechanism in the model. (p. 136)

Fourth, insofar as researchers do acquire knowledge, they often use this knowledge to add more complexity to technological or social systems, with one result being that they render themselves ignorant again. Bridge building offers one example. People have been building bridges for many, many millennia. Yet bridges collapse every year. They collapse because new knowledge induces bridge builders to go outside the envelope of experience, to experiment with designs that have not been used previously. The Challenger disaster presents a similar example (Starbuck and Milliken, 1988). As soon as NASA had a space vehicle that seemed to work well, they began to introduce modifications that made the vehicle able to carry heavier payloads. Each of these modifications was only a small increment to one feature, but each took the system slightly outside the envelope of experience, and three such modifications interacted to produce amplified effects.

Effective barriers to knowledge creation arise as limitations of people individually and collectively. As individuals, people have limited mental capacities that restrict their conceptualizations, so human knowledge has to be simplistic. Individual people also have limited experience and capacity to acquire, understand and incorporate knowledge. Collective barriers arise as people develop organizations, professions, and societies with cultures that impede some kinds of knowledge creation. These collectivities interact in complex relationships that make knowledge difficult to create and render simple forms of knowledge ineffective. Collectivities also have a propensity to change in ways that make existing knowledge obsolete and that complicate interactions until they exceed human capabilities to understand them or control them. Consider, for example, the US tax code or the legislative process that bundles unrelated issues into complex bills to secure sufficient support.

Barriers within individual researchers

The philosophy guiding scientific research relies very strongly on the correctness of rationality. However, rationality is a physiological property of human anatomy. Although people are comfortable with rational logic, it may not be adequate to the task it faces. The Law of Requisite Variety says that for people to understand their environments, human comprehension abilities must be as complex and diverse as the environments (Ashby, 1961). But human rationality is a rather crude and imperfect tool, with very limited powers of discrimination, so humans' environments could be more complex than people are able to grasp. Indeed, as observed above, when people do think they understand their environments, they proceed to introduce more complexity and more variety until the environments reach, or often exceed, comprehension.

Human rationality confers significant disadvantages. It seeks to classify almost everything into bifurcated categories, and in so doing it erases fine distinctions and converts faint relations into close ones. It warps humans' observations (Singer and Benassi, 1981). People see phenomena that their logic tells them they should see even when the phenomena do not actually occur. People remember events that never took place (Kiesler, 1971; Loftus, 1979; Nisbett and Wilson, 1977). Circumstances and environmental influences can dramatically impact human perception and information processing. Consider victims of severe abuse who begin to identify with their captors or abusers and the expressed views of cults and extreme religious or political factions. If applied without reservations, human rationality would extrapolate incomplete knowledge to impossible extremes (Starbuck, 1988).

Of course, much of the time, people do not actually follow the prescriptions for rational thought that guide scientific research. These deviations have both beneficial and harmful consequences. The deviations are beneficial insofar as they prevent people from carrying rationality to ridiculous extremes (Starbuck, 1983). Bazerman (1997) documented more than a dozen heuristics and biases that shape human thought. For instance, people tend to see themselves as causing events and they underestimate the effects of external causes. People especially emphasize their own impacts after they succeed, and they emphasize the effects of environmental causes after other people succeed. Similarly, notwithstanding the presumption of innocence, a criminal indictment labels the accused even before trial. Mahoney (1977) studied the justifications offered by reviewers for academic journals to support their editorial recommendations. Reviewers tended strongly to recommend rejection of manuscripts with findings that contradicted theories the reviewers had endorsed in print.

Summarizing such concerns, David Faust (1984) assessed errors of scientific judgment and the contributions of human cognition to scientific constructs of the world. He explained:

> We no longer believe that pure reason applied to pure facts provides pure knowledge. We no longer even believe that pure facts are possible, nor that there is a logic that can be used to decipher what the facts might mean. (p. 4)

While acknowledging that many scientific failures result from inadequate data, subjective biases, and inappropriate questions, Faust (1984: 116) said the most fundamental problem may be humans' insufficient cognitive ability: "scientists may have sufficient cognitive ability to comprehend simple configural relationships among cues or variables, but insufficient ability to comprehend more complex relationships." If nature were revealed to us, how much would we be able to understand?

Barriers in organizations

Organizations provide individual people with careers in hierarchies, they turn analyses and decisions into political actions, and they surround people with cultures that intensify the focus on formalized rationality.

When people see their statements and actions as influencing their career success and long-term economic welfare, they try to make their statements and actions defensible. Richard Faust (1978) explained that research scientists face a challenge of positioning proposed research to attract investment and funding. Researchers cannot rely on favorable outcomes to protect them because outcomes are not always favorable. Thus, organization members highlight the correctness of the analyses on which they base their statements and actions. Decision-makers try to demonstrate that they had good plans whether or not the plans were achieved. Researchers try to show that they used good methods whether or not these methods produce scientific progress. These effects become stronger when researchers attach their names to theories or decision-makers take ownership of projects.

Organizations also amplify the importance of rationality partly because communication emphasizes shared logic and partly because organizational decision processes often incorporate written rationalizations. Since it arises from human physiology, rationality is something that everyone can agree is good. Everyone can recognize the presence of rationality in an argument.

However, valid rationality is often insufficient to garner support for change, as political interests dominate rationality. Normann (1971) observed that senior managers welcome small incremental changes but they resist large dramatic changes. Incremental changes fit within current cognitive frameworks and current power structures, whereas dramatic changes might be incomprehensible or might call for new leaders (Starbuck, 1983). This bias toward incrementalism proves beneficial when rational logic suggests actions that would exceed the range of experience, and it proves detrimental when drastic changes become essential to continued survival (Quinn, 1980).

Barriers in professions

Professions differ from work organizations in the looseness of their structures and their emphasis on values. They have weak structures because their values guide their members' actions. However, professional values corrupt research efforts by defining methods ritualistically.

An old story illustrates the potential for professions to define proper methods ritualistically. During the 13th century, a professor at the University of Paris asked his colleagues whether oil would congeal if left outdoors on a very cold night. Other professors agreed that this was a very interesting question, so they began a joint project to discover the answer. But after many weeks and much work, they concluded that the question was unanswerable. They had searched all of the works of Aristotle and had found nothing on this subject.

Similar distortions of common sense occur today. For example, scholars in the field of management do not qualify their statistical findings by stating percentages such as "30 percent of companies do X" or "60 percent of managers are X." Instead, they routinely describe such observations by saying "companies do X" or "managers are X" as if the descriptions describe everyone or every situation. Much of the time, such statements have no bases beyond computed averages – that is, "an average manager is X." Another example is afforded by tests of statistical significance. Webster and Starbuck (1988) examined all of the pairs of variables observed in management studies, including both pairs that were the subjects of hypotheses and pairs that were unrelated to hypotheses. Two-thirds of the pairs of variables correlated "significantly" at the 5 percent level. Starting with a target variable, a researcher would need only three random trials to find another variable that correlates significantly with the target variable. Thus, significance tests are highlighting multitude correlations that have no theoretical meaning. Meaningful relations are being lost in clouds of random errors. Yet a third example is the use of ordinary least-squares regression with small samples. Because of the use of squared errors, which give extreme weight to low-probability observations, regression calculations are less reliable than a priori assumptions unless samples sizes are rather large. Simulation studies have shown that one needs at least 200 degrees of freedom even when the data have perfect normal distributions (Claudy, 1972; Schmidt, 1971). When data depart from normality, one might need several thousand observations. Yet, social scientists routinely publish least-squares regressions with small samples.

BARRIERS TO CONSENSUS BUILDING

> What is one psychologist's subject matter is another psychologist's error term. (Meehl, 1991: 5)

For knowledge to exist, people have to agree that it exists. In most cases, because the existence of knowledge is moot, knowledge can only exist where there is consensus. In a study of small companies, Jönsson and Lundin (1977) observed that people had waves of enthusiasm for ideas. After a new idea appeared, people gradually began to understand it and like it. More and more people joined the bandwagon. But then, people began to notice defects in the idea. It was less powerful than they had hoped, or less general, or possibly even disappointing. So enthusiasm waned and the idea gradually lost supporters. On a similar theme, Meehl (1991) reviewed the history of psychology and commented that theories fade away over time as people lose interest in them.

In order for research to create knowledge, researchers must agree that some beliefs and perceptions are correct. Kuhn (1970) argued that the development of some scientific fields has been marked by the existence of stable paradigms. These paradigms, he said (1970: 37), determine the criteria for choosing problems and issues and the methods of research.

As a result, knowledge develops for a long period within the confines of each paradigm. A novel theory and resulting new paradigm cannot emerge until a crisis creates widespread doubt about the validity of the existing paradigm.

But in many fields, certainly in the social and economic sciences, researchers' behavior indicates that they have not agreed that some beliefs and perceptions are correct. Almost every researcher discards prior "findings" and invents new "laws." Minor variations on existing theories receive distinctive new names and enthusiastic adherents. As a result, the process of creating knowledge often takes a dialectic form. A new assertion evokes a contrary assertion. Indeed, merely stating a conclusion is often sufficient to provoke a contrary hypothesis. These debates often lead to syntheses that combine the contending ideas and incorporate contingencies. Such integration broadens perceptions and increases understanding. For example, early in the 20th century, one widely accepted position was that leaders command: leaders have the ability to elicit compliance through their forceful personalities. This position elicited a contrary view – that leaders display friendliness and show concern for their subordinates. During the early years of the century, these two positions were seen as polar opposites, contenders for what is right. Then the Ohio State Leadership Studies found that subordinates' perceptions of leaders can be arrayed on two statistically independent dimensions: initiating structure and consideration. The two antitheses suddenly became two dimensions of a more complex phenomenon.

In a world where knowledge is often ephemeral, dialectic development can be useful. Contrasts between ideas help people to formulate concepts more clearly. Debates remind people of the ambiguities that surround evidence, assumptions, and analyses. But contrasting views tend to become political issues, with vocal proponents who have vested interests in the correctness of one side. Contrasting views can also prevent people from integrating concepts, as illustrated by the debate about leadership, where the existence of competing theories blocked vision of a greater possibility.

Unfortunately, the creation of knowledge does not always follow a fruitful trajectory. There are also often endless processes of empiricism that go nowhere, as illustrated by the studies in organizational behavior analyzed by Webster and Starbuck (1988). Thousands of studies follow one after another and the last embodies no more knowledge than the first because nothing occurs that elicits widespread agreement. As Dörner (1996: 99) observed, "The more we know, the more clearly we realize what we don't know."

But Do People Really Want to Create Knowledge?

Science becomes dangerous only when it imagines that it has reached its goal. (George Bernard Shaw, 1993: 406)

A more interesting question than what barriers exist may be: why do people create and tolerate barriers to the creation of knowledge? Researchers very often pursue personal goals that turn knowledge creation into a symbolic facade, organizations typically place higher priority on political stability than on the validity of knowledge, and professional associations routinely endorse method rituals that foster the creation of spurious knowledge. Such behaviors suggest that people believe knowledge is not essential or unimportant. Why is there so little dissatisfaction with such behaviors? Why are such behaviors widespread and acceptable? Is it possible that knowledge is not actually very important to human welfare? Is it possible that people can survive very well without useful knowledge? Do people recognize that barriers provide protection from dangerous inferential errors?

When a situation persists, even a situation that seems very undesirable, almost always someone is benefiting from it. So who benefits from barriers to the creation of knowledge? It is easy to spot beneficiaries. Knowledge is power, both for the current power holders and for those who aspire to power. Students often want formulas that they can apply that will yield career success; they want proven examples and recipes to follow. Doctoral students want to believe that the research methods they are studying really do work; they want to believe that the topics being discussed in journals really do matter. Dissertation committees want new theories to support their own work. Senior researchers have investments in existing methods and theories; they may even have endowed theories with their names. Senior managers are all too aware that their high statuses depend on their mastery of relevant knowledge, meaning the knowledge already at hand; radically new knowledge could render them obsolete and displace them from control (Normann, 1971; Starbuck, 1983). In the early 1990s as many law firms in Texas were having financial problems and dissolving, the largest law firm in Dallas elected to pay a consulting firm a significant fee to gather information about internal dissatisfaction that seemed to underlie growing productivity problems. After collecting and disseminating the results of the extensive study, management at the law firm ignored all recommendations that would have required significant changes by the firm's partners. Less than two years later, the internal strife exploded and the firm dissolved. Although new knowledge might have rescued the firm, accepting new knowledge appeared more costly.

People also draw value from the process of doing research whether or not the research produces useful results. Continuing to strive enables people to believe that they can someday comprehend. People must continue to "create knowledge" because the activity of trying to create knowledge gives them feelings of self-efficacy, self-confidence, and hope for future improvements. Consider, for instance, the innumerable articles in newspapers and magazines that describe current medical research and speculate about future treatments.

Why is it that people might think they are able to survive and live satisfying lives without effective processes for creating knowledge? There must be substitutes knowledge that make it unessential. Five substitutes come to mind.

First, most problem solving, possibly almost all problem solving, does not depend on having accurate knowledge of their current situations. People can act effectively without having accurate knowledge because they usually get evidence promptly about the effectiveness of their actions, at least in gross terms. When difficulties arise, people can usually change their actions quickly enough that their misperceptions cause only small errors. Mezias and Starbuck (2003) offered evidence that the great majority of managers lack accurate knowledge of their firms and of their firms' market environments; in fact, managers' beliefs are often wildly inaccurate. Large errors are not only prevalent, they are uncorrelated with the managers' job experience. The managers in these studies came from large well-known companies that have the resources to reduce or eliminate erroneous beliefs if these were causing serious problems. But these companies are not devoting substantial resources to error correction, so erroneous beliefs must not be causing serious problems.

For example, Mezias and Starbuck (2003) studied managers who were being urged to improve the quality of their company's products. The CEO had said quality improvement was his highest priority, and the company was spending large amounts of time and money to gather and disseminate information about quality performance. Most managers had attended training courses about quality, every division had a quality department, all managers received frequent reports about current measures of quality, and 74 percent of the managers expected to receive large personal rewards when their divisions reached higher quality. Yet, when asked about the current numerical measurements of quality, 49–91 percent of the managers said "I don't know." Indeed, the managers' responses showed rather strong halo effects: They described quality performance very similarly in all dimensions irrespective of the actual levels. Why did the managers lack knowledge of the current quality levels even though their company had taken great pains to make this knowledge available to them? Well, as a practical matter, the managers' ability to improve product quality depended hardly at all on their knowledge of current quality levels. Most managers had limited ranges of responsibility and they needed to identify actions that would produce improvements in those areas, whether or not these actions would affect the dimensions in which quality was most deficient.

Second, people who know they are acting without accurate knowledge expect to make mistakes so they can limit risks and hedge against mistakes. They attend to feedback about the actual results of their actions, and this alertness keeps errors small. They learn from surprises and disconfirmations. Doctors and patients make medical decisions with "informed consent" of the limitations and possibilities of error concerning treatments. Human action occurs with the constant presumption of underlying risk and potential for error.

However, many organizations have difficulty acknowledging and correcting errors. Managers in Executive MBA curricula said they fear the consequences of being wrong. Similarly, when asked to tell about instances in which their analyses corrected faulty policies, the managers of data-warehouse projects said that they were afraid that such stories would rouse the ire of superiors who do not want to admit that policies had been wrong. After studying organizations that had gotten into very serious trouble, Nystrom and Starbuck (1984) urged top managers to devote more attention to reacting promptly to early symptoms of trouble, to avoid superficial cover-ups, and to update and correct their perceptions on a continuous basis.

Third, people seem to exhibit some ability to allocate their knowledge-creation resources judiciously. Porrini (2001) found that high-tech firms are much more likely to form alliances than basic-tech firms. Corporate alliances enable firms to gather up-to-date information informally. This information generally does not rise to the level of knowledge because it is poorly documented and no consensus endorses its correctness. In fact, the very value of the information may arise from the fact that it is not well known and not public, and hence not knowledge. High-tech firms inhabit worlds that are in flux, where technologies and markets change often and rapidly, so high-tech firms dare not rely on knowledge. By contrast, basic-tech firms can rely on knowledge because they use well-known technologies and their markets are rather stable.

Fourth, people adhere to habits and concentrate their innovations on incremental moves, avoiding drastic innovations. Change is easier to accept in small doses. Since most environments remain stable for long periods, habitual behaviors almost always succeed and almost always produce expected outcomes. At the same time, to remain effective amid changing social and economic environments, people and organizations have to venture out of their familiar domains. Smaller innovations entail smaller risks because they place less reliance on current understanding of environments, and the outcomes from smaller innovations are more likely to resemble predicted outcomes (Hedberg et al., 1976; Quinn, 1980).

Fifth, disagreements sometimes help to surface implicit assumptions, debatable beliefs, alternative explanations, and unnoticed errors. The judicial systems of many countries rely on arguments between opponents to explicate key issues. Many widely accepted beliefs became knowledge through legal disputes in which the sides presented evidence in public. Such disagreements have disclosed dangerous products, deceptive business practices, and corruption by executives. Similarly, the governing systems of many countries seek to create moderate levels of disagreement. For example, the US Constitution assumes that the executive, legislative, and judicial branches will not act in complete harmony, but will counterbalance each other through processes involving both consensus and discord. Such counterbalancing has overturned or reinterpreted laws, blocked the enactment of laws, removed presidents or other officials from office, and stimulated new laws to curb litigation abuses.

People should welcome debates between alternative viewpoints because rationality is a limited and defective tool that serves people well only as long as they recognize its limitations and take notice of events that violate its logic (Starbuck, 1988, 1996). Research collaborators who disagree are probably both right; two tenable hypotheses are probably both correct; the converse of every proposition is probably equally valid. For people with imperfect knowledge, dialectical development can help to protect people from the dangers posed by knowledge. When perceptions and ideas are seen as facts and truths, not enough people are skeptical. When there is widespread consensus, not enough people are asking questions. Consensus about truths likely signals too much reliance on rationality, too much consistency among ideas.

However, people often have difficulty treating disagreements as opportunities for discovery. Advocates for a thesis usually find its antithesis implausible, and they usually regard those who espouse the antithesis as irrational opponents. As a result, disagreements tend to polarize and purify competing theses. Not only do the competing theses become more difficult to synthesize, the advocates on both sides grow less willing to appreciate opposing viewpoints. In the US, abortion, gun possession, drug legalization, condom distribution and school prayer have drawn ardent advocates on both sides – in some cases, to the point of violence. Although such highly polarized disagreements rarely lead to better understanding in the short run, they force new generations to reflect on their beliefs and to confront difficult issues. Many disagreements that once roused people to violence – slavery, women's right to vote, legality of alcoholic beverages – do so no longer.

Knowledge and error flow from the same mental sources, only the result distinguishes the two. (Ernst Mach, 1987: 116)

References

Armstrong, J.S. (1985) *Long-Range Forecasting: From Crystal Ball to Computer*, 2nd edn. New York: Wiley-Interscience.

Ashby, R.W. (1961) *Introduction to Cybernetics*. London: Chapman and Hall.

Bazerman, M.H. (1997) *Judgment in Managerial Decision Making*, 2nd edn. New York: Wiley.

Black, H.C. (1990) *Black's Law Dictionary: Definitions of the Terms and Phrases of American and English Jurisprudence, Ancient and Modern*, 6th edn. St. Paul, MN: West Publishing.

Blaug, M. (1980) *The Methodology of Economics: Or How Economists Explain*. Cambridge: Cambridge University Press.

Bonini, C.P. (1963) *Simulation of Information and Decision Systems in the Firm*. Englewood Cliffs, NJ: Prentice-Hall.

Brunsson, N. (1982) The Irrationality of Action and Action Rationality: Decisions, Ideologies, and Organisational Actions. *Journal of Management Studies*, 19: 29–44.

Cappelli, P. and Sherer, P.D. (1991) The Missing Role of Context in OB: The Need for a Meso-level Approach. *Research in Organizational Behavior*, 13: 55–110.

Circuits (2001) Birthing the Internet: Letters from the Delivery Room. *The New York Times*, Section G, November 22: G6.

Claudy, J.G. (1972) A Comparison of Five Variable Weighting Procedures. *Educational and Psychological Measurement*, 32: 311–22.

Cummings, L.L. and Schmidt, S.M. (1972) Managerial Attitudes of Greeks: The Roles of Culture and Industrialization. *Administrative Science Quarterly*, 17: 265–72.

Davis, M.S. (1971) That's Interesting! Towards a Phenomenology of Sociology and a Sociology of Phenomenology. *Philosophy of Social Science*, 1: 309–44.

Dörner, D. (1996) *The Logic of Failure*, translated by Rita and Robert Kimber. Reading, MA: Addison Wesley.

Dreeben, R. (1968) *On What Is Learned in School*. Reading, MA: Addison-Wesley.

Dutton, J.M. and Starbuck, W.H. (1971) *Computer Simulation of Human Behavior*. New York: Wiley.

Eisenhardt, K.M. and Schoonhoven, C.B. (1996) Resource-based View of Strategic Alliance Formation: Strategic and Social Effects in Entrepreneurial Firms. *Organization Science*, 7: 136–50.

Elliott, J.W. (1973) A Direct Comparison of Short-run GNP Forecasting Models. *Journal of Business*, 46: 33–60.

Faust, D. (1984) *The Limits of Scientific Reasoning*. Minneapolis: University of Minnesota Press.

Faust, R.E. (1978) Emerging Challenges for the Research Scientist. *Research Management*, 21 (3): 39–42.

Gaston, J. (1971) Secretiveness and Competition for Priority of Discovery in Physics. *Minerva*, 9 (October): 472–92.

Gilbert, N.G. (1977) Referencing as Persuasion. *Social Studies of Science*, 7 (February): 113–22.

Greenwald, A.G. (1975) Consequences of Prejudice against the Null Hypothesis. *Psychological Bulletin*, 82: 1–20.

Hafner, K. (2001) A Paternity Dispute Divides Net Pioneers. *The New York Times*, Section G, November 8: G1.

Haire, M., Ghiselli, E.E., and Porter, L.W. (1966) *Managerial Thinking*. New York: Wiley.

Hall, S.S. (2001) The Claritin Effect: Prescription for Profit. *The New York Times*, March 11: 40.

Hayek, F.A. von (1975) *The Pretence of Knowledge*. Stockholm: Nobel Foundation.

Hedberg, B.L.T., Nystrom, P.C., and Starbuck, W.H. (1976) Camping on Seesaws: Prescriptions for a Self-designing Organization. *Administrative Science Quarterly*, 21: 41–65.

Huxley, T.H. (1880) The Coming of Age of "The Origin of Species". *Nature*, 22: 1–4.

Jönsson, S.A. and Lundin, R.A. (1977) Myths and Wishful Thinking as Management Tools. In P.C. Nystrom and W.H. Starbuck (eds), *Prescriptive Models of Organizations*. Amsterdam: North-Holland, 157–70.

Kiesler, C.A. (1971) *The Psychology of Commitment*. New York: Academic Press.

Knorr-Cetina, K.D. (1981) *The Manufacture of Knowledge: Toward a Constructivist and Contextual Theory of Science*. Oxford: Pergamon.

Kuhn, T.S. (1970) *The Structure of Scientific Revolutions*, 2nd edn. Chicago: University of Chicago Press.

Kunda, G. (1992) *Engineering Culture: Control and Commitment in a High-Tech Corporation*. Philadelphia: Temple University Press.

Latour B. and Woolgar, S. (1979) *Laboratory Life*. Beverly Hills, CA: Sage.

Loftus, E.F. (1979) The Malleability of Human Memory. *American Scientist*, 67: 312–20.

Mach, E. (1987) *Erkenntnis und Irrtum: skizzen zur psychologie der forschung (Knowledge and Error: Outlines for the Psychology of Research)*. Darmstadt: Wissenschaftliche Buchgesellschaft. Originally published in 1905.

Mahoney, M.J. (1977) Publication Prejudices: An Experimental Study of Confirmatory Bias in the Peer Review System. *Cognitive Therapy and Research*, 1: 161–75.

Makridakis, S., Andersen, A., Carbone, R., Fildes, R., Hibon, M., Lewandowski, R., Newton, J., Parzen, E., and Winkler, R. (1982) *The Forecasting Accuracy of Major Time Series Methods*. Chichester, NY: Wiley.

Meehl, P.E. (1991) *Selected Philosophical and Methodological Papers*. Minneapolis: University of Minnesota Press.

Mezias, J. and Starbuck, W.H. (2003) Studying the Accuracy of Managers' Perceptions: A Research Odyssey. *British Journal of Management*, forthcoming.

Mitroff, I.I. (1974) Norms and Counter-norms in a Select Group of Apollo Moon Scientists: A Case Study of the Ambivalence of Scientists. *American Sociological Review*, 39 (August): 579–95.

Nisbett, R.E. and Wilson, T.D. (1977) Telling More than We Can Know: Verbal Reports on Mental Processes. *Psychological Review*, 84: 231–59.

Normann, R. (1971) Organizational Innovativeness: Product Variation and Reorientation. *Administrative Science Quarterly*, 16: 203–15.

Nystrom, P.C. and Starbuck, W.H. (1984) To Avoid Organizational Crises, Unlearn. *Organizational Dynamics*, 12 (4): 53–65.

Over, R. (1982) Collaborative Research and Publication in Psychology. *American Psychologist*, 37 (September): 996–1001.

Peter, J.P. and Olson, J.C. (1983) Is Science Marketing? *Journal of Marketing*, Fall: 111–25.

Platt, J.R. (1964) Strong Inference. *Science*, 146: 347–53.

Polanyi, M. (1962) *Personal Knowledge*. London: Routledge.

Popper, K.R. (1959) *The Logic of Scientific Discovery*. New York: Basic Books.

Porrini, P. (2001) Post-acquisition Performance: The Effect of Alliance Experience and Acquisition History. Manuscript, New York University.

Quinn, J.B. (1980) *Strategies for Change: Logical Incrementalism*, Homewood, IL: Irwin.Rindova, V. and Starbuck, W.H. (1997) Ancient Chinese Theories of Control. *Journal of Management Inquiry*, 6: 144–59.

Samuelson, F. (1980) J.B. Watson's Little Albert, Cyril Burt's Twins, and the Need for a Critical Science. *American Psychologist*, 35 (6): 19–25.

Schmidt, F.L. (1971) The Relative Efficiency of Regression and Simple Unit Predictor Weights in Applied Differential Psychology. *Educational and Psychological Measurement*, 31: 699–714.

Shaw, G.B. (1993) On Doctors: Preface to "The Doctor's Dilemma". In *Bernard Shaw: The Complete Prefaces, Volume 1: 1889–1913*. London: Allen Lane. Originally published in 1911.

Singer, B. and Benassi, V.A. (1981) Occult Beliefs. *American Scientist*, 69 (1): 49–55.

Solow, R.M. (1957) Technical Change and the Aggregate Production Function. *Review of Economics and Statistics*, 39 (3): 312–20.

Starbuck, W.H. (1976) Organizations and their Environments. In M.D. Dunnette (ed.), *Handbook of Industrial and Organizational Psychology*. Chicago: Rand McNally, 1069–123.

Starbuck, W.H. (1983) Organizations as Action Generators. *American Sociological Review*, 48: 91–102.

Starbuck, W.H. (1988) Surmounting our Human Limitations. In R. Quinn and K. Cameron (eds.), *Paradox and Transformation: Toward a Theory of Change in Organization and Management*. Cambridge, MA: Ballinger, 65–80.

Starbuck, W.H. (1992) Learning by Knowledge-intensive Firms. *Journal of Management Studies*, 29 (6): 713–40.

Starbuck, W.H. (1996) Unlearning Ineffective or Obsolete Technologies. *International Journal of Technology Management*, 11: 725–37.

Starbuck, W.H. and Milliken, F.J. (1988) Challenger: Changing the Odds until Something Breaks. *Journal of Management Studies*, 25: 319–40.

Stuart, E. (1998) Network Positions and Propensities to Cooperate: An Investigation of Strategic Alliance Formation in the Biotechnology Industry. *Administrative Science Quarterly*, 43: 668–98.

Webster, J. and Starbuck, W.H. (1988) Theory Building in Industrial and Organizational Psychology. In C.L. Cooper and I.T. Robertson (eds.), *International Review of Industrial and Organizational Psychology*. Chichester, NY: Wiley, 93–138.

Whitehead, A.N. (1926) *The Concept of Nature*. Cambridge: Cambridge University Press.

Zukav, G. (1979) *The Dancing Wu Li Masters: An Overview of the New Physics*. New York: Bantam.

Part IV

PROBLEMATIZING ORGANIZATIONAL LEARNING AND KNOWLEDGE

25

Discourses of Knowledge Management and the Learning Organization: Their Production and Consumption

Harry Scarbrough and Jacky Swan

Chapter Outline

This chapter seeks to place the discourses of knowledge management (KM) and the learning organization (LO) in the broader context of the institutional and organizational shifts of recent decades. KM and LO are seen as qualitatively different responses to a series of institutional changes confronting managers. These include the challenge to professional groups' control of knowledge resources and the advance of new technologies. Subsequently, it draws on a quantitative review of the management literature to highlight the diffusion of these concepts as management fashions. Evidence on the broad trends of diffusion underlines the role played by "knowledge entrepreneurs" such as management consultants in the spread of these concepts. A more detailed analysis of these trends, however, reveals the continuing role played by professional groups – specifically, information systems (IS) and human resources (HR) professionals – in mediating organizations' assimilation of these new discourses. Competition between the interpretations offered by different professional groups is one of the factors underpinning the spread of ambiguous concepts such as KM and LO. Our account therefore concludes not only that the consumption of management discourse is critical to patterns of assimilation, but that this is a more creative, reflexive, and politicized activity than is acknowledged by much of the existing literature.

Introduction

This chapter seeks to explore the current interest in knowledge and learning in organizations. While much writing in this area treats knowledge and learning as essentially native objects of study, our account of the discourses of knowledge management (KM) and the learning organization (LO) suggests the need to place these disciplines in the context of the interplay of discursive and social practices in society as a whole. More specifically, this chapter seeks to develop a more reflexive approach to the concepts of knowledge and learning by locating them within the new discursive space opened up by institutional and organizational shifts of recent decades. This is a space which has been both created and colonized by the discourses of LO and KM.

In relating KM and LO to these wider institutional and organizational changes, we drew on a quantitative review of the management literature which highlights the diffusion of these concepts. This review highlights two important elements of management discourse which are critical to locating KM and LO against their wider context. The first is the growing role of "knowledge entrepreneurs" in the production of knowledge, and the corresponding importance of fashion in promoting the spread of new discourses. Here our data on the rapid rise and subsequent decline of the KM and LO concepts highlights the bell curve pattern of diffusion which is a distinctive feature of management fashion. The second element, however, has to do with what can be termed the consumption of management discourse. Here we argue that it is important to consider the continuing role played by professional groups in mediating the assimilation of new management discourses. While KM and LO have certainly exploited the discursive space created by the erosion of professional power in organizations – specifically, the growing sense of knowledge as a corporate resource – we observe that the channels for the consumption of management knowledge are still heavily influenced by professional groupings. As our review of the literature underlines, the latter have retained their ability to act as the gatekeepers of new discourses. Thus, a more detailed examination of KM's diffusion in the literature shows the way in which this discourse has been shaped by the competing knowledge claims of different professional groups. In short, by analyzing the broad trends of KM and LO's diffusion in terms of specific professional interests and agendas, our account suggests that the consumption of management discourse is a more creative – indeed, reflexive – activity than is acknowledged by much of the existing literature. This focus on the process of knowledge consumption, and the different professional strategies within that process, represents the distinctive contribution of this chapter.

In developing this account, the chapter is structured as follows. The initial section is concerned with the emergence of KM and LO as management discourses. It seeks to explore the links between such discourses and the receptivity of the wider institutional and organizational context. The following section draws on our quantitative analysis of the literature to identify the major themes and concerns which characterize the KM and LO discourses respectively. This leads onto a discussion of the status of KM and LO as management fashions, and its implications for their adoption by organizations. The following section develops this argument further by relating the diffusion of KM and LO to the interests and activities of, on the one hand, "knowledge entrepreurs" such as consultants, and on the other professional groupings such as information technology (IT) specialists. While the role played by the former group is already well recognized in the literature, we observe that the influence of professional groupings on the consumption of knowledge is often neglected. Through an analysis of the adoption of KM, however, we show how the assimilation of new management discourse is subject to the gatekeeping roles and competing aspirations of different professional groups. This not only leads to some ironic conclusions about the clash between the rhetorics of KM and LO and the mechanics of their adoption, but also exposes the political character of the process through which such discourses become an accepted feature of organizational life.

KM AND LO AS MANAGEMENT DISCOURSES

A full exploration of the multi-faceted nature of discourse is beyond the scope of this chapter. However, we take as our reference point Fairclough's account, which views discourse as "being simultaneously a piece of text, an instance of discursive practice, and an instance of social practice" (1992: 4). Although a discourse cannot be readily summarized in its own terms, from this perspective the broad area of KM can be characterized as a complex of texts and practices concerned with creating, acquiring, capturing, sharing, and using knowledge to enhance performance in organizations. Similarly, the LO discourse can be summarized as texts and practices which seek to enhance an organization's ability to discover what is effective by reframing its own experiences and learning from that process (Pedler et al., 1991).

Although, as we describe later, there are important differences in emphasis and philosophy between KM and LO, in the first instance it is important to recognize the common features they share as management discourses shaped by the same historical and institutional context. Thus, in an historical perspective, the emergence of KM and LO can be readily linked to the acceptance of a world-view or hegemonic ideology which sees knowledge and learning as the defining characteristics of a new epoch. The influence of this world-view is reflected in the spread of a variety treatises dealing with the "Post-Industrial Era," the "Information Age," or the "Knowledge Society" (Stehr, 1994). To cite a recent example, consider the following extract from UK Prime Minister Tony Blair's speech to the Labour Party Conference on 28 September 1999:

> We know what a 21st century nation needs. A knowledge-based economy. A strong civic society. A confident place in the world. Do that and a nation masters the future. Fail and it is the future's victim.

In a speech that mentioned the word "socialism" just once, "knowledge" was mentioned four times. Clearly, as this kind of rhetoric indicates, the discourses of knowledge and learning seem cunningly designed to exploit the received history of our times; the perfect ideology for a post-ideological world.

Another common feature of the discourses of KM and LO is their shared affiliation with management authority and control. Both KM and LO embody the characteristic features of management discourse as identified by Huczynski (1993). That is, an understanding of the world of work as harmonious; an intellectual focus which reaffirms the nature and status of managers; and a concern to deliver useful outcomes for a managerial elite. Indeed, it is this intertwining of the texts of KM and LO with managerial practices and concerns, which helps to explain some of the substantive features in the way these discourses have evolved. For, within the broader historical and ideological trends of recent decades, managers of organizations remain the instruments of the owners and controllers of institutions (Thompson and McHugh, 1990). In that context, the managerial engagement with knowledge and learning has been subject to some specific institutional changes that have stimulated the kind of discursive innovations examined here. This is not to suggest a direct material relationship between institutional conditions and discursive practices. Rather, in the recent period we can identify patterns of institutional change which have helped to make managers a more receptive audience for discourses around knowledge and learning. The key elements of such change can be broadly defined as the challenge to the professional model within business firms, and the spread of network forms of organization.

On the first point, the challenge to the professional model as a template for managing knowledge was an important feature of the 1980s and 1990s business environment, particularly in the UK and USA. The professional model originally emerged out of scientific management primarily as a means of economizing on the deployment of knowledge through specialization (Grant, 1996). This involved concentrating expertise within the narrow silos of functional and disciplinary specializations. The professional bureaucracy represented a historic compromise between the demands of disciplinary knowledge and the commercial pressures of the business environment (Mintzberg, 1983). Over the last twenty years, however, this model has come under increasing attack from a variety of organizational and technological changes (Ackroyd and Lawrenson, 1996). The latter include, inter alia, the redesign of work flows into process-based and market-facing forms through a variety of three letter acronym-based initiatives including business process re-engineering (BPR), total quality management (TQM), and just-in-time (JIT); the rise of interdisciplinary project-based teamworking; and, more generally, the outsourcing of professional work in areas such as R&D and IT (Willcocks and Lacity, 1998). These developments have emphasized the assimilation of specialized knowledge within the business process through the codification of knowledge in IT systems (BPR), incorporation of specialist functions within mainstream tasks (TQM) and a move from hierarchical to horizontal systems of control (JIT, lean production). Knowledge which could not be metabolized within the business process was to be externalized through market-based outsourcing arrangements (Whittington, 1991).

These developments within organizations have also contributed to a wider restructuring of relationships between organizations (Lash and Urry, 1987). Thus, the recent period has seen the advance of the "network logic" (Castells, 1996) and the proliferation of network technologies and forms of organizing. Supply chain relationships, for example, have been aggressively integrated by large producer firms exploiting the control potential of EDI (Electronic Data Interchange) and the Internet (Harland, 1996). The cumulative effect of these developments represents an important change in the institutional context for management (Scarbrough, 2000).

These institutional changes have arguably served to make management's encounters with knowledge and learning problematic. First, new discourses such as BPR and TQM have sought to diffuse certain aspects of the management function to a widening circle of employee groups. Thus Sewell and Wilkinson (1992: 284) observe that:

> Although the flatter hierarchy of JIT/TQC suggests that the controlling function of middle management has completely disappeared, we would argue that, rather than being dispensed with, it has simply been incorporated into the consciousness of the members themselves.

In this context, the bases of management legitimacy seem to have shifted away from hierarchical control towards the dynamic and performance-based redesign of the operational environment. At the same time as managers were seeking to reconstruct the legitimacy of their roles, knowledge and learning were being progressively disembedded from existing local and professional settings. Knowledge was seen as leaking out through the loss of specialist expertise attendant on industrial restructuring and the impact of BPR. But, it was also being liberated from specific locales through changes in inter-organizational relationships and advances in IT networks outlined above. The growth of so-called knowledge–worker occupations (Drucker, 1993) and technological advances created by the convergence of computing and communications technology (Easterby-Smith et al., 1998) helped to create flatter structures, debureaucratization, and "virtual" or networked forms of organization. As businesses were increasingly stretched across time and space and restructured around virtual teams and networks, they endangered the kind of local work environments which were so conducive to the casual sharing of knowledge and learning. As Prusak (1997: xiii) puts it: "If the water cooler was a font of useful knowledge in the traditional firm, what constitutes a virtual one?"

In sum, the institutional and organizational shifts of recent decades have created a new discursive space for management, one which encompasses an admixture of different elements, including issues of managerial legitimacy, problems of loss of expertise and opportunities for the intensification of knowledge created by new technological and organizational forms. The discourses of LO and KM were important creators and colonizers of this new discursive space, and this is reflected in the common features described earlier. Having outlined these shared features, we now turn to the different positions which KM and LO have come to occupy within this new discursive space. In the following sections we draw on a review of the literatures on KM and LO (Scarbrough et al., 1999) which helps to illuminate the unfolding of these different positions.

A Review of KM and LO in the Management Literature

Three linked approaches were adopted for the literature review. Initially a quantitative analysis of search terms was carried out over the period 1990–2000, utilizing the search technology now available to users of comprehensive online journal databases such as ProQuest Direct (PQD) and BIDS. The timeframe for data analysis was designed to capture the major shifts in the relative popularity of KM and LO (Senge's seminal text on LO did not appear until 1990 and KM was relatively unheard of at that date). This analysis was then developed by categorization of those themes, topics, sectors, and approaches that emerged during such searches. In tandem with these approaches the review also followed a more traditional route, selecting from a highly variable literature the more influential work (based on frequency of citations) relevant to researchers in this area.

Discourse of KM

The quantitative analysis of the literature, outlined in figure 25.1, shows how interest in KM has soared since 1990, with the greatest number of articles appearing in 1998. By far

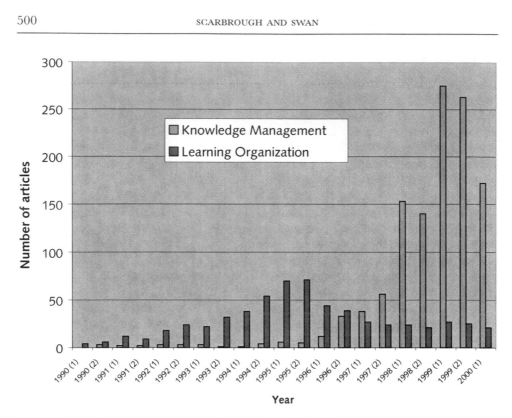

FIGURE 25.1   ProQuest references to KM and LO, 1990–2000

the majority of articles have appeared in the IS/IT literatures with, for example, nearly 70 percent of articles in 1998 appearing in these literatures. Much of the literature is practice, rather than theory driven, with many articles appearing in practitioner-oriented journals.

Interestingly, a number of these characteristics, including the explosive increase in interest, echo earlier experience with BPR (Tinaikar et al., 1995). Moreover, there are some substantive links between these discourses. Thus, there is evidence that KM has been adopted by some organizations as a response to the dissolution of traditional functional boundaries and loss of middle management expertise resulting from BPR programs (Coombs and Hull, 1996; Scarbrough, 1998). And, ironically in the light of this experience, it is also clear that many of the protagonists of BPR are involved with KM as well. These include the IT specialists, the consultancy firms and the management gurus such as Thomas Davenport (cf. Davenport and Prusak, 1997) who have driven many of the debates around KM. Indeed, KM is now a core component of the services provision and internal organization of major consultancies (for example, KPMG, CSC Consulting Group, IBM, Ernst and Young, McKinsey) and consultancies feature frequently as case examples in the literature (e.g., Hildebrand, 1994). In many of these consultancy firms, KM has been used as a means of repackaging IT products under a new label. This discursive affiliation between KM and IS is underlined when we review the range of journals in which KM articles appeared over the 1993 to 1999 period (that is, the period of its rise to popularity). Here we discover almost 50 percent of articles appearing in IS journals.

In terms of the inductive analysis of themes within the KM literature, it is possible to identify three themes which recur in a large number of the articles reviewed. The first and probably most pervasive theme is the almost universal concern in these articles with KM's critical role in business performance. The central assumption here is that firms are under growing pressures of complexity and globalization. In this context, it is argued, those firms that are effective at developing their KM capabilities will also develop a clear cost and performance advantage over their competitors (McKern, 1996). Thus, "KM is becoming a core competence that companies must develop to success in tomorrow's dynamic global economy" (Skyrme and Amidon, 1998). Many definitions of KM focus on this link with performance improvement: "KM is the process of creating, capturing, and using knowledge to enhance organizational performance" (Bassi, 1997). And in keeping with this emphasis on performance, core KM activities are said to include benchmarking and monitoring knowledge "assets" as well as processes for knowledge capture, creation and distribution (Drew, 1996).

The second recurring theme is to do with managing knowledge as a strategic resource. While the LO literature explores ways in which knowledge is acquired through developing a learning culture and self-motivated individuals, the KM literature focuses on how knowledge can be captured as a resource for the pursuit of competitive advantage. Roos and von Krogh (1996: 333) develop this argument as follows:

> Gone are the days when companies were seen only as physical entities that converted raw materials into tangible products. Today, physical capital is of less relative importance for creating and sustaining competitive advantage than intellectual capital.

Clearly, behind much of this thinking on KM lies a resource-based view of the firm which highlights the value of intellectual capital: "intellectual capital is accumulated knowledge which is useful to the firm in conducting its business, now or in the future' (Drew, 1996).

The third theme highlights the processing and storage of knowledge. Many of the articles focus on means of codifying knowledge through IT tools, including KM databases, decision support tools and Intranets. Computer networking technologies are seen as providing the tools for the creation of "knowledge bases," "knowledge webs," and "knowledge exchanges" (Bank, 1996). Indeed the practice of KM is frequently reduced to the implementation of new IT systems for knowledge sharing: "the idea behind KM is to stockpile workers' knowledge and make it accessible to others via a searchable application" (Cole-Gomolski, 1997). KM is equated to mining for data. Mining, digging, and drilling metaphors are frequently used (e.g., Finerty, 1997; Leonard-Barton, 1998).

To summarize, our analysis of the KM discourse highlights its development as a response both to the ideological ascendancy of knowledge and learning as well as to the shifting economic pressures and institutional contexts confronting managers. Thus the discourse of KM is polymorphous. The use of IT to "capture" knowledge is an important ingredient, but other elements such as the "intellectual capital" concept reflect the increasing need to organize, quantify and valorize knowledge to address problems of business restructuring and competitiveness.

Discourse of LO

The review of literature on the LO shows that general and strategic management theorists, organization theorists, PM and training specialists have led the debate and discourse of the LO. As the analysis of journal coverage outlined in table 25.1 indicates, a broad range of journals carry articles on the LO and these span a range of themes and disciplines. However, the dominant perspective is that of organization systems and design. This reflects the importance of one figure – Peter Senge – whose pre-eminence as a management guru is reflected in his continued presence (ranked number 11) in the *Financial Times* list of the top 50 gurus (*Financial Times*, 2001). Senge's book, *The Fifth Discipline: The Art and Practice of the Learning Organization*, defines the LO as an organization:

> where people continually expand their capacity to create the results they truly desire, where new and expansive patterns of thinking are nurtured, where collective aspiration is set free, and where people are continually learning how to learn together (Senge, 1990: 4).

As this definition suggests, a key theme of the LO literature is on creating the conditions in which individual and collective creativity may flourish, with the management of people – that is, their values, attitudes, collective beliefs, languages and discourses, being at the core of any LO initiative: "building LOs requires basic shifts in how people think and act" (Kofman and Senge, 1993). Indeed architecture and "building" (i.e. of people and organizations) are dominant metaphors in the LO. The emphasis is on organizations that are reflexive, not just responsive:

> Learning Organizations discover what is effective by reframing their own experiences and learning from that process. They are self aware, introspective organizations that constantly scan their environments. By contrast, other organizations merely adapt (McGill and Slocum, 1993).

A corollary theme to this is an emphasis on organization design to encourage flexibility in human resources (e.g., Hall and Parker, 1993). Attempts to become a LO are seen to involve some cultural change at the level of the organization, supported by top management and generating empowerment among employees. Thus leadership, visioning and the management of symbolic resources also feature as core elements in creating the LO. The LO is also depicted as a teaching organization where leaders play a key role in passing their expertise and knowledge on to others (Tichy and Cohen, 1998).

Third, where KM highlights knowledge processing, the LO focuses on what might be termed "people processing." Thus, training and development and human resource practices are central since a LO continuously transforms itself by developing the skills of all its people (Pedler et al., 1991).

A fourth theme in the LO is the importance of leadership in creating the right organizational environment. Strategic managers in general, and human resources managers in

TABLE 25.1 Source of publications of KM and LO articles for 1993 to December 1999

Type of publication	KM articles Count (%)	LO articles Count (%)
Computer/IT journals and magazines (e.g. *Computerworld*)	193 (47.7)	17 (5.0)
Personnel and human resource management journals and magazines (e.g. *People Management*)	28 (6.9)	128 (33.4)
Academic organization theory journals (e.g. *Organizational Dynamics*)	1 (0)	24 (6.3)
Academic general management journals (e.g. *British Journal of Management*)	15 (3.7)	43 (11.2)
Academic strategic management and technology strategy journals (e.g. *Strategic Management Journal*)	24 (5.9)	5 (1.3)
Miscellaneous academic journals (e.g. *Journal of Production and Operations Management*)	91 (22.5)	102 (26.7)
Miscellaneous popular magazines, trade magazines, newspapers (e.g. *CIO, Wall Street Journal*)	53 (13.1)	64 (16.7)

particular, therefore play a central role as leaders who facilitate the development of the LO through processes of strategic cultural change and empowerment. Thus the first phase in becoming a LO "should be oriented towards the attainment of an organizational culture which structurally endorses the vision of leadership and encourages collaborative learning and greater power sharing" (Dovey, 1997). A common theme captured in the literature is that the LO must be driven from the top.

In terms of its intellectual underpinnings, where the more eclectic literature of KM draws on a variety of concepts and perspectives, the LO discourse is more narrowly based on Senge's work. The latter identifies five disciplines which are seen as being necessary for becoming a LO. These are: personal mastery, mental models, shared vision, team learning, and systems thinking. The literature on the LO stems largely from organic systems approaches to the management of change. Although many authors argue that it is individuals and not organizations that learn, the main unit of analysis is the organization.

The dominance of Senge's work helps to sharpen intellectual divisions within the LO literature and with other literatures. Thus one major distinction within the LO literature is between descriptive and prescriptive approaches (Tsang, 1997). Prescriptive approaches (around half the articles) focus on the question of "how should an organization learn?" These approaches tend to offer unified universally applicable models or "best practice" guidelines to becoming the LO. Many of these are practice-driven, i.e.: "Targeting practitioners, these studies are usually based on the authors' consulting experience and seldom follow rigorous research methodologies" (Tsang, 1997). In contrast, the more descriptive approaches in the LO literature tackle the question of "how does an organization learn?" These approaches adopt a more critical academic stance (e.g., Starkey, 1998) recognizing

TABLE 25.2   Main foci of the literatures on the LO and KM

Learning organization	Knowledge management
Theory-driven	Practice-driven
Organization unit of analysis (and individual-organization interaction)	Specific project unit of analysis (and individual-project interaction)
"Building" metaphor	"Mining" metaphor
Emphasis on culture management and organization design	Emphasis on information systems management and systems design
Strategic/HR managers responsible for change	IS/IT managers and chief knowledge officers responsible for change
Sensitive to context (multiple practice techniques)	Independent of context ("best" practice techniques)
Major investment in people and management development	Major investment in systems and user training
Intangible gains	Tangible performance improvements
Emphasis on "internalization" and "socialization"	Emphasis on "externalization" and "combination"

organizational diversity and the social embeddedness of learning processes. Learning is seen as embedded in, and shaped by, the social context in which it occurs.

Moving beyond the more critical accounts within the LO literature takes us on to a wider division between the literature on LO and the literature on organizational learning (Easterby-Smith et al., 1998). In contrast to the LO, this literature sees learning as embedded in a wider institutional context of inter-organizational relationships:

> processes of organizational learning, both simple and complex, are tied to specifically institutional conditions. The conventional debate about organizational or managerial learning seems to explain only a specific part of these learning processes. In the managerial literature the often used metaphor of "the LO" describes learning as a self-centred process, in which the organization and its actors are separated from their institutional context and social embeddedness . . . it is also necessary to take into consideration the learning landscape of an organization. (Geppert, 1996)

While recognizing these divisions in the literature, it remains true that, in comparison with KM, the literature on the LO is more academically oriented in terms of coverage, with academic journals such as *Organizational Dynamics*, *Organization Studies*, and *Human Relations* featuring more strongly than practitioner-oriented journals. Although action research did feature as a core methodology in many articles, this was also driven by an interest in understanding "theories-in-use" which guide interpersonal behavior in organizations (Argyris and Schön, 1978).

Abstract thinking and research drives much of this literature and, as such, the implications for management practice in general are sometimes unclear. Articles that discuss the links between the broad themes identified in the LO literature and implications for management practice are rare. The relationship between the LO and the IT infrastructure of the organization is also rarely discussed, except in general terms reminiscent of a socio-technical systems approach. It is possible that the dwindling of interest in the LO since 1995 (in contrast with the surge of interest in KM) is in part a reflection of this lack of focus on practice and an apparent disregard of advances in IT systems which are reflected in KM.

Comparison of KM and LO discourses

In qualitative terms – see table 25.2 – it seems that the discourses of KM and LO have somewhat different foci. LO is more broadly based, being primarily concerned with the ways in which organizations design themselves to value, manage, and enhance the skills and career development of their people in order to ensure continuous organizational transformation. KM, on the other hand, is more narrowly focused on the ways in which firms facing highly turbulent environments can mobilize their knowledge base in order to ensure continuous innovation in projects.

The dominant discourse of KM (i.e., to capture, codify, use, and exploit the knowledge and experience of employees by developing better tools and methods) is fundamentally different to that of the LO (i.e. to harness the learning capability of the firm and individuals within it through people development, empowerment, leadership, and culture change). Also, the KM literature focuses mostly at the level of specific KM projects rather than at the level of broader change initiatives as considered by the LO. The emphasis on specific projects has advantages because it has meant that the practical implications and outcomes of KM projects have been easier to see (at least in terms of systems development) as compared to the more nebulous LO initiatives. For example ICL's use of an intranet to develop a cafe-style information sharing service (Lank, 1998) is cited as a successful KM project. However, while implications for IS development have received detailed attention in KM, implications for HRM practice have not.

The last two points in this comparison need further explanation. The penultimate point in table 25.2 refers to Nonaka and Takeuchi's (1995) theory of the knowledge creating company. Core to knowledge creation is the blending of tacit and explicit knowledge via processes of: socialization (tacit to tacit); externalization (tacit to explicit), internalization (explicit to tacit) and combination (explicit to explicit). The review here suggests that the LO and KM literatures have emphasized different aspects of the knowledge creation process (and correspondingly have de-emphasized others). Broadly, LO emphasizes culture management and leadership as means of encouraging socialization and the internalization of explicit knowledge into the values and tacit understandings of employees. In contrast KM emphasizes information systems as a means for the externalization of knowledge and the combination of different kinds of explicit knowledge.

The last point in table 25.1 refers to the ways in which knowledge is depicted in these literatures. Knowledge as cognition is a summary description of classical view of knowledge. It defines knowledge as a cognitive, analytical entity (i.e. know-what) which is possessed by individuals and which can be elicited and codified. This view of knowledge is strong in both KM and LO literatures. However, LO also stresses the links between cognition and action, seeing knowledge as something that is tacit and embedded in organizational routines, cultures, and languages. This literature recognizes the recursiveness in learning between acting and thinking. In contrast, the KM literature tends to see knowledge as a resource; a raw material to be leveraged, processed and utilized for the benefit of the organization. This transformation is achieved through the codification of tacit knowledge into explicit rules and procedures and its combination via the use of tools and technologies.

In sum then, what can be seen from this comparison is that within the discursive space around knowledge and learning, the KM and LO discourses embody qualitatively different responses to the institutional shifts confronting management. The discourse of KM presents such shifts in terms of the discovery of knowledge as an organizational resource. For the first time, it claims, knowledge has to be managed as a thing in itself. This reflects the way in which challenges to professionalism, coupled with organizational and technological innovations, have combined to reconstitute knowledge as a quasi-autonomous resource of the organization, divorced from particular groups or settings. In contrast, the LO interprets the critical challenge to management in terms not of resources but of actions – specifically, the increasingly dynamic and uncertain nature of the organization's interactions with its environment. We also conjecture that these different discursive positions give us an insight into the perceived failings of LO and KM: the first empowers action that is unrelated to the organization's cognitive resources (Tsang, 1997), and the second leads to the accumulation of knowledge that is unrelated to action (Pfeffer and Sutton, 1999). Significantly, some aspects of knowledge – particularly its socially constructed aspects and its political dimensions – are in the background in both literatures.

KM AND LO AS MANAGEMENT FASHION

Our analysis of the emergence of the KM and LO discourses highlights many characteristics that correspond to the model of management fashion.

This has been defined as "a relatively transitory collective belief, disseminated by management fashion setters, that a management technique leads to rational management progress" (Abrahamson, 1996: 257). As figure 25.1 indicates, the growth of interest in KM and LO seems to conform to the bell-shaped curve which has been found with earlier management fashions such as Quality Circles (Castorina and Wood, 1988). Figure 25.1 graphically illustrates the way in which the notion of the LO achieved most prominence earlier in the decade, rising to a peak in 1995. Since then there has been a clear decline in references to the LO; a decline mirrored in the sharp increase in references to KM. Indeed there were more references to the latter term in the first six months of 1998 than there were cumulatively in the previous five years. This is a classic example of the "bandwagon effect" noted of management fashions (Abrahamson, 1996).

A second characteristic feature of such fashions is the way in which each fashionable discourse will seek to distance itself from previous discourses. This raises the question of the discursive foci of KM and LO and the relationship or lack of it between each. In this context, the data in figure 25.1 on relative decline of LO and the rise of KM are intriguing. One possible interpretation is that KM is basically a relabelling of LO rather than a distinctive discourse needing its own explanation. However, as our earlier comparison indicated, there are important differences in focus between these discourses. This is reinforced by our analysis of the issues covered in KM and LO articles over the critical 1993–98 period when ascendancy shifted from one to the other. Here we find that the terms most frequently associated with KM were "information technology," "intellectual capital" and "information systems," whereas LO was frequently linked to "training," "organizational development," and "human resources." The conclusion seems inescapable: KM is not a development from the literature on the LO, but is explicitly differentiated as a discourse with a distinctive focus on tools and systems rather than on people and processes.

A final correspondence between the discourses of KM and LO and the management fashion model derives from the content of the discourse itself. A number of studies of management fashion suggest that successful discourses combine ambiguity with simplicity (Clark and Salaman, 1996). Thus, ambiguity is important because the idea can be interpreted and implemented in ways that are appropriate to the context of the potential adopter. Ambiguity thus increases the scope for an idea's diffusion. Cole notes of the TQM concept, for instance: "Because of the vagueness of the concept (TQM) . . . firms and industries were free within a certain range to interpret it, position it and adopt those practices that fit particular corporate traditions and industry imperatives" (Cole, 1999: 11). The corresponding vagueness in the KM and LO discourses is not difficult to identify – knowledge and learning being long on motherhood qualities but short on specifics.

In the same way, simplicity has long been recognized as a facilitator of diffusion (Rogers, 1983). In the case of KM, for example, simplicity is communicated by best practice case examples (these are numerous in KM). These provide "simple metaphors" of a generic kind of practice which can be creatively re-interpreted for almost any context. This kind of simplicity is also a point of differentiation between KM and LO. Thus, one of the above-noted features of the LO discourse is its more academic orientation and its holistic, organization-wide focus. This is seen to translate badly to the level of managerial action. According to Tsang (1997): "These are academic studies striving for scientific rigour. Nevertheless they often fail to generate useful implications for practitioners." In contrast, while KM is just as ambiguous about cause and effect relations as LO, it garners greater simplicity in application by appealing to technology as the enabler.

COMMODIFICATION AND COLONIZATION OF MANAGEMENT DISCOURSE

The fashion characteristics of KM and LO highlight the way in which these discourses are developed and diffused within a particular system of knowledge production. Abrahamson (1991; 1996) describes a management fashion setting process in which different management fashion setters – gurus, mass media, consulting firms, and business schools among others – create, process, and disseminate fashion propositions. KM and LO can clearly be seen as in part the products of this fashion-setting process, with the evident importance of consultants, academics, and gurus in developing and disseminating these discourses. At the same time, however, too much emphasis on the role of these "knowledge entrepreneurs" (Abrahamson and Fairchild, 1999) also risks overstating the importance of supply over demand, and of presenting fashions as being more homogeneous movements than they actually are. When we turn to the question of the consumption rather than the production of management fashions, we often encounter a much more fragmented and contradictory picture.

In the case of KM and LO, specifically, the fragmentation and contradiction arises from the continued importance of professional groups in the spread of management discourse. While the institutional changes of the 1980s and 1990s certainly challenged the political pretensions of these groups within organizations – imposing a much more unitary regimen of business strategy – they have continued to retain a critical role in the sensemaking activities of organizations (Barley, 1996). Thus, a number of studies have shown the continuing importance of professional groups in both disseminating and shaping the spread of new technologies and ideas (e.g. Swan and Newell, 1995). The early proponents of quality circles, for example, established a professional association – the International Association of Quality Circles – which took a leading role in disseminating quality circle discourse across the USA (Castorina and Wood, 1988). This evidence leads us to conjecture that the spread of new management discourses may be significantly influenced by the responses of a range of "speech communities" (Barley et al., 1988), in particular, the established professional groups such as accounting, information systems, and personnel/HRM specialists, who occupy strategic positions in the circuit of managerial knowledge production. While such groups are not motivated by the self-interest of knowledge entrepreneurs, they are able to act as "gatekeepers" of new discourses for many of their members, exerting a significant influence on the latter's spread and institutionalization.

This gatekeeping role for discourse can be related to the professional group's interest in assimilating emergent problems within their existing knowledge-base. Classification and abstraction are a crucial feature of a profession's ability to capture new problem fields. According to Abbott (1988: 9): "only a knowledge system governed by abstractions can redefine its problems and tasks, defend them from interlopers and seize new problems."

The role of professional groups in colonizing discourse is especially evident with KM which has been enthusiastically embraced by linked communities of IS consultants, vendors and practitioners. Although these communities are only weakly professionalized compared to the liberal professions of the law and medicine, this may actually confer advantages in terms of their ability to appropriate new management discourses. As Abbott (1988: 82–3) explains:

> In a peculiar way, relatively less organized professions have certain distinct advantages in workplace competition. Because they lack a clear focus and perhaps a clearly established cognitive structure, they are free to move to available tasks . . .

This opportunistic pattern of colonization by IS groups helps to explain a number of features of KM's development and diffusion. Thus, as table 25.2 indicates, there has been extensive coverage of KM in IS journals. Also, the greater spread of KM compared to the LO seems to be associated with the greater opportunities for commodification of the discourse in the form of consultancy projects and IT systems. Finally, and relatedly, the discourse of KM has helped IS specialists to legitimate and mobilize management support for organizational change programs aimed at using IT to capture and codify knowledge. The "softer" side of KM – that which focuses on the accumulation of intellectual capital through the development of skills and competencies – has often been lost in these initiatives. The KM banner has been assimilated within the IS community as an agenda for investment in new IT tools, and responsibility for KM has often fallen to those IS/IT experts who are equipped to develop IT strategy and to offer education and training in the application of the tools. The chief knowledge officer (CKO) role is often filled by a person (or group) with an IT background. Maglitta (1995) cites examples of KM projects in General Motors, Fidelity Inc., Hewlett Packard Co., and a number of other leading firms. In each case:

IS plays a key leadership or support role. IS's systemic thinking, technology know-how, and experience of working with many departments can be the perfect background for KM. Visions vary but duties include: mapping knowledge and information resources both on-line and off-line; training, guiding and equipping users with knowledge access tools; and monitoring outside news and information. (Maglitta, 1995)

The enthusiastic championing of KM by the IS community can be contrasted with the somewhat belated reaction of personnel or human resources specialists – with only a small percentage of KM articles appearing in HRM or Personnel journals compared to the coverage of LO (see table 25.1). The initially slow reaction of the HR community has been corrected latterly by greater attention to this topic – for example, since 1999 a number of articles on KM have appeared in *People Management* which is the magazine of the Chartered Institute of Personnel and Development. A provisional qualitative analysis of these articles suggests that KM is being reconstructed by the HR community as the creation of intellectual capital through the development of employees and the management of organizational culture (Scarbrough et al., 2000). The fact that KM is a popular term provides a convenient trigger with which to resurface and revitalize change processes associated with earlier LO initiatives.

Evidence from the IT and HR communities shows how the management discourses of KM and LO are appropriated in different ways according to the particular interests and professional agendas of different communities (Valentine and Knights, 1998). Moreover, it is highly ironic, given the rhetoric of both KM and LO discourses, that professional groups continue to play an important role in shaping this interplay between text and practices. It is ironic because the discursive space for KM and LO was created in part through the de-professionalizing tendencies of the 1980s and 1990s. LO, for instance, assumes a unified and reflexive response to the environment – not one mediated by the interests and perspectives of different functional groups. Likewise, the KM thesis that knowledge can become a collective resource for the organization is subtly contradicted by the technology-driven character of initiatives emanating from IS functions.

CONCLUSIONS

The discourses of KM and LO have much to tell us about the production of management knowledge. In particular, they highlight the complex interaction between changing contexts, texts and practices. The rise of KM and LO has been discussed in terms of changes in the societal and institutional context and the way that knowledge and learning have been disembedded and problematized. By mediating managerial responses to knowledge and learning, texts and talk about KM and LO have exerted a significant influence on practices. These discourses have been developed, however, not so much through the experience of managers themselves as through a fashion-setting complex – encompassing consultants, leading firms and academics – which provides organizations with a suitably simple yet ambiguous package of concepts and tools.

The imprint of the fashion-setting complex can be observed in the discourses of both KM and LO inasmuch as they have been developed and diffused by "knowledge entrepreneurs" whose marketing efforts involve carefully differentiating one discourse from another. The rise and fall of such discourses are therefore predictable, and indeed desirable, from the standpoint of the fashion-setting complex. At the same time, however, the pressures towards the commodification of management discourse are countered by the continuing role of professional groups such as IT and HRM specialists. Here – in contravention of the spirit of both KM and LO – we have found that professional groups such as IT experts exploit the ambiguity of management discourse to pursue their own professional agendas. Such groups thus help to extend the shelf-life of management discourses by importing them into the enduringly contested terrain of inter-professional competition (Abbott, 1988). One possible interpretation of this analysis is that the big new ideas in management are ultimately institutionalized less through formal initiatives than through their incorporation into the political life of the organization, and specifically through the advancing knowledge-claims of particular professional and managerial groupings.

REFERENCES

Abbott, A. (1988) *The System of the Professions*. London: University of Chicago Press.
Abrahamson, E. (1991) Managerial Fads and Fashions: The Diffusion and Rejection of Innovations. *Academy of Management Review*, 16: 586–612.
Abrahamson, E. (1996) Management Fashion. *Academy of Management Review*, 21 (1): 254–85.
Abrahamson, E. and Fairchild, G. (1999) Management Fashion: Lifecycles, Triggers, and Collective Learning Processes. *Administrative Science Quarterly*, 44 (4): 708–40.
Ackroyd, S. and Lawrenson, D. (1996) Knowledge Work and Organisational Transformation: Analysing Contemporary Change in the Social Use of Expertise. In R. Fincham (ed.), *New Relationships in the Organised Professions*. Aldershot: Avebury Press, 149–70.
Argyris, C. and Schön, D. (1978) *Organizational Learning: A Theory of Action Perspective*. Reading, MA: Addison Wesley.
Bank, D. (1996) Technology (a special report): The New Worker – Know-it-alls – Chief Knowledge Officers Have a Crucial Job: Putting the Collective Knowledge of a Company at Every Worker's Fingertips. *Wall Street Journal* Eastern Edition, November 18: R28.

Barley, S.R. (1996) *The New World of Work*. London: British-North American Committee.

Barley, S.R., Meyer, G.W., and Gash, D.C. (1988) Cultures of Culture: Academics, Practitioners and the Pragmatics of Normative Control. *Administrative Science Quarterly*, 33: 24–60.

Bassi, L.J. (1997) Harnessing the Power of Intellectual Capital. *Training and Development*, 51 (12): 25–30.

Castells, M. (1996) *The Rise of the Network Society*. Oxford: Blackwell.

Castorina, P. and Wood, B. (1988) Circles in the Fortune 500: Why Circles Fail. *Journal for Quality and Participation*, 11: 40–1.

Clark, T. and Salaman, G. (1996) The Management Guru as Organizational Witch Doctor. *Organization*, 3: 85–108.

Cole, R.E. (1999) *Managing Quality Fads*. Oxford: Oxford University Press.

Cole-Gomolski, B. (1997) Users Loathe to Share their Know-how. *Computerworld*, 31 (46): 6–15.

Coombs, R. and Hull, R. (1996) The Wider Research Context of Business Process Analysis. ESRC Business Process Resource Centre, Working Paper.

Davenport, T.H. and Prusak, L. (1997) *Information Ecology: Mastering the Information Knowledge Environment*. New York: Open University Press.

Dovey, K. (1997) The Learning Organization and the Organization of Learning – Power, Transformation and the Search for Form in Learning Organization. *Management Learning*, 28 (3): 331–49.

Drew, S. (1996) Strategy and Intellectual Capital. *Manager Update*, 7 (4): 1–11.

Drucker, P. (1993) *Post-Capitalist Society*. Oxford: Butterworth-Heinemann.

Easterby-Smith, M., Snell, R., and Gherardi, S. (1998) Organizational Learning: Diverging Communities of Practice. *Management Learning*, 29 (3): 259–72.

Fairclough, N. (1992) *Discourses and Social Change*. Cambridge: Polity Press.

Financial Times (2001) Financial Times website: www.ft.com

Finerty, L. (1997) Information Retrieval for Intranets: The Case for Knowledge Management. *Document World*, 2 (5): 32–4.

Geppert, M. (1996) Paths of Managerial Learning in the East German Context. *Organization Studies*, 17 (2): 249–68.

Grant, R. (1996) Prospering in Dynamically Competitive Environments: Organizational Capability as Knowledge Integration. *Organization Science*, 7 (4): 375–87.

Hall, D.T. and Parker, V.A. (1993) The Role of Workplace Flexibility in Managing Diversity. *Organizational Dynamics*, 22 (1): 5–18.

Harland, C.M. (1996) Supply Chain Management: Relationships, Chains and Networks. *British Journal of Management*, 7 (Special Issue): S63–S80.

Hildebrand, C. (1994) The Greater Good. *CIO*, 8 (4): 32–9.

Huczynski, A. (1993) *Management Gurus: What Makes Them and How to Become One*. London: Routledge.

Kofman, F. and Senge, P. (1993) Communities of Commitment: The Heart of Learning Organizations. *Organizational Dynamics*, 22 (2): 5.

Lank, E. (1998) Cafe Society. *People Management*, 4 (4): 40–3.

Lash, S. and Urry, J. (1987) *The End of Organised Capitalism*. Cambridge: Polity Press.

Leonard-Barton, D. (1998) *Wellsprings of Knowledge: Building and Sustaining the Sources of Innovation*. Cambridge, MA: Harvard Business School Press.

Maglitta, J. (1995) Smarten Up! *Computerworld*, 29 (23): 84–90.

McGill, M.E. and Slocum, J.W. Jr. (1993) Unlearning the Organization. *Organizational Dynamics*, 22 (2): 67–80.

McKern, B. (1996) Building Management Performance for the 21st Century. *The Practising Manager*, 17 (1): 13–19.

Mintzberg, H. (1983) *Structures in Fives: Designing Effective Organizations.* Englewood Cliffs: Prentice-Hall.

Nonaka, I. and Takeuchi, H. (1995) *The Knowledge Creating Company.* New York: Oxford University Press.

Pedler, M., Burgoyne, J., and Boydell, T. (1991) *The Learning Company: A Strategy for Sustainable Development.* London: McGraw-Hill.

Pffefer, J. and Sutton, R.I. (1999) *The Knowing-Doing Gap: How Smart Companies Turn Knowledge into Action.* Cambridge, MA: Harvard Business School Press.

Prusak, L. (1997) *Knowledge in Organizations.* Oxford: Butterworth-Heinemann.

Rogers, E. (1983) *Diffusion of Innovations*, 2nd edn. New York: Free Press.

Roos, J. and von Krogh, G. (1996) The Epistemological Challenge: Managing Knowledge and Intellectual Capital. *European Management Journal*, 14 (4): 333–8.

Scarbrough, H. (1998) BPR and the Knowledge-based View of the Firm. *Knowledge and Process Management: The Journal of Corporate Transformation*, 5 (3): 1–9.

Scarbrough, H. (2000) The HR Implications of Supply Chain Relationships. *Human Resource Management Journal*, 10 (1): 5–17.

Scarbrough, H., Swan, J., Mueller, F., and Carter, C. (2000) Professional Media and Management Fashion: The Case of Knowledge Management and "People Management" magazine. CEMP Conference, Barcelona, December.

Scarbrough, H., Swan, J., and Preston, J. (1999) *Knowledge Management: A Review of the Literature.* London: Institute of Personnel and Development.

Senge, P. (1990) *The Fifth Discipline: The Art and Practice of the Learning Organization.* London: Doubleday.

Sewell, G. and Wilkinson, B. (1992) Someone to Watch over Me: Surveillance, Discipline and the Just-in-time Labour Process. *Sociology*, 26 (2): 271–90.

Skyrme, D.J. and Amidon, D.M. (1998) New Measures of Success. *The Journal of Business Strategy*, 19 (1): 20–4.

Starkey, K. (1998) Durkheim and the Limits of Corporate Culture: Whose Culture? Which Durkheim? *Journal of Management Studies*, 35 (2): 125–36.

Stehr, N. (1994) *Knowledge Societies.* London: Sage.

Swan, J. and Newell, S. (1995) The Role of Professional Associations in Technology Diffusion. *Organization Studies*, 16 (5): 847–74.

Thompson, P. and McHugh, D. (1990) *The Nature of Work.* London: MacMillan.

Tichy, N.M. and Cohen, E. (1998) The Teaching Organization. *Training and Development*, 52 (7): 26–35.

Tinaikar, R., Hartman, A., and Nath, R. (1995) Rethinking Business Process Re-engineering: A Social Constructionist Perspective. In G. Burke and J. Peppard (eds.), *Examining Business Process Re-engineering: Current Perspectives and Research Directions.* London: Kogan Page, 107–16.

Tsang, E. (1997) Organizational Learning and the Learning Organization: A Dichotomy between Descriptive and Prescriptive Research. *Human Relations*, 50 (1): 73–89.

Valentine, R. and Knights, D. (1998) TQM and BPR – Can You Spot the Difference? *Personnel Review*, 27 (1): 78–85.

Whittington, R. (1991) Changing Control Strategies in Industrial R&D. *R&D Management*, 21: 43–53.

Willcocks, L. and Lacity, M. (1998) *The Strategic Sourcing of Information Systems.* Chichester: Wiley and Sons.

26

Stickiness: Conceptualizing, Measuring, and Predicting Difficulties in the Transfer of Knowledge within Organizations

GABRIEL SZULANSKI AND ROSSELLA CAPPETTA

CHAPTER OUTLINE

While, in general, all transfers of knowledge require some degree of effort, some transfers require significantly more effort than others. Those that require more effort are said to be stickier. The idea that sticky transfers might actually be the norm rather than the exception when it comes to transfer knowledge within organizations is beginning to be accepted by scholars and practitioners interested in knowledge management and organizational learning. That is because, so far, efforts to transfer knowledge have had a distinctly modest record of success. Regretfully, little is known about the nature of sticky transfers because they have been rarely studied. Perhaps, a useful starting point to begin to uncover the nature of the social processes that underlie the difficulty to transfer knowledge is provided by the fact that, in general, transfers of knowledge involve numerous actors. When a transfer proceeds as expected and yields the desired results, the transfer process in and of itself is barely noticed by organizational actors, except perhaps by those individuals that are directly involved in transfer related activities. However, when things do not go as smoothly, when the transfer poses unique problems that turn out to be difficult to resolve, the details of the process of transfer become suddenly more salient. When things do not go smoothly, the transfer is eventful. In this chapter we introduce and develop this notion of sticky transfers as eventful. Before introducing the notion of stickiness as eventfulness, however, we review prior conceptions of stickiness and discuss their limitations. Then, after introducing the notion of eventfulness, we develop a typology of stickiness based on current understanding of the process of transfer. Next, we review predictors of stickiness and conclude by sketching practical implications and some promising directions for future research.

INTRODUCTION

Major Hunter-Hunt let his emotion over the *stickiness* of the Treasury evaporate in a deep sigh. (C. Mackenzie, *Water on Brain* viii. 115)

He had not imagined . . . that there was anything more in Billson's recalcitrance . . . than his usual official *stickiness*. (N. Blake, *Minute for Murder* viii. 167)

The intense *stickiness* of the situation. (Wodehouse, *Spring Fever* xiii. 126)

You do seem to have involved her in some sort of *stickiness*. (J.D. MacDonald *Girl* xii. 186)

According to the *Oxford English Dictionary* (2nd edition, 1989, electronic version), the word "stickiness" describes social situations typified by hesitancy, stubbornness; awkwardness, and unpleasantness. In line with this interpretation of the word stickiness,[1] the notion of sticky transfers denotes transfers where vigilance and effort are required to detect and overcome difficulty. While, in general, all transfers of knowledge require some degree of effort, some transfers require significantly more effort than others. Those that require more effort are said to be stickier.

The idea that sticky transfers might actually be the norm rather than the exception when it comes to transfer knowledge within organizations is beginning to be accepted by scholars and practitioners interested in knowledge management and organizational learning. That is because, so far, efforts to transfer knowledge have had a distinctly modest record of success. Ruggles (1998) finds that only 12 percent are happy with how their organizations transfer knowledge. Tom Stewart (2001) reports that seven out of eight knowledge management projects fail to include return on investment considerations and that CKOs and CIOs come and go. Galbraith (1990) reports that transfers are invariably found more difficult than anticipated. Gupta and Govindarajan (2000) report that expectations vastly outperform reality when it comes to knowledge transfer. Rather than automatic, transfers of knowledge appear fraught with difficulty.

Regretfully, little is known about the nature of sticky transfers because they have been rarely studied. Indeed, the signaling metaphor (Shannon and Weaver, 1949) which underpins the vast majority of research in knowledge transfer (cf. Attewell, 1992) and organizational learning (cf. Brown and Duguid, 1991) is based on the idea that transfers are instantaneous and costless acts of signaling, rather than social processes that consist of costly and often protracted efforts to resolve technical and political problems. It follows from this conception of transfers as acts that information can be treated as a public good that is costly to create but virtually costless to reuse. Difficulty is characterized as noise, that is, as an undesirable anomaly that must be minimized or eliminated to restore transfers to their "normal" state of instantaneous acts of negligible marginal cost.

Perhaps, a useful starting point to begin to uncover the nature of the social processes that underlie the difficulty to transfer knowledge is provided by the fact that, in general, transfers of knowledge involve numerous actors. When a transfer proceeds as expected and yields the desired results, the transfer process in and of itself is barely noticed by organizational actors, except perhaps by those individuals that are directly involved in transfer related activities. However, when things do not go as smoothly, when the transfer poses unique problems that turn out to be difficult to resolve, the details of the process of transfer become suddenly more salient.

For example, in a typical transfer of systems and operating procedures to newly acquired banks, or "conversions" as they are known at Banc One (BO), senior management decides the timing and chooses general parameters for the conversion, such as the number of systems that will be implemented simultaneously in the acquired bank. Once the transfer is scheduled and the parameters are set, it is generally assumed that the implementation of the conversion will not require further intervention from senior management; because the vast experience with conversions has allowed BO to develop sophisticated and robust conversion procedures and because the cost of failure was prohibitive.

However, because BO acquired larger banks as it grew bigger, each conversion had broader scale and scope than earlier ones. Increased scale and scope bred new challenges. Such challenges were rare but dramatic, given the high cost of failure. When they surfaced during a conversion, efforts to resolve them often required additional resources and adjustments to the timetable. Transfer related problems that could not be resolved at the operational level required the special attention from higher-level executives.

During one of these rare but highly problematic conversions, serious operational clouds began gathering on the horizon from an early stage. Yet, problems that did not have a routine, mechanical resolution were left unresolved and any indication of the existence of these problems grew progressively muted as it was reported up the hierarchy so as to preserve a semblance of normalcy and close adherence to the original timetable. However, after the conversion weekend, when the newly acquired bank begun relying on BO systems to serve its clients and could no longer continue to do so properly, the attention to the transfer process escalated rapidly through the hierarchy, eventually featuring the active involvement of the President and the CEO, both located seven hierarchical levels above the operating personnel in charge of the transfer. In fact, at a certain point in the transfer, BO's CEO and the CEO of the newly acquired bank were exchanging daily telephone calls, weekly status reports, and bitter memos about that specific conversion. The transfer process came under close scrutiny. Difficulties were eventually resolved but only after a prolonged effort and the direct and costly intervention of high-level executives that would not have participated in the implementation of the transfer.

This dramatic example of the organizational dynamics that difficulty can trigger inspired the conception of sticky transfers as eventful that we present in this chapter. Before introducing the notion of stickiness as eventfulness, however, we review in the next session prior conceptions of stickiness and discuss their limitations. Then, after introducing the notion of eventfulness, we develop a typology of stickiness based on current understanding of the process of transfer. Next, we review predictors of stickiness and conclude by sketching practical implications and some promising directions for future research.

PRIOR CONCEPTIONS OF STICKINESS

Traditionally, the difficulty to transfer knowledge inside the firm was considered an anomaly slighted both by theorists and practitioners. This was largely a byproduct of the presumption that knowledge is a public good that while costly to produce could be transferred at negligible marginal cost (cf. Arrow, 1962: 614–15). Such disregard for difficulty can be detected in early studies of technological innovation where it was assumed that "new technology instantly diffuses across total capital" (cf. Nelson, 1981: 1049) and in early studies of international and domestic transfer of technology where it was assumed that the transmission of technologies between and within countries is costless (cf. Reddy and Zhao, 1990: 298; Teece, 1977: 242). Likewise, in the world of practice, Galbraith (1990) found that many corporations approached transfers and replications of advanced manufacturing technology as relatively straightforward undertakings and therefore assigned them to untested junior managers.

Evidence, however, showed a different reality, one in which difficulty was pervasive. As Galbraith reported, "almost unanimously, the employees he interviewed in his study – managers, engineers, and operators alike – acknowledged that their particular transfer had been far more complicated than originally imagined" (1990: 68).

Indeed, the success of a transfer is never guaranteed. In his study of 26 projects of international transfers of manufacturing capabilities by multinational corporations, Teece (1976) found that one transfer failed to match the quality of output of the source unit, two failed to match the material efficiency of the source unit and six failed to match the labor productivity of the source unit. Likewise, Galbraith's (1990) found that 16 out of 32 intra-firm complex technology transfers experienced severe productivity problems and 20 percent ultimately failed to achieve profitability. In yet another well-known example, General Motor's Van Nuys plant in California could not attain the same operational results achieved by GM's successful joint venture with Toyota, the Nummi car manufacturing plant in Fremont, California, which exhibits comparable productivity to its sister plant in Takaoda, Japan (cf. Brown and Reich, 1989). GM's Oldsmobile division failed in its attempt to take advantage of the practices developed by its Saturn division (Kerwin and Woodruff, 1992). Likewise, IBM experienced limited success in diffusing internally re-engineered processes among Business Units (Economist, 1993) most notably logistics and hardware design practices developed in its PC division.

In an effort to bring the notion of knowledge transfer closer to reality, Teece (1976) offered cost as a meaningful proxy for the difficulty to transfer technology. He defined technology transfer costs as the

> costs of transmitting and absorbing the relevant firm, system, and industry-specific knowledge to the extent that this is necessary for the effective transfer of the technology . . . [the cost of all the] other activities involved in establishing a plant abroad and bringing it on stream. (1976: 36)

He found that the resource cost of transfers of manufacturing capabilities averaged 19 percent of the total manufacturing project costs and it reached as high as 59 percent in one of the projects. The cost of those transfers in absolute terms averaged roughly $1.2 million, reaching as high as $7.4 million in a specific occasion. Teece (1976: 45) concluded from this evidence that "there seems to be little room for the notion that transfer costs are zero, or very nearly so." A few years later, Mansfield et al. (1983) reported a study of 26 projects of technology transfer where technology transfer costs averaged about 20 percent of the total costs of establishing an overseas plant (cf. Reddy and Zhao, 1990).

In a seminal paper, Von Hippel (1994) invoked the notion of stickiness to explain the loci of innovation-related problem solving. Focusing on the consequences of stickiness, he reasoned that information could be sticky, in the sense that the cost of transferring that information could be anticipated to be so significant as to influence the choice of location for innovation-related problem solving; that is, whether innovation-related problems will be resolved at the developer's or at the user's side, a prediction explored empirically by Ogawa (1998). In this line of work, cost is typically inferred from characteristics of the knowledge transferred, such as the degree of tacitness, which presumably make the transfer more costly.

Besides increasing cost, stickiness is often thought to slow down the movement of knowledge. Thus, for example, studies of the diffusion of innovation (Attewell, 1992; Rogers, 1983) and the utilization of knowledge in society (Glaser et al., 1983) consider the rate of diffusion of an innovation as the central indicator of the absence of obstacles for the diffusion. Besides monitoring cost overruns and unexpected delays, students of project management often consider the gap between expectations and realizations to be another possible indication of occurrence of difficulty (Pinto and Mantel, 1990).

STICKINESS AS EVENTFULNESS

Memory is attention in the past tense.

A process-based conception of stickiness can be derived from the fact that, in general, transfers of knowledge involve numerous actors. When a transfer proceeds as expected and yields the desired results, the transfer process is barely noticed by most organizational actors, except perhaps by those individuals that are involved directly in transfer-related activities. However, when things do not go as smoothly, when the transfer poses unique problems that turn out to be difficult to resolve, the details of the process of transfer become suddenly more salient.

Indeed, in a difficult transfer, problems are likely to escalate. Whereas some of the transfer-related problems will be diagnosed easily and resolved routinely by those directly involved with the transfer, other problems may transcend the resourcefulness of the organizational actor(s) who are normally affected by and routinely resolve transfer-related problems. This more complex level of problem is likely to require response in the form of additional deliberation, recourse to non-standard skills, allocation of supplemental resources and escalation of transfer-related decisions to higher hierarchical levels for resolution. Actors whose attention would not have been normally required, such as senior managers or consultants, are likely to be involved in efforts to identify and resolve this more complex level of problems. These actors will become involved on an exceptional basis to expedite the identification of possible solutions and to enable and coordinate their implementation.

This more complex level of problem is likely to be noticed more broadly because it interrupts the assumed flow of the transfer (Zeigarnik, 1967). In other words, this kind of problem is more likely to exceed the base rate of eventfulness of a typical transfer and thus is more likely to be noticed against a background of otherwise ambiguous and inconsistent organizational reality where anomalies go undetected and failure is typically concealed. This kind of problem is more likely to create a distinct moment of difficulty in the transfer (Gilovich, 1991) and thus is more likely to contribute to the overall perception of difficulty and to the intensity of efforts exerted to resolve the problem (cf. March and Simon, 1958). The assessment of the degree of difficulty experienced in a transfer is likely to reflect the number and intensity of those distinct moments of difficulty. Other things being equal, a transfer is more likely to be perceived as difficult or sticky when efforts to resolve transfer problems become noteworthy.

Eventfulness stems from critical incidents, that is, observable human activity that is sufficiently complete in itself to permit inferences and predictions to be made about the person performing the act. To be critical, an incident must occur in a situation where the purpose or intent of the act seems fairly clear to the observer and where its consequences are sufficiently definite to leave little doubt concerning its effects (Flanagan, 1954).

Measuring eventfulness thus entails identifying the minimal molar units of social behavior that could still be interpreted as the incidence of difficulty. Such a measure requires enumerating possible manifestations of difficulty during the transfer. If those critical events are properly defined then the measure intrinsically reflects stickiness.

This definition, however, still leaves ample room for variation in the scope of critical incidents that constitute the measure. Very specific critical incidents will enhance the timely identification of stickiness perhaps at the expense of making the measure specific to a narrow set of transfers. Conversely, very abstract definitions of micro-events may create either a noisy measure or one that requires waiting until sufficient evidence has been collected. Thus, it becomes necessary to strike a balance between generality and timeliness. A very specific measure will be very timely but possibly idiosyncratic to a specific transfer. Conversely, a very broad measure would apply more generally but will be less sensitive to small deviations. A common strategy to deal with this dilemma consists of breaking the transfer into stages and developing general measures of stickiness for *each* stage of the transfer. To this task we turn next.

A TYPOLOGY OF STICKINESS

Current understanding of knowledge transfer processes supports the notion that there are at least four distinct stages in a transfer of knowledge. The most frequent distinction made is that between the initiation and the implementation of a transfer. Within the implementation phase, further distinctions are often made among (a) the initial implementation effort, (b) the ramp-up to satisfactory performance, and (c) subsequent follow-through and evaluation efforts to integrate the practice with other practices of the recipient. Initial implementation of a new practice and the subsequent ramp-up to satisfactory performance involve a two-step sequence of first "learning before doing" (Pisano, 1996) – either by planning (Argote, 1999) or by experimenting in a contrived setting before knowledge is actually put to use by the recipient – and then "learning by doing" which entails the resolution of unexpected problems that arise when new knowledge is put to use by the recipient (von Hippel and Tyre, 1995). Follow-through efforts typically aim at maintaining and improving the outcome of the transfer after satisfactory results are initially obtained. Each of the four stages – initiation, implementation, ramp-up and integration – can be difficult in their own ways.

Initiation stickiness

Initiation stickiness is the difficulty in recognizing opportunities to transfer and in acting upon them. An opportunity to transfer exists as soon as the seed for that transfer is formed, that is, as soon as a gap and knowledge to address the gap is found within the organization. The discovery of a gap may trigger problemistic search (Cyert and March, 1963) for suitable solutions. Alternatively, slack search (Cyert and March, 1963) may uncover superior practices, thus revealing a previously unsuspected gap or creating a new one (Glaser et al., 1983; Rogers, 1983; Zaltman et al., 1973).

The eventfulness of the initiation stage depends on how difficult it is to find an opportunity to transfer and to decide whether or not to pursue it. This becomes more demanding when existing operations are inadequately understood or when relevant and timely measures of performance as well as internal or external yardsticks are missing. Furthermore, the opportunity may need further scrutiny in order to understand why or how superior results are obtained by the source. The original rationale for a practice and its nuances are gradually reduced to taken-for-granted beliefs and entrenched habits. Yet, before the transfer can be undertaken, the practice may need to be documented, for example, by creating process maps or flowcharts, and its rationale reconstructed in order to select what needs to be transferred. The initiation of a transfer may consequently require substantial effort to delineate the scope of that transfer, select the timing, assess the costs and establish the mutual obligations of the participants (Ounjian and Carne, 1987: 198).

The search for opportunities and the decision to proceed with a transfer inevitably occurs under some degree of irreducible uncertainty or causal ambiguity. The source's mastery and ability to articulate a practice is often incomplete as is the recipient's ability to specify the environment where new knowledge will be applied. Measures of performance used to identify opportunities are often imprecise and subject to fluctuation. It becomes more difficult to assess the real merit of an opportunity and to act upon it. However, this uncertainty is reduced when there is evidence that the knowledge to be transferred has proven robust in other environments and that the source is reputable. When the source is not perceived as reliable, initiating a transfer from that source will be more difficult and its advice and example are likely to be challenged and resisted (Walton, 1975).

Implementation stickiness

Following the decision to transfer knowledge, attention shifts to the exchange of information and resources between the source and the recipient. Transfer-specific ties are established between members of the source and the recipient, and information and resource flows will typically increase and possibly peak at this stage. Efforts are made to preempt problems through careful planning (Pisano, 1996), especially to avoid the recurrence of problems experienced in previous transfers of the same knowledge, and to help make the introduction of new knowledge less threatening to the recipient (Buttolph, 1992: 464; Rice and Rogers, 1980: 508–9).

The eventfulness of the implementation stage depends on how challenging it is to bridge the communications gap between the source and the recipient and to fill the recipient's technical gap. Bridging the communications gap may require solving problems caused by incompatibilities of language, coding schemes, and cultural conventions. Closing the technical gap may disrupt the normal activities of both source and recipient. It may distract the source from its main mission (unless its mission is to support the transfer) – especially when supporting the transfer means generating additional documents, constructing dedicated equipment, lending or donating its own skilled personnel, or training the recipient's personnel. It may also temporarily disrupt the recipient's operations because existing personnel may have to be retrained or reassigned, new personnel may be hired and trained, infrastructure may have to be modified and upgraded and consultants from the source unit or elsewhere may move temporarily to the recipient. Furthermore, when the recipient unit is large, transfer-related information may not reach all parts of the recipient, thus creating problems of coordination.

Further difficulty may also result from poor coordination between the source and the recipient, especially when the source or the recipient of knowledge deviates from agreed-upon responsibilities. The source or the recipient may do more or less than it is expected from them leading to situations where the recipient usurps roles of the source or where the source intrudes the domain of the recipient (Leonard-Barton, 1990).

The true motivations of the source and the recipient are likely to be revealed at this stage. The recipient may increase difficulty by ignoring the source's recommendations out of misunderstanding, resentment, or to preserve pride of ownership and status (Rice and Rogers, 1980). The extent of difficulty can be mitigated through planning. However, the extent to which implementation activities can be planned depends on the depth of understanding of the practice, that is, on causal ambiguity. Oversights during planning can be compensated through mutual adjustment. The effectiveness of planning, coordination and mutual adjustments is likely to depend on the quality of the relationship between the source and the recipient.

Ramp-up stickiness

Once the recipient begins using acquired knowledge – for example, starts up a new production facility, rolls over a new process, or cuts over to a new system – the main concern becomes identifying and resolving unexpected problems that keep the recipient from matching or exceeding a priori expectations of post-transfer performance. The ramp-up stage offers a relatively brief window of opportunity to rectify unexpected problems (Tyre and Orlikowski, 1994) where the recipient is likely to begin using new knowledge ineffectively (Adler, 1990; Baloff, 1970; Chew et al., 1991; Galbraith, 1990) ramping up gradually towards a satisfactory level of performance, often with external assistance.

The eventfulness of the ramp-up phase depends on the number and seriousness of unexpected problems and the effort required to solve them. Unexpected problems may surface because a new environment where the transferred knowledge is put to use reacts differently than expected, training of personnel turns out to be insufficient or incomplete, trained personnel leave the organization or prove unfit for new roles, or the new practices involve significant changes in the language system and in the shared norms and beliefs underlying the correct interpretation of work directives. Likewise, when the transition to the use of new knowledge is gradual rather than sharp, that is, when a new practice co-exists over time with the practice it was meant to replace, duplication of effort and resource contention is likely. Unexpected problems become more difficult to resolve the later they occur within the ramp-up stage because precarious versions of new practices may already have become habitualized and more difficult to modify. When new knowledge is put to use in broad scope, that is, simultaneously rather than sequentially, the scope of incidence of unexpected problems will generally be broader.

Difficulty during the ramp-up stage is thus likely to correspond primarily to the degree of causal ambiguity of the practice. Unexpected problems are easier to resolve when cause–effect relationships for the new practice are understood, and when it is possible to forecast and explain results. The absorptive capacity of the recipient, that is, the ability to utilize new knowledge, depends on its existing stock of knowledge and skills. Thus the presence of relevant expertise during the ramp-up stage, either from internal or external sources, is crucial to contain costs (Chew et al., 1991) and delays (Baloff, 1970).

Integration stickiness

Once satisfactory results are initially obtained, the use of new knowledge becomes gradually routinized. This progressive routinization is incipient in every recurring social pattern (Berger and Luckmann, 1966: 53) Unless difficulty is encountered in the process, the new practices will blend with the objective, taken-for-granted reality of the organization (Berger and Luckmann, 1966; Zucker, 1977). However, when difficulties are encountered, the new practices may be abandoned and, when feasible, reversal to the former status quo may occur.

The eventfulness of the integration phase depends on the effort required to remove obstacles and to deal with challenges to the routinization of the new practice. This involves maintaining a delicate and comprehensive truce in intraorganizational conflict (Nelson and Winter, 1982: 110), that is, a situation where members of the organization are "content to play their roles . . . [and where] . . . manifest conflict follows largely predictable paths and stays within predictable bounds." This truce may be disturbed by external events such as environmental changes, the arrival of new members, or the appearance of a clearly superior alternative (Goodman et al., 1980; Zaltman et al., 1973). Likewise, the truce may be disturbed by internal events such as individual lapses in performance, unmet expectations, unclear rationale for the practice, evidence of dysfunctional consequences of using new knowledge, or sudden change in the scale of activities. Each disturbance to the truce may compound difficulty because each time a contingency is resolved, the terms of the truce become more specific and likely to elicit some resistance.

PREDICTORS OF STICKINESS

The likelihood that a transfer will be eventful can be predicted to some extent by analyzing the properties of the transfer. It is useful to distinguish between the characteristics of knowledge transferred and the characteristics of the situation, social and others, in which the knowledge transfer occurs. Those characteristics are discussed below.

Characteristics of knowledge

Causal ambiguity   Successful replication of results, in a different setting, may be compromised by idiosyncratic features of the new context in which knowledge is put to use. The theory of uncertain imitability (Lippman and Rumelt, 1982; Rumelt, 1984) suggests that there may be irreducible uncertainty connected with an attempt to achieve results in a different setting. Such an effort falls short of complete success because irreducible uncertainty precludes complete understanding of how the features of a new context affect the results. Modeling the replication of results as the recreation of a production function, Lippman and Rumelt explain that uncertainty is most likely to result from ambiguity about what the factors of production are and how they interact during production. As Rumelt (1984: 562) explicates, "if the precise reasons for success or failure cannot be determined, even after the event has occurred, there is causal ambiguity and it is impossible to produce an unambiguous list of the factors of production, much less measure their marginal contribution." Therefore, he concludes that in the pure theory of uncertain imitability, the fundamental factor that hinders the achievement of the results from the use of knowledge is causal ambiguity (1984: 567).[2]

The process whereby causal ambiguity increases stickiness is explained by Jensen and Meckling (1992: 255):

> Uncertainty about what specific piece of idiosyncratic knowledge is valuable enlarges transfer costs in a subtle way. After the fact, it is often obvious that a specific piece of knowledge critical to a decision could have been transferred at low cost (for example, particular quirks of an organization, person, legal rule, or custom). But transferring this specific piece of knowledge in advance requires knowing in advance that it will be critical.

Costly omissions are more likely when there is causal ambiguity.

Routinized use of causally ambiguous knowledge is often accompanied by gaps between formal and actual patterns of use. Brown and Duguid (1991: 41), based on detailed ethnographic studies of service technicians, noted variance between formal descriptions of work, in training programs and manuals, and actual work practices as performed by the organization's members. Likewise, Nelson and Winter (1982: 108) distinguished between "nominal standards of the organization" and routine operation. Gaps between formal and actual patterns of use result from partial articulation of the espoused rules that govern behavior (Argyris and Schön, 1978), because of the partly tacit nature of individual skills (Polanyi, 1962), because of the partly tacit coordination principles that govern collective action (Kogut and Zander, 1992; Winter, 1987a), because incomplete knowledge of the production process precludes effective management (Bohn, 1994), because of the opacity of the organization to decision makers (Williamson, 1975) and because of the need to maintain a social truce to preserve routine operation (Nelson and Winter, 1982).

Essentially, more than absence of know-how, causal ambiguity signals the absence of know-why: why something is done, and why a given action results in a given outcome. If results cannot be precisely reproduced elsewhere because of differences in environmental conditions and if there exist causal ambiguity about the inner workings of productive knowledge then problems that arise in the new environment have to be solved *in situ* through costly trial and error. As Paul Adler (1990: 951) explains, when highly technologically sophisticated process knowledge is transferred, "its 'reach' into poorly mastered process techniques, is such that any substantial divergence of process designs risks multiplying operational problems beyond manageable levels." Thus, the higher the causal ambiguity, the more difficult it may prove to realize similar results by applying knowledge in a different context.

Unproven knowledge   When knowledge has been previously put to use for a brief period of time or on a limited scale or scope, the claim that it will be effective when used in a new situation may be somewhat speculative, due to lack of sufficient empirical substantiation. Lack of information may affect the expectations of potential recipients (Lenox, 1999) who may be more reluctant to engage in the recreation of that knowledge (Rogers, 1983) and who will question controversial integration efforts (Goodman et al., 1980; Nelson and Winter, 1982). Persuasion is often easier when there is a recurring working example of how to obtain results (Szulanski and Jensen, forthcoming).

Characteristics of the situation

Source lacks motivation   The motivation of the source of knowledge may impact the degree of difficulty experienced during a transfer. A source's agent can assume two roles: it can act as gatekeeper to a working example or it can supply a conception of such example. Consequently, the motivation of the source of knowledge to supply conceptions of the practice or to facilitate access to the recipient may impact the degree of difficulty experienced during a transfer. For example, the source may be reluctant to share crucial knowledge for fear of losing ownership, a position of privilege, of superiority, of becoming expendable or it may be resentful of not being adequately rewarded for sharing hard-won success. Furthermore, and especially in the first instances that knowledge is transferred, the source may have to make a special effort to support the recipient. This special effort may interfere with the source's ability to attend to its main mission, unless it is a part of it, and thus lower its motivation.

Source not perceived as trustworthy   It is generally believed that trustworthiness reduces stickiness. This belief can be traced back to Aristotle's seminal observation that the opinions of "good men" have more impact on other men's behavior. Well-known experiments show that immediately after the communication episode, a credible source substantially affects the recipient's attitude (e.g., Allen and Stiff, 1989; Capon and Hulbert, 1973; Hovland et al., 1949; Hovland and Weiss, 1951; Kelman and Hovland, 1953; for reviews see Perry, 1996). More generally, factors normally associated with credibility, such as trustworthiness (Zaheer, McEvily, and Perrone, 1998), status (Benjamin and Podolny, 1999) and social capital (Belliveau et al., 1996; Nahapiet and Ghoshal, 1998; Tsai and Ghoshal, 1998), are believed to contribute to the efficiency of social exchange.

When the source is perceived as trustworthy, the recipient will be less suspicious of the offered conception and thus more open and receptive to its detail (Hovland et al., 1949; Hovland and Weiss, 1951). This increases the amount of information that can be exchanged (Carley, 1991; Tsai and Ghoshal, 1998) and decreases the cost of the exchange (Curall and Judge, 1995; Zaheer et al., 1998). More detail can be communicated to the recipient, who can thus afford a better grasp of the source's conception of the practice. Furthermore, a recipient will expect little damage to ensue from interactions with a trustworthy source (Noteboom et al., 1997). When the source is not perceived as trustworthy, knowledge transfer can be expected to be stickier.

Recipient lacks motivation The motivation of a recipient to accept knowledge from an external source and engage in the activities necessary to recreate and apply that knowledge may prove critical to insure a non-eventful replication. The reluctance of some recipients to accept knowledge from the outside (the "not invented here" or NIH syndrome) is well documented (e.g., Hayes and Clark, 1985; Katz and Kahn, 1982). Lack of motivation may result in foot dragging, passivity, feigned acceptance, hidden sabotage, or outright rejection in the implementation of new knowledge (cf. Zaltman et al., 1973). This resistance may manifest itself during each one of the many activities that the recipient performs to support the recreation of knowledge, such as absorbing the source's understanding, analyzing the feasibility of the transfer, bridging the communication gap with the source unit, planning the transfer, implementing systems and facilities necessary to fruitfully absorb the new knowledge, assigning personnel for education and training, and solving unexpected problems that stem from the utilization of new knowledge.

Recipient lacks absorptive capacity The ability to exploit outside sources of knowledge is largely a function of the level of prior related knowledge (Capon and Hulbert, 1973; Cohen and Levinthal, 1990; Dewar and Dutton, 1986). At the most elementary level, this knowledge includes basic skills, a shared language, previous relevant experience, and up-to-date information on related knowledge domains (Cohen and Levinthal, 1990; Galbraith, 1990; Nord and Tucker, 1987; Pennings and Harianto, 1992a; Walton, 1975). Critical prior knowledge also includes awareness of the locus of useful complementary expertise within and outside the organization. Examples of this awareness are knowledge of who knows what, who can help with what problem, or who can exploit new information (Cohen and Levinthal, 1990; Nord and Tucker, 1987; Pennings and Harianto, 1992a, 1992b). The stock of prior related knowledge determines the "absorptive capacity" (Cohen and Levinthal, 1990: 128) of a recipient of knowledge.

A recipient that lacks absorptive capacity will be less likely to recognize the value of new knowledge, less likely to recreate that knowledge and less likely to apply it successfully. This may increase the cost, retard the completion and even compromise the success of a recreation effort.

Recipient lacks retentive capacity A transfer of knowledge is successful if there is long-term retention of the transferred knowledge (Druckman and Bjork, 1991), that is, to the extent that the recipient persists in using that knowledge when practicable (Glaser et al., 1983; Kostova, 1999). Persistence is more likely when recreated knowledge continues to be used until it sheds novelty and becomes a fact, a part of the objective, taken for granted reality of the recipient (Rogers, 1983; Zucker, 1977). This is more likely when use of new knowledge is fully extended, and when specific steps are taken to eradicate old knowledge (Glaser et al., 1983; Yin, 1979).[3] Studies of innovation (e.g. Nord and Tucker, 1987: 9; Rogers, 1983: 365) and of the persistence of planned organizational change (Glaser et al., 1983: 221–51 for a review; Goodman and Associates, 1982: 228; Yin, 1979) have documented instances where the use of superior technical and organizational knowledge is discontinued after successful implementation. The ability of a recipient to institutionalize the utilization of new knowledge reflects its "retentive capacity." Retentive capacity of a recipient is tested when initial difficulties experienced during the integration of recreated knowledge provide excuse for discontinuing its use, and reverting to the previous status quo when feasible (Zaltman et al., 1973).

Arduous relationship between the source and the recipient   Another important contextual aspect for both the source and the recipient of knowledge is the nature of their pre-existing relationship. A transfer of knowledge is rarely a singular event but more often it is an iterative process of exchange. A potential recipient may require explanations of the nature of knowledge to decide whether it would meet its needs. Likewise, once engaged in a transfer, the source may have to gain a closer appreciation of the needs of the recipient to select appropriate components to transfer and of its unresolved problems to support the initial period of utilization. The success of such exchange depends to some extent on the strength of the tie (Hansen, 1999), which is detectable in the ease of communication (Arrow, 1974) and in the "intimacy" of the relationship (cf. Marsden, 1990). Intimacy to some extent reflects a shared appreciation of the meaning of theories, puzzles, measures, and accepted results. This eases communication because, under conditions of intimacy, messages can be thought of as selections from a predefined set (Boland and Tenkasi, 1995: 355). Conversely, an arduous relationship might create additional hardship to transfer knowledge.

Barren context[1]   The organizational context may affect the gestation and evolution of an initiative to transfer. The same *transfer seed* that unfolds fully in one context, may grow timidly and yield ephemeral results in another or, in a third context, remain unrecognized. Insofar as the context nurtures the development of a transfer seed, the gestation and evolution of a transfer resembles the germination of a seed. Thus, an organizational context that facilitates the development of a transfer seed could be said to be *fertile*. Conversely, a context where transfer seeds mature no further could be said to be *barren*. Formal structure and systems (cf. Bower, 1970; Chakravarthy and Doz, 1992; Chew et al., 1990: 156–7; Hayes and Clark, 1985), sources of coordination and expertise (Argote et al., 1990; Chew et al., 1990) and behavior framing attributes (Ghoshal and Bartlett, 1994; Schein, 1985) of the organizational context can influence the number of attempts to recreate knowledge and the fate of those attempts.

SOME PRACTICAL IMPLICATIONS

The typology of stickiness and of its predictors may be used to plan knowledge transfers. First, timely identification of difficulty hinges on having proper measures for each stage.

Such measures are offered in the appendix. The four measures of stickiness may enable the detection of stickiness prior to the completion of the transfer. Such a timely and more specific detection may allow the design of more specific and possibly more effective action items to deal with incipient difficulties. Thus, for example, difficulties may be detected as early as the initiation stage so that remedies that are specifically meant for the initiation stage can be applied in a timely fashion.

Furthermore, the detection and prevention of stickiness at each stage may be enhanced by identifying the most likely predictors of stickiness for each stage. Such segmentation opens up the possibility that different barriers operate at different stages of the transfer. Thus, for example, the degree of proveness of the knowledge transferred is more likely to be a factor during the initiation of a transfer. Conversely, the absorptive capacity of the recipient may be more of a factor in later stages, after the implementation of the transfer has started. In fact, the analysis of the different types allows us to identify different sources of stickiness for each stage of the knowledge transfer and to plan the coherent mechanisms to reduce their impact.

AVENUES FOR FUTURE RESEARCH

That it could be difficult to transfer knowledge has been known for quite some time. Wisdom about possible sources of these difficulties has gradually formed. At first, motivational barriers were seen as the primary if not the sole culprit. Indeed, difficulties to transfer best practices internally are traditionally ascribed to interdivisional jealousy, lack of incentives, lack of confidence, insufficient priority, lack of buy-in, a heavy inclination to re-invent the wheel or to plow twice the same fields, refusal of recipients to do exactly what they are told, resistance to change, lack of commitment, turf protection and many other manifestations of what seem to be part of the popular definition of the NIH syndrome. These are sensible explanations.

Researchers who have looked at the phenomena from a general management perspective seem to agree. For example, Michael Porter (1985: 352) notes that "the mere hope that one business unit might learn something useful from another is frequently a hope not realized." He explains that "business units acting independently simply do not have the same incentives to propose and advocate strategies based on interrelationship as do higher level managers with a broader perspective." He blames both the recipient who can "rarely be expected to seek out know-how elsewhere in the firm," and also the source, who "will have little incentive to transfer [its know-how], particularly if it involves the time of some of their best people or involves proprietary technology that might leak out" (Porter, 1985: 368).

Yet, imperceptibly at first, the importance of knowledge-related factors was being increasingly recognized. Besides motivational factors, difficulty seemed to stem from the recipient's level of knowledge prior to the transfer, the depth of understanding of the practice by the source, the recipient's ability to unlearn prior practices, and the pre-existing social ties between the source and the recipient of knowledge are knowledge barriers.

The logic of barriers, however, is a logic that suggests that stickiness occurs in exceptional circumstances, and that normality may be restored by removing those barriers. Such logic is at odds with the observation that stickiness is pervasive, that stickiness is the rule, rather than the exception.

It is for this reason that perhaps the best starting point for a research agenda on stickiness lies in those theoretical perspectives that recognize the pervasive nature of stickiness, that is, that stickiness is a constant to be factored in any attempt to conceptualize the process of knowledge transfer. One such perspective is the so-called pragmatic view of knowledge (see Carlile, 2002, for a review).

Such perspective sees transfers in terms of the practical and political problems that they pose. The pragmatist starts from the presumption that social action requires effort, thus providing a way to reframe from difficulty as anomaly to difficulty as normalcy. That knowledge transfers would require effort is taken for granted. When that is the case, then the challenge of studying stickiness is the challenge of identifying the kinds of problems, the nature of the effort that has to be exerted to resolve them, and the consequences that resolving one kind of problem has on others.

Thus, a pragmatic perspective evokes a different view of transfers. Transfers of knowledge involve unending problem solving. For the pragmatists, problems are not just different in degree but also different in kind. Such line of thinking suggests that the emphasis of the research community then could be profitably directed to frame and articulate carefully a typology of problems that underlie stickiness, a task for which hopefully this chapter provides a useful starting point. Indeed, a series of critical incidents that increase the eventfulness of a transfer are identified in the discussion of each stage and a possible operationalization is reported in the appendix.

Therefore, a sensible partition of the problem of transfer into a set of qualitatively different problems seems a particularly promising way to move forward. The four stages identified in the process view of transfer could constitute a useful starting point. An example of the value of such an approach can be seen by examining a puzzling finding by Szulanski (2000). By analyzing the impact of the motivation of the recipient at different stages of the transfer, Szulanski found that even though it is normally expected to mitigate stickiness, the recipient's motivation has a more intricate effect on stickiness. On the one hand, a motivated recipient reduces the effort necessary during the early steps of the implementation. However, during ramp up a motivated recipient may create unnecessary eventfulness by doing too much too early. Thus, solving the problem of the recipient's motivation entails solving two very different kinds of problems, one that is mostly technical, and another that is political in essence.

In general, that means focusing on difficulty of specific parts of the transfer, rather than on the transfer as a whole. When we treated transfers as acts it was difficult to break them up into pieces and examine them. Now that many decades of careful study of innovation diffusion, organizational change and technology implementation have yielded an understanding of the stages of the transfer, perhaps a useful way forward is to study the different stages and take a closer look into the nature of difficulty at each stage, as the example of the recipient motivation suggests. This is in line not only with the spirit of the pragmatists but more broadly with the gist of evolutionary perspectives of organizations that stress the need to move into the micro-mechanisms behind observed macro-organizational phenomena (Dosi et al., 2000; Levinthal, 2000; Nelson and Winter, 1982) and the generalized widespread efforts in organizational research to open the black box of an organization. Indeed, perhaps the black box of knowledge transfer deserves, more than many other organizational phenomena, to be opened and scrutinized to understand mediating processes.

Perhaps, to conclude, it may be worthwhile to return to the notion of sticky transfers discussed in the introduction to highlight the fact that, stickiness, according to this conception, becomes a property of the transfer situation, not necessary of the knowledge transferred. While the attributes of knowledge are no doubt an important determinant in the transfer of knowledge (Kogut and Zander, 1992; Winter, 1987b), they are not necessarily the sole one. Such a view is implicit in von Hippel's (1994) seminal treatment of the stickiness of a given unit of information, because, as he points out, information stickiness involves not only attributes of the information itself, but attributes of and choices made by information seekers and information providers. For example, if a particular information seeker is inefficient or less able in acquiring information unit x (e.g., because of a lack of certain tools or complementary information), or if a particular information provider decides to charge for access to unit x, the stickiness of unit x will be higher than it might be under other conditions. The purpose of being inclusive with respect to causes of information stickiness in his definition is to direct researchers towards the impact of information stickiness independent of cause.

Yet, when it comes to manage stickiness, such distinctions of cause are significant. Stickiness may also be a result of situational characteristics in which the transfer takes place. Sticky information may yield sticky transfers. However, transfers of non-sticky information could be sticky as well. The intent of this chapter is to make such distinctions meaningful and tractable. Stickiness, that is, hesitancy, stubbornness; awkwardness, and unpleasantness during a transfer, either anticipated or experienced, is a property of each specific transfer and could result from attributes of the information transferred as well as from those of the situation in which it is transferred.

APPENDIX: MEASURING STICKINESS

Measures based on outcome

Stickiness was measured using a set of eight items corresponding to the so-called technical success indicators of a project (Pinto and Mantel, 1990, Randolph and Posner, 1988) – on time, on budget, and a satisfied recipient. Deviation in timing was measured as departure from the initial plan in reaching key milestones – the start of the transfer, the first day the practice became operational at the recipient and achievement of satisfactory performance. For these three items the five possible answers were: (1) Advanced by more than one month; (2) Advanced less than one month; (3) Not rescheduled; (4) Delayed less than one month; (5) Delayed more than one month.

Two items measured departure of actual cost from expected cost on the source side and the recipient side. For these two items the five possible answers were: (1) Much (>30 percent) more than expected; (2) Slightly more (<30 percent) than expected; (3) As expected; (4) Slightly (<30 percent) less than expected; (5) Much less (>30 percent) than expected.

Finally, three items measured recipient's satisfaction. One item measured adjustment in the recipient's expectations after gaining experience with the practice. The possible answers for this question were: (1) Dramatically upward; (2) Slightly upward; (3) No change; (4) Slightly downward; (5) Dramatically downward.

Two items measured whether the recipient was satisfied with the quality of the practice and with the quality of the transfer. For these two items, the possible answers were: (1) Very satisfied; (2) Somewhat satisfied; (3) Neither satisfied nor dissatisfied; (4) Somewhat dissatisfied; (5) Very dissatisfied.

Measures based on process: operationalization of the dependent variables

Unless indicated the answer is measured using the default scale (Y! y o n N!). Each sentence in the description of the scales below corresponds to one item of the questionnaire.

Stickiness during the initiation phase ($\alpha = 0.74$, Items = 8) default scale.

Ranking the performance of «company»'s units on their results on «practice» was straightforward. *Within «company»*, there existed consensus that «source» has obtained the best results with «practice». Compared to *external* benchmarks, «source» has obtained best-in-class results with «practice». «source» could easily explain how it obtained superior results with «practice». «source» could easily point to the key components of «practice». «source» was reluctant to share crucial knowledge and information relative to «practice». Distributing responsibility for the transfer between «source» and «recipient» generated much conflict. The transfer of «practice» from «source» to «recipient» was amply justified.

Stickiness during the implementation phase ($\alpha = 0.83$, Items = 13) default scale.

«recipient» recognized «source»'s expertise on «practice». The transfer of «practice» from «source» to «recipient» disrupted «source» normal operations. «recipient» could not free personnel from regular operations so that it could be properly trained. Communication of transfer related information broke down within «recipient». «recipient» was able to recognize inadequacies in «source»'s offerings. «recipient» knew what questions to ask «source». «recipient» knew how to recognize its requirements for «practice». «recipient» performed unnecessary modifications to the «practice». «recipient» modified the «practice» in ways contrary to expert's advice. «source» turned out to be less knowledgeable of the «practice» than it appeared before the transfer was decided. Much of what «recipient» should have done during the transfer was eventually completed by «source». «source» understood «recipient»'s unique situation. All aspects of the transfer of «practice» from «source» to «recipient» were carefully planned.

Stickiness during the ramp-up phase ($\alpha = 0.77$, Items = 9) default scale.

Initially «recipient» "spoon fed" the «practice» with carefully selected personnel and raw material until it got up to speed. At first «recipient» measured performance more often than usual, sometimes reacting too briskly to transient declines in performance. Some people left «recipient» after having been trained for their new role in the «practice», forcing «recipient» to hire hastily a replacement and train it "on the fly." Some people turned out to be poorly qualified to perform their new role in the «practice», forcing «recipient» to hire hastily a replacement and train it "on the fly." The «practice» had unsatisfactory side effects which «recipient» had to correct. By altering the «practice», «recipient» created further problems which had to be solved. «recipient»'s environment turned out to be different from that of «source» forcing «recipient» to make unforeseen changes to «practice». Outside experts (from «source», other units, or external consultants) could answer questions and solve problems about their specialty but did not have an overall perspective on the «practice». Teams put together to help «recipient» to get up to speed with the «practice» disbanded because their members had to attend to other pressing tasks.

Stickiness during the integration phase (α = 0.79, Items = 12) default scale unless indicated.

«recipient» has not yet solved all problems caused by the introduction of the «practice», because energy and resources were siphoned off by daily work pressures. Some of the "temporary workarounds" devised to help «recipient» get up to speed became habitual. For the «practice» today, the roles are well defined. «recipient» personnel are content to play their roles in «practice». The appropriateness of performing the «practice» in «recipient» has been *explicitly questioned* after its introduction. «recipient» has reconsidered its decision to adopt the «practice». «recipient»'s expectations created during the introduction of the «practice» have been met. Individual values favor performing the «practice». It is clear why «recipient» needs the «practice». The justification for performing the «practice» at «recipient» makes sense. The activities accompanying the «practice» are difficult. The activities accompanying the «practice» are: *(circle one option)* (1) Obviously functional; (2) Somewhat against the grain of existing work practices; (3) Arbitrary without a basis in reality.

ACKNOWLEDGMENTS

The authors acknowledge helpful comments and exchanges with Eric von Hippel, Marjorie Lyles, Yiorgos Mylonadis, Steve Postrel, and an anonymous referee. Financial support was graciously provided by the Jones Center of the University of Pennsylvania and the Mack Center for Technological Innovation. Errors and omissions are solely the authors' responsibility.

NOTES

1. The use of the word stickiness to describe the difficulties was inspired by Eric von Hippel's (1994) seminal use of the term "sticky information" to describe sticky transfers of information between users and developers (von Hippel, 1994).
2. Bohn (1994) has called causally ambiguous knowledge "incomplete." He suggested a practical definition of complete knowledge as a "model that will predict output characteristics to an accuracy of one-tenth of the tolerance band, for changes in inputs across a 2:1 range, and including all interactions" (1994: 70).
3. Make a quick connection to unlearning in the sense that retentive capacity includes the ability of unlearning.
4. This brief discussion of the organizational context is limited to an intra-firm setting.

REFERENCES

Adler, P.S. (1990) Shared Learning. *Management Science*, 36 (8): 938–57.

Allen, M. and Stiff, J. (1989) Testing Three Models for the Sleeper Effect. *Western Journal of Speech Communication*, 53: 411–26.

Argote, L. (1999) *Organizational Learning: Creating, Retaining, and Transferring Knowledge*. Boston: Kluwer Academic.

Argote, L., Beckman, S.L., and Epple, D. (1990) The Persistence and Transfer of Learning in Industrial Settings. *Management Science*, 36 (2): 140–54.

Argyris, C. and Schön, D.A. (1978) *Organizational Learning*. Reading, MA: Addison Wesley.

Arrow, K.J. (1962) Economic Welfare and the Allocation of Resources for Invention. In R. Nelson (ed.), *The Rate and Direction of Inventive Activity*. Princton, NJ: Princeton University Press, 609–25.

Arrow, K.J. (1974) *The Limits of Organization*. New York: Norton.

Attewell, P. (1992) Technology Diffusion and Organizational Learning: The Case of Business Computing. *Organization Science*, 3 (1): 1–19.

Baloff, N. (1970) Startup Management. *IEEE Transactions on Engineering Management*, EM-17 (4): 132–41.

Belliveau, M., O'Reilly, C., and Wade, J. (1996) Social Capital at the Top: Effects of Social Similarity and Status on CEO Compensation. *Academy of Management Journal*, 39 (6): 1568–93.

Benjamin, B. and Podolny, J. (1999) Status, Quality and Social Order in the California Wine Industry. *Administrative Science Quarterly*, 44 (3): 563–89.

Berger, P. and Luckmann, T. (1966) *The Social Construction of Reality*. New York: Doubleday.

Bohn, R.E. (1994) Measuring and Managing Technological Knowledge. *Sloan Management Review* (Fall): 61–73.

Boland, R.J. Jr. and Tenkasi, R.V. (1995) Perspective Making and Perspective Taking in Communities of Knowing. *Organization Science*, 6 (4): 350–72.

Bower, J.L. (1970) *Managing the Resource Allocation Process*. Boston, MA: Harvard University Press.

Brown, C. and Reich, M. (1989) When Does Union-Management Cooperation Work? A Look at NUMMI and GM- Van Nuys. *California Management Review*, 31 (4): 26–44.

Brown, J.S. and Duguid, P. (1991) Organizational Learning and Communities-of-Practice: Toward a Unified View of Working, Learning, and Innovation. *Organization Science*, 2 (1): 40–57.

Buttolph, D. (1992) A New Look at Adaptation. *Knowledge: Creation, Diffusion, Utilization*, 13 (4): 460–70.

Capon, N. and Hulbert, J. (1973) The Sleeper Effect: An Awakening. *Public Opinion Quarterly*, 37 (3): 333–58.

Carley, K. (1991) A Theory of Group Stability. *American Sociological Review*, 56 (3): 331–54.

Carlile, P.R. (2002) A Pragmatic View of Knowledge and Boundaries: Boundary Objects in New Product Development. *Organization Science*, 13 (4): 442–55.

Chakravarthy, B.S. and Doz, Y. (1992) Strategy Process Research: Focusing on Corporate Self-Renewal. *Strategic Management Journal*, 13 (Summer): 5–15.

Chew, W.B., Bresnahan, T.F., and Clark, K.B. (1990) Measurement, Coordination, and Learning in a Multiplant Network. In R.S. Kaplan (ed.), *Measures for Manufacturing Excellence*. Boston: Harvard Business School, 129–62.

Chew, W.B., Leonard-Barton, D., and Bohn, R.E. (1991) Beating Murphy's Law. *Sloan Management Review*, 32 (3): 5–16.

Cohen, W.M. and Levinthal, D. (1990) Absorptive Capacity: A New Perspective on Learning and Innovation. *Administrative Science Quarterly*, 35 (1): 128–52.

Curall, S. and Judge, T. (1995) Measuring Trust between Organizational Boundary Role Persons. *Organizational Behavior and Human Decision Processes*, 64: 151–70.

Cyert, R.M. and March, J.G. (1963) *A Behavioral Theory of the Firm*. Englewood Cliffs, NJ: Prentice-Hall.

Dewar, R.D. and Dutton, J.E. (1986) The Adoption of Radical and Incremental Innovations: An Empirical Analysis. *Management Science*, 32 (11): 1422–33.

Dosi, G., Nelson, R.R., and Winter, S.G. (eds.) (2000) *The Nature and Dynamics of Organizational Capabilities*. Oxford, UK: Oxford University Press.

Druckman, D. and Bjork, R.A. (eds.) (1991) *In the Mind's Eye: Enhancing Human Performance*. Washington, DC: National Academy Press.

Economist (1993) A Spanner in the Works. *The Economist*, 75–81.

Flanagan, J.C. (1954) The Critical Incident Technique. *Psychological Bulletin*, 51 (4): 327–58.

Galbraith, C.S. (1990) Transferring Core Manufacturing Technologies in High Tech Firms. *California Management Review*, 32 (4): 56–70.

Ghoshal, S. and Bartlett, C.A. (1994) Linking Organizational Context and Managerial Action: The Dimensions of Quality of Management. *Strategic Management Journal*, 15 (Special Issue, Summer): 91–112.

Gilovich, T. (1991) *How We Know What Isn't So: The Fallibility of Human Reason in Everyday Life*. New York: Free Press.

Glaser, E.M., Abelson, H.H., and Garrison, K.N. (1983) *Putting Knowledge to Use*. San Francisco: Jossey-Bass.

Goodman, P.S. and Associates (1982) *Change in Organizations*, 1st edn. London: Jossey-Bass.

Goodman, P.S., Bazerman, M., and Conlon, E. (1980) Institutionalization of Planned Organizational Change. In B.M. Staw and L.L. Cummings (eds.), *Research in Organizational Behavior*, Vol. 2. Greenwich, CT: JAI Press, 215–46.

Gupta, A. and Govindarajan, V. (2000) Knowledge Flows within Multinational Corporations. *Strategic Management Journal*, 21 (4): 473–96.

Hansen, M. (1999) The Search-transfer Problem: The Role of Weak Ties in Sharing Knowledge across Organization Subunits. *Administrative Science Quarterly*, 44: 82–111.

Hayes, R.H. and Clark, K.B. (1985) *Exploring the Sources of Productivity Differences at the Factory Level*. New York: Wiley.

Hovland, C., Lumsdaine, A., and Sheffield, F. (1949) *Experiments in Mass Communication*. New York: Wiley.

Hovland, C. and Weiss, W. (1951) The Influence of Source Credibility on Communication Effectiveness. *Public Opinion Quarterly*, 15 (4): 635–50.

Jensen, M.C. and Meckling, W.H. (1992) Specific and General Knowledge, and Organizational Structure. In L. Werin and H. Wijkander (eds.), *Contract Economics*. Cambridge, MA: Blackwell, 251–74.

Katz, D. and Kahn, R.L. (1982) *The Social Psychology of Organizations*. New York: Wiley.

Kelman, H. and Hovland C. (1953) Reinstatement of the Communication in Delayed Measurement of Opinion Change. *Journal of Abnormal and Social Psychology*, 45: 327–35.

Kerwin, K. and Woodruff, D. (1992) Can Olds Hitch its Wagon to Saturn's Star? *Business Week*, 74.

Kogut, B. and Zander, U. (1992) Knowledge of the Firm, Combinative Capabilities and the Replication of Technology. *Organization Science*, 3 (3): 383–97.

Kostova, T. (1999) Transnational Transfer of Strategic Organizational Practices: A Contextual Perspective. *Academy of Management Review*, 24: 308–24.

Lenox, M.J. (1999) *Agency and Information Costs in the Intra-firm Diffusion of Practice*. Boston: MIT Press.

Leonard-Barton, D. (1990) The Intraorganizational Environment: Point-to-Point versus Diffusion. In F. Williams and D.V. Gibson (eds.), *Technology Transfer: A Communication Perspective*. London: Sage, 43–62.

Levinthal, D. (2000) Organizational Capabilities in Complex Worlds. In G. Dosi, R.R. Nelson, and S.G. Winter (eds.), *The Nature and Dynamics of Organizational Capabilities*. New York: Oxford University Press.

Lippman, S.A. and Rumelt, R.P. (1982) Uncertain Imitability: An Analysis of Interfirm Differences in Efficiency under Competition. *Bell Journal of Economics*, 13: 418–38.

Mansfield, E., Romeo, A., Schwartz, M., Teece, D., Wagner, S., and Brach, P. (1983) New Findings in Technology Transfer, Productivity and Development. *Research Management* (March–April), 11–20.

March, J. and Simon, H. (1958) *Organizations*. New York.

Marsden, P.V. (1990) Network Data and Measurement. *Annual Review of Sociology*, 16: 435–63.

Nahapiet, P. and Ghoshal, S. (1998) Social Capital, Intellectual Capital and the Organizational Advantage. *Academy of Management Review*, 32 (2): 242–57.

Nelson, R. (1981) Research on Productivity Growth and Differences. *Economic Literature*, 19: 1029–64.

Nelson, R. and Winter, S. (1982) *An Evolutionary Theory of Economic Change*. Cambridge: Belknap Press.

Nord, W.R. and Tucker, S. (1987) *Implementing Routine and Radical Innovations*. Lexington, MA: Lexington Books.

Noteboom, N., Berger, H., and Noorderhaven, N. (1997) Effects of Trust and Governance on Relational Risk. *Academy of Management Journal*, 40 (2): 308–38.

Ogawa, S. (1998) Does Sticky Information Affect the Locus of Innovation? Evidence from the Japanese Convenience-store Industry. *Research Policy*, 26 (7,8): 777–90.

Ounjian, M.L. and Carne, E.B. (1987) A Study of the Factors which Affect Technology Transfer in a Multilocation Multibusiness Unit Corporation. *IEEE Transactions on Engineering Management*, EM-34 (3): 194–201.

Pennings, J.M. and Harianto, F. (1992a) The Diffusion of Technological Innovation in the Commercial Banking Industry. *Strategic Management Journal*, 13: 29–46.

Pennings, J.M. and Harianto, F. (1992b) Technological Networking and Innovation Implementation. *Organization Science*, 3 (3): 356–83.

Perry, D.K. (1996) *Theory and Research in Mass Communication: Contexts and Consequences*. Mahwah, NJ: Lawrence Erlbaum Associates.

Pinto, J.K. and Mantel, S.J.J. (1990) The Causes of Project Failure. *IEEE Transactions on Engineering Management*, 37 (4): 269–76.

Pisano, G.P. (1996) Learning-before-doing in the Development of New Process Technology. *Research Policy*, 25 (7): 1097–119.

Polanyi, M. (1962) *Personal Knowledge: Towards a Post-Critical Philosophy*. Chicago. IL: Chicago University Press.

Porter, M.E. (1985) *Competitive Advantage: Creating and Sustaining Superior Performance*. New York: Free Press.

Randolph, W.A. and Posner, B.Z. (1988) What Every Manager Needs to Know about Project Management. *Sloan Management Review*, Summer: 65–73.

Reddy, N.M. and Zhao, L. (1990) International Technology Transfer: A Review. *Research Policy*, 18 (1): 1–18.

Rice, R.E. and Rogers, E.M. (1980) Reinvention in the Innovation Process. *Knowledge: Creation, Diffusion, Utilization*, 1 (4): 499–514.

Rogers, E. (1983) *The Diffusion of Innovation*, 3rd edn. New York: Free Press.

Ruggles, R. (1998) The State of the Notion: Knowledge Management in Practice. *California Management Review*, 40 (3): 80–9.

Rumelt, R. (1984) Toward a Strategic Theory of the Firm. In R. Lamb (ed.), *Competitive Strategic Management*. Englewood Cliffs: Prentice Hall, 556–70.

Schein, E.H. (1985) *Organizational Culture and Leadership: A Dynamic View*, 1st edn. San Francisco: Jossey-Bass.

Shannon, C.E. and Weaver, W. (1949) *The Mathematical Theory of Communication*. Chicago: Illinois: University of Illinois Press.

Stewart, T.A. (2001) Intellectual Capital: Ten Years Later, How Far We've Come. *Fortune*, 143, May 28, 192–3.

Szulanski, G. (2000) The Process of Knowledge Transfer: A Diachronic Analysis of Stickiness. *Organizational Behavior and Human Decision Processes*, 82: 9–27.

Szulanski, G. and Jensen, R. (forthcoming) Templates and Stickiness: An Empirical Investigation of the Use of Working Examples in the Replication of Organizational Routines. *Managerial and Decision Economics*, forthcoming.

Teece, D.J. (1976) *The Multinational Corporation and the Resource Cost of International Technology Transfer*, 1st edn. Cambridge, MA: Ballinger Publishing Company.

Teece, D. (1977) Technology Transfer by Multinational Corporations: The Resource Cost of Transferring Technological Know-How. *Economic Journal*, 87: 242–61.

Tsai, W. and Ghoshal, S. (1998) Social Capital and Value Creation: The Role of Intrafirm Networks. *Academy of Management Journal*, 41 (4): 464–76.

Tyre, M.J. and Orlikowski, W.J. (1994) Windows of Opportunity: Temporal Patterns of Technological Adaptation in Organization. *Organization Science*, 5 (1): 98–118.

von Hippel, E. (1994) "Sticky Information" and the Locus of Problem Solving: Implications for Innovation. *Management Science*, 40 (4): 429–39.

von Hippel, E. and Tyre, M.J. (1995) How Learning by Doing Is Done: Problem Identification in Novel Process Equipment. *Research Policy*, 24: 1–12.

Walton, R.E. (1975) The Diffusion of New Work Structures: Explaining why Success Didn't Take. *Organizational Dynamics* (Winter): 3–21.

Williamson, O.E. (1975) *Markets and Hierarchies: Analysis and Antitrust Implications*. New York: Free Press.

Winter, S.G. (1987a) Knowledge and Competence as Strategic Assets. In D. Teece (ed.), *The Competitive Challenge-Strategies for Industrial Innovation and Renewal*. Cambridge, MA: Ballinger, 159–84.

Winter, S.G. (1987b) Natural Selection and Evolution. In J. Eatwell, M. Milgate and P. Newman (eds.), *The New Palgrave: A Dictionary of Economics*, Vol. 3. New York: Stockton Press, 614–17.

Yin, R.K. (1979) *Changing Urban Bureaucracies: How New Practices become Routinized*. Lexington, MA: Lexington Books.

Zaheer, A., McEvily, B., and Perrone, V. (1998) Does Trust Matter? Exploring the Effects of Interorganizational and Interpersonal Trust on Performance. *Organization Science*, 9 (2): 141–59.

Zaltman, G., Duncan, R., and Holbek, J. (1973) *Innovations and Organizations*. New York: John Wiley and Sons.

Zeigarnik, B. (1967) On Finished and Unfinished Tasks. In W.D. Ellis (ed.), *A Source Book of Gestalt Psychology*. New York: Humanities Press.

Zucker, L.G. (1977) The Role of Institutionalization in Cultural Persistence. *American Sociological Review*, 42 (October): 726–43.

27

Social Identity and Organizational Learning

JOHN CHILD AND SUZANA RODRIGUES

CHAPTER OUTLINE

This chapter explores the relevance of social identity for organizational learning. It discusses how the identities that people internalize as members of social groups can impact on the organizational learning process, and how in turn that process can contribute to the evolution of an organization's identity. Nationality and occupation are important sources of social identity in organizations. The range of national and occupational identities found within organizations raises the question of how management can transcend social identity boundaries with the aim of generating collective learning. When this is achieved, its integrative effect can contribute to the development of an organizational identity and at the same time enhance the identification of sub-groups with the organization as an entity. The chapter closes by examining the significance for social identity and learning of the new organizational forms that are now emerging.

INTRODUCTION

This chapter is concerned with the relevance of social identity for organizational learning. It explores how the identities that people internalize as members of social groups can impact on the organizational learning process, and how in turn that process can contribute to the evolution of an organization's identity. Organizational learning is understood to be the acquisition, conversion, and creation of knowledge aimed at facilitating the attainment of organizational goals.

Writers on organization are increasingly coming to recognize links between identity and learning (Brown and Starkey, 2000). However, with some exceptions such as Rothman and Friedman (2001), identity and learning are often treated as organizational-level phenomena in ways that are ontologically problematic and oversimplify analysis of the subject. As Edmondson (1999a: 300) has noted, "an implicit assumption in many accounts of organizational learning is that organizations are undifferentiated entities, such that within-organization variance is immaterial." Given that organizational learning is a socially constructed process, surprisingly little attention has been paid to the relevance of how organizations are socially constituted in terms of different groups and their identities (Child and Heavens, 2001). Variations in the configuration of group identities, and in their compatibility with what the organization stands for (organizational identity), may well contribute to differences in organizational learning performance.

In order to clarify the links between social identity and organizational learning, this chapter explores the constituent elements of both concepts. It begins by examining social identity and its sources, among which nationality and occupation are particularly relevant to organizations. This leads to a discussion of how social identity bears upon the process of organizational learning. Case examples of diverse occupational and national social identities raise the question of how managerial initiatives can transcend identity boundaries with the aim of generating a collective learning process. Successful initiatives of this kind can at the same time contribute to the development of organizational identity and reinforce identification with the organization. The closing section considers the significance for social identity and learning of the new organizational forms that are now emerging.

SOCIAL IDENTITY

The concept

Some economists view an organization, specifically the firm, as a nexus of contracts among individuals (e.g., Jensen and Meckling, 1976). This usefully draws attention to the economic interests of organizational members, and to the fact that these interests may conflict both among themselves and with those of the employer. Nevertheless, it is an inadequate perspective because it adopts an atomistic view of an organization, ignoring how they are socially constituted. Organizations are in fact complex systems of inter-group relations and networks. Some groups are employed within the organizational core; others contribute to value-chains through outsourcing, sub-contracting and various forms of partnership within a wider organizational network. The behavior and performance of these groups is not just defined in economic terms, but is also subject to logics of action that arise from what groups stand for in the eyes of the people who belong to them.

A sense of belonging to a group is reinforced when it possesses characteristics which are compatible with a person's own individual identity (Strauss, 1959). Indeed, such characteristics may contribute to the forming of that identity. They simultaneously make for uniformity within that group and for distinctiveness from other groups. Groups differ from one another in terms of values, experiences, and behaviors. The dynamics of social relations and the subtleties embedded in inter-personal interactions can encourage and reinforce the sense of belonging to a group.

Individual identity is related to the way that people conceive of themselves. Psychologists generally associate identity with those stable and enduring cognitive, emotional, and behavioral characteristics that are part of a person's biography and career (Weigert et al., 1986; Dubar, 1992). Identity is primarily informational and selective in the sense that it takes from the environment those sources of information considered useful or functional to the individual's self-concept (Tajfel, 1982; Turner, 1987). This self-concept is sustained importantly by what people value as their capabilities, including the competencies and knowledge they possess.

Various types of sources can inform the self: the activities individuals develop, the roles they perform in different contexts, and the groups they interact with. In order to inform their identity, people draw meaning from sources to which they attach an emotional and particular value – "the significant others" – whether they be a person, a group or an espoused value system (Foote, 1951). The notion of social identity builds upon this foundation by postulating that, while identity is an essentially subjective phenomenon, it normally has highly significant social referents. In other words, an individual's definition of the self is based (at least in part) on the group or other social categories to which he or she perceives they belong (Tajfel, 1982). Social identity is mostly relational and environmental in the sense that self-perception changes through the interaction of individuals with other people and with their environments. Goffman's (1959) concept of the "performed self" suggests that an individual's identity can change in the course of social interaction. People interpret and enact their social identities in response to the situations in which they find themselves (Weick, 2001).

Students of organization have become increasingly aware of the relevance of identity for the expectations and behavior of organizational members. Albert et al. (2000: 13) comment that "identity and identification . . . are root constructs in organizational phenomena and have been a subtext of many organizational behaviors." The significance of social identity for organizational behavior in general, and for the process of organizational learning in particular, lies in the way that identification with a particular social group can be a referent for people to surface certain cognitive assumptions about themselves in relation to others. These assumptions, and the sense that people make of situations, influence the extent to which they are prepared to relate positively with those others including sharing their tacit or specialized knowledge. Social identity thus impinges on the "meaning-based learning" that Corley and Gioia discuss in chapter 31 of this volume. The enactment of social identity, and the potential barriers to collective learning that this introduces, is likely to take place primarily under certain conditions, especially those that are interpreted as posing a threat to the people concerned and/or when dependence on their membership group is perceived to be high (Weick, 1988; Salk and Shenkar, 2001). Moreover, as Corley and Gioia argue, the identity people attach to an organization can be quite fluid and subject to change as they reinterpret what it means to be "us" as an organization.

The main challenge to organizational managements stems from the likelihood that individuals may be more inclined to identify with particular groups than with the organization itself (Martin, 1992). Identities can develop around a functional role, professional membership, gender, nationality, or a particular hierarchical status in an organization (Weigert et al., 1986; Ashforth and Mael, 1989). Occupational and national identities are of particular significance. Professionals, technical people and other specialists may identify more with their occupational peer group or external reference groups than with their employing organizations. Functional specialists who work across the interface between the organization and the environment, like sales personnel or purchasing officers, tend to identify strongly with clients and partners (Alvesson, 2000). Similarly, it is quite possible that the members of ethnic or national groups working within a multinational corporation (MNC) or an international strategic alliance (ISA) will identify more closely with their fellow-nationals, even those outside the organization, than with groups of different origin (Royce, 1982). Since people can belong to more than one group, it is possible for them to have multiple social identities, just as the pluralistic nature of organizations means that they will contain multiple social identities (Pratt and Foreman, 2000).

Occupationally based identity

It is widely agreed that the strongest occupationally based identity is to be found among the members of the recognized professions. Many professionals work in units where they regulate or partially regulate their own work and careers – in private practice, professional firms or public service organizations. This applies to most doctors, lawyers, and scientists, as well as to some accountants and engineers. However, many engineers and scientists are also employed within managerially led organizations such as business firms, where they play a vital role in one of the most important fields of learning, namely product and process innovation. Other less professionally recognized functional specialists such as HRM, IT and marketing personnel are often heavily involved in organizational learning and change projects within firms.

Alvesson notes (2000: 1109) that people who see themselves primarily as professionals, albeit broadly defined, are likely to have weaker ties to an employing company and may as a result be more disloyal to that employer. Evidence suggests, however, that this does not necessarily mean that there will be a conflict between occupational and organizational commitments. Professionals who remain with non-professional organizations appear willing to accommodate their value orientations and professional self-perception to managerial expectations (Child, 1982). A significant factor here is whether non-professional organizations can satisfy the aspirations that professionals have for career advancement (Wallace, 1995).

Nationality based identity

Nationality and ethnicity are two other bases for social identity that play an important role in contemporary organizations. Considerable attention has been paid to the cultural features that map onto different nationalities and their implications for behavior within organizations (Hofstede, 1991; Trompenaars, 1993). Nationality and ethnic group membership are strong life-long social points of reference for personal identity, and it is this identity that motivates adherence to the cultural values and behaviors associated with them (Weigert et al., 1986; Bloom, 1990; Sarup, 1996). As organizations increase their global reach, either through organic expansion or through mergers, acquisitions, and alliances, so their need to find a basis for people of different cultures to work together increases correspondingly. Given the intensity of global competition and the rapid rate of environmental change, much of this cross-cultural work will be directed towards the goals of innovation and learning.

A particular aspect of globalization concerns the international transfer of knowledge. When MNCs acquire local companies, they usually intend to transfer knowledge in the form of standard practices which are embedded in their domestic cultural contexts or that have been successful elsewhere. These practices extend beyond purely technical matters to involve particular ways of relating to people, authority, space, and time. These are sensitive issues because they impinge upon factors associated with social identity in the local context. What multinational managers understand as "rational and objective practice" may be viewed by local staff as inappropriate or even illegitimate in their social and political context (Markóczy and Child, 1995). Hence the argument that a transfer of practices across national cultural boundaries requires their adaptation to local norms, or "recontextualiztion" (Brannen et al., 1997). For this reason, managerial practices in areas like quality control and personnel selection are not necessarily imported by subsidiaries without modification. When foreign practices depend on group behavior and performance, it may be necessary to de-construct and re-construct those practices in order to prevent social identity conflict.

Organizational identity

When corporate strategies affront meaningful values for identity, or go against already embedded values, role performance is subject to a struggle between a subjective and an objective identity (Berger et al., 1973). People can show how they reject these changes by cognitively distancing themselves and withdrawing commitment from these roles or from the organization (Burke, 1980; Weigert et al., 1986; Snow and Anderson, 1987). The multiple attachments that people have to roles, institutions, and situations inside and outside the place of work may vary in intensity and in the degree to which they overlap. This allows space for accommodation of identity; by negotiating their involvement, people may be committed to their work and/or to colleagues in different groups, without necessarily being committed to the organization.

Faced with a plurality of group identities, managements endeavor to develop organizational identities that offer a basis for enhancing identification with, and loyalty to, the organization and accord with their definition of its goals (Alvesson, 2000). A classic definition of organizational identity is what is central, distinctive, and enduring about an organization's character (Albert and Whetten, 1985). This definition, however, presents two problems in relation to the analysis of organizational learning. First, the assumption that organizational identity is enduring is inconsistent with the need for contemporary organizations to adapt to rapid and substantial external changes, some of which may require a fundamental redefinition of their strategic missions. In the extreme case, when adaptation is accomplished through merger and acquisition, an organization's previous identity may be destroyed. Adaptation places a premium on the capacity of organizations to learn, including learning to develop a new or modified organizational identity. Second, and most germane to the theme of this chapter, there is the danger that a unitary conception of organizational identity overlooks the other social memberships that provide identities for people within an organization and the implications these alternative identities have for the process of learning.

Corporate cultures are designed to enhance organizational identity, and identification with it, by creating a notion of a common enterprise, a sense of belonging and a shared understanding. Most knowledge-creation and organizational learning requires the members of different groups to collaborate and also to commit to the organizational goals that inform the investment in learning. The task of those who manage organizational learning is therefore to reconcile group social identities with a wider organizational identity. This can pose a significant challenge. The relations between groups in organizations often involve competition for power, status, and reward (Hogg and Abrams, 1988). Therefore they do not necessarily cooperate easily. Moreover, the collective identity and sense of common interest among group members are not necessarily aligned to a given employer or network partner. As we have noted, professional and national groups may identify more strongly with their peers outside the organization in which they are employed or to which they are contracted.

ORGANIZATIONAL LEARNING AND SOCIAL IDENTITY

A manufacturing or service value chain relies on the ability to combine and recombine the distinct competencies provided by different groups (Teece et al., 1997). These groups provide the knowledge and skills that enable organizations both to perform effectively in the present and to learn in preparation for the future. Thus scientific professionals contribute knowledge essential to innovation, and foreign partners can provide invaluable knowledge for operating in new territories. However, while the source of their value resides in the differentiated competencies held separately by groups, its realization for effective organizational learning requires a degree of reconciliation and integration between them. Here social identity can present obstacles.

The social identity of organizational groups is vested in the systems and bodies of knowledge that they perceive they own. Their members attribute symbolic value to that knowledge and regard themselves as having a right to arbitrate over this value. The implications for the management of organizational learning are very significant. First, the identity of the groups party to an organization will be attached to, and manifest in, their existing practices, thus legitimizing such practices as acceptable conventions. Changes to practice implicit in a policy of promoting organizational learning may therefore be perceived as a threat to social identity, with the result that the people concerned exhibit a reluctance to undertake the "unlearning" that is a precondition for learning to proceed.

A second implication is that those involved in organizational learning will define its legitimate premises, such as learning goals, valid information and appropriate schemes for classifying knowledge, in terms consistent with their social identities. While this diversity provides a richer palette of resources for learning, the distinct definitions and classifications are quite likely to be contested between the different groups involved. For example, Scarbrough's study of learning about the possibilities presented by IT for organizational redesign in six Scottish financial organizations led him to conclude that each of the interested specialist groups fought to promote "classificatory world-views in which their own expertise is central" (1996: 200). If this conflict is not resolved, the willingness, indeed ability, of different groups to contribute to organizational learning will be compromised.

There is always a potential conflict between the values and interests signified by occupational, national, and organizational identities. The first two provide a basis for people to preserve some autonomy *vis-à-vis* the organization (even though this autonomy may in reality be primarily psychological). By contrast, the creation of an organizational identity forms part of a managerial armoury not only to encourage knowledge generation but also to ensure conformity and control. The case of "WorldDrug," a US-owned pharmaceutical MNC studied by McKinlay (2001) illustrates how this conflict can impinge on the capacity to generate organizational learning. In the pharmaceutical sector, accelerating the process of drug development is critical for competitive advantage. Over a five-year period, WorldDrug had focused on leveraging employee knowledge of drug project processes, but with little success. Much of this failure was due to the resistance of knowledge workers to managerial monitoring and attempts to capture their tacit knowledge. This tacit knowledge about the high-level coordinative and improvisational skills essential to successful projects constituted the expertise that defined the knowledge workers' identity as experts. To surrender that essential tacit knowledge would turn a private asset into a corporate one and threaten the core of the workers' self-image and interest. McKinlay notes the knowledge workers' sense of rootlessness within the company as a factor that contributed to their reluctance to cooperate with management in transforming their knowledge into an organizational property.

Organizational learning therefore does not occur naturally. It requires the active management of different social identities and of the conflict these differences may entail. Managers cannot assume that an existing organizational identity provides an acceptable psychological contract for group members willingly to contribute their specialized knowledge and competencies to the learning process. People are likely to be comfortable in sharing their knowledge with others in the social group or category they identify with, and this sharing may be facilitated by the use of a common national or technical language. They are likely to be far less comfortable in sharing their knowledge with people outside that group. Groups can acquire an identity by developing a unique knowledge about ways of working successfully (Penrose, 1979), and be reluctant to give this away. Nevertheless, cross-group knowledge sharing is a requirement for an organization to convert fragmented knowledge into a useful generalized form. This means that the knowledge held by, or accessible to, individuals or groups has to be transformed into an organizational property, namely knowledge held in a form that makes it potentially accessible to the organization as a whole.

Overall, organizational learning includes three main processes. The first concerns the *acquisition* of knowledge from external sources. Here the fact that some members of an organization share a social identity with such sources can facilitate the inward transfer of information and knowledge. For example, scientists employed by a firm will share a degree of professional identity with their specialist counterparts working in universities or research institutes, and this will often ease their access to information from these sources. Similarly, one of the reasons for joining with local joint venture partners in a different country is the expectation that they will enjoy favorable social ties to sources of local market and political information. The second process is the *conversion* of knowledge from a tacit to an explicit form. Rendering tacit knowledge explicit amounts to capturing it for wider organizational use and reducing management's dependence on a limited number of people who hold that knowledge. Even some explicit specialist knowledge is effectively tacit for the rest of the organization, and requires conversion to a form that is more generally accessible. In this way, knowledge already resident within an organization can be better exploited. The third process requires a collective contribution of different social groups towards the *creation* of new knowledge deriving from synergy between their distinct competencies. The acquisition of knowledge is similar to the process of knowledge "grafting" discussed by Huber (1991). The distinction between knowledge conversion and knowledge creation is consistent with the one March (1991) has made between exploitation of existing knowledge and exploration of new knowledge.

Knowledge acquired from external sources will need to be converted into a form that is intelligible and useful to the organization; in other words, it needs to be made more explicit to other organizational members, especially management. Moreover, imported knowledge may only contribute usefully to the organization's purposes if it can be brought together creatively and synergistically with knowledge held by other specialist groups. Here we arrive at the paradox that specialist group identity, when it spans the boundaries of an organization, is functional for the acquisition of knowledge but is potentially dysfunctional for the conversion and creation of knowledge. The identity boundaries between different groups within organizations or organized networks can render these last two processes problematic. Group members may be reluctant to release their tacit knowledge to management or to cooperate with people in other groups.

Learning within an organization therefore requires the bridging of identity boundaries on a basis that is acceptable to the parties concerned. For a learning process based on intergroup synergies to be accomplished, it is crucial that an integrating frame of reference be found. This higher order perspective will presumably reflect organizational goals and, if accepted by participants in the learning process, should serve to strengthen organizational identity and identification. If informed by learning, it will also adjust organizational strategies and practices to better suit the present and anticipated conditions for the organization's success and survival. Successful organizational learning thus strengthens organizational *identity* in the sense of providing a character (strategy and practices) for the organization that is compatible with its present and anticipated conditions. By providing a more convincing identity, the learning process should also make it easier for people to commit to what the organization stands for and so increase their organizational *identification*. Moreover, the experience of participating in goal-directed learning should enhance people's willingness to commit to the fruits of their knowledge creation, thus providing another means of enhancing organizational identification.

The alignment of group identities with organizational identity will be inhibited in circumstances where radical change is introduced in a purely top-down manner. Radical change requires new learning, but a forcing of the change is liable to inhibit identification with the new organizational mission except among the group(s) that take the lead in introducing the change. Such change implies a considerable adjustment of inter-subjective meanings for many organizational members, and this may be strenuously resisted (Corley and Gioia, this volume). Thus when the top management of Telemig, a major Brazilian telecommunications company, tried to introduce a completely new corporate culture and set of practices from the top, it merely succeeded in generating a counterculture (Rodrigues, 1996). It was regarded as manipulative and failed to create an effective climate for organizational learning to support the desired change. In such circumstances, many employees shifted the basis of their attachment to the company to one of contract and economic necessity rather than identification.

The sensitivity of social identity for organizational learning is liable to vary depending on (1) the type of knowledge involved and (2) whether the organization in question is unitary in form as opposed to being an alliance or network. Three categories of knowledge can be distinguished, each of which is likely to be perceived differently by the parties concerned in terms of their social identities. The three categories are, respectively, technical knowledge, knowledge about the design of systems and procedures (systemic knowledge), and strategic understanding (Child and Rodrigues, 1996).

Technical knowledge can range from explicit and routine techniques such as statistical quality control and market forecasting to more complex and new technologies that evolve through a process of innovation. The process of acquiring and learning routine techniques may be confined to individuals or small specialist groups, whereas the development of new technologies will typically involve the contributions of several specialist groups. Systemic knowledge is embodied in systems for budgeting, compensation and production control, in the definition of organizational responsibilities and reporting relationships, and in communication and information systems. This area of knowledge and its application impacts on relationships, across much, if not the whole, of the organization. Since new systems normally require a change in organizational behavior and relationships, they are liable to create considerable sensitivity for social identity. Strategic understanding concerns the mindsets of senior managers, especially their criteria of business success and their mental maps of factors that are significant for achieving such success. The prospect of acquiring new strategic understanding can threaten the self-perceived competencies of senior managers. Their social identity as organizational leaders is associated with the policies they have espoused and any substantial change in these promoted by strategic learning is liable to undermine the legitimacy of their position. It can be interpreted as a threat to the very basis of their social identity as senior managers, since this identity is nurtured by the claim to a special set of strategic competencies that identify them as a group of superior standing and privilege. The matter is made more sensitive insofar as the information speaking for strategic change typically comes from other parties, namely experts within and outwith the organization.

For these reasons, within a unitary organization, social identity is likely to be more sensitive for systemic and strategic knowledge than it is for knowledge of a technical nature. Systemic and strategic knowledge, and its application, impinges on a range of groups within an organization. It is largely generated within the organization, though often with the help of consultants, and its development requires the willing cooperation of several different groups or units. Such knowledge, concerning as it does strategy and role definitions, comes closer to the core of an organization's identity than does knowledge of a more technical nature. Technical knowledge is often transferred into an organization and does not always have to be shared with other specialities. Several of its characteristics reduce the social sensitivity of acquiring technical knowledge. One is that it is often expressed in a widely accessible, explicit standardized form, some of it as international standards. Another is that technical knowledge is readily accepted as valid by trained specialists who avoid the "not-invented-here" syndrome by virtue of their relatively cosmopolitan identity. Problems, however, tend to arise when the generation of new technology or new applications of technical knowledge requires the collaboration of people from different specialties, for then the presence of different externally validated technical standards and languages can increase the problem of integration.

The case of an alliance or international organizational network can be more complex. If the alliance or network partners are content to transfer technical knowledge between themselves, the fact that the gatekeepers for such transfer usually share a similar occupational identity can serve as a bridge between the organizations. As such, the transfer of technical knowledge is not likely to be perceived as carrying strong corporate values or involving a kind of imperialism by one national partner over the other. On the contrary, problems are more likely to arise when one partner is attempting to control access to its proprietary technology (cf. Hamel, 1991). This can place technical staff in a situation of dual loyalty and it may rapidly destroy trust between the partners and their staff.

The transfer of systemic knowledge from one partner to another, or pressure from one partner for an alliance to innovate in this area may be perceived as more threatening to the recipient organization's identity. This is especially likely in international alliances or networks. The more that systems introduced from abroad are concerned with ways of organizing and managing people, the stronger the implications for social identity. In these areas, systems and procedures brought in from another country impinge on issues that are deeply embedded in people's consciousness of the appropriate social order: on matters such as acceptance of responsibility, authority and power distance, relationships, personal dignity, and social equity. It can also be difficult to prove the superiority of foreign practices. One partner may take their superiority for granted and legitimize them as a reflection of "global standards"; other partners may resent and resist this.

The case of strategic learning is different again. Alliances and networks are formed in order to benefit from asset complementarity, scale economies or enhanced market power. To make economic sense they have to achieve a sufficient degree of strategic fit, which does not, however, mean that their objectives are identical (Child and Faulkner, 1998). If the underlying relationship between partner organizations remains a competitive one, or they regard its links to the other partners as a short-term phenomenon, it is unlikely that they will be willing to encourage any significant strategic learning by those partners. Defense of their own strategic identity will remain a paramount factor. Even with alliances between developed and developing or transition country partners, in which the latter explicitly state strategic learning to be one of their alliance objectives, the fact that they will be obliged to accept a learning role implies an inferior right to strategic control over the alliance. They may perceive this inferiority as threatening both their ability to protect their interests and their identity as a partner.

IDENTITY MANAGEMENT IN THE ORGANIZATIONAL LEARNING PROCESS

The implication of the above discussion is that the effective management of organizational knowledge acquisition, conversion, and creation speaks for policies that are sensitive to social identities and that can reconcile them with new organizational needs. There appear to be two key requirements for such policies to work. The first is to establish constructive relationships between the various participating groups based on trust and the preservation of what Edmondson (1999b) calls "psychological safety" for the persons involved – in other words assuaging their fears of failure and personal harm. The second is a search for acceptable overarching goals that integrate the participants' efforts and provide a sense of direction for the learning process. These points may be illustrated by examples from organizational learning processes, involving groups with respectively diverse occupational and national identities.

The use of teams as organizational learning vehicles that constructively reconcile identity differences is apparent in the examples. Senge (1993) observes that "teams, not individuals, are the fundamental learning unit in modern organizations" (p. 10). Marshall (2001) sees project teams, comprising members from several contributing social groups, as exemplary of the tension between seeking a team identity (homogeneity) and preserving member differences (heterogeneity). Heterogeneity reflects the different yet complementary competencies and knowledge-sets required to feed a constructive learning process. Homogeneity is required to unify diverse individuals and groups around a shared goal-directed activity. The managerial challenge is to resolve this tension in a manner that is conducive to organizational learning.

Learning and occupational identities

De Haen et al. (2001) offer the example of pharmaceutical companies that had to learn how to implement new regulations on Good Laboratory Practice (GLP). The first individuals in a pharmaceutical company to become familiar with GLP regulations were typically people with responsibility for pre-clinical drug safety assessment and regulatory compliance. However, compliance with GLP regulations required the cooperation of people from different specialities. Research protocols had to be endorsed by several investigators such as a pharmacotoxologist, veterinarian, statistician, manager, and a representative of a quality assurance unit. This degree of collective compliance threatened the identity of specialists who had previously conceived of themselves as individual researchers, especially as activities falling under GLP regulations became formalized into hierarchical systems of standard operating procedures (SOPs). The change was uncomfortable for researchers, for whom it sometimes lacked a scientific rationale, and who had been trained to conduct experiments with a degree of operational flexibility that fosters chance discovery.

Companies learned to become creative in fostering their employees' compliance with GLP regulations in ways that were consistent with the social identities of such personnel. For example, they encouraged research staff to take an expert role in the writing of SOPs, and attached acceptable symbols and incentives to the change in ways that met the need for peer recognition. They also endeavored to motivate acceptance among researchers by encouraging peer pressure within teams. De Haen et al. (2001) comment that: "The learning unit was always a group . . . This focus on groups signifies at least implicit acknowledgement of a social component in organizational learning needed for the implementation of GLP regulations" (p. 915).

In ways such as these, managers in the pharmaceutical companies studied were able to effect a cultural change among scientific staff that built upon rather than violated their social identity. In fact, the application of GLP regulations eventually encouraged the emergence of new corporate-wide attitudes towards quality assurance based on the way they promote accountability and transparency in the acquisition and manipulation of laboratory data. The learning process led to staff eventually accepting the regulations as an embedded norm that became, at least in part, tacit in nature. In this respect it provided a bridge from group to organizational identity in a way that changed an important aspect of the latter.

Learning and national identities

Many international acquisitions, alliances, and collaborations are made with knowledge acquisition or synergistic learning as one of their objectives. In the case of international technology partnerships, knowledge creation is the primary objective. Yet many such arrangements fail and this is often attributed to difficulties in reconciling the partners' different national cultures and identities. The role that can be attributed to national identity is, however, often difficult to isolate because other sources of friction may be present which also stand in the way of creating the conditions for knowledge transfer, let alone mutual learning. For example, the learning intentions of international partners can be motivated by a desire to acquire the other's proprietary knowledge for competitive reasons, or in the case of an acquisition to subsequently close down the unit supplying the knowledge. Differences in the partners' abilities to learn from each other can rapidly undermine trust between them and engender a defensive attitude toward sharing knowledge (Hamel, 1991). Differences in the partners' organizational cultures and modes of working can also inhibit the evolution of effective learning relationships between them, due to factors other than nationality, such as substantial differences in their size (Doz, 1996).

Heavens and Child (1999) examined the experience of six international project teams created to achieve specific knowledge-generating objectives. The cases pointed to problems caused by differences in national identity, and how the management of learning teams could reduce the gap created by these differences in the process of developing a new shared identity. The role of personal trust emerged as a vital facilitating factor for this process to take place, especially in terms of key relationships between individual team members. Trust informed the dynamics of team-generated knowledge and its transformation into organizational learning. It also helped the team members to transcend the factors defining their separate social identities, and that otherwise threatened to jeopardize the collective learning process. As closer relationships developed between team members, they gradually became more comfortable in sharing their views and knowledge and they became more aware of a common learning goal.

These observations can be illustrated by one of the cases, a water company. The scenario for cross-national team learning in this case developed through a series of takeovers. These were prompted by a desire on the part of the British company to expand in a certain business area, with the initial acquisition of a Swedish firm in possession of the required technology. Subsequently, this latter firm bought out a smaller, Norwegian company, whose patents therefore went to the British water company as overall owner. It was the work with this smaller company on new waste water processes that was studied, one of a number of collaborative projects with the Scandinavians.

Issues of group identity impacted on the work of the project team, especially in the initial stages. The company's head of technology innovation, who had been with the British company for 20 years, noted that team work with the Swedes and Norwegians, based on technology developed by the latter, took a long time to evolve. His mission was to establish the ground rules and research program, but was hindered by the fact that the Norwegian company was reluctant to tell him anything. There were two main reasons for this: first, the company, being small and therefore vulnerable, feared being "emptied out," with their patents being taken and sold on; second, and more generally, the Norwegians have a dislike of the English on account of contentious issues relating to their occupational identity as water engineers such as acid rain, and pollution from UK coastal outlets. It was only through withholding knowledge and distorting channels of information that the Norwegian subsidiary felt it could preserve its worth, and therefore its identity and security. A lack of trust held the Norwegians back from contributing to learning by the wider organization. It is significant that the initial formal framework of procedures and programs, devised for mutual working and intended also to promote mutual confidence, was insufficient to facilitate the learning process.

Barriers to knowledge sharing were becoming apparent about one year into the project. The initial barriers, created by fear and mistrust on the part of the Norwegian subsidiary, were overcome primarily through the personal relationship developed by the new project manager with his counterpart in Scandinavia. This relationship opened up communication between the British and Norwegian groups and enabled them to recognize mutual benefits and objectives. A joint R&D program also served importantly to assuage the Norwegians' fears and to provide a bridge across the national divide based on a sharing of their common scientific identities. This illustrates the importance of perceived goal congruence, a reconciliation of social identities and a sense of psychological safety as conditions for team members to share knowledge and so generate organizational learning. The joint R&D program enabled findings from the project to be applied throughout the British and Scandinavian companies. Informants agreed that both operational processes, concerning the day-to-day running of waste-water treatment works, and process knowledge – the actual technological processes of waste-water treatment – were considerably enhanced through the teamwork that was developed. The R&D program was also a symbolic indication of the new organizational identity that was being forged within the international corporate group.

National identities can clearly create sensitivities for learning within international partnerships, networks and MNCs. National identity can manifest itself in ideas of national superiority both through categorizing other partners' attitudes as negative and through conceiving of learning as a one-way process. This is particularly common among the managers of MNCs, which are more likely to transfer practices within ISAs unilaterally than other firms. Child and Rodrigues (1996: 53) report examples of this unilateralism and conclude that the definition of one partner as superior may, at worst, "lead to a situation in which exchanges are unbalanced, information is concealed and people are excluded from opportunities to learn." Even if there is a strong intention by the partners to learn from the strengths of each other's practices, their staff may consider the other's practices to be inappropriate or even illegitimate.

Salk conducted three detailed case studies of multi-management teams in international joint ventures (IJVs) that throw further light on the role of social identity as a referent for inter-personal attitudes and behavior (Salk, 1996; Salk and Brannen, 2000; Salk and Shenkar, 2001). While not focused explicitly on team learning, Salk's studies elucidate the problems that social identity can create for attaining the shared meanings and behaviors necessary for teams to succeed in achieving integrated knowledge conversion and creation. She found that although the three teams ultimately developed differently, in their first weeks and months they each passed through a similar phase of development which she terms the "encounter phase." During this phase, distinct social identities, primarily based on the members' nationalities, coexisted and sometimes competed with one another over how the team would work and the IJV would function. Cultural stereotyping and the creation of in-groups and out-groups characterized all three teams; this resulted from an enactment of social identity. In one of the IJVs, the dominant enactment of nationality based identities within the teams persisted for several years. Salk argues that this persistence was partly explicable in terms of reinforcing factors such as a heavy resource dependence on its two parent companies, staffing the IJV's management through secondment from the parents, and the threat of market downturn. However, she also draws attention to the way that in this case the nationality based social identities, once established, became "a lens mediating the impact of contextual change on the enactments of the IJV setting and functioning by its members" (Salk and Shenkar, 2001: 173).

The research we have reviewed points to the importance of attending carefully to the encounter phase in new teams composed of people who have different social identities. People coming together to work on a project create a discursive community which on the one hand enables them to compare their different perspectives and knowledge but, on the other hand, can give them a sense of being isolated, non-communicating and even in conflict with others (Gherardi and Nicolini, 2001). Management's aim must be to encourage them to reach as quickly as possible an accommodation that constructively combines their different frames of meaning and behavioral assumptions. It is important for this reason to minimize personal concerns and threats that can induce team members to retreat into the psychological refuge of their separate social identities as an excuse for defensive stereotyping of other members and/or of management.

In the specific context of teams established to generate organizational learning, assurances may have to be offered that a sharing of tacit knowledge will not be to the detriment of personal careers and employment, efforts made to surface and then constructively overcome social stereotypes, and care taken to offer the team members a clear objective for their work which they can understand and accept. Mixed identity teams can offer a rich mix of expertise, experience, and perspective to the learning process, but for this potential to be realized conditions of trust must prevail both within the team and in its relationship to management. If such teams are intended to have a continuing and evolving life, encouragement must be given to evolving trust to a point where the dominant social identity becomes one shared by the participants themselves (Child, 2001).

New Organizational Forms, Identity and Learning

The globalization of markets and rapid advance of new technology is making competition increasingly knowledge-based in terms of the premium attached to innovation and to an early awareness of changing market conditions. Non-business organizations are not immune either from pressures for new and improved services and responsiveness to public demands. These conditions clearly favor organizations that are fast learners and able to change quickly (March, 1995). As a result, there has been a search for new forms of organization that reduce internal identity barriers in the interest of improving learning capabilities and adaptability.

The new thinking on organization encompasses a move away from rigid bureaucratic structures toward the adoption of flexible unconventional forms. The contemporary design paradigm is shifting away from the hierarchy, in which it is assumed that the most valuable knowledge is held by top managers, and toward a "distributed network of minds" (Gibson, 1997: 8). Authority, power, responsibility, and resources are decentralized to semi-autonomous teams or work groups consisting of knowledgeable, professional, or multi-skilled, staff (Barley, 1996). They can also include relevant "outsiders" such as suppliers and customers. These teams and work groups operate with a high degree of local initiative, though it is recognized that their knowledge-creating activities need to be goal directed and contribute to the wider organization (Hedlund, 1986; Wellins et al., 1994). Organizational teams are today formed around different axes of social identity such as professional and disciplinary groupings, as well as nationality, ethnicity, gender, and hierarchical position. Cheney's (1991) observation, that in post-industrial societies organizational rhetoric is about the management of multiple identities, is very pertinent to these developments.

Many large organizations are also being deconstructed into systems of smaller components. This is expressed by the concept of the organizational network, which is regarded as a significant transformation away from "vertical bureaucracies" and into "horizontal corporations" (Castells, 1996). There is wide agreement about the virtue of small units in order to avoid the rigidity, lack of focus and anonymity of large-scale organization. It is recommended that the activities retained within any one organization be reduced to a minimal core, and other responsibilities outsourced or sub-contracted. It is similarly argued that small units can more readily become "self-organizing" than can larger units, and hence pursue their own learning initiatives when the need arises (Handy, 1992; Senge, 1997).

There is, however, a negative side to the adoption of new organization forms. The downgrading of hierarchy involves delayering and a hollowing out of middle management. The shift towards smaller units, combined with competitive pressures, has led to widespread downsizing and layoff. The push towards greater flexibility has shifted the focus of the employment relationship from career to contract, undermined employment security, and thrown the onus of ensuring a long-term income stream onto the shoulders of the individual. The distinction between core and non-core activities has also increased the differentiation between primary and secondary status employment.

This detachment of people from a long-term association with organizations creates insecurity and anxiety for many. It may weaken the sources of work-related social identity. Albert et al. (2000: 13–14) comment that,

> given the massive corporate downsizings of recent years, the decrease in long-term relational contracts in favor of shorter-term transactional ones, and the growth in boundaryless careers . . . the notion of identification with and loyalty to one's employer, workgroup, or occupation may seem quite quaint, even naive.

Insofar as identification with organizations is a condition for people to contribute to learning within them, this would be ironic because learning is one of the key processes that new organizational forms are intended to promote.

It certainly appears that some of the former supports for occupational identity are disappearing as new organizational forms are adopted. Previously, many specialists could rely on occupational credentialism (Collins, 1979) to provide an assured income stream and career progression within traditional functionally structured organizations. Today, many more people with specialized competencies have to rely on contract work secured on the basis of their standing in the labor market. The rise of a new educated managerial elite, and of new non-traditional specialties such as brand developers, software designers, and financial analysts, has added to the ranks of knowledge workers and further blurred the traditional lines of occupational identity. Some knowledge workers are typically located within the core of an organizational system, such as senior managers and key technical personnel. Others are today more usually hired on contract in a consulting capacity, and this can even apply to groups who used to occupy core roles such as HRM specialists and maintenance engineers. These developments move the source of specialist identity away from the organized profession, skilled trade union, or other occupational association and towards the self-standing individual or specialized firms through which people offer their services in the market. The shift away from a credentialist occupational identity may assist organizational learning by increasing the willingness of specialists to work flexibly with others in learning-directed inter-disciplinary teams and work units. On the other hand, the forced removal of people from core to periphery, or the fear that they may be the next to go, is not likely to motivate them to contribute enthusiastically to the organizational learning process. Marketization is likely to limit their loyalty to a given organization and may qualify the extent to which they are willing to disclose their proprietary knowledge and skills.

By contrast, national identity appears to have been enhanced rather than weakened by the impact of globalization, and the modern information and communication technologies that facilitate it. Paradoxically, at the same time as national transactional boundaries weaken, there is an increased awareness of cultural differences and a growing celebration of cultural diversity (Robertson, 1995). New technology dramatically improves communication between the members of cultural groups and provides opportunities for their self-expression. It also appears that people's awareness of their own culture and identity is promoted by the provision of more information about other societies or communities, which enables comparisons that clarify cultural distinctiveness. This enhanced awareness of national identity may add to the difficulties of achieving learning that relies upon integration between different national groups.

It thus appears that the nature and configuration of national and occupational identities are changing in the contemporary world. Much of this change is associated with the evolution of new organizational forms. They are presenting new challenges for aligning group social identities with the goal of organizational learning. Indeed, the greatest impact on organizational learning may actually come through the way that new forms reduce the identification people have with any one organization and the commitment they are willing to give to it. This puts people into a situation where they may have to devote considerable effort to re-establishing their identities through learning new inter-subjective meanings (Corley and Gioia, this volume). Many organizations are outsourcing activities and hollowing themselves out. This places a premium on the ability of the remaining core groups to achieve a requisite level and quality of learning through harnessing contributions from others that have become externalized. The issue becomes particularly acute with "virtual organization."

According to Mowshowitz (1994: 270),

> the essence of the virtual organization is the management of goal-oriented activity in a way that is independent of the means for its realization. This implies a logical separation between the conception and planning of an activity, on the one hand, and its implementation on the other.

This concept could readily deny any sense of identification with the collective activity to people in the system other than those in the leading core group. It is partly for this reason that many corporations have been devoting considerable effort to enhancing their public identities, in the form of corporate images and brand names. For, in addition to the market appeal of strong images and brands, it is essential for the leaders of virtual organizations to create some basis of identification with, and understanding of, their goals if they are to generate the will and purpose to compete with more integrated companies. More specifically, there is a danger that the further an organization moves towards a virtual form, with arms-length relationships based on contract rather than personal relationship, the less readily can it communicate the tacit knowledge that is essential for successful collective learning.

Experience to date suggests that the challenge of achieving learning through organized networks need not be insuperable. In some sectors such as bio-technology, the relevant knowledge for new product development is in any case scattered between research institutes, universities and bio-tech firms, while the cooperation of venture capital firms is required for financing and that of hospitals or firms specializing in clinical trials is necessary for product development and testing. It is proving possible to coordinate networks of these separate organizations into effective learning systems (Powell et al., 1996). Much depends on developing the managerial skills to handle the process so that people do not feel obliged to enact their social identities defensively.

CONCLUSION

This chapter has explored one of the lacunae in the field of organizational learning, namely how the process of such learning is conditioned by the social identities that people internalize as members of groups within organizations. A monolithic focus on organizational identity at the cost of overlooking that of constituent groups is seen to be theoretically inadequate and practically misleading. Many organizations today contain a wide range of groups with their own social identities, often based on occupation and nationality. These social identities are sustained importantly by what people value as the special capabilities of the groups or communities to which they belong. The knowledge they possess is intrinsic to these capabilities. They are therefore concerned to protect this personal asset and may be cautious about sharing it either with the members of other organizational groups or with management.

Their constituent groups contain potentially valuable learning resources for organizations. The translation of that potential into reality, however, requires certain attributes of managers. They have to be sensitive to the social identities of the relevant groups, establish constructive relationships between the parties to the learning process, and reconcile their perspectives with the organizational needs to which learning is directed. Evidence from case studies indicates that these requirements can be satisfied principally through two policies. The first is to create "psychological safety" for the participating groups as the basis for their willingness to contribute to learning. The second is to search for acceptable overarching goals that integrate the participants' efforts and provide a sense of direction for the learning process. Acceptance of organizational goals should also furnish an effective basis for promoting organizational identity, both in the sense of what an organization stands for and the willingness of its members to identify with that organization.

This chapter has also offered a number of analytical refinements that help to identify issues for further research. First, it indicated that social identity may impinge on organizational learning differently according to whether the latter involves acquiring knowledge from external sources or processes primarily internal to the organization, such as making tacit knowledge explicit and creating new knowledge. Second, it argued that the sensitivity of social identity for organizational learning depends on the type of knowledge involved. It postulated that the sensitivity of social identity for systemic and strategic knowledge is normally greater than it is for knowledge of a technical nature. Third, it recognized the additional complications introduced by hybrid organizations such as alliances or networks, which encompass a myriad of identities and interests, especially when they are international. Fourth, and most far-reaching of all, the chapter has signaled the many unknowns brought into the picture by the emergence and evolution of new organizational forms.

The emergence of new organizational forms, which attenuate the attachment that many people have to their employer, presents both opportunities and challenges to organizational learning. One of the prime justifications for the new forms lies in their claim to promote the capacity to innovate and adapt on the basis of a superior learning capability. It is claimed that opportunities for learning are promoted by the decentralization of initiative, the deconstruction of lethargic bureaucracies into smaller units, and a recourse to the market or external networks for accessing specialized knowledge. The challenge stems from the apparent consequences of these developments, particularly the ways in which the weakening of social ties to organizations and growing insecurity of employment jeopardize people's identification with their employer or even their occupation. The implications of new forms for organizational learning are a particularly urgent and little understood issue for practitioners, and they present a very large agenda for further research.

It is clear that the ways in which social identity and organizational learning interact are complex. They have to be examined at different levels: individual, group, organization, and network. The relationship cannot be regarded as simply one whereby social identity impacts on organizational learning. The process of learning, and achievement, can itself be a source of identity for people and the groups to which they belong (Corley and Gioia, this volume). When guided by clear goals, under non-threatening conditions, learning activities may serve to align the identities of groups with that of the organization as a whole. If, however, this alignment is not achieved, people are likely to adhere to their more immediate and longstanding social identities and may as a result choose to retain their knowledge rather than share it with the organization. We have suggested that this issue is becoming particularly acute in the changing circumstances of the contemporary organizational world.

REFERENCES

Albert, S. and Whetten, D. (1985) Organizational Identity. In L.L. Cummings and B.M. Staw (eds.), *Research in Organizational Behavior*, vol. 7. Greenwich, CT: JAI Press, 263–95.

Albert, S., Ashforth, B.E., and Dutton, J.E. (2000) Organizational Identity and Identification: Charting New Waters and Building New Bridges. *Academy of Management Review*, 25: 13–17.

Alvesson, M. (2000) Social Identity and the Problem of Loyalty in Knowledge-intensive Companies. *Journal of Management Studies*, 32: 1101–23.

Ashforth, B.E. and Mael, F. (1989) Social Identity Theory and the Organization. *Academy of Management Review*, 14: 20–39.

Barley, S.R. (1996) Technicians in the Workplace: Ethnographic Evidence for Bringing Work into Organization Studies. *Administrative Science Quarterly*, 41 (3): 404–41.

Berger, P.L., Berger, B., and Kellner, H. (1973) *The Homeless Mind: Modernization and Consciousness*. Harmondsworth: Penguin.

Bloom, W. (1990) *Personal Identity, National Identity and International Relations*. Cambridge: Cambridge University Press.

Brannen, M.Y., Liker, J.K., and Fruin, M. (1997) Recontextualization and Factory-to-factory Transfer from Japan to the US: The Case of NSK. Paper presented to the 1997 Annual Meeting of the Academy of International Business, Monterrey, Mexico, October 8–12.

Brown, A. and Starkey, K. (2000) Organizational Identity and Learning: A Psychodynamic Perspective. *Academy of Management Review*, 25: 102–20.

Burke, P. (1980) The Self: Measurement Requirements for an Interactionist Perspective. *Social Psychological Quarterly*, 43: 18–29.

Castells, M. (1996) *The Rise of the Network Society*. Cambridge, MA: Blackwell.

Cheney, G. (1991) *Rhetoric in an Organizational Society: Managing Multiple Identities*. Columbia, SC: University of South Carolina Press.

Child, J. (1982) Professionals in the Corporate World: Values, Interest and Control. In D. Dunkerley and G. Salaman (eds.). *The International Yearbook of Organization Studies 1981*. London: Routledge and Kegan Paul: 212–41.

Child, J. (2001) Trust – the Fundamental Bond in Global Collaboration. *Organizational Dynamics*, 29: 274–88.

Child, J. and Faulkner, D. (1998) *Strategies of Co-operation: Managing Alliances, Networks and Joint Ventures.* Oxford: Oxford University Press.

Child, J. and Heavens, S. (2001) The Social Constitution of Organizations and its Implications for Organizational Learning. In M. Dierkes, A.B. Antal, J. Child, and I. Nonaka (eds.), *Handbook of Organizational Learning and Knowledge.* Oxford: Oxford University Press, 308–26.

Child, J. and Rodrigues, S. (1996) The Role of Social Identity in the International Transfer of Knowledge through Joint Ventures. In S.R. Clegg and G. Palmer (eds.), *The Politics of Management Knowledge.* London: Sage, 46–68.

Collins, O. (1979) *The Credential Society: An Historical Sociology of Education and Stratification.* New York: Academic Press.

De Haen, C., Tsui-Auch, L.S., and Alexis, M. (2001) Multimodal Organizational Learning: From Misbehavior to Good Laboratory Practice in the Pharmaceutical Industry. In M. Dierkes, A.B. Antal, J. Child, and I. Nonaka (eds.), *Handbook of Organizational Learning and Knowledge.* Oxford: Oxford University Press, 902–18.

Doz, Y.L. (1996) The Evolution of Cooperation in Strategic Alliances: Initial Conditions or Learning Processes? *Strategic Management Journal,* 17: 55–83.

Dubar, C. (1992) Formes indentitaires et socialisation professionelle. *Revue Francaise de Sociologie,* XXXIII: 505–29.

Edmondson, A.C. (1999a) The View through a Different Lens: Investigating Organizational Learning at the Group Level of Analysis. In M. Easterby-Smith, L. Araujo, and J. Burgoyne (eds.), *Organizational Learning: 3rd International Conference.* Lancaster University, June, 6–8: 299–323.

Edmondson, A.C. (1999b) Psychological Safety and Learning Behavior in Work Teams. *Administrative Science Quarterly,* 44: 350–83.

Foote, N.N. (1951) Identification as a Basis for a Theory of Motivation. *American Sociological Review,* 16: 14–21.

Gherardi, D. and Nicolini, D. (2001) Learning in a Constellation of Interconnected Practices: Canon or Dissonance? *Journal of Management Studies,* 39: 419–37.

Gibson, R. (ed.) (1997) *Rethinking the Future.* London: Nicholas Brealey.

Goffman, E. (1959) *The Presentation of Self in Everyday Life.* London: Allen Lane.

Hamel, G. (1991) Competition for Competence and Inter-partner Learning within International Strategic Alliances. *Strategic Management Journal,* 12: 83–103.

Handy, C. (1992) Balancing Corporate Power: A New Federalist Paper. *Harvard Business Review,* November-December: 59–72.

Heavens, S. and Child, J. (1999) Mediating Individual and Organizational Learning: The Role of Teams and Trust. In M. Easterby-Smith, L. Araujo, and J. Burgoyne (eds.), *Organizational Learning: 3rd International Conference.* Lancaster University, June 6–8: 496–532.

Hedlund, G. (1986) The Hypermodern MNC – A Heterarchy? *Human Resource Management,* 25 (1): 9–35.

Hofstede, G. (1991) *Cultures and Organizations: Software of the Mind.* Maidenhead: McGraw-Hill.

Hogg, M.A. and Abrams, D. (1988) *Social Identifications: A Social Psychology of Intergroup Relations and Group Processes.* New York: Plenum.

Huber, G.P. (1991) Organizational Learning: The Contributory Processes and the Literatures. *Organization Science,* 2: 88–115.

Jensen, M.C. and Meckling, W.H. (1976) The Theory of the Firm: Managerial Behavior, Agency Costs, and Ownership Structure. *Journal of Financial Economics,* 3: 305–60.

McKinlay, A. (2001) The Limits of Knowledge Management. Paper presented to the 17th EGOS Colloquium, Lyon, July.

March, J.G. (1991) Exploration and Exploitation in Organizational Learning. *Organization Science,* 2: 71–87.

March, J.G. (1995) The Future, Disposable Organizations and the Rigidities of Imagination. *Organization*, 2: 427–40.

Markóczy, L. and Child, J. (1995) International Mixed Management Organizations and Economic Liberalization in Hungary: From State Bureaucracy to New Paternalism. In H. Thomas, D. O'Neal, and J. Kelly (eds.), *Strategic Renaissance and Business Transformation*. Chichester: Wiley: 57–79.

Marshall, N. (2001) Knowledge, Identity and Difference in Project Organizations. Paper presented to the 17th EGOS Colloquium, Lyon, July.

Martin, J. (1992) *Cultures in Organizations: Three Perspectives*. New York: Oxford University Press.

Mowshowitz, A. (1994) Virtual Organization: A Vision of Management in the Information Age. *The Information Society*, 10: 267–94.

Nonaka, I. and Takeuchi, H. (1995) *The Knowledge-Creating Company: How Japanese Companies Create the Dynamics of Innovation*. New York: Oxford University Press.

Penrose, E.T. (1979) *The Theory of the Growth of the Firm*. Oxford: Blackwell.

Powell, W.W., Koput, K.W., and Smith-Doerr, L. (1996) Interorganizational Collaboration and the Locus of Innovation: Networks of Learning in Biotechnology. *Administrative Science Quarterly*, 41: 116–45.

Pratt, M.G. and Foreman, P.O. (2000) Classifying Managerial Responses to Multiple Organizational Identities. *Academy of Management Review*, 25: 18–42.

Robertson, R. (1995) Glocalization: Time-space and Homogeneity-heterogeneity. In M. Featherstone, S. Lash, and R. Robertson (eds.), *Global Modernities*. London: Sage, 25–44.

Rodrigues, S.B. (1996) Corporate Culture and De-institutionalization: Implications for Identity in a Brazilian Telecommunications Company. In G. Palmer and S.R. Clegg (eds.), *Constituting Management, Markets, Meanings and Identities*. Berlin: De Gruyter, 115–33.

Rothman, J. and Friedman, V.J. (2001) Identity, Conflict and Organizational Learning. In M. Dierkes, A.B. Antal, J. Child, and I. Nonaka (eds.). *Handbook of Organizational Learning and Knowledge*. Oxford: Oxford University Press, 582–97.

Royce, A.P. (1982) *Ethnic Identity: Strategies of Diversity*. Bloomington, IN: Indiana University Press.

Salk, J.E. (1996) Partners and Other Strangers: Cultural Boundaries and Cross-cultural Encounters in International Joint Venture Teams. *International Studies of Management and Organization*, 26: 48–72.

Salk, J.E. and Brannen, M.Y. (2000) National Culture, Networks, and Individual Influence in a Multinational Management Team. *Academy of Management Journal*, 43: 191–202.

Salk, J.E. and Shenkar, O. (2001) Social Identities in an International Joint Venture: An Exploratory Case Study. *Organization Science*, 12: 161–78.

Sarup, M. (1996) *Identity, Culture and the Postmodern World*. Edinburgh: Edinburgh University Press.

Scarbrough, H. (1996) Strategic Change in Financial Services: The Social Construction of Strategic IS. In W.J. Orlikowski, G. Walsham, M.R. Jones, and J.I. DeGross (eds.), *Information Technology and Changes in Organizational Work*. London: Chapman & Hall, 197–212.

Senge, P.M. (1993) *The Fifth Discipline*. London: Century.

Senge, P.M. (1997) Through the Eye of the Needle. In R. Gibson (ed.), *Rethinking the Future*. London: Nicholas Brealey, 123–45.

Snow, A. and Anderson, L. (1987) Identity Work among the Homeless: The Verbal Construction and Avowal of Personal Identities. *American Journal of Sociology*, 92: 1336–71.

Strauss, A. (1959) *Mirrors and Masks: The Search for Identity*. Glencoe, IL: Free Press.

Tajfel, H. (1982) *Social Identity and Intergroup Relations*. Cambridge: Cambridge University Press.

Teece, D.J., Pisano, G., and Shuen, A. (1997) Dynamic Capabilities and Strategic Management. *Strategic Management Journal*, 18: 509–33.

Trompenaars, F. (1993) *Riding the Waves of Culture: Understanding Cultural Diversity*. London: The Economist Books.

Turner, J.C., with Hogg, M.A., Oakes, P.J., Reicher, S.D., and Wetherell, M.S. (1987) *Rediscovering the Social Group. A Self Categorization Theory*. Oxford: Blackwell.

Wallace, J.E. (1995) Organizational and Professional Commitment in Professional and Nonprofessional Organizations. *Administrative Science Quarterly*, 40: 228–55.

Weick, K.E. (1988) Enacted Sensemaking in Crisis Situations. *Journal of Management Studies*, 25: 305–17.

Weick, K.E. (2001) *Making Sense of the Organization*. Oxford: Blackwell.

Weigert, A.J., Teitge, J.S., and Teitge, D.W. (1986) *Society and Identity*. Cambridge: Cambridge University Press.

Wellins, R.S., Byham, W.C., and Dixon, G.R. (1994) *Inside Teams: How 20 World-Class Organizations Are Winning Through Teamwork*. San Francisco: Jossey-Bass.

28

Emotionalizing Organizational Learning

Stephen Fineman

Chapter Outline

The explosion of interest in organizational learning has failed to engage with another, highly relevant, development – emotion in organizations. This chapter brings together insights from both fields. Emotion, it is argued, is at the core of learning, as well as its product. Learning one's place in an organization, where one fits in the political and moral order, what is trustworthy, is substantively emotional. An emotion perspective raises key questions about dominant cognitive perspectives on learning, and the way organizational learning is foiled or favored by emotion. Emotion work and emotional labor shape profoundly the intense, micro performances, of work-life, sometimes under strict learning-controls. New management fashions, such as emotional intelligence, raise conceptual and moral questions about the emotional inculcation. And new organization forms, such as virtual organizations, contain hitherto unexplored emotional ramifications on the way we learn to construct our work identities.

Introduction

What would organizational learning look like if it was emotionalized?

Common experience would suggest that learning for both individuals and organizations (if "organizations" can learn) is emotional – driven, shaped and expressed through feeling and emotion. Accounts of fear, joy, excitement, ambivalence, gloom, tedium, apprehension, joy, shame, and pride are not hard to locate as people face new skills and tasks, respond to re-formed organizational cultures, adjust to crises, learn to adapt to new role demands, or simply "learn the ropes" as novices in a new job:

> One day we had tremendous problems finishing off the computing of the dollar position. Eventually I found the error and it was embarrassing to learn that it was my fault.

Shamefully I went to see my manager to explain why the process has been delayed and that I was the one to blame. "Listen", he started, "You haven't made a mistake, but the system has! Whenever something is wrong you must come and tell me that the accounts system has screwed up. The system will lose prestige and value, whereas you have gained recognition because you spotted the error. You see, this company likes winners." (Fineman and Gabriel, 1996: 116)

The implicit and explicit emotions of this "learning" incident would not be easy to place in the burgeoning literature on organizational learning which offers, in the main, an emotionally sanitized picture. While there is talk of "social" and "political" models of learning, emotion is relegated to the margins of concern, or is simply not mentioned. This is all the more remarkable given the recent growth of emotion in organizational studies, a field that embraces the very contexts where learning supposedly take place (Ashkenasy et al., 2000; Fineman, 2000c [1993]).

My purpose in this chapter is to bring together some of the insights on organizational learning with those on emotion in organizations. Core to my argument is that, despite the plethora of theoretical directions that inform organizational learning, most are substantively under-theorized because of their lack of attention to emotion. Specifically, the chapter will explore organizational learning and emotion as it bears upon controversies about cognition and rationality; socio-political perspectives on organization; the emotional labor process; organizational learning-zones; trust; emotional intelligence; and virtual organizations. The conclusion maps out some directions for future research.

WHERE DOES EMOTION BELONG IN THE LEARNING PROCESS?

Learning has been characterized in various ways – as a predominately cognitive process, as socially/culturally defined, and as politically formed (e.g., Easterby-Smith and Araujo, 1999). What people/organizations learn – explicitly or tacitly – can be conceptual skills and abilities; knowledge as encoded in books, manuals and computers; shared meanings and understandings; or knowledge through "doing" or "practice" (see Blackler et al., 1998).

Generally, emotion is hard to spot in these perspectives. The predominant emphasis on thinking skills and cognition is rooted in early psychological work on schemata, or representations "in the head" by Bartlett (1933). Bartlett's conceptual heirs in the management field speak of cognitive maps, mental models, paradigms and recipes for learning (e.g., Eden, 1988; Eden and Huxham, 2001). Learning and change is achieved through reframing and negotiating units of thought or perception, information processing, interpretation and memory (Huber, 1991). This orientation is evident in some of the most celebrated models of organizational learning, such as Argyris' (1977) "looped" learning cycles, adapted for "reflective practitioners" (Argyris, 1985; Argyris and Schön, 1978) where the effectiveness of the procedure depends on the potency and feedback of clear perceptions, uncluttered by "defensive" routines and feelings of threat. Karl Weick's "sensemaking" ideas are similarly cognitively based, but markedly more elaborate (Weick, 1995). He is concerned with interpretation and plausibility rather than the accuracy of meaning. His formulation hints at emotion in the "commitments" that are made with self and others, and, more explicitly, in the "positive" and "negative" emotions induced by interruptions in the sensemaking flow.

The above approaches raise questions about whether we can meaningfully speak of learning as "pure," cognition-free, or made free, of emotional form or nuance. In other words, are we able, aided or unaided, to "coolly" think our way through to new thoughts and ideas? The view that we indeed can, is strongly represented in rationalistic models of decision making and in formal educational practices where students are arranged to passively receive pre-packaged knowledge-as-facts. Such pedagogy is evident across all educational sectors as well as in the briefing-group style of instruction used in corporate settings. Indeed, curiously, few education writers have taken up the emotion-learning issue. Their dominant concern is with the finer details of cognitive psychology, separate from the social, physical and affective domains of learning (see Bendelow and Mayall, 2000; Ingleton, 1995).

Yet, those who have explored the possibility of emotion-learning nexus are firm in their view that emotion and learning *do* interconnect – sometimes positively, sometimes negatively, sometimes interactively. For example, Vail (1994) refers to emotion as the "on/off" switch to learning among children, where the child carries and reflects the different emotional agendas of their parents and teachers. Psychoanalytic educational writers speak of the emotions that interfere with effective learning among adults and children, especially emotional conflicts, anxiety, pain, fear, jealously, and envy (More, 1974; Salzberger-Wittenberg et al., 1983). In the tertiary sector of education, Ingleton (1995) uses "memory work" to elicit semi-structured recollections of the emotions of significant educational experiences. She found that the learnings of academically successful women were deeply embedded in their desire to avoid shame and to be positively affirmed. Ingleton highlights the socially constructed, gender-specificity, of learning and emotion, and concludes that "the split between the affective and cognitive aspects of a person's experience misses the significantly cognitive component of emotion and the affective component of cognition" (1995: 333). Snell's analysis of managers' experiences of their own learning suggests the intrinsic emotionality of the process, especially where learning is associated with pain, shock embarrassment, pleasure or novelty (Snell, 1988, 1992). Snell argues for ways of "thinking strategically" about the emotional experiences of learning in order to reduce pain and discomfort, and to amplify feelings of achievement and pleasure.

Restorative rationality?

These studies obviously sit uneasily with a view of learning that is exclusively cognitive. But do we take a position of restorative rationality, that learning can be made more effective by dealing with, managing, even removing, interfering emotions? Or are we better to conceptualize the inevitable entwinement of thinking and feeling in the learning process?

Such questions have exercised scholars of philosophy and psychology (e.g. see Elster, 1999; Fineman, 1996, 2000b; Johnson-Laird and Oatley, 2000). For example, the deleterious effects of blind commitment and passion to a course of action have frequently been

noted – "irrationalities" such as dogged adherence to hopeless battle plans; greedy acquisition of businesses, regardless of consequences; acts driven by hubris or revenge (Brody
and Lowe, 1995; Staw and Ross, 1987). In the eyes of many cognitive researchers these
are emotional responses that should be channeled and tamed to restore rationality to its
rightful, supreme, place (Cacioppo and Gardner, 1999). Most organizational psycho-
analysts are similarly minded, but wish to expose the "deeper" emotional roots of learning irregularities (e.g. Diamond, 1993; Gabriel, 1999; Kets de Vries, 1991). Brown and
Starkey (2000: 103) explain:

> Current accounts of the reasons why organizations fail to learn are incomplete because
> although they recognize cognitive limitations . . . as barriers to learning, they ignore the role
> of psychodynamic factors in individual and organizational identity maintenance and the neg-
> ative effects such factors can have on learning.

These authors proceed to outline how ego-defense mechanisms are mobilized to avoid
the "psychic pain" of challenges to individual and organizational identity. Dealing with
the fundamental anxiety that ego defenses defend against is the route to more "profound"
organizational learning, but it is a state that is "no easy task" to achieve. This notion of
"restricted" or "distorted" organizational learning is also developed by Vince (2001). He
argues that there are individual and collective emotions, especially anxiety-related, that
define the political tenor of organizations and their learning potential. Vince's case studies
reveal managers facing organizational change, anxious about failure and suppressing their
envy and mistrust. He is, however, unclear about how best to increase the transparency
of the politicized, conflicting, emotions that purportedly interfere with organizational
learning.

Restorative rationality has its appeal, especially in a Western culture that has long
privileged rationality and (male) reason. But there is a powerful counter-view in the
entwinement perspective. In essence, this proposes that, at the very least, thinking, knowing
and learning are steered and shaped through feelings. Feelings "tell" us what is worth learning, what should be ignored, how to evaluate alternatives, how to resolve tie-breaks. They
are an essential complement to "rational" processes (Blackler et al., 1998; Damasio, 1994;
Damasio, 2000; de Sousa, 1987; Frijda et al., 2000; Mumby and Putnam, 1992). It is a
view that Forgas (2000: 403) speaks of as "the fascinating phenomenon [of] the infusion
of affect into cognition," a process that lies at the heart of many professional applications
of psychology. Elsewhere, I have expressed the position as follows:

> Rationality is no longer the "master" process; nor is emotion. They both interpenetrate; they
> flow together in the same mould. From this perspective there is no such thing as a pure cog-
> nition; thinking is always brushed with emotion, however slight. This may be at the level of
> mood (gloom, excitement, tedium, anxiety) as we consider what to do, or what next. It can
> also be in terms of a myriad, micro, thinking/feeling adjustments as we scan alternatives, con-
> template possible outcomes, review interpretations, get stuck, get distracted . . . We may be
> dimly aware of these processes, or they may be unconscious. Moreover, we have different
> layers of thought and feeling, meta (or meta meta) processes where we contemplate, even
> interrogate, our (and others') feelings; have feelings about our feelings as well as feelings about
> our thoughts and ideas. (Fineman. 2000b: 11–12)

We can conclude that a strictly cognitive approach to learning, whether it be at the individual, group or organizational level is at best restrictive, at worst naive. Feeling and emotion are essential ingredients of what is learned and how it is learned (see also Fineman, 1997). Learning both reflects and produces emotion. Experientially, this is amply illustrated when we are engrossed in an endeavor, oblivious of time, external noise or interruptions. We are "focused," at one with the task – puzzling for hours at the computer screen, practicing a musical skill, trying to solve a complex engineering problem. Emotion is neither instrumental to what we are doing, nor an outcome – it infuses processes of doing and learning as a special sense of "flow," to use Czikszentmihalyi's (1977) terminology.

Ignoring emotion, or trying to remove it to achieve some emotionally unsullied state, is a seductive myth, best left to fictitious characters, such as Mr Spock of *Star Trek* fame. Moreover, the knowledge from learning "how," "of," "to," or "about," can shift in its emotional meanings according to time and social circumstances. So what was once boring can now feel exciting. The dull sense of proficiency with numerical skills can become enticing when applied to a new software project. The pride in mastering how to influence colleagues can turn to shame when accused of manipulation. In short, the social-emotional context of learning and knowledge is pivotal. Let us examine this in more detail.

THE SOCIO-POLITICALITY OF LEARNING AND EMOTION

There is a cluster of studies which firmly locate learning in the socially constructed organization. In other words, learning is produced, contested, and changed through a communal process rather than being atomized and individualized (e.g. see Brown and Duguid, 1991; Orr, 1990). In constructing the "real and the good" (Gergen, 1999), meaning and morality becomes a matter of implicit and explicit negotiations and the "trading" of interpretations, all of which are mediated by power relations and political interests (Blackler and McDonald, 2000; Coopey and Burgoyne, 2000). This approach is expressed in "communities of practice." Occupational identities – such as of meat cutters in supermarkets or construction workers – are formed through the collective learning of symbols and slogans of the trade, extant ideologies, local language, artifacts and status orders (e.g. see Fox, 2000; Gherardi et al., 1998; Lave and Wenger, 1991). The social-relational foundation is axiomatic, as is the mobility and "lived" nature of the learning. Sometimes more than one organizational setting contributes to the sense of community. This is nicely illustrated in Ackroyd and Crowdy's (1990) graphic observations of English slaughterhouse men learning their identity and place. A lively range of institutionalized, peer-determined, harassment and degradations punctuate the slaughterer's day and shape the working moralities of the group. But the men also join hands in out-of-work hobbies, such as hunting and taxidermy, all of which reinforce their exclusivity and sense of difference.

Emotionalizing the labor process

A socio-political frame markedly enriches our understanding of organizational learning, but the emotional "glue" is missing. With few exceptions, the writers fail to account, descriptively or analytically, for the way learning and meaning-making will also involve emotion as a part of the social-political process. In particular, we get little understanding of the emotion work, emotional labor and strategic deployment of emotion (i.e., performed to meet particular ends or objectives) that attends learning and organizational socialization (see Ashkenasy et al., 2000; Hochschild, 1979; Pinder, 1988).

Emotion *work* involves managing – by self and others – the everyday tension, or flip-flop, between emotion as felt and emotion as displayed. The art of sustaining social organization is significantly dependent on not always showing what you privately feel, an emotional hypocrisy that is *de rigeur*. Context/culturally specific rules and cues suggest the emotions that are appropriate to display and (to an extent) the private feelings that ought to be experienced. Both general life-experience and job-specific learnings hone the feigning process to create the "socially correct" individual. We come to know and value our own and others' feelings through the linguistic labels and value rhetorics and discourses that are around, such as on anger, shame, remorse, sadness, love, fear, embarrassment, disgust, joy, or pride. These may be transmitted in many different ways, such as through peer, parental, and colleague groups; in film presentations of emotional "episodes"; in popular music and song; or in magazine and newspaper descriptions of the emotionally good, bad, or ugly (see Heelas, 1986; Wetherall, 1966).

Emotion work can be contrasted with emotional *labor* when the "work" of emotional display – such as looking serious, sad, happy, smiling, sympathetic – is an explicit part of the job, or a strongly implicit feature of occupational competence. In other words, the prevalent smile, jollity, seriousness, passion, or petulance is an emotional demeanor that is expected and paid-for in the labor contract. Emotion sells the goods or services and is subject or learned regimes and organizational protocols. Emotional laborers such as hotel receptionists, waiters, fast-food workers, checkout clerks, flight attendants, call-center staff, theme-park "cast" and financial service workers, are often rigorously trained and scripted for emotional proficiency and are subject to close managerial surveillance. In the words of a headwaiter in Tracy's (2000) study of cruise ships: "When you wake up in the morning, turn your smile on. Don't turn it back off again until you go to sleep" (Tracy, p. 91). Sturdy and Fineman further illustrate the phenomenon. They report their observations of an insurance company training seminar for telephone sales personnel:

> New staff are initially subjected to twelve hours of service training to invoke positive feelings from customers – "making it easy for them to say 'yes'" [training course title]. Here, certain common words or expressions such as "sorry", "no problem" and "premium" are considered to have negative connotations – the wrong emotional tone. They are replaced by a range of positive, up-beat sounding, or "sexy" words such as "certainly", "rest assured", "immediate" and "great" which are to be used in all areas of work – and even at home – to avoid getting "out of the habit". This new language is not simply another rigid telephone sales script, but a new "empowering" vocabulary and dialogue structure developed partly in order to allow a measure of choice. It is, however, monitored through random eavesdropping of the salesperson's telephone calls. The aim is to leave customers with the impression that the salesperson was "genuine" and "natural" and, of course, to secure a sale. (Sturdy and Fineman, 2001: 140)

In Foucauldian logic, power is exercised in the way the very language and gestures of workers have been shaped by the organizational authorities (supervisors, managers) who watch over and measure them (Foucault, 1977). Scrutiny is technologized and routinized, such as through "mystery shoppers" (snoopers in disguise), recurrent training, computerized displays of "calls waiting," supervisory eavesdropping and covert video observation. When employees perform as desired with the minimum of such control ("it just feels natural") then we have a perfection of power, which renders its actual exercise unnecessary.

The organizational learning of emotion in this manner has worried some commentators because of the psychological damage that can accrue (e.g. alienation, cynicism, identity confusion) and the morality of such endeavors (Hochschild, 1979; Morris and Feldman, 1996). Others, however, have suggested that their dire effects have been overstated as employees find ways of insulating themselves from some, if not all, of the ravages of corporate scripts and others' control over their emotions (Adelman, 1995; Wharton, 1999). It would be wrong, however, to assume that emotion learning is all about unfettered managerial prerogative. Employee resistance is evident in a number of different forms (see Hopfl and Linstead, 1993; Kunda, 1992; Sturdy and Fineman, 2001). Thus we find cynicism, distancing, and even smile strikes among hotel receptionists and supermarket workers, objecting to the oppressiveness of regimes of control (Fuller and Smith, 1991; Zeidler, 1988).

Emotional learning zones

A tendency in discussions on learning in organizations is to treat the organizational space as an undifferentiated whole where "learning takes place." This is a part truth. While, in principle, learning is boundary free – it can happen anywhere and anytime – in practice, much learning is episodic and site specific. It takes place in formal "learning places" and events, such as lectures, briefings, team meetings, celebrations, board meetings, and negotiations. Less formally, organizational knowledge is gleaned vicariously "on-the-job," in rest rooms, offices, in coffee lounges, in car parks, and corridors. The various settings are important because of the way they become "zoned" emotionally, differentially appropriated and valued for sharing, displaying, divulging, contesting or practicing certain forms of knowledge (Fineman, 1996; Parkin, 1993). The settings are socio-emotionally constructed as private or public; safe or exposed; confronting or secure; back stage or front stage; requiring a tight or relaxed emotional posture; demanding more, or less, emotional labor; transient or permanent. Lim's story, as reported by Fineman and Gabriel (1996: 182–4), brings some of these points together. Lim, a corporate novice, tells of her first major "learning event" in her job with an oil company. She has to present her research findings to her superiors.

> The big occasion; a formal presentation of my research and ideas on future world energy production to an audience of energy experts at OilCo! Only ten minutes to go before my boss arrives. I could hear myself constantly questioning: are all my transparencies in order? Have I photocopied enough handouts? But more importantly, do I look presentable? Black velvet suit, hair tied back, understated make-up, uhm . . . perfect . . . I hoped!

Why the fuss and the feeling of nausea? Well this was my first opportunity to really show them what I was worth. I would either impress them and receive recognition or be branded as hopeless for the remaining twenty weeks. My objective, the former naturally.

10.30 am and a tap on the door heralded the entrance of my boss Steve. A quick smile and a nod of the head towards the lift meant that it was time to walk over to the downstream building for my presentation at 10.40 am. On entering the conference room, I was confronted by a mass of tables which were arranged in a square, with the projector at the far end of the room. A sense of panic as I began to realise the importance of the next hour. Again, anxieties and questions. How many people were going to come? There must have been seating capacity for at least 50 to 60, but although the room was large it had a comforting feeling, a sort of familiarity. Oceans of blue and grey suits then proceeded to enter. They seemed to be fairly relaxed, with coffee in one hand, files and paper in the other.

What seemed like a lifetime of waiting was in fact only a few minutes, before Peter Fallow, the Director, entered the room. All eyes turned towards him in the hope of making eye contact, followed by broad smiles and extended hands. The beginning of the presentation was marked by his step towards his chair. My onlookers followed and seated themselves one-by-one, positioning themselves near the head man.

A brief introduction was made by my boss but then it was up to me. The next forty minutes 'just happened'. I heard my own voice echoing around the room but it was their body language that said everything. Arms were folded, heads tilted, chins were rubbed, and eyebrows furrowed. I was being watched. I cleared my throat, took a deep breath, and smiled a smile as if to apologise for my pathetic existence. My every move was being scrutinized. Me under a microscope! Swarms of eyes were fixed on me and with a mixture of curiosity, bemusement and wariness. Shakily I placed my first slide up and began. I could hear my own voice resounding round the room but I knew my material inside out, so I was on autopilot.

During the presentation I had a demoralising feeling that managers have a reluctance to give any praise or feedback. I interpreted it as failure. Later, however, I realised that new ideas were absorbed slowly, and the time it took them to ask questions meant that I had sufficiently inspired them to think. This was a recognition of success by everyone. Approval was a significant factor as I was one of only three females among thirty-five men, at least half their age and of a different culture to myself. I was a representation of a somewhat unknown, and therefore threatening, group. Some positive gesture or comment from any one manager secured a certain amount of respect, but when it did come it came from Fallow, which meant I had passed the test and could enjoy the security of acceptance.

Lim's tale is emotionally revealing in a number of ways. Situationally, everything happening to her was new – it was a mega learning experience infused with private feelings – anxiety, doubt, panic, insecurity, relief. Her private and public identities were on the line. The physical setting had a pre-defined emotionalized architecture, shaped to elicit a confident, "presentable," smiling, demeanor from the speaker, someone firmly in control of her emotional display in the presence of a potentially critical audience. This much Lim understood, but her self-presentation was fragile, sustained only through considerable emotional labor. Lim constantly scans her audience's mood, which she reads as mostly cen-sorious. The setting is further politicized in two ways. First, through a culture of hierar-chical deference towards a male boss – Lim (and others) sought his acknowledgment and approval. Second, Lim's desire for affirmation as a young, ethnically distinctive, female. In this she is finally rewarded, enjoying the pleasure of her boss's public approval.

Knowledge sharing and trust

The intra and inter-organizational sharing of knowledge has become a prominent feature of new arrangements of work. The interpretive, political, power and structural features of such processes have been well noted (e.g. Knights et al., 1993; Oliver, 1991; Powell, 1990), where the rhetorics or trust and collaboration can thinly veil the realities of manipulation, capitulation and aggressive self-interest (Clegg and Hardy, 1996; Hardy and Phillips, 1995). Yet it appears that, for whatever motive, some *feelings* of, or about, trust, however transient, are important if knowledge is to be exchanged for mutual benefit.

In this respect the literature on trust mostly skirts around the emotional details, speak-ing more of the predictability of others' behaviors, risk and credibility (e.g. Gambetta, 1988; Lewis and Weigert, 1985; Luhmann, 1979), the frequency of interactions and norms of equity (Dasgupta, 1988; Ring and Van de Ven, 1992) and the degree of communality of goals (Pasquero, 1991; Westley and Vredenburg, 1991). Lewis and Weigert (1985) make some of the clearest claims for trust resting in "emotional bonds" along with cognitive expectations, a point developed by McAllister (1995). In these studies, however, little is revealed about the emotional texture of trust, nor an explicit link to learning. Andrews and Delahaye's (2000) qualitative study of medical scientists is, however, somewhat differ-ent. The scientists were required to share information with other scientists in partner organizations, a process fraught with anxieties – such as their comfort in dealing with rel-ative strangers; feeling intimidated when asking for information from a professional senior; and anticipated status loss in "giving away" important information. Knowledge in such settings is more than a dispassionate construct; it is an emotionalized commodity that is reframed and revalued in the politics of exchange.

Trust, we can conclude, is not something that is simply present or absent from a social relationship, but is negotiative and contextually/structurally specific. Its texture is essen-tially emotional, involving feelings of, for example, ease, suspicion, fear, confidence, comfort, or anxiety. In such terms, trust both frames and flavors what knowledge means to different people. It shapes the worth or value of new (or old) knowledge and learnings. This is sharply evident in organizational settings where trust is strained and injustice strongly felt (Harlos and Pinder, 2000). Instructions, rumors, or organizational changes are likely to be received cautiously, defensively or cynically when authority figures work by creating fear, anger, shame, or hopelessness.

LEARNING TO BE EMOTIONALLY INTELLIGENT

In 1995 the American Dialect Society selected emotional intelligence and emotional quo-tient (EQ) as the most useful of new words or phrases (Mayer et al., 2000: 92). Indeed, in

a relatively short period, emotional intelligence has become a major concept on both sides
of the Atlantic, attracting the attention of the popular press, academic researchers, edu-
cationalists, and management consultants. It bears all the hallmarks of a managerial
fashion with its attendant gurus, slick claims for organizational success, purchasable packages and measurement tools (Fineman, 2000a). Importantly, emotional intelligence
is offered not only as a panacea for many organizational ills, but as something that is
eminently learnable. In this respect, for Goleman (the major popularizer of emotional
intelligence) there is little room for doubt:

> our level of emotional intelligence is not fixed genetically, nor does it develop only in early
> childhood. Unlike IQ, which changes little after our teen years, emotional intelligence seems
> to be largely learned and it continues to develop as we go through life and learn through our
> experiences – our competence in it can keep growing. (Goleman, 1988: 7)

The explosion of interest in emotional intelligence has generated some jostling as to its
ownership (e.g. Bar-On, 2000; Sternberg, 1997) as well as wry observations on its popular
claims. For example, Salovey et al. (2000: 516) note:

> Some time after our initial work on the subject was published . . . a popular book on emo-
> tional intelligence appeared and skyrocketed up the best-seller list. With this book emotional
> competencies went almost overnight from a set of abilities worthy of further study (our view)
> to a wealth of personal assets capable of determining a person's character, life achievements,
> and health (Goleman's view). Truly extraordinary claims on behalf of emotional intelligence
> are now commonplace. . .

Pinning down the nature of emotional intelligence is not without controversy, and it
has certainly exercised psychologists. For Goleman (1966: 43–4), the emotionally intelligent know and manage their emotions, motivate themselves, recognize emotions in others,
and handle relationships. This is what helps them to be "stars" in their occupation or
calling. But, as Goleman's discussion unfolds, his view of emotional intelligence broadens
to include almost all features of personality. Mayer and Salovey (1997) are insistent that
emotional intelligence comprises particular *abilities* that span emotional and cognitive functions: the ability to perceive accurately, appraise, and express emotion; the ability to access
and/or generate feeling when they facilitate thought; the ability to regulate emotion and
to promote emotional and intellectual growth. Cooper and Sawaf's (1977) "EQ" map
expands emotional intelligence to include resilience, creativity, compassion and intuition,
while Bar-On (1997) speaks of reality testing, stress management and impulse control. The
picture is further complicated by discussions of emotional intelligence which refer to virtually any feature of social competence such as "the ability to integrate thinking, feeling,
and behaviour to achieve social tasks and outcomes valued in the host context and culture"
(Topping et al., 2000: 32).

Whether or not emotional intelligence can be individually or organizationally enhanced
depends on the notion of emotional intelligence one prefers. Contrary to Goleman's claims
of mutability, some scholars (echoing the old nature/nurture debate) argue that emotional
intelligence is so deeply rooted in early learning experiences and genetic predispositions

that later change is difficult or impossible (Mayer et al., 2000). Nevertheless, Cherniss (2000) concludes that workplace interventions to help workers improve their emotional intelligence have – under different labels – been in evidence since the Hawthorne studies of the 1920s. For a recent picture he cites the findings of the American Society for Training and Development that the majority of 50 leading US companies report that they are engaged in emotional intelligence training of their employees.

Cherniss takes the Goleman line that emotional competencies are critical for effective performance in most jobs. They are "what employers are looking for"; qualities such as adaptability in the face of setbacks, personal self-management, confidence, interpersonal effectiveness, teamwork, skill in negotiating disagreements and leadership potential. Cherniss refers to a poll of US employers which indicates that 40 percent of employees are not able to work cooperatively and 19 percent demonstrate insufficient self-discipline at the job-application stage. Here we see emotional intelligence stretched, uncritically, to serve a particular ideology about psychological health and job success. It is also taken to include just about any human resource management training program that deals with "people issues." And indeed, Cherniss cites a gamut of training practices that, he claims, are associated with emotional intelligence, such as communication and empathy training, conflict training, stress management, self-management, competency-based procedures for selecting high-performing employees, and self-confidence training for the unemployed.

We are left with a confusing picture of emotional intelligence. It is noteworthy more for its rhetorical flourish than its conceptual clarity. On the one hand it embraces fairly specific cognitive/affective personality features that are seen to be relatively immutable. On the other hand it is presented as an indefinite list of personal and interpersonal competencies that are more or less "emotional" and learnable. Critiques of its moral and political status are rare. To create "emotionally intelligent" people and organizations raises key questions about the values placed on different kinds of emotion and emotional performance; who defines and reinforces those values; and towards what or whose ends (see Fineman, 2000a; Mayer et al., 2000). Boler (1999: 61), for example, takes a critical feminist position: "None of the representations of emotional intelligence analyse how people are taught different rules of conduct for emotional behavior according to their gendered, radicalised, and social class status. Instead, we are all supposed to feel the same 'empathy' and 'optimism'."

If emotional intelligence is not to collapse into mystification, maybe it should be released from its essentialist roots, mired as they are in definitional and ownership controversy. Rather than being a property of an individual (an ability, trait, or competence) to be isolated by experts, measured and, perhaps, changed, we can cast emotional intelligence in a context-situated, constructivist, mold. Here the focus would shift from what the individual is or has, to the way emotionalities are performed and negotiated interrelationally with contextually located others – actual or imagined. The key point here is that emotionality is given meaning and substance through interactions, expressed through culturally available symbols, particularly language and stories. It is a process. Such a relational view (e.g., see Bouwen and Hosking, 2000; Gergen, 1999; McAdams, 1996) privileges active narrative construction and conversations as a means by which self and context are formed and re-formed. Organizational learning would spotlight the active *encounter*, and the constructed context that frames emotionally challenging action. How is the encounter negotiated, re-framed, politicized? Who is it with? What is the history of the relationship(s)? To what extent is the learning-setting predefined, or "zoned," for a particular form of emotional activity or display – such as muted expressiveness or more "frank" expressions of differ- ence and alliance? Cross-cutting such behaviors are collective, cultural processes, where the dominant, American, rendition of emotional intelligence will be less appropriate and the rules of emotional exchange differently defined.

Learning to Feel – Virtually

The re-shaping of work organizations over the last 10–15 years has been most apparent in its heavy dependency on communication technologies that, in effect, separate the worker from any tangible product or person. Many organizations have become splintered, the computer screen acting as a surrogate for workaday communities. The "tethered" office is being replaced by a centrally controlled office with dispersed employees connected through information technologies, where some people may enjoy considerable discretion over their work time, but where others are tightly monitored (Nolan and Galal, 1988).

The accoutrements of virtuality, or virtual "separation," include the laptop computer, computer-aided design, production control systems, e-mail, three-dimensional computer- ized representations and "multi-media kit" based on globally responsive mobile-phone technology. Conservatively, these artifacts can be regarded as add-ons, or enhancements, to the traditional, spatially fixed organization where, for example, the executive now uses a mobile phone instead of a landline, and e-mails rather than writes letters. More radi- cally, the very notion of organization is challenged as virtual space, or virtual processes, replace old certainties, structures and forms, colonizing interpersonal relationships, affec- tivity and learning (Jackson, 1999; Panteli and Dibben, 2001). The signifiers of "the organization" are markedly more ambiguous, dispersed, fleeting, or mediated. Virtuality privileges a "knowledge society" where its members work across time, space, and organi- zational boundaries (Lipnack and Stamps, 1977). The virtual worker confronts (and repro- duces) interdependencies and "teams," where information technology provides the prime medium for knowing others. For writers such as Turkle, this phenomenon is dramatic; life on the computer screen producing "new ways of thinking about evolution, relationships, sexuality, politics and identity" (1996: 26). In particular, she suggests that the computer dispenses with the demands of friendships while simultaneously offering illusions of companionship.

As the weak ties of modern institutional networks become further stretched and virtu- alized, how do we construct our emotional identities? How do we learn emotion codes, rules and presentation etiquette? The worker is faced with a very different sense of place and face when ephemeral, virtual, work relationships replace flesh-and-blood ones. How one appears to others, how to feel "appropriately," and the kind of cues relevant to bonding and trust, will operate on a different bandwidth and different, or non-existent, emotional vocabulary. At its crudest we see attempts to emotionalize e-mails and text messages with smiling, frowning or sad computer characters – impression management via new symbols and shorthands. We see home-working organizations attempting to bond their network of employees by arranging periodic get-togethers. The sense that something has been missing is evident in the anecdotal "conference embrace," as long-term e-mailers physically meet each other for the first time.

We may view such happening with a mix of pessimism and nostalgia. This is Sennett's (1998) position. He observes a new brand of alienation, or "corrosion of character." Once communities of workers learned mutual respect, honor and trust though hands-on cooperation and direct contact with the product. Now, there is little need for any such community as computer consoles at remote workstations replace the daily intimacy of working methods, dulling, or dumbing down, the experience of work. For example, the baker no longer has to know how to bake as the computer engineer is in overall command of the process. In the high-tech, flexible work of baking, "operationally, everything is so clear; emotionally, so illegible" (Sennett, 1998: 68). Others have noted the way loyalty is strained and conflict sharpened in virtual organizations (e.g., see De Sanctis and Monge, 1999). The status of trust is germane to such observations. As previously argued, learning to trust is a complex emotional process. It is one that sustains and shapes organizational linkages and underwrites promises. In virtual organizations the interpersonal play and the "touch" that typically forms trust (Handy, 1995) are replaced with "swift" surrogates. Remote messages, virtualized voices, texts, or pictures have to be read and interpreted for the "person" behind them. Overt signs of enthusiasm, excitement, optimism may be key to this process (Jarvenpaa and Leidner, 1999), although one would expect this to be highly moderated by national cultural differences in the way feelings are expressed and communicated.

Virtually mediated/defined work decreases the opportunity to create a coherent emotional identity and to negotiate a particular occupational sense of worth (e.g., see Wiesenfeld et al., 1999). The virtual world encourages a splintered self and emotional vicariousness. That is fine for fast, fragmented, remote operations (for which virtual organizations get praised). Less fine, perhaps, for old style communities, bonding and traditional emotion work. And there is the rub. It may be that virtuality presents a key test of what Gergen (1991) sees as a triumph of the saturated self, where diverse forms of relatedness replace a unitary sense of self, more in tune with unstable symbols, institutions and relationships (Lifton, 1993). So fragmentation enriches; relative isolation is to be celebrated; we will invent ways to get by and private/public codes of emotion will be reconfigured accordingly. A less up-beat conclusion is that such a transition will be fine for some, but like previous economic and technological revolutions, will leave many clinging to ways of knowing, being and feeling that are hard, if not impossible, to relinquish.

SOME FUTURE DIRECTIONS

In this chapter I have sought to demonstrate that an explicit consideration of emotion in organizational learning is essential. Not only is emotion a learning "product" in many personal and organizational displays, it also lies at the heart of the building of trust, competencies and the political and moral order of the enterprise. As such it demands the attention of the *critical* and *process* researcher as much, if not more, than the psychometrician. Our theories of organizational learning require emotionalizing to account for the way work meanings are formed and re-formed, not in more sophisticated units of cognition, but in sentient structures, passionate negotiations and emotion posturing. Phenomenologically, learning one's place in an organizational order has much to do with the feelings and emotion-deference patterns that are implied, forced upon one, and internalized. Given the intimate connection between the emotion order and the organizational order, we have still much to understand about how such patterns are shaped in "learning" terms. Future research in a social-constructivist vein is particularly promising as it embeds both learning and emotion in relational/political context. Finally, the extraordinary growth in virtuality raises exciting, and considerable, challenges for the learning theorist. Not least, because conventional notions of organization and self-identity are melting away. This is profoundly "about" the emotions that underpin notions of who we think we are and where we think we belong.

REFERENCES

Ackroyd, S. and Crowdy, P.A. (1990) Can Culture Be Managed? *Personnel Review*, 19 (5): 3–13.

Adelman, P.K. (1995) Emotional Labor as a Potential Source of Job Stress. In S.L. Sauter and L.R. Murphy (eds.), *Organizational Risk Factors for Job Stress.* Washington, DC: American Psychological Association.

Andrews, K.M. and Delahaye, B.L. (2000) The Influence on Knowledge Processes in Organizational Learning: The Psychosocial Filter. *Journal of Management Studies*, 37 (6): 797–810.

Argyris, C. (1977) Double-loop Learning in Organizations. *Harvard Business Review*, 55 (5): 115–25.

Argyris, C. (1985) How Learning and Reasoning Processes Affect Organizational Change. In P.S. Goodman (ed.), *Change in Organizations*. San Francisco: Jossey-Bass.

Argyris, C. and Schön, D. (1978) *Organizational Learning*. Reading, MA: Addison-Wesley.

Ashkenasy, N.M., Hartel, C.E.J., and Zerbe, W. (eds.) (2000) *Emotions in the Workplace: Research, Theory and Practice*. Westport, CT: Quorum.

Bar-On, R. (1997) *The Emotional Quotient Inventory (EQi): A Test of Emotional Intelligence*. Toronto: Multi-Health Systems.

Bar-On, R. (2000) Emotional and Social Intelligence. In R. Bar-On and J.D.A. Parker (eds.), *The Handbook of Emotional Intelligence*. San Francisco: Jossey-Bass.

Bartlett, F. (1933) *Remembering*. Cambridge: Cambridge University Press.

Bendelow, G. and Mayall, B. (2000) How Children Manage Emotion in Schools. In S. Fineman (ed.), *Emotion in Organizations* (2nd edn). London: Sage.

Blackler, F., Crump, N., and McDonald, S. (1998) Knowledge, Organizations and Competition. In G. Von Krogh, J., Roos and D. Kleine (eds.), *Knowing in Firms*. London: Sage.

Blackler, F. and McDonald, S. (2000) Power, Mastery and Organizational Learning. *Journal of Management Studies*, 37 (6): 833–51.

Boler, M. (1999) *Feeling Power*. New York: Routledge.

Bouwen, R. and Hosking, D.M. (2000) Reflections on Relational Readings Organizational Learning. *European Journal of Work and Organizational Psychology*, 9 (2): 267–74.

Brody, R.G. and Lowe, D.J. (1995) Escalation of Commitment in Professional Tax Preparers. *Psychological Reports*, 76 (1): 339–44.

Brown, A.D. and Starkey, K. (2000) Organizational Identity and Learning: A Psychodynamic Perspective. *Academy of Management Review*, 25 (1): 102–20.

Brown, J.S. and Duguid, P. (1991) Organizational Learning and Communities of Practice: Toward a Unified View of Working, Learning and Innovation. *Organization Science*, 2 (1): 40–57.

Cacioppo, J.T. and Gardner, W.L. (1999) Emotion. *Annual Review of Psychology*, 50: 191–214.

Cherniss, C. (2000) Social and Emotional Competence in the Workplace. In R. Bar-On and J.D.A. Parker (eds.), *The Handbook of Emotional Intelligence*. San Francisco: Jossey-Bass.

Clegg, S. and Hardy, C. (1996) Conclusions: Representations. In S. Clegg and C. Hardy (eds.), *Studying Organization: Theory and Method*. London: Sage.

Cooper, R. and Sawaf, A. (1977) *Executive EQ*. London: Orion Business.

Coopey, J. and Burgoyne, J. (2000) Politics and Organizational Learning. *Journal of Management Studies*, 37 (6): 869–85.

Czikszentmihalyi, M. (1977) *Beyond Boredom and Freedom*. San Francisco: Jossey-Bass.

Damasio, A.R. (1994) *Descartes' Error*. New York: G.P. Putman's Sons.

Damasio, A.R. (2000) *The Feeling of What Happens*. London: Heinemann.

Dasgupta, P. (1988) Trust as a Commodity. In D. Gambetta (ed.), *Trust: Making and Breaking Cooperative Relationships*. Oxford: Basil Blackwell.

De Sanctis, G. and Monge, P. (1999) Introduction to the Special Issue: Communication Processes for Virtual Organizations. *Organization Science*, 10 (6): 693–703.

de Sousa, R. (1987) *The Rationality of Emotion*. Cambridge, MA: MIT Press.

Diamond, M.A. (1993) *The Unconscious Life of Organizations: Interpreting Organizational Identity*. Westport: Quorum Books.

Easterby-Smith, M. and Araujo, L. (1999) Organizational Learning: Current Debates and Opportunities. In M. Easterby-Smith and L. Araujo (eds.), *Organizational Learning and the Learning Organization*. London: Sage.

Eden, C. (1988) Cognitive Mapping: A Review. *European Journal of Operations Research*, 36: 1–13.

Eden, C. and Huxham, C. (2001) The Negotiation of Purpose in Multi-organizational Collaborative Groups. *Journal of Management Studies*, 38(3): 373–91.

Elster, J. (1999) *Alchemies of the Mind*. Cambridge: Cambridge University Press.

Fineman, S. (1996) Emotion and Organizing. In S. Clegg, C. Hardy, and W. Nord (eds.), *Handbook of Organization Studies*, London: Sage.

Fineman, S. (1997) Emotion and Management Learning. *Management Learning*, 28 (1): 13–25.

Fineman, S. (2000a) Commodifying the Emotionally Intelligent. In S. Fineman (ed.), *Emotion in Organizations* (2nd edn). London: Sage, 101–39.

Fineman, S. (2000b) Emotional Arenas Revisited. In S. Fineman (ed.), *Emotion in Organizations* (2nd edn). London: Sage, 1–24.

Fineman, S (ed.) (2000c) *Emotion in Organizations* (2nd edn). London: Sage [1993].

Fineman, S. and Gabriel, Y. (1996) *Experiencing Organizations*. London: Sage.

Forgas, J.P. (2000) Introduction: The Role of Affect in Social Cognition. In J.P. Forgas (ed.), *Feeling and Thinking: The Role of Affect in Social Cognition*. Cambridge: Cambridge University Press.

Foucault, M. (1977) *Discipline and Punish*. London: Allen and Unwin.

Fox, S. (2000) Communities of Practice, Foucault and Actor-network Theory. *Journal of Management Studies*, 37 (6): 853–67.

Frijda, N.H., Manstead, S.R., and Bem, S. (eds.) (2000) *Emotions and Beliefs*. Cambridge: Cambridge University Press.

Fuller, L. and Smith, V. (1991) Consumers' Reports: Management by Customers in a Changing Economy. *Work, Employment and Society*, 5 (1): 1–16.

Gabriel, Y. (1999) *Organizations in Depth: The Psychoanalysis of Organizations*. London: Sage.

Gambetta, D. (ed.) (1988) *Trust: Making and Breaking Cooperative Relations*. Oxford: Blackwell.

Gergen, K. (1991) *The Saturated Self*. New York: Basic Books.

Gergen, K. (1999) *An Invitation to Social Construction*. London: Sage.

Gherardi, S., Nicolini, D., and Odella, F. (1998) Toward a Social Understanding of How People Learn in Organizations: The Notion of the Situated Curriculum. *Management Learning*, 29 (3): 273–97.

Goleman, D. (1966) *Emotional Intelligence.* London: Bloomsbury.

Goleman, D. (1988) *Working with Emotional Intelligence.* London: Bloomsbury.

Handy, C.B. (1995) Trust and the Virtual Organization. *Harvard Business Review*, 73 (3): 40–50.

Hardy, C. and Phillips, N. (1995) *Overcoming Illusions of Trust: Towards a Communicative Theory of Trust and Power.* McGill Working Papers, Montreal, Canada.

Harlos, K.P. and Pinder, C.C. (2000) Emotion and Injustice in the Workplace. In S. Fineman (ed.), *Emotion in Organizations* (2nd edn). London: Sage.

Heelas, P. (1986) Emotion Talk across Cultures. In R. Harre (ed.), *The Social Construction of Emotion.* Oxford: Basil Blackwell.

Hochschild, A. (1979) Emotion Work, Feeling Rules, and Social Structure. *American Journal of Sociology*, 39 (December): 551–75.

Hopfl, H. and Linstead, S. (1993) Passion and Performance: Suffering and the Carrying of Organizational Roles. In S. Fineman (ed.), *Emotion in Organizations.* London: Sage.

Huber, G.P. (1991) Organizational Learning: The Contributing Processes and the Literatures. *Organization Science*, 2: 88–115.

Ingleton, C. (1995) Gender and Learning: Does Emotion Make a Difference? *Higher Education*, 30 (3): 323–37.

Jackson, P. (1999) *Virtual Looking Social and Organisational Dynamics.* London: Routledge.

Jarvenpaa, S., and Leidner, D.E. (1999) Communication and Trust in Virtual Teams, *Organization Science*, 10 (6): 791–815.

Johnson-Laird, P.N. and Oatley, K. (2000) Cognitive and Social Construction in Emotions. In M. Lewis and J.M. Haviland-Jones (eds.), *Handbook of Emotions.* New York: The Guildford Press.

Kets de Vries, M.F.R. (ed.) (1991) *Organizations on the Couch: Clinical Perspectives on Organizational Behavior and Change.* San Francisco: Jossey Bass.

Knights, K., Murray, F., and Willmott, H. (1993) Networking as Knowledge Work: A Study of Strategic Interorganizational Development in the Financial Service Industry. *Journal of Management Studies*, 16 (4): 975–95.

Kunda, G. (1992) *Engineering Culture: Control and Commitment in a High-tech Corporation.* Philadelphia: Temple University Press.

Lave, J. and Wenger, E. (eds.) (1991) *Situated Learning: Legitimate Peripheral Participation.* Cambridge: Cambridge University Press.

Lewis, J.D. and Weigert, A. (1985) Trust as a Social Reality. *Social Forces*, 43 (4): 967–85.

Lifton, R.J. (1993) *The Protean Self: Human Resilience in an Age of Fragmentation.* New York: Basic Books.

Lipnack, J. and Stamps, J. (1977) *Virtual Teams: Reaching across Space, Time and Organizations with Technology.* New York: Wiley.

Luhmann, N. (1979) *Trust and Power.* Chichester: Wiley.

Mayer, J.D. and Salovey, P. (1997) What Is Emotional Intelligence? In P. Salovey and D.J. Sluyter (eds.), *Emotional Development and Emotional Intelligence.* New York: Basic Books.

Mayer, J.D., Salovey, P., and Caruso, D. (2000) Emotional Intelligence as Zeitgeist, as Personality and as Mental Ability. In R. Bar-On and J.D.A. Parker (eds.), *The Handbook of Emotional Intelligence.* San Francisco: Jossey-Bass.

McAdams, D.P. (1996) Alternative Futures for the Study of Human Individuality. *Journal of Research in Personality*, 30 (3): 374–88.

McAllister, D.J. (1995) Affect- and Cognition-based Trust as Foundations for Interpersonal Cooperation in Organizations. *Academy of Management Journal*, 38 (1): 24–59.

More, W.S. (1974) *Emotions and Adult Learning.* Westmead, Farnborough: Saxon House.

Morris, J.A. and Feldman, D.C. (1996) The Dimensions, Antecedents, and Consequences of Emotional Labor. *Academy of Management Review*, 21 (4): 986–1010.

Mumby, D.K. and Putnam, L.L. (1992) The Politics of Emotion: A Feminist Reading of Bounded Rationality. *Academy of Management Review*, 17 (3): 465–86.

Nolan, R.L. and Galal, H. (1988) Virtual Offices: Redefining Organizational Boundaries. In S.P. Bradley and R.L. Nolan (eds.), *Sense and Respond: Capturing Value in the Network Era*. Boston: Harvard Business Review Press.

Oliver, C. (1991) Strategic Responses to Institutional Processes. *Academy of Management Review*, 16: 145–79.

Orr, J. (1990) Sharing Knowledge and Celebrating Identity: War Stories and Community Memory in a Service Culture. In D. Middleton and D. Edwards (eds.), *Collective Remembering*. London: Sage.

Panteli, N. and Dibben, M.R. (2001) Revisiting the Nature of Virtual Organizations: Reflections on Mobile Communication Systems. *Futures*, 33: 379–91.

Parkin, W. (1993) The Public and the Private: Gender, Sexuality and Emotion. In S. Fineman (ed.), *Emotion in Organizations*. London: Sage.

Pasquero, J. (1991) Supraorganizational Collaboration: The Canadian Environmental Experiment. *Journal of Applied Behavioral Science*, 27 (1): 38–64.

Pinder, C.C. (1988) *Work Motivation in Organizational Behavior*. New Jersey: Prentice Hall.

Powell, W.W. (1990) Neither Market nor Hierarchy: Network Forms of Organization. In B.M. Staw and L.L. Cummings (eds.), *Research in Organizational Behavior*, Vol. 12. Greenwich CT: JAI Press, 295–336.

Ring, P.S. and Van de Ven, A.H. (1992) Structuring Cooperative Relationships between Organizations. *Strategic Management Journal*, 13: 483–98.

Salovey, P., Bedell, B.T., Detweiler, J.B., and Mayer, J.D. (2000) Current Directions in Emotional Intelligence Research. In M. Lewis and J.M. Haviland-Jones (eds.), *Handbook of Emotions*. New York: The Guilford Press.

Salzberger-Wittenberg, I., Henry, G., and Osborne, E.L. (1983) *The Emotional Experience of Learning and Teaching*. London: Routledge and Kegan Paul.

Sennett, R. (1998) *The Corrosion of Character*. New York: W.W. Norton.

Snell, R. (1988) The Emotional Cost of Managerial Learning at Work. *Management Education and Development*, 19 (4): 322–40.

Snell, R. (1992) Experiential Learning at Work: Why Can't it Be Painless. *Personnel Review*, 21 (4): 12–26.

Staw, B.M. and Ross, J. (1987) Understanding Escalations Situations: Antecedents, Prototypes and Solutions. In B.M. Staw and L.L. Cummings (eds.), *Research in Organizational Behaviour*, Vol. 9. Greenwich, CT: JAI Press.

Sternberg, R.J. (1997) *Successful Intelligence*. New York: Plume.

Sturdy, A. and Fineman, S. (2001) Struggles for the Control of Affect. In A. Sturdy, I. Grugulis, and H. Willmott (eds.), *Customer Service*. Basingstoke: Palgrave.

Topping, K., Bremner, W., and Holmes, E.A. (2000) Social Competence. In R. Bar-On and J.D.A. Parker (eds.), *The Handbook of Emotional Intelligence*. San-Francisco: Jossey-Bass.

Tracy, S.J. (2000) Becoming a Character for Commerce: Emotion Labor, Self-subordination, and Discursive Construction of Identity in a Total Institution. *Communication Quarterly*, 14 (1): 90–128.

Turkle, S. (1996) *Life on the Screen*. London: Weidenfeld and Nicolson.

Vail, P.L. (1994) *Emotion: The On/Off Switch for Learning*. Rosemont: Modern Learning.

Vince, R. (2001) Power and Emotion in Organisational Learning. *Human Relations*, 54 (10): 1325–51.

Weick, K.E. (1995) *Sensemaking in Organizations*. London: Sage.

Westley, F.R. and Vredenburg, H. (1991) Strategic Bridging: The Collaboration between Environmentalists and Business on the Marketing of Green Products. *Journal of Applied Behavioral Science*, 27. 65–90.

Wetherall, M. (1966) Romantic Discourse and Feminist Analysis: Interrogating Investment, Power and Desire. In S. Wilkinson and C. Kitzinger (eds.), *Feminism and Discourse: Psychological Perspectives.* London: Sage.

Wharton, A. (1999) The Psychosocial Consequences of Emotional Labor. *The Annals of the American Academy of Political and Social Science,* 561 (January): 158–75.

Wiesenfeld, B.M., Raghurma, S., and Garud, R. (1999) Managers in a Virtual Context: The Experience of Self-threat and its Effects on Virtual Organizations. In C. Cooper and D.M. Rousseau (eds.), *Trends in Organizational Behavior,* Vol. 6, *The Virtual Organization.* Chichester: Wiley.

Zeidler, S. (1988) Don't Have a Nice Day – Workers Protest Smile Rule. *Reuters,* November 16.

29

Learning from Organizational Experience

John S. Carroll, Jenny W. Rudolph,
and Sachi Hatakenaka

CHAPTER OUTLINE

Learning-in-action, the cyclical interplay of thinking and doing, is increasingly important for organizations as environments and required capabilities become more complex and interdependent. Organizational learning involves both a desire to learn and supportive structures and mechanisms. We draw upon three case studies from the nuclear power and chemical industries to illustrate a four-stage model of organizational learning: (1) local stage of decentralized learning by individuals and work groups; (2) control stage of fixing problems and complying with rules; (3) open stage of acknowledgement of doubt and motivation to learn; and (4) deep learning stage of skillful inquiry and systemic mental models. These four stages differ on whether learning is primarily single-loop or double-loop, that is, whether the organization can surface and challenge the assumptions and mental models underlying behavior, and whether learning is relatively improvised or structured. The case studies illustrate how organizations learn differently from experience, the details of learning practices, and the nature of stage transitions among learning practices.

INTRODUCTION

Learning-in-action, the cyclical interplay of thinking and doing (Argyris and Schön, 1996; Daft and Weick, 1984; Kolb, 1984) is increasingly important for organizations as they struggle to cope with rapidly changing environments and more complex and interdependent sets of knowledge. We define *learning* as a change in situation–action linkages, and *organizational* learning as an analogous change at an organizational level.[1] Whereas learning is a *process* of change, the *content* of that process, the situation-action linkages, is *knowledge* (broadly construed to include explicit information, tacit know-how, etc.). Organizational knowledge is embodied in physical artifacts (equipment, layout, databases, documents), organizational structures (roles, reward systems, procedures), and people (skills, values, beliefs, practices) (cf., Kim, 1993; Levitt and March, 1988; Schein, 1992). Although organizations may "fill knowledge reservoirs" (Argote and Ingram, 2000) from theoretical principles, by imaginative rumination, or by observing others, enactment or putting this knowledge to use requires combining component-level knowledge and filling gaps by improvisation (Weick, 1998). Enacting more unfamiliar, tacit, contextual, or contested knowledge requires a more iterative, unpredictable, and emergent learning process (Carlile, 2002; Nonaka and Takeuchi, 1995).

Characteristics that support organizational learning

Carrying out organizational learning activities involves complex interdependencies across people and groups (Crossan et al., 1999; Kim, 1993). Knowledge is more than lists of facts that can be summed together (e.g., Nonaka and Takeuchi, 1995). Different parts of the organization, such as plant operators and corporate executives, "know" different things about how work is done. Their knowledge is contained in different reservoirs (Argote and Ingram, 2000) and expressed in different languages by groups that live in different "thought worlds" (Dougherty, 1992). Bridging across these groups requires common experiences and common referents, which are developed in bridging practices (Carlile, 2002; Cook and Brown, 1999) including cooperative action, shared representations, collaborative reflection, and exchanges of personnel (Gruenfeld et al., 2000). Such sharing requires mutual trust or psychological safety (Edmondson, 1999) to reveal areas of doubt and vulnerability and invest scarce local resources for uncertain collective future benefits.

Theories of organizational learning are typically expressed as lists of characteristics and/or linked constituent sub-processes. For example, Popper and Lipshitz (1998) suggest that organizational learning involves both a desire to learn and a set of structures and mechanisms to enact learning. Some mechanisms are closely integrated with task performance, whereas others are off-line or delegated to designated learners. Crossan et al. (1999) offer a four-process theory of organizational learning that begins with individual improvisation and leads through shared interpretation and integration to organizational institutionalization. Many specific skills support these organizational activities, including conflict management skills to enable diverse group members to work with one another (Jehn et al., 1999), inquiry skills to enhance conversations and surface assumptions (Isaacs, 1999), and systems thinking skills to link a wider variety of information into actionable models (Senge, 1990).

A stage model of organizational learning

Although theorizing about organizational learning is rich with lists of characteristics, the dynamics of actually developing those characteristics is difficult to understand. Are all equally important? How can we move from a lower level of capability to a higher one? One possibility is to structure a stage model of organizational learning that suggests how organizations typically grow in their capacity to learn (cf. Cohen and Levinthal, 1990), including a description of the challenges faced at various stages and the ways they can be overcome. Such a model could be used to examine change in individual organizations and also to understand the historical development of organizational learning practices in industries.

In the context of a stage model, we can identify learning skills and mechanisms that appear earlier or later in a developmental sequence. For example, Argyris and Schön (1996) suggest that organizations typically enact single-loop learning processes in response to an unanticipated mismatch between expected or desired outcomes and reality. Feedback is used to adjust actions in order to reduce the gap between desired and actual results. In contrast, double-loop learning goes further to challenge the appropriateness of goals or the basic cultural assumptions and mental models for influencing human behavior and predicting results (Argyris et al., 1985; Schein, 1992; Senge, 1990). There are related distinctions, for example, between "fixing vs. learning" (Carroll, 1998) and "control vs. learning" (Sitkin et al., 1994). Although single-loop learning is often disparaged in contrast to double-loop learning, most learning is undoubtedly single loop, and single-loop learning can be very powerful (Argyris, 1996; Miner and Mezias, 1996). Presumably, double-loop learning emerges later in organizational life, if at all.

Setting and methods for our case studies of nuclear power and chemical plants

In this chapter, we draw upon several case studies of organizational learning from the nuclear power and chemical industries in order to illustrate a four-stage model of organizational learning. The case study data from three separate sites are part of the results of a ten-year project on high-hazard organizations. The first case study is based primarily on written questionnaire responses from members of an interdisciplinary team charged with investigating a workplace injury at a nuclear power plant, supported by questionnaires to manager sponsors of the investigation and our own analysis of the team's written report. Although the questionnaires were completed approximately one year after the event as part of a larger study of many such teams, the first author had visited the plant immediately after the incident and had additional interview data. The second case study examines an organizational transformation at a nuclear power plant. The first author visited this plant regularly as part of a team advising the board of directors of the parent utility. The case data includes first-hand observation, document review, and interviews with a wide range of employees and other key informants over a four-year period of time. The final case study is based primarily on direct observation of a team during its three-week investigation of a fire at a chemical plant. The data include follow-up interviews with team members and managers several months later, along with analysis of the written report.

The stage model emerged inductively over the course of several years of research on plant-level self-analysis and self-improvement efforts. We noted apparent long-term effects of industry-level phenomena such as disasters (Three Mile Island, Chernobyl, Bhopal) and anticipated deregulation, and corporate-level shifts in policies and resources following economic hardship (Marcus and Nichols, 1999). We began to observe patterns in the problems faced by different plants in the same and different industries as they struggled to increase their capability to find and correct current operating problems and forestall future problems. Again and again, it seemed that different plants were either confronting the same challenges, or were further along or further behind each other.

Nuclear power plants and chemical plants are examples of high-hazard organizations, that is, distinctive work settings that include potential harm or death to large numbers of individuals in a single event, such as an explosion or crash. The special importance of learning in high-hazard organizations was recognized early in both the research and policy literatures (e.g., the seminal work of Turner, 1978, and Perrow, 1984, and the investigation of Three Mile Island, Kemeny et al., 1979). As Weick (1987: 112) stated, "organizations in which reliability is a more pressing issue than efficiency often have unique problems in learning and understanding." Organization theorists argue vigorously regarding whether high-hazard organizations are distinctive because of the inherent normalcy of accidents (Perrow, 1984; Sagan, 1993; Vaughn, 1996) or because they achieve "high reliability" through special organizational features that allow people to handle hazardous tasks with remarkably few problems (LaPorte and Consolini, 1991; Roberts, 1990). Weick et al. (1999) and others argue that maintaining high reliability requires mindfulness consisting of attention to hazards and weak signals (Vaughn, 1996), a broad action repertoire (Westrum, 1988), and a willingness to consider alternatives (March et al., 1991; Schulman, 1993). Weick and Sutcliffe (2001: 91) theorize that such "inquiry and interpretation grounded in capabilities for action" is encouraged by distinctive organizational processes, including preoccupation with failure and reluctance to simplify interpretations.

STAGES OF ORGANIZATIONAL LEARNING

Research specifically on organizational learning and more generally on organizational growth and development suggests a progression in structure, goals, skills, and culture. Whether we use a biological metaphor to talk about individual growth and learning (e.g., Rooke and Torbert, 1998), organizational life-cycles (e.g., Quinn and Cameron, 1983), or an historical analysis of organizational forms over time (Chandler, 1962; Malone and Smith, 1988; Perrow, 1970), we repeatedly find a progression in size, complexity, and interdependence with a more intrusive and unpredictable environment. Bohn (1994) provides a stage model of increasing process control knowledge, and Reason (1997: 61–5) offers a stage model of organizational control that moves from predominantly feedforward embedding of anticipated problems into procedures, to predominantly feedback learning from experience.

The four stages in figure 29.1 are presented as a provocative guide to analysis, not as a rigid model of development. "As Weber noted, ideal types are useful not because they are descriptively accurate – actual instances rarely evince all of the attributes of an ideal type – but because they serve as models that assist in thinking about social phenomena" (Barley and Kunda, 2001: 83). The stage model illustrates distinctly different ways that organizations can learn from experience. In any organization, there will be examples of each stage in operation in different parts of the organization and at different moments in time. It is healthy for organizations to enact multiple learning orientations and processes at many organizational levels (individual, team, department, and so forth) in order to draw on a wide range of capabilities and enable a creative tension between different approaches (Crossan and Hurst, 2001; Crossan et al., 1999; Weick et al., 1999). However, the latter stages require shared understanding and collaborative effort across the organization, so

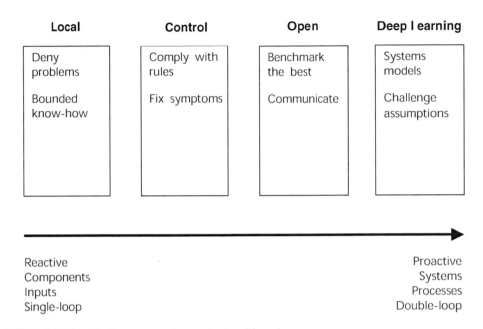

FIGURE 29.1   The four stages of organizational learning

these capabilities must become relatively widespread and commonly enacted if they are to be sustained. Although we propose that these stages and capabilities tend to emerge in a particular order, being "at" a stage means that there is relatively more behavior consistent with that stage and *earlier* stages.

Local stage

Most organizations begin their lives small, relatively unstructured, and personal or informal, like an entrepreneurial startup (Quinn and Cameron, 1983) or a craft shop (Perrow, 1970). Knowledge is based primarily on the experience and skill of individuals. Organization-specific and task-specific knowledge is local, contextual (Carlile, 2002), tacit (Nonaka and Takeuchi, 1995), and sticky or hard to transfer (von Hippel, 1994). Exceptions occur frequently, and the organization relies on technical expertise to cope with surprises and provide flexibility or resilience (Wildavsky, 1988). Decisions are made locally by those steeped in the details, and learning mostly occurs locally as well. Learning is decentralized in individuals or workgroups and primarily single-loop (Argyris and Schön, 1996), that is, behaviors are adjusted after comparison to performance standards or benchmark models, but underlying structures and assumptions are not challenged. The organization is minimal and hardly self-aware.

For example, from the beginning of the nuclear power industry, design engineers appear to have understood plant construction as a finite project that results in a production machine. Once built and debugged, the plants were expected simply to run, a belief echoed by nuclear utilities and regulators: "Technological enthusiasts heading the AEC [Atomic Energy Commission] believed most accidents were too unlikely to worry about" (Jasper, 1990: 52). Given this belief, little attention was paid to "minor" problems in a plant or other plants in the industry, unless those problems affected production. When a combination of minor problems and operators doing what they were trained to do produced the Three Mile Island (TMI) event in 1979, this constituted a "fundamental surprise"(Lanir, 1986) for the nuclear power industry. The information needed to prevent the TMI event had been available from similar prior incidents at other plants, recurrent problems with the same equipment at TMI, and engineers' critiques that operators had been taught to do the wrong thing in particular circumstances, yet nothing had been done to incorporate this information into operating practices (Marcus et al., 1989). In reflecting on TMI, the utility's president Herman Dieckamp said, "To me that is probably one of the most significant learnings of the whole accident [TMI] the degree to which the inadequacies of that experience feedback loop . . . significantly contributed to making us and the plant vulnerable to this accident" (Kemeny et al., 1979: 192). In the local stage, information necessary for learning does not travel easily beyond particular workgroups and contexts.

Control stage

Growth in terms of size and complexity is a major driver of formalization (e.g., Pugh et al., 1969). To achieve economies of scale, expertise is organized into workgroups and departments that often become classic "silos" of knowledge. To coordinate efficiently among workgroups and other sub-units, organizations generate standard operating procedures and other formal routines to make work uniform and predictable, and facilitate communication (Nelson and Winter, 1981; Levitt and March, 1988). Controls are instituted to encourage uniformity, including accounting controls, procedure manuals, training programs, planning processes, and so forth. The "machine" metaphor and technical logic dominates (Carroll, 1998), such that performance is viewed as a summation of component-level, often explicit and measurable, contributions. Learning itself is understood as a set of routines for training, performance feedback, statistical process control (Sitkin et al., 1994), after action review, procedure revision, and so forth. This learning is directed at further control through exploitation of the known rather than exploration of the unknown (March, 1991), single-loop evolutionary enhancements rather than double-loop revolutionary changes (Argyris and Schön, 1996).

For most of its history, the nuclear power industry attempted to improve operations and prevent accidents through creation and enforcement of bureaucratic controls. Elaborate probabilistic analyses were used to anticipate (Wildavsky, 1988) all possible failure paths and to design physical and procedural barriers to these paths. When problems occurred, incident reviews typically identified actions that failed to comply with the rules, such as operators who did not follow procedures or engineers who made erroneous calculations (Carroll, 1995; Reason, 1990). This single-loop learning tended to focus on causes proximal to the problem, with available solutions that could easily be enacted, and were acceptable to powerful stakeholders (Carroll, 1995; Tetlock, 1983). Line managers wanted concrete solutions that "fix" problems (Carroll, 1998) and avoided costly or unpredictable actions: they disparaged "trying to solve world hunger." The suggested corrective actions were usually to strengthen control mechanisms (more training, more supervision, more discipline), create more rules (more detailed procedures, more regulatory requirements), or design hazards and humans out of the system (according to technical design rules, e.g., "inherently safe" nuclear reactor designs). Compliance to industry standards, professional standards, and procedure manuals was backed up by layers of internal and external monitoring and record keeping.

Learning activities were separated from everyday work as part of training or a staff function to analyze problems or utilize industry experience. Staff specialists were accountable for investigation activity and corrective action programs without giving them any real authority. Problems stimulated blame that undermined information flow and learning (Morris and Moore, 2000; O'Reilly, 1978). For example, an inspector criticized one plant after he discovered a set of informal records of problems without a plan to address each problem. As one manager at a well-respected plant stated, "NRC [the US Nuclear Regulatory Commission] wants crisp problem identification and timely resolution." The plant's response was to stop documenting problems for which there were no immediate action plans, thus maintaining the "illusion of control" (Langer, 1975) but decreasing their potential for learning. Learning-in-action would represent a loss of control, both because it would acknowledge the unfinished nature of current routines (Schulman, 1993) and because the learning process itself is decentralized and informal.

Open stage

Large, conservative, bureaucratic organizations can be highly successful in stable environments, but in turbulent and unpredictable environments they do not learn or change fast enough. Bureaucratic controls over behavior fail when routines cannot be written and rewritten for all activities and when learning is restricted to specialized groups such as R&D. For example, Perron and Friedlander (1996) suggest that management systems for Process Safety Management "cannot yet be fully automated" (but notice the "yet"). Even when under pressure from new competitors with new products, rapidly changing technologies and customer preferences, deregulation, and so forth, large organizations may initially ignore these threats (Freeman, 1999). Eventually, increased pressure and enlightened employees at various levels may open the organization to self-analysis, elaboration of bureaucratic mechanisms, and innovation (Quinn and Cameron, 1983).

The open stage is marked by a climate of psychological safety (Edmondson, 1999) encouraging organization members to ask questions, explore, listen, and learn. Assumptions about authority and control give way to recognition of uncertainty and the need for collaborative learning. In the nuclear power industry, regulators and industry groups have long been calling for greater awareness of minor incidents and actions to avoid future trouble (Jackson, 1996; Rochlin, 1993). As Weick and Sutcliffe (2001: 91) state, "to move toward high reliability is to enlarge what people monitor, expect, and fear." Today, a typical nuclear power plant may identify over 2,000 problems or incidents per year, 90 percent of which would have been ignored in the past. Although efforts to accelerate learning may include technological initiatives such as web-based information exchanges and databases of new ideas and best-practice routines (Davenport and Prusak, 1997; Pan and Scarbrough, 1999), the open stage is based on attitudes and cultural values of involvement, sharing, and mutual respect. This goes beyond the typical response of adopting others' learning practices or buying consultants' solutions in an effort to treat learning as another activity to fix and control (cf. Sitkin et al., 1994).

Open stage plants are developing double-loop learning skills. Involvement of groups with different viewpoints provides feedback about varied assumptions and mental models and the impact of these assumptions on plant outcomes. With the stigma of reporting problems minimized, plants at the open stage are able to surface problems early and make the problems actionable. However, even the best plants still struggle with analyzing below the level of equipment problems, human error, and procedure inadequacies (Carroll, 1995, 1998, Carroll et al., 2001). Despite a desire to improve, investigators and managers seldom look for fundamental or deep systemic causes because they lack ready-made actions to address such issues and ways of evaluating their success (remnants of the control stage). The skills and discipline of deeper learning often develop later than the willingness to learn.

Deep learning stage

The final stage, as we envision it, would build upon the open stage by adding more capability for double-loop learning that promotes understanding of deep, systemic causes and creates a wider range of action possibilities to address such causes. Fundamental to double-loop learning is the recognition that one's view of external reality is shaped by internal cognitive frames. Organizations at this stage would be capable not only of mutual respect across internal and external boundaries, but also skillful inquiry and facility to gain insights, challenge assumptions, surface existing frames, and create comprehensive models (Argyris and Schön, 1996; Senge, 1990). Analyses would be based on facts but connect logically to systemic, organizational, cultural, and political viewpoints and experience with a repertoire of actions that can change these deep structures. Participants transcend component-level understanding and additive models of performance to develop systems thinking skills and more comprehensive mental models.

Deep learning practices are not widespread in the nuclear power and chemical industries. Carroll et al. (1998) relate one example of an innovative technique that introduced such practices to Du Pont chemical plants. As part of a company-wide cost-reduction effort, a benchmarking study showed that Du Pont spent more than its competitors on maintenance, yet had worse equipment availability. A culture of reactive firefighting had developed, with workers regularly pulled off jobs to do corrective maintenance. Responding to the benchmarking study, a series of cost-cutting initiatives were undertaken that had no lasting impact. Finally, one team questioned the tacit assumption that reducing maintenance costs could help reduce overall manufacturing costs; they thought that the effects of maintenance activities were tightly linked to so many aspects of plant performance that no one really understood the overall picture.

Du Pont was able to improve maintenance only after a collaborative conceptual breakthrough. An internal team developed a dynamic model of the system of relationships around maintenance (a "modeling for learning" exercise with the assistance of a researcher/consultant; Senge and Sterman, 1991). However, they were unable to transmit the systemic lessons of the model through ordinary means. Instead, the team created an experiential game in which plant employees play the roles of functional managers and discover new ways to think about plant activities, share their experiences and ideas, and test programs and policies. Having a broad range of employees with a system-wide understanding of the relationships between operations, maintenance, quality, and costs laid the groundwork for a successful pump maintenance pilot program. In the deep learning stage, the organization has the ability to surface assumptions, come up with alternative assumptions and models to guide action toward more desirable outcomes, experiment with the new ideas-in-action, and track feedback on their effectiveness.

In the remainder of this chapter, we present three case studies of organizations that made significant transitions from stage to stage. Presenting the cases as transitions clarifies the differences between stages and illustrates the challenges of changing behavior, emotions, and mental models. It also allows us to emphasize that organizations are now, and may always be, in transition. Following the case studies, we draw some lessons about learning-in-action and the stage model.

A Shift from Local to Control Stage

In the first case study, a nuclear power plant investigated an incident in which an employee was seriously hurt. This plant was attempting to improve safety and performance in part by using a newly upgraded incident investigation process. The investigation created an opportunity to raise collective awareness about local work practices and helped managers strengthen controls and increase conformity to rules.

Fall from roof

An electrical maintenance supervisor sent three men to replace light bulbs inside the "hot" machine shop, the area used to decontaminate equipment of radiological residue. The men headed off to the work area and discussed among themselves how to reach the light bulbs. They decided that one of them, whom we call Joe, would access the lights by climbing on the roof of a shed within the larger building. Joe and one co-worker dressed in anti-contamination suits and propped a ladder against the shed wall. Joe crawled up the ladder and onto the roof. As he was about to reach the lights, one of the roof panels gave way, dumping him 10 feet to the ground below. His injuries included a broken scapula, a broken rib, three fractures to the small bones near the spine, a lacerated lung and arm. His co-workers used a nearby phone to call for help. Emergency medical teams arrived shortly and took Joe to the hospital.

The plant's interpretation

For an event of this seriousness, a multi-discipline team was assembled to collect information, analyze causes, and make recommendations. The team noted that a number of standard operating procedures regarding safety assessment were not followed. When the electrical supervisor assigned three men to the job, no one was designated to be in charge. The supervisor did not conduct a pre-job brief (explaining the operational and safety issues involved in the job) and no one thought to walk down the job (conduct physical examination and discussion of the safety challenges at the work site) or plan the safest way to do the job. The workers failed to follow rules requiring fall protection (e.g., when aloft, wear a harness attached to a fixed support) and proper use of a folding ladder (unfold it, don't lean it against a wall).

The team's report noted that these actions and omissions may be part of a local culture of inappropriate risk-taking. The tone of the task was set, in part, by the most senior electrical worker of the three and the only one who had changed these light bulbs before. He told the others that they would "love this job 'cause it's kind of tight up there." Based on their interviews with Joe and others, the investigators speculated that this challenge struck Joe, who had just transferred to this department, as an "opportunity to succeed." Lastly, the workers ignored warning signs that the job was not routine. Nobody blinked when Joe was advised to stay on the one-and-a-half-inch steel framework of the building because it was the strongest part. Joe failed to reconsider the job when his hand slipped through a skylight and he nearly fell, shortly before slipping again and falling through.

The investigation team's report documented lack of compliance with established safety practices and suggested ways to enhance compliance with existing rules. The report concluded that:

> The cause of the accident was a failure of the employee, the employee in charge, and the supervisor to properly follow the Accident Prevention Manual requirements for working in elevated positions. The hazards associated with the job were not properly assessed; a stepladder was improperly used, and fall protection was not used when climbing on a structure.

The report then recommended that the plant should: (1) raise sensitivity to safety on routine jobs by appointing a full-time safety person; require managers to communicate to supervisors and supervisors communicate to employees the plant's expectations regarding industrial safety; and require department managers to provide feedback to the plant manager on each department's safety issues; (2) make more detailed guidelines on working aloft available to employees; (3) consider instituting a company-wide program on "Working in Elevated Positions," and (4) counsel all employees involved in the incident.

Making the transition between organizational learning stages

The incident investigation illustrates the plant's effort to shift its learning orientation from local to control. The report highlights the failure of the workers and the first line supervisor to comply with existing rules and procedures. The corrective actions aim to increase awareness and compliance with these rules by appointing a safety advocate, having superiors reinforce the safety message, and improving procedures. Information was generated about local work practices and compliance with rules that could be shared across groups, discussed openly, and used to institutionalize new work procedures. The focus is on changing actions to comply with rules in order to correct a mismatch between desired results (keep people safe) and actual results (Joe is hurt), that is, single-loop learning (Argyris and Schön, 1996).

Single-loop learning is very compatible with a desire for control and with the norms of the engineering profession that have shaped many industries such as nuclear power (Rochlin and von Meier, 1994). Carroll (1995: 187) argued that there is a "fixing" orientation dominated by analysis of complex situations into additive components, linear cause and effect thinking, a search among known solutions, a belief in the adequacy of current understanding, and an assumption that "any error is avoidable through engineering design and managerial controls."

In a control-oriented organization, managers are judged by their lack of problems or the speed with which problems are resolved and control reasserted. Challenges to that control are threatening and become political issues (Carroll, 1995; Tetlock, 1983). The investigation process itself is "delegated participation" (Nutt, 1999), a frequently ineffective process in which representatives suggest solutions to managers who may resist implementation (Carroll et al., 2002). One member of the investigation team commented, "When it was becoming apparent what the real problem was, I think the group became (temporarily) unsure where to go – what to do – it looked like a big step." It appears that the report writers had cause for concern. Another team member reported, "We put together three different drafts and each time someone in upper management disagreed with what we wrote. Finally the plant manager stepped in and accepted our answer."

The investigation team did not question their assumption that "compliance with safety rules will improve safety." A focus on compliance distinguishes those who make the rules from those who are being controlled. There is a contest for control between managers and engineers who are labeled as strategists and designers of the plant and operators and maintenance people who are labeled as implementers and doers (Carroll, 1998; Schein, 1996). The rules can become an empty ritual as alienated workers withdraw from the learning process. Without the opportunity to challenge underlying assumptions about why they work the way they do and the chance to reshape work accordingly, employees tend to feel that the corrective actions are simply another layer of control imposed from the outside. The investigators did not ask double-loop learning questions such as, "What frames do supervisors and workers hold that would allow a casual approach to safety develop and endure?"; "How does the status and career advancement system contribute to a culture of inappropriate risk taking?"; "What frames allowed management to have a design problem (lights in an unsafe place) exist for so long?"; or "How does the work system of separated functions and hierarchical authority inhibit mutual understanding?"

A SHIFT FROM CONTROL TO OPEN STAGE

The second case describes an organization-wide change effort in response to a crisis that shut down a large nuclear power station and nearly bankrupted the utility. It is a stark reminder of the importance of people in technically dominated companies.

The Millstone turnaround

In October 1996, the Millstone nuclear power station outside New London, Connecticut, received an unprecedented order from the US Nuclear Regulatory Commission (NRC) to keep its plants closed until they could demonstrate a "safety conscious work environment." The problem had come to public attention earlier through a cover story in *Time* magazine about harassment and intimidation of employees who brought safety concerns to management. An interviewee at Millstone (Carroll and Hatakenaka, 2001) labeled the management culture as "male . . . militaristic – control and command." The NRC review (Hannon et al., 1996) concluded that there was an unhealthy work environment, which did not tolerate dissenting views and stifled questioning attitudes among employees, and therefore discouraged learning and change. As the report said, "Every problem identified during this review had been previously identified to Northeast Utilities management . . . yet the same problems were allowed to continue."

New senior management was brought in to re-establish the trust of regulators, the public, and employees. Investments were made in physical improvements and extensive documentation to meet rising industry standards, but a critical component was culture change. Employees needed to feel safe about reporting concerns, to believe that managers could be trusted to hear their concerns and to take appropriate action. Managers had to believe that employees were worth listening to and worthy of respect. In short, the underlying values had to change from control to openness and trust. It took over two years to shift the culture and learning stage of the plant, but in June 1998 the internal oversight groups and external regulators certified that Millstone could restart its largest unit, and a second unit would restart a year later (the smallest and oldest unit was permanently decommissioned) (see Carroll and Hatakenaka, 2001 for more details).

The plant's interpretation

In September 1996, the new CEO for Nuclear Power, Bruce Kenyon, set the scene for change by an address to all employees on his first day, in which he introduced his values: high standards, openness and honesty, commitment to do what was right, and two-way communications. He immediately revamped the top management team and strengthened the employee concerns program.

His subsequent actions enacted and modeled openness and trust. Throughout the next months, Kenyon met regularly with small work groups and in large all-hands meetings to give information and encourage two-way communication: "It shocked them to get candid answers." Upon hearing Kenyon say publicly at his first NRC meeting that he found the organization "essentially dysfunctional," an interviewee from the NRC remembers thinking, "here's a fellow who at least recognizes the problem." Based on recommendations from an employee task force redesigning the employee concerns program, Kenyon agreed to create an Employee Concerns Oversight Panel (ECOP) to have an independent voice and report directly to him. ECOP was staffed with passionate advocates who argued with each other and with management, but over time they evolved a workable role. The panel's existence "sent a message to the work force that employees could act as oversight of management."

Kenyon allowed himself to be fallible and to enlist participation. When two contractors were terminated on the grounds of poor performance and the Director of the Employee Concerns Program provided evidence that the terminations had been improper, Kenyon quickly reversed his decision. As one of his senior managers recalls about their working relationship, Kenyon "went along with all my recommendations. He didn't always agree . . . [Sometimes he] swallowed hard." He called upon employees to voice their public support for Millstone to counterbalance media criticism: "when are you going to say what you think?" An *ad hoc* employee group self-organized, gathered over 1,500 signatures on a petition, attended public meetings, wrote to newspapers, and otherwise expressed their commitment to a management that trusted them to become part of the solution.

Individual managers experienced personal transformations that changed how they understood the nature of the problems. The case of the operations vice president was perhaps the most dramatic. Typical of the old-style management, he was weary of "whiners," and "didn't believe anyone would harass someone who brought forth safety concerns." When the two contractors were terminated and the employee concerns program offered their view that the terminations were improper, "It was one of those moments your perception changes . . . a watershed for me." He also remembers vividly his visit with several other Millstone managers to another nuclear power plant that had made a dramatic turnaround, where he learned that safety concerns could make business sense.

Millstone was typical of an industry in which managers are "not high on people skills, for example, few can read nonverbal signals." They had to appreciate that employees' perception was their reality. For example, when members of the training and operations departments were disciplined for inaccuracies in training documentation two years earlier, employees immediately assumed that the former training director was being punished because he had been an outspoken critic of management. Management had failed to anticipate reactions or to minimize the impression of retaliation. Managers had to learn new skills, including sensitivity to their own and others' emotions and perceptions. Through extensive new training programs and coaching by organizational development consultants, they had to "learn the difference between anger, hurt, and a chilling effect" and avoid confusing a fear of reprisal with a lack of confidence that management would take effective action.

Openness and trust emerged organically through multiple mechanisms and venues. We have already mentioned the Employee Concerns Program (ECP) that provided confidential ways to report issues for investigation and the Employee Concerns Oversight Panel (ECOP) that gave a direct connection between employee representatives and the CEO. The Executive Review Board was created after the contractor terminations to review all disciplinary actions, comprising senior managers and an ECOP representative as an observer. By opening up the management process, it helped restore employee trust in management, and created an environment for managers to learn and enact new values. The People Team, a coordinating group among human resources, legal department, ECP, ECOP, management, and organizational development consultants, met daily to respond to problems and to address issues and monitor progress. Internal Oversight groups and an independent third-party consulting group required by the NRC provided additional monitoring and advice. These multiple mechanisms and forums allowed broad participation so that managers and employees could share information, develop common language, learn by doing, and build trust by reacting well to challenges.

Making the transition between organizational learning stages

The NRC requirement that Millstone develop a "safety conscious work environment" and demonstrate this to the satisfaction of an independent third-party consultant was unprecedented in the industry. The NRC offered no guidance. Millstone had to find its own way to move from a control stage characterized by centralized authority and mutual suspicion to an open stage characterized by communication, trust, and participation.

Millstone managers were proud of Millstone's excellent record in the industry, built on technical leadership. Financial distress following the completion of the third unit led to an atmosphere of cost-cutting and production emphasis; the heroes were the ones who got the job done without breaking the budget. When employees complained about technical problems or the external regulators criticized them for lack of documentation or growing backlogs of work, managers ignored them or blamed the messengers. Managers believed that Millstone's design features and managerial controls were sufficient to operate the plant safety and reliably. Complaining employees and meddling regulators were annoying distractions that threatened their sense of control. In short, managers and employees lived in separate thought worlds (Dougherty, 1992) with strong cultural barriers and a perceived contest for control.

New senior management, external intervention, and an infusion of outside employees broke through some of that defensiveness. Management's basic assumption that "we know everything we need to know" was challenged (cf. Schulman, 1993). And so was employees' basic assumption that "management can't be trusted." Because senior management reacted well to critical events such as the contractor terminations, and independent voices were allowed to challenge the status quo, double-loop learning occurred. Multiple venues emerged for managers and employees to talk together and work on the common problem of rebuilding Millstone. Managers began to listen and trust the employees enough to act on what was being said; in turn, employees began to feel safer about speaking out (Edmondson, 1999) and to trust that management would listen and take action. The most powerful way to regain trust is to work together with a common purpose (Kramer, 1999; Whitener et al., 1998).

Managers not only became more open to information coming from employees and external observers, but also became aware of new kinds of information. Control-oriented managers, some of whom get their way by yelling and threatening, are generally unaware of their own emotionality and try to restrict any emotionality in their subordinates. They claim to value facts and rationality, even when they are using fear to exercise control. They did not realize that emotions and perceptions are reality. The more open environment at Millstone marked an increase in interpersonal skills and emotional intelligence (Goleman, 1995). Emotions and perceptions could be anticipated, considered, discussed, and managed.

A Shift to Deep Learning

The third case was part of a larger, plant-wide effort to begin using root cause analysis teams as a way to address, simultaneously, a recent history of financial losses, some dangerous incidents, and repeated equipment failures. The idea of using root cause analysis to address adverse incidents in the plant was introduced to plant management as a result of a merger with another petrochemical company, which used the root cause analysis process already. Two headquarters staff at this petrochemical company had been working for a decade to promote more strategic and systemic thinking at operational and executive levels, using root cause analysis as one of several approaches, and their progress was just beginning to accelerate. The Plant Manager had requested that they introduce their root cause analysis practice to his plant with a training intervention. The plant decided to train about 20 plant employees, operators, maintenance staff, engineers, and first line supervisors to conduct root cause analyses by exploring, in-depth, four significant recent incidents.

Each incident investigation team included some members from inside the plant and some from outside, and at least one experienced root cause facilitator. The overall process included training in investigation, analysis, and reporting methods during the course of a three-week time frame, culminating in reports to plant management. Training was timed to correspond to the needs of the teams as they collected maintenance and operations logs, reviewed physical evidence, interviewed involved parties and knowledgeable experts, analyzed causes, and prepared reports.

Charge heater fire

The charge heater fire investigation examined the explosion and fire in a charge heater that cost $16 million for lost production and repairs. Charge heaters are large gas-fueled burners used in the transformation of waste products from oil refining back into usable products through hydrocracking, a dirty and dangerous process requiring very high heat and pressure. The residue of this process is coke (coal dust), which can accumulate on the inside of heater tubes. In addition to unearthing causes of the explosion, plant managers also wanted to discover and ameliorate the conditions that led to this event and might lead to future events.

While the causal analysis presented below may seem extremely straightforward, its simplicity is the result of a rigorous and laborious root cause analysis process that involved four elements: a time line of events; an "Is/Is not" process that differentiates circumstances where the event occurred from similar circumstances where it did not (Kepner and Tregoe, 1981); a detailed causal event diagram; and a process of categorizing the quality of data used to draw inferences in the causal event diagram (as a verifiable fact, an inference, or a guess). In doing these analyses, members of the team argued with each other, built on each other's ideas, and alternated between stunned amazement and appreciation at the differences in each other's views of the refinery.

The plant's interpretation

Distilling and analyzing the information available, the team concluded that the explosion and fire were due to a tube rupture inside the charge heater that occurred when the tube's three-quarter inch steel skin got too hot and tore. The team found that three factors contributed to the heater explosion: (1) high heat input; (2) low heat removal; and (3) unawareness on the part of operators of the actual tube skin temperature. First, operators ran the burners in the charge heater unevenly to increase heat in order to achieve the desired production level, while avoiding alarms that would signal an unsafe condition. Second, heat was removed more slowly than usual from the tube skin because coke had adhered to the inside of the tubes and was acting as an insulator. There was more coke than usual because it was assumed that a new decoking process worked as well as the previous process and no one had checked for coke build up. Third, the combination of running some tubes hotter (at a higher gas pressure) and the build-up of coke moved the high-heat point up the tube. The thermocouple meant to detect temperature on the tube skin, set at a height specified in the heater design, was now below the hottest part of the tube, so that operators believed the tube temperature was acceptable. The tube ruptured above the thermocouple.

The team noted as a "key learning" that plant staff made decisions without questioning the assumptions that seemed to underlie them. First, the maintenance department changed decoking processes but did not know and never checked if the new process was effective. Second, operators increased the burner pressure in the charge heater to meet production goals but did not know the consequences of doing so. Third, operators changed the pattern of firing heater tubes (to fire hotter around the perimeter) but again did not know the consequences of doing so. On the basis of these insights, the team's lead recommendation for future action was that the plant identify "side effects" and be more aware of the broader "decision context" when changing production processes.

The team deepened their analysis as they discussed why assumptions about the effectiveness and safety of the new decoking process and the modified charge heater tube firing practices were never questioned at the time that changes were made. They speculated that their colleagues probably were unaware of the assumptions they were making. Our observations of the team's investigation and our *post hoc* interviews with team members highlight the team members' amazement and interest in "how quick we jump to conclusions about things." The team repeatedly mentioned the fact that, prior to learning the new investigation process, they rarely questioned their own conclusion-drawing processes and the assumptions that underlay them. One team member summarized his new approach by saying he now questions his co-workers: "I say, are you sure? Are you sure? Did you look at the initial aspects of what happened?"

As they worked on the investigation, the charge heater team frequently discussed their discovery of unanticipated and previously unknown interactions between apparently unrelated plant processes such as decoking and tube firing. When the team got to the bottom of their cause tree they noticed that each leg was a necessary but not sufficient contributor to the incident. In one of its verbal reports to other investigation teams during the training sessions, the charge heater team noted that, "We are seeing that several things combine over time to create an event." Independent decisions by maintenance to change decoking, the inspection service to trust that the new decoking was effective, and operators to change burner tube firing practices ended up interacting to produce the heater fire. The team described their learning to other teams by saying, "It appears that in most cases there are elements of human factors (systems) that show up if you dig deep enough."

Based on the insights from this team and from the other teams, the plant decided to implement a "Management of Change Process" to address the unanticipated side effects and interactions that caused problems. According to follow-up interviews with team members six months after their investigation, the actual results are mixed. One team member felt the plant management of change process had teeth:

> The biggest issue that came out [of the root cause analysis training] was management of change. MOC. Now people pay more attention to adhering to the MOC process. It may be that the RCA [root cause analysis] training helped focus attention on MOC. MOC is serious. It is real. If you don't do it, your job is on the line. If [you do] not do it, [you] have to explain why not.

However, another team member felt, "There are no legs on the management of change effort. It is just a lot of talk."

Making the transition between organizational learning stages

The charge heater investigation provides examples of an organization increasing both openness and deep learning. The independent decisions that changed decoking and heater tube firing practices illustrate aspects of the local stage of organizational learning. In our observations of the training session, it was evident that at least some participants were anxious about being open with colleagues in their own department or in other departments, or with management. Would operators talk to engineers? Would an operator working on this investigation be perceived as having sold out? Would managers listen to reports that were critical of their own behavior? The investigation could have blamed the operators for "getting around" the tube temperature alarms, ignored the role of management decisions about production goals, and instituted more monitoring and rules. A control approach to learning could have reinforced barriers to the open flow of information and discouraged participation, and failed to get at the underlying, systemic causes of the event.

However, plant management was not approaching its problems from the viewpoint of control. Instead, there was a desire to create more openness, and to demonstrate the value of openness and deep learning for achieving better performance. During the course of the training and investigation, teams experienced more openness and collaboration than they expected. There was a willingness to confront reality and to surface underlying assumptions about "how we do work around here." Support from a new plant manager helped encourage full participation. That support was itself an outcome of the training team who were working publicly with the investigation teams but privately meeting with management to reduce their defensiveness and enlist their visible engagement. And, it was evoked and reinforced by specific features of root cause analysis that require close attention to factual details, data quality, and cause–effect relationships.

The training team was very deliberate in bringing a deep learning approach to the plant. Their goal was to educate management by challenging their mental models with rich and compelling data and interpretations. The underlying concept was that managers establish the conditions for performance, that is, they manage the system. Managers do not control behavior, but rather provide the resources (people, time, money, equipment, plans, opportunities, legitimacy, procedures, etc.), shape the structures (e.g., silos vs. cross-functional teams), and set the values (e.g., "it's great we hit that production goal early, but how many safety corners did we cut to make it?") by which the system will operate.

The team investigation began to create deep learning when they started addressing operations at the plant from a systemic perspective and challenging assumptions. Paradoxically, the process of "drilling down" precisely and narrowly into causes of this incident allowed the team to develop new awareness of interdependencies across the system. They recognized interactions among components of the system and began to understand a central tenet of the quality movement (e.g. Goldratt and Cox, 1992) that working to optimize individual components does not automatically add up to an optimized system. Most importantly, they developed and practiced double-loop learning capabilities to recognize assumptions and mental models as separate from reality (Freidman and Lipshitz, 1992), understand that assumptions and mental models affect behaviors and outcomes, imagine alternative mental models to guide action toward more desirable outcomes, and take action with the new mental models (Argyris et al., 1985).

The process of root cause analysis encouraged awareness of mental models and ability to work *on* mental models rather than *through* them. The team became aware of their own mental models and the distinction between model and reality, which is a necessary step to double-loop learning (Friedman and Lipshitz, 1992). In our interviews with team members, they universally highlighted the benefit of having a diverse team because of the surprising differences among people's ways of looking at the same problem. The rigor of the root cause analysis process encouraged them to "hold their assumptions lightly" as the analysis held these views up to comparison and disconfirmation.

The cause–effect diagrams worked as a boundary object to help reveal tacit assumptions about plant processes that were key links in the causal chains leading to the heater explosion. The team's cause–event tree included the three assumptions: "[desired] charge rate [desired production rate] dictates heater firing"; "sandjetting works as well as steam air decoking [to remove coke from inside heater tubes]"; and "there are no 'hot spots' [overheated areas] on the tubes." Developing a gut sense that assumptions matter in shaping action and outcomes is important to overcome fears about "trying on" new mental models (Rudolph et al., 2000). Their recommendation that "identifying side effects and documenting decision context become a central part of decision making at [the plant]" implies a new insight: "Decisions made in one context may have side effects in other contexts and these are important to consider."

INSIGHTS ABOUT ORGANIZATIONAL LEARNING

A framework for the stages

The four organizational learning stages can be thought of as a progression, but the stages can also be examined for underlying dimensions and symmetries. In figure 29.2 we

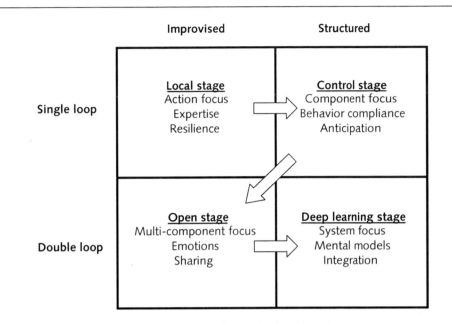

FIGURE 29.2 Attributes of the four stages of organizational learning

organize the four stages into a 2×2 table[2] representing two dimensions: (1) single- and double-loop learning; and (2) improvising and structuring. As we have discussed earlier in this chapter, single-loop learning adjusts goal-oriented actions based on feedback to better achieve the same goal (Argyris et al., 1985). In double-loop learning, a deeper inquiry surfaces and challenges underlying assumptions and values regarding the selection of that goal. Improvising is a process of acting intuitively into an emerging situation rather than following structured procedures or plans (Weick, 1998). In relation to the organizational learning framework of Crossan et al. (1999), improvising draws on processes of imagining and, to a lesser degree, interpreting and integrating. Structuring is about consistency and predictability embodied in routines and shared mental models. In relation to Crossan et al. (1999), structuring draws on processes of institutionalizing and, secondarily, integrating and interpreting. Brown and Duguid (2001) address the difficulties and benefits of simultaneously managing unstructured creative practices and explicit, structured processes.

The above analysis offers several important insights. First, it emphasizes the importance of the two dimensions. Although figure 29.1 suggests many differences among the four stages, the clearest underlying distinctions we have found seem to be the capabilities for single- and double-loop learning, improvising, and structuring. Local learning is single-loop and improvised, emerging from work practices and life experiences. Control is exercised by adding structure but it remains single-loop because underlying assumptions are rarely considered or changed. Open learning is double-loop and improvised, as individuals awaken to the limitations of the organization and challenge assumptions about separate domains of technical expertise, compliance with rules, hierarchy, and so forth. Deep learning is double-loop and adds structure as new tools for inquiry and collaboration spread through the organization.

Second, progress through the stages zigzags through the dimensions. In particular, the transition from controlled to open involves changing *both* dimensions, moving from structured single-loop learning to improvised double-loop learning. Perhaps this is a reason why the transition is so difficult and organizations seem to get stuck in the control stage. The most advanced of the companies we have studied are only beginning to transcend control, motivated by a few subversive visionaries and the intense pressures of competition and regulation. Anecdotal evidence suggests that companies adopt programs such as total quality management (TQM) and learning organization more to copy success stories and achieve legitimacy rather than through commitment and understanding.

Our third insight is more controversial – there will undoubtedly be arguments about whether the fourth stage should emphasize more rather than less improvisation. We came to our conclusions from a small number of case studies and a modicum of speculative analysis. However, we reiterate that organizations at the fourth stage have come through the earlier stages and are exhibiting behaviors and capabilities from the earlier stages. Thus, the deep learning stage *adds* structured, disciplined learning capabilities onto the learning values and improvisational capabilities of the open stage (as well as the capabilities of the local and control stages).

Progress through the stages

There appear to be multiple elements that must be brought together to support a transformation from one learning stage to another. Awareness and measurability are important, but so are cultural values and motives, supportive structures and resources, specific skills and tools, and concepts and mental models. The large, technologically driven organizations that we have studied do not appear to transform all these elements at once or even to change them gradually. Instead, there is a natural order to their focus. Control through measurement, monitoring, incentives, and other traditional bureaucratic mechanisms seems to come naturally to managers and engineers (Carroll, 1998; Schein, 1996) and enables movement from local learning to control. However, the control stage can become a competency trap that inhibits learning (Levitt and March, 1988).

Most of the organizations we have studied seem to move out of the control stage by recognizing the limitations of top-down control and promoting more participation and open exchange of information throughout the organization and between the organization and the outside world. The "questioning attitude" and "safety culture" advocated in these industries are directed at acknowledging doubt (Schulman, 1993), increasing awareness or mindfulness (Weick et al., 1999), creating psychological safety (Edmondson, 1999), respecting the contributions of others, and placing a positive value on teamwork and learning. Such trust can only be developed by observations of the experience of courageous pioneers who take early risks to tell the truth. When open behavior is validated by others, trust is built and openness spreads in a virtuous cycle.

The open stage is also characterized by an awareness of people as different from machines. An ability to acknowledge emotions, conflicts, and different perceptions that underlie work relationships and political contests allows for discussion of the human side of organization. Of course, some managers are uncomfortable and initially incompetent in this domain, but openness to its importance builds a greater emphasis on managers, employees, and consultants with people skills. Over time, people learn by doing and through feedback from colleagues and coaches.

Openness to learning becomes linked to a discipline for learning in the transition to what we call the deep learning stage. The complexity and pace of change of modern organizations requires more than a desire to learn. Special circumstances for learning and concepts and techniques that make learning more efficient are needed to break through long-held assumptions and cognitive habits. Deep learning is not simply the use of particular techniques such as root cause analysis. There are many versions of "root cause analysis," most of which are used with minimal training to find and fix problems (Carroll, 1995) rather than to challenge deep assumptions with rigorous and systemic thinking, just as TQM can be used for control rather than learning (Sitkin et al., 1994). It is not particular tools such as root cause analysis that lead to learning, but rethinking actions and assumptions in the context of new *concepts* that underlie the tools, such as data quality, rigorous cause–effect connections, systems thinking, mutual respect across groups, insight into personal and political relationships, and double-loop learning. The tools and the learning activities are only an opportunity to have new conversations, enact new behaviors, develop new skills, and build new relationships.

Learning-in-action

The cases reinforce the importance of learning through action. Although some kinds of knowledge are represented explicitly (numbers, words) and easy to store and transfer, many kinds of knowledge are difficult to represent or separate from their context. These kinds of knowledge have to be reconstructed by users, improvised, tried out and modified to suit the occasion. In the "Fall from roof" case, team members learned through their investigation process and interaction with management, and the organization learned from its failure (the accident) and by enacting the corrective action process. The "Millstone" case offers the clearest example of policy and culture change requiring an interactive and constructive process of learning and trying out new behaviors, then adjusting behaviors and mental models to the reactions of participants and the emerging definitions of success. The "Charge heater fire" investigation appears on the surface to be the introduction of new investigation and analysis techniques, but upon deeper reflection it represents a negotiated interaction among managers and workers, and among multiple worker groups, to achieve a new relationship of openness and collaborative engagement. Enactment is problematic, and learning is in the doing, individually and collectively. Learning is in the connection between action and reflection, in making knowledge actionable (implementation) and action knowledgeable (sensemaking) (Argyris et al., 1985; Crossan et al., 1999; Weick, 1995).

From this viewpoint, incident investigations involve both access to information and socially constructed processes such as imagination and negotiation. The collective analysis of factual details (with a disciplined logic that identified gaps) helped to drive a systemic understanding. The cause–effect diagrams were boundary objects (Carlile, 2002) negotiated by the team in a process of knowing (Cook and Brown, 1999) that helped surface previously unarticulated mental models of the work environment, compare them, and arrive at new, shared views. Some of the learning was articulated in the written report, another boundary object negotiated between the team and managers that initiates corrective actions and feeds databases, but much remained unwritten (although discussed as part of the reporting out process).

Experience with learning cycles increased tolerance for short-term difficulties and occasioned resource shifts away from production toward learning. A systemic view suggests that changes take time to unfold, that things get worse before they get better (since resources are shifted away from immediate needs), and that leverage points must be identified for selective investment in changes that are not simply ceremonial but actually transform practice. Problems are not simply someone's fault, but rather a feature of the system; altering that system takes deep understanding of which way to go and mobilization of broad support. This is more than "controlling" people. A good system may be difficult to understand; its principles may be hard to verbalize yet possible to learn through action or instruction. For example, a rigid grip of a rowing oar may increase the feeling of control but decrease absorption of the shock of uneven waters, thereby decreasing actual control. Managers may use "heavy-handed" incentives and authority to increase their feeling of control and drive non-compliance out of sight, simultaneously increasing the discrepancy between rules and actual behavior.

In summary, we have argued for the importance and difficulty of learning from experience, particularly when meaning must emerge from local bits and pieces and the enactment of new practices in complex and rapidly changing environments. Nuclear power plants and chemical plants are challenged by the hazards in their work processes to learn from problems and to overcome barriers to learning. The history of these industries and the case studies we have examined suggest that there is a common progression from local learning to a control orientation associated with single-loop learning, which is then held in place by managerial and professional culture. Yet problems continue to occur and many organizations seek to be more proactive by becoming a learning organization, which incorporates mutually reinforcing elements of attitudes and thinking patterns. Our results suggest that, to some degree at least, attitudes favorable to learning precede double-loop learning skills. The concepts and skills of deep learning seem to be difficult to master and to require significant commitment, discipline, and learning-in-action. Future research will undoubtedly put more flesh on the bones of this framework, and contribute alternative ways to think about organizational learning.

ACKNOWLEDGMENTS

This research was supported by National Science Foundation grants SBR96-1779 and SBR98-11451 and a Marvin Bower Fellowship at the Harvard Business School. Requests for reprints should be sent to the first author, 50 Memorial Drive, Cambridge, MA 02142. We greatly appreciate the cooperation of the nuclear power and chemical plant sites and the staff of their corrective action programs.

NOTES

1. This is similar to Argyris and Schön's (1996: 13) definition of theories of action as propositions of the form "if you intend to produce consequence C in situation S, then do [action] A". We preserve the form of these propositions but relax the focus on intentional learning to acknowledge that learning can occur without intention or awareness, and even without observable action (Glynn et al., 1994).

2. Because there were four stages, we wondered whether they could be placed into a 2×2 table. The dimensions of the table were induced from the case studies and should be treated as provisional.

REFERENCES

Argote, L. and Ingram, P. (2000) Knowledge Transfer: A Basis for Competitive Advantage in Firms. *Organizational Behavior and Human Decision Processes*, 82: 150–69.

Argyris, C. (1996) Unrecognized Defenses of Scholars: Impact on Theory and Research. *Organization Science*, 7: 79–87.

Argyris, C., Putnam, R., and Smith, D.M. (1985) *Action Science: Concepts, Methods and Skills for Research and Intervention*. San Francisco: Jossey-Bass.

Argyris, C. and Schön, D. (1996) *Organizational Learning II: Theory, Method, and Practice*. Reading MA: Addison-Wesley.

Barley, S.R. and Kunda, G. (2001) Bringing Work Back In. *Organization Science*, 12: 76–95.

Bohn, R.E. (1994) Measuring and Managing Technological Knowledge. *Sloan Management Review*, Fall: 61–73.

Brown, J.S. and Duguid, P. (2001) Creativity versus Structure: A Useful Tension. *MIT Sloan Management Review*, 42: 93–4.

Carlile, P.R. (2002) A Pragmatic View of Knowledge and Boundaries: Boundary Objects in New Product Development. *Organization Science*, 13: 442–55.

Carroll, J.S. (1995) Incident Reviews in High-hazard Industries: Sensemaking and Learning under Ambiguity and Accountability. *Industrial and Environonmental Crisis Quarterly*, 9: 175–97.

Carroll, J.S. (1998) Organizational Learning Activities in High-hazard Industries: The Logics Underlying Self-analysis. *Journal of Management Studies*, 35: 699–717.

Carroll, J.S. and Hatakenaka, S. (2001) Driving Organizational Change in the Midst of Crisis. *MIT Sloan Management Review*, 42: 70–9.

Carroll, J.S., Rudolph, J.W., and Hatakenaka, S., (2002) The Difficult Hand-over from Incident Investigation to Implementation: A Challenge for Organizational Learning. In B. Wilpert and B. Fahlbruch (eds.) *System Safety: Challenges and Pitfalls of Intervention*. Boston: Pergamon, 189–206.

Carroll, J.S., Rudolph, J.W., Hatakenaka, S., Wiederhold, T.L., and Boldrini, M. (2001) Learning in the Context of Incident Investigation Team Diagnoses and Organizational Decisions at Four Nuclear Power Plants. In E. Salas and G. Klein (eds.) *Linking Expertise and Naturalistic Decision Making*. Mahwah, NJ: Lawrence Erlbaum, 349–65.

Carroll, J.S., Sterman, J., and Marcus, A.A. (1998) Losing the Maintenance Game: How Mental Models Drive Organizational Decisions. In R.N. Stern and J.J. Halpern (eds.) *Debating Rationality: Nonrational Aspects of Organizational Decision Making*. Ithaca, NY: Cornell University ILR Press.

Chandler, A.D. (1962) *Strategy and Structure*. New York: Doubleday.

Cohen, W.M. and Levinthal, D.A. (1990) Absorptive Capacity: A New Perspective on Learning and Innovation. *Administrative Science Quarterly*, 35: 128–52.

Cook, S.D.N. and Brown, J.S. (1999) Bridging Epistemologies: The Generative Dance between Organizational Knowledge and Organizational Knowing. *Organization Science*, 10: 381–400.

Crossan, M.M. and Hurst, D. (2001) *Strategic Renewal as Improvisation: Reconciling the Tension Between Exploration and Exploitation*. London, Ontario: Richard Ivey School of Business, unpublished manuscript.

Crossan, M.M., Lane, H.W., and White, R.E. (1999) An Organizational Learning Framework: From Intuition to Institution. *Academy of Management Review*, 24: 522–37.

Daft, R.L. and Weick, K.E. (1984) Toward a Model of Organizations as Interpretation Systems. *Academy of Management Review*, 9: 284–95.

Davenport, T. and Prusak, L. (1997) *Working Knowledge*. Boston, Harvard Business School Press.

Dougherty, D. (1992) Interpretive Barriers to Successful Product Innovation in Large Firms. *Organization Science*, 3: 179–202.

Edmondson, A. (1999) Psychological Safety and Learning Behavior in Work Teams. *Administrative Science Quarterly*, 44: 350–83.

Freeman, S. F. (1999) Identity Maintenance and Adaptation: A Multilevel Analysis of Response to Loss. *Research in Organizational Behavior*, 21: 247–94.

Freidman, V.J. and Lipshitz, R. (1992) Teaching People to Shift Cognitive Gears: Overcoming Resistance on the Road to Model II. *Journal of Applied Behavioral Science*, 28 (1): 118–36.

Glynn, M.A., Lant, T.K., and Milliken, F.J. (1994) Mapping Learning Processes in Organizations: A Multi-level Framework Linking Learning and Organizing. *Advances in Managerial Cognition and Organizational Information Processing, Vol. 5*. Greenwich, CT: JAI Press, 43–83.

Goldratt, E.M. and Cox, J. (1992) *The Goal: A Process of Ongoing Improvement*. Great Barrington, MA: North River Press.

Goleman, D. (1995) *Emotional Intelligence*. New York: Bantam.

Gruenfeld, D.H., Martorana, P.V., and Fan, E.T. (2000) What Do Groups Learn from their Worldiest Members? Direct and Indirect Influence in Dynamic Teams. *Organizational Behavior and Human Decision Processes*, 82: 45–59.

Hannon, J.N. et al. (1996) *Handling of Employee Concerns and Allegations at Millstone Nuclear Power Station Units 1, 2, and 3 from 1985 – Present*. Millstone Independent Review Group, October 24.

Isaacs, W. (1999) *Dialogue and the Art of Thinking Together*. New York: Currency Doubleday.

Jackson, S.A. (1996) *Challenges for the Nuclear Power Industry and its Regulators: The NRC Perspective*. Speech presented at the Regulatory Information Conference, Washington, DC, April 9.

Jasper, J.M. (1990) *Nuclear Politics: Energy and the State in the United States, Sweden, and France*. Princeton, NJ: Princeton University Press.

Jehn, K.A., Northcraft, G.B., and Neale M.A. (1999) Why Differences Make a Difference: A Field Study of Diversity, Conflict, and Performance in Workgroups. *Administrative Science Quarterly*, 44: 741–63.

Kemeny, J.G., Babbitt, B., Haggerty, P.E. et al. (1979) *Report of the President's Commission on the Accident at Three Mile Island*. New York: Pergamon.

Kepner, C.H. and Tregoe, B.B. (1981) *The New Rational Manager*. Princeton, NJ: Princeton University Press.

Kim, D.H. (1993) The Link between Individual and Organizational Learning. *Sloan Management Review*, 35: 37–50.

Kolb, D.A. (1984) *Experiential Learning as the Source of Learning and Development*. Englewood Cliffs, NJ: Prentice-Hall.

Kramer, R.M. (1999) Trust and Distrust in Organizations: Emerging Perspectives, Enduring Questions. *Annual Review of Psychology*, 50: 569–98.

Langer, E.J. (1975) The Illusion of Control. *Journal of Personality and Social Psychology*, 32: 311–28.

Lanir, Z. (1986) *Fundamental Surprise*. Eugene, OR: Decision Research.

LaPorte, T.R. and Consolini, P.M. (1991) Working in Practice but not in Theory: Theoretical Challenges of "High-Reliability Organizations". *Journal of Public Administration Research*, 1 (1): 19–47.

Levitt, B. and March, J.G. (1988) Organizational Learning. *Annual Review of Sociology*, 14: 319–40.

Malone, T.W. and Smith, S.A. (1988) Modeling the Performance of Organizational Structures. *Operations Research*, 36: 421–36.

March, J.G. (1991) Exploration and Exploitation in Organizational Learning. *Organization Science*, 2: 71–87.

March, J.G., Sproull, L., and Tamuz, M. (1991) Learning from Samples of One or Fewer. *Organization Science*, 2: 1–13.

Marcus, A.A., Bromiley, P., and Nichols, M. (1989) *Organizational Learning in High Risk Technologies: Evidence from the Nuclear Power Industry*. Minneapolis: University of Minnesota Strategic Management Research Center, Discussion Paper #138.

Marcus, A.A. and Nichols, M. (1999) On the Edge: Heeding the Warnings of Unusual Events. *Organization Science*, 10: 482–99.

Miner, A.S. and Mezias, S.J. (1996) Ugly Duckling no More: Pasts and Futures of Organizational Learning Research. *Organization Science*, 7: 88–99.

Morris, M.W. and Moore, P.C. (2000) The Lessons We (don't) Learn: Counterfactual Thinking and Organizational Accountability after a Close Call. *Administrative Science Quarterly*, 45: 737–65.

Nelson, R. and Winter, S. (1981) *An Evolutionary Theory of Economic Change*. Cambridge, MA: Harvard University Press.

Nonaka, I., and Takeuchi, H. (1995) *The Knowledge-Creating Company: How Japanese Companies Create the Dynamics of Innovation*. New York: Oxford University Press.

Nutt, P.C. (1999) Surprising but True: Half the Decisions in Organizations Fail. *Academy of Management Executive*, 13: 75–90.

O'Reilly, C.A. (1978) The Intentional Distortion of Information in Organizational Communication: A Laboratory and Field Approach. *Human Relations*, 31: 173–93.

Pan, S.L. and Scarbrough, H. (1999) Knowledge Management in Practice: An Exploratory Case Study. *Technology Analysis and Strategic Management*, 11: 359–74.

Perrow, C. (1970) *Organizational Analysis: A Sociological View*. Belmont, CA: Wadsworth.

Perrow, C. (1984) *Normal Accidents*. New York: Basic Books.

Perron, M.J. and Friedlander, R.H. (1996) The Effects of Downsizing on Safety in the CPI/HPI. *Process Safety Progress*, 15 (1): 18–25.

Popper, M. and Lipshitz, R. (1998) Organizational Learning Mechanisms: A Structural and Cultural Approach to Organizational Learning. *Journal of Applied Behavioral Science*, 34: 161–79.

Pugh, D.S., Hickson, D.J., Hinings, C.R., and Turner, C. (1969) The Context of Organization Structures. *Administrative Science Quarterly*, 14: 19–114.

Quinn, R.E. and Cameron, K. (1983) Organizational Life Cycles and Shifting Criteria of Effectiveness: Some Preliminary Evidence. *Management Science*, 29: 33–51.

Reason, J. (1990) *Human Error*. New York: Cambridge University Press.

Reason, J. (1997) *Managing the Risks of Organizational Accidents*. Brookfield, VT: Ashgate.

Roberts, K.H. (1990) Some Characteristics of One Type of High Reliability Organization. *Organization Science*, 2: 160–76.

Rochlin, G.I. (1993) Defining "High Reliability" Organizations in Practice: A Taxonomic Prologue. In K.H. Roberts (ed.), *New Challenges To Understanding Organizations*. New York: Macmillan.

Rochlin, G.I. and von Meier, A. (1994) Nuclear Power Operations: A Cross-cultural Perspective. *Annual Review of Energy and the Environment*, 19: 153–87.

Rooke, D. and Torbert, W.R. (1998) Organizational Transformation as a Function of CEO's Developmental Stage. *Organization Development Journal*, 16: 11–28.

Rudolph, J.W., Taylor, S.S., and Foldy, E.G. (2000) Collaborative Off-line Reflection: A Way to Develop Skill in Action Science and Action Inquiry. In P. Reason and H. Bradbury (eds.), *Handbook of Action Research*. Thousand Oaks: Sage.

Sagan, S.D. (1993) *The Limits of Safety: Organizations, Accidents, and Nuclear Weapons*. Princeton, NJ: Princeton University Press.

Schein, E.H. (1992) *Organizational Culture and Leadership*, 2nd edn. San Francisco: Jossey-Bass.

Schein, E.H. (1996) The Three Cultures of Management: Implications for Organizational Learning. *Sloan Management Review*, 38: 9–20.

Schulman, P.R. (1993) The Negotiated Order of Organizational Reliability. *Administration and Society*, 25, 353–72.

Senge, P. (1990) *The Fifth Discipline*. New York: Doubleday.

Senge, P. and Sterman, J.D. (1991) Systems Thinking and Organizational Learning: Acting Locally and Thinking Globally in the Organization of the Future. In T. Kochan and M. Useem (eds.), *Transforming Organizations*. Oxford: Oxford University Press, 353–70.

Sitkin, S.B., Sutcliffe, K.M., and Schroeder, R.G. (1994) Distinguishing Control from Learning in Total Quality Management: A Contingency Perspective. *Academy of Management Review*, 18 (3): 537–64.

Tetlock, P.E. (1983) Cognitive Style and Political Ideology. *Journal of Personality and Social Psychology*, 45: 118–26.

Turner, B.A. (1978) *Man-Made Disaster*. London: Wykeham.

Vaughn, D. (1996) *The Challenger Launch Decision*. Chicago: Chicago University Press.

von Hippel, E. (1994) "Sticky Information" and the Locus of Problem Solving: Implications for Innovation. *Management Science*, 40 (4): 429–39.

Weick, K.E. (1987) Organizational Culture as a Source of High Reliability. *California Management Review*, Winter: 112–27.

Weick, K.E. (1995) *Sensemaking in Organizations*. Thousand Oaks, CA: Sage.

Weick, K.E. (1998) Improvisation as a Mindset for Organizational Analysis. *Organization Science*, 9: 543–55.

Weick, K.E. and Sutcliffe, K.M. (2001) *Managing the Unexpected: Assuring High Performance in an Age of Complexity*. Ann Arbor, MI: University of Michigan Press.

Weick, K.E., Sutcliffe, K.M., and Obstfeld, D. (1999) Organizing for High Reliability: Processes of Collective Mindfulness. *Research in Organizational Behavior*, 21: 81–123.

Westrum, R. (1988) Organizational and Inter-organizational Thought. Paper presented at the World Bank Conference on Safety Control and Risk Management.

Whitener, E.M., Brodt, S.E., Korsgaard, M.A., and Werner, J.M. (1998) Managers as Initiators of Trust: An Exchange Relationship Framework for Understanding Managerial Trustworthy Behavior. *Academy of Management Review*, 23: 513–30.

Wildavsky, A. (1988) *Searching for Safety*. New Brunswick, NJ: Transaction Press.

30

Deliberate Learning and the Evolution of Dynamic Capabilities*

Maurizio Zollo and Sidney G. Winter

Chapter Outline

This chapter investigates the mechanisms through which organizations develop dynamic capabilities, defined as routinized activities directed to the development and adaptation of operating routines. It addresses the role of (1) experience accumulation, (2) knowledge articulation and (3) knowledge codification processes in the evolution of dynamic, as well as operational, routines. The argument is made that dynamic capabilities are shaped by the co-evolution of these learning mechanisms. At any point in time, firms adopt a mix of learning behaviors constituted by a semi-automatic accumulation of experience and by deliberate investments in knowledge articulation and codification activities. The relative effectiveness of these capability-building mechanisms is analyzed here as contingent upon selected features of the task to be learned, such as its frequency, homogeneity, and degree of causal ambiguity. Testable hypotheses about these effects are derived. Somewhat counterintuitive implications of the analysis include the relatively superior effectiveness of highly deliberate learning processes, such as knowledge codification, at lower levels of frequency and homogeneity of the organizational task, in contrast with common managerial practice.

Introduction

Explaining the variation in the degree of success of business organizations by reference to different degrees and qualities of organizational knowledge and competence has been a major focus of recent theorizing in both strategic management and organizational theory. Concepts and labels coined to characterize the phenomenon abound. From pioneering

* This chapter first appeared in *Organization Science* (2002), Vol. 13, pp. 339–44. It is reproduced with permission from the publishers.

efforts, such as Selznick's (1957) "distinctive competence," to the more recent and refined notions of organizational routines (Nelson and Winter, 1982), absorptive capacity (Cohen and Levinthal, 1990), architectural knowledge (Henderson and Clark, 1990), combinative capabilities (Kogut and Zander, 1992), and, finally, dynamic capabilities (Teece et al., 1997) there are decades of investment in sorting out the traits and the boundaries of the phenomena. Recent contributions (Eisenhardt and Martin, 2000; Dosi et al., 2000) aim at clarifying distinctions among the various constructs. As the field progresses in the characterization of the phenomena, however, the need for a better understanding of the origins of capabilities becomes increasingly apparent. What ultimately accounts for the fact that one organization exhibits "competence" in some area, while another does not? And how do we explain the growth and decay of that particular competence, other than the simple repetition, or lack thereof, of decisions and behavior?

This chapter sets forth a theoretical account of the genesis and evolution of dynamic capabilities that focuses on the role of several learning mechanisms and their interaction with selected attributes of the organizational task being learned. We begin our discussion by presenting a general framework linking learning mechanisms to the evolution of dynamic capabilities, and these to the evolution of operating routines. We then draw on evolutionary economics to develop a more fine-grained representation of how organizational knowledge evolves at the level of operating routines as well as of dynamic capabilities. In the following section we discuss the different learning mechanisms in terms of a spectrum of learning investments and identify the contextual features that shape their roles. Finally, in the last section, we explore in detail how some key attributes of the organizational task under consideration affect the relative effectiveness of these learning mechanisms and develop testable hypotheses for future empirical work.

ORGANIZATIONAL LEARNING AND DYNAMIC CAPABILITIES

Our first objective is to develop a framework describing the linkages among the processes we intend to study. We describe a set of learning mechanisms encompassing both the relatively passive experiential processes of learning ("by doing") and more deliberate cognitive processes having to do with the articulation and codification of collective knowledge. These learning processes are responsible for the evolution in time of two sets of organizational activities: one geared towards the operational functioning of the firm (both staff and line activities) which we will refer to as *operating routines*; the other dedicated to the modification of operating routines, which we identify with the notion of *dynamic capabilities*.

Below, we provide a more detailed description of how we conceive of dynamic capabilities, and of the function of the identified learning mechanisms.

Dynamic capabilities

Building on Nelson and Winter's view of the organization as a set of interdependent operational and administrative routines, which slowly evolve on the basis of performance feedbacks, Teece et al. (1997) define the concept of "dynamic capabilities" as "the firm's ability to integrate, build and reconfigure internal and external competencies to address rapidly changing environments." While this suggests something of what dynamic capabilities are for and how they work, it leaves open the question of where they come from. Also, the definition seems to require the presence of "rapidly changing environments" for the existence of dynamic capabilities, but firms obviously do integrate, build, and reconfigure their competencies even in environments subject to lower rates of change. We propose the following alternative:

DEFINITION: *A dynamic capability is a learned and stable pattern of collective activity through which the organization systematically generates and modifies its operating routines in pursuit of improved effectiveness.*

In addition to avoiding the near-tautology of defining capability as ability, this definition has the advantage of specifically identifying operating routines, as opposed to the more generic "competencies," as the object on which dynamic capabilities operate. Also, it begins to spell out some of the characteristics of this construct. The words "learned and stable pattern" and "systematically" highlight the point that dynamic capabilities are structured and persistent; an organization that adapts in a creative but disjointed way to a succession of crises is not exercising a dynamic capability. Dynamic capability is exemplified by an organization that adapts its operating processes through a relatively stable activity dedicated to process improvements. Another example is given by an organization that develops from its initial experiences with acquisitions or joint ventures a process to manage such projects in a systematic and relatively predictable fashion. The ability to plan and effectively execute post-acquisition integration processes is another example of a dynamic capability, as it involves the modification of operating routines in both the acquired and the acquiring unit.

Figure 30.1 offers a generic picture of the organizational processes under consideration and of the linkages between them. Dynamic capabilities arise from learning; they constitute the firm's systematic methods for modifying operating routines. To the extent that the learning mechanisms are themselves systematic, they could (following Collis, 1994) be regarded as "second order" dynamic capabilities. Learning mechanisms shape operating routines directly as well as by the intermediate step of dynamic capabilities.

Learning mechanisms

What mechanisms are involved in the creation and evolution of dynamic capabilities? What features distinguish an organization capable of systematically developing new and enhanced understanding of the causal linkages between the actions it takes and the performance outcomes it obtains?

In the spirit of bridging the behavioral and cognitive approaches to the organizational learning phenomenon (Glynn et al., 1994), we attend both to the experience accumulation process and to more deliberate cognitive processes involving the articulation and codification of knowledge derived from reflection upon past experiences.[1] The three mechanisms focal to this analysis are introduced and discussed separately below.

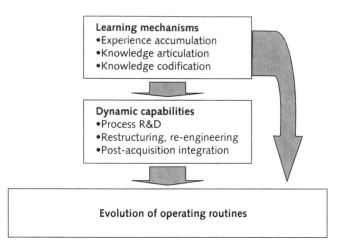

FIGURE 30.1   Learning, dynamic capabilities, and operating routines

Organizational routines and experience accumulation   Routines are stable patterns of behavior that characterize organizational reactions to variegated, internal or external stimuli. Every time an order is received from a customer, or a decision is made to upgrade a production process, for instance, a host of predictable and interrelated actions are initiated which will eventually conclude with the shipping of the ordered goods (and receipt of corresponding payment) or with the launch of the new production system. In spite of the superficial similarity between these two examples, though, the two patterns of behavior present a theoretically relevant distinction. The first type of routine involves the execution of known procedures for the purpose of generating current revenue and profit, while the second seeks to bring about desirable changes in the existing set of operating – in this case, production – routines, for the purpose of enhancing profit in the future. Routines of the second type are traditionally identified as *search* routines in evolutionary economics (Nelson and Winter, 1982), and are here regarded as constitutive of dynamic capabilities.

Routines of the two types have different effects on the generation and appropriation of rents, depending on the pace of change in the environment. Of course, effective operating routines are always a necessity, and superior operating routines are always a source of advantage. In a relatively static environment, a single learning episode may suffice to endow an organization with operating routines that are adequate, or even a source of advantage, for an extended period. Incremental improvements can be accomplished through the tacit accumulation of experience and sporadic acts of creativity. Dynamic capabilities are unnecessary, and if developed may prove too costly to maintain. But in a context where technological, regulatory and competitive conditions are subject to rapid change, persistence in the same operating routines quickly becomes hazardous. Systematic change efforts are needed to track the environmental change; both superiority and viability will prove transient for an organization that has no dynamic capabilities. Such capabilities must themselves be developed through learning. If change is not only rapid but also unpredictable and variable in direction, dynamic capabilities and even the higher-order learning approaches will themselves need to be updated repeatedly. Failure to do so turns core competencies into core rigidities (Leonard-Barton, 1992).

To our knowledge at least, the literature does not contain any attempt at a straight-forward answer to the question of how routines – much less dynamic capabilities – are generated and evolve. That is hardly surprising, for it seems clear that routines often take shape at the conjunction of causal processes of diverse kinds – for example, engineering design, skill development, habit formation, particularities of context, negotiation, coinci-dences, efforts at imitation and ambitions for control confronting aspirations for autonomy. In general, however, the literature that is relatively explicit on the question suggests that "routines reflect experiential wisdom in that they are the outcome of trial and error learn-ing and the selection and retention of past behaviors" (Gavetti and Levinthal, 2000: 113). This view is linked to an emphasis on the importance of tacit knowledge, since tacitness arises when learning is experiential. It is also linked to the notion that organizational rou-tines are stored as procedural memory (Cohen and Bacdayan, 1994), and to the image of routinized response as quasi-automatic. And it is consistent with the traditional view of organizational learning as skill building based on repeated execution of similar tasks that is implicit in much of the empirical literature on learning curves (see, e.g., Argote, 1999).

We incorporate this view in our discussion here, using the term "experience accumu-lation" to refer to the central learning process by which operating routines have tradi-tionally been thought to develop. In adopting this usage, we seek to provide a clear baseline for our analysis of some of the other learning processes that shape routines and dynamic capabilities. With respect to the latter, it seems clear that a theory of their development and evolution must invoke mechanisms that go beyond semi-automatic stimulus-response processes and tacit accumulation of experience.

Knowledge articulation   One of the recognized limitations of the behavioral tradition in the study of organizational learning consists in the lack of appreciation of the deliberative process through which individuals and groups figure out what works and what doesn't in the execution of a certain organizational task (Cangelosi and Dill, 1965: 196; Levinthal and March, 1981: 208; Narduzzo et al., 2000). Important collective learning happens when individuals express their opinions and beliefs, engage in constructive confrontations and challenge each other's viewpoints (Argyris and Schön, 1978; Duncan and Weiss, 1979). Organizational competence improves as members of an organization become more aware of the overall performance implications of their actions, and is the direct consequence of a cognitive effort more or less explicitly directed at enhancing their understanding of these causal links. We therefore direct attention to a second mechanism of development of col-lective competence, the process through which implicit knowledge is articulated through collective discussions, de-briefing sessions and performance evaluation processes. By sharing their individual experiences and comparing their opinions with those of their col-leagues, organization members can achieve an improved level of understanding of the causal mechanisms intervening between the actions required to execute a certain task and the performance outcomes produced. Organizational processes are often subject to signif-icant causal ambiguity with respect to their performance implications (Lippman and Rumelt, 1982), and particularly so in rapidly changing environmental contexts. Higher-level cognitive efforts and a more deliberate, collective, focus on the learning challenge can help to penetrate the ambiguity – although some part of it always persists. It is important to note that only a small fraction of articulable knowledge is actually articulated, and that organizations differ substantially on the degree to which they transform potentially articulable knowledge into articulated statements (Winter, 1987; Kogut and Zander, 1992; Cowan et al., 2000). While potentially requiring significant efforts and commitment on the part of the members of the organization, such articulation efforts can produce an improved understanding of the new and changing action-performance links, and therefore result in adaptive adjustments to the existing sets of routines or in enhanced recognition of the need for more fundamental change.

Knowledge codification   An even higher level of cognitive effort is required when individuals codify their understandings of the performance implications of internal routines in written tools, such as manuals, blueprints, spreadsheets, decision support systems, project management software etc. Knowledge codification is a step beyond knowledge articulation. The latter is required in order to achieve the former, while the opposite is obviously not true. The fact that in most cases articulated knowledge is never codified bears witness to additional costs incurred when stepping up the learning effort from a simple sharing of individual experience to developing manuals and other process-specific tools.

Note that, while some of these tools are deliberately aimed at uncovering the linkages between actions and performance outcomes (such as performance appraisals, post-mortem audits etc.) most of them are intended simply to provide guidelines for the execution of future tasks. Whatever the intentions motivating the codification effort, the process through which these tools are created and consistently updated implies an effort to understand the causal links between the decisions to be made and the performance outcomes to be expected, even though learning might not be the deliberate goal of the codification effort. To illustrate, both the readers and the authors of this article have certainly experienced the significant increase in the clarity of their ideas consequent to the act of writing the first draft of a research paper. Through the writing process, one is forced to expose the logical steps of one's arguments, to unearth the hidden assumptions and to make the causal linkages explicit. Similarly, a group of individuals who are in the process of writing a manual or a set of written guidelines to improve the execution of a complex task (think of the development of a new product, or the management of the post-acquisition integration process) will most likely reach a significantly higher degree of understanding of what makes a certain process succeed or fail, compared to simply telling "war stories" or discussing it in a de-briefing session.

Knowledge codification is, in our view, an important and relatively under-emphasized element in the capability-building picture. The literature has emphasized that codification facilitates the diffusion of existing knowledge (Winter, 1987; Zander and Kogut, 1992; Nonaka, 1994), as well as the coordination and implementation of complex activities. Having identified and selected the change in the operating routines or the new routine to be established, the organization should create a manual or a tool to facilitate its replication and diffusion. The principal benefits to the codification effort are seen as coming from the successful use of the manual or tool.

While this picture is clearly accurate in many cases, it may also exaggerate some benefits of codification while neglecting others. It overlooks, for example, important obstacles to the success of this type of use of codified knowledge, such as the difficulty of assuring that the codified guidance is both adequate and actually implemented. More importantly, this appraisal overlooks the learning benefits of the activities necessary for the creation and development of the tools. To develop a manual for the execution of a complex task, the individuals involved in the process need to form a mental model of what actions are to be selected under what conditions. By going through that effort, they will most likely emerge with a crisper definition of what works, what doesn't work, and why.

Codification, therefore, is potentially important as a supporting mechanism for the entire knowledge evolution process, not just transfer phase. It can, for instance, facilitate the generation of new proposals to change the currently available routines, as well as the identification of the strengths and the weaknesses in the proposed variations to the current set of routines. The cognitive simplification inherent in the act of synthesizing on paper (or in a computer program) the logic behind a set of instructions can therefore represent both an economizing on data processing requirements allowing more effective decision-making (Boisot, 1998; Gavetti and Levinthal, 2000) and a more-or-less deliberate form of retrospective sense-making with respect to the performance implications of a given set of activities (Weick, 1979, 1995). This sense-making typically draws upon a specialized language and causal understanding developed for and by other codification efforts of a similar type (Cowan and Foray, 1997; Cowan et al., 2000).

To be sure, these advantages do not come for free. There are specific costs attached to the knowledge codification process. Direct costs include the time, the resources and the managerial attention to be invested in the development and updating of task-specific tools, while indirect costs include a possible increase in the rate of "misfire" or inappropriate application of the routine (Cohen and Bacdayan, 1994) if the codification is poorly performed, and the more general increase in organizational inertia consequent to the formalization and structuring of the task execution. Concern with these costs is legitimate and familiar. A long debate, dating back to Weber's work, has engaged organizational theorists with respect to the advantages and disadvantages of formalization, a kindred phenomenon to knowledge codification. For a long time, the skeptics seemed to have the upper hand. More recently, there seems to be increasing willingness to see the formalization of operating routines in a positive light, e.g., as sometimes capable of producing an "enabling" rather than a "coercive" bureaucracy (Adler and Borys, 1996).

This contingency approach is consistent with the thrust of the current analysis: instead of rejecting knowledge codification processes tout-court as producers of inertial forces, our objective is to determine the conditions under which the learning and diffusion advantages attached to codification could more than offset its costs. We acknowledge, of course, that this is not likely to be true in all cases – and that codification, like many other things, is likely to produce bad results when done badly. In the concluding section, we discuss what seems to be involved in doing it well.

THE CYCLICAL EVOLUTION OF ORGANIZATIONAL KNOWLEDGE

Having offered our view on the notion of dynamic capabilities and the learning processes that might support their evolution, we now provide a more detailed description of the way in which dynamic capabilities and operating routines evolve in time.

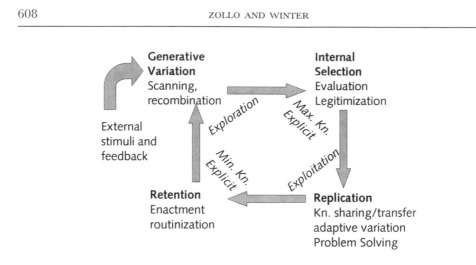

FIGURE 30.2   Activities in the knowledge evolution cycle

Figure 30.2 offers a graphical view of a "knowledge evolution cycle." It is a simple account of the development of collective understanding regarding the execution of a given organizational task. We have adapted for our purposes the classic evolutionary paradigm of variation-selection-retention.[2]

Organizational knowledge is here described as evolving through a series of stages, chained in a recursive cycle. The logical point of departure for each cycle lies in the variation stage, where individuals or groups of them generate a set of ideas on how to approach old problems in novel ways or to tackle relatively new challenges. This happens on the basis of a combination of external stimuli (competitors' initiatives, normative changes, scientific discoveries, etc.) with internally generated information derived from the organization's existing routines, and may involve substantial creativity. These sets of ideas, initially in embryonic and partly tacit form, are then subject to internal selection pressures aimed at the evaluation of their potential for enhancing the effectiveness of existing routines or the opportunity to form new ones (Nonaka, 1994). These pressures arise as new ideas are considered in relation to a shared understanding of the organization's prior experience, as well as in the context of established power structures and existing legitimization processes. Hypotheses as to the expected advantages from the application of the proposed changes are probed through a collective investment in articulation, analysis and debate of the merits and risks connected to the initiative.

The third phase of the cycle refers to the set of activities enacted by an organization for the purpose of diffusing the newly approved change initiatives to the relevant parties within the firm. This diffusion process requires the spatial replication of the novel solutions in order to leverage the newly found wisdom in additional competitive contexts (Winter and Szulanski, 2001). This mechanism is a relatively new addition to the standard variation-selection-retention triumvirate of evolutionary modeling borrowed from evolutionary biology (Campbell, 1969). Its rationale lies is the simple observation that organizations differ in a crucial way from biological entities in that they act simultaneously in spatially diverse contexts, posing the question of how novelties (ideas or change proposals in our case) that survive internal selection processes diffuse to the spatially dispersed parts of the organizations where the novel approach can be put to use.[3]

The replication phase, however, does not simply serve the function of diffusing the newly minted knowledge to the places and times where it is needed. Importantly for the purposes of this paper, the diffusion of knowledge through replication processes also contributes new (raw) information that can provide the diversity needed to start a variation phase of a new knowledge cycle. The application of the routines in diverse contexts generates new information as to the performance implications of the routines employed. The hypotheses constructed through the cognitive efforts of the selection phase can now (in theory) be tested with empirical evidence. This evidence, if properly collected and processed, can further illuminate the context-dependent cause-effect linkages between decisions and performance outcomes. It can thereby prime the initiation of a new knowledge cycle.

The qualification concerning collection and processing is important because replication and repetition processes tend to make knowledge evolve toward a more tacit form as it becomes highly embedded in the behavior of the individuals involved in the multiple executions of the task. Repetition leads to automaticity in the execution of a given task, and to a corresponding reduction in individual awareness and collective understanding of the action-performance linkages, as well as of the purpose of the execution criteria followed. The abundance of raw information potentially available due to the repeated execution of the new tasks is, in fact, typically unusable without significant cognitive efforts aimed at evaluating, classifying, analyzing and finally distilling the results into new initiatives to modify existing routines or create new ones.

The external environment plays two distinguishable roles in the process. It supplies diverse stimuli and substance for internal reflections on possible applications to the improvement of existing routines. Of course, it also functions as a selection mechanism in the classic evolutionary sense as it provides the feedback on the value and viability of the organization's current behaviors. While we fully recognize the fundamental relevance of both these roles, the focus of this chapter is on the set of internal processes located, from a temporal standpoint, between the two.

A few more observations can be made by entering some additional elements in the basic framework. First, the knowledge cycle proceeds, in March's (1991) terms, from an exploration phase to an exploitation one, potentially feeding back into a new exploration phase. Exploration activities are primarily carried out through cognitive efforts aimed at generating the necessary range of new intuitions and ideas (variation) as well as selecting the most appropriate ones through evaluation and legitimization processes. By contrast, exploitation activities rely more on behavioral mechanisms encompassing the replication of the new approaches in diverse contexts and their absorption into the existing sets of routines for the execution of that particular task. We suggest that exploitation can prime exploration, and propose that, in addition to the familiar tradeoff between exploration and exploitation processes, there can be a recursive and co-evolutionary relationship between them. This may indicate a way to conceptualize the managerial challenge of handling both processes simultaneously.

The second observation is that the nature of organizational knowledge changes over the cycle. In the first phases of generative variation and internal selection, the initial idea or novel insight needs to be made increasingly explicit in order to allow a debate on its merits, and the knowledge reaches a peak of explicitness as the cycle reaches the selection stage. Through the replication and retention phases, then, knowledge becomes increasingly embedded in human behavior, and likely gains in effectiveness while declining in abstraction (as it is applied to a wider variety of local situations) and in explicitness (as even the people involved in its application have difficulty in explaining what they are doing and why). The changing nature of knowledge throughout the evolutionary cycle is an issue of primary concern to us as well as some other scholars (Nonaka, 1994; Nonaka and Takeuchi, 1995; Boisot, 1998). We here identify as sources of such variations the different degrees of intentionality necessary at different stages of the cycle, and construct a theoretical argument about the conditions that warrant increasing efforts to turn implicit into explicit knowledge.

Learning Investments and Dynamic Capability Building

We now concentrate our analysis on the complex interplay of the learning mechanisms with the change processes that come under the heading of dynamic capabilities. The following proposition summarizes our view of the dynamic capability building process:

PROPOSITION: *Dynamic capabilities emerge from the co-evolution of tacit experience accumulation processes with explicit knowledge articulation and codification activities.*

The reference to co-evolution signals the importance of viewing the influence of the three mechanisms in terms of continuing interaction and mutual adjustment. Our emphasis is, however, not so much on the causal links among the three capability building mechanisms as on the way their interaction affects the firm's ability to improve the existing set of operating routines. In other words, firms learn systematic ways to shape their routines by adopting an opportune mix of behavioral and cognitive processes, by learning how to articulate and codify knowledge while at the same time they facilitate the accumulation and absorption of experiential wisdom. The ambition here is to begin an analytical effort aimed at providing a clearer sense of what an "opportune" mix of learning processes might mean. In this section, we frame the relationships among the mechanisms in terms of varying levels of investment in deliberate learning activities. We then attempt to identify the costs connected with these activities. Finally, we identify some of the most important contingencies that need to be considered in order to understand how costs and benefits vary in different contexts.

Learning investments

To study the relationships among the three learning mechanisms, we consider their positions on a continuum in the investment of resources (financial, temporal and cognitive) directed towards the purpose of improving the collective understanding of action–performance linkages.

The level of investment in developing dynamic capabilities will be the lowest when the firm counts on the experience accumulation process, as the learning happens in an essentially semi-automatic fashion on the basis of the adaptations that individuals enact in reaction to unsatisfactory performance. The effectiveness of this learning mechanism requires "*only*" the stability of personnel exposed to the experienced events, good performance monitoring systems and sufficiently powerful incentives to ensure that individuals will initiate the search routines when performance levels decay. Examples of activities that rely primarily on this type of learning mechanism include the creation of a specific function or department responsible for the process to be learned, and the hiring of "specialists" in the execution of the task under scrutiny (e.g., creating an M&A team, hiring a TQM expert, defining the function of the chief knowledge officer). These actions can be understood as efforts to provide a specific organizational locus where experience can accumulate.

The "learning investment" is likely to be higher when the organization (or the relevant unit) relies on knowledge articulation processes to attempt to master or improve a certain activity. In addition to the actions mentioned above as necessary to facilitate experience accumulation processes, the organization will have to incur costs due to the time and energy required for people to meet and discuss their respective experiences and beliefs (Ocasio, 1997). A meeting organized to de-brief the participants in a complex project can be expensive in terms of both the direct costs and, most importantly, the opportunity costs deriving from the sacrifice of time dedicated to working on active projects. Opportunity cost considerations have the somewhat paradoxical effect of tending to suppress learning when it is most valuable and needed: the higher the activity levels in the execution of a certain task, the higher the opportunity costs for the learning investments dedicated to that specific task, and therefore the lower the likelihood that the hyper-active team will afford the time to de-brief, despite the obvious advantages from the potential identification of process improvements (Tyre and Orlikowski, 1994).

The investment of time, effort, and resources will be the highest in the case of knowledge codification processes. Here, the team involved in the execution of the task not only has to meet and discuss, but also has to actually develop a document or a tool aimed at the distillation of the insights achieved during the discussion(s). If a tool (a manual or a piece of software) already exists, the team has to decide whether and how to update it, and then do it.

It is clear that, given a certain task, organizations might differ quite substantially in the degree to which they decide to invest in these kinds of deliberate, cognitively intense, learning activities. Consider, by way of example, the approaches taken by Hewlett Packard and Corning in developing their internal competence in the management of strategic alliances.[1] Both companies are considered to be among the most experienced and sophisticated players in the strategic alliance arena. The way they managed their capability development process, though, was at the opposite extremes of our learning investment continuum. Whereas Corning made a point of avoiding the codification of its alliance practices, preferring to rely on experience-based learning and apprenticeship systems, HP decided to invest in a large variety of collective learning mechanisms to both identify and diffuse best practices in this particular task. They started with the creation of a database of all their past alliances, for each of which they requested a written post-mortem analysis. They then proceeded to create what became a 400-page binder with the distilled wisdom on the criteria to follow and the pitfalls to avoid in each phase of the alliance process. Further, the expert team in charge of the alliance practice initiated a series of internal workshops/seminars open to any HP manager, to ensure the diffusion of their alliance management practices. In the language of our framework, HP combined support of behavioral learning mechanisms (the construction of a stable team of alliance experts) with deliberate investments in knowledge articulation (regular de-briefing sessions) and codification (written post-mortem analysis and updating of the alliance manual).

In terms of learning investments, HP's commitment of managerial resources is much higher than Corning's. But was the investment worthwhile? What kind of returns can organizations reap from higher levels of commitment to deliberate learning processes? And, most importantly, what factors influence those returns? What weight should be given to the fact that the Corning approach, relying heavily on tacit accumulation, is more vulnerable to personnel turnover? *Ex post*, both approaches seem successful, suggesting some degree of equifinality; but which one is preferable, *ex ante*, for a firm that is trying to develop a similar competence?

To start answering these questions, we need to examine some of the contingencies under which higher degrees of cognitive effort are likely to be justifiable in terms of greater learning effectiveness. Three broad categories of factors are particularly relevant to our purposes:

♦ *Environmental conditions*, such as the speed of technological development or the time-to-market lags required by customers. Consider the high-speed end: are investments in knowledge articulation and codification more justifiable in the context of high-tech industries? A trade-off is relevant here. On the one hand, the cognitive simplification afforded by knowledge codification has been argued to be advantageous and preferable to behavioral adaptations in these types of industries (Eisenhardt and Brown, 1997). On the other, speed requirements in operating routines raise the opportunity costs of deliberate learning investments, particularly codification. In less turbulent environments, learning processes based on craftsmanship, as in Brown and Duguid's (1991) notion of communities of practice, appear to be both more effective and cheaper than their highly inertial alternatives.

♦ *Organizational features*. Organizations differ in their dynamic capabilities partly because they inhabit environments with differing rates of change, but also partly because they place different bets, implicitly or explicitly, on the strategic importance of change in the future. Organizations that are culturally disposed toward betting on change, or whose managements have successfully instilled an acceptance of continual change practices, are likely to obtain higher returns from learning at any given level of learning investment because they are more effective in shifting behavior to exploit the novel understandings. From a design standpoint, the presence of structural barriers among the different activities, typical for example of multi-divisional firms, will raise the returns from deliberate learning investments, since experiential processes will tend to remain localized to the source of novel insights unless mobilized through explicit learning processes. Finally, scale economies in the use of information are certainly relevant, as the standard view of codification emphasizes. Hence, larger, more divisionized and diversified organizations, as well as firms with stronger change-prone cultures, are likely to have greater opportunities to benefit from deliberate learning investments.

♦   *Task features.* Returns to investments in deliberate learning mechanisms are likely to be influenced also by a number of dimensions characterizing the task that the organization is trying to master. A task of higher economic importance, for example, will clearly justify a relatively higher investment in cognitive activities aimed at developing competence and avoiding future failures. Another relevant dimension is the scope of the task, which determines whether a group, a department, or an entire organization is responsible for its execution. The larger the scope, the more compelling the recourse to more deliberate learning mechanisms, since individuals are able to experience, and therefore understand, only a small fraction of the task.

The implications of some other task features are less obvious, however. In the following section, we examine in detail three determinants of the returns to learning investments. We see substantial potential in the study of how knowledge accumulation, articulation, and codification processes interact with task features. First, the analysis is at a level amenable to strategic action on the part of the firm (while there is relatively little the firm can do to operate on its own cultural features, or change its environmental context). Second, this emphasis tends to correct a bias that has arguably distorted the organizational learning literature: the organization is typically considered to be engaged in highly frequent, relatively homogeneous types of tasks, reasonably well defined in their decisional alternatives and sometimes even in their action/performance linkages. This is the case with the vast majority of the learning studies conducted so far in organizational settings, where the task typically observed consists of manufacturing or service operations.

THE MODERATING ROLE OF TASK FEATURES

The central tenet of the present section is that the relative effectiveness of the learning mechanisms depends on the characteristics of the tasks that the organization is attempting to learn and of the operating routines that it is interested in adjusting or radically redesigning. We will focus our attention on three specific dimensions of the task or operating routines at hand. The first has to do with its frequency, or how often it gets triggered and executed within a specific period of time. The second is its degree of heterogeneity, or how novel the task appears each time to the unit that has to execute it. It is a matter of the dispersion in the defining traits of the task across multiple occurrences. The third dimension relates to the degree of causal ambiguity in the action-performance links, or how easy it is to derive clear indications as to what should or should not be done in the execution of the task. We will elaborate on each of these in turn.

Frequency

It is clear that organizational tasks vary immensely on this dimension. In principle, all of them, from extremely high frequencies, such as check processing in a bank, to rare events such as a reorganization or a CEO search process, are subject to learning mechanisms. The question of what mechanism(s) work better at different frequency levels has been substantially neglected, though March et al. (1991) have insightfully explored the situation at the very bottom of the spectrum. Based on the model presented above, we argue that at increasing frequency levels, the capability-building mechanism based on tacit accumulation of experiences in the minds of "expert" personnel becomes increasingly effective as a learning mechanism relative to the more explicit investments in knowledge articulation and knowledge codification processes. At lower frequency levels, while all the mechanisms will suffer significant losses in their capability-building power, we argue that the relative effectiveness ranking inverts, and knowledge codification becomes increasingly effective relative to knowledge articulation, which, in turn, becomes more effective than tacit experience accumulation.

The reasons are as follows.

◆ *Individual memory*. The experience accumulation mechanism relies on the memory of individuals exposed to previous occurrences. Other things equal, this suggests the more frequent the event is, the higher the likelihood that individuals will have retained their impressions as to what worked and what didn't work in the previous experiences. Indeed, the success of codification efforts may be limited because the results of tacit learning are too entrenched and people might believe the consultation and application of task-specific tools to be redundant.

◆ *Coordination costs*. The knowledge articulation and codification mechanisms become increasingly complex and costly to coordinate, as the frequency of the event increases. Individuals need to meet in order to brainstorm, and typically need face-to-face contact in order to coordinate the completion or upgrading of a manual or a decision-support system.

◆ *Opportunity costs*. Conducting de-briefing sessions and updating tools after the completion of the task cannot be done too often without diverting attention away from day-to-day operations. A balance between explicit learning activities and execution activities, between thinking and doing is essential (March, 1991; Mukherjee et al., 1999). March et al. (1991) argue that with highly infrequent events, organizations can learn from quasi-histories (i.e., "nearly happened" events) or from scenario analysis. Both mechanisms entail a substantial amount of investment in cognitive efforts and, most likely, rely on the creation of written output or on the use of electronic support systems in order to identify and make all the assumptions explicit.

These arguments can be expressed in a slightly more formal way by advancing the following hypothesis.

HYPOTHESIS 1: *The lower the frequency of experiences, the higher the likelihood that explicit articulation and codification mechanisms will exhibit stronger effectiveness in developing dynamic capabilities, as compared with tacit accumulation of past experiences.*

The comparison of the results obtained by a few recent studies on the effectiveness of learning processes in relatively low frequency tasks seem to lend some support to this contingency argument. As task frequency increases moving from re-engineering processes (Walston, 1998) to acquisitions (Zollo, 1998) to alliances (Kale, 1999) and finally to quality improvement projects (Mukherjee et al., 1999), the relative effectiveness of experience accumulation with respect to knowledge articulation and codification processes seems to increase. Whereas in re-engineering processes prior experiences do not affect the performance of the current project, while efforts to create written guidelines do (Walston, 1998), in the case of relatively more frequent quality improvement efforts, cognitive (modeling and simulation processes) and experiential (i.e., experiments) learning mechanisms show comparable (and statistically significant) effectiveness (Mukherjee et al., 1999). Acquisitions and alliances typically occur at intermediate frequency levels compared to re-engineering and quality improvement processes. Kale (1999) and Zollo (1998) show consistent results pointing to a weak but positive role for the experience accumulation mechanism, and a stronger performance effect for the knowledge codification proxy (number of task-specific tools developed by the focal firm).[5]

Heterogeneity

The variance in the characteristics of the task as it presents itself in different occurrences presents a different, albeit related, type of challenge with respect to the frequency problem. The issue here is that individuals have to make inferences as to the applicability of lessons learned in the context of past experiences to the task presently at hand. As task heterogeneity increases, inferences become more difficult to make and, when made, they are more likely to generate inappropriate generalizations and poorer performance (Cormier and Hagman, 1987; Gick and Holyoak, 1987; Holland et al., 1986; Holyoak and Thagard, 1995). How does the degree of task heterogeneity affect the relative effectiveness of the capability-building mechanisms? We submit that the more explicit mechanisms will be relatively more effective in developing dynamic capabilities, compared to tacit experience accumulation, at higher degrees of task heterogeneity. The rationale is that the hazards of inappropriate generalization can only be attenuated via an explicit cognitive effort aimed at uncovering the interdependence between the dimension(s) of heterogeneity and the action–performance relationships. For example, a firm that has made several acquisitions in a wide variety of sectors will probably find it more difficult to extrapolate rules of conduct in managing acquisition processes, compared to another one that has consistently acquired in its own domain. The former might find it comparatively more useful to invest in de-briefing sessions and in detailed post-mortem analyses as opposed to simply relying on its group of M&A experts. The need to understand what works and what doesn't in the different contexts experienced requires an explicit investment in retrospective sense-making, which fosters the development of specific capabilities to address the different contexts in which acquisitions might be completed in the future.

Empirical evidence unearthed in some recent studies of acquisition performance seems to support this line of reasoning. Haleblian and Finkelstein (1999) find a U-shaped learning curve connecting prior acquisition experience with the performance of the focal acquisition, whereas Zollo and Reuer (2000) replicate and extend this finding to the impact of prior alliance experience on the performance of the focal acquisition. The initially counterintuitive result represented by the declining portion of the U curve is plausibly interpreted as a consequence of the high heterogeneity in this kind of organizational task, which increases the likelihood of erroneous generalizations. Consistent with this interpretation, knowledge codification processes have been shown to be strongly related with performance in these conditions, and therefore relatively more effective than simple experience accumulation processes (Zollo, 1998).

These arguments suggest the following hypothesis for future empirical work.

HYPOTHESIS 2:   *The higher the heterogeneity of task experiences, the higher the likelihood that explicit articulation and codification mechanisms will exhibit stronger effectiveness in developing dynamic capabilities, as compared with tacit accumulation.*

Causal ambiguity

The third task dimension that we take into consideration is the level of causal ambiguity, or (conversely) the degree of clarity in the causal relationships between the decisions or actions taken and the performance outcomes obtained (Lippman and Rumelt, 1982). Irrespective of the degree of expertise developed in handling a certain task, there are a number of factors that obscure these cause–effect linkages. The number and the degree of interdependence of sub-tasks are obviously important considerations affecting the uncertainty as to the performance implications of specific actions. These, in fact, are the two key parameters of complexity addressed in the "NK" formal modeling approach, and it is complexity that poses the obstacle to learning by local "experiential" search (Gavetti and Levinthal, 2000). Another important factor is the degree of simultaneity among the sub-tasks. If the sub-tasks can be managed in a sequential fashion, it will be easier to pinpoint the consequences of each part for the performance of the entire process.

Again, the costs related to the "learning investments" described above will be justified and justifiable in the presence of high causal ambiguity, as the higher degrees of cognitive effort implicit in the articulation and codification of the lessons learned in previous experiences should help penetrate the veil of ambiguity and facilitate the adjustment of the routines.

We therefore submit this final hypothesis for testing in future empirical work:

HYPOTHESIS 3:   *The higher the degree of causal ambiguity between the actions and the performance outcomes of the task, the higher the likelihood that explicit articulation and codification mechanisms will exhibit stronger effectiveness in developing dynamic capabilities, as compared with tacit accumulation of past experiences.*

CONCLUSIONS

This chapter proposes a coherent structure for the study of the formation and evolution of dynamic capabilities within organizations. It does so by drawing on arguments derived from both the behavioral and cognitive traditions in organizational learning studies. Starting from a characterization of dynamic capabilities as systematic patterns of organizational activity aimed at the generation and adaptation of operating routines, we have proposed that they develop through the co-evolution of three mechanisms: tacit accumulation of past experience, knowledge articulation, and knowledge codification processes.

One implication of the analysis is the perhaps provocative suggestion that knowledge codification (and to a lesser extent knowledge articulation) activities become superior mechanisms with respect to the accumulation of expertise as the frequency and the homogeneity of the tasks are reduced. This learning-oriented appraisal runs counter to the logic of codification that now dominates both theory and practice. Ordinarily, a bank would copiously codify its branch operations (how to open an account, execute a wire transfer etc.), a manufacturer would do the same with its standard operating procedures, but neither would typically be prepared to do so when it comes to managing a re-engineering process or the acquisition of a company. This is the natural result of a habit of thinking that the costs of codification activities are justified only by their outputs, and not by the learning benefits of the codification process itself. In our perspective, the creation of a manual or a decision support tool aimed at the facilitation of a relatively infrequent and heterogeneous task may be more valid (or at least as valid) as a capability building exercise as for the benefit derived from the actual use of the tool. It can affect the level of performance on subsequent tasks, even if limited in number, and it can affect performance even if individual minds, and not the finished tool, are the key repository of the improved understanding. Codification efforts force the drawing of explicit conclusions about the action implications of experience, something that articulation alone (much less experience alone) does not do.

While the standard logic of codification correctly directs attention to the costs of codification and the scale of application, the learning perspective suggests other important desiderata for codification to be "done right." Applying the logic of our argument here, and drawing on a considerable amount of related empirical work and discussion,[6] we propose four guiding principles. First, codification should aim at developing and transferring "know why" as well as "know how." We have emphasized that codification efforts provide an occasion for valuable efforts to expose action-performance links. Aiming at process prescriptions alone forfeits this advantage and increases risks of inappropriate application. Second, codification efforts should be emphasized at an appropriate time in the course of learning. Attempted prematurely, codification efforts risk hasty generalization from limited experience, with attendant risks of inflexibility and negative transfer of learning. When codification is long deferred, attempts at careful examination of the causal relations may be frustrated by the entrenched results of tacit accumulation, which may have attained high acceptance for both superstitious (Levitt and March, 1988) and rational (March and Levinthal, 1993) reasons. What constitutes the "right time" depends on the overall heterogeneity of the tasks and the representativeness of the early sample; high heterogeneity and low representativeness urge deferral.

The third principle calls for the codified guidance to be tested by adherence. The implementation issues here are particularly delicate. It is clear, to begin with, that codification cannot be an instrument of continuing learning if the guidance developed after trial 7 is simply ignored at trial 8 and later. Subsequent application provides the experimental test for the causal understanding that the guidance is supposed to embody; the shortcomings of that understanding cannot be identified if the guidance is too easily dismissed. Since, however, it is implicit here that the guidance could be flawed, the desirability of testing by adherence is obviously qualified by the need to avoid inappropriate application. The need for judgment is inescapable, but the fourth and final point here is that there is also a need for some supporting structure. Significant departures from the guidance should not be entirely at the discretion of the task team, but should be subject to review and approval by a body that can assess the case in the light of the longer-term interest in capability building. At a minimum, such a process can serve the function of making sure that the subsequent discussion in the selection stage of the knowledge cycle is correctly informed about the path actually taken and can consider, for example, whether the departure should be adopted as part of the standard guidance. Such a review policy brings its own hazards, of course, particularly the risk that the review process may become a bottleneck. The processing of engineering change orders presents strong parallels with the organizational issues involved here.

In our view, a more nuanced assessment of knowledge codification and, more generally of deliberate learning processes, is just one example of the potential benefits, both for theory-building and management, of an inquiry into how competence is generated and evolves within an organization. The framework introduced in this chapter – particularly the knowledge evolution cycle and the relationships among learning, dynamic capabilities, and operating routines – constitutes, we believe, a significant clarification of the structure of the phenomena. This inquiry is, however, still in its infancy. We know little, for example, of how the characteristics of the organizational structure and culture interact with the features of the task to be mastered in determining the relative effectiveness of the various learning behaviors. Why is it that certain firms, with comparable levels of expertise, codify a set of activities more than others do? And under what conditions does that enable, as opposed to inhibit, performance? To what extent is intentionality necessary to produce adaptive adjustments in existing routines? The complexity of these questions, compounded by the fact that we have only recently started to converge on a parsimonious vocabulary for these concepts, is only comparable to the magnitude of the expected returns from the advancement of our knowledge on these issues.

Beyond theory-building, we hope that the present paper provides useful guidance for future empirical inquiry into the role that articulation and codification processes play in creating dynamic capabilities. That is its principal purpose, and although the existing empirical base is thin, we consider that there is already good reason to believe that significant progress in that direction is quite possible. More speculatively, we hope we have contributed in a small way to a major research thrust that seems to be emerging, the effort to expand our understanding of how cognitive activity of a deliberate kind shapes organizational learning, knowledge, and action. Although there have long been important voices urging a different course (Weick, 1979, 1995), too much of our theoretical understanding of organizations and competitive processes has been framed either by the unrealistic models of hyper-rationality favored in economics or by the more realistic but still distorting versions of bounded rationality favored in the behavioral tradition. People acting in organizational contexts often think imperfectly but constructively about what they are doing, and theorists of organizations urgently need to figure out how to think in a similar fashion about how to cope with that fact.

ACKNOWLEDGMENTS

The authors would like to acknowledge the support received from INSEAD's R&D department and the Reginald H. Jones Center of the Wharton School. We are also grateful for the many suggestions, comments and critiques generously offered by Ron Adner, Max Boisot, Tim Folta, Anna Grandori, Bruce Kogut, Arie Lewin, Bart Nooteboom, Gabriel Szulanski, Christoph Zott and three anonymous reviewers. Of course, we are responsible for any remaining errors and omissions. In its working paper version, this chapter was entitled "From Organizational Routines to Dynamic Capabilities."

NOTES

1. Of course, this is not to say that firms do not articulate and codify knowledge obtained from the external environment. As we will see below in the section "The Cyclical Evolution of Organizational Knowledge," environmental scanning activities are an important antecedent to generative variation processes. However, we argue that such activities are usually better understood as stimuli to the initiation of proposals to modify existing routines, rather than as mechanisms directly shaping the development of dynamic capabilities. To illustrate, a sound understanding of what competitors do and customers desire, represents a crucial element of any firm's competitive strategy, but, in and of itself, does not make it any more capable of creating and modifying its own set of operating routines. Also, operating routines typically involve tacit knowledge; hence they are highly unlikely to be developed or shaped simply by the observation of competitors, suppliers, customers or other external constituencies. Such knowledge has to be developed "in house" through a set of activities and cognitive processes focused on the organization's own routines.
2. This model has significantly benefited from many discussions had during the "Knowledge and Organization" workshop held at Warwick University. We would like to acknowledge the contributions of Arie Lewin, Anna Grandori, and Bart Nooteboom, among many other participants. The model is also closely related to Max Boisot's notion of the social learning cycle (Boisot, 1998), which influenced our thinking and spurred some of the insights that follow.
3. The justification for the explicit consideration of replication processes as distinct from the retention ones becomes considerably weaker as the nature and the size of the firm considered changes. Small, entrepreneurial start-ups, for example, might necessitate replication processes to a far lesser (and perhaps negligible) degree, compared to a multinational, multidivisional, organization.
4. For those interested in this specific empirical context, please refer to an article entitled "Two grandmasters at the extremes," which appeared in the *Alliance Analyst* on November 25, 1995.
5. Kale (1999) is the only empirical work, to our knowledge, that has measured all the three mechanisms theorized about in this paper. Knowledge articulation processes are positively and significantly correlated with alliance performance, with an overall explanatory power comparable to the knowledge codification proxy, and larger than experience accumulation.
6. See especially the discussion and references in Adler and Borys (1996), and empirical work cited in the section above.

References

Adler, P.S. and Borys, B. (1996) Two Types of Bureaucracy: Enabling and Coercive. *Administrative Science Quarterly*, 41: 61–89.

Argote, L. (1999) *Organizational Learning: Creating, Retaining and Transferring Knowledge*. Boston: Kluwer Academic Publishers.

Argyris, C. and Schön, D. (1978) *Organizational Learning*. Reading, MA: Addison-Wesley.

Boisot, M.H. (1998) *Knowledge Assets: Securing Competitive Advantage in the Information Economy*. Oxford, UK: Oxford University Press.

Brown, J.S. and Duguid, P. (1991) Organizational Learning and Communities of practice: Toward a Unified View of Working, Learning and Innovation. *Organization Science*, 2: 40–57.

Brown, S.L. and Eisenhardt, K. (1997) The Art of Continuous Change: Linking Complexity Theory and Time-paced Evolution in Relentlessly Shifting Organizations. *Administrative Science Quarterly*, 42: 1–34.

Campbell, D. (1969) Variation and Selective Retention in Socio-cultural Evolution. *General Systems*, 16: 69–85.

Cangelosi, V.E. and Dill, W.R. (1965) Organizational Learning: Observations Toward a Theory. *Administrative Science Quarterly*, 10: 175–203.

Cohen, M. and Bacdayan, P. (1994) Organizational Routines Are Stored as Procedural Memory: Evidence from a Laboratory Study. *Organization Science*, 5: 554–68.

Cohen, W.M. and Levinthal, D.A. (1990) Absorptive Capacity: A New Perspective on Learning and Innovation. *Administrative Science Quarterly*, 35: 128–52.

Collis, D. (1994) Research Note: How Valuable Are Organizational Capabilities? *Strategic Management Journal*, 15: 143–52.

Cormier, S. and Hagman, J. (1987) *Transfer of Learning: Contemporary Research and Applications*. San Diego: Academic Press.

Cowan, R. and Foray, D. (1997) The Economics of Codification and the Diffusion of Knowledge. *Industrial and Corporate Change*, 6: 595–622.

Cowan, R., David, P., and Foray, D. (2000) The Explicit Economics of Knowledge Codification and Tacitness. *Industrial and Corporate Change*, 9: 211–53.

Dosi, G., Nelson, R., and Winter, S. (eds.) (2000) *The Nature and Dynamics of Organizational Capabilities*. New York: Oxford University Press.

Duncan, R. and Weiss, A. (1979) Organizational Learning: Implications for Organizational Design. *Research in Organizational Behavior*, 1: 75–123.

Eisenhardt, K. and Martin, J. (2000) Dynamic Capabilities: What Are They? *Strategic Management Journal*, 21: 1105–21.

Gavetti, G. and Levinthal, D. (2000) Looking Forward and Look Backward: Cognitive and Experiential Search. *Administrative Science Quarterly*, 45: 113–37.

Gick, M. and Holyoak, K. (1987) The Cognitive Basis of Knowledge Transfer. In S.M. Cormier and J. Hagman (eds.), *Transfer of Learning: Contemporary Research and Applications*. New York: Academic Press.

Glynn, M.A., Lant, T.K., and Miliken, J.M. (1994) Mapping Learning Process in Organizations: A Multi-level Framework Linking Learning and Organizing. *Advances in Managerial Cognition and Organizational Information Processing*, Vol. 5. Greenwich, CT: JAI Press, 43–83.

Haleblian, J. and Finkelstein, S. (1999) The Influence of Organization Acquisition Experience on Acquisition Performance: A Behavioral Learning Theory Perspective. *Administrative Science Quarterly*, 44: 29–56.

Henderson, R.M. and Clark, K.B. (1990) Architectural Innovation: The Reconfiguration of

Existing Product Technologies and the Failure of Established Firms. *Administrative Science Quarterly*, 35: 9–30.

Holland, J., Holyoak, K., Nisbett, R., and Thagard, P. (1986) *Induction: Processes of Inference, Learning, and Discovery*. Cambridge, MA: MIT Press.

Holyoak, K.J. and Thagard, P. (1995) *Mental Leaps*. Cambridge, MA: MIT Press.

Kale, P. (1999) Building an Alliance Capability: A Knowledge-based Approach. Unpublished dissertation, University of Pennsylvania, Philadelphia.

Kogut, B. and Zander, U. (1992) Knowledge of the Firm, Combinative Capabilities, and the Replication of Technology. *Organization Science*, 3: 383–97.

Leonard-Barton, D. (1992) Core Capabilities and Core Rigidities: A Paradox in Managing New Product Development. *Strategic Management Journal*, 13: 111–25.

Levinthal, D. and March, J.G. (1981) A Model of Adaptive Organizational Search. In J.G. March (ed.), *Decisions and Organizations*. New York: Basil Blackwell, 187–218.

Levitt, B. and March, J.G. (1988) Organizational Learning. *Annual Review of Sociology*, 14: 319–40.

Lippman, S.A. and Rumelt, R.P. (1982) Uncertain Imitability: An Analysis of Interfirm Differences in Efficiency under Competition. *Bell Journal of Economics*, 13: 418–38.

March, J.G. (1991) Exploration and Exploitation in Organizational Learning. *Organization Science*, 2: 71–87.

March, J.G. and Levinthal, D. (1993) The Myopia of Learning. *Strategic Management Journal*, 14: 95–112.

March, J.G., Sproull, L.S., and Tamutz, M. (1991) Learning from Samples of One or Fewer. *Organization Science*, 2: 1–13.

Mukherjee, A., Lapré, M., and Van Wassenhove, L. (1999) Knowledge Driven Quality Improvement. *Management Science*, 44: 535–49.

Narduzzo, A., Rocco, E., and Warglien, M. (2000) Talking about Routines in the Field: The Emergence of Organizational Capabilities in a New Cellular Phone Network Company. In G. Dosi, R. Nelson, and S. Winter (eds.), *The Nature and Dynamics of Organizational Capabilities*. Oxford: Oxford University Press, 27–50.

Nelson, R. and Winter, S. (1982) *An Evolutionary Theory of Economic Change*. Cambridge, MA: Harvard University Press.

Nonaka, I. (1994) A Dynamic Theory of Knowledge Creation. *Organization Science*, 5: 14–37.

Nonaka, I. and Takeuchi, H. (1995) *The Knowledge-creating Company*. New York: Oxford University Press.

Ocasio, W. (1997) Towards an Attention-based View of the Firm. *Strategic Management Journal*, 18: 187–206.

Selznick, P. (1957) *Leadership in Administration: A Sociological Interpretation*. Evanston, IL: Row, Peterson and Co.

Teece, D.J., Pisano, G., and Shuen, A. (1997) Dynamic Capabilities and Strategic Management. *Strategic Management Journal*, 18: 509–33.

Tyre, M.J. and Orlikowski, W.J. (1994) Windows of Opportunity: Temporal Patterns of Technological Adaptation in Organizations. *Organization Science*, 5: 98–118.

Walston, S. (1998) Does Re-engineering Really Work? Paper extracted from an unpublished dissertation of the University of Pennsylvania and presented at the EGOS Conference in Maastricht, The Netherlands, July 1999.

Weick, K. (1979) *The Social Psychology of Organizing*, 2nd edn. Reading, MA: Addison-Wesley.

Weick, K. (1995) *Sensemaking in Organizations*. Thousand Oaks, CA: Sage Publications.

Wernerfelt, B. (1984) A Resource-based View of the Firm. *Strategic Management Journal*, 16: 171–80.

Winter, S. (1987) Knowledge and Competence as Strategic Assets. In D.J. Teece (ed.), *The Competitive Challenge: Strategies for Industrial Innovation and Renewal*. Cambridge, MA: Ballinger, 159–84.

Winter, S. and Szulanski, G. (2000) Replication as Strategy. *Organization Science*, 12: 730–43.

Zander, U. and Kogut, B. (1992) Knowledge and the Speed of Transfer and Imitation of Organizational Capabilities: An Empirical Test. *Organization Science*, 6: 76–92.

Zollo, M. (1998) Knowledge Codification, Process Routinization and the Development of Organizational Capabilities: Post-acquisition Integration in US the Banking Industry. Unpublished doctoral dissertation, University of Pennsylvania.

Zollo, M. and Reuer, J. (2000) Experience Spillovers across Corporated Development Activities. INSEAD Working Paper, Fontainebleau, France.

31

Semantic Learning as Change Enabler: Relating Organizational Identity and Organizational Learning

KEVIN G. CORLEY AND DENNIS A. GIOIA

CHAPTER OUTLINE

Contrary to recent portrayals, we argue that the relationship between organizational identity and organizational learning is not only a strong one, but also one that facilitates organizational adaptability to a constantly shifting competitive environment. The implications of this relationship are perhaps most powerful in the context of change because both learning and identity are essential to both the strategic and personal aspects of organizational change. Most relevant to this volume, this adaptive interrelationship has implications for current conceptualizations of organizational learning that include: (1) the specification of a type of organizational learning heretofore downplayed in the literature – *semantic learning* (i.e., learning based in meanings); and (2) the realization that organizational learning can be more subtle and tacit than previously conceptualized and, therefore, can occur out of conscious awareness or without explicit articulation. These implications provide the foundation for inquiry into other organizational phenomena closely linked to the learning–identity relationship.

INTRODUCTION

Organizational learning is intimately intertwined with organizational identity. The source of this assertion and the impetus for our inquiry into their mutual relationship arose from our research into the character of change in organizations grappling with issues of organizational identity. In this chapter we consider the nature of the learning/identity interrelationship and attempt to draw out some of the consequent implications for both concepts, as well as implications for theorists and researchers who study both phenomena.

Although it is an overused catchphrase in today's society, the notion that "change is everywhere; change is everything" still holds powerful sway over the modern organization. Because of fast-paced market changes confronting most industries, ever-accelerating technology cycles, insatiable desires for up-to-the-minute business news, and gyrating capital markets, as well as capricious terrorism, organizations are faced with tumultuous environmental relationships that require constant mindfulness and adaptability. Change *is*, in fact, everywhere in organizations and, to some extent, everything as well, in the sense that organizational well-being and even survival depend on organizational adaptability.

The emergent findings from our research emphasize the importance of organizational identity to the change process. Briefly, *organizational identity* involves perceptions or implicit theories shared by organization members about "who we are as an organization" (Albert and Whetten, 1985; Gioia, 1998; Stimpert et al., 1998). Issues of organizational identity arise not only as the members of an organization attempt to answer the question "Who are we?" but also the question of "Who should we be?" Attempting to answer these questions usually prompts the question "Who do others think we are?" which means that identity is closely interrelated with how insiders think outsiders perceive the organization (labeled as "construed external image" by Dutton et al., 1994) and how outsiders actually perceive the organization (or reputation, see Fombrun, 1996).

Researchers have argued that because organizational identity involves answers to such fundamental questions, it is inherently stable and resistant to change. Our research has demonstrated that this is not the case, however, and that, quite to the contrary, organizational identity can change over relatively short periods of time (Corley et al., 2000; Gioia et al., 2000; Gioia and Thomas, 1996). The underlying means by which identity change is possible while appearing to have endurance or continuity is that organization members maintain consistent labels for elements of their identity over time, but the meanings associated with these labels change to accommodate current needs (Corley, 2002; Gioia et al., 2000).

One major upshot of our theoretical and empirical efforts is the realization that processes of organizational learning are essential to the social construction and reconstruction of organizational identity in the now-common context of a fast-changing environment. In a general sense, identity construction and reconstruction are intertwined with a continuous process of organizational learning because an organization must continuously relearn its identity as its enacted environment recursively influences further action taking.

As our research has progressed, however, we have come to recognize that the type of learning involved in this dynamic process differs from the organizational learning typically described in management research. Learning associated with organizational identity change tends to be more subtle and based in changes to intersubjective meanings as compared to the overt, knowledge- and behavior-based changes fundamental to the individual-level origins of the psychology and management perspectives on organizational learning (Easterby-Smith, 1997; Huber, 1991; Miller, 1996). This emerging distinction has forced us to explore more deeply the relationship between organizational identity and organizational learning and, as a result, to reconsider organizational learning as a theoretical concept.

The basic premise of this chapter is that processes of organizational learning are more closely interrelated with organizational identity than previously presumed, and that this relationship is adaptive for the organization. This interrelationship is most evident in the milieu of organizational change, where both identity and learning play key roles strategically and contextually. The intersection between the two phenomena not only provides a powerful set of implications for the continued study of organizational change, but also produces a number of significant insights for reconceptualizing aspects of organizational learning that include:

◆ the formal recognition of a heretofore underspecified form of organizational learning based in intersubjective meanings: *semantic learning*;
◆ the appreciation that this form of learning provides the potential for organizational learning to be more subtle, and its effects more covert, than previously presumed;
◆ the pragmatically important insight that the influence an organization's identity has on learning processes can facilitate adaptability for the organization (as opposed to previous work depicting it as a constraint on adaptability).

We have two main purposes in writing this chapter that follow from these observations: (1) to act as interested outside observers who see value in bringing an identity perspective to the study of organizational learning (by highlighting and detailing the adaptive relationship between organizational identity and organizational learning); and (2) to explicate the argument that it is difficult to provide a definitive definition of organizational learning because learning takes so many different forms. Our contention here is parallel to Cook and Brown's (1999) argument that we should distinguish between different types of knowledge.

The remaining sections of this chapter explore more fully these expansions and reconsiderations of organizational learning, as well as exploring other implications of the interrelationship between organizational identity and learning. We begin with a discussion about the nature of organizational learning, followed by a more in-depth examination of how identity and learning are related at the organizational level. The chapter concludes with a discussion of both the theoretical and practical implications of this interrelationship, with particular attention paid to those implications involving organizational change.

The Nature of Organizational Learning

To explore the interrelationship between organizational identity and learning more deeply, it is first necessary to articulate our perspective on the nature of organizational learning. Similar to our arguments that organizational identity is more than just a collective version of individual identity (Corley et al., 2000), we believe that some types of organizational learning are more than just a collective version of individual learning.

Weick (1991) clearly articulates the strength of this position in his assertion that depicting organizational learning as following the same processes as individual learning limits our ability to gain insight into the phenomenon as a distinctive process in its own right. In its essence, Weick's argument contends that individual-level psychological theories of learning do not adequately describe the organizational learning process because the assumptions underlying those theories do not hold for organizations – organizations are a different type of entity than individuals and interact with environments differently than individuals.

To depict organizations as learning the same way that individuals do results in an overly micro-centric view that does not do justice to the unique nature of organizational learning as a macro concept.

Weick and Westley (1999) further support this perspective in their citing of Normann's (1985) and Argote and McGrath's (1993) work. These researchers embed organizational learning in the practices and structures of groups rather than solely in the cognitions of individuals. Learning does not become a macro concept because groups (or in our case organizations) have cognitive structures like humans. Rather, it becomes a macro concept because learning is embedded in action and social interaction; in becoming a macro concept, these researchers argue that learning must transcend individual cognition.

Finally, our view of organizational learning is informed by Cook and Yanow's (1993) conceptualization of organizational learning as a cultural process. Attempting to circumvent the problems they see with viewing organizations mainly as cognitive entities, Cook and Yanow examined the Powell Flute Company's encounter with a technological change as an instance of organizational learning. The Powell Flute Company was world famous for making "the best flutes in the world" using the Powell scale developed by the company's founder. When a new, highly demanded scale (the Cooper scale) was introduced, the members of the Powell Flute Company had to face questions about who they were and how that might change given the advent of this new scale. Essentially, they were faced with a question of identity: "Could the organization make a flute with a Cooper scale and still be the Powell organization?" (p. 383). Cook and Yanow focus on the organizational learning that occurs around this identity issue, especially on how the organization learns to "change without changing" and bring the new scale in to their operations without disrupting their sense of collective identity.

What emerges from their analysis is a depiction of organizational learning as "the acquiring, sustaining, or changing of intersubjective meanings though the artifactual vehicles of their expression and transmission and the collective actions of the group" (Cook and Yanow, 1993: 384). The crucial insight here is that organizational learning can involve "intersubjective meanings" created and sustained via cultural interaction – an insight that differs from those provided by discussions of practice-based learning (cf., Lave and Wenger, 1991), situated curricula (cf., Gherardi et al., 1998), and communities of practice (cf., Easterby-Smith et al., 1998) because these literatures maintain their primary focus on changes in knowledge and behavior. Similar to Weick and Robert's (1993) notion of collective mind embedded in group interaction, learning becomes collective when it is conceived at the level of social interaction, where cultural artifacts such as language, symbols, and rituals (all supra-individual notions) facilitate the expression and transmission of *shared understanding* of actions and events throughout the organization.

SEMANTIC ORGANIZATIONAL LEARNING

As Weick (1991) points out, conceptualizing organizational learning at a bona fide collective level opens up the possibility of seeing previously hidden or neglected aspects of the phenomenon that differ from learning at the individual level. One such aspect, and an important part of understanding the adaptive nature of the identity-learning relationship, involves the subtle nature of organizational learning that is based in meanings, or *semantic learning*. In choosing the label "semantic" to describe this form of learning, we are referring to the broad sense of the term as that which relates to meaning – i.e., not only the meanings of words, but symbols and actions as well. Semantic learning, then, involves changes to the intersubjective meanings underlying the labels and actions constituting the core of a collective's understanding of themselves. Instead of thinking of organizational learning as only involving changes in behavior and/or knowledge, this perspective acknowledges that changes in meaning also form a viable conceptualization of organizational learning.

The subtlety of semantic learning

By moving the locus of the learning process away from an emphasis on individual cognition and placing its emphasis on the social interactions and intersubjective meanings embedded within a collective, it becomes possible to conceive of organizational learning as taking place without the explicit awareness of learning, without the recognition of learning, or even without the intention to learn by the members of the collective. It thus becomes possible to account for organizational learning that occurs without overt acknowledgment because changes in intersubjective meanings can exist and affect future cognition and action without members of the collective overtly recognizing them.

If a socially shared sense of meaning changes among the members of a collective, no one member of the collective need articulate that change to the other members for it to be implemented. It can be more subtle because learning and meaning can exist independently of the individual, in the interactions of the collective. Thus, simply by acting differently and picking up subtle cues based on others' behaviors, it is possible for meanings to change even without linguistic interaction. Taking this argument even further, we can say that, at the extreme, changes in intersubjective meanings might be so subtle that not only are they not articulated and made explicit in the collective's interactions, but that they also remain at a tacit level for the individuals within the collective.

A clear example of this process involves the shifting meaning of what it is to be a team for the members of a software development group. As the individuals come together and begin interacting with one another, a shared sense emerges that they are a team because their interactions are based in a consensus-seeking, decision-making process in which everyone participates equally to achieve the collective's goals. Over time, however, as resource and time constraints arise, the interaction patterns of these individuals change such that each member takes on more autonomy, preferred task partnerships emerge, and important decisions are made individually, all the while accounting for the other members of the team and their shared goals. Even though the members of the collective might not be aware of the change or, if they are, do not articulate it in their verbal interactions, the meaning of what it is to be a team has changed for them. Not only have their individual and shared behaviors adapted to meet environmental constraints, but the meaning underlying their self-declaration as a "team" has shifted, even though they continue to use the same label.

Learning has occurred within the collective, even though they might never label it as such, or, if they do, it will not be labeled until an occasion for retrospective sensemaking occurs or until external feedback raises their awareness of the change. Once it is brought to the collective's attention, it can officially be labeled "learning" by those involved (Nicolini and Meznar, 1995) and become explicit in their actions and future meaning-making efforts. Nevertheless, the key point here is that conscious awareness and explicit articulation of the change in intersubjective meaning need not occur for organizational learning to take place.

It is even possible to argue that this form of subtle learning (and the subtle change often accompanying it) is the norm at the organizational level. We are accustomed to thinking about learning as an explicit, conscious process that leads to some noticeable change in either knowledge or action. Taken in the context of meaning-based learning, however, this assumption seems heavily rooted in individual-level cognitive models of learning and, therefore, not as easily applied to the organizational level. Instead, we might posit that at the organizational level, subtle learning based in meaning changes is the normal state and that explicit, conscious learning is the exception. Although this assertion might not be comforting for those of us intent on "capturing" and studying organizational learning in process, it might prove to be quite adaptive for those living the changes often accompanying organizational learning.

Meaning versus knowledge

It is also important to note that the distinction between knowledge and meaning is more than merely different labels for the same concept under the organizational learning scenario depicted in this chapter. An important theoretical difference exists between the two, in that any piece of knowledge must have meaning attached to it before it becomes useful. That is, knowledge can be thought of generally as "what we know," whereas meaning involves how that knowledge is applicable to us or how it relates to other knowledge.

Thus, for instance, it is not that we know a particular competitor is about to release a new product that is important, but that such knowledge has meaning in how it will affect our strategic planning for the coming year. Meaning-construction involves the interpretation of knowledge. Such interpretation involves discerning or constructing relationships between or among given pieces of knowledge and other pieces of knowledge. In a deep sense, then, we can only understand what a piece of knowledge means if we can relate it to some other piece of knowledge and its meaning. This distinction is also found in discussions about the differences between knowledge and information. Knowledge is often defined in practice as "that which is within and between the minds of individuals and is tacitly possessed" (Armbrecht et al., 2001: 29), whereas information is knowledge that makes a difference (Davenport and Prusak, 1998) or knowledge that has meaning attached to it "that informs the recipient of potential value" (Armbrecht et al., 2001: 29).

Building on this distinction, then, it is possible to conceive of two different levels of semantic learning, with the common foundation being that both involve interpretations about knowledge (i.e., about what something that is important to the collective means for the collective). At one level, semantic learning is about the meanings underlying particular knowledge, whether that knowledge involves an object, event, or person, or even a label used to describe an object, event, or person. Semantic learning thus involves a collectively shared sense of what specific knowledge means. At a more fundamental level, semantic learning involves the meanings underlying who we are as a collective; that is, coming to a collectively shared sense of what it means to be us. It is this deeper level that provides the strongest linkage between learning and identity, and where we next turn to provide a more in-depth discussion before exploring the implications of this interrelationship.

ORGANIZATIONAL IDENTITY ←→ ORGANIZATIONAL LEARNING

Building on the notion that organizational learning can involve subtle changes in inter-subjective meanings, it is possible to illustrate, both conceptually and empirically, how organizational identity and organizational learning are interrelated in an adaptive way. Based on a continuing line of research into the processes of organizational identity change, we suggest that instead of focusing on the potential for constraints to arise from identity and learning's mutual dependence (which inhibits adaptability), it is insightful to look at the enabling effects provided through their interrelationship (which facilitates adaptability).

Both Cook and Yanow (1993) and Nicolini and Meznar (1995) provide some insight into the relationship between learning and identity, albeit in a general sense. For example, in focusing on the cultural aspects of the learning undertaken by the Powell Flute Company, Cook and Yanow illustrate that learning can influence identity by strengthening or maintaining the current sense members have of who they are as a collective, or it can change that sense and lead to a redefinition of "who we are." Likewise, they also suggest that identity can either inhibit or facilitate learning, depending on how the organization's members deal with the potential for change in their collective sense of identity. In the end, Cook and Yanow posit that Powell Flute's learning about a new flute technology helped to strengthen their collective identity and that no change in identity occurred. We would argue, however, that through the meaning-based learning that occurred around Powell Flute's sense of collective self, their identity did in fact change in a subtle way that facilitated adaptation without loss of identity.

This is a key point, because more recent treatments of the identity-learning relationship have explicitly reduced it to its inhibiting aspects by emphasizing the constraints placed on identity and learning because of their interdependence. For instance, Brown and Starkey (2000: 102) argue from a psychodynamic perspective that "individuals and organizations are not primarily motivated to learn to the extent that learning entails anxiety-provoking identity change." They explain that "in practice, this means that individuals and organizations engage in learning activities and employ information and knowledge conservatively to preserve their existing identities." Thus, they strongly imply that both identity change and learning are constrained because of their mutual dependence on each other.

Likewise, Lant (1999: 185) explains that because identity "describes the boundaries of the collective [it] influences the interpretations of member firms and tends to constrain

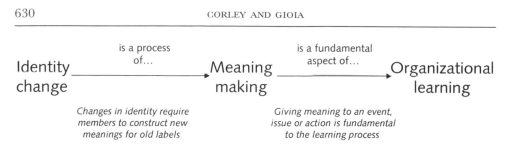

FIGURE 31.1   Illustration of the conceptual link between organizational identity and learning

the range of strategic actions taken . . . both interpretation and actions will tend toward congruence with this identity" while Weick and Ashford (2001: 711) suggest that "individuals learning about their own performance or that of their organization often make trade-offs between the desire for accurate information and the desire to defend the ego."

These perspectives on the identity-learning relationship, however, hinge on the assumption that organizational identity is stable and, therefore, changes in organizational identity can be disconcerting for an organization and anxiety-producing for its members. As our work on identity change has demonstrated, though, this conceptualization provides a rather incomplete picture of organizational identity, and in fact, prevents researchers from seeing complexities involved in its relationship with other key organizational phenomena. Nowhere is this more evident than in the relationship between organizational identity and organizational learning.

The fluidity of identity

Because organizational identity consists of collectively shared beliefs and perceptions of what it means to be "us" as an organization, any change in that collective sense necessarily involves changes in intersubjective meanings. As noted above, changes in intersubjective meanings form the basis of semantic learning (see figure 31.1). Yet, those changes are not always recognized by the members, nor explicitly labeled as learning, if recognized. Exploring why organizational identity changes and how this process comes about not only helps to illustrate the adaptive nature of the identity-learning relationship, it also provides a clear example of semantic learning.

Our original conceptualization of a malleable identity grew out of past research on organizational identity, image, and reputation that demonstrated the potential for identity to change over relatively short periods of time, but did not explicitly explain it (cf. Gioia and Thomas, 1996). In exploring these empirical examples, we posited that images of the organization communicated by outsiders are noticed by organization members and spur a social comparison process similar to James's (1918) "looking glass self" (Gioia et al., 2000).

Specifically, members of an organization (especially top management members) implicitly and explicitly assess how they see the organization (i.e., provide answers to such questions as "Who do we think we are?" and "Who do we think we should be?") in relation to how they think outsiders see the organization (i.e., provide answers to questions such as "Who do they think we are?" and "Who do they think we should be?"). Arising from this comparison is either a sense of discrepancy ("How we see ourselves does not match with how we think others see us") or a sense of alignment ("We see ourselves in a similar way to how we think they see us") (Corley et al., 2000). A perception of alignment feeds back to reinforce organizational identity, whereas a perception of discrepancy can either result in a sense that something must be done in response to the disparity or in an acceptance of the discrepancy if it falls within some "zone of indifference" (Barnard, 1938).

Regardless of whether a sense of alignment or discrepancy arises, identity is reconsidered and reconstructed (and thus destabilized to some degree) as organization members confront the implications of others' views of their organization. This instability of identity is actually adaptive, we argued, in that it allows an organization to cope better with the demands of an environment that itself is undergoing continuous change (Gioia et al., 2000). That is, an organizational identity that adapts to changing perceptions while maintaining a sense of continuity affords an organization the ability to cope with the changing expectations realized in interactions with a changing environment.

Perhaps the most useful aspect of our revised conceptualization of organizational identity, and the key to understanding its linkage with meaning-based organizational learning, was the recognition that changes in organizational identity can occur at the level of shared meanings, not just common language or labels. That is, an organization's identity consists of (1) the shared labels used to describe "who we are" among the members of the organization and to outsiders, and (2) the meanings associated with those labels by members. The seeming stability of an organization's identity resides in the stability of the consistent labels used to describe it, whereas the meanings associated with those labels often change over time to match external expectations and internal goals. Thus, an organization can claim a stable identity, for instance, as a service organization focused on "delivering the highest possible quality," but the significance of such words as "service," "quality," and "highest possible" can (and, in some circumstances, must) take on different meanings at different times for members of the organization.

Changing the meanings underlying identity is as much a process of organizational learning as a pronounced change to the descriptive labels would be. The biggest difference, and the reason why the relationship between identity and learning can be adaptive, is that the learning can take place below the level of articulation, and possibly even awareness, for the individuals within the collective. Organizational learning occurs subtly as members focus on the labels used to describe "who we are," while the more tacit and unexplored meanings underlying the labels change to match the shifting environment. This tacit process allows for a comforting sense of consensus, continuity, and stability among interested parties inside and outside the organization, while affording the organization the necessary adaptive learning to survive and grow in the face of changing environments. Thus, it is possible for learning to take place in the face of anxiety about changing identity because the identity change (and thus organizational learning) occurs at the level of intersubjective meanings embedded in social interaction.

In the context of Cook and Yanow's example of the Powell Flute Company, we suggest that, contrary to their original supposition, Powell Flute's identity did in fact change, albeit in a subtle manner that did not undermine the sense of continuity that was so important to its members. The concept of semantic learning as applied to organizational identity allows us the opportunity to see how an organization like Powell Flute can indeed "change without changing."

Changes in the external environment forced the organization to adapt and learn what
it meant to be Powell Flute by reinterpreting the labels used to describe themselves. Yes,
it was possible to continue making the best flutes in the world, regardless of whether the
flutes have the Powell scale or the Cooper scale. The labels used to describe who they were
remained the same, but their underlying meanings changed to reflect their new reality. The
power of the change resides in its subtlety – the fact that it was subtle precluded the kind
of anxiety often attributed to changes in identity. One might even posit that because the
change was successful and occurred without that anxiety that this event would normally
be expected to generate, it helped inculcate change into the culture and break down many
of the bases for resistance to change seen in other organizations.

IMPLICATIONS

The interrelationship between organizational identity and learning has a number of implications for organizations and for those of us studying them. Conceiving of organizational
learning as occurring subtly, at a tacit level of collective awareness, affords researchers
an opportunity to gain deeper insight into a diverse range of organizational phenomena.
Some of the more relevant areas for this handbook include conceptions of the "learning
organization," leadership and organizational change, knowledge management, and the
specification of the type of learning being examined in future conceptual and empirical
work on the subject.

The learning organization

One of the clearest implications of this interrelationship is found in discussions of the
"learning organization." As one might expect, the majority of definitions of the learning
organization revolve around the management literature's individualistic approach to
explicit organizational learning. Thus, some of the more traditional definitions include
Pedler et al.'s (1989: 2) definition as "an organization which facilitates the learning of all
of its members and continually transforms itself"; Senge's (1990: 3) original definition as
"organizations where people continually expand their capacity to create the results they
truly desire, where new and expansive patterns of thinking are nurtured, where collective
aspiration is set free, and where people are continually learning how to learn together";
and a modified version of this definition used by Garvin (1993: 80) as "an organization
skilled at creating, acquiring, and transferring knowledge, and at modifying its behavior to
reflect new knowledge and insights."

In reviewing this literature, our general expectation was that many of the insights
researchers have produced about "organizational learning" ought to translate into a better
understanding of "learning organizations," especially given the apparent intent to create
a more macro conceptualization of collective learning. Yet, this does not seem to be the
case (exceptions can be found among the contributors to this volume). We feel, however,
that the insights gained from examining the relationship between identity and learning,
and the semantic learning that arises through their relationship, are directly applicable to

our understanding of the learning organization. The following questions (and some answers) represent our attempt to do just that.

Perhaps the most obvious and enlightening place to start is with the observation that to become a learning organization, the organization must undergo some type of identity change. This is an implicit assumption of most treatments of the learning organization, but making it explicit provides some opportunities for discovery. For instance, must all identity changes involve formal, strategically planned efforts? No, as our discussions above have illustrated. What then happens to our notion of the learning organization if identity change, and thus organizational learning, occurs subtly and is more emergent than planned? One possibility is that the learning organization takes on a definition closer to *"an organization that is adaptive in its capacity for change"* rather than the grand definitions most often found among practitioner writings on the subject.

One of the original intentions behind the conceptualization of a "learning organization" was to make learning explicit and to bring it to a level of awareness so that learning in organizations and by organizations could be better studied, understood, and translated into practice. Our reconceptualization of organizational learning carries with it an interesting twist – that is, to understand learning organizations properly, we must account for their tacit, out-of-awareness dimensions, as well as their more explicit and evident dimensions. The upshot of this observation is that if we want to make manifest the subtlety of change and the critical role of meaning in the process, the best way to do so is to focus on the way that change occurs under the cover of stable labels.

A paradoxical question then arises: How can organizations maintain stability when stability itself is rooted in change? This paradox is evident in Barney's (1998) description of Koch Industries, an oil exploration company, whose ostensibly stable identity was that of a changing organization. The multiple-entendre meanings ascribable to Koch's own description of their organization ("We are a discovery company") vary on several enlightening levels (from the obvious "we discover oil," to the extensive "we discover new ways of doing," to the identity-reflective "we discover who we are," to the adaptive "we discover how to learn and how to change"). Similarly, 3M bases their stable conception of themselves on the premise that they continuously change. They continuously invent new products and continuously reinvent themselves so they can continuously invent new products. Change as both process and outcome is so frequent and so pervasive and so undramatic that it becomes part of the unnoticed landscape. Subtle identity change and learning are everywhere all the time so that changes in identity and learning are almost unremarkable, but are always occurring, in tandem.

Semantic leadership

Semantic learning also occurs in organizational processes other than organizational identity change, including the planning and implementing of strategic change initiatives, the development, growth, and intra-action of teams, and even the day-to-day practices that help define an organization's culture. All of these activities involve the sensemaking and sensegiving efforts associated with leadership (Gioia and Chittipeddi, 1991). Using Smircich and Morgan's (1982) portrayal of leadership as the management of meaning, it is easy to see how the existence of a meaning-based form of organizational learning would affect leadership.

One particularly promising area for insight that emerges from considering semantic learning concerns the role of leadership in organizational change. If learning does occur at the level of intersubjective meanings, and thus is subtle enough that it often is not noticed or articulated within an organization, then one important aspect of leadership is the act of noticing, articulating, or even instigating changes in intersubjective meanings. This noticing and articulation process can serve to heighten awareness among the organization's members that adaptive change is occurring and creates the opportunity to capture and codify valuable aspects of the change for future use. As this facet of leadership develops and progresses, semantic learning can become the basis for cultural change around learning processes, even helping the organization undergo the types of transformation necessary to become a learning organization.

There are important lessons to be learned on the other side of this coin, as well. Leaders too often presume that if change is to be successfully implemented, they must develop new labels and tout them explicitly to bring their followers' behavior and thinking into line with the proposed new paradigm. This approach often surprisingly produces not the hoped-for commitment, but rather an unexpected, increased resistance to change. Many organization members become weary and cynical about a "flavor of the month club" mentality concerning yet another planned change effort that comes complete with its own set of clever new labels. Resistance does not need to be an automatic response to change, however, as is evident in our examples of identity changes involving semantic learning.

An alternative approach building on these insights involves the leader focusing on maintaining continuity through the use of familiar and long-held labels, but subtly beginning a process of changing the meanings underlying those labels. Change that is more adaptive and subtle, as opposed to more "in-your-face," can avoid some of the usual cynicism and resistance and increase the opportunity for collective learning. (Of course, we would be remiss if we did not acknowledge the possible dark side contained in this approach to the leadership of change efforts. The subtlety of meanings confers extraordinary power to those in a position to manipulate them, so Lord Acton's famous dictum – power corrupts, and absolute power . . . – applies even to this apparently inconspicuous realm. Most worrisome is that motivated meaning management is a stealth process with the capability to circumvent healthy debates and preferences about the character of change. It therefore plays directly to critical theorists' worst fears that organizational elites too often manipulate the construction of reality to favor their own interests and ends at the expense of lower level members.)

Another area where leadership's role in the management of meaning is affected by the existence of semantic learning is in the area of knowledge management. Knowledge management is often associated with organizational learning, although usually from the perspective of the information systems and procedures an organization relies on to exploit the knowledge gained through its learning. If knowledge only becomes valuable once meaning is attributed it, however, then the management of meaning, and by extension the learning of that meaning, becomes a key aspect of knowledge management, so leaders have the responsibility to guide that process toward effectiveness. Although this dynamic is a direct outgrowth of recognizing a meaning-based form of organizational learning, it is not often discussed in current treatments of knowledge management.

On the need for specificity and clarity

Finally, our discussions of semantic learning raise important implications for future theoretical and empirical considerations of organizational learning. Perhaps one of the most important implications involves the use of the term "organizational learning" itself. In many ways, this term has become so broad and now subsumes so many varied notions that its usefulness as a concept has become limited in both research and practice. Based on our own research experiences on the relationship between organizational identity and organizational learning, we feel that it is imperative for researchers and practitioners to recognize and define multiple types of organizational learning, each differing in its structure and process, each fulfilling different functions within an organization, and each resulting in different types of knowledge.

For instance, we have discussed the subtle nature of semantic learning and the cultural processes involved in its occurrence. Semantic learning might also be more likely than other types of learning to lead to tacit, group level knowledge, or what Cook and Brown (1999: 392) refer to as "organizational genres." Organizational genres represent "the distinctive and useful meanings a given group attaches to its various literary artifacts [as well as] to its various physical and social artifacts." While "these genres are not explicitly learned or known," they represent knowledge "possessed or 'held in common' by that group" (p. 392) and confirmed or modified through continuing social interaction.

We believe that it is in our best interests as researchers, and in the best interests of the organizations we study and consult with, to be more specific and clear about the particular type(s) of organizational learning to which we are referring when we use this term. We hope our explication of semantic or meaning-based learning provides the impetus for this kind of specification. Although past research has discussed issues that relate to meanings associated with learning, in this chapter we have attempted (1) to specify semantic learning in some detail, (2) to discuss its role in forming a type of learning different from more traditional notions of knowledge- or behaviorally based learning, (3) to discuss its impact on the conceptualization of organizational learning, and (4) to label it in a fashion that allows researchers to see it as an interesting and useful domain for understanding and employing it in their work.

Although some might argue that specification of another form of organizational learning leads to further fragmentation of the concept, we feel that the inclusion of semantic learning within the spectrum of organizational learning types is a promising way for researchers to gain genuine insight into organizational phenomena related to organizational learning and to help the organizations they work with improve their learning processes. As researchers become more specific about the type of organizational learning they are describing and/or studying, our understanding of the role learning plays in organizational behavior and strategy will improve, thus enabling us as researchers to provide valuable knowledge for the organizations we study.

CONCLUSION

Our intent in this chapter has been to outline an argument for an adaptive relationship between organizational identity and learning. Contrary to (the few) current treatments of this relationship, we have attempted to articulate the case that changes in an organization's identity do not necessarily inhibit organizational learning, nor that organizational learning most often facilitates the maintenance of organizational identity. We believe, instead, that by focusing on changes to an organization's identity at the level of *meanings* (not language or labels), it is possible to see that organizational identity change and organizational learning are mutually facilitative and can help the organization in its adaptation to changing environments.

Focusing on this adaptive relationship has also led us to explicate a heretofore underspecified form of organizational learning, semantic learning. Semantic learning involves changes to the intersubjective meanings underlying a collective's labels and actions. Contrary to most treatments of organizational learning in the managerial literature, semantic learning is found only at a collective level, is more subtle and tacit than previously conceived types of organizational learning, and provides insight into alternative relationships between organizational phenomena (such as our example of the adaptive nature of the organizational identity – learning relationship).

The implications arising from semantic learning and the interrelationship between organizational identity and learning pertain to a wide spectrum of organizational phenomena. Our hope is that by clarifying this relationship and specifying the characteristics of semantic learning, future research can develop a more comprehensive picture of the complexities inherent in organizational learning. Instead of shying away from these complexities, we feel it is better to confront them head on. We hope this chapter constitutes a start to that process.

REFERENCES

Albert, S. and Whetten, D. (1985) Organizational Identity. In L.L. Cummings and B.M. Staw (eds.), *Research in Organizational Behavior*, Vol. 7. Greenwich, CT: JAI Press, 263–95.

Argote, L. and McGrath, J.E. (1993) Group Processes in Organization: Continuity and Change. In C.L. Cooper and I.T. Robertson (eds.), *International Review of Industrial and Organizational Psychology*. New York: Wiley.

Armbrecht, F.M.R.J., Chapas, R.B., Chappelow, C.C. et al. (2001) Knowledge Management in Research and Development. *Research – Technology Management*, July–August: 28–48.

Barnard, C.I. (1938) *The Functions of the Executive*. Cambridge: Harvard University Press.

Barney, J. (1998) Koch Industries: Organizational Identity as Moral Philosophy. In D. Whetten and P. Godfrey (eds.), *Identity in Organizations: Developing Theory through Conversations*. Thousand Oaks, CA: Sage, 106–9.

Brown, A.D. and Starkey, K. (2000) Organizational Identity and Learning: A Psychodynamic Perspective. *Academy of Management Review*, 25 (1): 102–20.

Cook, S.D.N. and Brown, J.S. (1999) Bridging Epistemologies: The Generative Dance between Organizational Knowledge and Organizational Knowing. *Organization Science*, 10 (4): 381–400.

Cook, S.D.N. and Yanow, D. (1993) Culture and Organizational Learning. *Journal of Management Inquiry*, 2: 373–90.

Corley, K. (2002) Breaking Away: An Empirical Examination of How Organizational Identity Changes during a Spin-off. Unpublished dissertation, The Pennsylvania State University.

Corley, K.G., Gioia, D.A., and Fabbri, T. (2000) Organizational Identity in Transition over Time. In C.L. Cooper and D.M. Rousseau (eds.), *Trends in Organizational Behavior*, Vol. 7. London: Wiley, 95–110.

Davenport, T. and Prusak, L. (1998) *Working Knowledge: How Organizations Manage what they Know*. Boston: Harvard Business School Press.

Dutton, J.E., Dukerich, J.M., and Harquail, C.V. (1994) Organizational Images and Member Identification. *Administrative Science Quarterly*, 39 (2): 239–63.

Easterby-Smith, M. (1997) Disciplines of Organizational Learning: Contributions and Critiques. *Human Relations*, 50 (9): 1085–113.

Easterby-Smith, M., Snell, R., and Gherardi, S. (1998) Organizational Learning: Diverging Communities of Practice. *Management Learning*, 29 (3): 259–72.

Fombrun, C.J. (1996) *Reputation: Realizing Value from the Corporate Image*. Boston: Harvard Business School Press.

Garvin, D.A. (1993) Building a Learning Organization. *Harvard Business Review*, 71 (4): 78–91.

Gherardi, S., Nicolini, D., and Odella, F. (1998) Toward a Social Understanding of How People Learn in Organizations: The Notion of Situated Curriculum. *Management Learning*, 29 (3): 273–97.

Gioia, D.A. (1998) From Individual to Organizational Identity. In D. Whetton and P. Godfrey (eds.), *Identity in Organizations: Developing Theory through Conversations*. Thousand Oaks, CA: Sage, 17–31.

Gioia, D.A. and Chittipeddi, K. (1991) Sensemaking and Sensegiving in Strategic Change Initiation. *Strategic Management Journal*, 12 (6): 443–58.

Gioia, D.A., Schultz, M., and Corley, K.G. (2000) Organizational Identity, Image and Adaptive Instability. *Academy of Management Review*, 25 (1): 63–81.

Gioia, D.A. and Thomas, J.B. (1996) Identity, Image, and Issue Interpretation: Sensemaking during Strategic Change in Academia. *Administrative Science Quarterly*, 41 (3): 370–403.

Huber, G.P. (1991) Organizational Learning: The Contributing Processes and the Literatures. *Organization Science*, 2 (1): 88–115.

James, W. (1918) *The Principles of Psychology*. New York: H. Holt and Company.

Lant, T.K. (1999) A Situated Learning Perspective on the Emergence of Knowledge and Identity in Cognitive Communities. In J.F. Porac and R. Garud (eds.), *Advances in Managerial and Organizational Information Processing*, Vol. 6. Greenwich, CT: JAI Press, 171–94.

Lave, J. and Wenger, E. (1991) *Situated Learning: Legitimate Peripheral Participation*. Cambridge: Cambridge University Press.

Miller, D. (1996) A Preliminary Typology of Organizational Learning: Synthesizing the Literature. *Journal of Management*, 22 (3): 485–515.

Nicolini, D. and Meznar, M.B. (1995) The Social Construction of Organizational Learning: Conceptual and Practical Issues in the Field. *Human Relations*, 48 (7): 727–46.

Normann, R. (1985) Developing Capabilities for Organizational Learning. In J.M. Pennings (ed.), *Organizational Strategy and Change*. San Francisco: Jossey-Bass, 217–48.

Pedler, M., Boydell, T., and Burgoyne, J. (1989) Towards the Learning Company. *Management Education and Development*, 20 (1): 1–8.

Senge, P.M. (1990) *The Fifth Discipline: The Art and Practice of the Learning Organization*. New York: Doubleday.

Smircich, L. and Morgan, G. (1982) Leadership: The Management of Meaning. *The Journal of Applied Behavioral Sciences*, 18 (3): 257–73.

Stimpert, J.L., Gustafson, L.T., and Sarason, Y. (1998) Organizational Identity within the Strategic Management Conversation: Contributions and Assumptions. In D. Whetten and P. Godfrey (eds.), *Identity in Organizations: Developing Theory through Conversations.* Thousand Oaks, CA: Sage, 83–98.

Weick, K.E. (1991) The Nontraditional Quality of Organizational Learning. *Organization Science*, 2 (1): 116–24.

Weick, K.E. and Ashford, S.J. (2001) Learning in Organizations. In F.M. Jablin and L.L. Putnam (eds.), *The New Handbook of Organizational Communication: Advances in Theory, Research, and Methods.* Thousand Oaks, CA: Sage, 704–31.

Weick, K.E. and Roberts, K.H. (1993) Collective Mind in Organizations: Heedful Interrelating on Flight Decks. *Administrative Science Quarterly*, 38 (3): 357–81.

Weick, K.E. and Westley, F. (1999) Organizational Learning: Affirming an Oxymoron. In S.R. Clegg, C. Hardy, and W.R. Nord (eds.), *Managing Organizations: Current Issues.* Thousand Oaks: Sage, 190–208.

32

Organizational Learning and Knowledge Management: Agendas for Future Research

MARJORIE A. LYLES AND MARK EASTERBY-SMITH

CHAPTER OUTLINE

This chapter provides a "look through the window" into the future for the area of organizational learning and knowledge management. We utilize the thoughts of the authors of our chapters and of a panel of experts drawn from the editorial boards of top journals to propose topics for a research agenda for the future.

INTRODUCTION

Organizational learning (OL) and knowledge management (KM) have gone through dramatic changes in the last ten years and without doubt, the field will undergo continuing change in the next ten years. Our research suggests that Cyert and March were the first authors to reference organizational learning in their publication of 1963 (see chapter 1). It was a little over ten years ago that a conference was held at Carnegie Mellon University to honor March and his contribution to the field of organizational learning. This conference brought together scholars to assist in defining the field, to discuss current theoretical development, and to identify the areas of research for the future. Many of these presentations were published in a special issue of *Organization Science* in 1991.

Since that time we have seen a rapid expansion in the number of journal articles – both academic and practitioner – devoted to organizational learning. Fields such as information technology and human resources have also jumped on the bandwagon. Doctoral programs are including seminars on organizational learning, and MBA courses on organizational learning are appearing. All of this reflects acceptance of the concept that organizations have knowledge, do learn over time, and consider their knowledge base and social capital as valuable assets. It also reaffirms the legitimacy of research on organizational learning and for its practical applications to organizations.

This chapter aims to identify areas of future research for organizational learning scholars. We build on the chapters in the book and extend them by querying experts in a

TABLE 32.1 Demographics of the expert panel

	Frequency
Years of teaching	
10 or more	51
5–9	10
1–4	2
Other	3
Teaching areas	
Strategic management	34
Organization behavior	19
International business	15
General management	6
Knowledge management	7
Other	4
Location of universities represented	
North America	37
Europe	15
South America	1
Asia	1
Australia	1
Middle East	1

systematic way to forecast the most promising research agendas for the future. The objectives are to build on the chapters in this Handbook, to report what topics some experts consider to be the most important issues for the future and to propose areas of future research in organizational learning and knowledge management. Given the diversity of constructs, measures, and theoretical perspectives, it is difficult to assess the cumulative contribution to a theory relating to organizational learning. This chapter provides an overview of the relevant research as seen by our chapter authors and members of the editorial boards of six top journals. We also provide their perspectives on future research areas and questions.

As a first step in pursuing an agenda for the future, we analyzed the topical areas of articles published in the last two years. Our assumption was that for a future view of what is to come, it was necessary to look slightly back in the literature. Second, we reviewed the chapters in this book to see what the authors consider that we know and what research questions still need to be addressed. In addition, we thought it important to ask experts to identify the topics that researchers should be addressing in the future. To do this we surveyed our authors and also the editorial boards of six journals (*Academy of Management Review, Academy of Management Journal, Journal of International Business Studies, Management Learning, Organization Science,* and *Strategic Management Journal*). The rest of this chapter reports on our findings.

TABLE 32.2 Areas of research of the expert panel[a,b]

Topic areas	Frequency	Percentage
1 Cognition, organizational identity, socio-political aspects, and tacitness of OL/KM	10	11.36
2 HRM and human capital	11	12.50
3 Knowledge creation and transfer	15	17.04
4 Learning capabilities, experience, and absorptive capacity	6	6.81
5 OL/KM across boundaries (e.g., MNCs, networks, alliances, and teams)	12	13.71
6 OL, unlearning, and innovation as processes	7	7.95
7 Practitioners and knowledge use	2	2.27
8 Specific contexts for OL/KM (e.g., transitional economies, eLearning, acquisitions, etc.)	11	12.50
9 Strategy, technology, and competitive advantage	14	15.90
Total	88	

[a] Other areas of study not related to organizational learning are not reported here.

[b] Some of the experts identified more than one topical area for their research.

SURVEY OF EXPERTS

We established a panel of experts to solicit their opinions about OL/KM research and the important areas for future research. The panel comprised members of the editorial review boards of the six journals mentioned above, plus our chapter authors. We received 66 responses, which was roughly 20 percent of the surveys mailed out, and table 32.1 represents a summary of the demographics of the experts. Over 50 universities in Asia, the Americas, and Europe are represented. The panel indicated that they were working in many different areas as well as those in OL/KM, but table 32.2 represents only the areas of OL/KM research for the panel. Three areas represent close to 50 percent of the responses: (1) "strategy, technology and competitive advantage", (2) "knowledge creation and transfer", and (3) "OL/KM across boundaries."

Panel members were asked to indicate: (1) their own areas of OL/KM research; (2) the published articles that would have the most impact on future OL/KM research; and (3) the topics or issues that will have the most impact on OL/KM research in the next five years.

Each response to each question was put on a separate piece of paper. Six of the experts were asked to combine the responses to each of the questions according to themes that they identified. They were then asked to name each theme and to sort the responses according to the themes. This served as a way of doing a qualitative factor analysis of the responses to each question, and these themes became the categories for the following tables. Thus ten topical categories were identified: "cognition, socio-political aspects, and tacitness," "HRM and human capital," "knowledge creation and transfer," "learning capabilities, experience and absorptive capacity," "OL/KM across boundaries (e.g., MNCs, networks, alliances, and teams)," "OL, unlearning, and innovation as processes," "practi-

TABLE 32.3   Articles that will have the most impact on academic debates in the next five years

Argote (1996)*	Leonard-Barton (1992)☐
Argote, Beckman, and Epple (1990)☐	Levinthal (1997)
Argyris (1994)	Levinthal and March (1993)☐
Bresman, Birkinshaw, and Nobel (1999)	Lyles and Salk (1996)
Burt (1997)	Lyles and Schwenk (1992)
Brown and Duguid (2001)*	Makadok (2001)
Cohen and Levinthal (1990)*☐	March (1991)*☐
Darr, Argote, and Epple (1995)*	March and Shapira (1992)
Edmondson and Moingeon (1998)	McDermott (1999)
Gherardi (2000)	Mowery, Oxley, and Silverman (1996)
Ghoshal and Moran (1996)*	Naphapiet and Ghoshal (1997)☐
Grant (1996)*☐	Nonaka (1994)*☐
Hansen (1999)	Pfeffer and Sutton (1999)
Henderson and Clark (1990)☐	Raelin (1999)
Hill and Matusik (1998)	Raelin (2001)
Hislop, Newell, Scarbrough, and Swan (2000)	Romme (1997)
Huber (1991)☐	Simon (1991)☐
Jacobson (1992)	Szulanski (1996)*☐
Khanna, Gulati, and Nohria (1998)	Teece (1997)*
Kogut and Zander (1996)*	Tsai and Ghoshal (1998)
Kogut and Zander (1998)*	Winter and Szulanski (2001)
Lane and Lubatkin (1998)	Yanow (2000)
Lane, Salk, and Lyles (2001)	Zack (1999)
	Zander and Kogut (1995)*

* Mentioned twice or more by panel of experts.
☐ Listed in table 1.1 of this Handbook.

tioners and knowledge use," "specific context and applications for OL/KM (e.g., transitional economies, eLearning, acquisitions, etc.)," "strategy, technology, and competitive advantage," and "theoretical foundations of OL/KM" (see figure 32.1).

When asked which articles would have the most impact in the next five years, several experts identified broad categories represented by particular authors, such as Argote, Kogut, Brown and Duguid, March, or Nonaka. Since the question asked specifically about "articles," any references to chapters or monographs are not included in our reporting. Several responses only gave partial information and therefore had to be eliminated. The responses resulted in 47 unique references that are shown in table 32.3. Those that were mentioned more than once are followed by an asterisk (*). The full references for these articles are in the appendix.

TOPICS OF ARTICLES PUBLISHED IN THE LAST TWO YEARS

We investigated what are regarded as topical areas in the field of OL/KM through an analysis of the titles of articles published in the above journals during the last two years.

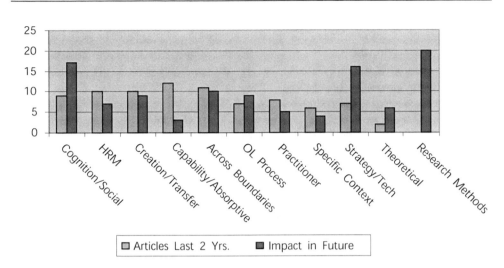

FIGURE 32.1   Topics of articles published in the last two years in six leading journals and research topics having the greatest impact in the next five years

A wider sampling of journals may provide more evidence of research, but for our objective of getting the general direction of research, we thought these six journals would be sufficient. The 82 articles were then categorized based on a content analysis of their titles with the themes identified by the expert panel (see figure 32.1).

Many of these topical areas overlapped. Frequently we found articles that addressed two or more topics, such as knowledge transfer across boundaries. In these cases we had to make a choice of which seemed the primary topic of the article. "Learning capabilities, experience, and absorptive capacity" is the largest category for the last two years and included several articles assessing the impact of learning on performance. These performance measures varied and ranged from survival, growth, cumulative returns, number of patents, and financial performance, to other more unique measures.

"OL/KM across boundaries," "knowledge creation and transfer," and "HRM and human capital" were the next largest categories for articles in the last two years, and seem to be frequently inter-related – 31 percent of the articles were in these three categories. These articles typically address the content of knowledge and how it is transferred across boundaries and/or what variables impact the creation and transfer of knowledge. The issues of human capital and people in various roles such as knowledge workers, boundary spanners, or expatriates were included in "HRM and human capital." Thus, HRM addresses social capital, knowledge workers, employees, and human competence and their relationships to OL and knowledge development.

Four other categories are next in terms of frequencies: "cognition, socio-political aspects, and tacitness," "practitioners, governance and knowledge use," "specific context and applications," and the "OL, unlearning and innovation processes." "Cognition, socio-political aspects, and tacitness" articles address topics such as communities of practice, socio-political processes, and the development of tacit knowledge or social identity. The

"OL, unlearning and innovation processes" area addresses research questions regarding the changes, unlearning, co-evolution, and sources of learning and innovation. A final category, "theoretical foundations," addresses the theoretical and economic foundations of OL/KM, often addressing topics such as markets versus hierarchies or the resource-based view versus the knowledge-based view.

Researchers used a variety of proxies for OL/KM in their empirical research. We find that generally these are based on: (1) content or kinds of knowledge, such as technological know-how, managerial knowledge, or distribution knowledge; (2) categories or numbers of past experiences, such as the number of joint ventures or acquisitions; (3) characteristics of the knowledge, such as tacitness, complexity, or specificity; or (4) outcomes of the knowledge, such as number of patents, innovations, new products, or strategies used.

In summary, treatments of OL/KM in the current literature often cover a range of topics and do not seem to be building upon clearly developed and tested streams of research. The dependent variables vary as do the independent variables. The theoretical perspectives are also confounding. The approach of Grant (1996) on the knowledge-based theory of the firm has provided a solid framework for the development of the field, and other approaches have included dynamic capabilities, evolutionary theory, institutional theory, agency theory, and the resource-based view. This leads to the conclusion that the field's theoretical development is still emerging and there is still much to do in terms of research. That said, the interest in OL/KM is increasing as shown by the number of articles on OL/KM in the top journals and the movement to test relationships empirically through both quantitative and qualitative studies.

A FUTURE RESEARCH AGENDA

Certainly much of the current research and writing on organizational learning is hard to compare since it is based on different measures, a variety of theories, and vastly different research methodologies. Yet there is an opportunity to speculate about what future research topics are important ones.

At this point, what cumulative knowledge can we say we have about organizational learning? First, organizational learning is multidimensional. It is a process that crosses organizational boundaries and affects and interacts with the human resources of the organization. It is affected by the governance of the organization and by the willingness of some to take on the role of "teacher" and "student" and even to exchange these roles. Second, although information technology has enhanced the capabilities for retrieving stored information, the value of learning and of knowledge depends to a great extent upon the human capital and its ability to recognize, assimilate, and utilize new knowledge.

The development of OL/KM as an area of academic interest has reinforced the importance of human resource perspectives within organizations seeking to enhance their ability to leverage knowledge and learning. There is an increasing emphasis on structures such as communities of practice as an important tool in enhancing organizational learning. Third, there is clear empirical evidence that organizational learning can impact the performance of the firm, but it is also appreciated that this relationship may not hold at all times, in all settings. The problem is that we know there are intervening variables, but it is still not clear which ones contribute the most, and under what circumstances, to organizational learning and performance.

Overall, we do not know how and when learning translates into improved performance. Related to this, we recognize that there is a relationship between learning and the exploitation or utilization of knowledge. Yet we do not know the constructs that influence knowledge or learning utilization. Few studies address when knowledge is used and the timeliness of that usage. Examining real-time learning poses many difficulties beyond access to organizations and data. Exceptions exist such as those studies that evaluate experience and how that experience affects future organizational strategies. We want to understand organizational learning, but lack research on actual learning processes and actual knowledge. These are difficult to measure accurately and to observe.

Figure 32.2 shows the research areas that the experts say will have the greatest impact in the next five years and compares them to the research areas of current work. The topic which the expert panel suggests will have the greatest impact in the future is "research methods and measures of OL/KM" and it represented 19 percent of the items. This reflects our above discussion for the development of better measures and research designs for addressing learning concepts. Among the remaining items, the next largest categories are "strategy, technology and competitive advantage," "cognitive, socio-political aspects, and tacitness," and the "learning across boundaries." The former two categories are ones in which less work has been done to date, as is evidenced by the difference between the number of articles in the columns. The other topic, "learning across boundaries," is one that is popular now and seems to have staying power for the future. "Learning capabilities, experience and absorptive capacity" is an area that our experts predict will be less popular in the future. Overall, the major future trends seem to be an increasing emphasis on social capital, cognitive approaches, networks and communities, and an increased emphasis on measures and research design.

Building upon chapter 1, we have mapped the research areas having the greatest impact in the four cells (see figure 32.2). Research methods seems to apply to all the four quadrants so it is not explicitly placed on the diagram but it does represent 19 percent of the items for future research. The others seem to fall into all four cells. Four areas are in *Organizational learning*, indicating the importance of greater understanding of the process and theories supporting learning in organizations. These represent about 36 percent of the items representing future research topics. The *Learning organization* encompasses "specific context and applications" and "OL/KM across boundaries" represent the intersection of process and practice. These comprise about 13 percent of items from figure 32.2. Developing "strategy, technology, and competitive advantage" and "theoretical foundations supporting OL/KM" are linked to *Organizational knowledge* and comprise about 21 percent. *Knowledge management* seems to entail "HRM and human capital" and "practitioners and knowledge use" for about 12 percent. The *Organizational learning* theme based on analyzing both process and theoretical development is the single area that will have the greatest impact. Next in order are *Organizational knowledge*, the *Learning organization* and then *Knowledge management*.

Building on these areas for future research are specific research questions raised in our chapters. Table 32.4 summarizes many but certainly not all of the suggested research questions by our authors. Our chapters by design were meant to approach OL/KM from

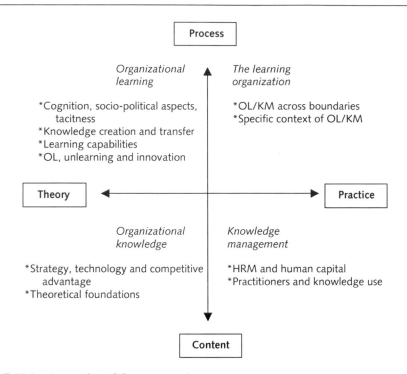

FIGURE 32.2   A mapping of future research areas

various perspectives and these are reflected in the suggested future research topics. We are struck by the fact that the future research questions vary with sub-disciplinary areas and that the idea of multiple agendas also is evident across many of the topics. There is little commonality in a narrow sense among these research questions raised by the chapters, but all seem to raise important issues about the variables, antecedents and theories appropriate for studying organizational learning.

SUMMARY

Experts in the field of organizational learning and knowledge management agree on many of the emerging areas for topics in future research. One area of critical importance is the development of better methods for measuring learning processes and knowledge and for evaluating the impact of learning on organizations and their performance. There seems to be agreement that process, content, and contextual issues will remain as important research topics in the future. Evaluating the effectiveness of learning is linked to addressing how learning capabilities are developed and the relationship between learning and performance. Dilemmas such as the lagged effect of learning and a latent effect remain as open areas for future research. Particularly salient is clarifying what is learning, what is learned, and in what context.

TABLE 32.4 Chapter authors' future research topics

Authors	Chapter title	Future research topics
Nicolai Foss and Volker Mahnke	Knowledge management: What can organizational economics contribute?	What are the incentive compatibility problems of investing in the production and sharing of knowledge? Under what conditions will the use of high-powered incentives to induce firm specific learning be most effective? Do firms that resolve incentive conflicts in knowledge production gain a competitive advantage?
Maryam Alavi and Amrit Tiwana	Knowledge management: The information technology dimension	How do technology tools impact the implementation of KM? What are the factors that influence knowledge storage and retrieval? How can an organization quantify the benefits of a KM system? How do communication support systems influence the effectiveness of knowledge transfer?
Dusya Vera and Mary Crossan	OL and KM: Toward an integrative framework	What are the aspects of co-alignment that would moderate the impact of knowledge and learning on performance? Does a multiparadigm approach to OL/KM create differences in enhancing performance?
Joshua Plaskoff	Intersubjectivity and community building: Learning to learn organizationally	What are the differences among communities of practice, learning communities, or networks? What are effective methods for encouraging the development of communities of practice?
Sully Taylor and Joyce Osland	The impact of inter-cultural communication on global organizational learning	To what extent does the marginality of expatriates affect their role in OL? What is the relationship between intercultural sensitivity and knowledge transfer in MNCs? Are ethnorelative firms more successful at OL than are ethnocentric firms?
Jane Salk and Berrard Simonin	Beyond alliances: Towards a meta-theory of collaborative learning	How can organizations calibrate learning and link it to performance? What are the drawbacks to collaborative learning? How do differences in the range of collaborative settings impact learning? What exogenous and contextual factors most affect learning in alliances?

Continues

TABLE 32.4 *Continued*

Authors	Chapter title	Future research topics
Bala Chakravarthy, Sue McEvily, Yves Doz, and Devaki Rau	Knowledge management and competitive advantage	If a firm has a more complex or more tacit knowledge base, is it easier to defend its competitive position? What characteristics of the knowledge base make it difficult to seek new opportunities? What encourages knowledge sharing within a firm?
Frans Van Den Bosch, Raymond Van Wijk, and Henk Volberda	Absorptive capacity: Antecedents, models and outcomes	What internal mechanisms influence absorptive capacity (AC)? What is the contribution of AC to various outcomes? How does co-evolution contribute to AC? What is the impact of managerial intentionality on AC?
Caroline Bartel and Raghu Garud	Narrative knowledge in action: Adaptive abduction as a mechanism for knowledge creation and exchange in organizations	How do individuals generate knowledge from narratives? What are the attributes that constitute a powerful knowledge-generating narrative? What elements of narratives provide an impetus for pursuing new knowledge? How do communities manage conflicting interpretations of narratives?
Richard Bettis and Sze-Sze Wong	Dominant logic, knowledge creation, and managerial choice	What is the interaction of dominant logic with processes of OL? Alternatively, does the learning process mediate the development of dominant logic? What is the relevance of complexity theory to OL?
George von Krogh	Knowledge sharing and the communal resource	Why and under what circumstances do people share knowledge? What are the processes within communities that facilitate transference? As the community evolves, what are the changes in the supporting structures? How do newcomers refresh viewpoints and new insights?

Raymond Van Wijk; Frans Van Den Bosch and Henk Volberda	Knowledge and networks	Is it possible to change the level of analysis from intra-organizational level to networks? How does interdependence in the network influence knowledge transfer? What are the barriers to knowledge transfer and learning in networks? What knowledge components and actors in networks influence knowledge use?
Rob Cross and Larry Prusak	The political economy of knowledge markets in organizations	Is the internal knowledge market efficient or inefficient? How does reciprocity or altruism impact internal transactions? Are informal networks or communities the most salient unit of analysis for learning and knowledge sharing? Is social network analysis the most salient methodology for studying knowledge markets?
Gabriel Szulanski and Rosella Cappetta	Stickiness: Conceptualizing, measuring, and predicting difficulties in the transfer of knowledge within organizations	What factors affect the successful transfer or the stickiness of knowledge? What are the political problems that affect knowledge transfer? What are the stages of knowledge transfer process? What are the difficulties at each stage?
John Child and Suzana Rodrigues	Social identity and learning	How does organizational learning interact with notions of social identity? In an environment of rapid change and new organizational forms, what is the impact on effective organizational learning?
Maurizio Zollo and Sidney Winter	Deliberate learning and the evolution of dynamic capabilities	What is the impact of knowledge codification on organizational learning dynamic capabilities? How should organizations address the co-evolution of tacit experience with explicit knowledge articulation? What is the degree of investment by firms into cognitive efforts versus codification processes and the impact on returns to learning investments?

Many of our authors are calling for more in-depth research studies while others are calling for more quantitative research that validates the qualitative studies. There is little agreement here except that there is room for more, and for more carefully designed studies.

The choice of an appropriate measure of OL/KM remains a debated topic and several of the authors in this volume lament the lack of agreement on appropriate measures for organizational learning. Few researchers have used multiple measures and there is a lack of emphasis on the validity and reliability of measures. Future research should consider several issues such as: Are retrospective reports as valid as real-time reports? Are real-time reports able to include issues about reflection and lagged timing? Are surveys or interviews better able to capture the true nature of learning? Finally, are the same learning measures comparable across firms, networks, time periods, and cultures? These questions raise important research design implications.

Learning typologies and the stages of learning also fit within the process and content categories. Several chapter authors and the expert panel members suggest that typologies such as "learning from experience," learning from "making it up," and "superstitious learning" may be useful for understanding how new learning and innovations are developed. Areas not readily found in current research are the aging of knowledge and when does knowledge need to be "unlearned" or "forgotten." These areas are inter-related to the stages of learning and what happens when the current knowledge is not sufficient, inappropriate, or out-of-date.

Learning in certain contexts and specific applications remain important particularly as emerging areas. The experts indicate that networks and learning capabilities remain as high potential topics for future research. Addressing such questions as whether nodal firms lose or develop capabilities over time or whether firms in networks unlearn or forget over time and, thus, lose some of their original internal capabilities are potential research topics for the future. How norms of reciprocity, cross-cultural differences, and instability affect learning processes are also areas for research and theoretical exploration.

Although often not addressed directly, many chapters and the expert panel do address some practical implications of learning and knowledge. Specifically, many suggest that linking learning and knowledge to performance is important. Although learning may influence performance, researchers should consider that there may be many cases in which a third variable may influence both learning and performance. Benchmarking, learning from failure, and best practices are learning from experience and can lead to developing routines from these experiences. Knowledge transfer has important practical implications for firms who want to transfer their knowledge of routines to their subsidiaries, alliances, or network members. Also of practical importance is determining if knowledge has been transferred and what enables this knowledge transfer. Building and leveraging knowledge resources will continue to be important to firms. Certainly important is the role of knowledge workers, their incentives, and their training. Finally, building on these other areas, a prescriptive literature needs to assist managers in assessing learning processes, knowledge management possibilities, and the importance of human capital.

Overall, organizational learning and knowledge management work has taken many important steps forward in the last ten years. We have progressed to a much better understanding of the complexities involved in assessing organizational learning and KM. At the same time, there remain sufficient gaps that are open to further analysis and development of the field.

Appendix

List of articles having the greatest impact in the next five years

Argote, L. (1996) Organizational Learning Curves: Persistence, Transfer and Turnover. *International Journal of Technology Management*, 11 (7/8): 759–69.

Argote, L., Beckman, S., and Epple, D. (1990) The Persistence and Transfer of Learning in Industrial Settings. *Management Science*, 36 (2): 140–54.

Argyris, C. (1994) Good Communication that Blocks Learning. *Harvard Business Review*, 72 (4): 77–86.

Bresman, H., Birkinshaw, J., and Nobel, R. (1999) Knowledge Transfer in International Acquisitions. *Journal of International Business Studies*, 30 (3): 439–63.

Burt, R.S. (1997) The Contingent Value of Social Capital. *Administrative Science Quarterly*, 42 (2): 339–66.

Brown, J.S. and Duguid, P. (2001) Knowledge and Organization: A Social-Practice Perspective. *Organization Science*, 12 (2): 198–213.

Cohen, W. and Levinthal, D. (1990) Absorptive Capacity: A New Perspective on Learning and Innovation. *Administrative Science Quarterly*, 35: 128–52.

Darr, E., Argote, L., and Epple, D. (1995) The Acquisition, Transfer, and Depreciation of Knowledge in Service Organizations: Productivity in Franchises. *Management Science*, 41 (11): 1750–62.

Edmondson, A. and Moingeon, B. (1998) From Organizational Learning to the Learning Organization. *Management Learning*, 29 (1): 5–20.

Gherardi, S. (2000) From Organizational Learning to Practice-based Knowing. *Human Relations*, 54 (1): 131–9.

Ghoshal, S. and Moran, P. (1996) Bad Practice: A Critique of the Transaction Cost Theory. *The Academy of Management Review*, 21 (1): 13–47.

Grant, R.M. (1996) Prospering in Dynamically-competitive Environments: Organizational capability as Knowledge Integration. *Organization Science*, 7: 375–87.

Hansen, M.T. (1999) The Search-Transfer Problem: The Role of Weak Ties in Sharing Knowledge Across Organization Subunits. *Administrative Science Quarterly*, 44 (1): 82–112.

Henderson, R.M. and Clark, K.B. (1990) Architectural Innovation: The Reconfiguration of Existing Product Technologies and the Failure of Established Firms. *Administrative Science Quarterly*, 35 (1): 9–31.

Hill, C.W.L. and Matusik, S.F. (1998) The Utilization of Contingent Work, Knowledge Creation, and Competitive Advantage. *Academy of Management Review*, 23 (4): 680–98.

Hislop, D., Newell, S., Scarbrough, H., and Swan, J. (2000) Networks, Knowledge and Power: Decision Making, Politics and the Process of Innovation. *Technology Analysis and Strategic Management*, 12 (3): 399–411.

Huber, G. (1991) Organizational Learning: The Contributing Processes and Literatures. *Organization Science*, 2: 71–87.

Jacobson, R. (1992) The "Austrian" School of Strategy. *Academy of Management Review*, 17 (4): 782–807.

Khanna, T., Gulati, R., and Nohria, N. (1998) The Dynamics of Learning Alliances: Competition, Cooperation, and Relative Scope. *Strategic Management Journal*, 19: 193–210.

Kogut, B. and Zander, U. (1996) What Firms Do? Coordination, Identity, and Learning. *Organization Science*, 7: 502–518.

Kogut, B. and Zander, U. (1998) Knowledge of the Firm, Combinative Capabilities, and the Replication of Technology. *Organization Science*, 3 (3): 383–97.

Lane, P.J. and Lubatkin, M.H. (1998) Relative Absorptive Capacity and Interorganizational Learning. *Strategic Management Journal*, 19 (8): 461–77.

Lane, P.J., Salk, J.E., and Lyles, M.A. (2001) Absorptive Capacity, Learning, and Performance in International Joint Ventures. *Strategic Management Journal*, 22: 1139–61.

Leonard-Barton, D. (1992) Core Capabilities and Core Rigidities: A Paradox in Managing New Product Development. *Strategic Management Journal*, 13 (Special Issue): 111–26.

Levinthal, D.A. (1997) Adaptation on Rugged Landscapes. *Management Science*, 43 (7): 934–50.

Levinthal, D.A. and March, J.G. (1993) The Myopia of Learning. *Strategic Management Journal*, 14: 95–112.

Lyles, M.A. and Salk, J. (1996) Knowledge Acquisition from Foreign Parents in International Joint Ventures. *Journal of International Business Studies*, 27 (5): 877–904.

Lyles, M.A. and Schwenk, C.R. (1992) Top Management, Strategy and Organizational Knowledge Structures. *Journal of Management Studies*, 29 (2): 155–74.

Makadok, R. (2001) Toward a Synthesis of the Resource-Based and Dynamic-Capability Views of Rent Creation. *Strategic Management Journal*, 22: 387–401.

March, J.G. (1991) Exploration and Exploitation in Organizational Learning. *Organization Science*, 2 (1): 71–87.

March, J.G. and Shapira, Z. (1992) Variable Risk Preferences and the Focus of Attention. *Psychological Review*, 99: 172–83.

McDermott, R. (1999) Why Information Technology Inspired but Cannot Deliver Knowledge Management. *California Management Review*, 41 (4): 103–17.

Mowery, D.C., Oxley, J.E., and Silverman, B.S. (1996) Strategic Alliances and Interfirm Knowledge Transfer. *Strategic Management Journal*, 17: 77–91.

Nahapiet, J. and Ghoshal, S. (1997) Social Capital, Intellectual Capital and the Creation of Value in Firms. *Academy of Management Best Paper Proceedings*, 3539.

Nonaka, I. (1994) A Dynamic Theory of Organizational Knowledge Creation. *Organization Science*, 5 (1): 14–37.

Pfeffer, J. and Sutton, R.I. (1999) Knowing "What" to Do is Not Enough: Turning Knowledge into Action. *California Management Review*, 42 (1): 83–108.

Raelin, J. (1999) Preface. *Management Learning*, 30 (2): 115–26.

Raelin, J. (2001) Public Reflection as the Basis of Learning. *Management Learning*, 32 (1): 11–30.

Romme, A.G.L. (1997) Organizational Learning, Circularity and Double-linking. *Management Learning*, 28 (2): 149–60.

Simon, H.A. (1991) Bounded Rationality and Organizational Learning. *Organization Science*, 2 (1): 125–34.

Szulanski, G. (1996) Exploring Internal Stickiness: Impediments to the Transfer of Best Practice within the Firm. *Strategic Management Journal*, 17: 27–44.

Teece, D.J. (1997) Technology Transfer by Multinational Firms: The Resource Cost of Transferring Technological Know-How. *The Economic Journal*, 87: 242–61.

Tsai, W. and Ghoshal, S. (1998) Social Capital and Value Creation: The Role of Intrafirm Networks. *Academy of Management Journal*, 41 (4): 464–77.

Winter, S. and Szulanski, G. (2001) Replication as Strategy. *Organization Science*, 12 (6): 730–43.

Yanow, D. (2000) Seeing Organizational Learning: A "Cultural" View. *Organization*, 7 (2): 247–68.

Zack, M.H. (1999) Developing a Knowledge Strategy. *California Management Review*, 41 (3): 125–45.

Zander, U. and Kogut, B. (1995) Knowledge and the Speed of the Transfer and Imitation of Organizational Capabilities: An Empirical Test. *Organization Science*, 6: 76–92.

Index

Printed in the United Kingdom by
Lightning Source UK Ltd., Milton Keynes
142546UK00001B/49/P